CONTENTS

W9-BFT-831

FROMMER'S

COMPREHENSIVE TRAVEL GUIDE

ENGLAND '94

by Darwin Porter
Assisted by Danforth Prince

PRENTICE HALL TRAVEL

NEW YORK • LONDON • TORONTO • SYDNEY • TOKYO • SINGAPORE

FROMMER BOOKS

Published by Prentice Hall General Reference
A division of Simon & Schuster Inc.
15 Columbus Circle
New York, NY 10023

ISBN 0-671-84898-4
ISSN 1055-5404

Design by Robert Bull Design
Maps by Geografix Inc.

Frommer's Editorial Staff
Editorial Director: Marilyn Wood
Editorial Manager/Senior Editor: Alice Fellows
Senior Editor: Lisa Renaud
Editors: Charlotte Allstrom, Thomas F. Hirsch, Peter Katucki, Sara Hinsey Raveret, Theodore Stavrou
Assistant Editors: Margaret Bowen, Christopher Hollander, Ian Wilker
Editorial Assistants: Gretchen Henderson, Bethany Jewett
Managing Editor: Leanne Coupe

Special Sales
Bulk purchases (10+ copies) of Frommer's Travel Guides are available to corporations at special discounts. The Special Sales Department can produce custom editions to be used as premiums and/or for sales promotion to suit individual needs. Existing editions can be produced with custom cover imprints such as a corporate logo. For more information write to: Special Sales, Prentice Hall Travel, 15 Columbus Circle, New York, New York 10023.

Manufactured in the United States of America

LIST OF MAPS

AN INVITATION TO OUR READERS

In researching this book, we have come across many wonderful establishments, the best of which we have included here. We are sure that many of you will also come across appealing hotels, inns, restaurants, guesthouses, shops, and attractions. Please don't keep them to yourself. Share your experiences, especially if you want to comment on places that have been included in this edition that have changed for the worse. You can address your letters to:

Darwin Porter
Frommer's England '94
c/o Prentice Hall Travel
15 Columbus Circle
New York, NY 10023

A DISCLAIMER

Readers are advised that prices fluctuate in the course of time and that travel information changes under the impact of the varied and volatile factors that affect the travel industry. Neither the authors nor the publisher can be held responsible for the experiences of readers while traveling. Readers are invited to write to the publisher with ideas, comments, and suggestions for future editions.

SAFETY ADVISORY

Whenever you're traveling in an unfamiliar city or country, stay alert. Be aware of your immediate surroundings. Wear a moneybelt and keep a close eye on your possessions. Be particularly careful with cameras, purses, and wallets, all favorite targets of thieves and pickpockets.

GETTING TO KNOW ENGLAND

Hundreds of millions of people around the world can trace their ancestry back to England, Scotland, or Wales. In ever growing numbers they come to visit the land of their forebears.

What's the big attraction?

England is not a big country—it's almost exactly the same size as New York State—but 2,500 years of eventful history have left their mark on its rich texture. Today it has moved far from the prim and-proper Puritanism of the mid-17th century and is an exciting land of change and experiment.

Why go to England? Many of the greatest writers of the world have placed this little country at or near the top of the list of places to savor and explore in a lifetime. Some of the world's greatest Anglophiles have no ancestral link to England at all, but they are inspired and ensnared by its cultural, historical, and spiritual heritage. Traveling in England is like experiencing a living, illustrated history book. You can ponder the ancient mystery of Stonehenge, relive the days of Roman Britain when you walk through an excavated villa, and hear the linguistic influence of Celtic, Norse, and Norman as well as Anglo-Saxon in words and place names.

It's a formidable task to condense the best of England between the covers of a guide. The best—not only hotels, restaurants, pubs, and nightspots, but also cities, towns, and sightseeing attractions—doesn't have to be the most expensive. Hence, my ultimate aim, after familiarizing you with the life of merrie old England, is to stretch your buying power, to show you that you need not always pay top dollar for charm, top-grade comfort, and food.

A lot of attention is devoted to the tourist meccas of London, Stratford-upon-Avon, and Oxford. But these ancient cities and towns do not come close to reflecting fully the complexity and diversity of the country. England defies a clear, logical, coherent plan of sightseeing. It's a patchwork quilt of treasures, with many of the most scenic items tucked away in remote corners—an Elizabethan country estate in Devon, a half-timbered thatched cottage by the sea in Dorset, a Regency manor in the Lake District.

Try to arrive with as few preconceptions about the English as possible; generalizing about their national character is fraught with hazards. Suffice it to say, they'll surprise you—particularly if you think of the English as a cold, snobbish, withdrawn people. A few visits to the haunts of Soho, or to a local pub for a "lager and lime," or even a look at the racy London tabloids will cure you of stereotypes.

1. GEOGRAPHY, HISTORY & POLITICS

GEOGRAPHY

England is a part of the British Isles, which lie in the Atlantic, separated from the European continent by the Channel and the North Sea.

The name United Kingdom refers to the political entity of England, Wales, Scotland, and Northern Ireland. Only 50,327 square miles, roughly comparable in size to New York State, England has an amazing amount of rural land and natural wilderness (easily observed from an airplane) and an astonishing regional physical and cultural diversity. The Pennine mountain chain is the backbone of the island, splitting the country in two with Lancashire on the west of the divide and Yorkshire on the east; other highland areas include the Cumbrian mountains (in the region better known as the Lake District) with the country's highest peak, Scafell Pike, at 3,210 feet. Several rivers empty into either the North Sea or the Irish Sea, like the Tyne at Newcastle and the Mersey at Liverpool, but the most famous of all is, of course, the 209-mile Thames, which empties into the Channel 20 miles downstream from London Bridge.

THE REGIONS IN BRIEF

The Cotswolds A ridge of limestone hills about a 2-hour drive west of London, dotted with honey-colored stone villages with such names as Stow-on-the-Wold and Moreton-in-Marsh—the most visited is Broadway.

East Anglia A region of fens and salt marshes, similar to the Netherlands, this is the name given to the semicircular bulge northeast of London composed of four very flat counties: Essex, Cambridge, Norfolk, and Suffolk. Its primary attraction is Cambridge University, followed by the cathedral at Ely, the recreational boating centers on the Norfolk Broads, and the landscape, made familiar by John Constable, which features also enchanting villages like Thaxted and Dedham.

East Midlands Primarily an industrial area consisting of Derbyshire, Leicestershire, Lincolnshire, Northamptonshire, and Nottinghamshire, it also has much to interest the visitor including several great houses like Chatsworth in Derbyshire, the seat of the dukes of Devonshire; and Sulgrave Manor, the ancestral home of George Washington; and Althorp House, the childhood home of the Princess of Wales, both in Northamptonshire. In Lincolnshire there's the old seaport town of Boston and the great cathedral at Lincoln, while Nottingham is famous for Robin Hood and Sherwood Forest.

The Midlands and Heart of England The Midlands consists of the potteries in Staffordshire with Birmingham as its industrial center. Neighboring Warwickshire and Worcestershire include Stratford-upon-Avon, Warwick, and Coventry. Herefordshire and Shropshire border the Welsh Marches.

Northwest England From Liverpool to the Scottish border, the Northwest includes the Lake District, where Shelley, Keats, Wordsworth, and Coleridge composed many of their great poems. Lake Windermere is the largest lake in England, but there are several others surrounded by magnificent peaks and hiking country. The region's most-visited cities are Chester, which has some fine medieval buildings, and Liverpool.

Hampshire and Wiltshire These two counties southwest of London possess two of England's greatest cathedrals—Salisbury and Winchester. Stonehenge, on the Wiltshire Downs, is another compelling attraction.

The Southeast Kent, Surrey, and the Sussexes are easily explored from London and contain such major attractions as Brighton, Canterbury, and Dover, as

well as such famous country homes and castles as Hever Castle and Leeds Castle. Rye and Winchelsea are two medieval seaport towns. The former attracted many famous folks, including Charles Lamb and Henry James.

The Southwest These four counties—Dorset, Somerset, Devon, and Cornwall—are the great vacation centers and retirement havens of England. Dorset, associated with Thomas Hardy, is a land of rolling downs, rocky headlands, well-kept villages, and rich farmlands. Somerset is associated with King Arthur and Camelot and such magical towns as Glastonbury. Devon has both Exmoor and Dartmoor and northern and southern coastlines with such famous resorts as Lyme Regis and such villages as Clovelly. In Cornwall you're never more than 20 miles from the rugged coastline, which ends at Land's End. Among the cities worth visiting in these counties are Bath, with its impressive Roman baths and Georgian architecture; Plymouth, departure point of the *Mayflower;* and Wells, site of a great cathedral.

The Thames Valley The Thames has influenced much of England's history and its banks are lined with such historical landmarks as Runnymede, where King John signed the Magna Carta, Windsor Castle, Eton, and Oxford, all within easy reach of London.

Yorkshire and Northumbria The first of these counties will be familiar to the readers of works by the Brontës (*Wuthering Heights* especially) and James Herriot. York with its immense cathedral is the most-visited city. Northumbria consists of Northumberland, Cleveland, Durham, and Tyne and Wear (the area around Newcastle upon Tyne). Durham is famous for its Romanesque cathedral, while the whole area echoes with the ancient border battles between the Scots and the English. Hadrian's Wall is a definite highlight.

DATELINE	HISTORY

DATELINE

- **54 B.C.** Julius Caesar invades England.
- **43 A.D.** Romans conquer England.
- **410** Jutes, Angles, and Saxons form small kingdoms in England.
- **500–1066** Anglo-Saxon kingdoms fight off Viking warriors.
- **1066** William, Duke of Normandy, invades England, defeats Harold at the Battle of Hastings.
- **1154** Henry II, first of the Plantagenets, launches their rule (until 1399).
- **1215** King John
  (continues)

HISTORY

Britain was probably split off from the continent of Europe some eight millennia ago by continental drift and other natural forces. Even after the split, some brave souls on the mainland made their way across the often-turbulent English Channel.

The earliest known inhabitants of the British Isles were the small, dark people known as Iberians (related to the early people of Spain, Portugal, and Sicily), also called Pre-Celts. These people are believed to have created Stonehenge before the massive invasions of iron-wielding, blond, often blue-eyed Celts around 500 B.C. The Iberians were driven back to the Scottish Highlands and Welsh mountains, where some of their descendants continue to live today.

In 54 B.C. Julius Caesar invaded. He wanted to eliminate a refuge for rebellious Gauls and also to investigate reports of precious metals, particularly tin. The Britons resisted, but lacking leadership and war experience they lost all of the southern part of the island to the Romans, from the Cheviot Hills in Scotland to the English Channel.

During almost four centuries of occupation, the Romans built roads, villas, towns, walls, and fortresses; farmed the land; and introduced first their pagan religions and then Christianity. Agriculture and trade flourished.

After the withdrawal of the Roman legions around A.D. 410, waves of Jutes, Angles, and Saxons flooded in, establishing themselves in small "kingdoms" throughout the formerly Roman colony. From the 8th through the 11th century, they contended with Danish raiders for control of the land.

In 1066 William the Conqueror invaded from Normandy and defeated and slew Harold, the last Anglo-Saxon king, at the Battle of Hastings. The Norman rulers were on the throne from 1066 to 1154, when the first of the Plantagenets, Henry II, was crowned. That line held power until 1399. A notable date here is 1215, when King John was forced by his nobles to sign the Magna Carta at Runnymede, guaranteeing certain rights to his subjects and the rule of law, beginning a process that led eventually to the development of parliamentary democracy.

In 1337 the Hundred Years' War began, impoverishing both England and France. A long period of civil strife ended at the battle of Bosworth Field with the victory of the first Tudor, Henry VII, who pacified the country and laid the foundations of a strong central monarchy. His work was continued by his son, Henry VIII, and his granddaughter, Elizabeth I. Under the Tudors England moved rapidly out of the Middle Ages. The Church of England established its independence from Rome. The country's wealth increased and so did its power, especially naval power. The New Learning of the Renaissance that spread from Italy stimulated a cultural movement that culminated in the works of Spenser, Bacon, and Shakespeare. In 1588 the Spanish Armada was defeated and English power firmly established.

The Stuarts ascended the throne in 1603 and held it, except for the 17-year interlude of Oliver Cromwell's Protectorate, through a century of civil war and religious dissension. The Puritans and other Dissenters, many of whom were in Parliament, began agitating for more power, and in 1629 Charles I dissolved Parliament, determined to rule the kingdom without it. Civil War followed. From 1642 to 1649 the Cavaliers and Roundheads (the Royalists and Parliamentarians) fought until the Parliamentarians triumphed and Charles I was executed in 1649. Cromwell became Lord Protector in 1653, establishing England's first and only dictatorship, which lasted until Charles II was restored in 1660. It was the beginning of a dreadful decade that saw London decimated by the Great Plague and destroyed by the Great Fire. The last male Stuart, James II, who tried to return the country to Roman Catholicism, was deposed in the "Glorious Revolution" of 1688, and succeeded by his daughter, Mary, and her husband, William of Orange, thus securing the Protestant succession that has continued to this day. These tolerant and levelheaded monarchs signed a Bill of Rights, establishing the principle that the monarch reigns by the will of Parliament, not by divine right from God.

When Queen Anne, last of the Stuarts, died childless, a Protestant, George I of Hanover, was invited to ascend the

DATELINE

signs the Magna Carta at Runnymede.

- **1337** Hundred Years' War between France and England begins.
- **1485** Battle of Bosworth Field ends War of the Roses between the Houses of York and Lancaster; Henry VII launches Tudor dynasty.
- **1509** Henry VIII brings the Reformation to England and dissolves the monasteries.
- **1558** The accession of Elizabeth I ushers in an era of exploration and a renaissance in science and learning.
- **1588** Spanish Armada defeated.
- **1603** James VI of Scotland becomes James I of England, uniting the crowns of England and Scotland.
- **1620** Pilgrims sail from Plymouth on the *Mayflower* to found colony in the New World.
- **1629** Charles I dissolves Parliament, ruling alone.
- **1642–49** Civil War between Royalists and Parliamentarians; the Parliamentarians win.
- **1649** Charles I beheaded, and England is a republic.

(continues)

DATELINE

- **1653** Oliver Cromwell becomes Lord Protector.
- **1660** Charles II restored to the throne with limited power.
- **1665–66** Great Plague and Great Fire decimate London.
- **1688** James II, a Catholic, is deposed, and William and Mary come to the throne, signing a Bill of Rights.
- **1727** The first of the Hanoverians, George I, assumes the throne.
- **1756–63** In the Seven Years' War, Britain wins Canada from the French.
- **1775–83** Britain loses its American colonies.
- **1795–1815** The Napoleonic Wars lead finally to the 1815 Battle of Waterloo and the defeat of Napoléon.
- **1837** Queen Victoria begins reign as Britain reaches the zenith of its empire.
- **1901** Victoria dies, and Edward VII becomes king.
- **1914–18** England enters World War I and emerges victorious on the Allied side.
- **1936** Edward VIII abdicates

(continues)

throne in 1727, the first in this 110-year dynasty. Under the Hanoverians the British empire was extended: Canada was won from the French in the Seven Years' War (1756–63), British control over India was affirmed and expanded, and Captain Cook claimed Australia and New Zealand for England. The American colonies, though, were lost and the British became embroiled in the Napoleonic Wars (1795–1815), achieving two of their greatest victories, Trafalgar by Admiral Lord Nelson and Waterloo by the Duke of Wellington.

Perhaps the single most important development from the mid- to late 18th century was the Industrial Revolution, which changed the lives of the laboring class, created a wealthy middle class, and changed England from a rural, agricultural society to an urban, industrial economy.

During the reign of Queen Victoria, which began in 1837, the first trade unions were formed, a public school system was developed, and the railroads were built. Benjamin Disraeli persuaded Parliament to declare Victoria Empress of India. When Edward VII succeeded to the throne in 1901, the country entered the 20th century at the height of its imperial power, while at home the advent of the motorcar and the telephone radically changed social life.

Edward's son, George V, ascended the throne in 1910 and led the nation through World War I. His oldest son, Edward VIII, abdicated before his coronation to marry the American divorcée, Wallis Simpson (he became the Duke of Windsor). George VI became king.

In 1939, World War II was declared and Britain's inspiring leader Winston Churchill, whose mother was an American, led the nation during its "finest hour." The Blitz, the Battle of Britain, the Dunkirk evacuation in 1940, and the D day invasion of German-occupied France are still remembered by many and are recorded in many documentaries and books.

After World War II, when Labour came into power in 1945, the welfare state was established and the empire was dismantled.

Upon the death of George VI, the "wartime king," Queen Elizabeth II ascended the throne to begin a long reign that has lasted until this day. Although the queen has remained steadfast, during the 1950s and 1960s political power seesawed back and forth between the Conservatives and Labour until Margaret Thatcher became prime minister in 1979. Her popularity soared as the economy revived and was at its height during the Falklands War. Afterward it declined, especially after the introduction of the poll tax. Eventually, the party forced her from power and John Major replaced her as prime minister in 1990. Major came into the world limelight in 1991 when he led Britain in a coalition with the United States in the desert war against Iraq.

But in 1992 it wasn't the prime minister who received

the most press coverage—rather, it was the House of Windsor. In a year that Queen Elizabeth II labeled *annus horribilis,* a devastating fire swept across Windsor Castle, the queen agreed to pay taxes for the first time, and the marriages of several of her children crumbled. Prince Charles and Princess Diana agreed to a separation, and there were ominous rumblings about the future of the House of Windsor.

POLITICS

The United Kingdom of Great Britain and Northern Ireland comprises England, Wales, Scotland, and Northern Ireland. It is a constitutional monarchy, the present head of state being Queen Elizabeth II. The head of government, however, is the prime minister, selected by the majority party in Parliament and then requested by the queen to form a government—in other words, to take charge and name cabinet members to head the various branches of government.

Parliament consists of the House of Lords and the House of Commons. The government consists of the prime minister and the cabinet members (who must be members of Parliament). The sovereign is Commander-in-Chief, but is "above politics," playing a ceremonial role only. There are two main political parties, Conservative and Labour. The Conservatives, currently led by John Major, support free enterprise, private ownership, and membership in the European Community. Labour advocates public ownership of important industries, with a maximum support structure for the individual. The Liberals and the Social Democrat party have joined in an uneasy alliance to form the middle-of-the-road Social Democratic and Liberal party.

2. ENGLAND'S FAMOUS PEOPLE

Baden-Powell, Robert Stephenson Smyth (1st Baron Baden-Powell) (1857–1941) A hero of the battle of Mafeking against the Boers, he is most famous for establishing, in 1908, the Boy Scouts. Two years later his sister, Agnes, established the Girl Guides (precursor to the Girl Scouts).

Beardsley, Aubrey Vincent (1872–98) A master of art nouveau. His romantically evocative illustrations were rediscovered during the 1960s and 1970s. Two of his most famous commissions were illustrations for Alexander Pope's *The Rape of the Lock* and Oscar Wilde's *Salome.*

Beaton, Cecil (1904–80) One of the most famous English designers and

DATELINE

throne to marry an American divorcée.

• **1939–45** Britain stands alone against Hitler until America enters the war in 1941; Dunkirk is evacuated in 1940, as Blitz bombs rain down on London.

• **1945** Churchill is defeated; the Labour Government introduces the welfare state and dismantles the empire.

• **1952** Queen Elizabeth II ascends the throne.

• **1973** Britain joins the EC.

• **1979** Margaret Thatcher becomes prime minister.

• **1982** Britain, led by Thatcher, defeats Argentina in the Falklands War.

• **1990** Thatcher is ousted; John Major becomes prime minister.

• **1991** Britain fights with Allies to defeat Iraq.

• **1992** In this *annus horribilis* of the House of Windsor, several royal marriages collapse, Windsor Castle burns, and the queen becomes a taxpayer.

photographers of his era. Everyone (yes, everyone) who mattered in the 1940s, '50s, and '60s was photographed by him, including Wallis Warfield Simpson, who designated him as the "official photographer" at her notorious wedding in France in 1936. American audiences knew him best for the sets he created for the New York City Ballet and for the costumes he designed for the Broadway production of *My Fair Lady.*

Beecham, Sir Thomas (1879–1961) The most famous English conductor of his era—heir to a fortune his father had earned marketing a health remedy known as "Beecham's Pills"—he was instrumental in introducing London audiences to Russian ballets, Richard Strauss's operas, and scores of musical works never before heard in England.

Besant, Annie (1847–1933) Popular opinion differed as to whether she was a harmless eccentric or a dangerous revolutionary. Coeditor (with Charles Bradlaugh) of the radical *National Reformer,* she was one of the best-known social reformers and occultists of her day. An advocate of both birth control and free speech, she promoted incendiary laborite and socialist causes.

Blake, William (1757–1827) Artist, illustrator, and mystical poet, he received critical acclaim for his illustrations of *The Book of Job,* Dante's *Divine Comedy,* and Milton's *Paradise Lost.* He is considered one of his era's most evocative catalysts of the exaltation of Spirituality through Art, using a complex religious symbolism that almost explodes from his illustrations and poetry.

Bligh, Capt. William (1754–1817) Sailor and sea captain, and inspiration for novels and film versions of *Mutiny on the Bounty.* When not inspiring rebellion at the hands of his sailors, being cast adrift into lifeboats in the midst of the Pacific Ocean, or acting as governor of New South Wales, Captain Bligh maintained a residence for almost 19 years in London's Lambeth Road.

Booth, Gen. William (1829–1912) Minister and social worker, he founded (in 1878) the Salvation Army in the East End of London. Much of his career was spent traveling to the United States, Australia, and India evangelizing the poor and sinful to the comforts and protection of basic Christian fellowship.

Britten, Benjamin (1st Lord) (1913–76) Son of a dentist father and an amateur musician mother, Britten became one of Britain's best-known composers with such works as *Billy Budd* and *Death in Venice.*

Brontë, Emily (1818–48) English novelist and poet, author of *Wuthering Heights,* and creator of Heathcliff as vividly depicted by Laurence Olivier in the film. Although Emily's novel in its day didn't sell as well as that of her sister's (Charlotte Brontë's *Jane Eyre*), *Wuthering Heights* is now listed among world masterpieces.

Brummel, George Bryan ["Beau"] (1778–1840) Supreme arbiter of fashion in Regency England and a fearsome (if foppish) wit, his whims, dress code, and values influenced the definition of social prestige in early 19th-century London. Inheriting a vast fortune in 1799, he was eventually ruined by gambling and by his many enemies. He died a pauper in a French asylum.

Byron, Lord George Noel Gordon (1788–1824) Romantic poet, Byron was born in London to ne'er-do-well parents and inherited a title and a modest fortune from his uncle. After a brief and disastrous marriage to Annabella Milbanke in 1815, Byron left London in 1816 and never returned, dying of fever in Greece.

Cartland, Barbara (1899–) Queen of the romance novel, Barbara Cartland has sold more than 500 million books. She dictated many of them with a

---

IMPRESSIONS

A mere whale's back insecurely anchored in the Atlantic.
—ARNOLD BENNETT, *PARIS NIGHTS,* 1913

white Pekingese, Twi-Twi, lying at her feet as she stretched out on a gold upholstered couch.

Chippendale, Thomas (1718–79) The most famous cabinetmaker in English history. Original highboys, lowboys, tables, and chairs bearing his signature today command price tags in the millions.

Churchill, Sir Winston (1874–1965) British statesman who became prime minister in 1940. He led his beloved country during World War II, rallying the people with his oratory when England stood alone against Hitler (1940–41). A prolific writer, he was knighted in 1953, the same year he received the Nobel Prize for literature. An Act of Congress in 1961 made him an honorary citizen of the United States.

Constable, John (1776–1837) Landscape artist whose works are considered the cream of dozens of English collections. His *View on the Stour* (1819) and his *Hay Wain* (1820) won Gold Medals at the Paris Salon of 1824 and now hang in London's National Gallery.

Coward, Noël (1899–1973) An international wit and a captivating gossip, this London-born prodigy wrote and produced such famous plays as *Private Lives*. His memorial stone, set into the floor of Westminster Abbey, is inscribed simply "a talent to amuse."

Disraeli, Benjamin (1st Earl of Beaconsfield) (1804–81) In 1837 he was elected a member of Parliament, having already authored five novels. As prime minister of the Tory party his greatest diplomatic victory was the securing of the Suez Canal for Britain in 1875, a route that cut the transit time to India almost in half.

Elgar, Sir Edward (1857–1934) Favorite composer of Victoria's son, King Edward VII, for whose coronation in 1902 he composed two of his *Pomp and Circumstance* marches. Many of his compositions reflected the power and majesty of the British Empire and arc invariably played at commencement exercises today at universities around the English-speaking world.

Fleming, Ian Lancaster (1908–64) Son of a member of Parliament and descended from a prosperous family of bankers, Ian Fleming joined the staff of Reuters and, from Moscow, covered the trials of alleged British spies during the height of the Cold War. He wrote the first of the "007" books (*Casino Royale*) in two months. Naming his fictional hero (coolheaded, suave, dashing, oversexed, and rich) James Bond after the author of a standard ornithological reference to birdwatching, Ian Fleming started an international industry.

Garrick, David (1717–79) The most famous actor of his era and honored for his craft with burial in the "Poets' Corner" of Westminster Abbey, he was the first important actor to interpret the characters of Shakespeare in a way that revitalized the interest of the British theatergoing public. His interpretations of Lear, Hamlet, and Macbeth (usually performed in the Drury Lane Theatre) were among the most famous ever.

Gibbons, Grinling (1648–1720) The most famous of the hundreds of brilliant wood-carvers employed by Sir Christopher Wren during the reconstruction of London after the Great Fire. The delicacy of Gibbons's designs has become legendary, especially flowers carved into wooden panels, which are so realistic that they seem to sway in the breeze.

Gladstone, William Ewart (1809–98) Liberal British politician and endless source of fretfulness for his monarch, Victoria, with whom he served contemporaneously for four terms as prime minister. A superb orator, he dominated the British Liberal Party between 1868 and 1894.

Hardy, Thomas (1840–1928) Forever associated with Dorset, his beloved county, Hardy, poet and novelist, has been called "the last of the Victorians." After the moral and critical hostility aroused by *Jude the Obscure* and *Tess of the D'Urbervilles,* he turned to poetry and drama, never again producing another novel.

Hogarth, William (1697–1764) Painter and engraver, Hogarth created works that satirized the social customs, hierarchies, and foibles of his era. His series of paintings, *The Rake's Progress* and *Marriage à la Mode,* are considered among the greatest British artistic works.

Hoyle, Edmond (1672–1769) An expert on gaming, he was the author of *Hoyle's Games* (1746), which reached an avid audience of dilettantes and gamblers during the Regency period. Hoyle's authority on the rules of cards and gambling is the standard throughout the world.

Keynes, John Maynard (1883–1946) Considered the most brilliant economist of the 20th century, largely because of his *The Economic Consequences of the Peace* (1919). He helped stimulate economic aid as a way of reviving the world economy after the Great Depression.

Langtry, Lillie (b. Emily Charlotte Le Brêton) (1852–1929) The greatest English beauty of her era, she rose to fame through the English stage and her discreet affairs with prominent men. Her greatest fame came as the publicly acknowledged mistress of the son of Queen Victoria (later king of England), Edward VII. Born on the Channel isle of Jersey (and known variously as "The Lily of Jersey" or "Jersey Lillie"), she reigned as one of the most famous arbiters of taste of her era from her town house near London's Cadogan Square.

Maugham, William Somerset (1874–1965) Author of novels, short stories, plays, and—later in his life—essays on writing. His most famous works include *Of Human Bondage, The Circle,* and *The Constant Wife.*

Milton, John (1608–74) This poet and prose writer, after losing his sight, composed what is considered the greatest epic poem in the English language, *Paradise Lost.* Other works include *Lycidas,* several dozen sonnets in the Italian style, and many different tracts supporting more liberal education and more realistic divorce laws.

Purcell, Henry (1659–95) Organist at Westminster Abbey from 1679 until shortly before his death, Purcell is considered the greatest English composer prior to the late 19th century.

Queensberry, Marquess of [John Sholto Douglas] (1844–1900) English aristocrat who formulated in 1865 the official rules of boxing and prizefighting. More famous, and far more notorious, was the libel suit brought against him by Oscar Wilde (which led to Wilde's eventual imprisonment for homosexuality).

Reynolds, Sir Joshua (1723–92) The most famous portrait painter in the history of English painting, Reynolds created works that included *The Strawberry Girl* and *Age of Innocence.*

Sullivan, Sir Arthur Seymour (1842–1900) Composer of comic operas, Sullivan worked with librettist W. S. Gilbert. Enormously popular throughout the English-speaking world, Gilbert and Sullivan operettas include *The Mikado, Pirates of Penzance,* and *HMS Pinafore.* In a distinctly different style, Sullivan also wrote one of the most famous hymns of the Anglican church, "Onward, Christian Soldiers." His obituary in the *Times* read, "The death of Sir Arthur Sullivan . . . may be said without hyperbole, to have plunged the whole of the Empire in gloom. . . ."

Waugh, Evelyn Arthur St. John (1903–66) This London-born author was a master of pessimistic and savage satire, often aimed at the pretensions of the English aristocracy, the institution of war, and the funeral business in America. Famous works include *Brideshead Revisited* and *The Loved One.*

Wesley, John (1703–91) After an involvement in a "romantic misunderstanding" during a brief sojourn in the American colony of Georgia, he returned to London where he experienced an evangelical conversion on May 24, 1738. Using London as his base, he traveled frequently, delivered as many as 40,000 sermons, established the Methodist branch of Protestantism, and wrote several works on grammar and history.

Woolf, Virginia (1882–1941) Novelist, essayist, and "literary priestess," she was the founder of the Hogarth Press and at the center of the brilliant group of intellectuals who formed the Bloomsbury Group. Her novels, which rely on the stream of consciousness, were extremely innovative and include *To the Lighthouse, Jacob's Room,* and *Orlando.* She was a supreme essayist, too, as proved by *The Common Reader.* She died by drowning herself.

Wren, Sir Christopher (1632–1723) Known for his masterly plans to rebuild London after the Great Fire of 1666, he is the most famous architect and designer in English history. The appearance of London today (including the design of St. Paul's Cathedral, Buckingham Palace, Marlborough House, and dozens of London churches) is a direct result of his influence. He was buried in the crypt of what is generally believed to be his finest creation, St. Paul's Cathedral.

3. ART, ARCHITECTURE, LITERATURE & MUSIC

ART

Any discussion of English art in this book obviously has to be brief and omit much. There are many Pre-Roman and Roman remains to visit like Stonehenge, Avebury Circle, Bath, and St. Albans, to name only a few. Art from the medieval period consists mainly of religious objects—intricately wrought crosses, religious statuary, and illuminated manuscripts. Ornate tombs with sculptured effigies marked the resting places of the nobility and the princes of the church of the Middle Ages, and the cathedrals became art galleries of awesome beauty. Little has survived from this period.

During the later Gothic period glorious stained-glass windows, religious paintings, and other church-related art became the primary art forms, and much can be seen at such cathedrals as Salisbury, Winchester, and Canterbury. Inevitably, such ornamentation overflowed into secular life as well.

During the Renaissance the primary secular painting was portraiture, as executed by the great Hans Holbein the Younger, a Swiss-born artist who became court painter to Henry VIII. The great miniaturist Nicholas Hilliard and his pupil Isaac Oliver rendered similar service to Queen Elizabeth I. Among the outstanding painters of the Stuart period, neither van Dyck nor Lely was English-born.

Native English painters came into their own by the 18th century. Among the great portrait artists of the period were Gainsborough and Reynolds, and they were supplemented by such remarkable social satirists as Hogarth, and such great landscape artists as Constable and Turner. The Royal Academy of Arts was established in 1768 and it still flourishes on Piccadilly, though it is considered rather stuffy by many.

Among 19th-century English painters great names include the multitalented William Blake and Pre-Raphaelites Sir Edward Burne-Jones, Dante Gabriel Rossetti, and Augustus John. Many of their works can be seen in the Tate Gallery, along with such famous 20th-century painters as Ben Nicholson, Francis Bacon, and Graham Sutherland.

Early British sculpture was mostly commissioned by the church. The religious conflicts of the 16th and 17th centuries temporarily ended the lavish ornamentation of churches, but in the late 17th and early 18th centuries, sculpture came back into vogue, producing such artists as Grinling Gibbons. In the 20th century sculpture became a serious competitor to painting in England when Henry Moore, Barbara Hepworth, Sir Jacob Epstein, and Kenneth Armitage all came to the fore.

ARCHITECTURE

The most stirring examples of early English architecture are the Pre-Celtic religious sites like Stonehenge; a few well-preserved Roman sites like Bath and Verulamium; a handful of Saxon churches; several Norman castles, the most famous being the White Tower at the Tower of London; and the great Romanesque cathedrals, like those at Durham, Norwich, and Ely.

In England the great Gothic period is usually divided into three periods spanning from the late 12th to the mid-16th century: Early English, Decorated, and Perpendicular—each more lavishly ornamented than the previous period. The finest example of the first is Salisbury Cathedral, closely followed by Wells and Lichfield cathedrals and the abbeys of Glastonbury and Fountains; of the second, the facades at Exeter Cathedral and York Minster and the Angel Choir at Lincoln Cathedral; of the last, the great chapels at Eton, King's College, Cambridge, and St. George's at Windsor. Hampton Court Palace and Bath Abbey are outstanding examples of Tudor Gothic. Other fine examples of 15th- and 16th-century architecture include Penshurst Place in Kent and such timber-frame buildings as the Guildhall at Lavenham and the Feathers Inn in Ludlow, Shropshire.

The Renaissance came late to England and, rather than following the Italian manner, tended to imitate the more Mannerist approach found in Germany and the Low Countries, using Flemish gabling and brickwork. The wealthy wool and other merchants built lavish mansions like Longleat House in Wiltshire and Hardwick Hall in Derbyshire. The Jacobean period in the early 17th century produced highly decorative domestic architecture like that of Hatfield House in Hertfordshire. It was Inigo Jones (1573–1652) who brought the formal classicism of the Italian Renaissance to England and the results can be seen at the Banqueting House in Whitehall, and parts of Wilton House in Wiltshire.

This classicism continued through the 17th century leaving the baroque and rococo with only a foothold in England compared to the Continent. Sir Christopher Wren, undoubtedly the leading 17th-century English architect, helped rebuild much of London after the Great Fire in 1666. He built a new St. Paul's and rebuilt 53 churches—two of the most famous being St. Bride's in Fleet Street and St. Mary-le-Bow. Other Wren masterpieces include the Royal Hospital at Greenwich, the Sheldonian Theatre in Oxford, and the library at Trinity College, Cambridge.

At the end of his life, Wren was eclipsed by such famous 18th-century architects as Sir John Vanbrugh (1664–1726), creator of Castle Howard and Blenheim Palace, and Sir Nicholas Hawksmoor (1661–1736). After 1720 the baroque influence declined and Palladianism took over, especially in domestic architecture. Great houses surrounded by parkland and natural landscapes dotted with classical sculptures and fountains like Holkham Hall were built by such architects as William Kent and Colen Campbell. Capability Brown was the foremost landscape artist of this period.

In the later 18th century a Classical Revival took place, led by such architects as Sir William Chambers and Robert Adam, whose Syon House near London and Kedleston Hall in Derbyshire are prime examples. The 18th century also saw the

---

IMPRESSIONS

This royall Throne of Kings, this sceptred Isle,
This earth of Majesty, this seate of Mars,
This other Eden, demy paradise . . .
—SHAKESPEARE, *RICHARD II*

England is the paradise of individuality, eccentricity, heresy, anomalies, hobbies and humours.
—GEORGE SANTAYANA, "THE BRITISH CHARACTER," *SOLILOQUIES IN ENGLAND,* 1922

laying out of whole terraces and crescents like Royal Crescent in Bath designed by John Wood. Similar schemes can be seen in Cheltenham and Brighton.

In the 19th century the types of buildings changed as a result of the Industrial Revolution. Factories, railroad stations, concert halls, and theaters were added to the roster of churches and domestic buildings. All kinds of earlier styles were interpreted—Romanesque, Byzantine, Gothic—new materials like glass and iron were used, and the mode of building changed, as many of the internal decorative elements like moldings were mass produced. England produced some fine architecture in the late Georgian and Regency periods by such architects as John Nash and Sir John Soane. From 1840 on, the English exhibited a preference for Gothic and Gothic Revival, which can be seen clearly in the Houses of Parliament, the Law Courts in London, the Natural History Museum, and the most controversial of all, the Albert Memorial. A few architects at the end of the century, like Charles Rennie Mackintosh, rejected the overdecoration and heaviness of this Victorian style and sought greater simplicity.

The famous architects of the early 20th century include Sir Edwin Lutyens (1869–1944) who built country houses, commercial buildings like the Reuters Building on Fleet Street, and laid out such grand schemes as the Cenotaph on Whitehall. He is also associated, of course, with the grand designs of British Delhi. Modern architecture as we know it really began after World War II. Many early modern buildings were created by immigrants en route to the United States including Walter Gropius. Much of modern British architecture is blockish and dull (just ask Prince Charles!), with some relief provided by such figures as Sir Hugh Casson and Sir Basil Spence.

LITERATURE

The most outstanding figure of all in England's literary heritage is William Shakespeare (1564–1616), but even without Shakespeare, English literature would still be among the richest in the world. From the Old English epic poem, *Beowulf*, to the works of the "angry young men" of the '50s, English literature is vast, and in this limited space I can only touch on the highlights.

The Old English poetry and historical prose found in such works as the *Anglo-Saxon Chronicle* of Alfred the Great's time gave way in the 13th and 14th centuries to so-called Middle English (Old Anglo-Saxon English enriched by the Norman) of which the great master was Geoffrey Chaucer, author of the *Canterbury Tales*, a rollicking series of often-bawdy tales. The literary highlight of the 15th century was *Le Morte d' Arthur*, Sir Thomas Malory's freehanded story about the legend of King Arthur and his court. Ballads were also popular storytelling devices in that century, a sort of continuation of the bardic epic tradition.

During the Tudor and Elizabethan era the literary stars were many—Sir Thomas More (*Utopia*), Edmund Spenser (*The Faerie Queen*), and Christopher Marlowe (*The Tragical History of Dr. Faustus*). Among poets the sonnet form adopted from an Italian verse model was popular and composed by such as Sir Philip Sidney and the greatest of them all, William Shakespeare.

The Elizabethan period was the golden era of the theater in England. London's first theater opened in 1576 in the Fields at Shoreditch, followed by the Curtain, and, in 1599, the most famous of all, the Globe, which belonged to Shakespeare and Marlowe.

The coming to the throne of the Stuarts ushered in the Jacobean period, when "rare Ben Jonson," who led the poets who met at the Mermaid Tavern in London, wrote some of his best satirical comedies, and John Donne ("never send to know for whom the bell tolls . . .") was at his finest. The translation of the Bible, known as the King James Version, was undertaken at this time under the auspices of James I, and it assumed its immortal place in literature.

By the mid-17th century, writers, like all English people, began to be divided in allegiance between the king and Parliament. The Cavalier poets, of whom Robert Herrick heads the list, wrote lyrical verse and backed the king. The literary giant of the mid-17th century was John Milton, a Pro-Parliamentarian and the author of *Paradise Lost,* who was considered even in his lifetime a genius. John Bunyan, a Baptist lay preacher also caught up in the Puritan cause, author of *Pilgrim's Progress,* an early prose work, was sent to prison after the restoration of the monarchy. After Charles II returned to the throne, theaters that had been closed by Cromwell were reopened, and literature took on a lighter, more lively tone, reflected in the plays of Sheridan and the diary of Samuel Pepys.

Throughout the 18th century, England's literary world was crowded with the output of geniuses and near-geniuses from the rising middle class. Among these were Daniel Defoe (*Robinson Crusoe* and *Moll Flanders*), Alexander Pope (*An Essay on Man*), Henry Fielding (*Tom Jones*), and a host of essayists and novelists. Most memorable in this period, however, is Samuel Johnson, whose *Dictionary of the English Language* made him the premier lexicographer and man of letters. His association with James Boswell from Scotland resulted in Johnson's becoming a major figure in literary annals, albeit through Boswell's writings. In Johnson's circle of close friends was another notable literary figure of the time, Oliver Goldsmith (*She Stoops to Conquer* and *The Vicar of Wakefield*).

To try to expound on the stars of the early 19th-century literary scene in England in limited space would be impossible, so I'll just mention several of the names known to everyone: William Blake, William Wordsworth, Samuel Taylor Coleridge, Lord Byron, John Keats, Percy Bysshe Shelley, Jane Austen, and Charles Lamb—but there are so many more. As you travel through the country, you will see birthplaces, residences, and burial places of many of these writers.

Now to the years that challenge a student of literature—the mid- and late 1800s when a broad literate middle-class public devoured the works of Charles Dickens, William Thackeray, the Brontë sisters, Matthew Arnold, Alfred Lord Tennyson, the Brownings, Lewis Carroll, George Eliot, George Meredith, Thomas Hardy, and Algernon Charles Swinburne, with a little heavier reading from John Ruskin thrown in.

Straddling the turn of the century but usually considered literary figures of modern times—from the early 1900s, it's true—are such notables as Rudyard Kipling, H. G. Wells, John Galsworthy, W. Somerset Maugham, Walter de la Mare, and Sir Arthur Conan Doyle. Writers of the 20th century include Robert Graves, Stephen Spender, W. H. Auden, Virginia Woolf, D. H. Lawrence, Aldous Huxley, Kingsley Amis, Graham Greene, George Orwell, E. M. Forster, Antonia Fraser, Ted Hughes, William Golding, Muriel Spark, and—not to be forgotten—Winston Churchill.

I could go on and on and on—and I still might well leave out your favorite English writer. In fact, I'm sure someone will ask, "But what about Jonathan Swift? George Bernard Shaw? Sir Walter Scott? Robert Burns? Robert Louis Stevenson? Joseph Conrad? Dylan Thomas? Doris Lessing?" My only defense might be that these novelists and poets are not English born, though they have certainly made their mark in English literature. There's no question about it—the British Isles are rich in literary greats, and I've only reminded you of *some* of them.

MUSIC

From the time the English monks' choirs surpassed those of Germany and France in singing the Gregorian chant (brought to this country in 597 by St. Augustine of Canterbury, Pope Gregory's missionary), and were judged second only to the choirs of Rome, music has been heard throughout England. Polyphonic music developed after the simple chant, and sacred vocal music was early accompanied by the organ. The first organ at Winchester was installed in the 10th century. One of the earliest written compositions was the polyphonic piece (a round), "Summer is Icumen In," with six parts.

Instruments commonly used in the Middle Ages—besides the organ found only in churches—were the fiddle, the lute, and the rebec, used in court circles for the entertainment of royalty and hangers-on. Plantagenet and Tudor monarchs had musicians at court, with Henry VIII in particular making himself known as a composer. He wrote sonnets for his lady loves and set them to music, the best known being "Greensleeves"; the British Museum contains some 34 manuscripts of Henry's compositions. So flourishing was music in England in the 16th century that Erasmus of Rotterdam reported after one of his visits: "They are so much occupied with music here that even the monks don't do anything else."

Music among the common people of the time may have been less polished but it was no less enthusiastic, as ditties and rounds were composed and heard in taverns and fields, the richness of the tunes compensating for the frequent vulgarity of the words. Some of the songs Shakespeare had his characters sing attest to the coarseness of the lyrics.

During the Tudor dynasty English cathedral music came into full flower. Also during these years masques—the forerunners of the opera—were frequently performed; these combined instrumental and vocal music, dancing, satire, recitations, and elaborate scenic effects.

Under Cromwell's Commonwealth, musicians were persecuted in the 1600s but they came back into glory with the restoration of the Stuart monarchy: Henry Purcell wrote the first English opera, *Dido and Aeneas*, in 1689. In the 18th century, Italian opera became the rage—even as John Gay satirized such productions in *The Beggar's Opera* in 1728. Handel, who became an English subject, composed many operas and oratorios in London, including *Messiah*, and other musicians followed (sometimes haltingly) in his train.

England's outstanding 19th-century contribution to the musical repertoire were the uniquely English operettas of Gilbert and Sullivan.

Many great names in the 20th-century music world are English: Sir Edward Elgar, Ralph Vaughan Williams, Sir William Walton, and Benjamin Britten, to name just a few.

Paul McCartney and John Lennon of the Beatles began what has been called in America "the British invasion." Since the 1960s, English rock musicians have often dominated the American music scene. Individual vocalists such as Phil Collins, David Bowie, Annie Lennox, and Sting, and guitarists such as Eric Clapton have been leading forces in popular music. But the biggest musical influence from England has been the rock bands: The Rolling Stones, The Who, Pink Floyd, Genesis, The Sex Pistols, and XTC. British rock's influence on Western popular music and culture has been and still is tremendous.

Boy George and George Michael continue the list of the music hall of fame. In the 1990s, many young British bands have looked to the 1960s for inspiration. Happy Mondays and Stone Roses are just two of the bands that have become household names in recent years. Manchester continues as a breeding ground for young bands. It is said that by the time many of these groups are "discovered" by the rest of the world they have already been washed up in the U.K.

4. LANGUAGE, RELIGION & FOLKLORE

LANGUAGE

Any visitor to England will surely experience communication problems. The already-mentioned William the Conqueror did more than transform Londor (or rather Westminster) into a royal capital. He and his nobles superimposed their Norman French on the country's original Anglo-Saxon language and thus originated English as it is spoken today. Both the richness and the maddening illogicality of our tongue are direct results of that concoction.

For an American it can be a minor shock to discover that the English in fact speak English. We Americans speak American. There are just enough differences between the two to result in crossed wires and occasional total communication breakdowns. For, although the British use words and phrases you think you understand, they often have quite different connotations from their U.S. equivalents.

When the British call someone "mean," they mean stingy. And "homely," meaning ugly or plain in America, becomes pleasant in England. "Calling" denotes a personal visit, not a phone call. But a person-to-person phone call is a "personal call." To "queue up" means to form a line, which they do at every bus stop. And whereas a "subway" is an underground pedestrian passage, the actual subway system is called "the Underground" or "the tube." The term "theatre" refers only to the live stage; movie theaters are "cinemas," and what's playing in them are "the pictures." And a "bomb," which suggests a disaster in America, means a success in England.

In a grocery store, canned goods become "tins," rutabagas become "swedes," eggplants become "aubergines," and endive is "chicory," while conversely chicory is "endive." Both cookies and crackers become "biscuits," which can be either "dry" or "sweet." That is, except graham crackers, which—unaccountably—are "digestives."

The going gets rougher when you're dealing with motor vehicles. When talking about the actual vehicle, very little means the same except for the word "car," unless you mean a truck, which is called a "lorry." In any case, gas is "petrol," the windshield is the "windscreen," and bumpers are "fenders." The trunk is the "boot" and what you do on the horn is "hoot."

Luckily most of us know that an English apartment is a "flat" and that an elevator is a "lift." And you don't rent a room or apartment, you "let" it. Although the ground floor is the ground floor, the second floor is the "first floor." And once you set up housekeeping, you don't vacuum, you "hoover."

Going clothes shopping? Then you should know that undershirts are called "vests" and undershorts are "pants" to the English, while long pants are called "trousers" and their cuffs are called "turn-ups." Panties are "knickers" and panty hose are "tights." Pullover sweaters can be called "jumpers" and little girls' jumpers are called "pinafores." If you're looking for diapers, ask for "nappies."

The education system offers such varied types of schools identified by an equally wide variety of terms that to explain them all to the general visitor would be too confusing. Briefly, however, the large English "public schools" (such as Eton) are similar to our large private prep schools (such as Andover). But the English also have other private, or "independent," schools on all levels. And all the above charge tuition. In addition, there are "state schools," which we would call public schools. These include "primary schools" and secondary "comprehensive schools," "modern schools," and "grammar schools" that are equivalent to our junior and senior high schools.

In school and elsewhere, the letter Z is pronounced "zed," and zero is "nought." And if you want to buy an after-school treat, a Popsicle is called an "iced lolly."

Please note that none of the above terms—except the last—are slang. If you really want a challenge in that arena, you can always take on cockney. The cockneys are indigenous Londoners, although strictly speaking the label refers only to people born within the sound of the bells of St. Mary-le-Bow in Cheapside.

The exact derivation of the word "cockney" is lost in the mist of antiquity, but it's supposed to have meant an "odd fellow." And the oddest feature about this fellow is undoubtedly the rhyming slang he concocted over the centuries, based on the rhyme—or the rhyme of a rhyme—that goes with a particular word or phrase. So take

IMPRESSIONS

For 'tis a low, newspaper, humdrum, law-suit Country.
—LORD BYRON, 1819–24

---

my advice and don't try to delve further, unless you happen to be Professor Higgins—pardon me—'iggins.

RELIGION

England is very different from the United States in that Church and State are inextricably intertwined. This relationship between Church and State dates back to the Reformation when Henry VIII broke with Rome in 1534, proclaimed himself "Supreme Head of the Church of England," confiscated Catholic treasuries and lands, and dissolved hundreds of monasteries and convents. After the religious conflicts of the 17th century, which defeated the attempts of the Stuarts to return England to Rome, the Church of England was secured and the law stated that the sovereign must be a member of the Church of England and must swear to uphold its doctrines. Thus today the monarch, Queen Elizabeth II, is the titular head of the Church of England or Anglican church while she reigns over a nation that grants freedom of worship to everyone. Britain is officially divided into two dioceses—Canterbury and York, the first the more powerful of the two. Besides these links between Church and State there are still others. The Church is not free to change either its doctrines or its form of worship, as originally defined in *The Book of Common Prayer* (compiled in 1549) without the specific assent of Parliament. Despite these legal and historical links, the Church of England is not fiscally subsidized by the State or by the Crown, but rather earns its income from its own capital, real estate, and communal contributions.

Although 60% of the population claim membership in the Church of England, only 8% of its baptized members attend on Easter Sunday. Contemporary Britain also contains a variety of Protestant and other sects: Baptists, Methodists, Quakers, Congregationalists, as well as Roman Catholics, Jews, and a growing number of Muslims and Hindus.

FOLKLORE

Although it's far too arcane to discuss here, England's history is rich in early myth and mystery, as anyone who has visited Stonehenge will have witnessed. The myth most often associated with England, though, is the Arthurian legend of Camelot, which originated in southwestern England and Wales. This story was published in literary form for the first time by Geoffrey of Monmouth in Norman France around 1135. It told of the birth of Arthur, his exploits with his knights of the Round Table, and the shattering of his idyllic kingdom by the adultery of Arthur's Queen Guinevere with his favorite knight, Lancelot, and by Arthur's search for the Holy Grail. Some historians even trace within the Arthurian legend certain exploits that, historically, were achieved by a mixture of Viking, Saxon, and even Roman military leaders. Every era, it seems, has produced its own version of the Arthurian legend from the medieval and Tudor versions by Sir Thomas Malory and Edmund Spenser, through the Victorian versions by William Morris, Tennyson, and Swinburne, to our very own 20th-century renderings by T. H. White and C. S. Lewis.

The other great legend that seems to have great resonance in England is the legend of Robin Hood and his merry men who stole from the rich and gave to the poor, and resisted the authority of the sheriff of Nottingham—a role model that seems to underlie the British love of justice and the fervor with which they root for the underdog.

5. FOOD & DRINK

FOOD

The reputation that Britain had for years for its soggy cabbage and tasteless dishes—which prompted the late British humorist George Mikes to write that "the Continentals have good food; the English have good table manners"—is no longer deserved. Contemporary London boasts many very fine restaurants indeed, and they're also found throughout the country.

MEALS & DINING CUSTOMS

Mealtimes are much the same as in the United States. Britain is famous for its enormous **breakfasts** of bacon, egg, grilled tomato, and fried bread—and although it has been replaced in some places by a continental variety, it can still be found at the finer hotels and other places. Kipper, which is the name given to a smoked herring, is also a popular breakfast dish. The finest come from the Isle of Man, Whitby, or Loch Fyne in Scotland. The herrings are split open and placed over oak chips and smoked slowly to produce a nice pale-brown smoked fish. **Lunch,** usually eaten between noon and 2pm, is often taken at the pub, or else consists of a sandwich on the run. **Afternoon tea** is still enjoyed by many and it may consist of a simple cup of tea or a formal tea that starts with tiny crustless sandwiches filled with cucumber or watercress, proceeds through scones or crumpets with jam and possibly clotted cream to cakes and tarts, all accompanied by a proper pot of tea. In London the tea at Brown's is quintessentially English, while the Ritz tea is an elaborate affair complete with orchestra and dancing. In the country teashops abound, and in Devon, Cornwall, and the West Country you'll find the best cream teas ever served, consisting of scones spread with jam and thick clotted Devonshire cream. A delicious treat indeed. It's a misconception to believe that "everything" stops for tea. People in Britain drink an average of four cups of tea a day, mainly at work. **Dinner** is usually enjoyed around 8pm and may consist of traditional English dishes or any number of ethnic cuisines that are currently found in London. **Supper** is traditionally a late-night meal usually eaten after the theater.

THE CUISINE

You don't have to travel around England to sample regional English dishes—you'll find them on many a London menu—but it's fun to see the regions and taste their bounty. On any pub menu you're likely to encounter such dishes as Cornish pasty and shepherd's pie. The first is traditionally made from the Sunday-meal leftovers consisting of chopped potato, carrot, onion, and seasoning mixed together and put into a pastry envelope and taken originally by the West Country fishermen on Monday for lunch. The second is a deep dish of chopped cooked beef mixed with onions and seasoning and covered with a layer of mashed potatoes and served hot. Another version is cottage pie, which is minced beef covered with potatoes and also served hot. The most common pub meal, though, is the ploughman's lunch—a traditional farm worker's lunch—consisting of a good chunk of local cheese, a hunk of homemade crusty white or brown bread, some butter, and a pickled onion or two, all washed down with ale. You will now find such variations as pâté and chutney replacing the onions and cheese. Cheese is still, however, the most common ingredient. Or you might find Lancashire hot pot, a stew of mutton, potatoes, kidneys, and onions (sometimes carrots). This concoction was originally put into a deep dish and set on the edge of the stove to cook slowly while the workers spent the day at the local mill.

Among appetizers, which are called "starters" in England, the most typical is potted shrimps (small buttered shrimps preserved in a jar), prawn cocktail, or smoked salmon. You might also be served pâté, or even "fish pie," which is very light fish pâté. If you're an oyster lover, try some of the famous Colchester oysters. Most menus will feature a variety of soups including cock-a-leekie (chicken soup flavored with leeks) and game soups that will often be flavored with sherry.

Among the best known and traditional of English dishes is, of course, roast beef and Yorkshire pudding. The pudding is made with a flour base and cooked under the joint, allowing the fat from the meat to drop onto it. The beef could easily be a large sirloin (rolled loin) which, so the story goes, was named by King James I (not Henry VIII as some claim) when he was a guest at Houghton Tower, Lancashire: "Arise, Sir Loin," he cried, as he knighted the joint with his dagger. Another dish that makes use of a batter similar to Yorkshire pudding is toad-in-the-hole, in which sausages are cooked in batter. Game, especially pheasant and grouse, is also a staple on British tables.

On the west coast, you'll find a not-to-be-missed delicacy, Morecambe Bay shrimp, and on any menu you'll find fresh seafood—cod, haddock, herring, plaice, and the aristocrat of flat fish, Dover sole. Cod and haddock are the most popular fish used in the making of that British tradition, fish-and-chips (chips, of course, are fried potatoes or french fries), which the true Briton covers with salt and vinegar.

The East End of London has quite a few interesting old dishes, among them tripe and onions. Dr. Johnson's favorite tavern, the Cheshire Cheese on Fleet Street, offers a beefsteak-kidney-mushroom-and-game pudding in a suet case in winter and a pastry case in summer. East Enders can still be seen on Sunday at the Jellied Eel stall by Petticoat Lane, eating eel or perhaps cockles (small clams), mussels, whelks, and winkles—all small shellfish eaten with a touch of vinegar. Eel-pie-and-mash shops can still be found in London purveying what is really a minced-beef pie topped with flaky pastry and served with mashed potatoes and a portion of jellied eel.

The British call desserts "sweets," or "pudding." Trifle is perhaps the most famous of English desserts—a sponge cake soaked in brandy or sherry, coated with fruit or jam, and topped with a cream custard. A "fool," such as gooseberry fool, is a light cream dessert whipped up from seasonal fruits. Regional sweets include such items as the northern "flitting" dumpling consisting of dates, walnuts, and syrup mixed with other ingredients and made into a pudding that can be sliced easily and carried along when one is "flitting" from one place to another. Similarly, "hurry pudding" or hasty pudding, a dish from Newcastle, is said to have been invented by those avoiding the bailiff. It consists of stale bread (some dried fruit and milk are added before it is put into the oven).

Cheese is traditionally served after dessert as a savory. There are many regional cheeses, the best known being Cheddar, a good, solid, mature cheese. Others are the semismooth-textured Caerphilly from a beautiful part of Wales, and Stilton, a blue-veined crumbly cheese, often enriched with a glass of port.

DRINK

Tea Most of the English drink tea in the morning, and it's usually superior to the American tea-bag-in-lukewarm-water variety. It usually comes in a pot accompanied by milk and sugar.

IMPRESSIONS

Even a boiled egg tastes of mutton fat in England.
—NORMAN DOUGLAS, *OLD CALABRIA,* 1915

Water and Soft Drinks   Tap water is safe to drink, but you will probably have to ask for water with your meal as it is not automatically served. Neither is ice. Popular brands of soda and soft drinks are available, but you may want to try some of Schweppes bottled waters such as "bitter lemon."

Liquor, Beer, and Wine   London pubs serve a variety of cocktails, but their stock in trade is beer—brown beer or "bitter," blond beer or lager, and very dark beer, which is called "stout." The standard English draft beer is (a) much stronger than American beer and (b) is served "with the chill off" because it doesn't taste good cold. Lager is always chilled and stout can be served either way. One of the most significant changes in English drinking habits has been the popularity of wine bars, and you will find many to patronize, some turning into discos late at night.

Britain is not known for its wine, although it does produce some medium-sweet fruity white wines. Its cider, though, is famous and very potent in contrast to the American variety.

Whisky (spelled without the "e") in England refers to scotch. Canadian and Irish whiskey are also available, but only the very best-stocked bars have American bourbon and rye. While you're in England you may want to try the very English drink Pimm's, a mixture developed by James Pimm, owner of a popular London oyster house in the 1840s. Though it can be consumed on the rocks, it's usually served as a Pimm's Cup—a drink that will have any number and variety of ingredients depending on which part of the world (read Empire) you're in. Here just for fun is a typical recipe: Take a very tall glass filled with ice. Add a thin slice of lemon (or orange), add a cucumber spike (or a curl of cucumber rind) and two ounces of Pimm's liquor, then fill with a splash of either lemon or club soda, 7-Up, or Tom Collins' mix.

6. SPORTS & RECREATION

SPORTS

Football—called soccer in the United States—is the most popular British sport (with about 35 million devotees) and it is taken so seriously that it has led to widely publicized riots in which people were killed. It's a fast game played by two teams of 11 for 90 minutes (two halves of 45 minutes each); they are allowed to use only their feet and their heads to move the ball and score goals by kicking it between two fixed goalposts.

Rugby, which supposedly originated at the famous public school in Warwickshire, is closer to American football insofar as both the ball and the goalposts are similarly shaped and the ball is thrown and kicked. In England it's primarily an upper-middle-class sport played at the private schools. Welsh rugby, though, is a more popular sport.

In summer, **cricket** and **tennis** are the main sports. Cricket is "the most English of games" conducted in a polite and gracious manner by two teams of 11 wearing white flannels, who adhere to the umpire's judgments without demur. From this game came such English phrases as "a sticky wicket" and "it's not cricket." An inning is one turn at bat by each side. Games can last for 1 or 5 days, as they do in the International Test Matches. Players bat in pairs from opposite ends of the pitch, a 22-yard-long patch of well-rolled and mowed grass at the center of the oval field that can be as big as a football field. The bowlers of the opposite team pitch the small hard ball with a straight arm so that the ball bounces in front of the batman, aiming to dislodge the wicket (an assemblage of three upright stumps with a "bail" slotted across the top of them). The intricacies of the game are many, but the whole performance on a sunny weekend afternoon—complete with picnic or afternoon tea—is quintessentially English.

The **fox hunt** is also traditionally English. Men and women on horseback sporting so-called "pink coats" (actually blood red) race across the fields of England following a pack of hounds in pursuit of their elusive but badly outnumbered fox or hare. Brits are great animal lovers, and many citizens view this as a cruel sport and loudly protest against it.

Horse racing is a distinctly royal pastime. The "flat" racing season lasts from late March until November and the classic race is the Derby run at Epsom Downs in early June. Steeplechasing, which involves jumping over fences and hedges, is more thrilling and certainly more dangerous than "flat" racing. The most famous steeplechase is the Grand National, held annually at Liverpool's Aintree.

RECREATION

BICYCLING   Bicycles are forbidden on most highways, trunk roads, and on what the English call "dual carriageways" (two-lane highways). In town, city, and country the bike is a great way to get around. If you're interested in a cycling holiday in England, contact the Cyclists' Touring Club, Cotterell House, 69 Meadrow, Godalming, Surrey GU7 3HS (tel. 0483/417217). Membership costs £22.50 ($33.80) a year.

BOATING   England is crisscrossed by historic canals and waterways, the most popular being the Norfolk Broads in East Anglia. You can also take canal and river cruises in Bath, York, Bristol, and Stratford-upon-Avon. For more information about boat rentals, contact the Association of Pleasure Craft Operators, 35A High St., Newport, Shropshire, TF10 8JW (tel. 0952/813572).

GOLFING   Hundreds of excellent courses are found all over England. If you're an avid golfer, consider buying *The Golf Course Guide to Great Britain and Ireland,* by Donald Steel (Collins, £7.95 [$11.90]), available in British bookstores.

HIKING   Hiking, or "rambling," is one of the most popular British activities. In England and Wales alone there are some 100,000 miles, maybe more, of footpaths and trails—many historical, like the Pennine Way in Yorkshire. Contact the Ramblers' Association, 1–5 Wandsworth Rd., London SW8 2XX (tel. 071/582-6878), which publishes a quarterly magazine and also lists B&Bs near the trails.

TENNIS   This is a favorite summer game and all cities and towns have municipal courts. Ask at local tourist offices for information.

WATER SPORTS   England has many lakes and rivers, and locals do fish and swim in them, but always check locally with the tourist office about whether they are indeed safe. Better to use indoor municipal pools or hotel pools.

The best beaches in England are found on the Cornish coast, but they're crowded in summer. Some visitors from hotter climes find the waters around Great Britain too cold for comfort.

IMPRESSIONS

England is one of the weird mysteries of God's afterthought.
—HENRY ADAMS, LETTER TO JOHN HAY, DECEMBER 1990

I take England "for better for worse"; that is the only way of making it better.
—G. K. CHESTERTON, LETTER TO A STRANGER WHO ASKED HIS ADVICE, c. 1909

7. RECOMMENDED BOOKS, FILMS & RECORDINGS

BOOKS

GENERAL & HISTORY

Anthony Sampson's *The Changing Anatomy of Britain* (Random House, 1982) still gives great insight into the idiosyncrasies of English society. Winston Churchill's *History of the English-Speaking Peoples* (Dodd Mead, 1956) is a tour de force in four volumes, while *The Gathering Storm* (Houghton-Mifflin, 1986) captures London and Europe on the brink of World War II.

My Love Affair with England, by Susan Allan Toth (Ballantine, 1992), tells of England's "many-layered past," and includes such little tidbits as why English marmalade tastes good only when consumed as part of a real (make that greasy) English breakfast. *Publishers Weekly* called it "the print equivalent of a nice cup of tea."

Britons: Forging the Nation (1707-1837), by Linda Colley (Yale University Press, 1992), took more than a decade to finish. Ms. Colley takes the reader from the date of the Act of Union (formally joining Scotland and Wales to England) up to the succession of the adolescent Victoria to the British throne. *Children of the Sun,* by Martin Green (Basic Books, 1976), portrays the "decadent" Twenties and the lives of such people as Randolph Churchill, Rupert Brooke, the Prince of Wales, and Christopher Isherwood.

In *A Writer's Britain* (Knopf, 1979), contemporary English author Margaret Drabble takes the reader on a tour of the sacred and haunted literary landscapes of England, places that inspired Hardy and Woolf, Spenser and Marvell. It's well illustrated, too.

Outsiders often paint more penetrating portraits than residents of any culture ever can. In England's case there are many who have expressed their views of the country at different periods. An early 18th-century portrait is provided by K. P. Moritz in his *Journeys of a German in England in 1782* (Holt, Rinehart & Winston, 1965), about his travels from London to the Midlands. Nathaniel Hawthorne recorded his impressions in *Our Old Home* (1863) as did Ralph Waldo Emerson in *English Traits* (1856). For a marvelous ironic portrait of mid-19th-century Victorian British morals, manners, and society, seek out *Taine's Notes on England* (1872). Henry James comments on turn-of-the-century England in his *English Hours.* In *A Passage to England* (St. Martins, 1959) Nirad Chaudhuri analyzes Britain and the British in a delightful, humorous book—a process continued today by such authors as Salman Rushdie, V. S. Naipaul, and Paul Theroux, among many. Among the more interesting portraits written by natives are Cobbet's *Rural Rides* (1830), depicting early 19th-century England; *In Search of England* (Methuen, 1927) by H. V. Morton; and *English Journey* by J. B. Priestley (Harper, 1934). For what's really going on behind that serene Suffolk village scene, read Ronald Blythe's *Akenfield: Portrait of an English Village* (Random House, 1969).

ART & ARCHITECTURE

For general reference, there's the huge multivolume *Oxford History of English Art* (Oxford University Press, 1982), and also the *Encyclopedia of British Art,* by David Bindman (Thames Hudson, 1988). *Painting in Britain 1530-1790* (Penguin, 1978) by Ellis Waterhouse covers British art from the Tudor miniaturists to Gainsborough, Reynolds, and Hogarth, while *English Art, 1870-1940* (Oxford University Press, 1979) by Dennis Farr covers the modern period.

On architecture, for sheer, amusing opinionated entertainment there's John Betjeman's *Ghastly Good Taste—the Rise and Fall of English Architecture* (St. Martin's Press, 1971). Betjeman is well known for his British TV programs on buildings. *A History of English Architecture* by Peter Kidson, Peter Murray, and Paul Thompson (Penguin, 1979) covers the subject from Anglo-Saxon to modern times. Nikolaus Pevsner's *The Best Buildings of England: An Anthology* (Viking, 1987) and his *Outline of European Architecture* (Penguin, 1960) are both eloquent. *Architecture in Britain 1530–1830,* by John Summerson (Penguin, 1971), concentrates on the great periods of Tudor, Georgian, and Regency architecture. Mark Girouard has written several books on British architecture including *The Victorian Country House* (Country Life, 1971) and *Life in the English Country House* (Yale University Press, 1978), a fascinating social/architectural history from the Middle Ages to the 20th century complete with handsome illustrations.

ABOUT LONDON

London Perceived (Hogarth, 1986), by novelist and literary critic V. S. Pritchett, is a witty portrait of the city—its history, art, literature, and life. Virginia Woolf's *The London Scene: Five Essays* (Random House, 1986) brilliantly depicts the London of the 1930s—a literary gem. *In Search of London* (Methuen, 1988), by H. V. Morton, is filled with anecdotal history and still well worth reading even though it was written in the 1950s.

In *London: The Biography of a City* (Penguin, 1980), popular historian Christopher Hibbert paints a very lively portrait. For some real 17th-century history, you can't beat the *Diary of Samuel Pepys* (written 1660–69), and for the flavor of the 18th century, try Daniel Defoe's *Tour Thro' London About the Year 1725* (Ayer, 1929).

Americans in London, by Brian N. Morton (William Morrow, 1986), is a street-by-street guide to the clubs, homes, and favorite pubs of more than 250 illustrious Americans—Mark Twain, Joseph Kennedy, Dwight Eisenhower, and Sylvia Plath—who made London a temporary home. The *Guide to Literary London* by George Williams (Batsford, 1988) charts a series of literary tours through London from Chelsea to Bloomsbury. *The Capital Companion* by Peter Gibson (Webb & Bower, 1985) contains more than 1,200 alphabetical entries, and is filled with facts and anecdotes about the streets of London and their inhabitants.

The Architect's Guide to London by Renzo Salvadori (Reed International, 1990) documents 100 landmark buildings with photographs and maps. *Nairn's London* by Ian Nairn (Penguin, 1988) is a stimulating, opinionated discourse on London's buildings. Donald Olsen's *The City as a Work of Art: London, Paris, and Vienna* (Yale University Press, 1986) is a well-illustrated text tracing the evolution of these great cities. *London One: The Cities of London and Westminster* and *London Two: South* (Penguin, 1984) are works of love by well-known architectural writers Bridget Cherry and Nikolaus Pevsner. David Piper's *The Artist's London* (Oxford University Press, 1982) does what the title suggests—captures the city that artists have portrayed. In *Victorian and Edwardian London* (Batsford, 1969), John Betjeman expresses his great love of those eras and their great buildings.

FICTION & BIOGRAPHY

Among English writers are found some of the greatest exponents of mystery and suspense novels from which a reader can get a good feel for English life both urban and rural. Agatha Christie, P. D. James, and Dorothy Sayers are a few of the familiar names, but the great London character is, of course, Sherlock Holmes of Baker Street, created by Arthur Conan Doyle. Any of these writers will give pleasure and insight into your London experience.

England's literary heritage is so vast that it's hard to select particular titles, but here are a few favorites. Master storyteller Charles Dickens re-creates Victorian London in such books as *Oliver Twist, David Copperfield,* and his earlier satirical *Sketches by Boz.*

Edwardian London and the '20s and '30s is captured wonderfully in any of Evelyn Waugh's social satires and comedies; any work from the Bloomsbury group will also prove enlightening, like Virginia Woolf's *Mrs. Dalloway,* which peers beneath the surface of the London scene. For a portrait of wartime London there's Elizabeth Bowen's *The Heat of the Day* (1949); for an American slant on England and London there's Henry James's *The Awkward Age.* Colin MacInnes's novels—*City of Spades* (1957) and *Absolute Beginners* (1959)—focus on more recent social problems.

Among contemporaries, Margaret Drabble and Iris Murdoch are both challenging, and there are so many more.

Among 18th-century figures, there's a great biography of Samuel Johnson by his friend James Boswell, whose *Life of Samuel Johnson* (Modern Library College Editions, 1964) was first published in 1791. Antonia Fraser has written several lively biographies of English monarchs and political figures, including Charles II and Oliver Cromwell. Her most recent is *The Wives of Henry VIII* (Knopf, 1992), telling the sad story of the six women foolish enough to marry the Tudor monarch.

Another great Tudor monarch, Elizabeth I, emerges in a fully rounded portrait: *The Virgin Queen, Elizabeth I, Genius of the Golden Age* (Addison-Wesley, 1992), by historian Christopher Hibbert.

Another historian, Anne Somerset, wrote *Elizabeth I* (St. Martin's, 1992), which was hailed by some critics as the most "readable and reliable" portrait of England's most revered monarch to have emerged since 1934.

No woman—or man, for that matter—had greater influence on London than did Queen Victoria during her long reign (1837–1901). The Duchess of York (Prince Andrew's estranged wife, "Fergie") along with Benita Stoney, a professional researcher, captures the era in *Victoria and Albert: A Family Life at Osborne House* (Prentice Hall, 1991). One reviewer said that HRH writes about "England's 19th-century rulers not as historical figures but as a loving couple and caring parents."

Another point of view is projected in *Victoria: The Young Queen,* by Monica Charlot (Blackwell, 1991), the first volume in a projected biographical series. This book has been praised for its "fresh information"; it traces the life of Victoria until the death of her husband, Prince Albert, in 1861. Queen Elizabeth II granted Charlot access to the Royal Archives.

In *Elizabeth II, Portrait of a Monarch* (St. Martin's, 1992), Douglas Keay drew on interviews with Prince Philip and Prince Charles to tell a lively story.

Each year sees new releases of biographies and autobiographies of English literary and theatrical figures. Most are quickly forgotten, but some remain to tantalize.

Richard Ellman's *Oscar Wilde* (Knopf, 1988) is a masterpiece revealing such Victorian-era personalities as Lillie Langtry, Gilbert and Sullivan, and Henry James along the way. Quintessential English playwright Noël Coward and the London he inhabited along with the likes of Nancy Mitford, Cecil Beaton, John Gielgud, Laurence Olivier and Vivien Leigh, Evelyn Waugh, and Rebecca West are captured in Cole Lesley's *Remembered Laughter* (Knopf, 1977). More recently *The Lives of John Lennon* by Albert Goldman (William Morrow, 1988) traces the life of this most famous of all '60s musicians.

The biography of an English great that captured the most attention in 1992 was *Laurence Olivier: A Biography,* by Donald Spoto (HarperCollins, 1992). The life of the century's greatest actor was filled with scandal and triumphs. The career of this son of an Anglican priest is traced through all his hits and disappointments, including three failed marriages. Spoto provides anecdote and analysis for Olivier's most famous roles, including Macbeth.

Dickens, by Peter Ackroyd (Harper Perennial, 1992), is a study of the painful childhood of the novelist. It's a massive volume, tracing everything from the reception of his first novel, *The Pickwick Papers,* to his scandalous desertion of his wife.

The most recent releases have included *Wild Spirit: The Story of Percy Bysshe Shelley,* by Margaret Morley (Hodder & Stoughton, 1992), a fictionalized biography of the poet (1792–1822). *Gertrude Jekyll,* by Sally Festing (Viking, 1992), paints a portrait of the woman (1843–1932) called "the greatest artist in horticulture." *Anthony Trollope,* by Victoria Glendinning (Knopf, 1993), is a provocative portrait of the English novelist (1815–1882). *Lawrence and the Women: The Intimate Life of D. H. Lawrence,* by Elaine Feinstein (HarperCollins, 1993), examines involvements with female friends and lovers of this passionately sensitive novelist (1885–1930).

FILMS

The British film industry used to be much more important than it is today, enjoying a golden era roughly from 1929 to 1939. The country's foremost director was Alfred Hitchcock, who made the first English talkie, *Blackmail,* in 1929. Other masterpieces followed, like *The Thirty-Nine Steps* (1935), *The Lady Vanishes* (1938), and *Jamaica Inn* (1939), all made before he left for Hollywood and even greater glory.

Another famous figure in English cinema was Hungarian Alexander Korda, who settled in London in 1933 and made such memorable movies as *The Private Life of Henry VIII,* starring Charles Laughton, and *The Private Life of Don Juan* (1934), the last film of Douglas Fairbanks.

In the '40s David Lean emerged as a major director, making such films as *Blithe Spirit* (1944), an adaptation of Noël Coward's play, and *Brief Encounter* (1945), which some feel is his paramount achievement.

After the war J. Arthur Rank formed the Rank Organization, which produced an array of films, among them Olivier's *Henry V* and *Hamlet,* which were acclaimed all over the world.

Carol Reed is remembered for the memorable *Odd Man Out* (1946), with a screenplay by Graham Greene, and *The Third Man* (1949), starring Orson Welles.

Many movies and British actors have portrayed the British scene. Among some of the great movies that you might want to see again are *Kind Hearts and Coronets,* in which Alec Guinness played all the members of the family; *The Lady Killers,* made in the '60s; and *The Mouse That Roared* and *I'm All Right Jack,* both starring Peter Sellers. *Oliver Twist* with Alec Guinness as Fagin and *Great Expectations* are two real classics. In the '60s Tony Richardson established himself with such English hits as *A Taste of Honey* and *The Loneliness of the Long Distance Runner.* Another '60s movie depicting the intellectual British middle class was *Sunday Bloody Sunday,* starring Glenda Jackson and Peter Finch. Ken Russell came on the scene at the same time with his lustrous *Women in Love.*

In the 1990s several English films have received world attention, including *Antonia & Jane* (1991), the work of a young English director, Beeban Kidron, who has been called an "English Woody Allen." This comedy explores the friendship between two unhappy Londoners.

The producing and directing team of "Merchant and Ivory," as they are known, continues to enchant the world after giving moviegoers *A Room with a View* and *Maurice.* Their latest—some say their greatest—is *Howards End,* which received nine Academy Award nominations, including best picture, best screenplay (adaptation), best actress, and best supporting actress. Released in 1992, this Merchant-Ivory adaptation is based on E. M. Forster's great novel. Vanessa Redgrave as Ruth Wilcox played the dying mistress of Howards End, a country farmhouse, Anthony Hopkins her husband. But Emma Thompson, playing Margaret Schlegel, generated the most attention, winning the Golden Globe Award and the New York Film Critics Circle's prize, among other acting honors.

Generating equal excitement in 1992 and 1993 is *The Crying Game,* which garnered six Oscar nominations (including best picture) in 1993. Often compared to James Mason's *Odd Man Out, The Crying Game* is a fearless romantic melodrama, with musings on race, sex, terrorism, and the IRA. It's set mainly in London. This tale of sexual obsession, starring Neil Jordan, is full of surprises—a sexy and violent film.

RECORDINGS

MEDIEVAL & RENAISSANCE MUSIC

For an English version of Gregorian chant, seek out *A Feather on the Breath of God,* featuring compositions (written in 1098) of Saint Hildegard, performed by a group called Gothic Voices. Directed by Christopher Page, it was recorded in the Church of St. Jude on the Hill in Hampstead, London, and produced by the Musical Heritage Society, Ocean, New Jersey (MHS-4889).

The courtly music of the troubadours is reputed to have been performed with skill (at least during his youth) by the Renaissance monarch Henry VIII, and by dozens of other musicians who composed and performed sophisticated and sometimes coyly flirtatious songs for the distraction and amusement of their aristocratic guests. Good examples of the music performed at the court of Elizabeth I are the works of composer Thomas Morley (1557-1602), which have been recorded by the Deller Consort on such titles as *Now Is the Month of Maying: Madrigal Masterpieces* (Vanguard BG 604).

For a taste of England's Renaissance church music, best exemplified by English composer William Byrd (1540-1632), listen to his *Cantiones Sacrae: 1589* performed by the Choir of New College, Oxford, and recorded in the New College Chapel on London Records (London CRD 3408).

ORCHESTRAL & OPERATIC WORKS

Henry Purcell's *Dido and Aeneas* is widely available with different performers. For an example of Purcell's orchestral music for horns, find *The Virtuoso Trumpet,* performed by trumpeter Maurice André, accompanied by the Academy of St. Martin-in-the-Fields, and conducted by Neville Marriner (RCA Red Seal CRL 3-1430).

John Gay's *The Beggar's Opera* (first performed in 1728) is available performed by Britain's National Philharmonic Orchestra and the London Opera Chorus on Polygram Records (London LDR 72008).

Although the debate continues about whether or not George Frideric Handel (brought to the English court by the German-born monarch George I) should be classified as an English composer, certainly his *Water Music,* first performed on July 17, 1717, during a royal procession along the Thames, conjures up 18th-century London. There's a fine recording by the English Chamber Orchestra, conducted by Raymond Leppard (Phillips 6500-047).

The works of the beloved British team of Sir Arthur Sullivan (composer) and Sir W. S. Gilbert (librettist) are widely available. *The Mikado,* for example, performed by the Pro Arte Orchestra and the Glyndebourne Festival Chorus, and conducted by Sir Malcolm Sargent, is available on Angel Records (3573 B/L).

The compositions of Sir Edward Elgar are musical tributes to the splendor and pageantry of the British Empire. The favorite composer of Edward VII, for whom he wrote two coronation marches, Elgar's music can be heard on a recording of *The Pomp and Circumstance Marches,* performed by Britain's Philharmonia Orchestra, conducted by Andrew Davis (CBS Records/Masterworks IM 37755).

England's modern master, Ralph Vaughan Williams, has been widely recorded.

The Symphony No. 3 (*Pastoral*), performed by the London Symphony Orchestra (Chandos Records CHAN 8594), and *A Sea Symphony,* performed by the London Symphony Orchestra and Chorus—with André Previn conducting, and Heather Harper, soprano, and John Shirley-Quirk, baritone—(RCA 6237-2RC), are both fine.

Benjamin Britten's *Ceremony of Carols* performed by the Choir of St. John's College, Cambridge (Argo Records ZRG 5440) and his *Variations for a String Orchestra,* performed by the London Philharmonic Orchestra, with Roger Best, viola (Chandos Records CHAN 8514), are both fine examples of this preeminent British composer.

RECENT RELEASES

In the 1960s, record impresarios claimed that for a pop recording to be noticed by American audiences, its chances were greatly increased if it originated in Britain. The U.S. airwaves were flooded with music by British-based musical artists whose names later became household words around the world. Later, punk rock and an entirely new generation of musical artists emerged. Their numbers are legion, their tastes range from mildly provocative to deliberately outrageous, and no list could possibly include them all. Here follows, however, a representational and highly subjective selection of some of the most visible:

The Beatles, *Past Masters* (Vols. I and II) (Capitol CDP 7-900-432 and CDP 7-900-442), is a retrospective collection of this influential group. Equally important is the Beatles's milestone album, *Sergeant Pepper* (Capitol 2653), released in 1967, which is considered both a musical watershed and a sociological landmark that altered the perceptions of a generation.

The Rolling Stones's *Flashpoint* (Sony/CBS Records CK 47-456) is a textbook study of the spirit of rock and roll, with Eric Clapton performing as a guest ace on a track entitled "Little Red Rooster." Another Rolling Stone great is *Exile on Main Street* (Sony/CBS CGK 40489).

Liquidizer (SBK Records CDP-944-80), by Jesus Jones, a British rock group, combines drums, bass guitar, keyboard, and vocal, meshing high-tech drumbeats with wild guitars. One of this album's tracks, "Right Here, Right Now," became a big hit on alternative radio stations.

FOLK MUSIC

Flower of Scotland is by the Corries (BBC ZCD 844), a leading Scottish folk-music group. The title song, appealing to Scottish pride, is now the unofficial national anthem of Scotland, and usually sung lustily by Scottish audiences at football (soccer) and tennis matches throughout Britain.

In the same folkloric vein is a celebration of Irish (and to a lesser degree, English) music compiled by the BBC, entitled *Bringing It All Back Home* (BBC CD844/REF 844). This is the recorded result of a $1.5-million study—funded partly by the BBC—tracing musical themes of American and Australian folk and blues music back to Irish, English, and Scottish roots. The recording includes tracks by such artists as Sinead O'Connor, the Everly Brothers, Kate Bush, Bob Dylan, Pete Seeger, the Waterboys, and Thin Lizzy, and is considered of major interest to sociologists, musical historians, and folk-music fans.

Richard Thompson, who performs on *Amnesia* (Capitol C4-48845), has been reviewed as one of the most unusual and iconoclastic of modern British folk performers. His melodies include the guitar, the mandolin, and the hammer dulcimer. His lyrics showcase both political and social satire, as well as soulfully nostalgic ballads.

The Pogues' *Rum, Sodomy, and the Lash* (Stiff Records 222701) was recorded by this half-English, half-Irish group, based in London. It's folk and rock music with a decidedly funky (sometimes shocking) twist.

On Benjamin Britten's *Song Cycles* (Chandos CHAN-8514), an unusual arrangement of folk songs and poems by mystic William Blake is performed by baritone Benjamin Luxon and pianist David Willison.

PLANNING A TRIP TO ENGLAND

This chapter is devoted to the where, when and how of your trip—the advance-planning issues required to get it together and take to the road.

After deciding where to go, most people have two fundamental questions: What will it cost? and How do I get there? This chapter will answer both these questions and also resolve other important issues such as when to go, what pretrip preparations are needed, where to obtain more information about the destination, and many more.

1. INFORMATION, ENTRY REQUIREMENTS & MONEY

SOURCES OF INFORMATION

In the U.S.A. & Canada

Before you go, you can obtain general information from the following British Tourist Authority Offices.

Atlanta: 2580 Cumberland Pkwy., Atlanta, GA 30339-3909 (tel. 404/432-9635).

Chicago: 625 N. Michigan Ave., Suite 1510, Chicago, IL 60611-1977 (tel. 312/787-0490).

Los Angeles: World Trade Center, 350 Figueroa St., Suite 450, Los Angeles, CA 90071 (tel. 213/628-3525).

New York: 551 Fifth Ave., New York, NY 10017 (tel. 212/986-2200).

Toronto: 111 Avenue Rd., Suite 450, Toronto, ON M5R 3J8 (tel. 416/925-6326).

A good travel agent can also provide tourist information. And always check out the travel sections of newspapers (such as the weekly section in the Sunday edition of *The*

New York Times) and magazines like *Travel & Leisure* and *Traveler*. If you feel like doing some library work, ask your librarian for the *Reader's Guide to Periodical Literature* (a comprehensive index of recently published magazine articles); look up England or your specific city of interest.

ENTRY REQUIREMENTS

DOCUMENTS All U.S. citizens, Canadians, Australians, New Zealanders, and South Africans must have a passport with at least 2 months' remaining validity. No visa is required. The Immigration officer will also want proof of your intention to return to your point of origin (usually a round-trip ticket) and visible means of support while you're in Britain. If you're planning to fly from, say, the U.S. to the U.K. and then on to a country that requires a visa (India, for example), it's wise to secure that visa before your arrival in Britain.

CUSTOMS Visitors from overseas entering England may bring in 200 cigarettes and 1 quart of liquor. If you come from the European Economic Community (EC), you're allowed 300 cigarettes and 1 quart of liquor, provided you bought these items and paid tax on them in that EC country. There is no limit on money, film, or other items for your own use, except that all drugs other than medical supplies are illegal. Commercial goods such as video films and nonpersonal items will require posting a bond and will take a number of hours to clear Customs. Importing live birds or animals is forbidden, and they will be destroyed.

U.S. citizens returning home who have been away for 48 hours or more are allowed to bring back, once every 30 days, $400 worth of merchandise duty free. You'll be charged a flat rate of 10% duty on the next $1,000 worth of purchases. Be sure to have your receipts handy. On gifts, the duty-free limit is $50.

MONEY

Before leaving home it's advisable to secure traveler's checks and a small amount of foreign currency to cover costs on arrival overseas. Also take along about $200 in cash.

CURRENCY/CASH

The British currency is the **pound sterling (£),** made up of 100 **pence (p),** which is used throughout the United Kingdom. Banknotes are issued in £1, £5, £10, £20, and £50 denominations. Coins come in 1p, 2p, 5p, 10p, 50p, and £1.

At this writing, $1 equals approximately 66p (or £1=$1.50), and this was the rate of exchange used to calculate the dollar values given in this guide (rounded to the nearest nickel). This rate fluctuates from time to time and may not be the same when you travel to the U.K., so please use the table on page 31 only as a general guide.

CURRENCY EXCHANGE

Many hotels in England simply will not accept a dollar-denominated check, and if they do, they'll certainly charge for the conversion. In some cases they'll accept countersigned traveler's checks or a credit card, but if you're prepaying a deposit for hotel reservations, it's cheaper and easier to pay with a check drawn upon a British bank.

This can be arranged by a large commercial bank or by a currency specialist like **Ruesch International,** 1350 Eye St. NW, Washington, DC 20005 (tel. 202/408-1200, or toll free 800/424-2923), which can perform a wide variety of conversion-related financial transactions for individual travelers. To place an order, call them and tell them the type and amount of the sterling-denominated check you need. Ruesch will quote a U.S. dollar equivalent, adding a $2 fee per check as their service fee. After receiving your dollar-denominated personal check for the agreed-upon amount, Ruesch will mail you a sterling-denominated bank draft, drawn at a British bank and payable to whatever party you specified, for the agreed-upon amount. Ruesch will also convert checks expressed in foreign currency into U.S. dollars, provide foreign currencies in cash from more than 120 countries, and sell traveler's checks payable in either dollars or any of six foreign currencies, including pounds sterling. In addition to its Washington, D.C., office, Ruesch maintains offices in New York, Los Angeles, Chicago, Atlanta, and Boston. Through phone orders, however, the Washington, D.C., office can supply any of the bank draft and traveler's check services mentioned above. Ruesch will mail brochures and information packets upon request.

TRAVELER'S CHECKS

Traveler's checks are the safest way to carry cash while traveling. Most banks will give you a better exchange rate for traveler's checks than for cash. If you can, purchase them in pound denominations. The following are the major issuers of traveler's checks:

American Express (tel. toll free 800/221-7282 in the U.S. and Canada) charges a 1% commission. Checks are free to members of the American Automobile Association.

Barclay's Bank/Bank of America (tel. toll free 800/221-2426 in the U.S. and Canada). Through Barclay's subsidiary, Interpayment Services, VISA traveler's checks are available in either U.S. dollars or British pounds.

THE BRITISH POUND & THE U.S. DOLLAR

£	U.S.$	£	U.S.$
.05	.08	15	22.50
.10	.15	20	30.00
.25	.38	25	37.50
.50	.75	30	45.00
.75	1.15	35	52.50
1	1.50	40	60.00
2	3.00	45	67.50
3	4.50	50	75.00
4	6.00	55	82.50
5	7.50	60	90.00
6	9.00	65	97.50
7	10.50	70	105.00
8	12.00	75	112.50
9	13.50	100	150.00
10	15.00	125	187.50

Citicorp (tel. toll free 800/645-6556 in the U.S. and Canada) issues checks in U.S. dollars, pounds, or German marks.

MasterCard International/Thomas Cook International (tel. toll free 800/223-9920 in the U.S., or 212/974-5695, collect, from the rest of the world).

Each of these agencies will refund your checks if they are lost or stolen, upon sufficient documentation of their serial numbers. When purchasing checks, ask about refund hotlines; American Express and Bank of America have the largest number of offices around the world.

CREDIT CARDS

Credit cards are useful in England, although one should be warned that many of the low-cost establishments, especially B&B houses, do not accept them. VISA is the most widely used card, along with Eurocard (which is the same as MasterCard). American Express is often accepted, mostly in the middle and upper bracket category. Diners Club, of the "big four," is the least accepted.

Credit cards can save your life when you're abroad. With American Express and VISA, for example, not only can you charge purchases in shops and meals in restaurants that take the card, but you can also withdraw sterling from bank automatic cash machines at many locations in England. Check with your credit-card company before leaving home.

Of course, you may make a purchase with a credit card thinking it will be at a certain rate, only to find that the dollar has declined by the time your bill arrives, and you're actually paying more than you bargained for. Credit-card companies base the rate on the date of posting of the charge, not on the date you actually made the transaction—but those are the rules of the game. It can also work in your favor if the dollar should unexpectedly rise after you make a purchase.

WHAT THINGS COST IN LONDON	U.S. $
Taxi from Victoria Station to a Paddington hotel	12.50
Underground from Heathrow Airport to central London	4.70
Local telephone call	.20
Deluxe double room (at the Ritz)	330.00
Moderate double room (at Durrants)	150.00
Budget double room (at Hallam Hotel)	127.00
Moderate lunch for one (at Bombay Brasserie)	20.25
Budget lunch for one (at Phoenicia)	13.50
Deluxe dinner for one, without wine (at Le Gavroche)	97.50
Moderate dinner for one, without wine (at Langan's Brasserie)	45.00
Budget dinner for one, without wine (at Porter's)	22.50
Pint of beer	2.50
Coca-Cola in a café	1.50
Cup of coffee	1.20
Roll of ASA 100 color film, 36 exposures	8.00
Admission to the British Museum	Free
Movie ticket	8.75
Inexpensive theater ticket	12.00

WHAT THINGS COST IN BATH	U.S. $
Taxi from Bath Rail Station to a centrally located hotel	5.00
Local telephone call	.20
Double room at the Priory Hotel (deluxe)	292.50
Double room at the Lansdown Grove (moderate)	165.00
Double room at the Laura Place Hotel (budget)	100.00
Lunch for one at Woods (moderate)	18.60
Lunch for one at the Pump Room (budget)	15.00
Dinner for one, without wine, at Pino's Hole in the Wall (deluxe)	63.00
Dinner for one, without wine, at The Olive Tree (moderate)	30.00
Dinner for one, without wine, at The Moon and Sixpence (budget)	18.00
Pint of beer	2.35
Coca-Cola in a café	1.40
Cup of coffee	1.20
Roll of ASA 100 color film, 36 exposures	7.80
Admission to the American Museum	6.80
Movie ticket	7.90
Theater ticket	11.00

2. WHEN TO GO — CLIMATE, HOLIDAYS & EVENTS

CLIMATE British temperatures can range from 30° to 110° Fahrenheit but they rarely drop below 35° or go above 78°. Evenings are cool even in summer. No Britisher will ever really advise you about the weather—it's far too uncertain. If you come here from a hot area, bring some warm clothes. If you're from cooler climes, you should be all right. Note that the British, who consider chilliness wholesome, like to keep the thermostats about 10° below the American comfort level. They are also hopelessly enamored of fireplaces, which warm little except whatever portion of your anatomy you turn toward them. Hotels have central heating but are usually kept just above the goose-bump (in English, "goose pimple") margin.

London's Average Daytime Temperatures & Rainfall

	Jan	Feb	Mar	Apr	May	June	July	Aug	Sept	Oct	Nov	Dec
Temp. °F	40	40	44	49	55	61	64	64	59	52	46	42
Rainfall "	2.1	1.6	1.5	1.5	1.8	1.8	2.2	2.3	1.9	2.2	2.5	1.9

HOLIDAYS New Year's Day, Good Friday, Easter Monday, May Day, spring and summer bank holidays (the last Monday in May and August, respectively), Christmas Day, and Boxing Day (December 26) are observed.

ENGLAND
CALENDAR OF EVENTS

For more information about these and other events, contact the various tourist offices throughout England.

FEBRUARY

☐ **Jorvik Viking Festival, York.** A month-long celebration of this historic cathedral city's role as a Viking outpost. For more information, call 0904/611944.

MARCH

◉ *THE SHAKESPEARE SEASON* *The Royal Shakespeare Company at Stratford-upon-Avon begins its annual season, presenting a varied program of works by the Bard in his hometown.*
Where: Royal Shakespeare Theatre, Waterside (tel. 0789/295623), in Stratford-upon-Avon. When: March–December. How: Tickets at box office or else through such agents as Keith Prowse (many locations) in London.

APRIL

☐ **Grand National Meeting.** This is the premier steeplechase event in England. Takes place over a 4-mile course at Aintree Racecourse, Aintree, outside Liverpool, Merseyside (tel. 051/523-2600).
☐ **Devizes to Westminster International Canoe Race.** A 125-mile race along the Avon and Kennet Canals and the River Thames. No tickets are needed. Call 0491/872042 for more information.

MAY

☐ **Chichester Festival Theatre.** Some of the best of classic and modern plays are presented at this West Sussex theater. For tickets and information, contact the Festival Theatre, Oaklands Park, West Sussex PO19 4AP (tel. 0243/781312).
☐ **Brighton International Festival.** This is England's largest multi-arts festival, which will celebrate its 27th anniversary in 1994 with some 400 different events. For information, write to Brighton International Festival, Dome Box Office, 29 New Rd., Brighton BN1 1UG. May 7–30.
☐ **The Royal Windsor Horse Show,** Home Park, Windsor, Berkshire. The country's major show-jumping presentation, attended by the queen herself. Call 0298/72272 for more information. Mid-May (dates vary).

◉ *BATH INTERNATIONAL FESTIVAL* *One of Europe's most prestigious international festivals of music and the arts. As many as 1,000 performers appear.*
Where: At various venues in Bath, Avon. When: Mid-May to late June. How: Full details can be obtained from the Bath Festival, Linley House, 1 Pierrepont Place, Bath BA1 1JY (tel. 0225/462231).

JUNE

☐ **Derby Day.** Famous horse-racing event at Epsom Racecourse, Epsom, Surrey.

For more details, contact United Racecourses Ltd., Racecourse Paddock, Epsom, Surrey KT18 5NJ (tel. 03727/463072).

☐ **Aldeburgh Festival of Music and the Arts.** Benjamin Britten, the late composer, lived near Aldeburgh and in 1948 launched this festival of music and the arts. For more information, write or call the Aldeburgh Foundation, High Street, Aldeburgh, Suffolk IP15 5AX (tel. 0728/452935). Mid- to late June.

☐ **Royal Ascot Week.** A premier horse-racing event and stellar social event, attracting such guests as Queen Elizabeth and Prince Philip. Information is available from The Secretary, Grand Stand Office, Ascot Racecourse, Ascot, Berkshire SL5 7JN (tel. 0344/22211).

JULY

☐ **Henley Royal Regatta.** An international rowing competition and premier event on the English social calendar. Takes place at Henley-on-Thames in Oxfordshire. For more information call 0491/572153. Early July.

AUGUST

☐ **Cowes Week.** A yachting festival held off the Isle of Wight (Hampshire). For details call 0983/295744. Early August.

SEPTEMBER

☐ **Burghley Horse Trials.** This annual event is staged on the grounds of the largest Elizabethan house in England, Burghley House, Stamford, Lincolnshire (tel. 0780/52982). Mid-September.

OCTOBER

☐ **Cheltenham Festival of Literature.** A Cotswold event, featuring readings, book exhibitions, and theatrical performances—all in this famed spa town of Gloucestershire. Call 0242/521621 for more details. Early to mid-October.

NOVEMBER

☐ **London-to-Brighton Veteran Car Run.** Begins in London's Hyde Park and ends in the seaside resort of Brighton in East Sussex. Tickets aren't necessary. Call 0753/681736 for more details. Early November.

DECEMBER

☐ **Christmas.** Observances throughout England's villages, towns, and cities.

LONDON
CALENDAR OF EVENTS

JANUARY

☐ **London International Boat Show,** Earl's Court Exhibition Centre, Warwick Road. The largest boat show in Europe. Call 0784/473377 for details. First 2 weeks in January.

☐ **The Charles I Commemoration.** Anniversary of the execution of King Charles I "in the name of freedom and democracy." Hundreds of cavaliers march through central London in 17th-century dress, and prayers are said at the Banqueting House in Whitehall. Free. Last Sunday in January.

☐ **Chinese New Year.** The famous Lion Dancers in Soho perform free. Late January or early February (based on the lunar calendar), celebrated on the nearest Sunday.

FEBRUARY

⊘ *CRUFT'S DOG SHOW* *The English, they say, love their pets more than their offspring. Cruft's offers an opportunity to observe the nation's pet lovers crooning over the 8,000 dogs representing 100 breeds that strut their stuff. An emotionally charged event for the English.*
Where: Earl's Court Exhibition Centre, Warwick Road (tel. 071/493-6651). When: First weekend in February. How: Tickets can be purchased from Keith Prowse or at the door.

APRIL—MAY

☐ **The Easter Parade.** Brightly colored floats and marching bands around Battersea Park, a full day of activities. Free.

☐ **The Chelsea Flower Show,** Chelsea Royal Hospital. The best of British gardening, with displays of plants and flowers of all seasons. Tickets are available abroad from overseas booking agents. Contact your local British Tourist Authority office to find out which agency is handling ticket sales this year, or write Chelsea Show Ticket Office, P.O. Box 1426, London W6 0LQ.

JUNE

☐ **Grosvenor House Antique Fair,** Grosvenor House. A prestigious antiques fair. Second week in June.

⊘ *TROOPING THE COLOUR* *The official birthday of the queen. Seated upon a horse for hours, the queen inspects her regiments and takes their salute as they parade their colors before her. A quintessential British event watched by the populace religiously on TV. The pageantry and pomp is exquisite. Depending on the weather the young men under the busbies have been known to pass out from the heat. They remain prostrate; nothing is allowed to mar the perfect regimentation of the day.*
Where: Horse Guards Parade. When: June 11, 1994. How: People often arrive before dawn to get a prime view.

⊘ *LAWN TENNIS CHAMPIONSHIPS* *Ever since the players took to the grass courts at Wimbledon in 1877, this tournament has drawn a socially prominent crowd. Although the courts are now crowded with all kinds of tennis fans, there's still an excited hush at the Centre Court and a certain thrill to being there. Savor the strawberries and cream that are still part of the experience.*
Where: Wimbledon, London. When: Last week in June and first week in July. How: Tickets are obtainable through a ballot, which opens January 1. Write to All England Lawn Tennis and Croquet Club, Church Road, Wimbledon, London SW19 5AE (tel. 081/946-2244).

JULY

- ☐ **Royal Tournament.** The British armed forces put on dazzling displays of athletic and military skill—an event of "military pomp, show biz, and outright jingoism." For information contact the Royal Tournament Exhibition Centre, Warwick Road, London SW5 9TA (tel. 071/373-8141). 2½ weeks in mid-July.
- ☐ **City of London Festival.** An annual art festival throughout the city. Call 081/377-0540 for information.

AUGUST

- ☐ **African-Caribbean Street Fair.** Held for 2 days in the community of Notting Hill Gate, it's one of the largest annual street festivals in Europe, attracting over half a million people. Live reggae and soul music plus great Caribbean food. Free. Late August.

SEPTEMBER

✪ *OPENING OF PARLIAMENT   Ever since the 17th century, when the English beheaded Charles I, the British monarch has been denied the right to enter the House of Commons. Instead, the monarch opens parliament in the House of Lords, reading an official speech which is in fact written for her by the Government of the day. She rides from Buckingham Palace to Westminster in a royal coach accompanied by the Yeoman of the Guard and the Household Cavalry.*
*   **Where:** Houses of Parliament. **When:** First Monday in September.*
*   **How:** Public Galleries are open on a first-come, first-served basis.*

NOVEMBER

- ☐ **Guy Fawkes Night.** Commemorates the anniversary of the "Gunpowder Plot," an attempt to blow up King James I and his parliament. Huge organized bonfires are lit throughout the city and Guy Fawkes, the plot's most famous conspirator, is burned in effigy. Free. Early November.

✪ *THE LORD MAYOR'S PROCESSION AND SHOW   The queen has to ask permission to enter the City's square mile—a right that has been jealously guarded by the merchants of London since the 17th century to this very day. Suffice to say that the lord mayor is a powerful character and the procession from the Guildhall to the Royal Courts is appropriately impressive.*
*   **Where:** The City. **When:** Second week in November. **How:** You can watch the procession from the street; the banquet is by invitation only.*

3. HEALTH & INSURANCE

HEALTH

You will encounter few health problems while traveling in England. The tap water is safe to drink, the milk is pasteurized, and health services are good. Occasionally the change in diet may cause some minor diarrhea, so you may want to take some antidiarrhea medicine along.

Chronic Illness If you suffer from a chronic illness, talk to your doctor before taking the trip. For such conditions as epilepsy, diabetes, or a heart condition, wear a **Medic Alert Identification Tag,** which will immediately alert any doctor to your condition and provide the number of Medic Alert's 24-hour hotline so that a doctor in a foreign country can obtain your medical records. For a lifetime membership, the cost is $35, $45, or $60. Contact the Medic Alert Foundation, P.O. Box 1009, Turlock, CA 95381-1009 (tel. toll free 800/432-5378).

Prescription Drugs Carry all your vital medicine in your carry-on luggage and bring enough prescribed medicines to sustain you during your stay. Bring along copies of your prescriptions that are written in the generic—not brand-name—form.

Immunization Be advised that immunizations are only required if you have been in an area infected with a contagious disease within 14 days prior to your arrival in Great Britain.

Finding a Doctor If you need a doctor, your hotel can recommend one or you can contact your embassy or consulate. Before you leave home, you can obtain a list of doctors in England from the International Association for Medical Assistance to Travelers (IAMAT). Contact **IAMAT** in the United States at 417 Center St., Lewiston, NY 14092 (tel. 716/754-4883); in Canada, at 40 Regal Rd., Guelph, ON N1K 1B5 (tel. 519/836-0102); or in Europe, at 57 Voirets, 1212 Grand-Lancy-Geneva, Switzerland.

INSURANCE

HEALTH Before leaving home, check to see if your health coverage extends to Europe. If it doesn't or if the coverage is inadequate, consider purchasing short-term travel insurance that will cover medical emergencies. Remember that Medicare covers U.S. citizens while traveling outside the U.S.A. in Mexico and Canada only.

PROPERTY Also check your homeowner or renter's insurance for coverage for off-premises theft. Again, if you need more coverage, consider a short-term policy.

CANCELLATION CHARGES If you are traveling as part of a tour, or are taking a charter or any other flight that has cancellation penalties, or have prepaid your vacation expenses, you may also want to purchase insurance that covers you if you have to cancel for any reason. However, your credit-card company may provide cancellation coverage if you have used your credit card to pay.

AUTOMOBILE If you are going to rent a car while in England, check to see whether your automobile insurance or automobile club covers personal accident insurance (PAI), collision damage waiver (CDW), or other insurance options. You may be able to avoid added charges by the car-rental companies if you are already covered.

Travel Clubs If you belong to a travel club, inquire about the insurance coverage or options to which your membership entitles you.

Documentation Note that to submit any claim, you must always have thorough documentation including all receipts, police reports, medical records, and the like.

COMPREHENSIVE POLICIES

Your best bet may be to purchase a comprehensive travel policy that covers all catastrophes, big and small—trip cancellation, health, emergency assistance, and lost luggage. A travel agent may sell you a policy (the price is small) or contact the following companies for more information.

Access America Located at 6600 W. Broad St., Richmond, VA 23230 (tel. 804/285-3300, or toll free 800/284-8300), Access America offers a comprehensive travel insurance and assistance package, including medical expenses, on-the-spot hospital payments, medical transportation, baggage insurance, trip cancellation/interruption insurance, and collision-damage insurance for a car rental. Their 24-hour hotline connects you to multilingual coordinators who can offer advice and help on medical, legal, and travel problems. Packages begin at $27.

Healthcare Abroad (MEDEX)   This company offers coverage for between 10 and 90 days at $3 per day; this policy includes accident and sickness coverage to the tune of $100,000. Medical evacuation is also included, along with a $25,000 accidental death and dismemberment compensation. Provisions for trip cancellation and lost or stolen luggage can also be written into this policy at a nominal cost. They can be contacted at Wallach & Co., 107 W. Federal St., P.O. Box 480, Middleburg, VA 22117-0480 (tel. 703/687-3166, or toll free 800/237-6615).

Mutual of Omaha (Tele-Trip)   This company offers insurance packages priced at from $113 for a 3-week trip. Included in the packages are travel-assistance services, and financial protection against trip cancellation, trip interruption, flight and baggage delays, accident-related medical costs, accidental death and dismemberment, and medical evacuation coverages. Application for insurance can be taken over the phone for major credit-card holders at toll free 800/228-9792. Their address is Mutual of Omaha Plaza, Omaha, NE 68175.

Travel Guard International   This company offers a comprehensive 7-day policy that covers basically everything, including lost luggage. It costs $52, including emergency assistance, accidental death, trip cancellation and interruption, medical coverage abroad, and lost luggage. There are restrictions, however, which you should understand before you accept the coverage. They can be reached at 1145 Clark St., Stevens Point, WI 54481 (tel. toll free 800/826-1300).

Travelers Insurance Company   Travel accident and illness coverage starts at $10 for 6 to 10 days; $500 worth of coverage for lost, damaged, or delayed baggage costs $20 for 6 to 10 days; and trip cancellation costs $5.50 for $100 worth of coverage. Written approval is necessary for cancellation coverage above $10,000. Contact the Travel Insurance Division, 1 Tower Sq., 10 NB, Hartford, CT 06183-5040 (tel. toll free 800/243-3174).

4. WHAT TO PACK

Always pack as light as possible. Sometimes it's hard to get a porter or a baggage cart in rail and air terminals. Also, airlines are increasingly strict about how much luggage you can bring—both carry-on and checked items. Checked baggage should not be more than 62 inches (width, plus length, plus height), or weigh more than 70 pounds. Carry-on luggage shouldn't be more than 45 inches (width, plus length, plus height) and must fit under your seat or in the bin above.

The most essential items of your English wardrobe are a good raincoat, a sweater or jersey, and, if possible, an umbrella.

Note also that conservative middle-age English people tend to dress up rather than down, and that they dress very well indeed, particularly at theaters and concerts. Nobody will bar you for arriving in sports clothes, but you may feel awkward, so include at least one smart suit or dress in your luggage.

Better-class restaurants usually demand that men wear ties and that women not wear shorts or jogging clothing, but those are the only clothing rules enforced.

Pack clothes that "travel well" because you can't always get pressing done at hotels. Be prepared to wash your underwear, etc., in your bathroom and hang it up to dry overnight.

The general rule of packing is to bring four of everything. For men, that means four pairs of socks, four pairs of slacks, four shirts, and four sets of underwear. At least two of these will always be either dirty or in the process of drying. Often you'll have to wrap semiwet clothes in a plastic bag as you head for your next destination. Women can follow the same rule.

Take at least one outfit for chilly weather and one outfit for warm weather. Even in the summer, you may experience suddenly chilly weather. Always take two pairs of walking shoes in case you get your shoes soaked and need that extra pair.

5. TIPS FOR SPECIAL TRAVELERS

FOR THE DISABLED
IN THE U.S.A.

Before you go on your trip, there are many agencies in the United States that can provide advance planning information. Knowing in advance which hotels, restaurants, and attractions are wheelchair accessible can save you a lot of frustration—firsthand accounts by other disabled travelers are the best. There are some companies that offer tours specifically designed for disabled travelers. See also "In England" below in this chapter.

Travel Information Service This service has prepared an information package that contains the names and addresses of accessible hotels, restaurants, and attractions—often based on reports of travelers who have been there. They can be contacted at **MossRehab,** 1200 W. Tabor Rd., Philadelphia, PA 19141 (tel. 215/456-9600).

Air Transportation of Handicapped Persons This free publication prepared by the U.S. Department of Transportation can be obtained by writing to Free Advisory Circular No. AC12032, Distribution Unit, U.S. Department of Transportation, Publications Division, M-4332, Washington, DC 20590.

The Society for the Advancement of Travel for the Handicapped This organization can provide a list of companies that operate tours for travelers with disabilities. The society can be contacted at 347 Fifth Ave., New York, NY 10016 (tel. 212/447-7284). Yearly membership dues are $45 or $25 for senior citizens and students.

Federation of the Handicapped This organization operates tours for members, who pay a yearly fee of $4. They can be contacted at 211 W. 14th St., New York, NY 10011 (tel. 212/727-4200).

American Foundation for the Blind This is the best information source for the blind. They can be contacted at 15 W. 16th St., New York, NY 10011 (tel. 212/620-2000, or toll free 800/232-5463).

IN ENGLAND

Many London hotels, museums, restaurants, and sightseeing attractions have wheelchair ramps. People disadvantaged are often granted special discounts (called "concessions") for attractions—and, in some cases, nightclubs—it always pays to ask.

The British Tourist Authority has a guide called *London Made Easy,* which offers advice and outlines facilities available to the handicapped; it costs £2.50 ($3.80). Bookstores often carry a copy of *Access in London* for £4 ($6), an even more helpful publication; it covers facilities for the handicapped at various shops, pubs, and theaters, among other information.

London's most visible organization for information about access to theaters, cinemas, subways, buses, and restaurants is **Artsline,** 5 Crowndale Rd., London NW1 1TU (tel. 071/388-2227). Funded by the London Arts Council, and staffed for the most part by disabled persons, it offers free information about wheelchair access, induction loops in theaters for hearing-aid hookups, and recommendations of restaurants and hotels that were designed with sensitivity for disabled clients. Although they'll mail information to North America, they are most effective when contacted from your hotel after you arrive in London. Call from 10am to 5:30pm Monday through Friday.

A second organization that cooperates closely with Artsline is **Tripscope,** The Courtyard, 4 Evelyn Rd., London W4 5JL (tel. 081/994-9294). Also staffed and managed by disabled persons, it offers advice on transport and travel for disabled persons in Britain and abroad.

FOR SENIORS

For so many people age 60 and older—retired, with the kids on their own, and the mortgage paid off—this is the time of their lives when they can relax and do some globe trotting. This growing segment of our population is well represented by organizations that offer discounts on airfares, accommodations, and car rentals. Be sure to ask for senior citizen discounts at attractions and have your identification ready as proof. Educational programs specially designed for seniors, as well as cruises and tours, are available.

AARP (American Association of Retired Persons) This is the best organization in the United States for seniors; members are offered discounts on car rentals, hotels, and airfares. The association group travel is provided by the AARP Travel Experience from American Express. Tours may be purchased through any American Express office or travel agent or by calling toll free 800/927-AARP. Cruises may be purchased only by telephone (tel. toll free 800/745-4567). Flights to the various destinations are handled by either of these toll-free numbers as part of land arrangements or cruise bookings. For more information, contact AARP at 601 E St. NW, Washington, DC 20049 (tel. 202/434-2277).

Mature Outlook Located at 6001 N. Clark St., Chicago, IL 60660 (tel. toll free 800/336-6330), this is a travel club for people more than 50 years of age. It's operated by Sears Roebuck & Co. Annual membership is available for $9.95, and the club issues a bimonthly newsletter featuring discounts at hotels.

Elderhostel This organization offers an array of university-based summer educational programs for seniors in England and other parts of the world. Most courses last around three weeks and are remarkable values—airfare, accommodations in student dormitories or modest inns, all meals, and tuition are included. Courses emphasize the liberal arts and include field trips—best of all there's no homework or grades.

Participants must be age 60 or older, but may take an under-60 companion. Meals are of the no-frills fare, typical of educational institutions worldwide. The program provides a safe and congenial environment for single "golden girls," who make up some 67% of the enrollment. The organization may be reached at 75 Federal St., Boston, MA 02110-1941 (tel. 617/426-7788).

SAGA International Holidays This organization offers all-inclusive tours for those age 60 and older. Insurance is included in the net price of the tours. They can be contacted at 222 Berkeley St., Boston, MA 02116 (tel. toll free 800/343-0273).

Publications: For a copy of *Travel Tips for Older Americans* (publication no. 8970, cost $1), contact the Superintendent of Documents, U.S. Government Printing Office, Washington, DC 20402 (tel. 202/783-5238). Another booklet—this one is free—*101 Tips for the Mature Traveler* is available from Grand Circle Travel, 347 Congress St., Suite 3A, Boston, MA 02210 (tel. 617/350-7500, or toll free 800/221-2610); this travel agency also offers escorted tours and cruises for seniors.

Information is also available from the **National Council of Senior Citizens,** 1331 F St. NW, Washington, DC 20005 (tel. 202/347-8800). A nonprofit organization, the council charges $12 per person/couple for which you receive a monthly newsletter, part of which is devoted to travel tips. Discounts on hotels and auto rentals are provided.

FOR SINGLE TRAVELERS

Unfortunately for the 85 million single Americans, the travel industry is far more geared to duos, and those adventuring about solo often wind up paying the penalty. It pays to travel with someone and split accommodations costs, which for those traveling solo can add up to more than half the price of a double room. There are, of course, dynamic and action-packed tours and vacations designed for the unattached, as well as companies that will match you with a compatible traveling partner.

Travel Companion   This company matches single travelers with like-minded companions. People seeking travel companions fill out a survey of their preferences and needs and receive a mini-listing of potential travel partners. Companions of the same or opposite sex can be requested. Individuals are then listed for 6 months on the company's well-publicized records; the charge is between $36 and $66. A bimonthly newsletter averaging 34 large pages also gives numerous money-saving travel tips of special interest to solo travelers. A sample copy is available for $4. For an application and more information, contact Jens Jurgen at Travel Companion, P.O. Box P-833, Amityville, NY 11701 (tel. 516/454-0880).

Singleworld   This travel agency, at 401 Theodore Fremd Ave., Rye, NY 10580 (tel. 914/967-3334, or toll free 800/223-6490), operates tours geared to singles. Two basic types of tours are available, either a youth-oriented tour for people in their 20s and 30s or jaunts for "all ages." Annual dues are $25.

FOR FAMILIES

Advance planning is the key to any successful overseas vacation—but this is especially true when you're traveling with infants, tots, or teenagers. For little ones, there's the supply of the bottles, food, diapers, etc., that you must carry at least for the passage over to England until you can buy more there. Recreational activities like splashing around in a pool or running off a little steam in a park are a welcomed break from museum-going for most kids. For accommodations, meals, and attractions, be sure to read the "Cool for Kids" features throughout this guide.

- If you have very small children, discuss your travel plans with your pediatrician. Take along children's aspirin, a thermometer, Band-Aids, etc.
- On airlines, a special menu for children must be requested at least 24 hours in advance. If baby food is required, bring your own and ask a flight attendant to warm it to the right temperature.
- Take along a "security blanket." For very young children, this can be a pacifier or a favorite book or toy. For older kids, a baseball cap, a favorite T-shirt, or some good-luck charm can make them feel at home in different surroundings.
- Make advance arrangements for cribs, bottle warmers, or car seats—in England small children aren't allowed to ride in the front seat.
- Ask the hotel if it stocks baby food; if not, take some with you and plan to buy the rest in local groceries.
- Draw up guidelines on bedtime, eating, keeping tidy, being in the sun, even shopping and spending—this will make the vacation more enjoyable.
- Babysitters can be found for you at most hotels, but insist that the babysitter have at least a rudimentary knowledge of English—this is no longer certain with the influx of foreign workers in England.

Family Travel Times is published 10 times a year by TWYCH, Travel With Your Children, and includes a weekly call-in service for subscribers. Subscriptions cost $55 a year and can be ordered by writing to TWYCH, 45 W. 18th St., 7th floor, New York, NY 10011 (tel. 212/206-0688). TWYCH also publishes two nitty-gritty information guides, *Skiing with Children* and *Cruising with Children*, which sell for $29 and $22, respectively, and are discounted to subscribers of the newsletter. An information packet describing TWYCH's publications, including a recent sample issue, is available by sending $3.50 to the above address.

FOR STUDENTS

Research is the key for students who want to take advantage of budget travel and study abroad. There are organizations and publications that will provide you with all the details of programs available specifically for students; see also "Educational/Study Travel" below in this chapter and "Networks and Resources: For Students" in Chapter 3. Of course, you'll want to carry an International Student Identity Card—good for discounts on travel fares and attractions. Youth hostels provide an inexpensive network of accommodations while trekking through the country.

Council Travel America's largest student, youth, and budget travel group has more than 60 offices worldwide. International Student Identity Cards are available to all bona fide students from any Council Travel office for $15 and entitle the holder to generous travel and other discounts.

Council Travel's London Centre is conveniently located in the West End at 28A Poland St., London W1V 3DB, just off Oxford Circus (tube: Oxford Circus).

Discounted international and domestic air tickets are available with special prices for student and youth travelers. Eurotrain rail passes, YHA passes, weekend packages, overland safaris, and hostel/hotel accommodations are all bookable from Council Travel.

Council Travel (a subsidiary of the Council on International Educational Exchange) also sells a number of publications for young people considering traveling abroad. Publications include: *Work, Study, Travel Abroad: The Whole World Handbook; Volunteer: The Comprehensive Guide to Voluntary Service in the U.S. and Abroad;* and *The Teenager's Guide to Study, Travel, and Adventure Abroad.*

Council Travel has offices throughout the United States, including the main office at 205 E. 42nd St., New York, NY 10017 (tel. 212/661-1414). Call toll free 800/GET-AN-ID to find the location nearest you. The London office telephone numbers are 071/287-3337 for European destinations, and 071/437-7767 for worldwide destinations.

IYHF (International Youth Hostel Federation) This organization was designed to provide bare-bones overnight accommodations for serious budget-conscious travelers. For information, contact American Youth Hostels (AYH)/Hostelling International, 733 15th St. NW, Suite 840, Washington, DC 20005 (tel. 202/783-6161). Membership costs $25 annually except for those under 18, who pay $10, and those over 54, who pay $15.

6. ALTERNATIVE/ADVENTURE TRAVEL

More and more seasoned travelers are looking for fresh, challenging vacation ideas. What follows is not meant to be an exhaustive list, only a place to start.

Caveat: Under no circumstances is the inclusion of an organization in this guide to be interpreted as a guarantee either of its creditworthiness or its competency. Information about the organizations listed below should be followed by your own investigation.

ADVENTURE/WILDERNESS

Whether by bicycle or on foot, the following organizations offer tours for the physically fit who want to explore "the wilds," or at least country roads, before they disappear forever.

English Lakeland Ramblers This company has designed its walking tours, which last 7 to 9 days, for the average active person in reasonably good physical shape. On its tour of the Lake District, you'll stay and have your meals in a charming 17th-century country inn near Ambleside and Windermere. A minibus takes hikers and sightseers daily to trails and sightseeing points throughout the region. Experts tell you about the culture and history of the area and highlight its natural wonders. They can be contacted at 18 Stuyvesant Oval, Suite 1A, New York, NY 10009 (tel. 212/505-1020, or toll free 800/724-8801 outside New York).

Outward Bound Founded in 1941 by Kurt Hahn, a German-English educator, Outward Bound aims to help people "go beyond their self-imposed limits, to use the wilderness as a metaphor for personal growth and self-discovery." Courses in wilderness training incorporate healthy doses of both mountain climbing and boating under challenging conditions. Courses last from 3 days to 3 months. There are now 56 Outward Bound schools and centers throughout the world.

The original Outward Bound was established—and still thrives—in the rugged mountains near Aberdovey, Wales; now there are about half a dozen more Outward Bound centers in various undeveloped regions of Britain. Some readers combine a hands-on experience of England's wilderness with an intensely cultivated museumgoer's visit to London in a single visit—thereby availing themselves of the best of both possible worlds. For information on the British (i.e., original) versions of Outward Bound, contact them at 384 Field Point Rd., Greenwich, CT 06830 (tel. 203/661-0797, or toll free 800/243-8520 outside Connecticut).

Vermont Bicycle Touring Often referred to as the "granddaddy of cycle tour operators," this company offers tours that range from 25 to 40 miles biked per day. The tours allow for different levels of cycling experience; extra guidance, assistance, and services are always available. A van transports your luggage (and tired cyclists). They can be contacted at P.O. Box 711, Bristol, VT 05443 (tel. 802/453-4811).

Wilderness Travel, Inc. Specializing in mountain tours and bicycle tours of Europe, this company also offers less strenuous walking tours of Cornwall and the Cotswolds, which combine transportation with walking sessions of no more than 3 hours at a time. They can be contacted at 801 Allston Way, Berkeley, CA 94710 (tel. 510/548-0420, or toll free 800/368-2794 outside California).

BOATING

For a completely new angle on travel in the British Isles, visitors can take boat trips on the network of inland waters threading through the country. You can choose between a skipper-yourself boat, equipped with food, comprehensive instructions, and suggested routes; or a hotel boat, on which you get good food, a helpful crew, and the companionship of fellow passengers. Boating holidays make sightseeing easy. You can either leave your luggage aboard as you spend the day exploring or you can take your boat right into the center of a city—such as Stratford-upon-Avon, London, or Milton Keynes, to mention a few.

For information and reservations, contact **Weltonfield Narrowboats** at Welton Hythe, Daventry, Northamptonshire, NN11 LG (tel. 0227/843773).

EDUCATIONAL/STUDY TRAVEL

What could be more enlightening for students of English literature than to do course work at such renowned universities as Oxford or Cambridge during the week and then to be able to take weekend excursions to the countryside where Shakespeare, Austen, Dickens, and Hardy—only to mention a few masters—set their work? While studying at these famed halls of learning, you can live with other students in the dormitories and dine in elaborate halls or the more intimate Fellows' clubs. It's quite a cultural education and you may develop friendships that will last a lifetime.

Study programs in England are not limited to the liberal arts, or to high school or college students. There's a wide variety of programs from which to choose, and some are designed specifically for teachers and senior citizens (see "For Seniors: Elderhostel" above in this chapter.) For more information, contact the organizations listed below or those mentioned above in "For Students" in this chapter.

American Institute for Foreign Study   Affiliated with Richmond College in London, this organization offers traveling programs of between 10 and 60 days to high-school students wishing to visit England, as well as academic programs for college students. College students can enroll in classes lasting for a summer, a semester, or a full year. They can also enroll in programs leading to the British equivalent of an MBA. The organization can be contacted at 102 Greenwich Ave., Greenwich, CT 06830 (tel. toll free 800/727-2437).

British Universities Summer Schools   Academic programs in literature are offered at the universities of Birmingham (at its Stratford-upon-Avon center), London, and Oxford. Programs are designed for graduates (particularly teachers), graduating seniors, and some undergraduates. Contact Oxford University, Department for Continuing Education, 1 Wellington Sq., Oxford OX1 2JA, England (tel. 0865/270378).

Earthwatch   Ecology-minded folks may be interested in the research projects sponsored by this nonprofit organization. Volunteers pay to work with teams during hands-on 2-week programs that are of educational, ecological, or sociological importance. Payments made by U.S. volunteers are considered tax-deductible contributions to a scientific project. Earthwatch publishes a magazine six times a year, listing more than 160 unusual opportunities, some of which are located in Great Britain. Projects range from tracking the migration habits of endangered species to excavating ancient archeological sites. Project costs range from $800 to $2,200 per person. No special skills are necessary. The U.S. headquarters is at 680 Mt. Auburn St., P.O. Box 403GB, Watertown, MA 02272 (tel. 617/926-8200, or toll free 800/776-8200).

IIE   (Institute of International Education) This organization is the largest international higher-education exchange agency in the U.S. It administers a variety of postsecondary academic, training, and grant programs for the U.S. Information Agency (USIA), with special stress on the management of predoctoral Fulbright grants. It is especially helpful in arranging enrollments for U.S. students in summer-school programs at Oxford, the University of London, and the University of Birmingham. For information, contact the U.S. Student Programs Division of IIE, 809 United Nations Plaza, New York, NY 10017-3580 (tel. 212/984-5330).

NRCSA   (National Registration Center for Study Abroad) This organization will register you at your school of choice in Great Britain. They will also arrange for room and board and make your airline reservations—all for no extra fee. Their catalog of schools in Great Britain is $3; ask for a free copy of their newsletter. NRCSA can be contacted at 823 N. Second St., Milwaukee, WI 53203 (tel. 414/278-0631).

UNIVAC   (University Vacations) This organization offers liberal arts programs at Oxford and Cambridge. Courses usually last 7 to 12 days and combine lectures, excursions, and guided walking tours; there's no pressure to prepare papers or take final exams. All adults over 18 are eligible and there are no formal academic requirements. You live at the colleges and eat either in an elaborate dining hall or the more intimate Fellows' dining rooms.

For information, contact UNIVAC, the International Building, 9602 NW 13th St., Miami, FL 33171 (tel. 305/591-1736, or toll free 800/792-0100). In Great Britain, the headquarters is at 8 Beaufort Place, Cambridge CB5 8AG; in summer, Brasenose College, Oxford OX1 4AJ, England.

HOMESTAYS/HOME EXCHANGES

Anyone would be enriched by a stay at the home of a friendly Brit. **Homestays** are an ideal way to gain greater insight into a culture, people, and country. Write to any of the BTA offices (see "Information, Entry Requirements, and Money" above in this chapter) and ask for their publications listing dozens of agencies and services providing homestays. See also "Promoting International Understanding" below in this chapter.

Another travel alternative is a **home exchange,** which is not only fun but can save you money. If you'd like to swap your house or apartment for a cottage or flat in England and live like a true Brit, contact the following organizations:

Intervac U.S. is part of the largest worldwide home-exchange network. It publishes three catalogs a year that list more than 8,800 homes in more than 36 countries. Members contact each other directly. The $62 cost, plus postage, includes the purchase of all three of the company's catalogs (which will be mailed to you), plus the inclusion of your own listing in whichever one of the three catalogs you select. If you want to publish a photograph of your home, it costs $11 extra. Hospitality and youth exchanges are also available. The organization can be contacted at P.O. Box 590504, San Francisco, CA 94119 (tel. 415/435-3497, or toll free 800/756-HOME).

The Invented City publishes home listings in February, May, and November each year, listing more than 200 homes in England alone. For a $50 fee, they will list your home with your preferred time for an exchange, your occupation, and hobbies. They can be contacted at 41 Sutter St., Suite 1090, San Francisco, CA 94104 (tel. 415/673-0347, or toll free 800/788-CITY).

Vacation Exchange Club, P.O. Box 650, Key West, FL 33041 (tel. 305/294-3720, or toll free 800/638-3841), will send you four directories a year—in one of which you're listed—for $60.

PROMOTING INTERNATIONAL UNDERSTANDING

It has long been a truth universally acknowledged that getting to know different peoples is the path for international understanding and peace. Listed below are organizations that foster friendship and goodwill through cultural exchanges, homestays, and educational and work programs. See also "Homestays/Home Exchanges" above in this chapter.

Friendship Force Founded in Atlanta, Georgia, under the leadership of then-governor Jimmy Carter, the Friendship Force exists for the sole purpose of encouraging friendship among disparate peoples around the world. Dozens of branch groups throughout North America meet regularly and arrange group tours, which take advantage of low-cost group rates. Each participant is required to spend 2 weeks in the host country, including 1 week in the home of a local family; most volunteers spend the second week traveling independently. No particular study regimen or work program is prescribed, but participants are asked to behave in a way that reflects well on the United States. Friendship Force can be contacted at 575 South Tower, 1 CNN Center, Atlanta, GA 30303 (tel. 404/522-9490).

People to People Established by President Eisenhower in the late 1950s, this organization promotes international understanding through educational and cultural exchanges. People to People organizes exchanges of adult professionals (in many different specialized fields) for 2- and 3-week programs. There is also a summer, 4-week high-school educational program. A summer collegiate study-abroad and internship program offers graduate and undergraduate credit opportunities abroad. Local chapters help to arrange homestays and other programs for members. Privileges include travel opportunities, newsletters, and a magazine. Annual fees are $25 for families, $15 for individuals, and $10 for students. People to People can be contacted at 501 E. Armour Blvd., Kansas City, MO 64109 (tel. 816/531-4701).

Servas A nonprofit, nongovernmental, international, interfaith network of travelers and hosts, Servas works to build world peace. Members of *Servas* (which is from the Esperanto word meaning "to serve") invite travelers to share living space, usually staying without charge for a visit of 2 days maximum. Day visits as well as a single shared meal can also be arranged. Members pay a $55 annual fee, fill out an application, and are interviewed for suitability. After they have been approved, they receive directories listing the names and addresses of hosts on six continents. Contact Servas at 11 John St., New York, NY 10038 (tel. 212/267-0252).

Work Camps After World War I, a work-camp program was established to promote "peace and understanding" through combinations of humanitarian work, study, and immersion by participants in foreign cultures. Participants arrange their own travel. The registration fee of $125 covers room and board for a 2- or 3-week program. For information, contact Volunteers for Peace, 43 Tiffany Rd., Belmont, VT 05730 (tel. 803/259-2759), which issues a complimentary newsletter. A work-camp directory, which covers 36 countries, is available for a tax-deductible contribution of $10.

OPERA TOURS

From the great classics to the light comic operas of Gilbert and Sullivan to new works premiered with flair and imagination, the English National Opera and the Royal Opera perform in London 5 or 6 nights each week 11 months a year. A high note for music lovers may be a tour of England that is filled with nights at the opera at either the splendid London Coliseum or the Royal Opera House, one of the most beautiful theaters in Europe. See also "The Performing Arts" in Chapter 7.

Probably the best-regarded organizer in the U.S.A. of music and opera tours, **Dailey-Thorp** is able to purchase blocks of otherwise unavailable tickets to the London opera—along with the Salzburg Festival, the Bayreuth Festival in Germany, and events in Vienna, Milan, Paris, regional Italy, and Eastern Europe. Tours range from 7 to 21 days, and include first-class accommodations and meals in top-rated European restaurants. They can be contacted at 330 W. 58th St., New York, NY 10019-1817 (tel. 212/307-1515).

7. GETTING THERE

BY PLANE

While the facts and figures below are as accurate as research can make them, the fast-moving economics of the airline industry, particularly since deregulation, make them all very tentative. Always check for the very latest flight and fare information.

Airlines compete fiercely on the North America–London route, one of the most heavily traveled in the world, and they offer a confusing barrage of options. The best strategy for securing the lowest fare is to shop around. Above all, remain as flexible about dates as possible. Keep calling the airlines or your travel agent—as the departure date nears, airlines will often discount seats if the flight is not fully booked.

Other general rules to keep in mind are that fares are usually lower during the week (Monday through Thursday noon) and that there are also seasonal fare differences (peak, shoulder, and basic). For transatlantic travel, peak season is summer, basic is winter, and shoulder is in between. Travel during Christmas and Easter weeks is usually more expensive than in the weeks just before or after those holidays.

In any season airlines offer regular first-class, business-class, and economy seating. Most airlines also offer discounted fares, like the Advance Purchase Excursion (APEX) fare, which carry restrictions (some severe), usually including advance purchase, a minimum stay abroad, and cancellation or alteration penalties.

THE MAJOR AIRLINES

Several airlines fly the enormously popular routes from North America to Great Britain. Below is a list of some of these carriers, arranged alphabetically.

Air Canada (tel. toll free 800/776-3000) For travelers departing from Canada, this carrier flies to London's Heathrow nonstop from both Calgary and Edmonton three to seven times a week, depending on the season. More importantly, from both Toronto and Montréal, Air Canada flies to Heathrow nonstop daily, with additional flights (between three and seven a week, depending on the season, between Toronto and Manchester). From Vancouver, daily flights either transfer through Edmonton or fly directly—about once a week—to London nonstop.

American Airlines (tel. toll free 800/624-6262) This carrier offers a total of 12 daily routes to London's Heathrow Airport from about a half-dozen different U.S. gateways: New York's JFK (four times daily); Chicago's O'Hare (twice daily); Miami (usually twice daily); and Los Angeles and Boston (each once a day).

British Airways (tel. toll free 800/AIRWAYS) Foremost among the carriers listed here, British Airways offers flights from at least 18 U.S. cities to London's Heathrow and Gatwick Airports, as well as many others to Manchester, Birmingham, and (within Scotland) Glasgow. All but a handful of its flights are nonstop. With more add-on options than any other airline, BA can make a visit to Britain cheaper than you might have expected. Of particular interest are the "Value Plus," "London on the Town," and "Europe Escorted" packages that include both airfare and hotel accommodations throughout Britain at heavily discounted prices—much lower than what you would have paid had you booked these various elements separately.

Attractive both for its coach class and for its well-respected club (business) class, newly privatized BA is probably the most popular and sought-after transatlantic airline in the world—with hundreds of connections between London and every other part of Europe, the Americas, and the British Commonwealth. Eager to compete effectively with the transatlantic services of other airlines, BA spent $150 million in 1992–93 to upgrade its own with bigger and more comfortable seats, lighter and more flavorful food, and more sophisticated in-flight audio programs. Good news for passengers who spend a lot of time in the air, BA fully participates in the frequent-flier programs of the most important U.S.-based airlines. (See also "Organized Tours," below, and "By Car" in "Getting Around," below in this chapter.)

Delta (tel. toll free 800/241-4141) Depending on the day of the week and the season, Delta makes either one or two daily nonstop flights between its headquarters in Atlanta and London's Gatwick. Delta also offers nonstop daily service to Gatwick from Cincinnati, Detroit, and Miami. (The last of these two were routes formerly controlled by USAir and the now-defunct Pan Am, respectively.)

Northwest Airlines (tel. toll free 800/447-4747) This carrier flies nonstop from both Minneapolis and Boston to Gatwick, with connections possible from such other cities as Detroit.

TWA (tel. toll free 800/221-2000) This carrier filed for a carefully planned corporate reorganization under the protection of Chapter 11 bankruptcy proceedings early in 1992. Under its new management, TWA has continued its nonstop routing to Gatwick every day from its hub in St. Louis. Connections are possible through St. Louis from virtually every other part of North America.

United Airlines   (tel. toll free 800/241-6522) This carrier flies nonstop from New York's JFK to Heathrow between two and three times a day, depending on the season. United also offers nonstop service twice a day from Washington, D.C.'s Dulles Airport, and service to Heathrow once a day from Newark, San Francisco, Seattle, and Los Angeles.

USAir   (tel. toll free 800/428-4322) This carrier flies daily nonstop to Gatwick from Philadelphia, Baltimore/Washington, and Charlotte, North Carolina.

Virgin Atlantic Airways   (tel. toll free 800/862-8621) This British carrier flies to London's Gatwick four times a week from Boston, Miami, and Orlando, and once a day to Heathrow from New York's JFK, New Jersey's Newark, and Los Angeles.

OTHER GOOD-VALUE CHOICES

BUCKET SHOPS   In the '60s, mainstream airlines in Britain gave this insulting name to resellers of blocks of unsold tickets consigned to them by major transatlantic carriers; it might be more polite to refer to them as "consolidators." They act as clearinghouses for blocks of tickets that airlines discount and consign during normally slow periods of air travel.

Tickets are usually priced 20% to 35% below the full fare. Terms of payment can vary—anything between last-minute and 45 days prior to departure. Tickets can be purchased through regular travel agents, who usually mark up the ticket 8% to 10%, maybe more, thereby greatly reducing your discount. A survey conducted of flyers who use consolidators voiced only one major complaint. Use of such a ticket doesn't qualify you for an advance seat assignment, and you are therefore likely to be assigned a "poor seat" on the plane at the last minute.

The survey revealed that most flyers estimated their savings at around $200 per ticket off the regular price. Nearly a third of the passengers reported savings of up to $300 off the regular price. But—and here's the hitch—many people who booked consolidator tickets reported no savings at all, as the airlines will sometimes match the consolidator ticket by announcing a promotional fare. The situation is a bit tricky and calls for some careful investigation on your part to determine just how much you are saving.

Bucket shops abound from coast to coast. Here are some recommendations. Look also for their ads in your local newspaper's travel section. They're usually very small and a single column in width.

In New York, try **TFI Tours International,** 34 W. 32nd St., 12th floor, New York, NY 10001 (tel. 212/736-1140 in New York State, or toll free 800/825-3834 elsewhere in the U.S.).

In Miami, it's **25 West Tours,** 2490 Coral Way, Miami, FL 33145 (tel. 305/856-0810 in Miami, or toll free 800/423-6954 in Florida, 800/225-2582 elsewhere in the U.S.).

Out West, you can try **Sunline Express Holidays, Inc.,** 607 Market St., San Francisco, CA 94105 (tel. 415/541-7800, or toll free 800/786-5463).

In New England, one of the best choices is **Travel Management International,** 18 Prescott St., Suite 4, Cambridge, MA 02138 (tel. toll free 800/245-3672), which offers a wide variety of discount fares, including youth fares. Often, its contract fares are lower than those offered by some rebators (see below).

Since dealing with unknown bucket shops might be a little risky, it's wise to call the Better Business Bureau in your area to see if complaints have been filed against the company from which you plan to purchase a fare.

CHARTER FLIGHTS For reasons of economy (never for convenience) some travelers opt for charter flights.

Strictly speaking, a charter flight occurs on an aircraft reserved months in advance for a one-time-only transit to some predetermined point. Before paying for a charter, check the restrictions on your ticket or contract. You may be asked to purchase a tour package and pay far in advance. You'll pay a stiff penalty (or forfeit the ticket entirely) if you cancel. Charters are sometimes canceled when the plane doesn't fill up. In some cases, the charter-ticket seller will offer you an insurance policy for your own legitimate cancellation (hospital confinement or death in the family, for example).

There is no way to predict whether a proposed flight to England will cost less on a charter or through a bucket shop. You must investigate at the time of your trip.

One company arranging charters is the **Council on International Educational Exchange (Council Travel),** 205 E. 42nd St., New York, NY 10017 (tel. 212/661-0311, or toll free 800/800-8222).

One of the biggest New York charter operators is **Travac,** 989 Sixth Ave., New York, NY 10018 (tel. 212/563-3303, or toll free 800/TRAV-800). Other Travac offices include 6151 W. Century Blvd., Los Angeles, CA 90045 (tel. 310/670-9692); 166 Geary St., San Francisco, CA 94108 (tel. 415/392-4610); and 2601 Jefferson St., Orlando, FL 32803 (tel. 407/896-0014).

REBATORS To confuse the situation even more, rebators also compete in the low-airfare market. These outfits pass along to the passenger part of their commission, although many of them assess a fee for their services. Most rebators offer discounts that range from 10% to 25% (but this could vary from place to place), plus a $25 handling charge. They are not the same as travel agents, although they sometimes offer similar services, including discounted land arrangements and car rentals.

Rebators include **Travel Avenue,** 641 W. Lake St., Suite 201, Chicago, IL 60606 (tel. 312/876-1116, or toll free 800/333-3335); and **The Smart Traveller,** 3111 SW 27th Ave., Miami, FL 33133 (tel. 305/448-3338, or toll free 800/448-3338).

STANDBYS A favorite of spontaneous travelers with absolutely no scheduled demands on their time, standby fares leave your departure to the whims of fortune and the hopes that a last-minute seat will become available. Most airlines don't offer standbys, although some seats are available to London and to Vienna.

Virgin Atlantic Airways (tel. toll free 800/862-8621) features both a day-of-departure and a day-prior-to-departure standby fare to London from JFK, Newark, Orlando, Miami, and Boston, but only between mid-October and late March.

GOING AS A COURIER This cost-cutting technique may not be for everybody. You travel as a passenger and courier, and for this service you'll secure a greatly discounted airfare or, in certain rare instances, even a free ticket.

You're allowed one piece of carry-on luggage only; your baggage allowance is used by the courier firm to transport its cargo (which, by the way, is perfectly legitimate). As a courier, you don't actually handle the merchandise you're "transporting" to Europe, you just carry a manifest to present to Customs.

Upon arrival, an employee of the courier service will reclaim the company's cargo. Incidentally, you fly alone, so don't plan to travel with anybody. (A friend may be able to arrange a flight as a courier on a consecutive day.) Most courier services operate from Los Angeles or New York, but some operate out of other cities, such as Chicago or Miami.

Courier services are often listed in the yellow pages or in advertisements in travel sections of newspapers.

For a start, check **Halbert Express,** 147-05 176th St., Jamaica, NY 11434 (tel. 718/656-8189 from 10am to 3pm daily).

Another firm to try is **Now Voyager,** 74 Varick St., Suite 307, New York, NY

(F) FROMMER'S SMART TRAVELER: AIRFARES

1. Take an off-peak flight. That means not only autumn to spring departures, but Monday to Thursday for those midweek discounts.
2. Avoid any last-minute change of plans (if you can) to avoid penalties airlines impose for changes in itineraries.
3. Keep checking the airlines and their fares. Timing is everything. A recent spot check of one airline revealed that in just 7 days it had discounted a New York–London fare by $195.
4. Shop all airlines that fly to your destination.
5. Always ask for the lowest fare, not just a discount fare.
6. Ask about frequent-flyer programs to gain bonus miles when you book a flight.
7. Check bucket shops for last-minute discount fares that are even cheaper than their advertised slashed fares.
8. Ask about air/land packages. Land arrangements are often cheaper when booked with an air ticket.
9. Check standby fares offered by Virgin Atlantic Airways.
10. Fly free or at a heavy discount as a courier.

10013 (tel. 212/431-1616). It has a 24-hour phone system. If you're interested in being a courier, you should probably contact Now Voyager first, as it works with six daily flights to London, one of which allows couriers a stay of up to 30 days *and* transport of a modest amount of personal luggage. (Halbert Express is actually one of Now Voyager's clients.) Now Voyager offers more flights to more destinations, including many to London.

The **International Association of Air Travel Couriers,** P.O. Box 1349, Lake Worth, FL 33460 (tel. 407/582-8320), for an annual membership of $35, will send you six issues of its newsletter, *Shoestring Traveler,* and about half a dozen issues of *Air Courier Bulletin,* a directory of air-courier bargains around the world. Other advantages of membership are photo identification cards, and the organization acts as a troubleshooter if a courier runs into difficulties.

BY SHIP

BY OCEAN LINER   The **Cunard Line,** 555 Fifth Ave., New York, NY 10017 (tel. 212/880-7500, or toll free 800/221-4770), boasts as its flagship the *Queen Elizabeth 2,* quite accurately billed as "the most advanced ship of the age." It is the only ocean liner providing regular transatlantic service—26 sailings a year between April and December—which docks at such cities as New York, Baltimore, and Fort Lauderdale, before sailing to the European ports of Cherbourg, France, and Southampton, England. Built along the Clyde River near Glasgow in the late 1960s, the *QE2* was totally modernized in 1987 at a cost of $152 million. On board, you'll find four swimming pools, a sauna, nightclubs, a balconied theater, cinema, chic boutiques (including the world's first seagoing branch of Harrods), five restaurants, paddle-tennis courts, and a children's playroom staffed with English nannies.

The lifestyle on the ship also includes an onboard "Spa at Sea," a computer learning center with 12 IBM personal computers, seminars by trained professionals on astrology, cooking, art, fitness, and health, and a Festival of Life series that introduces you to such personalities as James Michener, Carly Simon, Dick Cavett, or Ben Kingsley.

Fares are extremely complicated, based on cabin standard and location and the season of sailing. In thrift/superthrift season—roughly defined as late autumn—sailings usually cost a minimum of $2,170 in transatlantic class and around $3,515 in first class. Prices go steeply uphill from there, eventually reaching a maximum of $10,930 for a suite in high season. These prices are per person, based on double occupancy. All passengers pay a $155 port tax and handling charges, regardless of the class of cabin. Many different packages are promoted, most of which add on relatively inexpensive airfare from your home city to the port of departure, plus a return to your home city from London on British Airways.

BY FREIGHTER For an offbeat, often less expensive alternative (note, though, that a budget accommodation aboard the *QE2* can cost less), if you have time and an adventurous spirit, you can try to secure a cabin aboard a freighter. No freighter can carry more than 12 passengers because a full-time ship's doctor would be required. Your cabin will be adequate, but don't expect organized activities.

Most freighters dock at Le Havre, Rotterdam, or Bremerhaven, but a few make stops at such unlikely British ports as Felixstowe. The voyage takes 7 to 12 days from the U.S. East Coast. Sometimes the final port will change during crossing, throwing prearranged itineraries into confusion, so you need to be flexible.

In summer, cabins are often booked as much as a year in advance. Space is more likely to be available in winter.

For more information, contact **Ford's Freighter Travel Guide**, 19448 Londelius St., Northridge, CA 91324 (tel. 818/701-7414).

Lykes Brothers Steamship Co., Lykes Center, 300 Poydras St., New Orleans, LA 70130 (tel. toll free 800/235-9537), is owned and operated by a Florida-based family. This American-registered shipping company owns four freighters, one of which plies goods every 30 days between New Orleans, Antwerp (Belgium), and Bremerhaven (Germany). On the return trip from Bremerhaven, it stops at an English port (Felixstowe), at Le Havre (France), at Norfolk (Virginia), at Galveston (Texas), and then finally New Orleans. No more than six passengers can be accommodated at one time—there are three double cabins per vessel. There is no entertainment of any kind, no ship's doctor, and very little to do except watch the waves and read.

BY TRAIN OR CAR FROM THE CONTINENT OF EUROPE

BY TRAIN Britain's isolation from the rest of Europe has led to the development of an independent railway network with different rules and regulations than those observed on the Continent. If you're traveling to Britain from the Continent, your Eurailpass will *not* be valid when you get there. BritRail, however, offers its own pass if you plan to travel extensively in the British Isles.

If you're touring both Britain and France, consider using the BritFrance Railpass, which includes free access to round-trip Channel crossings. You may choose a total of any 5 days of unlimited rail travel during a 15-day consecutive period, or 10 days during a single month—on both the British and French rail networks. Adult first-class fares (any 5 days in 15) are $359; adult standard fares are $269. There is also a youth standard (ages 12 to 25), costing $229 for any 5 days in 15. Obtain the pass at RailEurope, Inc. (tel. toll free 800/848-7245) or at BritRail Travel International (tel. 212/575-2667).

The most popular rail crossing from the Continent to England departs from Paris's Gare du Nord and travels to Boulogne. There, you board a Seacat (a double-hulled catamaran powered by aircraft-style jet engines) for the Channel port of Folkestone. From there, you board a train to London. The entire transit takes 5½ hours.

BY FERRY/HOVERCRAFT For centuries, sailing ships and ferryboats have traversed the English Channel bearing supplies, merchandise, and passengers. Today, the major carriers are Sealink, Hoverspeed, and the P&O Channel Lines.

P&O maintains a North American sales agency at Scots-American Travel, 26 Rugen Dr., Harrington Park, NJ 07640 (tel. 201/768-5505), which can reserve passage on any of the P&O ferryboats into Britain. It will also issue ironclad reservations for portage of autos. (Advance reservations, particularly in summertime, are usually necessary for cars.)

P&O operates jetfoil service between Dover and Ostende, Belgium (for passengers only), and car and passenger ferries between Portsmouth and Cherbourg, France (three sailings a day, 4¾ hours each way); between Portsmouth and Le Havre (three sailings a day, 5¾ hours each way); between Dover and Calais (sailings every 90 minutes throughout the day, 75 minutes each way); between Dover and Ostende (between 6 and 8 sailings a day, 4 hours each way); and a somewhat less popular passage from Felixstowe to Zeebrugge (twice-daily, 5¾ hours each way). P&O also operates many of the ferries between the British mainland and the Scottish islands, ferries from Scotland to Northern Ireland, and a long-haul car-ferry between Portsmouth and Bilbao, Spain.

P&O's major competitors include Sealink and Hoverspeed, Ltd., either of which can carry both passengers and vehicles on all of their routings. Both companies are represented in North America by BritRail (tel. 212/595-2667).

By far the most popular routing across the Channel is between Calais and Dover. Hoverspeed operates 35-minute Hovercraft crossings, at least 12 a day, as well as slightly longer crossings via Seacat (a kind of double-hulled catamaran propelled by jet engines) between Boulogne and Folkestone. Seacats cross about four times a day and require 55 minutes.

Sealink operates conventional ferryboat service between Cherbourg and Southampton (usually one or two a day for a crossing of between 6 and 8 hours); and between Dieppe and Newhaven (four times a day for a crossing of 4 hours). Most popular of all are Sealink's conventional car-ferries between Calais and Dover. Departing 20 times a day in either direction, they require 90 minutes for the crossing, cost $42 each way for a passenger without a car, and between $123 and $300 for a car—depending on its size and the season—including up to five occupants.

If you plan to take a rented car across the Channel, check carefully about license and insurance requirements with the rental company before you leave. Sometime in late 1994 or early 1995 the long-heralded "Chunnel," or tunnel-under-the-Channel between Dover and Calais, might alter the above-mentioned ferryboat situation drastically.

ORGANIZED TOURS

Europe's largest tour operator, booking greater numbers of European hotel rooms and with more experience than almost anyone else in the travel industry, is Britain's national airline, **British Airways** (tel. toll free 800/AIRWAYS for details). Its selection of tours through the British Isles is gratifyingly extensive and often tailor-made for the specific wishes of potential clients. The company includes a full spectrum of what it calls "designer holidays," each of which is planned for participants with sometimes radically different interests. Some of the offerings include carefully structured, tightly scheduled motorcoach tours for clients who feel they need the most channeling, guidance, and well-informed running commentaries.

Equally popular are tours designed for bravely independent souls who need no more than discount vouchers for a rental car and reserved rooms at specific types of hotels. Depending on your tastes and your pocketbook, BA can arrange vouchers for discounted accommodations in everything from simple inns above a local pub to suites in the finest aristocratic mansions of England. The company can also arrange a reduced rate on a cost-conscious rented car so you can drive yourself over the hills and through the glens of England without interference from anyone except your chosen companion.

The array of options is huge: Tours can be as straightforward as a 1-day jaunt from London to Canterbury or Brighton, for example (with a return to London in time for a West End play); or they might include short excursions from London to the Edinburgh Music Festival (with difficult-to-obtain tickets included as part of the bargain), or a 9-day all-inclusive tour through the great houses and gardens of England. Clients preferring to travel alone should specify the area of their greatest interest and the dates of their intended visit; then a sales representative can tailor an itinerary specifically for them. (Possibilities for this type of excursion might include the West Country, the Lake District, or perhaps a spate of museum- and theater-going in London, with discounted rates on stays in a wide assortment of big-city hotels.)

For a free catalog and additional information, call British Airways at the toll-free number listed above *before you book your airline ticket,* since some of the company's available options are contingent upon the purchase of a round-trip transatlantic air ticket.

Chicago-based **Abercrombie & Kent International,** 1520 Kensington Rd., Oak Brook, IL 60521 (tel. 708/954-2944, or toll free 800/323-7308), books carefully organized 6-, 9-, or 13-day tours of Britain, using first-class rail transport and the accompanying presence of both a trained guide and a full-time baggage handler. Each night is spent in four- or five-star hotels—often buildings classified as stately homes of historical interest. Considered among the most posh and elegant tours in the business, they carry per-person tabs, without airfare, of from $2,460 for 6 days, from $3,845 for 9 days, and from $4,700 for 13 days.

8. GETTING AROUND

BY PLANE

British Airways (BA) (tel. toll free 800/AIRWAYS) flies to more than 20 cities outside London, including Manchester, Glasgow, and Edinburgh. British Airways telephone representatives in North America can give price and schedule information, and make reservations for flights, hotels, car rentals, and tours within the U.K. Ask about the British Airways Super Shuttle Saver fares, which can save you up to 50% on travel to certain key British cities. Trips must be reserved and ticketed 2 weeks in advance, and you can fly only during off-peak times. This usually (but not always) is restricted to anytime on weekends, or weekdays between 10am and 3:30pm, and any night flight after 7pm.

Other cost-conscious options include a 14-day round-trip APEX ticket that must be reserved and paid for 14 days in advance, and travel completed within 3 months of departure.

British Airways's U.K. airpass allows travel in a continuous loop to between 3 and 12 cities on BA's domestic routes. Passengers must end their journey at the same point they began. If such a ticket is booked (say, London to Manchester to Glasgow to Aberdeen to the Shetland Islands, with an eventual return to London), each segment of any itinerary will cost (subject to change) between $67 and $85. This is considerably less (as much as 50% less) than if each segment were booked individually. The pass is available for travel to about a dozen of the most-visited cities and regions of Britain. It must be booked and paid for at least 7 days before departure from the United States, and all sectors of the itinerary, including transatlantic passage from North America, must be booked simultaneously. Some changes are permitted in

flight dates (but not in the cities visited) after the ticket is issued. Check wi
full details and restrictions.

BY TRAIN

Eurailpass is not valid in Great Britain.

There are several special national passes for train travel outside London. For railroad information, go to the British Rail/Sealink office, 4–12 Lower Regent St., SW1 (tel. 071/928-5151), and at the British Rail Travel Centres in the main London railway stations—Waterloo, King's Cross, Euston, and Paddington—where each deals mainly with its own region.

BRITRAIL PASS This pass permits unlimited rail travel in England, Scotland, and Wales on all British Rail routes. (It is not valid for passage on ships between the U.K. and the rest of continental Europe, the Channel Islands, or Ireland.) An 8-day gold (first-class) pass costs $299; an 8-day silver (economy-class) pass costs $219. A 15-day pass costs $489 and $339, respectively; a 22-day pass costs $645 and $425; and a 1-month pass, $775 and $495. Kids 5 to 15 pay half fare; under-5s travel free.

Youth passes (for ages 16 to 25), all silver, are $179 for 8 days, $269 for 15 days. If you choose to go first class, you pay full adult fare.

BritRail also offers a Senior Citizen gold pass to people 60 and over. For 8 days, it's $279 in first class, $199 in second; for 15 days, $455 in first class, $305 in second; for 22 days, $599 in first class, $379 in second; and for 1 month, $725 in first class, $445 in second.

Note: Prices for BritRail Passes are higher for Canadian travelers because of the different conversion rate for Canadian dollars.

BritRail Passes cannot be obtained in Britain, but should be secured before leaving North America, either through travel agents or by writing or visiting BritRail Travel International, 1500 Broadway, New York, NY 10036 (tel. 212/575-2667). Canadians can write to P.O. Box 89510, 250 Eglinton Ave. East, Toronto, ON M4P 3EI. BritRail Passes do not have to be predated. Validate your pass at any British Rail station when you start your first rail journey.

BRITRAIL FLEXIPASS The Flexipass lets you travel anywhere on British Rail, with the understanding that many visitors like to alternate travel days with uninterrupted blocks of sightseeing time in a particular city or region. The 8-day Flexipass can be used for 4 days within any 8-day period, and costs $249 in first class, $189 in economy. Seniors pay $229 in first class or $169 in second class, and youths 16 to 25 pay $155 to travel economy class. Also available is a 15-day Flexipass that allows 8 days of travel within any 15-day period, and costs $389 in first class, $269 in economy. A senior pass costs $365 in first class, $245 in second class; the youth economy class costs $219.

LONDON EXTRA If you're planning to confine your explorations of England to easy day-trips from London, London Extra may make better sense than a BritRail Pass. It allows unlimited travel to accessible destinations on British Rail's "Network Southeast," which covers the area stretching southeastward from London to the sea and includes many of the most historic and appealing towns and villages of England (for example, Oxford, Cambridge, Dover, Canterbury, Salisbury, and Portsmouth). Frequent trains—41 daily from London to Brighton alone—let you leave early in the morning and return to London in time for the theater or dinner.

A 3-day London Extra Pass in first class costs $109 for adults, $55 for children aged 5 to 15; $85 for adults and $45 for children in second class. A 7-day London Extra Pass costs $189 for adults and $95 for children in first class, $155 for adults and $78 for children in second class. The pass is also issued in a 4-day version as well.

London Extra must be purchased from either your travel agent or from BritRail Travel International in the United States or Canada (see addresses above).

BRITAINSHRINKERS TOURS From early April to the end of October, Britainshrinkers, Ltd. operates a limited series of full-day escorted tours that include, in different combinations, visits to Bath, Stonehenge, Stratford-upon-Avon, Oxford, and sections of Wales and the Cotswolds. They include train transportation and sightseeing by bus. Tours include some free time to take lunch in a local pub, shop, and explore on your own. Tours return to London in time for dinner or the theater. Rates include entrance fees and VAT, but usually not the price of lunch.

The Britainshrinkers offer excellent value for the money, and if you use a valid BritRail Pass or Flexipass, you can save up to 60% of the cost of each tour you take. Britainshrinkers Tours can be purchased from either your travel agent or BritRail in the United States and Canada or in England at BritRail offices (see addresses above).

BY BUS

In Britain, a long-distance touring bus is called a "coach," and "buses" are taken for local transportation. There's an efficient and frequent express motorcoach network—operated by National Express and Scottish Citylink Coaches—that links most of Britain's towns and cities. Destinations off the main route can easily be reached by stopping and transferring to a local bus. Tickets are relatively cheap—often half the price of rail fare—and it's usually cheaper to purchase a round-trip (or "return") ticket than two one-way fares separately.

Victoria Coach Station, on Buckingham Palace Road (tel. 071/730-0202), is the departure point for most buses in London, as well as the large coach operators of National Express and Caledonian Express. The coach station is located just 1 block from the rail depot of Victoria Station. For credit card sales (MasterCard and VISA only), call 071/730-3499 from 8am to 9pm.

National Express Quite luxurious, National Express Rapides are long-distance coaches equipped with hostesses, light refreshments, reclining seats, toilets, and no-smoking areas. Details of all coach services can be obtained by phoning 071/730-0202 from 8am to 10pm daily. The National Express ticket office at Victoria Station is open from 6am to midnight daily.

The **Britexpress Card**—offered by both National Express and Caledonian Express—grants a discount of 33% off of all adult tickets purchased on Britain's Express Motorcoach network. The pass costs £12 ($18) and is good for travel to more than 1,500 destinations in England, Scotland, and Wales during any 30-day period.

You might also consider National Express's **Tourist Trail Pass** offering unlimited travel on their network within the United Kingdom. (Know in advance that this company's service is most extensive in England and Wales.) A 5-day pass costs £65 ($97.50); an 8-day pass, £90 ($135); a 15-day pass, £135 ($202.50); a 22-day pass, £160 ($240); and a 30-day pass, £190 ($285).

Green Line For journeys within a 35-mile radius of London, try the Green Line coach service. Their inquiry office is at 4A Fountain Sq., Bulleid Way, SW1 in Victoria (tel. 081/668-7261 for more information).

With a 1-day **Diamond Rover Ticket,** costing £6 ($9) for adults and £4 ($6) for children, you can visit many of the attractions of Greater London and the surrounding region, including Windsor Castle and Hampton Court. The pass is valid for 1 day on almost all Green Line coaches and Country buses Monday through Friday after 9am and all day on Saturday and Sunday. The 3-day Diamond Rover costs £16.50 ($24.80) for adults and £11 ($16.50) for children.

Green Line has bus routes called **Country Bus Lines** that circle through the periphery of London. Although they do not usually go directly into the center of the capital, they do hook up with the routes of the Green Line coaches and red buses that do. For information, contact Green Line Country Bus Lines, Lesbourne Rd., Reigate, Surrey RH2 7LE (tel. 081/668-7261).

BY CAR

Unless you buy a car in England or drive over from the Continent, you'll have to rent a car here if you plan to visit many of the rural corners of Britain without resorting to public transport. Note, however, that if you plan to remain in London during most of your stay in the U.K., a car might be an expensive and annoying hindrance rather than a helpmate. Many of the most interesting sights on the periphery of London can easily be reached by train. In contrast, if you're planning a get-away-from-the-crowds self-drive day-trip, or even a week's jaunt on your own, and if driving on the left appeals to your sense of adventure, here are some guidelines:

RENTALS   Partly because of the huge number of visitors to the United Kingdom, the car-rental market is among the most competitive in Europe. Nevertheless, car rentals are often relatively expensive, unless you avail yourself of one of the promotional deals that are frequently offered by such entities as British Airways (see below).

London has a large array of companies from which to choose (some of which are listed alphabetically below). Most of these will accept your U.S. driver's license, provided you're 23 years old (21 in rare instances) and have had the license for more than a year. Never forget, however, that cars in Britain travel on the left-hand side of the road and have their steering wheels positioned on the "wrong" side of the vehicle.

Many companies will grant discounts to clients who reserve their cars in advance (usually 48 hours) through the toll-free reservations offices in the renter's home country. Rentals of a week or more are almost always less expensive, per day, than day rentals.

When making reservations, be sure to ask if the price quoted includes the 17½% Value-Added Tax (VAT), personal accident insurance (PAI), collision-damage waiver (CDW), and/or any other insurance options. If not, ask what they will cost, because at the end of your rental, they can make a big difference in your bottom line. As in the United States, the CDW and some added insurance are sometimes offered free by certain credit-card companies if you use the card to pay for the rental. Check directly with your credit-card issuer to see if you are covered by your credit card so you can avoid the sometimes unnecessary coverage.

Avis   (tel. toll free 800/331-2112) This company offers a 1-day rental of the small but peppy Ford Fiesta with CDW and unlimited mileage for £83 ($124.50; taxes not included). At presstime, however, a full week's rental of a similar car, if reserved 14 days in advance, was a much better bargain at £98 ($147). Avis's main downtown office is in Mayfair at 8 Balderton St., London SW1 (tel. 071/917-6700).

British Airways   (tel. toll free 800/AIRWAYS) One of the least expensive ways to rent a car in Britain is through the reservations services of BA. As the largest renter of cars in the United Kingdom, BA can offer its passengers heavily discounted rates. Depending on their size, horsepower, amenities, and the season, cars range in price from a low of $14 to a maximum of $78 per day. VAT and insurance are extra. Child seats are available free. Understandably, these arrangements are offered only to passengers flying into Britain on BA. If your hotel accommodations are also reserved through the same toll-free number, booklets of valuable coupons (offering two-for-one nights at the theater and discounts on restaurants, shops, and museums) are also included in the deal.

Budget Rent-a-Car   (tel. toll free 800/472-3325) Depending on your needs and your airfare arrangements, you might want to try this reliable and cost-conscious company. Budget has eight offices in London, including one at the major airports and Victoria Railway Station, and about 100 others throughout the U.K. Their busiest London office is near Marble Arch at 89 Wigmore St., W1 (tel. 071/723-8038). If you reserve from North America at least 24 hours prior to pickup, cars will cost from £41 ($61.50) per day for short rentals, and from £145 ($217.50) per week (and less during certain promotions), with unlimited mileage, VAT, and CDW included as part of the net cost.

Hertz (tel. toll free 800/654-3001) This company offers an unlimited-mileage Ford Fiesta for as low as £119 ($178.50) per week, depending on the status of their seasonal promotions. (VAT, CDW, and PAI are extra, which will make this arrangement more expensive than it might seem at first.) Hertz's main London office is at 35 Edgware Rd., Marble Arch, W1 (tel. 071/402-4242).

DRIVING RULES & REQUIREMENTS In England, as you probably know, *you drive on the left* and pass on the right. Road signs are clear and the international symbols unmistakable.

To drive a car in Britain, your passport and driver's license must be presented when you rent a car. No special British license is needed. The prudent driver will secure a copy of the *British Highway Code,* available from almost any stationer or news agent. Wearing seat belts is mandatory in the British Isles.

Warning: Pedestrian crossings are marked by striped lines (zebra striping) on the road; flashing lights near the curb indicate that drivers must stop and yield the right of way if a pedestrian has stepped out into the zebra zone to cross the street.

ROAD MAPS Overall—and if you're trying to locate some obscure village in Britain—the best road map is *The Ordnance Survey Motor Atlas of Great Britain.* Revised annually, it's published by Temple Press. It's available at most bookstores, including W & G Foyle Ltd., 119 Charing Cross Rd., London, WC2 (tel. 071/439-8501).

BREAKDOWNS Membership in one of the two major auto clubs in England—the Automobile Association (AA) and the Royal Automobile Club (RAC)—can be helpful. Membership, which can be obtained through your car rental agent, entitles you to free legal and technical advice on motoring matters, as well as a whole range of discounts on motor-related products and services.

The AA is located at Fanum House, Basingstoke, Hampshire RG21 2EA (tel. 0256/20123). The RAC can be contacted at Spectrum, Bond Street (P.O. Box 700), Bristol, Avon BS99 1RB (tel. 0272/232340).

If your car breaks down on the highway, you can call for 24-hour breakdown service from roadside phones. The 24-hour number to call for AA is 0800/887766 and for RAC 0800/828282. All motorways are provided with special emergency phones that are connected to police traffic units, and the police can contact either of the auto clubs on your behalf.

GASOLINE Called "petrol," gasoline is sold by the liter with 4.5 liters to an imperial gallon. Prices are much higher than Stateside, and you'll probably have to serve yourself. In some remote areas stations are few and far between, and many all over the country are closed on Sunday.

HITCHHIKING

Hitchhiking in England is legal—except on motorways—but getting into a car with a stranger anywhere in the world can be extremely dangerous, especially for solo travelers. Always exercise caution. Generally, the cleaner and tidier you look, the better your chances for getting a ride. Have a sign with your destination written on it to hold up for drivers to see. Again, consider the great risk involved before you get into somebody's car. Women alone should never contemplate hitchhiking.

SUGGESTED ITINERARIES

CITY HIGHLIGHTS

The cities or towns below are not ranked in order of importance.

1. London
2. Windsor
3. Oxford
4. Canterbury
5. Portsmouth
6. Winchester
7. Plymouth
8. Salisbury
9. Glastonbury
10. Bath
11. Broadway
12. Stratford-upon-Avon
13. Cambridge
14. Lincoln
15. York
16. Windermere
17. Liverpool

PLANNING YOUR ITINERARY

IF YOU HAVE 1 WEEK

Days 1–4: London (for specific suggestions, see "Suggested Itineraries" in Chapter 6).

Day 5: Day-trip to Stratford-upon-Avon (try to see one of Shakespeare's plays performed).

Day 6: Day-trip to Windsor.

Day 7: Day-trip to Canterbury.

IF YOU HAVE 2 WEEKS

Days 1–7: Spend the first week as outlined above.

Day 8: Head for the West Country, visiting Winchester where you can stay overnight.

Day 9: Visit Salisbury and nearby Stonehenge.

Day 10: Head southwest to the coast to Plymouth.

Day 11: Continue west to Looe.

Day 12: Head north to Glastonbury and then to Wells for the night.

Day 13: To Bath for the night.

Day 14: Head west back to London.

IF YOU HAVE 3 WEEKS

Days 1–14: Spend your first 2 weeks as outlined above.

Day 15: From London, head north into East Anglia staying overnight at Cambridge.

Day 16: Visit Ely Cathedral and continue to Boston for lunch, with an overnight in Lincoln.

Day 17: Drive northwest from Lincoln to York for the night.

Days 18 and 19: From York, head across England on the A59 for lunch in Harrogate. Continue to the Lake District, with a 2-night stopover in Windermere. On Day 19 explore the lakes.

Day 20: Drive south to Liverpool and spend the night.

Day 21: Spend most of the day getting back to London, perhaps for a night at the theater, followed by a late supper in Soho.

---

9. WHERE TO STAY

CLASSIFICATIONS Unlike some countries, England doesn't have a rigid hotel-classification system. The tourist board grades hotels by crowns instead of stars, but note that crowns don't assess the quality of the hotel; therefore, crowns aren't a good barometer of whether the hotel is good or not.

Five crowns (deluxe) is the highest rating. Depending on their range of facilities, other hotels are rated four, three, two, or one crowns. There is even a classification of "listed" with no crowns. For the most part these are very modest accommodations with limited facilities.

In a five-crown hotel, all rooms must have a private bath; in a four-crown hotel, only 75%. In a one-crown hotel, buildings are required to have hot and cold running water in all the rooms. But in "listed" hotels hot and cold running water in the rooms is not mandatory. Crown ratings are posted outside the buildings.

The system is voluntary, and many hotels choose not to participate at all.

Many hotels—especially older ones—still lack private baths for all rooms; most have hot and cold running water; many have modern wings with all the amenities, as well as older sections that are less up-to-date. When making reservations, always ask what section of the hotel you'll be staying in, if it has extensions.

All hotels used to include a full English breakfast of bacon and eggs in the room price, but today only B&Bs continue that policy. The higher up the price ladder you go, the more likely you are to be charged extra for breakfast. A continental breakfast is commonly included, but it may mean just tea or coffee and toast, with extra charges for juice, etc.

RESERVATIONS Reservations are advised, even in the so-called slow hotel-booking months from November to March. Tourist travel to London peaks from May to October, when moderate and budget hotels are full. Only the most adventurous show up without a reservation.

It's easiest to reserve with a chain via their representatives in North America (and toll-free 800 numbers), but they might not be the type of accommodations you're seeking.

For hotels without representatives in North America, write or send a fax. If you write, send an International Reply Coupon, available at post offices. When seeking reservations, give alternative dates if possible. If a hotel accepts your request, you may be asked to send one night's deposit. At small places in England, many readers have reported great difficulty or even complete failure in getting their deposit returned if they were forced to cancel their reservations suddenly.

If you call a hotel right before your arrival, you may be lucky enough to secure a room because of a last-minute cancellation.

Like airlines, hotels traditionally overbook, counting on last-minute cancellations. When everybody shows up, however, they face irate customers shouting at the desk, waving a confirmed reservation. To avoid this, give the hotel a credit-card number and authorize management to add the cost to your bill even if you don't show up.

BED & BREAKFAST In towns, cities, and villages throughout England homeowners take in paying guests. Watch for the familiar B&B signs. Generally, these are modest family homes, but sometimes they are like small hotels, with as many as 15 or more rooms. If that big, they are more properly classified as a guesthouse. B&Bs are the cheapest places to stay comfortably and decently in England.

Hometours International, 1170 Broadway, New York, NY 10001 (tel. 212/689-0851, or toll free 800/367-4668), will make bed-and-breakfast reservations in England, Scotland, and Wales. This is the only company to guarantee reservations for more than 400 locations in Britain. Accommodations are paid for in the U.S. with dollars. Prices start as low as $33 per person per night but can go as high as $98 per person in London. The company also offers walking tours of Great Britain, with prices starting as low as $450 for 7 days, including meals. Tours are designed for families, single parents, and singles without children. In addition, Hometours can also arrange for apartments in London. The company also offers cottages in Great Britain that cost from $250 per week.

Another organization well equipped to arrange unusual accommodations in Britain is the **Barclay International Group (BIG),** 150 E. 52nd St., New York, NY 10022 (tel. 212/832-3777, or toll free 800/845-6636). They specialize in short-term rentals of apartments (they're called "flats") in London and cottages in the English countryside. Considered a viable alternative to traditional hotel stays, they may be appropriate for families, groups of friends, or businesspersons traveling together. Apartments are usually more luxurious than you might have imagined; furnished with kitchens, they offer a low-cost alternative to restaurant meals. Apartments suitable for one or two occupants begin, during low season, at around $500 a week (including tax) and can go much higher. Some travelers find that they are usually less expensive than equivalent stays in London hotels. For extended stays in the English countryside, BIG's country cottages are located in such areas as the Cotswolds, the Lake District, and Oxford, as well as farther afield in Scotland and Wales.

Reservations for B&B accommodations in London can also be made through the **British Travel Centre** (see "Tourist Information," in Chapter 3).

FARMHOUSES In many parts of the country, farmhouses have one, two, even three or four rooms set aside for paying guests, who usually arrive in the summer months. They don't have the facilities of most guesthouses, but they have a rustic appeal and charm, especially for motorists, as they tend to lie off the beaten path. Prices are generally lower than B&Bs or guesthouses, and sometimes you're offered some good country home-cooking (at an extra charge) if you make arrangements in advance. The British Tourist Authority will provide a booklet, *Stay on a Farm,* or you can ask at local tourist offices.

HOLIDAY COTTAGES Throughout England fully furnished studios, houses, cottages, "flats" (apartments), even trailers suitable for families and groups, are offered for rent (usually for a month). The British Tourist Authority offices and most tourist offices have lists available. *Note:* Sometimes from October to March, rents are slashed by 50%.

Ask the British Tourist Authority for the free *Apartments in London* and *Holiday Homes* listing rental agencies like **At Home Abroad,** 405 E. 56th St., Apt. 6H, New York, NY 10022 (tel. 212/421-9165). If interested parties write or fax (fax 212/752-1591) a description of their needs, At Home Abroad will send them free some appropriate listings.

British Travel Associates, P.O. Box 299, Elkton, VA 22827 (tel. 703/298-2232, or toll free 800/327-6097), represents between 8,000 and 10,000 rental properties in the U.K.—each of which is rented by the week (Saturday to Saturday) and requires a 50% payment in full at the time of booking. They publish a catalog with pictures of each of their offerings, which is available for a $4 fee, refundable with the payment of the deposit. They represent everything from the honey-colored, thatch-roofed cottage in the Cotswolds to condominiums in Britain's cathedral towns and university cities. The company also represents about 50 hotels in London, whose rates are discounted by 5% to 50%, depending on the season and market conditions. They are also the North American representative for the U.K.'s largest bus company, National Express.

YOUTH HOSTELS   England, Scotland, and Wales have some 350 youth hostels providing inexpensive accommodations with cooking facilities. No age restriction is imposed. Contact **YHA Headquarters,** Trevalyn House, 8 St. Stephen's Hill, St. Albans, Hertfordshire AL1 2DY (tel. 0727/55215).

FAST ENGLAND

For information on London, refer to "Fast Facts: London," in Chapter 3.

Business Hours   Business hours with many, many exceptions are Monday through Friday from 9am to 5pm. The lunch break lasts an hour, but most offices stay open all day. In general, stores are open Monday through Saturday from 9am to 5:30pm. In country towns, there is usually an early-closing day (often on Wednesday or Thursday), when the shops close at 1pm. The day varies from town to town.

Camera and Film   Film is readily available, especially in large cities. Processing takes about 24 hours although many places, particularly in London, will do it almost while you wait. There are few restrictions on the use of your camera, except where notices are posted, as in churches, theaters, and certain museums. If in doubt, ask.

Cigarettes   Most U.S. brands are available in major towns. *Warning:* More and more places now ban smoking. Make sure you enter a "smoker" on the train or Underground, and smoke only on the upper decks of buses or in the smoking area of single-deckers, theaters, and other public places. Some restaurants restrict smoking, as do many bed and breakfasts.

Climate   See "When to Go," in this chapter.

Crime   See "Safety," below.

Currency   See "Information, Entry Requirements, and Money," in this chapter.

Customs   See "Information, Entry Requirements, and Money," in this chapter.

Dentists   Outside London, ask the nearest sympathetic local resident— usually your hotelier—for information.

Doctors   Hotels keep lists of local practitioners, for whom you'll have to pay. Outside London, dial 100 and ask the operator for the local police, who will give you the name, address, and telephone number of a doctor in your area. Emergency treatment is free, but if you visit a doctor at his or her surgery (office), or if he or she makes a "house call" to your hotel, you will have to pay. It's wise to take out adequate medical/accident insurance coverage before you leave home.

Documents Required See "Information, Entry Requirements, and Money," in this chapter.

Driving Rules See "Getting Around," in this chapter.

Drug Laws Britain is becoming increasingly severe in enforcing antidrug laws. Persons arrested for possession of even tiny quantities of marijuana have been deported, forced to pay stiff fines, or sentenced to jail for 2 to 7 years. Possession of "white powder" drugs such as heroin or cocaine carry even more stringent penalties.

Drugstores In Britain they're called "chemists." Every police station in the country has a list of emergency chemists. Dial "0" (zero) and ask the operator for the local police, who will give you the name of the nearest.

Electricity British electricity is 240 volts AC, 50 cycles, roughly twice the voltage in North America, which is 115–120 volts AC, 60 cycles. American plugs don't fit British wall outlets. Always bring suitable transformers and/or adapters (some but definitely not all hotels will supply them). Be warned that you will destroy your appliance (and possibly start a fire as well) if you plug an American appliance directly into a European electrical outlet without a transformer. Tape recorders, VCRs, and other devices with motors intended to revolve at a fixed number of r.p.m. probably won't work properly even with transformers.

Embassies and Consulates See "Fast Facts: London," in Chapter 3.

Emergencies Dial 999 for police, fire, or ambulance. Give your name, address, and telephone number, and state the nature of the emergency. Misuse of the 999 service carries a heavy fine. Cardiac arrest, yes—sprained ankle, no. Accident injury, yes—dented fender, no.

Etiquette Be normal; be quiet. The British don't like hearing other people's conversations. In pubs you are not expected to buy a round of drinks unless someone has bought you a drink. Don't talk politics or religion in pubs.

Gasoline See "Getting Around," in this chapter.

Hitchhiking See "Getting Around," in this chapter.

Holidays See "When to Go," in this chapter.

Information See "Information, Entry Requirements, and Money," in this chapter, and individual city/regional chapters.

Laundry and Dry Cleaning Most stores and most hotels need 2 days to do the job. London and most provincial towns have launderettes where you can wash and dry your own clothes, but there are no facilities for ironing. Many launderettes also have dry-cleaning machines. One-day dry-cleaning service is available.

Legal Aid The American Services section of the U.S. Consulate (see "Fast Facts: London," in Chapter 3) will give advice if you run into trouble abroad. They can advise you of your rights and even provide a list of attorneys (for which you'll have to pay if services are used). But they cannot interfere on your behalf in the legal processes of Great Britain. For questions about American citizens who are arrested abroad, including ways of getting money to them, telephone the Citizens Emergency Center of the Office of Special Consulate Services in Washington, D.C. (tel. 202/647-5225).

Liquor Laws The legal drinking age is 18. Children under 16 aren't allowed in pubs, except in certain rooms, and then only when accompanied by a parent or guardian. Don't drink and drive. Penalties are stiff.

In England, pubs can be open Monday through Saturday from 11am to 11pm, and on Sunday from noon to 3pm and 7 to 10:30 or 11pm. Restaurants are also allowed to serve liquor during these hours, but only to people who are dining on the premises. The law allows 30 minutes for "drinking-up time." A meal, incidentally, is defined as "substantial refreshment." And you have to eat and drink sitting down. In hotels, liquor may be served from 11am to 11pm to both residents and nonresidents; after 11pm, only residents, according to the law, may be served.

Lost Property Report the loss to the nearest police station. For London information, see "Fast Facts: London," in Chapter 3.

Mail Letters and parcels for you may, as a rule, be addressed to you at any post office except a town sub-office. The words "To Be Called For" or "Poste Restante" must appear in the address. When claiming your mail, always carry some sort of identification. Airmail letters generally take 7 to 10 days to arrive from the U.S. Post Restante service is provided solely for the convenience of travelers, and it may not be used in the same town for more than 3 months. It can be redirected, upon request, for a 1-month period, or up to 3 months if so specified on the required application form. Post offices and sub-post offices are centrally located and open Monday through Friday from 9am to 5:30pm and on Saturday from 9:30am to noon; closed Sunday. To send an airmail letter to North America costs 39p (60¢), and postcards require a 33p (50¢) stamp. British mailboxes are painted red and carry a royal coat-of-arms as a signature. All post offices will accept parcels for mailing providing they are properly and securely wrapped.

Newspapers *The Times* is the newspaper of record. *The Telegraph* is white-collar oriented, the *Daily Mail* less so, and the *Guardian* intellectual-liberal. The *International Herald Tribune,* published in Paris, and an international edition of *USA Today* are available daily.

Pets It is illegal to bring in pets, except with veterinary documents, and then most are subject to 6 months in quarantine. Hotels have their own rules, but usually dogs are not allowed in restaurants or public rooms, and often not in bedrooms.

Police Dial 999 if the matter is serious. The British police have a helpful reputation and if the local police cannot help, they will know the address of the person who can. Losses, thefts, and other criminal matters should be reported to the police immediately.

Radio and TV There are 24-hour radio channels operating throughout the United Kingdom, with mostly pop music and talk shows during the night. TV starts around 6am with breakfast TV and educational programs. Lighter entertainment begins around 4 or 5pm, after the children's programs, and continues until around midnight. There are now four television channels—two commercial and two BBC without commercials.

Religious Services Times of services are posted outside houses of worship. Almost every creed is catered to in London and other large cities, but in the smaller towns and villages you are likely to find only Anglican (Episcopalian), Roman Catholic, Baptist, and Nonconformist churches.

Restrooms The signs usually say PUBLIC TOILETS. Women pay 5p (10¢) to enter a stall. Men pay nothing. Hotel restrooms are only grudgingly available to nonresidents. Garages (filling stations) also have facilities for customers only, and the key is often kept by the cash register.

Safety Stay alert. Be aware of your immediate surroundings. Don't sling your camera or purse over your shoulder; always lock your car and protect your valuables. Stay in well-lit areas and out of questionable neighborhoods. While Britain is a fairly safe country, every society has its criminals. It's your responsibility to be aware and alert even in the most heavily touristed areas, especially in London and other large cities.

Shoe Repairs Many of the large department stores in Britain have "heel bars" where repairs are done while you wait.

Taxes To encourage energy-saving, the British government levies a 25% tax on gasoline (petrol). There is also a national 17½% Value-Added Tax (VAT) that is added to all hotel and restaurant bills, and will have been included in the price of many of the items you purchase. This can be refunded if you shop at stores that participate in the Retail Export Scheme (signs are posted in the window). When you make a purchase, show your passport and request a Retail Export Scheme form (Form VAT 407) and a stamped, preaddressed envelope. Show the VAT form and your sales receipt to British Customs when you leave the country. They may also ask to see the merchandise. After Customs has stamped it, mail the form back to the shop in the envelope provided *before you leave the country.* Your VAT refund will be mailed to you.

Here are three organizing tips to help you through the Customs procedures: Keep your VAT forms with your passport, pack your purchases in a carry-on bag so you'll have them handy, and allow yourself enough time at your departure point to find a mailbox.

Telephone   British TeleCom is carrying out a massive improvement program of its public pay-phone service. During the transitional period, you could encounter four types of **pay phones:** The old-style (gray) pay phone is being phased out, but there are many still in use. You will need 10p (20¢) coins to operate such phones, but you should not use this type for overseas calls. Its replacement is a blue-and-silver push-button model that accepts coins of any denomination. The other two types of phones require cards instead of coins to operate. The Cardphone takes distinctive green cards especially designed for it. These cards are available in five values—£1 ($1.50), £2 ($3), £4 ($6), £10 ($15), and £20 ($30)—the cards are usable until the total value has expired. Cards can be purchased from news agencies and post offices. Finally, the credit-call pay phone operates on credit cards (AE, DC, MC, V) and is most common at airports and large railway stations.

Outside the major cities, **phone numbers** consist of an exchange code (like an area code) plus a local telephone number. To reach the number, you will need to dial both the exchange code and the number. The exchange codes are usually posted in the call box. If your code is not there, call the operator by dialing 100.

In major cities, phone numbers consist of the exchange code and the local number (seven digits or more). These local digits are all you need to dial if you are calling from within the same city. If you're calling from elsewhere, you'll also need to dial the exchange code for the city. Again, you will find these codes on the call box information sheets or call the operator by dialing 100.

If you don't have the telephone number of the person you want to call, to reach **directory assistance or "information,"** dial 142 for a number in London. For a number elsewhere in the country, dial 192 and then give the operator the name of the town and then the person's name and address.

To call London from the United States, dial the international code, 44 (Britain's country code), either 71 or 81 (London's area codes), and then the seven-digit local telephone number. To call outside London, dial the international code, 44, and then the exchange code and the local telephone number.

To make international calls from England, it's less expensive to dial them yourself from a post office or phone booth than from your hotel room. After you have inserted the coins, dial the international code, then the country code (for the United States, the code is 1), which is followed by the area code and the local number. If you're calling collect or need the assistance of an international operator, dial 155. Caller beware: Some hotels routinely add anywhere from 40% to 300% surcharges to local, national, and international phone calls made from your hotel room.

Telex and Fax   Both telex and fax are common in hotels and business premises, but are mostly restricted to these places. If your hotel has telex or fax facilities, they will send a message for you, but you may have to arrange in advance for the receipt of a reply. For telex bureaus, refer to the yellow pages. Or for information on faxes, dial 100 and ask for the Freefone Intelpost.

Time   England uses Greenwich mean time, 5 hours ahead of the U.S. East Coast. British summer time (GMT plus 1 hour) is in effect roughly from the end of March to the end of October.

Tipping   For **cab drivers,** add about 10% to 15% to the fare as shown on the meter. However, if the driver personally unloads or loads your luggage, add 25p (45¢) per bag.

In **hotels,** porters receive 75p ($1.10) per bag even if you have only one small suitcase. Hall porters are tipped only for special services. Maids receive £1 ($1.50) per day. In top-ranking hotels the concierge will often submit a separate bill, showing charges for newspapers, etc.; if he or she has been particularly helpful, tip extra.

Hotels often add a service charge of 10% to 15% to most bills. In smaller B&Bs, the tip is not likely to be included. Therefore, tip for special services, such as the waiter who serves you breakfast. If several people have served you in a B&B, many guests ask that 10% to 15% be added to the bill and divided among the staff.

In both **restaurants and nightclubs,** a 15% service charge is added to the bill. To that, add another 3% to 5%, depending on the quality of the service. Waiters in deluxe restaurants and nightclubs are accustomed to the extra 5%, which means you'll end up tipping 20%. If that seems excessive, you must remember that the initial service charge reflected in the fixed price is distributed among all the help. Sommeliers (wine stewards) get about £1 ($1.50) per bottle of wine served. Tipping in pubs is not common, although in cocktail bars the waiter or barmaid usually gets about 75p ($1.10) per round of drinks.

For **other services,** barbers and hairdressers expect 10% to 15%. Tour guides expect £2 ($3), although it's not mandatory. Gas station attendants are rarely tipped. Theater ushers also don't expect tips.

Weather   For London, call 071/246-8091; for Devon and Cornwall, 0392/8091; for the Midlands, 021/8091.

Yellow Pages   Throughout England, local phone books contain yellow pages at the back of the book. If you can't find what you're looking for, you may not be looking under the proper English equivalent. For example, instead of "drugstore," try "chemist" or "pharmacist."

GETTING TO KNOW LONDON

Europe's largest city is like a great wheel, with Piccadilly Circus at the hub and dozens of communities branching out from it. Since London is such a conglomeration of sections—each having its own life, hotels, restaurants, pubs—first-time visitors may be intimidated until they get the hang of it. Most visitors spend all their time in the West End, where most of the attractions are located, except for the historic part of London known as The City, including the Tower of London.

If you visit only two or three cities of the world in your lifetime, make one of them London. Stroll its streets, patronize its pubs, and visit its world-renowned museums and landmark buildings. It may not be the most beautiful or romantic of the world's cities, but it's near the top of the list as one of the most fascinating.

This chapter will help you get your bearings. It provides a brief orientation and a preview of the city's most important neighborhoods and answers questions you need to know about getting around London by transportation or on foot. It also presents an encapsulation of "Fast Facts" covering everything from babysitters to shoe repairs.

1. ORIENTATION

ARRIVING

BY PLANE

London is served by four airports. The one you'll arrive at will depend, to a certain extent, on the airline you're flying and your point of departure.

HEATHROW AIRPORT   Heathrow, west of London, in Hounslow (tel. 081/759-4321 for flight information), is one of the world's busiest airports, with staggering numbers of flights arriving from around the world, as well as throughout Britain. It is divided into four terminals, each of which is relatively self-contained. Terminal 4, the newest and most modern, contains the long-haul and transatlantic hub operations of British Airways. Most of the transatlantic flights of U.S.-based airlines arrive at Terminals 1 and 2. Terminal 3 receives the intra-European flights of several European airlines.

   Getting from Heathrow   There is an Underground (subway) connection from Heathrow Central to the center of London; the trip takes 50 minutes and costs

£3.10 ($4.70). There are also airbuses that will take you to central London in about an hour; they cost £5 ($7.50) for adults and £3 ($4.50) for children. A taxi is likely to cost more than £25 ($37.50).

GATWICK   This smaller and somewhat more remote airport (tel. 0293/535-353 for flight information) lies 25 miles south of London in West Sussex. Charter and many scheduled flights arrive here.

Getting from Gatwick   Trains leave for London every 15 minutes during the day and every hour at night, costing £8.50 ($12.80). There is also an express Flightline Bus (no. 777) from Gatwick to Victoria Station that departs every half hour from 6:30am to 8pm and every hour from 8 to 11pm; it costs £6 ($9) per person. A taxi from Gatwick to central London usually costs £40 to £45 ($60 to $67.50); however, you must negotiate a fare with the driver before you get into the cab—the meter does not apply since Gatwick lies outside the Metropolitan Police District.

LONDON CITY AIRPORT   Located about 6 miles east of The City in the Royal Docklands, this airport (tel. 081/474-5555) is used mainly for STOL (short takeoff and landing) and commuter-type flights to and from the Continent. You'll see mostly businesspeople from the Common Market countries passing through here. Among the STOL and commuter airlines that use this terminal are: Air France's link to Brymon Airlines, with routes to Lille, Strasbourg, and Nantes in France; Flex Air's flights to Rotterdam; London City Airways' (linked to Sabena) routes to Brussels; and UTA's flights to Paris.

Getting from London City   There are no direct subway or rail links connecting this airport to the center of London. It is possible to take a short taxi ride to the Plaistow station of the Underground's District Line. Most business passengers take a taxi into town at fares that run about £12 ($18) and up. However, it's a lot cheaper to go by river bus. The river bus landing pier is just a short walk from the airport terminal; boats leave every hour on the hour Monday through Friday from 7am to 7pm. There is a stop near the financial district at Swan Lane Pier (tube: Monument) and a final stop at Charing Cross Pier (tube: Embankment). A one-way ticket to Swan Lane Pier costs £4 ($6); to Charing Cross £5 ($7.50).

STANSTED AIRPORT   Located about 30 miles northeast of the center of London, Stansted is the city's newest airport (tel. 279/680-500) and often receives flights from the Continent.

Getting from Stansted   Cambridge Coach Service (tel. 22/344-0640) provides bus service into central London Monday through Saturday five times daily; on Sunday there are three buses. Buses also run to Heathrow and Gatwick airports in case you're making connecting flights from there. It's also possible to take the Stansted Express; this train will deliver you to London's Liverpool Street Station in about 45 minutes. Service runs daily from 5:30am to 11pm; a first-class seat costs £13.50 ($20.30), and a second-class seat £9 ($13.50).

BY TRAIN

Most arrivals on trains originating in Paris and traveling over the Channel are at **Victoria Station** in the center of London. Visitors from Amsterdam arrive at the **Liverpool Street Station,** and those journeying south by rail from Edinburgh arrive at **King's Cross Station.** Each of these stations is connected to London's vast bus and Underground (subway) network, and each has phones, restaurants, pubs, luggage-storage areas, and London Regional Transport Information Centres.

BY CAR

If you're taking a car-ferry across the Channel, you can quickly connect with a motorway into London. *Remember to drive on the left.* London is encircled by a ring road. Determine which part of the city you wish to enter and follow the signs there. You should confine your driving in London to the bare minimum, which means arriving and parking.

Parking is scarce and expensive. Before arrival in London, call your hotel and inquire if it has a garage (and what the charges are), or else ask the staff to give you the name and address of a garage close to the hotel.

TOURIST INFORMATION

The British Travel Centre, Rex House, 4–12 Lower Regent St., London SW1 4PQ (tel. 071/730-3400; tube: Piccadilly Circus), caters to walk-in visitors who arrive to pick up information on all parts of Britain. (If you're interested in making only a telephone inquiry, it's better to call 071/730-3488 for inquiries about London, and 071/824-8000 for inquiries about England and the rest of Britain.) On the premises you'll find a British Rail ticket office, a travel agency, a theater-ticket agency, a hotel-booking service, a bookshop, and a souvenir shop—all within one well-equipped and very modern facility. Hours are 9am to 6:30pm Monday through Friday, 10am to 4pm on Saturday and Sunday, with extended hours on Saturday from June through September.

Equally useful is the London Tourist Board's **Tourist Information Centre,** Victoria Station forecourt, SW1 (Tube: Victoria Station), which can help you with almost anything that might be of touristic interest to a visitor in the British capital. Staffed by courteous and patient people, the center deals chiefly with accommodations in all size and price categories, and can handle the whole spectrum of travelers, from singles, students, and family groups to large-scale conventions. It also arranges for travel, tour-ticket sales, and theater reservations, and it operates a shop offering a wide selection of books and souvenirs. The center is open for personal callers at the following times: between Easter and October, daily 8am to 7pm; November to Easter, Monday to Saturday 8am to 7pm, Sunday 8am to 5pm.

The tourist board also maintains offices in the basement of one of London's largest department stores, **Selfridges,** Oxford Street, W1 (tube: Bond Street), Duke Street entrance, open during store hours; at Heathrow Airport's Terminals 1, 2, and 3, Underground Concourse; and at the Liverpool Street Railway Station.

The tourist board also maintains a 24-hour recorded information service, "Visitorcall" (tel. 0839/123456), which, for a fee of between 36p (50¢) and 48p (70¢) per minute, depending on the time you call, will play a recorded message about sites of touristic interest that changes every day based on special events around London.

Written inquiries should be addressed to the Correspondence Assistant, Distribution Department, London Tourist Board and Convention Bureau, 26 Grosvenor Gardens, London SW1W ODU.

CITY LAYOUT

MAIN DISTRICTS, SQUARES & STREETS

There is—fortunately—an immense difference between the sprawling vastness of Greater London and the pocket-size chunk north of the River Thames that might be called "Tourist Territory."

Our London begins at **Chelsea,** on the north bank of the river, and stretches for roughly 5 miles north to **Hampstead.** Its western boundary runs through **Kensington,** while the eastern boundary lies 5 miles away at Tower Bridge. Within this 5- by 5-mile square, you'll find all the hotels and restaurants and nearly all the sights that are usually of interest to visitors.

Make no mistake: This is still a hefty portion of land to cover, and a really thorough exploration of it would take a couple of years. But it has the advantage of being flat and eminently walkable, besides boasting one of the best public transport systems ever devised.

The logical (although not geographical) center of this area is **Trafalgar Square,** which we'll therefore take as our orientation point.

If you stand facing the steps of the imposing National Gallery, you're looking northwest. That is the direction of **Piccadilly Circus**—the real core of tourist London—and the maze of streets that make up **Soho.** Farther north runs **Oxford Street,** London's gift to moderately priced shopping, and still farther northwest lies Regent's Park with the zoo.

At your back—that is, south—runs **Whitehall,** which houses or skirts nearly every British government building, from the Ministry of Defence to the official residence of the prime minister at **10 Downing Street.** In the same direction, a bit farther south, stand the Houses of Parliament and Westminster Abbey.

Flowing southwest from Trafalgar Square is the table-smooth **Mall,** flanked by magnificent parks and mansions and leading to Buckingham Palace, residence of the queen. Farther in the same direction lie **Belgravia** and **Knightsbridge,** the city's plushest residential areas, and south of them lies the aforementioned **Chelsea,** with its chic flavor, plus **King's Road,** principally a boulevard for shopping.

Due west stretches the superb and distinctly high-priced shopping area bordered by **Regent Street** and **Piccadilly Street** (as distinct from the Circus). Farther west lie the equally elegant shops and even more elegant homes of **Mayfair.** Then comes **Park Lane.** On the other side of Park Lane is Hyde Park, the biggest park in London and one of the largest in the world.

Charing Cross Road runs north from Trafalgar Square, past **Leicester Square,** and intersects with **Shaftesbury Avenue.** This is London's theaterland. A bit farther along, Charing Cross Road turns into a browser's paradise, lined with shops selling new and secondhand books.

Finally, it funnels into **St. Giles Circus.** This is where you enter **Bloomsbury,** site of the University of London, the British Museum, and erstwhile stamping ground of the famed Bloomsbury Group, led by Virginia Woolf.

Northeast of your position lies **Covent Garden,** known for its Royal Opera House and today a major shopping, restaurant, and café district.

Follow **The Strand** eastward from Trafalgar Square, and you'll come to **Fleet Street.** Beginning in the 19th century, this corner of London became the most concentrated newspaper district in the world. Where the Strand becomes Fleet Street stands Temple Bar, and only here do you enter the actual City of London, or "The City." Its focal point and shrine is the Bank of England on **Threadneedle Street,** with the Stock Exchange next door and the Royal Exchange across the street. In the midst of all the hustle and bustle rises St. Paul's Cathedral, a monument to beauty and tranquillity.

At the far eastern fringe of The City looms the Tower of London, shrouded in legend, blood, and history, and permanently besieged by battalions of visitors.

And this, as far as we will be concerned, concludes the London circle.

FINDING AN ADDRESS London's streets follow no pattern whatsoever, and both their naming and house numbering seem to have been perpetrated by a group of xenophobes with an equal grudge against postal carriers and foreigners. Don't think, for instance, that Southampton Row is anywhere near Southampton Street or that either of these places has any connection with Southampton Road.

London is checkered with innumerable squares, mews, closes, and terraces, which jut into or cross or overlap or interrupt whatever street you're trying to follow, usually without the slightest warning. You may be walking along ruler-straight Albany Street and suddenly find yourself flanked by Colosseum Terrace (with a different numbering system). Just keep on walking and after a couple of blocks you're right back on

Albany Street (and the original house numbers) without having encountered the faintest reason for the sudden change in labels.

House numbers run in odds and evens, clockwise and counterclockwise, as the wind blows. *That is, when they exist at all, and frequently they don't.* Many establishments in London, such as the Inn on the Park or Langan's Brasserie, *do not use house numbers,* although a building right next door might be numbered. Happily, Londoners are generally glad to assist a bewildered foreigner.

Every so often you'll come upon a square that is called a *square* on the south side, a *road* on the north, a *park* on the east, and possibly a something-or-other *close* on the west side. Your only chance is to consult a map or ask your way as you go along.

STREET MAPS If you're going to explore London in any depth, you'll need a good, detailed street map with an index—not one of those superficial overviews given away free at many hotels or at tourist offices. The best ones are published by *Falk,* and they're available at most newsstands and nearly all bookstores. If you can't find one, go to **W. & G. Foyle Ltd.,** 119 Charing Cross Rd., WC2 (tel. 071/439-8501; tube: Leicester Square).

NEIGHBORHOODS IN BRIEF

Mayfair Bounded by Piccadilly, Hyde Park, and Oxford and Regent Streets, this section of London is considered its most elegant, taking in Grosvenor Square and Berkeley Square.

St. James's Royal London begins at Piccadilly Circus, moving southwest. It basks in its associations with royalty, from the "merrie monarch," Charles II, to today's Queen Elizabeth II.

The Strand and Covent Garden Beginning at Trafalgar Square, the Strand runs east into Fleet Street and is flanked with theaters, shops, hotels, and restaurants. Covent Garden was until 1970 the fruit, flower, and vegetable market of London. Today it's a major shopping district, seat of dozens of restaurants and cafés, and site of the Royal Opera House on Bow Street.

Holborn The old borough of Holborn takes in the heart of legal London—home of the city's barristers, solicitors, and law clerks. It contains the ancient Inns of Court.

Westminster/Whitehall This area has been the seat of British government since the days of Edward the Confessor. It is dominated by the Houses of Parliament and Westminster Abbey.

Victoria Not an official district, Victoria takes its name from bustling Victoria Station, known as the "Gateway to the Continent." It lies directly south of Buckingham Palace in Belgravia, just west of Westminster.

Belgravia South of Hyde Park, this has been the longtime aristocratic quarter of London, rivaling Mayfair in grandness and money. It reached its pinnacle of prestige in the reign of Queen Victoria. It lies near Buckingham Palace Gardens and Brompton Road, and its center is Belgrave Square.

Knightsbridge Adjoining Belgravia, Knightsbridge is a top residential and shopping area, just south of Hyde Park. It is the center of the world's most famous department store, Harrods.

Chelsea A stylish district stretching along the Thames, Chelsea lies south of Hyde Park and South Kensington. It begins at Sloane Square, and its best-known and shop-flanked avenue is King's Road.

Kensington A royal borough, Kensington is traversed by Kensington High Street and takes in most of Kensington Gardens.

South Kensington Lying south of Kensington Gardens and Hyde Park, South Kensington is primarily residential and is often called "museumland" because of the preponderance of museums found here.

Paddington   This area around Paddington Station—where the famous bear was found by the Brown family—is separated from Hyde Park by pulsating Bayswater Road. Paddington is pleasantly residential yet lively enough to be interesting—it's close to sweeping parklands and some of the best shopping centers.

Bayswater   North of Kensington Gardens is an unofficial section of London known as Bayswater. Most of it lies north of Bayswater Road and west of Hyde Park. Once this area of London had a strong Russian influence—a memory that lives on in the St. Petersburg Place, considered by some the most charming street of Bayswater.

St. Marylebone   Below Regent's Park and northwest of Piccadilly Circus, St. Marylebone is primarily a residential section that faces Mayfair to the south, extending north of Marble Arch.

Soho   This section of narrow lanes and crooked streets, once the main foreign quarter of London, has some of the city's best international restaurants. Soho starts at Piccadilly Circus and stretches to Oxford Street.

Bloomsbury   To the northeast of Piccadilly Circus, beyond Soho, is Bloomsbury, heart of academic London and site of the British Museum.

The City   In the east of London, this was the original walled Roman city and is today the center of financial London.

The East End   One of London's poorest districts, the East End borders the richer area of the City. Many immigrants have found a home here, but it is most famous for its cockneys.

2. GETTING AROUND

BY PUBLIC TRANSPORTATION

If you know the ropes, transportation within London can be unusually easy and inexpensive. Both the Underground (subway) and bus systems are operated by London Transport—with Travel Information Centres in the Underground stations at King's Cross and Oxford Circus, as well as in the British Rail stations at Euston and Victoria, and in each of the terminals at Heathrow Airport. They take reservations for London Transport's **guided tours** and have free Underground and bus maps and other information leaflets. A **24-hour telephone information** service is available by calling 071/222-1234. Information is also available by writing London Transport, Travel Information Service, 55 Broadway, London SW1H 0BD.

London Transport offers **Travelcards** for use on bus, Underground, and British Rail services within Greater London. Available in a number of combinations of adjacent zones, Travelcards can be purchased for a minimum of 7 days or for any period (including odd days) from a month to a year. A Travelcard allowing travel in two zones for 1 week costs £8.50 ($12.80) for adults and £3.45 ($5.20) for children.

To purchase a Travelcard, you must present a Photocard. If you're 16 years old or older, bring along a passport-type picture of yourself when you buy your Travelcard and the Photocard will be issued free. Child-rate Photocards for Travelcards are issued only at main post offices in the London area, and in addition to a passport-type photograph, proof of age is required (for example, a passport or a birth certificate). Teenagers (14 or 15) are charged adult fares on all services unless in possession of one of the cards.

For shorter stays in London, you may want to consider the **One-Day Off-Peak Travelcard.** This Travelcard can be used on most bus, Underground, and British Rail services throughout Greater London after 9:30am Monday through Friday and at any time on weekends and bank holidays. The Travelcard is available from

Underground ticket offices, bus garages, Travel Information Centres, and some newsstands. For two zones, the cost is £2.50 ($3.80) for adults and £1.20 ($1.80) for children 5 to 15.

THE UNDERGROUND [SUBWAY]

Known locally as "the tube," this is the fastest and easiest (although not the most interesting) way to get from place to place. The tube has a special place in the hearts of Londoners: During the Blitz thousands of people used its subterranean platforms as air-raid shelters, camping down there all night in reasonable safety from the bombs.

All Underground stations are clearly marked with a red circle and blue crossbar. You descend either by stairways or escalators or by huge elevators, depending on the depth. Some Underground stations have complete subterranean shopping arcades and several boast high-tech gadgets such as pushbutton information machines.

You pick the station for which you're heading on the large diagram displayed on the wall, which has an alphabetical index to make it easy. You note the color of the line it happens to be on (Bakerloo is brown, Central is red, etc.). Then, by merely following the colored band, you can see at a glance whether and where you'll have to change and how many stops there are to your destination.

If you have British coins, you can get your ticket at one of the vending machines. Otherwise, you buy it at the ticket office. You can transfer as many times as you like so long as you stay in the Underground. The flat fare for one trip within the Central zone is 80p ($1.20). Trips from the Central zone to destinations in the suburbs range from £1.20 to £3.80 ($1.80 to $5.70).

Note: Be sure to keep your ticket; it must be presented when you get off. If you owe extra, you'll be asked to pay the difference by the attendant. And if you're out on the town and dependent on the Underground, watch your time carefully; many trains stop running at midnight (11:30pm on Sunday).

BUSES

London has just two types of buses, which you can't possibly confuse: the **red** double-decker monsters that bully their way through the inner-city areas, and the **green** single-deckers that link the center with the outlying towns and villages.

The first thing you learn about London buses is that nobody just gets on them. You "queue up"—that is, form a single-file line at the bus stop. The English do it instinctively, even when there are only two of them. It's one of their eccentricities, and you will grow to appreciate it during rush hours.

The comparably priced bus system is almost as good as the Underground, and you have a better view. To find out about current routes, pick up a free bus map at one of London Regional Transport's Travel Information Centres listed above. The map is available to personal callers only, not by mail.

London still has the old-style Routemaster buses, with both a driver and conductor. Once you're on the bus, a conductor will pass by your seat. You tell him or her your destination and pay the fare, receiving a ticket in return. This type of bus will eventually be phased out. Newer buses have only a driver. Pay the driver as you enter, then later exit through one of the rear doors. As with the Underground, the fares vary according to the distance traveled. Generally, they are 10p to 20p (15¢ to 30¢) lower than tube fares. If you go two or three stops, the cost is 60p (90¢); longer runs within Zone 1 cost 80p ($1.20). If you want to be warned when to get off, simply ask the conductor.

BY TAXI

London cabs are among the best-designed taxis in the world. You can pick one up from a cab rank or hail one on the street; if the red light on the roof is on, the taxi is free. Or for a radio cab, you can phone 071/272-0272, 071/253-5000, or 071/286-0286.

FARES The minimum fare is £1 ($1.50) for the first 1,152 yards or 3 minutes and 49.5 seconds, with increments of 20p (30¢) thereafter, based on distance or time. Each additional passenger is charged 20p (30¢). Passengers pay 10p (15¢) for each piece of luggage in the driver's compartment and any other item more than 2 feet long. Surcharges are imposed after 8pm and on weekends and public holidays. All these tariffs include VAT. Fares usually increase annually. It's recommended that you tip 10% to 15% of the fare.

Warning: If you phone for a cab, the meter starts running when the taxi receives instructions from the dispatcher. So you could find £1 ($1.50) or more already on the meter when you step inside.

Cab Sharing Now permitted in London by British law, cab sharing allows cabbies to offer rides for two to five people. The taxis accepting such riders display a sign on yellow plastic with the words SHARED TAXI. Each of two riders sharing is charged 65% of the fare a lone passenger would be charged. Three people pay 55%, four pay 45%, and five (the seating capacity of all new London cabs) pay 40% of the single-passenger fare.

COMPLAINTS/LOST & FOUND If you have a complaint about your taxi service or if you leave something in a cab, phone the **Public Carriage Office,** 15 Penton St., N1 (tel. 071/230-1631; tube: Angel Station). To file a complaint, you must have the cab number, which is displayed in the passenger compartment.

BY CAR

See "By Car" in "Getting Around," in Chapter 2, for information on car rentals; a description of driving rules and requirements; and information on gasoline, road maps, and breakdowns.

PARKING Driving around London is a tricky business. The city is a warren of one-way streets and parking spots are at a premium.

Besides strategically placed, expensive garages, central London also offers metered parking: But be aware that traffic wardens are famous for issuing substantial fines when the meter runs out. The time limit and the cost of metered parking are posted on the meter.

Zones marked "Permit Holders Only" are for local residents. If you violate these sacrosanct places, your vehicle is likely to be towed away.

A yellow line along the curb indicates "No Parking." A double yellow line signifies "No Waiting." However, at night—meters indicate exact times—and on Sunday, you're allowed to park along a curb with a single yellow line.

BY BICYCLE

You can rent bikes by the day or by the week from a number of outfits. One of the most popular is **On Your Bike,** 52–54 Tooley St., London Bridge, SE1 (tel. 071/378-6669; tube: London Bridge). It is open Monday through Friday from 9am to 6pm, on Saturday from 9:30am to 4:30pm. The staff has an inventory of around 50 bikes for men and women that they rent by the day or week. The 10-speed sports

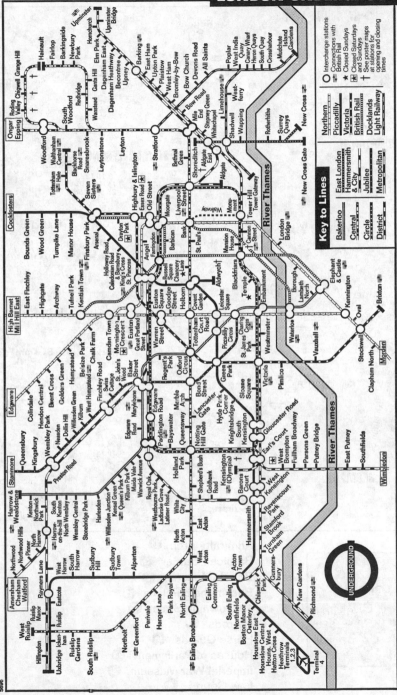

LONDON UNDERGROUND

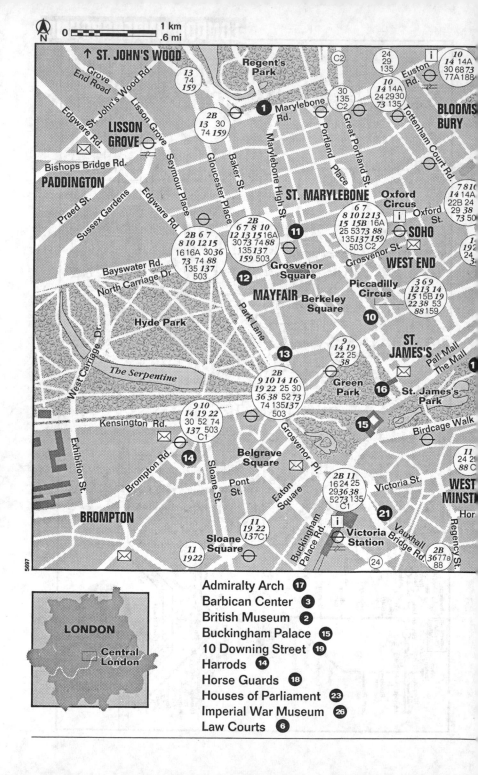

LONDON
Central London

Admiralty Arch **17**
Barbican Center **3**
British Museum **2**
Buckingham Palace **15**
10 Downing Street **19**
Harrods **14**
Horse Guards **18**
Houses of Parliament **23**
Imperial War Museum **26**
Law Courts **6**

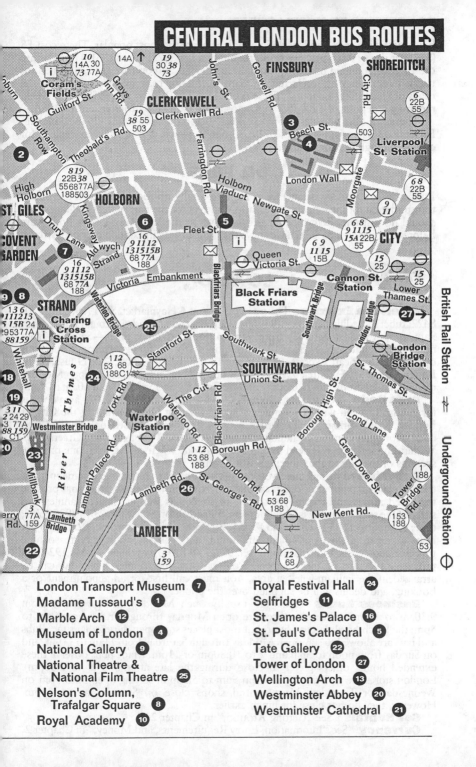

CENTRAL LONDON BUS ROUTES

London Transport Museum **7**
Madame Tussaud's **1**
Marble Arch **12**
Museum of London **4**
National Gallery **9**
National Theatre &
  National Film Theatre **25**
Nelson's Column,
  Trafalgar Square **8**
Royal Academy **10**

Royal Festival Hall **24**
Selfridges **11**
St. James's Palace **16**
St. Paul's Cathedral **5**
Tate Gallery **22**
Tower of London **27**
Wellington Arch **13**
Westminster Abbey **20**
Westminster Cathedral **21**

British Rail Station ≠

Underground Station ⊖

bikes, with high seats and low-slung handlebars, are the most popular. These cost £8 ($12) per day or £30 ($45) per week, requiring a £50 ($75) deposit. Also popular are the 18-gear mountain bikes, with straight handlebars and oversize gears; designed for rough terrain, they are preferred by many clients for their maneuverability on the roads of "backstreet London." These cost £15 ($22.50) a day or £60 ($90) per week, requiring a deposit of £200 ($300). Deposits are payable by MasterCard or VISA.

The store also operates a branch near Victoria Station at 22–24 Buckingham Palace Rd., Victoria, SW1 (tel. 071/630-6669), which is especially convenient for cycling through the royal parks.

ON FOOT

London is too vast and sprawling to explore totally on foot, but if you use public transportation for the long distances, and your feet for the narrow crooked lanes, you should do just fine. Remember that cars drive on the left. Always look both ways before stepping off a curb. Vehicles have the right-of-way in London over pedestrians.

FAST FACTS LONDON

American Express The main office is at 6 Haymarket, SW1 (tel. 071/930-8422; tube: Piccadilly Circus). Full services are available Monday through Friday from 9am to 5pm and on Saturday from 9am to noon. At other times—Saturday from noon to 6pm and Sunday from 10am to 4pm—only the foreign-exchange bureau is open. The American Express office at the British Travel Centre, Rex House, 4–12 Lower Regent St., SW1 (tel. 071/839-2682; tube: Piccadilly Circus), is open Monday through Friday from 9am to 6:30pm and on Saturday and Sunday from 10am to 4pm.

Area Code London has two area codes—071 and 081. The 071 area code is for central London within a 4-mile radius of Charing Cross (including the City of London, Knightsbridge, and Oxford Street, and as far south as Brixton). The 081 area code is for outer London (including Heathrow Airport, Wimbledon, and Greenwich). Within London, you will need to dial the area code when calling from one of these sections of the city to the other, but not within a section.

Babysitters Sometimes you can get your hotel to recommend someone, but there are also a number of organizations advertised in the yellow pages that provide registered nurses and carefully screened mothers—as well as trained nannies—as sitters. One such company is Childminders, 9 Paddington St., W1 (tel. 071/935-9763; tube: Baker Street). They charge £3.85 ($5.80) per hour in the daytime, £2.65 ($4) per hour at night. There is a 4-hour minimum, and you must also pay reasonable transportation costs. Universal Aunts (tel. 071/738-8937) was established in 1921 and provides child care, mother's helpers, proxy parents, and nannies. Interviews can be arranged in the Fulham-Chelsea area. You must call first for an appointment or a booking, and details will be supplied over the phone.

Business Hours Banks are usually open Monday through Friday from 9:30am to 3:30pm. Business offices are open Monday through Friday from 9am to 5pm; the lunch break lasts an hour, but most places stay open during that time. Pubs and bars are allowed to stay open Monday through Saturday from 11am to 11pm, and on Sunday from noon to 3pm and 7 to 10:30pm or 11pm. Many pubs observe these extended hours; others prefer to close during the late afternoon (3 to 5:30pm). London stores are generally open from 9am to 5:30pm, staying open until 7pm on Wednesday or Thursday. Most central shops close on Saturday around 1pm. However, they do not close for lunch earlier.

Car Rentals See "Getting Around," in Chapter 2.

Currency See "Information, Entry Requirements, and Money," in Chapter 2.

Currency Exchange In general, banks in London provide the best exchange rates, and you're likely to get a better rate for traveler's checks than for cash. At London's airports, there are branch offices of the main banks, but these charge a small fee. There are also bureaux de change at the airports, with offices around London, which charge a fee for cashing traveler's checks and personal U.K. checks, and for changing foreign currency into pounds sterling. Some travel agencies, such as American Express and Thomas Cook, also have currency-exchange services.

Dentists For dental emergencies, call Emergency Dental Service (tel. 071/752-0133), available 24 hours a day.

Doctors In an emergency, contact Doctor's Call (tel. 071/351-5312). Some hotels also have doctors on call. Medical Express, 117A Harley St., W1 (tel. 071/499-1991; tube: Great Portland Street), is a private British clinic; it's not part of the free British medical establishment. For filling the British equivalent of a U.S. prescription, there is a surcharge of £20 ($30) in addition to the cost of the medication; a British doctor must validate the U.S. prescription. The clinic is open Monday through Friday from 9am to 6pm and on Saturday from 9:30am to 2:30pm.

Drugstores In Britain they're called "chemist shops." Every police station in the country has a list of emergency chemists (dial "0" [zero] and ask the operator for the local police). One of the most centrally located chemists, keeping long hours, is Bliss The Chemist, 5 Marble Arch, W1 (tel. 071/723-6116; tube: Marble Arch), open daily from 9am to midnight. Every London neighborhood has a branch of the ubiquitous Boots, the leading pharmacist of Britain.

Embassies and High Commissions Passports, visas, whatever your problem, London has representatives in offices from nearly all the countries of the world. The **U.S. Embassy** is at 24 Grosvenor Sq., W1 (tel. 071/499-9000; tube: Bond Street). However, for passport and visa information, go to the U.S. Passport & Citizenship Unit, 55-56 Upper Brook St., London, W1 (tel. 071/499-9000, ext. 2563; tube: Marble Arch). Hours are Monday through Friday from 8:30am to noon and from 2 to 4pm. On Tuesday, the office closes at noon.

The **Canadian High Commission**, MacDonald House, 1 Grosvenor Sq., W1 (tel. 071/629-9492; tube: Bond Street), handles visa and passport problems for Canada. Hours are Monday through Friday from 9am to 5pm.

The **Australian High Commission** is at Australia House, The Strand, WC2 (tel. 071/379-4334; tube: Charing Cross or Aldwych), open Monday through Friday from 10am to 4pm. The **New Zealand High Commission** is at New Zealand House, 80 Haymarket at Pall Mall, SW1 (tel. 071/930-8422; tube: Charing Cross or Piccadilly Circus); open Monday through Friday from 10am to 4pm. The **Irish Embassy** is at 17 Grosvenor Pl., SW1 (tel. 071/235-2171; tube: Hyde Park Corner), open Monday through Friday from 9:30am to 5pm.

Emergencies In London, for police, fire, or an ambulance, dial 999.

Etiquette See "Fast Facts: England," in Chapter 2.

Eyeglasses Lost or broken? Try Selfridges Opticians on the street level of Selfridges Department Store, 400 Oxford St., W1 (tel. 071/629-1234, ext. 3889), open Monday through Saturday from 9:30am to 7pm, on Thursday until 8pm. Contact lenses are also usually available on the same day. Multifocal lenses sometimes take 2 to 3 working days to complete. It's always wise to carry a copy of your eyeglass prescription with you when you travel. Tube: Bond Street or Marble Arch.

Hairdressers and Barbers Hairdressers and hairstylists crop up on most major London street corners (a slight exaggeration), and range from grandly imperial refuges of English dowagers to punk-rock citadels of purple hair and chartreuse mascara. One of the most visible—and one of the best—is a branch of Vidal Sassoon, 11 Floral St., WC2 (tel. 071/240-6635; tube: Covent Garden). Unlike some other Sassoon outlets, this one caters to both men and women. The shop is open Monday through Friday from 10am to 7:45pm and on Saturday from 8:45am to 5:45pm.

Hospitals The following offer emergency care in London 24 hours a day, with the first treatment free under the National Health Service: **Royal Free Hospital,** Pond Street, NW3 (tel. 071/794-0500; tube: Belsize Park), and **University College Hospital,** Gower Street, WC1 (tel. 071/387-9300; tube: Warren Street). Many other London hospitals also have accident and emergency departments.

Hotlines   Capital Helpline (tel. 071/388-7575) answers almost any question you need to know about London. For police or medical emergencies, dial 999 (no coins required). If you're in some sort of legal emergency, call **Release** at 071/729-9904, 24 hours a day. The **Rape Crisis Line** is 071/837-1600, also in service 24 hours a day. **Samaritans,** 46 Marshall St., W1 (tel. 071/734-2800; tube: Oxford Circus), maintains a 24-hour crisis hotline that helps with all kinds of trouble, even threatened suicides. **Alcoholics Anonymous** (tel. 071/352-3001) answers its hotline daily from 10am to 10pm. The **AIDS** hotline is toll free 0800/567-123 24 hours a day.

Information   See "Information, Entry Requirements, and Money," in Chapter 2, and "Orientation," earlier in this chapter.

Laundry and Dry Cleaning   At Danish Express Laundry, 16 Hinde St., W1 (tel. 071/935-6306; tube: Marble Arch), they will clean, repair, or alter your clothes, even repair shoes. Open Monday through Friday from 8:30am to 5:30pm and on Saturday from 9:30am to 12:30pm, it's one of the best places in London for such services. One of the leading dry cleaners of London is Sketchley, 49 Maddox St., W1 (tel. 071/629-1292), with more than three dozen branches. Check the yellow pages of the London phone book for a location convenient to your hotel or call 081/300-5552. And if you're in the vicinity of the Bloomsbury B&Bs, you may choose Red and White Laundries, 78 Marchmont St., WC1 (tel. 071/387-3667; tube: Russell Square), open daily from 7am to 9pm.

Libraries   London's best collection of periodicals and reference materials is found at the Westminster Central Reference Library, St. Martin's Street, WC2 (tel. 071/798-2034), open Monday through Friday from 10am to 7pm and Saturday from 10am to 5pm. Tube: Leicester Square.

Lost Property   To find lost property, first report to the police and they will advise you where to apply for its return. Taxi drivers are required to hand over property left in their vehicles to the nearest police station. London Regional Transport's Lost Property Office will try to assist personal callers only at their office at the Baker Street Underground station. For items lost on British Rail, report the loss as soon as possible to the station on the line where the loss occurred. For lost passports, credit cards, or money, report the loss and circumstances immediately to the nearest police station. For lost passports, you should go directly to your embassy or high commission (see "Embassies and High Commissions," above). For lost credit cards, also report to the appropriate organization; the same holds true for lost traveler's checks.

Luggage Storage and Lockers   Places for renting lockers or storing luggage are widely available in London. Lockers can be rented at airports such as Heathrow or Gatwick and at all major rail stations, including Victoria Station. In addition, there are dozens of independently operated storage companies in the London area. The usual charge is £3 to £5 ($4.50 to $7.50) per item per week. Check the yellow pages for the luggage-storage establishment nearest you.

Maps   See "City Layout" in "Orientation," earlier in this chapter.

Newspapers and Magazines   The *Times* is tops, then the *Telegraph,* the *Daily Mail,* and the *Manchester Guardian,* all London papers carrying the latest news. The *International Herald Tribune,* published in Paris, and an international edition of *USA Today,* beamed via satellite, are available daily. Copies of *Time* and *Newsweek* are also sold at most newsstands. Small magazines, such as *Time Out* and *City Limits,* contain much useful data about the latest happenings in London, including theatrical and cultural events.

Photographic Needs   The Flash Centre, 54 Brunswick Centre, WC1 (tel.

071/837-6163; tube: Russell Square), is considered the best professional photographic equipment supplier in London. You can purchase your film next door at Leeds Film and Hire, which has a wide-ranging stock. Kodachrome is accepted for 48-hour processing.

Police   In an emergency, dial **999** (no coin required). You can also go to one of the local police branches in central London, including New Scotland Yard, Broadway, SW1 (tel. 071/230-1212; tube: St. James's Park).

Post Office   Post offices and sub-post offices are centrally located and open Monday through Friday from 9am to 5:30pm and on Saturday from 9:30am to noon. The Chief Post office in London, King Edward Street, EC1A 1AA, near St. Paul's Cathedral (tel. 071/239-5047; tube: St. Paul's), is open Monday through Friday from 8:30am to 6:30pm; closed Saturday and Sunday. The Trafalgar Square Post Office, 24–28 William IV St., WC2N 4DL (tel. 071/239-5047; tube: Charing Cross), operates as three separate businesses: inland and international postal service and banking (open Monday through Saturday from 8am to 8pm), philatelic postage stamp sales (open Monday through Friday from 10am to 7pm and on Saturday from 10am to 4:30pm), and the post shop, selling greeting cards and stationery (open Monday through Friday from 9am to 6:30pm and on Saturday from 9:30am to 5pm). Other post offices and sub-post offices are open Monday through Friday from 9am to 5:30pm and on Saturday from 9am to 12:30pm. Many sub-post offices and some main post offices close for an hour at lunchtime.

Radio   There are 24-hour radio channels operating throughout the United Kingdom, including London. They offer mostly pop music and "chat shows" during the night. Some "pirate" radio stations add more spice to the broadcasting selections. So-called "legal" FM stations are BBC1 (104.8), BBC2 (89.1), BBC3 (between 90 and 92), and the classical station, BBC4 (95). There is also the BBC Greater London Radio (94.9) station, with lots of rock; plus LBC Crown (97.3), with much news as well as reports of "what's on" in London. Pop/rock U.S. style is a feature of Capital FM (95.8), and if you like jazz, Jamaican reggae, or salsa, tune in to Choice FM (96.9). Jazz FM (102.2) is not just jazz, but offers sounds of the big-band era, the blues, and whatever.

Religious Services   Times of services are posted outside the various places of worship. Almost all major faiths are represented in London. The American Church in London is at 79 Tottenham Court Rd., W1 (tel. 071/580-2791; tube: Goodge Street). A service is conducted on Sunday from 11am to noon. The London Tourist Board has a fairly complete list of various churches. Protestants ideally might want to attend a Sunday-morning service at either Westminster Abbey (tel. 071/222-5152) or St. Paul's Cathedral (tel. 071/248-2705). If you're going to be in London on two separate Sundays, you might go to both landmarks. Services are held at varying hours at St. Paul's, so it's best to call for information first. At Westminster Abbey, Sunday services begin at 8am; other services are at 10am, 11:15am, 3pm, 5:45pm, and 6:30pm. Roman Catholics gravitate to Westminster Cathedral (not to be confused with Westminster Abbey), Ashley Place, SW1 (tel. 071/834-7452). Masses are conducted here on Sunday at 7am, 8am, 9am, 10:30am, noon, 5:30pm, and 7pm.

Restrooms   Often called "loos" by the English, they are usually found at signs saying PUBLIC TOILETS. Women should expect to pay from 5p (10¢); men usually pay nothing. Automatic toilets are found on many streets. They are sterilized after each use. The cost is just 10p (15¢).

Safety   See "Fast Facts: England," in Chapter 2.

Shoe Repair   Most of the major Underground stations, including the centrally located Piccadilly Circus, have "heel bars"—British for shoe-repair centers. Mostly, these are for quickie jobs. For more extensive repairs, go to one of the major department stores (see "Department Stores" in "Shopping A to Z," in Chapter 7). Otherwise, patronize Jeeves Snob Shop, 7 Pont St., SW1 (tel. 071/235-1101; tube: Knightsbridge).

Smoking Most U.S. brands of cigarettes are available in London. Antismoking laws are tougher than ever. Smoking is strictly forbidden in the Underground, including the cars and the platforms. It is allowed only in the back of the uppermost level of double-decker buses, and is increasingly frowned upon in many other places.

Taxis See "Getting Around," earlier in this chapter.

Telephone For directory assistance for London, dial 142; for the rest of Britain, dial 192. See "Fast Facts: England," in Chapter 2, for an overview of the telephone system. See also "Area Code," above.

Telex and Fax To send a fax, you can go to the Chesham Executive Centre at 50 Regent St., W1 (tel. 071/439-6288; tube: Piccadilly Circus). In addition to renting offices by the hour and providing secretarial and stenographic services, the center accepts walk-in business and will send fax messages. The cost of sending a one-page fax from London to anywhere in the world is £2.50 ($3.80), plus VAT and the cost of the phone call. Hours are 9am to 6pm Monday through Friday, 9am to noon on Saturday. See also "Fast Facts: England," in Chapter 2.

Tipping See "Fast Facts: England," in Chapter 2.

Transit Information Phone 071/222-1234, daily 24 hours.

Water Tap water in London is considered safe to drink, but because the water is different, you might still experience a stomach upset. If in doubt, order mineral water.

Weather Phone 071/246-8091.

Yellow Pages See "Fast Facts: England" in Chapter 2.

3. NETWORKS & RESOURCES

FOR GAY MEN & LESBIANS

London Lesbian and Gay Centre This center contains a bookstore, café, bar, and disco. There is one floor for women only. Located at 67–69 Cowcross St., EC1 (tel. 071/608-1471), it's open Sunday through Thursday from noon to 11pm, and on Friday and Saturday from noon to 2am. Tube: Farringdon.

Lesbian and Gay Switchboard You can call (tel. 071/837-7324) 24 hours a day for information about gay-related London activities and advice in general.

The **Bisexual Helpline** (tel. 081/569-7500) offers useful information but only Tuesday and Wednesday from 7:30 to 9:30pm. Harassment, gay-bashing, and other such matters are handled by **Gay and Lesbian Legal Advice** (tel. 071/253-2043) Monday through Friday from 7 to 10pm.

FOR WOMEN

London Rape Crisis Centre This center operates 24 hours a day. In addition to its counseling services, women are offered medical and legal advice, too. The center can even arrange to have another woman accompany you to the doctor, clinic, and the police station. Contact them at P.O. Box 69, WC1 (tel. 071/837-1600).

Silvermoon This is the leading feminist bookstore in London. It stocks thousands of titles by and about women—and sells tapes, videos, jewelry, T-shirts, and other items. It's located at 64–68 Charing Cross Rd. WC2 (tel. 071/836-7906). Tube: Leicester Square.

FOR STUDENTS

STA Travel This is one of the several London organizations that specialize in student discounts and youth fares. Located at 74–86 Old Brompton Rd., SW7, it's open Monday through Friday from 9am to 5:30pm and on Saturday from 10am to 4pm. For European sales, call 071/937-9921. Tube: Kensington.

The University of London Student Union Located at Malet Street (without number), WC1 (tel. 071/580-9551), this is the largest student union in the world and the best place to go to learn about student activities in the Greater London area. The union contains a swimming pool, fitness center, gymnasium, general store, sports shop, ticket agency, banks, bars, inexpensive restaurants, live events and discos, an office of STA Travel, and many other facilities. It is open Monday through Saturday from 9:30am to 11pm and on Sunday from 9:30am to 10:30pm. Take the tube to Goodge Street. Bulletin boards at the union provide a rundown on various events being sponsored, some of which it might be possible to attend, whereas others might be "closed door."

LONDON ACCOMMODATIONS

London boasts some of the most famous hotels in the world. These include such temples of luxury as Claridge's, Dorchester, the Ritz (where the term "ritzy" originated), Park Lane Hotel, the Savoy, and their recent-vintage rivals, the Inn on the Park, the Lanesborough, and the Langham Hilton.

All these establishments are superlative and budget hotels they are certainly not. It is in this bracket that you get the most fantastic contrasts, both in terms of architecture and comfort. Many of London's hotels were built around the turn of the century, which gives them a rather curlicued appearance. But whereas some have gone to no end of pain to modernize their interiors, others have remained at Boer War level, complete with built-in drafts and daisy-strewn wallpaper.

In between, however, you come across up-to-the-minute structures that seem to have been shifted bodily from Los Angeles. These aren't necessarily superior, but for what they lack in streamlining they frequently make up in personal service and spaciousness.

I have selected hotels that combine maximum comfort with good value in all price categories.

In most, but not all, of the places listed, there's a service charge ranging from 10% to 15% added to the bill. The British government also imposes a VAT (Value-Added Tax) that adds 17½% to your bill.

Again in many, although not all listings, the rates include breakfast, either a full English spread or a smaller continental one. You should be aware that what is termed "continental breakfast" consists of coffee or tea and some sort of roll or pastry. An "English breakfast" is a fairly lavish meal of tea or coffee; cereal; eggs; bacon, ham, or sausages; toast and jam.

All hotels, motels, inns, and guesthouses in Britain with four bedrooms or more (including self-catering accommodations) are required to display notices showing minimum and maximum overnight charges. The notice must be displayed in a prominent position in the reception area or at the entrance. The prices shown must include any service charge and may include VAT, and it must be made clear whether or not these items are included. If VAT is not included, it must be shown separately. If meals are provided with the accommodation, this must be made clear, too. If prices are not standard for all rooms, only the lowest and highest prices need be given.

RESERVATIONS

Most hotels require at least a day's deposit before they will reserve a room for you. This can be accomplished with an international bank draft or money order, a telephoned instruction in which the number of a valid credit card is transmitted, or, if agreed to in advance, a personal check. Usually you can cancel a room reservation 1 week ahead of time and get a full refund. A few hotelkeepers will return your money up to 3 days before the reservation date. There have also been reports of hotels that will take your deposit and never return it, even if you canceled far in advance. Many budget hotel owners operate on such a narrow margin of profit that they find just buying stamps for airmail replies too expensive by their standards. Therefore, it's most important that you enclose a prepaid International Reply Coupon, especially if you're writing to a budget hotel.

Because of the low phone charges of calling from North America to London, it might be better to call and speak to the hotel of your choice, or (and this grows increasingly more popular every year) send a fax.

July and August are the vacation months in England, when nearly two-thirds of the population strikes out for a long-awaited holiday. Many head for the capital, further exacerbating what is already a crowded hotel situation, particularly at the lower end of the price spectrum.

When summer vacations are over, "the season" in London begins, lasting through October. Therefore, in September and October, as in June, budget hotels are tight—although nothing like what they are in peak months. Many of the West End hotels have vacancies, even in peak season, between 9 and 11am, but by noon they are often packed solid again with fresh arrivals. Therefore, if you arrive without a reservation, begin your search for a room as early in the day as possible. If you arrive late at night—say, on a train from the Continent pulling into Victoria Station—you may have to take what you can get, often in a much higher price range than you'd like to pay.

Many times if you're booking into a chain hotel, such as one of the many Hiltons in Britain, you can call toll free in North America and easily make reservations over the phone. Whenever such a service is available, I have included the toll-free 800 numbers in the hotel write-up.

PRICE CATEGORIES

Classifying London hotels into a rigid price category is a bit tricky. For example, sometimes it's possible to find a moderately priced room in an otherwise "very expensive" hotel, or an expensive room in an otherwise inexpensive property. That's because most hotel rooms—at least in the older properties—are not standardized; therefore, the range of rooms goes from superdeluxe suites to the "maid's pantry," now converted into a small bedroom.

The following price categories are only for a quick general reference, and note that there will be many exceptions to this quick rule-of-thumb. It should also be noted that London is one of the most expensive cities in the world for hotels. Therefore, what might be viewed as expensive in your hometown could very likely be classified as "inexpensive" in London.

In general, very expensive suggests hotels offering double rooms ranging in price from £185 to £320 ($277.50 to $480). Most hotels ranked expensive charge anywhere from £100 to £185 ($150 to $277.50) for a double. Moderate hotels generally start at £80 ($120) for a double, although a few within this category sometimes contain far more expensive accommodations. The average is around £100 ($150) in a moderate double room. Inexpensive is anything under £80 ($120). In this category, it's usually possible to get a double room for around £55 ($82.50) and up per night.

BIJOU OR BOUTIQUE HOTELS Within the last decade, London has seen the emergence of a new breed of charming, small-scale hotel, known as *bijou* (jewel) or boutique hotels because of their small size and almost obsessive attention to detail. Many of the larger stately hotels originally built by the Edwardians, and long considered inviolable and permanent fixtures on the London hotel scene, are awakening to the new realities of increased competition from these elegant small-scale newcomers. In an era of declining standards and service, the old landmark hotels no longer command the awe they might have inspired decades ago.

My selection of London hotels has incorporated as many of these charming but expensive newcomers as possible, while retaining only a select handful of the best of the grand monuments of the past.

A TRAVELER'S ADVISORY If you've arrived in London as a first-time visitor and plan to seek low-cost lodgings, you should know that many of central London's B&B establishments and low-budget hotels are in very poor condition. In fact, since the last edition of this book was researched, I have received more complaints about B&B hotels in London than in any destination on the continent of Europe.

In this chapter, you'll find a list of what I consider adequate B&B lodgings for London, but I present most of them without any particular enthusiasm.

It is very easy for owners of small budget hotels to fill up their rooms every night—regardless of the condition of the room. Therefore, there is little incentive for many of them to improve their services, repair the broken plumbing, or renovate. You'll find far more reasonable and much better places to stay in the budget category once you leave London.

So, be duly warned: Don't expect too much when checking into your typical London B&B. There are a few good ones, but they also tend to be fully booked all year. In general, be prepared to pay more for a decent room in London than you would in many places, and save money perhaps on your restaurant and entertainment choices, where an array of reasonably priced offerings is available.

Unless otherwise noted, parking is not available within a hotel. Each establishment's staff, however, should be well informed about rules for streetside parking within the neighborhood, or at least know the location of the nearest public car park.

Hotel Savvy

- If you're making a reservation by telephone from North America, use the area codes 71 and 81. If you are calling from within Britain (including London), dial 071 and 081, respectively.
- If you want to remain undisturbed, don't forget to hang the DO NOT DISTURB sign on your doorknob. English hotel service personnel—most of whom aren't English—have a disconcerting habit of bursting in simultaneously with their knock.
- Elevators are called "lifts" and some of them predate Teddy Roosevelt's Rough Riders and act like it. They are, however, regularly inspected and completely safe.
- And don't forget that hotel rooms may be somewhat cooler than you're accustomed to—it's supposed to be healthier that way.

1. MAYFAIR

Mayfair is filled with elegant shops and even more elegant homes. This posh district is vaguely defined as lying between Oxford Street and Piccadilly (the street, not the circus). The neighborhood includes Park Lane and takes in both Grosvenor and Berkeley Squares.

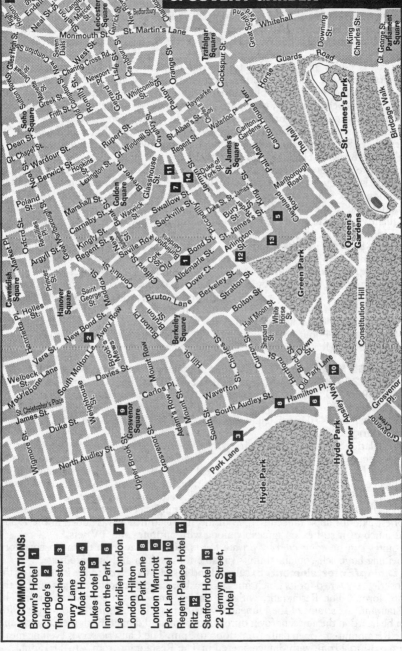

N

St. James's Park

Whitehall

Downing St.

King Charles St.

Gt. George St.

Parliament Square

Guards · Road

Horse Guards

Birdcage Walk

The Mall

Queen's Gardens

Green Park

Constitution Hill

Hyde Park

Hyde Park Corner

Apsley Way

Grosvenor Pl.

Grosvenor Cres.

Trafalgar Square

Cockspur St.

Great Scotland Yd.

Haymarket

Waterloo Pl.

Carlton House Terr.

Carlton Gardens

Pall Mall

Marlborough Road

St. James's Square

Regent St.

Jermyn St.

Duke of York St.

Carlton House Terr.

Piccadilly

Duke St. St. James's

Bury St.

King St.

St. James's St.

Arlington St.

Bennet St.

Park Pl.

Cleveland Row

Crown Passage

Regent St.

St. Alban's St.

Whitcomb St.

Orange St.

Pall Mall

Charing Cross Rd.

New Oxford St.

High Holborn

Drury Lane

Shorts Gardens

Endell St.

Neal St.

Long Acre

Mercer St.

Langley St.

Monmouth St.

Earlham St.

Shelton St.

Floral St.

Garrick St.

New Row

Bedfordbury

Chandos Pl.

Bedford St.

Maiden Lane

Exeter St.

Tavistock St.

Southampton St.

St. Martin's Lane

Bedford St.

Leicester Square

Lisle St.

Cranbourn St.

Newport Pl.

Gerrard St.

West St.

Seven Dials

Shaftesbury Ave.

Charing Cross Rd.

Denmark St.

Dean St.

Greek St.

Frith St.

Old Compton St.

Romilly St.

Moor St.

Bateman St.

Meard St.

Wardour St.

Berwick St.

Peter St.

Brewer St.

Poland St.

Lexington St.

Marshall St.

Carnaby St.

Kingly St.

Ganton St.

Beak St.

Golden Square

Great Windmill St.

Sherwood St.

Glasshouse St.

Warwick St.

Air St.

Swallow St.

Sackville St.

Vigo St.

Cork St.

Old Burlington St.

New Burlington St.

Savile Row

Clifford St.

Burlington Gardens

Bond St.

Grafton St.

Old Bond St.

Albemarle St.

Dover St.

Hay Hill

Berkeley St.

Stratton St.

Bolton St.

Half Moon St.

Clarges St.

Curzon St.

Shepherd St.

White Horse St.

Down St.

Brick St.

Hertford St.

Old Park Lane

Hamilton Pl.

Park Lane

Gt. Chapel St.

Noel St.

Berwick St.

Hopkins St.

Soho Square

Sutton Row

Compton St.

Gt. Marlborough St.

Argyll St.

Ramillies Pl.

Regent St.

Princes St.

Conduit St.

Maddox St.

George St.

Saint George St.

Hanover Square

Oxford St.

Market Pl.

Cavendish Square

Holles St.

Henrietta Pl.

Vere St.

Welbeck St.

Wigmore St.

Wimpole St.

Marylebone Lane

St. Christopher's Place

James St.

New Bond St.

Brook's Mews

Avery Row

Brook St.

Grosvenor St.

Maddox St.

Davies St.

South Molton St.

Weighhouse St.

Duke St.

Brook St.

Grosvenor Square

Upper Brook St.

Mount Row

Hill St.

Bruton Lane

Bruton St.

Berkeley Square

Carlos Pl.

Mount St.

Adam's Row

South Audley St.

Waverton St.

South St.

Charles St.

South Audley St.

Park St.

North Audley St.

Grosvenor St.

5698

VERY EXPENSIVE

BROWN'S HOTEL, 29–34 Albemarle St., London W1A 4SW. Tel. 071/ 493-6020, or toll free 800/435-4542 in the U.S. and Canada. Fax 071/493-9381. 133 rms, 6 suites. A/C MINIBAR TV TEL **Tube:** Green Park.

$ Rates: £193–£205 ($139.50–$307.50) single; £211–£223 ($316.50–$334.50) double; from £393 ($589.50) suite. Breakfast £13.75 ($20.60) extra. AE, DC, MC, V.

Brown's is highly recommended for those who want a fine hotel among the top traditional choices. This upper-crust, prestigious establishment was created by James Brown, a former manservant of Lord Byron. He and his wife, Sarah, who had been Lady Byron's personal maid, wanted to go into business for themselves. Brown knew the tastes of gentlemen of breeding and wanted to create a dignified, clublike place for them. His dream came true when the hotel, a former town house at 23 Dover St., opened in 1837, the year Queen Victoria ascended the throne of England.

Today, Brown's Hotel occupies some 14 historic houses on two streets, in an appropriate location—in Mayfair, just off Berkeley Square. To this day, old-fashioned comfort is dispensed with courtesy. A liveried doorman ushers you to an antique reception desk where you check in. The lounges on the street floor are inviting, including the Roosevelt Room, the Rudyard Kipling Room (the famous author was a frequent visitor here), and the paneled St. George's Bar for the drinking of "spirits."

The bedrooms vary considerably and are a tangible record of the history of England. Even the washbasins are semi-antiques. The rooms show restrained taste in decoration and appointments and beds are comfortable.

Dining/Entertainment: A good, old-fashioned English tea is served in the Albemarle Room. Men are required to wear jackets and ties for teas and for dining in the dining room, which has a quiet dignity and unmatched service. Most meals are à la carte, although there is also a set luncheon menu at £28 ($42) and a fixed-price dinner at £32 ($48), including service and VAT.

Services: 24-hour room service, laundry and dry cleaning, babysitting.

Facilities: Men's hairdresser, car-rental agency.

CLARIDGE'S, Brook St. (without number), London W1A 2JQ. Tel. 071/629-8860, or toll free 800/223-6800 in the U.S. and Canada. Fax 071/499-2210. 109 rms, 56 suites. A/C TV TEL **Tube:** Bond Street.

$ Rates: £185–£215 ($277.50–$322.50) single; £235–£280 ($352.50–$420) double; from £470 ($705) suite. Breakfast £15.75 ($23.60) extra. AE, DC, MC, V. **Parking:** £28 ($42).

Claridge's has been known from the mid-Victorian age under its present name, although an earlier "lodging house" complex occupied much of the hotel's area as far back as the reign of George IV. It has cocooned royal visitors in an ambience of discreet elegance since the time of the Battle of Waterloo. Queen Victoria visited Empress Eugénie of France here, and thereafter, Claridge's lent respectability to the idea of ladies dining out in public. The hotel took on its present modest exterior appearance in 1898. Inside, art deco decor was added in the 1930s, and much of it still exists agreeably along with antiques and TV sets.

Suites can be connected by private foyers closed away from the main corridors, providing large self-contained units suitable for a sultan and his entourage.

Dining/Entertainment: Excellent food is stylishly served in the intimacy of the Causerie, renowned for its lunchtime smörgåsbord and pretheater suppers, and in the more formal The Restaurant, with its English and French specialties. From The Restaurant, the strains of the Hungarian Quartet, a Claridge's institution since 1902, can be heard in the adjacent foyer during luncheon and dinner. Both the Causerie and The Restaurant are open daily from noon to 3pm. The Causerie serves evening meals from 5:30 to 11pm, with dinner offered in The Restaurant from 7 to 11:15pm.

Services: 24-hour room service, valet, laundry, babysitting.

Facilities: Hairdresser, car-rental agency, adjacent health club available to male clients.

THE DORCHESTER, 53 Park Lane, London W1A 2HJ. Tel. 071/629-8888, or toll free 800/727-9820 in the U.S. Fax 071/409-0114. 197 rms, 55 suites. A/C MINIBAR TV TEL **Tube:** Hyde Park Corner.

$ Rates: £180 ($270) single; £215–£240 ($322.50–$360) double; from £330 ($495) suite. VAT extra. Continental breakfast £10.50 ($15.80) extra. AE, DC, MC.

 A series of socially prominent manor houses and villas had stood on the site of this hotel for as long as anyone could remember, but in 1929, with an increased demand for hotel space in the expensive Park Lane district, a famous mansion—whose inhabitants had been known for everything from great debauchery to great aesthetic skills—was torn down. In its place was erected in 1931 the finest hotel London had seen in many years. Breaking from the neoclassical tradition which contemporary critics felt had forced the hidebound city into one homogenized unit, the most ambitious architects of the era designed a building of reinforced concrete clothed in terrazzo slabs.

Throughout the hotel, you'll find a 1930s interpretation of Regency motifs. The arrangements of flowers and the lavish elegance of the gilded-cage Promenade seem

---

Ⓕ FROMMER'S SMART TRAVELER: HOTELS

VALUE-CONSCIOUS TRAVELERS SHOULD TAKE ADVANTAGE OF THE FOLLOWING:

1. Price reductions in inexpensive or moderate hotels based on the plumbing. Rooms with showers are cheaper than rooms with private baths. Even cheaper is a room with hot and cold running water. For a bath you'll have to use the corridor bathroom, but you'll save a lot of money.
2. Package tours (or land arrangements that come with your air ticket). You'll often pay at least 30% less than individual "rack" rates (off-the-street, independent bookings).
3. A little on-the-spot bargaining to bring down the cost of a hotel room. Be polite. Ask if there's a "businessperson's rate," or if schoolteachers get a discount. This is a face-saving technique. Sometimes it works; sometimes it doesn't. If hotels are full, forget it. But you can try. The technique is best at night, when the hotel faces up to 40% vacancy and wants to fill some of those empty rooms.
4. Paying in cash. At cheaper hotels, it will often get you a reduction.
5. Long-term discounts if you'll be in London at least a week.

QUESTIONS TO ASK IF YOU'RE ON A BUDGET

1. Is there a garage? What's the charge?
2. Is there a surcharge on either local or long-distance calls? There usually is. In some places, it might be an astonishing 40%. Make your calls at the nearest post office.
3. Is service included in the rates quoted, or will a service charge be added on at the end of your stay?
4. Is the 17½% Value Added Tax (VAT) included, or will it be added on later?
5. Is breakfast (continental or English) included in the rates?

appropriate for a diplomatic reception, yet they convey a kind of sophisticated comfort with which guests from all over the world feel at ease. In the old days, those guests used to include General Eisenhower, Marlene Dietrich, and Bing Crosby; today's roster is likely to list Michael J. Fox, Cher, Tom Cruise, or Michael Jackson.

Owned by the Sultan of Brunei, who invested $192 million in its makeover, the Dorchester's bedrooms feature linen sheets, all the electronic gadgetry you'd expect from a world-class hotel, and double- and triple-glazed windows to keep the noise out. The bedrooms are filled with plump armchairs and cherrywood furnishings, and, in many cases, four-poster beds. In mottled gray Italian marble with Lalique-style sconces, even the bathrooms are stylish. The best rooms open onto views of Hyde Park.

Dining/Entertainment: Two of the hotel's restaurants—The Terrace and The Grill—are considered among the finest dining establishments in London, and the Dorchester Bar is a legend. The gray and green Terrace is a historic room outfitted in a Regency motif with an overlay of chinoiserie whose combination is especially sumptuous. When referring to its soaring columns capped with gilded palm fronds and mammoth swathes of filigree curtains, one English reviewer referred to it as "pure Cecil B. de Mille." The Terrace still features dancing, a tradition that goes back to the 1930s, when London's "bright young things" patronized the place. Today, unlike yesterday, there is a health-conscious *menu léger* to keep waistlines thin. In addition, the hotel also offers Cantonese cuisine in its Asian restaurant, The Oriental.

Services: 24-hour room service, laundry, dry cleaning, medical service.

Facilities: One of the best-outfitted health clubs in London, the Dorchester Spa; an exclusive nightclub; business center; barbershop; hairdresser.

INN ON THE PARK, Hamilton Place (without number), Park Lane, London W1A 1AZ. Tel. 071/499-0888, or toll free 800/332-3442 in the U.S. and Canada. Fax 071/493-1895. 201 rms, 26 suites. A/C MINIBAR TV TEL **Tube:** Hyde Park Corner.

$ Rates: £200 ($300) single; £245–£320 ($367.50–$480) double; from £400 ($600) suite. VAT extra. English breakfast £13.75 ($20.60) extra. AE, DC, MC, V. **Parking:** £12.25 ($18.40) extra.

The Inn on the Park, a member of the Toronto-based Four Seasons group, has captured the imagination of the glamourmongers of the world since it was inaugurated by Princess Alexandra in 1970.

Bordered with a smallish triangular garden and ringed by one of the most expensive neighborhoods in the world, it sits behind a tastefully modern facade. Its clientele includes heads of state, superstars, and business executives, among others. Howard Hughes, who could afford anything, chose it as a retreat, but his sprawling eighth-floor suite has since been subdivided into more easily rentable rooms.

Visitors enter a modern reception area, but acres of superbly crafted paneling and opulently conservative decor create the impression that the hotel is far older than it is. A gently inclined stairway leads in the grandest manner to a symmetrical grouping of Chinese and European antiques flanked by cascades of fresh flowers.

The rooms are large and beautifully outfitted with well-chosen chintz patterns, reproduction antiques, and plush upholstery, along with dozens of well-concealed electronic extras. Ten of the rooms contain private conservatories.

Dining/Entertainment: The Cocktail Bar is a piano bar that serves drinks in a room where Wellington might have felt at home. A pair of restaurants creates a most alluring rendezvous, including the highly acclaimed Four Seasons, which is both elegant and stylish, with views opening onto Park Lane. The finest wines and continental specialties dazzle guests either at lunch or at dinner, which is served until 11pm. The alternative dining choice is the less expensive Lanes Restaurant, which is rather popular with many members of London's business community. A coffee shop is open from 9am to 2pm.

Services: Valet, 24-hour room service, laundry.
Facilities: Shops, theater desk, garden, car-rental agency, concierge, and a health club.

LONDON HILTON ON PARK LANE, 22 Park Lane, London W1A 2HH. Tel. 071/493-8000, or toll free 800/445-8667 in the U.S. and Canada. Fax 071/493-4957. 448 rms, 54 suites. A/C MINIBAR TV TEL **Tube:** Hyde Park Corner.
$ Rates: £165–£210 ($247.50–$315) single or double; £240 ($360) single or double on Executive Floor; from £300 ($450) suite. Continental breakfast £12.50 ($18.80) extra. AE, DC, MC, V. **Parking:** £12.50 ($18.80).

The tallest building along Park Lane, and indeed one of the tallest structures in London, this hotel created an uproar when it was constructed in 1963. There were persistent allegations that residents of its uppermost floors were able to spy into the boudoirs of faraway Buckingham Palace.

Now considered a linchpin of the London hotel scene, and currently owned by Britain's Ladbroke chain, the Hilton is stylish and sophisticated. Graced with large picture windows overlooking London and Hyde Park, the bedrooms are decorated in tastefully restful colors, with fine copies of Georgian furniture.

Dining/Entertainment: Windows on the World restaurant on the 28th floor features a French/international cuisine and offers spectacular views over London. Reservations far in advance are needed for a window table. An international cuisine is served in the hotel's Café-Brasserie, and you can also order Polynesian food at Trader Vic's downstairs. St. George's Bar is a fashionable rendezvous, and there is dancing to a live band every night in Windows on the World.

Services: 24-hour room service, concierge, laundry and valet, babysitting, massage.

Facilities: Business center, sauna, solarium, Hertz Rent A Car desk, theater-ticket booking desk, six executive floors offering private check-in and a complimentary continental breakfast.

LONDON MARRIOTT, Grosvenor Sq. (without number), London W1A 4AW. Tel. 071/493-1232, or toll free 800/524-2000 in the U.S. and Canada. Fax 071/491-3201. 223 rms, 12 suites. A/C MINIBAR TV TEL **Tube:** Bond Street.
$ Rates: £160–£200 ($240–$300) single or double; from £300 ($450) suite. English breakfast £10.50 ($15.80) extra. AE, DC, MC, V. **Parking:** £25 ($37.50).

The property was built in a grander era as the very conservative Hotel Europa. After Marriott poured millions of dollars into its refurbishment, only the very best elements, and of course much of the tradition, remained. This triumph of the decorator's art sits proudly behind a red-brick and stone Georgian facade on one of the most distinguished parks in London, Grosvenor Square. Its polite battalions of porters, doormen, and receptionists wait near the entrance along a side street. The American embassy is just a few doors away.

Throughout the hotel's carefully crafted interior, combinations of pink, peach, ivory, and green are consistently used. Its breakfast room is a decorator's dream, filled with a cluster of Chippendale antiques and the kind of chintz that goes perfectly with masses of seasonal flowers. The accommodations are decorated in the Georgian style, and contain all the electronic extras you'd expect.

Dining/Entertainment: Guests enjoy the Regent Lounge, which is outfitted in an English country style. In the Diplomat, meals are served in an elegant yet comfortable setting. A contemporary cuisine, featuring dishes in the tradition of California, France, Tuscany, and England, are served.

Services: 24-hour room service, valet, laundry, concierge, babysitting.

Facilities: No-smoking rooms, health club facilities accessible from hotel, business center.

PARK LANE HOTEL, Piccadilly (without number), London W1Y 8BX. Tel. 071/499-6321, or toll free 800/223-5652 in the U.S. and Canada. Fax 071/499-1965. 322 rms, 54 suites. MINIBAR TV TEL **Tube:** Hyde Park Corner.
$ Rates: £147 ($220.50) single; £175–£205 ($262.50–$307.50) double; from £230 ($345) suite. Continental breakfast £8.50 ($12.80) extra. AE, DC, MC, V. **Parking:** £25 ($37.50) extra.

This is probably the most traditional and long-standing of the Park Lane deluxe hotels, proud of its loyal clientele and consistently winning new converts all the time. Flanked with neighbors who have sold their premises to well-heeled foreigners, the Park Lane is now the last of the Park Lane giants to be privately and staunchly owned by an English family. It was begun in 1913 by an enterprising former member of the Life Guards, who used advanced engineering techniques to construct the foundations and an intricately detailed iron skeleton. When its creator was tragically killed in World War I, local gossips mockingly referred to the echoing and empty shell as "the bird cage." In 1924 one of London's leading hoteliers, Bracewell Smith, completed the construction, and a short time later the Park Lane became one of the leading hotels of Europe.

Today you'll enter an intensely English hotel that sits behind a discreet stone-block facade. One of its gateways, the Silver Entrance, is considered such an art deco marvel that its soaring columns and mirrors have been used as a backdrop in many films, including *Brideshead Revisited, The Winds of War,* and *Shanghai Surprise.* Designed in a U shape, with a view overlooking Green Park, the Park Lane Hotel offers luxurious and comfortable accommodations, with double-glazed windows, that are among the least expensive of any of the other major Park Lane competitors. Many of the suites offer marble fireplaces and the original marble-sheathed bathrooms.

Dining/Entertainment: The hotel's restaurant, Bracewell's, is recommended in Chapter 5, "London Dining." Bracewell's Bar is one of London's most popular cocktail bars with a talented evening pianist and a decor lined with cinnabar-red Chinese lacquer. Less expensive but still very charming is the Brasserie, which changes the focus of its continental menu every month.

Services: 24-hour room service, concierge, valet, babysitting, laundry and dry cleaning.

Facilities: Business center, fitness center, safety-deposit boxes, gift and newspaper shop, barbershop, women's hairdresser.

2. PICCADILLY & ST. JAMES'S

PICCADILLY

HOTEL 22 JERMYN STREET, 22 Jermyn St., London SW1Y 6HL. Tel. 071/734-2353, or toll free 800/729-FLAG in the U.S. Fax 071/734-0750. 5 rms, 13 suites. MINIBAR TV TEL **Tube:** Piccadilly Circus.
$ Rates: £165 ($247.50) single or double; from £215 ($322.50) suite. English breakfast £11.50 ($17.30) extra. AE, DC, MC, V. **Parking:** Valet parking £20 ($30) extra.

Set behind a facade of gray stone with neoclassical embellishments, this structure was originally built in 1870 as an apartment house for English gentlemen doing business in London. Since 1915 it has been administered by three generations of the Togna family, whose most recent scion closed it for a radical restoration in 1990. Now reveling in its new role as a chic and upscale boutique hotel, it offers rooms that have masses of fresh flowers, chintzes, and traditional English furnishings. The rooms are furnished as in an elegant private English home. There are no dining facilities, but many restaurants are nearby.

Services: 24-hour room service, concierge staff, babysitting, laundry.

Facilities: Free use of Dictaphones and fax, two phone lines in each room, nearby health club (75 yards away).

LE MÉRIDIEN LONDON, 21 Piccadilly, London W1V 0BH. Tel. 071/734-8000, or toll free 800/543-4300 in the U.S. Fax 071/437-3574. 222 rms, 41 suites. A/C MINIBAR TV TEL **Tube:** Piccadilly Circus.

$ Rates: £190–£210 ($285–$315) single; £210–£230 ($315–$345) double; from £275 ($412.50) suite. English breakfast £12.75 ($19.10) extra. AE, DC, MC, V.
Parking: £20 ($30) extra.

At the time of this hotel's original opening in 1908, the Ionic arcade capping the limestone of its arched neoclassical facade was considered the height of Edwardian extravagance. It was instantly pronounced the grandest hotel in London, but its huge expense soon bankrupted its creator. New owners continued to make the hotel one of the most stylish in the world, receiving such luminaries as Mary Pickford accompanied by Douglas Fairbanks, and Edward VII. After World War II the hotel sank into a kind of musty obscurity until its lavish refurbishment during the revitalization of the Piccadilly theater district. In the late 1980s, it was radically restored and upgraded by the Air France–controlled Méridien chain, which considers the hotel its European flagship. It contains enough elaborately detailed plasterwork, stained glass, and limed oak paneling to make any Francophile feel at home, yet offers enough old-world service and style to satisfy even the most discerning British. Except for the intricate beauty of the skylit reception area, the centerpiece of the hotel is the soaring grandeur of the Oak Room Lounge, where gilded carvings and chandeliers of shimmering Venetian glass re-create Edwardian styles. Bedrooms are tasteful, exuding quality, comfort, and style.

Dining/Entertainment: The formal and very elegant Oak Room Restaurant is recommended in Chapter 5, "London Dining." The Terrace Restaurant is less formal, a sun-flooded aerie under the greenhouse walls of the facade's massive Ionic portico. There is, as well, a very British bar sheathed in hardwoods and filled with live piano music.

Services: 24-hour room service, laundry, hairdressing.

Facilities: The hotel's Champney's is one of the most exotic health clubs in London, featuring a large pool, saunas, steambaths, aerobic workshops, squash courts, billiard tables, and a private-membership clientele.

RITZ, 150 Piccadilly, London W1V 9DG. Tel. 071/493-8181, or toll free 800/544-7570 in the U.S. Fax 071/493-2687. 115 rms, 14 suites. MINIBAR TV TEL **Tube:** Green Park.

$ Rates: £190–£220 ($285–$330) single; £220–£290 ($330–$435) double; from £505 ($757.50) suite. English breakfast £14.50 ($21.80) extra. AE, DC, MC, V.
Parking: £35 ($52.50) extra.

Built in the French Renaissance style in 1906, overlooking the landscapes of Green Park, the Ritz is synonymous with luxury. The original color scheme of apricot, cream, and dusty rose enhances gold-leafed molding, marble columns, and potted palms. The oval Palm Court is dominated by a gold-leafed statue, *La Source*, adorning the fountain.

The bedrooms and suites, each with its own character, radios, and in-house films, are spacious and comfortable. Most are air-conditioned. The well-kept bedrooms often have marble fireplaces and elaborate gilded plasterwork. The decor is often in soft pastel hues.

Dining/Entertainment: It is still the most fashionable place in London to meet for afternoon tea, at which a selection of finger sandwiches, including cucumber and smoked salmon, are served, as well as specially made French pastries, scones, and cake.

The Ritz Restaurant, one of the loveliest dining rooms in the world, has been faithfully restored to its original splendor. Service is efficient yet unobtrusive, and the tables are spaced to allow the most private of conversations, perhaps the reason Edward and Mrs. Simpson dined so frequently at the Ritz.

Services: 24-hour room service, laundry, valet, babysitting.

Facilities: Garden, news kiosk, shopping boutiques, and access to the St. James's Health Club around the corner.

ST. JAMES'S

VERY EXPENSIVE

DUKES HOTEL, 35 St. James's Place, London SW1A 1NY. Tel. 071/ 491-4840. Fax 071/493-1264. 38 rms, 36 suites. TV TEL **Tube:** Green Park.

$ Rates: £180 ($270) single; £215–£275 ($322.50–$412.50) double; from £330 ($495) suite. English breakfast £11.75 ($17.60) extra. AE, DC, MC, V.

The Dukes provides elegance without ostentation. A hotel since 1908, it stands in a quiet courtyard off St. James's Street with its turn-of-the-century gas lamps. From the hotel it's possible to walk to Buckingham Palace, St. James's Palace, and the Houses of Parliament. Shoppers will be near Bond Street and Piccadilly, and literature buffs will be interested to note that Oscar Wilde lived and wrote at St. James's Place for a time.

Each of the well-furnished and centrally heated bedrooms is decorated in the style of a particular English period, ranging from Regency to Edwardian. In lieu of air conditioning, there are ceiling fans. Renovations are ongoing, covering one floor every year on a continuing basis.

Dining/Entertainment: Duke's Restaurant is small, tasteful, and elegant, combining both classic British and continental cuisine with nouvelle cuisine. Fixed-price lunches at £19.95 ($29.90) are an excellent value, although a three-course fixed-price dinner is more expensive, going for £28.50 ($42.80) per person. The hotel also has a clublike bar.

Services: 24-hour room service, laundry, babysitting.

STAFFORD HOTEL, 16–18 St. James's Place, London SW1A 1NJ. Tel. 071/493-0111, or toll free 800/222-0939 in the U.S. Fax 071/493-7121. 67 rms, 7 suites. TV TEL **Tube:** Green Park.

$ Rates: £184 ($276) single; £200–£245 ($300–$367.50) double; from £253 ($379.50) suite. English breakfast £10.75 ($16.10) extra. AE, DC, MC, V.

Famous for its American Bar and the warmth of its Edwardian decor, the Stafford was built late in the 19th century as a private home on a cul-de-sac off one of the most centrally located and busiest neighborhoods of London. It can be entered via St. James's Place or else via a cobble-covered courtyard which was originally designed as a mews and is known today as the Blue Ball Yard. Owned by the Cunard group, the Stafford has retained a homelike, country-house atmosphere with touches of antique charm and modern amenities.

The bedrooms and suites are individually decorated and of varying shapes and sizes that correspond to the original function of the building as a private home. A handful of the hotel's newest and plushest accommodations require transit across the cobblestones of the mews yard.

Dining/Entertainment: The Stafford Restaurant is an elegant dining room lit with handsome chandeliers and wall sconces and accented with flowers, candles, and white napery. You can lunch or dine on classic international dishes that are made from fresh, select ingredients. A lunch costs from £19.50 ($29.30); a dinner, from £25 ($37.50). The previously mentioned American Bar (actually more like a memento-packed library of an English country house) is an especially cozy attraction.

Services: 24-hour room service, babysitting, concierge, secretarial service, laundry.

INEXPENSIVE

REGENT PALACE HOTEL, Piccadilly Circus (without number), London W1A 4BZ. Tel. 071/734-7000. Fax 071/734-6435. 887 rms (none with bath). TV TEL **Tube:** Piccadilly Circus.
$ Rates (including English breakfast): £45 ($67.50) single; £67 ($100.50) double. AE, DC, MC, V.

Considered a major focal point since it was built in 1915 at the edge of Piccadilly Circus, this is one of the largest hotels in Europe. Today, it's known for its staunch loyalty to its original design whereby none of the rooms has a private bathroom. (Shared facilities in the hallways are adequate, and each room has a sink with hot and cold running water.) Some clients believe that this huge hotel's design provides a perspective on British life from another era.

If guests stay for 2 nights or more, charges are reduced to £33 ($49.50) in a single or £66 ($99) in a double, including breakfast. The hotel's Original Carvery makes a good place to dine, and The Dome bistro is open for pretheater meals. Drinks are served in the Half Sovereign and the Planters bars. Coffee, sandwiches, and snacks are available in Antonio's Coffee Bar.

3. BLOOMSBURY

"All I want is a room in Bloomsbury," sang Twiggy in Ken Russel's delightful movie musical *The Boyfriend* (1971). Between the world wars, this neighborhood—containing London University, the British Museum, and the Royal Academy of Dramatic Arts—was the stamping grounds of artists Duncan Grant and Vanessa Bell and writers Lytton Strachey and Leonard and Virginia Woolf, among other members of the Bloomsbury Group.

HOTEL RUSSELL, Russell Sq. (without number), London WC1 B5BE. Tel. 071/837-6470, or toll free 800/435-4542 in the U.S. Fax 071/837-2857. 308 rms, 19 suites. TV TEL **Tube:** Russell Square.
$ Rates: £105 ($157.50) single; £120 ($180) double; from £150 ($225) suite. English breakfast £10 ($15) extra. AE, DC, MC, V.

A late Victorian hotel facing the garden of this famous square, and within easy reach of theaters and shopping, the Russell is run by Forte Hotels. The immaculately maintained bedrooms, in contrast to the overall style of the hotel, are thoroughly modernized and up-to-date, with well-chosen fabrics.

Dining/Entertainment: The public rooms have been refurbished and include an excellent carvery restaurant and a brasserie. A grill restaurant, Virginia Woolf's, specializes in pasta. All the dining establishments offer good value for money. The Kings Bar serves cocktails in the atmosphere of a London club, and you can enjoy draft beer in the country-pub ambience of Benjamin's Bar.

Services: 24-hour room service, laundry, babysitting.
Facilities: Theater-ticket agent.

INEXPENSIVE

CENTRAL CLUB, 16–22 Great Russell St., London WC1B 3LR. Tel. 071/636-7512. Fax 071/636-5278. 100 rms. TV TEL **Tube:** Tottenham Court Road.
$ Rates: £31 ($46.50) single; £56 ($84) double; £17 ($25.50) per person in a triple or quad. Breakfast from £2.50 ($3.80) extra. MC, V.

This large and attractive building was designed by Sir Edwin Lutyens, the famous architect, and built around 1932 as a YWCA. Although still vaguely affiliated with YWCA, it now functions as a hotel and accepts men, women, families, and groups traveling together. Each of the simple but comfortable bedrooms contains a radio and beverage-making facilities. Included in the rate is use of the lounges, coin-operated laundry facilities, hair salon, gym, solarium, and a coffee shop.

4. THE STRAND & COVENT GARDEN

THE STRAND

This thoroughfare—chockablock with theaters, shops, hotels, and restaurants— begins at Trafalgar Square and runs east to Fleet Street.

SAVOY, The Strand (without number), London WC2R OEU. Tel. 071/ 836-4343, or toll free 800/223-6800 in the U.S. and Canada. Fax 071/240-6040. 156 rms, 48 suites. A/C MINIBAR TV TEL **Tube:** Charing Cross.

$ Rates: £158 ($237) single; £180–£240 ($270–$360) double; from £332 ($498) suite. English breakfast £15.75 ($23.60) extra. VAT extra. AE, DC, MC, V. **Parking:** £20 ($30) extra.

The Savoy is a London landmark, with eight stories behind a facade of light terra-cotta glazed tiles, rising majestically between the Strand and the Thames. The hotel, opened in 1889, was built by Richard D'Oyly Carte, impresario, for the use of people going to his theater to see the Gilbert and Sullivan operas he staged. Through the Savoy's portals have passed famous personages of yesterday and today, everybody from royalty to stars of stage, screen, TV, and rock. Today the hotel has regained the impeccable hospitality, service, and splendor of its early years.

Forty-eight of the hotel's bedrooms have their own sitting rooms. Each has a different decor, with color-coordinated accessories, and all have comfortable chairs, solid furniture, and large closets. The units contain a blend of antiques, an eclectic combination of such pieces as gilt mirrors, Queen Anne chairs, and Victorian sofas. Guests find fresh flowers and fruit in their rooms on arrival, and at night beds are turned down and a chocolate is placed on the pillows.

Dining/Entertainment: The world-famous Savoy Grill has long been popular with a theatrical clientele. Sarah Bernhardt was among its most celebrated customers in her time. The even-more-elegant River Restaurant is in a prime position, with tables overlooking the Thames; a four-person band plays in the evening for dancing.

Services: 24-hour room service, nightly turndown, limousine service, same-day laundry and dry cleaning, babysitting.

Facilities: Hairdresser, news kiosk, and a unique Health Club built on top of the historic Savoy Theatre, destroyed by fire in 1990 and rebuilt in 1993.

COVENT GARDEN

Covent Garden took its name from the garden that nuns once tended to on this site. The square was laid out by Inigo Jones in 1631 and housed London's fruit, vegetable, and flower market until the 1970s. This is where Professor Higgins found his Galatea, London flower girl Eliza Doolittle, in George Bernard Shaw's *Pygmalion* (1913). The Royal Opera House, also housing the Royal Ballet, is located here. The Theatre Museum, which opened in 1987, is in the Old Flower Market.

DRURY LANE MOAT HOUSE, 10 Drury Lane, High Holborn, London

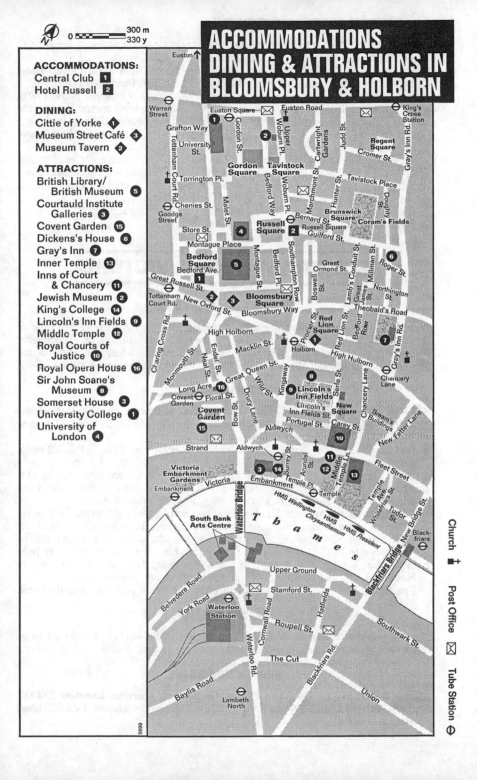

WC2B 5RE. Tel. 071/836-6666. Fax 071/831-1548. 146 rms, 7 suites. A/C TV TEL **Tube:** Holborn or Covent Garden.

$ Rates: £128–£148 ($192–$222) single or double; from £200 ($300) suite. English breakfast from £9.50 ($14.30). AE, DC, MC, V. **Parking:** £10 ($15).

A steel-and-glass structure, originally built in 1978, then later enlarged in the 1980s, with terraced gardens, its own plaza, and individually controlled central heating, the hotel is elegantly decorated in greens and beiges, its extensive planting evoking a garden effect. The well-decorated bedrooms—many for nonsmokers—have hairdryers, in-house videos, radios, trouser presses, and tea/coffee makers.

Dining/Entertainment: Maudie's Bar makes a good pretheater rendezvous, and Maudie's Restaurant is open for lunch and dinner 7 days a week specializing in a French cuisine. Who was the original Maudie? She's Sir Osbert Lancaster's famous arbiter-of-chic cartoon character, Maudie Littlehampton.

Services: 24-hour room service, laundry, baby-listening service.

Facilities: Garage.

5. WESTMINSTER & VICTORIA

WESTMINSTER

Proper Westminster has been the seat of the British government since the time of Edward the Confessor. Westminster encompasses Buckingham Palace, Westminster Abbey, the Houses of Parliament with Big Ben, Downing Street (the home of the prime minister at number 10), and the National Gallery and National Portrait Gallery.

EXPENSIVE

STAKIS ST. ERMINS HOTEL, Caxton St. (without number), London SW1H 0QW. Tel. 071/222-7888. Fax 071/222-6914. 290 rms, 7 suites. MINIBAR TV TEL **Tube:** St. James's Park.

$ Rates: £112 ($168) single; £145 ($217.50) double; from £275 ($412.50) suite. Continental breakfast £7.75 ($11.60) extra. AE, DC, MC, V.

A turn-of-the-century red-brick building, enlarged with a modern wing, this hotel is ideally located in the heart of Westminster and only a few minutes' walk from Buckingham Palace, the Houses of Parliament, and Westminster Abbey.

Dining/Entertainment: The hotel has two restaurants: the Caxton Grill offers an à la carte menu at excellent value, while the Carving Table has a fixed price for lunch and dinner, serving a selection of roast meats, salads, and international dishes. Lunch costs £14.75 ($22.10); dinner, £15.75 ($23.60). The lounge bar serves light snacks 24 hours a day, as well as an afternoon tea every day from 3 to 5:30pm.

Services: 24-hour room service, laundry, babysitting, guide services.

Facilities: The Queen Mother Sports Centre lies within a short walk of the hotel.

VICTORIA

Directly south of Buckingham Palace is a section in Pimlico often referred to as "Victoria," with its namesake—sprawling, bustling Victoria Station—as its center.

VERY EXPENSIVE

GORING HOTEL, 15 Beeston Place, Grosvenor Garden, London SW1W 0JW. Tel. 071/396-9000. Fax 071/834-4393. 75 rms, 5 suites. TV TEL **Tube:** Victoria Station.

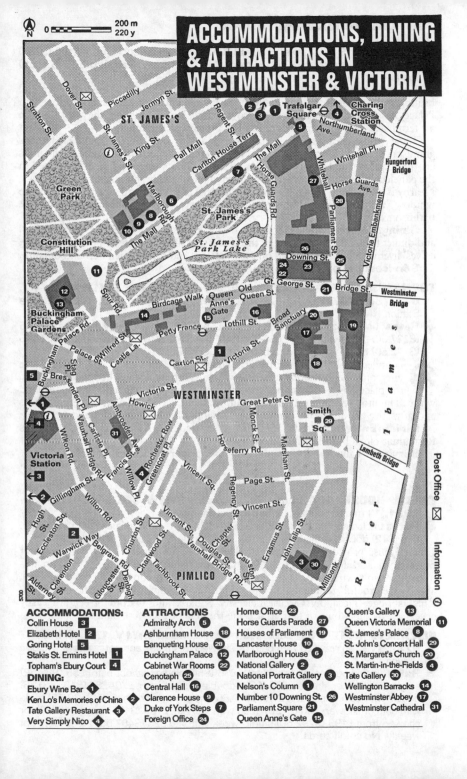

ACCOMMODATIONS, DINING & ATTRACTIONS IN WESTMINSTER & VICTORIA

ACCOMMODATIONS:
Collin House **3**
Elizabeth Hotel **2**
Goring Hotel **5**
Stakis St. Ermins Hotel **1**
Topham's Ebury Court **4**

DINING:
Ebury Wine Bar **1**
Ken Lo's Memories of China **2**
Tate Gallery Restaurant **3**
Very Simply Nico **4**

ATTRACTIONS
Admiralty Arch **5**
Ashburnham House **18**
Banqueting House **28**
Buckingham Palace **12**
Cabinet War Rooms **22**
Cenotaph **25**
Central Hall **16**
Clarence House **9**
Duke of York Steps **7**
Foreign Office **24**

Home Office **23**
Horse Guards Parade **27**
Houses of Parliament **19**
Lancaster House **10**
Marlborough House **6**
National Gallery **2**
National Portrait Gallery **3**
Nelson's Column **1**
Number 10 Downing St. **26**
Parliament Square **21**
Queen Anne's Gate **15**

Queen's Gallery **13**
Queen Victoria Memorial **11**
St. John's Concert Hall **29**
St. James's Palace **8**
St. Margaret's Church **20**
St. Martin-in-the-Fields **4**
Tate Gallery **30**
Wellington Barracks **14**
Westminster Abbey **17**
Westminster Cathedral **31**

$ Rates: £120 ($180) single; £150–£170 ($225–$255) double; from £190 ($285) suite. English breakfast £12 ($18) extra. AE, DC, MC, V. **Parking:** £15 ($22.50) extra.

Built in 1910 by Mr. O. R. Goring, this was the first hotel in the world to have central heating and a private bathroom in every bedroom. Located just behind Buckingham Palace, it lies within easy reach of the royal parks, Victoria Station, the West London air terminals, Westminster Abbey, and the Houses of Parliament.

Today, top-quality service is still provided, this time by the founding father's grandson, George Goring. The rooms here are called apartments. Some of the units are air-conditioned. The charm of a traditional English country home is reflected in the paneled drawing room, where fires burn in the ornate fireplaces on nippy evenings. Nearby is a sun room with a view of the gardens in the rear and a bar situated by the window. All the well-furnished bedrooms have been refurbished with marble bathrooms.

Dining/Entertainment: You can have a three-course luncheon for £20 ($30) and dinner from £30 ($45). Some of the chef's specialties include a fine duckling pâté, calves' liver with bacon and fried onions, venison, and roast boned best end of lamb.

Services: 24-hour room service, laundry, valet.

TOPHAM'S EBURY COURT, 28 Ebury St., London SW1W 0LU. Tel. 071/730-8147. Fax 071/823-5966. 42 rms (23 with bath). TEL **Tube:** Victoria Station.

$ Rates (including English breakfast): £55 ($82.50) single without bath, £85 ($127.50) single with bath; £65–£95 ($97.50–$142.50) double without bath, £115 ($172.50) double or twin with bath. AE, DC, MC, V.

Founded in 1937, this hotel was created when five small row houses were interconnected into one coherent whole. With its flower-filled windowboxes, the place has a country-house flavor and is brightly painted in turquoise and white. The little reception rooms are informal and decorated with flowery chintzes and attractive antiques. Most rooms have facilities for making coffee and tea.

Dining/Entertainment: Specializing in traditional English food, Tophams Restaurant offers both lunch and dinner.

Services: Laundry, dry cleaning, 24-hour porter service, babysitting.

INEXPENSIVE

COLLIN HOUSE, 104 Ebury St., London SW1W 9QD. Tel. 071/730-8031. 13 rms (8 with bath). **Tube:** Victoria Station.

$ Rates (including English breakfast): £34–£36 ($51–$54) single with private bath; £48 ($72) double without bath, £56 ($84) double with bath. No credit cards.

Collin House provides a good, clean B&B under the watchful eye of its resident proprietors, Mr. and Mrs. D. L. Thomas. Everything is well maintained in this mid-Victorian town house. There are a number of family rooms. The main bus, rail, and Underground terminals all lie about a 5-minute walk from the hotel. Knightsbridge, Piccadilly Circus, Leicester Square, and Oxford Street are easily accessible by tube, bus, or taxi, as are the theaters of the West End.

ELIZABETH HOTEL, 37 Eccleston Sq., London SW1V 1PB. Tel. 071/828-6812. 38 rms (20 with bath or shower), 8 studios and apts. **Tube:** Victoria Station.

$ Rates (including English breakfast): £36 ($54) single without bath, £55 ($82.50) single with bath or shower; £58 ($87) double without bath, £70–£84 ($105–$126) double with bath or shower; £75 ($112.50) triple without bath, £93 ($139.50) triple with bath or shower; £80 ($120) quad without bath, £104 ($156) quad with bath or shower; from £195 ($292.50) studio weekly; from £325 ($487.50) 2-bedroom apt weekly. No credit cards.

IMPRESSIONS

Till that day I never noticed one of the worst things about London—the fact that it costs money even to sit down.
—GEORGE ORWELL, DOWN AND OUT IN PARIS AND LONDON, 1933

$ The Elizabeth Hotel is an unpretentious, privately owned establishment overlooking the gardens of Eccleston Square, which was built by Thomas Cubitt, Queen Victoria's favorite builder. Located behind Victoria Station, it's an excellent place to stay, convenient to Belgravia and Westminster, not far from Buckingham Palace and just a few doors away from a house where Sir Winston Churchill once lived. Most of the accommodations are reached by elevator, and each is individually decorated in a Victorian motif. The original atmosphere of the place has been carefully preserved, as reflected in the furnishings, framed prints, and wallpaper. Some rooms have TVs. If you're going to be in London for a week, ask about leasing an apartment.

---

6. KNIGHTSBRIDGE & BELGRAVIA

KNIGHTSBRIDGE

A top residential and shopping district of London just south of Hyde Park, Knightsbridge is close in character to Belgravia, although much of this section to the west of Sloane Street is older, dating back in architecture and layout to the 18th century.

VERY EXPENSIVE

THE BEAUFORT, 33 Beaufort Gardens, London SW3 1PP. Tel. 071/584-5252, or 212/682-9191 in New York. Fax 071/589-2834. 21 rms, 7 suites. TV TEL **Tube:** Knightsbridge.

$ Rates (including continental breakfast): £110–£120 ($165–$180) single; £150–£220 ($225–$330) double or twin; £250 ($375) junior suite for two. AE, DC, MC, V. **Parking:** Free overnight on street.

The Beaufort, located only 100 yards from Harrods, sits behind two Victorian porticoes and an iron fence that was added when the buildings were constructed in the 1870s. The owner combined a pair of adjacent houses, ripped out the old decor, and created an updated ambience of merit and charm. You register at a small alcove extending off a bay-windowed parlor, and later you climb the stairway used by the queen of Sweden during her stay here several years ago.

Each bedroom features at least one well-chosen painting by a London art student, a thoughtfully modern color scheme, plush carpeting, and a kind of grace throughout. One added advantage of this place is the helpful staff and the inspired direction of its owner, Diana Wallis, a television producer. She created the feeling of a private house in the heart of London, putting earphone radios, flowers, and a selection of books to read in each room.

Dining/Entertainment: Snacks are available from room service; a complimentary 24-hour bar is also available.

Services: Food room service (7am to 9pm), 24-hour drink room service, babysitting, laundry, theater bookings.

Facilities: Free membership in a nearby health club.

THE CAPITAL, 22–24 Basil St., London SW3 1AT. Tel. 071/589-5171, or toll free 800/926-3199 in the U.S. Fax 071/225-0011. 48 rms, 8 suites. A/C MINIBAR TV TEL **Tube:** Knightsbridge.
$ **Rates:** £175 single; £210–£260 ($315–$390) double; from £300 ($450) suite. English breakfast £12.50 ($18.80) extra. AE, DC, MC, V. **Parking:** £15 ($22.50) extra.

The Capital is one of the most personalized hotels in the West End and is a member of Relais & Châteaux. Small and modern, it's a stone's throw from Harrods. The proud owner, David Levin, has created a warm town-house ambience, the result of an extensive refurbishment program. The elegant fin-de-siècle decoration is matched by the courtesy and professionalism of the staff. The corridors and staircase are all treated as an art gallery, with original oil paintings. Bedrooms are tastefully decorated, many with Ralph Lauren designs.

Dining/Entertainment: The Capital Restaurant is among the finest in London, offering exquisitely prepared main dishes. A fixed-price lunch costs £20 ($30); a set dinner, from £25 ($37.50). You can also order à la carte.

Services: 24-hour room service, laundry.

SHERATON PARK TOWER, 101 Knightsbridge, London SW1 X74N. Tel. 071/235-8050, or toll free 800/325-3535 in the U.S. Fax 071/235-8231. 295 rms, 22 suites. A/C MINIBAR TV TEL **Tube:** Knightsbridge.
$ **Rates:** £195 ($292.50) single; £230–£280 ($345–$420) double; from £450 ($675) suite. VAT extra. English breakfast £14.05 ($21.10) extra. AE, DC, MC, V. **Parking:** £9 ($13.50).

Rising like a concrete cylinder, the Sheraton Park Tower is not only one of the most convenient hotels in London, virtually at the doorstep of Harrods, but one of the best. Its unusual circular architecture provides a stark but interesting contrast to the well-heeled 19th-century neighborhood around it. From its windows guests have a magnificent view of Hyde Park. The front door isn't where you'd expect it—it's discreetly placed in the rear of the building, where taxis can deposit guests more conveniently.

Its busy travertine-covered lobby bustles with scores of international businesspeople, diplomats (the French embassy is across the street), and military delegations, who congregate on one of the well-upholstered sofas or amid the Edwardian comfort of the hideaway bar. Back in your room, you'll find such comforts as central heating, soundproof windows, in-house movies, and radios.

Ⓕ FROMMER'S COOL FOR KIDS: HOTELS

Sandringham Hotel (see p. 123) Out in Hampstead—children have plenty of room to play on the heath—this hotel offers both triple rooms and family rooms for four or five people.

Hart House Hotel (see p. 120) This small family-run B&B is right in the center of the West End near Hyde Park. Many of its rooms are triples, and special family suites with connecting rooms can be arranged.

Blandford Hotel (see p. 118) For the family on a budget, this hotel near Baker Street of Sherlock Holmes fame has a number of triple or family rooms (suitable for four or five guests). Kids can walk to Madame Tussaud's waxworks.

Dining/Entertainment: In the rotunda, near the ground-floor kiosks, you can enjoy afternoon tea. The champagne bar offers you the choice of either a glass or a silver tankard filled with bubbly, along with oysters, dollops of caviar, and iced vodka. The Restaurant 101, which has its own entrance onto Knightsbridge and is open daily from 7am to 11pm, offers exceptionally good food and is ideal for an after-theater supper. You can dine on such dishes as roasted sea bass with olives and crabmeat, lobster-stuffed ravioli, or filet of beef with horseradish-béarnaise sauce.

Services: 24-hour room service, laundry, babysitting.

Facilities: Business center, news kiosk, free access to a neighborhood health club.

EXPENSIVE

BASIL STREET HOTEL, 8 Basil St., London SW3 1AH. Tel. 071/581-3311. Fax 071/581-3693. 92 rms (74 with bath or shower), 1 suite. TV TEL **Tube:** Knightsbridge.

$ Rates: £59 ($88.50) single without bath, £110.50 ($165.80) single with bath; £90.50 ($135.80) double without bath, £156.50 ($234.80) double with bath; £238.25 ($357.40) suite. English breakfast £10.50 ($15.80) extra. AE, DC, MC, V. **Parking:** £23 ($34.50).

The Basil has long been a favorite little hotel for discerning British who make an annual pilgrimage to London to shop at Harrods and perhaps attend the Chelsea Flower Show. This Edwardian charmer is totally unmarred by modernization, and is preferred by guests who can appreciate a highly individualistic hotel.

There are several spacious and comfortable lounges, appropriately furnished with 18th- and 19th-century decorative accessories. Off the many rambling corridors are smaller sitting rooms. The hotel offers bedrooms that have been modernized and decorated in soft fabrics and harmonious color schemes. The standard of housekeeping is excellent. A three-course table d'hôte luncheon costs £15 ($22.50), and dinner is à la carte. Candlelight and piano music re-create the atmosphere of a bygone era. The Upstairs Restaurant serves lighter meals and snacks, and the Downstairs Wine Bar offers an excellent selection of wines and inexpensive food.

PARKES HOTEL, 41–43 Beaufort Gardens, London SW3 1PW. Tel. 071/581-9944. Fax 071/225-1442. 4 rms, 29 suites. MINIBAR TV TEL **Tube:** Knightsbridge.

$ Rates (including English breakfast): £90 ($135) single or double; from £120–£150 ($180–$225) suite. VAT extra. AE, MC, V. **Parking:** Free on street 6pm–8am; £12 ($18) at nearby garage.

A classy Edwardian-style town house, the Parkes is standing in one of the most desirable locations in London, close to Harrods. Facing a quiet and stately square, this is very much an individual private houselike hotel, with plenty of charm and style. Except for four standard bedrooms, each accommodation is a suite, complete with kitchenette. Each unit is individually decorated, sometimes in themes of blue and yellow. The staff does much to make guests feel at home.

MODERATE

CLAVERLEY HOTEL, 13–14 Beaufort Gardens, London SW3 1PS. Tel. 071/589-8541. Fax 071/584-3410. 32 rms (29 with bath). TV TEL **Tube:** Knightsbridge.

$ Rates (including English breakfast): £50 ($75) single without bath, £60–£90 ($90–$135) single with bath; £90–£150 ($135–$225) double with bath. MC, V. **Parking:** Free on street (6pm–8am).

Set on a quiet street in Knightsbridge, this tasteful hotel lies just a few blocks from

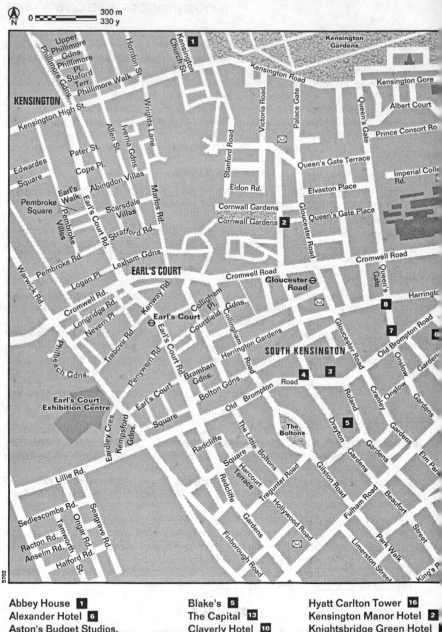

Abbey House **1**	Blake's **5**	Hyatt Carlton Tower **16**
Alexander Hotel **6**	The Capital **13**	Kensington Manor Hotel **2**
Aston's Budget Studios,	Claverly Hotel **10**	Knightsbridge Green Hotel
Aston's Designer Studios &	The Cranley **4**	The Lanesborough **15**
Aston's Luxury Apartments **3**	Diplomat Hotel **17**	Number Sixteen **6**
Basil Street Hotel **13**	Draycott **12**	Parkes Hotel **10**
The Beaufort **10**	The Fenja **12**	Pelham Hotel **9**
Blair House Hotel **11**	Hotel 167 **7**	Prince Hotel **6**

ACCOMMODATIONS IN KNIGHTSBRIDGE, KENSINGTON, SOUTH KENSINGTON, CHELSEA & BELGRAVIA

Regency Hotel **8**
Sheraton Park Tower **14**
5 Sumner Place **6**
Wilbraham Hotel **18**
Willett **19**

Harrods. In many ways it's one of the very best hotels in the neighborhood. It's a small, cozy place accented with Georgian-era accessories. The lounge is one of the hotel's most desirable features, containing 19th-century oil portraits, a Regency fireplace, and a collection of elegant antiques and leather-covered sofas—much like the ensemble you'd find in a private country house. Here, the hotel serves complimentary tea, coffee, hot chocolate, and cookies 24 hours a day. Awarded the British Tourist Authority's Certificate of Distinction for Bed-and-Breakfast Hotels in 1988, the Claverley continues to maintain the high standards that won it the award. Most rooms have Victorian-inspired wallpaper, wall-to-wall carpeting, and comfortably upholstered armchairs.

KNIGHTSBRIDGE GREEN HOTEL, 159 Knightsbridge, London SW1X 7PD. Tel. 071/584-6274. Fax 071/225-1635. 10 rms, 14 suites (all with bath). TV TEL **Tube:** Knightsbridge.
$ Rates: £75 ($112.50) single; £100 ($150) double; £125 ($187.50) suite. English breakfast £8.50 ($12.80) extra. AE, MC, V.

This unusual establishment was constructed a block from Harrods in the 1890s. In 1966, when it was converted into a hotel, the developers were careful to retain the wide baseboards, cove molding, high ceilings, and spacious proportions of the dignified old structure.

None of the accommodations contains a kitchen, but the result comes close to apartment-style living. Many of the doubles or twins are suites, each well furnished with access to the second-floor "club room" where coffee and pastries are available throughout the day. Rooms contain trouser press and hairdryer.

BELGRAVIA

The aristocratic quarter of London, Belgravia, south of Hyde Park, challenges its northern neighbor, Mayfair, for grandness. It reigned in glory with Queen Victoria, but today's aristocrats are more likely to be the top echelon in foreign embassies, along with a rising new monied class of actors and models. Belgravia is near Buckingham Palace Gardens and Brompton Road. Its center is Belgrave Square, one of the more attractive plazas in London. For those who prefer a residential address, Belgravia is choice real estate.

VERY EXPENSIVE

THE LANESBOROUGH, 1 Lanesborough Place, Hyde Park Corner, London SW1X 7TA. Tel. 071/259-5606, or toll free 800/999-1828 in the U.S. Fax 071/295-5606. 49 rms, 46 suites. A/C MINIBAR TV TEL **Tube:** Hyde Park Corner.
$ Rates: £165–£190 ($247.50–$285) single; £220–£275 ($330–$412.50) double; from £350 ($525) suite. English breakfast £16 ($24) extra. AE, DC, MC, V. **Parking:** £2 ($3) per hour.

Only a handful of other locations in London have elicited the kind of curiosity and loyalty that this building exerts on the public psyche. Originally built in 1719, when the neighborhood was still relatively uncrowded, as a country house by the second Viscount Lanesborough, it was demolished in 1827. Rebuilt soon after in the neoclassical style as St. George's Hospital, it was famous as the site of one of Florence Nightingale's crusades when she insisted on improvements and enlargements. During the darkest days of World War II, St. George's was one of the most visible beacons of hope as bombs fell on London, and many older Londoners were born or "patched up" within the hospital's severe and medicinal-smelling wards. In 1987, advances in technology had reduced the historic hospital into a hopelessly inefficient medical antique. The medical facilities were moved to newly built quarters in South London, and the grueling task of redefining the building began.

Soon after, a group of hoteliers, the Rosewood Group (famous for their management of such hotels as the Bel-Air in Los Angeles and The Mansion on Turtle Creek in Dallas), received permission from the London Planning Board to upgrade the building into a luxury hotel.

Most of the Georgian details of the historic building were retained, and the tacked-on machinery that was necessary for the maintenance of the building as a hospital was demolished. Into the echoing interior were added acres of Regency and Neo-Gothic details, ornate plasterwork reminiscent of some of the finest buildings in Britain, yards of mahogany paneling, and a discreet and well-polished aura similar to what you might have expected in a sumptuously decorated English country house. The bedrooms are as opulent and antique-drenched as you might have expected. Each has electronic sensors to alert the staff as to when a resident is in or out, a VCR, CD and videocassette players, personal safes, fax machines, 24-channel satellite TVs, bathrooms with every conceivable amenity, triple soundproofing, and the services of a personal butler. Security is tight; there are at least 35 surveillance cameras.

Dining/Entertainment: The Conservatory, an elegant coffee shop whose decor was inspired by the Chinese, Indian, and Gothic motifs of the Brighton Pavilion, is open daily from 7am to midnight. The Library Bar, which opens into a Victorian hideaway charmingly named "The Withdrawal Room," re-creates the atmosphere of a private and very elegant London club. Formal meals are served Monday to Saturday at lunch and dinner in The Dining Room.

Services: Personal butlers; concierges who can obtain virtually anything.

Facilities: Car-rental kiosk, news kiosk, and exercise equipment (Stairmasters and exercise bicycles) delivered directly to your room whenever you want them.

MODERATE

DIPLOMAT HOTEL, 2 Chesham St., London SW1X 8DT. Tel. 071/235-1544. Fax 071/259-6153. 27 rms (all with bath). TV TEL **Tube:** Sloane Square.
$ Rates (including English breakfast buffet): £65–£83 ($97.50–$124.50) single; £99–£135 ($148.50–$202.50) double. AE, DC, MC, V.

Part of the Diplomat Hotel's multifaceted allure lies in its status as a small, reasonably priced hotel in an otherwise prohibitively expensive neighborhood filled with privately owned Victorian homes and high-rise first-class hotels. It was originally built by one of the neighborhood's most famous architects in the 19th century on a wedge-shaped street corner near the site of today's Belgravia Sheraton. You register at a desk framed by the sweep of a partially gilded circular staircase beneath the benign gaze of cherubs looking down from a Regency-era chandelier.

Each of the comfortable high-ceilinged bedrooms boasts well-chosen wallpaper in Victorian-inspired colors, as well as a modern bath equipped with a hairdryer, among other accessories. The staff is very helpful. Each accommodation is named after one of the famous streets in this posh district.

THE CRANLEY, 10–12 Bina Gardens, London SW5 0LA. Tel. 071/373-0123, or toll free 800/553-2582 in the U.S. Fax 071/373-9497. 27 rms, 5 suites. A/C MINIBAR TV TEL **Tube:** South Kensington.
$ Rates (including continental breakfast): £104–£130 ($156–$195) single or double; £175–£230 ($262.50–$345) suite. AE, DC, MC, V.

Originally built as a trio of adjacent town houses around 1875, the Cranley became a hotel when its Michigan-based owners upgraded the buildings into one of the most charming hotels in South Kensington. Today, each of the high-ceilinged bedrooms has enormous windows, much of the original plasterwork, a scattering of antiques and plush upholstery, and a vivid sense of the 19th century. The public rooms have been described as a stage set for an ultra-English country house. There is no restaurant on the premises, although light snacks are served in the rooms upon request, and breakfast is a light continental affair in one of the public rooms. All but one of the accommodations are equipped with tiny kitchenettes.

Under the same ownership, about 4 blocks away, lies a similar hotel, One Cranley Place Hotel, charging the same rates. Originally built in the late 19th century as a private home, it features a stylish blend of antique and modern decorative accessories, and 10 rooms with the same amenities as, but slightly larger kitchenettes than, its larger sibling. Bookings can be made through the parent hotel.

7. CHELSEA & CHELSEA HARBOUR

CHELSEA

This stylish district stretches along the Thames, south of Hyde Park, Brompton, and South Kensington. It begins at the historic and charming Sloane Square. If you lodge here, you'll be close to the shopping districts of Knightsbridge and Sloane Street with the famous department store Harrods at your doorstep. Nearby is King's Road, with its boutiques, antique shops, and restaurants.

VERY EXPENSIVE

DRAYCOTT, 24–26 Cadogan Gardens, London SW3 2RP. Tel. 071/730-6466, or toll free 800/346-7007 in the U.S. Fax 071/730-0236. 25 rms, 6 suites. MINIBAR TV TEL **Tube:** Sloane Square.

$ Rates: £100–£150 ($150–$225) single; £195 ($292.50) double; £250 ($375) junior suite for two. English breakfast £10.50 ($15.80) extra. AE, DC, MC, V.

Located near Sloane Square in the heart of Chelsea, the Draycott opened in 1988 and has become a "secret address" known to fanciers of elegant but small hotels around the world. Here you might rest comfortably in a four-poster bed on fresh, crisp linen, as your champagne cools in a silver bucket. It's that kind of place. Check in with your most prestigious luggage. Out back the view opens onto a well-tended English garden, but inside the tone is set by chintz and a warming fire. Antiques are used discreetly. Staying here is like being a guest in a stately British home. There's even a bowl of apples set out so you can help yourself.

The main allure of the place is in its beautifully furnished bedrooms with private baths. In your room you are likely to find a copy of *An Innkeeper's Diary* by John Fothergill, but the Draycott doesn't take all his advice seriously—that is, his belief that boring clients should pay a higher tariff. Although there is no restaurant, there is room service that includes perfectly cooked and served breakfasts.

Services: 24-hour room service, laundry, babysitting.

Facilities: Complimentary use of a nearby health club, with sauna and solarium.

HYATT CARLTON TOWER, 2 Cadogan Place, London SW1 X9PY. Tel. 071/235-5411, or toll free 800/228-9000 in the U.S. Fax 071/235-9129. 164 rms, 60 suites. A/C MINIBAR TV TEL **Tube:** Knightsbridge.

IMPRESSIONS

London is a roost for every bird.
—BENJAMIN DISRAELI, *LOTHAIR*, 1870

$ Rates: £240 ($360) single or double; £320 ($480) suite. English breakfast £13 ($19.50) extra. AE, DC, MC, V. **Parking:** £20 ($30) extra.

Its location and height made this luxurious hotel a landmark even before Hyatt transformed it into its European flagship. An army of decorators, painters, and antiques dealers turned it into one of the most plushly decorated and best-maintained hotels in the city.

It overlooks one of London's most civilized gardens around which Regency-era town houses were built as part of an 18th-century planning initiative. The hotel's marble-floored lobby looks a lot like the private salon of an 18th-century merchant, complete with the lacquered and enameled treasures he might have brought back from the Far East. Even the pink-and-blue dragons and flowers that cover the thick wool carpets were made especially for the Hyatt in Hong Kong.

Its bedrooms are opulently outfitted, the beneficiaries of the many millions of dollars that the Hyatt spent on decor. Each contains all the modern comforts you'd expect, as well as marble-lined bathrooms, imaginative artwork, and in-house movies.

Dining/Entertainment: After the publicity it once received as "Britain's Tea Place of the Year," the hotel has been considered one of the capital's most fashionable corners in which to enjoy a midafternoon pick-me-up. Of course, scones, Devonshire clotted cream, arrays of pastries and delicate sandwiches, and music are all part of the experience. The Rib Room is for relatively informal meals in a warmly atmospheric setting. The Chelsea Room, considered one of the great restaurants of London, is covered separately in Chapter 5, "London Dining." On the upper floor, a Neo-Grecian bar serves light meals, and it's also popular as an early rendezvous place during the breakfast buffet.

Services: 24-hour room service, valet and laundry, hairdressing.

Facilities: Chic health club filled with state-of-the-art exercise machines and staffed by health and beauty experts.

EXPENSIVE

THE FENJA, 69 Cadogan Gardens, London SW3 2RB. Tel. 071/589-7333, or toll free 800/525-4800 in the U.S. Fax 071/581-4958. 14 rms. MINIBAR TV TEL **Tube:** Sloane Square.

$ Rates: £97.75 ($146.60) single; £130–£195 ($195–$292.50) double. English breakfast £11.75 ($17.60) extra. AE, MC, V. **Parking:** Free overnight on street; nearby garage £5 ($7.50).

Fenja is one of the most luxurious B&Bs in London, located near the Peter Jones Department Store and the fashionable boutiques of King's Road. It was originally built during the 19th century as a private house, and purchased from the estate of Lord Cadogan after World War II. Between 1985 and 1987, the building was completely restored and upgraded into a hotel. The rooms are named after famous writers and painters including, for example, the Turner Room. The bedrooms are decorated in an intensely traditional English style and furnished in part with antiques. The bathrooms, however, are modern, with all the amenities.

Dining/Entertainment: Light meals are available from a room-service menu, backed by a carefully selected wine list.

Services: Room service (7am to 11pm), laundry, shoe cleaning.

MODERATE

BLAIR HOUSE HOTEL, 34 Draycott Place, London SW3 2SA. Tel. 071/581-2323. Fax 071/823-7752. 17 rms (10 with bath). TV TEL **Tube:** Sloane Square.

$ Rates (including continental breakfast): £40 ($60) single without bath, £63 ($94.50) single with bath; £60 ($90) double without bath, £73 ($109.50) double with bath. AE, DC, MC, V.

⑤ This comfortable hotel is a good, reasonably priced choice in the heart of Chelsea. An old-fashioned building of architectural interest, it has been modified and completely refurnished, with every comfortable room sporting radios and tea- or coffee-making equipment. Breakfast is the only meal served. Babysitting and laundry can be arranged.

WILBRAHAM HOTEL, 1–5 Wilbraham Place (off Sloane St.), London SW1X 9AE. Tel. 071/730-8296. Fax 071/730-6815. 53 rms (40 with bath), 5 suites. TV TEL **Tube:** Sloane Square.

$ Rates: £38.50 ($57.80) single without bath, £52.50 ($78.80) single with bath; £54 ($81) double without bath, £64 ($96) double with bath; from £88 ($132) suite. English breakfast £6 ($9) extra. No credit cards. **Parking:** Nearby at £18 ($27).

This is a dyed-in-the-wool British hotel set on a quiet residential street just a few hundred yards from the endlessly trendy Sloane Square. It occupies three Victorian town houses that have been joined together. The bedrooms are furnished in an uncontroversial traditional style and are well maintained. On the premises is an attractive and old-fashioned lounge, The Bar and Buttery, where you can order drinks, simple lunches, and dinners.

WILLETT, 32 Sloane Gardens, Sloane Sq., London SW1W 8DJ. Tel. 071/824-8415. Fax 071/824-8415. 18 rms (15 with bath). TV TEL **Tube:** Sloane Square.

$ Rates (including English breakfast): £60.45 ($90.70) single without bath, £65.95 ($98.90) single with bath; £65.95 ($98.90) double without bath, £76.95 ($115.40) double with bath. VAT extra. AE, DC, MC, V.

A 19th-century town house opening onto gardens, the Willett is one of the nuggets of Chelsea. It has many architectural flourishes, including a Dutch roof and bay windows. While retaining its traditional charm, the hotel has been fully renovated with new furnishings in all the well-equipped bedrooms and in the public lounge areas. The breakfast room is especially inviting, with plush red velvet chairs. In fact, the hotel has rapidly become a favorite address with many discriminating English people who like a town-house address and who prefer being close to the restaurants, attractions, and good shops of Chelsea.

CHELSEA HARBOUR

This area is a new development lying beyond Chelsea in a marina complex of boutiques and restaurants, as well as some of the most desirable apartments in London.

HOTEL CONRAD, Chelsea Harbour, London SW10 OXG. Tel. 071/823-3000. Fax 071/351-6525. 160 suites, 7 penthouse suites. A/C MINIBAR TV TEL **Transportation:** Chelsea Harbour Hoppa Buses run to Chelsea Harbour from Earl's Court and Kensington High St. (bus C3) Mon–Sat, or a riverbus from Charing Cross Mon–Fri.

$ Rates: £200–£245 ($300–$367.50) single or double. AE, DC, MC, V. **Parking:** £10 ($15).

The Hotel Conrad, one of London's newest five-star deluxe hotels, may be the first all-suite hotel in Europe. A stunning modern architectural achievement, it's the linchpin of Chelsea Harbour's revitalization, rising high above the many yachts that bob at anchor in London's largest marina. Much of the elegant and comfortable decor inside was designed by David Hicks. Accommodations are elegant, streamlined, flooded with sunlight from large windows, and are equipped with a full line of toiletries, a hairdryer, and hypoallergenic pillows.

Dining/Entertainment: The hotel's dining and entertainment facilities include the Brasserie, whose stylish and cozy interior overlooks the Thames. The Lounge offers breakfast, light snacks, afternoon tea, and champagne by the glass in the evening (to the accompaniment of live piano music). Drakes Bar, as richly nautical as its name would imply, offers a view of the dozens of neatly moored yachts in the nearby marina.

Services: 24-hour room service, babysitting, luggage storage, laundry.

Facilities: Electronic safety locks, use of fax machines in each suite, personal computer, three phones with two-line capability; a health club with a heated swimming pool and saunas.

8. KENSINGTON & SOUTH KENSINGTON

KENSINGTON

The Royal Borough (W8) has some moderately priced accommodations, lying, for the most part, west of Kensington Gardens. It is considered one of the most desirable residential sections of London.

VERY EXPENSIVE

BLAKES, 33 Roland Gardens, London SW7 3PF. Tel. 071/370-6701, or toll free 800/926-3173 in the U.S. Fax 071/373-0442. 43 rms, 9 suites. MINIBAR TV TEL **Tube:** South Kensington or Gloucester Road.

$ Rates: £135–£155 ($202.50–$232.50) single; £185–£300 ($277.50–$450) double; from £485 ($727.50) suite. English breakfast £14.50 ($21.80) extra. AE, DC, MC, V. **Parking:** £18 ($27) extra.

Blakes is one of the best small hotels in London, certainly one of the most sophisticated. The neighborhood may be staunchly middle class, but this hotel is strictly an upper-class bastion of privilege. It's so glamorous, in fact, that guests might see Princess Margaret dining in its basement-level restaurant. The hotel is the creation of a talented actress, Anouska Hempel Weinberg. The richly appointed lobby is furnished with Victorian-era campaign furniture, probably brought back by some empire builder from a sojourn in India, or at least this is the kind of romantic thought it evokes. Bedrooms are highly individualized and come in many sizes. Some contain antiques.

Dining/Entertainment: London's parade of the young and stylish, including "rag trade" types, photographers, and actors, dine downstairs in what is one of the best-reputed restaurants in town. Reservations are strictly observed by a youthful maître d'hôtel. The menu might offer such appetizers as a salad of foie gras with Landais truffles and quail eggs on a purée of mushrooms. Main courses include deliciously flavored varieties of teriyaki, poached salmon in a champagne sauce, and roast partridge with juniperberries. None of this, of course, comes cheaply. The price of a meal, with wine and service, might come to £170 ($255) for two.

Services: 24-hour room service, laundry, babysitting.

Facilities: Access to a nearby health club, an "arrange anything" concierge.

INEXPENSIVE

ABBEY HOUSE, 11 Vicarage Gate, London W8 4AG. Tel. 071/727-2594. 15 rms (none with bath). TV **Tube:** Kensington High Street.

$ Rates (including English breakfast): £30 ($45) single; £52 ($78) double; £62 ($93) triple; £72 ($108) quad. No credit cards.

S Some hotel critics have rated this the best B&B in London. Thanks to renovations, this hotel, which was built in about 1860 on a typical Victorian square, is modern, though many of the original features have been retained. The spacious bedrooms have central heating, electrical outlets for shavers, vanity lights, and hot- and cold-water basins. The hotel offers shared baths, one to each two lodging units. The rooms are each refurbished annually, and each contains a color TV. Considering how well run and maintained it is, it gets top marks for value in its neighborhood.

SOUTH KENSINGTON

South of Kensington Gardens and Hyde Park, this district is essentially a residential area, though not as elegant as bordering Belgravia and Knightsbridge. South Kensington is, however, rich in museums and has a number of colleges.

EXPENSIVE

ALEXANDER HOTEL, 9 Sumner Place, London SW7 3EE. Tel. 071/581-1591. Fax 071/581-0824. 39 rms, 1 cottage suite. TV TEL **Tube:** South Kensington.

$ Rates (including English breakfast): £90.50 ($135.80) single; £116.35 ($174.50) double; £210 ($315) cottage suite with a garden entrance suitable for four or five occupants. VAT extra. AE, DC, MC, V.

Although it's probably the most expensive of the many hotels on Sumner Place, it's also the most elegant. Set within four interconnected town houses that were joined together in 1842, the hotel retains its mid-Victorian elegance thanks to an extensive program of ongoing refurbishment. The place is filled with artwork, both antique and modern, creating an ambience that encourages some guests to return again and again. A terrace leads to a walled garden, within which you'll find tables, chairs, and the most luxurious accommodation of all, a cottage suite. There's a residents' bar and lounge. The bedrooms have such extras as a hairdryer and a trouser press.

NUMBER SIXTEEN, 16 Sumner Place, London SW7 3EG. Tel. 071/589-5232. Fax 071/584-8615. 36 rms (34 with bath). MINIBAR TV TEL **Tube:** South Kensington.

$ Rates (including continental breakfast): £55–£75 ($82.50–$112.50) single without bath, £95 ($142.50) single with bath; £85–£130 ($127.50–$195) double without bath, £150 ($225) double with bath; £175 ($262.50) triple with bath. AE, DC, MC, V.

This is a select and elegant pension, composed of four Victorian row houses linked together into a dramatically organized whole, with an elevator. As each house was added, the front and rear gardens expanded, until their flowering shrubs and tulips now create one of the most idyllic spots on the street. The rooms contain an eclectic mixture of English antiques and modern paintings. There's an honor-system self-service bar in one of the elegantly formal sitting rooms, where a blazing fire is lit to remove the cold-weather chill. Extensive refurbishments took place in 1990. Babysitting is available, as is 24-hour laundry service on weekdays. Room service is available daily from 7:30am to 10pm. In 1992, the establishment was awarded a trophy as the best B&B in London.

PELHAM HOTEL, 15 Cromwell Place, London, SW7 2LA. Tel. 071/589-

8288. Fax 071/584-8444. 35 rms, 2 suites. A/C MINIBAR TV TEL **Tube:** South Kensington.

$ Rates: £115 ($172.50) single; £140–£165 ($210–$247.50) double; from £220 ($330) suite. English breakfast from £7 ($10.50) extra. AE, MC, V.

★ This place has charm, style, and class. Privately owned and small, it's one of the nuggets of London, suitable for everyone from your visiting movie star to your individualistic and discerning traveler. Personal service is the hallmark here. Kit and Tim Kemp, hoteliers extraordinaire, have made this hotel a gem. It is one of the most stunningly decorated hotels of London, formed from part of a row of early 19th-century terrace houses with a white portico facade. Inside, high ceilings and fine moldings create a backdrop for a luxurious decor, including richly draped fabrics, linens, and silks, and a collection of antiques, embracing Victorian oil paintings. The 18th-century paneling brought from a bank in Suffolk now lines the drawing room, making you feel as if you are in an elegant, private London town house. Mrs. Kemp, an inveterate collector, was the hotel decorator, filling Pelham with—among other fine trappings—needlepoint, rugs, and cushions for a homelike warmth.

Dining/Entertainment: The hotel's Pelham Restaurant is one of the finest in South Kensington. An honor bar in the drawing room creates a clublike atmosphere.

Services: "Solve-everything" concierge, room service when you want it, theater-ticket arrangements.

Facilities: Victorian "snuggery" for lounging and reading papers.

REGENCY HOTEL, 100 Queen's Gate, London SW7 5AG. Tel. 071/370-4595, or toll free 800/328-9898 in the U.S. Fax 071/370-5555. 210 rms, 11 suites. A/C MINIBAR TV TEL **Tube:** Gloucester Road or South Kensington.

$ Rates: £115 ($172.50) single; £145 ($217.50) double; £195 ($292.50) luxury suite for two; £235 ($352.50) duplex suite with Jacuzzi. English breakfast £10.50 ($15.80) extra. AE, DC, MC, V.

In many ways, this is one of the most appealing hotels in the neighborhood. It derives its name from the historical period of the Prince Regent, later King George IV. The hotel used this period to set the style for its gracious quarters close to museums, Kensington, and Knightsbridge. Five Victorian terrace houses were converted into one stylish hotel that offers tastefully elegant, modernized bedrooms. From the street, a glistening row of Doric columns reveals the bourgeois upper-class origins of the neighborhood's original occupants. The warmly decorated interior required the efforts of an army of construction engineers and decorators to turn the hotel into a seamless architectural whole. A Chippendale fireplace, flanked by wing chairs, greets guests near the polished hardwood of the reception area. One of the building's main stairwells contains one of London's most unusual lighting fixtures, consisting of five Empire chandeliers suspended vertically, one on top of the other. Since its opening, the hotel has hosted important artists and politicians, everybody from the late Margot Fonteyn to members of the British royal family.

Dining/Entertainment: The hotel's restaurant, The Pavilion, is both elegant and fun, and recommended separately in Chapter 5.

Services: 24-hour room service, laundry, babysitting.

Facilities: The basement-level Elysium Health Spa features Neo-Roman decor, steam rooms, saunas, and a sensory-deprivation "deprogramming" tank that is perfect for releasing the tensions of jet lag.

MODERATE

ASTON'S BUDGET STUDIOS, ASTON'S DESIGNER STUDIOS, and ASTON'S LUXURY APARTMENTS, 39 Rosary Gardens, London SW7 4NQ. Tel. 071/370-0737, or toll free 800/525-2810 in the U.S. Fax 071/835-1419. 60 studios and apts (38 with bath). A/C TV TEL **Tube:** Gloucester Road.

$ Rates: Aston's Budget Studios, £32–£38 ($48–$57) single; £42–£54 ($63–$81) double; £60–£72 ($90–$108) triple; £78–£90 ($117–$135) quad. Aston's Designer Studios, £75–£95 ($112.50–$142.50) single or double. Aston's Designer Suites, £125–£150 ($187.50–$225) for a 2-room suite for two to four occupants. AE, MC, V.

Located in a carefully restored row of interconnected Victorian town houses, this establishment offers a carefree alternative to the traditional hotel—which many readers find well suited for their needs. It features comfortably furnished studios and suites—usually but not always rented by the week—that combine the elegance and nostalgia of the 19th century with the convenience and economy of self-catering, under the personal management of Ms. Shelagh King. Heavy oak doors and collections of 18th-century hunting scenes give Aston's foyer a rich and traditional atmosphere.

Accommodations are available in several categories of size and luxury: Budget Studios, Designer Studios, and Designer Suites, with accessories and furnishings that grow increasingly opulent with each category. Regardless of its price, each unit has a fresh, colorful decor and lots of convenient extras which always include—concealed behind doors—a compact but complete kitchenette. The Budget Studios have fully serviced bathrooms which are shared with a strictly limited handful of other guests. The Designer Studios and two-room Designer Suites are lavishly decorated with rich fabrics and furnishings, contain marble-sheathed private shower and bathrooms, and have answering machines hooked up to the telephones, and a host of electronic accessories well suited to anyone doing business in London. Considering the amenities of this place (which has received very positive feedback from many Frommer readers), the cost of a London holiday here is considerably less than at a more standardized and traditional kind of hotel.

Services: Laundry service, secretarial service, private catering on request, car and limousine service. The Designer Studios and Suites have daily chamber service.

Facilities: A special guest's message line, highly capable staff who can also provide fax machines and touristic advice. The Designer Studios and Suites have a special welcome pack of essentials provided upon arrival and luxurious robes.

5 SUMNER PLACE, 5 Sumner Place, London SW7 3EE. Tel. 071/584-7586. Fax 071/823-9962. 14 rms (all with bath). MINIBAR TV TEL **Tube:** South Kensington.

$ Rates (including English breakfast): £75 ($112.50) single; £89–£98 ($133.50–$147) double. AE, DC, MC, V.

Winner of the British Tourist Authority award for Best B&B in Central London in 1991, this carefully restored 1850s Victorian town house is a delightful residence. Some of its traditionally furnished bedrooms have minibars, and all have private baths. Each room is immaculately maintained and refreshingly uncluttered. A buffet selection of foods is served within a 19th-century conservatory overlooking a sun terrace. The owners, John and Barbara Palgan, provide the kind of personal attention that makes their many visitors want to return.

HOTEL 167, 167 Old Brompton Rd., London SW5 0AN. Tel. 071/373-0672. Fax 071/373-3360. 19 rms (all with bath). MINIBAR TV TEL **Tube:** Gloucester Road.

$ Rates (including continental breakfast): £51–£61 ($76.50–$91.50) single; £64–£70 ($96–$105) double. Extra bed in room £12 ($18). MC, V.

Hotel 167 is one of the more fashionable guesthouses in the area, sheltered in a once-private Victorian town house, which, including the basement, has four floors of living space. While some of the bedrooms are in the basement, they have big windows for illumination. The decor is quite stylish, with such accents as metal, chrome, and pinewood, in Scandinavian modern and even Japanese styles, and the windows have venetian blinds, not curtains.

KENSINGTON MANOR HOTEL, 8 Emperor's Gate, London SW7 4HH.
   Tel. 071/370-7516. Fax 071/373-3163. 15 rms (all with bath), 2 suites.
   MINIBAR TV TEL **Tube:** Gloucester Road.
$ Rates (including English breakfast): £55–£59 ($82.50–$88.50) single; £69.95–
£80 ($104.90–$120) double; £105 ($157.50) suite. VAT extra. AE, DC, MC, V.
Located in a cul-de-sac, this hotel offers warmth and elegance in a stately late
Victorian building. Personal service of a high standard is the keynote of this place,
including room service, laundry service, and dry cleaning. Bedrooms in this small
lodging are individually decorated, each one named after a county of England. A
buffet breakfast is served.

PRINCE HOTEL, 6 Sumner Place, London SW7 3AB Tel. 071/589-6488.
   Fax 071/581-0824. 20 rms (all with shower, 15 with toilet). TV TEL **Tube:** South
   Kensington.
$ Rates (including English breakfast): £47 ($70.50) single with shower (no toilet),
£59 ($88.50) single with shower and toilet; £58 ($87) double with shower (no
toilet), £71 ($106.50) double with shower and toilet. AE, DC, MC, V.

⑤ The Prince has been successfully converted from an early Victorian terrace
house constructed about 1850. Decorated and restored in a classic English
style, it opens onto a greenhouse-style conservatory and garden in the rear. All
its bedrooms are individually decorated and designed. Breakfast, which is included in
the price, is served a few doors away at the more elegant (and more expensive)
Alexander Hotel (see previous recommendation).

---

9. EARL'S COURT & NOTTING HILL GATE

EARL'S COURT

This is one of the most popular hotel and rooming house districts in London, lying
below Kensington and bordering the western half of Chelsea. Before the mid-1970s, it
was virtually "occupied" by Australians. Earl's Court is considered one of the most
reasonable areas in London in which to seek lodgings.

BARKSTON HOTEL, 34–44 Barkston Gardens, London SW5 0EW. Tel.
   071/373-7851. Fax 071/370-6570. 80 rms (all with bath). TV TEL **Tube:** Earl's
   Court.
$ Rates: £54 ($81) single; £72 ($108) double; £85 ($127.50) triple. Continental
breakfast £4.50 ($6.80) extra. AE, DC, MC, V. **Parking:** £5 ($7.50) nearby.
The Barkston lies conveniently close to the Earl's Court tube stop, which has a direct
link to Heathrow airport. Composed of six harmoniously joined-together row houses,
it offered B&B at 5p (8¢) per person back in 1905. In the 1960s, it was the first hotel in
the chain that later developed into the megagiant, Forte Hotels. Today, the hotel is
privately owned, with its own restaurant and simple but comfortably furnished
bedrooms, each offering coffee-making facilities and hairdryers.

SWISS HOUSE HOTEL, 171 Old Brompton Rd., London SW5 0AN. Tel.
   071/373-2769. Fax 071/373-4983. 16 rms (11 with bath). TV TEL **Tube:**
   Gloucester Road.
$ Rates (including continental breakfast): £32 ($48) single without bath, £45
($67.50) single with bath; £48 ($72) double without bath, £58 ($87) double with
bath. MC, V.

The Swiss House is one of the more desirable B&Bs in the Earl's Court area. The hotel is a white-fronted Victorian row house festooned with flowers and vines. The rear windows overlook a communal garden with a view of the London skyline. Like its neighbors, Swiss House has a front-porch portico. Its country-inspired bedrooms are individually designed. Some also have working fireplaces. There's a snack menu, including hot dishes, which can be served in the bedrooms. Traffic is heavy outside, but windows are double-glazed. Room service is available from noon to 9pm, and babysitting is also offered.

NOTTING HILL GATE

Increasingly gaining in fashion and frequented by such personages as the Princess of Wales, Notting Hill Gate is bounded on the south by Bayswater Road and on the east by Gloucester Terrace. It is hemmed in on the north by West Way and on the west by the Shepherds Bush ramp leading to the M40. It has many turn-of-the-century mansions and small houses that sit on quiet, leafy streets.

THE ABBEY COURT, 20 Pembridge Gardens, London, W2 4DU. Tel. 071/221-7518. Fax 071/792-0858. 22 rms, 3 suites. TV TEL **Tube:** Notting Hill Gate.

$ Rates: £90 ($135) single; £130 ($195) double or twin; £160 ($240) suite with four-poster bed. Breakfast £9 ($13.50) extra. AE, DC, MC, V.

The Abbey Court is a small and rather luxurious choice. Situated in a white-fronted mid-Victorian town house, it has a flowery patio in front and a conservatory in back. The lobby is graciously decorated with a sunny bay window, flower-patterned draperies, and a comfortable sofa and chairs. You'll find fresh flowers in the reception area and the hallways. Each room offers carefully coordinated fabrics and fine furnishings, mostly 18th- and 19th-century country antiques. Bathrooms are equipped with Jacuzzi jets, heated towel racks, and Italian marble-lined baths. Light snacks and drinks are available from room service 24 hours a day. Kensington Gardens is a short walk away, as are the antiques stores along Portobello Road.

10. ST. MARYLEBONE

Below Regent's Park, northwest of Piccadilly Circus, is the district of St. Marylebone (pronounced *Mar*-li-bone), a residential section that faces Mayfair to the south and extends north of Marble Arch.

VERY EXPENSIVE

THE LANGHAM HILTON, 1 Portland Place, London W1V 3AA. Tel. 071/636-1000, or toll free 800/445-8667 in the U.S. and Canada. Fax 071/323-2340. 365 rms, 22 suites. A/C MINIBAR TV TEL **Tube:** Oxford Circus.

$ Rates: £165–£240 ($247.50–$360) single or double; £280–£1,000 ($420–$1,500) suite. English breakfast £13.50 ($20.30) extra. AE, DC, MC, V. **Parking:** £19 ($28.50).

When this hotel was originally inaugurated in 1865 by the Prince of Wales, its accommodations were considered suitable as the full-time London address for dozens of aristocratic squires seeking respite from their country estates. (Its guests included Antonín Dvořák, Toscanini, Oscar Wilde, Mark Twain, and Arnold Bennett.) After wartime bombing in 1940, it languished as a dusty office space for the BBC until the early 1990s, when Hilton International took over the premises as a historic and extremely well-located hotel.

Today, the hotel's public rooms reflect the power and majesty of the British Empire at its height in the 19th century. So visible is this painstaking restoration of a great Victorian hotel that Hilton International now considers it its European flagship. The bedrooms, although somewhat less opulent than the public rooms, are well furnished with French provincial furniture and red-oak trim—cozy enclaves from the restaurants, cinemas, and commercial bustle of nearby Leicester Square.

Dining/Entertainment: Afternoon tea is served amid the potted palms of the Edwardian-style Palm Court. Vodka, caviar, and glasses of champagne flow liberally amid the red velvet of the Tsar's Russian Bar and Restaurant, while drinks are served in the Chukka Bar, a green-toned re-creation of a polo players' private club. The most upscale restaurant is a high-ceilinged Victorian fantasy, Memories of the Empire, serving doses of patriotic nostalgia and cuisine from the far corners of the British Commonwealth.

Services: 24-hour room service, concierge.

Facilities: Health club with saunas and Jacuzzis; a business office, with full secretarial services and business equipment.

EXPENSIVE

DORSET SQUARE HOTEL, 39–40 Dorset Sq., London NW1 6QN. Tel. 071/723-7874, or toll free 800/543-4138 in the U.S. Fax 071/724-3328. 37 rms. MINIBAR TV TEL **Tube:** Baker Street or Marylebone.

$ Rates: £85 ($127.50) single; £110–£155 ($165–$232.50) double. English breakfast £10 ($15) extra. AE, MC, V.

A grand English country house, the Dorset Square is made up of two Georgian Regency town houses similar to their neighbors on the small square near Regent's Park. Hotelier Tim Kemp and his wife, Kit, have transformed the former dwellings into a hotel, with an interior so designed that the public rooms, luxurious bedrooms, and baths still give the impression of being in an elegant private home. The bedrooms are decorated in chintz or printed materials that complement the furniture, a mix of antiques and reproductions. Half the rooms are air-conditioned.

Dining/Entertainment: The hotel restaurant, the Dorset Square, is graced with a mural showing the square when it was the home of the Marylebone Cricket Club. The menu, featuring the best of English cuisine, changes seasonally, offering such dishes as Stilton venison (in season) and poached Scottish salmon with hollandaise sauce. The hotel's bar has a grand piano that is played every evening by a student from the Royal Academy of Music.

Services: 24-hour room service, laundry, babysitting.

MODERATE

BRYANSTON COURT HOTEL, 56–60 Great Cumberland Place, London W1H 7FD. Tel. 071/262-3141, or toll free 800/528-1234 in the U.S. Fax 071/262-7248. 54 rms (all with bath). TV TEL **Tube:** Marble Arch.

$ Rates: £70 ($105) single; £90 ($135) double; £105 ($157.50) triple. Continental breakfast £6.50 ($9.80) extra. AE, DC, MC, V. **Parking:** £18 ($27) extra.

Each of the three individual houses joined together to form this hotel was built about 190 years ago. Today this is one of the most elegant hotels on the street, thanks partly to the decorating efforts of its owners, the Theodore family. There's a gas fire burning in the Chesterfield-style bar, plus a stairway leading up to the comfortably furnished bedrooms.

DURRANTS HOTEL, George St., London W1H 6BJ. Tel. 071/935-8131. Fax 071/487-3510. 96 rms (all with bath), 3 suites. TV TEL **Tube:** Bond Street.

$ Rates: £65–£90 ($97.50–$135) single; £95–£150 ($142.50–$225) double; from £200 ($300) suite. English breakfast £8.50 ($12.80) extra. AE, MC, V.

Established in 1789, this historic hotel sits behind a sprawling facade of brown brick highlighted with Georgian detailing. During the 100 years it has been owned by the Miller family, several neighboring houses have been incorporated into the original structure, making a walk through the pine- and mahogany-paneled public rooms a tour through another century.

You'll find such 18th-century niceties as a letter-writing room sheathed with old paneling and a popular neighborhood pub with Windsor chairs, an open fireplace, and a decor that probably hasn't changed very much in 200 years. The establishment's oldest bedrooms face the front and have slightly higher ceilings than the newer ones. Even the most recent accommodations, however, have elaborate cove moldings, very comfortable furnishings, and a solid feeling of well-being. The in-house restaurant serves full afternoon teas and a satisfying French or traditional and English cuisine in one of the most beautiful Georgian rooms in the neighborhood. The less formal breakfast room is ringed with 19th-century political cartoons by a noted Victorian artist. Laundry service and babysitting are available. There is also 24-hour room service.

INEXPENSIVE

BLANDFORD HOTEL, 80 Chiltern St., London W1M 1PS. Tel. 071/486-3103. Fax 071/487-2786. 33 rms (all with bath). TV TEL **Tube:** Baker Street.

$ Rates (including English breakfast): £62 ($93) single; £77 ($115.50) double; £95 ($142.50) triple. AE, DC, MC, V.

Located only a minute's walk from the tube, this place on the street of Sherlock Holmes fame is a find and definitely one of London's better B&Bs for the price. Each room has a hairdryer and coffee-making equipment. Five rooms rented as triples are suitable for families. The hotel is family run, and each guest receives personal attention.

EDWARD LEAR HOTEL, 28–30 Seymour St., London W1H 5WD. Tel. 071/402-5401. Fax 071/706-3766. 31 rms (12 with bath), 4 suites. TV TEL **Tube:** Marble Arch.

$ Rates (including English breakfast): £37.50 ($56.30) single without bath, £55 ($82.50) single with bath; £49.50 ($74.30) double without bath, £62.50 ($93.80) double with bath; from £72.50 ($108.80) suite. MC, V.

(S) The Edward Lear is a popular hotel, made all the more desirable by the bouquets of fresh flowers set up around the public rooms. It's 1 block from Marble Arch in a pair of brick town houses, both of which date from 1780. The western house was the London home of the 19th-century artist and poet Edward Lear, whose illustrated limericks adorn the walls of one of the sitting rooms. Steep stairs lead up to the bedrooms. The cozy units are fairly small but have all the usual facilities.

HALLAM HOTEL, 12 Hallam St., Portland Place, London W1N 5LJ. Tel. 071/580-1166. Fax 071/323-4537. 25 rms (all with bath). TV TEL **Tube:** Oxford Circus.

$ Rates (including English breakfast): £55–£66 ($82.50–$99) single; £75–£88 ($112.50–$132) double. AE, DC, MC, V.

The Hallam is a heavily ornamented stone-and-brick Victorian house, one of the few on the street to escape bombing during World War II. Today, it's the property of the Baker family. Earl and his sons, Grant and David, maintain it well. The bedrooms are comfortably furnished, each with tea- or coffee-making facilities. In addition to 24-hour room service, there is a bar for residents and a bright breakfast room overlooking a pleasant patio.

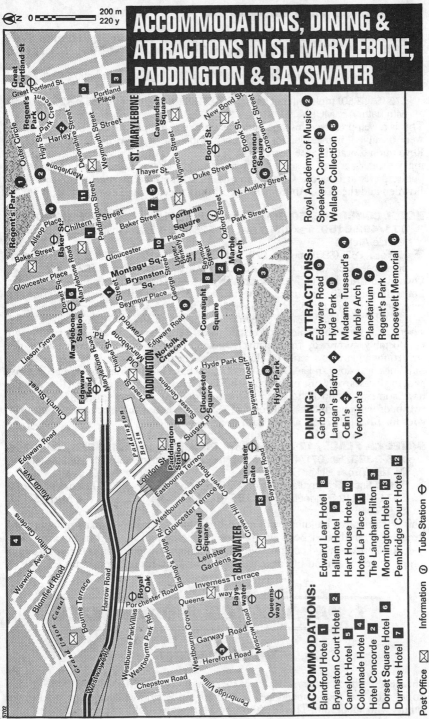

ACCOMMODATIONS, DINING & ATTRACTIONS IN ST. MARYLEBONE, PADDINGTON & BAYSWATER

ACCOMMODATIONS:
Blandford Hotel **1**
Bryanston Court Hotel **2**
Camelot Hotel **5**
Colonnade Hotel **4**
Hotel Concorde **2**
Dorset Square Hotel **6**
Durrants Hotel **7**
Edward Lear Hotel **8**
Hallam Hotel **9**
Hart House Hotel **10**
Hotel La Place **11**
The Langham Hilton **3**
Mornington Hotel **13**
Pembridge Court Hotel **12**

DINING:
Garbo's **1**
Langan's Bistro **2**
Odin's **4**
Veronica's **3**

ATTRACTIONS:
Edgware Road **9**
Hyde Park **8**
Madame Tussaud's **7**
Marble Arch **4**
Planetarium **1**
Regent's Park **1**
Roosevelt Memorial **6**
Royal Academy of Music **2**
Speakers' Corner **3**
Wallace Collection **5**

Post Office ⊠   Information ⓘ   Tube Station ⊖

HART HOUSE HOTEL, 51 Gloucester Place, Portman Sq., London SWH 3PE. Tel. 071/935-8516. 16 rms (10 with bath). TV TEL **Tube:** Marble Arch or Baker Street.

$ Rates (including English breakfast): £42 ($63) single without bath, £49 ($73.50) single with bath; £59 ($88.50) double without bath, £72 ($108) double with bath; £75 ($112.50) triple without bath, £80 ($120) triple with bath; £85 ($127.50) quad with bath. AE, MC, V.

This is a well-preserved historic building, part of a group of Georgian mansions that were occupied by members of the French nobility living in exile during the French Revolution. Located in the heart of the West End, it is within easy walking distance of many theaters, as well as some of the most sought-after concentrations of shops and public parks in London. Cozy and convenient, the hotel is run by Mr. and Mrs. Bowden and their son, Andrew. All bedrooms are clean and comfortable.

HOTEL CONCORDE, 50 Great Cumberland Place, London W1H 7FD. Tel. 071/402-6169. Fax 071/724-1184. 28 rms (all with bath). TV TEL **Tube:** Marble Arch.

$ Rates: £62 ($93) single; £72 ($108) double; £85 ($127.50) triple. English breakfast £6.50 ($9.80) extra. AE, DC, MC, V. **Parking:** £18 ($27) extra.

Owned and run by the Theodore family, this establishment was built as a private house in the 1850s and later converted into a small and stylish hotel. Inside, its reception desk, nearby chairs, and a section of the tiny bar area were at one time parts of a London church. A display case in the lobby has an array of reproduction English silver, each piece of which is for sale. The bedrooms are well maintained and comfortably furnished; this relatively quiet neighborhood is convenient to the attractions and traffic arteries of Marble Arch. The owners maintain 10 apartments in buildings next door and across the street. Each has a kitchen, one to three bedrooms, and, in all cases, only one bathroom. The decor is old-fashioned and most (but not all) have somewhat dowdy furniture. One-bedroom apartments cost £85 ($127.50), two-bedroom apartments rent for £95 ($142.50), and a three-bedroom apartment goes for £105 ($157.50), always with breakfast included.

HOTEL LA PLACE, 17 Nottingham Place, London W1M 3FB. Tel. 071/486-2323. Fax 071/486-4335. 24 rms; 2 family rooms (all with bath). MINIBAR TV TEL **Tube:** Baker Street.

$ Rates (including English breakfast): £55–£65 ($82.50–$97.50) single; £65–£75 ($97.50–$112.50) double; from £85 ($127.50) suite. DC, MC, V. **Parking:** £17 ($25.50) extra.

This Victorian-era building, with a red-brick facade similar to many others on its street, is a refurbished B&B hotel—one of the best of its kind in the area. The bedrooms are clean and comfortable, with traditional styling. On the premises, doing a healthy neighborhood business, is a chic little wine bar and restaurant.

11. PADDINGTON & BAYSWATER

PADDINGTON

This neighborhood is the namesake of that famous bear of Michael Bond's children's stories who was found abandoned at Paddington Station in London by the Brown family, who adopt him. This neighborhood—northwest of Kensington Gardens and

Hyde Park—is a center for budget travelers who fill up the B&Bs at Sussex Gardens and on Norfolk Square. Paddington is lively enough to be interesting and equally close to sweeping parklands and some of the best shopping centers.

MODERATE

COLONNADE HOTEL, 2 Warrington Crescent, London W9 1ER. Tel. 071/286-1052. Fax 071/286-1057. 48 rms (all with bath). TV TEL **Tube:** Warwick Avenue.

$ Rates (including English breakfast): £60.50–£82.50 ($90.80–$123.80) single; £80–£118 ($120–$177) double. AE, DC, MC, V. **Parking:** £7 ($10.50) extra.

The Colonnade is an imposing town house in a pleasant residential area, just a block from the tube station. Owned and managed for three generations by the Richards family, the hotel is run in a personal manner. Mr. Richards emphasizes: "Every bedroom, bathroom, and corridor is centrally heated 24 hours a day from the first chill wind of autumn until the last breath of retreating winter, even in summer if necessary." He's installed a water-softening plant as well. There are 16 special rooms with four-poster beds. Each room has a radio, hairdryer, and a trouser press; some are air-conditioned; and some have Jacuzzis. The hotel has a restaurant and a cocktail piano bar called Cascades, which has become so popular that sometimes you need a reservation.

MORNINGTON HOTEL, 12 Lancaster Gate, London W2 3LG. Tel. 071/262-7361, or toll free 800/528-1234 in the U.S. and Canada. Fax 071/706-1028. 68 rms (all with bath). TV TEL **Tube:** Lancaster Gate.

$ Rates (including Scandinavian buffet breakfast): £80 ($120) single; £90–£103 ($135–$154.50) double. AE, DC, MC, V.

Closely associated with a chain of hotels based in Stockholm, the Mornington brings a touch of Swedish hospitality to the center of London. Just north of Hyde Park and Kensington Gardens, the hotel has been completely redecorated with a Scandinavian-designed interior. The bedrooms are tastefully conceived and comfortable. In the library, visitors wind down—entertaining their friends or making new ones. In a well-stocked bar you can order snacks and, if you're back in time, afternoon tea. Considering what you get—especially the comfort and service, not to mention a genuine Finnish sauna—the price is competitive for London. The bedrooms are modern and comfortable.

INEXPENSIVE

CAMELOT HOTEL, 45–47 Norfolk Sq., London W2 1RX. Tel. 071/723-9118. Fax 071/402-3412. 44 rms (40 with bath or shower). TV TEL **Tube:** Paddington.

$ Rates (including English breakfast): £36.50 ($54.80) single without bath, £44–£50 ($66–$75) single with bath; £70 ($105) double with bath; £85.50 ($128.30) triple with bath; £110 ($165) quad with bath. MC, V.

 Originally built in 1850 as a pair of adjacent town houses, this simple but comfortable hotel stands at the center of an old tree-filled square, about 2 minutes' walk from Paddington Station. The hotel was refurbished in the late 1980s and now has an elevator. Floral curtains, framed prints, and matching bedspreads create a homelike environment. The comfortable and well-furnished guest rooms have radios and complimentary beverage trays. Families with children are welcome.

BAYSWATER

North of Kensington Gardens is an unofficial section of London known as Bayswater. Most of it lies north of Bayswater Road and west of Hyde Park. This section has a number of B&B hotels.

PEMBRIDGE COURT HOTEL, 34 Pembridge Gardens, London W2 4DX. Tel. 071/229-9977. Fax 071/727-4982. 21 rms. TV TEL **Tube:** Notting Hill Gate.

$ Rates (including English breakfast): £85–£120 ($127.50–$180) single; £110–£150 ($165–$225) double. AE, DC, MC, V.

Built in 1852 as a private house, this hotel presents an elegant cream-colored neoclassical facade to a residential neighborhood that has grown increasingly fashionable. Most of the comfortably outfitted bedrooms feature at least one antique, as well as 19th-century engravings and plenty of warmly patterned flowery fabrics. Some of the largest and most stylish rooms are on the top floor, their bathrooms tiled in Italian marble. Others include three exceptionally deluxe rooms overlooking Portobello Road. The Spencer and Church rooms, for example, are tastefully decorated in blues and yellows, while the Windsor room has a contrasting array of tartans.

Dining/Entertainment: In Caps, the hotel's brick-lined restaurant, good French and English food and drink, along with a well-chosen array of wines, is served. It's open only in the evening.

Services: 24-hour room service, laundry, same-day dry cleaning, babysitting.

Facilities: Lounge, car-rental agency.

12. HOLLAND PARK

HALCYON HOTEL, 81 Holland Park Ave., London W11 3RZ. Tel. 071/727-7288, or toll free 800/457-4000 in the U.S. Fax 071/229-8516. 44 rms, 19 suites. A/C MINIBAR TV TEL **Tube:** Holland Park.

$ Rates: £140–£165 ($210–$247.50) single; £185–£295 ($277.50–$442.50) double; from £375 ($562.50) suite. English breakfast £12.50 ($18.80) extra. AE, DC, MC, V.

⭐ As you arrive, you may think at first you're at the wrong address because only a small brass plaque distinguishes the aptly named Halcyon from other buildings on the street. Called "by far the grandest of London's small hotels," the Halcyon was formed by uniting a pair of Victorian mansions originally built in 1860. Today they constitute a hotel of charm, class, fashion, urban sophistication, and much comfort. Since the hotel opened in 1985, its clientele has included a bevy of international film and recording stars who like the privacy and anonymity provided here: the Rolling Stones, Bruce Willis, Sigourney Weaver.

Many of the accommodations are classed as suites, and each unit is lavishly outfitted with the kinds of furnishings and textiles you might find in an Edwardian country house. Several accommodations are filled with such whimsical touches as tented ceilings, and each has all the modern luxuries you'd expect in a hotel of this caliber. The public rooms are inviting oases, with trompe l'oeil paintings against backgrounds of turquoise. The designer of the hotel was an American, Barbara Thornhill.

Dining/Entertainment: The hotel's superb restaurant, The Room at the Halcyon, is recommended separately in Chapter 5.

Services: Complimentary limousine service, 24-hour room service, babysitting,

1-hour clothes pressing, message-paging system (for which they provide beepers) that extends 20 miles from the hotel.

Facilities: Garden patio, night safes, business center.

13. HAMPSTEAD

The old village of Hampstead, sitting high on a hill, is the most desirable residential suburb of London. The village borders a wild heathland, which contains sprawling acres of weeded dells and fields of heather. Yet the Northern Line of the Underground reaches the edges of the heath, making it possible for Londoners to enjoy isolated countryside while living only 20 minutes from the city's center. These advantages have led many artists to discover what Keats could have told them years ago: Hampstead is the place to live in if you can afford it. The expensive little Georgian houses have never received so much attention and love as they get now.

SANDRINGHAM HOTEL, 3 Holford Rd., London NW3 1AD. Tel. 071/ 435-1569. Fax 071/431-5932. 19 rms (9 with bath). MINIBAR TV TEL **Tube:** Hampstead.

$ Rates (including English breakfast): £39 ($58.50) single without bath, £46.50 ($69.80) single with bath; £60 ($90) double without bath, £65 ($97.50) double with bath; £90 ($135) family room with private bath. No credit cards.

 You'd never guess this is a hotel, because it stands on a residential street in one of the best parts of London. The Sandringham is a well-built, centrally heated house. The pretty breakfast room has been enlarged by the addition of a Victorian conservatory and overlooks a walled garden. From the upper rooms, you have a panoramic view over the heath to the center of London. You'll find a homelike lounge furnished with a color TV. Rooms are comfortably furnished and well maintained. Laundry, babysitting, and 24-hour room service are provided.

14. AIRPORT HOTELS

As major gateways to Europe (not to mention England), London's two major airports are among the busiest in the world. Many readers have expressed a desire to be near their point of departure, spending the night in ease before "taking off." With that in mind, I'd suggest the following accommodations.

NEAR GATWICK AIRPORT

GATWICK HILTON INTERNATIONAL HOTEL, Gatwick Airport, Gatwick, West Sussex RH6 0LL. Tel. 0293/518080, or toll free 800/HILTONS in the U.S. Fax 0293/528980. 550 rms, 18 suites. A/C TV TEL

$ Rates: £125–£130 ($187.50–$195) single; £135–£140 ($202.50–$210) double; from £210 ($315) suite. Breakfast £10–£12.95 ($15–$19.40) extra. AE, DC, MC, V. **Parking:** £12.50 ($18.80) extra.

The airport's most convenient resting place, this deluxe five-floor hotel is linked to the airport terminal with a covered walkway and offers trolleys to assist with luggage. There is also an electric buggy service between the hotel and the airport for the infirm, the elderly, or anyone with lots of suitcases. The most impressive part of the hotel is the first-floor lobby, whose glass-covered portico rises through four floors and contains a scale replica of the de Havilland Gypsy Moth airplane *Jason*, used by Amy Johnson on her solo flight from England to Australia in 1930. The reception desk is nearby, in an area with a lobby bar and lots of greenery. The rooms are equipped with triple-glazed, soundproofed windows, radios, color TVs, and hairdryers.

Dining/Entertainment: The American-themed restaurant Amy's serves buffet breakfasts, lunches, and dinners. The Garden Restaurant, outfitted in an English outdoor theme, serves drinks, full meals, and snacks as well. There's also the Lobby Bar, open 24 hours a day, and a watering hole with a polo-playing theme, The Jockey Bar.

Services: Same-day laundry and dry cleaning (if collected before 9am), up-to-date flight information channel, 24-hour room service, in-house hairdresser, bank, and gift shop.

Facilities: Health club with sauna, steam room, massage room, swimming pool, and gymnasium.

NEAR HEATHROW AIRPORT

SHERATON SKYLINE, A-4 Bath Rd., Hayes Middlesex UB3 5BP. Tel. 081/759-2535, or toll free 800/325-3535 in the U.S. Fax 081/750-9150. 352 rms, 5 suites. A/C MINIBAR TV TEL

$ Rates: £140–£160 ($210–$240) single; £150–£170 ($225–$255) double; from £310 ($465) suite. English breakfast £8.25 ($12.40) extra. AE, DC, MC, V.
Parking: Free to guests, £5 ($7.50) for nonguests.

This hotel's contemporary plushness and array of entertainment and dining facilities attract the experienced traveler, who checks in here either to recover from a long-distance flight or else to avoid London's morning traffic before an early flight the next day. This establishment—more a miniature village than a hotel—was voted the world's best airport hotel sometime during the 1980s. Each room sports a color TV with in-house video movies, massage-style shower, and a radio.

Set behind trees, the hotel operates on an international schedule, as business travelers from all over the world check in at all hours. The hotel was designed around an atrium where tropical plants and towering palms thrive beneath a translucent roof. The foundations of a cabana bar are set into the climate-controlled waters of a swimming pool.

Dining/Entertainment: In the Edwardian-style Colony Bar, a fireplace flickers late into the night, and in its adjacent well-upholstered restaurant, the Colony Room, where well-prepared food is served beneath massive ceiling timbers and heavy brass chandeliers. A French café offers light meals and full buffet breakfasts, and in Diamond Lil's, a Montana-style cabaret, the sight of showgirls enhances the flavor of charbroiled steaks and generous drinks.

Services: 24-hour room service, laundry, verification and confirmation of departures from Heathrow.

Facilities: Business center.

LONDON DINING

If you want to splurge in a big way, you have the London "greats" at your disposal: gourmet havens such as La Tante Claire, Le Gavroche, Nico at Ninety on Park Lane, or half a dozen others. The very top restaurants in London rank among those at the top anywhere. Usually they're French, or at least French-inspired. However, many chefs also do remarkable and inventive English dishes by making use of the very fresh produce available in the country. Wine tends to be very expensive in the leading restaurants of London.

If star eateries are too expensive for you, you'll find many more moderately priced restaurants and budget establishments. Among these are public houses, also known variously as the "local," the "watering hole," the "boozer," or the pub. Pubs are such a national institution that we ought to devote an entire section to it, but our space is limited. The pub represents far, far more than merely a place in which to drink. For millions of English people it's the regular lunchtime rendezvous. For an even-larger number, it also doubles as a club, front parlor, betting office, debating chamber, television lounge, or refuge from the family. It is not, by and large, a good "pickup" spot, but it's very nearly everything else.

At last count, there were some 5,000 to 6,000 pubs in metropolitan London, so our suggestions represent no more than a few random samplings of the field. Perhaps you could try an exploration safari of your own by moving on to possibly greener pastures next door after one drink. If repeated at length, the process evolves into a "pub crawl," possibly Britain's most popular national pastime.

Our selections are fine for both women and men, but should you strike out on your own, choose your pubs carefully. Some pubs are what the English call "downright grotty," a dirty, often tough drinking place that attracts what the English refer to as soccer-loving "lager louts." If you're well dressed for the evening and don't want to risk having a drink spilled on you in a crowded pub, a safer bet would be a hotel bar or cocktail lounge.

All restaurants and cafés in Britain are required to display the prices of the food and drink they offer in a place that the customer can see before entering the eating area. If an establishment has an extensive à la carte menu, the prices of a representative selection of food and drink currently available must be displayed as well as the table d'hôte menu, if one is offered. Charges for service and any minimum charge or cover charge must also be made clear. The prices shown must include 17½% VAT. Most restaurants add a 10% to 15% service charge to your bill. Look at your check to make sure of that. If nothing has been added, leave a 12% to 15% tip.

Finally, there's the matter of location. Once upon a time London had two traditional dining areas: Soho for Italian and Chinese fare, Mayfair and Belgravia for French cuisine. Today the gastronomical legions have conquered the entire heart of the metropolis, and you're liable to find any type of eatery anywhere, from Chelsea to Hampstead. The majority of our selections are in the West End, but only because this happens to be the handiest for most visitors.

RESERVATIONS Nearly all places, except pubs, cafeterias, and fast-food establishments (often chain run), prefer that you make a reservation. Almost invariably, you get a better table if you "book" in advance. Some restaurants absolutely require a reservation, and for a few of the really famous places Americans have been known to reserve tables weeks in advance, even before leaving home (such reservations need to be confirmed when you arrive in London). In the listings below, reservations policies of the various restaurants are noted.

HOURS Restaurants in London keep widely varied hours, depending on the establishment. In general, lunch is offered from noon to 2pm and dinner is served from 7:30 to 9:30pm. Many restaurants open an hour earlier, and of course, many others stay open later. Sunday is the typical closing day for London restaurants, but there are many exceptions to that rule.

PRICE CATEGORIES In this guide, meals that cost $75 or more are listed as "Very Expensive"; $50 to $75, "Expensive"; $30 to $50, "Moderate"; and under $30, "Inexpensive."

1. MAYFAIR & ST. JAMES'S

MAYFAIR

VERY EXPENSIVE

LE GAVROCHE, 43 Upper Brook St., W1. Tel. 071/408-0881.
  Cuisine: FRENCH. **Reservations:** Required, as far in advance as possible.
  Tube: Marble Arch.
$ Prices: Appetizers £15.50–£28.50 ($23.30–$42.80); main courses £25.50–£34.80 ($38.30–$52.20); fixed-price meal £29.50 ($44.30) at lunch, £59 ($88.50) at dinner. AE, DC, MC, V.
  Open: Lunch Mon–Fri noon–2pm; dinner Mon–Fri 7–11pm.

Le Gavroche has long stood for quality French cuisine, perhaps the finest in Great Britain. It's the creation of two Burgundy-born brothers, Michel and Albert Roux. Service is faultless, the ambience chic and formal without being stuffy. The menu changes constantly, depending on the availability of the freshest produce of the season and, more important, the inspiration of the Roux brothers, who began modestly in London at another location and went on to fame in the culinary world.

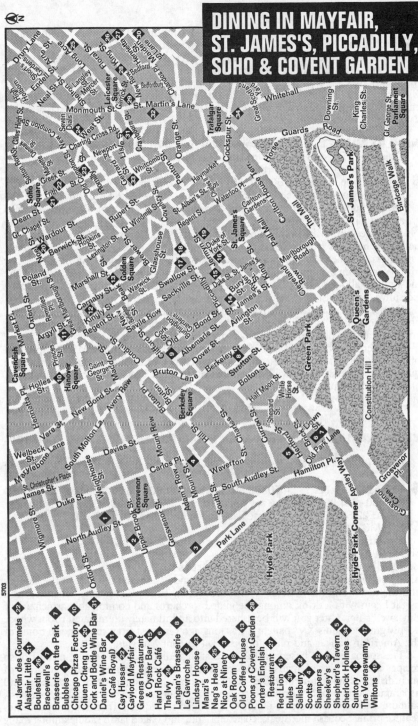

DINING IN MAYFAIR, ST. JAMES'S, PICCADILLY, SOHO & COVENT GARDEN

Au Jardin des Gourmets 22
Alastair Little 21
Boulestin 26
Bracewell's 7
Brasserie on the Park 1
Bubbles 10
Chicago Pizza Factory 20
Chuen Cheng Ku 31
Cork and Bottle Wine Bar
Daniel's Wine Bar
(Café Royal) 11
Gay Hussar 22
Gaylord Mayfair 9
Greens Restaurant
& Oyster Bar 15
Hard Rock Café 6
The Ivy 24
Langan's Brasserie 8
Le Gavroche 2
Lindsay House 23
Manzi's 25
Nag's Head 3
Nico at Ninety
Oak Room 18
Old Coffee House 13
Poons of Covent Garden 28
Porter's English
Restaurant 27
Red Lion 16
Rules 30
Salisbury 32
Scotts 4
Shampers 12
Sheekey's 29
Shepherd's Tavern 5
Sherlock Holmes 34
Suntory 14
The Veeraswamy
Wiltons 19

5703

Their wine cellar is among the most interesting in London, with many quality burgundies and Bordeaux. Try, if featured, their stuffed smoked salmon and their mousseline of lobster. Most main courses are served on a silver tray covered with a silver dome. Try such dishes as Bresse pigeon or veal kidneys in a sauce made with three mustards, perhaps sea bass with a champagne-cream sauce. The lid is lifted off with great flourish, and the platters, like a stage play, are artistically arranged. You can enjoy an apéritif upstairs while perusing the menu and enjoying the delectable canapés.

NICO AT NINETY, 90 Park Lane, W1. Tel. 071/409-1290.

Cuisine: FRENCH. **Reservations:** Required 2 days in advance for lunch, 10 days for dinner. **Tube:** Marble Arch.

$ Prices: Appetizers £12.50–£25 ($18.75–$37.50); main courses £22–£35 ($33–$52.50); fixed-price lunch £26 ($39); fixed-price dinner £42 ($63). AE, DC, MC, V.

Open: Lunch Mon–Fri noon–2pm; dinner Mon–Sat 7–11pm. **Closed:** 10 days around Christmas/New Year's.

No great restaurant in London has changed its location as often as this one, but dedicated habitués from around the world continue to seek out chef Nico Ladenis, regardless of where he moves. In a new setting under the umbrella of Grosvenor House, more impressive and stylish than ever before, chef Nico remains one of the most talked about chefs of Great Britain—the only one who is a former oil company executive, economist, and self-taught cook.

Dinners are profoundly satisfying and often memorable in the very best gastronomic tradition of "post-nouvelle cuisine," in which the tenets of classical cuisine are creatively and flexibly adapted to local fresh ingredients.

The menu, written in French, changes frequently and according to the inspiration of Mr. Ladenis. You might select, for example, sole with lobster sauce, a delectable quail pie, lobster-stuffed ravioli in truffled butter, and Bresse pigeon with foie gras. Desserts are sumptuous.

EXPENSIVE

BRACEWELL'S, in the Park Lane Hotel, Piccadilly W1. Tel. 071/499-6321.

Cuisine: BRITISH. **Reservations:** Required. **Tube:** Hyde Park Corner or Green Park.

$ Prices: Appetizers £4.50–£9.50 ($6.80–$14.30); main courses £9–£14.50 ($13.50–$21.80); 3-course set lunch menu £17.50 ($26.30); 3-course set dinner menu £22.50 ($33.80); 4-course gastronomique dinner menu £26.50 ($39.80). AE, DC, MC, V.

Open: Lunch Mon–Fri 12:30–2:30pm; dinner Mon–Sat 7–10:30pm.

Sheltered by the thick fortresslike walls of this previously recommended hotel, Bracewell's is one of chic London's better-kept secrets. The cuisine prepared by the highly acclaimed British-born chef, Simon Traynor, is among the best in the capital, and the decor and the five-star service are worthy of its distinguished clientele. You might begin with a drink among the gilded torchères and comfortable armchairs of Bracewell's Bar. Later you will be ushered into an intimately illuminated room whose deeply grained Louis XVI paneling was long ago removed from the London home of the American banker and philanthropist J. Pierpont Morgan.

The specialties are based on the freshest ingredients of the season, using British recipes and the best of British produce. The year-round menu features an array of such dishes as spinach-and-walnut soufflé with anchovies, terrine of baby leeks and asparagus, lobster and Cornish crab soup, a variety of fish from mullet, sea bass, salmon, and fish casserole to Dover sole cooked to request. Traditional meat dishes feature prime Scottish filet steak, chateaubriand, and baked lamb saddle among many other choices. All these traditional ingredients are interpreted creatively and in an attractively contemporary style by chef Traynor. Keep an eye on the three-course table d'hôte, which may feature asparagus, artichoke, and foie gras terrine with a sweet pickled pumpkin or poached chicken and sweetbreads served in a creamy mushroom sauce with toasted new potatoes. The desserts are irresistible; fight with your conscience over the pancake Belmonte flamed at your table with Armagnac and seasonal berries in an orange sauce. Linger over the array of offerings on the dessert trolley—you can always opt for a fruit salad that includes an abundance of exotic fruits. In the evenings a Menu Gastronomique is available offering four courses starting with, for instance, a smoked breast of guinea fowl served on a salad of greens with wild strawberries and black pepper, then a baked filet of halibut with a brioche-herb crust served on shredded cucumber with a light lemon-thyme sauce. As a meat course you may opt for the grilled loin of venison in a sweet peppercorn sauce served with shallots and herb-roasted new potatoes. A variety of wines is selected and recommended according to the menu.

OAK ROOM, in Le Méridien London, 21 Piccadilly, W1. Tel. 071/734-8000.

Cuisine: FRENCH. **Reservations:** Required. **Tube:** Piccadilly Circus.

$ Prices: Appetizers £12.50–£18 ($18.80–$27); main courses £17–£23 ($25.50–$34.50); fixed-price business lunch £24.50 ($36.80); menu gourmand £49 ($73.50). AE, DC, MC, V.

Open: Lunch Mon–Fri noon–2:30pm; dinner Mon–Sat 7–10:30pm.

The Oak Room is one of the finest restaurants in London and has been recognized as such with many culinary awards. The setting alone—said to be the most beautiful dining room in the center of London—would be worth the trip. But it's the refined cuisine that's the draw. Lavish in its appointments, this splendid period room where former and current greats of the world have dined has been restored to all its gilded splendor, including the ceiling and the original oak paneling. Averting your eye a moment from this gilded magnificence, you can preview the menu, a creation of French consultant chef Michel Lorain and resident executive chef David Chambers. You can select from "Cuisine Creative" or "Cuisine Traditionelle" menus, enjoying such dishes as gazpacho served with warm langoustines and zucchini quenelles, lightly smoked sea bass in a cream sauce flavored with Sevruga caviar, and glazed filet of turbot with balsamic vinegar and soy sauce, served with wild rice.

SCOTTS, 20 Mount St., W1. Tel. 071/629-5248.

Cuisine: SEAFOOD. **Reservations:** Required. **Tube:** Green Park.

$ Prices: Appetizers £5.50–£12 ($8.30–$18); main courses £13.50–£23 ($20.30–$34.50); fixed-price lunch £25 ($37.50). AE, DC, MC, V.

Open: Lunch Mon–Sat 1–3pm; dinner Mon–Sat 6–10:45pm, Sun 7–10pm.

Scotts is considered the most noted restaurant in the world for oysters, lobster, and caviar. In addition to the regular spacious dining room and cocktail bar, it has a special oyster, lobster, and caviar bar. Its origins are humble, going back to a fishmonger in Coventry Street in 1851. However, its fame rests on its heyday at Piccadilly Circus when the proprietors often entertained Edward VII and his guests in private dining rooms. Scotts has been at its present location since 1967, enjoying a chic address in the neighborhood of the swank Connaught Hotel and Berkeley Square. Its decor, with terra-cotta walls, has been called "Assyrian Monumental," and the wall panels are hung with English primitive pictures.

The restaurant's chef believes in British produce, and he handles the kitchen with consummate skill and authority. You get top-notch quality and ingredients. Lobster, crab, oysters, and perhaps smoked Ellingham eel are featured. The eel comes from Suffolk where it is "swum" (that is, kept alive) until it's ready for smoking. Dover sole is prepared "any way." The English prefer it "on the bone" and consider fileted fish food for sissies. A favorite appetizer is salad Chloe, and more down-to-earth dishes, such as fish cakes, appear regularly or at least weekly on the luncheon menu.

MODERATE

LANGAN'S BRASSERIE, Stratton St., W1. Tel. 071/491-8882.
 Cuisine: ENGLISH/FRENCH. **Reservations:** Required. **Tube:** Green Park.
$ Prices: Appetizers £4.50–£11 ($6.80–$16.50); main courses £11.50–£18 ($17.30–$27). AE, DC, MC, V.
 Open: Lunch Mon–Fri 12:30–3pm; dinner Mon–Fri 7–11:45pm, Sat 8pm–12:45am.

Langan's is a relaxed, café-style restaurant modeled after a Parisian brasserie, and it was *the* place to be in London in the '70s. It's still going strong. The brainchild of late restaurateur Peter Langan in partnership with actor Michael Caine and chef de cuisine Richard Shepherd—it has been a chic spot since its opening in 1976. The cuisine has many continental dishes, especially French ones, but always does English food as your English nanny did, including sausages and "mash" and black pudding. The potted palms and overhead fans create a faded '30s atmosphere; in the evening, you expect the musicians to break into "As Time Goes By" at any moment. Upstairs is a more formal and intimate but no more costly dining room.

THE VEERASWAMY, 99–101 Regent St., W1. Tel. 071/734-1401.
 Cuisine: INDIAN. **Reservations:** Recommended. **Tube:** Piccadilly Circus.
$ Prices: Appetizers £3.50–£6 ($5.30–$9); main courses £9.95–£18.95 ($14.90–$28.40); fixed-price 3-course dinner £17 ($25.50) for all-vegetarian, £20–£29 ($30–$43.50) for meat and vegetables; 3-course buffet lunch £13 ($19.50). AE, DC, MC, V.
 Open: Lunch Mon–Sat noon–2:30pm; dinner Mon–Sat 6–11:30pm.

When it was originally established in 1927 as the first Indian restaurant in Europe, every socialite in London came for the novel experience of tasting the cuisine of Britain's far-away colony. (Its founder, Edward Palmer, who had made a fortune in trading spices, was born in 1860 in India of English parents.) Beautifully restored in the mid-1980s, it is still one of London's leading choices for Indian regional and tribal dishes.

In the kitchen, each chef is a specialist in the cuisine of his region of the subcontinent. Whether from Gujarat or Goa (try the fiery coconut-flavored chicken), the food is often mouth-tingling. Vegetarians appreciate the thalis, the home-baked breads, and the array of well-seasoned vegetables, which some diners order in combinations as meals unto themselves. The Regent Street business crowd usually opts for the all-you-can-eat lunchtime buffet, while the evening crowd opts for pre- or posttheater dinners, before or after a West End play. (Some diners prefer drinks and appetizers before the play, and then return for their main courses after the play is over—an accommodation that the management here usually schedules gracefully.)

INEXPENSIVE

BRASSERIE ON THE PARK, in the Park Lane Hotel, Piccadilly (without number), W1. Tel. 071/499-6321.
 Cuisine: INTERNATIONAL. **Reservations:** Recommended. **Tube:** Hyde Park Corner.
$ Prices: Appetizers £3.25–£6.50 ($4.90–$9.80); main courses £4.25–£10.75 ($6.40–$16.10); fixed-price menus £11.95 ($17.90) and £14.95 ($22.40). AE, DC, MC, V.
 Open: Lunch Mon–Fri noon–3pm; dinner Mon–Fri 6–11pm, Sat–Sun noon–11pm.

The Brasserie on the Park in the Park Lane Hotel is bright and breezy, decorated in an art deco style in continuity of theme with the hotel's famous ballroom. There are three menus offering international brasserie dishes pleasing to every kind of mood, appetite, and wallet.

There is a standard menu featuring appetizers such as smoked salmon and sliced avocado served on a whole-meal crouton with hollandaise sauce. The main courses feature classic brasserie dishes such as a choice of omelets to more exotic dishes such as the grilled tiger prawns with chili mayonnaise or three-bone rack of lamb roasted with marinated and barbecued green vegetables. A special fixed-price menu changes weekly (for instance, dishes may include stir-fried sea scallops or grilled quail with wild mushrooms). Popular dishes include such favorites as Cumberland sausages and beefburgers. The Brasserie has also introduced the idea of offering a choice of wines, *available by the glass,* that have been carefully selected to "marry" with your food. During the year the Brasserie frequently holds special festivals of foods and wines from specific regions of countries—southwest France, Veneto in northern Italy, or California, for example.

CHICAGO PIZZA FACTORY, 17 Hanover Sq., W1. Tel. 071/629-2669.

Cuisine: AMERICAN. **Reservations:** Recommended for lunch. **Tube:** Oxford Circus.

$ Prices: Appetizers £2.75–£3.75 ($4.10–$5.60); main courses £6.50–£10 ($9.80–$15); pizzas for two £7.50–£12 ($11.30–$18). AE, V.

Open: Mon–Sat 11:45am–11:30pm, Sun noon–10:30pm.

 This place specializes, as its name suggests, in deep-dish pizza covered with everything we are used to in all possible combinations. The regular-size pizza is enough for two or three diners, and the large one is suitable for four or five. The menu also includes stuffed mushrooms, garlic bread, salads, and homemade cheesecakes.

The restaurant was introduced to London by former advertising executive Bob Payton, an ex-Chicagoan. It's one of the few places providing doggy bags. It also has a large bar with a wide choice of U.S. beers and cocktails, including a specialty known as St. Valentine's Day Massacre. A video over the bar shows continuous American baseball, football, and basketball games. The 275-seat restaurant is full of authentic Chicago memorabilia, and the staff wears *Chicago Sun Times* newspaper-sellers' aprons. Dress is casual.

GAYLORD MAYFAIR, 16 Albermarle St., W1. Tel. 071/629-9802.

Cuisine: INDIAN. **Reservations:** Not required. **Tube:** Green Park.

$ Prices: Appetizers £7.95–£10.75 ($11.90–$16.10); main courses £8.25–£10.95 ($12.40–$16.40); dinner with meat dish £18.25 ($27.40); vegetarian fixed-price lunch or dinner £14.50 ($21.80). AE, DC, MC, V.

Open: Lunch daily noon–3pm; dinner Mon–Sat 6–11:30pm.

Actually there are two Gaylords in London, but this is the newer one and it has established an enviable reputation among local connoisseurs of Indian cuisine. One reason for this is that the Gaylord offers samplings of several regional cooking styles, so that you can feast on Kashmiri and Mughlai as well as on the usual tandoori delicacies. The menu is downright dazzling in its variety. The best idea here is for several people to go and order as many small dishes as possible, so that you can taste a variety. Try the *keema nan* (leavened bread stuffed with delicately flavored minced meat) and certainly the little spiced vegetable pastries known as samosas. For a main course, you might choose *goshtaba* (lamb "treated and beaten beyond recognition"), or the *murg musallam* (diced chicken sautéed with onions and tomatoes). If you don't happen to like curry, the staff will help you select a meal of any size totally devoid of it, but flavored with a great many spices. You'll find the manager helpful in guiding you through the less familiar Kashmiri dishes.

HARD ROCK CAFE, 150 Old Park Lane, W1. Tel. 071/629-0382.
  Cuisine: AMERICAN. **Reservations:** Not accepted. **Tube:** Green Park or Hyde Park Corner.
  $ Prices: Appetizers £2.25–£5.25 ($3.40–$7.90); main courses £5.45–£13.95 ($8.20–$20.90). AE, MC, V.
  Open: Sun–Thurs 11:30am–12:30am, Fri–Sat 11:30am–1am. **Closed:** Dec 25–26.

This is a down-home southern-cum-midwestern American roadside diner with good food at reasonable prices, taped music, and service with a smile. It was established on June 14, 1971, and since then more than 12 million people have eaten there. Almost every night there's a line waiting to get in, as this is one of the most popular places in town with young people, visiting rock and film stars, and tennis players from America.

Generous portions are served, and the price of a main dish includes not only a salad but also fries. Their specialties include a smokehouse steak, filet mignon, and a T-bone special. They also offer charbroiled burgers and hot chili. The dessert menu is equally tempting, including homemade apple pie and thick cold shakes. There's also a good selection of beer.

PUBS & WINE BARS

BUBBLES, 41 N. Audley St., W1. Tel. 071/491-3237.
  Cuisine: ENGLISH/CONTINENTAL/VEGETARIAN. **Reservations:** Recommended. **Tube:** Marble Arch or Bond Street.
  $ Prices: Appetizers £3–£5 ($4.50–$7.50); main courses £6.50–£12 ($9.80–$18); fixed-price dinner £9.50–£14.50 ($14.30–$21.80); fixed-price vegetarian menus £6.75–£7.50 ($10.10–$11.30); wine by the glass £1.90 ($2.90). MC, V.
  Open: Lunch daily 11am–6pm; dinner daily 6–11pm.

Bubbles is an interesting wine bar lying between Upper Brook Street and Oxford Street (in the vicinity of Selfridges). The owners attach equal importance to their food and their impressive wine list. Some selections of wine are sold by the glass. On the ground floor guests enjoy fine wines but also draft beer and liquor, along with a limited but well-chosen selection of bar food, such as mussels marinara and meat and fish salads, including one made with honey-roast ham. Downstairs is an à la carte restaurant serving both English and continental dishes, including a selection appealing to vegetarians. Begin, for example, with French onion soup, followed by roast rack of English lamb or perhaps roast duckling with a lemon-and-tarragon sauce.

SHEPHERD'S TAVERN, 50 Hertford St., W1. Tel. 071/499-3017.
  Cuisine: BRITISH. **Reservations:** Recommended. **Tube:** Green Park.
  $ Prices: Appetizers £1.10–£3 ($1.70–$4.50); main courses £2.95–£7.95 ($4.40–$11.90). AE, DC, MC, V.
  Open: Lunch Mon–Sat noon–3pm; dinner Mon–Sat 6–11pm, Sun 7–10:30pm. Pub, Mon–Fri 11am–11pm, Sat noon–3pm and 5:30–11pm, Sun noon–3pm and 7–10:30pm.

This tavern is a nugget, attracting a congenial mixture of patrons. There are many luxurious touches, including a collection of antique furniture. Chief among these is a sedan chair that once belonged to the son of George III, the Duke of Cumberland. Many of the local habitués recall the tavern's association with the pilots of the Battle of Britain. Bar snacks and hot dishes include shepherd's pie or fish pie with vegetables. Upstairs, the owners operate a cozy restaurant, Georgian in style with cedar paneling, serving a classic British cuisine such as shepherd's pie, steak-and-kidney pie, or Oxford ham.

You can visit just for drinks, of course, with beer prices beginning at £1.65 ($2.50) or wine by the glass at £1.75 ($2.60).

ST. JAMES'S
VERY EXPENSIVE

SUNTORY, 72–73 St. James's St., SW1. Tel. 071/409-0201.
Cuisine: JAPANESE. **Reservations:** Required. **Tube:** Green Park.
$ Prices: Appetizers £3.60–£12.50 ($5.40–$18.80); main courses £22–£42 ($33–$63); fixed-price meals £22–£32 ($33–$48) at lunch, £49.50–£64 ($74.30–$96) at dinner. AE, DC, MC, V.
Open: Lunch Mon–Sat noon–1:30pm; dinner Mon–Sat 7–9:30pm.

Suntory is the most elite, expensive, and best Japanese restaurant in London. Owned and operated by the Japanese distillers and brewers, it offers a choice of dining rooms in a setting evocative of a Japanese manor house. Most first-time visitors prefer the teppanyaki dining room downstairs, where iron grills are set in each table and you share the masterful skills of the high-hatted chef, who is amazingly familiar with a knife. You can also dine in other rooms on such fare as sukiyaki and tempura, perhaps selecting sushi, especially the fresh raw tuna fish delicately sliced. You can also enter one of the private dining rooms, but only if shoeless. Waitresses in traditional dress serve you with all the highly refined ritualistic qualities of the Japanese, including the presentation of hot towels. You may prefer a salad of shellfish and seaweed or a superb squid. Appetizers are artful and delicate, and even the tea is superior.

PUBS & WINE BARS

RED LION, 2 Duke of York St., off Jermyn St., SW1. Tel. 071/930-2030.
Cuisine: BRITISH. **Reservations:** Not required. **Tube:** Piccadilly Circus.
$ Prices: Sandwiches £1.50 ($2.30); main courses £1.50–£3.75 ($2.30–$5.60). No credit cards.
Open: Mon–Sat 11am–11pm; hot food Mon–Sat noon–2:30pm.

Ian Nairn compared the Red Lion's spirit to that of Edouard Manet's painting *A Bar at the Folies-Bergère* (see the collection at the Courtauld Institute Galleries). The food is pub grub: chips, pork sausages, cheese-and-onion pie, fish-and-chips, and chicken pies. The food is prepared in upstairs kitchens and sent down in a century-old dumbwaiter. Food orders are placed at the bar. Everything is washed down with Ind Coope's fine ales in this little Victorian pub with its early 1900s decorations, one of London's few remaining gin palaces, with mirrors 150 years old. The house's special beer is Burton's, an unusual brew made from spring water from the Midlands town of Bourton-on-Trent.

SHAMPERS, 4 Kingly St., W1. Tel. 071/437-1692.
Cuisine: CONTINENTAL. **Reservations:** Recommended. **Tube:** Oxford Circus.
$ Prices: Appetizers £3.20–£5.50 ($4.80–$8.30); main dishes £5.50–£13.50 ($8.30–$20.30); glass of wine from £2.10 ($3.20). AE, DC, MC, V.
Open: Mon–Fri 11am–11pm, Sat 11am–3pm; hot food, Mon–Sat noon–3pm, Mon–Fri 5–11pm. **Closed:** Easter and Christmas.

For a number of years now, this has been a favorite of West End wine bar aficionados who gravitate to its location between Carnaby Street of '60s fame and Regent Street of shoppers' fame. The entire complex consists of a street level and a basement dining room. The basement is exclusively a restaurant, and the upstairs is the wine bar. In the restaurant you can order such main dishes as braised leg and breast of guinea fowl, but in the bar you can enjoy food designed to accompany the wine. Salads are especially popular, including tuna and pasta with a spicy tomato sauce, or chicken salad with a tarragon-cream dressing. A platter of Irish mussels cooked in white wine seems to be everybody's favorite. The restaurant is closed in the evening but the bar serves an extended menu, incorporating not only the luncheon menu, but such dishes as grilled calves' liver, grilled pork sausages, or homemade duck sausages with lentils.

2. PICCADILLY, LEICESTER SQUARE & TRAFALGAR SQUARE

PICCADILLY

EXPENSIVE

WILTONS, 55 Jermyn St., SW1. Tel. 071/629-9955.
Cuisine: BRITISH. **Reservations:** Required. **Tube:** Green Park or Piccadilly Circus.
$ Prices: Appetizers £4–£14.50 ($6–$21.80); main courses £13.50–£20 ($20.30–$30). AE, DC, MC, V.
Open: Lunch Mon–Fri 12:30–2:30pm; dinner Mon–Sat 6:30–10:30pm.
Closed: 2 weeks in Aug.

Wiltons is one of the leading exponents of cookery called "as British as a nanny." In spite of its move into new quarters, its developers re-created the lush ambience of the original premises. You might be tempted to have an apéritif or drink in the bar near the entrance, where photos of the royal family alternate with oil portraits of the original owners. One of them, the legendary Jimmy Marks, or so it is said, used to "strike terror into the hearts of newcomers if he took a dislike to them." However, those days, still fondly recalled by some, are gone forever, and today a wide array of international guests are warmly welcomed by what I consistently find to be the most sensitive serving staff in the West End.

The thoroughly British menu of this restaurant, which opened in 1941, is known for its fish and game. You might begin with an oyster cocktail and follow with Dover sole, plaice, salmon, or lobster, prepared in any number of ways. In season, you can enjoy such delights as roast partridge, roast pheasant, or roast grouse. The chef might ask you if you want them "blue" or "black," a reference to roasting times. In season, you might even be able to order roast widgeon, a wild, fish-eating river duck. Game is often accompanied by bread sauce (made of milk thickened with breadcrumbs). To finish, if you want to seem truly British, you may order a savory such as Welsh rarebit or soft roes, even anchovies. But if that's too much, try the sherry trifle or syllabub.

MODERATE

GREENS RESTAURANT AND OYSTER BAR, 36 Duke St., SW1. Tel. 071/930-4566.
Cuisine: SEAFOOD. **Reservations:** Recommended for dinner. **Tube:** Piccadilly Circus or Green Park.
$ Prices: Appetizers £3.50–£7.25 ($5.30–$10.90); main dishes £8.50–£17.50 ($12.80–$26.30); Sun brunch from £12.50 ($18.80). AE, DC, MC, V.
Open: Lunch Mon–Sat 12:30–2:45pm; dinner Mon–Sat 6–11pm; brunch Sun 11:30am–3:30pm.

This is a good choice for the excellence of its menu, the charm of its staff, and its central location. This busy place has a cluttered entrance leading to a crowded bar where you can stand at what the English call "rat-catcher counters," if the tables are full, to sip fine wines and, from September to May, enjoy oysters. Other foods to encourage the consumption of the wines are quails' eggs, king prawns, smoked Scottish salmon, "dressed" crab, and baby lobsters. If you choose to go on into the dining room, you can select from a long menu with a number of fish dishes or such grilled foods as calves' liver and bacon, kedgeree, and Greens fish cakes with parsley sauce. Desserts include Duke of Cambridge tart, black-currant sorbet, and banana fritters.

A WINE BAR

DANIEL'S WINE BAR [CAFE ROYAL], 68 Regent St., W1. Tel. 071/437-9090, ext. 277.
   Cuisine: BRITISH. **Reservations:** Not required. **Tube:** Piccadilly Circus.
$ **Prices:** Appetizers £2.50–£2.80 ($3.80–$4.20); main courses £5 ($7.50); glass of wine from £2 ($3). AE, DC, MC, V.
   Open: Lunch Mon–Fri noon–2:30pm; wine bar Mon–Fri noon–3pm and 5:30–11pm.

The deliberately unpretentious annex of the chillingly expensive Café Royal Grill, Daniel's dates from 1865. Both are accessible from the marble-floored lobby of a watering hole where the literary greats of 19th-century England have trod, including Oscar Wilde. Despite its opulent design with art nouveau moldings, oaken half-paneling, and lots of framed cartoons and illustrations, the café is very informal and has a resident pianist whose melodies seem to make the wine ever-so-more drinkable. Platters of food such as beef Stroganoff are served at lunchtime. The rest of the day, until late into the night, only wine and drinks are served.

LEICESTER SQUARE

MODERATE

MANZI'S, 1–2 Leicester St., off Leicester Sq., WC2. Tel. 071/734-0224.
   Cuisine: SEAFOOD. **Reservations:** Required for dinner. **Tube:** Leicester Square.
$ **Prices:** Appetizers £4–£5.20 ($6–$7.80); main courses £10.50–£17.50 ($15.80–$27). AE, DC, MC, V.
   Open: Lunch Mon–Sat noon–2:40pm; dinner Mon–Sat 5:30–11:15pm, Sun 6–10pm.

 **FROMMER'S SMART TRAVELER:
RESTAURANTS**

VALUE-CONSCIOUS TRAVELERS SHOULD
TAKE ADVANTAGE OF THE FOLLOWING:

1. London's best-kept dining secret: Some of the great restaurants of London offer a fixed-price luncheon at such a reasonable price that the kitchen actually loses money.
2. Many fixed-price luncheons or dinners represent at least a 30% savings off à la carte menus.
3. Daily specials on any à la carte menu. They're invariably fresh and often carry a lower price tag than regular à la carte listings.
4. The house wine. Served in a carafe, it's only a fraction of the price of bottled wine.
5. The price of alcohol. Wine and liquor are both expensive in London, and your tab will rise rapidly.

Manzi's is London's oldest seafood restaurant, where you can dine either in the simply decorated ground-floor restaurant or in the Cabin Room upstairs. Famous for its Whitstable and Colchester oysters among other specialties, it has a loyal patronage, drawn to its moderately priced fare and fresh ingredients. If you'd like something less expensive than their legendary oysters, I suggest a prawn cocktail, even fresh sardines. If it's a luncheon stopover, you might happily settle for the crab salad. Main-course specialties include Dover sole and grilled turbot. Steaks are also available. The house has a good selection of wines and sherries.

SHEEKEYS, 28–32 St. Martin's Court, WC2. Tel. 071/240-2565.

Cuisine: SEAFOOD. **Reservations:** Required. **Tube:** Leicester Square.

$ Prices: Appetizers £5.50–£11 ($8.30–$16.50); main courses £11–£22 ($16.50–$33). AE, DC, MC, V.

Open: Lunch Mon–Fri 12:30–3pm; dinner Mon–Fri 6–11:15pm, Sat 5:30–11:15pm.

Since it was established in 1896 by an Irish-born vaudevillian, Sheekeys has always been closely associated with London's theater district. Contained within a series of small but intimate dining rooms, its walls are almost completely covered with the photographs of British and North American stage and screen stars, many of them autographed. A formally dressed staff caters to the culinary needs of a conservative and well-heeled clientele who feels comfortable with the restaurant's sense of tradition and polite good manners. Seafood is the specialty here, one of the few places in London that almost never (and only when specifically requested) fries its food. Instead, the delicate and fresh ingredients are steamed, grilled, or stewed, and then laden with such ingredients as sherry, cream, garlic, lemon, and herbs. The result is usually rich and delicious. Specialties include lobster and langoustine bisque, lobster thermidor, Dover sole prepared in the style of Joseph Sheekey, jellied eels (a British delicacy), fish cakes, and a concoction identified as Sheekeys' fisherman's pie. Desserts include apple tart with calvados.

PUBS & WINE BARS

CORK AND BOTTLE WINE BAR, 44–46 Cranbourn St., WC2. Tel. 071/734-7807.

Cuisine: INTERNATIONAL. **Reservations:** Recommended. **Tube:** Leicester Square.

$ Prices: Appetizers £2.95–£4.25 ($4.40–$6.40); main courses £5.50–£8.95 ($8.30–$13.40); glass of wine from £2 ($3). AE, DC, MC, V.

Open: Mon–Sat 11am–midnight, Sun noon–10:30pm.

The Cork and Bottle is just off Leicester Square. The most successful dish is a raised cheese-and-ham pie. It has a cream-cheesy filling, and the well-buttered pastry is crisp—not your typical quiche. (In just 1 week the bar sold 500 portions of this alone.) The kitchen also offers a spicy chicken salad, smoked chicken with avocado-and-grape salad, tandoori chicken, and lamb in ale. The expanded wine list features an excellent selection of beaujolais cru and wines from Alsace, as well as some 30 selections from "Downunder," 30 champagnes, and a good selection of California labels.

SALISBURY, 90 St. Martin's Lane, WC2. Tel. 071/836-5863.

Cuisine: BRITISH. **Reservations:** Not accepted. **Tube:** Leicester Square.

$ Prices: Buffet meal £3.50–£4.95 ($5.30–$7.40); beer from £1.76 ($2.60). AE, DC, MC, V.

Open: Mon–Sat 11am–11pm, Sun noon–3pm and 7–10:30pm.

Salisbury's glittering cut-glass mirrors reflect the faces of English stage stars (and hopefuls) sitting around the curved buffet-style bar. If you want a less prominent place to dine, choose the old-fashioned wall banquette with its copper-top tables and art nouveau decor. The light fixtures, veiled bronze girls in flowing robes holding up clusters of electric lights concealed in bronze roses, are appropriate. In the saloon, you'll see and hear the Oliviers of yesterday and tomorrow. But don't let this put you off your food. The pub's specialty, an array of homemade pies set out on a buffet table with salads, is really quite good and inexpensive. Food is served from noon until 7:30pm.

TRAFALGAR SQUARE

A PUB

SHERLOCK HOLMES, 10 Northumberland St., WC1. Tel. 071/930-2644.

Cuisine: BRITISH. **Reservations:** Recommended for restaurant. **Tube:** Charing Cross or Embankment.

$ Prices: Appetizers £2.50–£5 ($3.80–$7.50); main dishes £6.95–£12.95 ($10.40–$19.40); ground-floor snacks from £3 ($4.50). AE, DC, MC, V.

Open: Restaurant, Mon–Sat 9am–9:30pm; lunch Sun noon–2pm; dinner Sun 7–9:30pm. Pub, Mon–Sat 11am–11pm, Sun noon–3pm and 7–10:30pm.

It would be rather strange if Sherlock Holmes were not the old gathering spot for "The Baker Street Irregulars," a once-mighty clan of mystery lovers who met here to honor the genius of Arthur Conan Doyle's most famous fictional character. Upstairs you'll find a re-creation of the living room at 221B Baker St. and such "Holmesiana" as the cobra of *The Speckled Band* and the head of *The Hound of the Baskervilles*. The downstairs is mainly for drinking, but upstairs you can order complete meals with wine. Main dishes are reliable, including roast beef and Yorkshire pudding and chicken Sherlock Holmes with red wine and mushroom sauce. You select a dessert from the trolley. There's also a good snack bar downstairs, with cold meats, salads, cheese, and wine sold by the glass, if you wish.

3. SOHO

EXPENSIVE

THE IVY, 1–5 West St., WC2. Tel. 071/836-4751.

Cuisine: ENGLISH. **Reservations:** Required. **Tube:** Leicester Square.

$ Prices: Appetizers £4–£11 ($6–$16.50); main courses £8–£18.50 ($12–$27.80). AE, DC, MC, V.

Open: Lunch daily noon–3pm; dinner daily 5:30pm–midnight (last order).

Effervescent and sophisticated, the Ivy has been intimately associated with the West End theater district since it was originally established in 1911. Since then, its clientele has included Prime Ministers Lloyd George and Sir Winston Churchill (both of whom knew a lot about viands and wines), Noël Coward, Gracie Fields, Dame Sybil Thorndike, and Rex Harrison. Renovated in the early 1990s, it features a tiny bar near the entrance where guests might be asked to wait until their table is ready, and a paneled decor that seems deliberately designed to encourage discreet stargazing. Meals go on until very late, a graceful acknowledgment of the allure of after-theater suppers. Most importantly, the place, with its ersatz 1930s look, is fun, humming, and throbbing with the energy of London's glamour.

Although menu items appear deceptively simple, they mask a solid appreciation for fresh ingredients and skillful preparation. They include oysters Rockefeller, sautéed squid with tiger prawns, langoustines mayonnaise, an appetizer of ham hock with lentils, Mediterranean fish soup, salmon fish cakes with sorrel sauce, one of the best-received mixed grills in the neighborhood, salads, and such all-English desserts as sticky toffee pudding and bitter-chocolate ice cream.

MODERATE

ALASTAIR LITTLE, 49 Frith St., W1. Tel. 071/734-5183.

Cuisine: BRITISH. **Reservations:** Recommended. **Tube:** Leicester Square.

$ Prices: Appetizers £6.50–£12 ($9.80–$18); main courses £14–£18 ($21–$27); fixed-price 3-course lunch £18 ($27). AE, MC, V.

Open: Lunch Mon–Fri noon–3pm; dinner Mon–Sat 6–11:30pm.

Contained in a circa-1830 brick-fronted town house—which for a brief period is said to have housed the art studio of John Constable—this pleasantly monochromatic restaurant provides an informal and cozy place for a well-prepared lunch or dinner. Owned by the British-Danish-Spanish trio of Alastair Little, his wife, Kirsten Pedersen (who directs the dining room), and Mercedes Downend—it features a well-chosen menu whose offerings reflect whatever is available that day from the market. Examples might include roast baby brill with *cèpes* (flap mushrooms); filet of red snapper with parsley and a grilled vegetable salad; breast of chicken wrapped in collard greens and prosciutto and served with a truffle sauce; a bouillabaisse of sliced fish and shellfish; and Chinese-style squab with crispy vegetables. Dessert might consist of a lemon and goat-cheese tart or a prune-and-almond galette served with vanilla ice cream. A full complement of wines (mostly Californian and Australian) might accompany your meal.

AU JARDIN DES GOURMETS, 5 Greek St., W1. Tel. 071/437-1816.

Cuisine: FRENCH. **Reservations:** Required. **Tube:** Tottenham Court Road.

$ Prices: Appetizers £5–£8.95 ($7.50–$13.40); main courses £14–£19 ($21–$28.50); fixed-price 3-course lunch or dinner £19.75 ($29.60). AE, DC, MC, V.

Open: Lunch Mon–Fri 12:15–2:30pm; dinner Mon–Sat 6:15–11:15pm.

In an "Ile de France" off Soho Square, devotees of Gallic cuisine have been gathering to enjoy traditional specialties since 1931. Today, Soho Square and Greek Street have been largely rebuilt and are back in fashion again. The Jardin itself has climbed to a level never previously attained, what with new kitchens and wine cellars, lavatories that can be reached without climbing two floors, and, most important of all, an air-conditioned restaurant that separates smokers and nonsmokers in the two adjacent rooms on the ground floor. There is a comprehensive à la carte menu with such specialties as feuillette of braised lamb's tongue, sauté of fresh foie gras Aigre-Doux, noisettes of lamb with sauce Riches, and breast of pigeon roasted with cloves of garlic. A masterful selection of vintage Bordeaux and burgundies is expertly served.

LINDSAY HOUSE, 21 Romilly St., W1. Tel. 071/439-0450.

Cuisine: BRITISH. **Reservations:** Required. **Tube:** Leicester Square or Tottenham Court Road.

$ Prices: Appetizers £4–£7.75 ($6–$11.60); main courses £11.50–£15 ($17.30–$22.50); fixed-price lunch £14.75–£16.75 ($22.10–$25.10). AE, DC, MC, V.

Open: Lunch Mon–Sat 12:30–2:30pm, Sun 12:30–2pm; dinner Mon–Sat 6pm–midnight, Sun 7–10pm. **Closed:** Dec 25–26.

Lindsay House bases many of its dishes on 18th-century English recipes, although several platters are designated Tudor or nouvelle. Everyone from royalty to film stars, from diplomats to regular people show up here, including an array of discerning Americans. Since it begins serving dinner early, you might want to consider it for a pretheater dinner before a stage presentation at a Shaftesbury Avenue theater. The owners, Roger Wren and Malcolm Livingston—who already run some of the most fashionable restaurants in London, including Waltons of Walton Street, the English House, and the English Garden—decided to open this eating house in the heart of Soho. Welcoming fireplaces and fresh flowers give it class and style.

The food lives up to the decor. For what is called "first dishes," you might begin with potted spinach with herbs (studded with chicken livers, ham, and tongue, and served with a Cumberland sauce). To follow, you might try roast rack of Southdown lamb or a traditional fish pie with cubes of halibut, salmon, scallops, and quail eggs in a creamy sauce. Summer puddings are often featured—packed with such traditional fruits as strawberries, red currants, and raspberries, all served with a raspberry "cullis" with Devonshire clotted cream. You might also order floating islands, one of 18th-century-England's best confections, light poached meringues floating in a rose-scented custard.

INEXPENSIVE

CHUEN CHENG KU, 17 Wardour St., W1. Tel. 071/437-3281.
    Cuisine: CHINESE. **Reservations:** Recommended on weekend afternoons.
    Tube: Piccadilly Circus or Leicester Square.
$ Prices: Appetizers £1.85–£9 ($2.80–$13.50); main courses £9.50–£15 ($14.30–$22.50); fixed-price menu from £18 ($27). AE, DC, MC, V.
    Open: Daily 11am–11:45pm. **Closed:** Dec 24–25.

    This is one of the finest eateries in Soho's "New China," seating 400 diners. A large restaurant on several floors, Chuen Cheng Ku is noted for its Cantonese food and is said to have the longest and most interesting menu in London. Specialties are paper-wrapped prawns, rice in lotus leaves, steamed spareribs in black-bean sauce, and shredded pork with cashew nuts, all served in generous portions. Other featured à la carte dishes include fried oysters with ginger and scallions, sliced duck with chili and black-bean sauce, steamed pork with plum sauce, and Singapore noodles (thin rice noodles, sometime mixed with curry and pork or shrimp with red and green peppers, reflecting a Chinese-Malaysian inspiration). Dumplings are served from 11am to 6pm.

THE GAY HUSSAR, 2 Greek St., W1. Tel. 071/437-0973.
    Cuisine: HUNGARIAN. **Reservations:** Required, especially for lunch. **Tube:** Tottenham Court Road.
$ Prices: Appetizers £4.50–£7.50 ($6.80–$11.30); main courses £12.50–£25 ($18.80–$37.50); fixed-price lunch £15 ($22.50). AE.
    Open: Lunch Mon–Sat 12:30–2:30pm; dinner Mon–Sat 5:30–11pm.

The Gay Hussar has been called "the best Hungarian restaurant in the world." The "last of the great Soho restaurants," it's an intimate place, where diners can begin with a chilled wild-cherry soup or a hot spicy redfish soup in the style of Szeged, in Hungary's southern Great Plain. Main courses are likely to include stuffed cabbage, roast saddle of carp, half a perfectly done chicken served in a mild paprika sauce with a cucumber salad and noodles, and, of course, veal goulash with egg dumplings. For dessert, select either a raspberry-and-chocolate torte or lemon-cheese pancakes.

A PUB

OLD COFFEE HOUSE, 49 Beak St., W1. Tel. 071/437-2197.
    Cuisine: BRITISH. **Reservations:** Not accepted. **Tube:** Oxford Circus or Piccadilly Circus.
$ Prices: Main courses £3–£4 ($4.50–$6); beer from £1.70 ($2.60). No credit cards.
    Open: Daily 11am–11pm; meals at lunchtime only, daily noon–3pm.

Once honored as Soho Pub of the Year, the Old Coffee House takes its name from the coffeehouse heyday of 1700s London, when coffee was called "the devil's brew." The pub—heavily decorated with bric-a-brac, including such items as old musical instruments and World War I recruiting posters—still serves pots of filtered coffee. Have your drink at a long, narrow bar, where a lager costs from £1.80 ($2.70), or retreat to the restaurant upstairs where you can enjoy good pub food at lunch, including such typically English dishes as steak-and-kidney pie, three vegetarian dishes, and scampi and chips.

4. BLOOMSBURY & FITZROVIA

BLOOMSBURY

MODERATE

MUSEUM STREET CAFE, 47 Museum St., W1. Tel. 071/405-3211.
   Cuisine: MODERN BRITISH. **Reservations:** Required. **Tube:** Tottenham Court Road.
$ **Prices:** Lunch appetizers £3.50–£4.50 ($5.30–$6.80); lunch main courses £7–£9 ($10.50–$13.50); fixed-price 3-course lunch £14 ($21); fixed-price 3-course evening menu £19.50 ($29.30). No credit cards.
   Open: Lunch Mon–Fri 12:30–2:15pm (last order); dinner Mon–Fri 7:30–9:15pm (last order).

In an undistinguished building located within a 2-minute walk from the British Museum, this small-scale but unpretentiously charming dining room was the neighborhood's least appealing "greasy spoon" until it was transformed by Boston-born Gail Koerber and her English partner, Mark Nathan. Today—in a deliberately underfurnished setting filled with simple tables and chairs and lined with primitive paintings—you can enjoy an array of up-to-date dishes based on the freshness of available ingredients and the inspiration of the chefs. Examples might include maize-fed and charcoal-grilled chicken served with pesto sauce; portions of risotto studded with porcini mushrooms; a homemade sausage of lean pork served with an aromatic salsa verde; and kebabs of salmon and tuna with an onion and red wine sauce. Dessert might include a crusty *tarte tatin* (apple pie) or whatever else originated as a gleam in the eye of the owners on the morning of your arrival.

A PUB

MUSEUM TAVERN, 49 Great Russell St., WC1. Tel. 071/242-8987.
   Cuisine: ENGLISH. **Reservations:** Not accepted. **Tube:** Holborn or Tottenham Court Road.
$ **Prices:** Bar snacks £3.25–£4.95 ($4.90–$7.40); pint of lager £1.80 ($2.70). AE, DC, MC, V.
   Open: Mon–Sat 11am–11pm, Sun noon–10:30pm.

On a corner opposite the British Museum, the Museum Tavern is a pub dating from 1703. However, its Victorian trappings—velvet, oak paneling, and cut glass—are from 1855. It's right in the center of the London University area, and frequented by writers and publishers. Very crowded at lunchtime, it's also popular with researchers at the museum, and it's said that Karl Marx wrote in the pub over a meal. At lunch you can order such real, tasty, low-cost English food as shepherd's pie or beef in beer with two vegetables. There's also a cold buffet, including smoked mackerel, turkey and ham pies, a selection of salads, and English cheeses.

FITZROVIA

MODERATE

NICO CENTRAL, 35 Great Portland St., W1. Tel. 071/436-8846.
   Cuisine: FRENCH. **Reservations:** Required. **Tube:** Oxford Circus.
$ **Prices:** Appetizers £4.60–£12 ($6.90–$18); main courses £7.70–£13 ($11.60–$19.50). AE, MC, V.

Open: Lunch Mon–Fri noon–2pm; dinner Mon–Sat 6:45–11:15pm.

In this brasserie, founded and inspired by London's most legendary chef, Nico Ladenis, who now cooks at Nico at Ninety (see above), this brasserie delivers earthy French cuisine. Of course, everything is handled with considerable culinary urbanity. Guests sit on bentwood chairs at linen-covered tables. Nearly a dozen appetizers—called "starters," the pride of the chef—tempt you, especially Mediterranean fish soup with rouille and croutons. Deep fried squid salad with garlic mayonnaise is another signature dish, but nothing can quite top the pan-fried foie gras on toasted brioche with caramelized orange. For a main course, I take delight in the pot-roasted guinea fowl with white *coco* beans (French white beans), as do many members of the London "rag trade" who lunch here. Red mullet with a basil-flavored potato purée is yet another temptation. All "puddings" (desserts) cost £5 ($7.50) and range from an Armagnac parfait to a Bakewell tart.

5. THE STRAND, COVENT GARDEN & HOLBORN

THE STRAND

MODERATE

SIMPSON'S-IN-THE-STRAND, 100 The Strand, WC2. Tel. 071/836-9112.

    Cuisine: BRITISH. **Reservations:** Required. **Tube:** Charing Cross or Embankment.

$ Prices: Appetizers £2.75–£14 ($4.10–$21); main courses £9–£18.50 ($13.50–$27.80); fixed-price lunch £21.25 ($31.90); fixed-price dinner (6–7pm only) £21.25 ($31.90). AE, DC, MC, V.

    Open: Lunch Mon–Sat noon–3pm, Sun noon–2pm; dinner Mon–Sat 6–11pm, Sun 6–9pm.

Simpson's is more of an institution than a restaurant. Located next to the Savoy Hotel, it has been in business since 1828. All this very Victorian place needs is an empire. It has everything else: Adam paneling, crystal, and an army of grandly formal waiters hovering about. On most first-time visitors' lists, there is this notation: "See the changing of the guard, then lunch at Simpson's." One food critic wrote that "nouvelle cuisine here means anything after Henry VIII." However, there is one point on which most diners agree: Simpson's serves the best roasts (joints) in London. Huge roasts are trolleyed to your table and you can have slabs of beef carved off and served with traditional Yorkshire pudding. The classic dishes are roast sirloin of beef, roast saddle of mutton with red-currant jelly, roast Aylesbury duckling, and steak, kidney, and mushroom pie. Remember to tip the tail-coated carver, and men should wear a jacket and tie. For dessert, you might order the treacle roll and custard or Stilton with a vintage port.

JOE ALLEN'S, 13 Exeter St., WC2. Tel. 071/836-0651.

    Cuisine: AMERICAN. **Reservations:** Required. **Tube:** Covent Garden or Embankment.

$ Prices: Appetizers £4–£7 ($6–$10.50); main courses £6.50–£12.50 ($9.80–$18.80). No credit cards.

    Open: Mon–Sat noon–1am, Sun noon–midnight.

This fashionable American restaurant attracts primarily theater crowds. It lies north of the Strand in the vicinity of the Savoy Hotel. The restaurant has other branches in Paris and New York. The decor is inspired by the New York branch, with theater posters, gingham tablecloths in red-and-white check, and a menu offering such specialties as black-bean soup, barbecued ribs with black-eyed peas, Cajun chicken breast, and a bowl of chili.

COVENT GARDEN

EXPENSIVE

BOULESTIN, 1A Henrietta St., WC2. Tel. 071/836-7061.

Cuisine: FRENCH. **Reservations:** Required. **Tube:** Covent Garden.

$ **Prices:** Appetizers £4.50–£15.50 ($6.80–$23.30); main courses £16.75–£18.95 ($25.10–$28.40); fixed-price lunch £18.75 ($28.10). AE, DC, MC, V.

Open: Lunch Mon–Fri 12:30–3pm; dinner Mon–Sat 7:30–11:15pm. **Closed:** Bank holidays and last 3 weeks of Aug.

This famous old restaurant was founded more than half a century ago by Marcel Boulestin, the first Fleet Street restaurant critic. It's reached by a side door, which goes down into the basement beneath a bank. Kevin Kennedy, who is now both the manager and the chef, is one of the new British-bred cuisine experts who has style, flair, and imagination in the kitchen.

The chandeliers are still there, and the menu still has many of the old Boulestin dishes. Seared foie gras is served with sliced apples and balsamic vinegar as an appetizer, or you might sample Scottish chanterelles with a baby leek terrine. Poached filet of baby turbot comes with a sauce of white wine and shallots, or breast of pheasant is offered with chestnuts and a cranberry and calvados sauce. For dessert, a selection of Boulestin sorbets and ice creams is presented along with other choices, including an orange, chocolate, and pistachio terrine.

RULES, 35 Maiden Lane, WC2. Tel. 071/379-0258.

Cuisine: ENGLISH. **Reservations:** Recommended. **Tube:** Covent Garden.

$ **Prices:** Appetizers £4.25–£9 ($6.40–$13.50); main courses £13–£15.50 ($19.50–$23.30). AE, MC, V.

Open: Daily noon–midnight.

By anyone's estimate, this might be the most quintessentially British restaurant in London. Originally established in 1798 as an oyster bar, and lined with the framed memorabilia of the British Empire at its height, it rambles through a series of Edwardian dining rooms dripping in patriotic nostalgia. In fact, it lays claim to being the oldest restaurant in London still operating on the site of its original premises. Around the turn of the century, Edward VII, portly future king of England, used to arrive here quite frequently with his infamous mistress, Lillie Langtry, before heading up to a private red-velvet dining room on the second floor. Their signed portraits still embellish the yellowing walls, along with that of Charles Dickens, who crafted several of his novels here. Brilliant writer and curmudgeon Graham Greene made a visit to Rules an unchangeable condition of each of his birthdays despite his long-term residence in the south of France. Other artists and actors who appreciated Rules included Thackeray, John Galsworthy, H. G. Wells, Evelyn Waugh, John Barrymore, Clark Gable, and Laurence Olivier.

Today, amid cartoons executed by George Whitelaw in the 1920s, you can order such classic dishes as Irish or Scottish oysters, jugged hare, and Aylesbury duckling in orange sauce. Depending on the season, you can also order wild Scottish salmon or wild sea trout, wild Highland red deer, or any of any array of game birds such as grouse, snipe, partridge, pheasant, and woodcock. These might be followed by those unusual British savories, angels on horseback (oysters wrapped in bacon on toast).

MODERATE

CHRISTOPHER'S, 18 Wellington St., WC2. Tel. 071/240-4222.

Cuisine: AMERICAN. **Reservations:** Recommended. **Tube:** Covent Garden.
$ Prices: Appetizers £5–£12 ($7.50–$18); main courses £8–£18 ($12–$27). AE,
DC, MC, V.
Open: Lunch Mon–Fri noon–3pm; dinner Mon–Sat 6–11:30pm.

This is the most stylish, crowded, and sought-after American restaurant in London,
favored by everyone from stage and film stars to the youthful and monied successes of
London's financial district. It is housed in a Victorian-baroque building that was
originally built in 1820 as a papier-mâché factory. After 1864, it was London's first
licensed casino.

Many visitors are tempted to remain in the street-level bar, where steaks,
hamburgers, oysters, and fresh salads are served, and where no one minds if you while
away the time just drinking. More serious diners climb an elaborate corkscrew-shaped
stone staircase beneath a lavishly frescoed ceiling to reach a pair of Italianate dining
rooms. There, simple but flavorful American-inspired dishes are served, including
such vernacular dishes as smoked tomato soup with fresh pesto, rack of lamb, grilled
breast of chicken, filet of beef, stewed red cabbage with onions, mashed potatoes with
nutmeg, baby scallops in cream sauce, and key lime pie.

The establishment's owner and namesake is British-born Christopher Gilmour,
who spent 11 years in Los Angeles and Chicago trading commodities futures before
returning to London with his vision of a smart and sassy urban American restaurant.

POONS OF COVENT GARDEN, 41 King St., WC2. Tel. 071/240-1743.
  Cuisine: CHINESE. **Reservations:** Recommended. **Tube:** Covent Garden.
$ Prices: Appetizers £2.30–£6.90 ($3.50–$10.40); main courses £6.90–£21
  ($10.40–$31.50); fixed-price meal £13.50 ($20.30) at lunch, £23.50 ($35.30) at
  dinner. AE, DC, MC, V.
  Open: Daily noon–11:30pm.

This is one of the best Chinese restaurants in London. The place is run by Bill and
Cecilia Poon. Mr. Poon's great-great-grandfather cooked for the Chinese emperors,
and succeeding generations of the family have all interested themselves in traditional
Chinese cookery. The decor is reminiscent of a 1920s Raffles Hotel in Singapore.
Tables surround an island see-through kitchen. Two of the most recommendable
courses include Poons special crispy duck and Poons special wind-dried meat,
including sausage, which is quite different in flavor from smoked. For serious and
dedicated gourmets of Cantonese cuisine, Mr. and Mrs. Poon will arrange special
menus for parties of 10 or more, featuring dishes not on the à la carte menu (24 hours'
notice required).

INEXPENSIVE

**PORTER'S ENGLISH RESTAURANT, 17 Henrietta St., WC2. Tel. 071/
836-6466.**
  Cuisine: ENGLISH. **Reservations:** Not required. **Tube:** Covent Garden or
  Charing Cross.
$ Prices: Main courses £7.25–£7.70 ($10.90–$11.60); fixed-price menu £15
  ($22.50). AE, MC, V.
  Open: Mon–Sat noon–11:30pm, Sun noon–10:30pm.

(S) This place is owned by the current Earl of Bradford, who is a frequent visitor. It
has a friendly, informal, and lively atmosphere in comfortable surroundings on
two floors. Porter's specializes in classic English pies, including steak and
kidney, lamb and apricot, chicken and broccoli, and steak, oyster, and clam. Main
courses are so generous that the menu wisely eliminates appetizers. The traditional
roast beef with Yorkshire pudding is served on weekends. With whipped cream or
custard, the "puddings" come hot or cold, including bread-and-butter pudding or
steamed syrup sponge. The English call all desserts puddings, but at Porter's they are
the real puddings, as the word is known in the American sense. The bar does quite a

few exotic cocktails, and you can also order cider by the half pint, even English wines or traditional English mead. A traditional English tea is also served.

A PUB

NAG'S HEAD, 10 James St., WC2. Tel. 071/836-4678.
   Cuisine: ENGLISH. **Reservations:** Not accepted. **Tube:** Covent Garden.
$ Prices: Sandwiches £2.50 ($3.80); salads £3.95 ($5.90); main courses £5.50 ($8.30); pint of lager £1.80 ($2.70). No credit cards.
   Open: Lunch only, daily 11:30am–2:30pm. Pub 11am–11pm.

The Nag's Head is one of the most famous Edwardian pubs of London. In days of yore, patrons had to make their way through lorries of fruit and flowers for a drink here. Elegantly dressed operagoers in the evening used to mix with cockney cauliflower peddlers at the bar—and 300 years of British tradition happily faded away. With the moving of the market, all that has long ago changed, and the pub is patronized mainly by young people who seem to fill up all the tables every evening, including drinking space around the bar counter. Try a draft Guinness for a change of pace. Lunch is typical pub grub: sandwiches, salads, pork cooked in cider, and garlic prawns.

HOLBORN

A PUB

CITTIE OF YORKE, 22–23 High Holborn, WC1. Tel. 071/242-7670.
   Cuisine: ENGLISH. **Reservations:** Not accepted. **Tube:** Holborn or Chancery Lane.
$ Prices: Appetizers £2–£3 ($3–$4.50); main courses £2.50–£7 ($3.80–$10.50); fixed-price menu £9.50 ($14.30); wine by the glass £1.80 ($2.70). MC, V.
   Open: Mon–Fri 11am–11pm, Sat 11:30am–3pm and 5:30–11pm.

The Cittie of Yorke stands near the Holborn Bars, the historic entrance to London marked by dragons holding the coat-of-arms of the City between their paws. Persons entering and leaving London were checked and paid tolls here. A pub has stood on this site since 1430. This pub's principal hall, said to have the longest bar counter in England, has handsome screenwork, comfortable little compartments, a long row of huge vats, and a high trussed roof. The place is popular with barristers and judges. Lunch is a bar-snack type of thing, not formal in any way. You get a choice of four different hot platters. Other fare includes burgers, goulash, and casseroles. Dinner is slightly more formal and includes ham steak, fresh fish, lasagne, or rumpsteak. Appetizers are served only at dinner.

6. THE CITY & FLEET STREET

THE CITY

EXPENSIVE

LE POULBOT, 45 Cheapside, EC2. Tel. 071/236-4379.
   Cuisine: FRENCH. **Reservations:** Required. **Tube:** St. Paul's.
$ Prices: In the brasserie, appetizers £3.60–£5.65 ($5.40–$8.50); main dishes

£4.65–£9.95 ($7–$14.90). In the restaurant, fixed-price lunch £31.50 ($47.30).
DC, MC, V.
Open: Restaurant, lunch only, Mon–Fri noon–2:30pm. Brasserie, lunch only,
Mon–Fri noon–2:30pm.

Le Poulbot is a French restaurant par excellence. Founded by the Roux brothers of Le
Gavroche fame (the best restaurant in London), it was launched in 1969 and ever since
has been an attraction for the movers and shakers of the high-profile business world of
The City. The fixed-price menu is seasonally adjusted depending on what is best at the
market. Only a set menu (no à la carte) is offered in the restaurant. While ensconced
on a high-backed banquette, you can peruse a menu of sheer delight, selecting your
favorites from among light new-style continental dishes or longtime favorites, such as
a turbot fricassée or lamb cooked in its own juice and flavored with mint.

Upstairs, Le Poulbot offers what the French call a *casse-croûte* bar, which enjoys
great renown among City workers less well heeled than those who patronize the
expensive basement restaurant. Here you can order from a limited à la carte menu or
enjoy French "snacks."

LE SOUS-SOL, 32 Old Bailey, EC4. Tel. 071/236-7931.
Cuisine: FRENCH. **Reservations:** Required. **Tube:** St. Paul's.
$ Prices: Fixed-price lunch £19.95 ($29.90) for 2 courses, £24.50 ($36.80) for 3
courses. AE, MC, V.
Open: Lunch only, Mon–Fri noon–3pm.

Acclaimed by some critics as one of the finest restaurants in The City, this
air-conditioned and spacious restaurant serves a French cuisine that is creative and
prepared with fresh, quality ingredients. It has a pronounced Gallic decor, with
French food and impeccable service even when it's rushed. Guests sit down with a
glass of Kir and examine the fixed-price luncheon menu, which is changed daily. You
might begin with game terrine with grapes, perhaps a crab-and-fennel bisque, then
follow with roast guinea fowl with ginger and lime, or perhaps a filet of lamb sautéed
with herbs. Each day of the week a traditional plat du jour is offered, evoking
memories of an old-fashioned Anglo-French cuisine. These range from braised pig's
trotters to a traditional French lamb stew.

PUBS & WINE BARS

BOW WINE VAULTS, 10 Bow Churchyard, EC4. Tel. 071/248-1121.
Cuisine: ENGLISH. **Reservations:** Recommended. **Tube:** Bank or St. Paul's.
$ Prices: "The Restaurant," appetizers £2.50–£5.95 ($3.80–$8.90); main dishes
£5.50–£13.50 ($8.30–$20.30); glass of wine from £2 ($3). AE, DC, MC, V.
Open: Lunch only, Mon–Fri 11:30am–3pm. Pub, Mon–Fri 11:30am–8pm.

The Bow Wine Vaults has existed since long before the current wine-bar fad that
began in the 1970s and is now a firmly entrenched institution on the London scene.
One of the most famous wine bars of London, it attracts cost-conscious diners and
drinkers from the financial district who head below ground to its vaulted cellars.
Menu choices in the Cellar Grill, as it's called, include such traditional fare as
deep-fried Camembert, chicken Kiev, and a mixed grill, along with fish. More elegant
meals are served in the street-level dining room, called "The Restaurant," which offers
an English-inspired menu, including, perhaps, mussels in cider sauce, English wild
mushrooms in puff pastry, and individual servings of beef Wellington. Try the steak
with brown-butter sauce. Adjacent to the restaurant is a cocktail bar, popular with
City employees after work.

THE JAMAICA WINE HOUSE, St. Michael's Alley, off Cornhill, EC3. Tel.
071/626-9496.
Cuisine: ENGLISH. **Reservations:** Not accepted. **Tube:** Bank.

$ Prices: Bar snacks £1–£3 ($1.50–$4.50); lager £1.65–£1.95 ($2.50–$2.90). AE, MC, V.
Open: Lunch only, Mon–Fri 11:30am–3pm. Pub, Mon–Fri 11:30am–8pm.

The Jamaica Wine House is one of the first coffeehouses to be opened in England, and, reputedly, in the Western world. For years London merchants and daring sea captains came here to lace deals with rum and coffee. Nowadays, the two-level house dispenses beer, ale, lager, and fine wines, among them a variety of ports, to appreciative drinkers. The oak-paneled bar is at street level, attracting a jacket-and-tie crowd of investment bankers, whereas the basement bar is an even cozier retreat. You can order game pie and baked potatoes, toasted sandwiches, and such old English favorites as Lancashire hot pot or shepherd's pie, even Créole fish pie or goulash.

OLDE WINE SHADES, 6 Martin Lane, Cannon St., EC4. Tel. 071/626-6876.
Cuisine: ENGLISH. **Reservations:** Not required. **Tube:** Cannon Street.
$ Prices: Appetizers £2.50–£4.25 ($3.80–$6.40); main courses £3.50–£12 ($5.30–$18); wine by the glass £2.50 ($3.80). MC, V.
Open: Lunch only, Mon–Fri 11:30am–3pm. **Closed:** Bank holidays.

Dating from 1663, the Olde Wine Shades survived the Great Fire of 1666 and Hitler's bombs. It is the oldest wine house in The City. Near the Monument (a famous London landmark designed by Christopher Wren to commemorate the Great Fire of 1666), it is decorated with oil paintings and 19th-century political cartoons. It's also one of the many London bars that Dickens used to patronize. There is a restaurant downstairs, and you can order light meals upstairs, including Breton pâté and French bread with ham "off the bone." You can order jacket potatoes filled with cheese, venison pie with a salad garnish, or a large beef salad. Simple fare notwithstanding, men must wear jackets, collars, and ties.

YE OLDE WATLING, 29 Watling St., EC4. Tel. 071/248-6252.
Cuisine: ENGLISH. **Reservations:** Not accepted. **Tube:** Mansion House.
$ Prices: Fixed-price lunch £3.95–£5 ($5.90–$7.50); bar snacks from £1.60 ($2.40); beer from £1.70 ($2.60). AE, MC, V.
Open: Lunch only, Mon–Fri noon–2:30pm. Pub, Mon–Fri 11am–9pm.

Ye Olde Watling was built after the Great Fire of London. On the ground level is a mellow pub, and upstairs an intimate restaurant where, under oak beams and at trestle tables, you can have a simple choice of English main dishes for lunch. The menu varies daily by including the choice of four hot dishes, such as beef-and-ale pie, steak-and-kidney pie, seafood Mornay, lasagne, chili con carne, and usually a vegetarian dish. All are served with two vegetables or a salad, rice, or potatoes.

FLEET STREET

INEXPENSIVE

THE CHESHIRE CHEESE, Wine Office Court, 145 Fleet St., EC4. Tel. 071/353-6170.
Cuisine: ENGLISH. **Reservations:** Not required. **Tube:** St. Paul's.
$ Prices: Appetizers £2–£3.50 ($3–$5.30); main courses £6.25–£9 ($9.40–$13.50). AE, DC, MC, V.
Open: Lunch daily noon–2:30pm; dinner daily 6–9:30pm. Drinks and bar snacks, daily 11am–11pm.

 Set within a recently remodeled, carefully preserved building whose foundation was originally laid in the 13th century, this is one of the most famous of the old City chophouses and pubs. It was established in 1667, and claims to be the spot where Dr. Samuel Johnson (who lived within shooting distance) entertained his

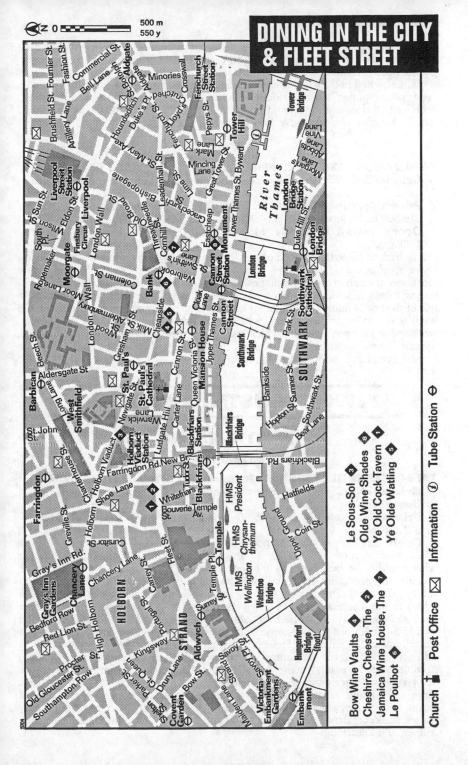

DINING IN THE CITY & FLEET STREET

N 0 — 500 m / 550 y

Bow Wine Vaults ◆4
Cheshire Cheese, The ◆2
Jamaica Wine House, The ◆7
Le Poulbot ◆6

Le Sous-Sol ◆3
Olde Wine Shades ◆8
Ye Old Cock Tavern ◆1
Ye Olde Watling ◆5

Church ✝   Post Office ⊠   Information ⓘ   Tube Station ⊖

admirers with his acerbic wit. Later, many of the ink-stained journalists and scandalmongers of 19th- and early 20th-century Fleet Street made its four-story premises their "local."

Within, you'll find six bars and three dining rooms. The house specialties include "ye famous pudding"—(steak, kidney, mushrooms, and game)—and Scottish roast beef, with Yorkshire pudding and horseradish sauce. Sandwiches, salads, and such standby favorites as steak-and-kidney pie are also available.

A PUB

YE OLD COCK TAVERN, 22 Fleet St., EC4. Tel. 071/353-8570.

Cuisine: ENGLISH. **Reservations:** Recommended. **Tube:** Temple or Chancery Lane.

$ Prices: Appetizers £2.50–£5.25 ($3.80–$7.90); main courses £8–£11 ($12–$16.50); buffet lunch £9.95 ($14.90); beer from £1.75 ($2.60). AE, DC, MC, V.

Open: Carvery, lunch only, Mon–Fri noon–3pm. Pub, Mon–Fri 11:30am–10:30pm.

Dating back to 1549, this tavern boasts a long line of such ghostly literary comrades as Dickens, who once favored this ancient pub with their presence. Samuel Pepys mentioned the pub in one of his diaries, and Lord Tennyson referred to it in one of his poems, a copy of which is framed and proudly displayed near the front entrance. It's one of the few buildings in London to have survived the Great Fire in 1666. At street level, you can order a pint as well as snack-bar food. You can also order steak-and-kidney pie or a cold chicken-and-beef plate with salad. At the Carvery upstairs, a meal includes a choice of appetizers, followed by all the roasts you can carve—beef, lamb, pork, or turkey.

7. WESTMINSTER & VICTORIA

WESTMINSTER

MODERATE

TATE GALLERY RESTAURANT, Millbank, SW1. Tel. 071/834-6754.

Cuisine: ENGLISH. **Reservations:** Required 2 days in advance. **Tube:** Pimlico. **Bus:** 88.

$ Prices: Appetizers £3.75–£6 ($5.60–$9); main courses £9.25–£14.50 ($13.90–$21.80). MC, V.

Open: Lunch only, Mon–Sat noon–3pm.

The restaurant in the Tate Gallery is particularly attractive to wine fanciers, offering what may be the best bargains for superior wines to be found anywhere in the country. It is especially strong on Bordeaux and burgundies. Management keeps the markup on wines ranging from 40% to about 65%, rather than the 100% to 200% added to the wholesale price in other restaurants. In fact, the prices here are even lower than they are in most retail wine shops. Wines begin at £8.50 ($12.80) per bottle or £1.75 ($2.60) per glass. Wine connoisseurs frequently come here for lunch and never look at the paintings. However, if you're looking for food instead of (or in addition to) wine, the restaurant specializes in English cuisine. You can choose "umbles paste" (a pâté), "hindle wakes" (cold stuffed chicken and prunes), "pye with fruyt ryfshews" (fruit tart topped with meringue), or perhaps just one of "Joan Cromwell's grand sallets," made of raisins, almonds, cucumbers, olives, pickled beans, and shrimp, among other ingredients. Or you might prefer more customary dishes: steak, omelets, ham, roasts of beef and lamb, fish, and the traditional steak, kidney, and mushroom pie.

VICTORIA

MODERATE

KEN LO'S MEMORIES OF CHINA, 67–69 Ebury St., SW1. Tel. 071/730-7734.

Cuisine: CHINESE. **Reservations:** Required. **Tube:** Victoria Station.

$ **Prices:** Appetizers £3.65–£8.80 ($5.50–$13.20); main courses £8.40–£26.50 ($12.60–$39.80); fixed-price meal £18.50 ($27.80) at lunch, £24–£27 ($36–$40.50) at dinner. AE, DC, MC, V.

Open: Lunch Mon–Sat noon–2:30pm; dinner Mon–Sat 7–10:45pm.

Ken Lo's is considered the finest Chinese restaurant in London by many food critics. The restaurant was founded by Ken Lo, whose grandfather was the Chinese ambassador to the Court of St. James (he was knighted by Queen Victoria in 1880). Mr. Lo has written more than 30 cookbooks and once had his own TV cooking show. His "Memories" in Belgravia has been called "a gastronomic bridge between London and China." Against a modern minimalist decor, such dishes as Cantonese quick-fried beef in oyster sauce, lobster with handmade noodles, pomegranate prawn balls, and "bang bang chicken" (a Szechuan dish) are served.

VERY SIMPLY NICO, 48A Rochester Row, SW1. Tel. 071/630-8061.

Cuisine: FRENCH. **Reservations:** Required. **Tube:** Victoria Station.

$ **Prices:** 3-course fixed-price meal £23 ($34.50) at lunch, £25 ($37.50) at dinner. AE, MC, V.

Open: Lunch Mon–Fri noon–2pm; dinner Mon–Sat 6:45–11:15pm.

This place was created in a moment of whimsy by Nico Ladenis, the owner of a grander and more expensive restaurant, Nico at Ninety (see "Mayfair," above). Run by his sous-chef, Very Simply Nico is, in the words of Nico, "cheap and cheerful." Wood floors seem to reverberate with the din of contented diners, who pack in here daily at snug tables. The food is often simply prepared and invariably French inspired, with fresh ingredients handled deftly in the kitchen. The fixed-price menu changes frequently.

A WINE BAR

EBURY WINE BAR, 139 Ebury St., SW1. Tel. 071/730-5447.

Cuisine: CONTINENTAL. **Reservations:** Recommended. **Tube:** Victoria Station or Sloane Square.

$ **Prices:** Appetizers £2.50–£4.75 ($3.80–$7.10); main courses £7.25–£11 ($10.90–$16.50); fixed-price Sun lunch £8.95 ($13.40); glass of wine from £2.20 ($3.30). AE, DC, MC, V.

Open: Lunch Mon–Sat 11am–3pm, Sun noon–2:45pm; dinner daily 6–10:30pm.

The Ebury is a wine bar and bistro, convenient for dining or drinking, that attracts a youthful clientele to its often-crowded but always-atmospheric precincts. Wine is sold either by the glass or bottle. You can always get an enticing plat du jour, such as traditional beef Wellington or perhaps one of the grilled filet steaks.

8. KNIGHTSBRIDGE & BELGRAVIA

KNIGHTSBRIDGE

EXPENSIVE

WALTONS OF WALTON STREET, 121 Walton St., SW3. Tel. 071/584-0204.

Cuisine: INTERNATIONAL. **Reservations:** Recommended. **Tube:** South Kensington or Knightsbridge.

$ Prices: Appetizers £6–£16.50 ($9–$24.80); main courses £13.50–£17.50 ($20.30–$26.30); "Simply Waltons" fixed-price lunch £14.75 ($22.10); 3-course fixed-price Sun lunch £16.50 ($24.80); late-night fixed-price supper £22 ($33). AE, DC, MC, V.

Open: Lunch Mon–Sat 12:30–2:30pm, Sun 12:30–2pm; dinner Mon–Sat 7:30–11pm, Sun 7:30–10:30pm; late-night supper daily from 10pm.

Waltons is elegant and intimate, serving some of the best food in London. A posh rendezvous place, it offers the best-quality fresh produce from local and European markets served with flair in surroundings of silk walls and floral decorations. Its chefs prepare a refined international cuisine, featuring such British dishes as roast breast of Norfolk duckling or roast filet of Welsh lamb with crab. Specialties include terrine of truffled foie gras, whole roast lobster with coriander and ginger, and orange mousse on a white-chocolate sauce. Waltons, long a favorite with the Harrods lady-shoppers crowd, has a reputation for being expensive. However, it has special-value fixed-price menus. The wine list, which features the best champagne list in London, is wide ranging, from Australia to California.

MODERATE

GEORGIAN RESTAURANT, in Harrods Department Store, 87–135 Brompton Rd., SW1. Tel. 071/581-1656.

Cuisine: ENGLISH. **Reservations:** Recommended but accepted only for lunch. **Tube:** Knightsbridge.

$ Prices: 3-course fixed-price lunch £18.50 ($27.80); appetizers £3.15–£10.50 ($4.70–$15.80); main courses £10.95–£15.95 ($16.40–$23.90); sandwiches and pastries at teatime £8.95 ($13.40). AE, DC, MC, V.

Open: Lunch Mon–Sat noon–2:45pm; tea Mon–Sat 3:45–5:15pm.

 The Georgian Restaurant lies on the top floor of this fabled emporium, under elaborate ceilings and Belle Epoque skylights. It's one of the neighborhood's most appealing lunchtime restaurants. Lunch and afternoon tea are served. One of the rooms, big enough for a ballroom, features a pianist, whose music trills among the crystals of the chandeliers.

At lunchtime there's a sprawling buffet filled with cold meats and an array of fresh salads. Guests who want a hot meal can head for the carvery section where a uniformed crew of chefs dish out such offerings as Yorkshire pudding with roast beef, poultry, fish, and pork. First courses and desserts are brought to your table.

SAN LORENZO, 22 Beauchamp Place, SW3. Tel. 071/584-1074.

Cuisine: ITALIAN. **Reservations:** Required. **Tube:** Knightsbridge.

$ Prices: Appetizers £4.50–£8 ($6.80–$12); main courses £9.50–£17 ($14.30–$25.50). No credit cards.

Open: Lunch Mon–Sat 12:30–3pm; dinner Mon–Sat 7:30–11:30pm.

This fashionable modern place, a 1987 debutant, is by now firmly established on the London scene, not only among artists and writers, but among models and photographers as well. It is the favorite of Princess Di. Reliability is the keynote of the cuisine, that and good-quality produce, often seasoned with fresh herbs. Nearly everything on the menu is delectable, from the homemade fettuccine with salmon to the carpaccio, and certainly the risotto with fresh asparagus. You can also order such traditional regional Italian dishes as salt cod with polenta or a bollito misto, going on to fried calamari or partridge in a white wine sauce. The veal piccata is exceptionally good.

PUBS & WINE BARS

BILL BENTLEY'S, 31 Beauchamp Place, SW3. Tel. 071/589-5080.

Cuisine: ENGLISH. **Reservations:** Recommended. **Tube:** Knightsbridge.
$ Prices: Appetizers £3.50–£7.75 ($5.30–$11.60); main courses £7–£16 ($10.50–$24); glass of wine from £1.80 ($2.70). MC, V.
Open: Lunch Mon–Sat noon–2:30pm; dinner Mon–Sat 6–10:30pm.

Bill Bentley's stands right on this fashionable restaurant- and boutique-lined block. Its wine list is varied and reasonable, including a good selection of Bordeaux. Many visitors come here just to sample the wines, including some "New World" choices along with popular French selections. In summer, a garden patio is used. If you don't care for the formality of the restaurant, you can order from the wine-bar menu which begins with half a dozen oysters, or else you can enjoy the chef's fish soup with croutons and rouille. Main dishes include Bill Bentley's famous fish cakes, served with tomato sauce, and the day's specialties are written on a blackboard. In keeping with contemporary trends in London dining, the menu has been simplified and is somewhat less expensive than before. The carte is changed frequently, but typical dishes might include duck breast salad with a beetroot vinaigrette as an appetizer, followed by pan-fried wing of skate with lemon and capers, or salmon *en croûte* with hollandaise sauce. All main dishes are served with a selection of fresh vegetables.

LE METRO, 28 Basil St., SW3. Tel. 071/589-6286.
Cuisine: CONTINENTAL. **Reservations:** Accepted only for large parties.
Tube: Knightsbridge.
$ Prices: Appetizers £2.75–£4.65 ($4.10–$7); main courses £5.35–£8.55 ($8–$12.80); glass of wine £1.95 ($2.90). AE, MC, V.
Open: Mon–Fri noon–10:30pm, Sat 7:30am–4pm.

Standing around the corner from Harrods department store, Le Metro draws a fashionable crowd to its precincts in the basement. You can order special wines by the glass instead of by the bottle. A *cruover* preserves their freshness. This wine bar, owned by David and Margaret Levin, serves good, solid, and reliable food prepared with flair. The menu is frequently changed, but might include an intriguing squid-and-mussel risotto with pine nuts and basil, or grilled *gambas* (shrimp) with garlic, olive oil, and herbs, perhaps spicy baby chicken with turmeric and a warm potato salad.

THE NAG'S HEAD, 53 Kinnerton St., SW1. Tel. 071/235-1135.
Cuisine: ENGLISH. **Reservations:** Not required. **Tube:** Knightsbridge.
$ Prices: Appetizers £1.95–£2.85 ($2.90–$4.30); main dishes £3.50–£3.95 ($5.30–$5.90); beer from £1.80 ($2.70). No credit cards.
Open: Mon–Sat 11am–11pm, Sun noon–3pm and 7–10:30pm.

The Nag's Head is snuggled on a "back street," a short walk from the deluxe Berkeley Hotel. Dating from 1780, it is said to be the smallest pub in London, although others also claim that distinction. The pub is housed in what was previously a jail. In 1921 it was sold for £12 and 6p—what might be called a steal. Take your drink up front or wander to a tiny little bar in the rear. The pub is warm and cozy, with a welcoming staff. Here, in the midst of a cosmopolitan clientele, you might enjoy "real ale sausage" (made with pork and ale), or perhaps shepherd's pie, steak-and-mushroom pie, even quiche of the day. The pub is patronized by newspaper people, musicians, and what one columnist called "mechanics and gay young things."

BELGRAVIA

EXPENSIVE

OLIVO, 21 Eccleston St., SW1. Tel. 071/730-2505.
Cuisine: ITALIAN. **Reservations:** Required. **Tube:** Victoria Station.
$ Prices: Appetizers £3.50–£5.50 ($5.30–$8.30); main courses £8–£15.50 ($12–$23.30); fixed-price lunch £13–£15 ($19.50–$22.50). AE, MC, V.

Open: Lunch Mon–Fri noon–2:30pm; dinner Mon–Fri 7–11pm. **Closed:** Last 3 weeks in Aug.

Located on the periphery of Belgravia, Olivo is the choice of many a discriminating London diner. The artfully simple decor mingles high-tech elements with bright colors, flowers, and imaginative lighting. The menu offers flavorful combinations whose ingredients are impeccably fresh. Vegetables—too often neglected in England—are perfectly cooked and beautifully served by the polite waiters. The restaurant's owners have set for themselves a lofty goal: to become the best Italian restaurant in London.

The menu is wisely limited but carefully chosen so that all ingredients will be fresh. You might begin with a grilled cuttlefish salad, perhaps even grilled vegetables flavored with basil. Several pasta dishes, including pumpkin ravioli with sage, can be ordered as an appetizer. Main dishes include grilled loin of pork with lentils, pan-fried calves' liver with marsala, and rabbit cooked in red wine with polenta. For dessert, try the pear cooked in red wine with cinnamon, followed by an espresso.

MODERATE

DRONES, 1 Pont St., SW1. Tel. 071/235-9638.

Cuisine: INTERNATIONAL. **Reservations:** Required. **Tube:** Sloane Square or Knightsbridge.

$ Prices: Appetizers £3.80–£5 ($5.70–$7.50); main courses £9.95–£16 ($14.90–$24). AE, DC, MC, V.

Open: Lunch Mon–Sat 12:30–2:45pm; dinner Mon–Sat 7:30–11pm.

Drones was labeled by one newspaper columnist as "the unofficial club for bright people at least half of whom seem to know each other." The late David Niven and friends launched this two-floor restaurant some years ago, and its reputation for charm and chic has spread. There is no elaborate menu and there are no fancy sauces—just simple but good food. At lunch have the cheese soufflé or salmon fish cakes and parsley sauce. For dinner, the calves' liver with bacon is superb (have it cooked pink if you prefer). As an appetizer, baby leaf spinach and bacon salad with shaved parmesan or scallops and frisée salad with garlic oil are good. Main-dish specialties are veal Pojarsky, or roast sea bass with a fondue of braised fennel or alternatively a Cornish crab salad. For your attention in the dessert department, try steamed ginger-and-treacle pudding or warm mango soufflé. The menu is wisely limited and changes monthly. Two plats du jour are featured. If you are lingering at the bar while waiting for a table (a likely possibility), take a look at the baby pictures of famous movie stars and pictures by award-winning young British artists—all of which are for sale. The decor is that of an Edwardian conservatory.

PUBS & WINE BARS

ANTELOPE, 22 Eaton Terrace, SW1. Tel. 071/730-7781.

Cuisine: ENGLISH. **Reservations:** Recommended for the upstairs dining room. **Tube:** Sloane Square.

$ Prices: Appetizers £1.75–£2.75 ($2.60–$4.10); main courses £7.85–£9 ($11.80–$13.50); Sun brunch £9.50 ($14.30); wine by the glass £2.20 ($3.30). MC, V.

Open: Lunch Mon–Sat 11am–3pm; brunch Sun noon–3pm. Pub, Mon–Sat 11am–11pm, Sun noon–3pm and 7:30–10:30pm.

Antelope is located on the fringe of Belgravia, at the gateway to Chelsea. This eatery caters to a hodgepodge of clients, aptly described as "people of all classes, colours, and creeds who repair for interesting discussion on a whole gamut of subjects, ranging from port to medieval, mid-European wicker-work, bed-bug traps, and for both mental and physical refreshment." It is also a base for English rugby aficionados (not to be confused with those who follow soccer).

At lunchtime, the ground-floor bar provides hot and cold pub food, but in the evening only drinks are served there. On the second floor (British first floor), food is served at lunch. The food is principally English, with steak-and-kidney pie and jugged hare among the specialties. Steaks are also served. On Sunday a two-course carvery meal costs £9.50 ($14.30).

GRENADIER, 18 Wilton Row, SW1. Tel. 071/235-3074.
   Cuisine: ENGLISH. **Reservations:** Recommended. **Tube:** Hyde Park Corner.
$ Prices: Appetizers £3.50–£8 ($5.30–$12); main courses £9.95–£17.55 ($14.90–$26.30); fixed-price lunch or dinner £25 ($37.50); wine by the glass £2 ($3). AE, DC, MC.
   Open: Lunch daily noon–3pm; dinner daily 5:30–11pm. **Closed:** Dec 24–26 and Jan 1.
Tucked away in a mews, Grenadier is one of London's numerous reputedly haunted pubs. Apart from the poltergeist, the basement also houses the original bar and skittles alley used by the Duke of Wellington's officers on leave from fighting Napoléon. The scarlet front door of the one-time officers' mess is guarded by a scarlet sentry box and shaded by a vine. The bar is nearly always crowded. Luncheons and dinners are offered daily—even on Sunday, when it is a tradition to drink Bloody Marys here. In the stalls along the side, you can order good-tasting fare based on seasonal ingredients. Filet of beef Wellington is a specialty; other good dishes include pork Grenadier and chicken-and-Stilton roulade. Snacks are available at the bar if you don't want a full meal.

STAR TAVERN, 6 Belgrave Mews West, SW1. Tel. 071/235-3019.
   Cuisine: ENGLISH. **Reservations:** Not accepted. **Tube:** Knightsbridge or Hyde Park.
$ Prices: Pub snacks £2.50–£4 ($3.80–$6) at lunch, £4.50–£5.50 ($6.80–$8.30) at dinner; wine by the glass £1.75 ($2.60). No credit cards.
   Open: Lunch Mon–Fri 11:30am–3pm; dinner Mon–Fri 6:30–8:45pm. Pub, Mon–Thurs 11:30am–3pm and 5–11pm, Fri 11:30am–11pm, Sat 11:30am–3pm and 6:30–11pm, Sun noon–3pm and 7–10:30pm. **Closed:** Dec 25.
Set in a Georgian mews, the Star Tavern is one of the most colorful pubs in the West End, lying behind a picture-postcard-type facade. In winter it's one of the coziest havens around, with two fireplaces going. Groups of office workers descend after work, staking out their territory. The place is attractive inside, with Victorian walls and banquettes beneath 19th-century Victorian moldings. You can order such dishes as baby spring chicken, sirloin steak, or, perhaps, a vegetable quiche. There is no table service; patrons place their orders at the bar.

9. CHELSEA & CHELSEA HARBOUR

CHELSEA

VERY EXPENSIVE

LA TANTE CLAIRE, 68–69 Royal Hospital Rd., SW3. Tel. 071/352-6045.
   Cuisine: FRENCH. **Reservations:** Required. **Tube:** Sloane Square.
$ Prices: Appetizers £17.50–£19.50 ($26.30–$29.30); main courses £22.50–£26 ($33.80–$39); fixed-price lunch £23.50 ($35.30). Minimum charge £45 ($67.50) per person. AE, DC, MC, V.

Open: Lunch Mon–Fri 12:30–2pm; dinner Mon–Fri 7–11pm. **Closed:** Dec 25 and Jan 1.

★ The quality of its cuisine is so legendary that this "Aunt Claire" has become, in the eyes of many critics, the leading choice among the capital's gaggle of French restaurants. It's considered a culinary monument of the highest order. A discreet doorbell, set into the Aegean-blue-and-white facade, prompts an employee to usher you politely inside. There, birchwood and chrome trim, bouquets of flowers, and a modernized, vaguely Hellenistic decor complements an array of paintings that might have been inspired by Jean Cocteau.

Pierre Koffman is the celebrated chef, creating such specialties as ravioli stuffed with frog meat. Every gastronome in London talks about the pigs' trotters stuffed with morels and the exquisite sauces that complement many of the dishes. These include grilled scallops served on a bed of squid-ink sauce, baked filet of turbot with cabbage and fresh vegetables cooked in a consommé with preserved duck, or duck in red-wine sauce and confit. For dessert, try a caramelized ice cream soufflé with hazelnuts and a coulis of raspberries or the pistachio soufflé.

EXPENSIVE

CHELSEA ROOM, in the Hyatt Carlton Tower, 2 Cadogan Place, SW1. Tel. 071/235-5411.

Cuisine: FRENCH. **Reservations:** Required. **Tube:** Knightsbridge.

$ **Prices:** Appetizers £4–£11 ($6–$16.50); main courses £16–£32 ($24–$48); fixed-price lunch £22.50 ($33.80); fixed-price dinner £30.50 ($45.80). AE, DC, MC, V.

Open: Lunch daily 12:30–2:45pm; dinner Mon–Sat 7–11pm, Sun 7–10pm.

The Chelsea Room is a superb restaurant, one of the best in London, lying inside the walls of one of Hyatt's finest international properties (recommended in Chapter 4, "London Accommodations"). The dining room's combination of haute cuisine, stylish clientele, and elegant decor make it a much sought-after place for lunch or dinner. It's one floor above the lobby level of the hotel at the end of a paneled hallway reminiscent of something in a private Edwardian house. The color scheme is tasteful and subdued in grays, beiges, and soft greens.

The kitchen is run by maître cuisinier de France Bernard Gaume. Monsieur Gaume has pleased palates at some of the leading and most famous hotels in Europe, including L'Abbaye in Tallories in the French Alps, the Savoy in London, and Hôtel des Bergues in Geneva. His portions are large and satisfying, and their presentation shows his extraordinary flair. Highly professional dishes, original offerings, time-tested classics, and very fresh ingredients are his forte. The menu will change by the time of your visit, but to give you an idea, you are likely to be served baked sea bass in a light sauce with leeks and a garnish of salmon and Russian caviar, roast partridge served on a bed of savoy cabbage, or small filets of venison in a game sauce with port and a medley of multicolored peppercorns with juniperberries. His desserts require a separate menu, ranging from a light chestnut mousse with ginger sauce to a chilled hazelnut parfait in a light Cointreau sauce. Wedgwood plates with the restaurant's cockerel motif adorn each place setting.

MODERATE

ENGLISH GARDEN, 10 Lincoln St., SW3. Tel. 071/584-7272.

Cuisine: ENGLISH. **Reservations:** Required. **Tube:** Sloane Square.

$ **Prices:** Appetizers £3.60–£11.60 ($5.40–$17.40); main courses £12.75–£15.60 ($19.10–$23.40); 3-course fixed-price lunch £14.75 ($22.10). AE, DC, MC, V.

Open: Lunch Mon–Sat 12:30–2:30pm, Sun 12:30–2pm; dinner Mon–Sat 7:30–11:30pm, Sun 7–10pm. **Closed:** Dec 25–26.

Here in this historic Chelsea town house, the decor is pretty and lighthearted. The

Garden Room on the ground floor is whitewashed brick with panels of large stylish flowers. The attractive pelmets are in vivid flower colors with stark-white curtains. Rattan chairs in a Gothic theme and candy-pink napery complete the scene. With the domed conservatory roofs and banks of plants, the atmosphere is relaxing and pleasant.

The menu is extensive and includes plenty of salads and fish. Interesting dishes are a checkerboard of freshwater fish, including a steamed fish of the day, or roast rack of Welsh lamb with a hazelnut-bread crust. The chef's daily choices are included in a special luncheon menu. A comprehensive wine list is available, and an excellent French house wine is always obtainable.

ENGLISH HOUSE, 3 Milner St., SW3. Tel. 071/584-3002.
   Cuisine: BRITISH. **Reservations:** Required. **Tube:** Sloane Square.
$ **Prices:** Appetizers £3.50–£9.75 ($5.30–$14.60); main courses £8.75–£15.60 ($13.10–$23.40); 3-course fixed-price lunch £14.75 ($22.10). AE, DC, MC, V.
   Open: Lunch Mon–Sat 12:30–2:30pm, Sun 12:30–2pm; dinner Mon–Sat 7:30–11:30pm, Sun 7–10pm. **Closed:** Dec 25–26.

This is another design creation of Michael Smith, who did the English Garden, previewed above. The English House is a tiny restaurant in the heart of Chelsea, where dining is like being a guest in an elegant private house, its decor providing both spectacle and atmosphere. Blues and terra-cotta predominate. The walls are clad in a printed cotton depicting a traditional English design of autumn leaves and black currants. The fireplace creates a homelike environment, and the collection of interesting and beautiful furniture adds to the background. Attention has been paid to detail, and even the saltcellars are Victorian in origin.

The food is British, with such succulent offerings as roast rack of Welsh lamb with minted apple jelly, seared breast of duck with a spicy plum sauce, or filet of beef with a wild mushroom and Madeira cream sauce. Summer berries predominate on the "pudding" menu in season, including a bowl of fresh berries laced with elderflower syrup. Another offering is "A Phrase of Apples," the chef's adaptation of a 17th-century recipe for a delectable apple pancake.

GAVVERS, 61–63 Lower Sloane St., SW1. Tel. 071/730-5983.
   Cuisine: FRENCH. **Reservations:** Required. **Tube:** Sloane Square.
$ **Prices:** Fixed-price meal £12.50–£14.75 ($18.80–$22.10) at lunch, £22.65–£28.25 ($34–$42.40) at dinner. DC, MC, V.
   Open: Lunch Mon–Fri noon–2:30pm; dinner Mon–Sat 7–11pm.

S This was the location of the original Le Gavroche (now the premier restaurant of London). But Le Gavroche moved to Mayfair in 1981, and the owners, the Roux brothers, turned their former premises into this winning choice for truly French dining in an informal atmosphere. It is chic and sophisticated, and its atmosphere is soft and inviting. Considering the quality of the food, this is one of the best value-for-money dining choices among the French restaurants in London. Fixed-price menus change daily but are likely to include such main dishes as lightly roasted salmon with fresh spring vegetables, breast of duck stuffed with black olives, or rolled, boned, and stuffed quail with braised chicory.

PUBS & WINE BARS

THE FRONT PAGE, 35 Old Church St., SW3. Tel. 071/352-0648.
   Cuisine: CONTINENTAL. **Reservations:** Not required. **Tube:** Sloane Square or South Kensington.
$ **Prices:** Bar snacks £2.50–£5.70 ($3.80–$8.60); main courses £4.70–£5.70 ($7.10–$8.60). MC, V.
   Open: Food service, daily noon–2:15pm and 7–10:15pm. Pub, daily 9am–3pm and 5:30–11pm. **Closed:** Dec 24–26.

The Front Page is favored by young Chelsea professionals who like the mellow atmosphere provided by its wood paneling, wooden tables, and pews and benches. In one section an open fire burns on cold nights. The pub stands in an expensive residential section of Chelsea and is a good, safe place to go for a drink, with lager beginning at £1.80 ($2.70). You can also order bottled Budweiser. Look at the blackboard for a listing of the daily specials, which might include ratatouille au gratin or lamb curry, perhaps even mackerel with a kumquat sauce. You might begin with a homemade soup du jour. Place your order at the bar and a waiter will bring the food to you.

KING'S HEAD AND EIGHT BELLS, 50 Cheyne Walk, SW3. Tel. 071/352-1820.

Cuisine: ENGLISH. **Reservations:** Not accepted. **Tube:** Sloane Square.

$ Prices: Appetizers £2–£4.50 ($3–$6.80); main courses £4–£8.90 ($6–$13.40). AE, MC, V.

Open: Pub, Mon–Sat noon–11pm; Sun noon–3pm and 7–10:30pm. Food, Mon–Sat noon–3pm and 7–10pm, Sun noon–2:30pm and 7–10pm.

This is a historic Thames-side pub. Many distinguished personalities once lived in this area. A short stroll in the neighborhood will take you to the former homes of such personages as Carlyle, Swinburne, and George Eliot. In other days, press-gangs used to roam these parts of Chelsea seeking long travelers to abduct for a life at sea. Today it's popular with stage and TV celebrities as well as writers.

The best English beers are served here, as well as a good selection of reasonably priced wines. A refrigerated display case holds cold dishes and salads, and a hot counter features the homemade specials of the day, including at least one vegetable main dish.

CHELSEA HARBOUR

MODERATE

KEN LO'S MEMORIES OF CHINA, Harbour Yard, Chelsea Harbour, SW10. Tel. 071/352-4953.

Cuisine: CHINESE. **Reservations:** Required. **Transportation:** Chelsea Harbour Hoppa Bus C3 from Earl's Court or Kensington High Street Mon–Sat, or riverbus from Charing Cross Pier Mon–Fri; on Sun take a taxi.

$ Prices: Appetizers £3.85–£7 ($5.80–$10.50); main courses £5–£10 ($7.50–$15); fixed-price meal £10.85 ($16.30) at lunch, £24 ($36) at dinner. AE, DC, MC, V.

Open: Lunch Mon–Sat noon–2:30pm; dinner 7–10:45pm; brunch Sun noon–2:30pm; dim sum bar Mon–Fri noon–2:30pm.

This is the far-flung branch of Ken Lo's (see above). Many people like to make an excursion to this modern "village" of London, with its marina complex. Mr. Lo chose a riverside site for his second restaurant, perhaps recalling in his "memory bank" his boyhood in Foochow on the banks of the Ming River. The restaurant is decorated in blue and gold, the colors of the Ming Dynasty. The cuisine wanders from region to region of China, with an emphasis on fish and seafood. Specialties include steamed sea bass, Mongolian barbecued lamb, and chicken in a hot black-bean sauce.

INEXPENSIVE

DEALS RESTAURANT AND DINER, Harbour Yard, Chelsea Harbour, SW10. Tel. 071/352-5887.

Cuisine: INTERNATIONAL. **Reservations:** Recommended. **Transportation:**

Chelsea Harbour Hoppa Bus C3 from Earl's Court or Kensington High Street
Mon–Sat, or riverbus from Charing Cross Mon–Fri; on Sun take a taxi.
$ Prices: Appetizers £3–£5 ($4.50–$7.50); main courses £5–£14 ($7.50–$21).
AE, MC, V.
Open: Mon–Sat 11am–11pm.

After the Queen Mother arrived here on a barge to order a Dealsburger, the success of
the place was assured. Deals is co-owned by Princess Margaret's son, Viscount Linley,
and Lord Lichfield. The early 1900s atmosphere includes ceiling fans and bentwood
banquettes. The food is American diner style with a strong Eastern influence: try
teriyaki burgers, prawn curry, spareribs, a vegetarian dish, and finish with New
England apple pie.

A WINE BAR

**BOATERS WINE BAR, Harbour Yard, Chelsea Harbour, SW10. Tel.
071/352-3687.**
Cuisine: ENGLISH. **Reservations:** Not required. **Transportation:** Riverbus
from Charing Cross Mon–Fri, or a Chelsea Harbour Hoppa Bus (C3) from Earl's
Court or Kensington High Street Mon–Sat; on Sun take a taxi.
$ Prices: Sandwiches, cheese plates, and salads £2–£3 ($3–$4.50); main courses
£4–£5 ($6–$7.50). AE, MC.
Open: Mon–Fri 11am–11pm, Sun noon–3pm.

Boaters occupies premises in one of London's new "villages," Chelsea Harbour.
Well-heeled local flat dwellers who own the soaringly expensive apartments in this
complex often come here to drink champagne by the bottle while munching from
complimentary bowls of popcorn on the long wooden bar counter. Visitors from all
over the world pour in here as well. Most of the emphasis at the bar is on an impressive
array of bottled beers, beers on tap, and wine by either the bottle or the glass; only a
minimum array of liquor is available. Sandwiches, cheese plates, salads, and such main
dishes as chili con carne and mushroom-and-leek Stroganoff are available throughout
the day. An impressive carte offers wine by the glass, costing from £1.95 ($2.90) for the
house version.

10. KENSINGTON & SOUTH KENSINGTON

KENSINGTON

MODERATE

**LAUNCESTON PLACE RESTAURANT, 1A Launceston Place, W8. Tel.
071/937-6912.**
Cuisine: BRITISH. **Reservations:** Required. **Tube:** Gloucester Road.
$ Prices: Appetizers £4–£7.50 ($6–$11.30); main courses £12–£14.50 ($18–
$21.80); fixed-price lunch £12.50 ($18.80) and £15.50 ($23.30). MC, V.
Open: Lunch Sun–Fri 12:30–2:30pm; dinner Mon–Sat 7–11:30pm.

Launceston Place has a kind of urban chic, situated in an affluent, almost villagelike
neighborhood, a place where many Londoners would like to live if only they could
afford it. The restaurant is a series of uncluttered Victorian parlors illuminated in the
rear by a skylight at lunch.

Since its opening in the spring of 1986, Launceston Place has been known for its new British cuisine, including such dishes as curried parsnip soup, Lancashire hot pot, roast mallard with cranberries, noisettes of hare with grapes and chanterelles, or stuffed breast of guinea fowl with chestnut purée and celery. Roast grouse is also featured. For an appetizer, try such delights as a galette of wood pigeon with leeks, foie gras, and oyster mushrooms, or ravioli of braised oxtails, a first for many diners.

INEXPENSIVE

PERSEPOLIS, 39 Kensington High St., W8. Tel. 071/937-3555.
   Cuisine: PERSIAN. **Reservations:** Not required. **Tube:** High Street Kensington.
   $ Prices: Appetizers £2–£3 ($3–$4.50); main courses £6–£15 ($9–$22.50). AE, DC, MC, V.
   Open: Daily noon–11pm.

Persepolis is a good representative sample of Iranian cooking, which is still called Persian in many culinary circles. The restaurant is sleek, modern, and thoroughly tasteful. A small, subtly lit place, it features picture windows viewing the street. The only distinctive Persian features are friezes on the walls showing winged lions and spade-bearded ancient kings illuminated by colored lanterns.

Appetizers include homemade creamy yogurt with either chopped-mint-flavored cucumber or chopped spinach flavored with fried onions. For a main dish, you might choose such traditional dishes as a quarter chicken cooked with grated walnuts and served with a pomegranate purée, or finely chopped lamb, eggplant, and split peas cooked with tomato purée. Baklava and *halva shekari* (a sesame-seed concoction) are among the desserts.

PHOENICIA, 11 Abingdon Rd., W8. Tel. 071/937-0120.
   Cuisine: LEBANESE. **Reservations:** Required. **Tube:** High Street Kensington.
   $ Prices: Appetizers £2.40–£4.85 ($3.60–$7.30); main courses £6.70–£10.70 ($10.10–$16.10); buffet lunch £8.95 ($13.40); fixed-price dinner £14.50–£26.50 ($21.80–$39.80). AE, DC, MC, V.
   Open: Daily 12:15–11:45pm.

Phoenicia is highly regarded, both for the quality of its Lebanese cuisine and its moderate prices. The food is outstanding in its presentation and freshness. For the best value, go for lunch when you can enjoy a buffet of more than a dozen *meze* (appetizers), which are presented in little pottery dishes. Each day at lunch the chef prepares two or three home-cooked dishes to tempt your taste buds, including, for example, chicken in garlic sauce or stuffed lamb with vegetables. Many Lebanese patrons begin their meal with the apéritif "arak," a liqueur some have compared to ouzo. You can select as an appetizer such classic Middle Eastern dishes as hummus or stuffed vine leaves. In a clay oven the kitchen staff bakes its own bread and makes two different types of pizza. Minced lamb, spicy and well flavored, is the eternal favorite. Various charcoal-grilled dishes are also offered.

SOUTH KENSINGTON

EXPENSIVE

BIBENDUM/THE OYSTER BAR, 81 Fulham Rd., SW3. Tel. 071/581-5817.
   Cuisine: FRENCH/MEDITERRANEAN. **Reservations:** Required in Bibendum; not accepted in Oyster Bar. **Tube:** South Kensington.
   $ Prices: Appetizers £8.50–£18.50 ($12.80–$27.80); main courses £12–£19 ($18–$28.50); 3-course fixed-price lunch £25 ($37.50); cold shellfish platter in Oyster Bar £18.50 ($27.80) per person. MC, V.

Open: Bibendum, lunch daily 12:30–2:30pm; dinner daily 7–11:30pm. Oyster Bar, Mon–Sat noon–10:30pm, Sun noon–3pm and 7–11:30pm.

★ Considered one of the most gastronomically desirable restaurants in London, this fashionable eating place occupies two floors of a building that is considered one of the art deco masterpieces of London. Built in 1911, it housed the British headquarters of the Michelin tire company. Bibendum, the more visible eatery, lies one floor above street level in a white-tiled art deco–inspired room whose stained-glass windows, streaming sunlight, and chic clientele make meals extremely pleasant. Menu items are carefully planned interpretations of seasonal ingredients, known for their freshness and simplicity. The menu on the day of your arrival might include porcini risotto, deep-fried spinach cakes with anchovy-flavored hollandaise, grilled focaccia, smoked eel with potato pancakes and horseradish sauce, boeuf bourguignonne, rabbit with polenta and aïoli, superfresh preparations of fish-and-chips, roasted rabbit in pepper sauce, pink duck slices with cotechino sausages and rosemary-flavored lentils, and grilled veal kidneys with mustard sauce and bacon.

Simpler meals and cocktails are available on the building's street level, in the Oyster Bar. The bar-style menu and 1930s-style decor stress fresh shellfish presented in the traditional French style, on ice-covered platters occasionally adorned with strands of seaweed.

TURNER'S, 87–89 Walton St., SW3. Tel. 071/584-6711.

Cuisine: CONTINENTAL. **Reservations:** Required. **Tube:** South Kensington.

$ **Prices:** Fixed-price lunch £15.75–£18.50 ($23.60–$27.80) Mon–Fri, £18.50 ($27.80) Sun; 4-course fixed-price dinner £23.50 £32 ($35.30–$48). AE, DC, MC, V.

Open: Lunch Sun–Fri 12:30–2:45pm; dinner Mon–Sat 7:30–11pm, Sun 7:30–10pm. **Closed:** 1 week at Christmas.

This restaurant is named after Brian J. Turner, the accomplished London chef who gained fame at a number of establishments he didn't own, including the Capital Hotel. As one critic aptly put it, his food comes not only fresh from the market that day but "from the heart." He had early roots in Yorkshire, but he surely didn't learn his refined cuisine working in his father's transport "caff" in Leeds. In London, he paid his dues, so to speak, working in such hotels as the Savoy and Claridge's before achieving his own place in the culinary sun.

His cooking has been called "cuisine à la Brian Turner," meaning he doesn't seem to imitate anyone, but sets his own goals and standards. Try, for example, his pigeon breasts in a red-wine sauce, English duck with Thai herbs, or a roast rack of lamb with an herb crust. You might begin with a hot crab mousse or a cold creamy smoked haddock.

MODERATE

BOMBAY BRASSERIE, Courtfield Close, adjoining Bailey's Hotel, SW7. Tel. 071/370-4040.

Cuisine: INDIAN. **Reservations:** Required. **Tube:** Gloucester Road.

$ **Prices:** Appetizers £3.50–£5.50 ($5.30–$8.30); main courses £10.50–£20.50 ($15.80–$30.80); buffet lunch £13.50 ($20.30). MC, V.

Open: Buffet lunch daily 12:30–3pm; dinner Mon–Sat 7:30pm–midnight, Sun 7:30–11:30pm. **Closed:** Dec 26–27.

By anyone's estimation, this is the finest, most popular, and most talked-about Indian restaurant in London. Established in 1982, with a cavernous trio of rooms, it is staffed with one of the capital's most accommodating teams of Indian waiters, each one willing and very able to advise you on the spice-laden delicacies that thousands of years of Indian culinary tradition have developed. Lattices cover the windows, dhurrie rugs the floors, and sepia Raj pictures of imperial Britain at its height adorn the walls.

Before heading in to dinner, you might enjoy a drink amid the wicker chairs of the pink-and-white bar; the atmosphere there has often been compared to Singapore's Raffles. The bartender's specialty is a mango Bellini.

One look at the menu and you're launched on "A Passage to India," a grand culinary tour of the subcontinent: tandoori scallops, fish with mint chutney, chicken tikka (a dish from the Hindu Kush mountains), *sali boti* (mutton with apricots, a famous Parsi wedding dish), and whole meals for vegetarians. One corner of the menu is reserved for Goan cookery, that part of India that was seized from Portugal in 1961. The cookery of North India is represented by Mughlai specialties. Reflecting royal traditions of the Mughal emperors, it includes the famous Muslim pilaf specialty, chicken biryani. Under the category "Some Like It Hot," you'll find such dishes as mirchi korma Kashmiri style, a favorite of frequent customer Faye Dunaway.

HILAIRE, 68 Old Brompton Rd., SW7. Tel. 071/584-8993.

Cuisine: FRENCH. **Reservations:** Recommended. **Tube:** South Kensington.

$ Prices: Appetizers £4–£12.50 ($6–$18.80); main courses £12.50–£18 ($18.80–$27); 3-course fixed-price lunch £20 ($30); 3-course fixed-price dinner £25.50 ($38.30). AE, DC, MC, V.

Open: Lunch Mon–Fri noon–2:30pm; dinner Mon–Sat 7:30–11:30pm. **Closed:** Bank holidays.

Hilaire is a jovially cramped restaurant, housed in what was originally a Victorian storefront. Ceiling fans, apple-green walls, fresh flowers, and twin Corinthian columns provide the setting within which elegant French specialties are served. Chef Bryan Webb prepares a mixture of classical French and cuisine moderne that has made this one of the most stylish restaurants in London. An apéritif bar, extra tables, and a pair of semiprivate alcoves are in the lower dining room. A typical lunch might begin with a potato, *cèpes* (flap mushrooms), and truffle soup, then follow with pan-fried strips of calves' liver with sweetbreads, cream, and wild mushrooms, ending with a plum sorbet. The menu always reflects the best of the season's offerings, and main courses at dinner might include noisettes of venison with polenta, roast grouse with bread sauce, or sea bass with lentils.

ST. QUENTIN, 243 Brompton Rd., SW3. Tel. 071/581-5131.

Cuisine: FRENCH. **Reservations:** Required. **Tube:** Knightsbridge or South Kensington.

$ Prices: Appetizers £3.50–£9.80 ($5.30–$14.70); main courses £10.50–£14.50 ($15.80–$21.80); 3-course fixed-price lunch £12.50 ($18.80); 4-course fixed-price dinner £15.25 ($22.90). AE, DC, MC, V.

Open: Lunch Mon–Fri noon–3pm, Sat–Sun noon–4pm; dinner Sun–Fri 7pm–midnight, Sat 6:30pm–midnight.

Founded in 1980, St. Quentin is probably the most authentic-looking French brasserie in London. Modeled on the famous La Coupole in Paris (with its memories of "The Lost Generation"), it attracts many members of the French community in London (a good sign). The decor of mirrors and crystal chandeliers has been aptly named "glitzy," a word that might on occasion describe the clientele as well. Try such dishes as rack of lamb perfectly roasted and served very pink in the French style, roast quail with truffle and a foie gras sauce, and potted duck with a mustard sauce. Look also for the plats du jour. For an hors d'oeuvre, you might ask for a mixed salad with grilled goat's cheese or raw salmon marinated in lime and olive oil.

SYDNEY STREET, 4 Sydney St., SW3. Tel. 071/352-3433.

Cuisine: AUSTRALIAN. **Reservations:** Recommended. **Tube:** South Kensington.

$ Prices: Appetizers £3.50–£8.80 ($5.30–$13.20); main courses £13.80–£17.20 ($20.70–$25.80). AE, DC, MC, V.

Open: Lunch Mon–Fri noon–2:30pm; dinner Mon–Sat 7–11:30pm (last order).

Reeking of Australian bonhomie, and dedicated to the proposition that the Land Down Under can successfully appeal to a clientele of Londoners, this restaurant— better than perhaps any other in the northern hemisphere—combines the allure of a Grand Bistro with the earthy colors and themes of the Australian outback. The street level contains an affable bar where an array of whisky, Australian beers, and Australian and New Zealand wines might make an attractive prelude to a meal in the basement-level dining room. There, in an oceanic decor lined with fish tanks, postmodern metal tables and chairs padded with pink, green, and aquamarine vinyl, you can enjoy some of the most startling specialties in town. (Their creation requires an importation of most ingredients directly from Sydney, Australia, to Sydney Street.) The result might include a spicy version of Australian bouillabaisse made with sea creatures from the Barrier Reef; an Asian-style tartare of (raw) tuna and salmon served with *wasabi* (Japanese horseradish) and kumquats; roast filet of kangaroo stuffed with a nut-and-herb niçoise; a quick-seared filet of barramundi (a meaty and aromatic South Pacific sea fish) served with braised pineapple chutney, squid ink noodles, and spicy essence of carrots; many different preparations of Australian beef; and an Australian version of a freshwater crayfish known Down Under as a yabbie.

11. FULHAM

EXPENSIVE

BLUE ELEPHANT, 4–6 Fulham Broadway, SW6. Tel. 071/385-6595.
    Cuisine: THAI. **Reservations:** Required. **Tube:** Fulham Broadway.
$ Prices: Appetizers £5.75–£7.50 ($8.60–$11.30); main courses £6.50–£14.50 ($9.80–$21.80); fixed-price dinner £25–£28 ($37.50–$42). AE, DC, MC, V.
    Open: Lunch Sun–Fri noon–2:30pm; dinner daily 7pm–12:30am.
This is the counterpart of the famous L'Eléphant Bleu in Brussels. Located in a converted factory building, London's Blue Elephant has been all the rage since it opened in 1986; in fact, it's the leading Thai restaurant in the capital, where the competition is growing.

In an almost-magical-garden setting of lush tropical foliage, diners are treated to an array of ancient and modern MSG-free Thai food. You can begin with a "floating market" (shellfish in clear broth flavored with chili paste and lemongrass), going on to a splendid and varied selection of main courses, for which many of the ingredients have been flown in from Thailand. For a main course, you might try roast duck curry served in a clay cooking pot. The most popular choice is the £25 ($37.50) a head Royal Thai banquet.

MODERATE

TALL ORDERS, 676 Fulham Rd., SW6. Tel. 071/371-9673.
    Cuisine: MEDITERRANEAN. **Reservations:** Required. **Tube:** Parson's Green.
$ Prices: All dishes £3.50 ($5.30); 5-course fixed-price menu £15.75 ($23.60). AE, MC, V.
    Open: Dinner Mon–Fri 6:30pm–midnight, Sat–Sun noon–midnight.
The decor features an eye-catching, very large mural covering one entire wall, showing the crumbs and dregs of a completed and satisfying banquet. There's a central bar and minimalist trappings in dark blue and beige. The Mediterranean-inspired cuisine deliberately blurs the distinctions between appetizer and main course. Food is served in steamers, stacked high (thus "tall orders") on top of one another. Tables are tiny, making a balancing act necessary from time to time. Dishes include salad of smoked chicken with cherry tomatoes and balsamic vinaigrette, quail eggs with freshly

poached salmon and new potatoes, polenta with a creamy porcini mushroom sauce, chargrilled lamb with flageolet beans and a rosemary *jus,* and free-range chicken (roasted) with rosemary potatoes and aïoli. Four fixed-price menus, each consisting of five courses and costing the same, include a varied assortment called "multistory." The Emerald Tower is all vegetarian, and the Pudding Tower is all desserts. "The Fairy Storey," at £7.95 ($11.90), is for "the young gourmet" under 12.

12. EARL'S COURT, NOTTING HILL GATE & HOLLAND PARK

EARL'S COURT

EXPENSIVE

LA CROISETTE, 168 Ifield Rd., SW10. Tel. 071/373-3694.
  Cuisine: SEAFOOD. **Reservations:** Required. **Tube:** Earl's Court.
$ Prices: Appetizers £4.25–£15 ($6.40–$22.50); main courses £9.50–£15.50 ($14.30–$23.30); fixed-price menu £26 ($39). AE, DC, MC, V.
  Open: Lunch Wed–Sun 1–2:30pm; dinner Tues–Sun 7–11:30pm.

La Croisette lies in an unlikely neighborhood in southwestern London. Yet because of its French decor, you might believe you're in the south of France once you go inside. You enter a turn-of-the-century apéritif bar, then descend a wraparound iron staircase into an intimate dining room inspired by Cannes. The fixed-price menu offers an amazingly wide choice of seafood. For example, your first course might include one of five different kinds of oysters, three preparations of mussels, five of scallops, or frogs' legs provençal, six appetizer salads, and many more. Most visitors opt for the plateau des fruits-de-mer, where all the bounty of the sea's shellfish is served from a cork platter dripping with garlands of seaweed. A handful of dishes, notably lamb, is offered for meat lovers, but by far the strongest tempters are the imaginative array of red snapper, sea bass, stingray, monkfish, or sole.

INEXPENSIVE

CHAPTER 11, 47 Hollywood Rd., SW10. Tel. 071/351-1663.
  Cuisine: CALIFORNIAN. **Reservations:** Recommended. **Tube:** Earl's Court.
$ Prices: Appetizers £2.20–£5.50 ($3.30–$8.30); main courses £6.50–£10.50 ($9.80–$15.80). AE, DC, MC, V.
  Open: Lunch Mon–Sat noon–3pm; dinner Mon–Sat 6:45pm–midnight. **Closed:** Dec 24–26.

Once the best cuisine you could hope to find in this neighborhood was bangers and mash. But today some of the most fashionable members of young London gravitate here, drawn by shops selling some of the most exclusive and costly goods in town. Chapter 11 has a small garden terrace in back, although London's gray skies usually encourage diners to head for the lower dining room instead. The menu is wisely limited, but dishes are well prepared, based on fresh ingredients. You might select duck-breast salad with a rice-wine vinaigrette, roasted red peppers with grilled goat's cheese, or red cabbage and pork sausages with Bubble & Squeak (a combination of cabbage and potatoes).

NOTTING HILL GATE

MODERATE

CLARKE'S, 124 Kensington Church St., W8. Tel. 071/221-9225.

Cuisine: BRITISH. **Reservations:** Recommended. **Tube:** Notting Hill Gate or High Street Kensington.

$ Prices: Fixed-price lunch £22–£26 ($33–$39); 4-course fixed-price dinner £22–£37 ($33–$55.50). MC, V.

Open: Lunch Mon–Fri 12:30–2pm; dinner Mon–Fri 7–10pm.

Named after its owner, English chef Sally Clarke—who is considered one of the finest in London—this is one of the hottest restaurants in Notting Hill Gate. Clarke trained in California at Michael's in Santa Monica and the West Beach Café in Venice (California, that is). In this excellent restaurant, everything is bright and modern, with wood floors, discreet lighting, and additional space in the basement where tables are more spacious and private. Here you get a fixed-price menu with no choice, but the food is so well prepared "in the new style" that diners rarely object. The menu is changed daily. You might begin with an appetizer such as hot soup of roasted red peppers with parmesan and rosemary breadsticks, then follow with charcoal-grilled lamb sausage with chili mayonnaise. Desserts are likely to include a strawberry and vanilla ice-cream trifle.

HOLLAND PARK

EXPENSIVE

THE ROOM AT THE HALCYON, in the Halcyon Hotel, 81 Holland Park Ave., W11. Tel. 071/727-7288.

Cuisine: INTERNATIONAL/ITALIAN. **Reservations:** Required. **Tube:** Holland Park.

$ Prices: Appetizers £4–£6.50 ($6–$9.80); main courses £10.50–£15 ($15.80–$22.50). AE, DC, MC, V.

Open: Lunch daily 12:30–2:30pm; dinner daily 7:30–11:30pm.

Part of the previously recommended hotel, this is an exciting dining possibility. On the hotel's lower level, management has installed a restaurant that attracts the rich and famous, including royalty. To reach the restaurant, you pass a medley of colorful and whimsical trompe l'oeil murals. You might enjoy an apéritif in the pink-tinted bar before heading for a meal in the tastefully uncluttered restaurant. Lattices and a garden view create an image of springtime even in winter.

The menu is sophisticated and highly individualized. One food critic wrote that the menu "reads like a United Nations of cuisine," although it leans heavily toward Italy. The menu is based on the inspiration of the chef and the vagaries of shopping, as only the freshest ingredients are used. You might begin with ravioli filled with crab, coriander, and ricotta before going on to roast breast of guinea fowl with noodles, prunes, and leek or salmon baked in pastry with pesto, or a perfectly prepared steamed sea bass with ginger and fennel. Desserts are worth saving room for, as exemplified by a ginger parfait with mango coulis or a dark-chocolate pudding with coffee-bean sauce.

13. ST. MARYLEBONE & BAYSWATER

ST. MARYLEBONE

MODERATE

LANGAN'S BISTRO, 26 Devonshire St., W1. Tel. 071/935-4531.

Cuisine: FRENCH/ENGLISH. **Reservations:** Required. **Tube:** Regent Park.
$ Prices: Appetizers £4–£5.50 ($6–$8.30); main courses £9.50–£10.50 ($14.30–$15.80). AE, DC, MC, V.
Open: Lunch Mon–Fri 12:30–2:30pm; dinner Mon–Sat 7–11:30pm.

Langan's Bistro has been a busy fixture on the London restaurant scene since the mid-1960s. Like its neighbor, Odin's Restaurant (see below), it's owned by actor Michael Caine, among others. The bistro is less expensive than the better-known Langan's Brasserie in Mayfair. You'll find it behind a buttercup-yellow storefront in a residential neighborhood. Inside, almost every square inch of the high ceiling is covered with fanciful clusters of Japanese parasols. Rococo mirrors accent the black walls, setting off surrealistic paintings and old photos guaranteed to create a warmly nostalgic kind of excitement.

The French-inspired menu changes frequently, and only the best and freshest seasonal ingredients are used in the tempting specialties. These might include smoked monkfish with tomato, fennel, and Pernod sauce; veal with Pommery mustard and tarragon; and pork with prunes and brandy. On one occasion I enjoyed sautéed calves' liver with cranberries and kumquats. The dessert extravaganza is known as "Langan's chocolate pudding."

ODIN'S, 27 Devonshire St., W1. Tel. 071/935-7296.
Cuisine: CONTINENTAL. **Reservations:** Required. **Tube:** Regent's Park.
$ Prices: Appetizers £4.25–£6.50 ($6.40–$9.80); main courses £11–£13.50 ($16.50–$20.30). AE, DC, MC, V.
Open: Lunch Mon–Fri 12:30–2:30pm; dinner Mon–Sat 7–11:30pm.

Odin's is a particularly appealing, elegant restaurant owned by actor Michael Caine and others. Amid an eclectic decor of gilt-touched walls, art deco armchairs, Japanese screens, ceiling fans, and evocative paintings, you can enjoy well-prepared specialties of the chef. The menu offers an excellent wine list and selections from many culinary traditions. Selections change every day, depending on the availability of fresh ingredients at the market. You might begin your meal with such typical fare as pigeon breast in puff pastry, marinated salmon with lemon, or a chicken-liver mousse. Main courses include a filet of turbot with prawns from Dublin Bay, steamed Dover sole with ginger and pink peppercorns, wild salmon with sorrel sauce, and a Scottish sirloin with garlic and breadcrumbs.

INEXPENSIVE

GARBO'S, 42 Crawford St., W1. Tel. 071/262-6582.
Cuisine: SWEDISH. **Reservations:** Required. **Tube:** Baker Street, Edgware Road, or Marylebone.
$ Prices: Appetizers £2.50–£5.95 ($3.80–$8.90); main courses £5.95–£10.45 ($8.90–$15.70); buffet lunch £8 ($12). AE, DC, MC, V.
Open: Lunch daily noon–3pm; dinner daily 6pm–midnight.

Garbo's is the most engaging and appealing Swedish restaurant in London, taking its theme from that country's most celebrated export, the late star herself. Lying south of Marylebone Road, it attracts patrons from the Swedish embassy on Montagu Place. The best value—in fact, one of the finest lunchtime values in St. Marylebone—is the "mini-smörgåsbord" which may be called "mini," but in fact has a range of perfectly prepared hot and cold dishes and is most satisfying and filling. Reading the evening menu might even tempt you to visit Scandinavia. You could begin with gravlax with a dill-mustard sauce prepared in the old Viking manner, or else enjoy smoked eel or Swedish pea soup. Various meat courses are featured, including Swedish meatballs in a cream sauce or white cabbage stuffed with beef and pork. Watch also for the specialties of the day, and finish with a dessert from the sweets trolley or ask for crêpe Garbo, filled with ice cream and coated with a Melba sauce.

BAYSWATER

INEXPENSIVE

VERONICA'S, 3 Hereford Rd., W2. Tel. 071/229-5079.
  Cuisine: ENGLISH. **Reservations:** Required. **Tube:** Bayswater or Queensway.
$ Prices: Appetizers £3.50–£5.50 ($5.30–$8.30); main courses £5.50–£13.50
  ($8.30–$20.30); fixed-price meals £10 ($15). AE, DC, MC, V.
  Open: Lunch Mon–Fri noon–3pm; dinner Mon–Sat 7pm–midnight.

⑤ Called the "market leader in café salons," Veronica's offers some of the finest British cuisine in London at tabs you don't mind paying. In fact, it's like a celebration of British food, including some dishes based on recipes used in medieval or Tudor times. For example, your appetizer might be a salad enjoyed by Elizabeth I and called salmagundy, made with crunchy pickled vegetables. Another concoction might be watersouchy, a medieval stew crammed with mixed seafood. However, each dish is given today's imaginative interpretation by Veronica Shaw, the owner. One month she'll focus on Scotland; another month, Victorian foods; yet another month, Wales. Many dishes are vegetarian, and everything tastes better when followed with one of the selections of British farmhouse cheeses or a "pudding." The restaurant is brightly and attractively decorated, and service is warm and ingratiating.

14. AWAY FROM THE CENTER

PIMLICO

MODERATE

POMEGRANATES, 94 Grosvenor Rd., SW1. Tel. 071/828-6560.
  Cuisine: INTERNATIONAL. **Reservations:** Required. **Tube:** Pimlico.
$ Prices: Fixed-price meal £14.50–£20.50 ($21.80–$30.80) at lunch, £17.75–
  £26.50 ($26.60–$39.80) at dinner. AE, DC, MC, V.
  Open: Lunch Mon–Sat 12:30–2:15pm; dinner Mon–Sat 7:30–11:15pm.
This is a basement restaurant by the river in Pimlico. Owner Patrick Gwynn-Jones has traveled far and collected recipes for dishes throughout the world. Asian and Indonesian delicacies vie for space on the fixed-price menus along with European and North American dishes: West Indian curried goat, escargot-and-mushroom pie, Welsh salt duck with a white-onion sauce, or Créole-Cajun jambalaya. The decor is *fin de siècle,* with mirrors and well-laid tables. House wines are reasonably priced, and there is also a good wine list. You have a wide range of choices on the set menus, which begin with *crudités* and might end with homemade honey-and-cognac ice cream.

HAMPSTEAD HEATH

MODERATE

KEATS, 3–4 Downshire Hill, Hampstead, NW3. Tel. 071/435-3544.
  Cuisine: ENGLISH/CONTINENTAL. **Reservations:** Required. **Tube:** Hampstead.
$ Prices: Appetizers £3.50–£5.50 ($5.30–$8.30); main courses £7–£12 ($10.50–
  $18); 3-course fixed-price lunch £9 ($13.50). AE, DC, MC, V.

Open: Lunch Sun–Fri noon–3pm; dinner daily 7–11:30pm.

Named after Keats's house in Hampstead, which lies within a 3-minute walk, this pleasant restaurant is the 1992 reincarnation of a famous restaurant, Keats, which used to thrive in the same premises after World War II. Set on the ground floor of a stone-fronted 18th-century house, it offers an elegant pair of dining rooms richly and theatrically outfitted with Victorian-inspired fabrics, furniture, and accessories. Menu items include a frequently changing array of seasonal dishes of the day, such as mussels prepared in the French style with white wine, garlic, and shallots, or a sauté of wild mushrooms. Items that are usually available throughout the year include Keats salad (studded with asparagus, artichokes, red peppers, and quail eggs), a filet of pepper steak in a brandy and cream sauce, Jamaican jerk chicken, grilled Dover sole in clarified butter sauce, marinated lamb steak, and an array of vegetarian dishes.

PUBS & WINE BARS

JACK STRAW'S CASTLE, North End Way, NW3. Tel. 071/435-8885.

Cuisine: ENGLISH. **Reservations:** Not required. **Tube:** Hampstead.

$ Prices: Appetizers £1.25–£2.75 ($1.90–$4.10); main courses £9.15–£11.55 ($13.70–$17.30); fixed-price Sun lunch £10.15 ($15.20); beer from £1.80 ($2.70). AE, DC, MC, V.

Open: Carvery, lunch daily noon–2pm; dinner Mon–Sat 6–10pm, Sun 7–9:30pm. Pub, Mon–Fri 11am–3pm and 5:30–11pm, Sat 11am–11pm, Sun noon–2pm and 7–10:30pm.

This place was named for one of the leaders of the peasants who, along with Wat Tyler, revolted successfully against what was, basically, a wage freeze in 1381. The pub was rebuilt on the site of Jack's house and is now a bustling place with a large L-shaped bar and quick-snack counter where there are cold salads, meats, and pies, plus three hot dishes with vegetables served every day. You can eat in the bar or on the large patio overlooking part of the heath.

SPANIARDS INN, Spaniards Rd., NW3. Tel. 081/455-3276.

Cuisine: ENGLISH. **Reservations:** Not required. **Tube:** Hampstead or Golders Green.

$ Prices: Appetizers £2.25–£3.50 ($3.40–$5.30); main courses £4.25–£6.75 ($6.40–$10.10); beer from £1.60 ($2.40). MC, V.

Open: Food service, Mon–Fri noon–3pm and 6–9:30pm, Sat noon–10pm, Sun noon–3pm and 7–9:30pm. Pub, Mon–Sat 11am–11pm, Sun noon–3pm and 7–10:30pm.

This is a Hampstead Heath landmark, opposite the old tollhouse, a bottleneck in the road where people had to pay the toll to enter the country park of the bishop of London. The notorious highwayman, Dick Turpin, leaped over the gate on his horse when he was in flight from the law. The pub was originally built in 1585, and the present building dates from 1702. It still contains some antique benches, open fires, and cozy nooks in its rooms with their low, beamed ceilings and oak paneling.

The pub serves traditional but above-average food. In summer, customers can sit at slat tables on a terrace in a garden beside a flower-bordered lawn and aviary. Byron, Shelley, Dickens, and Galsworthy patronized the pub. Even Keats may have quaffed a glass here.

ST. JOHN'S WOOD

A PUB

THE CLIFTON HOTEL, 96 Clifton Hill, NW8. Tel. 071/624-5233.

Cuisine: ENGLISH. **Reservations:** Not required. **Tube:** St. John's Wood or Maida Vale.
$ Prices: Appetizers £2.25–£7.25 ($3.40–$10.90); main courses £7–£11 ($10.50–$16.50). MC, V.
Open: Food service, Mon–Fri noon–2:30pm and 6–10pm, Sat noon–3pm and 6–10pm, Sun noon–3pm. Pub, Mon–Fri 11am–3pm and 5–11pm, Sat 11am–11pm, Sun noon–3pm and 7–10:30pm.

This longtime favorite, one of the most charming pubs in London, stands in an expensive residential area in the northern part of town. Built in 1837, Clifton was a hotel renowned for its fine ports and wines. Edward VII discovered it, and used it as a hideaway with his mistress, Lillie Langtry. Restored in 1984, it's now a pub and restaurant, although it still calls itself a hotel, attracting a lively crowd with its glowing fireplace and mellow atmosphere enhanced by many Victorian and Edwardian touches. Look for the daily specials, such as beef-and-Guinness stew with dumplings, or order a steak sandwich, perhaps preceded by smoked mackerel pâté.

WATERLOO

MODERATE

RSJ, 13A Coin St., SE1. Tel. 071/928-4554.
Cuisine: ENGLISH/FRENCH. **Reservations:** Required. **Tube:** Waterloo.
$ Prices: Appetizers £4.25–£6.95 ($6.40–$10.40); main courses £11.95–£12.95 ($17.90–$19.40); fixed-price lunch or dinner £13.95 ($20.90) for 2 courses, £15.95 ($23.90) for 3 courses. AE, MC, V.
Open: Lunch Mon–Fri noon–2pm; dinner Mon–Sat 6–11pm.

Set on the traditionally unglamorous south bank of the Thames, this restaurant has clients so loyal that they travel from many different parts of London to reach it. Others dine here after seeing a program at the South Bank cultural center. Named after a type of construction material (rolled structural joists) used during its restoration, the restaurant occupies the 250-year-old premises of what was originally a stable for the Duke of Cornwall. You'll enter from a nondescript street, perhaps order a drink from the stand-up apéritif bar, and be led upstairs to a table in a room that used to be the hayloft for the horses downstairs. Nigel Wilkenson, the sophisticated owner of this place, personally selects from the vast array of excellent French (especially Loire Valley) wines that fill his impressive and reasonably priced wine list.

Food is prepared in the tradition of modern British cuisine, and includes such specialties as a bavarois of salmon, a brace of quails stuffed with smoked ham and sweetbreads, filet of Scottish beef with a fricassée of pink mushrooms, tortellini of shellfish, and French duck marinated in sherry vinegar.

ELEPHANT & CASTLE

A PUB

THE GOOSE & FIRKIN, 47 Borough Rd., SE1. Tel. 071/403-3590.
Cuisine: ENGLISH. **Reservations:** Not accepted. **Tube:** Elephant & Castle.
$ Prices: Sandwiches from £1.90 ($2.90); small pies from £1.60 ($2.40); hot platters £3.15 ($4.70); wine by the glass £1.50 ($2.30). No credit cards.
Open: Mon–Fri noon–11pm, Sat–Sun noon–3pm and 7pm–midnight.

Established in 1979 on the premises of a much older, unsuccessful pub, this was the first member of a chain, the Goose & Firkin, which later spread throughout the British Isles. Food is a simple assortment of "big baps" (rolls stuffed with ham, turkey, or tuna), or crock pots filled with chili, or platters of such pub staples as lasagne. Aside from that, most of the clientele comes to drink, converse, and meet with newcomers and other regulars. Goose & Firkin brews its own beer in three special strengths:

Goose, Borough Bitter, and the potent Dogbolter. A guitarist performs 3 nights a week, usually Wednesday, Friday, and Saturday, from 9 to 11pm.

EAST END
INEXPENSIVE

BLOOM'S, 90 Whitechapel St., E1. Tel. 071/247-6001.
   Cuisine: KOSHER. **Reservations:** Recommended. **Tube:** Aldgate East.
$ Prices: Appetizers £2.75–£4.50 ($4.10–$6.80); main courses £4.50–£9.50 ($6.80–$14.30). AE, DC, MC, V.
   Open: Sun–Thurs 11:30am–9:30pm, Fri 11:30am–3pm (to 2pm Dec–Feb).
This is London's most famous Jewish restaurant, originally established in 1920. But to reach it, you have to take the tube to the East End near the Tower of London. This large, bustling restaurant is in the back of a delicatessen. The cooking is strictly kosher. Sunday lunchtime is extremely busy, as many visitors come here after shopping on Petticoat Lane. The cabbage borscht is the traditional opening course, although you may prefer chicken blintzes. Main-dish specialties run to sauerbraten and salt beef (corned). For dessert, the apple strudel is a favorite.

A PUB

THE PROSPECT OF WHITBY, 57 Wapping Wall, E1. Tel. 071/481-1095.
   Cuisine: ENGLISH/FRENCH. **Reservations:** Required. **Tube:** Wapping.
$ Prices: Appetizers £2.75–£8.95 ($4.10–$13.40); main courses £9.95–£16.50 ($14.90–$24.80). AE, DC, MC, V.
   Open: Restaurant, lunch daily noon–2pm; dinner Mon–Sat 7–10pm. Pub, Mon–Sat 11:30am–3pm and 5:30–11pm, Sun noon–3pm and 7–10:30pm.
The Prospect of Whitby was founded in the days of the Tudors, taking its name from a coal barge which made weekly trips from Yorkshire to London. Come here for a tot, a noggin, or whatever it is you drink and soak in its traditional pubby atmosphere.
   Downstairs you can enjoy beer and snacks. Upstairs you can dine in the Pepys Room, which honors the diarist, who may—just may—have visited the Prospect in rowdier days, when the seamy side of London dock life held sway here. You can enjoy such food items as veal champagne, Prospect of Whitby pie, or beef Wellington.

ST. KATHARINE'S DOCK
INEXPENSIVE

CARVERY RESTAURANT, in the Tower Thistle Hotel, St. Katharine's Way, E1. Tel. 071/481-2575.
   Cuisine: ENGLISH. **Reservations:** Not required. **Tube:** Tower Hill.
$ Prices: Fixed-price menu £16.75 ($25.10). AE, DC, MC, V.
   Open: Lunch Mon–Sat 12:15–2:30pm, Sun 12:15–3pm; dinner Sun–Thurs 5:30–10:30pm, Fri–Sat 5:30–11pm.
 At the Carvery Restaurant at this modern hotel built overlooking the Thames, you can enjoy all you want of some of the most tempting roasts in the Commonwealth. Everything is served buffet style. Before going to the carving table you'll be served either a shrimp cocktail, a bowl of soup, or a cold slice of melon. Then you can select (rare, medium, or well done) from standing ribs of prime beef with Yorkshire pudding, horseradish sauce, and the drippings; or from tender roast pork with cracklings accompanied by a spiced bread dressing and applesauce; or perhaps the roast spring Southdown lamb with mint sauce—and help yourself to the roast potatoes, the green peas, the baby carrots. Or you may prefer a selection of cold meats and salads from the buffet table. You can end the meal with a selection from the dessert list and you also receive a large cup of American-style coffee.

DICKENS INN BY THE TOWER, St. Katharine's Way, E1. Tel. 071/488-2208.

Cuisine: ENGLISH. **Reservations:** Recommended. **Tube:** Tower Hill.

$ Prices: Appetizers £2–£5 ($3–$7.50); main courses £5–£19.95 ($7.50–$29.90); snacks £4 ($6); hot dish of the day £5 ($7.50); pizzas £6.50–£18 ($9.80–$27); Sun lunch £11.95 ($17.90). AE, DC, MC, V.

Open: Bar, Mon–Sat 11am–11pm, Sun noon–3pm and 7–10:30pm. Restaurant, Mon–Sat noon–3pm and 6:30–10:30pm, Sun noon–3pm and 7–10pm.

This three-floor restaurant is contained within the solid brick walls of what was originally built around 1830 as a warehouse for the spices then pouring into London from Britain's far-flung empire. Its main decorative allure derives from the massive redwood timbers of its original construction. It is deliberately devoid of carpets, curtains, or anything that might conceal its unusual antique trusses. Large windows overlook a sweeping view of the nearby Thames and Tower Bridge.

On the ground level, you'll find a bar and the Tavern Room, serving sandwiches, platters of lasagne or smoked mackerel, steaming bowls of soup or chili, and bar snacks. One floor above street level is a pizza restaurant, serving three sizes of pizzas ranging from 12 inches wide to a much-accessorized 18-inch behemoth known as "The Beast." Above that, you'll find a relatively formal dining room, The Pickwick Grill, serving more elegant meals. Specialties there include roast lamb or roast beef with Yorkshire pudding, fresh seafood, and salads.

BUTLER'S WHARF
MODERATE

LE PONT DE LA TOUR, 36 Shad Thames, Butler's Wharf, SE1. Tel. 071/403-8403.

Cuisine: INTERNATIONAL. **Reservations:** Not accepted in the Bar & Grill; recommended in The Restaurant. **Tube:** Tower Hill.

$ Prices: In the Bar & Grill, appetizers £3–£7 ($4.50–$10.50); main courses £7.50–£17.50 ($11.30–$26.30). In The Restaurant, appetizers £6–£9 ($9–$13.50); main courses £14.50–£19 ($21.80–$28.50); 3-course fixed-price lunch £25 ($37.50) per person. AE, DC, MC, V.

Open: Lunch daily noon–3pm, dinner Sun–Fri 6–11pm, Sat 6pm–midnight. Cold platters and snacks available in the Bar & Grill, daily 3–6pm.

These two restaurants are considered the most interesting and unusual of those within a newly developed waterfront complex of shops and cafés near Tower Bridge. Both of them are on the ground floor of a brick-and-sandstone warehouse (Butler's Wharf) that was originally built during the 19th century, and that was gutted and remodeled in 1992. Today, the complex includes condominiums, at least three extremely sophisticated food shops, and a sweeping view of some of the densest river traffic in Europe.

Many visitors prefer the brash hubbub of the Bar & Grill. Its hard surfaces, live entertainment, and widely diverse choice of alcoholic drinks create one of the most animated and convivial places in the neighborhood. Although such dishes as fish-and-chips, black pudding with sausages, pâté of chicken livers, and grilled pork chops with an onion compote are ordered and enjoyed, the culinary star is a platter of fresh shellfish (*fruits de mer*) that is copious, flavorful, and very much a meal in itself. For two people it's perfect together with a bottle of wine.

In bold contrast is the enormous and more formal room known simply as The Restaurant. Quieter, and filled with white linen, burl oak, and framed reproductions of French cartoons from the 1920s, it offers excellent food and a polite but undeniable English reserve. Menu items include best end of English lamb in a parsley-cream sauce, Bayonne ham with a celeriac rémoulade, lobster à la nage, eggplant with pesto sauce, filet steaks, oysters, and different preparations of venison.

Unfortunately, tables beside the windows are much in demand and at a highly competitive premium.

15. SPECIALTY DINING

DINING ON THE WATER

MY FAIR LADY, 250 Camden High St., NW1. Tel. 071/485-4433 or 071/485-6210.

    Cuisine: ENGLISH/FRENCH. **Reservations:** Required. **Tube:** Camden Town.

$ Prices: Lunch trip £17.95 ($26.90); dinner trip £25.95 ($38.90). MC, V.

    Open: Dinner trip departs at 8pm Tues–Sat; lunch trip departs at 1pm Sun only.

This cruise-while-you-dine establishment, a motor-driven barge, noses through Regent's Canal for 3 hours, passing through the zoo, Regent's Park, and Maida Hill tunnel before it reaches Robert Browning's Island at Little Venice, where a popular singer-guitarist joins you for the return journey. The menu, which is based on fresh seasonal ingredients, consists of such traditional English fare as prime roast rib of beef, chicken suprême, and filet of beef.

HISPANIOLA, Victoria Embankment, Charing Cross, WC2. Tel. 071/ 839-3011.

    Cuisine: ENGLISH. **Reservations:** Required. **Tube:** Embankment.

$ Prices: Appetizers £3–£7 ($4.50–$10.50); main courses £7–£12 ($10.50–$18). AE, DC, MC, V.

    Open: Lunch Mon–Sat noon–2pm; dinner Mon–Sat 6:30–10pm (last order).

    Closed: Mon Nov–Easter.

This large, luxurious ship was originally built in the 1960s to haul passengers around the islands of Scotland. (Two similar vessels built at the same time still carry passengers between Naples, Italy, and the island of Capri.) Today, stripped of its engine, the ship is permanently moored to the side of the Thames, providing good food and excellent views of the passing river traffic. There are tables on two different levels and, throughout, a certain elegance prevails. The menu offers many different meat, game, and vegetarian dishes, including roasted quail with grapes and chestnuts, Barbary duck with lime-and-honey sauce, and Dover sole meunière. A pianist or harpist provides evening music.

HOTEL DINING

PAVILION RESTAURANT, in the Regency Hotel, 100 Queen's Gate, SW7. Tel. 071/370-4595.

    Cuisine: INTERNATIONAL. **Reservations:** Not required. **Tube:** Gloucester Road or South Kensington.

$ Prices: Appetizers £3.50–£7.95 ($5.30–$11.90); main courses £9.50–£14.50 ($14.30–$21.80); buffet lunch £15.50 ($23.30). AE, DC, MC, V.

    Open: Lunch Mon–Fri 12:30–2:30pm; dinner daily 5:30–10:30pm.

The Pavilion is a glamorous but reasonably priced choice if you're staying at one of the many hotels in South Kensington and would like to come here for meals and drinks. Diners look forward to an enjoyable choice of modern dishes based on prime seasonal produce. For example, lamb is roasted to pink perfection with a flavor of rosemary, or prime beef is cut into strips and flavored with spices and sizzled in butter before a brandy flambé finish. Sea bass, grilled in butter, is served on a bed of beetroot with lemon on the side. Sole can be grilled or pan-fried to your request, and you can always order tender steaks from the charcoal grill. Vegetarian dishes are also available. Care and attention also go into the appetizers, which feature unusual "New Wave" surprises, such as the chef's baked avocado and mango glazed with a ginger-wine sabayon or parfait of duck livers and truffles combined with orange and coriander into a salad.

PELHAM RESTAURANT, in the Pelham Hotel, 15 Cromwell Place, SW7. Tel. 071/589-8288.
Cuisine: ENGLISH. **Reservations:** Required. **Tube:** South Kensington.
$ **Prices:** Appetizers £5–£8.50 ($7.50–$12.80); main courses £8–£15 ($12–$22.50); fixed-price lunch £15.50 ($23.30) Mon–Fri, £16.50 ($24.80) Sun. AE, DC, MC, V.
Open: Lunch Sun–Fri 12:30–2:30pm; dinner Sun–Fri 6:30–10:30pm.

The Pelham is one of the dining "secrets" of London. On the ground floor of this previously recommended elegant little hotel is one of London's finest restaurants. Decorated with a subtle racing motif, the restaurant is accented with sophisticated lighting, cove moldings, a blue-and-white decor, and a large mahogany bar. It provides uniformed and impeccable French service at its limited number of well-attended tables, which are often filled with London luminaries.

Fashion aside, it's the food that attracts diners. Seasonal menus glean the "pick of the market," as the English say. Dishes are expertly prepared, and represent an interpretation of modern French cuisine. Making for very exciting eating are such selections as a tartlet of sautéed sweetbreads and foie gras or perhaps a terrine of escargot or a leek quiche with essence of tomatoes. For your main course, your selection might be fricassée of chicken breast with grapes and a basil-flavored sauce (the pure essence, with no starchy thickener), or a blanquette of lamb. Desserts are sumptuous, often presented like portrait miniatures, including a dark-chocolate mousse on a mint sauce or a gratin of exotic fruits.

AFTERNOON TEA

BROWN'S HOTEL, 29–34 Albemarle St., W1. Tel. 071/493-6020.
Reservations: Not accepted. **Tube:** Green Park.
$ **Prices:** Afternoon tea £12.95 ($19.40); "high tea" £15.50 ($23.30). AE, DC, MC, V.
Open: Daily 3–6pm.

Ranking along with the Ritz Hotel as a chic venue for tea in London, Brown's Hotel offers afternoon tea in its lounge. The room is decorated with English antiques, wall panels, oil paintings, and floral chintz, much like a private English country estate. Give

---

Ⓕ FROMMER'S COOL FOR KIDS: RESTAURANTS

Tall Orders *(see p. 161)* Dishes here are brought to the table stacked in Chinese-style bamboo steamers. If you're really hungry, order a "skyscraper." "The Fairy Storey" is a minitower for the young gourmet under 12.

Deals Restaurant *(see p. 156)* Kids love to take the boat down to Chelsea Harbour to enjoy food of North America, including "Dealsburgers." Reduced-price children's portions are available.

Chicago Pizza Factory *(see p. 131)* If your kids are nostalgic for the food back home, they'll find it here at a place whose regular-size pizzas are big enough for two or three diners.

your name to the concierge upon arrival; arrangements will be made for you to be seated on clusters of sofas and settees or at low tables. The regular afternoon tea includes a choice of 10 different teas, sandwiches, and pastries, which are rolled around on a trolley for your selection. Scones with jam and clotted cream are also included. Some pretheater tea-drinkers opt for a "high tea," which is more expensive, but includes all the ingredients for a regular tea plus a warm dish. This dish might be fish cakes with a medley of relishes, or something called a "Brown's griddle," a mixed English grill.

OAK ROOM LOUNGE, in Le Méridien London, 21 Piccadilly, W1. Tel. 071/734-8000.
Reservations: Recommended. **Tube:** Piccadilly Circus or Green Park.
$ Prices: Average tea from £11 ($16.50). AE, DC, MC, V.
Open: Daily 3–6pm.

The Oak Room Lounge has been restored to its former Edwardian glory and welcomes nonresidents for the very British tradition of afternoon tea. Formal but unstuffy, the soothing elegance of this oak-paneled room is augmented by comfortable armchairs and background music by a resident harpist. A complete tea includes a selection of sandwiches and tarts. The menu lists a tempting array of more exotic teas, some of which you may never have tried before.

PALM COURT, in the Waldorf Hotel, Aldwych, WC2. Tel. 071/836-2400.
Reservations: Required. **Tube:** Covent Garden.
$ Prices: Regular afternoon tea £11.50 ($17.30); afternoon tea dance £17.75 ($26.60). AE, DC, MC, V.
Open: Daily 3:30–6:30pm.

The Palm Court combines afternoon tea with afternoon dancing (such as the fox-trot, quickstep, and the waltz) Friday through Sunday; on other days, a pianist entertains as you enjoy your Earl Grey. The Palm Court is aptly compared to a 1920s movie set, which is in fact what it's been several times in its long life. Art directors would find it difficult to duplicate such a natural setting. You can order tea on a terrace or in a pavilion the size of a ballroom lit by skylights. On tea-dancing days, the orchestra leader will conduct such favorites as "Ain't She Sweet" and "Yes, Sir, That's My Baby," as a butler in a cutaway inquires if you want a cucumber sandwich. Of course, men must wear jacket and tie.

PALM COURT LOUNGE, in the Park Lane Hotel, Piccadilly W1. Tel. 071/499-6321.
Reservations: Not required. **Tube:** Hyde Park Corner or Green Park.
$ Prices: Average tea menu £9.90 ($14.90); club sandwich £7.80 ($11.70). AE, DC, MC, V.
Open: Daily 24 hours.

One of the great favorites of London for tea, it has an atmosphere straight from 1927. Restored to its former charm by John Siddeley, one of the world's leading interior designers, the lounge has a domed yellow-and-white glass ceiling, torchères, and palms in Compton stoneware jardinières. A delightful tea of three scones, Devonshire cream and thick jam, sandwiches, and a selection of cakes is served daily. Many guests come here after the theater for a sandwich and a drink, since food is served 24 hours a day. During the week a pianist plays every afternoon and evening. A harpist plays on Sunday afternoons.

RITZ PALM COURT, in the Ritz Hotel, Piccadilly, W1. Tel. 071/493-8181.
Reservations: Required, at least a week in advance. **Tube:** Green Park.
$ Prices: Afternoon tea £14.50 ($21.80). AE, DC, MC, V.
Open: Daily at 3 and 4:30pm.

★ This is the most fashionable place in London to order afternoon tea, and perhaps the hardest to get in without reservations far in advance. The atmosphere is one of marble steps and columns, along with a baroque fountain. It's strictly a setting from the 1920s and 1930s. You have your choice of the widest possible variety of teas, served with those delectable little sandwiches on white bread or one of the luscious pastries to follow. Here men are required to wear jacket and tie and women are encouraged to wear hats. Jeans and sneakers are not acceptable.

BREAKFAST

THE FOX AND ANCHOR, 115 Charterhouse St., EC1. Tel. 071/253-4838.
    Cuisine: ENGLISH. **Reservations:** Required. **Tube:** Farringdon or Barbican.
$ Prices: "The full house" breakfast £6.50 ($9.80); steak breakfast £11.50 ($17.30). MC, V.
    Open: Breakfast Mon–Fri 7–10:30am; lunch Mon–Fri noon–2:15pm.

For breakfast at its best, try this place which has been serving traders from the nearby famous Smithfield meat market since the pub was built in 1898. Breakfasts are gargantuan, especially if you order "the full house," which will have at least eight different items on your plate, including sausage, bacon, mushrooms, kidney, eggs, beans, black pudding, and a fried slice of bread, to mention just a few, along with unlimited tea or coffee, toast and jam. If you want a more substantial meal, you can order a filet steak with mushrooms, chips, tomatoes, and salad. Add a Black Velvet (champagne with Guinness) and the day is yours. Of course, in the modern British view, Guinness ruins champagne, but some people order it anyway—just to be traditional. More fashionable is a Bucks fizz, with orange juice and champagne. The Fox and Anchor is noted for its range of fine English ales, all available at breakfast. Butchers from the meat market, spotted with blood, still appear, as do nurses getting off their shift and clerks and tycoons from The City who have been working at bookkeeping chores all night. Ale flows freely from 6 to 10:30am, since many of the drinkers are ending their night shifts.

PICNIC FARE & WHERE TO FIND IT

Because of its "green lungs" (public parks), London is a great place for a picnic. Virtually any neighborhood you stay in has a supermarket or a deli where you can purchase cold cuts, cheeses, and soft drinks to take out for a picnic.

    However, if you'd like to do as the queen of England might do if she were inviting guests for a picnic, there is no better place to go than **Fortnum & Mason,** 181 Piccadilly (tel. 071/734-8040), the world's most famous grocery store. Here you can find a wide array of food stuff to take away to your favorite park. See "The Parks of London" in "More Attractions," Chapter 6, to decide where you'd like to enjoy the makings of your picnic.

    Remember, the English disapprove mightily of littering in their public parks, and you could be fined, so clean up after you've enjoyed your picnic.

CHAPTER 6

LONDON ATTRACTIONS

Dr. Johnson said, "When a man is tired of London, he is tired of life, for there is in London all that life can afford." In this chapter, we'll survey only a fraction of that life: ancient monuments, literary shrines, museums, walking tours, Parliament debates, royal castles, waxworks, palaces, cathedrals, and parks. Some of what we're about to see was known to Johnson and Boswell, even Shakespeare, but much of it is new.

SUGGESTED ITINERARIES

IF YOU HAVE 1 DAY Even on the most rushed of itineraries, no first-time visitor dares leave London without a visit to Westminster Abbey. See Poets' Corner in the abbey where everybody from Robert Browning to Alfred Tennyson are buried. After a visit inside, walk over to see Big Ben and the Houses of Parliament. Also see the changing of the guard and walk over to 10 Downing Street, home of the prime minister. Have dinner at one of the little restaurants in Covent Garden.

IF YOU HAVE 2 DAYS Spend your first day as above. Devote a good part of the second day to exploring the British Museum, considered the biggest and best in the world. Spend the afternoon visiting the Tower of London and seeing the collection of Crown Jewels (expect slow-moving lines).

IF YOU HAVE 3 DAYS Spend Days 1 and 2 as above. On the third day, go to the National Gallery, facing Trafalgar Square, in the morning. In a lighter vein, enjoy an afternoon at Madame Tussaud's Waxworks.

IF YOU HAVE 5 DAYS Spend the first 3 days as above. On the morning of the fourth day, head for The City, the financial district of London in the East End. Your major sightseeing goal here will be Sir Christopher Wren's St. Paul's Cathedral. Take our walking tour of The City and visit such attractions as the Guildhall (the City's city hall). In the late afternoon, head down King's Road in Chelsea for some boutiquehopping and have dinner at one of Chelsea's many restaurants.

On the fifth and final day, explore the Victoria and Albert Museum in the morning, then head for the Tate Gallery for lunch at its restaurant. Spend the rest of the afternoon wandering through the gallery enjoying its masterpieces. Attend the theater that evening, or cram in as many West End shows as you can on the first 4 nights.

1. THE TOP ATTRACTIONS

London is not a city to visit hurriedly. It is so vast, so stocked with treasures that, on a cursory visit, a person will not only miss many of the highlights but will also fail to grasp the spirit of London and to absorb fully its unique flavor. Still, faced with an infinite number of important places to visit and a time clock running out, the visitor will have to concentrate on a manageable group.

Here are the top sights of London. Try to see them even if you have to skip all the rest, saving them for next time.

THE TOWER OF LONDON, Tower Hill, on the north bank of the Thames, EC3. Tel. 071/709-0765.

⭐ This ancient fortress continues to pack 'em in because of its macabre associations with all the legendary figures who were imprisoned or executed here (or both). James Street once wrote, "There are more spooks to the square foot than in any other building in the whole of haunted Britain. Headless bodies, bodiless heads, phantom soldiers, icy blasts, clanking chains—you name them, the Tower's got them." Many visitors consider the Tower to be the highlight of their sightseeing in London—so schedule plenty of time for it.

The fortress is actually a compound, in which the oldest and finest structure is the White Tower, begun by William the Conqueror. Here you can view the Armouries, which dates from the reign of Henry VIII. A display of instruments of torture and execution will recall some of the most ghastly moments in the history of the Tower. At the Bloody Tower, the Little Princes (Edward V and the Duke of York) were allegedly murdered by their uncle, Richard III. Through Traitors' Gate passed such ill-fated, but romantic, figures as Robert Devereux, known as the second Earl of Essex, a favorite of Elizabeth I. At Tower Green, Anne Boleyn and Catherine Howard, two wives of Henry VIII, lost their lives. The 9-day queen, Lady Jane Grey, and her husband, Dudley, also were executed but at Tower Hill, as well as such figures as Sir Thomas More.

To see the **Jewel House,** where the Crown Jewels are kept, go early in the day during summer because long lines usually form by late morning. Get one of the Yeoman Warders, the so-called Beefeaters in Tudor dress, to tell you how Colonel Blood almost made off with the crown and regalia in the late 17th century. Of the three English crowns, the Imperial State Crown is the most important—in fact, it's probably the most famous crown on earth. Made for Victoria in 1837, it is worn today by Queen Elizabeth when she opens Parliament. Studded with some 3,000 jewels (principally diamonds), it contains the Black Prince's Ruby, worn by Henry V at Agincourt, the 1415 battle where the English defeated the French. Don't miss the 530-carat Star of Africa, a cut diamond on the Royal Sceptre with Cross.

The Tower of London has an evening ceremony called the **Ceremony of the Keys.** It is the ceremonial locking up of the Tower. The Beefeater will explain to guests the significance of the ceremony. For free tickets, write to the Resident Governor, Queen's House, Tower of London, London EC3N 4AB, and request a specific date, but also list alternative dates. At least 6 weeks' notice is required. All requests must be accompanied by a stamped, self-addressed envelope (British stamps only) or two International Reply Coupons. With ticket in hand, you'll be admitted by a Yeoman Warder around 9:35pm.

There are also the ravens. Six of them, plus two spares, are all registered as official Tower residents and each is fed exactly 6 ounces of rations per day. According to a legend, London will stand as long as those black, ominous birds remain in the Tower and so, to be on the safe side, they have had their wings clipped.

Tours of approximately an hour in length are given by the Yeoman Warders at frequent intervals, starting from the Middle Tower near the main entrance. The tour includes the Chapel Royal of St. Peter and Vincula. The last guided walk starts about 3:30pm in summer, 2:30pm in winter.

Admission: £6.70 ($10.10) adults, £4.40 ($6.60) children, free for children under 5; family ticket for five (but no more than two adults) £19 ($28.50).

Open: Nov–Feb, Mon–Sat 9:30am–5pm; Mar–Oct, Mon–Sat 9:30am–6pm, Sun 10am–6pm. **Closed:** Jan 1, Good Friday, Dec 24–26. **Tube:** Tower Hill. **Boat:** From Westminster Pier.

WESTMINSTER ABBEY, Broad Sanctuary, SW1. Tel. 071/222-7110.

Nearly every figure in English history has left his or her mark on Westminster Abbey. In 1065 the Saxon king, Edward the Confessor, founded the Benedictine abbey and rebuilt the old minster church on this spot, overlooking Parliament Square. The first English king crowned in the abbey was Harold in 1066, who was killed at the Battle of Hastings that same year. The man who defeated him, Edward's cousin, William the Conqueror, was also crowned at the abbey; the coronation tradition has continued to the present day, broken only twice (Edward V and Edward VIII). The essentially Early English Gothic structure existing today owes more to Henry III's plans than to those of any other sovereign, although many architects, including Wren, have contributed to the abbey.

Built on the site of the ancient lady chapel in the early 16th century, the **Henry VII Chapel** is one of the loveliest in Europe, with its fan vaulting, Knights of Bath banners, and Torrigiani-designed tomb of the king himself over which is placed a 15th-century Vivarini painting, *Madonna and Child.* Also buried here are those feuding half-sisters, Elizabeth I and Mary Tudor ("Bloody Mary"). In one end of the chapel you can stand on Cromwell's memorial stone and view the RAF chapel containing the Battle of Britain memorial stained-glass window, unveiled in 1947 to honor the RAF.

You can also visit the most hallowed spot in the abbey, the shrine of Edward the Confessor (canonized in the 12th century). In the saint's chapel is the Coronation Chair, made at the command of Edward I in 1300 to contain the Stone of Scone. Scottish kings were once crowned on this stone (in 1950 the Scots stole it back, but it was later returned to its position in the abbey).

Another noted spot in the abbey is **Poets' Corner,** to the right of the entrance to the Royal Chapel, with monuments to everybody—Chaucer, Shakespeare, "O Rare Ben Johnson" (his name misspelled), Samuel Johnson, the Brontë sisters, Thackeray, Dickens, Tennyson, Kipling, even the American Longfellow. The most stylized monument is Sir Jacob Epstein's sculptured bust of William Blake. One of the more recent tablets commemorates poet Dylan Thomas.

Statesmen and men of science—such as Disraeli, Newton, Charles Darwin—are also interred in the abbey or honored by monuments. Near the west door is the 1965 memorial to Sir Winston Churchill. In the vicinity of this memorial is the tomb of the Unknown Soldier, symbol of British dead in World War I. Some totally obscure personages are also buried in the abbey, including an abbey plumber.

Don't overlook the 13th-century **chapter house,** where Parliament used to meet. And even more fascinating are the treasures in the **museum** in the Norman undercroft (crypt), part of the monastic buildings erected between 1066 and 1100. The collection includes effigies—figures in wax, wood carvings of early English royalty, ancient documents, old religious vestments, the sword of Henry V, and the famous Essex Ring that Elizabeth I is supposed to have given to her favorite earl.

Off the Cloisters, the **College Garden** is the oldest garden in England, under cultivation for more than 900 years. Surrounded by high walls, flowering trees dot the lawns, and park benches provide comfort where you can hardly hear the roar of passing traffic.

The only time photography is allowed in the abbey is Wednesday evening in the Royal Chapels. On Sunday the Royal Chapels are closed, but the rest of the church is open unless service is being conducted. For times of services, phone the Chapter Office (tel. 071/222-5152). Up to six supertours of the abbey are conducted by the vergers Monday through Friday, beginning at 10am.

Admission: Abbey free; £1.35 ($2) donation suggested. Royal Chapels, Royal Tombs, Coronation Chair, Henry VII Chapel, £3 ($4.50) adults, £1 ($1.50) children; Royal Chapels, free Wed evenings.

Open: Mon–Fri 9:20am–4pm, Sat 9:30am–2pm and 3:45–5pm; Royal Chapels, Wed 6–7:45pm. **Tube:** Westminster or St. James's Park.

HOUSES OF PARLIAMENT, Westminster Palace, Old Palace Yard, SW1. Tel. 071/219-4272 for the House of Commons, or 071/219-3107 for the House of Lords.

⭐ These are the spiritual opposite of the Tower; they are the stronghold of Britain's democracy, the assemblies that effectively trimmed the sails of royal power. Both Houses (Commons and Lords) are in the formerly royal Palace of Westminster, the king's residence until Henry VIII moved to Whitehall.

The debates are often lively and controversial in the House of Commons (seats are at a premium during crises). The chances of getting into the House of Lords when it's in session are generally better than they are in the more popular House of Commons—where even the queen isn't allowed. The old guard of the palace informs me that the peerage speak their minds more freely and are less likely to adhere to party line than their counterparts in the Commons.

The present Houses of Parliament were built in 1840, but the Commons chamber was bombed and destroyed by the Luftwaffe in 1941. The 320-foot tower that houses Big Ben, however, remained standing and the "symbol of London" continues to strike its chimes. Big Ben, incidentally, was named after Sir Benjamin Hall, a cabinet minister distinguished only by his long-windedness.

Except for the Strangers' Galleries, the two Houses of Parliament are closed to tourists. To be admitted to the Strangers' Galleries, join the public line outside the St. Stephen's entrance; often there is a delay before the line is admitted. You might speed matters up by applying at the American embassy or the Canadian High Commission for a special pass. Be aware, though, that the embassy has only four tickets for daily distribution, so you might as well stand in line.

Admission: Free.

IN THEIR FOOTSTEPS

Sir Walter Raleigh (c. 1552–1618) Known for his charm and dashing personality, he was the favorite of Elizabeth I until he was accused of having an affair with one of her maids of honor.

• **Accomplishments:** He wrote many prose works, notably a *History of the World*, but perhaps is best remembered for introducing tobacco and the potato to England. He sponsored various colonization projects in America.

• **Least Favorite Haunt:** The Tower of London, where he was imprisoned on trumped-up charges of plotting against the king. He stayed there for 13 years.

• **Resting Place:** St. Margaret's Church in London.

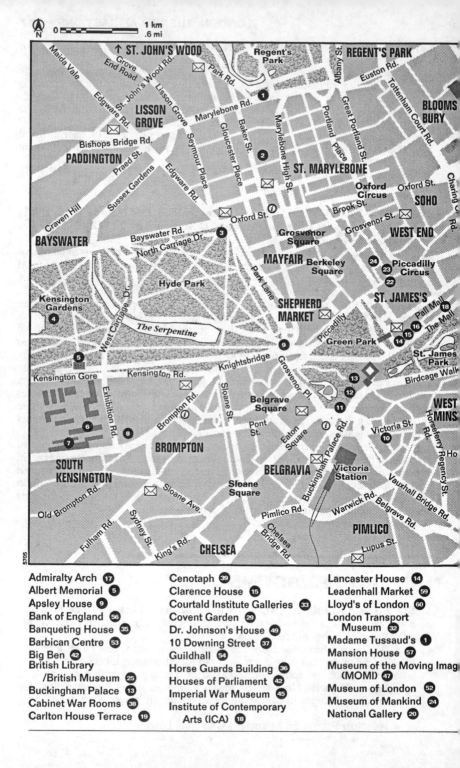

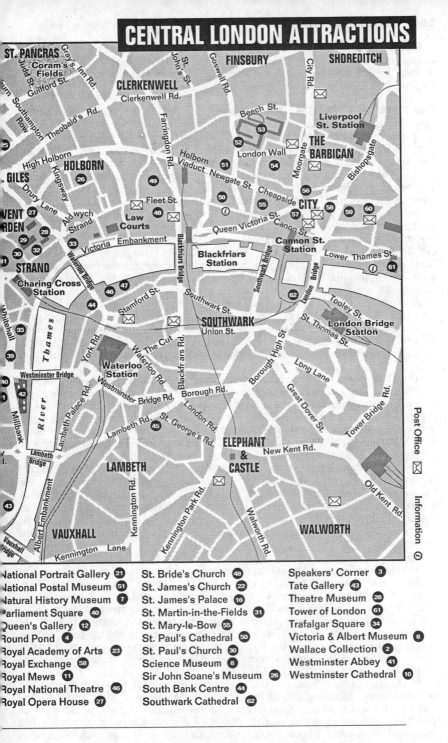

CENTRAL LONDON ATTRACTIONS

Post Office ⊠ Information ⊙

Open: House of Lords, open to the public Mon–Thurs about 3pm and sometimes on Fri (call to check). House of Commons, open to the public Mon–Thurs at 4pm, Fri 9:30am–3pm. Join the line at St. Stephen's entrance. Debates often continue into the night. **Tube:** Westminster.

THE BRITISH MUSEUM, Great Russell St., WC1. Tel. 071/636-1555.

The British Museum shelters one of the most comprehensive collections of art and artifacts in the world, including countless treasures of ancient and modern civilizations. Even on a cursory first visit, be sure to see the Asian collections (the finest assembly of Islamic pottery outside the Islamic world), the Chinese porcelain, the Indian sculpture, and the Prehistoric and Romano-British collections. The overall storehouse splits basically into the national collections of antiquities; prints and drawings; coins, medals, and banknotes; and ethnography.

As you enter the front hall, you may want to head first to the Assyrian Transept on the ground floor, where you'll find the winged and human-headed bulls and lions that once guarded the gateways to the palaces of Assyrian kings. Nearby is the Black Obelisk of Shalmaneser III (858–824 B.C.) depicting Jehu, king of Israel, paying tribute. From here you can continue into the angular hall of Egyptian sculpture to see the Rosetta Stone, whose discovery led to the deciphering of hieroglyphs.

Also on the ground floor is the Duveen Gallery, housing the Elgin Marbles, consisting chiefly of sculptures from the Parthenon, on the Acropolis in Athens.

The classical sculpture galleries house a caryatid from the Erechtheum, also on the Acropolis, a temple started in 421 B.C. and dedicated to Athena and Poseidon. Displayed here, too, are sculptures from the Mausoleum at Halicarnassus (around 350 B.C.).

The Department of Medieval and Later Antiquities has its galleries on the first floor (second floor to Americans), reached by the main staircase. Of its exhibitions, the Sutton Hoo Anglo-Saxon burial ship, discovered in Suffolk, is, in the words of an expert, "the richest treasure ever dug from English soil," containing gold jewelry, armor, weapons, bronze bowls and cauldrons, silverware, and the inevitable drinking horn of the Norse culture. No body was found, but the tomb is believed to be that of a king of East Anglia who died in the 7th century A.D.

The featured attractions of the upper floor are the Egyptian Galleries, especially the mummies. Egyptian Room 63 is extraordinary, looking like the props for *Cleopatra*, with its cosmetics, domestic utensils, toys, tools, and other work. Items of Sumerian art, unearthed from the Royal Cemetery at Ur (southern Iraq), lie in a room beyond, some dating from about 2500 B.C. In the Iranian room rests "The Treasure of the Oxus," a hoard of riches, perhaps a temple deposit, dating from the 6th to the 3rd century B.C.

See also the galleries of the City of Rome and its Empire, which include exhibitions of art before the Romans. The Portland Vase is one of the most celebrated possessions of the British Museum, having been found in 1582 outside Rome. This vase is the finest example of ancient cameo carving and was made about 25 B.C. It was so named after it was purchased by the Duchess of Portland in the 18th century and later sold to the British Museum. The interpretation of the vase remains controversial; there are two main schools of thought: one claiming that the scenes include references to contemporary events such as the birth of the emperor Augustus and the Battle of Actium, the other suggesting that the subjects were drawn from classical mythology, in particular the story of Peleus and Thetis.

In the Manuscript "Saloon" (yes, that's right) are manuscripts of historical and literary interest, including two of the four surviving copies of King John's Magna Carta (1215) and the Lindisfarne Gospels (an outstanding example of the work of Northumbrian artists in the earliest period of English Christianity, written and illustrated about 698). Almost every major literary figure, such as Dickens, Austen,

Charlotte Brontë, and Yeats, is represented in the English literature section, plus autographs of historical personages.

In the King's Library—where the library of King George III is housed—the history of the book is illustrated by notable specimens of early printing, including the Gutenberg Bible (1455), the first book ever printed from movable type.

Admission: Free.

Open: Mon–Sat 10am–5pm, Sun 2:30–6pm (the galleries start to close 10 minutes earlier). **Closed:** Jan 1, Good Friday, first Mon in May, Dec 24–26. **Tube:** Holborn, Tottenham Court Road, or Russell Square.

BUCKINGHAM PALACE, at the end of The Mall (the street running from Trafalgar Sq.). Tel. 071/930-4832.

⭐ This massively graceful building is the official residence of the queen, and you can tell whether Her Majesty is at home by the Royal Standard flying at the masthead. During most of the year, you can't visit the palace unless you're officially invited, but you can do what thousands of others do: peep through the railings into the front yard.

However, in the spring of 1993, Queen Elizabeth II agreed to allow visitors to tour her state apartments and picture galleries, at least for the next five years. The palace will be open to the public for eight weeks in August and September, when the royal family is away on vacation. The queen decided on these Buckingham Palace tours to help defray the massive cost of fire damage at Windsor Castle.

The tours will include not only the state apartments, but a number of other rooms used by King George IV and designed by John Nash in the 1800s, including the Throne Room and the grand staircase. The queen's picture gallery contains some world class masterpieces rarely if ever seen by the public, including Van Dyck's celebrated equestrian portrait of Charles I.

The red-brick palace was built as a country house for the notoriously rakish Duke of Buckingham. In 1762 it was bought by King George III, who (if nothing else) was prolific; he needed room for his 15 children. From then on, the building was expanded, remodeled, faced with Portland stone, and twice bombed (during the Blitz). Today in a 40-acre garden, it stands 360 feet long and contains 600 rooms.

Every morning from early April to mid-August and every other morning the rest of the year—always at 11:30am—Buckingham Palace puts on its most famous spectacle, the **Changing of the Guard.** This ceremony, which lasts half an hour, is perhaps the finest example of military pageantry extant. The new guard, marching behind a band, comes from either the Wellington or Chelsea Barracks and takes over from the old guard in the forecourt of the palace.

At 11am Monday through Saturday and at 10am on Sunday, another guard-changing takes place a few minutes' walk away, on the far side of St. James's Park, at the Horse Guards Parade, Whitehall, SW1.

Both these ceremonies are curtailed in winter, between October 1 and March 31. During those months, the Changing of the Guard officially takes place on even calendar days in October, December, and February, and on odd calendar days in November, January, and March. Call 071/730-3488 for information on the ceremony if the weather is uncertain. (Two other places in London also get ritual Guards protection: St. James's Palace and the Tower of London.)

Admission: £8.30 ($12.50) adults; £4.20 ($6.25) children under 17; £4.40 ($6.60) senior citizens over 60 years of age.

Open: From the second week in August for 8 weeks. Check with tourist offices or local publications such as *Time Out* for exact days and hours.

Tube: St. James's Park or Green Park.

MADAME TUSSAUD'S, Marylebone Rd., NW1. Tel. 071/935-6861.

In 1770, an exhibition of life-size wax figures was opened in Paris by Dr. Curtius. He was soon joined by his niece, Strasbourg-born Marie Tussaud, who learned the secret of making lifelike replicas of the famous and the infamous. During the French Revolution, the head of almost every distinguished victim of the guillotine was molded by Madame Tussaud or her uncle.

While some of the figures on display today come from molds taken by Madame Tussaud, who continued to make portraits until she was 81, the exhibition also introduces new images of whoever is *au courant*. An enlarged Grand Hall continues to house years of royalty and old favorites, as well as many of today's heads of state and political leaders. In the Chamber of Horrors, you can have the vicarious thrill of walking through a Victorian London street where special effects include the shadow terror of Jack the Ripper. The instruments and victims of death penalties contrast with present-day criminals portrayed within the confines of prison. You are invited to mingle with the more current stars in the garden party, "meeting" Dudley Moore and Jane Seymour.

"Super Stars" offers latest technologies in sound, light, and special effects combined with new figures in a celebration of success in the fields of film and sports. A popular attraction—200 years of Tussaud's treasures—opened in 1990.

Admission: £6.75 ($10.10) adults, £4.40 ($6.60) children under 16.

Open: Mon–Fri 10am–5:30pm, Sat–Sun 9:30am–5:30pm (doors open earlier in summer). **Closed:** Dec 25. **Tube:** Baker Street.

TATE GALLERY, beside the Thames on Millbank, SW1. Tel. 071/821-1313.

The Tate houses the best groupings of British paintings from the 16th century on, as well as England's finest collection of modern art, the works of British artists born after 1860, together with foreign art from the impressionists onward. The number of paintings is staggering. Try to schedule at least two visits—the first to see the classic English works, the second to take in the modern collection. Since only a portion of the collections can be shown simultaneously, the works on display vary from time to time.

The first giant among English painters, William Hogarth (1697–1764), is almost invariably well represented, particularly by his satirical *O the Roast Beef of Old England* (known as *Calais Gate*). Two other famous 18th-century British painters are Sir Joshua Reynolds (1723–92) and Thomas Gainsborough (1727–88).

In the art of J. M. W. Turner (1775–1851), the Tate possesses its greatest collection of the works of a single artist. Most of the paintings and watercolors exhibited here were willed to the nation by Turner. In 1987, a new wing at the Tate, called the Clore Gallery, was opened so that the entire bequest of the artist can be seen.

In a nation of landscape painters, John Constable (1776–1837) stands out. American-born Sir Jacob Epstein became one of England's greatest sculptors, and some of his bronzes are owned and occasionally displayed by the Tate.

The Tate also has the works of many major painters from both the 19th and 20th centuries, including Paul Nash. The drawings of William Blake (1757–1827), the incomparable mystical poet and illustrator of such works as *The Book of Job, The Divine Comedy,* and *Paradise Lost,* attract the most attention.

In the modern collections, the Tate contains works by Matisse, Dalí, Modigliani, Munch, Ben Nicholson, and Picasso.

Truly remarkable is the room devoted to several enormous, somber, but rich abstract canvases by Mark Rothko; the group of paintings and sculptures by Giacometti (1901–66); and the paintings of one of England's best-known modern artists, the late Francis Bacon. Sculptures by Henry Moore and Barbara Hepworth are also displayed.

Downstairs is the internationally renowned gallery restaurant (see Chapter 5, "London Dining"), with murals by Rex Whistler, as well as a coffee shop.

Admission: Free, except special exhibitions.

Open: Mon–Sat 10am–5:50pm, Sun 2–5:50pm. **Tube:** Pimlico. **Bus:** 77A, C10, or 88.

NATIONAL GALLERY, on north side of Trafalgar Sq., WC2. Tel. 071/389-1785.

✪ In an impressive neoclassical building the National Gallery houses one of the most comprehensive collections of Western paintings, representing all the major schools from the 13th to the early 20th century. The largest part of the collection is devoted to the Italians, including the Sienese, Venetian, and Florentine masters, now housed in the new Sainsbury Wing.

Of the early Gothic works, the *Wilton Diptych* (French school, late 14th century) is the rarest treasure; it depicts Richard II being introduced to the Madonna and Child by John the Baptist and the Saxon king, Edward the Confessor.

A Florentine gem by Masaccio is displayed, as well as notable works by Piero della Francesca, Leonardo da Vinci, Michelangelo, and Raphael.

Among the 16th-century Venetian masters, the most notable works include a rare *Adoration of the Kings* by Giorgione, *Bacchus and Ariadne* by Titian, *The Origin of the Milky Way* by Tintoretto, and *The Family of Darius Before Alexander* by Veronese.

A number of satellite rooms are filled with works by major Italian masters of the 15th century—such as Andrea Mantegna of Padua, Giovanni Bellini, and Botticelli. The painters of northern Europe are well represented. For example, there is Jan van Eyck's portrait of G. Arnolfini and his bride, plus Pieter Brueghel the Elder's Bosch-influenced *Adoration*. The 17th-century pauper, Vermeer, is rich on canvas in a *Young Woman at a Virginal*. Fellow Delftite Pieter de Hooch comes on sublimely in a *Patio in a House in Delft*.

One of the big drawing cards of the National is its collection of Rembrandts. His *Self-Portrait at the Age of 34* shows him at the pinnacle of his life; his *Self-Portrait at the Age of 63* is more deeply moving and revealing.

Five of the greatest of the homegrown artists—Constable, Turner, Reynolds, Gainsborough, and Hogarth—have masterpieces here, as do three giants of Spanish painting. Velázquez's portrait of the sunken-faced Philip IV, El Greco's *Christ Driving the Traders from the Temple*, and Goya's portrait of the Duke of Wellington (once stolen) and his mantilla-wearing *Dona Isabel de Porcel* are on display.

Other rooms are devoted to early 19th-century French painters, such as Delacroix and Ingres; the later 19th-century French impressionists, such as Manet, Monet, Renoir, and Degas; and postimpressionists such as Cézanne, Seurat, and van Gogh.

Admission: Free.

Open: Mon–Sat 10am–6pm, Sun 2–6pm. **Closed:** Jan 1, Good Friday, May Day, Dec 24–26. **Tube:** Charing Cross or Leicester Square.

KENSINGTON PALACE, The Board Walk, Kensington Gardens, W8. Tel. 071/937-9561.

Home of the state apartments, some of which were used by Queen Victoria—the palace is located at the far western end of Kensington Gardens; the entrance is from The Board Walk. The palace was acquired by William III (William of Orange) in 1689 and was remodeled by Sir Christopher Wren. George II, who died in 1760, was the last king to use it as a royal residence.

The most interesting chamber to visit is Queen Victoria's bedroom. In this room, on the morning of June 20, 1837, she was aroused from her sleep with the news that she had ascended the throne, following the death of her uncle, William IV. In the anteroom are memorabilia from Victoria's childhood—a dollhouse and a collection of her toys. As you wander through the apartments, be sure to admire the many fine paintings from the Royal Collection.

A special attraction is the Court Dress Collection, which shows restored rooms from the 19th century, including Queen Victoria's birthroom and a series of room settings with the appropriate court dress of the day, from 1760 to 1950. However, a more modern dress captures the attention of most visitors—the wedding dress worn by the Princess of Wales on July 29, 1981.

The palace gardens, originally the private park of royalty, adjoin Hyde Park and are open to the public for daily strolls around Round Pond, near the heart of Kensington Gardens. Also in Kensington Gardens is the Albert Memorial, honoring Queen Victoria's consort. Facing Royal Albert Hall, the statue reflects the ostentation of the Victorian era.

Admission: £4 ($6) adults, £2.75 ($4.10) children.

Open: Mon–Sat 9am–5pm, Sun 1–5pm. **Tube:** Queensway or Bayswater on the north side of the gardens, or High Street Kensington on the south side; then you'll have to walk a lot.

ST. PAUL'S CATHEDRAL, St. Paul's Churchyard, EC4. Tel. 071/248-2705.

✪ During World War II, newsreel footage reaching America showed the dome of St. Paul's Cathedral lit by fires burning after bombings all around it. That it survived at all is miraculous, as it was badly hit twice in the early years of the Nazi bombardment of London. But St. Paul's is accustomed to calamity, having been burned down three times and destroyed once by invading Norsemen. It was in the Great Fire of 1666 that the old St. Paul's was razed, making way for a new Renaissance structure designed (after many mishaps and rejections) by Sir Christopher Wren and built between 1675 and 1710.

The classical dome of St. Paul's dominates The City's square mile. Inside, the cathedral is laid out like a Greek cross, containing few art treasures (Grinling Gibbons's choir stalls are an exception) but many monuments—including one to the "Iron Duke" and a memorial chapel to American service personnel who lost their lives in World War II while stationed in the United Kingdom. Encircling the dome is the Whispering Gallery, where discretion in speech is advised. In the crypt lie not only Wren but also the Duke of Wellington and Lord Nelson. A fascinating Diocesan Treasury was opened in 1981.

You can climb to the very top of the dome for a spectacular 360° view of London.

St. Paul's is an Anglican cathedral, with daily services held at 7:30am and 5pm. Sunday services are at 10:30 and 11:30am and 3:15pm.

Admission: Cathedral, adults £2.50 ($3.75), £1.50 ($2.30) children under 16; galleries, £2.50 ($3.75) adults, £1.50 ($2.30) children under 16. When the crypt is closed the entrance charge is reduced by 50p (80¢). Tours, excluding the entrance charge but including the galleries, £3 ($4.50) adults, £1 ($1.50) children under 16.

Open: Cathedral, Mon–Sat 7:15am–6pm; crypt and galleries, Mon–Sat 8:45am–4:15pm. **Tube:** St. Paul's.

VICTORIA AND ALBERT MUSEUM, Cromwell Rd., SW7. Tel. 071/589-6371.

✪ Located in South Kensington, this museum is one of the liveliest and most imaginative in London. It's named after the queen and her consort but not run in their spirit. The general theme here is the fine and decorative arts, but adhered to in a pleasantly relaxed fashion.

The medieval holdings include many treasures, such as the Eltenberg Reliquary (Rhenish, second half of the 12th century); the Early English Gloucester Candlestick; the Byzantine Veroli Casket, with its ivory panels based on Greek plays; and the Syon Cope, a highly valued embroidery made in England in the early 14th century. The Gothic tapestries, including the Devonshire ones depicting hunting scenes, are displayed in another gallery. An area devoted to Islamic art contains the Ardabil carpet from 16th-century Persia (320 knots per square inch).

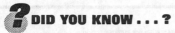**DID YOU KNOW . . . ?**

- A romance between one of the queen's corgis and one of Princess Margaret's dachshunds produced three royal "dorgis" for the queen.
- St. Paul's Cathedral is the fifth church dedicated to the patron saint of London to be constructed on the same spot, and the first English cathedral built by one architect.
- A grocer's daughter from Lincolnshire, Margaret Thatcher lived at 10 Downing Street longer than any other prime minister.
- Covent Garden once had so many Turkish baths and brothels it was called "the great square of Venus."
- The richest man in the world, the Sultan of Brunei, owns the landmark art deco Dorchester Hotel. He issued orders to restore it until it was "the greatest hotel in the world."
- FDR (1882–1945) honeymooned with Eleanor at Brown's Hotel, which had been launched by a manservant of Lord Byron.
- Nash's Marble Arch (1827), one of the most famous London landmarks, was banned from Buckingham Palace because it was too narrow for the royal coaches to pass through.

The Victoria and Albert houses the largest collection of Renaissance sculpture outside Italy, including a Donatello marble relief, *The Ascension;* a small terra-cotta statue of the Madonna and Child by Antonio Rossellino; a marble group, *Samson and a Philstine,* by Giovanni Bologna; and a wax model of a slave by Michelangelo. The highlight of 16th-century art from the continent is the marble group *Neptune with Triton,* by Bernini. The cartoons by Raphael, which were conceived as designs for tapestries for the Sistine Chapel, are owned by the queen and can also be seen here.

A most unusual, huge, and impressive exhibit is the Cast Courts, life-size plaster models of ancient and medieval statuary and architecture.

Asiatic art is represented by stunning carpets from Persia and from every part of the Muslim world. The museum also has the greatest collection of Indian art outside India. Recently it opened Chinese and Japanese galleries as well. In complete contrast are suites of English furniture, metalwork, and ceramics dating beyond the 16th century, and a superb collection of portrait miniatures, including the one Hans Holbein the Younger made of Anne of Cleves for the benefit of Henry VIII, who was again casting around for a suitable wife.

A restaurant serves traditional English snacks and meals, and two museum shops sell gifts, posters, cards, and books.

Admission: Free, but donations of £3.50 ($5.30) suggested.
Open: Mon–Sat 10am–5:50pm, Sun 2:30–5:50pm. **Tube:** South Kensington.

2. MORE ATTRACTIONS

ROYAL LONDON

In the **Queen's Gallery,** entrance on Buckingham Palace Road, SW1. (tel. 071/799-2331), you can see a sampling of the royal family's art collection. I can't predict what exhibition you're likely to see, since they are changed yearly, but I can tell you that the queen's collection contains an unsurpassed range of royal portraits, including the well-known profile of Henry V; the companion portraits of Elizabeth I as a girl and her brother, Edward VI; four fine Georgian pictures by Zoffany; two portraits of Queen Alexandra from Sandringham; plus paintings of Queen Elizabeth II and other members of the royal family. Admission to the gallery is £2 ($3) for adults, £1 ($1.50) for children. It's open early March to late December Tuesday through Saturday and bank holidays from 10am to 5pm, and on Sunday from 2 to 5pm; closed Monday, except bank holidays. Tube: Green Park, Victoria, or St. James's.

You can get a close look at Queen Elizabeth II's coronation carriage at the **Royal**

⭐ **FROMMER'S FAVORITE LONDON EXPERIENCES**

Watching the Sun Set at Waterloo Bridge Waterloo Bridge is the best place in London to watch the sun set over Westminster in the west. The last rays can also be seen bouncing off The City's spires in the East End.

Enjoying a Pub Lunch Taking lunch in the bustling, overcrowded atmosphere of a London pub is totally uncomfortable but totally fun.

Enjoying a Traditional English Tea Nothing rounds out an afternoon quite like it—and nothing is more typically British.

Brass Rubbing You can re-create England's age of chivalry—all those costumed ladies and knights in armor—in medieval brasses. You can spend hours rubbing wax over paper taped over the brass to produce a picture to frame.

A Night at a West End Theater The West End was the stage for Shakespeare and Marlowe, and today it's also the stage for next year's Broadway hit.

Mews, on Buckingham Palace Road, SW1. (tel. 071/799-2331). Her Majesty's State Coach, built in 1761 to the designs of Sir William Chambers, has emblematic and other paintings on the panels and doors executed by Cipriani. The coach, traditionally drawn by eight gray horses, was formerly used by sovereigns when they traveled to open Parliament in person and on other state occasions. Queen Elizabeth used it in 1953 for her coronation and in 1977 for her Silver Jubilee Procession.

Admission is £2 ($3) for adults, £1 ($1.50) for children. It's open October through March, on Wednesday from noon to 4pm; from April to July 11, on Wednesday and Thursday, from noon to 4pm; and from July 17 through September, Wednesday through Friday from noon to 4pm. Tube: Green Park, Victoria, or St. James's.

OFFICIAL LONDON

Whitehall, SW1, the seat of the British government, grew up on the grounds of Whitehall Palace and was turned into a royal residence by Henry VIII, who snatched it from its former occupant, Cardinal Wolsey. Whitehall extends south from Trafalgar Square to Parliament Square. Along it you'll find the Home Office, the Old Admiralty Building, and the Ministry of Defence.

Visitors today can see the **Cabinet War Rooms,** the bombproof bunker suite of rooms, just as they were left by Winston Churchill and the British government at the end of World War II. You can see the Map Room with its huge wall maps, the Atlantic map a mass of pinholes (each hole represents at least one convoy). Next door is Churchill's bedroom-cum-office, which has a bed and a desk with two BBC microphones on it for his broadcasts of those famous speeches that stirred the nation.

The Transatlantic Telephone Room, to give it its full title, is little more than a broom closet, but it had the Bell Telephone Company's special scrambler phone, called Sig-Saly, and it was where Churchill conferred with Roosevelt. A system of boards with such laconic phrases as "wet," "very wet," "hot and sunny," "dry and dull" was used to indicate weather conditions around the world before maneuvers were planned. All visitors are provided with a step-by-step personal sound guide, providing a detailed account of the function and history of each room.

The entrance to the War Rooms is by Clive Steps at the end of King Charles Street,

SW1 (tel. 071/930-6961), off Whitehall near Big Ben. Visitors receive a cassette-recorded guided tour, and admission is £3.80 ($5.70) for adults and £1.90 ($2.90) for children. The rooms are open daily from 10am to 6pm (last admission at 5:25pm); they're closed on New Year's Day, Christmas holidays, and state occasions (sometimes on short notice). Tube: Westminster.

At the **Cenotaph** (honoring the dead from two world wars), turn down unpretentious Downing Street to the modest little town house at **No. 10,** flanked by two bobbies. Walpole was the first prime minister to live here, Churchill the most famous. But Margaret Thatcher was around longer than any of them.

Nearby is the **Horse Guards Building,** Whitehall, SW1 (tel. 071/930-4466, ext. 2396), now the headquarters, Household Division and London District. There has been a guard change here since 1649, when the site was the entrance to the old Palace of Whitehall. You can watch the Queen's Life Guards ceremony at 11am (10am on Sunday). You can also see the hourly smaller change of the guard, when mounted troopers are changed. And at 4pm you can watch the evening inspection, when 10 unmounted troopers and 2 mounted troopers assemble in the courtyard. Tube: Westminster.

Across the street is Inigo Jones's **Banqueting House,** Palace of Whitehall, Horse Guards Avenue, SW1 (tel. 071/930-4179), site of the execution of Charles I. William and Mary accepted the crown of England here, but they preferred to live at Kensington Palace. The Banqueting House was part of Whitehall Palace, which burned to the ground in 1698, but the ceremonial hall escaped razing. Its most notable feature today is an allegorical ceiling painted by Peter Paul Rubens. Admission to the Banqueting House is £2.75 ($4.10) for adults and £1.90 ($2.90) for children. It's open Monday through Saturday from 10am to 5pm and on Sunday from 2 to 5pm. Tube: Westminster.

Finally, stroll to Parliament Square for a view of **Big Ben,** the world's most famous timepiece and the symbol of the heart and soul of England. Big Ben is actually the name of the deepest and loudest bell, but it's become the common name for this clock tower on the Houses of Parliament. Opposite, in the gardens of Parliament Square, stands the statue of Churchill by Oscar Nemon. Tube: Westminster.

LEGAL LONDON

The smallest borough in London, bustling **Holborn** (pronounced Ho-burn) is often referred to as Legal London, home of the city's barristers, solicitors, and law clerks. It also embraces the university district of Bloomsbury. Holburn, which houses the ancient Inns of Court—Gray's Inn, Lincoln's Inn, Middle Temple, and Inner Temple—was severely damaged in World War II bombing raids. The razed buildings were replaced with modern offices, but the borough still retains pockets of its former days.

MIDDLE TEMPLE TUDOR HALL, Middle Temple Lane, EC4. Tel. 071/353-4355.

Going away from the Victoria Embankment, Middle Temple Lane leads between Middle and Inner Temple Gardens in the area known as **The Temple,** named after the medieval order of the Knights Templar (originally formed by the Crusaders in Jerusalem in the 12th century). It was in the Middle Temple Garden that Henry VI's barons are supposed to have picked the blooms of red and white roses and started the War of the Roses in 1430; today only members of the Temples and their guests are allowed to enter the gardens. But the Middle Temple contains a Tudor hall, completed in 1570, that is open to the public. It is believed that Shakespeare's troupe played *Twelfth Night* here in 1602. A table on view is said to have come from timber from Sir Francis Drake's *The Golden Hind*.

Admission: Free.
Open: Hall, Mon–Fri 10am–noon and 3–4pm. **Tube:** Temple.

TEMPLE CHURCH, The Temple, within the precincts of the Inner Temple, EC4. Tel. 071/353-1736.

One of three Norman "round churches" left in England, this was first completed in the 12th century—not surprisingly, it has been restored. Look for the knightly effigies and the Norman door, and take note of the circle of grotesque portrait heads, including a goat in a mortar board.

On Inner Temple Lane, about where the Strand becomes Fleet Street going east, is the memorial pillar called **Temple Bar,** which marks the boundary of the City.

Admission: Free.

Open: Mon–Sat 10am–4pm. **Tube:** Temple.

ROYAL COURTS OF JUSTICE, The Strand, WC2. Tel. 071/936-6751.

The Royal Courts of Justice stand north across the Strand. The building, which was completed in 1882 but designed in the 13th-century style, was the home of such courts as admiralty, divorce, probate, chancery, appeals, and Queen's Bench. Leave the Royal Courts building by the rear door and you'll be on Carey Street, not far from New Square.

Admission: Free.

Open: Mon–Fri 10am–4:30pm. **Tube:** Temple.

LINCOLN'S INN, Carey St., WC2.

This 14th-century inn evokes colleges at Cambridge or Oxford and forms an important link in the architectural maze of London. The chapel was rebuilt around 1620 by Inigo Jones, and Cromwell lived here at one time.

West of the inn lies the late 17th-century square, one of the few such London areas still complete, called Lincoln's Inn Fields.

Admission: Free.

Open: Chapel and gardens, daily noon–2:30pm. **Tube:** Holborn.

STAPLE INN, High Holborn St., WC1.

This half-timbered old inn near the Chancery Lane tube stop and eight other former Inns of Chancery are no longer in use in the legal world. Now lined with shops, it was built between 1545 and 1589 and has been rebuilt many times. Dr. Johnson moved here in 1759, the year *Rasselas* was published.

Tube: Chancery Lane.

GRAY'S INN, Gray's Inn Rd. (entrance on Theobald's Rd.), WC1. Tel. 071/405-8164.

Gray's Inn, north of High Holborn, is the fourth of the ancient Inns of Court still in operation. As you enter, you'll see a late Georgian terrace lined with buildings that, like many of the other houses in the inns, are combined residences and offices. Gray's was restored after suffering heavy damage in World War II bombings. Francis Bacon, scientist and philosopher (1561–1626), was its most eminent tenant. The inn contains a rebuilt Tudor Hall, but its greatest attraction is the tree-shaded lawn and handsome gardens, considered the best in the inns. The 17th-century atmosphere exists today only in the square.

Admission: Free.

Open: Mon–Sat 9am–5pm. **Tube:** Chancery Lane.

OLD BAILEY [CENTRAL CRIMINAL COURT], on the corner of Old Bailey and Newgate St., EC4. Tel. 071/248-3277.

This courthouse replaced the infamous Newgate Prison, once the scene of public hangings and other forms of public "entertainment." Entry is strictly on a first-arrival basis, and guests line up outside (where, incidentally, the final public execution took place in the 1860s). Courts 1 to 4, 17, and 18 are entered from Newgate Street, and the balance from Old Bailey (the street). To get here, travel east on Fleet Street, which

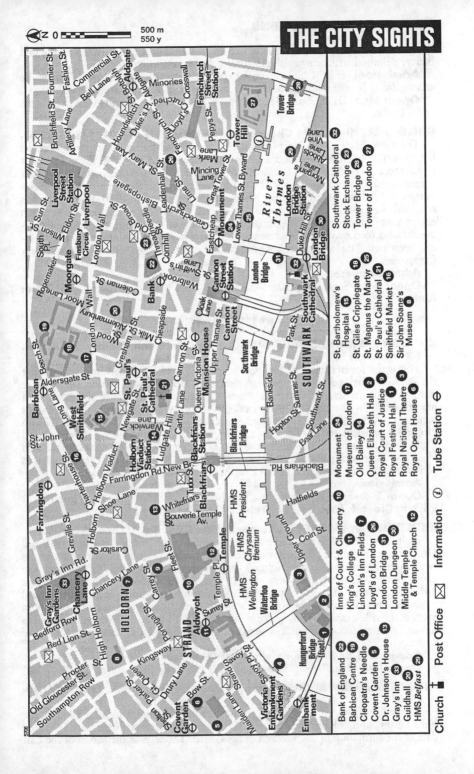

THE CITY SIGHTS

Bank of England ② Monument ⑰ St. Bartholomew's Hospital ㉒
Barbican Centre ⑲ Museum of London ㉔ St. Giles Cripplegate ⑮
Cleopatra's Needle ④ Old Bailey ⑭ St. Magnus the Martyr ⑱
Covent Garden ⑤ Queen Elizabeth Hall ⑨ St. Paul's Cathedral ㉑
Dr. Johnson's House ⑬ Royal Court of Justice ① Smithfield Market ⑯
Gray's Inn ㉝ Royal Festival Hall ③ Sir John Soane's Museum ⑧
Guildhall ⑳ Royal National Theatre ② Southwark Cathedral ㉜
HMS Belfast ㉙ Royal Opera House ⑥ Stock Exchange ㉓
Hungerford Bridge (foot) ① Inns of Court & Chancery ⑩ Tower Bridge ㉘
Victoria Embankment Gardens ④ King's College ⑪ Tower of London ㉗
Lincoln's Inn Fields ⑦
Lloyd's of London ㉖
London Bridge ㉛
London Dungeon ㉚
Middle Temple & Temple Church ⑫

Church ♦   Post Office ■   Information ⓘ   Tube Station ⊖

along the way becomes Ludgate Hill. Cross Ludgate Circus and turn left to the Old Bailey, a domed structure with the figure of *Justice* standing atop it.

Admission: Free. Children under 14 not admitted; ages 14–17 must be accompanied by a responsible adult. No cameras or tape recorders allowed.

Open: Mon–Fri 10:20am–1pm and 1:50–4pm. **Tube:** Temple, Chancery Lane, or St. Paul's.

GUILDHALL, King St. in Cheapside, The City, EC2. Tel. 071/606-3030.

The Civic Hall of the Corporation of London has had a rough time since its beginnings in 1411, notably in the Great Fire of 1666 and the 1940 Blitz. The most famous tenants of the rebuilt Guildhall are Gog and Magog, two giants standing over 9 feet high. The present giants are third generation, because the original effigies burned in the London fire, and the next set were destroyed in 1940. Restoration has returned the Gothic grandeur to the hall, which is replete with a medieval porch entranceway; monuments to Wellington, Churchill, and Nelson; stained glass commemorating lord mayors and mayors; and banners honoring fishmongers, haberdashers, merchant "taylors," ironmongers, and skinners—some of the major Livery Companies.

Admission: Free.

Open: May–Sept, daily 10am–5pm; Oct–Apr, Mon–Sat 10am–5pm. **Tube:** Bank.

MUSEUMS

SIR JOHN SOANE'S MUSEUM, 13 Lincoln's Inn Fields, WC2. Tel. 071/430-0175.

This is the former home of Sir John Soane (1753–1837) an architect who rebuilt the Bank of England (not the present structure). With his multilevels, fool-the-eye mirrors, flying arches, and domes, Soane was a master of perspective and a genius of interior space (his picture gallery, for example, is filled with three times the number of paintings a room of similar dimensions would be likely to hold). Don't miss William Hogarth's satirical series, *The Rake's Progress,* containing his much-reproduced *Orgy,* and the satire on politics in the mid-18th century, *The Election.* Soane also filled his house with paintings and classical sculpture. Be sure to see the sarcophagus of Pharaoh Seti I, found in a burial chamber in the Valley of the Kings.

Admission: Free.

Open: Tues–Sat 10am–5pm; first Tues of each month 6–9pm. Tours given Sat at 2:30pm. **Closed:** Bank holidays. **Tube:** Chancery Lane or Holborn.

IMPERIAL WAR MUSEUM, Lambeth Rd., SE1. Tel. 071/416-5000.

Built around 1815, this large domed building, the former Bethlehem Royal Hospital for the Insane, or Bedlam, houses the museum's collections relating to the two world wars and other military operations involving the British and the Commonwealth since 1914. There are four floors of exhibitions, including the Large Exhibits Gallery, a vast area showing historical displays, two floors of art galleries, and a dramatic re-creation of London at war in the Blitz. You can see a Battle of Britain Spitfire, the rifle carried by Lawrence of Arabia, Hitler's political testament, as well as models, decorations, uniforms, photographs, and paintings. It's located just across the Thames.

Admission: £3.70 ($5.60) adults, £1.85 ($2.80) children.

Open: Daily 10am–6pm. **Tube:** Lambeth North or Elephant & Castle.

NATIONAL ARMY MUSEUM, Royal Hospital Rd., SW3. Tel. 071/730-0717.

Located in Chelsea, this museum traces the history of the British land forces, the Indian army, and colonial land forces. The collection starts with the year 1485, the date of the formation of the Yeomen of the Guard. The saga of the forces of the East

India Company is also traced, from its beginning in 1602 and to Indian independence in 1947. The gory and glory is all here—everything from Florence Nightingale's lamp to the cloak wrapped around the dying Wolfe at Québec. Naturally, there are the "cases of the heroes," mementos of such outstanding men as the Duke of Marlborough and the Duke of Wellington. But the field soldier isn't neglected either: The Nation in Arms Gallery tells the soldier's story in two world wars, including an exhibit of the British Army in the Far East from 1941 to 1945.

Admission: Free.

Open: Daily 10am–5:30pm. **Closed:** Jan 1, Good Friday, May bank holiday, Dec 24–26. **Tube:** Sloane Square.

APSLEY HOUSE, the Wellington Museum, 149 Piccadilly, Hyde Park Corner, W1. Tel. 071/499-5676.

This former town house of the Iron Duke, the British general (1769–1852) who defeated Napoléon at the Battle of Waterloo and later became prime minister, was opened as a public museum in 1952. The building was designed by Robert Adam and was built in the late 18th century. Wellington once had to retreat behind the walls of Apsley House, fearing an attack from Englishmen outraged by his autocratic opposition to reform. In the vestibule, you'll find a colossal marble statue of Napoléon by Canova—ironic, to say the least; it was presented to the duke by King George IV.

In addition to the famous *Waterseller of Seville* by Velázquez, the Wellington collection includes works by Correggio, Jan Steen, and Pieter de Hooch. A large porcelain and china collection consists of a magnificent Sèvres porcelain Egyptian service originally made for Empress Joséphine and given to Wellington by Louis XVIII.

Admission: £2 ($3) adults, £1 ($1.50) children. The museum, closed at presstime, is slated to reopen in mid-1994. Call before going there.

Open: Daily 11am–5pm. **Closed:** Jan 1, May Day, Dec 24–26. **Tube:** Hyde Park Corner.

MUSEUM OF LONDON, 150 London Wall, EC2. Tel. 071/600-3699.

In London's Barbican district near St. Paul's Cathedral, the Museum of London allows visitors to trace the history of London from prehistoric times to the present—through relics, costumes, household effects, maps, and models. Anglo-Saxons, Vikings, Normans—they're all here, arranged on two floors around a central courtyard. The exhibits are arranged so that visitors can begin and end their chronological stroll through 250,000 years at the main entrance to the museum, and exhibits have quick labels for museum sprinters, more extensive ones for those who want to study, and still deeper details for scholars.

You'll see the death mask of Oliver Cromwell; the Great Fire of London in living color and sound; reconstructed Roman dining rooms with kitchen and utensils; cell doors from Newgate Prison made famous by Charles Dickens; and an amazing shop counter with pre–World War II prices on the items. But the pièce de résistance is the lord mayor's coach, built in 1757 and weighing 3 tons. Still used each November in the Lord Mayor's Procession, this gilt-and-red horse-drawn vehicle is like a fairy-tale coach.

The museum, which opened in 1976, overlooks London's Roman and medieval walls and was built at a cost of some $18 million. It's an enriching experience for everybody—at least an hour should be allowed for a full (but still quick) visit. Free lectures on London's history are often given during lunch hours; ask at the entrance hall if one will be given the day you're there. You can reach the museum by going up to the elevated pedestrian precinct at the corner of London Wall and Aldersgate, 5 minutes from St. Paul's. There is also a restaurant, which overlooks a garden.

Admission: £3 ($4.50) adults, £1.50 ($2.40) children.

Open: Tues–Sat 10am–6pm, Sun noon–6pm. **Tube:** St. Paul's or Barbican.

LONDON TRANSPORT MUSEUM, The Piazza, Covent Garden, WC2. Tel. 071/379-6344.

This splendidly restored Victorian building used to house the flower market. Horse buses, motorbuses, trams, trolleybuses, railway vehicles, models, maps, posters, photographs, and audiovisual displays illustrate the fascinating evolution of London's transport systems and how it has affected the growth of London. There are also a number of unique working displays: You can put yourself in the driver's seat of a tube train, a tram, and a bus, and also operate full-size signaling equipment. The exhibits include a reconstruction of George Shillibeer's omnibus of 1829, a steam locomotive that ran on the world's first underground railway, and a coach from the first deep-level electric railway. The museum sells a variety of souvenirs of London Transport (see Chapter 7 "London Shopping & Evening Entertainment").

Admission: £4 ($6) adults, £2 ($3) children.

Open: Daily 10am–6pm (last entry at 5:15pm). **Closed:** Dec 24–26. **Tube:** Covent Garden, Leicester Square, or Charing Cross.

NATIONAL POSTAL MUSEUM, King Edward Building, King Edward St., EC1. Tel. 071/239-5420.

This museum houses the most important collection of Victorian stamps from the Phillips collection as well as the public record collection of the artwork, essays, and registration sheets of all British stamps. It also features postage stamps from around the world issued since 1878.

Admission: Free.

Open: Mon–Fri 9:30am–4:30pm. **Tube:** St. Paul's or Barbican.

ROYAL AIR FORCE MUSEUM, Grahame Park Way, Hendon, NW9. Tel. 081/205-2266.

The Royal Air Force Museum, Britain's national museum of aviation, contains one of the world's finest collections of historic aircraft, and tells the story of flight through the display of more than 60 aircraft. The museum stands on 15 acres of the former airfield at Hendon in North London, and its main aircraft hall occupies two large hangars from World War I. The complex also includes a collection of famous bomber aircraft, including the Lancaster, Wellington, B17 Flying Fortress, Mosquito, and Vulcan.

In 1990, to celebrate the 50th anniversary of the Battle of Britain, the museum launched a major exhibition, the Battle of Britain Experience. Aircraft on display include the Spitfire, Hurricane, Gladiator, Blenheim, and Messerschmitt BF109. Features include cassette-tape tour guides and a flight simulator that allows visitors to experience flying an RAF Tornado.

The nearest British Rail station to the museum is Mill Hill Broadway. Access by road is via the A41, the A1, and the M1 (southbound), Junction 4.

Admission: £5 ($7.50) adults, £2.50 ($3.75) children.

Open: Daily 10am–6pm. **Closed:** Jan 1, Dec 24–26. **Tube:** Colindale.

SCIENCE MUSEUM, Exhibition Rd., SW7. Tel. 071/938-8000.

This museum traces the development and influence of science and industry. The collections are among the largest, most comprehensive, and most significant anywhere. On display is Stephenson's original *Rocket,* the tiny locomotive that beat all competitors in the Rainhill Trials and became the world's prototype railroad engine. You can also see Whittle's original jet engine and the Gloster aircraft, the first jet-powered British plane. A cavalcade of antique cars from the Stanley steam car to the yellow Rolls-Royce can be seen, side by side with carriages and vintage bicycles and motorcycles.

To aid the visitor's understanding of many scientific and technological principles, there are working models and video displays, including a hands-on gallery, called Launch Pad.

Admission: £4 ($6) adults, £2.10 ($3.20) children 5–15.
Open: Mon–Sat 10am–6pm, Sun 11am–6pm. **Tube:** South Kensington. **Bus:** 9, 10, 14, 52, or 74.

LINLEY SAMBOURNE HOUSE, 18 Stafford Terrace, W8. Tel. 081/994-1019.

You'll step back into the days of Queen Victoria when you visit this house, which has remained unchanged for more than a century. Part of a terrace built between 1868 and 1874, this is a five-story, Suffolk brick structure to which Linley Sambourne, a draftsman who later became a cartoonist for *Punch,* brought his bride. From the moment you step into the entrance hall, you see a mixture of styles and clutter that typified Victorian decor, with a plush portière, a fireplace valance, stained glass in the backdoor, and a large set of antlers vying for attention. The drawing room alone contains an incredible number of items.
Admission: £3 ($4.50) adults, £1.50 ($2.25) children under 16.
Open: Mar–Oct, Wed 10am–4pm, Sun 2–5pm. **Tube:** High Street Kensington.

DESIGN MUSEUM, Butlers Wharf, Shad Thames, SE1. Tel. 071/403-6933.

This is the only museum in Europe that explains why and how mass-produced objects work and look the way they do and how design contributes to the quality of our lives. The museum comprises: a collection of objects that include cars, furniture, domestic appliances, graphics, and ceramics; the Review, with its changing displays of new products and prototypes from around the world; a library, a shop; a café/bar; and the Blueprint Café, which serves lunch and dinner, plus brunch on Sunday. Located at Butlers Wharf, on the riverbank with views of the Tower Bridge and the River Thames, the Design Museum is a showcase of past and present design.
Admission: £3.50 ($5.30) adults, £2.50 ($3.80) children.
Open: Daily 9:30am–5:30pm. **Tube:** Tower Hill or London Bridge.

GALLERIES

NATIONAL PORTRAIT GALLERY, St. Martin's Place, WC2. Tel. 071/306-0055.

The National Portrait Gallery was founded in 1856 to collect the likenesses of famous British men and women. Today the collection is the most comprehensive of its kind in the world and constitutes a unique record of the men and women who created (and are still creating) the history and culture of the nation. A few paintings tower over the rest, including Sir Joshua Reynolds's portrait of Samuel Johnson ("a man of most dreadful appearance"). Among the best are Nicholas Hilliard's miniature of a handsome Sir Walter Raleigh and a full-length Elizabeth I, along with the Holbein cartoon of Henry VIII (sketched for a family portrait that hung, before it was burned, in the Privy Chamber in Whitehall Palace). You'll also see a portrait of William Shakespeare (with gold earring, no less), which is claimed to be the most "authentic contemporary likeness" of its subject of any work yet known. One of the most unusual pictures in the gallery—a group of the three Brontë sisters was painted by their brother, Branwell. For a finale, Diana, Princess of Wales, is on the Royal Landing.

The entrance to the museum is around the corner from the National Gallery on Trafalgar Square.
Admission: Free, except for special exhibitions.
Open: Mon–Fri 10am–5pm, Sat 10am–6pm, Sun 2–6pm. **Tube:** Charing Cross or Leicester Square.

WALLACE COLLECTION, Hertford House, Manchester Sq., W1. Tel. 071/935-0687.

This outstanding collection of artworks bequeathed to the nation by Lady Wallace in 1897 is still displayed in the house of its founders, off Wigmore Street. There are important pictures by artists of all European schools, including Titian, Rubens, van Dyck, Rembrandt, Hals, Velázquez, Murillo, Reynolds, Gainsborough, and Delacroix. Representing 18th-century France are paintings by Watteau, Boucher, and Fragonard, and sculpture, furniture, goldsmiths' work, and Sèvres porcelain. Also found are valuable collections of majolica and European and Asian arms and armor. Frans Hals's *Laughing Cavalier* is the most celebrated painting in the collection, but Pieter de Hooch's *A Boy Bringing Pomegranates* and Watteau's *The Music Party* are also well known. Other notable artists include Canaletto, Rembrandt, Gainsborough, and Boucher.

Admission: Free.

Open: Mon–Sat 10am–5pm, Sun 2–5pm. **Closed:** Jan 1, Good Friday, first Mon in May, Dec 24–26. **Tube:** Bond Street.

COURTAULD INSTITUTE GALLERIES, Somerset House, The Strand, WC2. Tel. 071/873-2526.

The home of the University of London's art collection, the Courtauld is noted for its superb impressionist and post-impressionist works. It has eight works by Cézanne alone, including his *A Man with a Pipe*. Other notable art includes Seurat's *Woman Powdering Herself,* van Gogh's self-portrait (with bandaged ear), a nude by Modigliani, Gauguin's *The Dream,* Monet's *Fall at Argenteuil,* Toulouse-Lautrec's delicious *Tête-à-Tête,* and Manet's *Bar at the Folies-Bergère.* The galleries also feature Renaissance works, including Giovanni Bellini's *The Assassination of St. Peter Martyr;* a Botticelli; a Veronese; a triptych by the Master of Flemalle; works by Pieter Brueghel the Elder, Massys, and Parmigianino; 32 oils by Rubens; oil sketches by Tiepolo; three landscapes by Kokoschka; and old-master drawings.

Admission: £3 ($4.50) adults, £1.50 ($2.30) children.

Open: Mon–Sat 10am–6pm, Sun 2–6pm. **Tube:** Charing Cross, Temple, or Covent Garden.

COMMONWEALTH INSTITUTE, Kensington High St., W8. Tel. 071/603-4535.

Why come just to London when you can visit the Caribbean, see Canada from a Skidoo, climb Mount Kenya, and take a ricksha across Bangladesh? The history, landscapes, wildlife, and crafts of the 50 Commonwealth countries are presented in this tent-shaped building next to Holland Park. Something's always happening here, ranging from special exhibitions, shows for children, or cultural festivals. The Commonwealth Shop is a source for gifts and other items, including food and wine, from around the world; light refreshments are sold at Flags Restaurant.

Admission: Free.

Open: Mon–Sat 10am–7pm; Sun 2–5pm. **Closed:** Dec 24–26, Jan 1, Good Friday, and May Day. **Tube:** High Street Kensington, Earl's Court, or Holland Park. **Bus:** 9, 10, 27, 28, 31, or 49.

ROYAL ACADEMY OF ARTS, Burlington House, Piccadilly, W1. Tel. 071/439-7438.

Founded in 1768, this is the oldest established society in Great Britain devoted solely to the fine arts. The academy is made up of a self-supporting, self-governing body of artists, who conduct art schools, hold exhibitions of the work of living artists, and organize loan exhibits of the arts of past and present periods. A summer exhibition, which has been held annually for an unbroken 225 years, presents contemporary paintings, drawings, engravings, sculpture, and architecture. The academy occupies Burlington House, which was built in Piccadilly in the 1600s and is opposite Fortnum and Mason.

Admission: Price depends on the exhibit.

Open: Royal Academy Shop, restaurant, and exhibition, daily 10am–6pm; framing workshop, Mon–Fri 10am–5pm. **Tube:** Piccadilly Circus or Green Park. **Bus:** 9, 14, 19, 22, or 38.

HAYWARD GALLERY, South Bank Centre, Belvedere Rd., SE1. Tel. 071/928-3144, or 071/261-0127 for recorded information.

Opened by Queen Elizabeth II in 1968, this gallery presents a changing program of major exhibitions. The gallery forms part of the South Bank Centre, which also includes the Royal Festival Hall, the Queen Elizabeth Hall, the Purcell Room, the National Film Theatre, and the National Theatre. The gallery is closed between exhibitions, so check before crossing the Thames.

Admission: £5 ($7.50) adults, £3.50 ($5.30) children, £12 ($18) family ticket.

Open: Thurs–Mon 10am–6pm, Tues–Wed 10am–8pm. **Tube:** Waterloo Station.

HAMPSTEAD & HIGHGATE

HAMPSTEAD HEATH

Located about 4 miles north of the center of London, Hampstead Heath consists of hundreds of acres of wild and unfenced royal parkland. On a clear day you can see St. Paul's Cathedral and even the hills of Kent south of the Thames from here. For years, Londoners have come here for kite flying, sunning, fishing in the ponds, swimming, picnicking, and jogging. In good weather, it's also the site of big 1-day fairs. Tube: Hampstead Heath.

HAMPSTEAD VILLAGE

When the Underground came to this town in 1907, its attraction as a place to live became widely known, and writers, artists, architects, musicians, and scientists— some from the City—came to join earlier residents. Keats, D. H. Lawrence, Rabindranath Tagore, Shelley, and Robert Louis Stevenson all once lived here, and Kingsley Amis and John Le Carré still do.

The Regency and Georgian houses in this village are just 20 minutes by tube from Piccadilly Circus. There's a palatable mix of historic pubs, toy shops, and chic boutiques along Flask Walk, a pedestrian mall. The original village, on the side of a hill, still has old roads, alleys, steps, courts, and groves to be strolled through.

KEATS HOUSE, Wentworth Place, Keats Grove, Hampstead, NW3. Tel. 071/435-2062.

The famous romantic poet John Keats lived here for only 2 years, but that was something like two-fifths of his creative life, because he died in Rome of tuberculosis at the age of 25 (1821). In Hampstead, Keats wrote some of his most celebrated odes—in praise of a Grecian urn and to the nightingale. His Regency house is well preserved and contains the manuscripts of his last sonnet ("Bright star, would I were steadfast as thou art"), and a portrait of him on his deathbed in a house on the Spanish Steps in Rome.

Admission: Suggested donation, £1.50 ($2.30) adults, 75p ($1.10) children.

Open: Apr–Oct, Mon–Fri 10am–1pm and 2–6pm, Sat 10am–1pm and 2–5pm, Sun 2–5pm; Nov–Mar, Mon–Fri 1–5pm, Sat 10am–1pm and 2–5pm, Sun 2–5pm. **Tube:** Belsize Park or Hampstead. **Bus:** 24 from Trafalgar Square.

KENWOOD [IVEAGH BEQUEST], Hampstead Lane, NW3. Tel. 081/348-1286.

Kenwood was built as a gentleman's country home in the early 18th century. In 1754 it became the seat of Lord Mansfield and was enlarged and decorated by the famous Scottish architect Robert Adam from 1764. In 1927 Lord Iveagh gave it to the nation, along with his art collection. The rooms contain some fine neoclassical furniture, but the main attractions are the works by old masters and British artists. You can see paintings by Rembrandt (*Self-Portrait in Old Age*), Vermeer, Turner, Frans Hals, Gainsborough, Reynolds, Romney, Raeburn, Guardi, and Angelica

Kauffmann, plus a portrait of the Earl of Mansfield, Lord Chief Justice, who made Kenwood such an important home. A 19th-century family coach that comfortably carried 15 people stands in the Coach House, where there is also a cafeteria.
Admission: Free.
Open: Apr–Sept, daily 10am–6pm; Oct–Maundy Thursday, daily 10am–4pm.
Closed: Dec 24–25. **Tube:** Golders Green, then bus 210.

FENTON HOUSE, Windmill Hill, NW3. Tel. 071/435-3471.

This National Trust property is on the west side of Hampstead Grove, just a short distance north of Hampstead Village. You pass through beautiful wrought-iron gates to reach the red-brick house in a walled garden. Built in 1693, it's one of the earliest, largest, and finest houses in the Hampstead section. The original main staircase, some door frames, and chimneypieces remain of the early construction. Paneled rooms contain furniture, pictures, English, German, and French porcelain from the 18th century, and the outstanding Benton-Fletcher collection of early keyboard musical instruments. Exhibits of these date from 1540 to 1805 and include a 17th-century Flemish harpsichord on loan from the Queen Mother, other harpsichords, spinets, clavichords, and a virginal. Occasional concerts are held at the house.
Admission: £3 ($4.50) adults, £1.50 ($2.30) children.
Open: Mar, Sat–Sun 2–6pm; Apr–Oct, Mon–Wed 1–7pm, Sat–Sun 11am–6pm.
Closed: Good Friday and Nov–Feb. **Tube:** Hampstead.

FREUD MUSEUM, 20 Maresfield Gardens, NW3. Tel. 071/435-2002.

After he and his family left Nazi-occupied Vienna as refugees, Sigmund Freud lived, worked, and died in this spacious three-story red-brick house in northern London. On view are rooms containing original furniture, letters, photographs, paintings, and personal effects of Freud and his daughter, Anna. A focal point of the museum is the study and library, where you can see the famous couch and Freud's large collection of Egyptian, Roman, and Asian antiquities. This domestic and working environment offers a unique perspective on the contribution that Freud made to the understanding of the human mind.
Admission: £2.50 ($3.80) adults, free for children under 12.
Open: Wed–Sun noon–5pm. **Tube:** Finchley Road.

BURGH HOUSE, New End Sq., NW3. Tel. 071/431-0144.

A Queen Anne structure built in 1703 in the middle of the village, this was at one time the residence of the daughter and son-in-law of Rudyard Kipling, who often visited here. It's now used for local art exhibits, concerts, recitals, and talks and public meetings on many subjects, and the house is the home of several local societies, including the Hampstead Music Club and the Hampstead Scientific Society.

The **Hampstead Museum** is also in Burgh House and displays and illustrates the area's local history. It has a room devoted to reproductions by the great artist John Constable, who lived nearby for many years and was buried in the local parish church. There is also a bookstall, well stocked with souvenirs and postcards, plus a licensed buttery (tel. 071/431-2516), popular for lunch or tea (its prices are the lowest in Hampstead).
Admission: Free.
Open: House and museum, Wed–Sun noon–5pm; buttery, Wed–Sun 11am–5:30pm. **Tube:** Hampstead.

HIGHGATE VILLAGE

A stone's throw east of Hampstead Heath, Highgate Village has a number of 16th- and 17th-century mansions, as well as small cottages, lining three sides of the now-pondless Pond Square. Its most outstanding feature, however, is **Highgate Cemetery**—entered from Swain's Lane, N6 (tel. 071/340-1834)—the ideal setting for a collection of Victorian sculpture. Once described in the British press as everything from "walled romantic rubble" to "an anthology of horror," the 37-acre burial ground attracts tombstone fanciers. Highgate's most famous grave is that of Karl Marx, who died in Hampstead in 1883; on the tomb is a huge bust of Marx, inscribed with his quotation, "Workers of the world, unite."

The Western Cemetery can be visited only on a guided tour, leaving April through October Monday through Friday at noon, 2pm, and 4pm, and on Saturday and Sunday hourly from 11am to 4pm. In winter, tours are conducted Tuesday through Friday at noon, 2pm, and 3pm, and on Saturday and Sunday hourly from 11am to 3pm. The Eastern Cemetery can be visited on your own any time daily from 10am to 4:45pm, April through October. In winter, it is open daily from 10am to 3:45pm. For a tour, a donation of £4 ($6) is requested. Tube: Archway, then walk through Waterlow Park.

THE PARKS OF LONDON

London's parklands easily rate as the greatest system of "green lungs" of any large city on the globe. Not as rigidly laid out as the parks of Paris, London's are maintained with a loving care and lavish artistry that puts their American equivalents to shame. Above all, they've been kept safe from land-hungry building firms and city councils. Maybe there's something to be said for inviolate "royal" property, after all. Because that's what most of London's parks are.

Largest of them—and one of the biggest in the world—is **Hyde Park,** W2. With the adjoining Kensington Gardens, it covers 636 acres of central London with velvety lawns interspersed with ponds, flowerbeds, and trees. Hyde Park was once a favorite deer-hunting ground of Henry VIII. Running through the width is a 41-acre lake known as the Serpentine. Rotten Row, a 1½-mile sand track, is reserved for horseback riding and on Sunday attracts some skilled equestrians.

Kensington Gardens, W2, blending with Hyde Park, border on the grounds of Kensington Palace. These gardens contain the celebrated statue of Peter Pan, with the bronze rabbits that toddlers are always trying to kidnap. The Albert Memorial is also here.

East of Hyde Park, across Piccadilly, stretch **Green Park** and **St. James's Park,** W1, forming an almost-unbroken chain of landscaped beauty. This is an ideal area for picnics, which you'll find hard to believe was once a festering piece of swamp near the leper hospital. There is a romantic lake, stocked with a variety of ducks and pelicans, descendants of the pair that the Russian ambassador presented to Charles II in 1662.

IN THEIR FOOTSTEPS

Oscar Wilde (1854–1900) Born in Dublin, this British poet, novelist, and dramatist was noted for his epigrammatic wit. Eccentric in taste and dress, he served 2 years in prison on a conviction of homosexuality before retreating— bankrupted and disgraced—to Paris, where he died.

• **Accomplishments:** Best remembered for his plays, Wilde was a genius of the English theater, as exemplified by *The Importance of Being Earnest* and *Lady Windermere's Fan.* His *The Picture of Dorian Gray* became in its time a notorious novel.

• **Favorite Haunts:** Café Royale in London; various boy brothels.

• **Residences:** In London: 1 Tite St., SW3; 34 Tite St., SW3; and 10–11 St. James's St., SW1.

• **Resting Place:** Père-Lachaise (Paris).

Regent's Park, NW1, covers most of the district by that name, north of Baker Street and Marylebone Road. Designed by the 18th-century genius John Nash to surround a palace of the prince regent that never materialized, this is the most classically beautiful of London's parks. The core is a rose garden planted around a small lake alive with waterfowl and spanned by humped Japanese bridges. The Open-Air Theatre and the London Zoo are here, and, as in all the local parks, there are hundreds of deck chairs on the lawns in which to sunbathe. The deck-chair attendants, who collect a small fee, are mostly college students on vacation.

MARBLE ARCH & SPEAKERS' CORNER

At the northwest extremity of Mayfair, head for **Marble Arch,** an enormous *faux pas* that the English didn't try to hide but turned into a monument. Originally it was built by John Nash as the entrance to Buckingham Palace, but it was discovered that it was too small for carriages to pass through. In this part of Hyde Park (Tube: Marble Arch) is **Speakers' Corner,** where you will see English free speech in action. Everybody from terrorists to Orgone theorists mounts the soapbox to speak their minds. The speeches reach their most vehement pitch on Sunday, the best day to visit Marble Arch.

LANDMARK CHURCHES

St. Martin-in-the-Fields, overlooking Trafalgar Square, WC2 (tel. 071/930-0089), is the Royal Parish Church, dear to the hearts of many English people, especially the homeless. The present classically inspired church, with its famous steeple, dates from 1726; James Gibbs, a pupil of Wren's, is listed as the architect. The first known church on the site dates from the 13th century; among the congregation in years past was George I, who was actually a churchwarden, unique for an English sovereign. From St. Martin's vantage position in the theater district, it has drawn many actors to its door—none more notable than Nell Gwynne, the mistress of Charles II. On her death in 1687, she was buried in the crypt. Throughout the war, many Londoners rode out uneasy nights in the crypt, while Blitz bombs rained down overhead. One, in 1940, blasted out all the windows. Today the crypt contains a pleasant restaurant, a bookshop, and a gallery. Tube: Charing Cross.

St. Etheldreda's, Britain's oldest Roman Catholic church, lies on Ely Place, Clerkenwell, EC1 (tel. 071/405-1061), leading off Charterhouse Street at Holborn Circus. Built in 1251, it was mentioned by the Bard in both *Richard II* and *Richard III*. One of the survivors of the Great Fire of 1666, the church was built by and was the property of the diocese of Ely in the days when many bishops had their episcopal houses in London as well as in the actual cathedral cities in which they held their sees. Until this century, the landlord of Ye Olde Mitre public house near Ely Place had to obtain his license from the Justices of Cambridgeshire rather than in London, and even today the place is still a private road, with impressive iron gates and a lodge for the gatekeeper, all administered by six elected commissioners.

St. Etheldreda, whose name is sometimes shortened to St. Audrey, was a 7th-century king's daughter who left her husband and turned to religion, establishing an abbey on the Isle of Ely. The word *tawdry* comes from the cheap trinkets sold at the annual fair honoring St. Audrey. St. Etheldreda's is made up of a crypt and an upper church and caters to working people and visitors who come to pray. It has a distinguished musical tradition, with an 11am Latin mass on Sunday. Other mass times are on Sunday at 9am and 6pm, Monday through Friday at 8am and 1pm, and on Saturday at 8am. Lunches are served Monday through Friday from noon to 2pm in the Pantry, with a varied choice of hot and cold dishes. Tube: Farringdon or Chancery Lane.

ALONG THE THAMES

All of London's history and development is linked to this winding ribbon of water—which connects the city with the sea—from which London drew its wealth and its power. For centuries the river was London's highway and main street, and today there is a row of fascinating attractions lying on, across, and alongside the River Thames.

Some of the bridges that span the Thames are household words. **London Bridge,** which, contrary to the nursery rhyme, has never "fallen down," but was dismantled and shipped to the United States in 1971 and was immediately replaced by a new London Bridge; it ran from the Monument (a tall pillar commemorating the Great Fire of 1666) to Southwark Cathedral, parts of which date from 1207.

Its neighbor to the east is the still-standing **Tower Bridge,** E1. (tel. 071/407-0922), one of the city's most celebrated landmarks and possibly the most photographed and painted bridge on earth. The Tower Bridge was built during 1886–94 with two towers 200 feet apart, joined by footbridges that provide glass-covered walkways for the public, who can enter the north tower, take the elevator to the walkway, cross the river to the south tower, and return to street level. The bridge is a photographer's dream, with interesting views of St. Paul's, the Tower of London, and in the distance, a part of the Houses of Parliament.

You can also visit the main engine room with Victorian boilers and steam-pumping engines, which used to raise and lower the roadway across the river. Among the exhibitions that trace the history and operation of this unique bridge are models showing how the 1,000-ton arms of the bridge can be raised in 1½ minutes to allow ships' passage. Nowadays, electric power is used to raise the bridge, an occurrence that usually happens about once a day, more often in summer. When it's going to open, a bell sounds throughout the bridge and road traffic is stopped. Admission to exhibits is £3.50 ($5.30) for adults and £2.50 ($3.80) for children. It's open daily in summer from 10am to 6:30pm (to 4:45pm in winter). Tube: Tower Hill.

The piece of river between the site of the old London Bridge and the Tower Bridge marks the city end of the immense row of docks stretching 26 miles to the coast. Although most of them are no longer in use, they have long been known as the **Port of London.**

Particular note should be taken of the striking removal of pollution from the Thames in the past decades. The river, so polluted in the 1950s that no marine life could exist in it, can now lay claim to being "the cleanest metropolitan estuary in the world," with many varieties of fish, even salmon, living in its waters.

THE THAMES FLOOD BARRIER

From time to time throughout centuries, the Thames estuary has brought tidal surges that have on occasion caused disastrous flooding at Woolwich, Hammersmith, Whitehall, Westminster, plus other areas within the river's flood reaches. Furthermore, the flooding peril has increased during this century due to natural causes: the unstoppable rise of tide levels in the Thames; surge tides from the Atlantic; and the down-tilt of the country by some 12 inches a century.

All this led to the construction, beginning in 1975, of the Thames Flood Barrier with huge piers linking mammoth rising sector gates, smaller rising sector gates, and falling radial gates, all of which can make a solid steel wall about the height of a five-story building, which completely dams the waters of the Thames, keeping the surge tides from passage up the estuary. The gates are operated every month to remove river silt and be sure they work smoothly.

Since its official opening in 1984, the engineering spectacle has drawn increasing crowds to the site, at a point in the river known as Woolwich Reach in east London, where the Thames is a straight stretch about a third of a mile in width. **London Launches** (tel. 071/930-3373) offers trips to the barrier, operating from Westminster Pier. At the Barrier Centre, an audiovisual show depicts the need for the barrier and its operation, and there are also a souvenir shop, a snack bar, and a cafeteria. London Launches leave five times daily from Westminster Pier, with returns from Barrier Pier. Adults pay £5.40 ($8.10) round-trip or £3.80 ($5.70) one way. Children under 14 are charged £2.75 ($4.10) round-trip or £2.20 ($3.30) one way.

It's also possible to take the boat over and then return by train; the tube stop is Charlton Station. Trains there depart for central London every 30 minutes, and the ride takes only 15 minutes.

The **Thames Barrier Visitors' Centre,** Unity Way, Woolwich, SE18 (tel. 081/854-1373), is open Monday through Friday from 10:30am to 5pm and on Saturday and Sunday from 10:30am to 5:30pm. Admission is £2.25 ($3.40) for adults and £1.40 ($2.10) for children.

A FLOATING MUSEUM

HMS *Belfast,* Morgan's Lane, Tooley Street, SE1 (tel. 071/407-6434), Europe's largest historic warship, is permanently moored on the Thames, opposite the Tower of London. This World War II veteran was among the first to open fire against German fortifications on D day. It also served with distinction during the Korean War, where it earned the name "that straight-shooting ship" from the United States Navy. By exploring the ship from the bridge right down to the engine and boiler rooms, seven decks below, you can discover how Royal Navy sailors lived and fought during the past 50 years. Visitors can explore the bridge, operations room, 6-inch gun turrets, living quarters, and galley. The HMS *Belfast* is open daily from 10am to 6pm in summer and from 10am to 4:30pm in winter. Last boardings are 30 minutes before closing. Admission is £4 ($6) for adults, £2 ($3) for children, with a discounted ticket of £10 ($15) for two adults and two children. Tube: London Bridge or Tower Hill. A ferry runs daily in summer from Tower Pier (Tower of London) directly to the ship; in off-season, it operates only on Saturday and Sunday, and does not run at all from mid-December through January.

LONDON DOCKLANDS

What was once a dilapidated 8 square miles of property surrounded by water—some 55 miles of waterfront acreage within a sailor's cry of London's major attractions—has been reclaimed and restored. Today London Docklands is coming into its own as a leisure, residential, and commercial lure.

Included in this complex are Wapping, the Isle of Dogs, the Surrey and Royal Docks, and more, all with Limehouse at its heart. A visit to the **Exhibition Centre** on the Isle of Dogs offers an opportunity to see what the Docklands past, present, and future include. Already the area has provided space for overflow from the City of London's square mile, and it looks as though the growth and development is more than promising. A shopping village at Tobacco Dock, a new home at Shadwell Basin for the Academy of St. Martin-in-the-Fields Orchestra, and the London Arena (largest human-made sport-and-leisure complex in the country) at the tip of the Isle of Dogs are being joined by luxury condominiums, offices, hotels, museums, and theaters; these and all the other amenities aimed at making the East End of London a desirable place to live and visit have been or soon will be completed.

The former urban wasteland of deserted warehouses and derelict wharves can be visited by taking the **Docklands Light Railway** that links the Isle of Dogs and London Underground's Tower Hill station, via several new local stations. To see the whole complex, take the railway at the Tower Gateway near Tower Bridge for a short journey through Wapping and the Isle of Dogs. Get off at Island Gardens and pass through the 100-year-old Greenwich Tunnel under the Thames to see the attractions at Greenwich described below in "Easy Excursions from London." A regular waterbus service connects Greenwich with Charing Cross in a river voyage of about half an hour, and other tunnels are planned to link the Docklands with port points and motorways.

3. COOL FOR KIDS

The following attractions are fun places to which you can take youngsters without having to worry about their safety. However, you don't need a juvenile escort to have fun visiting them—it's even possible that you'll enjoy them more than any kid around. This isn't to say that the other sights listed in this chapter aren't fun for kids—at the British Museum, for example, I've watched group after group of kids stand absolutely spellbound in front of the Egyptian mummies, while their parents tug at them to trot along.

SIGHTS

THE LONDON DUNGEON, 28-34 Tooley St., SE1. Tel. 071/403-7221.

Set under the arches of London Bridge Station, the dungeon is a series of tableaux, more grizzly than Madame Tussaud's, that faithfully reproduces the ghoulish conditions of the Middle Ages. The rumble of trains overhead adds to the spine-chilling horror of the place. Bells toll, and there is constant melancholy chanting in the background. Dripping water and live rats (caged!) make for even more atmosphere. The heads of executed criminals were stuck on spikes for onlookers to observe through glasses hired for the occasion. The murder of Thomas à Becket in Canterbury Cathedral is also depicted. Naturally, there's a burning at the stake, as well as a torture chamber with racking, branding, and fingernail extraction. The Great Fire of London is brought to crackling life by a computer-controlled spectacular that re-creates Pudding Lane, where the fire started.

Of course this experience may not be to every child's (or adult's) taste. If you survive, there is a souvenir shop selling certificates to testify that you have been through the works.

Admission: £5.50 ($8.30) adults, £3.50 ($5.30) children under 14.

Open: Apr–Sept, daily 10am–5:30pm; Oct–Mar, daily 10am–4:30pm. **Closed:** Dec 24–25. **Tube:** London Bridge.

NATURAL HISTORY MUSEUM, Cromwell Rd., SW7. Tel. 071/938-9123.

This is the home of the national collections of living and fossil plants, animals, minerals, rocks, and meteorites, with lots of magnificent specimens on display. Exciting exhibitions designed to encourage people of all ages to enjoy learning about modern natural history include "Human Biology—An Exhibition of Ourselves," "Man's Place in Evolution," "British Natural History," and "Discovering Mammals." The exhibition that attracts the most attention is a 13,000-square-foot dinosaur exhibit, displaying 14 complete dinosaur skeletons. The center of the show depicts a trio of ripping, clawing, chewing, moving, full-size robotic Deinonychus caught having a freshly killed Tenontosaurus for lunch.

Admission: £4 ($6) adults, £2 ($3) children.

Open: Mon–Sat 10am–6pm, Sun 1–6pm. **Closed:** Dec 23–26 and Jan 1. **Tube:** South Kensington.

BETHNAL GREEN MUSEUM OF CHILDHOOD, Cambridge Heath Rd., E2. Tel. 081/980-3204.

Here you'll find displays of toys from the past century. The variety of dolls alone is staggering, some of them dressed in elaborate period costumes. The dollhouses range from simple cottages to miniature mansions, complete with fireplaces, grand pianos, carriages, furniture, kitchen utensils, and household pets. In addition, the museum displays optical toys, toy theaters, marionettes, puppets, and an exhibit of soldiers and battle toys of both world wars. There is also a display of children's clothing and furniture.

Admission: Free.

Open: Mon–Thurs and Sat 10am–5:50pm, Sun 2:30–5:50pm. **Tube:** Bethnal Green.

ROCK CIRCUS, London Pavilion, 1 Piccadilly Circus, W1. Tel. 071/734-7203.

Run by the Tussaud's Group of Madame Tussaud's waxworks, this place tells the story of rock and pop music from the 1950s through the present day, using a combination of wax and "moving" bionic likenesses of all the big names in rock from the past four decades. Very young children might not understand it, but preteens and teenagers will love it. Visitors also get to hear the famous songs from rock history. The highlight of the Rock Circus is a show using Audio Animatronic techniques, in which the Beatles, Elvis Presley, Madonna, Bruce Springsteen, and other perform "live."

Admission: £6.50 ($9.80) adults, £4.50 ($6.80) children ages 15 or under.

Open: Daily 10am–10pm. **Tube:** Piccadilly Circus.

ENTERTAINMENT

UNICORN THEATRE FOR CHILDREN, the Arts Theatre, 6–7 Great Newport St., WC2. Tel. 071/379-3280, or 071/836-3334 for the box office.

Situated in the heart of London's "Theatreland," the Unicorn, founded in 1947 and going stronger than ever, is the city's only theater just for children. The adult actors and actresses present a season of plays for 4- to 12-year-olds each year. A program includes specially commissioned plays, adaptations of old favorites, and entertainment of the highest quality.

Admission: Tickets, £3.50 ($5.30), £5 ($7.50), and £6.50 ($9.80) adults or children, depending on seat locations.

Open: Performances, Sept–June, Sat–Sun and school holidays at 2:30pm. **Tube:** Leicester Square.

LITTLE ANGEL MARIONETTE THEATRE, 14 Dagmar Passage, Cross St., N1. Tel. 071/226-1787.

Specially constructed for presentation of puppetry in all its forms, this theater is open to the general public and has 200 to 300 performances each year. The theater is the focal point of a loosely formed group of some 20 professional puppeteers who present their own shows or help with performances of the resident company. These vary in style and content from *The Soldier's Tale,* using 8-foot-high figures, to *The Nine Pointed Crown* and *Lancelot the Lion,* written especially for the humble glove puppet. Many of the plays, such as Hans Christian Andersen's *The Little Mermaid,* are performed with marionettes. You'll be enthralled by the exquisite lighting and the skill with which the puppets are handled.

The theater is beautifully decorated and is well equipped. There's a coffee bar in the foyer and a workshop where the settings and costumes, as well as the puppets, are made. To find out what's playing and to reserve your seats, call the number above. Also, there are many special programs during the Christmas season.

Admission: £4.50–£6 ($6.80–$9) adults, £4–£5 ($6–$7.50) children.

Open: Shows, Sat–Sun at 11am and 3pm. **Tube:** Angel Station (then walk up Upper St. to St. Mary's Church and down the footpath to the left of the church), Highbury and Islington Station; or go by car or taxi to Essex Rd. and then up to Dagmar Terrace.

OUTDOOR ACTIVITIES

Battersea Park, SW11 (tel. 081/871-7530), is a vast patch of woodland, lakes, and lawns on the south bank of the Thames, opposite Chelsea Embankment between Albert Bridge and Chelsea Bridge. Formerly known as Battersea Fields, the present park was laid out in 1852–58 on an old dueling ground (the most famous duel fought here was between Lord Winchelsea and the Duke of Wellington in 1829). The park, which measures three-quarters of a mile on each of its four sides, has a lake for boating, a fenced-in deer park with wild birds, and fields for tennis and football (soccer). There's even a children's zoo.

The park's architectural highlight is a Peace Pagoda—built of stone and wood—that was donated in 1986 to the now-defunct Council of Greater London by an order of Japanese monks.

The park, open May through September daily from 7:30am until dusk, is not well serviced by public transportation. The nearest tube is in Chelsea on the right bank (Sloane Square); from there it's a brisk 15-minute walk. If you prefer to ride the bus, take no. 137 from the Sloane Square station, exiting at the first stop after the bus crosses the Thames.

One of the greatest zoos in the world, the **London Zoo,** Regent's Park, NW1 (tel. 071/722-3333), is more than 150 years old. Run by the Zoological Society of London, the 36-acre garden houses some 8,000 animals, including some of the rarest species on earth. Separate houses are reserved for some species: the insect house (incredible bird-eating spiders, a cross-sectioned ant colony); the reptile house (huge dragonlike monitor lizards and a fantastic 15-foot python); and other additions, such as the Sobell Pavilion for Apes and Monkeys and the Lion Terraces.

Designed for the largest collection of small mammals in the world, the Clore Pavilion has a basement called the Moonlight World, where special lighting effects simulate night for the nocturnal beasties, while rendering them clearly visible to onlookers. You can see all the night rovers in action.

Many families spend an entire day with the animals, watching seals being fed, enjoying an animal ride in summer, and meeting the young elephants on their walks. There are two fully licensed restaurants—one self-service and the other with waiters.

Zoo admission is £6 ($9) for adults, £3.70 ($5.60) for children 4 to 14, free for children under 4. The zoo is open daily from 10am to dusk (last entrance is 1 hour before closing). Take the tube to Camden Town or bus no. 274 or Z1 in summer only.

Hampstead Heath, the traditional playground of the Londoner, was dedicated "to the use of the public forever" by a special Act of Parliament in 1872. This 800-acre expanse of high heath entirely surrounded by London is a chain of continuous park, wood, and grassland that contains just about every known form of outdoor amusement, with the exception of deep-sea fishing and big-game hunting. There are natural lakes for swimmers who don't mind goose bumps, bridle paths for horseback riders, athletic tracks, hills for kite flying, and a special pond for model yachting. At the shore of Kenwood Lake, in the northern section, is a concert platform devoted to symphony performances on summer evenings. In the northeast corner, in Waterlow Park, ballets, operas, and comedies are staged at the Grass Theatre in June and July. Tube: Hampstead or Belsize Park.

4. SPECIAL-INTEREST SIGHTSEEING

FOR THE LITERARY ENTHUSIAST

See the discussion of Hampstead Village, under "More Attractions," above, for details on Keats's House.

SAMUEL JOHNSON'S HOUSE, 17 Gough Sq., EC4. Tel. 071/353-3745.

Dr. Johnson and his copyists compiled his famous dictionary in this Queen Anne house, where the lexicographer, poet, essayist, and fiction writer lived from 1748 to 1759. Although Johnson also lived at Staple Inn in Holborn and at a number of other houses, the Gough Square house is the only one of his London residences remaining. The 17th-century building has been painstakingly restored, and it's well worth a visit.

Admission: £2 ($3) adults, £1.50 ($2.30) children.

Open: May–Sept, Mon–Sat 11am–5:30pm; Oct–Apr, Mon–Sat 11am–5pm. **Tube:** Blackfriars (when you come out of the tube station, walk up New Bridge St. and turn left onto Fleet St.; Gough Square is a tiny, hidden square, north of Fleet) or Temple.

CARLYLE'S HOUSE, 24 Cheyne Row, SW3. Tel. 071/352-7087.

From 1834 to 1881 the author of *The French Revolution* and his letter-writing wife took up abode in this modest 1708 terraced house. Furnished essentially as it was in Carlyle's day, the house is located about three-quarters of a block from the Thames, near the Chelsea Embankment and King's Road. It was described by his wife as being "of most antique physiognomy, quite to our humour; all wainscotted, carved and queer-looking, roomy, substantial, commodious, with closets to satisfy any Bluebeard." The second floor features the drawing room of Mrs. Carlyle, but the most interesting chamber is the not-so-soundproof "soundproof" study in the skylit attic. Filled with Carlyle memorabilia—his books, a letter from Disraeli, a writing chair, even his death mask—this is where the author labored over his *Frederick the Great* manuscript.

Admission: £2.50 ($3.80) adults, £1.25 ($1.90) children.

Open: Easter Sat–Oct, Wed–Sun 11am–5pm. **Tube:** Sloane Square. **Bus:** 11, 19, 22, or 49.

DICKENS'S HOUSE, 48 Doughty St., WC1. Tel. 071/405-2127.

IN THEIR FOOTSTEPS

Samuel Johnson (1709–84), lexicographer and savant. The son of an unsuccessful bookdealer, Johnson never finished college at Oxford. In 1735, the brillant author, critic, and conversationalist married Elizabeth Porter, an older woman whom he called Tetty. When he was 28, Johnson came to London. James Boswell, a Scot, helped immortalize him by becoming his biographer.

- **Accomplishments:** His *A Dictionary of the English Language* was by far the best in its field for nearly a century. *Lives of the Poets* stands as a memorial to his genius.
- **Favorite Haunts:** Ye Olde Cheshire Cheese.
- **Residences:** His most famous was at 17 Gough Sq. (now a museum).
- **Resting Place:** Westminster Abbey (Poets' Corner).

The great English novelist, born in 1812 in what is now Portsmouth, lived here from 1837 to 1839. Unlike some of the London town houses of famous men (Wellington, Soane), the Bloomsbury house is simple—the embodiment of middle-class restraint. The house has an extensive library, including manuscripts and letters second in importance only to the Forster Collection in the Victoria and Albert Museum. Dickens's drawing room on the first floor has been reconstructed, as have the still room, wash house, and wine cellar in the basement.

Admission: £3 ($4.50) adults, £2 ($3) students, £1 ($1.50) children, £5 ($7.50) families.

Open: Mon–Sat 10am–5pm. **Tube:** Russell Square.

FOR VISITING AMERICANS

Despite the fact that they fought two wars against each other, no two countries have stronger links than America and Britain. The common heritage cuts right across political and economic conflicts.

In London, mementos of this heritage virtually crowd in on you. Stand in front of the National Gallery and you'll find a bronze **statue of George Washington** gazing at you over Trafalgar Square.

Visit **Westminster Abbey** and you'll see a memorial tablet to President F. D. Roosevelt, a bust of Longfellow in the Poets' Corner, and the graves of Edward Hyde and James Oglethorpe.

Grosvenor Square, in the heart of the West End, is known as "Little America." Watched over by a statue of FDR, it is the site of the modern U.S. Embassy and the home of John Adams when he was minister to Britain.

Norfolk House, St. James's Square, was General Eisenhower's headquarters during World War II, the spot from which he directed the Allies in the Normandy landing in 1944.

At 36 Craven St., just off the Strand, stands **Benjamin Franklin's London residence.** And in **St. Sepulchre,** at Holborn Viaduct, is the grave of Capt. John Smith of Pocahontas fame—he who had been prevented from sailing on the *Mayflower* because the other passengers considered him an "undesirable character."

The most moving reminder of national links is the American Memorial Chapel at **St. Paul's Cathedral.** It commemorates the 28,000 U.S. service personnel who lost their lives while based in Britain during World War II. The Roll of Honor containing their names was handed over by General Eisenhower on the Fourth of July 1951, and the chapel—with the Roll encased in glass—has become an unofficial pilgrimage place for visiting Americans.

5. WALKING TOURS

The best way to discover London is on foot, using your own shoe leather. This section is organized into a series of walking tours of some major attractions and districts.

WALKING TOUR — WESTMINSTER/WHITEHALL

Start: Tate Gallery. **Tube:** Pimlico.
Finish: Trafalgar Square. **Tube:** Charing Cross or Leicester Square.

Time: About 3 hours, excluding interior visits.
Best Times: Monday through Thursday, when Parliament is in session.
Worst Times: Evenings, or Sunday, when the district becomes almost deserted except for fast-moving traffic.

Begin your tour in front of the grand Palladian entrance to one of the finest art museums in the world, the:

1. **Tate Gallery.** Built in 1897 and donated to London by the scion of a sugar manufacturer, it's jammed with the works of virtually every great painter in British history (see "The Top Attractions," above). Return to browse the collections at your leisure, but for the moment, turn north along the west bank of the Thames (the embankment here is known as Millbank), beside the river that made British history, with the Houses of Parliament looming skyward ahead of you. At the first left-hand turn after the first bridge you'll see (Lambeth Bridge), turn inland onto Dean Stanley Street, which in a block will lead to the symmetrical elegance of:

2. **Smith Square,** whose centerpiece is St. John's Church. Designed with a highly personalized kind of neoclassicism by Thomas Archer in 1728, it was heavily damaged by bombs in 1941. Rebuilt (but not reconsecrated), it now serves as concert hall for some of the greatest musicians of the Western world.

   Retrace your steps back to the Thames, turn left (north) toward the Neo-Gothic regularity of the Houses of Parliament, and enter the verdant triangular park before its southern entrance. A tranquil oasis rich with sculpture is the:

3. **Victoria Tower Garden,** which contains a 1915 replica of Rodin's 1895 masterpiece, *The Burghers of Calais,* and A. G. Walker's monument to Emmeline Pankhurst, early 20th-century leader of the British suffragettes, who was frequently imprisoned for her actions and beliefs. Near the northern perimeter to the garden, turn left onto Great College Street and walk about a block, noticing on your right:

4. **The Abbey Garden.** Continuously cultivated over the past 900 years, and associated with nearby Westminster Abbey, it's the oldest garden in England, rich with lavender and ecclesiastical ruins. Even if the gate is locked, parts of this charming historic oddity are visible from the street outside.

   Retrace your steps along Great College Street to Millbank (which on some maps at this point might be referred to as Abingdon Street), turning left (north), remaining on the opposite side of Millbank from the Houses of Parliament. The tower on your left, completed in 1366 by Edward III for the storage of treasure, is the:

5. **Jewel Tower,** all that remains of the domestic portions of the once-mighty Palace of Westminster. It contains a small museum showing the dramas connected with the construction of the Houses of Parliament. Exiting from the Jewel Tower, continue north along Millbank (Abingdon Street) for 2 blocks, passing on your left the semicircular apse of the rear side of one of Britain's most densely packed artistic and cultural highlights:

6. **Westminster Abbey.** The spiritual heart of London, completed in 1245, and steeped in enough tradition, sorrow, majesty, and blood to merit an entire volume of its own, this is one of the most majestic and most-visited sights in Europe. Turn left, skirting the building's northern flank, and enter via its western facade.

   After your visit, leave the abbey through the Cloisters, emerging into Dean's Yard, site of Westminster School. Look for an arch straight ahead and on the right. It leads back to the west door of the abbey and to:

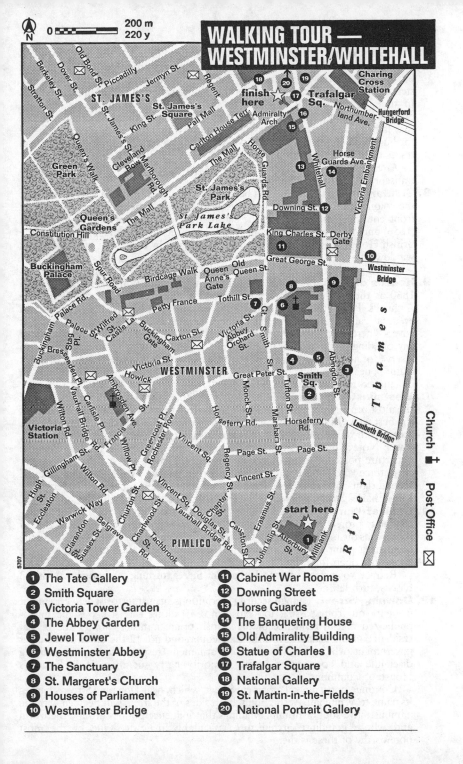

WALKING TOUR — WESTMINSTER/WHITEHALL

1. The Tate Gallery
2. Smith Square
3. Victoria Tower Garden
4. The Abbey Garden
5. Jewel Tower
6. Westminster Abbey
7. The Sanctuary
8. St. Margaret's Church
9. Houses of Parliament
10. Westminster Bridge
11. Cabinet War Rooms
12. Downing Street
13. Horse Guards
14. The Banqueting House
15. Old Admirality Building
16. Statue of Charles I
17. Trafalgar Square
18. National Gallery
19. St. Martin-in-the-Fields
20. National Portrait Gallery

7. The Sanctuary, which consists of two streets, called Broad Sanctuary and Little Sanctuary. In medieval days, the Sanctuary was actually a jumbled mass of buildings and narrow winding lanes. Enclosed by the precinct wall of Westminster, this complex offered a haven for the downcast and the odd political refugee. In time, the Sanctuary was said to shelter a "mire of cutthroats, whores, pickpockets, and murderers." It became so disease-ridden and crime-oriented that James I shut it down. Although the slums which this place generated lasted for hundreds of years, urban renewal has been successful in removing the final traces of this once-notorious haven.

After a walk around, look to your right, just beyond the abbey's north transept, to see the much-restored:

8. St. Margaret's Church. Built between 1504 and 1523, it contains the body of the colonizer of Virginia, Sir Walter Raleigh (who was beheaded just outside its front entrance), and served as the site for the marriages of both John Milton (1656) and Sir Winston Churchill (1908). Considered the parish church for the British House of Commons, it contains a noteworthy collection of stained-glass windows.

When you exit from St. Margaret's, the Neo-Gothic bulk of the:

9. Houses of Parliament will almost overwhelm you. Built between 1840 and 1860 as the result of a competition won by architects Sir Charles Barry and Augustus Pugin (both of whom suffered several nervous breakdowns and eventual early deaths as a result of the overwork and stress it caused them), it covers 8 acres and has what might be the greatest volume of ornate stonework of any building in the world. Your tour of the interior (which you might want to reserve for another day) begins at the base of Big Ben (its clock tower and tallest feature), near the building's northwest corner. One of Parliament's best views can be enjoyed from a position on the:

10. Westminster Bridge. Built in 1862 in the then-popular cast iron, and one of the most ornate bridges in London, it gives, from midway across its span, some of the best views of Parliament anywhere. To reach the bridge, turn right on Bridge Street from your position in front of the misnamed but very visible Big Ben clock tower. Note at the western base of the bridge, aptly named Westminster Pier, the departure point for many boat trips down the Thames.

Retrace your footsteps along Bridge Street, passing by Big Ben, and take the second right-hand turn along the busy Parliament Street. Take the first left along King Charles Street, where, on the left-hand side, you'll reach the:

11. Cabinet War Rooms, Clive Steps, King Charles Street. Set 17 feet underground to protect its occupants from Nazi air raids, this unpretentious handful of rooms was the meeting place for Churchill's cabinet during World War II, and the originating point of many of his most stirring speeches. A half dozen of the rooms are open for visits.

Retrace your steps back to Parliament Street, turning left (north). Within 2 blocks, turn left at:

12. Downing Street. Though security precautions against terrorist activities might prevent you from passing too close, no. 10 along this street is the much-publicized official residence of the British prime minister, no. 11 the official residence of the chancellor of the Exchequer, and no. 12 the office of the chief government whip, the Member of Parliament responsible for maintaining discipline and cooperation among majority party members in Parliament's House of Commons.

Continue north along Parliament Street, which, near Downing Street, changes its name to Whitehall. At this point, both sides of the street will be lined with the administrative soul of Britain, buildings that influence politics around the world and whose grandiose architecture is suitably majestic. One of the most noteworthy of these is the:

13. Horse Guards. Completed in 1760 and designed by William Kent, it's one of the most symmetrically imposing of the many buildings along Whitehall, and the venue of a ceremony (held Monday through Saturday at 11am and on Sunday at 10am) known as the Mounting of the Guard (which is the first step of an equestrian ceremony that continues, daily at 11:30am, with the Changing of the Guard in front of Buckingham Palace.)

Across the avenue rises the pure proportions of one of London's most superlative examples of Palladian architecture, the:

14. Banqueting House. Commissioned by James I, and designed by Inigo Jones in the early 1600s, it's considered one of the most aesthetically and mathematically perfect buildings in England. Containing a mural by Peter Paul Rubens, its facade was the backdrop for perhaps the most disturbing and unsettling execution in British history, that of King Charles I by members of Parliament.

REFUELING STOP One of the most famous pubs of London, beloved of Parliamentarians throughout England, **the Clarence Pub,** at 53 Whitehall St., W1 (tel. 071/930-4808), was originally opened in the 18th century and has been cosseting the taste buds of government administrators ever since. With gaslights, oak ceiling beams, antique farm implements dangling from the ceiling, and battered wooden tables ringed with churchlike pews, it contains at least half a dozen choices of real ale, and pub grub.

After your drinks with members of Parliament, notice the building that sits almost directly across Whitehall from the pub, the:

15. Old Admiralty Building, at Spring Gardens. Designed in 1725 by Sir Thomas Ripley, and strictly closed except for official business, it served for almost two centuries (until it was replaced by newer quarters between the wars) as the administrative headquarters of the British navy.

Continue walking north until you see what might be the finest and most emotive equestrian statue in London, the:

16. Statue of Charles I. Isolated on an island in the middle of a sea of speeding traffic, it commemorates one of the most tragic kings of British history and the beginning of:

17. Trafalgar Square. Centered around a soaring monument to the hero of the Battle of Trafalgar, Lord Nelson, who defeated Napoléon's navy off the coast of Spain in 1805, it is the single grandest plaza in London. Against the square's northern perimeter rises the grandly neoclassical bulk of the:

18. National Gallery, whose works cannot possibly be catalogued here, but which definitely merits a detailed tour of its own.

The church that flanks the eastern edge of Trafalgar Square is one of London's most famous:

19. St. Martin-in-the-Fields, the home of one of London's greatest chamber orchestras. Designed in the style of Sir Christopher Wren in 1726 by James Gibbs, it has a Corinthian portico and a steeple whose form has inspired the architects of many American churches. It was the christening place of English King Charles II, and the burial place of his infamous but fun-loving mistress, Nell Gwynne.

Finally, for an overview of the faces that altered the course of Britain and the world, walk to the right-hand (east) side of the previously mentioned National Gallery, where the greatest repository of portraits in Europe awaits your inspection at the:

20. National Portrait Gallery, at 2 St. Martin's Place. They're all here—kings, cardinals, mistresses, playwrights, poets, coquettes, dilettantes, and other historical personages. Their assemblage in one gallery celebrates the subject of each painting rather than the artist who created it.

WALKING TOUR — THE CITY

Start: The southern terminus of London Bridge.
Tube: Monument.
Finish: St. Paul's Cathedral.
Tube: St. Paul's.
Time: About 3 hours, excluding interior visits.
Best Times: Weekday mornings, when the financial district is functioning but its churches are the most unvisted.
Worst Times: Weekends, when the district is almost deserted.

Our tour begins on the southern edge of the Thames, directly to the west of one of the world's most famous bridges. Facing the Thames rises the bulk of:

1. **Southwark Cathedral.** When it was built in the 1200s, it was an outpost of the faraway diocese of Winchester. Deconsecrated after Henry VIII's Reformation, it later sheltered bakeries and pig pens. Much of what you'll see is a result of a sorely needed 19th-century rebuilding, but a view of its Gothic interior, with its multiple commemorative plaques, gives an idea of the religious power of London's medieval church. After your visit, walk across the famous masonry of:

2. **London Bridge.** Originally designed by Henry de Colechurch under the patronage of Henry II in 1176—but replaced several times since, the last time in 1971—it's probably the most famous bridge in the world. Until as late as 1729, it was the only bridge across the Thames. During the Middle Ages, it was lined with shops and houses crowded close upon its edges, and served for centuries as the showplace for the severed heads—preserved in tar—of enemies of the British monarchs. (The most famous of these included the head of Sir Thomas More, the highly vocal lord chancellor of England.) From Southwark Cathedral, cross the bridge. At its northern end, notice the first street that descends to the right (east), Monument Street. Detour down it a short distance to read the commemorative plaques attached to the:

3. **Monument.** Commemorating the Great Fire of 1666, this soaring Doric column is appropriately capped with a carved version of a flaming urn. The disaster that it memorializes erupted in a bakery in nearby Pudding Lane, raged for 4 days and nights, and destroyed 80% of the City. A cramped and foreboding set of stairs spirals up to the top's view over the cityscape so heavily influenced after the fire by architect Sir Christopher Wren.

   Retrace your steps toward London Bridge, but before you actually step onto it, detour to the left (south, toward the river) at Monument Street's first intersection, Fish Hill Street. Set near the edge of the water, within its shadow of the bridge, is one of Wren's many churches:

4. **St. Magnus the Martyr.** Completed in 1685 (with its tower added in 1705), it has a particularly magnificent interior which at one time was devoted to the neighborhood's many fishmongers.

   After your visit, continue walking east along Lower Thames Street. At the corner of Idol Lane (the fifth narrow street on your left), turn left to see the bombed-out remains of another of Sir Wren's churches:

5. **St. Dunstan-in-the-East.** Its unexpectedly verdant garden, the only part of the complex that regenerated itself after the Nazi blitz of World War II, offers a comforting oasis amid a sea of traffic and masonry. After your visit, continue walking north. Where Idol Lane dead-ends at Great Tower Street, look straight ahead to the spire of another of Wren's churches, this one in substantially better shape:

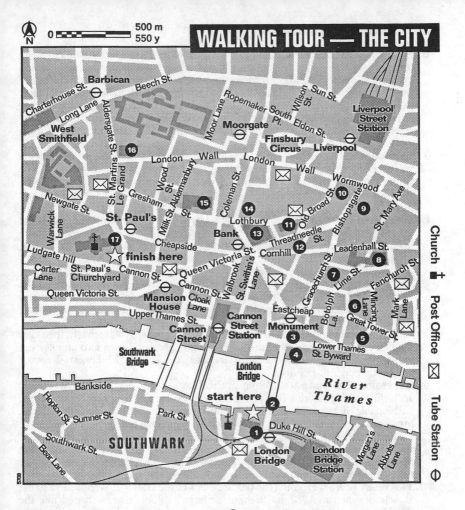

① **Southwark Cathedral**
② **London Bridge**
③ **Monument**
④ **St. Magnus the Martyr**
⑤ **St. Dunstan-in-the-East**
⑥ **St. Margaret Pattens**
⑦ **Leadenhall**
⑧ **Lloyd's of London Building**
⑨ **St. Helen Bishopsgate**
⑩ **NatWest Tower**
⑪ **London Stock Exchange**
⑫ **Royal Exchange**
⑬ **Bank of England**
⑭ **St. Margaret's, Lothbury**
⑮ **Guildhall**
⑯ **Museum of London**
⑰ **St. Paul's Cathedral**

6. St. Margaret Pattens. Built between 1684 and 1689, it has much of its original paneling and interior fittings, and a narrow and slender spire which inspired, in one form or another, many later churches. After your visit, walk to the west side of the church, and take Rood Lane north 1 block to Fenchurch. Go left (west) for 2 blocks, then right on Gracechurch Street, into the dusky and narrow streets of Europe's largest financial capital. Within a very short walk, on your right, you'll reach the Victorian arcades of one of the neighborhood's most densely packed shopping centers:

7. Leadenhall. Designed in 1881 by Horace Jones, it contains the accoutrements you'd need for either a picnic or a full gourmet dinner. Browse at will, but once you've finished return to Gracechurch Street, walk north about a block, then go right (east) on Leadenhall Street. Take the second right-hand (south) turn on Lime Street, where you can admire the soaring and iconoclastically modern:

8. Lloyd's of London Building. Designed by Richard Rogers in 1986, this is the most recent home of a company originally founded in the 1680s as a marine insurance market. This is the most famous insurer in the world, with a hypermodern headquarters built atop the heart of the ancient Roman community (Londinium) whose builders launched London's destiny more than 2,000 years ago. Note that within just a few blocks of your position are headquartered the London Metal Exchange, the London Futures and Options Exchange, and hundreds of financial institutions whose clout is felt as far away as the Pacific Basin.

Emerge from Lime Street back onto Leadenhall, where you turn left, then take the first right on Bishopsgate, then the second right-hand turn into an alleyway known as Great St. Helen's. Near its end, you'll find the largest surviving medieval church in London:

9. St. Helen Bishopsgate. Begun in the 1400s, it was dedicated to St. Helen, according to legend the British mother of the Roman emperor Constantine. Fashionable during the Elizabethan and Jacobean periods, its monuments, memorials, and grave markers are especially interesting.

Exit back onto Bishopsgate, turning right (north). Two blocks later, turn left onto Wormwood Street. At the first left (Old Broad Street), go left. Towering above you—the most visible building on its street—rises the modern bulk of the tallest building in Britain, and the second-tallest building in Europe, the:

10. NatWest Tower. Housing the headquarters of the National Westminster Bank, it was designed in 1981 by Richard Seifert. Its floor plan is shaped like the NatWest logo. Built upon massive concrete foundations above a terrain composed mostly of impervious clay, it was designed to sway gently in the wind. Unfortunately, there is no public observation tower in the building, so visitors must admire it from afar.

Continue south along Old Broad Street, noticing on your right the bulky headquarters of the:

11. London Stock Exchange. The center was built in the early 1960s to replace its outmoded original quarters. Its role has become much quieter (and somewhat redundant) since 1986, when the nature of most of the City's financial operations changed from a face-to-face agreement between brokers to a computerized clearinghouse conducted electronically.

Continue southwest along Old Broad Street until it merges with Threadneedle Street. Cross over Threadneedle Street, jog a few paces to your left, and head south along the narrow confines of Finch Lane. Cross the busy traffic of Cornhill to the south side of the street. Follow it east to St. Michael's Alley.

REFUELING STOP **Jamaica Wine House,** St. Michael's Alley, EC3 (tel. 071/626-9496). According to claims, this was one of the first coffeehouses to open in the Western world. Historically favored by London merchants and the sea captains who imported their goods, it today dispenses beer, ale, lager, wine, and other refreshments, including bar snacks and soft drinks from its historic precincts.

After you tipple, explore the labyrinth of narrow alleyways that shelter you within an almost medieval maze from the district's roaring weekday traffic. Eventually, however, head for the major boulevard (Cornhill), a few steps north of the site of your earlier refueling stop. There, near the junction of five major streets, rises the:

12. Royal Exchange. Designed by William Tite in the early 1840s, its imposing neoclassical pediment is inset with Richard Westmacott's sculpture of a victorious *Commerce*. Launched by a partnership of merchants and financiers during the Elizabethan Age, its establishment was a direct attempt to lure European banking and trading functions from Antwerp (then the financial capital of northern Europe) to London. Separate markets and auction facilities for raw materials were conducted in frenzied trading here until 1982, when the building became the headquarters of the London International Financial Futures Exchange (LIFFE).

On the opposite side of Threadneedle Street rises the massive bulk of the:

13. Bank of England. Originally established "for the Publick Good and Benefit of Our People" in a charter granted in 1694 by William and Mary, it's a treasure trove both of gold bullion, British banknotes, and historical archives. The only part of this massive building open to the public is the Bank of England Museum, whose entrance is on a narrow side street, Bartholomew Lane (tel. 071/601-4878). Open Monday through Friday from 10am to 5pm. Entrance is free.

From the Bank of England, walk northwest along Prince's Street to the intersection of Lothbury. From the northeast corner of the intersection rises another church designed and built by Sir Christopher Wren between 1686 and 1690:

14. St. Margaret's, Lothbury. Filled with statues of frolicking cupids, elaborately carved screens, and a soaring eagle near the altar, it's worth a visit inside.

After you exit, cross Prince's Street and head west on Gresham Street. After traversing a handful of alleyways, you'll see on your right the gardens and the grandly historical facade of the:

15. Guildhall. The power base for the lord mayor of London since the 12th century (and rebuilt, adapted, and enlarged many times since), it was the site of endless power negotiations throughout the Middle Ages between the English kings (headquartered outside the City of Westminster) and the guilds, associations, and brotherhoods of the City's merchants and financiers. Today, the rituals associated with the lord mayor are almost as elaborate as those of the monarchy itself. The medieval crypt of the Guildhall is the largest in London, and its east facade was rebuilt by Sir Christopher Wren after the Great Fire of 1666.

After your visit to the Guildhall, continue walking west on Gresham, and take the second right-hand turn onto Wood Street. Walk 2 blocks north to London Wall, go left for about a block, where you'll see the modern facade of the:

16. Museum of London. Here in new quarters built in 1975, it presents an assemblage of London memorabilia gathered from several earlier museums, as well as one of the best collections of period costumes in the world. Built on top of the Western Gate of the ancient Roman colony of Londinium, it is especially strong on archeological remnants unearthed during centuries of London building. There are also tableaux portraying the Great Fire and Victorian prison cells.

After your visit to the museum, head south on Aldersgate, whose name soon changes to St. Martins-le-Grand. After you cross Newgate Street, you'll see before you the enormous and dignified dome of one of Europe's most famous and symbolic churches:

17. St. Paul's Cathedral. Considered the masterpiece of Sir Christopher Wren, and the inspiration for the generation of Londoners who survived the firebombings of World War II, it was the scene of the state funerals of Nelson, Wellington, and Churchill, and the wedding celebration of Prince Charles. It is the only church in England built with a dome, the country's only church in the English baroque style, and the first English cathedral to be designed and built by a single architect. Designated as the cathedral church for the sprawling diocese of London, its role as a church for Londoners contrasts distinctly with the national role of the Royal Church of Westminster Abbey.

WALKING TOUR — ST. JAMES'S

Start: The Admiralty Arch. **Tube:** Charing Cross.
Finish: Buckingham Palace. **Tube:** St. James's Park or Green Park.
Time: About 2 hours, not including stops.
Best Times: Before 3pm, after which the setting sun might glare into your eyes.
Worst Times: After dark.

Begin your tour near the southwest corner of Trafalgar Square, at the monumental eastern entrance of the:

1. Admiralty Arch. Commissioned by Queen Victoria's son, King Edward VII (who died before it was completed), it was designed in 1911 by Sir Aston Webb. Piercing its center are a quintet of arches faced with Portland stone, whose assemblage marks the first (and widest) stage of a majestic processional route leading from Buckingham Palace eastward to St. Paul's Cathedral. The centermost of the five arches is opened only for ceremonial occasions, the two side arches are for vehicular traffic, and the two smallest arches are for pedestrians.

Pass beneath the arch and enter the wide panoramic thoroughfare that leads to Buckingham Palace. With your back to the Admiralty Arch, you'll see the wide and verdant expanse of:

2. The Mall, the only deliberately planned avenue in London. Designed by Sir Aston Webb in 1910 as a memorial to the recently departed Queen Victoria, and lined with plane trees, it was originally the garden of the nearby Palace of St. James's, and was used for the aristocratic game *paille maille* (a precursor of croquet) by the courtiers of Charles II. On Sunday, the Mall often becomes a pedestrian extension of the adjacent expanse of St. James's Park. The Mall's wide boundaries are a favorite exercise area for London's equestrians and their mounts. Immediately to your left (keeping your back to the arch) are the interconnected buildings of the:

3. New and Old Admiralties. Considered one of the most important nerve centers of the British military, they have seen their share of drama since they were originally built and enlarged.

As you stroll in a southwesterly direction down the Mall, the right-hand side will reveal one of the most regal ensembles of town houses in London, the:

4. Carlton House Terrace. These buildings replaced the once-palatial home of the 18th-century prince regent, who later became George III. He built (and subsequently demolished) at staggering expense what was considered the most

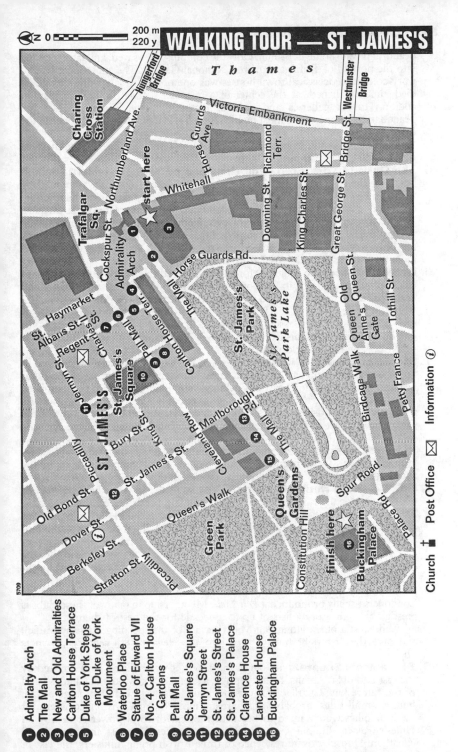

WALKING TOUR — ST. JAMES'S

0 200 m / 220 y

Thames

Hungerford Bridge
Westminster Bridge

Charing Cross Station

Victoria Embankment

Northumberland Ave.
Horse Guards Ave.
Richmond Terr.
Bridge St.

start here

Whitehall

Downing St.
King Charles St.
Great George St.

Trafalgar Sq.

Cockspur St.
Admiralty Arch

Horse Guards Rd.

Old Queen St.
Queen Anne's Gate
Tothill St.

Haymarket
St. Albans St.
Regent St.
Charles St.

The Mall

St. James's Park

St. James's Park Lake

Jermyn St.
Carlton House Terrace
Pall Mall

St. JAMES'S
St. James's Square

King St.
Bury St.
Birdcage Walk
Petty France

Piccadilly
Old Bond St.
Cleveland Row
Marlborough Rd.

St. James's St.

The Mall

Dover St.
Berkeley St.
Stratton St.

Queen's Walk

Green Park

Queen's Gardens
Spur Road.
Constitution Hill
Palace Rd.

finish here

Buckingham Palace

Church ✝   Post Office ☒   Information *i*

1. Admiralty Arch
2. The Mall
3. New and Old Admiralties
4. Carlton House Terrace
5. Duke of York Steps and Duke of York Monument
6. Waterloo Place
7. Statue of Edward VII
8. No. 4 Carlton House Gardens
9. Pall Mall
10. St. James's Square
11. Jermyn Street
12. St. James's Street
13. St. James's Palace
14. Clarence House
15. Lancaster House
16. Buckingham Palace

5709

beautiful private home in Britain. Only the columns were saved, and later recycled into the portico of Trafalgar Square's National Gallery. The subsequent row of ivory-colored neoclassical town houses was one of Nash's last works before he died, much maligned, at the center of a financial scandal in 1835. Today, in addition to art galleries and cultural institutions, the Terrace houses the headquarters of one of the most highly reputed scientific bodies in the world, the Royal Society.

Midway along the length of Carlton House Terrace, its evenly symmetrical neoclassical expanse is pierced with:

5. The Duke of York Steps and the Duke of York Monument. Built in honor of the second son of George III, the massive sculpture was funded by withholding one day's pay from every soldier in the British Empire. The resulting column was chiseled from pink granite, and the statue was created by Sir Richard Westmacott in 1834. Contemporary wits, knowing that the duke died owing massive debts to his angry creditors, joked that placing his effigy on a column was the only way to keep him away from their grasp. This soaring column and monument (the statue weighs 7 tons) dominates:

6. Waterloo Place, the square before it. Considered one of the most prestigious pieces of urban planning in London, it reeks with both aristocratic elegance and nostalgia for England's grand military victories over Napoléon. No. 107 Waterloo Place (designed in 1830 and considered one of the finest examples of early 19th-century neoclassical architecture in London) is the headquarters for one of the most distinguished men's clubs in Britain, the Athenaeum Club.

Notice, within Waterloo Place, the:

7. Statue of Edward VII. It was crafted in 1921 by Sir Bertram Mackennal in honor of the man who gave the world the Edwardian Age and much of the grand neighborhood to the northeast of Buckingham Palace. The son of the long-lived Victoria, he ascended the throne at the age of 60, only 9 years before his death. As if to balance the position of his statue, a statue dedicated to the victims of the Crimean War, part of which honors Florence Nightingale, stands at the opposite end of Waterloo Place.

History buffs will appreciate Carlton House Gardens, which run into Carlton House Terrace's western end. Lovers of France and French history especially appreciate the plaques that identify the facade of:

8. No. 4 Carlton House Gardens. These were the London headquarters of Charles de Gaulle's French government-in-exile, and site of many of his French-language radio broadcasts to the French Underground during World War II. (Another facade of this same building faces the Mall, on the opposite side of the block.)

One of the streets intersecting Waterloo Place is an avenue rich in the headquarters of many exclusive private clubs. Not to be confused with the longer and broader expanse of the Mall, this is:

9. Pall Mall. Despite its variant pronunciation in different parts of the empire, Londoners usually pronounce it *Pell-Mell*. Membership in many of these clubs is prestigious, with waiting lists of up to a decade for the best of them.

Walk west a block along Pall Mall (beware of the speeding one-way traffic), and take the first right (north) turn into the elegant 18th-century precincts of:

10. St. James's Square. Laid out in the 1660s, it was built on land donated by the first Earl of St. Albans, Henry Jermyn, a friend of the widow of Charles I and of the future king Charles II. It was originally designed with very large private houses on all sides, probably with artistic input by Sir Christopher Wren, for noble families who wanted to live near the seat of royal power at nearby St. James's Palace. Buildings on the square of special interest include no. 10 (Chatham House), private residence of three British prime ministers, the last of which was Queen Victoria's nemesis, William Gladstone. At no. 32, General Eisenhower and his subordinates planned the 1942 invasion of North Africa and the 1944 Allied invasion of Normandy. At no. 16, the announcement of the climactic defeat by Wellington of Napoléon's forces at Waterloo was delivered (along with the captured eagle-shaped symbols of Napoléon's army) by a bloodstained officer, Major Percy, to the British Regent.

Circumnavigate the square, eventually exiting at its northern edge via Duke of York Street. One block later, turn left onto:

11. **Jermyn Street,** perhaps the most prestigious shopping street in London. Expensive, upscale, with shop attendants who are usually very, very polite, the street offers shops whose windows and displays show a mixture of what is considered inviolable British tradition mingled with the perceived necessities for The Good Life.

REFUELING STOP Much about the facade and paneled decor of **Green's Restaurant and Oyster Bar**—at 36 Duke St., SW1 (tel. 071/93-4566)—might remind you of the many men's clubs you've already passed within the surrounding neighborhood. This one, however, welcomes nonmembers and a healthy dose of the clientele is female. There's a battered bar for the consumption of glasses of wine, platters of oysters, dollops of caviar, shrimp, or crabmeat (which you can consume either standing at the bar or sitting at a table), and a wide variety of English-inspired appetizers and main courses. The place is especially popular at lunchtime.

Exit from Duke Street onto Jermyn Street, turn right (west), and continue to enjoy the shops. Two blocks later, turn left onto:

12. **St. James's Street.** As you have by now grown to expect, it contains its share of private clubs, the most fashionable of which is, arguably, White's, at no. 37. Its premises were designed in 1788 by James Wyatt. Prince Charles celebrated his stag party here with friends the night before his marriage to Diana. Past members include Evelyn Waugh (who received refuge here from his literary "hounds of modernity"). Even if you're recommended for membership (which is unlikely), the waiting list is 8 years.

At the bottom (south end) of St. James's Street is one of the most historic buildings of London:

13. **St. James's Palace.** Birthplace of many British monarchs, it served as the principal royal residence from 1698 (when Whitehall Palace burned down) until the ascent of Queen Victoria (who moved into Buckingham Palace) in 1837. Originally enlarged from a Tudor core built by Henry VIII for one of his ill-fated queens, it was altered by Sir Christopher Wren in 1703. The palace, rich in history and connotation, gave its name to the entire neighborhood you've just surveyed. After your visit, walk southwest along Cleveland Row, then turn left (southeast) onto Stable Yard Row. On your left rises the side of:

14. **Clarence House.** Designed in 1829 by John Nash, it's the official London home of the Queen Mother. On the opposite side of Stable Yard Row rises the side of the very formal:

15. **Lancaster House.** Designed in 1827 by Benjamin Wyatt, it has, during its lifetime, been known variously as York House and Stafford House. Chopin performed his ballads and nocturnes for Queen Victoria here and Edward VIII lived here during his tenure as the Prince of Wales. Heavily damaged by World War II bombings, it has been gracefully restored, furnished in the French Louis XV style, and now serves as a setting for state receptions and dinners.

Within a few steps, when you arrive at the multiple plane trees of the Mall, turn right for a vista of the front of:

16. **Buckingham Palace.** The official London residence of every British monarch

since Victoria, it exerts a pull and allure that is mystical, magical, carefully cultivated, and vital.

WALKING TOUR —— CHELSEA

Start: Chelsea Embankment at the Battersea Bridge.
Tube: Sloane Square.
Finish: Chelsea's Old Town Hall, or any nearby pub.
Tube: Sloane Square.
Time: 2 hours, not counting stops, pub time, or visits.
Best Times: Anytime, except rainy days.
Worst Times: Any rainy day.

Begin your tour above the massive masonry buttresses known as the Chelsea Embankment, at the northern terminus of the:

1. **Battersea Bridge,** which will align and orient you to an understanding of Chelsea's vital link to the Thames. Here begins a beautiful walk eastward through a historic neighborhood marred only by the roar of the riverside traffic. Across the water rises the district of Battersea, a rapidly gentrifying neighborhood.

   The street beside the Thames will soon be identified as Cheyne Walk. Rich with Georgian and Victorian architecture (and containing some of the most expensive houses of a very expensive neighborhood), it is considered an architectural treasurehouse. Although the bulk of your exploration along this street will be eastward, for the moment detour from the base of Battersea Bridge westward to:

2. **Turner's House,** at 119 Cheyne Walk. Its tall and narrow premises sheltered England's greatest painter, J. M. W. Turner (1775–1851), during the last years of his life. Although contemporary with the French impressionists, he painted in a style distinctly and originally different, and his work is uniquely recognizable by its use of shimmering colors. When he died in one of this house's bedrooms, his very appropriate final words were "God is Light."

   Just to the east of Turner's House, at nos. 96–100 Cheyne Walk, is a building considered one of Chelsea's most beautiful:

3. **Lindsey House,** completed in the 1670s. Built by the Swiss-born physician to two British kings (James I and Charles II), it became the British headquarters of the Moravian church around 1750. Later divided and sold as four separate residences, it housed the American-born painter James Whistler (at no. 96 between 1866 and 1879). The gardens of no. 99 and no. 100 were designed by Britain's most celebrated Edwardian architect, Sir Edwin Lutyens (1869–1944).

   At this point, retrace your steps eastward to Battersea Bridge and begin what will become a long eastward ramble along Cheyne Walk. Midway between the heavy traffic of Beaufort Street and the much quieter Danvers Street, you'll see:

4. **Crosby Hall.** Designated by no identifying street number, its original brick-and-stone construction (resembling a chapel) is prefaced with a modern wing of gray stone added in the 1950s. It was originally built in the early 1400s and owned successively by King Richard III and Sir Thomas More. It was transported in the early 1900s stone by stone from Bishopsgate, partly under the financial incentive of American-born Nancy Astor. Today it provides apartments and dining facilities for the British Federation of University Women. Parts of its interior (which contain paintings by Holbein, a gracefully trussed roof, and some

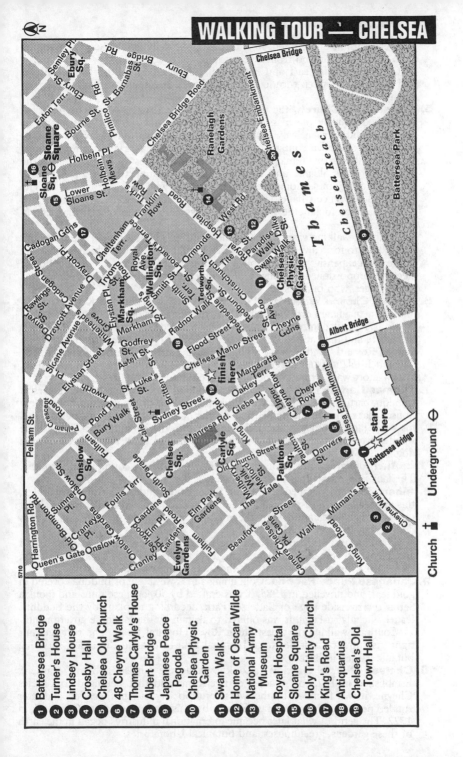

WALKING TOUR — CHELSEA

① Battersea Bridge
② Turner's House
③ Lindsey House
④ Crosby Hall
⑤ Chelsea Old Church
⑥ 48 Cheyne Walk
⑦ Thomas Carlyle's House
⑧ Albert Bridge
⑨ Japanese Peace Pagoda
⑩ Chelsea Physic Garden
⑪ Swan Walk
⑫ Home of Oscar Wilde
⑬ National Army Museum
⑭ Royal Hospital
⑮ Sloane Square
⑯ Holy Trinity Church
⑰ King's Road
⑱ Antiquarius
⑲ Chelsea's Old Town Hall

Church ⊞ Underground ⊖

Jacobean furniture) are open, free, to the public daily except Sunday morning, from 10am to noon and from 2:15 to 5pm.

Continue walking east on Cheyne Walk. After crossing both Danvers Street and Old Church Street, turn left on Old Church Street and walk a few steps to reach:

5. Chelsea Old Church, the parish church of Sir Thomas More. Its beauty is diminished only by the masses of traffic outside and the fact that it and its neighborhood were heavily damaged by Nazi bombs during World War II. Gracefully repaired, it contains a chapel partly designed by Hans Holbein, an urn containing the earthly remains of a man who owned most of Chelsea during the 1700s, Sir Hans Sloane, and a plaque commemorating the life of American novelist Henry James, a longtime Chelsea resident, who died nearby in 1916. The building's Lawrence Chapel is reputed to have been the scene of Henry VIII's secret marriage to Jane Seymour several days before their official marriage in 1536.

Continue walking east along Cheyne Walk. In about a block, the pavement will branch to form a verdant copse of trees and lawn, behind which stand some of the most expensive and desirable town houses of Chelsea. Occupants of these elegantly proportioned buildings have included some very famous people, such as Mick Jagger, who purchased:

6. No. 48 Cheyne Walk. Jagger's neighbors included guitarist Keith Richard, publishing magnate Lord Weidenfeld, and the grandson of oil industry giant Paul Getty, Jr. Artistic denizens of an earlier age included George Eliot who lived part of her life and died at no. 19. The star of the Pre-Raphaelite movement, Dante Gabriel Rossetti, lived in what is considered the street's finest building, no. 16.

Branch inland from the Thames, heading north along Cheyne Row, where, after a short walk, at no. 5 Cheyne Row you'll see:

7. Thomas Carlyle's House. Considered one of the most interesting houses in London, particularly to literary enthusiasts, it is one of the neighborhood's few houses that's open to the public. The former home of "the sage of Chelsea" and his wife, Jane, it offers a fascinating insight into the Victorian era. Notice the small gravestone in the garden marking the burial place of the author's favorite dog.

After your visit, retrace your steps to Cheyne Walk and continue walking east. The lacy iron bridge that looms into view is the:

8. Albert Bridge. Matched only by the Tower Bridge and the Westminster Bridge, this might be the most-photographed bridge in London. Created at the height of the Victorian fascination with the multiple possibilities of cast iron, it was designed in 1873 by R. M. Ordish.

Continue walking east beneath the trees of Cheyne Walk, heading inland along Royal Hospital Road. Before you leave the banks of the Thames, however, look across the river and try to see the Buddhist-inspired:

9. Japanese Peace Pagoda. Containing a massive statue of Buddha covered in gold leaf, and unveiled in 1985, it was crafted by 50 Japanese nuns and monks. Set at the riverside edge of Battersea Park, according to plans by the Buddhist leader Nichidatsu Fugii, it was offered to Britain by the Japanese government.

Continue walking northeast along Royal Hospital Road. The turf on your right (its entrance is at 66 Royal Hospital Rd.) belongs to the oldest surviving botanic garden in Britain, the:

10. Chelsea Physic Garden (also known as the Chelsea Botanic Garden). Established in 1673 on 4 acres of riverfront land that belonged to Charles Cheyne, it was founded by the Worshipful Society of Apothecaries, and later funded permanently by Sir Hans Sloane, botanist and physician to George II, in 1722. The germ of what later became international industries began in the earth of these gardens, greenhouses, and botanical laboratories.

Continue your walk northeast along Royal Hospital Road, and turn right at the first cross street onto:

11. Swan Walk. Known for its 18th-century row houses, it's an obscure yet charming part of Chelsea. Walk down it, taking your first left onto Dilke Street. At its dead end, turn left onto Tite Street. (From here, your view of the Japanese Peace Pagoda on the opposite bank of the Thames might be even better than before.) At 34 Tite St. you'll see a plaque commemorating the:

12. Home of Oscar Wilde, where Wilde wrote many of his most charming plays, including *The Importance of Being Earnest* and *Lady Windermere's Fan.* After Wilde was arrested and imprisoned during the most famous trial for homosexuality in British history, the house was sold to pay his debts. The plaque was presented in 1954, a century after Wilde's birth. A few steps away on the same street lie houses that once belonged to two of America's most famous expatriates. No. 31 was the home and studio of John Singer Sargent and no. 35 was the home of James McNeill Whistler.

At the end of Tite Street, turn right onto Royal Hospital Road. Within a block, you'll reach the fortresslike premises of the:

13. National Army Museum. Its premises contain galleries devoted to weapons, uniforms, and art, with dioramas of famous battles and such memorabilia as the skeleton of Napoléon's favorite horse.

Next door to the museum, a short distance northeast, is the building that contains the world's most famous horticultural exhibition, the Chelsea Flower Show, held every year on the vast premises of the:

14. Royal Hospital. Designed in 1682 in the aftermath of the Great Fire of London by Sir Christopher Wren (and considered, after St. Paul's cathedral, his masterpiece) it may have been built to compete with Louis XIV's construction of Les Invalides in Paris. Both were designed as a home for wounded or aging soldiers, and both are grandiose and immense.

Pass the Royal Hospital and turn left (northeast) 4 blocks later at Chelsea Bridge Road. This street's name changes in about a block to Lower Sloane Street, and leads eventually to:

15. Sloane Square. Considered the northernmost gateway to Chelsea, it was laid out in 1780 on land belonging to Sir Hans Sloane. His collection of minerals, fossils, and plant specimens was the core of what eventually became the British Museum. Detour half a block north of Sloane Square (its entrance is on Sloane Street) to visit:

16. Holy Trinity Church, known as a triumph of the late 19th century's arts-and-crafts movement. Completed in 1890, it contains windows by William Morris following designs by Burne-Jones and embellishments in the Pre-Raphaelite style.

Exit from Sloane Square's southwestern corner, and stroll down:

17. King's Road, one of the most variegated and interesting commercial streets in London. It's filled with antiques stores, booksellers, sophisticated and punk clothiers, restaurants, coffeehouses, tearooms, and diehard adherents of the "Sloane Ranger" mystique. Dozens of possibilities for food, sustenance, and companionship exist.

REFUELING STOP Luring the homesick Yankee, **Henry J. Bean's (But His Friends All Call Him Hank) Bar & Grill**—195–197 King's Rd. (tel. 071/352-9255)—has been compared to a "Cheers"-style bar. Big burgers and meaty dogs are part of the American fare, and you can order such drinks as a Tequila Sunrise. In summer, you can eat and drink in the rose garden in back. Happy hour with reduced drink prices is daily from 5:30 to 7:30pm.

After your refreshment (which can be found at any of the neighborhood's other pubs and cafés along the way), continue walking southwest along King's Road. Midway between Shawfield Street and Flood Street lies a warren of antiques sellers, all clustered together into a complex known as:

18. Antiquarius, at 131–141 King's Rd., SW3. Browse at will; maybe you'll buy an almost-heirloom or perhaps at least something of lasting value.

As you continue down King's Road, you'll see oval-shaped blue and white plaques identifying buildings of particular interest. One to watch for is:

19. Chelsea's Old Town Hall. Set on the southern side of King's Road, midway between Chelsea Manor and Oakley Street, its Georgian grandeur is the favorite hangout of everyone from punk rockers to soon-to-be-married couples applying for a marriage license. Many wedding parties are photographed in front of it.

The energetic and/or still curious might transform the finale of this walking tour into a pub crawl, as the neighborhood is filled with many enticing choices.

WALKING TOUR — DICKENS'S LONDON

Start: Russell Square. **Tube:** Russell Square.
Finish: The Old Deanery. **Tube:** St. Paul's.
Time: 2½ hours.
Best Time: Any daylight hours. Early Saturday or anytime on Sunday might entail the least amount of traffic.
Worst Time: Morning and afternoon rush hours Monday through Friday.

The writings of Charles Dickens have international appeal. The author's scenes and settings within certain neighborhoods are intimately linked to such works as *Little Dorrit, The Pickwick Papers,* and *David Copperfield.* Follow this walking tour and try to imagine an earlier era: the overcrowded alleyways and grimy buildings; the workplaces which, during the 19th century, were infinitely more polluted from constant coal smoke and dust; and the streets littered with excretions from thousands of horses that hauled passengers and freight through the narrow streets.

Begin your tour amid the regular symmetry of a neighborhood in the shadow of the British Museum:

1. Russell Square. In addition to inspiring Dickens, this square and its side streets were inhabited by such other writers as Ralph Waldo Emerson, T. S. Eliot, and an adolescent Edgar Allan Poe. From the square's eastern edge, walk east along Guilford Street where, to the left, you'll see:

2. Coram's Fields. This is the site where the Foundling Hospital stood in Victorian times (before it was moved to another part of London), the place where several of Dickens's characters—including a rebellious servant named Tattycoram in *Little Dorrit*—were raised. Of the Foundling Hospital, originally established around 1740, only the ornate gateway survives to remind passersby of the formerly influential organization that brought up many of London's abandoned children.

Turn right onto Doughty Street (but do not confuse this with Doughty Mews, which you'll reach first). At no. 48 Doughty Street, you'll find one of London's most potent homages to Dickens:

3. Dickens's House. The author rented it between 1837 and 1839, producing within its walls three of his most famous novels, *The Pickwick Papers, Oliver Twist,* and *Nicholas Nickleby.* Today, it's the headquarters of the Dickens Fellowship, and contains a collection of Dickens memorabilia, including one of

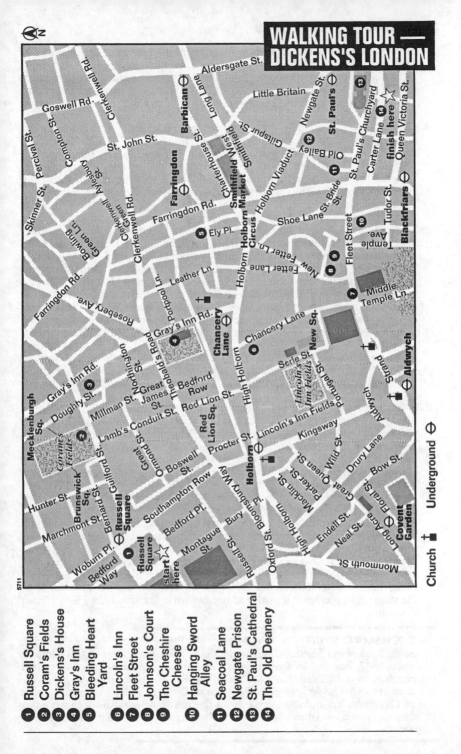

**WALKING TOUR —
DICKENS'S LONDON**

Aldersgate St.
Little Britain
St. Paul's Churchyard
Goswell Rd.
Clerkenwell Rd.
Barbican
Newgate St.
Carter Lane
finish here
Queen Victoria St.
Compton St.
Percival St.
Skinner St.
St. John St.
Long Lane
Charterhouse St.
Smithfield West
Giltspur St.
Old Bailey
St. Paul's
Blackfriars
Farringdon
Charterhouse St.
Smithfield Market
Holborn Viaduct
St. Bride St.
Tudor St.
Aylesbury St.
Clerkenwell Green
Farringdon Rd.
Holborn Circus
Shoe Lane
Fleet Street
Temple Ave.
Ely Pl.
Bowling Green Ln.
Farringdon Ave.
Leather Ln.
Holborn
New Fetter Ln.
Fetter Lane
Roseberry Ave.
Gray's Inn Rd.
Chancery Lane
Chancery Lane
Middle Temple Ln.
Gray's Inn Rd.
Northington St.
Great James St.
Bedford Row
High Holborn
Serle St.
New Sq.
Lincoln's Inn Fields
Portugal St.
Strand
Aldwych
Doughty St.
Millman St.
Theobald's Road
Red Lion St.
Lincoln's Inn Fields
Mecklenburgh Sq.
Lamb's Conduit St.
Procter St.
Kingsway
Wild St.
Drury Lane
Bow St.
Coram's Fields
Great Ormond St.
Boswell St.
Southampton Row
Holborn
New Kingsway
Bloomsbury Pl.
Macklin St.
Parker St.
Great Queen St.
Covent Garden
Hunter St.
Brunswick Sq.
Guilford St.
Bedford Pl.
Bury Pl.
Oxford St.
Endell St.
Neal St.
Long Acre
Floral St.
Marchmont St.
Bernard St.
Russell Square
Montague St.
Russell St.
High Holborn
Monmouth St.
Woburn Pl.
Bedford Way
Russell Square
start here

Church ✝   Underground ⊕

1. Russell Square
2. Coram's Fields
3. Dickens's House
4. Gray's Inn
5. Bleeding Heart Yard
6. Lincoln's Inn
7. Fleet Street
8. Johnson's Court
9. The Cheshire Cheese
10. Hanging Sword Alley
11. Seacoal Lane
12. Newgate Prison
13. St. Paul's Cathedral
14. The Old Deanery

his writing desks, and a creation in its cellar of a kitchen he described in *The Pickwick Papers*.

Doughty Street soon becomes John Street. Continue south along John Street until it dead-ends at Theobald's Road, where you turn left. Two blocks later, turn right on Gray's Inn Road. The complex of buildings that have been on your right-hand side is:

4. Gray's Inn. Theoretically, the loosely defined official function of this sprawling collection of buildings was to provide offices and residential flats for lawyers and to admit applicants to the practice of law in England. In *The Uncommercial Traveller,* Dickens called this warren of offices, residences, and dark cubbyholes, "one of the most depressing institutions in brick and mortar known to the children of men." This unattractive description was probably inspired by Dickens's unhappy experience when, at age 15, he worked as a clerk in no. 1. Later, other addresses within Gray's Inn were used as settings in *David Copperfield* and served as inspiration for similarly depressing locales in other novels. Continue walking south on Gray's Inn Road until you reach the wide and busy expanse of High Holborn. (It might be referred to at this point as simply "Holborn.") Turn left, walking eastward, along the left-hand (northern) edge of the avenue, turning very soon left again onto Brooke Street. Here you'll be in a warren of alleyways and narrow streets whose original layout was altered by the erection of several modern buildings since the bombings of World War II. If you can imagine these streets teeming with residents and permeated with the choking pall of coal smoke, you might gain an insight into the settings described by Dickens.

In 1 short block, turn right onto Fox Court, which soon changes its name to Greville Street (the narrow streets run into one another here), and walk eastward until, on your right, you reach a dignified courtyard stained black by a century of industrial grime:

5. Bleeding Heart Yard. This opening in the neighborhood's mass of masonry was made famous by Dickens in *Little Dorrit* as the locale of Doyce and Clennam's factory, and the grimy, underprivileged home of the Plornish family. Its evocative name was attributed to a very old inn whose trademark was a brokenhearted virgin, but the place was also associated with a certain Lady Hatton. She entered into an alliance with the Devil who—when the fun was over—came embodied as a dashing swain dressed entirely in black to claim her. Spiriting her off to hell, he left only her bleeding heart beside the pump in a courtyard later known as Bleeding Heart Yard.

Although street urchins of a century ago could take shortcuts through the winding hallways and cellars of the district's slums, you'll have to walk almost completely around the block to reach your next objective. Exit from Bleeding Heart Yard onto Greville, turning right (east). Two blocks later, turn right (south) onto Farringdon Street and walk for a block. Then, turn right (west) onto Charterhouse Street. Walk for a block on the right-hand side of the street until you reach a small and narrow street known as Ely Place. Herein lies your:

REFUELING STOP   Ye Old Mitre, Ely Place, EC1 (tel. 071/405-4751). Some kind of inn has stood beside the dingy brick-lined sides of this alleyway since 1547, but the incarnation you'll see today has dark-stained Victorian paneling and battered wooden floors, tables, and benches well worn by characters who might have filled the pages of Dickens. Today's clientele consists of City financiers and salespeople from the nearby jewelry district who enjoy uncomplicated food (place your order at the bar) and countless mugs of Burton's ale.

After your tipple, continue south along Ely Place, then turn right into the roundabout known as Holborn Circus, which funnels into High Holborn Street. Proceed westward, walking along the south (left-hand) side of the street for 6 blocks to Chancery Lane. On the junction's southwest corner lies another group of weathered buildings, used a century ago as a complex of Victorian apartments and legal offices:

6. Lincoln's Inn. Originally built during the 1400s, it's pervaded with associations of Dickens. Its Old Hall was the setting for the opening scene of *Bleak House.* Some 2½ labyrinthine blocks to the west is an open space, Lincoln's Inn Fields. Betsey Trotwood of *David Copperfield* took lodgings in a building that flanked it. On Lincoln's Inn Fields' western border sits no. 58, a town house that belonged to John Foster, who entertained the author from time to time within its precincts.

Retrace your steps eastward to Chancery Lane, then head south past several narrow alleyways and covered passageways until you reach the traditional headquarters of British publishing and journalism:

7. Fleet Street. Although its grip on British journalism is now a memory, many of Dickens's characters met or interacted with one another along Fleet Street. At no. 1, you'll find the Williams and Glyn Bank, which in an earlier incarnation was Child's Bank—the model for Tellson's Bank in *A Tale of Two Cities.* Fleet Street was crucially important to the author's career. In 1833, Chapman & Hall, the publishers of *Monthly Magazine,* published Dickens's first manuscript. To see the offices that launched one of England's most important writers, turn north off Fleet Street into the postage-stamp-size confines of:

8. Johnson's Court. Farther along, from an entrance located at 145 Fleet St. (near the corner of Wine Office Court), is a restaurant and pub that was familiar to Dickens and that provided a setting for some of his scenes:

9. The Cheshire Cheese. One of the greatest of the old City chophouses, it's been in business since 1667. It claims to be the place where Samuel Johnson dined and entertained his friends.

Now cross to the south side of Fleet Street and retrace your steps, walking west for a block. Extending south of Fleet Street is Whitefriars Street which, if you'll enter, soon provides access to:

10. Hanging Sword Alley. Here, Dickens housed Jerry Cruncher, one of the more gruesome characters in *A Tale of Two Cities.*

Fleet Street soon empties into a traffic circle known as Ludgate Circus. Continue your walk eastward onto a street called Ludgate Hill. The first street on your left is:

11. Seacoal Lane. This street was the site of one of the Victorian era's most feared and loathed prisons, the long-ago demolished Fleet Prison, where Mr. Pickwick was incarcerated for debt. Continue walking northeast on Seacoal Lane, which merges after about a block with Old Bailey, where you turn left. There, a grim-looking judicial building—the Central Criminal Court—occupies the site of an even more infamous Victorian jail:

12. Newgate Prison. Incarceration in one of its dank cells was perhaps the greatest fear of Fagin and his band of adolescent pickpockets in *Oliver Twist;* Dickens later portrayed the prevalent despair of its inmates in sections of *Great Expectations.* Although Newgate was demolished in 1902, its reputation as one of the most truly horrible prisons of 19th-century Europe lingers on in the neighborhood even today.

Turn south along Old Bailey for about a block, then go left (eastward) along Ludgate Hill until you come to a monument rich in associations for both Dickens and dozens of other writers:

13. St. Paul's Cathedral. Dickens set some of the pivotal scenes of *David Copperfield* here, including episodes where Betsey Trotwood meets secretly with a man who is later revealed as her estranged husband. South of the cathedral, in a short alleyway called Dean's Court, stands the:

14. Old Deanery, where Dickens worked for a brief period as a legal reporter in 1829.

WALKING TOUR —— THE BRITISH MUSEUM

Start: Assyrian Transept. **Tube:** Holborn, Russell Square, or Tottenham Court Road.
Finish: The King's Library.
Time: 2½ hours.
Best Time: Monday through Friday, when the museum opens at 10am.
Worst Times: Saturday and Sunday, when it's overcrowded.

As you enter the front hall of the British Museum, Great Russell Street, WC1 (tel. 071/636-1555), head immediately for one of its most monumental vistas, Room 26. Set near the main entrance, it's better known as the:

1. Assyrian Transept. There, you'll find the winged and human-headed bulls that once guarded the gateways to the palaces of Assyrian kings.

From here, you can continue north into the long and echoing Hall of Egyptian Sculpture (Room 25) to see the:

2. Rosetta Stone, whose discovery during one of Napoléon's campaigns led to the deciphering of hieroglyphs, explained in a wall display behind the stone.

Within a parallel room to the east (Room 19, the Nimrud Gallery) rises the:

3. Black Obelisk of Shalmaneser III (858–824 B.C.), an ancient tribute from Jehu, king of Israel.

Several galleries to the west of the Nimrud Gallery sprawls one of the largest and most famous rooms of the British Museum, the Duveen Gallery (Room 8), housing the:

4. Elgin Marbles, which include some of the finest sculptures ever produced in ancient Greece, most notably fragments from the frieze of the Parthenon in Athens. Of the 92 metopes from the Parthenon, 15 are housed today in the British Museum. They depict the to-the-death struggle between the handsome Lapiths and the grotesque, drunken Centaurs. The head of the horse from the chariot of Selene, goddess of the moon, is one of the pediment sculptures.

Directly northeast of the Duveen Gallery in Room 9 (Room of the Caryatid) is the:

5. Caryatid from the Erechtheum (421 B.C.), a gracefully robed depiction of a maiden whose body supported part of a temple dedicated to Athena and Poseidon. Displayed nearby, in Room 12, are sculptures from the:

6. Mausoleum at Halicarnassus, which, after its construction around 350 B.C., was considered one of the Seven Wonders of the Ancient World. It was intended to house the remains of Mausollus, ruler of Caria.

Funneling off from Room 12 rise the museum's West Stairs. Climb them to reach the upper floor, then walk south through four galleries until you reach Room 70. There, you'll find:

7. The Portland Vase, considered the finest example of ancient cameo carving in the world today. Dating from around 25 B.C., using techniques imported to Rome from Egypt, it's named after the Dowager Duchess of Portland, who acquired it from a family of Italian cardinals (the Barberinis) in 1784. Smashed to

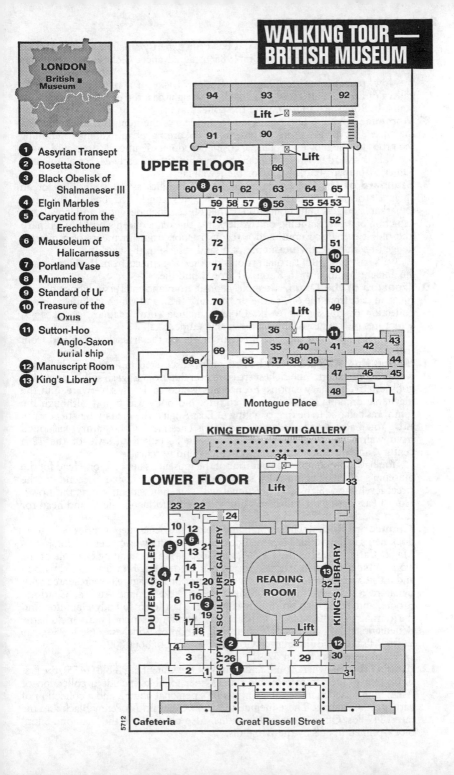

pieces by a British vandal in 1845, it has been expertly repaired and dismantled twice since then, most recently in 1985 using advanced techniques and epoxy resins.

Now, retrace your steps through Room 71 (site of a recently refurbished gallery of Etruscan artifacts) and continue straight past the entrance to the West Stairs. In Rooms 61 and 60, note the collection of:

8. Mummies, ghoulish and mysterious reminders of the hopes for an afterlife of the ancient Egyptians. Adjacent, in Room 63, are Egyptian exhibits resembling the props for the movie *Cleopatra;* cosmetics, domestic utensils, toys, and tools.

Walk eastward to Room 56, devoted to objects from early Mesopotamia and Sumeria (southern Iraq). Look for the jewellike:

9. Standard of Ur. Crafted from lapis-lazuli mosaics as the soundbox for an ancient stringed instrument in 2,500 B.C., it's considered one of the most remarkable objects in its collection. Other objects include a gold and lapis-lazuli depiction of a goat standing on two legs in a thicket, a queen's bull-headed harp (the oldest ever discovered) and a reconstruction from fragments of a queen's sledge (the oldest-known example of a land vehicle in the world).

Walk east and south through rooms devoted to artifacts from the Hittites and the ancient Anatolians. In Room 51, you'll find the:

10. Treasure of the Oxus, a temple deposit from ancient Persia whose objects range in date from the 6th to the 3rd century B.C., and which include a unique collection of goldsmith's work. Objects include votive plaques, signet rings, sculptures of a nude youth and a fish-shaped pedestal.

Several galleries to the south, in Room 41, are the artifacts unearthed from the:

11. Sutton-Hoo Anglo-Saxon burial ship, discovered in Suffolk. It is, in the words of one expert, "the richest treasure ever dug from English soil," containing gold jewelry, armor, weapons, bronze bowls and caldrons, silverware, and the inevitable drinking horn of Norse culture. No body was found, although the tomb was believed to be that of a king of East Anglia who died in the 7th century A.D. You'll also see the bulging-eyed Lewis chessmen (12th century) fashioned from walrus ivory, Romanesque carvings in Scandinavian style of the 12th century, and the Ilbert collection of clocks and watches.

You have now completed your tour of the museum's upper floor. Head for the museum's Main Stairs, a very short walk to the west, and descend to the street-level floor. (Signs and personnel will sometimes identify it as the Lower Floor.) Pass beside the museum's gift shop and information desk, and head for Room 30, the:

12. Manuscript Room, where you'll find one of the richest depositories of historic documents in the world. They include one of two surviving copies of King John's Magna Carta, as well as the Lindisfarne Gospels (an outstanding example of the work of Northumbrian artists in the early period of English Christianity, written and illustrated about 698). Almost every major literary figure is represented with signatures, including those of Shakespeare, Dickens, Jane Austen, Charlotte Brontë, and Yeats. Also on display is Nelson's last letter to Lady Hamilton and the journals of Captain Cook. Other notable exhibitions in the library include the Benedictional (in Latin) of St. Ethelwold, bishop of Winchester (963–984); the Luttrell Psalter; and the Harley Golden Gospels of about 800.

Head north into Room 32, the very large:

13. King's Library, where you'll find a copy of the Gutenberg Bible (1455), the first book ever printed from movable type. Other exhibits include a collection of Asian illuminated manuscripts, George III's personal library, and a collection of early postage stamps. These include the 1840 Great British Penny Black and the rare 1847 Post Office issues of Mauritius. Also on display is the Diamond Sutra, block-printed in 868 by the Moghuls.

6. ORGANIZED TOURS

In addition to touring London by foot or tube, you can take one of several coach tours to see the sights, plus there are dozens of fascinating trips offered along the Thames.

BUS TOURS

For the first-timer, the quickest and most economical way to bring the big city into focus is to take a 2-hour, 20-minute circular tour of the West End and the City of London on the guided **Original London Transport Sightseeing Tour,** which passes virtually all the major places of interest in central London. Operated by London Coaches, part of the city's official bus company, the journeys leave at frequent intervals daily from Victoria, Piccadilly Circus, Marble Arch, and Baker Street. Tickets cost £9 ($13.50) for adults and £5 ($7.50) for children, and they're available from the conductor. Tickets can also be purchased from London Transport's Travel Information Centres, where you can get a discount of £1 ($1.50) off each ticket. Locations of the Travel Information Centres are listed under "Getting Around" in Chapter 3.

London Transport also offers a 3-hour guided **Royal Westminster Tour,** passing Westminster Abbey, the Houses of Parliament, the Horse Guards, a view of the Changing of the Guard at Buckingham Palace, Trafalgar Square, and Piccadilly Circus. Tickets for this tour cost £12.50 ($18.80) for adults and £11.50 ($17.30) for children under 14.

Another excellent choice would be London Transport's 3-hour City tour that includes guided trips to the Tower of London and St. Paul's Cathedral. The cost of this tour is £16.50 ($24.80) for adults, £15.50 ($23.30) for children under 14. The City tour leaves at noon Monday through Saturday.

These two tours are also combined to form the **London Day tour,** which costs £27 ($40.50) for adults and £25 ($37.50) for children under 14, including lunch.

A **London Plus** tour lets you get off and on as you like, at more than 30 different places around central London. London Plus is operated with traditional "old-fashioned" Routemaster-type double-deck buses (open top in summer). Buses run every quarter hour in summer and every half hour in winter, daily from about 10am to 5pm—exact times vary from point to point, depending on traffic. Tickets cost £12 ($18) for adults and £6 ($9) for children.

The West End and City tours begin at London Transport's Coach Station, 195 Victoria St., SW1, which lies adjacent to Victoria Railway Station. To reserve seats or for information, phone 071/828-6449, or go to one of the London Transport Travel Information Centres.

HARRODS SIGHTSEEING BUS A double-decker air-conditioned coach in the discreet green-and-gold livery of **Harrods** takes sightseeing tours around London's attractions. The first departure from door no. 8 of Harrods on Brompton Road is at 10:30am and there are also tours at 1:30 and 4pm. Tea, coffee, and orange juice are served on board. The tour costs £15 ($22.50) for adults, £7 ($10.50) for children under 12. All-day excursion tours to Bath, Windsor, Stratford-upon-Avon, plus around all of London are available. You can purchase tickets at Harrods, Sightseeing Department, lower ground floor (tel. 071/581-3603). Tube: Knightsbridge.

BOAT TRIPS

Touring boats operate on the Thames all year and can take you to various places within Greater London. Main embarkation points are Westminster Pier, Charing Cross Pier, and Tower Pier—a system that enables you, for instance, to take a "water taxi" from the Tower of London to Westminster Abbey. Not only are the boats energy-saving, bringing you painlessly to your destination, but they also permit you to sit back in comfort as you see London from the river.

Pleasure boats operate all year down the Thames from Westminster Pier to the Tower of London, Greenwich, and the Thames Barrier; they operate from 10am to 4pm and depart every 20 minutes in summer, and every 30 minutes in winter. It takes 20 minutes to reach the Tower and 40 minutes to arrive at Greenwich. In the summer, services operate upriver to Kew, Richmond, and Hampton Court from Westminster Pier. There are departures every 30 minutes from 10:30am to 4pm for the 1½-hour journey to Kew; and there are three departures daily for the 2½-hour Richmond trip and three departures daily for the 3- to 5-hour trip to Hampton Court.

The multitude of small companies operating boat services from Westminster Pier have organized themselves into the **Westminster Passenger Service Association,** Westminster Pier, Victoria Embankment (tel. 071/930-4097). Boats leave the pier for cruises of varying lengths throughout the day and evening.

CANAL CRUISES The London canals were once major highways. Since the Festival of Britain in 1951, some of the traditional painted canal boats have been resurrected for Venetian-style trips through these waterways. One of them is *Jason,* which takes you on a 90-minute trip from Blomfield Road in Little Venice through the long Maida Hill tunnel under Edgware Road, through Regent's Park, passing the mosque, the London Zoo, Lord Snowdon's Aviary, past the Pirate's Castle to Camden Lock, and returns to Little Venice.

The season begins on Good Friday and lasts through October. During April, May, and September, the boat runs at 10:30am, 12:30pm, and 2:30pm. In June, July, and August, there is an additional trip during the afternoon, but always telephone first, and in October the boat runs at 12:30 and 2:30pm only.

There is a canalside café at the moorings, where lunches and teas are freshly made to order, and can either be served on the boat or in the courtyard (booking essential for the boat). The round-trip fare is £4.75 ($7.10) for adults and £3.50 ($5.30) for children. To inquire about bookings get in touch with **Jason's Trip,** opp. 60 Blomfield Road, Little Venice, W9 (tel. 071/286-3428). Tube: Paddington Station.

Also offered are one-way trips to Camden Lock with its craft shops and flea market. Every Tuesday a romantic evening cruise is organized with traditional fish-and-chips, soft music, and a full bar, cost £13.50 ($20.30) per person excluding the bar.

WALKING TOURS

ORGANIZED LONDON WALKS John Wittich, of **J. W. Promotions,** 66 St. Michael's St., W2 (tel. 071/262-9572), started walking tours of London in 1960. He is a Freeman of the City of London and a member of two of the ancient guilds of London, as well as the author of several books on London walks. There's no better way to search out the unusual, the beautiful, and the historic than to take a walking tour. The company concentrates on personal walking tours for families and groups who have booked in advance. John Wittich conducts all tours. The cost for 1½-hour walks is £15 ($22.50) minimum for one or two adults.

The **Original London Walks,** 87 Messina Ave., NW6 (tel. 071/624-3978 or 071/794-1764), is London's oldest—and premier—walking tour. Its guides include author Donald Rumbelow, leading authority on Jack the Ripper; a distinguished BBC producer, the foremost authority on Regent's Canal; the author of a classic guidebook (*London Walks*), and a London Historical Society official, along with prominent actors and actresses. Some 50 walks a week are featured year-round, ranging from Ghost Walks to Bloomsbury, from Dickens to the footsteps of the Beatles, even

Shakespeare to Soho. Walks cost £4 ($6) for adults and £3 ($4.50) for students and senior citizens. Children go free. Call for more information.

7. SPORTS & RECREATION

SPORTS

London can be as exciting for sports enthusiasts as for theater fans. That is, if they happen to be British sports enthusiasts. The trouble is that Britain's two main sporting obsessions—soccer and cricket, respectively—are unknown and incomprehensible to the average American visitor.

Soccer is the national winter sport. The London teams that set British pulses racing—Arsenal, Chelsea, Tottenham Hotspurs—sound like so many brands of cheese spread to a Statesider.

In summer there's cricket, played at the **Foster's Oval Cricket Ground,** The Oval, Kennington, SE11 (tel. 071/582-6660). During the international test matches between England and Australia, the West Indies, or India (equivalent in importance to the World Series), the country goes into a state of collective trance, hanging glassy-eyed on every ball as described over the radio or on TV. Bus: 36.

At the **All England Lawn Tennis & Croquet Club,** Church Road, Wimbledon, SW19 (tel. 081/946-2244), you can see some of the world's greatest tennis players in action. The annual championship Fortnight—the famous **Wimbledon**—comprises the last week in June and the first in July, with matches lasting from noon till dark (the gates open at 10:30am). Although the British founded the All England Lawn Tennis & Croquet Club back in 1877, they now rarely manage to win against latecomers to the game from other countries. Tube: Southfields Station; then a special bus from there.

Within easy reach of central London, there are horse-racing tracks at **Kempton Park, Sandown Park,** and the most famous of them all, **Epsom,** where the **Derby** is the main feature of the meeting in early June. Racing takes place both midweek and on weekends, but not continuously. Sometimes during the summer there are evening race meetings, so you should contact **United Racecourses Ltd.,** The Grandstand, Epsom, Surrey (tel. 0372/726311), for information of the next meeting at Epsom, Sandown Park, or Kempton Park. You can drive yourself or, if you want to travel by rail, call 071/928-5100 in London for details of train service. Bus no. 406 from Victoria Coach Station also goes there.

Finally, we come to a spectacle for which it is difficult to find a comprehensive tag—the **Royal Tournament,** which some viewers describe as a series of indoor parades paying homage to the traditions and majesty of the British armed forces. Performed every year in late July, usually for a 2½-week run, it's a long-running spectacle that has been viewed enthusiastically by thousands. The show includes massed bands presenting stirring music, the Royal Navy field-gun competition, the Royal Air Force with their dogs, the Royal Marines in action, the King's Troop Royal Horse Artillery, the Household Cavalry, and a series of visiting military-style exhibitions from throughout the British Commonwealth.

There are two performances Tuesday through Saturday, at 2:30 and 7:30pm, at the Earl's Court Exhibition Centre, Warwick Road, SW5. There are no evening performances on Sunday, and no matinees on Monday. Seats cost from £9 to £23 ($13.50 to $34.50), with discounts of around 40% for children 5 to 14 and senior citizens over 65. For tickets and other information, write to the **Royal Tournament Exhibition Centre,** Warwick Road (without number), London SW5 9TA (tel.

071/373-8141). Tube: Earl's Court. For any other information, contact the **Royal Tournament Horse Guards,** Whitehall (without number), London SW1 2AX (tel. 071/930-4288). Tube: Westminster.

RECREATION

SWIMMING **Brittania Leisure Centre,** 40 Hyde Rd., N1 (tel. 071/729-4485), is a sports and recreation center operated and paid for by one of the eastern boroughs of London. It houses a swimming pool with a wave machine, fountains, badminton and squash courts, and soccer and volleyball fields. Admission is 55p (80¢) for adults and 25p (40¢) for children. The complex is open Monday through Friday from 9am to 8:15pm, and on Saturday and Sunday from 9am to 5:45pm. Tube: Old Street.

HEALTH & FITNESS CENTERS **Jubilee Hall Sports Centre,** 30 The Piazza, Covent Garden, WC2 (tel. 071/836-4835), is the result of a radical makeover during the 1980s of a Victorian-era fish and flower market into a modern gym. Today, it's one of the best and most centrally located sports centers in London, with the capital's largest weight room and an avid corps of bodybuilding regulars. It also offers badminton, basketball, aerobics, gymnastics, martial arts, self-defense training (for women), tennis, and weight training. Maintained by the City of Westminster, it is open Monday through Friday from 7am to 10pm, on Saturday and Sunday from 8am to 5pm. The admission is £5 ($7.50) for use of the weight room and £4 ($6) for participation in an aerobics class. Tube: Covent Garden.

8. EASY EXCURSIONS FROM LONDON

It would be sad to leave England without ever having ventured into the countryside, at least for a day. The English are the greatest excursion travelers in the world, forever dipping into their own rural areas to discover ancient abbeys, 17th-century village lanes, shady woods for picnic lunches, and stately mansions. From London, it's possible to take advantage of countless tours—coach, boat, or a do-it-yourself method on bus or train. On many trips, you can combine two or more methods of transportation; for example, you can go to Windsor by boat and return by coach or train.

I highly recommend the previously described Green Line Coaches, operated by London Country Bus Services Ltd. (see "Getting Around," in Chapter 2).

For longer tours, say, to Stratford-upon-Avon, you'll find the trains much more convenient. Often you can take advantage of the many bargain tickets outlined in Chapter 2 under "Getting Around." For further information about trains to a specific location, go to the British Rail offices on Lower Regent Street.

HAMPTON COURT PALACE

On the north side of the Thames, 13 miles west of London in East Molesey, Surrey (tel. 081/781-9500), this 16th-century palace of Cardinal Wolsey can teach us a lesson: Don't try to outdo your boss—particularly if he happens to be Henry VIII. The rich cardinal did just that, and he eventually lost his fortune, power, and prestige, and ended up giving his lavish palace to the Tudor monarch. Henry took over, even outdoing the Wolsey embellishments. The Tudor additions included the Anne Boleyn gateway, with its 16th-century astronomical clock that even tells the high-water mark at London Bridge. From Clock Court, you can see one of Henry's major contributions, the aptly named great hall, with its hammer-beam ceiling. Also added by Henry were the tiltyard, a tennis court, and kitchen.

To judge from the movie *A Man for All Seasons,* Hampton Court had quite a retinue to feed. Cooking was done in the great kitchens. Henry cavorted through the various apartments with his wives of the moment—everybody from Anne Boleyn to Catherine Parr (the latter reversed things and lived to bury her erstwhile spouse). Charles I was imprisoned here at one time and temporarily managed to escape his jailers.

Although the palace enjoyed prestige and pomp in Elizabethan days, it owes much of its present look to William and Mary—or rather to Sir Christopher Wren, who designed and had built the Northern or Lion Gates, intended to be the main entrance to the new parts of the palace. The fine wrought-iron screen at the south end of the south gardens was made by Jean Tijou around 1694 for William and Mary. You can parade through the apartments today, filled as they are with porcelain, furniture, paintings, and tapestries. The King's Dressing Room is graced with some of the best art. In Queen Mary's closet, you'll find Pieter Brueghel the Elder's macabre *Massacre of the Innocents*. Tintoretto and Titian deck the halls of the King's Drawing Room. Finally, be sure to inspect the royal chapel (Wolsey wouldn't recognize it). To confound yourself totally, you may want to get lost in the serpentine shrubbery maze in the garden, also the work of Sir Christopher Wren.

The gardens—including the Great Vine, King's Privy Garden, Great Fountain Gardens, Tudor and Elizabethan Knot Gardens, Board Walk, Tiltyard, and Wilderness—are open daily year round from 7am until dusk (but not later than 9pm), and can be visited free. The cloisters, courtyards, state apartments, great kitchen, cellars, Hampton Court exhibition, and Mantegna paintings gallery are open daily from 9:30am to 6pm mid-March to mid-October, and 9:30am to 4:30pm mid-October to mid-March. The Tudor tennis court and banqueting house are open the same hours as above, but only from mid-March to mid-October. Admission to all these attractions is £5.90 ($8.90) for adults, £3.90 ($5.90) for children (children under 5, free).

A garden café and restaurant is in the Tiltyard Gardens.

You can get to Hampton Court by bus, train, boat, or car. London Transport buses no. 111, 131, 216, 267, and 461 make the trip, as do Green Line Coaches (ask at the nearest London Country Bus office for routes 715, 716, 718, and 726). Frequent trains from Waterloo Station (Network Southeast) go to Hampton Court Station. Boat service is offered to and from Kingston, Richmond, and Westminster.

KEW

Kew is 9 miles southwest of central London, near Richmond.

ROYAL BOTANIC GARDENS, KEW GARDENS, Kew, Surrey. Tel. 081/940-1171.

These are among the best-known botanic gardens in Europe and contain thousands of varieties of plants. But Kew is no mere pleasure garden—rather, it's essentially a vast scientific research center that happens to be beautiful. A pagoda, erected in 1761–62, represents the "flowering" of chinoiserie. The Visitor Centre at Victoria Gate houses an exhibit telling the story of Kew, as well as a bookshop where guides to the garden are available.

The gardens cover a 300-acre site encompassing lakes, greenhouses, walks, garden pavilions, and museums, together with fine examples of the architecture of Sir William Chambers. At whatever season you visit Kew, there's always something to see: in spring, the daffodils and bluebells, through to the coldest months when the Heath Garden is at its best. Among the 50,000 plant species are notable collections of arum lilies, ferns, orchids, aquatic plants, cacti, mountain plants, palms, and tropical water lilies.

The least expensive and most convenient way to visit the gardens is to take the District line tube to Kew Gardens on the south bank of the Thames. The most romantic way to come in summer is via a steamer from Westminster Bridge to Kew Pier.

Admission: £3.50 ($5.30) adults, £1.30 ($2) children, £9 ($13.50) family ticket.
Open: Mon–Sat 9:30am–4 (Apr–Oct, to 6:30pm), Sun and public holidays 9:30am–8pm. **Closed:** Jan 1, Dec 25.

KEW PALACE, Kew Gardens, Kew, Surrey. Tel. 081/940-3321.

Much interest focuses on the red-brick palace (dubbed the Dutch House), a former residence of King George III and Queen Charlotte. Now a museum, it was built in 1631 and contains memorabilia of the reign of George III, along with a royal collection of furniture and paintings. It is reached by walking to the northern tip of the Broad Walk.

Admission: £1.10 ($1.70) adults, 75p ($1.10) children.
Open: Apr–Sept, daily 11am–5:30pm.

QUEEN CHARLOTTE'S COTTAGE, Kew Gardens, Kew, Surrey. Tel. 081/940-1171.

Built in 1771, this cottage is half-timbered and thatched; George III is believed to have been the architect. The house has been restored to its original splendor in great detail, including the original Hogarth prints that hung on the downstairs walls.

Admission: 75p ($1.10) adults, 60p (90¢) children.
Open: Apr–Sept, Sat–Sun and bank holidays 11am–5:30pm.

KEW BRIDGE STEAM MUSEUM, Green Dragon Lane, Brentford, Middlesex. Tel. 081/568-4757.

This museum houses what is probably the world's largest collection of steam-powered beam engines. These were used in the Victorian era and up to the 1940s to pump London's water, and one engine has a capacity of 700 gallons per stroke. There are seven restored engines that are steamed on weekends, plus other unrestored engines, a steam railway, and a working forge. The museum has a tearoom, plus free parking for cars.

The museum is north of Kew Bridge, under the tower, a 10-minute walk from Kew Gardens. You can reach it by a British Rail train from Waterloo Station to Kew Bridge Station; by bus no. 65, 237, 267, or 391 (no. 7 on Sunday); or by tube to Gunnersbury or South Ealing, and then by bus.

Admission: On steam days, £2.50 ($3.80) adults, £1.40 ($2.10) children; on other days, £1.70 ($2.60) adults, 90p ($1.40) children.
Open: Steam exhibits, Sat–Sun and Mon holidays 11am–5pm; static exhibition, Mon–Fri 11am–5pm.

GREENWICH

Greenwich mean time is the basis of standard time throughout most of the world, the zero point used in the reckoning of terrestrial longitudes since 1884. But Greenwich is also home of the Royal Naval College, the National Maritime Museum, and the Old Royal Observatory. In dry dock at Greenwich Pier is the clipper ship *Cutty Sark,* as well as Sir Francis Chichester's *Gipsy Moth IV.*

About 4 miles from the City, Greenwich is reached by a number of methods, and part of the fun of making the jaunt is getting there. Ideally, you'll arrive by boat, as Henry VIII preferred to do on one of his hunting expeditions. In summer, launches depart at regular intervals from the pier at Charing Cross, Tower Bridge, or Westminster. The boats leave daily for Greenwich about every half hour from 10am to 7pm (times are approximate, depending on the tides). Bus no. 1 runs from Trafalgar Square to Greenwich; bus no. 188 goes from Euston through Waterloo to Greenwich. From Charing Cross Station, the British Rail train takes 15 minutes to reach Greenwich, and there is now the new Docklands Light Railway, running from Tower

Gateway to Island Gardens on the Isle of Dogs. A short walk under the Thames through a foot tunnel brings you out in Greenwich opposite the *Cutty Sark*.

WHAT TO SEE & DO

On Saturday and Sunday in Greenwich, there are arts, crafts, and antiques markets. Ask at the **tourist information center** by the pier and *Cutty Sark* (tel. 081/858-6376), open Friday through Wednesday from 2:30 to 5pm.

CUTTY SARK, Cutty Sark Gardens, King William Walk, Greenwich Pier, SE10. Tel. 081/853-3589.

Unquestionably, the last of the great clippers holds the most interest and has been seen by millions. At the spot where the vessel is now berthed stood the 19th-century Ship Inn, where Victorians came for whitebait dinners. Ordered built by Capt. Jock Willis ("Old White Hat"), the clipper was launched in 1869 to sail the China tea-trade route. It was named after the Witch Nannie in Robert Burns's *Tam o' Shanter* (note the figurehead). Yielding to the more efficient steamers, the *Cutty Sark* later was converted to a wool-carrying clipper and plied the route between Australia and England. Before its retirement in 1954, it knew many owners, and even different names.

Admission: £3.25 ($4.90) adults, £2.25 ($3.40) children.
Open: Summer, Mon–Sat 10am–6pm, Sun noon–6pm; winter, Mon–Sat 10am–5pm, Sun noon–5pm.

GIPSY MOTH IV, Cutty Sark Gardens, King William Walk, Greenwich Pier, SE10. Tel. 081/853-3589.

Next to the clipper—and looking like a sardine beside a shark—lies the equally famous *Gipsy Moth IV*. This was the ridiculously tiny sailing craft in which Sir Francis Chichester circumnavigated the globe—solo! You can go on board and marvel at the minuteness of the vessel in which the gray-haired old sea dog made his incredible 119-day journey. His chief worry—or so he claimed—was running out of ale before he reached land.

Admission: 60p (90¢) adults, 40p (60¢) children under 16.
Open: Apr–Oct, Mon–Sat 10am–6pm, Sun noon–6pm. **Closed:** Nov–Mar.

ROYAL NAVAL COLLEGE, King William Walk, Greenwich, SE10. Tel. 081/858-2154.

This college grew up on the site of the Tudor palace in Greenwich in which Henry VIII and Elizabeth I were born. William and Mary commissioned Wren to design the present buildings in 1695 to house naval pensioners, and these became the Royal Naval College in 1873. The buildings are baroque masterpieces, in which the Painted Hall (by Thornhill from 1708 to 1727) and the chapel are outstanding.

Admission: Free.
Open: Fri–Wed 2:30–5pm (last entrance 4:30pm). **Closed:** Some public holidays (days are published in the daily papers).

NATIONAL MARITIME MUSEUM, Romney Rd., Greenwich, SE10. Tel. 081/858-4422.

Built around Inigo Jones's 17th-century Palladian Queen's House, this museum portrays Britain's maritime heritage. Actual craft, marine paintings, ship models, and scientific instruments are displayed, including the uniform coat that Lord Nelson wore at the Battle of Trafalgar. Other treasures include the chronometer (or sea watch) used by Captain Cook when he made his Pacific explorations in the 1770s.

The **Old Royal Observatory**, Greenwich Park (tel. 081/858-4422), part of the museum, is also worth exploring. Sir Christopher Wren was the architect; in fact, he was interested in astronomy even before he became famous. The observatory overlooks Greenwich and the Maritime Museum from a park laid out to the design of Le Nôtre, the French landscaper. Here you can stand at 0° longitude, as the Greenwich Meridian, or prime meridian, marks the first of the globe's north-south divisions. See also the big red time-ball used in olden days by ships sailing down the river from London to set their timepieces by. There's a fascinating bewilderment of astronomical and navigational instruments; time and travel become more realistic after a visit here.

Admission: £3.75 ($5.60) adults, £2.75 ($4.10) children 7–16, £13.95 ($20.90) family tickets.

Open: Apr–Sept, Mon–Sat 10am–6pm, Sun noon–6pm; Oct–Mar, Mon–Sat 10am–5pm, Sun 2–5pm. **Closed:** Dec 24–26.

WHERE TO DINE

CUTTY SARK FREE HOUSE, Ballast Quay, Lassell St., Greenwich, SE10. Tel. 081/858-3146.
    Cuisine: ENGLISH. **Reservations:** Not required. **Transportation:** BritRail's Greenwich train from Charing Cross Station to Maze Hill.
    $ Prices: Pub snacks £2–£5 ($3–$7.50). No credit cards.
    Open: Mon–Sat 11am–11pm, Sun noon–3pm and 7–10:30pm.

With plenty of local color, this English riverside tavern is one of the most historic pubs in the environs of London, established in 1698. Today it's a preferred watering hole of a bevy of pop music stars who live in the area. There is sometimes live music on Tuesday night. Pub snacks are served in the bar, including sandwiches, steak sandwiches, salads, vegetable lasagne, and four kinds of fish platters (cod, plaice, whitebait, and scampi).

TRAFALGAR TAVERN, Park Row, Greenwich, SE10. Tel. 081/858-2437.
    Cuisine: ENGLISH. **Reservations:** Recommended for restaurant. **Transportation:** BritRail's Greenwich train from Charing Cross Station to Maze Hill.
    $ Prices: Appetizers £2.50–£4.20 ($3.80–$6.30); main courses £6–£11 ($9–$16.50). MC, V.
    Open: Daily 11am–11pm.

The Trafalgar Tavern, a 2-minute walk north of Greenwich Pier, overlooks the Thames at Greenwich and is surrounded by many attractions; directly opposite the tavern is the Royal Naval College. Ringed with nautical paintings and engravings, lots of heavy dark wood, and brass artifacts, the restaurant invites you to enjoy traditional English specialties that go well with the 18th-century naval memorabilia. Try the steak-and-kidney pie, one of the succulent steaks, or perhaps chateaubriand. Pheasant and venison are also on the menu. You can also order daily specials, with freshly prepared vegetables. In the rear is a separate restaurant section specializing in fish. The full menu is available during opening hours. You can also visit for pub snacks, priced at £3.50 to £5.50 ($5.30 to $8.30). Platters of roast beef are a specialty.

RUNNYMEDE

Two miles outside Windsor is the 188-acre meadow on the south side of the Thames, in Surrey, where King John put his seal on the Great Charter. Today Runnymede is also the site of the **John F. Kennedy Memorial,** an acre of English ground given to the United States by the people of Britain. The memorial, a large block of white stone, is hard to see from the road. The pagoda that you can see from the road was placed there by the American Bar Association to acknowledge the fact that American law stems from the English system.

    The historic site, to which there is free access all year, lies on the Thames, half a mile west of Runnymede Bridge on the south side of the A308. If you're taking the

M25, exit at Junction 13. The nearest rail connection is at Egham, half a mile away. For bus information for the surrounding area, call 081/668-7261.

SYON PARK

Syon Park lies in Brentford, Middlesex, 9 miles from Piccadilly Circus, on 5 acres of the Duke of Northumberland's Thames-side estate. It is one of the most beautiful spots in all of Great Britain; there's always something in bloom. Called "The Showplace of the Nation in a Great English Garden," Syon Park was opened to the public in 1968. A nation of green-thumbed gardeners is dazzled here, and the park is also educational, showing amateurs how to get the most out of their small gardens. The vast flower- and plant-studded acreage betrays the influence of "Capability" Brown, who laid out the grounds in the 18th century.

Particular highlights include a 6-acre rose garden, a butterfly house, and the great conservatory, one of the earliest and most famous buildings of its type, built in 1822–29. There's a quarter-mile-long ornamental lake studded with water lilies and silhouetted by cypresses and willows, even a gardening supermarket. Syon is also the site of the first botanical garden in England, created by the father of English botany, Dr. William Turner in 1548. Trees include a 200-year-old Chinese juniper, an Afghan ash, Indian bean trees, and liquidambars.

On the grounds is **Syon House,** built in 1431, the original structure incorporated into the Duke of Northumberland's present home. The house was later remade to the specifications of the first Duke of Northumberland in 1762–69. The battlemented facade is that of the original Tudor mansion, but the interior is from the 18th century, the design of Robert Adam. Basil Taylor said of the interior feeling: "You're almost in the middle of a jewel box." In the Middle Ages, Syon was a monastery, later suppressed by Henry VIII. Catherine Howard, the king's fifth wife, was imprisoned in the house before her scheduled beheading in 1542.

The combined house and gardens admission price is £4.50 ($6.80) for adults and £3.25 ($4.90) for children.

The house is open from Easter to the end of September, Sunday through Thursday from noon to 5pm. The gardens are open all year except for Christmas and Boxing Day (Dec 26). The gates open at 10am and close at dusk or 6pm. After October, the winter closing hour is 4pm. For more information, phone 081/560-0882. Syon Park lies 2 miles west of Kew Bridge (the road is signposted from the A315/310 at Busch Corner). By public transport, from Waterloo Station in London, take British Rail to Kew Bridge Station. From there, catch bus no. 237 or 267 to the pedestrian entrance to Syon House. It's faster, however, to take the tube to Gunnersbury.

THORPE PARK

One of Europe's leading family leisure parks, Thorpe Park, Staines Road, Chertsey, Surrey (tel. 0932/569393), lies only 21 miles from central London on the A320 between Staines and Chertsey, with easy access from Junctions 11 and 13 on the M25. The entrance fee of £9.95 ($14.90) for adults and £8.95 ($13.40) for children under 14 includes all rides, shows, attractions and exhibits. Additional charges are made only for coin-operated amusements. Just a few of the favorite rides and shows are Loggers Leap, Thunder River, Treasure Island, Magic Mill, Phantom Fantasia, the Family Tea Cup Ride, Cinema 180, and the Palladium Theatre. Newer attractions are the Flying Fish, an outdoor roller coaster, Carousel Kingdom, an undercover entertainment area, and A Drive in the Country, a vintage track ride, and the U.K.'s first four-lane water slide. Free transport is provided around the 500 acres by railway and waterbus.

Guests can picnic on the grounds or patronize one of the restaurants or fast-food areas. The park is open daily from April 3 through October from 10am to 5pm. The nearest main-line station is Staines, from Waterloo Station in London. Many bus services also operate directly from Victoria Coach Station in London to Thorpe Park.

WOBURN ABBEY

✪ Few tourists visiting Bedfordshire miss the Georgian mansion of Woburn Abbey, Woburn, Bedfordshire MK43 0TP (tel. 0525/290666), the seat of the dukes of Bedford for more than three centuries. It lies 44 miles north of London. The much-publicized 18th-century estate is signposted half a mile from the village of Woburn, which itself lies 13 miles southwest of Bedford. Its state apartments are rich in furniture, porcelain, tapestries, silver, and a valuable art collection, including paintings by van Dyck, Holbein, Rembrandt, Gainsborough, and Reynolds. A series of paintings by Canaletto, showing his continuing views of Venice, grace the walls of the Canaletto Room, an intimate dining room. (Prince Philip said the duke's collection was superior to the Canalettos at Windsor—but Her Royal Highness quickly corrected him.) Of all the paintings, one of the most notable from a historical point of view is the *Armada Portrait* of Elizabeth I. Her hand rests on the globe, as Philip's invincible armada perishes in the background.

Queen Victoria and Prince Albert visited Woburn Abbey in 1841; Victoria's Dressing Room contains a fine collection of 17th-century paintings from the Netherlands. Among the oddities and treasures at Woburn Abbey are a Grotto of Shells, a Sèvres dinner service (gift of Louis XV), and a chamber devoted to memorabilia of "The Flying Duchess." Wife of the 11th Duke of Bedford, she was a remarkable woman who disappeared on a solo flight in 1937 (the same year as Amelia Earhart). The duchess, however, was 72 years old at the time.

In the 1950s the present Duke of Bedford opened Woburn Abbey to the public to pay off millions of pounds in inheritance taxes. In 1974 he turned the estate over to his son and daughter-in-law, the Marquess and Marchioness of Tavistock, who reluctantly took on the business of running the 75-room mansion. And what a business it is, drawing hundreds of thousands of visitors a year and employing more than 300 people to staff the shops and grounds.

Today Woburn Abbey is surrounded by a 3,000-acre deer park that includes the famous Père David deer herd, originally from China and saved from extinction at Woburn. The Woburn Wild Animal Kingdom contains lions, tigers, giraffes, camels, monkeys, Przewalski horses, bongos, elephants, and other animals.

The house and park are open only on Saturday and Sunday from January 1 to March 28; visiting times for the house are 11am to 4:45pm, and for the park, 10:30am to 3:45pm. From March 29 to October 31, the abbey is open daily; the house can be visited Monday through Saturday from 11am to 5:45pm and on Sunday from 11am to 6:15pm, and the park is open Monday through Saturday from 10am to 4:45pm and on Sunday from 10am to 5:45pm. Admission is £6 ($9) for adults and £2 ($3) for children.

Light meals are available at the Flying Duchess Pavilion Coffee Shop.

In summer, travel agents can book you on organized coach tours out of London. Otherwise, motorists take the M1 (motorway) north to Junction 12 or 13, where Woburn Abbey directions are signposted.

HUGHENDEN MANOR

Outside High Wycombe, in Buckinghamshire, sits a country manor that not only gives us insight into the age of Victoria, but also acquaints us with a remarkable man. In Benjamin Disraeli we meet one of the most enigmatic figures of 19th-century England. At age 21 Dizzy published anonymously his five-volume novel *Vivian Grey*. Then he went on to other things and in 1839 married an older widow for her money, although they apparently developed a most successful relationship. He entered politics in 1837 and continued writing novels; his later ones met with more acclaim.

In 1848 Disraeli acquired Hughenden Manor, a country house that befitted his fast-rising political and social position. He served briefly as prime minister in 1868, but his political fame rests on his stewardship as prime minister from 1874 to 1880. He became Queen Victoria's friend—and in 1877 she paid him a rare honor by visiting him at Hughenden. In 1876 Disraeli became the Earl of Beaconsfield: he had arrived, but his wife was dead, and he was to die in 1881. Instead of being buried at Westminster Abbey, he preferred the simple little graveyard of Hughenden Church.

Today Hughenden contains an odd assortment of memorabilia, including a lock of Disraeli's hair, letters from Victoria, autographed books, and a portrait of Lord Byron, known to Disraeli's father.

If you're driving to Hughenden Manor on the way to Oxford, continue north of High Wycombe on the A4128 for about 1½ miles. If you're relying on public transportation from London, take coach no. 711 to High Wycombe, then board a Beeline bus (High Wycombe–Aylesbury no. 323 or 324). The manor house and garden are open April to October, Wednesday through Saturday from 2 to 6pm and on Sunday and bank holidays from noon to 6pm; in early March, on Saturday and Sunday only, from 2 to 6pm. It's closed from November to the end of March and on Good Friday. Admission is £3.30 ($5) for adults, £1.65 ($2.50) for children. For more information, call 0494/532580.

HATFIELD HOUSE

✪ West of Hertford, Hatfield House, Hatfield, Hertfordshire AL9 5NQ (tel. 0707/262823), is one of the great English country houses. Only the banqueting hall of the original Tudor palace remains; the remainder is Jacobean.

Hatfield was much a part of the lives of both Henry VIII and his daughter, Elizabeth I. In the old palace, built in the 15th century, Elizabeth romped and played as a child. Although Henry was married to her mother, Anne Boleyn, at the time of Elizabeth's birth, the marriage was later nullified (Anne lost her head and Elizabeth her legitimacy). Henry also used to stash away his oldest daughter, Mary Tudor, at Hatfield. But when Mary became Queen of England and set about earning the dubious distinction of "Bloody Mary," she found Elizabeth a problem. For a while she kept her in the Tower of London but eventually let her return to Hatfield. In 1558, while at Hatfield, Elizabeth learned of her ascension to the throne of England.

The Jacobean house that exists today contains much antique furniture, tapestries, and paintings, as well as three often-reproduced portraits, including the ermine and rainbow portraits of Elizabeth I. The great hall is suitably medieval, complete with a minstrel's gallery. One of the rarest exhibits is a pair of silk stockings, said to have been worn by Elizabeth herself, the first woman in England to don such apparel. The park and the gardens are also worth exploring. Luncheons and teas are available from 11am to 5pm in the converted coach house in the old palace yard.

Hatfield is open from March 25 to the second Sunday in October, Tuesday through Saturday from noon to 4pm, on Sunday from 1:30 to 5pm, and on bank-holiday Mondays from 11am to 5pm; it's closed Good Friday. Admission is £4.50 ($6.80) for adults, £3 ($4.50) for children. The house is across from the station in Hatfield. From London, take the fast trains from King's Cross or Moorgate.

Elizabethan banquets are staged in the banqueting hall of Hatfield House Tuesday and Thursday through Saturday, with much gaiety and music. Guests are invited to drink in an anteroom, then join the long tables for a feast of five courses with continuous entertainment from a group of Elizabethan players, minstrels, and jesters. Wine is included in the cost of the meal, but you're expected to pay for your before-dinner drinks yourself. The best way to get there from London for the feast is to book a coach tour for an inclusive fee starting at £37 ($55.50). The Evan Evans agency has tours leaving from Russell Square or from 41 Tottenham Court Rd. in London. The coach returns to London after midnight. If you get there under your own steam, the cost is £24.50 ($36.80) on Tuesday and Thursday, £25.50 ($38.30) on Friday, and £26.50 ($39.80) on Saturday. For reservations, call 0707/262055.

CHAPTER 7

LONDON SHOPPING & EVENING ENTERTAINMENT

1. THE SHOPPING SCENE

2. SHOPPING A TO Z

3. EVENING ENTERTAINMENT

When Prussian Field Marshal Blücher, Wellington's stout ally at Waterloo, first laid eyes on London, he allegedly slapped his thigh and exclaimed, "Herr Gott, what a city to plunder!"

He was gazing at what, for the early 19th century, was an overwhelming number of shops and stores. Since those days, other cities have come up to London's level as shopping centers, but none has ever surpassed it.

And when night falls, the pickings are equally rich, since London has one of the most varied spectrums of after-dark diversions of any city in the world.

1. THE SHOPPING SCENE

London displays an enormous variety of wares. You can pick up bargains ranging from a still-functioning hurdy-gurdy to a replica of the crown jewels. For the best buys, search out new styles in clothing, as well as traditional and well-tailored men's and women's suits, small antiques and curios, woolens, tweeds, tartans, rare books, Liberty silks, Burberrys, English china, silver, even arms and armor, to name just a few.

London stores keep fairly uniform hours, usually shorter than their American equivalents. Most stores are open Monday through Saturday from 9am to 5:30pm, with late shopping on Wednesday or Thursday to 7 or 8pm; however, many central shops close at around 1pm on Saturday. In the East End, around Aldgate and Whitechapel, many shops are open on Sunday from 9am to 2pm. There are a few all-night stores, mainly in the Bayswater section, and shops seldom close for lunch.

Bargains—that magic word in every traveler's dictionary—are everywhere, but they are likely to be limited by the U.S. Customs regulations. According to the latest rules, you—and everyone traveling with you—are entitled to bring back $400 worth of foreign-made merchandise per person without paying U.S. duty. This applies only to goods accompanying you. You can quite legitimately stretch that amount by mailing unsolicited gifts home; however, no gift can be worth more than $50, and you are not permitted to send more than one present per day to the same address.

Many London shops will help you beat the whopping purchase tax levied on much of England's merchandise. By presenting your passport, you can frequently purchase goods tax-free, but only if you have your purchase sent directly to your home address or to the plane you're taking back.

The huge purchase taxes imposed on so-called luxury goods are responsible for the extremely high cost of items such as wines, spirits, tobacco, cigarettes, and gasoline.

SHOPPING AREAS

London's retail stores tend to cluster in certain areas, a holdover from the times when each guild or craft had its own street, so you can often head in a certain direction to find a certain type of merchandise. The following is a very rough outline of the main shopping districts (not including the "Specialty Shopping Streets," which I will detail below) to help get you started.

Regent Street Curving down elegantly from Oxford Circus to Piccadilly Circus, this stylish thoroughfare is crammed with fashionable stores, selling everything from silks to silverware. It has both department stores and boutiques, but the accent is on the medium-size establishment in the upper-medium price range. Tube: Oxford Circus or Piccadilly Circus.

Oxford Street The main shopping artery of the metropolis, Oxford Street runs from St. Giles Circus to Marble Arch and is an endless, uninspiring but utility-crammed band of stores, stores, and more stores. It contains six of London's major department stores, apart from just about every kind of retailing establishment under the sun. Tube: Tottenham Court Road.

Piccadilly Unlike the circus, Piccadilly Street is distinctly in the upper bracket, specializing in automobile showrooms, travel offices, art galleries, plus London's poshest grocery store, Fortnum & Mason. Tube: Piccadilly Circus.

Bond Street Divided into New and Old, Bond Street connects Piccadilly and Oxford Street and is synonymous with the luxury trade. Here are found the very finest—and most expensive—of tailors, hatters, milliners, cobblers, and antiques dealers. Tube: Bond Street.

Knightsbridge Together with Kensington and Brompton Roads, this forms an extremely svelte shopping district south of Hyde Park. It's patronized for furniture, antiques, jewelry, and Harrods department store. Tube: Knightsbridge.

The Strand Stately, broad, and dignified, the Strand runs from Trafalgar Square into Fleet Street. It's lined with hotels, theaters, and specialty stores that you could spend a whole day peeking into. Tube: Charing Cross or Aldwych (weekdays only).

Kensington High Street This has been called "the Oxford Street of West London." Stretching for about 1½ miles, it includes many shops, such as the House of Fraser department store. You'll also find lots of stores on the side streets, such as Earl's Court Road and Abingdon Road, and Thackeray and Victoria Streets retain some of the old village atmosphere. From Kensington High Street, you can walk up Kensington Church Street, which, like Portobello Road, is one of the city's main shopping avenues, selling everything from antique furniture to impressionist paintings. Tube: High Street Kensington.

SPECIALTY SHOPPING STREETS

If you think London has unique department stores, wait until you see its equally unique shopping streets.

Carnaby Street Just off Regent Street is the legendary Carnaby Street. Alas, it no longer dominates the world of fashion as it did in the '60s, but it's still visited by the young, especially punkers, and some of its shops display lots of claptrap and

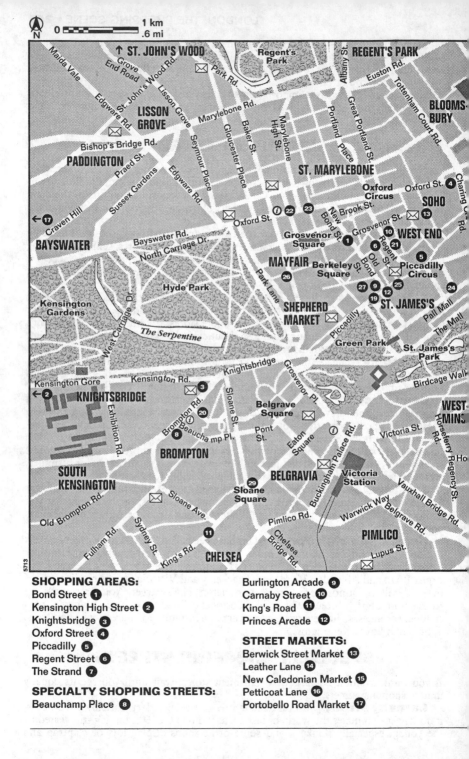

SHOPPING AREAS:
Bond Street ❶
Kensington High Street ❷
Knightsbridge ❸
Oxford Street ❹
Piccadilly ❺
Regent Street ❻
The Strand ❼

SPECIALTY SHOPPING STREETS:
Beauchamp Place ❽

Burlington Arcade ❾
Carnaby Street ❿
King's Road ⓫
Princes Arcade ⓬

STREET MARKETS:
Berwick Street Market ⓭
Leather Lane ⓮
New Caledonian Market ⓯
Petticoat Lane ⓰
Portobello Road Market ⓱

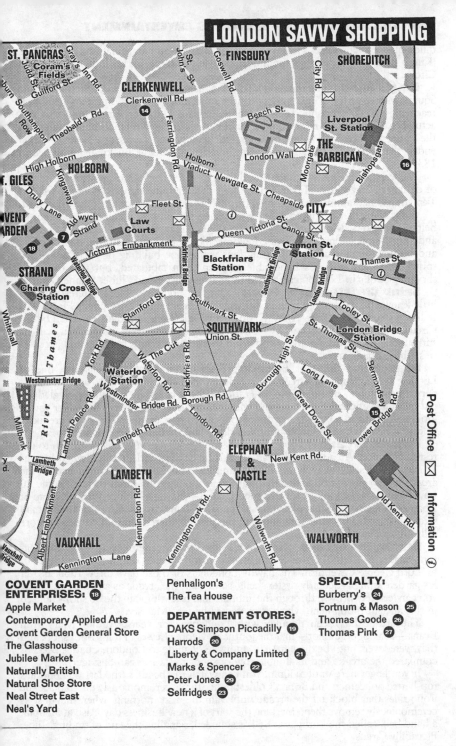

LONDON SAVVY SHOPPING

COVENT GARDEN ENTERPRISES: 18

Apple Market
Contemporary Applied Arts
Covent Garden General Store
The Glasshouse
Jubilee Market
Naturally British
Natural Shoe Store
Neal Street East
Neal's Yard
Penhaligon's
The Tea House

DEPARTMENT STORES:
DAKS Simpson Piccadilly 19
Harrods 20
Liberty & Company Limited 21
Marks & Spencer 22
Peter Jones 29
Selfridges 23

SPECIALTY:
Burberry's 24
Fortnum & Mason 25
Thomas Goode 26
Thomas Pink 27

Post Office ⊠ Information ⓘ

quick-quid merchandise. However, for value, style, and imagination, the Chelsea (King's Road) and Kensington boutiques have left Carnaby far behind. Tube: Oxford Circus.

King's Road The formerly villagelike main street of Chelsea starts at Sloane Square with Peter Jones's classy department store, and meanders on for a mile until it reaches a swank new shop-filled complex, Chelsea Harbour. Until 1830 this was actually a king's private road, running from the palaces at Whitehall or St. James's to the country places at Hampton Court, Richmond, and Chelsea. (Queen Victoria ended that when she became the first sovereign to inhabit Buckingham Palace in 1837.)

The leap of King's Road to the "mod throne" in the late '60s came with the advent of designer Mary Quant. Fashion boutiques, including the famous "Granny Takes a Trip" (it had half a motor car crashing through its window), once lined the boulevard.

Today the street is still crowded with young people and it can still lay claim to being outrageous. More and more in the 1990s, King's Road is a lineup of markets and "multi-stores," large or small conglomerations of in- and outdoor stands, stalls, and booths fulfilling all sorts of functions within one building or enclosure. They spring up so fast that it's impossible to keep them tabulated, but few thorough shopping strolls in London can afford to ignore King's Road. Tube: Sloane Square.

Saint Christopher's Place One of London's most interesting and little-known (to the foreign visitor) shopping streets is Saint Christopher's Place, W1. It lies just off Oxford Street: Walk down Oxford from Selfridges toward Oxford Circus, ducking north along Gees Court across Barrett Street. There you will be surrounded by antiques markets and good shops for women's clothing and accessories. Tube: Bond Street.

Beauchamp Place Beauchamp Place (pronounced "*Bee*-cham"), one of London's top shopping streets, is a block off Brompton Road, near Harrods department store. The *International Herald Tribune* called it "a higgledy-piggledy of old-fashioned and trendy, quaint and with-it, expensive and cheap." Whatever you're looking for—from a pâté de marcassin to a carved pine mantelpiece—you are likely to find it here. It's pure fun, even if you don't buy anything. Tube: Knightsbridge.

Princes Arcade If you like "one-stop" shopping, you may be drawn to the restored Princes Arcade, which was opened by Edward VII in 1883, when he was Prince of Wales. Between Jermyn Street and Piccadilly, in the heart of London, the arcade has wrought-iron lamps that light your way as you search through some 20 bow-fronted shops, looking for that special curio—maybe a 16th-century nightcap or a pair of shoes made by people who have been satisfying royal tastes since 1847. Small signs hanging from metal rods indicate the kind of merchandise a particular store sells. Tube: Piccadilly Circus.

Burlington Arcade Next door to the Royal Academy of Arts, the Burlington Arcade, W1 (tel. 071/427-3568), is more than 150 years old; it was built in 1819 by Lord George Cavendish. The bawdy Londoners of those days threw rubbish over his garden wall, particularly oyster shells, so he built the arcade as a deterrent. Today you can leisurely browse through the antiques and bric-a-brac in the 38 shops housed in this ancient monument, which is protected by Her Majesty.

The arcade has been popular with Londoners for years. Author Mary Ann Evans—alias George Eliot—met the journalist George Lewes in Jeff's Bookshop, and they were lovers until he died in 1878. In his 1879 guide to London, Charles Dickens compared the arcade and its double row of shops to "a Parisian passage."

If you linger here until 5:30pm, you can watch the beadles (the last of London's top-hatted policemen and Britain's oldest police force) ceremoniously put in place the iron grilles that block off the arcade until 9am the next morning, when they just as ceremoniously remove them, marking the start of a new business day. Also at 5:30pm, a hand bell, called the Burlington Bell, is sounded, signaling the end of trading. Tube: Piccadilly Circus.

COOL FOR KIDS

CHILDREN'S BOOK CENTRE, 237 Kensington High St., W8. Tel. 071/ 937-7497.

This is the best place to go for children's books—it has thousands of titles. Fiction is arranged according to age, up to the 14 or 16 age group. It also sells videos and toys for children. Open Monday through Saturday from 9:30am to 6:30pm (on Thursday to 7pm). Tube: High Street Kensington.

HAMLEYS OF REGENT STREET, 188–196 Regent St., W1. Tel. 071/ 734-3161.

This is an Ali Baba's cave of toys and games, with merchandise ranging from electronic games and Star Wars robots on the ground floor to toys for all age groups on each of the other floors. Open Monday through Saturday from 10am to 6:30pm (on Thursday to 8pm). Tube: Oxford Circus.

2. SHOPPING A TO Z

ANTIQUES

ALFIES ANTIQUE MARKET, 13–25 Church St., NW8. Tel. 071/723-6066.

The biggest and one of the cheapest covered markets in London, this is where many dealers come to buy. The market contains more than 370 stalls, showrooms, and restoration on 35,000 square feet of floor, plus there's an enormous 70-unit basement area. Open Tuesday through Saturday from 10am to 6pm. Tube: Edgware Road.

ANTIQUARIUS, 131–141 King's Rd., SW3. Tel. 071/351-5353.

Antiquarius echoes the artistic diversity of the street on which it is located. More than 150 stallholders offer specialized merchandise, such as period clothing, porcelain, silver, antique books, boxes, clocks, prints, and paintings, with an occasional piece of antique furniture. You'll also find a lot of items dating from around 1950. Open Monday through Saturday from 10am to 6pm. Tube: Sloane Square.

CHELSEA ANTIQUES MARKET, 245–253 King's Rd., SW3. Tel. 071/ 352-1720.

Sheltered in a rambling old building, this market offers endless browsing possibilities for the curio addict. About one-third of the market is given over to old or rare books. You're likely to run across Staffordshire dogs, shaving mugs, Edwardian buckles and clasps, ivory-handled razors, old velours and lace gowns, wooden tea caddies, antique pocket watches, wormy Tudoresque chests, silver snuff boxes, grandfather clocks, and jewelry of all periods. Open Monday through Saturday from 10am to 6pm. Tube: Sloane Square.

CHENIL GALLERIES, 181–183 King's Rd., SW3. Tel. 071/351-5353.

These galleries specialize in art nouveau and art deco objects, along with lots of jewelry. A permanent exhibition of an Epstein statue reflects the long association of the galleries with the arts. The merchandise includes Asian carpets, collector's dolls, and teddy bears, as well as prints and maps, fine porcelain, chess sets, some period furniture, and 17th- and 18th-century paintings. Open Monday through Saturday 10am to 6pm. Tube: Sloane Square.

GRAYS AND GRAYS, in the Mews Antique Markets, 58 Davies St. and 1–7 Davies Mews, W1. Tel. 071/629-7034.

Just south of Oxford Street and opposite the Bond Street tube station, you'll find Grays and Grays in a triangle formed by Davies Street, South Molton Lane, and Davies Mews. The two old buildings have been converted into walk-in stands with independent dealers. The term "antique" here covers items from oil paintings to, say, the 1894 edition of the *Encyclopaedia Britannica*. Also sold here are exquisite antique jewelry, silver, gold, maps and prints, bronzes and ivories, arms and armor, Victorian and Edwardian toys, furniture, antique luggage, antique lace, scientific instruments, crafting tools, and Chinese, Persian, and Islamic pottery, porcelain, miniatures, and antiquities. There is also a whole floor of repair workshops, an engraver, and a bureau de change. Tube: Bond Street.

MALL ANTIQUES ARCADE, at Camden Passage, Islington, N1.

Here you'll find one of Britain's greatest concentrations of antiques businesses. The some 35 dealers specialize in fine furniture, porcelain, and silver and are housed in individual shop units. There is no central phone. Open on Tuesday, Thursday, and Friday from 10am to 5pm, on Wednesday from 7:30am to 5pm, and on Saturday from 9am to 6pm. Tube: Angel.

ARTS & CRAFTS

On Sunday morning along **Bayswater Road,** pictures, collages, and craft items are hung on the railings along the edge of Hyde Park and Kensington Gardens—for more than a mile. If the weather is right, start at Marble Arch and walk and walk, shopping or just sightseeing as you go along. Along Piccadilly, you'll see much of the same thing by walking along the railings of **Green Park** on a Saturday afternoon.

CRAFTS COUNCIL, 44A Pentonville Rd., Islington, N1. Tel. 071/278-7700.

This is the national body for the promotion of fine craftsmanship, encouraging high standards of work and an increased public awareness of contemporary crafts. Here you can discover some of the most creative work in Britain today. The center houses the largest public gallery for contemporary crafts in Britain, plus a shop selling craft objects, books, and magazines. There's also a picture library, information center, education workshop, and café. Open Tuesday through Saturday from 11am to 6pm, Sunday 2 to 6pm. Tube: Angel.

BOOKS

W. & G. FOYLE LTD., 119 Charing Cross Rd., WC2. Tel. 071/439-8501.

Claiming to be the world's largest bookstore, W. & G. Foyle has an impressive array of hardcovers and paperbacks. The shop also sells travel maps, records, videotapes, and sheet music. Open Monday through Wednesday and Friday and Saturday from 9am to 6pm, Thursday 9am to 7pm. Tube: Leicester Square.

HATCHARDS LTD., 187–188 Piccadilly, W1. Tel. 071/439-9921.

On the south side of Piccadilly, Hatchards is one of the oldest and most famous bookshops in the world. It is a landmark for the tourist, a paradise for the browser and the book collector, and a British institution for account holders and mail-order customers throughout the world. In 1797 John Hatchard, having acquired 15 years' experience in the book trade, opened the store. Hatchards has traditionally served the royal families of Europe and is now one of only 12 establishments to hold all four royal warrants. Among early customers were Queen Charlotte, wife of George III, and Queen Adelaide, wife of William IV. It is filled with books ranging from popular fiction to specialized reference. There are shelves of guidebooks, atlases, cookbooks, paperbacks, plus puzzle books to occupy you on train and plane trips. Open Monday through Friday from 9am to 6pm and on Saturday from 9am to 5pm. Tube: Piccadilly Circus.

HISTORY BOOKSHOP, 2 Broadway, N11. Tel. 081/368-8568.
This shop for history buffs stands at the corner of Friern Barnet Road and MacDonald Road. Behind its 1890s facade, this is one of the largest repositories of secondhand books in London and contains some 40,000 volumes scattered over three floors. It specializes in military history, and catalogs are issued at regular intervals. Open Wednesday through Friday from 10am to 4pm. Tube: Arnos Grove.

STANFORDS, 12–14 Long Acre, WC2. Tel. 071/836-1321.
Established in 1852, this is not only the world's largest map shop, but it is also the best travel-book store in London (naturally, it carries a complete selection of the Frommer guides, in case you're going on to some other country after a tour of Britain). Open Monday, Wednesday, Friday, and Saturday from 10am to 6pm; Tuesday and Thursday from 9am to 7pm. Tube: Leicester Square.

BRASS RUBBING

LONDON BRASS RUBBING CENTRE, at St. Martin-in-the-Fields Church, Trafalgar Sq., WC2. Tel. 071/437-6023.
The center is in the big, brick-vaulted 1730s crypt, alongside the Café-in-the-Crypt, a bookshop, and an art gallery. The center has 88 exact copies of bronze portraits ready for use. Paper, rubbing materials, and instructions on how to begin are furnished, and classical music is played for visitors' enjoyment as they proceed. The charges range from £1.50 ($2.30) for a small copy to £11.50 ($17.30) for the largest, a life-size Crusader knight.

There is also a gift area, where you can buy brass-rubbing kits for children, budget-priced ready-made rubbings, and a wide variety of books, souvenirs, posters, and postcards. For those who wish to make brass rubbings in the countryside churches, the center offers instructions and sells guidebooks and the necessary materials. Open Monday through Saturday from 10am to 6pm and on Sunday from noon to 6pm. Tube: Charing Cross.

LONDON BRASS RUBBING CENTRE, at All Hallows by the Tower, Byward St, EC3. Tel. 071/481-2928.
The same company as above operates this brass-rubbing center at this fascinating church, next door to the Tower—which has a crypt museum, Roman remains, and traces of early London, including a Saxon wall predating the Tower. Samuel Pepys, the famed diarist, climbed to the spire of this church to watch the raging fire of London in 1666. Material and instruction are supplied, and the charges range from £1.50 ($2.30) to £11.50 ($17.30) for the largest.

The center is open Monday through Friday from 11am to 4pm, Saturday 11am to 4pm, and Sunday from 1 to 4pm. Tube: Tower Hill.

CHINA

THOMAS GOODE, 19 S. Audley St., W1. Tel. 071/499-2823.
Established in 1827, 10 years before Queen Victoria came to the throne, this is perhaps the most famous china and glass shop in the world, with three royal warrants, and has Minton majolica elephants gracing its front windows. The main entrance, with its famous mechanical doors, leads you to the china, glass, and silverware displayed in the 14 showrooms. A Thomas Goode catalog is available. Open on Monday and Wednesday through Friday from 9am to 5pm, on Tuesday from 9:30am to 5pm, and on Saturday from 9:30am to 1pm. Tube: Hyde Park Corner.

LAWLEYS, 154 Regent St., W1. Tel. 071/734-3184.
A wide range of English bone china, as well as crystal and giftware, is sold here.

The firm specializes in Royal Doulton, Minton, Royal Crown Derby, Wedgwood, and Aynsley china; Royal Doulton, Stuart, Waterford, and Swarovski; Lladró figures; David Winter Cottages; Border Fine Arts; and other famous giftware ranges. They also sell cutlery. Open Monday through Saturday from 9:30am to 7pm. Tube: Piccadilly Circus or Oxford Circus.

CHOCOLATES

CHARBONNEL ET WALKER LTD., 1 Royal Arcade, 28 Old Bond St., W1. Tel. 071/491-0939.

Here you'll find what may be the finest chocolates in the world. The staff of this bow-fronted shop, on the corner of the Royal Arcade off Old Bond Street, will send messages spelled out on the chocolates themselves. The prices are determined by weight. Create your own box of candy or select one of their ready-made presentation boxes. Open Monday through Friday from 9:30am to 5:30pm and on Saturday from 10am to 4pm. Tube: Green Park.

PRESTAT, 14 Princes Arcade, SW1. Tel. 071/629-4838.

Prestat is chocolate maker "to Her Majesty the Queen by appointment." Why not take home a box of assorted Napoléon truffles? Or a wide assortment of other flavors may tempt you: coffee-flavored chocolate, mint-flavored chocolate, or chocolate-coated brandy cherries. All boxes are elegantly gift wrapped. Open Monday through Friday from 9:30am to 5:30pm, and Saturday 10am to 5:30pm. Tube: Piccadilly Circus.

CLOCKS

STRIKE ONE ISLINGTON LIMITED, 33 Balcombe St., NW1. Tel. 071/224-9719.

This store sells clocks, music boxes, and barometers. Strike One clearly dates and prices each old clock—from Victorian dial clocks to early English long-case timepieces—and every purchase is guaranteed worldwide for a year against faulty workmanship. Strike One specializes in Act of Parliament clocks. It also issues an illustrated catalog, which is mailed internationally to all serious clock collectors. On top of that, the firm undertakes to locate any clock a customer might request if no suitable example is in stock. Open by appointment only. Tube: Baker Street.

CONTEMPORARY ART

BERKELEY SQUARE GALLERY, 23A Bruton St., W1. Tel. 071/493-7939.

Originally established as a branch office of Christie's, specializing in limited edition prints, today this independent gallery offers etchings, lithographs, and screen-prints by up-and-coming artists. It also offers major works, by such world masters as Henry Moore, Hockney, Chagall, and Matisse. The gallery is considered innovative and creative, even within the competitive world of London galleries. Open Monday through Friday from 10am to 6pm and on Saturday from 10am to 4pm. Tube: Green Park.

COVENT GARDEN ENTERPRISES

An impressive array of shops, pubs, and other attractions can be found in the Central Market Building at Covent Garden. For the shops listed below, take the tube, of course, to Covent Garden.

APPLE MARKET, Covent Garden Piazza, WC2. Tel. 071/836-9136.

A fun, bustling place, the Apple Market almost qualifies as street entertainment and is filled with traders selling . . . well, everything. Much is what the English call "collectible nostalgia." You'll have to sift through some of the worthless items to find the genuinely worthy ones, such as brass door knockers. Be sure to keep your resistance up as you wander; some of the vendors are mighty persuasive.

On Monday, the antiques section of Apple Market overflows into the Jubilee Market, Jubilee Hall, Covent Garden Piazza, WC2. Antiques are sold from 7am to 5pm (go early). The general market operates Tuesday through Friday from 9am to 5pm. Crafts take over on Saturday and Sunday from 9am to 5pm. This ever-changing market has a wide array of merchandise. Among the inevitable junk is some really good merchandise, ranging from perfumes to household goods.

CONTEMPORARY APPLIED ARTS, 43 Earlham St., WC2. Tel. 071/836-6993.

This association of craftspeople encourages both traditional and progressive contemporary artwork. The galleries at the center house a diverse retail display that includes glass, rugs, lights, ceramics, fabric, clothing, paper, metalwork, and jewelry—all created by the most outstanding artisans currently producing in the country. There is also a program of special exhibitions that focuses on innovations in the crafts; these are solo or small-group shows from the membership. Many of Britain's best-established makers, as well as promising, lesser-known ones, are represented in this association. Open Monday through Wednesday and Friday and Saturday from 10am to 6pm, Thursday 10am to 7pm.

COVENT GARDEN GENERAL STORE, 111 Long Acre, WC2. Tel. 071/240-0331.

This offers thousands of ideas for gifts and souvenirs ranging in price from a few pence to several pounds. It is ideally situated in Covent Garden, and because of the entertainment nature of the area, the store offers extended trading hours: Monday through Saturday from 10am to 11:30pm and on Sunday from 11am to 7pm. The store also features the Covent Garden General Store Restaurant, which serves salads from a salad bar, jacket potatoes, chili con carne, and macaroni and cheese, among other items; the restaurant is downstairs and is open Monday through Saturday from 10:30am to 7pm and on Sunday from noon to 6pm.

THE GLASSHOUSE, 65 Long Acre, WC2. Tel. 071/836-9785.

Not only can visitors buy beautiful glass here, but they can also watch the craftspeople producing glass works of art in the workshop. Open Monday through Friday from 10am to 6pm and on Saturday from 11am to 5pm.

JUBILEE MARKET, Covent Garden Piazza, WC2.

At this small open-air general market, antiques are sold on Monday, crafts on Saturday, and various other items on other days by dozens of independent dealers who arrive early to set up their stalls. Open Monday through Saturday from 9am to 5pm.

NATURALLY BRITISH, 13 New Row (by Covent Garden), WC2. Tel. 071/240-0551.

This shop has a traditional British ambience with old wooden floors and antique furniture. A wide range of English, Welsh, and Scottish goods is sold, including toys, clothes, ceramics, jewelry, and food. Many items can be made to order, including rocking horses, painted christening spoons, and furniture. Open Monday through Saturday from 11am to 7pm, Sunday noon to 5pm. Tube: Leicester Square or Covent Garden.

NATURAL SHOE STORE, 21 Neal St., WC2. Tel. 071/836-5254.

Shoes for both men and women are stocked in this shop, which also does shoe repairs. The selection includes all comfort and quality footwear—from Birkenstock to the best of the British classics. Open Monday, Tuesday, and Saturday from 10am to 6pm, and Wednesday through Friday from 10am to 7pm.

NEAL STREET EAST, 5 Neal St., WC2. Tel. 071/240-0135.

In this vast shop devoted to Asian or Asian-inspired merchandise, you can find dried and silk flowers, pottery, baskets, chinoiserie, toys, calligraphy, modern and antique clothing, textiles, and ethnic jewelry. There is also an extensive cookware department and bookshop. Open Monday through Saturday from 10am to 7pm, Sunday noon to 6pm.

NEAL'S YARD, off Neal St., WC2.

Behind the warehouse off Neal Street runs a narrow road leading to Neal's Yard, a mews of warehouses that retain some of the old London atmosphere. The open warehouses display vegetables, health foods, fresh-baked breads, cakes, sandwiches, and, in an immaculate dairy, the largest variety of flavored cream cheeses you are ever likely to encounter.

PENHALIGON'S, 41 Wellington St., WC2. Tel. 071/836-2150.

A Victorian perfumery established in 1870, Penhaligon's holds royal warrants to HRH Duke of Edinburgh and HRH Prince of Wales. It offers a large selection of perfumes, aftershaves, soaps, and bath oils for women and men, and the antique silver perfume bottles make perfect gifts. Open Monday through Friday from 10am to 6pm and on Saturday from 10am to 5:30pm.

THE TEA HOUSE, 15A Neal St., WC2. Tel. 071/240-7539.

This shop sells everything associated with tea, tea drinking, and teatime. It boasts more than 70 quality teas and tisanes, including whole-fruit blends, the best tea of China (gunpowder, jasmine with flowers), India (Assam leaf, choice Darjeeling), Japan (Genmaicha green), and Sri Lanka (pure Ceylon), plus such longtime favorite English blended teas as Earl Grey. The shop also offers novelty teapots and mugs among other items. Open Monday through Saturday from 10am to 7pm and on Sunday from 11am to 6pm.

DEPARTMENT STORES

DAKS SIMPSON PICCADILLY, 203 Piccadilly, W1. Tel. 071/734-2002.

Simpson Piccadilly, which opened in 1936 as the international home of DAKS clothing and accessories for men and women, also offers distinctive designer clothing from famous names suitable for every conceivable occasion. Simpson also offers jewelry from Christian Dior, accessories by Cartier, chocolates by Leonidas, and a wide selection of gifts from Saville-Edells Objets Extraordinaires. The store has a good restaurant that offers traditional English food; an English breakfast is served from 9 to 11:30am; lunch from noon to 2:30pm; afternoon tea from 3:30 to 5:15pm; the Sushi Bar is open from noon to 2:30pm. For light meals, try the Gallery Wine Bar, overlooking Jermyn Street. Open Monday through Saturday from 9am to 6pm (on Thursday until 7pm). Tube: Piccadilly Circus.

HARRODS, 87–135 Brompton Rd., Knightsbridge, SW1. Tel. 071/730-1234.

✪ As firmly entrenched in English life as Buckingham Palace and the Ascot Races, Harrods is an elaborate emporium, at times as fascinating as a museum. In a magazine article about Harrods, a salesperson called it "more of a sort of way of life than a shop." The store underwent refurbishment to restore it to the elegance and luxury of the '20s and '30s.

Aside from the fashion department (including high-level tailoring), you'll find such incongruous sections as a cathedral-ceilinged and arcaded meat market, even a funeral service. Harrods has everything: men's custom-tailored suits, tweed overcoats, cashmere or lambswool sweaters for both men and women, hand-stitched traveling bags, raincoats, mohair jackets, patterned ski sweaters, scarves of handwoven Irish wool, pewter reproductions, a perfumery department, "lifetime" leather suitcases, and pianos.

You have a choice of 11 restaurants and bars at Harrods. One of the highlights for visitors is the Food Hall. Harrods began as a grocer in 1849 and it's still the heart of the business. Among other offerings, Harrods has 500 different cheeses, 130 different types of bread, along with exotic fruits and vegetables, game, flowers, confectionery items, whatever. The motto is, "If you can eat or drink it, you'll find it at Harrods." In the basement you'll find Harrods Bank, a theater-booking service, a Travel Bureau, and Harrods Shop with a range of souvenirs, including the famous green-and-gold bags.

The whole fifth floor is devoted to sports and leisure, with all of the equipment and costumes you need for participating in everything from tennis to polo, from horseback riding to angling. The Toy Kingdom is on the fourth floor, along with departments devoted to children's wear. The whole floor has everything a child could need, even hairdressing. The Egyptian Hall, which opened in 1991 on the ground floor, focuses on crystal from the likes of Lalique and Baccarat to porcelain and antique jewelry. The setting re-creates ancient Egyptian architecture of the 18th dynasty, with carved stone pillars, sphinx heads, and a frieze with authentic hieroglyphic scriptures and scenic drawings. Open Monday through Tuesday and Saturday from 10am to 6pm, and Wednesday through Friday from 10am to 7pm. Tube: Knightsbridge.

LIBERTY PUBLIC LIMITED COMPANY, 210–220 Regent St., W1. Tel. 071/734-1234.

Renowned worldwide for selling high-quality, stylish merchandise in charming surroundings, this chain has its flagship store on Regent Street, with six floors of fashion, fabrics, china, and home furnishings. The personal "corner shop" service is staffed with helpful and informed assistants. In addition to the famous Liberty Print fashion fabrics, furnishing fabrics, scarves, ties, luggage, and gifts, the shop sells well-designed high-quality merchandise from all over the world. The company also has outlets in Bath, Cambridge, Canterbury, Edinburgh, Glasgow, Manchester, Norwich, York, and Oxford. Open Monday, Tuesday, Friday, and Saturday from 9:20am to 6pm; Wednesday 10am to 6pm; and Thursday 9:20am to 7:30pm. Tube: Tottenham Court Road.

MARKS & SPENCER, 458 Oxford St., W1. Tel. 071/935-7954.

Marks & Spencer attracts the thrifty British, who get fine buys here, especially in woolen goods. This chain has built a reputation for quality and value and now clothes some 70% of British workers—wholly or partially; it is said that 25% of the socks worn by men in Britain come from M&S. The prices are competitive, even for women's cashmere sweaters. The main department store is 3 short blocks from Marble Arch. However, there are a number of branches in London as well as in most towns of any size in Britain. Open Monday through Wednesday and Friday from 7am to 8pm, on Thursday from 9am to 8pm, and on Saturday from 9am to 6pm. Tube: Marble Arch.

PETER JONES, Sloane Sq., SW1. Tel. 071/730-3434.

Founded in 1877 and rebuilt in 1936, Peter Jones is well known for its fashions and for its household departments, including china, glass, perfumery, soft furnishings, and linens. The store also displays a constantly changing selection of antiques. On the ground floor you face an abundance of gift ideas, ranging from framed pictures to small objets d'art. The store also has a coffee shop and a first-class licensed restaurant, both with extensive views over London rooftops. Open Monday, Tuesday, Thursday, Friday, and Saturday from 9am to 5:30pm; Wednesday from 9:30am to 7pm. Tube: Sloane Square. Bus: 11, 19, 137, 219, or C1.

SELFRIDGES, 400 Oxford St., W1. Tel. 071/629-1234.

Much more economical than Harrods, Selfridges is one of the biggest department stores in Europe, with more than 300 divisions, selling everything from artificial flowers to groceries. The specialty shops are particularly enticing, with good buys in Irish linen, Wedgwood, leather goods, silver-painted goblets, and cashmere and woolen scarves. There's also the Miss Selfridge Boutique, for the young. To help you travel light, the Export Bureau will air-freight your purchases to anywhere in the world, completely tax free. In the basement Services Arcade, the London Tourist Board will help you find your way around London's sights with plenty of maps, tips, and advice. Open Monday through Wednesday and on Friday and Saturday from 9:30am to 6pm, and on Thursday from 10am to 8pm. Tube: Oxford Street.

DESIGNER CLOTHING [SECONDHAND]

PANDORA, 16–22 Cheval Place, SW7. Tel. 071/589-5289.

A London institution since it was first established in the 1940s, Pandora is located in fashionable Knightsbridge, a stone's throw from Harrods. The store carries the finest merchandise in London, including dozens of hand-me-down designer dresses. Several times a week, chauffeurs drive up with bundles from the anonymous gentry of England that are likely to include dresses, jackets, suits, and gowns that the ladies wish to sell. Entire generations of London women have clothed themselves at this store. One woman, voted best dressed at Ascot several years ago, was wearing a secondhand dress acquired at Pandora's. Identities of the owners are strictly guarded, but many buyers are thrilled with the thought of wearing a royal hand-me-down. Prices are generally one-third to one-half their retail value. Chanel, Anne Klein, and Valentino are among the designers represented. Outfits are no more than two seasons old. Open Monday through Saturday from 10am to 5pm. Tube: Knightsbridge.

FASHIONS

AUSTIN REED, 103–113 Regent St., W1. Tel. 071/734-6789.

Offering both British and international designers, Austin Reed is known for quality clothing. The suits of Chester Barrie, for example, are said to fit like bespoke (tailored) models. The store always has a wide variety of top-notch jackets and suits, both from its own line as well as such designer names as Hugo Boss. Men can outfit themselves from dressing gowns to overcoats. The entire third floor is devoted to women's clothing, with carefully selected suits, separates, coats, shirts, knitwear, and accessories offered. Open: Monday through Wednesday and Friday and Saturday from 9:30am to 6pm, Thursday 9:30am to 7pm. Tube: Piccadilly Circus.

Men's

The selection of menswear in England is perhaps the finest in the world and ranges from Savile Row (at celestial prices) to bargain-basement wear. Your best buys are in ready-to-wear, instead of the superexpensive tailored clothing.

AQUASCUTUM, 100 Regent St., W1. Tel. 071/734-6090.

The popular *Time Out* said that this shop is "about as quintessentially British as you'll get this side of Savile Row, and it's a popular stop-off for American tourists wanting to look more British than the Brits." On four floors, the classic shop sells high-quality British and imported clothing for men and women desiring the classic look. It also offers leisure wear. On the third floor is the Seasons Café. Open Monday through Wednesday and Friday from 9:30am to 6pm, Thursday 9am to 7pm, and Saturday 9:30am to 6:30pm. Tube: Piccadilly Circus.

BURTON, 311 Oxford St., W1. Tel. 071/491-0032.

Since tailor-made British suits tend to be beyond the wallets of most men, a much cheaper alternative is to go to one of the Burton stores found all over Britain; there are 66 branches in the Greater London area alone. Ready-made suits, where a man selects first his jacket, then the trousers to match in his size, come in a number of economical price ranges. Open on Monday, Tuesday, and Saturday from 9am to 6pm, Wednesday through Friday from 9:30am to 7pm, and on Thursday from 9:30am to 8pm. Tube: Oxford Circus.

GIEVES & HAWKES, 1 Savile Row, W1. Tel. 071/434-2001.

Despite Gieves & Hawkes' prestigious address on Savile Row and a list of clients that includes the Prince of Wales, the prices here are not the lethal tariffs of other stores along this street. It's expensive, but you get good quality, as befits its reputation as a supplier to the British Royal Navy since the days of Lord Nelson. Cotton shirts, silk ties, Shetland sweaters, and exceptional suits—both ready-to-wear and tailor made—are sold. Open Monday through Saturday from 9am to 5:30pm. Tube: Piccadilly Circus.

HARRODS, 87–135 Brompton Rd., Knightsbridge, SW1. Tel. 071/730-1234.

Harrods is a worthy choice for just about everything (see "Department Stores," above). Don't overlook its men's store, which has a huge array of high-quality ready-to-wear suits and all the accessories, including shoes, knitwear, socks, shirts, and pajamas. Tube: Knightsbridge.

HILDITCH & KEY, 37 and 73 Jermyn St., SW1. Tel. 071/930-5336 or 071/734-4707.

Perhaps the finest name in men's shirts, Hilditch & Key has been in business since 1899. There are two shops on this street, at no. 37 and at no. 73. Hilditch also has an outstanding tie collection. Open Monday through Wednesday and Friday from 9:30am to 6pm, on Thursday from 9:30am to 7pm, and on Saturday from 9:30am to 5:30pm. Tube: Green Park or Piccadilly Circus.

THOMAS PINK, 35 Dover St., W1. Tel. 071/493-6775.

✪ These Dover Street shirtmakers, named after an 18th-century Mayfair tailor, gave the world the phrases "Hunting pink" and "In the pink." They have an excellent reputation for their well-made cotton shirts, for both men and women. The shirts are made of the finest two-fold pure cotton poplin, coming in a wide range of patterns, plain colors, stripes, or checks. Some patterns are classic; others are constantly changing with unusual designs. All are generously cut with extra-long tails and finished with a choice of double cuffs or single-button cuffs. Open Monday through Friday from 9:30am to 5:30pm and on Saturday from 9:30am to 5pm. Tube: Green Park.

Women's

For raincoats, see **Burberry's** under "Raincoats," below, which also has a selection of other coats for women, along with scarves and handbags. For sporting wear, refer to **Lillywhites** under "Sporting Goods," below. Listed under "Department Stores," **DAKS Simpson Piccadilly**, once exclusively a men's store, now offers a variety of fashions for women. And of course, you must preview the fashions at the world's most famous department store, **Harrods,** listed above under "Department Stores."

The following are a few suggestions, but of course there are hundreds of women's clothing stores in all parts of town.

BRADLEY'S, 85 Knightsbridge, SW1. Tel. 071/235-2902.

Bradley's is the best-known lingerie store in London. Even some members of the royal family shop here. Bradley's fits "all sizes" in silk, cotton, lace, polycotton, whatever. You'll love the fluffy slippers and its satin or silk nightgowns will make you feel like Myrna Loy enticing William Powell in the old "Thin Man" flicks. Open Monday, Tuesday, Thursday, and Friday from 9:30am to 6pm, Wednesday 9:30am to 7pm, and Saturday 10am to 6pm. Tube: Knightsbridge.

THE CHANGING ROOM, 10A Gees Court, St. Christopher's Place, W1. Tel. 071/408-1596.

This is a small but well-staffed shop that stocks the clothing and accessories of at least a dozen different designers. The establishment's expertise lies in its ability to coordinate items from different lines to create unusual and unique fashion statements for all types of women. Among the designers featured are Issey Mikaye, Betty Jackson, Helen Storey, and many others. Open Monday through Wednesday and Friday and Saturday from 10:30am to 6:30pm, Thursday 10:30am to 7:30pm. Tube: Bond Street.

FENWICK OF BOND STREET, 63 New Bond St., W1. Tel. 071/629-9161.

Fenwick is a small department store that offers an excellent collection of womenswear, ranging from moderately priced ready-to-wear items to designer fashions. A wide range of lingerie (in all price ranges) is also sold here. The store dates from 1891. Open Monday through Saturday from 9:30am to 6pm (on Thursday until 7:30pm). Tube: Bond Street.

HYPER-HYPER, 26–40 Kensington High St., W8. Tel. 071/938-4343.

Showcasing young and talented British fashion designers since 1983, Hyper-Hyper displays the work of nearly 70 designers at all times. From sportswear to eveningwear, with plenty of accessories thrown in, including shoes, Hyper-Hyper will thrill and intrigue. Menswear is also sold here. Open Monday through Wednesday and Friday and Saturday from 10am to 6pm, Thursday 10am to 7pm. Tube: High Street Kensington.

LAURA ASHLEY, 256–258 Regent St., W1. Tel. 071/437-9760.

This famous store will outfit you with flower-print Victorian dresses or easy-to-wear jersey and knitwear. They also sell a wide range of accessories, including belts and handbags. Open on Monday and Tuesday from 9:30am to 6pm, on Wednesday and Friday from 9:30am to 7pm, on Thursday from 9:30am to 8pm, and on Saturday from 9am to 6pm. Tube: Oxford Circus.

FOOD

FORTNUM & MASON LTD., 181 Piccadilly, W1. Tel. 071/734-8040.

✪ Fortnum and Mason is no mere grocery store—it has been a British tradition since 1707. Down the street from the Ritz, it draws the carriage trade, those from Mayfair or Belgravia who come seeking such tinned treasures as pâté de foie gras or boar's head. Today this store exemplifies the elegance and style one would expect from an establishment with two royal warrants. Enter the doors and be transported to another world of deep-red carpets, crystal chandeliers, spiraling wooden staircases, and unobtrusive, tail-coated assistants.

The grocery department is renowned for its impressive selection of the finest foods from around the world—the best champagne, the most scrumptious Belgian chocolates, and succulent Scottish smoked salmon. You might choose one of their wicker baskets of exclusive foods to have shipped home, perhaps through their telephone and mail-order service. You can wander through the other four floors and inspect the bone china and crystal cut glass, perhaps find the perfect present in the leather or stationery department, or reflect on the changing history of furniture, paintings, and ornaments in the antiques department. Dining choices include Patio & Buttery, St. James's Restaurant, and the Fountain Restaurant. Open Monday through Saturday from 9:30am to 6pm. Tube: Piccadilly Circus or Green Park.

IRISH WARES

IRISH SHOP, 11 Duke St., W1. Tel. 071/935-1366.

For more than 25 years this small family business has been selling a wide variety of articles shipped directly from Ireland. The staff will be happy to welcome you and answer any questions on the selection of out-of-the-ordinary tweeds, traditional linens, hand-knit Aran fisherman's sweaters, and Celtic jewelry. Merchandise includes Belleek and Royal Tara china, tapes of Irish music, souvenirs, and gift items. Waterford crystal in all styles and types is a specialty. Open Monday through Saturday from 9:30am to 5:30pm (on Thursday until 7pm). Tube: Bond Street.

JEWELRY

LONDON DIAMOND CENTRE, 10 Hanover St., W1. Tel. 071/629-5511.

This establishment provides an opportunity to discover the world of diamonds. Guides are on hand to demonstrate the various stages of diamond manufacturing and to escort you through a life-size diamond mine into one of the largest jewelry showrooms in the world. Here you can select a diamond and ring mounting to suit your budget and watch it being set by a resident goldsmith, or choose from a vast array of ready-made jewelry. Prices start at £50 ($75). Admission is free; the hours are Monday through Saturday from 9:30am to 5:30pm. Tube: Oxford Circus. Bus: 3, 6, 12, 15, 53, 88, or 159.

MAPS & ENGRAVINGS

GREATER LONDON RECORD OFFICE AND HISTORY LIBRARY, 40 Northampton Rd., EC1. Tel. 071/606-3030.

Here you'll find archives, maps, books, and photographs on the history of London, and reproductions of old maps and prints of London are for sale. Open on Tuesday from 9:30am to 7:30pm and Wednesday through Friday from 9:30am to 4:45pm. Tube: Farringdon or Angel.

MAP HOUSE, 54 Beauchamp Place, SW3. Tel. 071/589-4325.

An ideal place to find an offbeat souvenir of your visit to London, the Map House was established in 1907 during the height of the Edwardian age. It sells antique maps and engravings, as well as items from a vast selection of old prints of London and England, both original and reproduction. An original engraving, guaranteed to be more than a century old, can cost as little as £5 ($7.50), although some rare and/or historic items sell for a massive £50,000 ($75,000). Open Monday through Friday from 9:45am to 5:45pm, Saturday 10:30am to 5pm. Tube: Knightsbridge.

MUSIC

VIRGIN MEGASTORE, 14 Oxford St., W1. Tel. 071/631-1234.

If a record's just been released—and if it's worth hearing in the first place—chances are this store carries it. It's like a giant "grocery store" of records, and you get to hear the release on a headphone before making a purchase. Even the rock stars themselves come here on occasion to pick up new releases. A large selection of classical and jazz recordings are also sold. In between selecting your favorites, you can enjoy a coffee at the café, perhaps purchase a ticket from the Virgin Atlantic ticket office. Open Monday through Saturday from 9:30am to 8pm. Tube: Tottenham Court Road.

NOTIONS

FLORIS, 89 Jermyn St., SW1. Tel. 071/930-2885.

⭐ A variety of toilet articles and fragrances is found in the floor-to-ceiling mahogany cabinets that line Floris's walls, considered architectural curiosities in their own right. The walls were installed relatively late in the establishment's history (that is, 1851), long after the shop had received its royal warrants as suppliers of toilet articles to the king and queen. The business was established in 1730 by a Minorcan entrepreneur, Juan Floris, who brought from his Mediterranean home a technique for extracting fragrances from local flowers. Fashionable residents of St. James's flocked to the shop to purchase his soaps, perfumes, and grooming aids. Today, you can buy essences of flowers grown in English gardens, including stephanotis, rose geraniums, lily-of-the-valley, and carnation. Open Monday through Friday from 9:30am to 5:30pm and on Saturday from 9:30am to 4pm. Tube: Piccadilly Circus.

PHILATELY

NATIONAL POSTAL MUSEUM, King Edward Building, King Edward St., EC1. Tel. 071/239-5420.

Not only does the museum house a magnificent collection of postage stamps and allied material, but it also sells postcards illustrating the collection and has a distinctive Maltese Cross postmark first used on the Penny Black. A letter mailed from Heathrow Airport is franked at Hounslow with an attractive Concorde cancellation. In country areas, the post office provides a postbus service between many remote and otherwise isolated villages. Often passenger tickets are cancelled with a special stamp of collector interest, and postcards depicting places of interest along the routes are issued and mailed from these buses. More specialized, many of the narrow-gauge and privately owned railroads in the country issue and cancel their own stamps. Open Monday through Thursday from 9:30am to 4:30pm and on Friday from 9:30am to 4pm. Tube: St. Paul's.

POSTERS

LONDON TRANSPORT MUSEUM SHOP, Covent Garden, The Piazza, WC2. Tel. 071/379-6344.

This unique shop carries a wide selection of posters, books, cards, T-shirts, and other souvenir items. The London Underground maps can be purchased here, as well as massive pictorial posters as seen at tube stations (size: 40 by 60 inches). Open daily from 10am to 5:45pm; closed Christmas Day and December 26. Tube: Covent Garden.

RAINCOATS

BURBERRY'S, 18 Haymarket, SW1. Tel. 071/930-3343.

⭐ The word Burberry has been synonymous with raincoats ever since King Edward VII publicly ordered his valet to "bring my Burberry" when the skies threatened rain. Its circa-1912 Haymarket store connects three lavishly stocked floors to an oak-lined staircase upon which have trod some of the biggest names in politics, the stage, and the screen. An impeccably trained staff sells the famous raincoat, along with a collection of excellent men's shirts, sportswear, knitwear, and accessories. Women's raincoats are also available. Don't think you'll get anything cheap from such a world-famous retailer; you'll get prestige and quality. But sometimes there are sales. Open Monday through Saturday from 9am to 5:30pm (on Thursday until 7pm). Tube: Piccadilly Circus.

SHOES

London is called the footwear capital of the world, and somewhere in this city you can find what you're looking for. In addition to the following, see the recommendation of **Natural Shoe Store** under "Covent Garden Enterprises," above, if you like your shoes wholesome—that is, made from natural materials; they stock shoes for both men and women.

CHARLES JOURDAN, 39–43 Brompton Rd., SW3. Tel. 071/581-3333.

This carries one of the largest range of women's shoes in London, including a variety of styles. Open Monday through Saturday from 10am to 6:30pm (on Wednesday until 7pm). Tube: Knightsbridge.

CHURCH'S, 143 Brompton Rd., SW3. Tel. 071/589-9136.

Top-quality shoes have been turned out by these famous shoemakers since 1873, when the company was founded at Northampton. A trio of brothers (Alfred, Thomas, and William) started what has become a tradition among well-outfitted English gents. Of course, the company has changed with the times and now offers more stylish selections along with their traditional footwear. There is also a fashionable selection of shoes for women. Open Monday through Friday from 9am to 5:30pm and on Saturday from 9am to 5pm. Tube: Knightsbridge.

LILLEY & SKINNERS, 360 Oxford St., W1. Tel. 071/629-6381.

The biggest shoe store in the world, Lilley & Skinners displays its merchandise across four floors and markets shoes with both its own label and designer labels. All sizes of feet are fitted here, including extra-small, or extra-large, for both men and women. Prices, likewise, are wide ranging. Open Monday through Wednesday and Friday from 9:30am to 6:30pm, on Thursday from 9:30am to 8pm, and on Saturday from 9am to 6pm. Tube: Bond Street.

SILVER

LONDON SILVER VAULTS, Chancery Lane, WC2. Tel. 071/242-5506.

Established in 1882, these are the largest silver vaults in the world. You can shop in vault after vault for that special treasure. Open Monday through Friday from 9am to 5:30pm and on Saturday from 9am to 12:30pm. Tube: Chancery Lane.

STANLEY LESLIE, 15 Beauchamp Place, SW3. Tel. 071/589-2333.

Here you'll find an array of high-quality Georgian, Victorian, and early 20th-century silver. It's just the place to spend hours ferreting around for a special present. Open Monday through Friday from 9am to 5pm and on Saturday from 9am to 1pm. Tube: Knightsbridge.

SPORTING GOODS

LILLYWHITES LTD., Piccadilly Circus, SW1. Tel. 071/930-3181.

Established in 1863, Lillywhites offers everything connected with sport, together with fashionable leisure-wear for both men and women. This is Britain's biggest sports store and has floor after floor of sports clothing, equipment, and footwear. Open Monday through Saturday from 9:30am to 6pm (on Thursday until 7pm). Tube: Piccadilly Circus.

STREET MARKETS

Street markets have played an important role in London, and I recommend them not only for bric-a-brac but also for a low-cost adventure. In fact, you don't have to buy a thing; but be warned—some of the stallkeepers are mighty persistent. Here are the best ones.

BERWICK STREET MARKET This may be the only street market in the world that is flanked by two rows of strip clubs, porno stores, and adult-movie dens; however, don't let that put you off. This array of stalls and booths sells probably the best and cheapest fruit and vegetables in town, as well as ancient records that may turn out to be collector's items, tapes, books, and old magazines. The market is in action Monday through Saturday 8am to 5pm. Tube: Tottenham Court Road.

LEATHER LANE At this lively market, open Monday through Saturday from 11am to 3pm, you'll find a good variety of items for sale: fruit, vegetables, books, men's shirts and sweaters, and women's clothing. There are no try-ons at this outdoor market, so you have to inspect the size of the clothing carefully. Tube: Chancery Lane.

NEW CALEDONIAN MARKET This is commonly known as the **Bermondsey Market,** because of its location at Bermondsey Square, SE1, at the corner of Long Lane and Bermondsey Street; the extreme east end of the market is at Tower Bridge Road. This is one of Europe's outstanding street markets in size and quality of goods offered. The stalls are well known, and many dealers come into London from the country. The market is held on Friday from 7am until noon, and the most serious bargain hunters get here early; antiques plus other items are generally lower in price here than they are at Portobello Road and the other street markets, but bargains are gone by 9am. Tube: Elephant and Castle; then take bus no. 1 or 188.

PETTICOAT LANE On Sunday between 9am and 2pm (go before noon), throngs of shoppers join the crowds on Petticoat Lane (also known as Middlesex Street, E1), where you can buy inferior clothing, food, and plenty of junk. Despite the street's reputation, many readers have found that a Sunday morning trip here is no longer worth the effort. The area is surrounded by a maze of lanes that begin at the Liverpool Street Station on the Bishopsgate side. Tube: Liverpool Street, Aldgate, or Aldgate East.

PORTOBELLO ROAD MARKET ✪ A magnet for collectors of virtually everything, Portobello Market, Portobello Road, W11, is mainly a Saturday happening from 8am (it's best to go early) to 5pm. The name came from Admiral Vernon's capture of a Caribbean city, Puerto Bello, in 1739. A farm once stood here, but by the 1860s a market had grown up. Once known mainly for fruit and vegetables (still sold, incidentally, throughout the week), Portobello in the past four decades became synonymous with antiques (but don't take the stallholder's word for it). You can also browse around for jewelry, weapons (modern and antique), toys, kitchenware, scientific instruments, china, books, movie posters, magazines long defunct, watches, pens, music boxes, whatever.

The market is divided into three major sections, including the most crowded, the southern antiques section, running between Colville Road and Chepstow Villas. The greatest concentration of pickpockets is in this area, so be duly warned. The second sector (and the oldest part) is the "fruit and veg" market, which lies between Westway and Colville Road. In the third and final section, Londoners operate a flea market, selling bric-a-brac and lots of secondhand goods.

In addition to stalls, many permanent shops are found both on and off Portobello Road—mostly between Westway and Colville Road—and can be visited throughout the week. From many of the stores, the serious collector can pick up a copy of a helpful official guide, *Saturday Antique Market: Portobello Road & Westbourne Grove,* published by the Portobello Antique Dealers Association. It lists where to find what, ranging from music boxes to militaria, from lace to 19th-century photographs. The serious collector can visit any of the 90-odd antiques and art shops during the week when the temporary market is closed.

Many art galleries can also be found in and around the area, such as on Kensington

Park Road, Blenheim Crescent, and in the fruit and vegetable section of Portobello Road. Tube: Ladbroke Grove or Notting Hill Gate.

TRAVEL CENTER

BRITISH AIRWAYS, 156 Regent St., W1. Tel. 071/434-4700.

The retail flagship of British Airways, housed on three floors, offers not only worldwide travel and ticketing, but also a wide range of services and shops—including a travel clinic for immunization and a pharmacy selling first-aid kits and travel medication. There's also a bureau de change, plus a passport and visa service, as well as a theater-booking desk. The ground floor offers luggage and other quality goods, plus travel accessories, and a coffee shop serves teas, coffee, and pastries. Other services include a change machine, photobooth, phones, toilets, public fax, and photocopying facilities. Passengers with hand baggage only can check in here for a BA flight. Open Monday through Friday from 9am to 7pm and on Saturday from 9am to 5pm. Tube: Piccadilly Circus.

WOOLENS

BERK, 46 Burlington Arcade, W1. Tel. 071/493-0028.

Berk, the cashmere specialist, is one of those irresistible "fancy shops" for which London is famous. To shelter your precious cashmere from the elements, the shop also carries Burberry's raincoats, golf jackets and caps, and rain hats. All this is displayed in the 150-year-old Burlington Arcade, an attraction in its own right. Open Monday through Friday from 9am to 5:30pm and on Saturday from 9am to 5pm. Tube: Piccadilly Circus.

SCOTCH HOUSE, 84 Regent St., SW1. Tel. 071/734-5966.

The Scotch House is renowned worldwide for its comprehensive selection of top-quality cashmere and wool knitwear for both men and women. Also available is a wide range of tartan garments and accessories, as well as Scottish tweed classics. The children's collection covers ages 2 to 13 and also offers excellent value and quality. Open Monday through Wednesday from 10am to 6pm, Thursday 10am to 7pm, Friday 10am to 6:30pm, and Saturday 9am to 6:30pm. Tube: Piccadilly Circus.

WESTAWAY & WESTAWAY, opposite the British Museum, 62–65 Great Russell St., WC1. Tel. 071/405-4479.

A visit here is a substitute for a shopping trip to Scotland. They stock an enormous range of kilts, scarves, waistcoats, capes, dressing gowns, and rugs in authentic clan tartans. What's more, they are knowledgeable on the subject of these minutely intricate clan symbols. They also sell superb—and untartaned—cashmere, camel's hair, and Shetland knitwear, along with Harris tweed jackets, Burberry raincoats, and cashmere overcoats for men. Another branch is at 92–93 Great Russell St., WC1. Open Monday through Saturday from 9am to 5:30pm. Tube: Tottenham Court Road.

3. EVENING ENTERTAINMENT

Nowhere else but in London will you find such a panorama of legitimate theaters, operas, concerts, nightclubs, folk music cafés, and ballrooms—along with vaudeville at Victorian music halls, striptease joints, and gambling clubs. Your choices are countless—from the dives of Soho to the elegant jazz clubs—and so much depends on your taste, pocketbook, and even the time of year.

THE ENTERTAINMENT SCENE About 90% of London's bright lights burn in the area roughly defined as the West End. The core of this region is Piccadilly Circus, with Coventry Street running down to Leicester Square. To the north lies Soho, chockablock with entertainment in various hues of scarlet. To the east is the theaterland of Covent Garden, to the south Trafalgar Square, and to the west the fashionable and expensive night world of Mayfair.

INFORMATION   Ask a newsstand dealer for a copy of *Time Out* or *What's On in London*, both of which contain listings of theaters and nightclubs.

THE PERFORMING ARTS
THEATER

In London, you'll have a chance to see the world-renowned English theater on its home ground. You may want to spend a classical evening at the National Theatre, catch up on that Broadway musical you missed in the United States, or scout out a new play—perhaps next year's big Stateside hit. Matinees are on Wednesday (Thursday at some theaters) and on Saturday. It's impossible to describe all of London's theaters in this space, so below are listed just a few from the treasure trove.

RESERVATIONS   Several evenings at the London theater is an essential part of a trip to Britain for many people. If you want to see specific shows—especially hit ones—purchase your tickets in advance. The most recommended method is to purchase your ticket from the theater's box office. Many theaters will accept bookings by telephone if you give your name and credit-card number when you call; then all you have to do is go to the theater before the performance to collect your tickets, which will be sold at the theater price. If you don't show up they charge your account anyway. A few theaters will even reserve tickets for the gallery—the cheapest seats.

TICKET AGENTS   You can also make theater reservations through ticket agents. Before going through a ticket agent, it's wise to call the theater directly to see if any tickets are available at the regular price. In the case of hit shows, only brokers may be able to get you a seat, but you'll pay for the privilege.

Under a British voluntary code, ticket brokers should disclose the face value of a ticket as well as their fee. But since the requirement is voluntary, many brokers don't bother to disclose this information. Their markup is usually 20% to 25%, but spot checks in London have revealed markups as high as 80% of the face value of the ticket.

With offices in London and the United States, **Keith Prowse/First Call** can reserve tickets for hit shows weeks or even months in advance. In the United States, contact them at 234 W. 44th St. New York, NY 10036 (tel. 212/398-1430, or toll free 800/669-8687). In London their number is 071/836-9001. The fee for booking a ticket in the U.S.A. is $10 to $20; in London, it's £2.30 to £7 ($3.50 to $10.50).

One of the most reliable ticket agents is **British Airways,** which has some of the best seats available for London productions (including musicals), Stratford-upon-Avon, and the Edinburgh Festival. The reservation service is only available to BA customers. For information and reservations, call toll free 800/AIRWAYS.

Visitors interested in ordering theater tickets days, weeks, or months in advance can contact **Edwards & Edwards,** 156 Shaftesbury Ave., WC2 (tel. 071/379-5822). Tickets to almost anything in London can be arranged in advance by telephone (a personal visit is seldom necessary). Tickets will be mailed or delivered to the box office of any particular theater, usually after imposing a service charge of about 10% to 20%.

Some North Americans prefer to order tickets for London plays through Edwards & Edwards's New York office, 1 Times Square Plaza, New York, NY 10036 (tel. 212/944-0290 in New York City, or toll free 800/223-6108 from elsewhere in the U.S.). In some cases, if they're available, tickets to certain London theaters can be pre-ordered using a credit card. A service charge is added to the final bill.

On the day of any particular London performance, tickets are sometimes reduced in price and sold through such discount outlets as **Theatre Tonight** (tel. 071/753-0333), a division of Edwards & Edwards. Personal visits to Theatre Tonight are not encouraged or necessary, and only tickets for performances of that day are sold, but with a telephone and a credit card (only VISA or MasterCard) you'll pay only the cost of the ticket, and sometimes less, depending on the popularity of the show. Tickets are then picked up directly at the theater before the show begins. This company has a larger range of seats than the Leicester Square Half-Price Ticket Booth (see below), which rarely has tickets for the big musicals. Theatre Tonight's switchboard is open Monday to Saturday from 11am to 5:45pm.

GALLERY & DISCOUNT TICKETS London theater tickets are priced quite reasonably when compared with those in the U.S. Prices vary greatly depending on the seat—from £10 to £35 ($15 to $52.50). Sometimes gallery seats (the cheapest) are sold only on the day of the performance, so you'll have to head to the box office early in the day and return an hour before the performance to queue up, since they're not reserved seats.

Discounted tickets are sometimes offered—but usually only to long-running plays on their last legs or to new "dogs," which you may not want to see anyway. Reduced tickets are more likely to be available for matinees—Wednesday or Thursday, and Saturday. A really hot musical—or "bomb" to the Brits—in its early life almost never offers discounted tickets.

Over on Leicester Square, there's a long line—but it moves quickly and it's well worth the effort if you want to save money—for half-price tickets (cash only) on the day of performance at the **Leicester Square Half-Price Ticket Booth.** Operated by the Society of West End Theatre, it's open Monday through Saturday from noon to 2pm for matinees and from 2:30 to 6:30pm for evening shows. A list of shows for which tickets are available is displayed; hit productions are rarely offered.

Warning: Beware of scalpers who hang out in front of theaters with hit shows. There are many reports of scalpers selling forged tickets, and their prices are outrageous.

OLD VIC, Waterloo Rd., SE1. Tel. 071/928-2651.
The Old Vic is a 170-year-old theater whose facade and much of the interior have been restored to their original early 19th-century style, but most of the modernization is behind the scenes. The proscenium arch has been moved back, the stage has tripled in size, and more seats and stage boxes have been added. Fully air-conditioned and containing five bars, it presents short seasons of varied plays, and several subscription offerings have been introduced. Tube: Waterloo.

THE MAJOR CONCERT & PERFORMANCE HALLS

The following is a quick-reference list of major performance spaces in London, with box office telephone numbers. Details are provided in the listings below.

Barbican Centre (tel. 071/638-8891)
London Coliseum (tel. 071/836-3161 or 240-5258)
Royal National Theatre (tel. 071/928-2033)
Royal Albert Hall (tel. 071/589-8212)
Royal Court Theatre (tel. 071/730-1745)
Royal Opera House (tel. 071/240-1911)
South Bank Centre (including Royal Festival Hall) (tel. 071/928-8800)

Admission: Plays, £5–£20 ($7.50–$30); musicals, £8–£30 ($12–$45).

OPEN AIR, Inner Circle, Regent's Park, NW1. Tel. 071/486-2431.

This outdoor theater is right in the center of Regent's Park. The setting is idyllic, and the longest theater bar in London provides both drink and food. Presentations are mainly Shakespeare, usually in period costume, and both seating and acoustics are excellent. If it rains, you're given tickets for another performance. Performances are from May 28 to September 11, daily at 8pm, plus Wednesday, Thursday, and Saturday at 2:30pm. Tube: Baker Street.

Admission: Tickets, £6.50–£15.50 ($9.80–$23.30).

ROYAL COURT THEATRE, Sloane Sq., SW1. Tel. 071/730-1745.

The English Stage Company has operated this theater for nearly 40 years, with an emphasis on new playwrights. John Osborne got his start here with the 1956 production of *Look Back in Anger*. Also on the premises is the Theatre Upstairs, a studio theater devoted to new and experimental works. Shows are Monday through Saturday at 8pm, plus Saturday at 4pm; in the upstairs theater, they're Monday through Saturday at 7:30pm, plus Saturday at 3:30pm. Tube: Sloane Square.

Admission: Tickets, Upstairs, £5 ($7.50); downstairs, £5 ($7.50) Mon, £9–£12 ($13.50–$18) Tues–Sat, £5–£18 ($7.50–$27) Sat matinees.

ROYAL NATIONAL THEATRE, South Bank, SE1. Tel. 071/928-2033.

Occupying a prime site on the South Bank of the River Thames is the flagship of British theater, the Royal National Theatre. Winner of 175 top drama awards since its opening in 1976, and home to one of the world's greatest stage companies, the National houses not one but three theaters. The largest, named after Lord Laurence Olivier, is the **Olivier,** with 1,200 seats and a style reminiscent of the Greek amphitheater with its fan-shaped open stage. The more traditional proscenium-arch auditorium, the **Lyttelton,** seats 900 people, while the **Cottesloe** is a small box-shaped studio theater with flexible seating and staging, with space for up to 400 people. Across its three stages the National presents a repertoire of the finest in world theater from classic drama to award-winning new plays, and from comedy to musicals to shows for young people.

The National is also a full-time theater center which is open to everyone, with or without a ticket, Monday to Saturday from 10am till 11pm. The National features three bookshops, free foyer exhibitions and live music, backstage tours, short early-evening events when theater professionals discuss their work, two restaurants, seven bars, a coffee bar, and three buffets, plus riverside walks and terraces. Tube: Waterloo, Embankment, or Charing Cross.

Admission: Tickets, £9–£20 ($13.50–$30); midweek matinees, Sat matinees, and previews cheaper.

ROYAL SHAKESPEARE COMPANY [RSC], Barbican Centre, Silk St., Barbican, EC2. Tel. 071/638-8891 (box office).

One of the world's finest theater companies is based in Stratford-upon-Avon and here at the Barbican Centre. The central core of the company's work remains the plays of William Shakespeare, but it also presents a wide-ranging program of three different productions each week in the Barbican Theatre—the 1,200-seat main auditorium, which has excellent sightlines throughout, thanks to a raked orchestra—and the Pit, the small studio space where much of the company's new writing is presented.

In recent years, the RSC has had great success in transferring its hit shows, such as *Les Misérables* and *Les Liaisons Dangereuses* to West End theaters, while continuing its diverse repertoire both in London and Stratford. Tube: Barbican or Moorgate.

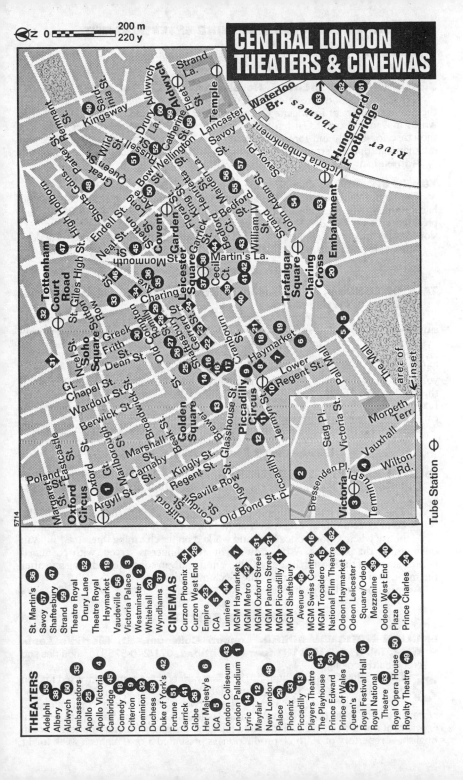

CENTRAL LONDON THEATERS & CINEMAS

200 m
220 y

Tube Station ⊕

5714

THEATERS

Adelphi	55
Albery	38
Aldwych	60
Ambassadors	35
Apollo	25
Apollo Victoria	4
Cambridge	45
Comedy	18
Criterion	9
Dominion	32
Duchess	58
Duke of York's	42
Fortune	51
Garrick	41
Globe	26
Her Majesty's	6
ICA	5
London Coliseum	43
London Palladium	1
Lyric	14
Mayfair	12
New London	48
Palace	29
Phoenix	33
Piccadilly	13
Players Theatre	53
The Playhouse	54
Prince Edward	30
Prince of Wales	17
Queen's	27
Royal Festival Hall	61
Royal National Theatre	63
Royal Opera House	50
Royalty Theatre	49
St. Martin's	36
Savoy	57
Shaftesbury	47
Strand	59
Theatre Royal Drury Lane	52
Theatre Royal Haymarket	19
Vaudeville	56
Victoria Palace	3
Westminster	2
Whitehall	20
Wyndhams	37

CINEMAS

Curzon Phoenix	34
Curzon West End	28
Empire	23
ICA	5
Lumiere	44
MGM Haymarket	7
MGM Metro	22
MGM Oxford Street	31
MGM Panton Street	21
MGM Piccadilly	11
MGM Shaftesbury Avenue	46
MGM Swiss Centre	16
MGM Trocadero	15
National Film Theatre	62
Odeon Haymarket	8
Odeon Leicester Square/Odeon Mezzanine	39
Odeon West End	40
Plaza	10
Prince Charles	24

Admission: Barbican Theatre, £7–£21.50 ($10.50–$32.30); The Pit, £11.50 ($17.30) matinees, £13.50 ($20.30) evening performances.

SADLER'S WELLS THEATRE, Rosebery Ave., EC1. Tel. 071/278-8916.

A theater has stood here since 1683, on the site of a well that was once known for the healing powers of its waters. Once the home of the famed Sadler's Wells Ballet which moved to Covent Garden to become the Royal Ballet, the theater today is a showcase for British and foreign modern ballet and modern dance companies and international opera. Performances usually begin at 7:30pm. Tube: Angel.

Admission: Tickets, £6–£35 ($9–$52.50).

YOUNG VIC, 66 The Cut, Waterloo, SE1. Tel. 071/928-6363.

The Young Vic presents classical and modern plays for theatergoers of all ages and backgrounds, with the priority of attracting young people aged 16 to 25. Recent productions have included Shakespeare, Ibsen, Arthur Miller, and specially commissioned plays for young people. Performances usually begin at 7:30pm. Tube: Waterloo.

Admission: Tickets, £14 ($21) adults, £7 ($10.50) students and children.

Dinner Theater

TALK OF LONDON, New London Theatre, Parker St., off Drury Lane, WC2. Tel. 071/568-1616.

A unique theater restaurant in a unique setting, that's the Talk of London. It is situated in the heart and soul of the city's theaterland. The restaurant is ingeniously designed so that every guest gets "the best seat in the house." Sitting in a circular layout on varying floor levels, everyone has an uninterrupted view of the show. The Talk of London offers a complete evening's entertainment: a three-course dinner of your choice, dancing to a top show band, and an international cabaret at 9:45pm. All this and coffee, service, and VAT are included in the price. Drinks are extra. Reservations are essential. It's open 6 nights a week (different nights each week—so call) from 7:30pm to midnight.

Admission (including dinner): £36 ($54) Sun–Thurs, £45 ($67.50) Fri–Sat.

Gilbert and Sullivan Evenings

GILBERT AND SULLIVAN EVENINGS, Mansion House at Grim's Dyke, Old Redding, Harrow Weald, Middlesex HA3 6SH. Tel. 081/954-4227.

The English Heritage Singers present Gilbert and Sullivan programs in the context of a dinner event. You arrive for cocktails in the Library Bar of the house where Gilbert once lived and worked on his charming operettas. Sullivan once visited the premises. A full Edwardian-style dinner is served, with costumed performances of the most beloved of Gilbert and Sullivan songs both during and after the meal. You can request your favorite G&S melodies.

Admission (including dinner): £32 ($48) per person.

OPERA & BALLET

ENGLISH NATIONAL OPERA, London Coliseum, St. Martin's Lane, WC2. Tel. 071/836-3161 for reservations, 071/240-5258 for inquiries and credit-card booking.

The London Coliseum, built in 1904 as a variety theater and converted into an opera house in 1968, is London's largest and most splendid theater. The English National Opera is one of the two national opera companies and performs a wide range of works, from great classics to Gilbert and Sullivan to new and experimental works, staged with flair and imagination, and with every performance in English. A repertory of 18 to 20 productions is presented 5 or 6 nights a week for 11 months of the year. Although the balcony seats are cheaper, many visitors prefer the Upper Circle or Dress Circle. Tube: Charing Cross or Leicester Square.

Admission: Tickets, £6–£10 ($9–$15) balcony, £10.50–£42.50 ($15.80–$63.80) upper dress circle or stalls. About 100 discount balcony tickets are sold on the day of performance from 10am during the opera season (Aug–June).

ROYAL OPERA HOUSE, Bow St., WC2 (Box Office, 48 Floral St., WC2). Tel. 071/240-1911.

⭐ This classical building is on the northeast corner of Covent Garden, which was London's first square, laid out by Inigo Jones as a residential piazza. Until a few years ago the whole area was a thriving fruit and vegetable market, originally started by nuns selling surplus stocks from their convent garden. In the 16th century the section became fashionable to live in, and was soon to become one of the centers of London nightlife. The first theater was built on the present site in 1732. The existing opera house, one of the most beautiful theaters in Europe, was built in 1858 and is now the home of **The Royal Opera** and **The Royal Ballet,** which are leading international companies. Newspapers give full details of performances. Open Monday through Saturday from 10am to 8pm. Tube: Covent Garden.

Admission: Tickets, £3.30–£124 ($5–$186) ballet, £1.65–£54 ($2.50–$81) opera.

CONCERT & MULTIPURPOSE HALLS

BARBICAN CENTRE, Silk St., The Barbican, EC2. Tel. 071/638-8891.

Considered the largest art and exhibition center in western Europe, the Barbican was created to make a perfect setting in which to enjoy good music and theater from comfortable, roomy seating. The theater is now the London home of the Royal Shakespeare Company (see description above), and the Concert Hall is the permanent home of the **London Symphony Orchestra** and host to visiting orchestras and performers.

In addition to the hall and theater, the Barbican Centre has The Pit, a studio theater; Barbican Art Gallery, a showcase for the visual arts; the Concourse Gallery and foyer exhibition spaces; Cinemas One and Two, which show recently released mainstream films, and seasons related by theme or subject; Barbican Library, a general lending library that also places a strong emphasis on the arts; a Conservatory, one of London's largest plant houses; and four restaurants as well as bars. The box office is open Monday through Saturday from 9am to 11pm and on Sunday from noon to 11pm. Tube: Barbican.

Admission: Tickets, £5–£28 ($7.50–$42).

LONDON PALLADIUM, Argyll St., W1. Tel. 071/494-5100.

It's hard to encapsulate the prestige of this show-business legend in a paragraph. Performers from Britain, Europe, and America consider that they have "arrived" when they've appeared here. The highlight of the season is the Royal Command Performance, held before the queen, which includes an introduction of the artists to Her Majesty.

In days of yore, the Palladium has starred Frank Sinatra, Shirley MacLaine, Andy Williams, Perry Como, Julie Andrews, Tom Jones, Sammy Davis, Jr., and so on. The Palladium is usually closed on Sunday. Tube: Oxford Circus.

Admission: Tickets, depends entirely on the show.

ROYAL ALBERT HALL, Kensington Gore, SW7. Tel. 071/589-8212.

Opened in 1871 and dedicated to the memory of Queen Victoria's consort, Prince Albert, this building encircles one of the world's largest and finest auditoriums with a seating capacity of 5,200. Home since 1941 to the BBC Promenade Concerts, the famous 8-week annual festival of classical music, it's also a popular venue for light music plus the latest in rock and pop. Sporting events such as boxing and tennis also figure strongly here. For Royal Albert Hall 24-hour events information, call 0898/500252, a service updated daily. Ticket availability is also given. Rates for calling this number range from 36p to 48p (50¢ to 70¢) a minute. Tube: South Kensington, Kensington High Street, or Knightsbridge.

Admission: Tickets, £2.50–£35 ($3.80–$52.50), but this could vary considerably, depending on the event.

SOUTH BANK CENTRE, ROYAL FESTIVAL HALL, at South Bank, SE1. Tel. 071/928-8800.

In recent years, the musical focus of London has shifted to a uniquely specialized complex of buildings on the South Bank side of Waterloo Bridge, called the South Bank Centre.

The complex houses three of the most stylish, comfortable, and acoustically perfect concert structures in the world: the Royal Festival Hall, Queen Elizabeth Hall, and the Purcell Room. Here, more than 1,200 performances a year are presented, including classical music, ballet, jazz, popular classics, pop and contemporary dance. The center also accommodates the internationally famous Hayward Gallery whose exhibitions include both contemporary and historical art. Recent exhibitions have included Andy Warhol, Renoir, Jasper Johns, Leonardo da Vinci, Diego Rivera, and Le Corbusier.

The Royal Festival Hall is open from 10am every day and offers an extensive range of things to see and do. There are free exhibitions in the foyers and free lunchtime music from 12:30pm. The Poetry Library is open from 11am to 8pm, as well as shops that provide a wide selection of books, records, and crafts.

The Festival Buffet offers a wide variety of food at reasonable prices, and there are numerous bars throughout the foyers. The Review Restaurant serves both lunch and dinner and offers a spectacular view of the Thames. A preconcert meal is available well before concerts begin.

Reservations are recommended by calling 071/921-0800. The box office is open 10am to 9pm. Tube: Waterloo or Embankment Station.

Admission: Tickets, £5–£30.50 ($7.50–$45.80); credit cards accepted.

WIGMORE HALL, 36 Wigmore St., W1. Tel. 071/935-2141.

An intimate auditorium, Wigmore Hall is where you'll hear excellent recitals and concerts. There are regular series of song recitals, piano, and chamber music, along with early music and baroque concerts. A free list of the month's programs is available from the hall. Performances are given nightly, plus Sunday Morning Coffee Concerts and additional concerts on Sunday at 4 or 7pm.

Admission: Tickets, £4.50–£40 ($6.80–$60).

THE CLUB & MUSIC SCENE

Midnight divides the world of bright lights like a curtain. This "midnight curtain" prevents you from just dropping into a place for a nightcap—you must order something to eat when you have an alcoholic drink after 11pm. The midnight curtain doesn't exempt you from a cover charge—frequently disguised as a membership fee. After hours, you can still enjoy a stage show, take a spin on the dance floor, and try your luck at a gaming table. And you can devour a five-course meal while drinking yourself into oblivion.

About this front-door mumbo-jumbo that passes as membership enrollment: what it amounts to is so-called temporary membership, which satisfies the letter—if not the spirit—of the law and allows you to get in without delay. In many cases, the temporary membership is deducted from the cost of dinner, but there is no hard-and-fast rule.

At this point, I'd better add a word for the benefit of male travelers. London's club world is full of "hostesses." These ladies intend to get you to buy things—from drinks to dolls to cigarettes—which can shoot up your tab far beyond what you budgeted to spend. Recognized meeting places for the young—like discos and ballrooms—do not employ hostesses.

NIGHTCLUBS & CABARETS

CAMDEN PALACE, 1A Camden High St., NW1. Tel. 071/387-0428.

Camden Palace is housed inside what was originally a theater. It draws an over-18 crowd who flock there in various costumes and energy levels according to the night of the week. Since it offers a rotating style of music, it's best to phone in advance to see if that evening's musical genre appeals to your taste. Styles range from rhythm and blues to what young rock experts call "boilerhouse," "garage music," "acid funk," "hip-hop," and "twist & shout." A live band performs only on Tuesday. There's a restaurant if you get the munchies, and a pint of lager goes for £2.20 ($3.30). Open Tuesday, Wednesday, Friday, and Saturday 9pm to 2:30am. Tube: Camden Town or Mornington Crescent.

Admission: £5 ($7.50) Tues–Wed, £10 ($15) Fri–Sat.

CSAR RICARDO, 9 Young St., W8. Tel. 071/937-9403.

Just off Kensington High Street, this is a good place to go for a widely varied repertoire of music, including rock. Likewise, the patrons come from many different countries and backgrounds, and span a wide age spectrum as well. Beer costs about £2.50 ($3.80). Open Monday through Saturday 10pm to 12:30am, Sunday 9pm to 2am. Tube: Kensington High Street.

Admission: £3–£7 ($4.50–$10.50).

L'HIRONDELLE, 99–101 Regent St., W1. Tel. 071/734-6666.

L'Hirondelle stands in the heart of the West End and puts on some of the most lavishly gorgeous floor shows in town. What's more, you can dine, drink, and dance without taking out a "temporary membership." Neither is there an entrance fee. The shows are really full-scale revues and go on at 11pm and 1am. Dancing to one of the few live bands in London is from 9:30pm. Dancing-dining partners are available. The club offers a three-course dinner for £30 ($45) per person, including VAT and service charges, or you can choose from their very large à la carte menu. A bottle of wine begins at £23 ($34.50). Open Monday through Saturday from 8:30pm to 3:30am. Tube: Piccadilly Circus.

Admission: £10 ($15) cover charge for nondiners.

RHEINGOLD CLUB, Sedley Place, off 361 Oxford St., W1. Tel. 071/629-5343.

The Rheingold, founded in 1959, is the oldest and most successful "singles club" in London, existing long before the term was coined. It's a safe place for men to take their wives or girlfriends, and single women are welcome and safe here.

This spot thrives in a century-old wine cellar and has a restaurant, two bars, and a good-size dance floor. The main attraction is a top-class band playing every evening except Sunday and bank holidays. There is also an occasional cabaret, usually with big-time guest stars.

The club offers a tasty German dish called Champignonschnitzel, a tender escalope of Dutch veal served with rice and peas in a cream-and-mushroom sauce, costing £9 ($13.50). There is a strong German draft beer at £1.50 ($2.30) for a half pint and excellent French and German wines from £10 ($15) for an *appellation contrôlée*. Open on Monday and Tuesday from 7:30pm to 1:30am, on Wednesday and Thursday (cabaret nights) from 7:30pm to 2am, and on Friday and Saturday from 7:30pm to 2:30am. Tube: Bond Street.

Admission: £6 ($9), including temporary membership.

TIDDY DOLS, 55 Shepherd Market, Mayfair, W1. Tel. 071/499-2357.

Housed in nine small atmospheric Georgian houses, circa 1741, this club is named for the famous gingerbread baker and eccentric. Guests come to Tiddy Dols to enjoy such dishes as jugged hare, cock-a-leekie, plum pudding, and the original gingerbread of Tiddy Dol. While dining they are entertained with madrigals, Noël Coward, Gilbert and Sullivan, music-hall songs, and a town crier. In the summer there is a large pavement café with parasols and a view of the "village" of Shepherd Market. During winter there are open fires. An à la carte dinner, costing £28 ($42) and up, is served nightly. Dancing is nowadays restricted to special evenings. All year there is a café and wine bar serving a full menu, at lower prices, and offering sandwiches as well. Drinks begin at £2.75 ($4.10). Open daily from 6pm to 1am (11:30pm last arrivals); café and wine bar, noon to midnight. Tube: Green Park.

Admission: £1.55 ($2.30) cover charge.

A COMEDY CLUB

THE COMEDY STORE, corner of Coventry St. and Oxendon, off Leicester Sq., W1. Tel. 0426/914433 for a recorded message.

This is London's most visible showcase for both established and emerging comic talent, set in the heart of the city's nighttime district. Even if the performers are unfamiliar to you, you will still enjoy the spontaneity of live British comedy. Visitors must be more than 18. There is no particular dress code at this place, and many clients wear jeans. Reservations are accepted, and the club opens 1 hour before each show. Open Wednesday, Thursday, and Sunday (shows at 8pm), and on Friday and Saturday (shows at 8pm and midnight). Tube: Leicester Square or Piccadilly Circus.

Admission: £8 ($12).

ROCK

GULLIVER'S, 15–21 Ganton St., W1. Tel. 071/499-0760.

Established more than 20 years ago at another location, this well-rooted club sits in a very modern black and gold-colored cellar off Carnaby Street. It specializes in American and British soul music, although a highly appealing blend of other styles is presented at each of its opening nights. The venue ranges from "old soul" night (the Supremes, Otis Redding, for example) to evenings that include swing, beat, and rap music, with doses of Caribbean calypso, reggae, and "soca music" (you heard right) thrown in. At the long bar, you can order a Budweiser for £2.50 ($3.80). Open on Thursday from 10pm to 3:30am, Friday and Saturday from 10pm to 4:30am, and Sunday from 7pm to midnight. Tube: Oxford Circus.

Admission: £6–£8 ($9–$12).

MARQUEE, 105 Charing Cross Rd., WC2. Tel. 071/437-6603.

The Marquee is considered one of the best-known centers for rock in the world. Its reputation goes back to the 1950s and another location, but it remains forever young, in touch with the sounds of the future. Famous groups such as the Rolling Stones played at the Marquee long before their names spread beyond the shores of England. You don't have to be a member—you just pay at the door. Live bands perform Monday through Thursday from 7pm to midnight. On Friday, live bands perform from 7 to 10:30pm, then disco takes over until 3am. On Saturday, you get only recorded music from 10:30pm to 3:30am. Sunday night is comedy night, with comedians performing live from 7pm to midnight. That's when a £18 ($27) cover charge is imposed. Many well-known musicians frequent the place regularly on their nights off. The club occupies a building that was once a cinema. Open Monday through Thursday from 7pm to midnight, Friday 7pm to 3am, and Saturday 10:30pm to 3:30am. Tube: Leicester Square or Tottenham Court Road.

Admission: £5.50–£18 ($8.30–$27), depending on the performer.

ROCK GARDEN RESTAURANT & ROCK MUSIC VENUE, 6–7 The Piazza, Covent Garden, WC2. Tel. 071/836-4052.

This is the place where new bands are launched, where such renowned groups as Dire Straits, The Police, U2, and The Stanglers all played before becoming famous. In summer the restaurant offers outside seating in the heart of Covent Garden. A wide range of meals is offered, beginning at £7 ($10.50). Both the restaurant and the Venue have licensed bars, with drinks for £2 ($3) and up. The restaurant is open Monday through Thursday and on Sunday from noon to midnight, and on Friday and Saturday from noon to 1am; the Venue is open Monday through Saturday from 7:30pm to 3am and on Sunday from 7:30pm to midnight. Tube: Covent Garden; night buses from neighboring Trafalgar Square.

Admission: The Venue, £3–£6 ($4.50–$9).

JAZZ & BLUES

THE BASS CLEF/THE TENOR CLEF, 58 Hoxton Sq., N1. Tel. 071/729-2476.

Both of these jazz clubs are in the same sprawling brick-fronted building, the former site of a prominent 19th century hospital—a treatment for Parkinson's disease was reputedly its specialty. The Bass Clef (located in the cellar with an entrance on Coronet Street) is a multimusic venue, while the Tenor Clef (located one floor above street level) presents somewhat more traditional jazz and "fusion jazz." Both of these smoke-filled places are frequented by London's nighttime crowds. A complicated series of stairs and hallways interconnect the two clubs, although on certain nights each club has a separate admission price. Both the Bass and Tenor contain restaurants, where full meals cost around £12 ($18) and drinks start at £2.50 ($3.80). Both clubs are open Monday through Saturday from 7:30pm to 2am, Sunday 8pm to midnight. Call for show times.

Admission: £3.50–£7 ($5.30–$10.50).

THE BULL'S HEAD, 373 Lonsdale Rd., Barnes, SW13. Tel. 081/876-5241.

The Bull's Head has presented live modern jazz concerts every night of the week for more than 30 years. One of the oldest hostelries in the area, it was a staging post in the mid-19th century where travelers on their way to Hampton Court and beyond could eat, drink, and rest while the coach horses were changed. Today the place is known for its jazz, performed by musicians from all over the world. Jazz concerts are presented on Sunday from 1 to 2:30pm and 8:30 to 10:30pm. Monday through Saturday, you can hear music from 8:30 to 11pm. You can order good food at the Carvery in the Saloon Bar daily and dine in the 17th-century Stable Restaurant. The restaurant, in the original, restored stables, specializes in steaks, fish, and other traditional fare. Meals cost £7.50 ($11.30) and up. Beer begins at £1.40 ($2.10). Open Monday through Saturday from 11am to 11pm and on Sunday from noon to 3pm and 7 to 10:30pm. Tube: Hammersmith, then bus no. 9A the rest of the way; or take the Hounslow Look train from Waterloo Station and get off at Barnes Bridge Station, then walk 5 minutes to the club.

Admission: £4–£7 ($6–$10.50).

100 CLUB, 100 Oxford St., W1. Tel. 071/636-0933.

Although less plush and cheaper, the 100 Club is considered a serious rival of the above among many dedicated jazz gourmets. Its cavalcade of bands includes the best British jazz musicians, as well as many touring Americans. Drinks start at £1.80 ($2.70). Open on Friday from 8:30pm to 3am, on Saturday from 7:30pm to 1am, and on Sunday from 7:30 to 11:30pm. Tube: Tottenham Court Road or Oxford Circus.

Admission: Fri £7 ($10.50) for everybody; Sat £7 ($10.50) members, £8 ($12) nonmembers; Sun £5 ($7.50) members, £6 ($9) nonmembers.

RONNIE SCOTT'S, 47 Frith St., W1. Tel. 071/439-0747.

⭐ Mention the word "jazz" in London and people immediately think of Ronnie Scott's, long the citadel of modern jazz in Europe where the best English and American groups are booked. Featured on almost every bill is an American band, often with a top-notch singer. It's in the heart of Soho, a 10-minute walk from Piccadilly Circus via Shaftesbury Avenue, and worth an entire evening. Not only can you saturate yourself in the best of jazz, you get reasonably priced drinks and dinners as well. There are three separate areas: the Main Room, the Upstairs Room, and the Downstairs Bar. You don't have to be a member, although you can join if you wish. If you have a student ID you are granted entrance Monday through Thursday for £6 ($9). In the Main Room you can either stand at the bar to watch the show or sit at a table, where you can order dinner. The Downstairs Bar is more intimate, a quiet rendezvous where you can meet and talk with the regulars, often some of the world's most talented musicians. The Upstairs Room is separate and it has a disco called the Club Latino. Drinks begin at £2.50 ($3.80); a half pint of beer, £1.20 ($1.80). Both the Main Room and the Upstairs Room are open Monday through Saturday from 8:30pm to 3am. Tube: Tottenham Court Road or Leicester Square.

Admission: From £12 ($18), depending on the performers.

DANCE CLUBS & DISCOS

BARBARELLA 2, 43 Thurloe St., SW7. Tel. 071/584-2000.

This place combines a first-class Italian restaurant with a carefully controlled disco. So that diners can converse in normal tones, the flashing lights and electronic music of the disco are separated from the dining area by thick sheets of glass. Full meals, costing from £20 ($30), include an array of Neapolitan-inspired dishes. Only clients of the restaurant are allowed into the disco, which prevents hordes of late-night revelers from cramming into the place when the regular pubs close. Drinks start at £2.50 ($3.80); beer, at £1.80 ($2.70). Open Monday through Saturday from 7:30pm to 3am (last food orders at 12:45am). Tube: Kensington.

Admission: Free.

EQUINOX, Leicester Sq., WC2. Tel. 071/437-1446.

New and flashy, the Equinox opened in 1992, rising from the ashes of the empire, a once-famous dance emporium. More than £7 million was spent to create an elaborate labyrinth where you can shake off your dance fever. Presumably something or someone is available for every taste. Thursday is traditionally a live concert night. Drinks begin at £2.35 ($3.50) each. Open Tuesday to Saturday from 9pm to 4am. Closed on Christmas night. Tube: Leicester Square.

Admission: £5–£12 ($7.50–$18), depends on night of week and whether there is live entertainment.

HIPPODROME, Leicester Sq., WC2. Tel. 071/437-4311.

⭐ Here you will find one of London's greatest discos, an enormous place where light and sound beam in on you from all directions. Revolving speakers even descend from the roof to deafen you in patches, and you can watch yourself on closed-circuit video. Golden Scan lights are a spectacular treat. There are six bars, together with an à la carte balcony restaurant. Lasers and a hydraulically controlled stage for visiting international performers are only part of the attraction of this place. Drinks run £3 ($4.50) and up. Open Monday through Saturday from 9pm to 3:30am. Tube: Leicester Square.

Admission: £5–£12 ($7.50–$18).

ROYAL ROOF RESTAURANT, in the Royal Garden Hotel, 24 Kensington High St., W8. Tel. 071/937-8000.

Situated on the top floor of the hotel, the Royal Roof Restaurant is elegant and refined, and overlooks Kensington Gardens and Hyde Park. From your table you will see the lights of Kensington and Knightsbridge, with a view of London's West End skyline. In a romantic candlelit aura, you can dance to the resident band on Thursday, Friday, and Saturday and enjoy a five-course dinner costing £35 ($52.50). On other nights there's live piano music. Reservations are vital. Open Monday through Saturday from 7pm to 1am (last order at 10:30pm Monday through Friday and at 11:30pm on Saturday). Tube: Kensington High Street.

Admission: Free.

SMOLLENSKY'S ON THE STRAND, 105 The Strand WC2. Tel. 071/497-2101.

This American eatery and drinking bar is a cousin of Smollensky's Baloon at 1 Dover St. (see "The Bar Scene," below, for my recommendation). At the Strand location, there is dancing on Friday and Saturday nights. On Sunday nights there is a special live jazz session, in association with Jazz F.M., an English radio station devoted to jazz. Many visit just for drinks, ordering everything from house cocktails to classic cocktails to deluxe cocktails. Beer costs from £2.05 ($3.10), drinks from £3.95 ($5.90). Meals, ranging from barbecue loin of pork to corn-fed chicken, cost from £12 ($18). Open Monday through Saturday noon to midnight and Sunday noon to 10:30pm. Tube: Charing Cross or Embankment.

Admission: Free except music charge of £3 ($4.50) imposed when live music is offered.

STRINGFELLOWS, 16–19 Upper St. Martin's Lane, WC2. Tel. 071/240-5534.

This is one of London's most elegant nighttime rendezvous spots. It is said to have $2 million (U.S.) worth of velvet and high-tech gloss and glitter. In theory, it's a members-only club, but—and only at the discretion of management—nonmembers may be admitted. It offers two lively bars and a first-class restaurant. Its disco has a stunning glass dance floor and a dazzling sound-and-light system. It's been called "an exquisite oasis of elegance," and its food "the best in London" (for a nightclub, that is). Drinks run £3.25 ($4.90), and beer goes for £2.25 ($3.40). It's open for dinner Monday through Saturday from 8pm to 3am, with dancing from 11pm to 3am. Tube: Leicester Square.

Admission: Mon–Wed £8 ($12), Thurs £10 ($15), Fri–Sat £11–£15 ($16.50–$22.50).

WAG CLUB, 35 Wardour St., W1. Tel. 071/437-5534.

This popular dance club is set behind an innocuous-looking brick facade in one of the most congested neighborhoods of London's entertainment districts. Its two levels are decorated with unusual murals, some with themes from ancient Egypt, others with snakes, whose shapes seem to enhance the perceptions of the many mixed groups who come in here. Clients all seem to love to dance and hail from throughout the world. Live bands are sometimes presented on the street level, while the upstairs is reserved for highly danceable recorded music. Drinks run £2.20 ($3.30). Open Monday through Thursday 10:30pm to 3:30am, Friday and Saturday 10:30pm to 6am. Tube: Piccadilly Circus or Leicester Square.

Admission: £3–£9 ($4.50–$13.50).

GAY & LESBIAN CLUBS

The most reliable source of information on gay clubs and activities is the **Gay Switchboard** (tel. 071/837-7324). The staff runs a 24-hour service for information on places and activities catering to homosexual men and women. See also "Gay Bars," below in this chapter.

HEAVEN, The Arches, Craven St., WC2. Tel. 071/839-3852.

Heaven is the biggest gay venue not only in Great Britain but perhaps in Europe as well. It also has the most sophisticated sound-and-laser system of any gay club in Europe. A London landmark, set in the vaulted cellars of Charing Cross Railway Station and painted a universal black inside, Heaven is divided into at least four distinctly different areas, each of these connected by a labyrinth of catwalks, stairs, and hallways, allowing for different activities within the club at the same time. It features different theme nights. For example, Wednesday is for gay men and women; Thursday is "straight night," and Saturday leaves you guessing since the clients are 50% straight and 50% gay. Open Tuesday through Saturday from 10:30pm to 3:30am. Tube: Charing Cross or Embankment.

Admission: £5–£9 ($7.50–$13.50).

MADAME JO JO'S, 8 Brewer St., W1. Tel. 071/734-2473.

Set side by side with some of Soho's most explicit girlie shows, Madame Jo Jo also presents "girls," but they're in drag. This is London's most popular transvestite show, with revues staged nightly at 12:15am and 1:15am and a popular piano bar. Drinks cost about £2.75 ($4.10). Open Monday through Saturday from 10pm to 3am. Tube: Piccadilly Circus.

Admission: £8–£10 ($12–$15).

ROY'S, 306B Fulham Rd., SW10. Tel. 071/352-6828.

Roy's is the leading gay restaurant of London. People come here not only for the good food but also for the entertaining and relaxing ambience. The fixed-price menu of freshly prepared ingredients is only £17.50 ($26.30) at this basement restaurant. Open Monday through Saturday from 7:30 to 11:30pm, and on Sunday from 1:30 to 3pm and 7:30 to 11pm. Tube: Earl's Court or South Kensington.

STEPH'S, 39 Dean St., W1. Tel. 071/734-5976.

Looking like a stage set for *Pink Flamingos*, Steph's is one of the most charming restaurants of Soho, near the exclusive Groucho Club. Its owner is Stephanie Cooke, a much-traveled former British schoolteacher who is today the sophisticated host of this little well-run restaurant. A theatrical clientele, among others, is attracted to the place. The clientele is mixed—straight, gay, bi, or whatever.

You could conceivably come here just to have fun, but the food is worthy in its own right. Everything is cooked fresh, so sit back, relax, and enjoy such specialties as Snuffy's chicken, beef-and-oyster pie, or selections from the charcoal grill, including filet steak with barbecue sauce. Steph might even suggest her own "diet"—a plate of wild Scottish smoked salmon and a bottle of champagne. The ubiquitous burger also appears on the menu, as do salads and even a vegetarian club sandwich (how fashionable can you get?). Meals begin at £15 ($22.50). Open Monday through Thursday from noon to 3pm and 5:30 to 11:30pm, Friday noon to 3pm and 5:30pm to midnight, and Saturday only from 5:30pm to midnight. Tube: Piccadilly Circus.

WILD ABOUT OSCAR, in the Philbeach Hotel, 30–31 Philbeach Gardens, SW5. Tel. 071/373-1244.

Catering to a mostly gay clientele, this restaurant is situated on the garden level of an interconnected pair of Victorian row houses. Decorated in blues and greens, and with portraits of Oscar Wilde (the restaurant's namesake), the establishment overlooks the brownstone's garden and offers well-prepared French cuisine, with three-course fixed-price menus costing £13 to £20 ($19.50–$30). There's a small cocktail bar open only to restaurant patrons and residents of the adjoining gay hotel. Open Monday through Saturday for dinner only from 7 to 10:30pm. A Sunday brunch is served from 1:30 to 4pm. Tube: Earl's Court.

THE BAR SCENE

PUBS, WINE BARS & BARS

AMERICAN BAR, in the Savoy Hotel, The Strand, WC2. Tel. 071/836-4343.

The American Bar is still one of the most sophisticated places in London. The bartender is known for such special concoctions as Royal Silver and Savoy 90. Many people enjoy the fruity champagne cocktails. From Monday to Saturday evenings jazz and piano music are featured. The après-theater crowd flocks here (it's near many West End theaters) to listen to show tunes. Men should wear a jacket and tie. Drinks begin at £5 ($7.50). Open Monday through Saturday from 11am to 3pm and 5:30 to 11pm, Sunday noon to 3pm and 7 to 10:30pm. Tube: Charing Cross or Embankment.

BRACEWELL'S BAR, in the Park Lane Hotel, Piccadilly, W1. Tel. 071/499-6321.

Chic, nostalgic, and elegant, it's the kind of bar where Edward VII and his stylish companion, Ms. Langtry, might have felt very much at home. Its plush, comfortable decor contains touches of Chinese lacquer, upholstered sofas, soft lighting, and an ambience like that of an elegant private club. The bar adjoins Bracewell's (see Chapter 5), one of the finest hotel restaurants in London. Mixed drinks begin at £5 ($7.50); beer, at £2.50 ($3.80). Open Monday through Saturday from 11am to 3pm and 5:30 to 11pm, and on Sunday from noon to 2:30pm and 7 to 10:30pm. Tube: Green Park.

COCKTAIL BAR, in the Café Royal, 68 Regent St., W1. Tel. 071/437-9090.

In business since 1865, this bar was once patronized by Oscar Wilde, James Whistler, and Aubrey Beardsley. Decorated in a 19th-century rococo style, it is one of the more glamorous places in London where one can order a drink. Café Royal cocktails, including the Golden Cadillac and the Prince William, begin at £5.50 ($8.30); mixed drinks at £2.50 ($3.80). Nonalcoholic drinks are also served, and you can order wine by the glass from the superb wine cellars. A traditional English tea, served between 3 and 5pm, costs £9.50 ($14.30). Open Monday through Saturday from noon to 11:30pm and on Sunday from noon to 10:30pm. Tube: Piccadilly Circus.

THE DORCHESTER BAR, in the Dorchester, Park Lane, W1. Tel. 071/629-8888.

This is a fun and sophisticated modern hideaway on the lobby level of one of the most lavishly decorated hotels in the world. Amid its champagne-colored premises, you'll find a clientele from all over the world who share certain assumptions about the pleasures that only taste and lots of money can buy. You can order upscale bar snacks, lunches, and suppers throughout the day and evening, including lobster cream soups, Scottish smoked salmon, fried filet of sea bass with seasonal salads, and "fine chocolate layers with a chocolate mousse." Otherwise, the bartender can make any drink ever conceived on the planet Earth. A pianist plays suitable background music every evening after 6:30pm. Open Monday through Saturday from 11:30am to 11pm, Sunday noon to 3pm and 6:30 to 10:30pm. Entrance is free. Drinks are priced from £6 ($9). Tube: Hyde Park Corner.

LILLIE LANGTRY BAR, in the Cadogan Hotel, Sloane St., SW1. Tel. 071/235-7141.

This spot epitomizes some of the charm and elegance of the Edwardian era. Lillie Langtry, actress and society beauty at the turn of the century (notorious as the mistress of Edward VII), used to live here. She became known as "Jersey Lily." The bar, next to Langtry's Restaurant, exudes a 1920s aura. Oscar Wilde was arrested on charges of sodomy here. But that unfortunate event is long forgotten, and the great playwright is honored on the drink menu with "Hock and Selzer," his favorite drink at the Cadogan, according to Sir John Betjeman's poem, "The Arrest of Oscar Wilde at the Cadogan Hotel." We'd call it a white wine spritzer today. The most popular drink is a Cadogan Cooler. Still another drink—champagne, cognac, and strawberry liqueur—honors Queen Victoria. Cocktails, beginning at £3.75 ($5.60), are served from 11am to 11pm daily. A glass of wine costs £2.75 ($4.10). Tube: Sloane Square.

RUMOURS, 33 Wellington St., WC2. Tel. 071/836-0038.

Rumours is the kind of place where you might expect Tom Cruise to turn up as a bartender. Called the "granddaddy of modern American cocktail-style bars," it is a spacious, pillared bar, enveloped by mirrors. Once this was a flower market in the heyday of Covent Garden, but today it dispenses about 10 pages of cocktail suggestions; at least three dozen of these are considered originals and worthy of carrying a copyright. On Friday and Saturday nights, the place is packed. Cocktails with generous measures cost £3.75 ($5.60) and up. Open Monday through Saturday from 5 to 11pm and on Sunday from 7 to 10:30pm. Tube: Covent Garden.

SMOLLENSKY'S BALLOON, 1 Dover St., W1. Tel. 071/491-1199.

A basement restaurant, this American eatery and drinking bar is packed during happy hour from 5:30 to 7pm with Mayfair office workers fortifying themselves before heading home. The place has a 1930s piano bar atmosphere, with polished wood and a mirrored ceiling. Steaks and french fries are its favorite fare, although you can also order well-prepared vegetarian dishes. Meals start at £12 ($18); house cocktails (good measures), at £2.85 ($4.30); beer, at £2.05 ($3.10). A pianist/singer entertains Monday through Saturday evenings. Open Monday through Saturday from noon to midnight and on Sunday from noon to 10:30pm. Tube: Green Park.

SPECIALTY BARS

Bouzouki

ELYSÉE, 13 Percy St., W1. Tel. 071/636-4804.

Elysée is for *Never on Sunday* devotees who like the reverberations of bouzouki and the smashing of plates. The domain of the Karegeorgis family, it offers hearty fun at moderate tabs. You can dance nightly to the music by Greek musicians. At two different intervals (last one at 1am) a cabaret is provided, highlighted by an altogether amusing act of balancing wine glasses (I'd hate to pay the breakage bill). You can book a table on either the ground floor or the second floor, but the Roof Garden is a magnet in summer. The food is good too, including the house specialty, the classic moussaka, and the kebabs from the charcoal grill. A complete meal with wine costs £30 ($45), and there is a £3 ($4.50) cover charge. Open Monday through Saturday from 7pm to 2:45am. Tube: Goodge Street or Tottenham Court Road.

Gay Bars

BRIEF ENCOUNTER, 41 St. Martin's Lane, WC2. Tel. 071/240-2221.

This aptly named place that stands across from the Duke of York's Theatre is in the very heart of West End theaterland. In fact, it's the most frequented West End gay pub. Bars are on two levels, but even so it's hard to find room to stand up, much less drink. Some men are in jeans, leather, or whatever, whereas others are dressed in business suits from their stockbroker jobs in The City. Lager begins at £1.72 ($2.60). Open Monday through Saturday from 11am to 11pm and on Sunday from 7 to 10:30pm. Tube: Leicester Square or Charing Cross.

COLEHERNE, 261 Old Brompton Rd., SW5. Tel. 071/373-9859.

This denim-and-leather bar must be featured in every gay guide to Europe ever written, and consequently it's often jammed. Lunch and afternoon tea are served upstairs. Lager starts at £1.72 ($2.60). Open Monday through Saturday 11am to 11pm, and on Sunday from noon to 3pm and 7 to 10:30pm. Tube: Earl's Court.

THE DUKE OF WELLINGTON, 119 Balls Point Rd., N1. Tel. 071/249-3729.

The most popular lesbian bar in London, this pub was originally built in the late 19th century. The "Women's Room," an inner sanctum with art deco lighting, has a bar and pool table—there is an outer bar also open to gay men. Pints of lager start at £1.70 ($2.60) and vegetarian snacks, at £2 ($3). Live bands perform every Friday and Saturday, and many special events are often staged here (check the local gay press for details). The outer bar is open Monday to Friday from 6pm to midnight, Saturday 3pm to midnight, and Sunday 7 to 10:30pm. The inner bar is open Monday to Saturday 8pm to midnight, and Sunday 7 to 10:30pm. Tube: Highbury.

HALFWAY TO HEAVEN, 7 Duncannon St., WC2. Tel. 071/930-8312.

Contained in century-old premises whose beamed ceiling evokes something out of a novel by Charles Dickens, this is perhaps the most popular and least frenetic gay bar in the Trafalgar Square neighborhood. Most clients wear jackets and ties, perhaps dropping in after work for a pint of ale and some conversation before setting off for their evening's activities. Lager from £1.72 ($2.60). Open Monday through Saturday from 3 to 11pm and on Sunday from 7:30 to 10:30pm. Tube: Charing Cross or Embankment.

MORE ENTERTAINMENT
CASINOS

London was a gambling metropolis long before anyone had ever heard of Monte Carlo and when "pre-Bugsy" Las Vegas was an anonymous sandpile in the desert.

Queen Victoria's reign changed all that, as usual by jumping to the other extreme. For more than a century, games of chance were so rigorously outlawed that no bartender dared to keep a dice cup on the counter.

However, according to the 1960 "Betting and Gaming Act," gambling was again permitted in "bona fide clubs" by members and their guests.

There are at least 25 of them in the West End alone, with many more scattered throughout the suburbs. But I cannot make specific recommendations. Under a new law, casinos aren't allowed to advertise, which in this context would mean appearing in a guidebook. It isn't illegal to gamble, only to advertise a gambling establishment. Most hall porters can tell you where you can gamble in London.

You will be required to become a member of your chosen club, and in addition you must wait 24 hours before you can play at the tables . . . and then strictly for cash. The most common games are roulette, blackjack, punto banco, and baccarat.

MOVIES

MGM CINEMA, Panton St., off Leicester Sq., SW1. Tel. 071/930-0631.

This streamlined, black-and-white block houses four superb theaters under one roof. They share one sleekly plush lobby, but each runs a separate program, always including at least one European film, along with the latest releases, often from the United States. Tube: Leicester Square or Piccadilly Circus.

Admission: Tickets, £2.50 ($3.80) all day Mon; £3.50 ($5.30) Tues–Fri before 6pm, otherwise £5 ($7.50).

NATIONAL FILM THEATRE, South Bank, Waterloo, SE1. Tel. 071/928-3232.

This cinema is in the South Bank complex. More than 2,000 films a year from all over the world are shown here, including features, shorts, animation, and documentaries. Tube: Waterloo.

Admission: 40p (60¢) daily membership, £4.35 ($6.50) screenings with membership.

ODEON LEICESTER SQUARE AND ODEON MEZZANINE, Leicester Sq., SW1. Tel. 0426/915-683.

The Odeon is another major London film theater, with one main screen and a mezzanine complex comprising another five screens. All screens feature the latest international releases. Tube: Leicester Square.

Admission: Tickets, £6.50–£9 ($9.80–$13.50).

MUSEUM OF THE MOVING IMAGE [MOMI], underneath Waterloo Bridge, SE1. Tel. 071/401-2636.

MOMI is also part of the South Bank complex. Tracing the history of the development of cinema and television, it takes the visitor on an incredible journey from cinema's earliest experiments to modern animation, from Charlie Chaplin to the operation of a TV studio. There are artifacts to handle, buttons to push, and a cast of actors to tell visitors more. Allow 2 hours for a visit. Open daily from 10am to 6pm. Tube: Waterloo.

Admission: £5.50 ($8.30) adults, £4 ($6) children, £16 ($24) family ticket.

STRIP SHOWS

Soho has many strip shows, sometimes two in one building. Along Frith Street, Greek Street, Old Compton Street, Brewer Street, Windmill Street, Dean and Wardour Streets, and the little courts and alleys in between, the disrobing establishments jostle cheek by jowl. Big ones and small ones, fancy and dingy, elaborate and primitive, they all sport outsize photos of the inside attractions, gloriously exotic names, and bellowing speakers to draw your attention.

RAYMOND REVUEBAR, Walker's Court, Brewer St., W1. Tel. 071/734-1593.

The Revuebar dates from 1958. Proprietor Paul Raymond is considered the doyen of strip society and his young, beautiful, hand-picked strippers are among the best in Europe. This strip theater occupies the much-restored premises of a Victorian dance hall, with a decor of flaming red velvet. There are two bars, which allow clients to take their drinks to their seats. Whisky costs £3 ($4.50) for a large measure. The club presents two shows nightly: at 8 and 10pm. Tube: Piccadilly Circus.

Admission: £17 ($25.50).

STORK CLUB, 99 Regent St., W1. Tel. 071/734-3686.

This first-class nightclub incorporates good food, a Las Vegas–style cabaret with a lineup of attractive dancers who don't believe in overdressing, and an ambience noted for its good taste and theatrical flair. Located near the corner of Swallow Street in the upscale heart of Mayfair, it welcomes diners and drinkers to a royal blue-and-peach–colored decor of art deco inspiration. Two shows are staged nightly, one at 11:30pm, another at 1am. Foreign visitors don't have to go through the tedium of obtaining membership. Clients who don't want dinner can sit at the bar and pay a £10 ($15) cover charge to see the show. Drinks begin at £4 ($6). Open Monday through Saturday from 8:30pm to 3:30am. Tube: Piccadilly Circus.

Admission: 3-course dinner and show, £35 ($52.50).

CHAPTER 8

WINDSOR & OXFORD

1. WINDSOR
- **WHAT'S SPECIAL ABOUT WINDSOR & OXFORD**

2. ASCOT

3. HENLEY-ON-THAMES

4. OXFORD

5. WOODSTOCK (BLENHEIM PALACE)

The historical Thames Valley and Chiltern Hills lie so close to London that they can easily be reached by automobile, train, or Green Line coach. In fact, you can explore here during the day and return to London in time to see a West End show.

The most-visited historic site in England is Windsor Castle, 21 miles west of London, one of the most famous castles in Europe and the most popular day trip for visitors venturing out of London for the first time.

Certainly your principal reason for visiting Oxfordshire is to explore the university city of Oxford, about an hour's ride from London by car or train. But Oxford is not the only attraction in the county; the shire is a land of great mansions, old churches of widely varying architectural styles, and rolling farmland.

In a sense, Oxfordshire is a kind of buffer zone between the easy living in the southern towns and the industrialized cities of the heartland. Southeast are the chalky Chilterns, and in the west you'll be moving toward the wool towns of the Cotswolds. The Upper Thames winds its way across the southern parts of the country.

SEEING WINDSOR & OXFORD
A SUGGESTED ITINERARY

Day 1: Explore Windsor and its castle and visit Eton College across the bridge.

Day 2: Either still based in London or from a hotel in Oxford, explore the major colleges of this university city.

1. WINDSOR

21 miles W of London

GETTING THERE   By Train   The train from Waterloo or Paddington Station in London (tel. 071/262-6767) does the trip in 30 minutes. More than a dozen trains per day make the run, costing £4 ($6) for a same-day round-trip.

By Bus   Green Line coaches (tel. 071/668-7261) no. 704 and 705 from Hyde Park Corner in London take about 1½ hours. A same-day round-trip costs £3.80 ($5.70).

By Car   Take the M4 west from London.

ESSENTIALS   The **telephone area code** is 0753. A **Tourist Information Centre** is in the Central Station, Thames Street (tel. 0753/852010), the railway station at the top of the hill, opposite the castle. There is also an information booth in the tourist center at Windsor Coach Park.

WHAT'S SPECIAL ABOUT WINDSOR & OXFORD

Great Towns/Villages
- [ ] Oxford, one of the world's greatest universities and a seat of learning since the 12th century.
- [ ] Windsor, site of the castle founded by William the Conqueror (ca. 1070), the world's largest inhabited castle.
- [ ] Henley-on-Thames, a small town and resort at the foothills of the Chilterns, famed for its High Street and Royal Regatta.

Castles
- [ ] Windsor Castle, steeped in royal associations, where the royal family spends Christmas.

- [ ] Blenheim Palace, majestic palace of the Duke of Marlborough at Woodstock, with decorative work by Grinling Gibbons. Churchill was born here.

Architectural Highlights
- [ ] St. George's Chapel, Windsor Castle, a notable example of Perpendicular architecture and rich vaulting, with several royal tombs.
- [ ] New College, Oxford, founded in 1379 by William of Wykeham; its initial quadrangle formed the architectural design for the other colleges.

Windsor, the site of England's greatest castle and its most famous boys' school, was called "Windlesore" by the ancient Britons, who derived the name from winding shore—so noticeable as you walk along the Thames here.

WHAT TO SEE & DO

The bus will drop you near the Town Guildhall, to which Wren applied the finishing touches. It's only a short walk up Castle Hill to the top sights.

CASTLE SIGHTS

WINDSOR CASTLE, Castle Hill. Tel. 831118.

When William the Conqueror ordered a castle built on this spot, he began a legend and a link with English sovereignty that has known many vicissitudes: King John cooled his heels at Windsor while waiting to put his signature on the Magna Carta at nearby Runnymede; Charles I was imprisoned here before losing his head; Queen Bess did some renovations; Victoria mourned her beloved Albert, who died at the castle in 1861; the royal family rode out much of World War II behind its sheltering walls; and when Queen Elizabeth II is in residence, the royal standard flies.

The apartments contain many works of art, porcelain, armor, furniture, three Verrio ceilings, and several 17th-century Gibbons carvings. Several Rubens adorn the King's Drawing Room and in his relatively small dressing room is a Dürer, along with Rembrandt's portrait of his mother, and Van Dyck's triple portrait of Charles I. Of the apartments, the grand reception room, with its Gobelin tapestries, is the most spectacular.

In November 1992, a fire swept through part of Windsor Castle, severely damaging it. It has since reopened, but naturally until restoration is complete visitors aren't able to see all the rooms they did before.

The Windsor changing of the guard is a much more exciting and moving experience, in my opinion, than the London exercises. In Windsor when the court is in residence, the guard marches through the town, stopping the traffic as it wheels into the castle to the tune of a full regimental band; when the queen is not there, a drum-and-pipe band is mustered. From May to August, the ceremony takes place Monday through Saturday at 11am. In winter, the guard is changed every 48 hours Monday through Saturday, so call the number listed above to find out which days the ceremony will take place. In fact, it's always advisable to call ahead and check what's open before visiting. The castle is in the town center.

Admission: £4.20 ($6.30) adults, £1.60 ($2.40) children.

Open: Jan–Feb and Nov–Dec, daily 10:30am–3pm; Mar and Oct, daily 10:30am–4pm; Apr–Sept, daily 10:30am–5pm. Ticket sales cease about 30 minutes before closing; last admissions are 15 minutes before closing. **Closed:** Periods in Apr, June, and Dec when the royal family is in residence.

QUEEN MARY'S DOLLS' HOUSE, Windsor Castle. Tel. 831118.

A palace in perfect miniature, the Dolls' House was given to Queen Mary in 1923 as a symbol of national goodwill. The house, designed by Sir Edwin Lutyens, was created on a scale of 1 to 12. It took 3 years to complete and involved the work of 1,500 tradesmen and artists. Every item is a miniature masterpiece; each room is exquisitely furnished, and every item is made exactly to scale. Working elevators stop on every floor, and there is running water in all five bathrooms. There is electric lighting throughout the house.

Admission: £1.60 ($2.40) adults, 80p ($1.25) children.

Open: Same as Windsor Castle (see above).

⭐ ST. GEORGE'S CHAPEL, The Cloisters, Windsor Castle. Tel. 865538.

A gem of the Perpendicular style, this chapel shares the distinction with Westminster Abbey of being a pantheon of English monarchs (Victoria is a notable exception). The present St. George's was founded in the late 15th century by Edward IV on the site of the original Chapel of the Order of the Garter (Edward III, 1348). You first enter the nave, which has fan vaulting (a remarkable achievement in English architecture) and contains the tomb of George V and Queen Mary, designed by Sir William Reid Dick. Off the nave in the Urswick Chapel, the Princess Charlotte memorial provides an ironic touch; if she had survived childbirth in 1817, she—and not her cousin, Victoria—would have ruled the British Empire. In the aisle are the tombs of George VI and Edward IV. The Edward IV "Quire," with its imaginatively carved 15th-century choir stalls (crowned by lacy canopies and Knights of the Garter banners), evokes the pomp and pageantry of medieval days. In the center is a flat tomb, containing the vault of the beheaded Charles I, along with Henry VIII and his third wife, Jane Seymour. Finally, you may want to inspect the Prince Albert Memorial Chapel, reflecting the opulent tastes of the Victorian era.

Historical note: Queen Victoria died on January 22, 1901, and was buried beside her beloved Prince Albert in a mausoleum at **Frogmore** (a private estate), a mile from Windsor (open only August 5 to September 27, daily from 11am to 5pm). The prince consort died in December 1861. Call 483/211-535 for more details.

Admission: £3 ($4.50) adults, £1.80 ($2.70) children.

Open: Mon–Sat 10am–4pm, Sun 2–3:45 or 4pm (call first to check hours). **Closed:** During services, Jan, and a few days in mid-June.

THE ROYAL MEWS, St. Albans St., Tel. 868286.

The red-brick buildings of the Royal Mews and Burford House were built for Nell Gwynne in the 1670s and were named for King Charles II's natural son by her, the Earl of Burford. When the child was 14 years old, he was created Duke of St. Albans, from which the street outside takes its name.

Housed in the mews is the exhibition of the Queen's Presents and Royal Carriages. Displayed are pictures of several members of the royal family, including those of Queen Elizabeth II as Colonel-in-Chief of the Coldstream Guards riding in the grounds of Buckingham Palace, the Duke of Edinburgh driving his horses through a water obstacle at Windsor, and the Queen Mother with Prince Edward, Viscount Linley, and Lady Sarah Armstrong-Jones in the Scottish State Coach. There is also a full-size stable with model horses showing stable kit, harnesses, and riding equipment. A magnificent display of coaches and carriages kept in mint condition and in frequent use is in the coach house. The exhibition of the Queen's Presents includes unique items of interest given to Her Majesty and the Duke of Edinburgh throughout her reign. There is also a collection of pencil drawings of the queen and family with horses and dogs. The mews is just outside entrance to the castle.

Admission: £1.60 ($2.40) adults, 80p ($1.25) children.

Open: Nov–Mar, Mon–Sat 10:30am–3pm; Apr–Oct, Mon–Sat 10:30am–5pm (plus Mar–Oct, Sun 10:30am–3pm).

OTHER SIGHTS

The **town** of Windsor is largely Victorian, with lots of brick buildings and a few remnants of Georgian architecture. In and around the castle are two cobblestone streets, Church and Market, which have antiques shops, silversmiths, and pubs. One shop on Church Street was supposedly occupied by Nell Gwynne, who needed to be within call of Charles II's chambers. After lunch or tea, you may want to stroll along the 3-mile, aptly named Long Walk.

On Sunday, there are often polo matches in **Windsor Great Park**—and at Ham Common—and you may see Prince Charles playing and Prince Philip serving as umpire. The queen often watches. The queen goes riding in the park and on Sunday attends a little church near the Royal Lodge. Traditionally, she prefers to drive herself there, later returning to the castle for Sunday lunch. For more information, call 860633.

The famous company founded by Madame Tussaud in 1802 has taken over part of the Windsor and Eton Central Railway Station on Thames Street (tel. 857837) to present an exhibition of **"Queen Victoria's Diamond Jubilee 1837–1897."** At one of the station platforms is a replica of *The Queen,* the engine used to draw the royal coaches; disembarking are the life-size wax figures of guests arriving at Windsor for the Jubilee celebration. Seated in the Royal Waiting Room are Queen Victoria and her family. In one of the carriages, the Day Saloon, are Grand Duke Serge and the Grand Duchess Elizabeth (the queen's granddaughter) of Russia. Waiting in the anteroom is the queen's faithful Indian servant, Hafiz Abdul Karim, the Munshi. Among the famous guests portrayed are the Prince and Princess of Wales (Edward VII and Alexandra), the Empress Frederick of Prussia (Queen Victoria's eldest daughter), and the prime minister, Lord Salisbury. The platform is busy with royal servants, a flower seller, a newsboy, an Italian with a barrel organ, and others who have come to see the arrival of the train. Drawn up on the ceremonial parade ground are the troops of the Coldstream Guards and the horse-drawn carriage that would take the party to the castle. With the sound of military bands in the background and the voices of officers commanding their troops, you really feel you are present for Her Majesty's arrival.

The entire visit takes about 45 minutes. The exhibition is open daily from 9:30am to 5:30pm (closed Christmas Day). Admission is £4.50 ($6.80) for adults, £3.50 ($5.30) for children.

TOURS

BUS TOURS   Guide Friday runs the best bus tours in Windsor, carefully tailored on a "come and go as you please" basis which is enormously appealing. Tours depart 7 days a week between 10:45am and 4:40pm opposite the main entrance to Windsor Castle on Castle Hill. Tours run only between March 15 and late October daily. For reservations and information, call 855755 in Windsor.

Tours cover a distance of 9 miles, and incorporate the best sights of Windsor, Eton, and Datchet (Datchet is a charming English village 4 miles east of Windsor, which lies at the end of a road loaded with sights and history). Tours are conducted in open-top buses, and if no one gets off the bus, the tour takes an hour. However, tours are designed to allow visitors to get on and off at their whim, along any stage of the way, so the tour can become a half-day outing.

Tours cost £5 ($7.50) for adults, £1.50 ($2.30) for children 5 to 11, free for children under 5. No credit cards.

BOAT TOURS Tours depart from the main embarkation point along The Promenade, Barry Avenue, for a 35-minute ride to Boveney Lock. The cost is £1.90 ($2.90) for adults and half price for children. However, you can also take a 2-hour tour through the Boveney Lock and up past stately private riverside homes, the Bray Film Studios, Queens Eyot, and Monkey Island, all for a cost of £4.20 ($6.30) for adults and half price for children. Finally, you can take a 35-minute tour from Runnymede on board the *Lucy Fisher,* a replica of a Victorian paddle steamer. You pass Magna Carta Island, among other sights. The cost is £1.90 ($2.90) for adults and half price for children. In addition, a range of longer tours is also offered. The boats offer light refreshments and have a licensed bar. The decks are covered in case of an unexpected shower. Tours are operated by **French Brothers Ltd.,** Clewer Boathouse, Clewer Court Rd., Windsor (tel. 0753/851900).

WHERE TO STAY

You may choose to make Windsor your base for London sightseeing. Trains leave London as late as 10:30 or 11pm, so it's quite easy to take in an early theater and dinner before returning to Windsor for overnight. *Warning:* During the Ascot races and Windsor Horse Show, reservations are necessary far in advance.

EXPENSIVE

THE CASTLE HOTEL, High St., Windsor, Berkshire SL4 1LJ. Tel. 0573/ 851011, or toll free 800/435-4542 in the U.S. Fax 0753/830244. 102 rms, 1 suite. TV TEL

$ Rates: £95 ($142.50) single; £140 ($210) double; from £155 ($232.50) suite. Breakfast £9.50 ($14.30) extra. AE, DC, MC, V. **Parking:** £6.50 ($9.80).

Near Windsor Castle, on the main street, is this solid and long-established hotel with a dignified Georgian facade. It was originally built in the 15th century to shelter the hundreds of workers laboring on the town's foundations and the royal buildings. By the 17th century it had changed its name from the Mermaid to the Castle and benefited from the heavy stagecoach traffic that often deposited visitors at its doorstep. In 1986 the entourage of the royal family of Spain was housed in 17 of its best rooms; Princess Anne has dropped in for breakfast; and the Duke of Edinburgh has been a guest speaker at functions. Centuries ago the grounds in back of the hotel served as the stable yard for Windsor Castle, but now they support a modern bedroom wing.

SIR CHRISTOPHER WREN'S HOUSE HOTEL, Thames St., Windsor, Berkshire SL4 1PX. Tel. 0753/861354. Fax 0753/860172. 38 rms, 2 suites. TV TEL

$ Rates: £89 ($133.50) single; £114 ($171) double; from £124 ($186) suite. Breakfast £9.50 ($14.30) extra. AE, DC, MC, V. **Parking:** £5 ($7.50).

★ Designed by Christopher Wren in 1676 as his own home, this former town house, between Eton and Windsor, just a 3-minute walk from the castle, occupies a prime position on the Thames, its gardens overlooking swans and boats. The central hall is impressive, with a Queen Anne black marble refectory table. Wren's white-paneled former study contains his Empire desk, a fireplace, and shield-back Hepplewhite chairs. The bay-windowed main drawing room, decorated with mirrors, sconces, and a formal marble fireplace, opens into a garden and a riverside flagstone terrace for after-dinner coffee and drinks. Some of the bedrooms have fine old furniture, and all are equipped with trouser presses. Several overlook the river. Room 2, which was Sir Christopher Wren's bedroom, is said to be haunted. Open to nonresidents, the hotel restaurant, the Orangerie, is recommended below.

MODERATE

ROYAL ADELAIDE HOTEL, 46 Kings Rd., Windsor, Berkshire SL4 2AG. Tel. 0753/863916. Fax 0753/830682. 42 rms (all with bath). TV TEL
$ Rates (including English breakfast): £50 ($75) single; £60 ($90) double. AE, DC, MC, V. **Parking:** Free.
This interesting Georgian building is opposite the famous Long Walk leading to Windsor Castle, 5 minutes away. It was named for Queen Adelaide who visited the premises during her reign, thereby dubbing it "royal." All the well-furnished bedrooms, which vary in size, have radios, alarm clocks, and hot-beverage facilities. A fixed-price dinner is available at £15.25 ($22.90) for three courses. The cuisine is both English and French.

YE HARTE & GARTER HOTEL, 31 High St., Windsor, Berkshire SL4 1LR. Tel. 0753/863426. Fax 0753/830527. 50 rms (43 with bath). TV TEL
$ Rates (including English breakfast): £30 ($45) single without bath, £45 ($62.50) single with bath; £70 ($105) double with bath. AE, DC, MC, V.
On Castle Hill opposite Windsor Castle, the old Garter Inn, named for the Knights of the Garter, was the setting for scenes in Shakespeare's *Merry Wives of Windsor*. The Garter burned down in the 1800s and was rebuilt as part of one hostelry that included the Hart. From the front bedrooms you can watch the guards marching up the High Street every morning on their way to change the guard at the castle. The rooms contain trouser presses, hot-beverage equipment, and other amenities. You can dine in the Apéritif Restaurant or have a drink in the café.

A NEARBY PLACE TO STAY

THE OAKLEY COURT HOTEL, Windsor Rd., Water Oakley, Windsor, Berkshire SL4 5UR. Tel. 0628/74141. Fax 0628/37011. 92 rms (all with bath), 11 suites. MINIBAR TV TEL **Directions:** Take the river road, the A308, 3 miles from Windsor toward Maidenhead.
$ Rates: £125–£150 ($187.50–$225) single; £145–£175 ($217.50–$262.50) double; from £245 ($367.50) suite. English breakfast £11.50 ($17.30) extra. AE, DC, MC, V. **Parking:** Free.
★ On the A308 between Windsor and Maidenhead this attractive riverside hotel is about 20 minutes from Heathrow. The Gothic house with its turrets and chimneys is where the reception, the living rooms, and the restaurants are located. One modern wing of bedrooms extends from the old house; another, built beside the river, is a 30-foot walk from the main building. The rooms in the old house have high ceilings, interesting shapes, and big baths, and one still has the original paneling. In the two modern wings, the rooms are of generous size and have baths. There is 24-hour room service.
At Oakley Court's Oakleaf Restaurant, you can enjoy terrine de homard et turbot (terrine of lobster and turbot encased in spinach and served with a mint-and-honey

cream) and suprême de volaille blanquette (breast of chicken stuffed with a chicken mousse, prunes, and orange zest, served with a cream and white wine sauce). A fixed-price lunch costs £18.75 ($28.10), and a fixed-price dinner goes for £29 ($43.50). If you order à la carte, expect to pay £50 ($75) and up. The culinary expertise of the chef has made this a popular dining spot, with such notables as Prince Charles and Prince Philip among the customers. Open daily: for lunch from 12:30 to 2:15pm and for dinner from 7:30 to 10:15pm. Another less formal restaurant, the Boaters, is much less expensive, offering main courses that begin at £5 ($7.50).

WHERE TO DINE

Many visitors prefer to dine in Eton across the bridge. The well-heeled gourmet will patronize the Oakley Court Hotel (see above), which has the best cuisine in the Greater Windsor area.

EXPENSIVE

THE ORANGERIE, at Sir Christopher Wren's House Hotel, Thames St. Tel. 861354.
   Cuisine: CONTINENTAL. **Reservations:** Not required.
$ Prices: Appetizers £1.75–£5.75 ($2.60–$8.60); main courses £4.95–£12.95 ($7.40–$19.40). AE, DC, MC, V.
   Open: Lunch Sun–Fri noon–2pm; dinner daily 7–10:30pm.
Already recommended as a hotel, this location, a 3-minute walk from the castle, boasts the most elegant and charming restaurant in Windsor, with garden terraces and a conservatory. The dining room is designed a bit like a greenhouse, with cabriole-legged furniture, lots of chintz, and views of the garden through tall French windows. At dinner a pianist entertains. Specialties include salmon filet (poached with a tomato and tarragon cream sauce), or strips of beef filet in a horseradish and peppercorn sauce. In summer, guests can dine in the garden on an Italian terrace beside the Thames.

EASY EXCURSIONS

ETON

To visit Eton, home of what is arguably the most famous public school (Americans would call it a private school) in the world, you can take a train from Paddington Station, go by car, or take the Green Line bus to Windsor. By car, take the M4 motorway to Exit 5 to go straight to Eton. However, parking is likely to be a problem, so I advise turning off the M4 at Exit 6 to Windsor; you can park there and take an easy stroll past Windsor Castle and across the Thames bridge. Follow Eton High Street to the college. (From Windsor Castle's ramparts, you can look down on the river and on the famous playing fields of Eton.)

What to See and Do

Eton College (tel. 671177) was founded by an adolescent boy himself, Henry VI, in 1440. Some of England's greatest men, notably the Duke of Wellington, have played on these fields. Twenty prime ministers were educated here, as well as such literary figures as George Orwell, Aldous Huxley, and Ian Fleming. If it's open, take a look at the Perpendicular chapel, with its 15th-century paintings and reconstructed fan vaulting.

The history of Eton College since its inception in 1440 is depicted in the **Museum of Eton Life,** Eton College (tel. 671177), located in vaulted wine cellars under College Hall, which were originally the storehouse for use of the college's masters. The displays, ranging from formal to extremely informal, include a turn-of-the-century boy's room, school books, sports trophies, canes used by senior boys to apply punishment they felt needful to their juniors, and birch sticks used by masters for the same purpose. Also to be seen are letters written home by students describing day-to-day life at the school, as well as samples of the numerous magazines produced by students over the centuries, known as ephemera because of the changing writers and ideas. Many of the items to be seen were provided by Old Etonians.

Admission to the school and museum, including guided tours, costs £3 ($4.50) for adults, £2.50 ($3.80) for children. The college is open from Easter to September, daily from 2 to 4:30pm (during the summer holidays from 10:30am to 5pm); guided tours are given at 2:15 and 3:15pm. Call the above number for the museum's hours—they're based on the school year and vary widely.

Where to Dine

ANTICO, 42 High St. Tel. 863977.

Cuisine: ITALIAN. **Reservations:** Strongly recommended.

$ Prices: Appetizers £3.50–£9.30 ($5.30–$14); main courses £8.50–£14 ($12.80–$21). AE, DC, MC, V.

Open: Lunch Mon–Fri noon–2:30pm; dinner Mon–Sat 7–10:30pm. **Closed:** Bank holidays.

This is a first-rate Italian restaurant, so go to a fast-food chain for pizza. People have been dining here for 200 years, although not from an Italian menu. In a traditional English setting, dating from 1787, and decorated with artifacts of bygone days, the restaurant has definitely turned to the Mediterranean for its cuisine. On your way to the tiny bar you pass a cold table, displaying an array of hors d'oeuvres, fresh fish, and cold meats. There is a wide choice of fish dishes, such as grilled fresh sardines, sole Colbert, or sole with mushrooms, capers, and prawns. Beef filet is a favorite dish. Desserts from the trolley are offered.

ETON WINE BAR, 82–83 High St. Tel. 854921.

Cuisine: FRENCH/ENGLISH/CONTINENTAL. **Reservations:** Recommended.

$ Prices: Appetizers £2.50–£3.95 ($3.80–$5.90); main courses £5.25–£8.50 ($7.90–$12.80); 2-course fixed-price menu £8.95 ($13.40); 3-course fixed-price menu £11.50 ($17.30). MC, V.

Open: Lunch Mon–Fri noon–3pm, Sat–Sun noon–2pm; dinner Mon–Thurs 6–10:30pm, Fri 6–11pm, Sat–Sun 6–10pm.

Just across the bridge from Windsor, this charming place set on the main street among the antiques shops has pinewood tables and old church pews and chairs, and there's a glassed-in conservatory out back. You might begin with one of the well-prepared soups, or Cumbrian air-dried ham with melon, perhaps one of several different salads, including warm goat's cheese. Main dishes include English beef pie and either a vegetarian lasagne or vegetarian risotto. Wine can be ordered by the glass.

HOUSE ON THE BRIDGE, 71 High St. Tel. 860914.

Cuisine: ENGLISH/INTERNATIONAL. **Reservations:** Recommended.

$ Prices: Appetizers £3.25–£24.50 ($4.90–$36.80); main courses £11.50–£16.95 ($17.30–$25.40). AE, DC, MC, V.

Open: Lunch daily noon–2:30pm; dinner daily 6–11pm.

This restaurant is charmingly contained in a red-brick and terra-cotta Victorian house, set adjacent to the bridge, beside the river at the edge of Eton. Near the handful of outdoor tables is an almost vertical garden whose plants cascade into the Thames. Some of the well-prepared main dishes are crispy duckling with calvados and Seville oranges, chicken suprême flavored with tarragon and served with mushrooms, and chateaubriand. Some specialties such as roast rack of herb-flavored lamb are served only for two diners. Desserts, such as flambées or crêpes Suzette, are elaborate concoctions.

SAVILL GARDEN

Savill Garden, Wick Lane, Englefield Green, Egham, Surrey (tel. 860222), is in Windsor Great Park and is signposted from Windsor, Egham, and Ascot. Started in 1932, the 35-acre garden is considered one of the finest of its type in the northern hemisphere. The display starts in spring with rhododendrons, camellias, and daffodils beneath the trees; then throughout the summer there are spectacular displays of flowers and shrubs presented in a natural and wild state. It's open all year (except at Christmas) from 10am to 6 or 7pm; admission is £3 ($4.50) for adults, free for children under 16. It's located 5 miles from Windsor along the A30; turn off at Wick Road and follow the signs to the gardens. The nearest rail station is at Egham; from there you'll need to take a taxi a distance of 3 miles. There's a licensed, self-service restaurant on the premises.

Adjoining the Savill Garden are the **Valley Gardens,** full of shrubs and trees in a series of wooded natural valleys running down to the water. It's open daily throughout the year. Entrance to the gardens is free, although the car parking costs £2 ($3) per vehicle.

2. ASCOT

28 miles W of London

GETTING THERE   By Train   Trains travel between Waterloo in London and Ascot Station, which is about 10 minutes from the racecourse. Service is about every 30 minutes during the day (trip time: 30 min.).

By Bus   Frequent buses depart throughout the day from Victoria Coach Station in London.

By Car   From Windsor, take the A332 for a 13-minute drive.

ESSENTIALS   The **telephone area code** is 0344.

While following the royal buckhounds through Windsor Forest, Queen Anne decided to have a racecourse on Ascot Heath. The first race meeting at Ascot, which is directly south of Windsor at the southern end of Windsor Great Park, was inaugurated in 1711. Since then, the Ascot Racecourse has been a symbol of high society as pictures of the royal family, including the queen and Prince Philip, have been flashed around the world. Nowadays instead of Queen Anne, you are likely to see Princess Anne, an avid horsewoman.

The ✪ **Ascot Racecourse,** High Street (tel. 22211), the largest racecourse in the United Kingdom, is open from September to July. There are three enclosures: Tattersalls is the largest, Silver Ring the least expensive, and the third is the Members Enclosure. There are bars and restaurants to suit everybody's taste. Tickets cost £3 to

£20 ($4.50 to $30) for adults; children under 16 are admitted free if accompanied by an adult. The highlight of the Ascot social season—complete with fancy hats and white gloves—is Royal Week in late June, but there is excellent racing on the fourth Saturday in July and the last Saturday in September, with more than a million pounds in prize money.

Advance booking for the grandstand and paddock opens on January 1 every year. Write for tickets to the Secretary, Grandstand, Ascot Racecourse, Ascot, Berkshire SL5 7JN. For admission to the Royal Enclosure, write to Her Majesty's Representative, Ascot Office, St. James's Palace, London SW1 (tel. 071/930-9882). First-timers have a difficult time being admitted to the Royal Enclosure, as their application must be endorsed by someone who has been admitted to the Royal Enclosure at least eight times before.

WHERE TO STAY & DINE

VERY EXPENSIVE

THE ROYAL BERKSHIRE, London Rd., Sunninghill, Ascot, Berkshire SL5 OPP. Tel. 0344/23322, or toll free 800/445-8667 in the U.S. Fax 0344/27100. 75 rms, 6 suites. TV TEL **Directions:** Take the A322 2 miles northeast of Ascot.
$ Rates: £105 ($157.50) single; £145 ($217.50) double; from £215 ($322.50) suite. Breakfast £11.50 ($17.30) extra. AE, DC, MC, V. **Parking:** Free.

The interior of this elegant hotel does justice to its history. Built of russet-colored bricks in the Queen Anne style in 1705, it housed the Churchill family for many years. Harmonious color schemes and well-chosen furnishings set a stylish tone in the bedrooms, which are divided between the main house and an annex that is also furnished in good taste and with style. Many people visit only for a meal in the Stateroom Restaurant, overlooking the lawns and gardens of the hotel. The food, some of the finest in the area, is made with quality ingredients, often reflecting artistic flair. Set luncheons are featured for both £12.95 ($19.40) and £19.95 ($29.90). There's a good à la carte menu that changes frequently and offers a range of contemporary English dishes. Meals are served daily from 12:30 to 2:30pm and 7:15 to 9:30pm.

EXPENSIVE

BERYSTEDE COUNTRY HOUSE HOTEL, Bagshot Rd., Sunninghill, Ascot, Berkshire SL5 9JH. Tel. 0344/23311. Fax 0344/872301. 91 rms, 1 suite. TV TEL **Directions:** Take the A330 1½ miles south of Ascot.
$ Rates: £95 ($142.50) single; £120 ($180) double; from £180 ($270) suite. Breakfast £10.50 ($15.80) extra. AE, DC, MC, V. **Parking:** Free.
This hotel is a Victorian fantasy of medieval towers, half-timbering, steeply pitched roofs, and a landscaped garden. The entrance hall incorporates a huge stone fireplace that, if the weather's cool enough, might be blazing. Bedrooms, with their high ceilings and chintz, evoke the aura of a private country house. The suite boasts mahogany reproductions of 18th-century antiques. Fixed-price lunches cost £16.50 ($24.80); fixed-price dinners, £20 ($30).

MODERATE

BROCKENHURST, Brockenhurst Rd., South Ascot, Berkshire SL5 9HA. Tel. 0344/21912. Fax 0344/873252. 11 rms (all with bath). TV TEL

$ Rates (including continental breakfast): £65–£85 ($97.50–$127.50) single; £75–£100 ($112.50–$150) double. AE, DC, MC, V. **Parking:** Free.

A small, tactfully improved Edwardian hotel of charm and distinction, Brockenhurst is conveniently located near shops and the train station. The most expensive rooms are called "executive," and include whirlpool baths, trouser presses, and hairdryers. The hotel has a bar and offers a room-service menu. The owners serve mainly a French cuisine, and, if given 24 hours' notice, will try to prepare a meal of your choice, costing £20 ($30) and up.

---

3. HENLEY-ON-THAMES

35 miles W of London

GETTING THERE   By Train   Trains depart from London's Paddington Station but require a change at the junction in Twyford. More than 20 trains make the journey daily, requiring about 54 minutes to an hour for the total trip.

By Bus   About 10 buses depart every day from London's Victoria Coach Station for Henley. Although no changes or transfers are required, bus travel is actually slower (about 1¾ hr.) than the train because of the multiple stops along the way.

By Car   From London, take the M4 toward Reading, cutting northwest onto the A423.

ESSENTIALS   The **telephone area code** is 0491. A summer-only **Tourist Information Centre** is at Town Hall, Market Place (tel. 0491/578034).

SPECIAL EVENTS   The **Henley Royal Regatta** (July 1–5) is one of the premier racing events of England. If you want a closeup view from the Stewards' Enclosure, you'll need a guest badge, which is obtainable through a member only. In other words, you have to know someone, but admission to Regatta Enclosure is open to all. Information is available from the Secretary, Henley Royal Regatta, Henley-on-Thames, Oxfordshire RG9 2LY (tel. 0491/572153).

At the eastern edge of Oxfordshire, Henley-on-Thames, a small town and resort on the river at the foothills of the Chilterns, is the headquarters of the Royal Regatta held annually in late June and early July. The regatta is the number-one event among European oarsmen and dates back to the first years of the reign of Victoria.

The Elizabethan buildings, the tearooms, and the inns along the town's High Street live up to one's conception of what an English country town should look like. Cardinal Wolsey is said to have ordered the building of the tower of the Perpendicular and Decorated parish church.

Henley-on-Thames makes for an excellent stopover en route to Oxford. However, readers on the most limited of budgets will appreciate the much less expensive lodgings in Oxford; the fashionable inns of Henley-on-Thames (Charles I slept here) are far from cheap.

WHERE TO STAY & DINE

During the Royal Regatta, rooms are difficult to secure unless you've made reservations months in advance.

RED LION HOTEL, Hart St., Henley-on-Thames, Oxfordshire RG9 2AR.
Tel. 0491/572161. Fax 0491/410039. 26 rms (22 with bath or shower). TV
TEL
$ Rates: £43 ($64.50) single without bath, £70 ($105) single with bath; £83
($124.50) double with bath, £95 ($142.50) deluxe double with bath. Breakfast £8
($12) extra. AE, MC, V. **Parking:** Free.

This 16th-century ivy-covered, red-brick coaching inn near Henley Bridge used to
keep a bedchamber ready for the Duke of Marlborough, who would stop on his way
to Blenheim. The guest list reads like a hall of fame—Johnson and Boswell, and even
George IV, who, it is said, consumed 14 mutton chops one night. Most of the
well-furnished bedrooms overlook the Thames. The hotel also offers laundry service.

The last dinner is served at 10pm, but 24-hour room service is provided. Guests
congregate in the low-beamed lounge and take meals in the Riverside Restaurant,
where a three-course table d'hôte dinner costs £25.50 ($38.30).

EASY EXCURSIONS

MAPLEDURHAM HOUSE ON THE THAMES The Elizabethan mansion home
of the Blount family (tel. 0734/723350) lies beside the Thames in the unspoiled
village of Mapledurham and can be reached by car from the A4074 Oxford-Reading
road. A much more romantic way of reaching the lovely old house is to take the boat
that leaves the promenade next to Caversham Bridge at 2pm on Saturday, Sunday, and
bank holidays from Easter through September. The journey upstream takes about 40
minutes, and the boat leaves Mapledurham again at 5pm for the journey back to
Caversham. This gives you plenty of time to walk through the house and see the
Elizabethan ceilings and the great oak staircase, as well as the portraits of the two
beautiful sisters with whom the poet Alexander Pope, a frequent visitor here, fell in
love. The family chapel, built in 1789, is a fine example of modern Gothic
architecture. Cream teas with homemade cakes are available at the house, costing
£2.50 ($3.80). On the grounds, the last working watermill on the Thames still
produces flour.

The house is open Easter to September, on Saturday, Sunday, and public holidays
from 2:30 to 5pm; the entrance charge is £3 ($4.50) for adults, £1.50 ($2.30) for
children 5 to 14. The mill is open only from Easter to September on Saturday, Sunday,
and public holidays from 1:30 to 5pm; admission is £2.50 ($3.80) for adults, £1.25
($1.90) for children.

The round-trip boat ride from Caversham costs £3.80 ($5.70) for adults, half price
for children. Further details about the boat can be obtained from **D & T Scenics
Ltd.,** Pipers Island, Bridge Street, Caversham Bridge, Reading (tel. 0734/481088).

THE WELLINGTON DUCAL ESTATE This trip to **Stratfield Saye House,**
Stratfield Saye, Reading, Berkshire RG7 2BT (tel. 0256/882882), 7 miles south of
Reading on the A33 to Basingstoke, takes you a little farther afield. It has been the
home of the dukes of Wellington since 1817, when the 17th-century house was
bought for the Iron Duke to celebrate his victory over Napoléon at the Battle of
Waterloo. Many memories of the first duke remain in the house, including his billiard
table, battle spoils, and pictures. The funeral carriage that since 1860 had rested in St.
Paul's Cathedral crypt is now in the ducal collection. In the gardens is the grave of
Copenhagen, the charger ridden to battle at Waterloo by the first duke. There are also
extensive pleasure grounds together with a licensed restaurant and gift shop.

A short drive away is the **Wellington Country Park** (tel. 0734/326444) with a
National Dairy Museum, where you can see relics of 150 years of dairying. Other
attractions include a riding school, nature trails, and boating and sailing on the lake. In
addition, there are a miniature steam railway, the Thames Valley Time Trail, and a
deer park.

Stratfield Saye is open from May to the last Sunday in September, Saturday through Thursday from 11:30am to 4pm. Admission is £4 ($6) for adults and £2.85 ($4.30) for children. Wellington Country Park is open March to September, daily from 10am to 5pm. Admission is £2.85 ($4.30) for adults, £1.35 ($2) for children. A combined ticket for the house and park costs £6 ($9) for adults, £3.50 ($5.30) for children.

4. OXFORD

54 miles NW of London, 54 miles S of Coventry

GETTING THERE   By Train   Trains from Paddington Station (tel. 071/262-6767) reach Oxford in 1¼ hours. Service is every hour. A cheap same-day round-trip ticket costs £13.20 ($19.80).

By Bus   Oxford City Link provides coach services from London's Victoria Coach Station (tel. 071/730-0202) to the Oxford Bus Station. Three buses per hour make the 1½-hour trip at a round-trip cost of £6.50 ($9.80).

By Car   Take the M40 west from London and just follow the signs.

ORIENTATION   Park & Ride   Traffic and parking are a disaster in Oxford, and not just during rush hours. However, there are three large parking lots on the north, south, and west of the city's ring road, all well marked. Parking is free at all times, but at any time from 9:30am on, and all day on Saturday, you pay about 75p ($1.15) for a bus ride into the city, which drops you off at St. Aldate's or Queen Street to see the city center. The buses run every 8 to 10 minutes in each direction. There is no service on Sunday. The parking lots are on the Woodstock road near the Peartree traffic circle, on the Botley road toward Farringdon, on the Abingdon road in the southeast, and on the A40 toward London.

Information   The **telephone area code** is 0865. The **Oxford Information Centre** is at St. Aldate's Chambers, St. Aldate's, opposite the town hall, near Carfax (tel. 0865/726871).

Tours and Tourist Services   The best way to get a running commentary on the important sightseeing attractions is to go to the **Oxford Information Centre,** St. Aldate's Chambers, St. Aldate's, opposite the town hall, near Carfax (tel. 0865/726871). Two-hour walking tours through the city and the major colleges leave daily in the morning and afternoon and cost £3.20 ($4.80) adults, £1 ($1.50) children; the tours do not include New College or Christ Church. The center sells a comprehensive range of maps, brochures, souvenir items, as well as the famous Oxford University T-shirt. It's open Monday through Saturday from 9:30am to 5pm and on Sunday from 10am to 3:30pm.

A walk down the long sweep of The High, one of the most striking streets in England; a mug of cider in one of the old student pubs; the sound of a May Day dawn when choristers sing in Latin from Magdalen Tower; the Great Tom bell from Tom Tower, whose 101 peals traditionally signal the closing of the college gates; towers and spires rising majestically; the barges on the upper reaches of the Thames; nude swimming at Parson's Pleasure; the roar of a cannon launching the bumping races; a tiny, dusty bookstall where you can pick up a valuable first edition. All that is

Oxford—home of one of the greatest universities in the world, and also an industrial center of a large automobile business.

At any time of the year you can enjoy a tour of the colleges, many of which represent a peak in England's architectural kingdom, as well as a valley of Victorian contributions. The Oxford Information Centre (see above) offers guided walking tours daily throughout the year. Just don't mention the other place (Cambridge) and you shouldn't have any trouble.

The city predates the university—in fact, it was a Saxon town in the early part of the 10th century. By the 12th century, Oxford was growing in reputation as a seat of learning, at the expense of Paris, and the first colleges were founded in the 13th century. The story of Oxford is filled with conflicts too complex and detailed to elaborate here. Suffice it to say, the relationship between town and gown wasn't as peaceful as it is today. Riots often flared, and both sides were guilty of abuses. Nowadays, the young people of Oxford take out their aggressiveness in sporting competitions.

Ultimately, the test of a great university lies in the caliber of the people it turns out. Oxford can name-drop a mouthful: Roger Bacon, Sir Walter Raleigh, John Donne, Sir Christopher Wren, Samuel Johnson, Edward Gibbon, William Penn, John Wesley, William Pitt, Matthew Arnold, Lewis Carroll, Arnold Toynbee, Harold Macmillan, Graham Greene, A. E. Housman, T. E. Lawrence, and many others.

Many Americans arriving in Oxford ask: "Where's the campus?" If a local shows amusement when answering, it's because Oxford University is, in fact, made up of 35 colleges. To tour all of these would be a formidable task. Besides, a few are of such interest that they overshadow the rest.

WHAT TO SEE & DO

SEEING THE UNIVERSITY

A Word of Warning The main business of a university, is, of course, to educate—and this function at Oxford has been severely interfered with by the number of visitors who disturb the academic work of the university. So, unfortunately, visiting is restricted to certain hours and small groups of six or fewer. In addition, there are areas where visitors are not allowed at all, but the tourist office will be happy to advise you when and where you may "take in" the sights of this great institution.

AN OVERVIEW For a bird's-eye view of the city and colleges, climb **Carfax Tower** at Carfax. This is the one with the clock and figures that stroke the hours. Carfax is the tower that remains from St. Martin's Church, where William Shakespeare once stood as godfather for William Davenant, who also became a playwright. A church stood on this spot from 1032 until 1896. The tower used to be higher, but after 1340 it was lowered, following complaints to Edward III that townspeople threw stones and fired arrows from it during town-and-gown disputes. Admission is 80p ($1.25) for adults, 40p (60¢) for children. The tower is open from late March to late October, Monday through Saturday from 10am to 6pm and on Sunday from 2 to 6pm. For information, call 726871.

The **Oxford Story,** 6 Broad St. (tel. 790055), helps the visitor to understand the complexities of Oxford University. Insight into the structure of the colleges and a look at some of the architectural and historical features that might otherwise be missed are highlighted. Visitors are also filled in on the general background of the colleges and the deeds of some of the famous people who have passed through its portals. The audiovisual presentation is given daily, with an admission charge of £4.25 ($6.40) for adults and £2.95 ($4.40) for children. Open April to June, September, and October, daily from 9:30am to 5pm; in July and August, daily from 9:30am to 7pm; and November to March, daily from 10am to 4pm.

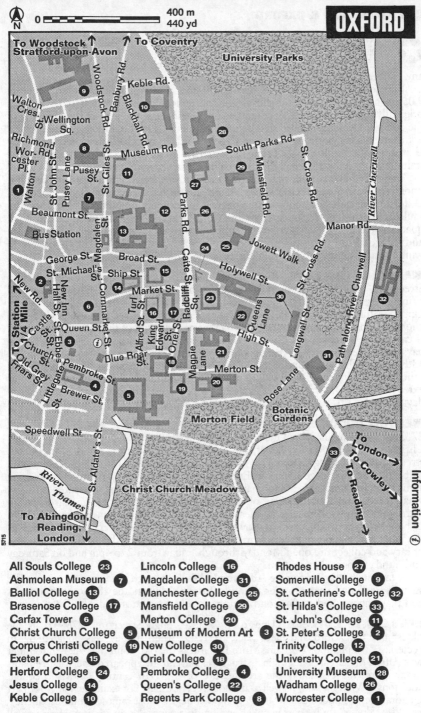

OXFORD

All Souls College ㉓	Lincoln College ⑯	Rhodes House ㉗
Ashmolean Museum ⑦	Magdalen College ㉛	Somerville College ⑨
Balliol College ⑬	Manchester College ㉕	St. Catherine's College ㉜
Brasenose College ⑰	Mansfield College ㉙	St. Hilda's College ㉝
Carfax Tower ⑥	Merton College ⑳	St. John's College ⑪
Christ Church College ⑤	Museum of Modern Art ③	St. Peter's College ②
Corpus Christi College ⑲	New College ㉚	Trinity College ⑫
Exeter College ⑮	Oriel College ⑱	University College ㉑
Hertford College ㉔	Pembroke College ④	University Museum ㉘
Jesus College ⑭	Queen's College ㉒	Wadham College ㉖
Keble College ⑩	Regents Park College ⑧	Worcester College ①

✪ **CHRIST CHURCH** Begun by Cardinal Wolsey as Cardinal College in 1525, Christ Church (tel. 276499), known as the House, was founded by Henry VIII in 1546. Facing St. Aldate's Street, Christ Church has the largest quadrangle of any college in Oxford.

Tom Tower houses Great Tom, the 18,000-pound bell referred to earlier. It rings at 9:05pm nightly, signaling the closing of the college gates. The 101 times it peals originally signified the number of students in residence at the time of the founding of the college. The student body number changed, but Oxford traditions live on forever. Some interesting portraits are in the 16th-century great hall, including works by Gainsborough and Reynolds. Prime ministers are pictured, as Christ Church was the training ground for 13 prime ministers. There is a separate picture gallery.

The cathedral was built over a period of centuries, beginning in the 12th century. (Incidentally, it's not only the college chapel, but also the cathedral of the diocese of Oxford.) The cathedral's most distinguishing features are its Norman pillars and the vaulting of the choir, dating from the 15th century. In the center of the great quadrangle is a statue of Mercury mounted in the center of a fish pond. The college and cathedral can be visited from 9:30am to 6pm in summer, 9:30am to 4:30pm in winter. Entrance fee is £1.50 ($2.30) for adults, 50p (75¢) for children.

MAGDALEN COLLEGE Pronounced "*maud*-lin," Magdalen College, High Street (tel. 276000), was founded in 1458 by William of Waynflete, bishop of Winchester and later chancellor of England. Its alumni range from Wolsey to Wilde. Opposite the botanic garden, the oldest in England, is the bell tower, where the choristers sing in Latin at dawn on May Day. The reflection of the 15th-century tower is cast in the waters of the Cherwell below. On a not-so-happy day, Charles I—his days numbered—watched the oncoming Roundheads from this tower. Visit the 15th-century chapel, in spite of many of its latter-day trappings. Ask when the hall and other places of special interest are open. The grounds of Magdalen are the most extensive of any Oxford college; there's even a deer park. You can visit Magdalen each day from 2 to 6:15pm. Admission is £1.25 ($1.90) in summer; free otherwise.

MERTON COLLEGE Founded in 1264, Merton College, Merton Street (tel. 276310), is among the trio of the most ancient at the university. It stands near Corpus Christi College on Merton Street, the sole survivor of Oxford's medieval cobbled streets. Merton College is noted for its library, built between 1371 and 1379 and said to be the oldest college library in England. There was once a tradition of keeping some of its most valuable books chained. Now only one book is so secured, to show what the custom was like. One of the treasures of the library is an astrolabe (an astronomical instrument used for measuring the altitude of the sun and stars) thought to have belonged to Chaucer. You pay £1 ($1.50) to visit the ancient library, as well as the Max Beerbohm Room (the satirical English caricaturist who died in 1956). The library and college are open Monday through Friday from 2 to 4pm and on Saturday and Sunday from 10am to 4pm.

A favorite pastime is to take **Addison's Walk** through the water meadows. The stroll is so named after a former alumnus, Joseph Addison, the 18th-century essayist and playwright noted for his contributions to *The Spectator* and *The Tatler*.

UNIVERSITY COLLEGE University College, High Street (tel. 276602), is the oldest one at Oxford and dates back to 1249, when money was donated by an ecclesiastic, William of Durham. More fanciful is the old claim that the real founder was Alfred the Great. The original structures have all disappeared and what remains today represents essentially the architecture of the 17th century, with subsequent additions in Victoria's day as well as in more recent times. For example, the Goodhart Quadrangle was added as late as 1962. The college's most famous alumnus, Shelley, was "sent down" for his part in collaborating on a pamphlet on atheism. However, all is forgiven today, as the romantic poet is honored by a memorial erected in 1894. The hall and chapel of University College can be visited daily during vacations from 2 to 4pm for a charge of £1.25 ($1.90) for adults, 50p (75¢) for children.

NEW COLLEGE   New College, New College Lane, off Queen's Lane (tel. 279555), was founded in 1379 by William of Wykeham, bishop of Winchester and later lord chancellor of England. His college at Winchester supplied a constant stream of students. The first quadrangle, dating from before the end of the 14th century, was the initial quadrangle to be built in Oxford and formed the architectural design for the other colleges. In the antechapel is Sir Jacob Epstein's remarkable modern sculpture of *Lazarus* and a fine El Greco painting of St. James. One of the treasures of the college is a crosier (pastoral staff of a bishop) belonging to the founding father. In the garden, you can see the remains of the old city wall and the mound. The college (entered at New College Lane) can be visited in July through September, daily from 11am to 5pm. In winter, hours are daily from 2 to 5pm. Admission is £1 ($1.50) from July to September; free off-season.

A LOCAL SPORT — PUNTING

At **Punt Station,** Cherwell Boathouse, Bardwell Road (tel. 515978), you can rent a punt for £5 ($7.50) per hour, plus a £25 ($37.50) deposit. Similar charges are made on rentals at Magdalen Bridge Boathouse and at the Folly Bridge Boathouse. Hours are 10am to 10pm daily, June to September.

SHOPPING

An arcade of first-class shops and boutiques, the **Golden Cross** lies between Cornmarket Street and the Covered Market (or between High Street and Market Street). Parts of the arcade date from the 12th century. Many buildings remain from the medieval era, along with some 15th- and 17th-century structures. The market also has a reputation as the Covent Garden of Oxford, where live entertainment takes place on Saturday mornings in summer. In the arcade shops you'll find a wide selection of merchandise, including handmade Belgian chocolates, specialty gifts, clothing for both women and men, and luxury leather goods.

WHERE TO STAY

Accommodations in Oxford are limited, although the addition of motels on the outskirts has aided the plight of those who require modern amenities. Recently, some of the more stalwart candidates in the city center have been refurbished. In addition, motorists may want to consider country houses or small B&Bs on the outskirts of town, which offer the best living in Oxford if you don't mind commuting.

Oxford Information Centre, St. Aldate's Chambers, St. Aldate's (tel. 0865/ 726871), operates a year-round room-booking service for a fee of £2.50 ($3.80) and an 8% refundable deposit. If you'd like to seek lodgings on your own, the staff at the center will provide, for a fee, a list of accommodations, maps, and guidebooks.

EXPENSIVE

OLD PARSONAGE HOTEL, 1 Banbury Rd., Oxford OX2 6NN. Tel. 0865/ 310210. Fax 0865/311362. 30 rms, 4 suites. MINIBAR TV TEL **Bus:** 7.
$ Rates (including English breakfast): £95 ($142.50) single; £115–£140 ($172.50–$210) double; from £190 ($285) suite. AE, MC, V. **Parking:** Free.

This massively renovated hotel near St. Giles Church and Keble College is so old (1660) it looks like an extension of one of the ancient colleges. Originally a 13th-century hospital named Bethleen, it was restored in the early 17th century. Oscar Wilde once lived here for a time and is famed for a remark "Either this wallpaper goes, or I do." In the 20th century a modern wing was added, and in 1990 it was completely done over and made into a luxurious hotel. Bedrooms are individually designed, with such amenities as remote-control radio and hairdryer. The marble bathrooms are air-conditioned, with their own phone extensions. All the suites and some bedrooms have sofa beds. Bedrooms open onto the private gardens, and 10 bedrooms are on the ground floor. The Parsonage Bar serves everything from cappuccino to mixed drinks. Here in lieu of a restaurant you can order from a well-prepared menu of continental and English food from 7am until "late at night." There is also 24-hour room service.

OXFORD MOAT HOUSE, Godstow Rd., Wolvercote Roundabout, Oxford, Oxfordshire OX2 8AL. Tel. 0865/59933. Fax 0865/310259. 155 rms, 4 suites. TV TEL **Bus:** 60.

$ Rates (including English breakfast): £87 ($130.50) single; £105 ($157.50) double; from £175 ($262.50) suite. AE, DC, MC, V. **Parking:** Free. **Closed:** Dec 24–Jan 2.

One of the Queens Moat Houses Group, incorporating the principles of motel design, with an emphasis on spacious, glassed-in areas and streamlined bedrooms. Its position, at the northern edge of Oxford 2 miles away, is hidden from the traffic at the junction of the A40 and the A34. It is generally patronized by motorists. Each room contains a radio, video, trouser press, and hot-beverage equipment. The Moat House has a swimming pool, squash courts, a whirlpool bath, a sauna, a solarium, and a snooker (billiards) room. Its Oxford Blue Restaurant serves an English menu, with a table d'hôte dinner reasonably priced at £18 ($27).

RANDOLPH HOTEL, Beaumont St., Oxford, Oxfordshire OX1 2LN. Tel. 0865/247481, or toll free 800/435-4542 in the U.S. Fax 0865/791678. 109 rms, 8 suites. TV TEL **Bus:** 7.

$ Rates: £115 ($172.50) single; £140 ($210) double; from £155 ($232.50) suite. Breakfast £11.50 ($17.30) extra. AE, DC, MC, V. **Parking:** Free.

For more than a century the Randolph has been overlooking St. Giles, the Ashmolean Museum, and the Cornmarket. The lounges, although modernized, are still cavernous enough for dozens of separate conversational groupings. The furnishings are contemporary, and all rooms have private bath.

The hotel's Spires Restaurant presents both a time-tested English and a modern cuisine in a high-ceilinged Victorian dining room. An à la carte dinner costs about £35 ($52.50) per person, while a fixed-price dinner goes for £32.50 ($48.80). The restaurant serves daily: lunch from 12:30 to 2pm and dinner from 7 to 10pm. There is also a coffee shop with an entrance off the street, serving from 10am to 6pm daily. The hotel's Chapters Bar has a tradition-laden atmosphere. The drink list offers everything from "textbook classics" to "epilogue."

MODERATE

COTSWOLD LODGE HOTEL, 66A Banbury Rd., Oxford, Oxfordshire OX2 6JP. Tel. 0865/512121. Fax 0865/512490. 52 rms (all with bath). TV TEL **Directions:** See below.

$ Rates (including English breakfast): £79.50 ($119.30) single; £102.50 ($153.80) double. AE, DC, MC, V. **Parking:** Free.

A 19th-century building set on a wide avenue lined with stately trees, the Cotswold Lodge is about a mile east of the town center. In the older section, a scattering of units have flowered wallpaper and some Victoriana. English and French lunches and dinners are served in the hotel's restaurant daily from noon to 2:30pm and 6:30 to 10:30pm.

To get here, leave the M40 at Junction 8 for Oxford and follow the A40; about a mile after passing through a set of traffic lights at the Park & Ride car park, you come to a large traffic circle; turn left here, signposted SUMMERTOWN CITY CENTRE. This is

Banbury Road; the hotel is about 2 miles down on the left-hand side, on the corner of Norham Road and Banbury Road.

EASTGATE HOTEL, 23 Merton St., The High, Oxford, Oxfordshire OX1 4HE. Tel. 0865/248244, or toll free 800/435-4542 in the U.S. Fax 0865/141681. 43 rms (all with bath), 1 suite. TV TEL **Bus:** 7.

$ Rates: £93 ($139.50) single; £110 ($165) double; from £130 ($195) suite. Breakfast £8.50 ($12.80) extra. AE, DC, MC, V. **Parking:** Free.

The Eastgate stands opposite the ancient Examination Halls, within walking distance of Oxford colleges and the city center. Recently refurbished, it offers modern facilities while retaining somewhat the atmosphere of an English country house. All rooms have radios, as well as tea and coffee makers. The Shires Restaurant offers a selection of roasts and traditional English fare, complemented by a choice of wines. A three-course table d'hôte dinner is priced at £15.50 ($23.30).

ROYAL OXFORD HOTEL, Park End St., Oxford, Oxfordshire OX1 1HR. Tel. 0865/248432. Fax 0865/250049. 25 rms (12 with bath). TV TEL

$ Rates: £60 ($90) single without bath, £85 ($127.50) single with bath; £80 ($120) double without bath, £100 ($150) double with bath. Breakfast £8.50 ($12.80) extra. AE, DC, MC, V.

Built in 1933, the Royal Oxford Hotel has been given a new lease on life by a renovation of its interior. Near Oxford Station, about a 10-minute walk from the center of the city, it is a comfortable and convenient place at which to stay. The bedrooms are well kept, with modern, compact furnishings. Ask about "weekend breaks" when booking.

WELCOME LODGE, Peartree Roundabout, Woodstock Rd., Oxford, Oxfordshire OX2 8JZ. Tel. 0865/54301, or toll free 800/435-4542 in the U.S. Fax 0865/513474. 95 rms (all with bath). TV TEL **Bus:** Park & Ride bus (blue and white), with frequent trips from downtown Oxford to a public parking lot nearby.

$ Rates (including English breakfast): £54 ($81) single Mon–Thurs, £36.50 ($54.80) Fri–Sun; £65.50 ($98.30) double Mon–Thurs, £38 ($57) Fri–Sun. AE, DC, MC, V. **Parking:** Free.

Located 3 miles north of Oxford, near the beginning of the A34 highway leading away from town, this large commercial hotel is suitable for motorists who want to be within easy reach of the university and the shopping districts of Oxford. Easy to spot, near a large bus stop, the lodge invites with international flags fluttering in the breezes. Its lower-level bedrooms open onto private terraces. The furnishings are in the typical motel style, with compact, built-in necessities. Each room has a picture-window wall, radio, individually controlled heating, and tea-making facilities. Special rooms for nonsmokers are also offered. On the grounds are a swimming pool (summer only), the Lodgekeepers Restaurant and bar, the Little Chef Grill, the Granary Self-Service Restaurant, and a family shop.

INEXPENSIVE

From Friday through Sunday night the **Welcome Lodge** (recommended above) becomes a budget-priced hotel—and it contains 95 rooms.

ADAMS GUEST HOUSE, 302 Banbury Rd., Oxford, Oxfordshire OX2 7ED. Tel. 0865/56118. 6 rms (all with shower). TV **Bus:** 7, 20, 21, or 22.

$ Rates (including English breakfast): £22–£26 ($33–$39) single; £32–£40 ($48–$60) double. No credit cards.

 In Summertown, 1¼ miles from Oxford, is the Adams Guest House, operated by John Strange, and one of the best B&Bs in the northern Oxford area. The comfortable and cozy rooms have hot and cold running water and private showers. Breakfast is served in a dining room decorated in an old-world style. Mr.

Strange will provide touring tips. A bus runs every few minutes to the city center. The Adams Guest House is located opposite the Midland Bank, and in its neighborhood are seven restaurants, shops, a post office, a swimming pool, a cycle-rental shop, and a launderette.

DIAL HOUSE, 25 London Rd., Headington, Oxford, Oxfordshire OX3 7RE. Tel. 0865/69944. 8 rms (all with bath). TV **Bus:** 7, 7A, 20, 21, or 22. **$ Rates:** £35–£40 ($52.50–$60) single; £45–£50 ($67.50–$75) double. No credit cards. **Parking:** Free.

Two miles east of the heart of Oxford, beside the main highway leading to London, this country-style house was originally built between 1924 and 1927. Graced with mock Tudor half-timbering and a prominent blue-faced sundial (from which it derives its name), it contains cozy and recently renovated bedrooms, each of which has tea-making facilities and hairdryers. No smoking is permitted in the bedrooms, although smoking is allowed in a small guest lounge. The owners, Julie and Tony Lamb, serve only breakfast in their bright dining room.

NEARBY PLACES TO STAY

WESTON MANOR, Weston-on-the-Green, Oxfordshire OX6 8QL. Tel. 0869/50621. Fax 0869/50901. 34 rms (all with bath or shower), 3 suites. MINIBAR TV TEL **Directions:** Take the A43 8 miles from Oxford toward Northampton. **$ Rates** (including English breakfast): £80–£85 ($120–$127.50) single; £105–£110 ($157.50–$165) double; from £125 ($187.50) suite. AE, DC, MC, V. **Parking:** Free.

Ideal as a center for touring the district (Blenheim Palace is only 5 miles away), the manor, owned and run by the Osborn family, has existed since the 11th century; portions of the present building date from the 14th and 16th centuries. The estate was an abbey until abbeys were abolished by Henry VIII. Of course, there are ghosts: Mad Maude, the naughty nun who was burned at the stake for her "indecent and immoral" behavior, returns to haunt the Oak Bedrooms. Prince Rupert, during the English Civil War, hid from Cromwell's soldiers in one of the fireplaces, eventually escaping in drag as the "maiden of the milk bucket."

As you enter the driveway, you pass two elm trees dating back to 1672 on your way to the parking area. The reception lounge is dominated by a Tudor fireplace and a long refectory table. Most of the bedrooms are spacious, furnished with antiques (often four-posters), old dressing tables, and chests. The Great Hall is one of the most beautiful dining rooms in England, with an open-rafter and beamed ceiling, the lower portion solidly paneled with a rare example of linenfold. There's a minstrels' gallery and a large wrought-iron chandelier. The English food is first rate. A la carte meals average £25 ($37.50), and the big Sunday lunch costs £17.50 ($26.30). In warm weather, you can enjoy an open-air swimming pool surrounded by gardens.

STUDLEY PRIORY HOTEL, Main St., Horton-cum-Studley, Oxfordshire OX9 1AZ. Tel. 0865/351203. Fax 0865/351613. 18 rms (all with bath or shower), 1 suite. TV TEL **Directions:** See below. **$ Rates** (including English breakfast): £88 ($132) single; £150 ($225) double; from £210 ($315) suite. AE, DC, MC, V. **Parking:** Free.

The Studley Priory Hotel may be remembered by those who saw the movie *A Man for All Seasons*. The former Benedictine priory, a hotel since 1961, was used for background shots for the private residence of Sir Thomas More. It's a stunning example of Elizabethan architecture, although it originally dates from the 12th century. Located on 13 acres of wooded grounds and occupied for around 300 years by the Croke family, the manor is only 7 miles from Oxford. It is built of stone in the manorial style, with large halls and long bedroom wings and gable with mullioned windows. The rooms are large and the furnishings tasteful. Room service is provided all day, as is laundry service. Even if you're not staying over, you may want to visit for lunch or dinner, with a four-course, rather sophisticated meal averaging around £21.50 ($32.30).

Getting here is a bit complicated—so be armed with a good map when you strike out from Oxford. From Oxford, travel to the end of Banbury Road. At the traffic circle take the third exit (toward London). Travel approximately 3½ miles. At the next traffic circle, take the first exit (signposted Horton-cum-Studley) and travel 4½ miles. Go through the estate and stay on the same road till you come to "staggered crossroads." Go straight across, signposted Horton-cum-Studley 2½ miles. This road will bring you straight into the village, and the hotel is at the top of the hill on the right-hand side.

WHERE TO DINE
VERY EXPENSIVE

LE MANOIR AUX QUAT' SAISONS, Great Milton, Oxfordshire OX9 7PD. Tel. 0844/278881.

Cuisine: FRENCH. **Reservations:** Required. **Directions:** Take Exit 7 off the M40 and head along the A329 toward Wallingford; look carefully for signs about a mile later.

$ Prices: Appetizers £16–£25 ($24–$37.50); main courses £25.50–£30 ($38.30–$45); lunch *menu du jour* £29.50 ($44.30); lunch or dinner *menu gourmand* £59.50 ($89.30). AE, DC, MC, V.

Open: Lunch daily 12:15–2:30pm; dinner daily 7:15–10:30pm.

Some 12 miles southeast of Oxford, Le Manoir aux Quat' Saisons enjoys a reputation for offering the finest cuisine in the Midlands. The gray- and honey-colored stone manor house was originally built by a Norman nobleman in the early 1300s, and over the years attracted many famous visitors. The connection with France has been masterfully revived by the Gallic owner and chef, Raymond Blanc. His reputation for comfort and cuisine attracts guests from as far away as London—gastronomes who regard the 1-hour trek as a delicious excuse for a day in the country.

The main focus of the establishment is a pair of beamed-ceiling dining rooms whose mullioned windows offer views of the garden. You can enjoy such specialties as a soup of Cornish lobster with cumin, a mousse of asparagus with chervil sauce, zucchini flowers stuffed with a sabayon of wild mushrooms, veal cutlet with truffles, breast of wild duck with pear and apples, and scallops poached with herbs. After-dinner coffee is served beside the fire in the lounge. If you call, an employee will provide travel directions.

The gabled house was built in the 1500s and improved and enlarged in 1908. An outdoor swimming pool, still in use, was added much later. Inside, 19 luxurious bedrooms, each decorated boudoir style with lots of flowery draperies, ruffled canopies, radio, color TV, phone, private bath, springtime colors, and high-quality antique reproductions, cost £165 to £375 ($247.50 to $562.50), double occupancy.

EXPENSIVE

BATH PLACE HOTEL, 4–5 Bath Place, at Holywell St., Oxford OX1 3SU. Tel. 0865/791812.

Cuisine: ENGLISH. **Reservations:** Required. **Bus:** 7.

$ Prices: Appetizers £3.50–£6 ($5.30–$9); main courses £12.50–£17 ($18.80–$25.50); 3-course fixed-price lunch £14.50 ($21.80); 4-course fixed-price dinner £24.50 ($36.80). AE, DC, MC, V.

Open: Lunch Tues–Sun noon–2pm; dinner Tues–Sat 7–10:30pm.

Well-known to Oxonians, the Bath Place Hotel, off Holywell Street, is a discovery for foreigners. It is like a French *restaurant avec chambres,* serving tasty continental meals. Most people seek out these 17th-century, converted cottages for the excellent restaurant run by the Fawsitt family. Bath Place was launched in 1989, and has won a devoted following. The menu reflects the availability of seasonal produce: breast of young guinea fowl poached in marsala and served with spring vegetables or braised Dublin Bay prawns served on a bed of young spinach leaves with light leek-butter sauce.

Even though the food is the main attraction, there are 10 accommodations on the premises, each with bath or shower. B&B charges range from £70 to £80 ($105 to $120) daily in a single, £84 to £100 ($126 to $150) in a double. Rooms have TVs and phones.

15 NORTH PARADE, 15 North Parade. Tel. 513773.
Cuisine: INTERNATIONAL. **Reservations:** Not required. **Bus:** 7.
$ Prices: Appetizers £4–£7.75 ($6–$11.60); main courses £10.50–£16.50 ($15.80–$24.80); fixed-price meals £14.75 ($22.10) at lunch, £15.75 ($23.60) at dinner. MC, V.
Open: Lunch Mon–Sat noon–2pm, Sun noon–2pm; dinner Mon–Sat 7–10:30pm.

15 North Parade, located off Banbury Road, continues to win respect and praise from its patrons; the continental cookery here is first-rate. Wicker chairs, subtle lighting, and plenty of photos provide the proper background for the presentation of the ever-changing cuisine. You might begin with a fish soup (similar to what you'd be served in Nice), then follow with roast guinea fowl in a sherry sauce. Care also goes into the vegetables, such as the fresh, crisp-cooked French beans. Wines are reasonably priced for the most part.

RESTAURANT ELIZABETH, 84 St. Aldate's. Tel. 242230.
Cuisine: CONTINENTAL. **Reservations:** Required. **Bus:** 7.
$ Prices: Appetizers £3.50–£7.50 ($5.30–$11.30); main courses £10.50–£15 ($15.80–$22.50); fixed-price lunch £15.50 ($23.30). AE, DC, MC, V.
Open: Lunch Tues–Sun 12:30–2:30pm; dinner Tues–Sat 6:30–11pm, Sun 7–10:30pm.

This intimate, special restaurant, opposite Christ Church College, owes the inspiration of its cuisine to the Continent, notably Spain, France, and Greece. It attracts Oxonians who appreciate good food served in an inviting atmosphere. Try the pipérade, prawns with rice and aïoli, or salmon in a white wine sauce. The rack of lamb with gratin dauphinois and duck à l'orange are also excellent selections. Wine by the liter, both burgundy and Bordeaux, is available.

MODERATE

AL-SHAMI, 25 Walton Crescent. Tel. 310066.
Cuisine: LEBANESE. **Reservations:** Recommended. **Bus:** 7.
$ Prices: Appetizers £3.50–£6.50 ($5.30–$9.80); main courses £8.50–£12.50 ($12.80–$18.80). MC, V.
Open: Daily noon–midnight.

Ideal for meals all afternoon and late into the evening, this Lebanese restaurant has awakened the sleepy taste buds of Oxford. Before its opening, after the theater you were faced with only Chinese or Indian restaurants. Many diners rarely make it beyond the appetizers, as they consist of more than 35 delectable hot and cold selections, everything from falafels to a salad made with lamb's brains. Charcoal-grilled chopped lamb, chicken, or beef comprise most of the main-dish selections. In between selections, guests nibble on uncut raw vegetables such as fresh tomatoes. A dessert selection is made from the trolley. Vegetarian meals are also available.

CHERWELL BOATHOUSE RESTAURANT, Bardwell Rd. Tel. 391800.
   Cuisine: FRENCH. **Reservations:** Recommended. **Bus:** Banbury Rd. bus.
$ Prices: Main courses £8–£12 ($12–$18); fixed-price dinner from £15.75 ($23.60); Sun lunch £11.75 ($17.60). MC, V.
   Open: Lunch Sun 12:30–2pm; dinner daily 7:30–11:30pm. **Closed:** Dec 24–31.
This virtual Oxford landmark on the River Cherwell is owned by Anthony Verdin, who has the help of a young crew. A fixed-price menu is offered and the cooks change the menu every 2 weeks to take advantage of the availability of fresh vegetables, fish, and meat. Appetizers aren't served separately. There is a very reasonable, even exciting, wine list. If they don't order a full meal, children are charged half price. In summer, the restaurant also serves on the terrace. Before dinner, you can try "punting" on the Cherwell; punts are rented on the other side of the boathouse.

INEXPENSIVE

MUNCHY MUNCHY, 6 Park End St. Tel. 245710.
   Cuisine: SOUTHEAST ASIAN/INDONESIAN. **Reservations:** Required. **Bus:** 52.
$ Prices: Main courses £4.35–£6.85 ($6.50–$10.30). No credit cards.
   Open: Lunch Tues–Sat noon–2pm; dinner Tues–Sat 5:30–10pm. **Closed:** Jan, 3 weeks in Aug, 3 weeks in Dec.

 Some Oxford students, who frequent this location near the station, claim that this restaurant offers the best food value in the city. Main dishes depend on what's available in the marketplace, and appetizers are not offered. Ethel Ow is adept at herbs and seasoning, and often uses fresh fruit inventively, as reflected by such dishes as scallops sautéed with ginger and lamb with passion-fruit sauce. Indonesian and Malaysian dishes are popular. Sometimes, especially on Friday and Saturday, long lines form at the door. Children under 6 are not allowed on Friday and Saturday evenings.

SPECIAL PUBS

THE BEAR INN, Alfred St. Tel. 244680.
   Cuisine: ENGLISH. **Reservations:** Not accepted. **Bus:** 2A or 2B.
$ Prices: Snacks and bar meals £2.25–£4.50 ($3.40–$6.80). No credit cards.
   Open: Mon–Sat noon–11pm, Sun noon–3pm and 7–10:30pm.
A short block from The High, overlooking the north side of Christ Church College, this is the village pub and an Oxford tradition. Its swinging inn sign depicts the bear and ragged staff, old insignia of the earls of Warwick, who were among the early patrons. Built in the 13th century, the inn has been known to many famous people who have lived and studied at Oxford. Over the years it's been mentioned time and time again in English literature.

   The Bear has served a useful purpose in breaking down social barriers, bringing a wide variety of people together in a relaxed way. You might talk with a raja from India, a university don, a titled gentleman—and the latest in a line of owners that goes back more than 700 years. Some former owners developed an astonishing habit: clipping neckties. Around the lounge bar you'll see the remains of thousands of ties, which have been labeled with their owners' names. For those of you who want to leave a bit of yourself, a thin strip of the bottom of your tie will be cut off (with your permission, of course). After this initiation, you may want to join in some of the informal songfests of the undergraduates.

THE TROUT INN, 195 Godstow Rd., Wolvercote. Tel. 54485.
   Cuisine: ENGLISH. **Reservations:** Not required. **Bus:** 520 or 521 to Wolvercote; then walk.
$ Prices: Appetizers £2.05–£7.25 ($3.10–$10.90); main courses £10–£21.50

($15–$32.30); Sun barbecue grills £2.75–£5.50 ($4.10–$8.30); snacks £2.25–£5.75 ($3.40–$8.60). AE, DC, MC.
Open: Restaurant, lunch daily noon–2pm; dinner Mon–Sat 7–10pm, Sun barbecue 7–9:30pm. Pub, Mon–Fri 11am–3pm and 6–11pm, Sat 11am–11pm, Sun noon–3pm and 7–10:30pm.

Lying 2½ miles north of Oxford and hidden away from visitors and townspeople, the Trout is a private world where you can get ale and beer—and standard fare. Have your drink in one of the historic rooms, with their settles, brass, and old prints, or go out in sunny weather to sit on a stone wall. On the grounds are peacocks, ducks, swans, and herons that live in and around the river and an adjacent weir pool, that will join you if you're handing out crumbs. Take an arched stone bridge, stone terraces, architecture with wildly pitched roofs and gables, add the Thames River, and you have the Trout. The Stable Bar, the original 12th-century part, complements the inn's relatively new 16th-century bars. Daily specials are featured, and there is a cold snack bar. Hot meals are served all day in the restaurant; salads are served in summer, and there are grills in winter. On your way there and back, look for the view of Oxford from the bridge.

THE TURF TAVERN, 4 Bath Place, at Holywell St. Tel. 243235.
 Cuisine: ENGLISH. **Reservations:** Not accepted. **Bus:** 52.
$ Prices: Appetizers £1.30 ($2); salads £3.55 ($5.30); main dishes £4.85 ($7.30). No credit cards.
 Open: Mon–Sat 11am–11pm, Sun noon–3pm and 7–10:30pm.

This 13th-century tavern lies on a very narrow passageway in the area of the Bodleian Library. Thomas Hardy used the place as the setting of *Jude the Obscure*. It was "the local" of Burton and Taylor when they were in Oxford many years ago making a film, and today's patrons might include Kris Kristofferson or John Hurt, as well as a healthy sampling of the university's students and faculty. At night, the nearby old tower of New College and part of the old city wall are floodlit, and during warm weather you can select a table in any of the three separate gardens that radiate outward from the pub's central core. For wintertime warmth, braziers are lighted in the courtyard and in the gardens.

A separate food counter, set behind a glass case, displays the day's fare. (If you're hungry, present yourself to the employee behind the case, and carry your food back to your table.) Menu choices include salads, soups, sandwiches, and platters of such traditional dishes as English beef pie, roast chicken, lasagne, and mutton. Local ales (including one with a relatively high-alcohol content named Headbanger) are served, as well as a range of wines. The pub is reached via St. Helen's Passage, which stretches between Holywell Street and New College Lane. (You'll probably get lost, but any student worth his beer can direct you.)

5. WOODSTOCK (BLENHEIM PALACE)

8 miles N of Oxford, 63 miles NW of London

GETTING THERE   By Train   Take the train to Oxford (see above).

By Bus   The Gloucester Green bus (no. 20) leaves Oxford about every 30 minutes during the day (trip time: 36 min.). Call 0865/722333 for details.

By Car   Take the A44 from Oxford.

ESSENTIALS   The **telephone area code** is 0993. The **information office** is on Hensington Road (tel. 0993/811038).

The small country town of Woodstock, the birthplace in 1330 of the Black Prince, ill-fated son of King Edward III, lies on the edge of the Cotswolds. Some of the stone houses here were constructed when Woodstock was the site of a royal palace, which had so suffered the ravages of time that its remains were demolished when Blenheim Palace was built. Woodstock was once the seat of a flourishing glove industry.

BLENHEIM PALACE

This extravagant baroque palace regards itself as England's answer to Versailles. Blenheim is the home of the 11th Duke of Marlborough, a descendant of John Churchill, the first duke, an on-again, off-again favorite of Queen Anne's. In his day (1650–1722), the first duke became the supreme military figure in Europe. Fighting on the Danube near a village named Blenheim, Churchill defeated the forces of Louis XIV, and the lavish palace of Blenheim was built for the duke as a gift from the queen. It was designed by Sir John Vanbrugh, who was also the architect of Castle Howard; landscaping was carried out by Capability Brown.

The palace is loaded with riches: antiques, porcelain, oil paintings, tapestries, and chinoiserie. North Americans know Blenheim as the birthplace of Sir Winston Churchill. His birthroom forms part of the palace tour, as does the Churchill exhibition, four rooms of letters, books, photographs, and other relics. Today the former prime minister lies buried in Bladon Churchyard, near the palace.

Blenheim Palace (tel. 811091) is open from mid-March to October, daily from 10:30am to 4:45pm. Admission costs £6.30 ($9.50) for adults, £3.10 ($4.70) for children age 5 to 15.

WHERE TO STAY & DINE

THE BEAR HOTEL, Park St., Woodstock, Oxfordshire OX7 1SZ. Tel. 0993/811511, or toll free 800/435-4542 in the U.S. Fax 0993/813380. 41 rms (all with bath), 4 suites. TV TEL

$ Rates: £90–£108 ($135–$162) single; £115 ($172.50) double; from £178 ($267) suite. Breakfast £7.95 ($11.90) extra. AE, DC, MC, V. **Parking:** Free.

Reputed to be one of the six oldest coaching inns in England, dating from the 16th century, the half-stone structure stands in the center of Woodstock. Look for the sign in front with the picture of a huge brown bear. History surrounds you here, even relatively recent history like the hiding away here of Richard Burton and Elizabeth Taylor. They stayed in the Marlborough suite, an attractively decorated sitting room with a minibar, plus a bedroom and bath. One of the chambers of the hotel is haunted, legend says. Modern amenities are combined with antiques in the bedrooms, which have hairdryers, trouser presses, radios, and private baths. Blazing hearth fires are found throughout the hotel when the days and nights are cool. You can relax in the big, black-beamed bar or the comfortable lounge for drinks, and enjoy traditional dishes in the dining room. Meals cost £19.50 ($29.30) and up.

FEATHERS, Market St., Woodstock, Oxfordshire OX20 1SX. Tel. 0993/812291. Fax 0993/813158. 17 rms (all with bath), 1 suite. TV TEL

$ Rates (including continental breakfast): £75 ($112.50) single; £90–£125 ($135–$187.50) double; from £165 ($247.50) suite. AE, DC, MC, V. **Parking:** Free.

The bedrooms in this beautifully furnished hotel just a short walk from Blenheim Palace are individually decorated and have private baths. The two lounges have wood fires. One boasts fine china and valuable old books; the other is oak-paneled with sturdy beams. A multitude of stuffed birds from which the house gets its name adorn the bar; from there you can go into the delightful garden in the courtyard.

The food at Feathers is of high quality. Whether you are here for lunch or for a candlelit dinner, you're sure to enjoy the well-prepared, simple dishes or such specialties as hot lobster soufflé and English game pie. An exceptionally good fixed-price lunch costs £17.95 ($26.90), while a fixed-price dinner goes for £19.95 ($29.90) and up. In summer, you can have a light lunch or afternoon tea in the courtyard garden. Lunch is served daily from 12:30 to 2:15pm; dinner, from 7:30 to 9:30pm.

CHAPTER 9

KENT & SURREY

- **WHAT'S SPECIAL ABOUT KENT & SURREY**
1. **CANTERBURY**
2. **DOVER**
3. **WESTERHAM & SEVENOAKS**
4. **ROYAL TUNBRIDGE WELLS**
5. **MAIDSTONE**
6. **DORKING**
7. **GUILDFORD**
8. **HASLEMERE**

Lying to the south and southeast of London are the shires (counties) of Kent and Surrey—both fascinating areas to explore are within easy commuting distance of the capital. Of all the tourist centers, Canterbury in Kent is of foremost interest.

Once the ancient Anglo-Saxon kingdom of Kent, this county is on the fringes of London yet is far removed in spirit and scenery. Since the days of the Tudors, cherry blossoms have pinkened the fertile landscape. Not only orchards, but hop fields abound, and the conical oasthouses with kilns for drying the hops dot the rolling countryside. Both the hops and orchards have earned for Kent the title of the garden of England—and in England, the competition's rough.

Kent suffered severe destruction in World War II, as it was the virtual alley over which the Luftwaffe flew in its blitz of London. But in spite of much devastation, it is still filled with interesting old towns, mansions, and castles. The county is also rich in Dickensian associations—in fact, Kent is sometimes known as Dickens Country. His family once lived near the naval dockyard at Chatham.

Long before William the Conqueror marched his pillaging Normans across its chalky North Downs, Surrey was important to the Saxons. In fact, early Saxon kings were once crowned at what is now Kingston-on-Thames (their Coronation Stone is still preserved near the guildhall).

More recently, this tiny county has for some time been in danger of being gobbled up by the growing boundaries of London and turned into a sprawling suburb. But although it is densely populated in the area bordering the capital, Surrey still retains much unspoiled countryside, largely because its many heaths and commons form undesirable land for postwar suburban houses. Essentially, Surrey is a county of commuters (Alfred Lord Tennyson was among the first), since a worker in the city can travel to the remotest corner of Surrey from London in anywhere from 45 minutes to an hour.

SEEING KENT & SURREY

GETTING THERE

British Rail's Network Southeast offers frequent service to all the major towns and cities of Kent and Surrey through its Victoria Station or Charing Cross Station. National Express buses serve the region from Victoria Coach Station (for specific bus routes in Surrey, call 071/5419365, and for information in Kent dial 0622/671411). Motorists take the A2/M2 connections east from London to Canterbury and Dover.

A SUGGESTED ITINERARY

Day 1: Head east for an overnight in Royal Tunbridge Wells, with stopover visits at Churchill's former home (Chartwell) and Knole. Before going to Canterbury the next morning, visit Penshurst Place and Hever Castle.

✓

WHAT'S SPECIAL ABOUT KENT & SURREY

Great Towns/Villages
- [ ] Canterbury, a cathedral city and the headquarters of the Anglican church, a center of international pilgrimage.
- [ ] Dover, Britain's historic "gateway" to continental Europe, famed for its white cliffs.

Castles
- [ ] Knole, one of the largest private houses of England, a great example of purely British Tudor architecture.
- [ ] Hever Castle, dating from the end of the 13th century, a gift from Henry VIII to the "great Flanders mare," Anne of Cleves.
- [ ] Penshurst Place, a magnificent English Gothic mansion, one of the outstanding country houses of Britain.

- [ ] Leeds Castle, near Maidstone, dating from A.D. 857 and once called "the loveliest castle in the world."
- [ ] Dover Castle, whose keep was built at the command of Henry II in the 12th century.

Gardens
- [ ] Chilham Castle Gardens, landscaped by Capability Brown on former royal property 6 miles west of Canterbury.

Historic Homes
- [ ] Chartwell House, former country home of Sir Winston Churchill, with much memorabilia.

Day 2: Arrive in the late afternoon at Canterbury and visit its cathedral the following morning.

Day 3: Head for Dover to see its white cliffs and castle.

Day 4: Return to London via Maidstone for a visit to Leeds Castle.

Day 5: Those with an extra day may want to continue west to Surrey, visiting Dorking and staying overnight at Guildford. One or two historic homes nearby can be included.

---

1. CANTERBURY

56 miles E of London

GETTING THERE   By Train   By train from Victoria, Charing Cross, Waterloo, or London Bridge Station, the journey takes 1½ hours. There is frequent service.

By Bus   The bus from Victoria Coach Station takes 2 to 3 hours. Buses leave twice daily.

By Car   From London, take the A2, then the M2. Canterbury is signposted all the way. The city center is closed to cars, but it's only a short walk from several parking areas to the cathedral.

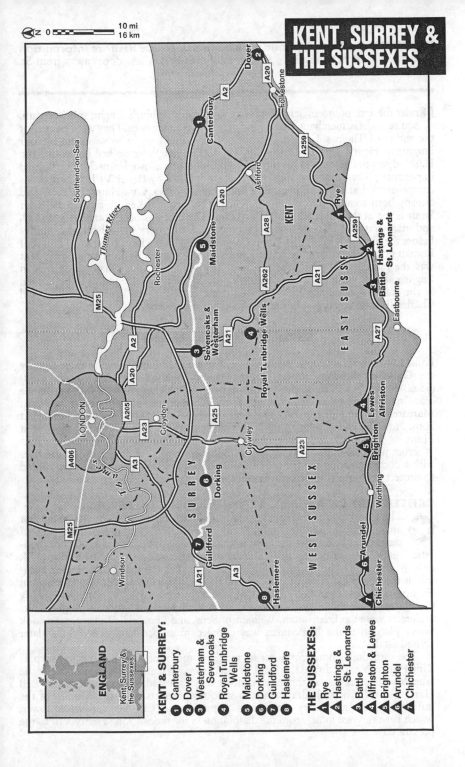

KENT, SURREY &
THE SUSSEXES

0   10 mi
     16 km

Southend-on-Sea

Thames River

Dover

Canterbury

A2

A20

Folkestone

A259

Ashford

A20

KENT

A28

Rye

A259

Maidstone

A262

A21

Hastings &
St. Leonards

Rochester

Sevenoaks &
Westerham

A21

Royal Tunbridge
Wells

EAST SUSSEX

Battle

Eastbourne

M25

A2

A20

A25

Crawley

A23

Lewes
Alfriston

A27

LONDON

A205

A23

Croydon

Brighton

A406

SURREY

Dorking

WEST SUSSEX

Worthing

M25

A3

Guildford

Arundel

Windsor

A21

A3

Haslemere

Chichester

ENGLAND

Kent; Surrey &
the Sussexes

KENT & SURREY:
1 Canterbury
2 Dover
3 Westerham &
   Sevenoaks
4 Royal Tunbridge
   Wells
5 Maidstone
6 Dorking
7 Guildford
8 Haslemere

THE SUSSEXES:
1 Rye
2 Hastings &
   St. Leonards
3 Battle
4 Alfriston & Lewes
5 Brighton
6 Arundel
7 Chichester

ESSENTIALS The **telephone area code** is 0227. The **Visitors Information Centre** is at 34 St. Margaret's St. (tel. 0227/766567), a few doors away from St. Margaret's Church.

Under the arch of the ancient West Gate journeyed Chaucer's knight, solicitor, nun, squire, parson, merchant, miller, and others—spinning tales. They were bound for the shrine of Thomas à Becket, archbishop of Canterbury, who was slain by four knights of Henry II on December 29, 1170. (The king later walked barefoot from Harbledown to the tomb of his former friend, where he allowed himself to be flogged in penance.) The shrine was finally torn down in 1538 by Henry VIII, as part of his campaign to destroy the monasteries and graven images. Canterbury, by then, had already been an attraction of long standing. The medieval Kentish city on the River Stour is the ecclesiastical capital of England. The city was once completely walled, and many traces of its old fortifications remain. Canterbury was inhabited centuries before the birth of Jesus Christ. Julius Caesar arrived on the Kent coast in 54 B.C., but Roman occupation didn't begin until much later. Although its most famous incident was the murder of Becket, the medieval city witnessed other major moments in English history, including Bloody Mary's ordering of nearly 40 victims to be burned at the stake. Richard the Lion-Hearted came back this way from crusading, and Charles II passed through on the way to claim his crown.

WHAT TO SEE & DO

From Easter to early November, daily guided tours of Canterbury are organized by the **Guild of Guides,** Arnett House, Hawks Lane (tel. 459779), costing £2.40 ($3.60) for adults and £1.40 ($2.10) for students and children over 12. Don't go to the office to take the tours; rather, meet at the Visitors Information Centre at 34 St. Margaret's St., in a pedestrian zone near the cathedral, daily (including Sunday) at 2pm. From the end of May to mid-September, there is also a daily morning tour at 11am.

From just below the Weavers House, boats leave for half-hour trips on the river with a commentary on the history of the buildings you pass. Umbrellas are provided to protect you against inclement weather.

CANTERBURY CATHEDRAL, 11 The Precincts. Tel. 762662.

The foundation of this splendid cathedral dates back to the coming of the first archbishop, Augustine, from Rome in A.D. 597, but the earliest part of the present building is the great Romanesque crypt built circa 1100. The monastic "quire" erected on top of this at the same time was destroyed by fire in 1174, only 4 years after the murder of Thomas à Becket on a dark December evening in the northwest transept, still one of the most famous places of pilgrimage in Europe. The destroyed "quire" was immediately replaced by a magnificent early Gothic one, the first major expression of that architectural style in England. Its architects were the Frenchman, William of Sens, and "English" William, who took Sens's place after the Frenchman was crippled in an accident in 1178 that later proved fatal.

The cathedral is noteworthy for its medieval tombs of royal personages, such as King Henry IV and Edward the Black Prince, as well as numerous archbishops. To the later Middle Ages belong the great 14th-century nave and the famous central "Bell Harry Tower." The cathedral stands in spacious precincts amid the remains of the buildings of the monastery—cloisters, chapter house, and Norman water tower, which have survived intact from the dissolution in the time of King Henry VIII to the present day.

Becket's shrine was destroyed by the Tudor king, but the site of that tomb is in Trinity Chapel, near the high altar. The saint is said to have worked miracles, and the cathedral contains some rare stained glass depicting those feats. Perhaps the most miraculous event is that the windows escaped Henry VIII's agents of destruction as well as Hitler's bombs. The windows were removed as a precaution at the beginning of the war. During the war, a large area of Canterbury was flattened, but the main body of the church was unharmed. However, the cathedral library was damaged by a German air raid in 1942. The replacement windows of the cathedral were blown in, which proved the wisdom of having the medieval glass safely stored away. East of the Trinity Chapel is "Becket's Crown," in which is a chapel dedicated to "Martyrs and Saints of Our Own Time." St. Augustine's Chair, one of the symbols of the authority of the archbishop of Canterbury, stands behind the high altar.

Admission: Free. Guided tours, based on demand, £2.40 ($3.60) adults, 70p ($1.10) children 12 and under.

Open: Easter–Oct, daily 8:45am–7pm; Nov–Apr, daily 8:45am–5pm.

THE CANTERBURY TALES, St. Margaret's St. Tel. 454888.

Pilgrim's Way re-creates the Thomas à Becket pilgrimage of Chaucerian England. Visitors are taken on a tour through England's Middle Ages and meet some of Chaucer's pilgrims, including the Wife of Bath. Audiovisual techniques bring these characters to life, and stories of jealousy, pride, avarice, and love are recounted. It's off the High Street near the cathedral.

Admission: £4.25 ($6.40) adults, £2.95 ($4.40) children.

Open: Daily 9:30am–5:30pm.

WHERE TO STAY

Before you can begin any serious exploring, you'll need to find a hotel. You have several possibilities, both in the city and on the outskirts, ranging from craggy Elizabethan houses of historic interest to modern studio-type bedrooms with private baths.

EXPENSIVE

CHAUCER HOTEL, 63 Ivy Lane, Canterbury, Kent CT1 1TT. Tel. 0227/ 464427. Fax 0227/450397. 42 rms.

$ Rates: £79 ($118.50) single; £98 ($147) double. Breakfast £8 ($12) extra. AE, DC, MC, V. **Parking:** Free.

On a historic street, off Lower Bridge Street, the Chaucer Hotel is within a few minutes' walk of the cathedral and the Micawber house made famous in *David Copperfield*. Originally it was a Georgian house, although it was extensively rebuilt following bomb damage during World War II. Your comfortably furnished room will lie at the end of a labyrinth of stairs, narrow hallways, and doors. (The hotel staff will carry luggage and park your car.) Don't overlook the possibility of a drink in the Pilgrim's Bar, with its Regency mantelpieces and French windows open to outdoor terraces in summer. The hotel also has a good restaurant, the Geoffrey Chaucer, serving English meals until 9:45pm, and it provides 24-hour room service. A table d'hôte dinner costs £15.95 ($23.90).

COUNTY HOTEL, High St., Canterbury, Kent CT1 2RX. Tel. 0227/ 766266. Fax 0227/451512. 72 rms, 1 suite. TV TEL

$ Rates: £65–£71 ($97.50–$106.50) single; £71.50–£94 ($107.30–$141) double; from £170 ($255) suite. Breakfast £8 ($12) extra. AE, DC, MC, V. **Parking:** £3 ($4.50).

This place has been a hotel since the closing years of Victoria's reign, with a recorded history going back to the end of the 12th century. Bedrooms are equipped with tea and coffee makers, radios, and bowls of fruit. Some are period rooms with either Georgian or Tudor four-posters. For gourmet dining, go to Sully's Restaurant, the hotel's fully air-conditioned dining room (see "Where to Dine," below). For snacks, vegetarian specialties, salads, and hot dishes, the coffee shop may be your best bet. There is also the Tudor Bar, where you can have apéritifs or after-dinner libations.

FALSTAFF HOTEL, 8–10 Dunstan's St., Canterbury, Kent CT2 8AF. Tel. 0227/462138. Fax 0227/463525. 25 rms. TV TEL
$ Rates (including English breakfast): £55–£68 ($82.50–$102) single; £68–£80 ($102–$120) double. AE, DC, MC, V. **Parking:** Free.
The Falstaff, located 400 yards from West Station, is a classic Canterbury hostelry that pilgrims of old entered through a flagstone courtyard, as they do today. Even though small, the bedrooms are well maintained and neatly arranged. The hotel also operates a good restaurant, where meals begin at £14.50 ($21.80).

HOWFIELD MANOR, Chartham Hatch, Canterbury, Kent CT4 7HQ. Tel. 0227/738294. Fax 0227/731535. 13 rms, 1 suite. TV TEL
Directions: Take the A28 3¼ miles from Canterbury.
$ Rates (including English breakfast): £60 ($90) single; £80 ($120) double; from £90 ($135) suite. AE, DC, MC, V. **Parking:** Free.

⭐ The oldest section of this brick manor house, which dates from 1181, is now used as a restaurant called the Old Well. An ancient well remains from when it was built as a chapel for an Augustinian priory. Set on 5 acres of rolling meadows, the house offers tastefully furnished bedrooms containing such amenities as alarm clocks, trouser presses, and hairdryers. Drinks are served from the Priory Bar and can be taken into the warm, comfortable lounge. The hotel's restaurant is one of the best in Canterbury. A table d'hôte costs £18.95 ($28.40).

MODERATE

CATHEDRAL GATE HOTEL, 36 Burgate, Canterbury, Kent CT1 2HA. Tel. 0227/464381. Fax 0227/462800. 24 rms (12 with bath). TV TEL
$ Rates (including continental breakfast): £24 ($36) single without bath, £32.50 ($48.80) single with shower only; £44 ($66) double without bath, £66 ($99) double with bath. AE, DC, MC, V. **Parking:** £2 ($3).
The Cathedral Gate is for modern-day pilgrims who want to rest their bones at an inn shouldering up to the cathedral's gateway. Built in 1438, adjoining Christchurch Gate and overlooking the Buttermarket, the hotel has views of the cathedral. In 1620 this former hospice became one of the earliest of the fashionable coffeehouses and teahouses of England, and the interior reveals many little architectural details of the 17th century. The rooms are comfortably furnished, and some with private bath have minibars. Afternoon tea and supper are served. The hotel is a 10-minute walk from the train station.

SLATTERS, St. Margaret's St., Canterbury, Kent CT1 2TR. Tel. 0227/463271. Fax 0227/764117. 31 rms (all with bath). TV TEL
$ Rates (including English breakfast): £65 ($97.50) single; £75 ($112.50) double. AE, DC, MC, V. **Parking:** Free.
In the heart of Canterbury, 200 yards from the cathedral, this building is historic but the bedrooms are motellike. Most of them convert into sitting areas during the day, with armchairs. Each room is furnished with a color TV, radio, direct-dial phone, trouser press, hairdryer, and a welcome tray with tea- or coffee-making facilities. The fully licensed French restaurant serves lunch and dinner. Bar snacks are also available at lunchtime.

INEXPENSIVE

EBURY HOTEL, 65–67 New Dover Rd., Canterbury, Kent CT1 3DX. Tel. 0227/768433. Fax 0227/459187. 15 rms (all with bath). TV TEL **Directions:** Follow the signs to the A2, Dover Road.

$ Rates (including English breakfast): £41–£48 ($61.50–$72) single; £59–£62 ($88.50–$93) double. AE, MC, V. **Parking:** Free. **Closed:** Dec 14–Jan 14.

⑤   Acclaimed as one of the finest B&B hotels in Canterbury, this gabled Victorian house stands at the edge of the city. It is important to reserve here, as this owner-operated hotel is quite popular. Its rooms are well furnished, roomy, and pleasantly decorated. The hotel has a heated, indoor swimming pool and spa, as well as a spacious lounge and a licensed restaurant serving good meals prepared with fresh vegetables.

THREE TUNS INN, 24 Watling St., Canterbury, Kent CT1 2UD. Tel. 0227/767371. 7 rms (3 with bath). TV TEL

$ Rates (including English breakfast): Mon–Thurs £30 ($45) per person single or double, with or without private bath; Fri–Sun (2-night minimum), £15 ($22.50) per person, with or without private bath. AE, DC, MC, V. **Parking:** Free.

⑤   In the center of town, just off Castle Street, this old-fashioned inn derives most of its business from its exceptionally busy pub. However, many readers appreciate the handful of antique bedrooms upstairs, which impart a feeling of old-world charm. The inn occupies a fine 15th-century building on the site of an ancient Roman theater. William and Mary, who later became king and queen of England, stopped here in 1679, and you can follow their example, even going so far as to stay in the same room. Today, that room is attractively furnished and has a four-poster bed. The pub downstairs serves a buffet-style "tavern fare" lunch Monday to Saturday from noon to 6pm, and Sunday from noon to 3pm. You choose from a row of steaming hot plates, paying upward from £7 ($10.50) for a full meal. The spillover from the pub gravitates into a side room, The Chapel Restaurant, which was the setting for illegal Catholic masses during the Civil War. It still has the entrance to a secret passageway that allowed the celebrants to leave quickly in case of danger.

WHERE TO DINE

MODERATE

GEORGE'S BRASSERIE, 71–72 Castle St. Tel. 765658.
    Cuisine: FRENCH. **Reservations:** Recommended.

$ Prices: Appetizers £4–£6 ($6–$9); main courses £8–£14 ($12–$21); fixed-price meal £12.50 ($18.80) at lunch, £20 ($30) at dinner. AE, DC, MC, V.

    Open: Mon–Thurs 10am–10pm, Fri–Sat 10am–10:30pm (with last order time extended for theatergoers).

This attractive establishment, in the center of town east of Stour Street, is run by brother and sister Simon Day and Beverley Holmes, who pride themselves on the cleanliness of their restaurant and the quality of their food, made only of fresh ingredients. They serve everything from coffee and a croissant to gourmet meals. A la carte, numerous appetizers are offered including a fresh anchovy salad and George's terrines, all served with a basket of French bread. The selection of main dishes changes with the season, but it always includes fish and meat dishes served with new potatoes or french fries. Try, for example, roast duck with green olives and rosemary, venison filet with port and juniper, fresh wild salmon with watercress sauce, or Scottish steak cut from the bone with garlic and mushrooms.

SULLY'S, in the County Hotel, High St., Tel. 766266.

Cuisine: ENGLISH/CONTINENTAL. **Reservations:** Recommended.

$ **Prices:** Appetizers £3–£4.50 ($4.50–$6.80); main courses £8–£14 ($12–$21); 3-course fixed-price lunch £14.50 ($21.80); 4-course fixed-price dinner £18.50 ($27.80). AE, DC, MC, V.

Open: Lunch daily 12:30–2:20pm; dinner daily 7–10pm.

The most distinguished restaurant in Canterbury is located in its most distinguished hotel (see "Where to Stay," above). The seating and comfort level are first-rate, and both visitors and locals (the latter usually celebrating some special occasion) frequent this establishment. Considering the quality of the ingredients, the menu offers good value. You can always count on a selection of plain, traditional English dishes, but try one of the more imaginatively conceived platters instead. Dishes are backed by a respectable wine list.

TUO E MIO, 16 The Borough. Tel. 761471.

Cuisine: ITALIAN. **Reservations:** Recommended, especially at lunch.

$ **Prices:** Appetizers £3–£5.50 ($4.50–$8.30); main courses £6.50–£11.50 ($9.80–$17.30). AE, DC, MC, V.

Open: Lunch Wed–Sun noon–2:30pm; dinner Tues–Sun 7pm–midnight.

Closed: Last 2 weeks in Aug and last 2 weeks in Feb.

Tuo e Mio is a bastion of zesty Italian cookery, the finest in town in its category. Signor R. P. M. Greggio, known locally as Raphael, sets the style and plans the menu at his casual bistro. Some dishes are standard, including the pastas, beef, and veal found on most Italian menus, but the daily specials have a certain flair, based on the shopping for fresh and good quality ingredients on any given day. Try especially the fish dishes, including skate, which is regularly featured. A selection of reasonably priced Italian wines accompanies your food selection.

---

2. DOVER

76 miles SE of London, 84 miles E of Brighton

GETTING THERE By Train Frequent trains run between Victoria Station or Charing Cross Station in London and Dover daily from 5am to 10pm. Arrivals in Dover are at Priory Station (tel. 0304/45-4411), off Folkestone Road. During the day two trains per hour depart Canterbury East Station heading for Dover.

By Bus Frequent buses throughout the day leave from London's Victoria Coach Station bound for Dover. The local bus station is on Pencester Road (tel. 0304/240024). There is also frequent daily service between Canterbury and Dover.

By Car From London, head first to Canterbury (see above), then continue along the A2 southeast until you reach Dover on the coast.

ESSENTIALS The **telephone area code** for Dover is 0304. The **Tourist Information Centre** is on Townwall Street (tel. 0304/205108).

One of the ancient Cinque Ports, Dover is famed for its white cliffs. In Victoria's day, it basked in popularity as a seaside resort, but today it's known as the port for major cross-Channel car and passenger traffic between England and France (notably Calais). Dover was one of England's most vulnerable and easy-to-hit targets during World War II; repeated bombings destroyed much of its harbor.

WHAT TO SEE & DO

DOVER CASTLE, Castle Hill. Tel. 201628.

Hovering nearly 400 feet above the port is one of the oldest and best-known castles in England. Its keep was built at the command of Becket's fair-weather friend, Henry II, in the 12th century. The ancient castle was called back to active duty as late as World War II. The "Pharos" on the grounds is a lighthouse built by the Romans in the first half of the 1st century. The Romans first landed at nearby Deal in 54 B.C., but after 6 months they departed and did not return until nearly 100 years later, in A.D. 43, when they stayed and occupied the country for 400 years. The castle houses a military museum and a film center, and the restaurant is open all year.

Admission: £5 ($7.50) adults, £2.50 ($3.80) children, £14 ($21) family ticket.

Open: Apr–Sept, daily 10am–6pm; Oct–Mar, daily 10am–4pm. **Bus:** 90 bound for Deal.

HELLFIRE CORNER, Dover Castle, Castle Hill. Tel. 201628.

These secret tunnels were used during the evacuation of Dunkirk in 1940 and the Battle of Britain. Two hundred feet below ground, they were the headquarters of Operation Dynamo, which saw the evacuation of more than 300,000 troops from Dunkirk. For years they were on the top-secret list, but now can be explored on a guided tour. They were originally excavated to house cannons to counter the threat of an invasion by Napoléon.

Admission: Free with castle admission (see above).

Open: Same hours as the castle (see above). **Bus:** 90.

ROMAN PAINTED HOUSE, New St. Tel. 203279.

This spectacular 1,800-year-old Roman structure has exceptionally well preserved walls and an underfloor heating system. It's famous for its unique Bacchic murals and is the winner of four national awards for presentation. You'll find it in the town center near Market Square.

Admission: £1.50 ($2.30) adults, 50p (80¢) children.

Open: Apr–Oct, Tues–Sun 10am–5pm.

WHERE TO STAY

Because of the cross-Channel traffic, Dover operates in a sellers' market, so hotel prices tend to run high.

DOVER MOAT HOUSE, Townwall St., Dover, Kent CT16 1SZ. Tel. 0304/203270. Fax 0304/213230. 79 rms (all with bath and shower). TV TEL

$ Rates: £63.20–£85 ($94.80–$127.50) single; £76–£102 ($114–$153) double. Breakfast £8.75 ($13.10) extra. AE, DC, MC, V. **Parking:** Free.

In the center of town, just a few minutes away from the train station, the seafront, and the international ferry terminal and Hoverport, the Dover Moat House features rooms with queen-size beds, radios, in-house movies, and hairdryers. On the premises are an indoor heated swimming pool and Braid's Restaurant, with a carvery and salad bar, plus coffee-shop facilities and an English-style bar. Laundry and 24-hour room service are available.

THE WHITE CLIFFS, Waterloo Crescent, Dover, Kent CT17 9BP. Tel. 0304/203633. Fax 0304/216320. 56 rms (all with bath or shower). TV TEL

$ Rates (including English breakfast): £45–£55 ($67.50–$82.50) single; £72 ($108) double. AE, DC, MC, V. **Parking:** £1 ($1.50).

The facade of Dover's standard choice is impressive, built like a string of attached town houses, with an unbroken seafront balcony and a glass-enclosed front veranda. The rooms, many of which face the Channel, are comfortable and tranquil, and all have radios and hot-beverage facilities. Meals and light snacks are available 24 hours a day; dinner costs £12 ($18) and up. The hotel is close to the eastern and western docks and the Hoverport for travel to and from Europe.

WHERE TO DINE

INEXPENSIVE

BRITANNIA, 41 Townwall St. Tel. 203248.
   Cuisine: ENGLISH. **Reservations:** Recommended for restaurant.
$ Prices: Appetizers £3–£5 ($4.50–$7.50); main courses £4.50–£10 ($6.80–$15); fixed-price lunch £6.50–£8.25 ($9.80–$12.40). AE, MC, V.
   Open: Restaurant, lunch Mon–Sat noon–2pm; dinner Mon–Sat 3–9pm, Sun noon–9pm. Pub, Mon–Sat 11am–11pm, Sun noon–3pm and 7–10:30pm.

If you gravitate to typically English, pub-style meals, try this restaurant, whose windows overlook the ferry terminal and the many ships arriving from Calais and Boulogne. Its well-maintained facade has a bow window and lots of gilt and brass nautical accents. The popular pub is on the ground floor and the restaurant on the upper level. Try a prawn cocktail or a pâté for an appetizer, followed by rumpsteak or a mixed grill. Many different salads are offered, including one made with salmon, another with ham. Dover sole is a specialty.

English breakfast, priced at £3.95 ($5.90) per person, is a morning specialty, served every day from 8 to 11am.

RISTORANTE AL PORTO, 43 Townwall St. Tel. 204615.
   Cuisine: ITALIAN. **Reservations:** Required.
$ Prices: Appetizers £1.75–£5.20 ($2.60–$7.80); main courses £4.75–£9.80 ($7.10–$14.70); fixed-price lunch £7.50 ($11.30). AE, DC, MC, V.
   Open: Lunch Mon–Sat noon–2:30pm; dinner Mon–Sat 7–10:30pm. **Closed:** First 2 weeks in Oct.

One block from the landing dock of the ferryboats, this Italian-owned restaurant is decorated in a nautical style, with fishnets hanging from the ceiling. It offers one of the largest menus in town, featuring such specialties as tagliatelle alla Porto, along with homemade lasagne al forno, or chateaubriand Vesuviano in a succulent garlic butter with fresh mushrooms. For dessert, try the chef's specialty, tiramisu.

3. WESTERHAM & SEVENOAKS

Westerham: 20 miles SE of London
Sevenoaks: 26 miles SE of London

GETTING THERE   By Train   Trains run daily from London's Victoria Station to both Westerham and Sevenoaks. Taxis wait at the station.

By Car   Head east along the M25, taking the exit to Westerham where the B2026 leads to Chartwell (the road is signposted).

WESTERHAM

The Westerham area abounds with homes of famous men, which have now been preserved as museums and memorials. Chartwell, where Sir Winston Churchill lived for many years, displays personal mementos, the world leader's paintings, and gifts from people around the world. On the lake at Chartwell swim black swans. Down House is where Darwin wrote his still controversial *On the Origin of Species*. Here you can amble down the scientist's "Thinking Path." Québec House, the boyhood home of General Wolfe, and Squerryes Court are of particular interest to Canadians.

WHAT TO SEE & DO

CHARTWELL (Churchill's home), 2 miles south of Westerham (signposted from the B2026). Tel. 0732/866368.
Chartwell was the late prime minister's home from 1922 and is now a museum. Not as grand as Blenheim Palace where Sir Winston was born in 1874, the rooms of Chartwell remain as the Conservative politician left them; they include maps, documents, photographs, pictures, and other personal mementos. Two rooms display a selection of gifts that the prime minister received from people all over the world. There is also a selection of many of his well-known uniforms. Terraced gardens descend toward the lake, where you'll find black swans swimming. Many of Churchill's paintings are displayed in a garden studio. A restaurant on the grounds serves from 10:30am to 5pm on days when the house is open.

Admission: House, Mar–Nov £2.30 ($3.50); house and garden, Apr–Oct, £4.20 ($6.30); gardens, £2.20 ($3.30); Churchill's studio, 50p (80¢). Children enter for half price.

Open: Apr–Oct, Tues–Thurs noon–5pm, Sat–Sun 11am–5pm; Mar and Nov (house and garden only), Wed and Sat–Sun 11am–4pm.

QUÉBEC HOUSE, Québec Sq. Tel. 0959/562206.
This square, red-brick, gabled house is the boyhood home of Gen. James Wolfe, who led the English in their victory over the French in the battle for Québec. Wolfe was born in Westerham on January 2, 1727, and lived here until he was 11 years old. A National Trust property, Québec House contains an exhibition about the capture of Québec and memorabilia associated with the military hero.

Admission: £2 ($3) adults, £1 ($1.50) children.

Open: Apr–Oct, Sun–Wed and Fri 2–6pm. **Directions:** At the junction of Edenbridge and Sevenoaks roads (the A25 and the B2026).

SQUERRYES COURT, just west of Westerham (signposted from the A25). Tel. 0959/562345.
Built in 1681 and owned by the Warde family for 250 years, this William and Mary–period manor house has—besides a fine collection of paintings, tapestries, and furniture—pictures and relics of the family of General Wolfe. The military hero received his commission on the grounds of the house—the spot is marked by a cenotaph.

Admission: £3 ($4.50) adults, £1.50 ($2.30) children.

Open: House and grounds, Mar, Sun 2–6pm; Apr–Sept, Wed, Sat–Sun, and bank holidays 2–6pm.

In Nearby Downe

DOWN HOUSE (Darwin's home), Luxted Rd., Downe, Orpington. Tel. 0680/859119.
The famous naturalist/evolutionary theorist lived here from 1842 until his death in 1882. The drawing room and old study are restored to how they were when Darwin was working on his famous—and still controversial—book *On the Origin of Species,* first published in 1859. The museum also includes collections and memorabilia from Darwin's voyage on the HMS *Beagle.* There is a room dedicated to his famous grandfather, Dr. Erasmus Darwin, and a modest exhibit on evolution is in the new study, the last room to be added to the house. An important feature of the museum is the garden, which retains original landscaping and a glass house, beyond

which lies the Sand Walk or "Thinking Path," where Darwin took his daily solitary walk. The village of Downe is 5½ miles south of Bromley off the A233.

Admission: £1.50 ($2.30) adults, 50p (80¢) children 5–15.

Open: Mar–Dec 15, Wed–Sun and Sat 1–6pm. **Transportation:** From London's Victoria Station, take a daily train to Bromley South, then go by bus no. 146 to Downe (note that the bus does not run on Sunday). Down House lies a quarter mile southeast of the village of Downe along Luxted Road.

SEVENOAKS

The architecture enthusiast will find the area of Sevenoaks a veritable treasure trove. In nearby Knole (just 1½ miles away), you'll find one of the finest examples of Tudor architecture, the palace of Knole. The ancient home of Ightham Mote is well worth a visit to see its Great Hall; you'll cross a stone bridge over a moat to its central courtyard.

WHAT TO SEE & DO

KNOLE, at south end of town of Knole, east of the A225, opposite St. Nicholas Church. Tel. 0732/450608.

Begun in the mid-15th century by Thomas Bourchier, archbishop of Canterbury, Knole is one of the largest private houses in England and is considered one of the finest examples of purely British Tudor-style architecture. It is set in a 1,000-acre deer park, 5 miles north of Tonbridge, at the Tonbridge end of the town of Sevenoaks. Virginia Woolf, often a guest of the Sackvilles, used Knole as the location for her novel *Orlando*.

Henry VIII liberated the former archbishop's palace from the church in 1537. He spent considerable sums of money on Knole, but there is little record of his spending much time here after extracting the place from the reluctant Archbishop Cranmer; history records one visit only, in 1541. It was then a royal palace until Queen Elizabeth I granted it to Thomas Sackville, first Earl of Dorset, whose descendants have lived here ever since. The Great Hall and the Brown Gallery are Bourchier rooms, early 15th century, both much altered by the first earl, who made other additions in about 1603. The earl was also responsible for the Great Painted Staircase. The house covers 7 acres and has 365 rooms, 52 staircases, and seven courts. The elaborate paneling and plasterwork provide a background for the 17th- and 18th-century tapestries and rugs, Elizabethan and Jacobean furniture, and the collection of family portraits. The building was given to the National Trust in 1946.

Admission: House, £4 ($6) adults, £2 ($3) children.

Open: House, Apr–Oct, Wed–Sun and bank holidays 11am–5pm (last admission 1 hour before closing). Gardens, May–Sept, the first Wed of the month. Park, daily to pedestrians; open to cars when the house is open. **Transportation:** Frequent train service is available from London (about every 30 min.) to Sevenoaks, and then you can take a taxi or walk the remaining 1½ miles to Knole.

IGHTHAM MOTE, Ivy Hatch, Sevenoaks. Tel. 0732/810378.

This National Trust property is well worth a stop if you're in the area visiting other stately homes and castles. It was extensively remodeled in the early 16th century, and the Tudor chapel with its painted ceiling, the timbered outer walls, and the ornate chimneys reflect that period. A stone bridge crosses the moat and leads into the central courtyard overlooked by the magnificent windows of the Great Hall. The rest of the house is built around the courtyard. From the Great Hall, a Jacobean staircase leads to the old chapel on the first floor, where you go through the solarium, with an oriel window, to the Tudor chapel.

Unlike many other ancient houses of England that have been lived in by the same family for centuries, Ightham Mote passed from owner to owner, each family leaving its mark on the place. When the last private owner, an American who was responsible for a lot of the restoration, died, he bequeathed the house to the National Trust.

Admission: £4 ($6) adults, £2 ($3) children.

Open: Apr–Oct, Mon and Wed–Fri noon–5pm, Sun 11am–5pm. **Closed:** Nov–Mar and Tues and Sat throughout the year. **Directions:** Take the A227 6 miles east of Sevenoaks to the small village of Ivy Hatch; the estate is 2½ miles south of Ightham. It's also signposted from the A25.

---

4. ROYAL TUNBRIDGE WELLS

36 miles SE of London, 33 miles NE of Brighton

GETTING THERE By Train Two to three trains per hour leave London's Charing Cross Station during the day bound for Hastings, but going via the town center of Royal Tunbridge Wells (trip time: 50 min.).

By Bus There are no direct bus links with Gatwick Airport or London. However, there is hourly service during the day between Brighton and Royal Tunbridge Wells (call 0273/606605 for the bus schedule). You can purchase tickets aboard the bus.

By Car After reaching the ring road around London, from whichever part of London you're in, continue east along the M25, cutting southeast at the exit for the A21 to Hastings.

ESSENTIALS The **telephone area code** is 0892. The **Tourist Information Centre,** Old Fishmarket, The Pantiles (tel. 0892/515675), provides a full accommodations list and offers a room-reservations service.

Dudley Lord North, courtier to James I, is credited with the accidental discovery in 1606 of the mineral spring that led to the creation of a fashionable resort. Over the years the "Chalybeate Spring" became known for its curative properties and was considered the answer for everything from too many days of wine and roses to failing sexual prowess. It is still possible to "take the water" today.

The spa resort reached its peak in the mid-18th century under the foppish patronage of "Beau" Nash (1674–1761), a dandy and final arbiter on how to act, what to say, and even what to wear (for example, he got men to remove their boots in favor of stockings).

Tunbridge Wells continued to enjoy a prime spa reputation through to the reign of Queen Victoria, who used to holiday here as a child, and in 1909 Tunbridge Wells received its Royal status.

WHAT TO SEE & DO

The most remarkable feature of Royal Tunbridge Wells is The Pantiles, a colonnaded walkway for shoppers, tea drinkers, and diners, built near the wells. The town boasts many other interesting and charming spots which can be viewed on a walk around the town, and a wide variety of entertainment is presented at the Assembly Hall and Trinity Arts Centre.

Canadians touring in the area may want to seek out the grave of the founder of their country's capital. Lt. Col. John By of the Royal Engineers (1779–1836) died at Shernfold Park in Frant, East Sussex, near Tunbridge Wells, and is buried in the churchyard there. His principal claim to fame is that he established the city of Ottawa, and built the Rideau Canal.

Within easy touring distance from Royal Tunbridge Wells are a number of castles, gardens, and stately homes, all with their own history and beauty; for example, Sissinghurst Castle, the home of novelist Vita Sackville-West, and Chartwell, former home of Sir Winston Churchill.

WHERE TO STAY

RUSSELL, 80 London Rd., Royal Tunbridge Wells, Kent TN1 1DZ. Tel. 0892/544833, or toll free 800/832-2957 in the U.S. Fax 0892/515846. 21 rms (all with bath), 5 suites. TV TEL
$ Rates (including English breakfast): £62 ($93) single; £76 ($114) double; from £80 ($120) suite. AE, DC, MC, V. **Parking:** Free.
One of the best places for accommodations at the old spa, within an easy walk of The Pantiles, is the reasonably priced Russell, near the intersection of the A26 and the A264. Bedrooms are comfortably furnished and well maintained. You should take your meals here, as they offer good value for your money—a four-course dinner, for example, costs £16 ($24). A tourist menu costs only £8.45 ($12.70).

THE SPA HOTEL, Mount Ephraim, Royal Tunbridge Wells, Kent TN4 8XJ. Tel. 0892/520331. Fax 0892/510575. 76 rms (all with bath). TV TEL **Directions:** From The Pantiles, take Major Yorke Rd.
$ Rates: £74–£84 ($111–$126) single; £90–£110 ($135–$165) double. Breakfast £8 ($12) extra. AE, DC, MC, V. **Parking:** Free.
Standing on 14 acres, this building dates back to 1766; once a private home, it was converted to a hotel in 1880. This is the kind of place where many guests check in for long stays. Facilities include a sauna, a solarium, tennis courts, and an indoor swimming pool. The Chandelier Restaurant serves a combination English and French cuisine, with a fixed-price lunch at £17 ($25.50), a fixed-price dinner going for £22 ($33).

WHERE TO DINE

THACKERAY'S HOUSE, 85 London Rd. Tel. 511921.
Cuisine: ENGLISH/FRENCH. **Reservations:** Required.
$ Prices: Appetizers £5.25–£8.50 ($7.90–$12.80); main courses £12.50–£18.75 ($18.80–$28.10); fixed-price meals from £14.95 ($22.40) at lunch, £19.85 ($29.80) at dinner. MC, V.
Open: Lunch Tues–Sun 12:30–2:30pm; dinner Tues–Sat 7–10pm.
✪ Thackeray's, located at the corner of Mount Ephraim Road, serves the finest food in Royal Tunbridge Wells. You get a little history here as well, as this second-oldest house in the spa was once inhabited by novelist William Makepeace Thackeray. He wrote *Tunbridge Toys* here. The house is circa 1660. Bruce Wass, the owner-chef, worked at one of my favorite restaurants in London, Odin's, before coming here to set up his own place. He has created an elegant atmosphere, backed by attentive service, for his specialties.

Care goes into all his dishes, and many have flair, including an occasional salad with fresh flowers. He reaches perfection with such dishes as tender duck breast served with citrus, or fresh-herb-flavored lamb with baby turnips. For dessert, he is most often cited for his chocolate Armagnac loaf, served with a walnut-liqueur sauce.

EASY EXCURSIONS

PENSHURST PLACE, at Penshurst, near Tonbridge. Tel. 0892/870307.

★ This stately home 6 miles west of Tonbridge is one of the outstanding country houses in Britain. In 1338, Sir John de Pulteney, four times lord mayor of London, built the manor house whose Great Hall still forms the heart of Penshurst—after more than 600 years. The boy king, Edward VI, presented the house to Sir William Sidney, and it has remained in that family ever since. It was the birthplace in 1554 of Sir Philip Sidney, the soldier-poet. In the first half of the 17th century Penshurst was known as a center of literature and attracted such personages as Ben Jonson, who was inspired by the estate to write one of his greatest poems. Today it is the home of the second Viscount De L'Isle. The Nether Gallery, below the Long Gallery, which contains a suite of ebony-and-ivory furniture from Goa, houses the Sidney family collection of armor. Visitors can also view the splendid state dining room. In the Stable Wing is an interesting toy museum.

On the grounds are nature and farm trails plus an adventure playground for children.

Admission: House and grounds, £4.50 ($6.80) adults, £2.50 ($3.80) children.
Open: Mar 27–Oct 3, daily; house noon–5:30pm, grounds 11am–6pm.

HEVER CASTLE AND GARDENS, 3 miles southeast of Edenbridge, off B2026, between Sevenoaks and East Grinstead. Tel. 0732/865244.

★ Hever Castle dates back to 1270 when the massive gatehouse, the outer walls, and the moat were first constructed. Some 200 years later the Bullen (or Boleyn) family added a comfortable Tudor dwelling house inside the walls. Hever Castle was the childhood home of Anne Boleyn, the second wife of Henry VIII and mother of Queen Elizabeth I. The castle holds many memories of her.

In 1903, William Waldorf Astor acquired the estate and invested time, money, and imagination in restoring the castle, building the "Tudor Village" and creating the gardens and lake. The Astor family's contribution to Hever's rich history can be appreciated through the collections of furniture, paintings, and objets d'art and through the quality of workmanship employed, particularly in the wood carving and plasterwork.

The gardens at Hever Castle were created between 1904 and 1908. They have now reached their maturity and are a blaze of color throughout most of the year. The spectacular Italian Garden contains statuary and sculpture dating from Roman to Renaissance times. William Waldorf Astor acquired these items in Italy and brought them to Hever where they form a magnificent sight among the displays of shrubs and climbing and herbaceous plants. The formal gardens include a walled Rose Garden, fine topiary work, and a maze. There is a 35-acre lake and throughout the gardens there are streams, cascades, and fountains.

Admission: Castle and gardens, £4.80 ($7.20) adults, £2.40 ($3.60) children 5–16; gardens only, £3.40 ($5.10) adults, £2 ($3) children.
Open: Mar 16–Nov 7, gardens, daily 11am–6pm (last entry at 5pm); castle, daily noon–6pm. For further information, call the Hever Castle Estate Office. **Directions:** Follow the signs northwest of Royal Tunbridge; it's 3 miles southeast of Edenbridge, midway between Sevenoaks and East Grinstead, and 20 minutes from Exit 6 of the M25.

---

5. MAIDSTONE

36 miles SE of London, 64 miles NE of Brighton

GETTING THERE   By Train   Trains run frequently from London's Victoria Station to Maidstone.

By Bus   Daily buses run from London's Victoria Coach Station to Maidstone.

By Car From London's ring road, continue east along the M26 and the M20.

ESSENTIALS The **telephone area code** is 0622. The **Tourist Information Centre** is at The Gatehouse, The Old Palace Gardens, Mill Street (tel. 0622/673581).

LEEDS CASTLE

Once described by Lord Conway as the loveliest castle in the world, Leeds Castle, Maidstone, Kent ME17 1PL (tel. 0622/765400), dates from A.D. 857. Originally built of wood, it was rebuilt in 1119 in its present stone structure on two small islands in the middle of the lake, and it was an almost impregnable fortress before the importation of gunpowder. Henry VIII converted it to a royal palace.

The castle has strong links with America through the sixth Lord Fairfax who, as well as owning the castle, owned five million acres in Virginia and was a close friend and mentor of the young George Washington. The last private owner, the Hon. Lady Baillie, who restored the castle with a superb collection of fine art, furniture, and tapestries, bequeathed it to the Leeds Castle Foundation. Since then, **royal apartments,** known as "Les Chambres de la Reine" (the chambers of the queen), in the Gloriette, the oldest part of the castle, have been open to the public. The Gloriette, the last stronghold against attack, dates from Norman and Plantagenet times, with later additions by Henry VIII.

Within the surrounding parkland is a wildwood garden and duckery where rare swans, geese, and ducks can be seen. The redesigned aviaries contain a superb collection of birds, including parakeets and cockatoos. Dogs are not allowed here, but dog lovers will enjoy the **Dog Collar Museum** at the gatehouse, with a unique collection of collars dating from the Middle Ages. A nine-hole golf course is open to the public. The **Culpepper Garden** is a delightful English country flower garden. Beyond are the castle greenhouses, the maze centered on a beautiful underground grotto, and the vineyard recorded in the *Domesday Book,* now again producing Leeds Castle English white wine.

From mid-March to October, Leeds Castle is open daily from 11am to 5pm; from November through the first 2 weeks of March, it is open on a daily basis between 10am and 3pm, with guided tours of the castle leaving every 30 minutes. The castle is closed for annual open-air concerts on the last Saturday in June and the first Saturday in July. Admission to the castle and grounds is £6.50 ($9.80) for adults or £4.50 ($6.80) for children. Car parking is free, with a free ride on a fully accessible minibus available for persons who cannot manage the half mile or so walk from the car park to the castle.

Snacks, salads, cream teas, and hot meals are offered daily at a number of places on the estate, including Fairfax Hall, a restored 17th-century tithe barn with a self-service carvery restaurant and bar.

Kentish Evenings are presented in Fairfax Hall most Saturdays throughout the year, except in August, starting at 7pm, with a sherry cocktail reception, then a guided tour of the castle. Guests feast on Kentish pâté, followed by broth and roast beef carved at the table, plus seasonal vegetables. The meal is rounded off by dessert, cheese, and coffee. A half bottle of wine is included in the overall price of £35.50 ($53.30) per person. During the meal, musicians play a selection of music suitable to the surroundings and the occasion. Advance reservations are required, made by calling the castle. Kentish Evenings finish at 12:30am, and accommodation is available locally.

If you are not driving during your trip, British Rail and several London-based bus-tour operators offer inclusive day excursions to Leeds Castle. The castle is 4 miles east of Maidstone at the junction of the A20 and the M20 London-Folkestone roads.

6. DORKING

26 miles S of London

GETTING THERE By Train There is frequent daily train service from London's Victoria Station to Dorking (trip time: 35 min.).

By Bus Green Line buses (no. 714) leave from London's Victoria Coach Station daily, heading for Kingston with a stop at Dorking (trip time: 1 hr.).

By Car Take the A3 south from London.

ESSENTIALS The **telephone area code** is 0306.

This town, birthplace of Lord Laurence Olivier, lies on the Mole River at the foot of the North Downs. Within easy reach are some of the most scenic spots in the shire, including Silent Pool, Box Hill, and Leith Hill.

Three miles to the northwest and 1½ miles south of Great Bookham, off the A246 Leatherhead-Guildford road, stands **Polesden Lacey** (tel. 0372/452048), a former Regency villa built in 1824. It contains the Greville collection of antiques, paintings, and tapestries. In the early part of this century it was enlarged to become a comfortable Edwardian country house when it was the home of a celebrated hostess, who frequently entertained royalty. The estate consists of 1,000 acres, and the 18th-century garden is filled with herbaceous borders, a rose garden, and beech walks.

The house is open April to October, Wednesday through Sunday from 1:30 to 5:30pm; March and November, on Saturday and Sunday from 1:30 to 4:30pm. The charge to visit the house on Sunday and bank holiday Mondays is £3.50 ($5.30); on other days, £2.50 ($3.80). To visit the garden from April until the end of October costs £2.50 ($3.80). Children under 17 pay half price, and those under 5 are admitted free. A licensed restaurant on the grounds is open from 11am on the days the house can be visited.

WHERE TO STAY & DINE

BURFORD BRIDGE HOTEL, Box Hill, Dorking, Surrey RH5 6BX. Tel. 0306/884561. Fax 0306/880386. 48 rms (all with bath). TV TEL **Directions:** Take the A24 1½ miles north of Dorking.
$ Rates: £98 ($147) single; £115–£128 ($172.50–$192) double. Breakfast £8.95 ($13.40) extra. AE, DC, MC, V. **Parking:** Free.

The Burford Bridge Hotel offers stylish living in a rural town from which a train will zip you into London in less than half an hour. At the foot of beautiful Box Hill, the hotel has many historical associations. Lord Nelson was a frequent patron, and Keats completed *Endymion* here in 1817. Wordsworth and Robert Louis Stevenson also visited the hotel occasionally. You get the best of both the old and the new here, including a tithe barn (ca. 1600) as well as a large bedroom.

The restaurant serves good English food, and a bar opens onto a flowered patio with a fountain. In summer, you can enjoy the garden swimming pool and frequent barbecues.

WHITE HORSE HOTEL, High St., Dorking, Surrey, RH4 1BE. Tel. 0306/881138, or toll free in the U.S. 800/435-4542. Fax 0306/887241. 68 rms (all with bath or shower).
$ Rates: £78 ($117) single; £110 ($165) double. Breakfast £8.35 ($12.50) extra. AE, DC, MC, V. **Parking:** Free.

Just 10 miles from Gatwick Airport you can dine or lodge at a hotel that is supposed to have been the "Marquis of Granby" in the *Pickwick Papers*. At least Dickens was known to have frequented the bar parlor. All the well-furnished rooms have radio and beverage facilities. Some are in a modern annex. Often called "the most interesting house in Dorking," the inn has a restaurant as well as a Pickwick Bar offering à la carte meals for £16.75 ($25.10) and up. There's also a heated outdoor pool.

7. GUILDFORD

33 miles S of London

GETTING THERE   By Train   The train departs from London's Waterloo Station (trip time: 40 min.).

By Bus   National Express operates buses from London's Victoria Coach Station daily, with a stopover at Guildford on its runs from London to Brighton. It's usually more convenient to take the train.

By Car   From London, head south along the A3.

ESSENTIALS   The **telephone area code** is 0483. The **Tourist Information Centre** is at The Undercroft, 72 High St. (tel. 0483/444007).

The guildhall in this country town, which lies on the Wey River, has an ornamental projecting clock that dates from 1683, and Charles Dickens considered the High Street, which slopes to the river, one of the most beautiful in England.

Lying 2½ miles southwest of the city, **Loseley House,** Loseley Park, Guildford (tel. 0483/304440), a beautiful and historic Elizabethan mansion visited by Queen Elizabeth I, James I, and Queen Mary, has been featured on TV and in five films. Its works of art include paneling from Henry VIII's Nonsuch Palace, period furniture, a unique carved chalk chimneypiece, magnificent ceilings, and cushions made by the first Queen Elizabeth. The mansion is open from the end of May to the end of September, Wednesday through Saturday from 2 to 5pm, charging £3.50 ($5.30) for adults, £2 ($3) for children. Lunches and teas are served in the 17th-century tithe barn from 11am to 5pm, and you can tour the farm and visit the farm shop.

WHERE TO STAY & DINE

FORTE CREST HOTEL, Egerton Rd., Guildford, Surrey GU2 5XZ. Tel. 0483/574444, or toll free 800/435-4542 in the U.S. Fax 0483/302960. 109 rms (all with bath), 2 suites. MINIBAR TV TEL **Directions:** Head about 2 miles southwest of the center of Guildford, just off the A3 London-Portsmouth road.

$ Rates: £95 ($142.50) single; £100–£140 ($150–$210) double; from £130 ($195) suite. Breakfast £8.95 ($13.40) extra. AE, DC, MC, V. **Parking:** Free.

In this 1987 hostelry, surrounded by landscaped grounds, a feeling of heritage is conveyed by natural red elm joinery, polished brass fittings, and marble floors. Bedrooms incorporate both living and sleeping areas, and all contain radios and hot-beverage facilities. The needs of disabled guests have been taken into consideration.

The restaurant features traditional English roasts and international dishes. Guests find the hot and cold buffet to be a good value. The coffee shop, open daily from 6:30

to 11pm, offers family favorites served in an informal atmosphere. There's a health and fitness club with an indoor heated swimming pool and a sun terrace.

A NEARBY PLACE TO STAY

INN ON THE LAKE, Ockford Rd., Godalming, Surrey GU7 1RH. Tel. 0483/415575. Fax 0483/860445. 20 rms (17 with bath). TV TEL **Directions:** From Guildford, take the A3100 south.

$ Rates (including English breakfast): £45 ($67.50) single without bath, £75 ($112.50) single with bath; £85 ($127.50) double with bath. AE, DC, MC, V. **Parking:** Free.

This haven of landscaped gardens with ducks drowsing on pools beside the lake is only 5 miles from Guildford. The rooms are decorated with pretty country prints and simple furniture, each with a tea and coffee maker and radio. Excellent snacks are served in a real old-world bar, where some of the timbers date from Tudor times. In summer, barbecues are held in the garden. For more substantial dinners, fixed-price menus are offered at £16.50 ($24.80) plus à la carte with a varied selection of grills, English favorites, and continental dishes. The house was listed in the *Domesday Book* and has Tudor, Georgian, and Victorian associations.

AN EASY EXCURSION

One of the great gardens of England, **Wisley Garden,** Wisley, Woking (tel. 0483/224234), stands in Wisley near Ripley just off the M25 (junction 10) on the A3 London-Portsmouth road. Every season of the year, this 250-acre garden has a profusion of flowers and shrubbery, ranging from the New Alpine House with its delicate blossoms in spring, to the walled garden with formal flowerbeds in summer, to the heather garden's colorful foliage in the fall, to a riot of exotic plants in the glasshouses in winter. This garden is the site of a laboratory where botanists, plant pathologists, and an entomologist experiment and assist amateur gardeners. There is a large gift shop with a wide range of gardening books and a licensed restaurant and cafeteria. Open all year, Monday through Saturday from 10am to 7pm (or sunset if earlier). Admission is £4.20 ($6.30) for adults, and £1.75 ($2.60) for children ages 6 to 16.

---

8. HASLEMERE

42 miles S of London, 37 miles NW of Brighton

GETTING THERE By Train Haslemere is an hour's train ride from Waterloo Station in London.

By Bus There is no bus service from London to Haslemere because the train service is so excellent. Once in Haslemere, local buses connect the town to such nearby villages as Farnham and Grayshott.

By Car From Guildford (see above), continue south on the A3100, going via Godalming and branching onto the A286.

ESSENTIALS The **telephone area code** is 0428.

In this quiet, sleepy town, early English musical instruments are made by hand, and an annual music festival (see below) is the town's main drawing card. Over the years, the Dolmetsch family has been responsible for the acclaim that has come to this otherwise unheralded little Surrey town, which lies in the midst of some of the shire's finest scenery.

THE FESTIVAL

It isn't often that one can hear such exquisite music played so skillfully on the harpsichord, recorder, lute, or any of the instruments created to play the music of earlier centuries. Throughout the year the Dolmetsch family makes and repairs these instruments and welcomes visitors to their place on the edge of Haslemere. They rehearse constantly, preparing for the concerts that are held in July and last 6 days.

You can get specific information and arrange for the purchase of tickets by contacting Haslemere Hall, Bridge Road, Haslemere, Surrey GU27 2AS (tel. 0428/642161). Hours are Monday to Friday 9am to noon and 2 to 4pm, Saturday 9am to 1am. During the festival, matinees begin at 3:15pm, evening performances at 7:30pm. Balcony seats cost £6 to £8 ($9 to $12), and stall seats cost £4 to £7 ($6 to $10.50).

WHERE TO STAY

LYTHE HILL HOTEL, Petworth Rd., Haslemere, Surrey GU27 3BQ. Tel. 0428/651251, or toll free 800/323-5463 in the U.S. Fax 0428/644131. 40 rms (all with bath), 12 suites. TV TEL **Directions:** Take the B2131 1½ miles east from Haslemere.

$ **Rates:** £78–£90 ($117–$135) single; £90 ($135) double; from £120 ($180) suite. Breakfast £8 ($12) extra. AE, MC, V. **Parking:** Free.

This 14th-century farmhouse of historic interest on the outskirts of Haslemere is situated on 20 acres of parkland overlooking National Trust woodlands—just an hour from London, Heathrow, and Gatwick. Across the courtyard is the main hotel, with luxuriously appointed bedrooms and suites, as well as an English restaurant. In the black-and-white timbered farmhouse are five elegant period units with marble-tile baths. One has a four-poster bed dated 1614.

Downstairs in the farmhouse is the renowned, oak-beamed and paneled Auberge de France Restaurant, offering a classic French cuisine served by candlelight on polished oak tables. Specialties include turbot, fresh Scottish salmon, tournedos de boeuf, and a cellar of fine wines. Dinner costs around £30 ($45). Open from 7 to 9:45pm Tuesday through Sunday; on Sunday, for lunch as well (noon to 2pm).

WHERE TO DINE

MOREL'S, 23 Lower St. Tel. 651462.
   Cuisine: FRENCH. **Reservations:** Required.
$ **Prices:** Appetizers £4.50–£7.30 ($6.80–$11); main courses £13.50–£15.50 ($20.30–$23.30); fixed-price meals £19.50 ($29.30) at lunch, £25 ($37.50) at dinner. AE, DC, MC, V.
   Open: Lunch Tues–Fri 12:30–2pm; dinner Tues–Sat 7–10pm. **Closed:** Last 2 weeks in Sept and last 2 weeks in Feb.

Surrey's preeminent French restaurant showcases the talents of a remarkable chef, Jean-Yves Morel. He represents the best of yesterday, yet he's not afraid to experiment with new ideas (mainly those that work). His main-street establishment, created from a row of terraced cottages, is bright and furnished in modern overtones, but there's nothing about the decor that detracts from the cuisine. Londoners flock here.

M. Morel, appropriately, uses morels in some of his dishes. His menu, adjusted to the seasons and market conditions, changes every 30 days or so, so it's difficult to recommend specific dishes. A typical one might be chargrilled pigeon breast subtly flavored with a light sauce made with juices of langoustine. Vegetables are done to perfection, and the cheese-board selection rivals those of France. The assiette du chef is a festival for the palate, a perfectly balanced selection of his finest desserts.

- **WHAT'S SPECIAL ABOUT THE SUSSEXES**
1. **RYE**
2. **HASTINGS & ST. LEONARDS**
3. **BATTLE**
4. **ALFRISTON & LEWES**
5. **BRIGHTON**
6. **ARUNDEL**
7. **CHICHESTER**

If King Harold hadn't loved Sussex so much, the course of English history might have been changed forever. Had the brave Saxon waited longer in the north, he could have marshaled more adequate reinforcements before striking south to meet the Normans. But Duke William's soldiers were ravaging the countryside he knew so well, and Harold rushed down to counter them.

Harold's enthusiasm for Sussex is understandable. The landscape rises and falls like waves. The county is known for its downlands and tree-thickened weald, from which came the timbers to build England's mighty fleet in days gone by. The shires lie south of London and Surrey, bordering Kent in the east, Hampshire in the west, and opening directly onto the sometimes sunny, seaside-town-dotted English Channel.

Like the other sections in the vulnerable south of England, Sussex witnessed some of the biggest moments in the country's history. Apart from the Norman landings at Hastings, the most life-changing transformation occurred in the 19th century, as middle-class Victorians flocked to the seashore, pumping new spirit into Eastbourne, Worthing, Brighton, even old Hastings. The cult of the saltwater worshipers flourished, and has to this day. Although Eastbourne and Worthing are much frequented by the English, I'd place them several fathoms below Brighton and Hastings, which are much more suitable if you're seeking a vacation by the sea.

The old towns and villages of Sussex, particularly Rye and Winchelsea, are far more intriguing than the seaside resorts. No Sussex village is lovelier than Alfriston (and the innkeepers know it, too); Arundel is noted for its castle; the cathedral city of Chichester is a mecca for theater buffs. Traditionally, and for purposes of government (and this book), Sussex is divided into East Sussex and West Sussex.

SEEING THE SUSSEXES

GETTING THERE

If you're heading straight for the region, it's best to land at Gatwick Airport (tel. 0293/531299), which has convenient rail, bus, and road connections to all of the southeast. The airport is close to such major highways as the A23 and the M23. The area is well served by British Rail's Network Southeast, with frequent departures from London's Victoria or Charing Cross Station for the east or Waterloo Station for West Sussex. National Express buses (tel. 071/730-0202 in London) serve the region from London's Victoria Coach Station. A network of private bus companies also operates in the region. For East Sussex, call 0273/481000 for bus information, and for West Sussex destinations, call 0243/777556.

WHAT'S SPECIAL ABOUT THE SUSSEXES

Great Towns/Villages

- □ Rye, former Cinque Port, now considered one of England's best-preserved medieval villages.
- □ Alfriston, ancient town in the Cuckmere Valley and a former smugglers' haunt.
- □ Brighton, first and largest seaside resort in the southeast, with its famed Royal Pavilion.

Castles

- □ Arundel Castle, ancestral home of the dukes of Norfolk, with an exceptional collection of paintings in this Georgian town.
- □ Hastings Castle, first of the Norman castles to be built in England (ca. 1067).
- □ Battle Abbey, the setting for the Battle of Hastings in 1066.

Ace Attractions

- □ The Royal Pavilion at Brighton, a John Nash version of an Indian mogul's palace.
- □ The Hastings Embroidery, a commemorative needlework tracing 900 years of English history.

Literary Shrines

- □ Bateman's, northwest of Battle, home of Rudyard Kipling and filled with mementos of English days of empire in India.
- □ Monks House, outside Lewes, a National Trust property, home to Virginia and Leonard Woolf from 1919 to Leonard's death in 1969.

A SUGGESTED ITINERARY

Day 1: Head for Rye and Winchelsea for the night.

Day 2: Explore Hastings in the morning, Battle Abbey in the afternoon, and stay overnight in the little village of Alfriston.

Day 3: Go west to Brighton for a day's fun and a visit to the Royal Pavilion.

Day 4: Explore Arundel Castle and stay overnight in the area, perhaps taking in a theatrical presentation in the evening at Chichester.

---

1. RYE

62½ miles S of London

GETTING THERE   By Train   From London, the Southern Region Line offers trains south from Charing Cross or Cannon Street Station, with a change at Ashford, before continuing on to Rye. You can also go via Tunbridge Wells with a change in Hastings. Trains run every hour during the day, arriving at the Rye Train Station off Cinque Ports Street (trip time: 1½–2 hr.).

By Bus   You need to take the train to get to Rye, but once you're there you'll find bus coaches departing for many destinations, including Hastings. Schedules of the various bus companies are posted on signs in the parking lot. For bus connections information throughout the region, call 0797/223343.

By Car   From London, take the M23, M26, and M20 east to Maidstone, going southeast along the A20 to Ashford. At Ashford, continue south along the coast on the A2070.

ESSENTIALS   The **telephone area code** is 0797. The **Tourist Information Centre** is at The Strand Quay (tel. 0797/226696).

"Nothing more recent than a Cavalier's Cloak, Hat and Ruffles should be seen in the streets of Rye," said Louis Jennings. This ancient town, formerly an island, was flourishing in the 13th century. Rye, near the English Channel, and neighboring Winchelsea were once part of the "Antient" Cinque Port Confederation. Rye in its early days was a smuggling center, its denizens sneaking in contraband from the marshes to stash away in little nooks.

But the sea receded from Rye, leaving it perched like a giant whale out of water, 2 miles from the Channel. Its narrow, cobblestone streets twist and turn like a labyrinth, with buildings jumbled along them whose sagging roofs and crooked chimneys indicate the town's medieval origins. The old town's entrance is **Land Gate,** where a single lane of traffic passes between massive, 40-foot-high stone towers. The parapet of the gate contains holes through which boiling oil used to be poured on unwelcome visitors, such as French raiding parties.

Attacked several times by French fleets, Rye was practically razed in 1377. But it rebuilt itself sufficiently, decking itself out in the Elizabethan style, so that Queen Elizabeth I, during her visit in 1573, bestowed upon the town the distinction of Royal Rye. This has long been considered a special place and over the years has attracted the famous, such as novelist Henry James.

Today the town has lots of sites of architectural interest, notably the mid-12th-century **St. Mary's Parish Church,** Church Square (tel. 224935), with its 16th-century clock flanked by two gilded cherubs, known as Quarter Boys from their striking of the bells on the quarter hour. The church is often referred to as "the Cathedral of East Sussex" because of its size and beauty. If you're courageous, you can climb a set of wooden stairs and ladders to the bell tower of the church, from which an impressive view is afforded. It's open daily from 9:30am to 8pm June through September, from 9:30am to dusk off-season. Contributions are appreciated to enter the church. Admission to the tower costs £1.50 ($2.30) for adults and 75p ($1.10) for children.

WHAT TO SEE & DO

LAMB HOUSE, West St., at the top of Mermaid St. Tel. 224982.
Henry James lived in Lamb House from 1898 to 1916. There are many James mementos in the house, which is set in a walled garden. Its former owner rushed off to join the Gold Rush in North America but perished in the Klondike, and James was able to buy the freehold for a modest £2,000. Some of his well-known books were written here.

   Admission: £2 ($3) adults and children.
   Open: Apr–Oct, Wed–Sat 2–5:30pm.

RYE MUSEUM, Ypres Tower, Gungarden. Tel. 226728.
   This stone-built fortification was constructed about 1250 by King Henry III to

defend the coast against attack by the French. For 300 years, it was the town jail, but has long since been converted into a museum. A wealth of local and Cinque Ports history comes alive here, along with the saga of Romney Marsh and its legendary smugglers.

Admission: £1.50 ($2.30) adults, 50p (80¢) children.
Open: Easter–Oct, daily 10:30am–5:30pm.

A NEARBY ATTRACTION

The neighbor Cinque Confederation port to Rye, **Winchelsea** has also witnessed the water's ebb. It traces its history back to Edward I and has experienced many dramatic moments, such as sacking by the French. In the words of one 19th-century writer, Winchelsea is "a sunny dream of centuries ago." The finest sight of this dignified residential town is a badly damaged 14th-century church, containing a number of remarkable tombs.

On the outskirts of Winchelsea, you can visit **Smallhythe Place,** Smallhythe, near Tenterden (tel. 05806/2334), for 30 years the country house of Dame Ellen Terry, the English actress acclaimed for her Shakespearean roles who had a long theatrical association with Sir Henry Irving; she died in the house in 1928. This timber-framed house, known as a "continuous-jetty house," was built in the first half of the 16th century and is filled with Terry memorabilia. The house is on the B2082 near Tenterden, about 6 miles to the north of Rye, and is open April to October, Saturday through Wednesday from 2 to 6pm. Adults pay £2.50 ($3.80) admission; children, £1.30 ($2). Take bus no. 312 from Tenterden.

WHERE TO STAY

MODERATE

THE GEORGE, High St., Rye, East Sussex TN31 7JP. Tel. 0797/222114, or toll free 800/435-4542 in the U.S. Fax 0797/224065. 22 rms (all with bath). TV TEL
$ **Rates:** £68 ($102) single; £105 ($157.50) double. Breakfast £7.95 ($11.90) extra. AE, DC, MC, V. **Parking:** Free.

This coaching inn has a 400-year history. In the 18th century it drew a diverse clientele: some traveling by horse-drawn carriage, others by boat, between London and France. This is one of the most charming small inns in the region, with half-timbered architecture. Some of the timbers are said to have come from the wreck of an English ship broken up in Rye Harbour after the defeat of the Spanish Armada.

On the premises, tucked away at the end of narrow hallways and twisted stairwells, is the John Crouch pub, with about eight different kinds of beer and cider on tap. The hotel also has an old-fashioned restaurant and at least two blazing fireplaces in cold weather.

MERMAID INN, Mermaid St., Rye, East Sussex TN31 7EU. Tel. 0797/ 223065. Fax 0797/226995. 29 rms (all with bath). TV TEL
$ **Rates** (including English breakfast): £70 ($105) single; £95–£115 ($142.50–$172.50) double. AE, DC, MC, V. **Parking:** Free.

⭐ The Mermaid Inn, between West Street and the Strand, is one of the most famous of the old smugglers' inns of England, known to that band of cutthroats, the real-life Hawkhurst Gang, as well as to Russell Thorndike's fictional character, Dr. Syn. One of the present rooms, in fact, is called Dr. Syn's

Bedchamber, and is connected by a secret staircase—set in the thickness of the wall—to the bar. The most sought-after rooms are in the building overlooking the cobblestone street. One, the Smugglers Room, has an oak four-poster and all have private bath or shower.

When Elizabeth came to Rye and the Mermaid in 1573, the inn had already been operating nearly 150 years. A covered carriageway leads to the parking area. In the center of the hotel is a courtyard, where you'll see a pedestal fountain with water flowing down on the heads of water lilies. The Mermaid has also taken over the 16th-century Ship Inn at the foot of Mermaid Street, which, with its 12 bedrooms and restaurant on the first floor, complements the Mermaid.

INEXPENSIVE

DURRANT HOUSE HOTEL, East St., Rye, East Sussex TN31 7LA. Tel. 0797/223182. 10 rms (all with bath), 1 suite. TV

$ Rates (including English breakfast): £30–£40 ($45–$60) single; £40–£60 ($60–$90) double; from £80 ($120) suite. DC, MC, V. **Parking:** Free.

This beautiful Georgian house is set on a quiet residential street, at the end of Market Street off High Street. The hotel possesses much charm and character and has a cozy lounge with an arched, brick fireplace and, across the hall, a residents' bar. Over the years, it has attracted many famous personages. In more recent times, the renowned artist Paul Nash lived next door until his death in 1946; in fact, his celebrated view, as seen in his painting, *View of the Rother,* can be enjoyed from the River Room of the hotel. The house is named for a previous owner, Sir William Durrant, a friend of the Duke of Wellington, who bought it in the 18th century. At one time the house was used as a relay station for carrier pigeons; these birds brought news of the victory at Waterloo. The Durrant House Restaurant serves a traditional English cuisine, specializing in seafood. French and Italian specialties are also served. A five-course table d'hôte menu costs £15 ($22.50).

HOLLOWAY HOUSE, High St., Rye, East Sussex TN31 7JF. Tel. 0797/224748. 7 rms (all with bath). TEL

$ Rates (including English breakfast): Sun–Thurs, £39–£60 ($58.50–$90) single; £50–£90 ($75–$135) double. Fri–Sat, £70–£90 ($105–$135) single or double. MC, V.

Winner of several awards for the beauty of its small front garden and the quality of its restoration, this charming house was originally built in 1568 above a much older vaulted cellar. (Local historians suspect that the cellar was the foundation of a prominent medieval inn, the White Vine, which is frequently mentioned in historical archives.) Restored from an almost derelict shell in 1987 by Sheila Brown, the capable owner, it carefully maintains the Georgian detailing of the formal public rooms and the Tudor-style wall and ceiling beams of the antique bedrooms. An in-house restaurant, strictly separated into smoking and no-smoking sections, serves evening meals priced from around £8 ($12) each.

HOPE ANCHOR HOTEL, Watchbell St., Rye, East Sussex TN31 7HA. Tel. 0797/222216. Fax 0797/223796. 14 rms (9 with bath). TV

$ Rates (including English breakfast): £36 ($54) single without bath, £40 ($60) single with bath; £50 ($75) double without bath, £60–£62 ($90–$93) double with bath. MC, V. **Parking:** Free.

At the end of a cobblestone street on a hill dominating the town stands this 17th-century hostelry, which enjoys panoramic views of the surrounding countryside and overlooks the Strand Quay where yachts can be seen at their moorings. Oak beams and open fires in winter make this a most inviting place to spend a few days.

The bedrooms are comfortable, all with hot-beverage facilities. Some contain four-poster beds.

Bar meals are served at lunch, and the Hope Anchor Restaurant offers an English cuisine, featuring fresh fish caught locally. A dinner in the restaurant costs £12.50 ($18.80).

WHERE TO DINE

MODERATE

FLUSHING INN, 4 Market St. Tel. 223292.
   Cuisine: SEAFOOD/ENGLISH. **Reservations:** Required.
$ **Prices:** Appetizers £3–£11 ($4.50–$16.50); main courses £7.50–£21.50 ($11.30–$32.30); fixed-price meals £11 ($16.50) at lunch, £19 ($28.50) at dinner. AE, DC, MC, V.
   Open: Lunch Wed–Mon 12:15–1:45pm; dinner Wed–Sun 6:45–9pm. **Closed:** First 2 weeks in Jan.

In a 16th-century inn on a cobblestone street near Rye Parish Church, the Flushing Inn has preserved the best of the past, including a wall-size fresco in the restaurant dating from 1544 and depicting a menagerie of birds and heraldic beasts. A rear dining room overlooks a carefully tended flower garden. A special feature is the Sea Food Lounge Bar, where sandwiches and plates of seafood are available for £7 to £11 ($10.50 to $16.50). Besides these lunches and dinners, gastronomic evenings are held at regular intervals between October and April. For one of these specialty meals, including your apéritif, wine, and after-dinner brandy, you pay £44 ($66) per person. Fine-wine evenings cost £48 to £60 ($72 to $90). The Flushing Inn has been run by the Mann family since 1960, with the second generation now fully active in the business.

THE LANDGATE BISTRO, 5–6 Landgate. Tel. 222829.
   Cuisine: ENGLISH. **Reservations:** Required.
$ **Prices:** Appetizers £3.50–£7 ($5.30–$10.50); main courses £9.50–£14 ($14.30–$21); fixed-price dinner £14.50 ($21.80). DC, MC, V.
   Open: Dinner only, Tues–Fri 7–9:30pm, Sat 7–10pm. **Closed:** One week in Oct.

Toni Ferguson-Lees is known for fresh local fish, wild duck, rabbit, pigeon, and jugged hare. It's all there in pies, casseroles, and stews, accompanied by fresh seasonal vegetables properly cooked or a salad. The fixed-price dinner is featured from Tuesday to Thursday only. Service is both polite and efficient. The restaurant occupies two small converted Landgate shops and is lined with brick, very much in the old cottagelike style of Rye.

THE OLD VICARAGE IN EAST STREET, East St., Rye, East Sussex TN31 7JY. Tel. 0797/225131.
   Cuisine: FRENCH/INTERNATIONAL. **Reservations:** Usually required.
$ **Prices:** Appetizers £1.90–£3.40 ($2.90–$5.10); main courses £8–£9.80 ($12–$14.70); 3-course fixed-price dinner £10.95 ($16.40). DC, MC, V.
   Open: Dinner only, daily 7–9pm. **Closed:** Jan.

Once the Georgian vicarage for St. Mary's Church, this charming establishment off High Street was converted into a French-style *restaurant avec chambres* in 1979. Although the owners, Sarah and Bill Foster, maintain four beautifully decorated bedrooms upstairs, the establishment is best known for its elegant restaurant. After an apéritif in the cocktail bar, dinner guests proceed into the blue-and-white dining room, where, within sight of a carved fireplace, they enjoy a selection of dishes from the classic French and international cuisine. The menu changes monthly to make the most of the best in local fish and meat. A typical meal listing might include shrimp-and-spinach soup, hot deviled crab, Romney Marsh lamb grilled with rosemary, filet of Rye Bay plaice stuffed with prawns in a fresh cream-and-herb sauce, and escalope of pork in a vermouth sauce, followed by desserts such as vacherin aux fruits and a selection of unusual homemade ice creams.

Each of the bedrooms is suitable for one or two people and rents, with breakfast included, for £28 to £39 ($42 to $58.50) daily per person. Units contain private baths, color TVs, phones, and a carefully assembled kind of panache. This establishment is not to be confused with a nearby B&B also called the Old Vicarage.

2. HASTINGS & ST. LEONARDS

63 miles SE of London, 45 miles W of Dover

GETTING THERE **By Train** Daily trains run from London's Victoria Station or Charing Cross to Hastings hourly. Trip time is 1½ to 2 hours, depending on the train.

By Bus Hastings is linked by bus to Maidstone, Folkestone, and Eastbourne, which has direct service with scheduled departures. National Express operates regular daily service from London's Victoria Coach Station.

By Car From the M25 ring road around London, head southeast to the coast and Hastings on the A21.

ESSENTIALS The **telephone area code** is 0424. The **Tourist Information Centre** is at 4 Robertson Terrace (tel. 0424/718888).

The world has seen bigger battles, but few are as well remembered as the Battle of Hastings in 1066. When William, Duke of Normandy, landed on the Sussex coast and lured King Harold (already fighting Vikings in Yorkshire) southward to defeat, the destiny of the English-speaking people was changed forever. The actual battle occurred at what is now Battle Abbey (9 miles away), but the Norman duke used Hastings as his base of operation.

Linked by a 3-mile promenade along the sea, Hastings and St. Leonards were given a considerable boost in the 19th century by Queen Victoria, who visited several times. Neither town enjoys such royal patronage today; rather, they do a thriving business with the English on vacation. Hastings and St. Leonards have the usual shops and English sea-resort amusements.

WHAT TO SEE & DO

HASTINGS CASTLE, Castle Hill Rd., West Hill. Tel. 718888.
In ruins now, the first of the Norman castles to be built in England sprouted up on a western hill overlooking Hastings, circa 1067. Precious little is left to remind us of the days when proud knights, imbued with a spirit of pomp and spectacle, wore bonnets and girdles. The fortress was defortified by King John in 1216, and later served as a church. Owned by the Pelham dynasty from the latter 16th century to modern times, the ruins have been turned over to Hastings. There is now an audiovisual presentation of the castle's history, including the famous battle of 1066. From the mount, you'll have a good view of the coast and promenade.

Admission: £2.30 ($3.50) adults, £1.60 ($2.40) children.
Open: Feb 13–Apr 1, daily 11am–4pm; Apr 2–Sept 26, daily 10am–5:30pm.
Transportation: The West Cliff Railway takes you from George St. to the castle for 55p (80¢) adults, 35p (50¢) children.

THE HASTINGS EMBROIDERY, Town Hall, Queen's Rd. Tel. 718888.

★ A commemorative work, the Hastings Embroidery is a remarkable achievement that traces 900 years of English history through needlework. First exhibited in 1966, the 27 panels, 243 feet in length, depict 81 historic scenes, including some of the nation's greatest moments and legends: the murder of Thomas Becket, King John signing the Magna Carta, the Black Plague, Chaucer's pilgrims going to Canterbury, the Battle of Agincourt with the victorious Henry V, the War of the Roses, the Little Princes in the Tower, Bloody Mary's reign, Drake's *Golden Hind,* the arrival of Philip II's ill-fated armada, Guy Fawkes's gunpowder plot, the sailing of the *Mayflower,* the disastrous plague of 1665, the great London fire of 1666, Nelson at Trafalgar, the Battle of Waterloo, the Battle of Britain, and the D-day landings at Normandy. Also exhibited is a scale model of the battlefield at Battle, with William's inch-high men doing in Harold's model soldiers.

Admission: £1.25 ($1.90) adults, 75p ($1.10) children.

Open: May–Sept, Mon–Fri 10am–5pm; Oct–Apr, Mon–Fri 11:30am–3:30pm.

SMUGGLERS ADVENTURE, St. Clements Caves, West Hill. Tel. 422964.

Here you can descend into the once-secret underground haunts of the smugglers of Hastings. In these chambers, where the smugglers stashed their bounty away from Customs authorities, you can see an exhibition and museum, a video in a theater, and take a subterranean adventure walk with 50 life-size figures, along with dramatic sound and lighting effects.

Admission: £3.50 ($5.30) adults, £2.25 ($3.40) children, £9.95 ($14.90) family ticket.

Open: Easter–Sept, daily 10am–5:30pm; Oct–Easter, daily 11am–4:30pm.

Transportation: The West Cliff Railway from George St., for 55p (80¢) adults, 35p (50¢) children.

WHERE TO STAY

BEAUPORT PARK HOTEL, Battle Rd. (A2100), Hastings, East Sussex TN38 8EA. Tel. 0424/851-222, or toll free 800/528-1234 in the U.S. and Canada. Fax 0424/852465. 23 rms (all with bath), 2 suites. TV TEL Directions: Head 3½ miles northwest of Hastings, at the junction of the A2100 and the B2159. Bus: 52 from Hastings.

$ Rates (including English breakfast): £62 ($93) single; £90 ($135) double; from £94 ($141) suite. AE, DC, MC, V. **Parking:** £1.50 ($2.30).

Originally the private estate of General Murray, former governor of Québec (who had previously served under General Wolfe), the building was destroyed by fire in 1923 and reconstructed in the old style. It is surrounded by beautiful gardens (the Italian-style grounds in the rear contain statuary and flowering shrubbery). The living room and lounge are tastefully furnished, and the French windows in the dining room open onto the parklike rear.

The hotel offers well-prepared and handsomely served cuisine. Some of the produce comes from the hotel's own gardens. A fixed-price lunch is offered at £14 ($21) with many choices available. The fixed-price dinner is £16 ($24), again with a wide selection.

THE ROYAL VICTORIA, Marina, St. Leonards, East Sussex TN38 0BD. Tel. 0424/445544. Fax 0424/721995. 52 rms (all with bath). MINIBAR TV TEL

$ Rates (including English breakfast): £57.50–£67.50 ($86.30–$101.30) single; £75–£95 ($112.50–$142.50) double. AE, DC, MC, V. **Parking:** Free.

The seafront hotel, constructed in 1828, has the most impressive architecture of any establishment in town, and offers the best accommodation in Hastings or St. Leonards. Since a complete refurbishing in 1988, the Royal Victoria is back to its premier position. The hotel is attractively furnished and decorated, and offers some of the best food at the resort in its restaurant, which accepts nonresidents who reserve. A fixed-price lunch begins at £13 ($19.50), and a fixed-price dinner goes for £17 ($25.50). Service is daily from noon to 1:45pm and 7:30 to 9:45pm.

WHERE TO DINE

RÖSER'S, 64 Eversfield Place. Tel. 712218.
    Cuisine: FRENCH. **Reservations:** Required.
$ Prices: Appetizers £2.95–£7.95 ($4.40–$11.90); main courses £11.50–£14.95 ($17.30–$22.40); fixed-price lunch £15.95 ($23.90). AE, DC, MC, V.
    Open: Lunch Tues–Fri noon–2pm; dinner Tues–Sat 7–10pm. **Closed:** Last week in Aug.

This is a pleasant surprise in what is often considered one of the gastronomic wastelands of southern England. Most diners come to Röser's, opposite the pier, to enjoy the seafood dishes of Gerald Röser, who shows considerable skill in his choice of food offerings, including everything from the classic Dover sole to lamb from Romney Marsh. In season, game dishes are also featured. Try the wild boar chop with lentil sauce. The service is first-rate. The wine list is chosen with discretion, and prices tend to be reasonable since this is not a resort for big spenders.

---

3. BATTLE

55 miles S of London, 34 miles NE of Brighton

GETTING THERE   **By Train**   The train station at Battle is a stop on the London-Hastings rail link, with departures from both Charing Cross and Victoria Stations in London. For more information, call 04246/429325. Trip time: 1 hour, 20 minutes.

By Bus   It's best to go from London to Battle by train. However, if you're in Rye or Hastings in summer, you can take one of several frequent buses that run to Battle. For information and schedules, call 04246/431770.

By Car   From the M25 (the ring road around London), cut south to Sevenoaks and continue along the A21 to Battle via A2100.

ESSENTIALS   The **telephone area code** is 0424. The **Tourist Information Centre** is at 88 High St. (tel. 0424/773721).

Seven miles from Hastings, in the heart of the Sussex countryside, is the old market town of Battle, famed in history as the setting for the Battle of Hastings in 1066. King Harold, last of the Saxon kings, encircled by his housecarls, fought bravely, not only for his kingdom but for his life. He was killed by William, Duke of Normandy, and his body was dismembered. To commemorate the victory, William the Conqueror founded Battle Abbey at the south end of Battle High Street (tel. 0424/773792); some of the construction stone was shipped from his own lands at Caen in northern France.

During the dissolution of the monasteries from 1538 to 1539 by King Henry VIII, the church of the abbey was largely destroyed. Some buildings and ruins, however, remain in what Tennyson called "O Garden, blossoming out of English blood." The principal building still standing is Abbot's House, which is leased to a private school for boys and girls and is open to the general public only during summer holidays. Of architectural interest is the gatehouse, which has octagonal towers and stands at the top of the Market Square. All of the north Precinct Mall is still standing, and one of the most interesting sights of the ruins is the ancient Dorter Range, where the monks once slept.

The town of Battle grew up around the abbey; even though it has remained a medieval market town, many of the old half-timbered buildings regrettably have lost much of their original character because of stucco plastering carried on by past generations.

The abbey is open April through September, daily from 10am to 6pm; October to March, daily from 10am to 4pm. Admission is £2.70 ($4.10) for adults and £1.30 ($2) for children. The abbey is located a 5-minute walk from the rail station.

WHERE TO STAY & DINE

GEORGE HOTEL, 23 High St., Battle, East Sussex TN33 0EA. Tel. 0424/774466. Fax 0424/774853. 22 rms (all with bath). TV TEL
$ Rates (including continental breakfast): £40 ($60) single; £54 ($81) double. AE, DC, MC, V. **Parking:** Free.

An inn has stood on this site for more than 600 years, and today the George combines modern comfort and a historic building. The owners offer well-furnished rooms with private bath and hot-beverage facilities.

The hotel has a comfortable bar, with a full snack menu. Open log fires make the place cozy in winter. The spacious restaurant, the Brasserie, features English and continental dishes. Lunch costs £6.95 ($10.40), and dinner begins at £10 ($15). There is a private parking area.

NETHERFIELD PLACE, Netherfield Rd., Battle, East Sussex TN33 9PP. Tel. 0424/774455, or toll free 800/828-5572 in the U.S. Fax 0424/774024. 14 rms (all with bath or shower), 1 suite. TV TEL **Directions:** Take the A2100 1¾ miles northwest of Battle.
$ Rates (including English breakfast): £50–£65 ($75–$97.50) single; £85–£115 ($127.50–$172.50) double; from £190 ($285) suite. AE, DC, MC, V. **Parking:** £5 ($7.50). **Closed:** Dec 15–Jan 15.

★ Built in 1924 on 30 acres of parkland, this is by far the best place to stay. The symmetrical wings of this brick-fronted Georgian mansion extend toward flowering gardens on all sides. Once you pass beneath the cornices of the entrance, you'll discover a world of plush upholstery, comfortable bedrooms, and sun-flooded panoramas.

You can enjoy tea or a drink in the glassed-in lounge overlooking the trees outside. The international cuisine is also good and carefully served, prepared with fresh, wholesome produce. Fresh fruit and vegetables come from the hotel's garden. Dinners cost £18.50 ($27.80) and up.

4. ALFRISTON & LEWES

60 miles S of London

GETTING THERE By Train Rail service is available from London's Victoria Station and London Bridge Station heading for Lewes. One train per hour makes the trip during the day (trip time: 1¼ hr.). Trains are more frequent during rush hours. There is no rail service to Alfriston.

By Bus Buses run daily to Lewes from London's Victoria Coach Station, although there are many, many stops along the way (trip time: 3 hr.)—it's better to take the train. Once in Lewes, you can connect with a bus in Lewes run by the Southdown Bus Company which will take you to Alfriston in 30 minutes. The bus station at Lewes is on East Street in the center of town.

By Car Head east along the M25 (the London ring road), cutting south along the A26 via East Grinstead to Lewes. Once at Lewes, follow the A27 east to the signposted turnoff for the village of Alfriston.

ESSENTIALS The **telephone area code for Alfriston** is 0323; the **area code for Lewes** is 0273. The **Tourist Information Centre** is in Lewes at 32 High St. (tel. 0273/483448).

Nestled on the Cuckmere River, **Alfriston** is one of the most beautiful villages of England and has several old inns. Its High Street, with its old market cross, looks like one's idea of what an English village should be. Some of the old houses still have hidden chambers where smugglers stored their loot.

The village lies northeast of Seaford on the English Channel, in the vicinity of the resort of Eastbourne and the modern port of Newhaven. During the day, Alfriston is likely to be overrun by coach tours (it's that lovely, and that popular).

Only about a dozen miles along the A27 toward Brighton, **Lewes,** an ancient Sussex town centered in the South Downs, is worth exploring. Since the home of the Glyndebourne Opera is only 5 miles to the east, the accommodations of Lewes are difficult to reserve during the Glyndebourne Opera festival. The town has many historical associations, listing such residents as Thomas Paine, who lived at Bull House, High Street, now a restaurant.

WHAT TO SEE & DO

IN ALFRISTON

Drusilla's Park, off the A27 (tel. 0323/870656), has won awards. It lies 1 mile outside Alfriston. It's not large, but is fascinating nonetheless with a flamingo lake, Japanese garden, and unusual breeds of some domestic animals, among other attractions. Children are especially delighted, as there is a playland covering more than an acre. The park is open daily from 10am to 5pm (until dusk in winter), charging £4.80 ($7.20) for adults and £4.20 ($6.30) for children. It is closed December 24–26.

IN LEWES

The half-timbered **Anne of Cleves House,** 52 Southover High St. (tel. 0273/474610), was part of Anne of Cleves's divorce settlement from Henry VIII, but Anne of Cleves never lived in the house, and there is no proof that she ever visited Lewes. Today the house is a Museum of Local History and is cared for by the Sussex Archaeological Society. The museum has a furnished bedroom and kitchen and displays of furniture, local history of the Wealden iron industry, and other local crafts. Admission is £1.60 ($2.40) for adults, 80p ($1.20) for children. It's open April to October, Monday through Saturday from 10am to 5pm and on Sunday from 2 to 5pm. Bus: no. 123.

Lewes, of course, grew up around its Norman castle. Adjacent to the castle is the **Museum of Sussex Archaeology,** 169 High St. (tel. 0273/486290). A 20-minute audiovisual show is also presented. A joint admission ticket to both the castle and the museum costs £2.50 ($3.80) for adults, £1.25 ($1.90) for children. They're both open Monday through Saturday from 10am to 5:30pm and on Sunday from 11am to 5:30pm. Bus: no. 27, 28, 121, 122, 166, 728, or 729.

KIPLING'S HOME IN SUSSEX

Rudyard Kipling, the British writer famous for his stories about the days of empire in India, lived his last 34 years (1902–36) at **Bateman's,** a country house northwest of Battle and half a mile south of Burwash, on the A265, the Lewes-Etchingham road (tel. 0435/882302). The sandstone house, built in 1634, was bequeathed, together with its 300 acres of land and its contents, to the National Trust by Kipling's widow. The interior is filled with Asian rugs, antique bronzes, and other mementos the writer collected in India and elsewhere. Kipling's library is among the points of interest to be visited. The house is open April to October, Saturday through Wednesday from 11am to 5:30pm. Admission to the house and garden is £3.50 ($5.30) for adults and £1.80 ($2.70) for children Monday through Wednesday; on Saturday, Sunday, and bank holidays, it's £4 ($6) for adults and £2 ($3) for children.

WHERE TO STAY

IN ALFRISTON

STAR INN, High St., Alfriston, East Sussex BN26 5TA. Tel. 0323/ 870495, or toll free 800/435-4542 in the U.S. Fax 0323/870922. 34 rms (all with bath). TV TEL
$ Rates: £80 ($120) single; £95 ($142.50) double. Breakfast £8.50 ($12.80) extra. AE, DC, MC, V. **Parking:** Free.

The Star Inn occupies a building dating from 1450, although it was originally founded in the 1200s, perhaps to house pilgrims en route to Chichester and the shrine of St. Richard. In the center of the village, its carved front still unchanged, it boasts an overhanging second story of black-and-white timbers and bay windows. The lounges are on several levels, a forest of old timbers. Out back is a motel wing, with studio rooms. All units have radios, heating, and built-in wardrobe. A three-course dinner is priced from £17.95 ($26.90).

WHITE LODGE COUNTRY HOUSE HOTEL, Sloe Lane, Alfriston, East Sussex BN26 5UR. Tel. 0323/870265. Fax 0323/870284. 20 rms (all with bath). TV TEL **Bus:** Southdown no. 712.
$ Rates (including English breakfast): £50 ($75) single; £75–£110 ($112.50–$165) double. AE, MC, V. **Parking:** Free.

This converted private home, a 5-minute walk from the town center off the A27, is now one of the most opulently furnished hotels in the region, run by the original owners. It stands on 5 acres of gardens. The public rooms are outfitted like French salons, with carved 18th- and 19th-century antiques, many of them gilded. Bronze statues inspired by classical Greek myths are placed about. Each of the beautifully furnished bedrooms has a color TV, hairdryer, lots of tasseled curtains, and countryside views.

The daytime dining room is French, with Louis XV furniture centered around a chiseled fireplace of violet-tinged marble. Dinner is served below the reception area in an Edwardian room. A four-course lunch, served daily from 12:15 to 2pm, goes for £12.50 ($18.80); a four-course dinner, served from 7:15 to 9:45pm, costs £16.95 ($25.40). Menu specialties include corners of smoked salmon, grilled lemon sole, and, in season, marinated venison.

IN LEWES

SHELLEYS HOTEL, High St., Lewes, East Sussex BN7 1XS. Tel. 0273/ 472361. Fax 0273/483152. 21 rms (all with bath or shower). TV TEL
$ Rates: £72.50 ($108.80) single; £114–£145 ($171–$217.50) double. Breakfast £9.50 ($14.30) extra. AE, DC, MC, V. **Parking:** Free.

This 1526 manor house was owned by the Earl of Dorset before it was sold to the Shelley family, distant relatives of the famous poet. Radical changes were made to the architecture in the 18th century. Nowadays, the standards of the management are reflected in the fine antiques, the bowls of flowers, the paintings and prints, the well-kept gardens, and most important, the staff. In the rear is a sun terrace and lawn for tea and drinks; horse chestnuts and copper beech shade the grounds. The central hall is characterized by Ionic columns, a domed ceiling, and the family coat-of-arms. The bay windows of the front drawing room open onto the rear gardens, and the lounge is paneled. The bedrooms are personal, individually furnished, usually spacious, and most comfortable. Room 11 has a 16th-century frieze of bacchanalian figures and a design of entwining grapes and flowers. You can order meals at Shelleys, beginning at £13.50 ($20.30) for lunch or £18 ($27) for dinner.

WHERE TO DINE

IN ALFRISTON

MOONRAKERS, High St. Tel. 870472.
  Cuisine: ENGLISH. **Reservations:** Recommended.
$ Prices: Fixed-price dinner £20.90 ($31.40). No credit cards.
  Open: Dinner only, Tues–Fri 7–9:15pm, Sat 6:45–9:45pm. **Closed:** Mid-Jan to mid-Feb.

⭐ The welcome is warm at this charming little 14th-century restaurant with old beams and a well-prepared cuisine. Elaine Wilkinson is the chef, and she operates the restaurant with her husband, Barry. The fixed-price menu (there is no à la carte) is changed every few weeks, but fresh fish appears frequently on the menu, and duck dishes are prepared with flair. Count yourself lucky if you're there on the night Elaine decides to prepare beef Wellington. Fresh herbs are used discreetly, and Moonrakers' wine list is the finest in town. Log fires in the inglenook burn in winter, and tables in summer are placed in the patio garden for before-dinner drinks. Try, if featured, burgundy pie, ragoût of lamb with celery and walnuts, or duck served with a rich sauce of red wine and orange liqueur.

IN LEWES

PAILIN, 20 Station St. Tel. 473906.
  Cuisine: THAI. **Reservations:** Recommended.
$ Prices: Appetizers £2.50–£4 ($3.80–$6); main courses £8.50–£13.50 ($12.80–$20.30); fixed-price lunch or dinner £13–£15.50 ($19.50–$23.30). AE, DC, MC, V.
  Open: Lunch Mon–Sat noon–2:30pm; dinner Mon–Sat 6:30–10:30pm. **Closed:** Nov 5 and Dec 25–26.

The spicy hot cuisine of Thailand has come to Lewes. Prices are moderate, and the cuisine is well flavored, with fresh ingredients. Begin perhaps with the lemon-chicken soup with lemongrass, typical of Thai cuisine, and follow with a crab-and-prawn "hotpot." A special favorite with local residents is the barbecued chicken which has been carefully marinated. It's served with a sweet-and-sour plum sauce—quite hot but delectable. Many dishes are flavored with a sweet-and-sour sauce. Vegetarian meals are served, and children are also welcomed and given small portions at reduced prices.

EASY EXCURSIONS

RODMELL   This small downland village lies midway between Lewes and the port of Newhaven on the C7 road. Its chief claim to fame is **Monks House** (tel. 0273/479274), a National Trust property that was bought by Virginia and Leonard Woolf in 1919 and was their home until his death in 1969. Virginia wrote of the profusion of fruit and vegetables produced by the garden and of the open-water meadows looking out on the downs. Much of the house was furnished and decorated by Virginia's sister, Vanessa Bell, and the artist Duncan Grant. The house is open May through September on Wednesday and Saturday from 2 to 6pm; October to April, Wednesday and Saturday from 2 to 5:30pm. Last entry is half an hour before closing time. Admission is £2 ($3); children under 5 enter free. More information is available by calling the headquarters of the National Trust in East Sussex at 0892/890651.

Rodmell also has a 12th-century church, a working farm, and a tiny Victorian school still in use. Take Southdown bus no. 123 from the Lewes rail station.

THE BLUEBELL RAILWAY   This all-steam railway starts at Sheffield Park Station in East Sussex (tel. 0825/723777) on the A275 between East Grinstead and Lewes. The name is taken from the spring flowers that grow alongside the track, running from Sheffield Park to Kingscote. It is a delight for railway buffs, with locos dating from the 1870s through the 1950s, when British Railways ended steam operations. You can visit loco sheds and a small museum, then later patronize the bookshop or lunch in a large buffet, bar, and restaurant complex. The round-trip is 1 hour and 30 minutes, as the train wanders through a typical English countryside. The cost is £8 ($12) for adults or £4 ($6) for children, with a family ticket going for £20 ($30). Trains run throughout the year, daily from June through September, but only weekends from October through May.

5. BRIGHTON

52 miles S of London

GETTING THERE   By Train   London's favorite seaside resort lies on the Sussex coast. Fast trains—41 a day—leave from Victoria or London Bridge Station (trip time: 55 min.).

By Bus   Buses from Victoria Coach Station take around 2 hours.

By Car   The M23 (signposted from Central London) leads to the A23, which will take you into Brighton.

ESSENTIALS   The **telephone area code** is 0273. At the **Tourist Information Centre,** Marlborough House, 54 Old Steine (tel. 0273/323755), by the Royal Albion Hotel and the bus terminal, you can make hotel reservations, reserve tickets for National Express coaches, and pick up a list of current events.

Brighton was one of the first of the great seaside resorts of Europe. The village on the sea from which the present town grew was named Brighthelmstone, and the

English eventually shortened it to Brighton. The original swinger who was to shape so much of its destiny arrived in 1783, after just turning voting age; he was the then Prince of Wales, whose presence and patronage gave immediate status to the seaside town.

Fashionable dandies from London, including Beau Brummell, turned up. The construction business boomed, as Brighton blossomed with charming and attractive town houses and well-planned squares and crescents. From the Prince Regent's title came the voguish word "Regency," which was to characterize an era, but more specifically refers to the period between 1811 and 1820. Under Victoria, and in spite of her cutting off the patronage of her presence, Brighton continued to flourish.

Alas, earlier in this century, as the English began to discover more glamorous spots on the Continent, Brighton lost much of its old *joie de vivre*. It became more aptly tabbed as tatty, featuring the usual run of fun-fair-type English seaside amusements. However, that state of affairs has been changing, owing largely to the huge numbers of Londoners moving in (some of whom have taken to commuting); the invasion is making Brighton increasingly lighthearted and sophisticated. For instance, a beach east of the town attracts nude bathers, which was Britain's first such venture.

WHAT TO SEE & DO

The Lanes, a closely knit section of alleyways off North Street in Brighton (many of the present shops were formerly fisherman's cottages), were frequented in Victoria's day by style-setting curio and antique collectors. Some are still there, although they now share space with boutiques.

THE ROYAL PAVILION   Among the royal residences of Europe, the Royal Pavilion at Brighton (tel. 603005), a John Nash version of an Indian mogul's palace, is unique. Ornate and exotic, it has been subjected over the years to the most devastating wit of English satirists and pundits; but today we can examine it more objectively as one of the outstanding examples of the orientalizing tendencies of the romantic movement in England.

The pavilion was originally built in 1787 by Henry Holland, but it no more resembled its present look than a caterpillar does a butterfly. By the time Nash had transformed it from a simple classical villa into an orientalist fantasy, the Prince Regent had become King George IV, and the king and one of his mistresses, Lady Conyngham, lived in the palace until 1827.

A decade passed before Victoria, then queen, arrived in Brighton. Although she was to bring Albert and the children on a number of occasions, the monarch and Brighton just didn't mix. The very air of the resort seemed too flippant for her. By 1845, Victoria began packing, and the royal furniture was carted off. Its tenants gone, the pavilion was in serious peril of being torn down, but by a narrow vote, Brightonians agreed to purchase it. Gradually it was restored to its former splendor, enhanced in no small part by the return of much of its original furniture on loan by the present tenant at Buckingham Palace.

Of exceptional interest is the domed **Banqueting Hall,** with a chandelier of bronze dragons supporting lilylike glass globes. In the great kitchen, with its old revolving spits, is a collection of Wellington's pots and pans, his *batterie de cuisine,* from his town house at Hyde Park Corner. In the state apartments, particularly the domed salon, dragons wink at you, serpents entwine, lacquered doors shine. The music room, with its scalloped ceiling, is a salon of water lilies, flying dragons, sunflowers, reptilian paintings, bamboo, silk, and satin.

In the second-floor gallery, look for Nash's views of the pavilion in its elegant heyday. Other attractions include Queen Victoria's Apartments, beautifully re-created, and the impressively restored South Galleries, breakfast rooms for George

IV's guests. Refreshments are available in the Queen Adelaide Tea room, which has a balcony overlooking the Royal Pavilion Gardens.

The pavilion is open October to May, daily from 10am to 5pm; June to September, daily from 10am to 6pm; closed Christmas and Boxing Day (December 26). Admission is £3.60 ($5.40) for adults, £1.90 ($2.90) for children 5 to 15. Bus: no. 1, 2, 3, 5, or 6.

WHERE TO STAY

VERY EXPENSIVE

THE GRAND, Kings Rd., Brighton, East Sussex BN1 2FW. Tel. 0273/ 321188. Fax 0273/202694. 195 rms, 5 suites. A/C TV TEL **Bus:** 1, 2, or 3.

$ Rates (including English breakfast): £65–£123 ($97.50–$184.50) single; £130– £158 ($195–$237) double; from £225 ($337.50) suite. AE, DC, MC, V. **Parking:** £10 ($15).

This is the premier hotel of Brighton. The original Grand was constructed in 1864, and it entertained some of the most eminent Victorians and Edwardians.

This landmark was massively damaged following a terrorist attack on Margaret Thatcher and key figures in the British government. Several colleagues were killed, Mrs. Thatcher narrowly escaped, and entire sections of the hotel looked as if they had been hit by an air raid. That gave its present owners, De Vere Hotels, the challenge to create a new Grand, and frankly, the new one is better than the old. It's the most elegant Georgian re-creation in town.

You enter via a glassed-in conservatory and register in a grandiose public room, with soaring ceilings and elaborate moldings. The hotel has plushly comfortable furniture in traditional tastes with well-chosen accessories. The rooms, of a very high standard, are generally spacious with many amenities, including private baths, radios, hospitality trays, trouser presses, and hairdryers. The sea-view rooms contain minibars. There are also units designed for "lady executives," as well as "romantic rooms" with double whirlpool baths. Some accommodations have been provided with additional facilities for the disabled.

Dining/Entertainment: Both British and continental cuisine are served in the King's Restaurant, with superb ingredients masterfully handled by the kitchen staff. The Victoria Bar is an elegant rendezvous, and Midnight Blues is considered the most sophisticated club at the resort.

Services: 24-hour room service, laundry, babysitting.

Facilities: Hobden's Health Spa (complete with spa pool, steam room, sauna, solarium, and massage and exercise arena), hairdressing salon, beautician.

EXPENSIVE

BRIGHTON METROPOLE, 106 King's Rd., Brighton, East Sussex BN1 2FU. Tel. 0273/775432. Fax 0273/207764. 328 rms, 16 suites. TV TEL **Bus:** 1, 2, or 3.

$ Rates (including English breakfast): £122 ($183) single; £160 ($240) double; from £360 ($540) suite. AE, DC, MC, V. **Parking:** £10.50 ($15.80).

Centrally located on the seafront, the Metropole offers recently refurbished and luxurious bedrooms with private baths and showers, radios, in-house movies, hairdryers, trouser presses, and tea and coffee makers.

On the premises is a leisure club, including an indoor swimming pool, plus an array of dining and drinking facilities, among them the Arundel and Windsor restaurants, the Canon Pub, and the Metro Night Club.

HOSPITALITY INN, King's Rd., Brighton, East Sussex BN1 2GS. Tel.

0273/206700, or toll free 800/44-UTELL in the U.S. Fax 0273/820692. 200 rms, 4 suites. TV TEL **Bus:** 1, 2, or 3.

$ Rates: £115 ($172.50) single; £160 ($240) double; from £275 ($412.50) suite. Breakfast £9.75 ($14.60) extra. AE, DC, MC, V. **Parking:** £10 ($15).

The Hospitality Inn is one of the finest accommodations in the south of England. Rising from the seafront, it has been stylishly and rather luxuriously designed for maximum comfort. Guests wander at leisure through an array of tastefully furnished public rooms.

Dining/Entertainment: Its restaurant, La Noblesse, is outstanding, and merits a separate recommendation (see "Where to Dine," below). The Promenade restaurant, overlooking the sea, has an imaginative and well-planned menu. Nonresidents can enjoy meals in the restaurants Monday through Saturday from noon to 2pm and 7 to 11pm. There's also a coffee shop that remains open until 11pm and a bar.

Services: 24-hour room service, laundry, babysitting.

Facilities: The hotel is perhaps the best equipped in the town, certainly for the athletic, with a gym, an indoor swimming pool, along with a solarium and sauna.

MODERATE

OLD SHIP HOTEL, King's Rd., Brighton, East Sussex BN1 1NR. Tel. 0273/329001. Fax 0273/820718. 149 rms (all with bath), 3 suites. TV TEL **Bus:** 1, 2, or 3.

$ Rates (including English breakfast): £90–£100 ($135–$150) single; £95–£135 ($142.50–$202.50) double; from £150 ($225) suite. AE, DC, MC, V. **Parking:** £7.50 ($11.30).

In a central position on the seafront, the Old Ship boasts a paneled interior, comfortable sea-view lounges, an oak-paneled bar, and a spacious sea-facing restaurant, the Great Escape, that, naturally, specializes in seafood. A well-organized kitchen serves good-tasting meals with selections from an impressive wine list. In 1651 the owner of an inn on this site saved the life of King Charles II by spiriting him away in his ship. Laundry, babysitting, and 24-hour room service are available.

TOPPS HOTEL, 17 Regency St., Brighton, East Sussex BN1 2FG. Tel. 0273/729334. Fax 0273/203679. 14 rms (all with bath). MINIBAR TV TEL **Bus:** 1, 2, 3, 5, or 6.

$ Rates (including English breakfast): £47 ($70.50) single; £82–£92 ($123–$138) double. AE, DC, MC, V. **Parking:** £5 ($7.50). **Closed:** Christmas and the first week in Jan.

 Flowerboxes fill the windows of this cream-colored town house, whose owners, Paul and Pauline Collins, have devoted years to upgrading it. The hotel enjoys a diagonal view of the sea from its position beside the sloping lawn of Regency Square. Each of the differently shaped and individually furnished accommodations has a radio and a trouser press. A small restaurant in the basement serves dinners to clients who reserve by giving the room number.

INEXPENSIVE

PASKINS HOTEL, 19 Charlotte St., Brighton, East Sussex BN2 1AG. Tel. 0273/601203. Fax 0273/621973. 18 rms (16 with bath). TV TEL **Bus:** 7 or 52.

$ Rates (including English breakfast): £20 ($30) single without bath, £30 ($45) single with bath; £45–£55 ($67.50–$82.50) double with bath. 50% discount for children up to 11 years sharing with two adults. MC, V. **Parking:** Free.

This well-run small hotel owned by Michael Paskins is only a short walk from the Palace Pier and Royal Pavilion. The rates depend on the plumbing and furnishings; the most expensive units are fitted with four-poster beds. The hotel is licensed and provides bar food most evenings; it's also surrounded by lots of restaurants.

REGENCY HOTEL, 28 Regency Sq., Brighton, East Sussex BN1 2FH. Tel. 0273/202690. Fax 0273/220438. 14 rms (10 with shower), 1 suite. TV TEL **Bus:** 1, 2, 3, 5, or 6.

$ Rates (including English breakfast): £30–£37 ($45–$55.50) single; £50–£62 ($75–$93) double; from £75 ($112.50) suite. AE, DC, MC, V. **Parking:** £8 ($12).

 This typical Regency town house was built in 1820 with bow windows, a canopied balcony, and a porticoed entrance. The property was once the home of Jane, Dowager Duchess of Marlborough, and grandmother of Sir Winston Churchill. This landmark building contains fine cornices, paneled doors, and a fireplace. It was skillfully converted into a family-managed hotel with a licensed bar and modern comforts. Each bedroom has a direct-dial phone, color TV, and hairdryer, and many rooms enjoy window views across the square and out to the sea. The Regency Suite has a half-tester bed (1840) and antique furniture, along with a huge bow window dresssed with ceiling-to-floor swagged curtains and a balcony facing the sea and West Pier. Gail and Ambrose Simons welcome guests from all over the world.

TWENTY-ONE HOTEL, 21 Charlotte St., Marine Parade, Brighton, East Sussex BN2 1AG. Tel. 0273/686450. 7 rms (6 with shower). TV TEL **Bus:** 7 or 52.

$ Rates (including English breakfast): £40 ($60) single without bath, £50 ($75) single with bath; £46–£68 ($69–$102) double with bath. AE, MC, V.

One of the most sophisticated—perhaps *the* most sophisticated—of the smaller hotels of Brighton, this early Victorian white house is a block from the sea. Janet and David Power rent attractive and well-furnished bedrooms with radios and hot-beverage facilities. The basement-level garden suite opens directly onto an ivy-clad courtyard.

Dinner is available, with a minimum notice of 24 hours. A set three-course meal is served for £15 ($22.50) Monday through Thursday, rising to £22 ($33) Friday and Saturday. Closed Sunday. Possible main courses are breast of duck with cherry brandy and orange sauce or poached salmon with a prawn and lobster sauce. A good selection of wines is available.

IN NEARBY HOVE

COURTLANDS HOTEL, 19–27 The Drive, Hove, East Sussex BN3 3JE. Tel. 0273/731055. Fax 0273/28295. 60 rms (all with bath or shower). TV TEL **Bus:** 52.

$ Rates (including English breakfast): £30–£60 ($45–$90) single; £60–£78 ($90–$117) double. AE, DC, MC, V. **Parking:** Free.

The Courtlands is 400 yards from the sea, opening onto the wide thoroughfare known as "The Drive," about a mile from the center of Brighton. It's a comfortable Victorian building, recently modernized. In the complex are five particularly agreeable rooms with minibars in the cottage and coach-house annex. Bedrooms are spacious and harmonious, with prices set according to plumbing.

This traditional hotel has more than adequate facilities, including the Golden Dolphin lounge bar and a dining room opening onto gardens. A good cuisine, both international and English, is assured. The hotel has a small children's playground, a solarium, and a heated swimming pool, as well as a games room.

THE DUDLEY, Lansdowns Place, Hove, Brighton, East Sussex BN3 1HG. Tel. 0273/736266. Fax 0273/729802. 80 rms (all with bath), 2 suites. TV TEL **Bus:** 52.

$ Rates: £65 ($97.50) single; £75 ($112.50) double; from £120 ($180) suite. Breakfast £8.50 ($12.80) extra. AE, DC, MC, V. **Parking:** Free.

Near the seafront, in Hove, the Dudley is just a few blocks from the resort's bronze statue of Queen Victoria. Going up marble steps, you register beneath crystal chandeliers and within view of 18th-century antiques and oil portraits of Edwardian-era debutantes. The large, high-ceilinged public rooms emphasize the deeply comfortable chairs, the thick cove moldings, and the chandeliers. The bedrooms contain radios, coffee-making equipment, tall windows, and conservatively stylish furniture.

A bar precedes the entrance to the dining room, where candles and paneling add to the allure of the British and international cuisine. Laundry, babysitting, and 24-hour room service are available.

SACKVILLE HOTEL, 189 Kingsway, Hove, Brighton, East Sussex BN2 4GU. Tel. 0273/736292. Fax 0273/205759. 45 rms (all with bath), 2 suites. TV TEL **Bus:** 52.

$ Rates (including English breakfast): £65 ($97.50) single; £85 ($127.50) double; from £95 ($142.50) suite. AE, DC, MC, V.

Its lime- and cream-colored neobaroque facade was built across the road from the beach in 1902. Today, in a comfortably updated form, the Sackville welcomes visitors with high-ceilinged bedrooms featuring big windows, sea views, and an assortment of Queen Anne furnishings. All units have terraces.

A large ground-floor dining room offers a warm, masculine formality, with views of the sea and good service and food. An adjacent bar, Winston's, is filled with photographs of Churchill in war and peace.

WHERE TO DINE

EXPENSIVE

LA NOBLESSE, in the Hospitality Inn, King's Rd. Tel. 206700.
Cuisine: CLASSIC CONTINENTAL. **Reservations:** Required.
$ Prices: Appetizers £7–£12.50 ($10.50–$18.80); main courses £15–£17.50 ($22.50–$26.30); fixed-price meals £16.95 ($25.40) at lunch, £21.95 ($32.90) at dinner; menu gourmand £32 ($48). AE, DC, MC, V.
Open: Lunch Mon–Fri noon–2:30pm; dinner Mon–Sat 7–9:30pm.

This is the flagship restaurant of this previously recommended hotel (see "Where to Stay," above). The chefs are in fine form, as reflected in their menu of classic dishes, relying on such expensive ingredients as smoked salmon, langoustines, foi gras (can be pan-fried with ginger and mango), and oysters. The elegant surroundings in pink, blue, and brass form a proper backdrop for this "night out on the town" choice for Brighton. A continental staff is perfectly trained, serving such dishes as rack of lamb roasted à point (served with morels) and smoked goose breast served on a bed of citrus. The sauces are generally excellent, cooked to bring out natural flavors. Vegetarian meals, such as a vegetable stir-fry medley, are also available. Wear your "Brighton best" outfit here.

MODERATE

CHINA GARDEN, 88 Preston St. Tel. 325124.
Cuisine: CHINESE. **Reservations:** Recommended.
$ Prices: Appetizers £3–£4 ($4.50–$6); main courses £8.50–£11.50 ($12.80–$17.30); fixed-price menu £15.50 ($23.30). AE, DC, MC, V.
Open: Daily noon–11:30pm. **Closed:** Dec 25–26.

The menu at China Garden, located in the center off Western Road, is large and satisfying. Dim sum (a popular luncheon choice) is offered only until 4pm. Try such dishes as chicken feet in a black-bean sauce, duck's web, and mixed meat, perhaps sliced pork Szechuan style. Most of the dishes are in the Peking style.

ENGLISH'S OYSTER BAR AND SEAFOOD RESTAURANT, 29–31 East St. Tel. 327980.

Cuisine: SEAFOOD. **Reservations:** Not required.

$ Prices: Appetizers £1.95–£8.95 ($2.90–$13.40); main courses £8.25–£16.35 ($12.40–$24.50); fixed price 2-course menu £5.95 ($8.90) lunch or dinner. AE, DC, MC, V.

Open: Mon–Sat noon–10:15pm, Sun 12:30–9:30pm.

My leading choice for superbly cooked fish, this place near the bus station combines an inviting setting with good food. For years diners have been making such wise selections as half a dozen Colchester native oysters or a hot seafood en croûte with lobster sauce. The chef is known for such specialties as Dover sole and fresh, locally caught plaice. He also offers a seasonal menu, which is available for lunch and dinner every day. You're given a selection of appetizers, plus a choice from at least six main courses.

LA MARINADE, 77 St. George's Rd., Kemp Town. Tel. 600992.

Cuisine: FRENCH. **Reservations:** Recommended.

$ Prices: Appetizers £2.50–£6.50 ($3.80–$9.80); main courses £11.50–£20 ($17.30–$30); fixed-price meals £13.50 ($20.30) at lunch, £15.95–£20.95 ($23.90–$31.40) at dinner. AE, MC, V.

Open: Lunch Tues–Fri and Sun 12:15–2pm; dinner Tues–Sat 7:15–10pm.

The cuisine here is inspired by the regions of Normandy and Brittany and shows a certain subtle sophistication. You get a good range of sensitively cooked dishes, where care has been taken to preserve natural flavors. The white-butter sauce, for example, on my recently sampled fish dish was just as good as that served in the Loire Valley. La Marinade is off King's Cliff along the seafront.

LANGAN'S BISTRO, 1 Paston Place. Tel. 606933.

Cuisine: FRENCH. **Reservations:** Required.

$ Prices: Appetizers £3.95–£5.50 ($5.90–$8.30); main courses £10.95–£13.50 ($16.40–$20.30); fixed-price 3-course lunch £13.50 ($20.30). AE, DC, MC, V.

Open: Lunch Tues–Fri and Sun 12:30–2:30pm; dinner Tues–Sat 7:30–10:30pm.

Closed: Two weeks in Aug.

This is the latest—and most welcome—branch of this minichain of restaurants, which gained fame in London. The venture onto the Brighton scene has improved the restaurant lineup here considerably. A meal at Brighton's version of Langan's, near the waterfront off King's Cliff, is not unlike a meal across the Channel in France.

The menu is wisely limited, but it's based on the freshest of ingredients available at the market. You might, for example, begin with a salad made from tiger prawns and scallops, then follow with halibut meunière or a gigot of perfectly done lamb. Vegetarian meals are also available. Desserts are often sumptuous, as reflected by the Grand Marnier–and–orange-flavored crème brûlée.

OLD SHIP HOTEL RESTAURANT, in the Old Ship Hotel, King's Rd. Tel. 329001.

Cuisine: ENGLISH. **Reservations:** Recommended. **Bus:** 1, 2, or 3.

$ Prices: Appetizers £3.50–£5 ($5.30–$7.50); main courses £7–£14 ($10.50–$21); 3-course fixed-price lunch £12 ($18); 4-course fixed-price dinner £17.50 ($26.30). AE, DC, MC, V.

Open: Lunch daily 12:30–2:30pm; dinner Sun–Thurs 7–9:30am, Fri–Sat 7–10pm.

A long-enduring favorite, the Old Ship Restaurant in the center of town on the seafront enjoys an ideal location, with premises opening onto the waterfront. Whenever possible, locally caught fish appears on the menu. Try such dishes as moules marinières (mussels) or fresh salmon from Scotland grilled with saffron. Vegetables, which accompany main dishes, are always fresh and cooked "new style." Sometimes local dishes such as turkey from Sussex appear on the menu, but with a French sauce. The wine list is excellent. Stop in the adjoining pub for a pre- or postdinner drink.

6. ARUNDEL

58 miles S of London, 21 miles W of Brighton

GETTING THERE By Train Trains leave hourly during the day from London's Victoria Station (trip time: 1¼ hr.).

By Bus Most bus connections are through Littlehampton, opening onto the English Channel west of Brighton. From Littlehampton, you can leave the coastal road by taking bus no. 212, which runs between Littlehampton and Arundel hourly during the day.

By Car From London, follow the signposts to Gatwick Airport and from there head south toward the coast along the A29.

ESSENTIALS The **telephone area code** is 0903. The **Tourist Information Centre** is at 61 High St. (tel. 0903/882268).

This small town in West Sussex nestles at the foot of one of England's most spectacular castles. The town was once an Arun River port, and its denizens enjoyed the prosperity of considerable trade and commerce. However, today the harbor traffic is replaced with buses filled with tourists.

WHAT TO SEE & DO

ARUNDEL CASTLE, Mill Rd. Tel. 883136.

The ancestral home of the dukes of Norfolk, this ducal estate is a much-restored mansion of considerable importance. Its legend is associated with some of the great families of England—the Fitzalans and the powerful Howards of Norfolk.

Arundel Castle has suffered destruction over the years, particularly during the Civil War, when Cromwell's troops stormed its walls, perhaps in retaliation for the 14th Earl of Arundel's (Thomas Howard) sizable contribution to Charles I. In the early 18th century the castle virtually had to be rebuilt, and in late Victorian times it was remodeled and extensively restored again. Today it is filled with a good collection of antiques, along with an assortment of paintings by old masters, such as van Dyck and Gainsborough.

Surrounding the castle, in the center off High Street, is a 1,100-acre park (scenic highlight: Swanbourne Lake).

Admission: £4 ($6) adults, £3 ($4.50) children 5–15.
Open: Apr–Oct, Sun–Fri 11am–5pm.

ARUNDEL CATHEDRAL, London Rd. Tel. 882297.

A Roman Catholic cathedral, the Cathedral of Our Lady and St. Philip Howard stands at the highest point in town. It was constructed for the 15th Duke of Norfolk by A. J. Hansom, who invented the Hansom taxi. However, it was not consecrated as a cathedral until 1965. The interior includes the shrine of St. Philip Howard, featuring Sussex wrought ironwork.

Admission: Free, but donations are appreciated.

Open: June–Sept, daily 9am–6pm; Oct–May, daily 9am–dusk. **Directions:** From the town center, continue west from High St.

ARUNDEL TOY AND MILITARY MUSEUM, at "Doll's House," 23 High St. Tel. 882908.

In a Georgian cottage in the heart of historic Arundel, this museum displays an intriguing family collection spanning many generations of old toys and games, small militaria, dolls, dollhouses, tin toys, musical toys, famous stuffed bears, Britain's animals and model soldiers, arks, boats, rocking horses, crested military models, an eggcup collection, and other curiosities. The museum is opposite Treasure House Antiques and Collectors Market.

Admission: £1.50 ($2.30) adults, £1.25 ($1.90) children.
Open: June–Aug, daily 10:45am–5pm; Sept–May, Sat–Sun 10:45am–5pm.

BRASS RUBBING CENTRE/HERITAGE OF ARUNDEL MUSEUM, 61 High St. Tel. 882268.

Both of these attractions are situated in the same stone-sided house as the town's tourist office. The **Brass Rubbing Centre** is in the cellar, where a collection of movable plaques and gravestones, each of historic and artistic interest, awaits the chalk and heavy paper of those who would like to trace their forms. You're charged according to the stone you choose to copy, usually about £1 ($1.50) per item.

Open: Tues–Sun 10am–5pm.

On the street level, adjacent to the rooms housing the tourist information office, is the **Heritage of Arundel Museum.** It displays postcards, memorabilia, antique costumes, and historic documents relating to the history of Arundel and its famous castle.

Admission: Free.
Open: May to mid-Oct, Tues–Sat 11am–1pm and 2–5pm, Sun 2–5pm.

WHERE TO STAY

THE NORFOLK ARMS, 22 High St., Arundel, West Sussex BN18 9AD. Tel. 0903/882101. Fax 0903/884275. 34 rms (all with bath). TV TEL

$ Rates: £45 ($67.50) single; £60 ($90) double. Breakfast from £7.50 ($11.30) extra. AE, DC, MC, V. **Parking:** Free.

A former coaching inn, the Norfolk Arms is on the main street just a short walk from the castle. The lounges and dining room are in the typically English country-inn style—not ostentatious but unquestionably comfortable. The hotel has been restored with many modern amenities blending with the old architecture. The bedrooms are handsomely maintained and furnished, each with personal touches.

In the restaurant you can order good English food, with a luncheon for £10 ($15). When available, fresh local produce is offered. You can also order dinner for £15 ($22.50), which includes many traditional English dishes.

NEARBY IN AMBERLEY

AMBERLEY CASTLE HOTEL, Amberley, near Arundel, West Sussex BN18 9ND. Tel. 0798/831992, or toll free 800/525-4800 in the U.S. Fax 0798/831998. 14 rms (all with bath). TV TEL **Directions:** Take the B2139 north of Arundel, 1½ miles southwest of Amberley.

$ Rates (including English breakfast): £100 ($150) single; £130–£225 ($195–$337.50) double. AE, DC, MC, V. **Parking:** Free.

⭐ The best place for food and lodging is near the village of Amberley. Joy and Martin Cummings have operated this deluxe establishment since 1988, in a 14th-century castle, with portions dating from the 12th. From the battlements you'll have views of weald and downland. Elizabeth I herself once held the lease on this castle (1588–1603), and Cromwell's forces attacked it during the Civil War. Charles II visited the castle on two occasions. Each of the sumptuous rooms, all doubles, is named after a castle in Sussex, and each has a private Jacuzzi bath as well as a video library.

Dining/Entertainment: Nonresidents who reserve can attend the 12th-century Queen's Room Restaurant, the finest dining room in the area. Service is under a barrel-vaulted ceiling with lancet windows, and the food is classic French and traditional English. Among the exquisite repertoire is everything from zucchini flowers filled with crab to a citrus-flavored dish of smoked lambs' tongues. Service is from 7 to 10pm, with meals costing from £25.50 ($38.30) on the table d'hôte, from £37.50 ($56.30) if ordered à la carte.

WHERE TO DINE

CHINA PALACE, 67 High St. Tel. 883702.

Cuisine: CHINESE. **Reservations:** Recommended on weekends.

$ Prices: Appetizers £1.70–£3.75 ($2.60–$5.60); main courses £5.50–£8 ($8.30–$12), fixed-price 3-course dinner for two £24 ($36). AE, DC, MC, V.

Open: Lunch daily noon–2:15pm; dinner daily 5:30–11pm.

The most prominent Chinese restaurant in the region sits incongruously beneath an elaborately carved 17th-century ceiling imported by a former owner long ago from a palace in Italy. With an interior decorated with the artfully draped sails from a Chinese junk, it occupies a painted stone building across the road from the crenellated fortifications surrounding Arundel's castle. The Beijing and Szechuan cuisine includes such classic dishes as Peking duck, crispy lamb, king prawns Kung Po, and lobster with fresh ginger and spring onions.

THE WINCHESTER BAR/THIRTIES RESTAURANT, 25 Tarrant St. Tel. 882222.

Cuisine: ENGLISH. **Reservations:** Not required.

$ Prices: In the Winchester, sandwiches £1.50–£2 ($2.30–$3). In Thirties, lunch appetizers 90p–£1.75 ($1.40–$2.60); lunch main courses £3–£7.50 ($4.50–$11.30); 3-course set dinner £11 ($16.50). AE, MC, V.

Open: Winchester, Mon–Sat 11am–11pm, Sun noon–3pm and 7–10:30pm. Thirties, lunch daily noon–2:30; dinner daily 7–10:30pm.

Located in the center of town near the castle, this establishment is comprised of a popular bar and pub (The Winchester) on its street level and a cost-conscious, art deco–style restaurant upstairs. You can order a sandwich amid the oaken paneling of the bar, although most people come just to drink and gossip. Upstairs, a mostly English menu offers steak-and-kidney pie and such bistro fare as soups, pastas, salads, and an occasional slice of quiche. The building that houses these establishments was originally constructed in the 18th century and converted from a chemist's shop (pharmacy) in the 1960s.

7. CHICHESTER

69 miles SW of London, 31 miles W of Brighton

GETTING THERE By Train Trains depart for Chichester from London's Victoria Station once every hour during the day (trip time: 1½ hr.). However, if you visit Chichester to attend the theater, plan to stay over—the last train back to London is at 9pm.

By Bus   Buses to Chichester leave from London's Victoria Coach Station four times per day.

By Car   From London's ring road, head south along the A3, turning onto the A286 for the final approach to Chichester.

ESSENTIALS   The **telephone area code** is 0243. The **Tourist Information Centre** is at St. Peter's Market, West Street (tel. 0243/775888).

According to one newspaper, Chichester might have been just a market town if the Chichester Festival Theatre had not been established in its midst. One of the oldest Roman cities in England, Chichester draws a crowd from all over the world who come to see its theater's presentations.

Only a 5-minute walk from the Chichester Cathedral and the old Market Cross, the 1,400-seat theater, with its apron stage, stands on the edge of Oaklands Park. It opened in 1962 (first director: Lord Laurence Olivier), and its reputation has grown steadily, pumping new vigor and life into the former walled city.

WHAT TO SEE & DO

CHICHESTER FESTIVAL THEATRE & MINERVA STUDIO THEATRE   The Chichester Festival Theatre offers plays and musicals with all-star casts during the summer season (May to September) and in the winter and spring months orchestras, jazz, opera, theater, ballet, and a Christmas show for the entire family. Matinee performances begin at 2:30pm and evening performances at 7:30pm, except first nights, which begin at 7pm.

The Minerva is a studio theater that offers one of the most adventurous programs during the year in the south and houses a theater restaurant (tel. 782219), society clubroom, and shop. Performances here begin at 2:45pm and 7:45pm.

Theater reservations made over the telephone will be held for a maximum of 4 days (call 0243/781312). It's better to mail inquiries and checks to the Box Office, Chichester Festival Theatre, Oaklands Park, Chichester, West Sussex PO19 4AP. MasterCard, VISA, and American Express are accepted. Season ticket prices range from £8 to £20 ($12 to $30). Unreserved seats, sold only on the day of performance, cost from £5 to £6 ($7.50 to $9).

EASY EXCURSIONS

FISHBOURNE   A worthwhile sight that's only 1½ miles from Chichester is the remains of the **Roman Palace,** Salthill Road, Salthill (tel. 0243/785859), the largest Roman residence yet discovered in Britain. Built around A.D. 75 in villa style, it has many mosaic-floored rooms and even an underfloor heating system. The gardens have been restored to their original 1st-century plan. The story of the site is told both by an audiovisual program and by text in the museum. There is a cafeteria.

The museum charges £3.20 ($4.80) for adults, £1.50 ($2.30) for children, or £8 ($12) for a family ticket. From mid-December to mid-February it is open only on Sunday from 10am to 4pm. For the rest of the year, it is open daily. Hours are March, April, and October, 10am to 5pm; May through September, 10am to 6pm; February, November, and December, 10am to 4pm. The museum is situated to the north of the A259, off Salthill Road, and signposted from Fishbourne. Parking is free. Buses stop regularly at the bottom of Salthill Road, and the museum is within a 5-minute walk of British Rail's station at Fishbourne.

OLD BOSHAM ✪ Bosham, 4 miles west of Chichester by the A259, is one of the most charming villages in West Sussex and is principally a sailing resort, linked by good bus service to Chichester. It was the site of the first establishment of Christianity on the Sussex coast. The Danish King Canute made it one of the seats of his North Sea empire, and it was the site of one of the last of England's Saxon kings, Harold, who sailed from here to France on a journey that finally culminated in the invasion of England by William the Conqueror in 1066.

Bosham's little church was depicted in the Bayeux Tapestry. Its graveyard overlooks the boats, and the church is filled with ship models and relics, showing the villagers' link to the sea. A daughter of King Canute is buried inside. Near the harbor, it is reached by a narrow lane.

WEALD & DOWNLAND OPEN AIR MUSEUM In the beautiful Sussex countryside at Singleton, 6 miles north of Chichester on the A286 (London road), historic buildings that have been saved from destruction are being reconstructed on a 40-acre downland site. The structures show the development of traditional building from medieval times to the 19th century in the weald and downland area of southeast England.

Exhibits include a Tudor market hall, a medieval farmstead and other houses dating from the 14th to the 17th century, a working watermill producing stone-ground flour, a blacksmith's forge, plumbers' and carpenters' workshops, a toll cottage, a 17th-century treadwheel, agricultural buildings including thatched barns and an 18th-century granary, a charcoal burner's camp, and a 19th-century village school.

The museum is open March through October, daily from 11am to 6pm; November to February, on Wednesday and Sunday from 11am to 5pm. Admission is £4 ($6) for adults, £2 ($3) for children. For further information, call 024363/348. Bus: no. 260 from Chichester.

WHERE TO STAY

THE DOLPHIN & ANCHOR, West St., Chichester, West Sussex PO19 1QE. Tel. 0243/785121, or toll free 800/435-4542 in the U.S. Fax 0243/533408. 51 rms (all with bath). TV TEL

$ Rates: £75–£82.50 ($112.50–$123.80) single; £85–£115 ($127.50–$172.50) double. Breakfast £8.50 ($12.80) extra. AE, DC, MC, V.

Two old inns joined together, right at the historic 15th-century Market Cross and opposite the Chichester Cathedral, the Dolphin & Anchor is in the center off South Street, a 10-minute walk from the Festival Theatre. The setting blends 19th-century architectural features, including an old coaching entrance, with 20th-century comforts. A more up-to-date wing of bedrooms is also offered.

There are lounges, bars, the Whig and Tory Restaurant, and the Roussillon Coffee Shop, which serves light meals and grills until 8pm.

SHIP HOTEL, North St., Chichester, West Sussex PO19 1NH. Tel. 0243/782028. Fax 0243/774254. 37 rms (32 with bath). TV TEL

$ Rates (including English breakfast): £36 ($54) single without bath, £46–£60 ($69–$90) single with bath; £46 ($69) double without bath, £66–£80 ($99–$120) double with bath. AE, DC, MC, V.

One of the classic Georgian buildings of the city, the Ship is only a few minutes' walk from the cathedral, the Chichester Festival Theatre, and many fine antique shops. It was built as a private house in 1790 for Adm. Sir George Murray (one of Nelson's commanders) and still retains an air of elegance and comfort. A grand Adam staircase leads from the main entrance to the bedrooms, which are all named after historic ships. Hornblower's Lounge, relatively formal with its own fireplace and rows of books, is an elegant place for a drink. Murray's Restaurant offers good value for money, and features a special four-course dinner menu every evening for £14.50 ($21.80).

PLACES TO STAY NEARBY

MILLSTREAM HOTEL, Bosham Lane, Bosham, Chichester, West Sussex PO18 8HL. Tel. 0243/573234. Fax 0243/573459. 29 rms (all with bath). TV TEL **Directions:** Take the road to the village of Bosham and its harbor, off the A27. **Bus:** Bosham bus from Chichester.
$ Rates (including English breakfast): £56–£66 ($84–$99) single; £90–£107 ($135–$160.50) double. AE, DC, MC, V. **Parking:** Free.
Completely redecorated, the rooms here have different colors, but all are outfitted with floral-patterned wallpaper. The decor is in keeping with the country cottage-type hotel. Beds are comfortable.

The cocktail bar at the entrance to the restaurant is tastefully furnished with white bamboo chairs and tables. At the adjoining restaurant, you can order such à la carte dishes as moules (mussels) marinières and roast Sussex lamb with fresh herbs. Dinner begins at £16.75 ($25.10); lunch, at £12.50 ($18.80).

SPREAD EAGLE HOTEL, South St., Midhurst, West Sussex GU29 9NH. Tel. 0730/816911. Fax 0730/815668. 41 rms (all with bath), 1 suite. TV TEL **Bus:** Midhurst bus from Chichester.
$ Rates (including English breakfast): £78 ($117) single; £90–£130 ($135–$195) double; from £150 ($225) suite. AE, DC, MC, V. **Parking:** Free.

The inn and the market town of Midhurst are so steeped in history that the room you sleep in and the pavement you walk on have a thousand tales to tell. The rooms have beams, small mullioned windows, and unexpected corners.

Dining/Entertainment: Dinner is served in the dining hall, the Coal Hole, lit by candles that flicker on the gleaming tables. In the winter, log fires blaze. Meals cost £27.50 ($41.30) and up. The lounge with its timbered ceiling is where Elizabeth I and her court might have sat to watch festivities in the Market Square outside. The eagle in the lounge is the actual one that decorated the back of Hermann Goering's chair in the Reichstag. It was acquired for its apt illustration of the hotel's name. There are several bars.

WHERE TO DINE

COMME ÇA, 67 Broyle Rd. Tel. 788724.
Cuisine: FRENCH. **Reservations:** Required.
$ Prices: Appetizers £3.50–£5.50 ($5.30–$8.30); main courses £7.70–£12.50 ($11.60–$18.80). MC, V.
Open: Lunch Tues–Fri and Sun 12:15–2pm; dinner Tues–Sat 6–10:30pm.
This is the best French restaurant in town—in fact, the best restaurant, period. The decor is unpretentious, with a certain French provincial quality. The chef is French, as a look at the menu offerings will reveal. Try feuilletté of salmon with chives, sole Comme Ça, perhaps filet of beef with a Dijon mustard sauce. Good-quality ingredients are used. You'll find Comme Ça just a 5-minute walk from the center.

NEARBY AT CHILGROVE

WHITE HORSE, 1 High St., Chilgrove. Tel. 0243/359219.
Cuisine: ENGLISH/FRENCH. **Reservations:** Required. **Directions:** Head 6½ miles north of Chichester on the B2141 to Petersfield.

$ Prices: 3-course fixed-price lunch £17.50 ($26.30); 4-course fixed-price dinner £24.50 ($36.80). AE, MC, V.

Open: Lunch Tues–Sat noon–2pm; dinner Tues–Sat 7–11pm. **Closed:** Last week in Oct and Dec 25–26.

The wine cellar at this informally elegant country restaurant is one of the most comprehensive in Britain. This is partly because of the careful attention the owners pay to the details of their 18th-century inn, whose patina has been burnished every day since it was first built in 1765. The trio of dining rooms contains old beams, lots of hardwood, and a close attention to the gleaming silver of the table settings. Typical dishes include wild duck with a black-cherry and port sauce, wild mushroom and chicken vol-au-vent, and veal with a vermouth-and-sorrel sauce.

CHAPTER 11
HAMPSHIRE & DORSET

This countryside is reminiscent of scenes from Burke's *Landed Gentry,* from fireplaces where stacks of logs burn to wicker baskets of apples freshly brought in from the orchard. Old village houses, now hotels, have a charming quality. Beyond the pear trees, on the crest of a hill, you'll find the ruins of a Roman camp. A village pub, with two rows of kegs filled with varieties of cider, is where the hunt gathers.

You're in Hampshire and Dorset, two shires jealously guarded by the English, who protect their special rural treasures. Everybody knows of Southampton and Bournemouth, but less known is the hilly countryside farther inland. You can travel through endless lanes and discover tiny villages and thatched cottages untouched by the industrial invasion.

The area is rich in legend and in literary and historical associations. Here Jane Austen and Thomas Hardy wrote and set their novels. Here, too, King Arthur held court at the Round Table. And from here sailed such famous ships as the *Mayflower,* Lord Nelson's *Victory,* the D-day invasion flotilla, and the *QE2.*

HAMPSHIRE This is the county Jane Austen wrote of—firmly middle class, largely agricultural, its inhabitants doggedly convinced that Hampshire is the greatest place on earth. Austen wrote six novels, including *Pride and Prejudice* and *Sense and Sensibility,* that earned her a permanent place among the great 19th-century writers. Her books provide an insight into the manners and mores of the English who were to build up a powerful empire. Although the details of the life she described have now largely faded, much of the mood and spirit of the Hampshire depicted in her books remains.

Hampshire encompasses the South Downs, the Isle of Wight (Victoria's favorite retreat), and the naval city of Portsmouth. The more than 90,000 acres of the New Forest was preserved by William the Conqueror as a private hunting ground. William lost two of his sons in the New Forest—one killed by an animal, the other by an arrow. Today it is a vast woodland and heath, ideal for walking and exploring.

Although Hampshire is filled with many places of interest, for our purposes I've concentrated on two major areas: Southampton for convenience of transportation and accommodations and Winchester for history.

WHAT'S SPECIAL ABOUT HAMPSHIRE & DORSET

Great Towns/Villages

☐ Winchester, the ancient capital of England, with a cathedral built by William the Conqueror.

☐ Portsmouth, the premier port of the south (the first dock built in 1194); home to HMS *Victory*, Nelson's flagship.

☐ Lyme Regis, with its famed Cobb, a favorite of Jane Austen and a setting for *The French Lieutenant's Woman*.

Literary Shrines

☐ Chawton Cottage, where novelist Jane Austen lived.

☐ Thomas Hardy's Cottage at Higher Bockhampton.

Buildings

☐ Beaulieu Abbey, Lord Montagu's estate west of Southampton, a sumptuous private home from 1538 surrounded by gardens.

☐ Osborne House, Queen Victoria's most cherished residence, where she died on January 22, 1901.

☐ Broadlands, an elegant Palladian house on the River Test, former home of the late Lord Mountbatten.

☐ Winchester Cathedral, dating from 1079, the longest medieval cathedral in Britain.

Beaches

☐ Bournemouth, the premier seaside resort of Dorset, set among pines with sandy beaches and fine coastal views.

☐ Chesil Beach, a 20-mile-long wall-like bank of shingle running from Abbotsbury to the Isle of Portland; great beachcombing.

Natural Spectacles

☐ The New Forest, 145 square miles of heath and woodland, once the hunting ground of Norman kings.

DORSET   This is Thomas Hardy country. Some of the towns and villages in Dorset, although altered considerably, are still recognizable from his descriptions. "The last of the great Victorians," as he was called, died in 1928 at the age of 88. His tomb is in a position of honor in Westminster Abbey.

One of England's smallest shires, Dorset encompasses the old seaport of Poole in the east and Lyme Regis in the west (known to Jane Austen). Dorset is a southwestern county and borders the English Channel. It's known for its cows, and Dorset butter is served at many an afternoon tea. This is mainly a land of farms and pastures, with plenty of sandy heaths and chalky downs.

The most prominent tourist center of Dorset is the Victorian seaside resort of Bournemouth. If you don't anchor there, you might also try a number of Dorset's other seaports, villages, and country towns; I mostly stick to the areas along the impressive coastline. Dorset, as the vacation-wise English might tell you, is a budget traveler's friend.

SEEING HAMPSHIRE & DORSET

GETTING THERE

The south is linked to London by excellent motorways, notably the M3 to Winchester, the M3 and A33 to Southampton, and the A3 to Portsmouth. British Rail serves the area frequently from London's Waterloo Station (call 071/928-5100 for specific schedules of London departures). It takes only 1 hour and 15 minutes to reach Southampton, 2 hours to Bournemouth, and 1 hour and 40 minutes to Portsmouth.

A SUGGESTED ITINERARY

Day 1: Arrive in Portsmouth early for a full day's sightseeing of its many attractions. Stay overnight here.

Day 2: Using Southampton as a base, explore the sights of the New Forest.

Day 3: Visit Winchester and explore its attractions, including its cathedral, and stay overnight here.

Day 4: Devote this day to the Isle of Wight and visit Queen Victoria's Osborne House.

Day 5: Begin your tour of Dorset with an overnight stopover in the premier seaside resort of Bournemouth.

Day 6: End your tour of Dorset with an overnight stay at Lyme Regis.

---

1. PORTSMOUTH & SOUTHSEA

70 miles SE of London; 21 miles E of Southampton

GETTING THERE   By Train   Trains from London's Waterloo Station stop at Portsmouth and Southsea Station frequently throughout the day (trip time: 1½ hr.).

By Bus   National Express coaches operating out of London's Victoria Coach Station make the run to Portsmouth and Southsea every 1½ hours during the day (trip time: 2½ hr.).

By Car   From London's ring road, cut south on the A3.

ESSENTIALS   The **telephone area code** is 0705. The **Tourist Information Centre** is at The Hard in Portsmouth (tel. 0705/826722).

Virginia, New Hampshire, even Ohio, may have a **Portsmouth,** but the forerunner of them all is the old port and naval base on the Hampshire coast. German bombers in World War II leveled the city, hitting about nine-tenths of its buildings. But the seaport has recovered admirably.

Its maritime associations are known around the world. From Sally Port, the most interesting district in the Old Town, countless naval heroes have embarked to fight England's battles. That was certainly true on June 6, 1944, when Allied troops set sail to invade occupied France.

Southsea, adjoining Portsmouth, is a popular seaside resort with fine sands, gardens, bright lights, and a host of vacation attractions. Many historic monuments can be seen along the stretches of open space, where you can walk on the Clarence Esplanade and look out on the Solent and view the busy shipping activities of Portsmouth harbor.

WHAT TO SEE & DO

You might want to begin your tour on the Southsea front, where you can see a number of **naval monuments.** These include the big anchor from Nelson's ship *Victory,* plus a commemoration of the officers and men of HMS *Shannon* for heroism in the Indian Mutiny. An obelisk with a naval crown honors the memory of the crew of HMS *Chesapeake,* and a massive column, the Royal Naval memorial, honors those lost at sea in the two world wars. A shaft is also dedicated to men killed in the Crimean War. There are also commemorations of those who fell victim to yellow fever in Queen Victoria's service in Sierra Leone and Jamaica.

The **Southsea Common,** between the coast and houses of the area, known in the 13th century as Froddington Heath and used for army bivouacs, is a picnic and play area today. Walks can be taken along Ladies' Mile if you want to be away from the common's tennis courts, skateboard and roller-skating rinks, and other activities.

THE *MARY ROSE* SHIP HALL AND EXHIBITION, College Rd., Portsmouth Naval Base. Tel. 750521.

⭐ The *Mary Rose,* flagship of the fleet of wooden men-of-war of King Henry VIII, sank in the Solent in 1545 in full view of the king. In 1982 the heir to the throne, Charles, Prince of Wales, watched the *Mary Rose* break the water's surface after almost four centuries on the ocean floor, not exactly shipshape and Bristol fashion but surprisingly well preserved nonetheless. Now the remains are on view, but the hull must be kept permanently wet.

The hull and the more than 10,000 items brought up by divers constitute one of the major archeological discoveries in England in many years. Among the artifacts on permanent exhibit are the almost complete equipment of the ship's barber, with surgeon's cabin saws, knives, ointments, and plaster all ready for use; long bows and arrows, some still in shooting order; carpenters' tools; leather jackets; and some fine lace and silk. Close to the dock, near the hull, is the *Mary Rose* exhibition in Boathouse 5, where artifacts rescued from the ship are stored. It features an audiovisual theater and a spectacular two-deck reconstruction of a segment of the ship, including the original guns. A display with sound effects recalls the sinking of the vessel.

For more information, write the *Mary Rose* Trust, College Road, H.M. Naval Base, Portsmouth, Hampshire PO1 3LX.

Admission: £4 ($6) adults, £2.50 ($3.80) children; £10.50 ($15.80) family (two adults and up to four children).

Open: Mar–Oct, daily 10am–5:30pm; Nov–Feb, daily 10:30am–5pm. **Closed:** Dec 25. **Directions:** Use the entrance to the Portsmouth Naval Base through Victory Gate (as for HMS *Victory*), and follow the signs.

HMS *VICTORY*, No. 2 Dry Dock, in Portsmouth Naval Base. Tel. 839766.

Of major interest is Lord Nelson's flagship, a 104-gun, first-rate ship. Although it first saw action in 1778, it earned its fame on October 21, 1805, in the Battle of Trafalgar when the English scored a victory over the combined Spanish and French fleets. It was in this battle that Lord Nelson lost his life. The flagship, after being taken to Gibraltar for repairs, returned to Portsmouth with Nelson's body on board (he was later buried at St. Paul's in London).

Admission: £4 ($6) adults, £2.50 ($3.80) children.

Open: Mar–June and Sept–Oct, 10am–5pm; July–Aug, 10am–6:45pm; Nov–Feb, 10am–5pm. **Closed:** Dec 25. **Directions:** Use the entrance to the Portsmouth Naval Base through Victory Gate.

ROYAL NAVAL MUSEUM, in the dockyard, Portsmouth Naval Base. Tel. 733060.

The museum is next to Nelson's flagship, HMS *Victory,* and the *Mary Rose* in the heart of Portsmouth's historic naval dockyard. The only museum in Britain devoted

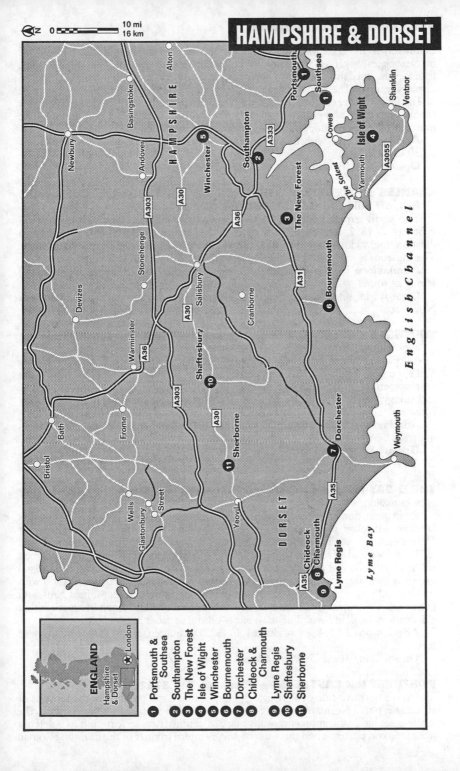

exclusively to the general history of the Royal Navy, it contains relics of Nelson and his associates, together with unique collections of ship models, naval ceramics, figureheads, medals, uniforms, weapons, and other naval memorabilia. Special displays feature "The Rise of the Royal Navy" and "HMS *Victory* and the Campaign of Trafalgar." Other exhibits include the Victorian navy, the navy in the 20th century, the modern navy, and representations of the sailor in popular art and culture. The museum complex includes a buffet and souvenir shop.

Admission: Free with ticket for HMS *Victory;* otherwise £1.80 ($2.70) adults, £1.30 ($2) children.

Open: Daily 10:30am–5pm.

CHARLES DICKENS'S BIRTHPLACE MUSEUM, 393 Old Commercial Rd., off Mile End Rd. (M275). Tel. 827261.

The small terrace house of 1804 in which the famous novelist was born on February 7, 1812, and lived for a short time, has been restored and furnished to illustrate the middle-class taste of southwestern counties of the early 19th century. The museum is near the center of Portsmouth off Kingston Road.

Admission: £1 ($1.50) adults, 60p (90¢) students and children, £2.60 ($3.90) family of four.

Open: Mar–Oct, daily 10:30am–5:30pm (last entrance at 5pm). **Closed:** Nov–Feb.

SOUTHSEA CASTLE, Clarence Esplanade, Southsea. Tel. 827261 for information.

A fortress built of stones from Beaulieu Abbey in 1545 as part of King Henry VIII's coastal defense plan, the castle is now a museum. Exhibits trace the development of Portsmouth as a military stronghold, as well as naval history and the archeology of the area. The castle is in the center of Southsea near the D-Day Museum.

Admission: £1 ($1.50) adults, 75p ($1.10) children 13–18, free for children under 13.

Open: Mar–Oct, 10am–5:30pm; Nov–Feb, 10am–4:30pm. **Closed:** Dec 24–26.

THE D-DAY MUSEUM, Clarence Esplanade, Southsea. Tel. 827261 for information.

Right next door to Southsea Castle, the museum—devoted to the Normandy landings—displays the Overlord Embroidery, which shows the complete story of Operation Overlord. The appliquéed embroidery, believed to be the largest of its kind (272 feet long and 3 feet high), was designed by Sandra Lawrence and took 20 women of the Royal School of Needlework 5 years to complete. There is a special audiovisual program with displays, including reconstructions of various stages of the mission with models and maps. You'll see a Sherman tank in working order, Jeeps, field guns, and even a DUKW (popularly called a Duck), that incredibly useful amphibious truck that operated on land and sea. The museum is on the seafront at Southsea.

Admission: £3 ($4.50) adults, £1.80 ($2.70) children, £7.80 ($11.70) family of four.

Open: Daily 10am–5:30pm. **Closed:** Dec 24–26.

PORTCHESTER CASTLE, Near Farnham. Tel. 378291.

On the northern side of Portsmouth Harbour on a spit of land are the remains of this castle, plus a Norman church. Built in the late 12th century by King Henry II, the castle is set inside the impressive walls of a 3rd-century Roman fort built as a defense against Saxon pirates, when this was the northwestern frontier of the declining Roman

Empire. By the end of the 14th century, Richard II had modernized the castle and had made it a secure small palace. Among the ruins are the hall, kitchen, and great chamber of this palace. Portchester was popular with medieval kings, who stayed here when they visited Portsmouth. The last official use of the castle was as a prison for French seamen during the Napoleonic Wars.

Admission: £1.50 ($2.30) adults, 75p ($1.10) children 5–16.

Open: Apr–Sept, daily 10am–6pm; Oct–Mar, Tues–Sun 10am–4pm. **Directions:** Head west toward Southampton on the M27.

ROYAL NAVY SUBMARINE MUSEUM, Haslar Jetty Rd., Gosport. Tel. 510354.

Cross Portsmouth Harbour by one of the ferries that bustle back and forth all day to Gosport. Some departures go directly from the station pontoon to HMS *Alliance* for a visit to the submarine museum, which traces the history of underwater warfare and life from the earliest days to the present nuclear age and contains excellent models, dioramas, medals, and displays from all ages. There is also as much about submariners themselves as about the steel tubes in which they make their homes, and although the museum focuses on English boats, it includes much of international interest.

The principal exhibit is HMS *Alliance,* and after a brief audiovisual presentation, visitors are guided through the boat by ex-submariners. Midget submarines, not all of them English, including an X-craft, can be seen outside the museum. Also on display is HM *Torpedo Boat No. 1,* better known as *Holland I,* launched in 1901, which sank under tow to the breaker's yard in 1913 and was salvaged in 1982.

Admission: £3 ($4.50) adults, £2 ($3) children.

Open: Apr–Oct, daily 10am–4:30pm; Nov–Mar, daily 10am–3:30pm. **Transportation:** Ferry from The Hard in Portsmouth to Gosport; or bus no. 9.

WHERE TO STAY

HOSPITALITY INN, South Parade, Southsea, Hampshire PO4 0RN. Tel. 0705/731281. Fax 0705/817572. 113 rms (all with bath), 2 suites. TV TEL **Bus:** Southsea bus.

$ Rates (including English breakfast): £70 ($105) single; £84 ($126) double; from £125 ($187.50) suite. AE, DC, MC, V. **Parking:** Free.

The balconied Victorian facade of this hotel directly east of Southside Common rises above the boulevard running beside the sea. Restored by its owners, the hotel contains an interior decor that, depending on the room, ranges from contemporary to full-curtained traditional. Each of the bedrooms has been renovated with built-in furniture and equipped with such extras as a trouser press and tea-making facilities. A restaurant serves dinner for £13.50 ($20.30) and up.

PORTSMOUTH MARRIOTT, North Harbour, Cosham, Portsmouth, Hampshire PO6 4SH. Tel. 0705/383151, or toll free 800/534-2000 in the U.S.; 800/228-2990 in Canada. Fax 0705/388701. 168 rms (all with bath), 2 suites. TV TEL **Bus:** Take the bus marked "Fresham" from Portsmouth's center.

$ Rates: £95–£103 ($142.50–$154.50) single; £107–£115 ($160.50–$172.50) double; £205 ($307.50) suite. English breakfast £10.25 ($15.40) extra. AE, DC, MC, V. **Parking:** Free.

Located 2 miles southeast of Portsmouth's center, a short walk from the ferryboat terminal for ships arriving from Le Havre and Cherbourg in France, this seven-story building towers above everything in its district. Originally built as a Holiday Inn in 1980, it was acquired by Marriott in 1992. Some of the public areas are sheltered by a steel-and-glass domelike structure known as the "Holidome" whose big windows create an effect resembling that of a greenhouse or conservatory. The bedrooms are clean, comfortable, and modern, with tiled bathrooms and such electronic amenities as video movies.

Dining/Entertainment: There's a cocktail lounge and a lunch and dinner restaurant on the ground floor, The Occasions Restaurant, serving international food.

Services: 24-hour room service, concierge, babysitting, valet and laundry service.

Facilities: An indoor swimming pool, sauna, solarium, exercise equipment, a snooker room, children's playroom and playground.

IN NEARBY WICKHAM

THE OLD HOUSE HOTEL, The Square, Wickham, Fareham, Hampshire PO17 5JG. Tel. 0329/833049. Fax 0329/833672. 12 rms (all with bath). TV TEL **Directions:** Head 9 miles from Portsmouth, at the junction of the B2177 and the A32, or 2 miles north of the M27 motorway linking Brighton through Portsmouth to Bournemouth. **Bus:** 69 from Fareham.

$ Rates (including English breakfast): £70–£80 ($105–$120) single; £80–£90 ($120–$135) double. AE, DC, MC, V. **Parking:** Free.

A handsome early Georgian (1715) house, thought to have been the first of its architectural type in the village, the Old House is surrounded by low, medieval timber structures around the square. The paneled Georgian rooms on the ground and first floors of the hotel contrast with the beamed bedrooms on the upper floors, once the servants' quarters. All nine bedrooms contain period furniture, many pieces original antiques; an additional three rooms, in an annex 50 yards from the main property in a building dating from the 16th century, have all the facilities of the main hotel, including private baths.

Dining/Entertainment: The restaurant occupies what was once a timber-frame outbuilding with stables, adjacent to a garden overlooking the Meon River. It serves a French provincial cuisine, with a complete meal costing from £23 ($34.50) up. The menu changes weekly, and care goes into the selection of the freshest vegetables and seasonal produce. Lunch is served Tuesday through Friday from 12:30 to 1:45pm and dinner Monday through Saturday from 7:30 to 9:30pm. The hotel's bar, with a French provincial ambience, is open exclusively for hotel and restaurant guests. Owners Richard and Annie Skipwith, who converted a private residence into this fine hotel in 1970, recommend making reservations in advance.

WHERE TO DINE

BISTRO MONTPARNASSE, 103 Palmerston Rd., Southsea. Tel. 816754.

Cuisine: BRITISH/FRENCH. **Reservations:** Required Sat. **Directions:** Follow the signs to the D-Day Museum, and at the museum turn left and go to the next intersection; the restaurant is on the right. **Bus:** Southsea bus.

$ Prices: 3-course fixed-price dinner £18.90 ($28.40). MC, V.

Open: Dinner only, Tues–Sat 7–10pm. **Closed:** Two weeks in Jan (dates vary). Generally conceded to serve the best food in the area, this bistro offers background music to get you in the mood for a well-rounded selection of dishes served in a fixed-price format. Fresh produce is delicately prepared. The cooking is familiar fare, and some of the dishes, such as veal flavored with calvados and cream, betray a Norman influence. Fresh fish—caught locally—is also served. Although the menu changes, you might try such dishes as a ragoût of local seafood with basil or crisp breast of duck with pineapple and a mild curry cream sauce.

2. SOUTHAMPTON

87 miles SW of London, 161 miles E of Plymouth

GETTING THERE **By Plane** There is a small airport outside Southampton, which is used mainly for flights to the Channel Islands. For information, call 0703/629600.

By Train British Rail serves the south, with departures from London's Waterloo Station several times daily (trip time: 66 min.).

By Bus National Express operates hourly departures from London's Victoria Coach Station, heading for Southampton (trip time: 2½ hr.).

By Car Take the M3 southwest from London.

ESSENTIALS The **telephone area code** is 0703. The **Tourist Information Centre** is at Above Bar Precinct (tel. 0703/221106).

To many North Americans, England's number-one passenger port, home base for the *Queen Elizabeth 2*, is the gateway to Britain. Southampton is a city of wide boulevards, parks, and shopping centers. During World War II, some 31½ million men set out from here (in World War I, more than twice that number passed through Southampton).

Its supremacy as a port dates from Saxon times, when the Danish conqueror, Canute, was proclaimed king here in 1017. Southampton was especially important to the Normans and helped them keep in touch with their homeland. Its denizens were responsible for bringing in the bubonic plague, which wiped out a quarter of the English population in the mid-14th century. On the Western Esplanade is a memorial tower to the Pilgrims, who set out on their voyage to the New World from Southampton on August 15, 1620. Both the *Mayflower* and the *Speedwell* sailed from here but were forced by storm damages to put in at Plymouth, where the *Speedwell* was abandoned. The memorial is a tall column with an iron basket on top—the type used as a beacon before lighthouses.

If you're waiting in Southampton between boats, you may want to explore some of the major sights of Hampshire on the periphery of the port—the New Forest, Winchester, the Isle of Wight, and Bournemouth in neighboring Dorset.

WHAT TO SEE & DO

In addition to the tours and museums listed below, **Ocean Village** and the **town quay** on Southampton's waterfront are bustling with activity and are filled with shops, restaurants, and entertainment possibilities.

TOURS Southampton has a long and varied history, as witnessed by the Roman settlement at Bitterne, the Saxon port of Hamvic, and the Norman town with town walls, some of which still stand. City tourist guides offer a wide range of free guided walks and regular city bus tours. **Free guided walks** of the medieval town are offered throughout the year on Sunday and Monday at 10:30am and in July, August, and September twice daily at 10:30am and 2:30pm. Tours start at Bargate. **City bus tours** run from mid-July to mid-September every Monday, Wednesday, and Friday in August. These tours depart at 2pm from outside the art gallery on the north side of the Civic Centre. Charges are £3.50 ($5.30) for adults and £3 ($4.50) for children. Boat cruises around the docks and Solent run from Ocean Village most afternoons at 2:30pm. For more details, check with the tourist center (see above).

MUSEUMS

TUDOR HOUSE MUSEUM, Bugle St., St. Michael's Sq. Tel. 332513.

The museum is housed in a late medieval timber-framed house with a banqueting hall furnished in a 16th-century style. It features exhibitions of Victorian and Edwardian domestic and social life and also sponsors temporary shows. Its garden, based on 16th-century texts and illustrations, is unique in southern England and has 50 species of herbs and flowers.

Admission: Free, but charges may be introduced in 1994.
Open: Tues–Fri 10am–noon and 1–5pm, Sat 10am–noon and 1–4pm, Sun 2–5pm. **Bus:** 2, 6, 8, or 13.

MUSEUM OF ARCHAEOLOGY, God's House Tower, Winkle St. Tel. 220007.

Housed in part of the town's 15th-century defenses, the exhibitions here trace the history and portray the daily life of the Roman, Saxon, and medieval eras. The lives of the inhabitants are depicted in exhibitions.

Admission: Free.
Open: Tues–Fri 10am–noon and 1–5pm, Sat 10am–noon and 1–4pm, Sun 2–5pm. **Bus:** 2, 6, 8, or 13.

SOUTHAMPTON MARITIME MUSEUM, The Wool House, Town Quay. Tel. 223941.

This museum is housed in an impressive 14th-century stone-built warehouse, with a magnificent timber ceiling. Its exhibits trace the history of Southampton, including a model of the docks as they looked at their peak in the 1930s. Also displayed are artifacts from some of the great ocean liners whose home port was Southampton.

Admission: Free, but charges might be imposed sometime in 1994.
Open: Tues–Fri 10am–1pm and 2–5pm, Sat 10am–1pm and 2–4pm, Sun 2–5pm. **Bus:** 2, 6, 8, or 13.

WHERE TO STAY

Finding an accommodation right in Southampton isn't as important as it used to be. Very few ships now arrive, and the places to stay just outside the city are, in the main, superior to what one finds in the city itself. For accommodations in the area, refer to "The New Forest" section, below. However, I'll provide some accommodation listings for those who for transportation or other reasons may want to stay in the city center.

MODERATE

DOLPHIN HOTEL, 35 High St., Southampton, Hampshire SO9 2DS. Tel. 0703/339955, or toll free 800/435-4542 in the U.S. Fax 0703/333650. 71 rms (all with bath), 2 suites. TV TEL **Bus:** 2, 6, or 8.

$ Rates: £60 ($90) single; £70 ($105) double; from £110 ($165) suite. Breakfast £7.95 ($11.90) extra. AE, DC, MC, V. **Parking:** Free.

This bow-windowed Georgian coaching house on the main street, dating back to the 13th century, was Jane Austen's choice, and even Thackeray's when he was writing

Pendennis. Even Queen Victoria came in her horse-drawn carriage. It's in the center of the city, and is approached through an arched entrance, over which rests a coat-of-arms of William IV and Queen Adelaide. The bedrooms vary widely in size, but are generally spacious and well furnished. The open staircase holds a rare collection of naval uniform prints.

French and English meals at the Dolphin are quite good, with a table d'hôte dinner beginning at £14.95 ($22.40). Drinks are served in the Nelson Bar. The hotel has health and fitness facilities.

FORTE POST HOUSE, Herbert Walker Ave., Southampton, Hampshire SO1 0HJ. Tel. 0703/330777, or toll free 800/435-4542 in the U.S. Fax 0703/332510. 130 rms (all with bath), 2 suites. TV TEL **Bus:** 2, 6, or 8.
$ Rates: £39.50–£49.50 ($59.30–$74.30) single or double; from £115 ($172.50) suite. Breakfast £6.95 ($10.40) extra. AE, DC, MC, V. **Parking:** £6 ($9).

This 10-floor high-rise across from Mayflower Park was built near the new docks to overlook the harbor, but is only 5 minutes away from the city center. You can unload your luggage under a sheltered drive and walk into the reception area. The rooms are handsome and spacious, with fine built-in pieces, private baths, and picture-window walls.

Among the facilities of the hotel are a heated, open-air swimming pool and a residents' lounge with color TV. The Harbour Bar adjacent to the restaurant offers an intimate atmosphere.

POLYGON HOTEL, Cumberland Place, Southampton, Hampshire SO9 4GP. Tel. 0703/330055, or toll free 800/435-4542 in the U.S. Fax 0703/332435. 117 rms (all with bath), 2 suites. MINIBAR TV TEL **Bus:** 2, 6, or 8.
$ Rates: £55 ($82.50) single or double; from £125 ($187.50) suite. Breakfast £8.50 ($12.80) extra. AE, DC, MC, V. **Parking:** £6 ($9).

The Polygon is a favorite with tourists and business travelers. It bears the name of a district known as the Polygon that was popular with visiting nobility in the 18th century. The present hotel has been modernized and refurbished to a good standard. The bedrooms all have radios, private baths, and hot-beverage facilities. The Polygon overlooks the town's Watts Park and civic center, and is within easy reach of the main shopping area and the train station.

SOUTHAMPTON MOAT HOUSE, 119 Highfield Lane, Portswood, South-ampton, Hampshire SO9 1YO. Tel. 0703/559555. Fax 0703/583910. 71 rms (all with bath). TV TEL **Bus:** 11 or 13.
$ Rates (including English breakfast): £53.50 ($80.30) single; £63.50 ($95.30) double. AE, DC, MC, V. **Parking:** Free.

In a residential area on the northern outskirts of the city, this modern hotel off Portswood Road, a member of Queens Moat Houses group, offers comfortable accommodations with private baths and efficient service.

Its restaurant, Hamilton's, serves both table d'hôte and à la carte menus, complemented by a comprehensive wine list. Lunch and dinner cost £15 ($22.50) and up for a three-course meal.

WHERE TO DINE

KUTI'S, 70 London Rd. Tel. 221585.
   Cuisine: INDIAN. **Reservations:** Recommended Fri–Sat. **Bus:** 11 or 17.
$ Prices: Appetizers £2.35–£3.10 ($3.50–$4.70); main courses £5.95–£6.70 ($8.90–$10.10); fixed-price buffet lunch £6.50 ($9.80). AE, MC, V.
   Open: Lunch daily noon–2:30pm; dinner daily 6–11:30pm.

The best Indian restaurant in Hampshire, flamboyantly decorated with murals from India, Kuti's pays homage to the subcontinent's many different cuisines, with a special emphasis on the vegetarian cuisines of Bangladesh. Sample a vegetarian thali or tandoori chicken slow-cooked in an earthenware pot, along with a host of other dishes available at the luncheon buffet. Some items may be familiar to you; others come as delightful, zesty surprises.

PORTER'S, Town Quay. Tel. 221159.
　　Cuisine: SEAFOOD. **Reservations:** Recommended for the restaurant; not required for the wine bar. **Bus:** 2, 6, or 8.
　$ Prices: 3-course lunches and dinners in the restaurant £19.50 ($29.30); platters in the wine bar £3.50–£10 ($5.30–$15). AE, DC, MC, V.
　　Open: Lunch Mon–Sat noon–3pm; dinner Mon–Sat 7pm–11:30pm (last order).
Considered the best restaurant in town, Porter's was designed by Scottish-born architect John Geddes as a warehouse and boatyard. At the time, the sea came up to its foundations and boats could unload their cargoes directly into its cavernous interior. Today, although the exterior is rustic and weathered, its interior is stylishly decorated in shades of rose and turquoise, with French Regency accessories. The restaurant has a wine cellar with 600-year-old walls, once part of the medieval wall that ringed Southampton. Meals feature preparations of mussels, lobster, trout, plaice, and oysters, with a changing array of specialties that might include a platter of fresh shellfish on a bed of seaweed, a timbale of seafood mousse wrapped in slices of smoked salmon, grilled salmon in a hollandaise sauce, and such meat dishes as filet mignon in red wine sauce and roasted rib of beef.

In 1992, the restaurant added an informal wine bar much favored by local businesspersons at lunch, and by relatively informal diners in the evening. It features wines from around £1.80 ($2.70) per glass, and less formal versions of the food served in the nearby restaurant.

AN EASY EXCURSION

Eight miles northwest of Southampton in Romsey on the A31 stands ✪ **Broadlands** (tel. 0794/516878), the home of the late Earl Mountbatten of Burma, who was assassinated in 1979. Lord Mountbatten, who has been called "the last war hero," lent the house to his nephew, Prince Philip, and Princess Elizabeth as a honeymoon haven in 1947, and in 1981 Prince Charles and Princess Diana spent the first nights of their honeymoon here.

Broadlands is owned by Lord Romsey, Lord Mountbatten's eldest grandson, who has created a fine exhibition and audiovisual show that depicts the highlights of his grandfather's brilliant career as a sailor and statesman. The house, originally linked to Romsey Abbey, was purchased by Lord Palmerston in 1736 and was later transformed into an elegant Palladian mansion by Capability Brown and Henry Holland. Brown landscaped the parkland and grounds and made the river (the Test) the main object of pleasure. The house and riverside lawns are open from Easter until the last Sunday in September; it's closed on Friday except Good Friday or any Friday in August. Hours are noon to 4pm. Adults pay £5 ($7.50) admission; children 12 to 16 £3.40 ($5.10). Free for children under 12.

---

3. THE NEW FOREST

95 miles SW of London, 10 miles W of Southampton

GETTING THERE By Train Go to Southampton (see above) where rail connections can be made to a few centers in the New Forest, depending on where you're going. Where the train leaves off, bus connections are possible to all the towns and many villages.

By Bus   Southampton and Lymington have the best bus connections to New Forest villages.

By Car   Head west from Southampton along the A35.

ESSENTIALS   The **telephone area code** depends on the town or village (see individual write-ups). The **information office** is at The New Forest Visitor Centre, Lyndhurst (tel. 0703/282269).

Encompassing about 92,000 acres, the New Forest is a large tract that was created by William the Conqueror, who laid out the limits of this then-private hunting preserve. Successful poachers faced the executioner if they were caught, and those who hunted but missed had their hands severed.

Henry VIII loved to hunt deer in the New Forest, but he also saw an opportunity to build up the British naval fleet by supplying oak and other hard timbers to the boatyards at Buckler's Hard on the Beaulieu River. Today you can visit the old shipyards and also the museum with its fine models of men-of-war, pictures of the old yard, and dioramas showing the building of these ships, their construction, and their launching. It took 2,000 trees to build one man-of-war.

Nowadays, a motorway cuts through the area, and the once-thick forest has groves of oak trees separated by wide tracts of common land that is grazed by ponies and cows, hummocked with heather and gorse, and frequented by rabbits. But away from the main roads, where signs warn of wild ponies and deer, you'll find a private world of peace and quiet.

WHAT TO SEE & DO

BEAULIEU ABBEY—PALACE HOUSE, Beaulieu, on the B3056 in the New Forest. Tel. 0590/612345.

✪   The abbey and house, as well as the National Motor Museum, are on the property of Lord Montagu of Beaulieu (pronounced "*Bew*-ley"), at Beaulieu, 5 miles southeast of Lyndhurst and 14 miles west of Southampton. A Cistercian abbey was founded on this spot in 1204, and the ruins can be explored today. The Palace House was the great gatehouse of the abbey before it was converted into a private residence in 1538 and is surrounded by gardens.

On the grounds, the **National Motor Museum,** one of the best and most comprehensive motor museums in the world, with more than 250 vehicles, is open to the public. It traces the story of motoring from 1895 to the present. Famous autos include four land-speed record holders, among them Donald Campbell's Bluebird. The collection was built around Lord Montagu's family collection of vintage cars. A special feature is called "Wheels." In a darkened environment, visitors can travel in specially designed "pods," each of which carries up to two adults and one child along a silent electric track. They move at a predetermined but variable speed, and each pod is capable of rotating almost 360°. This provides a means by which the visitor is introduced to a variety of displays spanning 100 years of motor development. Sound and visual effects are integrated into individual displays. In one sequence, visitors experience the thrill of being involved in a Grand Prix race. For further information, contact the visitor reception manager, John Montagu Building (tel. 0590/612345).

Admission: £7 ($10.50) adults, £5 ($7.50) children.

Open: Easter–Sept, daily 10am–6pm; Oct–Easter, daily 10am–5pm. **Closed:**

Dec 25. **Transportation:** Buses run from the Lymington bus station Mon–Sat; Sun you'll need a taxi or private car.

THE MARITIME MUSEUM, Buckler's Hard. Tel. 0590/616203.

Buckler's Hard, a historic 18th-century village 2½ miles from Beaulieu on the banks of the River Beaulieu, is where ships for Nelson's fleet were built, including the admiral's favorite, *Agamemnon,* as well as *Eurylus* and *Swiftsure.* The Maritime Museum reflects the shipbuilding history of the village. Its displays include shipbuilding at Buckler's Hard; Henry Adams, master shipbuilder; Nelson's favorite ship; Buckler's Hard and Trafalgar; and models of Sir Francis Chichester's yachts and items of his equipment. The cottage exhibits are a re-creation of 18th-century life in Buckler's Hard. Here you can stroll through the New Inn of 1793 and a shipwright's cottage of the same period, or look in on the family of a poor laborer at home. All these displays include village residents and visitors of the late 18th century. The walk back to Beaulieu, 2½ miles along the riverbank, is well marked through the woodlands. During the summer, you can take a half-hour cruise on the River Beaulieu in the present *Swiftsure,* an all-weather catamaran cruiser.

Admission: £2.40 ($3.60) adults, £1.60 ($2.40) children, family ticket £6.30 ($9.50).

Open: Easter–May, daily 10am–6pm; June–Sept, daily 10am–9pm; Sept–Easter, daily 10am–4:30pm.

WHERE TO STAY

IN NEW MILTON

CHEWTON GLEN HOTEL, Christchurch Rd., New Milton, Hampshire BH25 6QS. Tel. 0425/275341. Fax 0425/272310. 45 rms (all with bath), 13 suites. TV TEL **Directions:** After leaving the village of Walkford, follow signs off the A35 New Milton–Christchurch road, through parkland.

$ **Rates:** £178–£280 ($267–$420) double; from £298 ($447) suite. Breakfast £14 ($21) extra. AE, DC, MC, V. **Parking:** Free.

A gracious country house on the fringe of the New Forest, the Chewton Glen is within easy reach of Southampton and Bournemouth. In the old house, the magnificent staircase leads to well-furnished chambers, each a double, opening onto lovely views over the spacious grounds. In the new wing, you find yourself on the ground level with French doors opening onto your own private patio. Here the decor is in muted colors, the rooms named for the heroes of novels written by Captain Marryat (author of *The Children of the New Forest).* Everywhere log fires burn and fresh flowers add fragrance. The garden sweeps down to a stream and then to rhododendron woods.

Dining/Entertainment: In the dining room, the standards of cooking and presentation are high. Particular emphasis is placed on fresh ingredients. The chef favors a modern cuisine, complemented by excellent sauces and velvety smooth desserts. The fixed-price meal of three courses is changed daily. A fixed-price lunch is £25 ($37.50), going up to £30 ($45) on Sunday. A fixed-price dinner costs £40 ($60) and up.

Services: 24-hour room service, valet and laundry service.

Facilities: Guests can swim in an open-air, heated swimming pool. In addition there are two indoor tennis courts, a nine-hole golf course, a health club, an indoor swimming pool, a sauna, and a Jacuzzi.

IN LYNDHURST

CROWN HOTEL, 9 High St., Lyndhurst, Hampshire SO43 7NF. Tel. 0703/282922. Fax 0703/282751. 39 rms (all with bath), 1 suite. MINIBAR TV

TEL **Directions:** Exit the M27 motorway at Junction 1 and drive 3 miles due south. **Bus:** 56 or 56A.

$ **Rates** (including English breakfast): £56–£61 ($84–$91.50) single; £89–£99 ($133.50–$148.50) double; from £110 ($165) suite. AE, DC, MC, V. **Parking:** Free.

Though the present building is only 100 years old, there has been a hostelry here on the main street of the New Forest village of Lyndhurst, opposite the church with its tall spire, for centuries. Rooms are comfortable and traditionally furnished.

Much local produce is used in the dining room, including venison. The food is not only good but reasonable in price. A fixed-price lunch or dinner begins at £14.50 ($21.80), and there are also à la carte selections. Sunday lunch is well patronized by the local people. The hotel also does substantial bar meals.

LYNDHURST PARK HOTEL, 68 High St., Lyndhurst, Hampshire SO43 7NL. Tel. 0703/283923. Fax 0703/283019. 59 rms (all with bath). TV TEL **Bus:** 56 or 56A.

$ **Rates** (including English breakfast): £45–£57.50 ($67.50–$86.30) single; £60–£85 ($90–$127.50) double. AE, DC, MC, V. **Parking:** Free.

 A large Georgian country house set in 5 acres of beautiful gardens, this hotel boasts an outdoor heated swimming pool and an all-weather tennis court. The bedrooms all have radio alarms, tea and coffee makers, hairdryers, and trouser presses. There is a bar, plus an oak-paneled restaurant, where a wide selection of dishes is offered at lunch and dinner. A four-course dinner with coffee will cost about £14 ($21).

IN BROCKENHURST

BALMER LAWN HOTEL, Lyndhurst Rd., Brockenhurst, Hampshire SO42 7ZB. Tel. 0590/23116. Fax 0590/23864. 58 rms (all with bath). TV TEL **Directions:** Take the A337, the Lyndhurst-Lymington road, about a mile outside Brockenhurst.

$ **Rates** (including English breakfast): £50–£60 ($75–$90) single; £80–£97 ($120–$145.50) double. AE, DC, MC, V. **Parking:** Free.

The Balmer Lawn Hotel is a former hunting lodge, set back from the main highway, its grounds blending with those of the New Forest. It has both an indoor and an outdoor swimming pool, along with a sauna and a gym. Its bedrooms, in a variety of styles and shapes, are comfortable and well kept, all with bath or shower. The hotel is also a good choice for dining. It offers bar meals at lunch and full-course meals at night, costing £25 ($37.50) and up.

CAREY'S MANOR, Lyndhurst Rd., Brockenhurst, Hampshire SO42 7RH. Tel. 0590/23551. Fax 0590/22799. 80 rms (all with bath). TV TEL **Directions:** From the center, head toward Lyndhurst on the A337.

$ **Rates** (including English breakfast): £70–£80 ($105–$120) single; £99–£190 ($148.50–$285) double. AE, DC, MC, V. **Parking:** Free.

This manor house dates back to Charles II, who used to come here when Carey's was a hunting lodge. Greatly extended in 1888, the building became a country hotel in the 1930s. Much improved in recent years, it's better than ever. The old house is still filled with character, as exemplified by its mellow, timeworn paneling and carved oak staircase. Each bedroom, whether in the restored main building or in the garden wing, has a private bath or shower, radio, hairdryer, and trouser press. The hotel also serves good food, a modern British and French cuisine. Carey's is ideal as a resort, with an indoor swimming pool, gym, solarium, and sauna, all on 5 acres of landscaped grounds. It's about a 90-minute drive from London.

NEW PARK MANOR, Lyndhurst Rd., Brockenhurst, Hampshire SO42

7QH. Tel. 0590/23467. Fax 0590/22268. 26 rms (all with bath). TV TEL
Directions: Head half a mile off the A337 Lyndhurst-Brockenhurst road past the 500-year-old thatched lodge to the manor.

$ Rates (including English breakfast): £68–£75 ($102–$112.50) single; £104–£124 ($156–$186) double. AE, DC, MC, V. **Parking:** Free.

This former royal hunting lodge, dating from the days of William the Conqueror and a favorite of Charles II, is the only hotel in the New Forest itself. Now a modern country hotel, the original rooms have been preserved, including such features as beams and open log fires. The owners have installed central heating throughout. Each room is comfortable and well kept (10 contain minibars). Included in the tariff is the use of a swimming pool in a sheltered corner of the garden (heated in summer) and a hard tennis court. Riding from the hotel's stables is available.

The candlelit restaurant, with its log fire, specializes in flambé cookery. The chef often uses fresh garden produce, which is backed up by a good wine list. A table d'hôte meal costs £19.50 ($29.30).

IN BEAULIEU/BUCKLER'S HARD

MASTER BUILDERS HOUSE HOTEL, Buckler's Hard, Beaulieu, Hampshire SO42 7XB. Tel. 0590/616253. Fax 0590/616297 23 rms (all with bath). TV TEL

$ Rates (including English breakfast): £45 ($67.50) single; £95 ($142.50) double. AE, DC, MC, V. **Parking:** Free.

About 2½ miles south of Beaulieu is this lovely 18th-century main house, once the home of master shipbuilder Henry Adams, who was responsible for many of the wooden hulls that dominated the seaways of the world. A modern wing with well-furnished rooms now accommodates guests, while the space in the main building is devoted to the Yachtsman Buffet Bar, which provides good, ample snack meals, and to the restaurant with its wide windows overlooking the busy river. Meals begin at £16.50 ($24.80).

MONTAGU ARMS, Palace Lane, Beaulieu, Hampshire, SO42 7ZL. Tel. 0590/612324. Fax 0590/612188. 22 rms (all with bath), 2 suites. TV TEL

$ Rates (including English breakfast): £67.90–£75.90 ($101.90–$113.90) single; £95.90–£109.90 ($143.90–$164.90) double; from £165.90 ($248.90) suite. AE, DC, MC, V. **Parking:** Free.

This time-tested favorite combines the comfort of a country manor house with the cozy hospitality of a mellow wayside inn, which dates in part from the 18th century. The hotel staff keeps up an old English garden, which is well sheltered and filled with a number of rare plants.

The main lounge overlooks this garden, and the dining room, serving good food and wine, is oak beamed and paneled. In one of the three bars, the counter was fashioned with an old wine press. The bedrooms are immaculately kept and modernized. Each is a double, but rates for single occupancy are quoted. You can have a fixed-price lunch in the dining room for £14.95 ($22.40); a fixed-price dinner begins at £24 ($36).

WHERE TO DINE

LE POUSSIN, The Courtyard, rear of 49–55 Brookley Rd., Brockenhurst. Tel. 23063.
Cuisine: GAME/FISH. **Reservations:** Recommended.
$ Prices: Fixed-price menus £20 ($30) for 2 courses, £25 ($37.50) for 3 courses;

4-course "no-choice" gastronomic menu (dependent solely on the chef's inventories and whims) £25 ($37.50). MC, V.

Open: Lunch Tues–Sun noon–2pm; dinner Tues–Sat 7–10pm. **Closed:** 2 weeks in Jan, 1 week in Sept.

★ Considered one of the most sophisticated and famous small restaurants in the region, Le Poussin is located in what was originally a 19th-century stable and workshop for an itinerant craftsman known as a tinker. To reach it, pass beneath the arched alleyway (located midway between nos. 49 and 55 Brookley Rd.) and enter stylishly simple premises directed by English-born chef Alexander Aitken and his wife, Caroline.

Amid a decor accented with framed 19th-century poems and illustrations celebrating, in one form or another, the gastronomic pleasures of poultry, the staff will offer an array of fish and game dishes whose ingredients usually come fresh from the nearby New Forest. In season, you'll find several different versions of venison, the most visible of which is called "Fruits of the New Forest." (It contains individually cooked portions, encased in puff pastry of pigeon, wild rabbit, hare, and venison served with game sauce.) Your meal might begin with a *pithivier* of lobster (a dome-shaped puff pastry traditionally prepared as a dessert but in this case served as an appetizer and filled with chunks of lobster encased in a lobster mousse). Dessert choices change with the season but will usually include a festival of wild strawberries served with an elderflower sorbet.

4. ISLE OF WIGHT

91 miles SW of London, 4 miles S of Southampton

GETTING THERE   By Train   There is a direct train from London's Waterloo Station to Portsmouth, which deposits travelers directly at the pier for a ferry crossing to the Isle of Wight; ferries are timed to meet train arrivals. Travel time from London to the arrival point of Ryde on the Isle of Wight (including ferry-crossing time) is 2 hours. One train per hour departs during the day from London to Portsmouth.

By Car   Drive to Southampton (see above) and take the ferry, or leave Southampton and head west along the A35, cutting south on the A337 toward Lymington on the coast where the ferry crossing to Yarmouth (Isle of Wight) is shorter than the trip from Southampton.

By Ferry   A car-ferry from Town Quay in Southampton goes to East Cowes (Isle of Wight). The fare for a car and its passengers varies slightly according to its size, but the average round-trip fare is £38 ($57) for a crossing that takes about an hour each way, depending on the weather.

More popular with train travelers is the passenger-only high-speed ferryboat (a double-hulled catamaran) that travels between Southampton and West Cowes. Its price is £10.50 ($15.80) for adults and £5.50 ($8.30) for children round-trip. Trip time is around 25 minutes. Another passenger ferry operates between Portsmouth and Ryde, taking 20 minutes and costing £8.60 ($12.90) for adults and £4.30 ($6.50) for children round-trip. Daytime departures leave every 30 minutes in summer, and every 60 minutes in winter. A final option involves a Hovercraft that travels from Southsea (Portsmouth's neighbor) to Ryde, charging £8.20 ($12.30) for adults and £4.10 ($6.20) for children. For information on departure times and schedules, call the tourist office in Shanklin (see below) or 0983/293383 for car-ferries and 0983/811000 for passenger ferries.

GETTING AROUND   By Bus and Train   Visitors can explore the Isle of Wight just for the day on an Around the Island Rover bus trip. Tickets may be purchased on the bus, and you can board or leave the bus at any stop on the island. The price of a Day Rover is £5.90 ($8.90) for adults and £3 ($4.50) for children. It also entitles you to passage on the island's only railway, which runs from the dock to Ryde and to the center of Shanklin, a distance of 8 miles. For further information, call the Newport Bus Station (tel. 0983/523831).

ESSENTIALS   The **telephone area code** is 0983. The **information office** is at 67 High St., Shanklin (tel. 0983/862942).

The Isle of Wight is known for its sandy beaches and its ports, favored by the yachting set. The island, which long attracted such literary figures as Alfred Lord Tennyson and Charles Dickens, is compact in size, measuring 23 miles from east to west, 13 miles from north to south. **Ryde** is the railhead for the island's communications system. **Yarmouth** is something else—a busy little harbor providing a mooring for yachts and also for one of the lifeboats in the Solent area.

Cowes is the premier port for yachting in Britain. Henry VIII ordered the castle built here, but it is now the headquarters of the Royal Yacht Squadron. The seafront, the Prince's Green, and the high cliff road are worth exploring. Hovercraft are built in the town, which is also the home and birthplace of the well-known maritime photographer, Beken of Cowes. It's almost *de rigueur* to wear oilskins and wellies, leaving a wet trail behind you.

Newport, a bustling market town in the heart of the island, is the capital and has long been a favorite of British royalty. Along the southeast coast are the twin resorts of **Sandown,** with its new pier complex and theater, and **Shanklin,** at the southern end of Sandown Bay, which has held the British annual sunshine record more times than any other resort. Keats once lived in Shanklin's Old Village. Farther along the coast, **Ventnor** is called the "Madeira of England," because it rises from the sea in a series of steep hills.

On the west coast are the many-colored sand cliffs of Alum Bay. The Needles, three giant chalk rocks, and the Needles Lighthouse, are further features of interest at this end of the island. If you want to stay at the western end of Wight, consider **Freshwater Bay.**

WHAT TO SEE & DO

OSBORNE HOUSE, 1 mile southeast of East Cowes. Tel. 200022.

IN THEIR FOOTSTEPS

Queen Victoria (1819–1901) The woman who sat on the British throne longer than any other monarch and who became the Empress of India. Ruling over the "golden age" of the British Empire, she lent her name to the Victorian era and was the mother of the future King Edward VII. She married her cousin, Prince Albert of Saxe-Coburg-Gotha, in 1840.

• **Accomplishments:** She was a powerful monarch, influencing British imperial policies. She liked Disraeli's policies, but not those of the liberal Gladstone. Most of the Empire, certainly Great Britain, admired and respected her to the end.

• **Favorite Residences:** Osborne House on the Isle of Wight and her "beloved" Balmoral in Scotland.

• **Resting Place:** Frogmore (a private estate) near Windsor.

⭐ Queen Victoria's most cherished residence, a mile southeast of East Cowes, was built at her own expense. Prince Albert, with his characteristic thoroughness, contributed to many aspects of the design of the Italian-inspired mansion, which stands amid lush gardens, right outside the village of Whippingham. The rooms have remained as Victoria knew them, right down to the French piano she used to play and all the cozy clutter of her sitting room. Grief-stricken at the death of Albert in 1861, she asked that Osborne House be kept as it was, and so it has been. Even the turquoise scent bottles he gave her, decorated with cupids and cherubs, are still in place. It was in her bedroom at Osborne House that the queen died on January 22, 1901.

Admission: £5.40 ($8.10) adults, £2.70 ($4.10) children.
Open: Apr–Oct, daily 10am–6pm. **Bus:** 4 or 5.

CARISBROOKE CASTLE, Carisbrooke, 1¼ miles southwest of Newport. Tel. 522107.

This is where Charles I was imprisoned by the Roundheads in 1647. The fine medieval castle is in the center of the island. Everybody heads for the Well House, concealed inside a 16th-century stone building. Donkeys take turns treading a large wooden wheel connected to a rope that hauls up buckets of water.

Admission: £3 ($4.50) adults, £1.50 ($2.30) children.
Open: Mid-Mar to Oct, Mon–Sat 10am–6pm; Nov to mid-Mar, Mon–Sat 10am–4pm. **Bus:** 91A.

WHERE TO STAY

IN RYDE

BISKRA HOUSE BEACH HOTEL, 17 St. Thomas's St., Ryde, Isle of Wight PO33 2XX. Tel. 0983/567913. Fax 0983/616976. 9 rms (all with bath or shower). MINIBAR TV TEL

$ Rates (including English breakfast): £29.50–£32.50 ($44.30–$48.80) single; £47.50–£57.50 ($71.30–$86.30) double. MC, V. **Parking:** Free.

 You'll find some of the best dining on the island at Biskra House, which also offers rooms. The rooms are furnished in a comfortable, slightly old-fashioned way, with tea- or coffee-making facilities and hairdryers. The most expensive double room in the house has a private balcony with views over the Solent where occupants gather to watch sunsets.

Giuseppe's Cellar Restaurant is Italian, serving full meals daily from noon to 2pm and 7 to 10:30pm, costing £13.50 ($20.30) and up per person. A large cocktail bar opens onto gardens fronting the beach.

HOTEL RYDE CASTLE, The Esplanade, Ryde, Isle of Wight PO33 1JA. Tel. 0983/563755. Fax 0983/568925. 19 rms (all with bath), 1 suite. TV TEL Bus: 1 or 1A.

$ Rates (including English breakfast): £69–£79 ($103.50–$118.50) single; £80–£95 ($120–$142.50) double; from £109 ($163.50) suite. MC, V. **Parking:** Free.

This seafront hotel, looking out on the Solent, makes a fine base for exploring the island. The original castle (ca. 1540) was ordered built by Henry VIII as part of the defenses against a possible invasion which came in his daughter's reign—the Spanish Armada. With its crenellated, ivy-clad exterior and its well-kept public rooms and bedrooms, the hotel attracts families as well as single visitors. The bedrooms all have radios, hairdryers, and tea and coffee makers; double bedrooms have four-poster beds.

Both table d'hôte and à la carte meals are offered in the dining room, where full use is made of fresh fish caught locally and island farm produce. Meals cost £17.50 ($26.30) and up. The bar/lounge offers a wide range of inexpensive snacks for lunch.

IN SHANKLIN

BOURNE HALL COUNTRY HOTEL, Luccombe Rd., Shanklin, Isle of Wight PO37 6RR. Tel. 0983/862820. 30 rms (all with bath). TV TEL **Bus:** 12A. **$ Rates** (including English breakfast): £35.70 ($53.60) single; £61 ($91.50) double. AE, DC, MC, V. **Parking:** Free.

Many visitors prefer to base themselves at Shanklin because of its old village, with its thatched cottages and the Chine, two of the leading attractions on the island. At Bourne Hall they receive a warm welcome from the owners, who have one of the best-equipped hotels in the area, complete with two swimming pools, a sauna, a solarium, and a Jacuzzi. Each room is well furnished and comfortably maintained.

LUCCOMBE CHINE HOUSE, Luccombe Chine, Shanklin, Isle of Wight PO37 6RH. Tel. 0983/862037. 8 rms (all with bath or shower). TV **Directions:** Take the A3055 Shanklin-Ventnor road to the signposted private driveway. **Bus:** 12A. **$ Rates** (including English breakfast): £27–£34 ($40.50–$51) per person. MC, V. **Parking:** Free. **Closed:** Dec–Jan.

Luccombe Chine House stands on some 10 acres of grounds opening onto Luccombe Bay. Each room is immaculately kept and well furnished, with hot-beverage facilities and hairdryer; six have four-poster beds. It's a good base from which to explore the Isle of Wight. The food is also good, with meals beginning at £12 ($18).

IN SANDOWN

ST. CATHERINE'S HOTEL, 1 Winchester Park Rd., Sandown, Isle of Wight PO36 8HJ. Tel. 0983/402392. Fax 0983/402392. 20 rms (all with bath or shower). TV TEL **Bus:** 16 from Ryde. **$ Rates** (including English breakfast): £21 ($31.50) single; £42 ($63) double. MC, V. **Parking:** Free.

Just a few minutes' walk from Sandown's sandy beach, leisure center, and pier complex, with its sun lounges and theater, St. Catherine's was built in 1860 of creamy Purbeck stone and white trim for the dean of Winchester College. A modern extension was added for streamlined and sunny bedrooms. The brightly redecorated lounge has matching draperies at the wide bay windows. There are card tables and a small library of books. Adjacent is a cozy, fully stocked bar and a spacious, comfortable dining room, serving high-quality English food, with a meal costing £10.50 ($15.80). The bedrooms have duvets, white furniture, and built-in headboards.

IN CHALE

THE CLARENDON HOTEL AND WIGHT MOUSE INN, Newport Rd. (B3399), Chale, Isle of Wight PO38 2HA. Tel. 0983/730431. 13 rms (all with bath), 1 suite. TV **Directions:** Lies 50 yards off Military Rd.; it's signposted. **$ Rates** (including English breakfast): £37–£39 ($55.50–$58.50) single; £74–£78 ($111–$117) double; from £98 ($147) suite. MC. **Parking:** Free.

This old coaching inn lies on the most southerly part of the island, where the vegetation is almost tropical. From here, you have views over the Channel to the mainland coast. The Clarendon is a cheerful place at which to spend the night. Some of the rooms are beautifully furnished with antiques, and all have tea and coffee makers. Children are most welcome here.

The meals are ample, with many fresh ingredients. In the pub, the Wight Mouse Inn, open all day every day for hot meals and drinks, they serve a large selection of beers, including real ales, and 365 scotch whiskies (one for every day of the year), in addition to the more usual drinks. Live entertainment is provided nightly year-round. Traditional English dishes are served in the more formal Clarendon Restaurant.

WHERE TO DINE

THE COTTAGE, 8 Eastcliff Rd., Shanklin. Tel. 862504.
  Cuisine: ENGLISH/FRENCH. **Reservations:** Required.
$ **Prices:** Fixed-price 3-course lunch £7.95 ($11.90); dinner appetizers £1.90–£5 ($2.90–$7.50); dinner main courses £12.95 ($19.40). MC, V.
  Open: Lunch Tues–Sat noon–2pm; dinner Tues–Sat 7:30–9:45pm. **Closed:** Feb and Oct.

Established in 1973, this restaurant is within a 200-year-old stone-sided cottage that is set among the thatch-covered buildings of the center of Shanklin. Inside, two floors of pink and blue dining rooms have lace tablecloths and heavy oaken beams. Lunches are fixed-price affairs that feature such dishes as chicken with green peppercorns or a roast of the day (pork, lamb, or beef) served with new potatoes and two vegetables. Dinners are more elaborate, and include such recipes as tournedos of beef with a grape and port wine sauce, or poached filet of fresh lemon sole stuffed with smoked salmon and served with lobster sauce.

---

5. WINCHESTER

72 miles SW of London, 12 miles N of Southampton

GETTING THERE By Train From London's Waterloo Station there is frequent daily train service to Winchester (trip time: 1 hr.).

By Bus National Express buses leaving from London's Victoria Coach Station depart every 2 hours for Winchester during the day (trip time: 2 hr.).

By Car From Southampton, drive north along the A335; from London take the M3 motorway west.

ESSENTIALS The **telephone area code** is 0962. The **Tourist Information Centre** is at the Winchester Guildhall, The Broadway (tel. 0962/840500).

The most historic city in all of Hampshire, Winchester is big on legends—it's even associated with King Arthur and the Knights of the Round Table. In the Great Hall, all that remains of Winchester Castle, a round oak table, with space for King Arthur and his 24 knights, is attached to the wall. But all that spells undocumented romance. What is known, however, is that when the Saxons ruled the ancient kingdom of Wessex, Winchester was the capital.

The city is also linked with King Alfred, who is believed to have been crowned here and is honored today by a statue. The Danish conqueror, Canute, came this way too, as did the king he ousted, Ethelred the Unready (Canute got his wife, Emma, in the bargain). The city is the seat of the well-known Winchester College, whose founding father was the bishop of Winchester, William of Wykeham. Established in 1382, it is reputed to be the oldest public (private) school in England.

Traditions are strong in Winchester. You can still go to St. Cross Hospital—dating from the 12th century—now an almshouse. There you'll get ye olde pilgrim's dole of ale and bread (and if there's no bread, you can eat cake). You must arrive, however, on a weekday before 11am. Winchester is essentially a market town, on the downs on the Itchen River.

WHAT TO SEE & DO

For centuries, ✪ **Winchester Cathedral,** The Square (tel. 853137), has been one of the great churches of England. The present building, the longest medieval cathedral in Britain, dates from 1079, and its Norman heritage is still in evidence. When a Saxon church stood on this spot, St. Swithun, bishop of Winchester and tutor to young King Alfred, suggested modestly that he be buried outside. When he was later buried inside, it rained for 40 days. The legend lives on: Just ask a resident of Winchester what will happen if it rains on St. Swithun's Day, July 15, and you'll get a prediction of rain for 40 days.

In the present building, the nave with its two aisles is most impressive, as are the chantries, the reredos (late 15th century), and the elaborately carved choir stalls. Of the chantries, that of William of Wykeham, founder of Winchester College, is perhaps the most visited (it's found in the south aisle of the nave). The cathedral also contains a number of other tombs, notably those of Jane Austen and Izaak Walton (exponent of the merits of the pastoral life in *The Compleat Angler*). The latter's tomb is to be found in the Prior Silkestede's Chapel in the South Transept. Jane Austen's grave is marked with a commemorative plaque. Winchester Cathedral contains in chests the bones of many of the Saxon kings and the remains of the Viking conqueror, Canute, and his wife, Emma, in the presbytery. The son of William the Conqueror, William Rufus (who reigned as William II), is also buried at the cathedral. There are free guided tours April through October, Monday through Saturday at 11am and 3pm.

The crypt is flooded during winter months but part of it may be seen from a viewing platform. When it's not flooded, there are two regular tours, Monday through Saturday at 10:30am and 2:30pm. The cathedral library and the Triforium Gallery are open from Easter to September on Monday from 2 to 4:30pm and Tuesday through Saturday from 10:30am to 1pm and 2 to 4:30pm; from October to Easter, on Saturday from 10:30am to 4pm. The library comprises Bishop Morley's 17th-century book collection and an exhibition room containing the 12th-century Winchester Bible. The Triforium shows sculpture, woodwork, and metalwork from 11 centuries and affords magnificent views over the rest of the cathedral. Admission to the library and Triforium Gallery is £1.50 ($2.30) for adults and 50p (80¢) for children. No admission fee is charged for the cathedral, but a donation of £2 ($3) is suggested.

WHERE TO STAY

VERY EXPENSIVE

LAINSTON HOUSE, Sparsholt, Winchester, Hampshire SO21 2LT. Tel. 0962/863588. Fax 0962/72672. 38 rms, 3 suites. MINIBAR TV TEL **Directions:** Take the A272 3½ miles northwest of Winchester.

$ Rates: £95 ($142.50) single; £115–£180 ($172.50–$270) double; from £225 ($337.50) suite. Breakfast £9.50 ($14.30) extra. AE, DC, MC, V. **Parking:** Free.

✪ The beauty of this fine, restored William and Mary red-brick manor house strikes visitors as they approach via a long, curving, tree-lined drive. It is situated on 63 acres of rolling land, linked with the name Lainston in the *Domesday Book* of 1086. Inside the stately house, elegance is the keynote, with Delft-tile fireplaces, oak and cedar paneling, molding, and cornices of the original owners preserved, set off with period pieces. The largest and most elegant rooms are in the main house, with traditional English furnishings and color-coordinated decors. Other rooms, less spacious, but also comfortable and harmoniously furnished, are in a nearby annex.

In either of the two dining rooms, you can order such French and English specialties as roast partridge or roast loin of lamb rolled with a herb stuffing. Dinners cost £27.50 to £40 ($41.30 to $60).

EXPENSIVE

ROYAL HOTEL, St. Peter St., Winchester, Hampshire SO23 8BS. Tel. 0962/840840, or toll free 800/528-1234 in the U.S. Fax 0962/841582. 75 rms (all with bath or shower), 3 suites. TV TEL

$ Rates: £78 ($117) single; £110 ($165) double; from £120 ($180) suite. Breakfast £6.50 ($9.80) extra. AE, DC, MC, V. **Parking:** Free.

This fine old hotel was built at the end of the 17th century as a private house. It has a modern extension overlooking gardens. All rooms have traditional English styling. For 50 years it was used by nuns from Brussels as a convent before being turned into a hotel—when it soon became the center of the city's social life. It's only a few minutes' walk to the cathedral, yet still enjoys a secluded position. Best of all is the garden hidden behind high walls. Meals are served in a small, formal dining room with a view of the private garden, where a fixed-price dinner costs £17.50 ($26.30). Shoe cleaning, valet service, and 24-hour room service constitute some of the amenities.

MODERATE

WYKEHAM ARMS, 75 Kingsgate St., Winchester, Hampshire SO23 9PE. Tel. 0962/853834. Fax 0962/854411. 7 rms (all with bath). TV TEL MINIBAR

$ Rates (including English breakfast): £62.50 ($93.80) single; £72.50 ($108.80) double. AE, MC, V.

This is one of the most enduring recommendations in Winchester, known to almost everyone in town for its food and bar facilities. It lies behind a 200-year-old brick facade in the historic center of town, near the cathedral. The bedrooms are comfortably and traditionally furnished with antiques or reproductions and such lighthearted touches as fresh flowers and baskets of potpourri. The bathrooms are modern.

Most of the establishment's income and prestige derive from its paneled pub and restaurant, where carefully flavored food is served in historic surroundings. Lunches (served Monday to Saturday from noon to 3pm) are informal affairs where pub snacks and platters are served after clients place their orders at the bar. Sandwiches, ploughman's lunches, and such platters as Thai chicken with rice and chutney are priced from £2.50 to £5.50 ($3.80 to $8.30). Evening meals (served Monday to Saturday from 6:30 to 8:45pm) are more elaborate, with waitresses taking orders directly at the tables. Menu items, priced from £2 to £4 ($3 to $6) for a starter and from £9 to £11 ($13.50 to $16.50) for main dishes, are more elegant than you might have imagined. They include, for example, poached filet of salmon served with a salmon mousse and a warm mint and cucumber vinaigrette; creamy Swiss-style chicken layered with Gruyère and mushrooms and served on a bed of Rösti potatoes; and such vegetarian main dishes as a leek-and-mushroom strudel.

INEXPENSIVE

STRATTON HOUSE, Stratton Rd., St. Giles Hill, Winchester, Hampshire SO23 8JQ. Tel. 0962/863919. Fax 0962/842095. 6 rms (4 with bath). TV

Transportation: Free pickup available from the train or bus station.

$ Rates (including English breakfast): £22 ($33) single without bath, £30 ($45) single with bath; £44 ($66) double without bath, £47 ($70.50) double with bath. No credit cards. **Parking:** Free. **Closed:** Dec 24–Jan 1.

 This lovely old Victorian house (ca. 1890) is situated on an acre of St. Giles Hill, overlooking the city. It's about a 5- to 10-minute walk from the center. All the comfortably furnished bedrooms have TVs and hot-beverage facilities. A three-course evening meal can be arranged for £10 ($15). There is ample parking in a private courtyard.

WHERE TO DINE

NINE THE SQUARE, 9 Great Minster St. Tel. 864004.
Cuisine: CONTINENTAL. **Reservations:** Recommended.
$ Prices: In wine bar, appetizers £2.20–£3.90 ($3.30–$5.90); main courses £4.95 ($7.40). In upstairs restaurant, appetizers £3.75–£10 ($5.60–$15); main courses £15–£17.50 ($22.50–$26.30); 3-course fixed-price restaurant lunch £12.95 ($19.40). AE, MC, V.
Open: Lunch Mon–Sat noon–2:30; dinner Mon–Sat 7–10:30pm.

One of the assets of this establishment is its enviable view of Winchester Cathedral. Clients may either head upstairs to the comfortably formal restaurant, or remain at street level in the likable wine bar. Casual dress is not frowned upon, but management prefers for men to wear jackets upstairs during the evening meal.

The wine-bar offers at least four kinds of freshly made pastas, including a homemade parsley tagliatelle with fresh pesto sauce, and *brodetto,* an Italian fish stew containing salmon, mussels, mullet, and tomatoes. Wine prices begin at around £1.80 ($2.70) per glass. Upstairs, the fare is more serious, with terrine of wood pigeon and venison served with an orange chutney; "hand-dived" (i.e., not commercially dredged) scallops in a citrus beurre blanc sauce; poached marinated saddle of venison in a juniperberry sauce, and pan-fried mignons of pork in a kumquat sauce.

ELIZABETHAN RESTAURANT, 18 Jewry St. Tel. 853566.
Cuisine: ENGLISH/FRENCH. **Reservations:** Recommended.
$ Prices: Appetizers £1.95–£4.95 ($2.90–$7.40); main courses £7.50–£12.75 ($11.30–$19.10); fixed-price lunch and early-evening menu £9.50 ($14.30). AE, DC, MC, V.
Open: Lunch daily noon–2:30pm; dinner daily 6:30–10:30pm.

In the atmosphere of another century, the Elizabethan Restaurant offers you an opportunity to dine under hand-hewn beams by candlelight. The street-level bar is for drinks and snacks, while the more formal dining room is one floor above. The restaurant sits in the upper reaches of the village, in a building originally dating from 1509. Well run, the kitchen offers an excellent English cuisine with many French-inspired dishes. Try, for example, roast beef or lobster thermidor. A tourist menu costs only £9.50 ($14.30) for three courses, but you must order it by 8pm. After that, à la carte dinners cost from £18 ($27).

AN EASY EXCURSION

If you love Jane Austen, you might want to make a trip to see **Chawton Cottage,** Jane Austen's House, in Chawton, a mile southwest of Alton off the A31 and the B3006 (tel. 0420/83236). The location is 15 miles east of Winchester. The cottage is signposted at Chawton. Born in 1775, Jane Austen was the daughter of the Oxford-educated rector, the Rev. Mr. George Austen, a typical Hampshire country gentleman, who had lots of charm but little money. In keeping with a custom of the time, the Austens gave their third son, Edward, to a wealthy, childless family connection, Thomas Knight. As Knight's heir, it was Edward who let his mother and sisters live in the house.

Visitors can see the surroundings in which the novelist spent the last 7½ years of her life, her period of greatest accomplishment. In the unpretentious but pleasant cottage, you can see the table on which Jane Austen penned new versions of three of her books and wrote three more, including *Emma*. You can also see the rector's George III mahogany bookcase and a silhouette likeness of the Reverend Austen presenting his son to the Knights. It was in this cottage that Jane Austen became ill in 1816 with what would have been diagnosed by the middle of the 19th century as Addison's disease.

There is an attractive garden in which visitors are invited to have picnics and an old bakehouse with Austen's donkey cart. Visitors can also browse through a bookshop. The home is open April to October, daily from 11am to 4:30pm for £1.50 ($2.30) admission; children 8 to 18 pay 50p (80¢). It is closed Monday and Tuesday in November, December, and March; Monday through Friday in January and February; and Christmas Day and Boxing Day (Dec 26).

---

6. BOURNEMOUTH

104 miles SW of London, 15 miles W of the Isle of Wight

GETTING THERE By Train An express train from Waterloo Station takes 2 hours. There is frequent service throughout the day.

By Bus Buses leave London's Waterloo Station every 2 hours during the day, heading for Bournemouth (trip time: 2½ hr.).

By Car Take the M3 southwest from London to Winchester, then the A31 and the A338 south to Bournemouth.

ESSENTIALS The **telephone area code** is 0202. The **information office** is at Westover Road (tel. 0202/789789).

The south-coast resort at the doorstep of the New Forest didn't just happen: It was carefully planned and executed, a true city in a garden. Flower-filled, park-dotted Bournemouth contains a great deal of architecture inherited from those arbiters of taste, Victoria and her son, Edward. (The resort was discovered back in Victoria's day, when seabathing became an institution.) Bournemouth's most distinguished feature is its chines (narrow, shrub-filled, steep-sided ravines) along the coastline.

It is estimated that of Bournemouth's nearly 12,000 acres, about one-sixth is comprised of green parks and flowerbeds, such as the Pavilion Rock Garden, which amblers pass through day and night. The total effect, especially in spring, is striking and helps explain Bournemouth's continuing popularity with the garden-loving English.

Bournemouth, along with Poole and Christchurch, forms the largest urban area in the south of England. It makes a good base for exploring a historically rich part of England; on its outskirts are the New Forest, Salisbury, Winchester, and the Isle of Wight. It also has some 20,000 students attending the various schools or colleges, who explore, in their off-hours, places made famous by such poets and artists as Shelley, Beardsley, and Turner.

The resort's amusements are varied. At the Pavilion Theatre, for example, you can see West End–type productions from London. The Bournemouth Symphony Orchestra is justly famous in Europe. And there's the usual run of golf courses, band concerts, variety shows, and dancing. The real walkers might strike out at Hengistbury Head and make their way past sandy beaches, the Boscombe and Bournemouth piers—all the way to Alum Chine, a distance of 6 miles.

WHERE TO STAY

EXPENSIVE

THE CARLTON HOTEL, Meyrick Rd., East Overcliff, Bournemouth, Dorset BH1 3DN. Tel. 0202/552011. Fax 0202/299573. 64 rms, 6 suites. A/C TV TEL

$ Rates (including English breakfast): £98 ($147) single; £150 ($225) double; from £200 ($300) suite. AE, DC, MC, V. **Parking:** £6 ($9).

Better defined as a vacation resort than as an ordinary hotel, the Carlton sits atop a seaside cliff lined with private homes and other hotels. Many of the better rooms are quite spacious, offering king-size beds, along with armchairs and writing desks. All bathrooms are contemporary, with a number of amenities (including both a bathtub and a shower) and a bidet. The Carlton boasts a luxury restaurant and cocktail bar, elegant lounges, a boutique, a swimming pool, and a health and beauty spa. There, a sudsy whirlpool, a gymnasium, and a trained staff contribute to healthy vacations. Lunch goes for £17.50 ($26.30), and dinner costs £29.50 ($44.30). Laundry and 24-hour room service are available.

ROYAL BATH HOTEL, Bath Rd., Bournemouth, Dorset BH1 2EW. Tel. 0202/555555. Fax 0202/554158. 124 rms, 7 suites. TV TEL

$ Rates (including English breakfast): £91.50–£105 ($137.30–$157.50) single; £140 ($210) double; from £215 ($322.50) suite. AE, DC, MC, V. **Parking:** £6 ($9).

This early Victorian version of a French château, with towers and bay windows looking out over the bay and Purbeck Hill, opened on June 28, 1838, the very day of Victoria's coronation. After the adolescent Prince of Wales (later—a long time later—Edward VII) stayed here, the hotel added "Royal" to its name. Over the years it has attracted everybody from Oscar Wilde to Rudolf Nureyev, and the great prime minister, Disraeli. Each luxuriously furnished bedroom has a private bath, and the larger rooms have sitting areas.

The table d'hôte lunch at Oscar's is £14.50 ($21.80), and a fixed-price dinner is £23 ($34.50). The resident band plays for a dinner-dance Saturday evenings. For health enthusiasts, there is a sauna, as well as Swedish massages and special diets. Amid its 3 acres of clifftop gardens is a heated swimming pool.

MODERATE

LANGTRY MANOR HOTEL, 26 Derby Rd., East Cliff, Bournemouth, Dorset BH1 3QB. Tel. 0202/553887. Fax 0202/290115. 27 rms (all with bath or shower), 3 suites. MINIBAR TV TEL

$ Rates (including English breakfast): £49.50–£69 ($74.30–$103.50) single; £79 ($118.50) double; from £145 ($217.50) suite. AE, DC, MC, V. **Parking:** Free.

North of Christchurch Road (A35) is the Red House, as it was originally called, built in 1877 for Lillie Langtry, the famous Jersey Lily, as a gift from Edward VII to his favorite mistress. The house contains all sorts of reminders of its illustrious inhabitants, including initials scratched on a windowpane and carvings on a beam of the entrance hall. On the half-landing is the peephole through which the prince could scrutinize the assembled company before coming down to dine, and one of the fireplaces bears his initials. The bedrooms range from ordinary twins to the Lillie Langtry suite, Lillie's own room, with a four-poster bed draped in Nottingham lace and a double heart-shaped bathtub; or you can rent the Edward VII suite, furnished as it was when His Royal Highness lived in this spacious room. The huge carved-oak fireplace has hand-painted tiles depicting scenes from Shakespeare. The four-poster bed can be made up as either twins or a large double bed.

The owner has furnished the hotel in the Edwardian style. There is no menu; the dishes are just produced for inspection. A three-course dinner begins at £20 ($30).

NORFOLK ROYALE HOTEL, Richmond Hill, Bournemouth, Dorset BH2 6EN. Tel. 0202/551521. Fax 0202/299729. 90 rms (all with bath), 5 suites. MINIBAR TV TEL
$ Rates: £71.50–£106.50 ($107.30–$159.80) single; £99–£165 ($148.50–$247.50) double; from £192.50 ($288.80) suite. Breakfast £8.75 ($13.10) extra. AE, DC, MC, V. **Parking:** Free.

One of the oldest prestige hotels of the resort, a few blocks from the seafront and the central shopping area, has undergone a major £5-million renovation program, restoring it to its former Edwardian elegance. Disregarding what lies on its periphery, it's like a country estate, with a formal entrance and a rear garden and fountain shaded by trees. The public rooms are geared to holiday guests, with two bars. The rooms and suites have been luxuriously appointed with the traditional styles of the Edwardian period blending with modern comforts such as private baths, phones, and TVs. Among the special features of the hotel are the swimming pool covered with a glass dome and the Orangery restaurant set in the terraced gardens. Meals cost £18.50 ($27.80) and up.

MODERATE

SWALLOW HIGHCLIFF HOTEL, 105 St. Michael's Rd., West Cliff, Bournemouth, Dorset BH2 5DU. Tel. 0202/557702. Fax 0202/292734. 154 rms (all with bath), 3 suites. TV TEL
$ Rates (including English breakfast): £82–£97 ($123–$145.50) single; £120 ($180) double; from £195 ($292.50) suite. AE, DC, MC, V. **Parking:** Free.

The high-ceilinged interior of this 19th-century cliffside hotel has been tastefully renovated into a subtly updated format, retaining most of the elegant ceiling moldings but replacing the antiques with conservatively modern counterparts. Many of the bedrooms have beautiful views of the sea. Bedrooms, each well furnished and maintained, are either in the main building or else in converted coastguard cottages on the grounds. The hotel premises offer a heated swimming pool, tennis court, sauna, solarium, putting green, and games room. An elegant restaurant serves well-prepared food in a grand manner, with formal service. Dinners cost £16.95 ($25.40).

IN NEARBY POOLE

THE MANSION HOUSE, 7–11 Thames St., Poole, Dorset BH15 1JN. Tel. 0202/685666. Fax 0202/665709. 28 rms (all with bath), 1 suite. A/C TV TEL
$ Rates (including English breakfast): £50–£75 ($75–$112.50) single; £80–£100 ($120–$150) double; from £130 ($195) suite. AE, DC, MC, V. **Parking:** Free.

The Mansion House, 4 miles west of Bournemouth, was built more than 200 years ago by an English entrepreneur engaged in cod-fishing off the coast of Newfoundland. The neoclassical detailing and fan-shaped windows that pierce the red brick of the establishment's facade are the pride and well-maintained joy of the owners. You'll probably be offered a glass of sherry as you register, near the sweeping staircase of the entrance vestibule.

A pair of bars are decorated with formal and rustic decors. An upstairs lounge and graciously furnished bedrooms provide plenty of quiet, well-decorated corners for relaxation. Excellent modern English cuisine is served at £25 ($37.50) for dinner.

WHERE TO DINE

BOURNE RESTAURANT, in the Hampshire House, Bourne Ave., The Square. Tel. 551430.

Cuisine: ENGLISH/FRENCH. **Reservations:** Recommended.

$ Prices: Appetizers £3.50–£5.50 ($5.30–$8.30); main courses £8.50–£14.95 ($12.80–$22.40); 3-course fixed-price lunch £7.95 ($11.90). MC, V.

Open: Lunch daily noon–2:30pm; dinner daily 6–11pm.

One of the best centrally located restaurants in Bournemouth has awakened sleepy local taste buds with some really good food at fair prices. Look for the daily specials on a blackboard menu. You might begin with moules marinières or Stilton mushrooms with garlic mayonnaise, then follow with king prawns wrapped in bacon and cooked in garlic butter or poached halibut with crab-and-lobster sauce.

SOPHISTICATS, 43 Charminster Rd. Tel. 291019.

Cuisine: FRENCH/INTERNATIONAL. **Reservations:** Required.

$ Prices: Appetizers £2.85–£6.75 ($4.30–$10.10); main courses £9.75–£11.95 ($14.60–$17.90). No credit cards.

Open: Dinner only, Tues–Sat 7–10pm. **Closed:** Two weeks in Feb, two weeks in Nov.

Among the leading restaurants at this south-coast resort, Sophisticats is worth a repeat visit. In a shopping section, about 1½ miles north of Bournemouth, Sophisticats tempts its diners with its excellent fresh fish, and you can order any number of veal and beef dishes (sometimes the latter will be prepared in the Indonesian style). Appetizers are filled with flavor and texture, and a highly desirable finish to a meal is a dessert soufflé (but let the waiter know in time).

EASY EXCURSIONS

KINGSTON LACY

An imposing 17th-century mansion, Kingston Lacy, at Wimborne Minster, on the B3082 Wimborne-Blandford road, 1½ miles west of Wimborne (tel. 0202/883402), was the home for more than 300 years of the Bankes family, who had as guests such distinguished persons as King Edward VII, Kaiser Wilhelm, Thomas Hardy, George V, and Wellington. The house contains a magnificent collection of works of art by such old masters as Rubens, Titian, and Van Dyck. There is also an important collection of Egyptian artifacts.

The present house was built to replace Corfe Castle, the Bankes' family's home that was destroyed in the Civil War. During her husband's absence while performing duties as chief justice to King Charles I, Lady Bankes led the defense of the castle, withstanding two sieges before being forced to surrender to Cromwell's forces in 1646 through the actions of a treacherous follower. The keys of Corfe Castle hang in the library at Kingston Lacy.

The house, set in 250 acres of wooded park, is open from April to the end of October, Saturday through Wednesday from noon to 5:30pm. The park is open from

11:30am to 6pm. Admission to the house is £5 ($7.50) for adults, £2.50 ($3.80) for children. Admission to the garden is £2 ($3) for adults, £1 ($1.50) for children.

WAREHAM

This historic little town on the Frome River 2 miles west of Bournemouth is a good center for touring the South Dorset coast and the Purbeck Hills. It contains remains of early Anglo-Saxon and Roman town walls, plus the Saxon church of St. Martin, with its effigy of T. E. Lawrence (Lawrence of Arabia), who died in a motorcycle crash in 1935. His former home, **Clouds Hill** (tel. 0305/262366), lies 7 miles west of Wareham (a mile north of Bovington Camp) and is extremely small. It's open April to October, on Wednesday, Friday, and Sunday from 11am to 1pm; November to March, only on Sunday from 1 to 4pm. Admission is £2.50 ($3.80) for adults; children under 5 free.

Aficionados of Lawrence and/or military history should probably also head for **The Tank Museum,** which lies within the village and army base of Bovington Camp (tel. 0929/403463), an installation maintained by the British military. Among the dozens of rare and historic armed vehicles are exhibitions and memorabilia on the life of T. E. Lawrence. Admission is £4 ($6) for adults and £2 ($3) for children 5 to 16. It's open daily from 10am to 4:30pm (last admission).

Where to Stay and Dine

THE PRIORY HOTEL, Church Green, Wareham, Dorset BH20 4ND. Tel. 0929/551666. Fax 0929/554519. 15 rms (all with bath), 4 suites. MINIBAR TV TEL

$ Rates (including English breakfast): £80–£95 ($120–$142.50) single; £110–£150 ($165–$225) double; from £175 ($262.50) suite. AE, DC, MC, V. **Parking:** Free.

Beside the River Frome and near the village church, this hotel has a well-tended garden adorned by graceful trees. Inside, a warmly paneled bar and a sumptuous lounge filled with antiques open onto views of the lawn. The bedrooms are tastefully furnished with antiques and complementary textiles, and have many extras. In the hotel's restaurant, dishes are cooked to order, and every effort is made to make use of the abundant local produce. The headwaiter will always advise of daily specials. Meals cost £22.50 to £26.50 ($33.80 to $39.80) and are likely to include such dishes as quails stuffed with pistachio nuts and ham in a champagne-cream sauce and médaillons of venison with chestnuts and celeriac in a port wine sauce.

7. DORCHESTER

120 miles SW of London, 27 miles W of Bournemouth

GETTING THERE By Train Trains run from London's Waterloo Station during the day at the rate of one per hour (trip time: 2½ hr.).

By Bus Several National Express coaches a day depart from London's Waterloo Station heading for Dorchester (trip time: 3 hr.). In Dorchester, Bere Regis, 7 Bridport Rd. (tel. 0305/62992), sells tickets both for National Express buses for London and for local buses.

By Car From London, take the M3 motorway southwest, but near the end get onto the A30 in the direction of Salisbury, where you should connect with the A354 for the final approach to Dorchester.

ESSENTIALS The **telephone area code** is 0305. The **Tourist Information Centre** is at 1 Acland Rd. (tel. 0305/267992).

———————————————

Thomas Hardy, in his 1886 novel *The Mayor of Casterbridge,* gave Dorchester literary fame. Actually, Dorchester was notable even in Roman times, when Maumbury Rings, considered the best Roman amphitheater in Britain, was filled with the sounds of 12,000 spectators screaming for the blood of the gladiators. Dorchester, a county seat, was the setting of another bloodletting, the "Bloody Assize" of 1685, when Judge Jeffreys condemned to death the supporters of the Duke of Monmouth's rebellion against James II.

WHAT TO SEE & DO

IN TOWN

DORSET COUNTY MUSEUM, High West St. (next to St. Peter's Church). Tel. 262735.

This museum has a gallery devoted to memorabilia of Thomas Hardy's life. In addition, you'll find an archeological gallery with displays and finds from Maiden Castle, Britain's largest Iron Age hill fort, plus galleries on the geology, local history, and natural history of Dorset.

Admission: £2 ($3) adults, £1 ($1.50) children 5–16, free for children under 5.
Open: Mon–Sat 10am–5pm.

IN NEARBY HIGHER BOCKHAMPTON

HARDY'S COTTAGE, Higher Bockhampton. Tel. 0305/262366.

Thomas Hardy was born in 1840 at Higher Bockhampton, 3 miles northeast of Dorchester, and half a mile south of Blandford Road (A35). His home, now a National Trust property, may be visited by appointment. You approach the cottage on foot—it's a 10-minute walk after parking your vehicle in the space provided in the wood. Write in advance to Hardy's Cottage, Higher Bockhampton, Dorchester, Dorset DT2 8QJ, England, or call the number above.

Admission: £2.30 ($3.50).
Open: Apr–Oct, Fri–Wed 11am–6pm or dusk.

ATHELHAMPTON, on the A35, 1 mile east of Puddletown. Tel. 0305/848363.

This is one of England's great medieval houses and considered to be the most beautiful and historic in the south. Thomas Hardy mentioned the place in some of his writings, but called it Athelhall. It was begun in the reign of Edward IV on the legendary site of King Athelstan's palace. A family home for more than 500 years, it is noted for its 15th-century Great Hall, Tudor great chamber, state bedroom, and King's Room. The house is on 10 acres of formal and landscaped gardens, with a 15th-century dovecote, river gardens, fish ponds, fountains, and rare trees. It's a mile east of Puddletown.

In 1992, the same year as the more famous fire at Windsor Castle, a dozen of the house's rooms were damaged by an accidental fire due to faulty wiring in the attic. Six have since been repaired and can be visited, whereas the remaining half dozen are still undergoing restoration. Today, an exhibition is on display documenting this tragedy.

Admission: £3.80 ($5.70) adults, £1.90 ($2.90) children.

Open: Apr 7–Oct, Wed–Thurs and Sun noon–5pm; Tues (May–Sept only), noon–5pm; Mon and Fri (Aug only), noon–5pm. **Directions:** Take the Dorchester-Bournemouth road (A35) east of Dorchester for 5 miles.

WHERE TO STAY & DINE

IN DORCHESTER

KINGS ARMS HOTEL, 30 High East St., Dorchester, Dorset DT1 1HF. Tel. 0305/265353. Fax 0305/260269. 31 rms (all with bath), 2 suites. TV TEL
$ Rates (including English breakfast): Mon–Thurs, £55.50 ($83.30) single; Fri–Sun, £25 ($37.50) single. Mon–Thurs, £79 ($118.50) double; Fri–Sun, £45 ($67.50) double. Suites Mon–Thurs, £99 ($148.50); Fri–Sun, £145 ($217.50). AE, MC, V.
Parking: Free.

In business for more than three centuries, the Kings Arms has great bow windows above the porch and a swinging sign hanging over the road, a legacy of its days as a coaching inn. An archway leads to the courtyard and parking area at the back of the hotel. All the rooms have been refurbished and have radios and hot-beverage facilities. Note that unlike the standard bedrooms, suites are less expensive weekdays and more expensive on weekends. A pub-style food emporium is also on the premises, dispensing platters-cum-bar-snacks priced from £6 to £7 ($9 to $10.50).

IN NEARBY EVERSHOT

SUMMER LODGE, Summer Lane, Evershot, Dorset DT2 OJR. Tel. 0935/83424. Fax 0935/83005. 17 rms (all with bath). TV TEL **Directions:** Head north from Dorchester on the A37.
$ Rates (including English breakfast, afternoon tea, and 6-course dinner): £122–£135 ($183–$202.50) single; £184–£245 ($276–$367.50) double. AE, MC, V.
Parking: Free.

In this country-house hotel 15 miles north of Dorchester, the resident owners, Nigel and Margaret Corbett, provide care, courtesy, and comfort. Once home to the heirs of the earls of Ilchester, the country house, in the village of Evershot, stands on 4 acres of secluded gardens. Evershot appears as Evershed in *Tess of the D'Urbervilles*, and author Thomas Hardy designed a wing of the house. In this relaxed, informal atmosphere, bedrooms have views either of the garden or over the village rooftops to the fields beyond. Although centrally heated, the hotel offers log fires in winter. Guests sit around the fire getting to know each other in a convivial atmosphere.

The chefs specialize in traditional English dishes the way they should be done, placing the emphasis on home-grown and local produce. In addition to the dining room with its French windows, opening onto a terrace, the Corbetts have a bar, plus a heated outdoor pool and an all-weather tennis court.

IN NEARBY CHEDINGTON

CHEDINGTON COURT, Chedington, near Beaminster, Dorset DT8 3HY. Tel. 0935/891265. Fax 0935/891442. 10 rms (all with bath). TV TEL **Directions:** Lies 4½ miles east of Crewkerne, just off the A356, at Winyard's Gap.
$ Rates (including half board): £76–£95 ($114–$142.50) single; £132–£170 ($198–$255) double. AE, MC, V. **Parking:** Free.

The village of Chedington, 17 miles from Dorchester, is known to mapmakers and geographers as the source of two of England's famous rivers, the Axe and the Parrett. The legendary King Alfred is said to have found solace in this countryside from the pressures of ruling his kingdom. This Jacobean manor house set in 10 acres of terraces, gardens, and lawns contains mullioned windows, boldly angled gables, and steep slate roofs. The manor was converted into a 10-room hotel in 1981 by the establishment's owners, Philip and Hilary Chapman. Much of the style and some of the grandeur of the Victorians have been preserved. There's a glassed-in conservatory laden with mimosa. The bedrooms are individually furnished, sometimes with antiques, canopied beds, and fireplaces, along with some elegant accessories. One contains satinwood furniture that once adorned a suite aboard the *Queen Mary*.

The fresh and flavorful meals served in the dining room from 7 to 9pm are a high point of the day. Each is carefully prepared and served in a room with a view over the garden. The hotel has its own 9-hole, par-74 golf course nearby.

IN NEARBY LOWER BOCKHAMPTON

YALBURY COTTAGE COUNTRY HOUSE HOTEL AND RESTAURANT, Lower Bockhampton, near Dorchester, Dorset DT2 8PZ. Tel. 0305/ 262382. 8 rms (all with bath). TV TEL **Directions:** Head 2 miles east of Dorchester (A35) and watch for signs to Lower Bockhampton.
$ Rates (including English breakfast): £61.50 ($92.30) single; £84–£90 ($126–$135) double. AE, MC, V. **Parking:** Free.
This thatch-roofed cottage with inglenooks and beamed ceilings is in a small country village within walking distance of Thomas Hardy's cottage and Stinsford Church, where his heart is buried. The comfortably furnished and equipped bedrooms overlook the gardens or fields beyond, reflecting a mood of tranquillity. Each has hot-beverage facilities, ironing center, hairdryer, bathrobes, and other small touches for guests' added comfort.

The restaurant is open, evenings only, for both residents and nonresidents. Well-flavored sauces and lightly cooked fresh vegetables enhance traditional English and continental dishes. Meals begin at £22 ($33).

8. CHIDEOCK & CHARMOUTH

157 miles SW of London, 1 mile W of Bridport

GETTING THERE   By Train   The nearest connection is Dorchester (see above).

By Bus   Buses run frequently throughout the day west from both Dorchester and Bridport.

By Car   From Bridport, continue west along the A35.

ESSENTIALS   The **telephone area code** for Chideock and Charmouth is 0297.

Chideock is a charming village hamlet of thatched houses with a dairy farm in the center. About a mile from the coast, it's a gem of a place for overnight stopovers, and even better for longer stays. The countryside, with its rolling hills, may tempt you to go exploring.

On Lyme Bay, Charmouth, like Chideock, is another winner. A village of Georgian houses and thatched cottages, Charmouth provides some of the most dramatic coastal scenery in West Dorset. The village is west of Golden Cap, which, according to the adventurers who measure such things, is the highest cliff along the coast of southern England.

WHERE TO STAY & DINE

IN CHIDEOCK

CHIDEOCK HOUSE HOTEL, Main St., Chideock, Dorset DT6 6JN. Tel. 0297/89242. 9 rms (8 with bath). **Bus:** 6 from Bridport.

$ Rates (including English breakfast): £30 ($45) single without bath, £36 ($54) single with bath; £46 ($69) double without bath, £50 ($75) double with bath. MC, V. **Parking:** Free. **Closed:** Dec 20–Mar 15.

In a village of winners, this 15th-century thatched house is perhaps the prettiest. The house was used by the Roundheads in 1645, and the ghosts of the village martyrs still haunt the house since their trial was held here. The resident owners are Derek and Jenny Hammond. Set near the road, with a protective stone wall, the house has a garden in back, and a driveway leads to a large parking area. The beamed lounge has two fireplaces, one an Adam fireplace with a wood-burning blaze on cool days. All the bedrooms have hot-beverage facilities. The hotel offers a good table d'hôte or à la carte French and English menu, served from 7 to 9pm daily. The dessert table is the best in town. Meals cost £13.50 ($20.30) and up.

IN CHARMOUTH

WHITE HOUSE, 2 Hillside, The Street, Charmouth, Dorset DT6 6PJ. Tel. 0297/60411. 10 rms (all with bath or shower), 1 suite. TV TEL **Bus:** Charmouth bus from Bridport.

$ Rates (including English breakfast): £48.50–£65 ($72.80–$97.50) single; £77–£110 ($115.50–$165) double; from £106–£120 ($159–$180) suite. AE, DC, MC, V. **Parking:** Free. **Closed:** Dec.

The White House is a Georgian home, with much of its period architecture, including bow doors, well preserved. It is tastefully furnished in a traditional style in keeping with the character of the house. Mr. and Mrs. Balfour took this place, constructed in 1827, and turned it into a most comfortable place at which to stay. Each of their handsomely furnished bedrooms has hot-beverage facilities. Bar lunches are available during the day, and at night home-cooked dishes, with a selection of carefully chosen wines are offered. West Country regional dishes are featured. Dinners begin at £24 ($36).

---

9. LYME REGIS

160 miles SW of London, 25 miles W of Dorchester

GETTING THERE **By Train** Take the London-Exeter train, getting off at Axminster and continuing the rest of the way by bus.

By Bus Bus no. 31 runs from Axminster to Lyme Regis at the rate of one coach per hour during the day. There is also National Express bus service (no. 705) daily in summer at 9:50am from Exeter to Lyme Regis, the run taking 1¾ hours.

By Car From Bridport, continue west along the A35, cutting south to the coast at the junction with the A3070.

ESSENTIALS The **telephone area code** for Lyme Regis is 0297. The **Tourist Information Centre** is next to The Guildhall, on Bridge Street (tel. 0297/442138).

On Lyme Bay near the Devonshire border, the resort of Lyme Regis is one of the most attractive centers along the south coast. For those who shun big, commercial holiday centers Lyme Regis is ideal—it's the true English coastal town with a highly praised mild climate. Sea gulls fly overhead; the streets are steep and winding; walks along Cobb Beach are brisk and stimulating; the views, particularly of the craft in the harbor, are so photogenic that John Fowles, a longtime resident of the town, selected it as the site for the 1980 filming of his novel, *The French Lieutenant's Woman*. During its heyday, the town was a major seaport. (The Duke of Monmouth returned from his exile in Holland in 1685, during an unsuccessful attempt to overthrow the regime of his father, Charles II.) Later, Lyme developed into a small spa, including among its clientele Jane Austen. She penned her final novel, *Persuasion* (published posthumously and based partly on the town's life), after staying here in 1803 and 1804.

Today, one of the town's most visible spokespersons is Richard J. Fox, three-time winner of Britain's cherished Town Crier Award. Famed for his declamatory delivery of official (and sometimes irreverent) proclamations, he follows a 1000-year-old tradition of newscasting. Every Tuesday at 3pm, beginning at the Guildhall, mentioned below, he leads visitors on a 2-hour walk around the town. No reservations are necessary, and the price is £1 ($1.50) for adults and 60p (90¢) for children. Mr. Fox can be reached at the premises of **Tales of Lyme, The Experience,** at Marine Parade (tel. 443039). Highly recommended, it is a 22-minute multimedia exhibition of the town of Lyme Regis from its prehistoric origins up to the present. Open daily from Easter to October from 10am to 5pm (with a 10pm closing in July and August), its cost is £2.20 ($3.30) for adults and £1 ($1.50) for children under 15.

Another famous building is **The Guildhall,** Bridge Street (call the tourist office) whose Mary and John Wing (built in 1620) houses the completed sections of an enormous tapestry woven by local women. Depicting Britain's colonization of North America, it's composed of a series of 11- by 4-foot sections, each of which took a team of local women 11 months to weave. Admission is free, but if anyone wants to add a stitch to the final tapestry as a kind of charitable donation, it costs £1 ($1.50). It's open Monday to Friday from 10:30am to 4pm.

The surrounding area is a fascinating place for botanists and zoologists because of the predominance of blue lias, a sedimentary rock well suited to the formation of fossils. In 1810 Mary Anning (at the age of 11) discovered one of the first articulated ichthyosaur skeletons. She went on to become one of the first professional fossilists in England. Books outlining walks in the area and the regions where fossils can be studied are available at the local information bureau, mentioned above.

WHERE TO STAY & DINE

EXPENSIVE

ALEXANDRA HOTEL, Pound St., Lyme Regis, Dorset DT7 3HZ. Tel. 0297/442010. Fax 0297/443229. 26 rms. TV TEL
$ Rates (including English breakfast): £40–£44 ($60–$66) single; £64–£98 ($96–$147) double. AE, DC, MC, V. **Parking:** Free.
Built in 1735, this hotel, situated on a hill about 5 minutes from the center of town, was originally the home of the dowager Countess Poulett and was later owned by the Duke de Stacpoole. But by the turn of the century it had reverted from an aristocratic address to a hotel with well-furnished bedrooms. Today it has been discreetly

modernized but with an awareness of its original character; it has 1½ acres of garden. Both table d'hôte and à la carte meals are offered in the hotel's excellent dining room, with dinner from £18 ($27).

MODERATE

ROYAL LION, Broad St., Lyme Regis, Dorset DT7 3QF. Tel. 0297/ 445622. Fax 0297/445859. 30 rms (all with bath). TV TEL
$ Rates (including English breakfast): £33 ($49.50) single; £66 ($99) double. AE, DC, MC, V. **Parking:** Free.

An old coaching inn known 200 years ago as the White Lion, the Royal Lion is situated in the center of town on a hillside climbing up from the sea. There are country furnishings in the oak-beamed bar and lounge; the bedrooms are also country style, including one with a canopied bed used regularly by Edward VII when he was Prince of Wales. On the second floor is a cocktail lounge. A street-level pub dispenses bar snacks daily from noon to 2pm, costing £2 to £4 ($3 to $6).

INEXPENSIVE

KERSBROOK HOTEL AND RESTAURANT, Pound Rd., Lyme Regis, Dorset DT7 3HX. Tel. 0297/442596. 10 rms (all with bath or shower).
$ Rates (including half board): £47–£62 ($70.50–$93) single; £87 ($130.50) double. AE, MC, V. **Parking:** Free. **Closed:** Dec–Jan.

 Built of stone in 1790 and crowned by a thatch roof, the Kersbrook sits on a ledge above the village, which provides a panoramic view of the coast, on 1½ acres of gardens landscaped according to the original 18th-century plans. The public rooms have been refurnished with antique furniture, re-creating old-world charm yet with modern facilities. Mr. and Mrs. Eric Hall Stephenson are the resident proprietors.

The hotel is justifiably proud of its pink, candlelit restaurant, serving table d'hôte and à la carte meals daily from 7:30 to 9:30pm, with an extensive wine list. The chef is known as an artist in the kitchen. A traditional Old English and French cuisine is served, with dinner costing from £16.50 ($24.80).

10. SHAFTESBURY

115 miles SW of London, 29 miles N of Dorchester

GETTING THERE By Train There is no direct access. Take the Exeter train leaving from London's Waterloo Station to Gillingham in Dorset, where a 4-mile bus or taxi ride to Shaftesbury awaits you. Trains from London run hourly.

By Bus Connections are possible from London's Victoria Coach Station once a day. There are also two or three daily connections from Bristol, Bath, and Bournemouth.

By Car Head west from London along the M3, continuing along the A30 for the final approach.

ESSENTIALS The **telephone area code** is 0747. The **Tourist Information Centre** is at 8 Bell St. (tel. 0747/53514), and is open only from June to September.

The origins of this typical Dorsetshire market town date back to the 9th century when King Alfred founded the abbey and made his daughter the first abbess. King

Edward the Martyr was buried here, and King Canute died in the abbey but was buried in Winchester. Little now remains of the abbey, but the ruins are beautifully laid out. The museum adjoining St. Peter's Church at the top of Gold Hill provides a good idea of what the ancient Saxon hilltop town was like.

Today, ancient cottages with thatched roofs and tiny paned windows line the steep cobbled streets, and modern stores compete with the outdoor market on the High Street and the cattle market off Christy's Lane. The town is an excellent center from which to visit Hardy Country (it appears as Shaston in *Jude the Obscure*), Stourhead Gardens, and Longleat House.

WHERE TO STAY & DINE

IN SHAFTESBURY

ROYAL CHASE HOTEL, Royal Chase Roundabout, Shaftesbury, Dorset SP7 8DB. Tel. 0747/53355. Fax 0747/51969. 35 rms. TV TEL
$ Rates (including English breakfast): £68.25 ($102.40) single; £88 ($132) double. AE, DC, MC, V. **Parking:** Free.

This was once a button-making factory and later a monastery, but now it's a delightfully informal hotel at the junction of the A30 and the A350. Early-morning tea and a newspaper are complimentary. Bedrooms are comfortably furnished and well equipped. The hotel offers an indoor swimming pool and a Turkish steam room.

A meal in the elegant Byzant Restaurant, which costs from £19.50 ($29.30), includes several local dishes such as local trout, seasonal game, and venison marinated in sherry. Dinner is served nightly from 7 to 10:30pm. A more informal restaurant, the Country Restaurant, serves light meals, snacks, and children's favorites throughout the day. They serve Thomas Hardy's Ale, featured in the *Guinness Book of Records* as the strongest beer available in a bottle. Even for less fanatical drinkers, the bar, dominated by an open-kitchen range and decorated with Dorsetshire bygones, is an attraction. There are traditional bar games, shove ha'penny, and table skittles at which to pitch your skill.

IN NEARBY STURMINSTER NEWTON

PLUMBER MANOR, Hazelbury Bryan Rd., Sturminster Newton, Dorset DT10 2AF. Tel. 0258/72507. Fax 0258/73370. 16 rms (all with bath). TV TEL **Directions:** Head less than 2 miles southwest of Sturminster Newton off the A357 and on Hazelbury Bryan Rd.
$ Rates (including English breakfast): £57.50–£70 ($86.30–$105) single; £60–£110 ($90–$165) double. AE, DC, MC, V. **Parking:** Free. **Closed:** Feb.

This Jacobean manor house, on 600 acres of farmland, has been lived in by the Prideaux-Brune family since the early 17th century. The present inhabitants, Richard Prideaux-Brune and his wife, Alison, open the lovely old place to guests. Downstairs, a large hall from which the staircase rises is decorated with family portraits. A comfortable lounge is furnished with antiques. There's a bar to serve the restaurant, made up of three connecting dining rooms where guests can sample the excellent cooking of Brian Prideaux-Brune, Richard's brother. Upstairs, a gallery leads to some of the bedrooms, opening onto views over the gardens and the countryside. The others, in a long, low stone barn across the stable block (large umbrellas are provided to make the crossing if necessary), are well designed, with wide window seats, views over the gardens, and well-chosen furnishings.

Dinner is a three-course meal beginning at £19.50 ($29.30). Try the English lamb or roast pheasant in port sauce. All main courses are served with fresh vegetables. The restaurant may be closed to nonresidents on Monday in winter. On those days, a fixed-price meal is served. Plumber Manor has a family atmosphere, with the Prideaux-Brunes treating their clientele as houseguests.

AN EASY EXCURSION

OLD WARDOUR CASTLE   The ruined 14th-century English Heritage castle has a lakeside setting on the landscaped grounds of New Wardour Castle, a 1776 Palladian mansion that is now a private home. Old Wardour Castle (tel. 0747/870487), built in 1392 by Lord Lovel, was acquired in 1547 by the Arundell family and modernized in 1578. After being besieged during the Civil War, however, it was abandoned. Today it houses displays on the war sieges and the landscape, as well as an architectural exhibition. It lies 1½ miles north of the A30 going west out of Salisbury, 2 miles southwest of Tisbury. Admission is £1.30 ($2) for adults, 70p ($1.10) for children 5 to 16, and it's open from March 24 to October 1, daily from 10am to 6pm; October 2 to March 23, on Saturday and Sunday from 10am to 4pm.

Three miles west of Wardour is a privately owned manor house, Hook Manor, which North Americans might like to know was built by Cecil Culvert, the second Lord Baltimore, the staunchly Catholic cofounder of Maryland. Today, the city of Annapolis, Maryland, bears a historic center known as the Wardour District, whose name derives from the famous nearby castle. Wardour, translated from the Celtic, means "defensive riverbank." Wardour Castle and the district around it remained Catholic throughout the Cromwellian Wars, its peerage abandoned by the largely Protestant monarchists throughout later periods of English history.

---

11. SHERBORNE

128 miles SW of London, 19 miles N of Dorchester

GETTING THERE   By Train   Frequent trains throughout the day depart from London's Waterloo Station (trip time: 2 hr.).

By Bus   There is one National Express coach departure daily from London's Victoria Coach Station.

By Car   Take the M3 motorway west from London, continuing southwest along the A30.

ESSENTIALS   The **telephone area code** is 0935. The summer-only **Tourist Information Centre** is on Hound Street (tel. 0935/815341).

A little gem of a town, with well-preserved medieval, Tudor, Stuart, and Georgian buildings, Sherborne is in the heart of Dorset in a setting of wooded hills, valleys, and chalk downs. It was here that Sir Walter Raleigh lived before his fall from fortune.

WHAT TO SEE & DO

In addition to the attractions listed below, you can go to **Cerne Abbas,** a village south of Sherborne, to see the Pitchmarket, where Thomas and Maria Washington, uncle and aunt of America's George Washington, once lived.

SHERBORNE OLD CASTLE, Castleton, off the A30, half a mile east of Sherborne. Tel. 812730.

The castle was built in the early 12th century by the powerful Bishop Roger de Caen, but it was seized by the Crown at about the time of King Henry I's death in 1135 and Stephen's troubled accession to the throne. The castle was given to Sir Walter Raleigh by Queen Elizabeth I. The gallant knight built Sherborne Lodge in the deer park close by (now privately owned). The buildings were mostly destroyed in the Civil War, but you can still see a gatehouse, some graceful arcades, and decorative windows.

Admission: £1.20 ($1.80) adults, 60p (90¢) children 5–16.

Open: Apr–Sept, daily 10am–6pm; Oct–Mar, Tues–Sun 10am–4pm. **Closed:** Jan 1 and Dec 24–26. **Directions:** Follow the signs 1 mile east from the town center.

SHERBORNE CASTLE, Cheap St. Tel. 813182.

Sir Walter Raleigh built this castle in 1594, when he decided that it would not be feasible to restore the old castle to suit his needs. This Elizabethan residence was a square mansion, to which later owners added four Jacobean wings to make it more palatial. After King James I had Raleigh imprisoned in the Tower of London, the monarch gave the castle to a favorite Scot, Robert Carr, and banished the Raleighs from their home. In 1617 it became the property of Sir John Digby, first Earl of Bristol, and has been the Digby family home ever since. The mansion was enlarged by Sir John in 1625, and in the 18th century the formal Elizabethan gardens and fountains of the Raleighs were altered by Capability Brown, who created a serpentine lake between the two castles. The 20 acres of lawns and pleasure grounds around the 50-acre lake are open to the public. In the house are fine furniture, china, and paintings by Gainsborough, Lely, Reynolds, Kneller, and Van Dyck, among others. The castle is off New Road a mile east of the center.

Admission: Castle and grounds, £3.60 ($5.40) adults, £1.80 ($2.70) children; grounds only, £1.50 ($2.30) adults, 80p ($1.20) children.

Open: Easter–Sept, Thurs, Sat–Sun, and bank holidays 2–5:30pm.

SHERBORNE ABBEY, Half Moon St. Tel. 812452.

The abbey is worth a visit to see the splendid fan vaulting of the roof, as well as the many monuments, including Purbeck marble effigies of medieval abbots and the Elizabethan four-posters and canopied Renaissance tombs. A baroque statue of the Earl of Bristol standing between his two wives dates from 1698. A public school operates out of the abbey's surviving medieval monastic buildings and was the setting of a novel by Alec Waugh, *The Loom of Youth,* and for MGM's film *Goodbye, Mr. Chips.*

Admission: Free.

Open: June–Sept, daily 9am–6pm; Oct–May, daily 9am–4pm.

WHERE TO STAY & DINE

EASTBURY HOTEL, Long St., Sherborne, Dorset DT9 3BY. Tel. 0935/ 813131, or toll free 800/444-1545 in the U.S. Fax 0935/817296. 15 rms (all with bath). TV TEL

$ Rates (including English breakfast): £72.50 ($108.80) single; £98–£108 ($147–$162) double. MC, V. **Parking:** Free.

This Georgian town-house hotel lies in its own walled garden near the 8th-century abbey and Sherborne's two castles. Built in 1740 in the reign of George II, it has a traditional ambience, with its own library of antiquarian books. Beautifully restored, it still maintains its 18th-century character. The best, fresh English produce is served in the dining room, which has an extensive wine list. Meals begin at £20 ($30).

FORTE POST HOUSE HOTEL, Horsecastles Lane, Sherborne, Dorset DT9 6BB. Tel. 0935/813191, or toll free 800/435-4542 in the U.S. Fax 0935/816493. 60 rms (all with bath). TV TEL

$ Rates (including English breakfast): £55 ($82.50) single or double. AE, DC, MC, V. **Parking:** Free.

This modern hotel is convenient to motorists because of its location on the A30. Accommodations are comfortable, carpeted, and attractively upholstered, with newly renovated bathrooms. A bar and restaurant are on the premises. Meals cost £15 ($22.50) and up. The staff is helpful.

CHAPTER 12

DEVON

- **WHAT'S SPECIAL ABOUT DEVON**
1. **EXETER**
2. **DARTMOOR**
3. **CHAGFORD**
4. **TORQUAY**
5. **TOTNES**
6. **DARTMOUTH**
7. **PLYMOUTH**
8. **CLOVELLY**
9. **LYNTON-LYNMOUTH**

The great patchwork quilt area of southwest England, part of the "West Countree," abounds in cliffside farms, rolling hills, foreboding moors, semitropical plants, and fishing villages that provide some of the finest scenery in England. The British approach sunny Devon with the same kind of excitement one would normally reserve for hopping over to the Continent. Especially along the coastline—the English Riviera—the names of the seaports, villages, and resorts have been synonymous with holidays in the sun: Torquay (Torbay), Clovelly, Lynton-Lynmouth.

It's easy to get involved in the West Country life. You can go pony trekking across moor and woodland, past streams and sheep-dotted fields, or stop at local pubs to soak up atmosphere and ale.

Devon is a land of jagged coasts—the red cliffs in the south face the English Channel. In south Devon, the coast from which Drake and Raleigh set sail, the tranquil life prevails, and on the bay-studded coastline of north Devon, pirates and smugglers used to find haven. The heather-clad uplands of Exmoor, with its red deer, extend into north Devon from Somerset—a perfect setting for an English mystery. Much of the district is already known to those who have read Victorian novelist R. D. Blackmore's romance of the West Country, *Lorna Doone.* Aside from the shores, many of the scenic highlights are in the two national parks: Dartmoor in the south, Exmoor in the north.

Almost every hamlet is geared to accommodate tourists. However, many small towns and fishing villages do not allow cars to enter; these towns have car parks on their outskirts, but this can involve a long walk to reach the center of the harbor area. From mid-July to mid-September the more popular villages get quite crowded, and one needs reservations since the number of hotels is limited. Perhaps your oddly shaped bedroom will be in a barton (farm) mentioned in the *Domesday Book,* or in a thatched cottage.

The two main bus companies of Devon and Cornwall combine to offer a **Key West** bus ticket, granting unlimited travel anywhere on the two networks for any 7 consecutive days at a cost of £20.80 ($31.20) for adults and £15.30 ($23) for children under 14. A family ticket—two adults and two children—costs £40.60 ($60.90). You can plan your journeys from the maps and timetables available at any Western National/Devon General office when you purchase your ticket. Further information may be obtained from Devon General Ltd., Belgrave Road, Exeter, Devon EX1 2LB (tel. 0392/56231).

SEEING DEVON

GETTING THERE

There are airports at Plymouth and Exeter, but many visitors arrive by rail instead. British Rail runs trains to the area from London's Paddington Station, arriving in

WHAT'S SPECIAL ABOUT DEVON

Beaches
- ☐ The English Riviera, 22 miles of Devonshire coastline and 18 beaches, with Torquay at the center; there are even palm trees growing here.

Great Towns/Villages
- ☐ Exeter, a university city rebuilt after the 1940s bombings around its venerable cathedral, with notable waterfront buildings.
- ☐ Plymouth, the largest city in Devon; from this major port and sea base, the Pilgrims set sail on the *Mayflower* for the New World.
- ☐ Torquay, Devon's premier seaside resort which grew from a small fishing village; it's set against a backdrop of colorful cliffs and beaches.

- ☐ Clovelly, considered the most charming village in England by many; the village cascades down a mountainside.

Natural Spectacles
- ☐ Dartmoor, a national park northeast of Plymouth, a landscape of gorges and moors filled with gorse and purple heather, and home of the Dartmoor pony.

Buildings
- ☐ Exeter Cathedral, dating from Saxon times and built in the "Decorated" style of the 13th and 14th centuries.
- ☐ Buckland Abbey, near Yelverton, the former home of the dashing Sir Francis Drake, hero to the English, "pirate" to the Spanish.

Exeter in 2¼ hours and in Plymouth in 3¼ hours. National Express coaches from London also service the area from London's Victoria Coach Station, arriving in Exeter in 3¾ hours and in Plymouth in 4½ hours. From London, the M4 and the M5 quickly connect you with Devon.

A SUGGESTED ITINERARY

Day 1: Visit Exeter; walk its old streets and see its cathedral.

Day 2: Spend a day touring the national park of Dartmoor, which is more sensibly done by car. Stay overnight in Moretonhampstead.

Day 3: Go to Torquay for a night at a major English seaside resort.

Day 4: Continue west to Plymouth, following in the footsteps of the Pilgrims.

Day 5: Head north from Plymouth for a luncheon stopover at Clovelly before continuing west to the twin resorts of Lynton-Lynmouth for the night.

---

1. EXETER

201 miles SW of London, 46 miles E of Plymouth

GETTING THERE   By Plane   The Exeter Airport (tel. 0392/67433) serves the southwest. It is also used for charter flights by the English heading south on a holiday.

Monday through Friday it offers flights on Brymon Airways to and from London's Gatwick Airport where worldwide connections can be made. For reservations on Brymon Airways, call 0345/717383.

By Train   Trains from London's Paddington Station depart every hour during the day (trip time: 2½ hr.). Trains also run during the day between Exeter and Plymouth at the rate of one per hour (trip time: 1¼ hr.).

By Bus   A National Express coach departs from London's Victoria Coach Station every 30 minutes during the day (trip time: 4 hr.). You can also take bus no. 38 or 39 between Plymouth and Exeter. During the day two coaches depart per hour (trip time: 1 hr.).

By Car   From London, take the M4 motorway west, cutting south to Exeter at the junction with the M5.

ESSENTIALS   The **telephone area code** is 0392. The **Tourist Information Centre** is at the Civic Center, Paris Street (tel. 0392/265700).

The county town of Devonshire, on the banks of the River Exe, Exeter was a Roman city founded in the 1st century A.D. Two centuries later it was encircled by a mighty stone wall, traces of which remain today. Conquerors and would-be conquerors, especially the Vikings, stormed the fortress in later centuries; none was more notable than William the Conqueror. Irked at Exeter's refusal to capitulate (perhaps also because it sheltered Gytha, mother of the slain Harold), the Norman duke brought Exeter to its knees on short notice.

Under the Tudors, the city grew and prospered. Sir Walter Raleigh and Sir Francis Drake were two of the striking figures who strolled through Exeter's streets. In May 1942 the Germans bombed Exeter, destroying many of the city's architectural treasures. Exeter was rebuilt, but the new, impersonal-looking shops and offices couldn't replace the Georgian crescents and the black-and-white timbered buildings with their plastered walls. Fortunately, much was spared.

WHAT TO SEE & DO

Just off "The High," at the top of Castle Street stands an impressive **Norman Gate House** from William the Conqueror's Castle. Although only the house and walls survive, the view from here and the surrounding gardens is spectacular.

IN TOWN

EXETER CATHEDRAL, 1 The Cloisters. Tel. 55573.

The Roman II Augusta Legion made their camp on the site where the Cathedral Church of Saint Peter now stands in Exeter. It has been occupied by Britons, Saxons, Danes, and Normans. The English Saint Boniface, who converted North Germany to Christianity, was trained here in 690 A.D. Bishop Leofric was installed here as bishop for Devon and Cornwall in 1050 A.D. by Edward the Confessor. The conqueror's nephew, Bishop Warelwast, began building the present cathedral about 1112 A.D. and the twin Norman towers still stand. Between the towers runs the longest uninterrupted true Gothic vault in the world, at a height

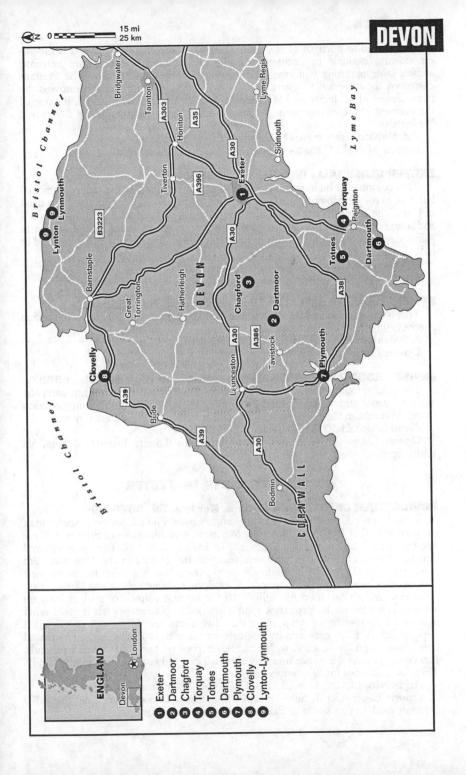

DEVON

N
0 | 15 mi
25 km

Bristol Channel

Bridgwater
Taunton
A303
Honiton
A35
A30
Lyme Regis
Sidmouth

Lyme Bay

A396
Exeter
Tiverton
① Exeter

Torquay
④ Paignton
Dartmouth
⑥
Totnes
⑤

Lynton
⑨ Lynmouth
⑨

B3223

Barnstaple

DEVON

Great
Torrington
Hatherleigh
Chagford ③
② Dartmoor

A30
A386
Tavistock

A38

Clovelly
⑧
A39
Launceston

Plymouth ⑦

Bude
A30

A39

CORNWALL

Bodmin

Bristol Channel

ENGLAND
London
★
Devon

① Exeter
② Dartmoor
③ Chagford
④ Torquay
⑤ Totnes
⑥ Dartmouth
⑦ Plymouth
⑧ Clovelly
⑨ Lynton-Lynmouth

of 66 feet and to a length of 300 feet. This was completed in 1369 and is the finest existing example of decorated Gothic architecture, featuring rare tierceron arches, large matching windows, and decorated corbels and bosses. The Puritans destroyed the cathedral Cloisters in 1650 A.D. and a German bomb destroyed the twin Chapel of St. James and St. Thomas in May 1942. Now restored, it's one of the prettiest churches anywhere. Its famous choir sings evensong every day except Wednesday.

Admission: Free; requested donation £1 ($1.50) adults.
Open: Mon–Fri 7:15am–5:30pm, Sat–Sun 8:30am–6:30pm.

EXETER GUILDHALL, High St. Tel. 265500.

This colonnaded building on the main street is regarded as the oldest municipal building in the kingdom; the earliest reference to the guildhall is contained in a deed of 1160. The Tudor front that straddles the pavement was added in 1593. Inside you'll find a fine display of silver, plus a number of paintings, including one of Henrietta Anne, daughter of Charles I (born in Exeter in 1644). The ancient hall is paneled in oak.

Admission: Free.
Open: Tues–Sun 10am–4pm.

ST. NICHOLAS PRIORY, The Mint, off Fore St. Tel. 265858.

This is the guest wing of a Benedictine priory founded in 1070. You will see fine plaster ceilings and period furniture.

Admission: 50p (80¢) adults, free for children.
Open: Easter–Oct, Tues–Sat 10am–5pm.

UNDERGROUND PASSAGES, Boots Corner, off High St. Tel. 265887.

The Underground Passages, accessible from High Street, were built to carry the medieval water supply into the city. By entering the new underground interpretation center, visitors can view a video and exhibition before taking a guided tour.

Admission: £1.50 ($2.30) adults, £1 ($1.50) children.
Open: Easter–Oct, Tues–Sat 10am–5pm; Nov–Easter, Tues–Fri 2–5pm, Sat 10am–5pm.

ON THE OUTSKIRTS OF EXETER

POWDERHAM CASTLE, Powderham, Kenton. Tel. 0626/890243.

A castle was built here in the late 14th century by Sir Philip Courtenay, sixth son of the second Earl of Devon, and his wife, Margaret, granddaughter of Edward I. Their magnificent tomb is in the south transept of Exeter Cathedral. The castle suffered damage during the Civil War and was restored and altered in the 18th and 19th centuries. The castle contains many family portraits and fine furniture, including a remarkable clock that plays full tunes at 4pm, 8pm, and midnight, some 17th-century tapestries, and a chair used by William III for his first council of state at Newton Abbot. The staircase hall contains some remarkable plasterwork set in bold relief against a turquoise background, more than two centuries old, as well as a detailed pedigree of the Courtenay family, a document more than 12 feet high. The chapel dates from the 15th century, with hand-hewn roof timbers and carved pew ends. Powderham Castle is a private house lived in by Lord and Lady Courtenay and family. There is a tearoom for light refreshments.

Admission: £3.95 ($5.90) adults, £2.95 ($4.40) children 5–17.
Open: Easter–Oct 1, Sun–Fri 9:30am–5:30pm. **Directions:** Take the A379 Dawlish road 8 miles south of Exeter. The castle is signposted.

WHERE TO STAY

IN EXETER

BUCKERELL LODGE, Topsham Rd., Exeter, Devon EX2 4SQ. Tel. 0392/ 52451, or toll free 800/528-1234 in the U.S. and Canada. Fax 0392/412114. 54 rms (all with bath). TV TEL **Directions:** Take the B3182 1 mile southeast, off Junction 30 of the M5. **Bus:** K, T, or R.

$ Rates (including English breakfast): £46–£79.50 ($69–$119.30) single; £68–£87 ($102–$130.50) double. AE, DC, MC, V. **Parking:** Free.

Buckerell Lodge is perhaps the finest place to stay in the area. The origins of the house go back to the 12th century, but it has been altered and changed beyond recognition over the years. Often a choice of commercial travelers, it's also a tourist favorite, especially in summer. The look today is Regency, and the bedrooms are well decorated and nicely equipped and come in a range of styles and sizes.

On the premises, Raffles Restaurant is one of the finer dining choices in the area. Taking its name from the famed hotel in Singapore, it specializes in fresh fish, game, steaks, and poultry, and there's always something for the vegetarian. Both a table d'hôte and an à la carte menu are featured. During the day you can dine on light fare such as soups and salads, and in the evening you can order such traditional English fare as roast beef and Yorkshire pudding, served from 7 to 9:45pm, costing £14.95 ($22.40) for a complete meal.

DEVON MOTEL, Exeter Bypass, Matford, Exeter, Devon EX2 8XU. Tel. 0392/59268. Fax 0392/413142. 41 rms (all with bath). TV TEL

$ Rates (including English breakfast): £48–£55 ($72–$82.50) single; £60–£70 ($90–$105) double. AE, DC, MC, V. **Parking:** Free.

The Devon Motel lies on the outskirts of the city at the western sector of the bypass on the A38. It's convenient to the airport and as a stopping-off point for those headed for the West Country. You drive your car into your own open garage, and your bedroom and private bath are directly overhead. Inside, all is compact and built-in, with a picture window overlooking the meadows beyond.

On the premises are a restaurant and bars. An à la carte dinner begins at £13 ($19.50).

ROUGEMONT HOTEL, Queen St., Exeter, Devon EX4 3SP. Tel. 0392/ 54982. Fax 0392/420928. 88 rms (all with bath), 2 suites. A/C TV TEL

$ Rates (including English breakfast): £69 ($103.50) single; £79 ($118.50) double; from £115 ($172.50) suite. AE, DC, MC, V. **Parking:** £5 ($7.50).

The Rougemont Hotel, opposite the train station, is imbued with a stylish flair that none of its competitors provides. Fairly recently, this great, old-fashioned Victorian hotel, opposite the central railway station, underwent renovations. Its neoclassical architecture is a background for the contemporary furnishings. Much of the comfort and tasteful decor are found in the bedrooms. Amenities include radios.

A fixed-price dinner costs £14.95 ($22.40). Guests gather in the Adam-style Drake's Bar for drinks. A good stock of wine comes from the cellar, which, incidentally, was once a debtors' prison.

ROYAL CLARENCE HOTEL, Cathedral Yard, Exeter, Devon EX1 1HD. Tel. 0392/58464. Fax 0392/439423. 56 rms (all with bath), 2 suites. TV TEL

$ Rates (including English breakfast): £70–£77.50 ($105–$116.30) single; £95– £110 ($142.50–$165) double; from £130 ($195) suite. AE, DC, MC, V. **Parking:** Free.

The Royal Clarence Hotel is a Georgian building that escaped destruction during the war. Recently refurbished, it's full of history. Many of the well-furnished bedrooms overlook the 14th-century cathedral. Comfortable lounges display a mixture of antiques, gilt mirrors, and modern pieces. In the restaurant, a table d'hôte lunch costs £14.95 ($22.40) and a fixed-price dinner costs £19.95 ($29.90). You can also order à la carte.

ST. OLAVES COURT HOTEL, Mary Arches St., Exeter, Devon EX4 3AZ. Tel. 0392/217736. Fax 0392/413054. 15 rms (all with bath). TV TEL
$ Rates (including English breakfast): £45–£75 ($67.50–$112.50) single; £55–£90 ($82.50–$135) double. AE, DC, MC, V. **Parking:** Free.

The St. Olaves Court Hotel is such a favorite that it's almost considered a special address. A Georgian mansion, it lies in the center of Exeter, off High Street, having been constructed as a home by a rich merchant, circa 1830. The location is ideal, within a short walk of the cathedral. You can hear the church bells. The house has been discreetly furnished, in part with antiques. Each of the bedrooms has been individually decorated and has such amenities as hot-beverage facilities and radios. A trouser press, hairdryer, and what the English call a "hospitality tray" are found in every room, some of which are equipped with Jacuzzis.

The hotel also features an excellent English cuisine in its Golsworthy Restaurant, serving meals until 9:30pm. See separate recommendation in "Where to Dine," below.

WHITE HART HOTEL, 65–66 South St., Exeter, Devon EX1 1EE. Tel. 0392/79897. Fax 0392/50159. 68 rms (all with bath). TV TEL
$ Rates (including English breakfast): £34–£58.50 ($51–$87.80) single; £48–£78 ($72–$117) double. AE, DC, MC, V. **Parking:** Free.

The White Hart Hotel, in the center of town, a coaching inn in the 17th and 18th centuries, is one of the oldest inns in the city. It is said that Cromwell stabled his horses here. The hotel is a mass of polished wood, slate floors, oak beams, and gleaming brass and copper. The bedrooms combine old and new and have baths or showers. Guests are housed in either the old wing or a more modern one. Some units are considered deluxe.

The dining room offers good English and continental dishes in a well-appointed atmosphere. The hotel has a wine cellar, which supplies the Ale & Port House (a bar with waiter service where you can feast on traditional English fare), plus the well-known Bottlescreu Bills wine bar, which offers beefsteak-and-oyster pie or, in summer, barbecued steak in the wine garden. You may want to patronize the bar even if you're not a guest. It's open Monday through Saturday from 11am to 11pm and on Sunday from 11am to 3pm and 6 to 10:30pm.

IN NEARBY BICKLEIGH

Perhaps the finest way to enjoy the cathedral city of Exeter, especially if you have a car, is to stay on the outskirts, 10 to 19 miles from the heart of the city. In the Exe Valley, 4 miles south of Tiverton and 10 miles north of Exeter, lies **Bickleigh,** a hamlet with a river, an arched stone bridge, a mill pond, and thatch-roofed cottages—the epitome of English charm, one of the finest spots in all of Devon.

BICKLEIGH COTTAGE COUNTRY HOTEL, Bickleigh Bridge, Bickleigh, Devon EX16 8RJ. Tel. 0884/855230. 9 rms (7 with bath). **Bus:** 354 from Exeter.
$ Rates (including English breakfast): £22.50 ($33.80) single without bath; £42 ($63) double without bath, £48 ($72) double with bath. MC, V. **Parking:** Free. **Closed:** Nov–Mar.

This is a thatched, 17th-century hotel with a riverside garden leading down to the much photographed Bickleigh Bridge. Add to this image swans and ducks gliding by. Inside, the rooms are cozy with oak beams and old fireplaces. Mr. and Mrs. Stuart Cochrane, the owners, provide good and nourishing meals. The raspberries and gooseberries come fresh from the garden and are topped with generous portions of Devonshire cream. Dinner is priced from £11.50 ($17.30). Inside, the rooms are cozy, with oak beams and old fireplaces.

WHERE TO DINE

COOLINGS WINE BAR, 11 Gandy St. Tel. 434184.
Cuisine: ENGLISH. **Reservations:** Not required. **Bus:** N.
$ Prices: Soup £1.50 ($2.30); main courses £3.85 ($5.80); 3-course fixed-price lunch £7.85 ($11.80). MC, V.
Open: Mon–Sat 8am–11pm.

Situated in a Victorian building on a short, cobblestone street that intersects Exeter's High Street near the center of town, is this beckoning place with beams, checkered tablecloths, and tables that spill over into the cellar. Wine by the glass includes many dozens of vintages from throughout Europe. The food is prepared on the premises and includes a plentiful selection of meats, pies, and quiches, as well as such changing specialties as chicken Waldorf and sugar-baked ham, each served with freshly prepared salads. Hot platters are listed on a blackboard, along with the featured wine of the day.

GOLSWORTHY RESTAURANT, in St. Olaves Court Hotel, Mary Arches St. Tel. 217736.
Cuisine: CONTINENTAL. **Reservations:** Recommended.
$ Prices: Appetizers £3–£4.50 ($4.50–$6.80); main courses £11 ($16.50); fixed-price "light lunch" £10.50 ($15.80); fixed-price lunch or dinner £13.50 ($20.30). AE, DC, MC, V.
Open: Lunch Sun–Fri noon–1:45pm; dinner daily 6:30–9:30pm.

Acknowledged as the finest restaurant in Exeter, this establishment lies within a previously recommended hotel that was originally built as the home of a merchant (James Golsworthy) and later served briefly as a nunnery. Guests enjoy a predinner drink in a paneled bar that overlooks a verdant garden. The cuisine, which reflects the sophisticated Europeanized palate of the congenial owners, might include breast of wood pigeon with creamed leeks and fried celeriac, sautéed lamb's liver with caramelized orange and olive oil, breast of Devon chicken with a mushroom-and-ginger mousse served with a sage sauce, a parfait of herring with a mustard and dill dressing and a salad of croutons, sliced salmon with saffron-butter sauce, and filet of sole with a sauce of Noilly Prat and creamed leeks. Any of these might be followed by a salad of Stilton cheese with walnuts, or a hot pear and frangipani tart and vanilla sauce.

THE SHIP INN, St. Martin's Lane. Tel. 72040.
Cuisine: ENGLISH. **Reservations:** Recommended.
$ Prices: Appetizers £1.25–£2.95 ($1.90–$4.40); main courses £5.25–£8.25 ($7.90–$12.40). AE, DC, MC, V.
Open: Restaurant, lunch daily noon–2pm; dinner Mon–Sat 6:30–10pm, Sun 7–9pm. Bar, lunch Mon–Sat 11am–2:30pm, Sun noon–2pm; dinner Mon–Sat 5–11pm, Sun 7–10:30pm.

The Ship Inn was often visited by Sir Francis Drake, Sir Walter Raleigh, and Sir John Hawkins. Of it Drake wrote: "Next to mine own shippe, I do most love that old 'Shippe' in Exon, a tavern in Fyssh Street, as the people call it, or as the clergie will have it, St. Martin's Lane." The pub still provides tankards of real ale, lager, and stout, and is still loved by both young and old. A large selection of snacks is offered in the bar every day, while the restaurant upstairs provides more substantial English fare. At either lunch or dinner, you can order from a wide selection including French onion soup, whole grilled lemon sole, and five different steaks. The price of the main courses includes vegetables, a roll, and butter. Portions are large, as in Elizabethan times.

2. DARTMOOR

213 miles SW of London, 13 miles W of Exeter

GETTING THERE By Train Take the train down from London to Exeter (see above), then depend on local buses to connect you with the various villages of Dartmoor.

By Bus Transmoor Link, a public transport bus service, usually operates throughout the summer and is an ideal way to get onto the moor. Information on the Transmoor Link and on the bus link between various towns and villages on Dartmoor is available from the Transport Co-ordination Centre (tel. 0392/272123).

By Car Exeter is the most easily reached "gateway" by highway. From Exeter, continue west along the B3212 to such centers of Dartmoor as Easton, Chagford, Moretonhampstead, or North Bovey. From these centers, tiny roads—often not really big enough for two cars—cut deeper into the moor.

ESSENTIALS See individual recommendations for phone area codes. Accommodation information is operated by the **Dartmoor Tourist Association,** Duchy Building, Princetown, Yelverton, Devon PL20 6QF (tel. 082289/567). Local information centers will also provide a list of accommodations.

This national park lies northeast of Plymouth, stretching from Tavistock and Okehampton on the west to Exeter in the east, a granite mass that sometimes rises to a height of 2,000 feet above sea level. The landscape offers vistas of gorges with rushing water, gorse and purple heather ranged over by Dartmoor ponies—a foreboding landscape for the experienced walker only.

Some 13 miles west from Exeter, the peaceful little town of **Moretonhampstead,** perched on the edge of Dartmoor, makes a good center. Moretonhampstead contains an old market cross and several 17th-century colonnaded almshouses.

The much visited Dartmoor village of **Widecombe-in-the-Moor** is only 7 miles from Moretonhampstead. The fame of the village of Widecombe-in-the-Moor stems from an old folk song about Tom Pearce and his gray mare, listing the men who were supposed to be on their way to Widecombe Fair when they met with disaster: Bill Brewer, Jan Stewer, Peter Gurney, Peter Davy, Daniel Whiddon, Harry Hawke, and Old Uncle Tom Cobley. Widecombe also has a parish church worth visiting. Called the **Cathedral of the Moor,** with a roster of vicars beginning in 1253, the house of worship in a green valley is surrounded by legends. When the building was restored, a wall-plate was found bearing the badge of Richard II (1377–99), the figure of a white hart.

In Dartmoor, you'll find 500 miles of footpaths and bridleways and more than 90,000 acres of common land with public access. The country is rough, and on the high moor you should always make sure you have good maps, a compass, and suitable clothing and shoes. Don't be put off, however. Unless you're an experienced hiker, it's unlikely that you'll go far from the well-trodden paths.

WHAT TO SEE & DO

Dartmoor National Park Authority (DNPA) runs guided walks of varying difficulty, ranging from 1½ to 6 hours for a trek of some 9 to 12 miles. All you have to do is turn up suitably clad at your selected starting point. Details are available from DNP information centers or from the **Dartmoor National Park Authority Headquarters,** Parke, Haytor Road, Bovey Tracey, Devon TQ13 9JQ (tel. 0626/832093). The charge for walks is £1.50 to £3 ($2.30 to $4.50).

Throughout the area are stables where you can arrange for a day's trek across the moors. For ✪ **horseback riding** on Dartmoor there are too many establishments to list. All are licensed, and you are accompanied by an experienced rider/guide. The moor can be dangerous, as sudden fogs descend without warning on treacherous marshlands. Prices are around £6 ($9) per hour, £13 ($19.50) for a half day, and £22 ($33) for a full day. Most riding stables are listed in a useful free publication, *The Dartmoor Visitor,* which also contains details of guided walks, places to go, accommodation, local events, and articles about the national park. *The Dartmoor Visitor* is obtainable from DNP information centers and tourist information centers or by mail. Send an International Reply Coupon to the DNPA headquarters (address above).

The market town of Okehampton owes its existence to the Norman castle built by Baldwin de Bryonis, sheriff of Devon, under orders from his uncle, William the Conqueror, in 1068, just 2 years after the Conquest. The Courtenay family lived there for many generations until Henry VIII beheaded one of them and dismantled the castle in 1538. The **Museum of Dartmoor Life,** at the Dartmoor Centre, 3 West St., Okehampton (tel. 0837/52295), is housed in an old mill with a water wheel and is part of the Dartmoor Centre, a group of attractions around an old courtyard. Also here are working craft studios, a Victorian Cottage Tea Room, and a Dartmoor National Park information center. Museum displays cover all aspects of Dartmoor's history from prehistoric times, including geology industries, living conditions, crafts, farm tools and machinery, and some old vehicles—a Devon box wagon of 1875, a 1922 Bullnose Morris motorcar, a 1937 motorcycle. There is a reconstructed cider press, a blacksmithy, and a tourist information center. The museum is open only from Easter to October 31, Monday through Saturday from 10am to 5pm (daily from June to September). Admission is £1.50 ($2.30) for adults, 75p ($1.10) for children.

WHERE TO STAY & DINE

IN ASHBURTON

HOLNE CHASE HOTEL, Two Bridges Rd., Ashburton, near Newton Abbot, Devon TQ13 7NS. Tel. 0364/471. Fax 0364/453. 19 rms (all with bath), 1 suite. TV TEL
$ Rates (including English breakfast): £45–£60 ($67.50–$90) single; £82–£111 ($123–$166.50) double; from £130 ($195) suite. AE, DC, MC, V. **Parking:** Free.
The Holne Chase Hotel is a white-gabled country house, 3 miles northwest of the center of town, within sight of trout- and salmon-fishing waters. You can catch your lunch and take it back to the kitchen to be cooked. Although the mood of the moor predominates, Holne Chase is surrounded by trees, lawns, and pastures, a perfect setting for walks along the Dart. It's off the main Ashburton-Princetown road, between Holne Bridge and New Bridge. Every bedroom in the house is named after a tributary of the River Dart.

The house is furnished in period style, a refurbished bar also being done in the style of the rest of the hotel. The cooking combines the best of English fare with specialty dishes that are made all the better whenever produce from the gardens is used or fresh fish from the Dart River and Torquay. Devon beef and lamb are also featured. The old cellars hold a good selection of wines. Meals cost from £15 to £25 ($22.50 to $37.50).

IN LYDFORD

THE CASTLE INN, Lydford, near Okehampton, Devon EX20 4BH. Tel. 082282/242. Fax 082282/454. 8 rms (5 with bath), 1 suite.

$ Rates (including English breakfast): £25 ($37.50) single without bath, £35 ($52.50) single with bath; £37.50 ($56.30) double without bath, £52.50 ($78.80) double with bath. AE, MC, V. **Parking:** Free.

The Castle Inn is a 16th-century structure next to Lydford Castle, 1 mile off the A386 midway between Okehampton and Tavistock. The inn, with its pink facade and row of rose trellises, is the hub of the village. The owners have maintained the character of the commodious rustic lounge with its collection of old furniture and accessories. One room is called the "Snug," containing a group of high-backed oak settles arranged in a circle.

In the Foresters' Bar, meals are served from noon to 2:30pm daily. The cost depends on your selection of a main course. Bar snacks are available as well. Lunches are bar meals priced from £3 to £6.50 ($4.50 to $9.80) each. Dinners include the bar meals described above, but also include more elaborate restaurant meals priced at £14.50 ($21.80) for a three course table d'hôte dinner, with an à la carte main course priced at £9.95 to £13.95 ($14.90 to $20.90). Hours are daily from 7 to 9pm. The bedrooms are not large but are well planned and attractively furnished, often with mahogany and marble Victorian pieces.

IN TWO BRIDGES

CHERRYBROOK HOTEL, Two Bridges, Yelverton, Devon PL20 6SP. Tel. 0822/88260. 7 rms (all with shower). TV

$ Rates (including English breakfast): £25.50 ($38.30) single; £51 ($76.50) double. No credit cards. **Parking:** Free. **Closed:** Dec 22–Jan 2.

The Cherrybrook Hotel, on the B3212 between Postbridge and Two Bridges, is a small family-run hotel in the center of the Dartmoor National Park, on the high moor but within easy driving distance of Exeter and Plymouth. It was built in the early 19th century by a friend of the Prince Regent, who received permission to enclose a large area of the forest of Dartmoor for farming. Part of the farm was later leased to a gunpowder-manufacturing company, whose remains can still be seen. The lounge and bar with their beamed ceiling and slate floors are a reminder of these times. Andy and Margaret Duncan rent comfortably furnished and well-maintained rooms. You can also dine here, paying around £12.50 ($18.80) for a four-course dinner and coffee.

3. CHAGFORD

218 miles SW of London; 13 miles W of Exeter;
20 miles NW of Torquay; 6 miles NE of Postbridge

GETTING THERE   By Train   Go to Exeter, then take a local bus to Chagford.

By Bus   From Exeter, take the Transmoor Link National Express bus no. 82.

By Car   From Exeter, drive west on the A30, then south on the A382 to Chagford.

ESSENTIALS   The **telephone area code** is 0647.

Six hundred feet above sea level, Chagford is an ancient Stannary Town, and with the moors all around, it's a good base for your exploration of north Dartmoor. Chagford overlooks the Teign River in its deep valley and is itself overlooked by the high granite tors. There's good fishing in the Teign (ask at your hotel). From Chagford, the most popular excursion is to Postbridge, a village with a prehistoric clapper bridge.

WHAT TO SEE & DO

CASTLE DROGO, in the hamlet of Drewsteignton. Tel. 0647/433306.

This massive granite castle was designed and built by Sir Edwin Lutyens and the castle's owner, Julius Drewe, in the early 20th century. It stands high above the River Teign, with views over the moors. The family can trace its origins back to the Norman Conquest. Drewe, who wanted to create a home worthy of his noble ancestors, found the bleak site high above the moors, and he and Lutyens created a splendid modern castle. The tour includes the elegant library, the drawing room, the dining room with fine paintings and mirrors, and a chapel, along with a vaulted-roof gunroom and a garden. There is also a restaurant.

Admission: Castle and grounds, £4.60 ($6.90) adults, £2.30 ($3.50) children; grounds only, £2 ($3) adults, £1 ($1.50) children.

Open: Castle, Apr–Oct, Sat–Thurs 11am–5pm (closed Nov–Mar); grounds, daily 10:30am–5:30pm. **Directions:** Take the A30 and follow the signs; the castle lies 4 miles northeast of Chagford and 6 miles south of the Exeter-Okehampton road (A30).

SIR FRANCIS DRAKE'S HOUSE, Buckland Abbey, Yelverton. Tel. 0822/853607.

Constructed in 1278, Sir Francis Drake's House was originally a Cistercian monastery. The monastery was dissolved in 1539 and became the country seat of sailors Sir Richard Grenville and, later, Sir Francis Drake. The house remained in the Drake family until 1946, when the abbey and grounds were given to the National Trust. The abbey is now a museum and houses exhibits including Drake's drum, banners, and other artifacts. Light snacks are available daily.

Admission: £4 ($6) adults, £2 ($3) children.

Open: Apr–Sept, Fri–Wed 10:30am–5:30pm; Oct, Fri–Wed 10:30am–5pm; Nov–Mar, Wed and Sat–Sun 2–5pm. **Directions:** Go 3 miles west of Yelverton off the A386.

WHERE TO STAY & DINE

EASTON COURT HOTEL, Easton Cross, Chagford, Devon TQ13 8JL. Tel. 0647/433469. 7 rms (all with bath). TV TEL **Directions:** Take the A382 1½ miles northeast of Chagford. **Bus:** 359 from Exeter.

$ Rates (including English breakfast): £44 ($66) single; £76–£82 ($114–$123) double. AE, MC, V. **Parking:** Free. **Closed:** Jan.

Ever since it was established as a hotel in the 1920s by an American, Carolyn Cobb, this Tudor house has been known to discerning visitors, including many literary and theatrical celebrities. Alec Waugh wrote *Thirteen Such Years* here, and Patrick Leigh Fermor penned *The Traveller's Tree*. But it is best known as the place where Evelyn Waugh wrote *Brideshead Revisited*. The guestbook reads like a Who's Who of yesteryear: Robert Donat, Margaret Mead, Ralph Richardson, C. P. Snow, Richard Widmark, John Steinbeck. Here is the atmosphere that usually fits in with a preconceived impression of a country place in England: an ancient stone house with a thatched roof, heavy oak beams, an inglenook where log fires burn in cold weather, and a high-walled flower garden. The bedrooms are snug and comfortable, sheltering 15 guests at a time. British and international dishes are served, including coq au vin, steak-and-mushroom pie, and curried prawns. Meals, open to nonresidents who reserve, cost £22 ($33) and up.

GIDLEIGH PARK HOTEL, 2 miles by Gidleigh Rd., Chagford, Devon TQ13 8HH. Tel. 0647/432367. Fax 0647/432574. 14 rms (all with bath), 1 cottage. TV TEL **Directions:** See below.

$ Rates (including English breakfast, morning tea, newspaper, dinner, service, and tax): £160–£310 ($240–$465) single; £260–£350 ($390–$525) double; £350 ($525) cottage. MC, V. **Parking:** Free.

⭐ A visit to this Tudor-style hotel, a Relais & Châteaux, is highly recommended. Its American owners, Kay and Paul Henderson, have renovated and refurnished the house with flair and imagination. In a park of 40 acres, large beech and oak trees abound. Inside, the oak-paneled public rooms and the open log fires invite a return to yesterday. The windows open onto views of the garden and the Teign Valley, with Dartmoor lying beyond. Most of the bedrooms are on the second floor and are approached by a grand staircase; all have a private bath. The hotel has a three-room thatched cottage with two bathrooms across the river, 350 yards from the hotel. It is available for two, three, or four people.

Excellent meals (for nonguests the cost is £45 to £50 [$67.50 to $75]) are served in an oak-paneled dining room. The menu is changed daily, and only the best and freshest products are used. Dining here has been called a memorable experience. In fact, this restaurant has been called "one of the best in the West Country," and its wine list has received numerous awards.

To get here, from Chagford Square turn right onto Mill Street at Lloyds Bank. After 200 yards, turn right and go down the hill to the crossroads. Cross straight over onto Holy Street, following the lane passing Holy Street Manor on your right and shifting into low gear to negotiate two sharp bends on a steep hill. Over Leigh Bridge, turn a sharp right into Gidleigh Park. A half-mile drive will bring you to the hotel.

GREAT TREE HOTEL, Sandy Park, Chagford, Devon TQ13 8JS. Tel. 0647/432491. 12 rms (all with bath). TV TEL **Directions:** Take the A30 to the traffic circle at Whiddon Down, and drive 2 miles south along the A382.

$ Rates (including English breakfast): £48–£58 ($72–$87) single; £76–£88 ($114–$132) double. AE, DC, MC, V. **Parking:** Free.

Formerly an old hunting lodge, the Great Tree Hotel is a comfortable country house located on 18 acres of private grounds. Bedrooms are country style, with radios and tea and coffee makers. Beverley and Nigel Eaton-Gray, the proprietors, offer a five-course dinner made, so far as possible, with homegrown produce, costing £19.50 ($29.30). English and continental meals are served in their Whitewater Restaurant. There are bar snacks at lunch and Devonshire cream teas on the terrace or by the log fire in winter.

---

4. TORQUAY

223 miles SW of London, 23 miles S of Exeter

GETTING THERE By Plane The nearest connection is Exeter Airport (see above), 40 minutes away.

By Train Frequent trains run throughout the day from London's Paddington Station to Torquay (trip time: 2½ hr.).

By Bus National Express coach links from London's Victoria Coach Station leave every 2 hours during the day for Torquay.

By Car   From Exeter (see above), head west along the A38, veering south at the junction with the A380.

ESSENTIALS   The **telephone area code** is 0803. The **Tourist Information Centre** is at Vaughan Parade (tel. 0803/297428).

In 1968, the towns of Torquay, Paignton, and Brixham joined to form "The English Riviera" as part of a plan to turn the area into one of the super three-in-one resorts of Europe. The area today—the birthplace of mystery writer Agatha Christie—opens onto 22 miles of coastline and 18 beaches.

Torquay is set against a backdrop of the red cliffs of Devon, with many sheltered pebbly coves. With its parks and gardens, including numerous subtropical plants and palm trees, it's often compared to the Mediterranean. At night, concerts, productions from the West End (the D'Oyly Carte Opera appears occasionally at the Princess Theatre), vaudeville shows, and ballroom dancing keep the vacationers—and many honeymooners—entertained.

WHERE TO STAY

IN TORQUAY

HOMERS, Warren Rd., Torquay, Devon TQ2 5TN. Tel. 0803/213456.
Fax 0803/213458 14 rms (all with bath), 1 suite. TV TEL **Directions:** Turn left from the Sea Front along the front (inside lane) straight up the hill. Warren Rd. is on the right (very tight turn by St. Luke's Church).
$ Rates (including full breakfast): £45 ($67.50) single; £128 ($192) double; from £130 ($195) suite. AE, DC, MC, V. **Parking:** Free. **Closed:** Jan 2–Feb 7.

The Victorians who built this house in the 1850s situated it near the top of steeply inclined gardens overlooking Tor Bay. The bedrooms are furnished with such touches as antique mirrors and patterned wallpaper. International specialties are served in the hotel's restaurant, Les Ambassadeurs, the dishes prepared with fresh ingredients. A fixed-price dinner costs £28 ($42).

THE IMPERIAL, Park Hill Rd., Torquay, Devon TQ1 2DG. Tel. 0803/294301, or toll free 800/435-4542 in the U.S. Fax 0803/298293. 146 rms (all with bath), 17 suites. MINIBAR TV TEL
$ Rates (including English breakfast, use of sporting facilities, and dancing in the ballroom Mon–Sat): £90–£100 ($135–$150) single; £160–£180 ($240–$270) double; from £260 ($390) suite. AE, DC, MC, V. **Parking:** Garage, £8 ($12); parking lot, free.

This leading five-star hotel in the West Country dates from the 1860s. It sits on 5½ acres of subtropical gardens opening onto rocky cliffs, with views of the Channel. Inside, a world unfolds of soaring ceilings, marble columns, and ornate plasterwork, enough to make a former visitor, Edward VII, feel at home. Each of the bedrooms enjoys lots of well-ordered space, traditional furniture, private bath, and a radio. Each accommodation has a private balcony suspended high above a view taking in offshore islands with black rocks and sheer sides.

Dining/Entertainment: The elegant Regatta Restaurant serves either table d'hôte at £32 ($48) or à la carte, of both British and international dishes, supplemented by a fine wine list. Hours are daily from 12:30 to 2:30pm for lunch. If you go for dinner, served from 7:30 to 9:30pm, it's important to reserve a table.
Services: 24-hour room service, hairdresser, laundry service, babysitting.

Facilities: The hotel also boasts one of the most modern sports facilities in town, complete with Jacuzzi, a pair of all-weather tennis courts, two squash courts, and an exercise room.

PALACE, Babbacombe Rd., Torquay, Devon TQ1 3TG. Tel. 0803/ 200200. Fax 0803/299899. 135 rms (all with bath), 6 suites. TV TEL **Directions:** From the center take the B3199 east. **Bus:** 32.

$ Rates (including English breakfast): £55–£76 ($82.50–$114) single; £110 ($165) double; from £152 ($228) suite. AE, DC, MC, V. **Parking:** £5 ($7.50).

This Victorian hotel was built when life was on a grand scale, as reflected by its spacious public rooms with their molded ceilings and columns. With all its many improvements in recent years, it should ride into the next century in a premier position. A four-star hotel, it is luxurious in appointments and facilities. Its public facilities, in fact, are the most impressive in Torquay, with both in- and outdoor swimming pools along with in- and outdoor tennis courts, even a nine-hole golf course. All its bedrooms are well furnished. The hotel occupies 25 choice acres of real estate in Torquay, sweeping down to Anstey's Cove.

PALM COURT HOTEL, Sea Front, Torquay, Devon TQ2 5HD. Tel. 0803/ 294881. Fax 0803/211199. 64 rms (52 with bath). TV TEL

$ Rates (including English breakfast): £26.50–£33 ($39.80–$49.50) single with bath; £44–£57 ($66–$85.50) double without bath, £53–£66 ($79.50–$99) double with bath. DC, MC, V. **Parking:** £3 ($4.50).

 The Palm Court Hotel, facing south onto the esplanade overlooking Torquay, offers style and good living. The original row of Regency-era houses became interconnected to form a hotel in the 1920s. Two lounges are wood-paneled with leaded-glass windows. In the dining room is a minstrels' gallery. There are two up-to-date bars and a coffee shop, open all day. All rooms have been modernized and have hot-beverage facilities, central heating, and radios. Each single has a private bath, although some doubles are without bath. With garden chairs and tables on the sun terrace outside the coffee shop, the Palm Court becomes a social center. At night the colored floodlighting around the bay evokes a Riviera atmosphere.

IN MAIDENCOMBE

ORESTONE MANOR, Rockhouse Lane, Maidencombe, Torquay, Devon TQ1 4SX. Tel. 0803/328098. Fax 0803/328336. 18 rms (all with bath). TV TEL **Directions:** Drive 3½ miles north of Torquay on the A379.

$ Rates (including English breakfast): £35 ($52.50) single; £160 ($240) double. AE, DC, MC, V. **Parking:** Free. **Closed:** Jan.

Orestone Manor lies in a small village north of Torquay. Sometimes the best way to enjoy a bustling seaside resort is from afar, nestling in a country home. Orestone Manor provides such an opportunity from February to December. In one of the loveliest valleys in south Devon, this gabled manor house, constructed in the early 17th century as a private home, enjoys a tranquil rural setting, standing on 2 acres of well-landscaped gardens. The bedrooms are handsomely and comfortably furnished and have beverage-making facilities. Tasty bar lunches are provided Monday through Saturday, and a fixed-price dinner, correctly prepared and using fresh ingredients, is £23.50 ($35.30).

WHERE TO DINE

REMY'S, 3 Croft Rd. Tel. 292359.

Cuisine: FRENCH. **Reservations:** Required. **Directions:** From the Sea Front, head north on Shedden Hill. **Bus:** 32.

$ Prices: Fixed-price menu £14.85 ($22.30). MC, V.

Open: Dinner only, Tues–Sat 7:30–9:30pm.

 Considered by some the finest independent dining spot in town, Remy's serves food at reasonable prices, offering a fixed-price menu of three courses which is changed daily. Owner and chef de cuisine Remy Bopp, of France, sets great store by his raw ingredients, whether they be fresh fish from a local fisherman or vegetables from the market. Everything is homemade, including bread, ice cream, sorbet, and pastries. Food-wise guests also enjoy his carefully selected collection of French wines.

A Restaurant with B&B

MULBERRY ROOM, 1 Scarborough Rd., Torquay, Devon TQ2 5UJ. Tel. 0803/213639.

Cuisine: ENGLISH. **Reservations:** Not required. **Directions:** From the Sea Front, turn up Belgrave Rd.; Scarborough Rd. is the first right. **Bus:** 32.

$ Prices: Appetizers £2–£3.50 ($3–$5.30); main courses £5–£7.50 ($7.50–$11.30); fixed-price lunch £7 ($10.50) for 2 courses, £8.50 ($12.80) for 3 courses; 6-course fixed-price dinner £18.50 ($27.80). No credit cards.

Open: Lunch Wed–Sun 12:15–2:30pm; dinner Fri–Sat 7:30–9:30pm.

Lesley Cooper is an inspired cook, and she'll feed you well in her little dining room, seating some two dozen diners at midday. The restaurant is situated in the dining area of one of Torquay's Victorian villas, facing a patio of plants and flowers, with outside tables for summer lunches and afternoon teas. The vegetarian will find comfort here, while regular diners feast on her baked lamb or honey-roasted chicken among other dishes such as grilled natural smoked haddock with brown lentils. Traditional roasts draw the Sunday crowds. The choice is wisely limited so that everything served will be fresh.

You can even stay here in one of three bedrooms, each comfortably furnished and well kept, with private bath. B&B charges range from £14.50 to £18.50 ($21.80 to $27.80) per person daily, making it one of the bargains of the resort.

5. TOTNES

224 miles SW of London, 12 miles N of Dartmouth

GETTING THERE By Train Totnes is on the main London-Plymouth line. Trains leave London's Paddington Station frequently throughout the day.

By Bus Totnes is served locally by the Western National and Devon General bus companies (tel. 0803/63226 in Torquay for information about individual routings).

By Boat Many visitors approach Totnes by river steamer from Dartmouth. Contact Dart Pleasure Craft, River Link (tel. 0803/2277 for information).

By Car From Torquay, head west along the B3210.

ESSENTIALS The **telephone area code** is 0803. The summer-only **Tourist Information Centre** is at the Plains (tel. 0803/863168).

One of the oldest towns in the West Country, the ancient borough of Totnes rests quietly in the past, seemingly content to let the Torbay area remain in the vanguard of the building boom. On the River Dart, upstream from Dartmouth, Totnes is so totally removed in character from Torquay that the two towns could be in different countries. Totnes has several historic buildings, notably the ruins of a Norman castle, an ancient guildhall, and the 15th-century church of St. Mary, constructed of red sandstone. In the Middle Ages the old cloth town was encircled by walls, and the North Gate serves as a reminder of that period.

WHERE TO STAY

IN TOTNES

ROYAL SEVEN STARS, The Plains, Totnes, Devon TQ9 5DD. Tel. 0803/ 862125. Fax 0803/867925. 18 rms (12 with bath). TV TEL
$ Rates (including English breakfast): £39.50 ($59.30) single without bath, £49.50 ($74.30) single with bath; £49.50 ($74.30) double without bath, £69.50 ($104.30) double with bath. DC, MC, V. **Parking:** Free.
A historic former coaching inn in the center of town, the Royal Seven Stars largely dates back to 1660. The hotel has an interesting porch over its entrance and overlooks a square in the town center, near the banks of the River Dart. The interior courtyard, once used for horses and carriages, is now enclosed in glass, with an old pine staircase. With antiques and paintings, the hotel's own heraldic shield, hand-carved chests, and a grandfather clock, the courtyard forms an inviting entrance to the inn. The bedrooms have been modernized and have built-in furniture. Each has comfortable beds and hot-beverage facilities. Some rooms contain four-poster beds.
A buffet bar is open for lunch all year as well as for supper May to September. A three-course lunch or four-course dinner can be enjoyed in the Brutus Room, open all year. Lunch costs £7.95 ($11.90), and dinner, £12.95 ($19.40).

IN NEARBY STOKE GABRIEL

GABRIEL COURT HOTEL, Stoke Gabriel, near Totnes, Devon TQ9 6SF. Tel. 080428/206. Fax 080428/333. 20 rms (all with bath and shower), 3 family rms. TV TEL **Directions:** Take the A385 toward Paignton; after a mile, turn right and follow the signs for Stoke Gabriel. **Bus:** 625 from Paignton.
$ Rates (including English breakfast): £50–£57 ($75–$85.50) single; £77–£84 ($115.50–$126) double; from £97 ($145.50) family rm. AE, DC, MC, V. **Parking:** Free. **Closed:** Feb.
⑤ The Gabriel Court Hotel was a manor house owned by the same family from 1487 until 1928, when it was converted into a hotel. Michael and Eryl Beacom run a hotel of quality, offering good value. The hotel, on the banks of the Dart River, standing in a terraced Elizabethan garden, has a heated swimming pool and a lawn tennis court. The 3-acre site is a setting for the white-painted house, which offers well-furnished rooms. Eight of these accommodations are in a modern extension.
Gabriel Court enjoys a reputation for its well-cooked English food, enhanced all the more by fruit and vegetables from the garden, as well as trout and salmon from the Dart and poultry from nearby farms. The hotel also has a bar. In winter, there are log fires in the lounges, and the house is also centrally heated.

IN NEARBY DARTINGTON

COTT INN, Dartington, near Totnes, Devon TQ9 6HE. Tel. 0803/

863777. Fax 0803/866629. 6 rms (5 with bath). TV TEL **Transportation:** Bus X80 travels from Totnes to Dartington, but most hire a taxi for the 1½-mile journey.
$ Rates (including English breakfast): £45 ($67.50) single without bath, £55 ($82.50) single with bath; £50 ($75) double without bath, £60 ($90) double with bath. MC, V. **Parking:** Free.

Built in 1320, this hotel is the second-oldest inn in England. It is a low, rambling two-story building of stone, cob, and plaster, with a thatched roof and walls 3 feet thick, on the old Ashburton-Totnes turnpike. Steve and Gill Culverhouse rent low-ceilinged, double rooms upstairs, with modern conveniences, including hot and cold running water. The inn is a gathering place for the people of Dartington, and you'll feel the pulse of English country life. In winter, log fires keep the lounge and bar snug. You'll surely be intrigued with the tavern, where you can also order a meal. A buffet is laid out at lunchtime, priced according to your choice of dish. The à la carte dinners feature local produce prepared in interesting ways; scallops, duck, steak, or fresh salmon may be available. A set dinner costs £17 ($25.50). Even if you're not staying over, at least drop in at the pub (seven beers are on draft). Pub hours are Monday to Saturday from 11am to 2:30pm and 6 to 11pm, and Sunday from noon to 2:30pm and 7 to 10:30pm.

WHERE TO DINE

IN TOTNES

THE ELBOW ROOM, 6 North St. Tel. 863480.
    Cuisine: INTERNATIONAL. **Reservations:** Required.
$ Prices: Appetizers £2.75–£5.40 ($4.10–$8.10); main courses £7.50–£10.50 ($11.30–$15.80). AE, DC, MC, V.
    Open: Lunch Tues–Sat noon–2pm; dinner Tues–Sat 7–9:30pm.

An intimate rendezvous for diners, the Elbow Room is in a converted one-time cider press and adjoining cottage in the center adjacent to the Castle Car Park. The original 300-year-old stone walls have been retained and decor matched to them to give a unique atmosphere. Mr. and Mrs. R. J. Savin provide a standard of food and service that attracts gourmets. Mrs. Savin combines technical skill with inspiration and a flair for the unusual in the selection, preparation, and presentation of her appetizers, main courses, and homemade desserts. Main courses include fresh vegetables. The menu is restricted to a maximum of 10 dishes, ranging from chicken with almonds (a suprême of fresh chicken served in a fresh cream and Grand Marnier sauce, garnished with flaked almonds and apple) to whisky steak dijonnaise (prime filet of English beef served in a whisky, herb mist, and mushroom sauce). The lunch menu offers a selection of roasts. Mr. Savin presides over the restaurant with charm and expertise.

---

6. DARTMOUTH

236 miles SW of London, 35 miles S of Exeter

GETTING THERE By Train Dartmouth is not easily reached by public transport. British Rail trains run to Totnes (see above) and Paignton.

By Bus There is one bus a day from Totnes to Dartmouth.

By Car From Exeter, take the A38 southwest, cutting southeast to Totnes along the A381. Follow the A381 to the junction with the B3207.

By Boat There are river boats making the 10-mile run from Totnes to Dartmouth, but these depend on tide and operate only during Easter to the end of October. Check at the Totnes tourist office—see below—for details about possible boat schedules.

ESSENTIALS The **telephone area code** is 0803. The **Tourist Information Centre** is at 11 Duke St. (tel. 0803/834224).

At the mouth of the Dart River, this ancient seaport is the home of the Royal Naval College. Traditionally linked to England's maritime greatness, Dartmouth sent out the young midshipmen who saw to it that "Britannia ruled the waves." You can take a river steamer up the Dart to Totnes (book at the kiosk at the harbor); the scenery along the way is breathtaking, as the Dart is Devon's most beautiful river.

Dartmouth's 15th-century castle was built during the reign of Edward IV. The town's most noted architectural feature is the Butterwalk, which lies below Tudor houses. The Flemish influence in some of the houses is pronounced.

WHERE TO STAY

DART MARINA HOTEL, Sandquay, Dartmouth, Devon TQ6 9PH. Tel. 0803/832580, or toll free 800/435-4542 in the U.S. Fax 0803/835040. 31 rms (all with bath). TV TEL

$ Rates: £70–£100 ($105–$150) single; £90–£128 ($135–$192) double. Breakfast £8.50 ($12.80) extra. AE, DC, MC, V. **Parking:** Free.

The Dart Marina Hotel is an ocher-walled establishment at the edge of its own marina, within a 3-minute walk of the center of town. Originally built as a clubhouse for the marina, it was later expanded into a full-fledged hotel. From the bar, the yachting set can view their craft through large windows. Several of the comfortable bedrooms feature balconies, radio, and coffee-making equipment; all have private baths.

ROYAL CASTLE HOTEL, 11 The Quay, Dartmouth, Devon TQ6 9PS. Tel. 0803/833033. Fax 0803/835445. 25 rms (all with bath). TV TEL

$ Rates (including English breakfast): £48–£64 ($72–$96) single; £74–£128 ($111–$192) double. MC, V. **Parking:** £2 ($3).

A coaching inn since 1639, the Royal Castle Hotel has hosted Sir Francis Drake, Queen Victoria, Charles II, and Edward VII (bedrooms named after them commemorate their visits). Horse-drawn carriages (as late as 1910) dispatched passengers in a carriageway, now an enclosed reception hall. The glassed-in courtyard, with its winding wooden staircase, has the original coaching horn and a set of 20 antique spring bells connected to the bedrooms. Many of the rooms opening off the covered courtyard and the rambling corridors have antiques. All units have been recently restored and have central heating and private baths. Some are air-conditioned.

The meals, taken in the restaurant under a beautiful Adam ceiling, are excellent, in the best English tradition. Dinner costs £19.95 ($29.90). A favorite place to settle in is the Galleon Bar, once two old kitchens, with double fireplaces and large hand-hewn beams said to have been salvaged from armada ships. There is another pub-style bar, with settles, popular with the locals. Guests lounge on the second floor in a room with a bay window overlooking the harbor.

WHERE TO DINE

THE CARVED ANGEL, 2 South Embankment. Tel. 832465.
Cuisine: CONTINENTAL. **Reservations:** Required.

$ Prices: Appetizers £7.50–£9 ($11.30–$13.50); main courses £19.50 ($29.30);

3-course fixed-price meals £27.50 ($41.30) at lunch, £42.50 ($63.80) at dinner. No credit cards.
Open: Lunch Tues–Sun 12:30–1:45pm; dinner Mon–Sat 7:30–9:30pm.
Closed: Jan–Feb 15, Oct 1–7.

✪   Considered the best restaurant in town, the Carved Angel serves specialties that are usually more akin to the creative cuisine of the Continent than to the traditional cookery of England. Co-owner and chef Joyce Molyneux welcomes visitors to her stylishly simple riverside restaurant, the kitchen of which is partially screened from the dining room by plants. It was a former Victorian storefront. The restaurant is behind a half-timbered, heavily carved facade rising opposite the harbor. Inside, a central statue of a carved angel is ringed with a decor of neutral colors. Typical dishes include lobster soup with lemongrass, coconut, and chili; Dart salmon in pastry with currants and ginger; and, for dessert, hot chocolate soufflé with homemade ice cream.

HORN OF PLENTY, in the Tamar View House, Gulworthy, Devon PL19 8JD. Tel. 0822/832528.
   Cuisine: INTERNATIONAL. **Reservations:** Required. **Directions:** Drive 3 miles west of Tavistock on the A390.
$ **Prices:** Appetizers £6–£8 ($9–$12); main courses £16–£18 ($24–$27); fixed-price meals £17.50 ($26.30) at lunch, £23.50 ($35.30) at dinner. AE, MC, V.
   Open: Lunch Tues–Sun noon–2pm; dinner daily 7–9:30pm. **Closed:** Christmas Day.

As you drive from Tavistock to Callington, you will see a small sign pointing north along a leafy drive to the solid Regency house where the owners operate what the French call a *restaurant avec chambres*. It was built by a local miner in the early 1800s as a private home. After a day of touring the country, guests enjoy well-prepared dinners, which might include filet of lemon sole with a coating of chopped shrimp; scallops and fresh coriander cooked in a tempura batter and served on a delicate herb-flavored salad; or roast partridge garnished with a cabbage leaf filled with mushrooms, foie gras, bacon, and shallots, all in a port wine sauce.

   You can stay in one of the spacious, warm, and elegant bedrooms, seven in all, which have been installed over the old stables of the house. With English breakfast included, depending on the season, singles cost from £58 to £70 ($87 to $105) and double rooms rent for £78 to £90 ($117 to $135). All accommodations have color TVs, hot-beverage facilities, phone, and a well-stocked minibar.

---

7. PLYMOUTH

142 miles SW of London, 161 miles W of Southampton

GETTING THERE   **By Plane**   Plymouth Airport lies 4 miles from the center of the city. Brymon Airways has direct service from the London airports at Heathrow and Gatwick to Plymouth. For service, call Brymon (tel. 0752/707023).

By Train   Frequent trains run from London's Paddington Station to Plymouth in 3 to 3½ hours, depending on the train.

By Bus   National Express has frequent daily bus service between London's Victoria Coach Station and Plymouth (trip time: 4½ hr.).

By Car   From London, take the M4 motorway west to the junction of the M5 going south to Exeter. From Exeter, head southwest on the A38 to Plymouth.

ESSENTIALS The **telephone area code** is 0752. The **Tourist Information Centre** is at the Civic Centre, Royal Parade (tel. 0752/264849).

The historic seaport of Plymouth is more romantic in legend than in reality. But this was not always so. During World War II, the blitzed area of greater Plymouth lost at least 75,000 buildings. The heart of present-day Plymouth, including the municipal civic center on the Royal Parade, has been entirely rebuilt—the way that it was done is the subject of much controversy.

For the old you must go to the Elizabethan section, known as the Barbican, and walk along the quay in the footsteps of Sir Francis Drake (once the mayor of Plymouth) and other Elizabethan seafarers, such as Sir John Hawkins, English naval commander and slave trader. It was from here in 1577 that Drake set sail on his round-the-world voyage. An even more famous sailing took place in 1620, when the Pilgrims left their final port in England for the New World.

Of special interest to visitors from the United States is the final departure point of the Pilgrims in 1620, the already-mentioned Barbican. The two ships, *Mayflower* and *Speedwell,* that sailed from Southampton in August of that year put into Plymouth after they suffered storm damage. Here the *Speedwell* was abandoned as unseaworthy, and the *Mayflower* made the trip to the New World alone. The Memorial Gateway to the Waterside on the Barbican marks the place, tradition says, whence the Pilgrims' ship sailed.

WHAT TO SEE & DO

The **Barbican** is a mass of narrow streets, old houses, and quayside shops selling antiques, brasswork, old prints, and books. Fishing boats still unload their catch at the wharves, and passenger-carrying ferryboats run short harbor cruises. A trip includes a visit to Drake's Island in the sound, the dockyards, and naval vessels, plus a view of the Hoe from the water. A cruise of Plymouth Harbour costs £3 ($4.50) for adults and £1.50 ($2.30) for children. Departures are February to November, with cruises leaving every half hour from 10:30am to 3pm daily. These Plymouth Boat Cruises are booked at the Phoenix Wharf, the Barbican (tel. 822797).

WHITE LANE GALLERY, 1 White Lane, The Barbican. Tel. 221450.
This gallery specializes in contemporary art and crafts, with changing exhibitions of paintings and ceramics. It also has three resident craftspeople, including a potter, furniture maker, and silk painter. It's a 5-minute walk from the town center in Plymouth's historic Barbican, near Mayflower Steps.
   Admission: Free.
   Open: Mon noon–4pm, Tues–Sat 10am–5pm. **Bus:** 39.

PLYMOUTH DRY GIN, Black Friars Distillery, 60 Southside St. Tel. 667062.
Plymouth Gin has been produced here for 200 years on a historic site that dates back to a Dominican monastery built in 1425. Although this is a working distillery, there are public guided tours. A Plymouth Gin Shop is on the premises. The gin factory lies next to a historic monument, now part of the Distillery Beefeater Restaurant. These premises, one of Plymouth's oldest surviving buildings, was where the Pilgrims met prior to sailing for the New World.
   Admission: £1.50 ($2.30) adults, 80p ($1.20) children under 10.
   Open: Easter–Sept, Mon–Sat 10:30am–4pm. **Bus:** 54.

PRYSTEN HOUSE, Finewell St. Tel. 0752/661414.

Built in 1490 as a town house close to St. Andrew's Church, it is now a church house and working museum. Rebuilt in the 1930s with American help, it displays a model of Plymouth in 1620 and tapestries depicting the colonization of America. At the entrance is the gravestone of the captain of the U.S. brig *Argus,* who died on August 15, 1813, after a battle in the English Channel.

Admission: 50p (80¢) adults, 25p (40¢) children.

Open: Apr–Oct, Mon–Sat 10am–4pm.

WHERE TO STAY

ASTOR HOTEL, 14–22 Elliott St., The Hoe, Plymouth, Devon PL1 2PS. Tel. 0752/225511. Fax 0752/251994. 56 rms (all with bath). TV TEL

$ Rates (including English breakfast): £45–£55 ($67.50–$82.50) single; £50–£69 ($75–$103.50) double. AE, DC, MC, V. **Parking:** Free overnight; daytime parking in public lot nearby, £1.50 ($2.30).

 The hotel building was originally constructed during the Victorian era as the private home of a prosperous sea captain. In 1987 it underwent a major restoration, and today it has comfortable bedrooms, each with radio and coffee-making facilities. The hotel lies near the Hoe on a street lined with 19th-century buildings. On the premises are well-decorated public lounges and a cozy and accommodating bar—open to residents and nonresidents alike—separated from the reception desk by a fan-shaped trio of glass doors. Fixed-price three-course meals in the hotel's restaurant cost £8.50 ($12.80) at lunch and £13.50 ($20.30) at dinner. Otherwise, less expensive bar snacks, priced at £3 to £6 ($4.50 to $9) per platter, can be ordered over the countertop of the bar.

DUKE OF CORNWALL HOTEL, Millbay Rd., Plymouth, Devon PL1 3LG. Tel. 0752/266256. Fax 0752/600062. 70 rms (all with bath). TV TEL

$ Rates (including English breakfast): £50–£90 ($75–$135) single; £60–£125 ($90–$187.50) double. AE, DC, MC, V. **Parking:** Free.

The Duke of Cornwall Hotel is a Victorian Gothic building that survived World War II bombings. Constructed in 1863, it was regarded by Sir John Betjeman as the finest example of Victorian architecture in Plymouth. The refurbished bedrooms all have radios and coffee-making facilities. Some rooms have an antique four-poster bed.

The hotel dining room is of an elegant contemporary style with a circular ceiling supporting a fine chandelier. Lunch costs £9.50 ($14.30), and dinner starts at £18 ($27).

FORTE POSTHOUSE, Cliff Rd., The Hoe, Plymouth, Devon PL1 3DL. Tel. 0752/662828, or toll free 800/435-4542 in the U.S. Fax 0752/660974. 104 rms (all with bath), 4 suites. TV TEL

$ Rates: £39.50–£69.50 ($59.30–$104.30) single or double; from £95 ($142.50) suite. Breakfast £6.95 ($10.40) extra. AE, DC, MC, V. **Parking:** Free.

The hotel is situated on a hilltop above the bay. The nine-story hotel was constructed in 1970, its clientele divided equally between tourists and business travelers. The hotel has well-furnished rooms, all but a dozen of which face the sea. Each unit has a radio.

On the premises is a pub, the Boston Bar, with a separate entrance, along with a free-form, heated outdoor pool (open daily April to October) and a restaurant with wide-angle views of the sea. Meals cost £16 ($24) and up.

NOVOTEL PLYMOUTH, 270 Plymouth Rd., Marsh Mills Roundabout, Plymouth, Devon PL6 8NH. Tel. 0752/221422. Fax 0752/221422. 100 rms (all with bath or shower). A/C TV TEL **Bus:** 21 or 22.

$ Rates: £49.50 ($74.30) single; £54.50 ($81.80) double. Two children under 16

stay free in parents' room. Breakfast £7.50 ($11.30) extra. AE, DC, MC, V. **Parking:** Free.

The Novotel Plymouth, lying at the entrance to the city on the A38, is suitable for motorists, especially those with children. With landscaped gardens and plenty of parking, it offers an ample number of soundproofed bedrooms. Two children under 16 sharing a room with their parents also receive free breakfast. There's a swimming pool and a children's play area. A grill restaurant is open daily from 6am to midnight. Meals begin at £12.50 ($18.80).

PLYMOUTH MOAT HOUSE HOTEL, Armada Way, Plymouth, Devon PL1 2HJ. Tel. 0752/662866. Fax 0752/673816. 213 rms (all with bath), 2 suites. A/C TV TEL
$ Rates: £89 ($133.50) single; £119 ($178.50) double; from £175 ($262.50) suite. Breakfast £9.75 ($14.60) extra. AE, DC, MC, V. **Parking:** Free.

One of the most distinguished hotels in the West Country, overlooking the harbor and the Hoe, the Plymouth Moat House Hotel rises like a midget high-rise. The good-sized rooms are well furnished with long double beds and have wide picture windows and radios. Babysitting is available. A covered swimming pool is on the grounds, and there's a sauna and sun terrace as well, with garden tables set up for poolside refreshments.

In the Blue Riband Restaurant, with its panoramic sea views, both à la carte and a table d'hôte menu are served. Seafood is a specialty, some of the catch brought fresh each day from the Barbican.

WHERE TO DINE

CHEZ NOUS, 13 Frankfort Gate. Tel. 266793.
Cuisine: FRENCH. **Reservations:** Required.
$ Prices: Appetizers £7.50–£8 ($11.30–$12); main courses £17–£36 ($25.50–$54); fixed-price dinner £26.50 ($39.80). AE, DC, MC, V.
Open: Lunch Tues–Sat 12:30–2pm; dinner Tues–Sat 7–10:30pm. **Closed:** First 3 weeks in Feb and Sept.

The most distinguished restaurant in Plymouth is Chez Nous, situated directly off Western Approach. Owner and chef Jacques Marchal borrows heavily from the past, but also dares to express his creative talent. His type of cooking is called *la cuisine spontanée*—using fresh produce that changes with the seasons. Chez Nous is quite pretty and cozy, situated in a shopping complex. Look for the specials of the day on the blackboard menu. Aided by a classic and rather elegant wine list, the food is likely to include such dishes as scallops steamed with ginger, seaman's pie, and pork with prunes. Fish, generally, is the preferred main dish to order here. Desserts and appetizers are also prepared with care. Fresh, quality ingredients are a hallmark of the cuisine.

GREEN LANTERNS, 31 New St., the Barbican. Tel. 660852.
Cuisine: ENGLISH. **Reservations:** Recommended for dinner. **Bus:** 54.
$ Prices: Appetizers £1.40–£3.30 ($2.10–$5); main courses £4.80–£10.25 ($7.20–$15.40). AE, MC, V.
Open: Lunch Mon–Sat 11:45am–2:15pm; dinner Mon–Sat 6:30–10:45pm.

A 16th-century eating house on a Tudor street, the Green Lanterns lies 200 yards from the *Mayflower* Steps. The lunch menu offers a selection of grills, chicken, and fish—all served with vegetables. The kitchen also features blackboard specials such as Lancashire hot pot. Several unusual dishes are on the dinner menu such as goose breasts in breadcrumbs, wild duck (teal), and venison in red wine. Chicken, beef, turkey, plaice, and mackerel are also available—all served with vegetables. Family owned, the Green Lanterns is run by Sally M. Russell and Kenneth Pappin, who are fully aware that tourists like the Elizabethan atmosphere, traditional English fare, and personal service. The restaurant is near the municipally owned Elizabethan House.

8. CLOVELLY

240 miles W of London, 11 miles W of Bideford

GETTING THERE   By Train   From London's Paddington Station, trains depart for Exeter frequently. At Exeter, passengers transfer to a train headed for the end destination of Barnstable. Travel time from Exeter to Barnstable is 1¼ hours. From Barnstable, passengers transfer to Clovelly by bus.

By Bus   From Barnstable, about one bus per hour, operated by either the Red Bus Company or the Filers Bus Company, goes to Bideford (trip time: 40 min.). At Bideford, connecting buses (with no more than a 10-minute wait between the arrival and the departure) continue on for the 30-minute drive to Clovelly. Two Land Rovers make continuous round-trips to the Red Lion inn from the top of the hill, costing 50p (80¢) per person each way.

By Car   From London, head west along the M4 motorway, cutting south at the junction of the M5 motorway. At the junction near Bridgwater, continue west along the A39 in the direction of Lynton. The A39 runs all the way to the signposted turnoff for Clovelly.

ESSENTIALS   The **telephone area code** is 0237. Clovelly doesn't have a tourist office, but information about the area is available at the summer-only **Tourist Information Centre** at The Quay (tel. 0237/477676), in nearby Bideford.

This is the most charming of all Devon villages and one of the main attractions of the West Country. Starting at a great height, the village cascades down the mountainside, with its narrow, cobblestone High that makes travel by car impossible—you park your car at the top and make the trip on foot; supplies are carried down by donkeys. Every step of the way provides views of tiny cottages, with their terraces of flowers lining the main street. The village fleet is sheltered at the stone quay at the bottom.

Tips: To avoid the tourist crowd, stay out of Clovelly from around 11am until teatime. Visit nearby villages during the middle of the day when the congestion here is at its height. Also, to avoid the climb back up the slippery incline, go to the rear of the Red Lion inn and queue up for a Land Rover. In summer the line is often long, but considering the alternative, it's worth the wait.

WHERE TO STAY

NEW INN, High St., Clovelly, Devon EX39 5TQ. Tel. 0237/431303. Fax 0237/431636. 20 rms (5 with bath).

$ Rates (including English breakfast): £19.50 ($29.30) single without bath; £39 ($58.50) double without bath, £48 ($72) double with bath. AE, DC, MC, V.

 About halfway down High Street is the village pub, a good meeting place at sundown. It offers the best lodgings in the village, in two buildings on opposite sides of the steep street (but only a 12-foot leap between their balconies). Five of the bedrooms are furnished with TV and phone.

This little country inn is also recommended for meals. A wide choice of moderately priced meals is offered in the oak-beamed dining room. The local fare, including Devonshire cream, is featured whenever possible. Locally caught lobsters are also prepared by the chef. Motorists can park in the lot at the entrance to the town. It's advisable to pack an overnight case, since the luggage has to be carried down (but is returned to the top by donkey).

RED LION, The Quay, Clovelly, Devon EX39 5TF. Tel. 0237/431237. 12 rms (all with bath). TV
$ Rates (including English breakfast): £37.50 ($56.30) single; £59 ($88.50) double. MC, V.
At the bottom of the steep cobbled street, right on the stone seawall of the little harbor, the Red Lion occupies the jewel position in the village. Rising three stories with gables and a courtyard, it's actually an unspoiled country inn, where life centers around an antique pub and village inhabitants, including sea captains, who gather to satisfy their thirst over pints of ale. Most of the bedrooms look out directly to the sea, and all of them have hot and cold running water and adequate furnishing. Dinner is available in the sea-view dining room for £14.50 ($21.80), with a choice of four main dishes, two of which are always fresh local fish, then a selection from the dessert trolley. The manager suggests that the Red Lion is not suitable for children under 7 years of age.

9. LYNTON-LYNMOUTH

206 miles W of London, 59 miles N of Exeter

GETTING THERE   By Train   The resort is rather remote, and the local tourist office recommends that you rent a car. However, local daily trains from Exeter arrive at Barnstable.

By Bus   From Barnstable, bus service is provided to Lynton at a frequency of one about every 2 hours.

By Car   Take the M4 west from London to the junction of the M5, then head south to the junction of the A39. Continue west on the A39 to Lynton-Lynmouth.

ESSENTIALS   The **telephone area code** for Lynton-Lynmouth is 0598. The **Tourist Information Centre** is at the Town Hall, Lee Road (tel. 0598/52225).

The north coast of Devon is set off dramatically in Lynton, a village some 500 feet high, which is a good center for exploring the Doone Valley and that part of Exmoor that overflows into the shire from neighboring Somerset. The Valley of the Rocks, west of Lynton, offers the most spectacular scenery.

The town is joined by a cliff railway to Lynmouth, about 500 feet lower. The length of the track is 862 feet with a gradient of 1 inch which gives a vertical height of approximately 500 feet. The two passenger cars are linked together with two steel cables, and the operation of the lift is on the counterbalance system, which is simply explained as a pair of scales where one side, when weighted by water ballast, pulls the other up.

The East Lyn and West Lyn rivers meet in Lynmouth, a popular resort with the British. For a panoramic view of the rugged coastline, you can walk on a path halfway between the towns that runs along the cliff. From Lynton, or rather from Hollerday

Hill, you can look out onto Lynmouth Bay, Countisbury Foreland, and Woody Bays in the west.

WHERE TO STAY & DINE

BATH HOTEL, Sea Front, Lynmouth, Devon EX35 6EL. Tel. 0598/52238.
24 rms (all with bath). TV TEL
$ Rates (including English breakfast): £31–£42 ($46.50–$63) single; £54–£74 ($81–$111) double. AE, DC, MC, V. **Parking:** Free. **Closed:** Nov–Feb.

The Bath Hotel is a solid building between the busy street and the towering cliffs. Many of the comfortably furnished bedrooms have views over the river and out to the sea. A good fixed-price dinner is served in the restaurant for £14 ($21), with lobster and salmon specialties. Sunday lunch offers cuts from a roast, traditional vegetables, and an old-fashioned dessert.

HEWITT'S HOTEL AND RESTAURANT, North Walk, Lynton, Devon EX35 6HJ. Tel. 0598/52293. Fax 0598/52489. 8 rms (all with bath). TV TEL
$ Rates (including English breakfast): £45 ($67.50) single; £84 ($126) double. MC, V. **Parking:** Free.

Hewitt's Hotel and Restaurant is named for Sir Thomas Hewitt, who helped construct the funicular rail that links the twin resorts. In the late 19th century, he also built a home for himself, and that place today is one of the most successful little inns in Lynton. Situated on some two dozen acres, it opens onto beautiful vistas of Lynmouth Bay (best enjoyed while seated on a sunny terrace). The old house is filled with architectural character, as exemplified by its grand staircase, time-mellowed paneling, antiques, and stained-glass windows. All rooms are well furnished and comfortably appointed, with sea views and some with private balconies. The hotel is "for all seasons," and has a country-house atmosphere.

The quality of the bar lunches is far above average, and dinner is among the best served at the resort. In fact, it's reason enough to stay here, and you won't be overcharged either since meals begin at £21.50 ($32.30). A medley of British and continental dishes is served.

THE RISING SUN HOTEL, The Harbour, Lynmouth, Lynton, Devon EX35 6EQ. Tel. 0598/53223. Fax 0593/53480. 16 rms (all with bath), 1 cottage. TV TEL
$ Rates (including English breakfast): £39.50–£43 ($59.30–$64.50) single; £79–£86 ($118.50–$129) double; Shelley's Cottage, £110 ($165) for two. AE, DC, MC, V. **Parking:** Free.

The Rising Sun Hotel is a thatched inn right at the end of the quay at the mouth of the Lyn River. Not only is the harbor life spread before you, but you can bask in the wonder and warmth of an inn in business for more than 600 years. All the bedrooms, with crazy levels and sloping ceilings, offer views of the water, the changing tides, and bobbing boats. It's a lovely old place, where the staircase is so narrow and twisting that it requires care to negotiate. Ceilings are low and floorboards creak. Behind the inn, halfway up the cliff, is a tiny garden bright with flowers in summer, where you can sit and gaze out over the thatch roofs to the sea. The owner has refurbished the place and added more rooms by joining two adjacent properties, and he has rooms available nearby in Shelley's Cottage, where the poet honeymooned in 1812. R. D. Blackmore wrote part of *Lorna Doone* while staying at the hotel. Two of the rooms have four-poster beds. It's a delight to dine at the Rising Sun since everything is 101% British in the dining room, with its deeply set window and fireplace. See the original 14th-century fireplace in the bar.

TORS HOTEL, Lynmouth, Lynton, Devon EX35 6NA. Tel. 0598/53236.
35 rms (all with bath). TV TEL

$ Rates (including English breakfast): £37–£77 ($55.50–$115.50) single; £67–£97 ($100.50–$145.50) double. AE, DC, MC, V. **Parking:** Free. **Closed:** Jan–Feb. Set high on a cliff, the Tors Hotel opens onto a view of the coastline and the bay of Lynmouth. It was built in the fashion of a Swiss château, with more than 40 gables, Tyrolean balconies jutting out to capture the sun (or the moon), black-and-white timbered wings, and some 30 chimneys. Surrounding the hotel are a terrace and a heated swimming pool. The interior has been modernized, and much attention has been lavished on the comfortable bedrooms. A fixed-price lunch costs £8 ($12), and a fixed-price dinner goes for £25 ($37.50).

CHAPTER 13

CORNWALL

- **WHAT'S SPECIAL ABOUT CORNWALL**
1. **LOOE**
2. **POLPERRO**
3. **ST. MAWES**
4. **PENZANCE**
5. **THE ISLES OF SCILLY**
6. **NEWLYN, MOUSEHOLE & LAND'S END**
7. **ST. IVES**
8. **PORT ISAAC**
9. **TINTAGEL**
10. **BOLVENTOR**

The ancient duchy of Cornwall is in the extreme southwestern part of England, often called "the toe." This peninsula is a virtual island—spiritually if not geographically. Encircled by coastline, it abounds in rugged cliffs, hidden bays, fishing villages, sandy beaches, and sheltered coves where smuggling was once rampant. Although many of the little seaports with hillside cottages resemble towns along the Mediterranean, Cornwall retains its own distinctive flavor.

The Celtic-Iberian origin of the Cornish people is apparent in superstition, folklore, and fairy tales. When Cornish people speak of King Arthur and his Knights of the Round Table, they're not just handing out a line to tourists. To them, Arthur and his knights really existed, roaming around Tintagel Castle, now in ruins.

The ancient land had its own language up until about 250 years ago, and some of the old words (*pol* for pool, *tre* for house) still survive. The Cornish dialect is more easily understood by the Welsh than by those who speak the Queen's English.

I suggest berthing at one of the smaller fishing villages, such as East or West Looe, Polperro, Mousehole, or Portloe—where you'll experience the true charm of the duchy. Many of the villages, such as St. Ives, are artists' colonies. Except for St. Ives and Port Isaac, some of the most interesting places lie on the southern coast, often called the Cornish Riviera, which strikes many foreign visitors as being the most intriguing. However, the north coast has its own peculiar charm as well.

SEEING CORNWALL

GETTING THERE

The fastest way to Cornwall by car is via the M4 and M5 motorways. Eventually, the M5 links up with the A30 and goes all the way to Land's End at the tip of Cornwall. British Rail offers frequent service to the southwest from London's Paddington Station, arriving at Penzance and the end of the line in 5 hours. National Express coaches also service the region from London's Victoria Coach Station (8 hours to Penzance).

A SUGGESTED ITINERARY

Day 1: Spend the day exploring both Looe and Polperro, staying overnight in either resort.

✓

WHAT'S SPECIAL ABOUT CORNWALL

Beaches
☐ A majestic coastline—both north and south—studded with fishing villages and hidden coves for swimming, with Penzance and St. Ives the major meccas.

Great Towns/Villages
☐ Penzance, granite resort and fishing port on Mount's Bay, with a Victorian promenade.
☐ St. Ives, old fishing port and artists' colony, with a good surfing beach.
☐ Mousehole, considered the most charming old fishing port in Cornwall, filled with twisting lanes and granite cottages.

Natural Spectacles
☐ The Isles of Scilly, 27 miles off the Cornish coast, with only five islands inhabited out of more than 100.

☐ Land's End, where England comes to an end, 9 miles west of Penzance.

Castles
☐ Tintagel Castle, on a wild stretch of the Atlantic coast, the legendary castle of King Arthur, Lancelot, and Merlin.
☐ St. Michael's Mount, off the coast of Penzance, rising 250 feet from the area—part medieval, part 17th century.

Gardens
☐ The Abbey Gardens of Tresco on the Isles of Scilly, 735 acres with 5,000 species of plants from some 100 countries.

Day 2: Head for Penzance along the southern coast and visit St. Michael's Mount.

Day 3: After leaving Penzance, spend a leisurely day exploring little fishing villages and Land's End before journeying to St. Ives for the night.

Day 4: After a look at St. Ives in the morning, drive along the north Cornish coast to Port Isaac for lunch, staying overnight in Tintagel after a visit to King Arthur's legendary castle.

1. LOOE

20 miles W of Plymouth, 264 miles SW of London

GETTING THERE   By Train   Daily trains run from Plymouth, and rail connections can also be made from Exeter (Devon) and Bristol (Avon).

By Bus   Local bus companies have various routings from Plymouth into Looe. Ask at the tourist office in Plymouth for a schedule (see Chapter 12).

By Car   From Plymouth, take the A38 west, then the B3253.

ESSENTIALS   The **telephone area code** is 0503. The **Tourist Information Centre** (summer only) is at The Guildhall, Fore Street (tel. 0503/262072).

The ancient twin towns of East and West Looe are connected by a seven-arched stone bridge that spans the river. Houses on the hills are stacked one on top of the other in terrace fashion. In both fishing villages you can find good accommodations.

Fishing and sailing are two of the major sports, and the sandy coves, as well as East Looe Beach, are spots for seabathing. Beyond the towns are cliff paths and downs worth a ramble. Looe is noted for its shark fishing, but you may prefer simply walking the narrow, crooked medieval streets of East Looe, with its old harbor and 17th-century guildhall.

WHERE TO STAY & DINE

COMMONWOOD MANOR HOTEL, St. Martin's Rd., East Looe, Cornwall PL13 1LP. Tel. 0503/262929. 10 rms (all with bath), 1 suite. TV TEL
$ Rates (including English breakfast): £37 ($55.50) single; £66 ($99) double; from £80 ($120) suite. AE, MC, V. **Parking:** Free. **Closed:** Dec.
A family-operated, country-house hotel on the main Plymouth-Looe road (B3253) on the edge of town at the entrance to Looe, about a 12-minute walk from the harbor and the center of the resort, Commonwood Manor stands on a wooded hillside in some 3 acres of private grounds opening onto the Looe River Valley, with a heated swimming pool. Guests receive a warm welcome and are shown to one of the well-furnished and comfortably appointed bedrooms.

The meals are good, prepared with fresh ingredients, and dinners cost between £10 and £13 ($15 to $19.50).

FIELDHEAD HOTEL, Portuan Rd., Hannafore, West Looe, Cornwall PL13 2DR. Tel. 0503/262689. Fax 0503/264114. 14 rms (all with bath or shower). MINIBAR TV TEL
$ Rates (including English breakfast): £29–£37 ($43.50–$55.50) single; £58–£74 ($87–$111) double. AE, MC, V. **Parking:** Free. **Closed:** Jan.

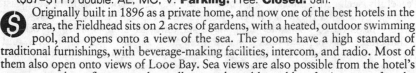 Originally built in 1896 as a private home, and now one of the best hotels in the area, the Fieldhead sits on 2 acres of gardens, with a heated, outdoor swimming pool, and opens onto a view of the sea. The rooms have a high standard of traditional furnishings, with beverage-making facilities, intercom, and radio. Most of them also open onto views of Looe Bay. Sea views are also possible from the hotel's restaurant where flowers and candles on the tables add a festive note for the home-cooked English and continental cuisine. A five-course meal costs £13 ($19.50) and up.

HANNAFORE POINT HOTEL, Marine Dr., Hannafore, West Looe, Cornwall PL13 2DG. Tel. 0503/263273. Fax 0503/263272. 37 rms (all with bath or shower). TV TEL
$ Rates (including English breakfast): £49.50–£51.50 ($74.30–$77.30) single; £93–£103 ($139.50–$154.50) double. AE, DC, MC, V. **Parking:** Free.
This rambling, gabled structure commands a fine prospect of the harbor, overlooking miles of Cornish coastline and one of the most beautiful bays in England. Hannafore Point is in the main center for shark and deep-sea fishing, and is ideal for exploring either Cornwall or parts of Devon.

In addition to the older bay-windowed rooms, newer sections have glass walls for viewing the harbor and St. George's Island. The entrance opens onto several levels of comfortable lounges and bars, with cantilevered stairs and balconies. The hotel has an elevator, and there is a comprehensive activity center with an indoor pool on the premises. Most of the front bedrooms have balconies, and each has a radio, hairdryer, and hot-beverage facilities. The panoramic view adds to the pleasure of dining in the

Headland Restaurant, where fresh ingredients are used in the fine Cornish and French cuisine. A table d'hôte meal in the restaurant costs £17.50 ($26.30) per person. The hotel also has a health club with a sauna.

TALLAND BAY HOTEL, Talland-by-Looe, Cornwall PL13 2JB. Tel. 0503/ 72667. Fax 0503/72940. 24 rms (all with bath), 1 suite. TV TEL **Directions:** Take the A387 4 miles southwest of Looe.
$ Rates (including half board): £53.50–£75.50 ($80.30–$113.30) single; £124–£171 ($186–$256.50) double; from £146 ($219) suite. AE, DC, MC, V. **Parking:** Free. **Closed:** Jan.
A country house dating from the 16th century, situated on 2½ acres, this hotel is the domain of Polly and Ian Mayman, who will direct you to local beaches and the croquet lawn. Its rectangular swimming pool is ringed with flagstones and a semitropical garden. Views from the tastefully furnished bedrooms include the sea and rocky coastline. Some of the bedrooms are in an annex.

Dining/Entertainment: The food is the best in the area, featuring excellently prepared seafood. Even if you aren't staying here, you may want to reserve a table. A la carte meals cost from £19.50 ($29.30) per person. A popular buffet lunch is served by the pool in summer. The restaurant is open for lunch Monday through Saturday from 12:30 to 2pm and on Sunday from 12:45 to 1:30pm; for dinner, daily from 7:30 to 9pm.

IN NEARBY ST. KEYNE

THE OLD RECTORY COUNTRY HOUSE HOTEL, Duloe Rd., St. Keyne, near Liskeard, Cornwall PL14 4RL. Tel. 0579/342617. 8 rms (all with bath or shower). TV **Directions:** From Liskeard, take the B3254 to St. Keyne, go through St. Keyne, and make a left turn at the sign.
$ Rates (including English breakfast): £25–£30 ($37.50–$45) single; £60 ($90) double. MC, V. **Parking:** Free.
Peacefully secluded 5 miles from Looe in the beautiful countryside of southeast Cornwall, the hotel overlooks 3 acres of gardens with views across the valley. The owners have raised the hotel to a high standard to complement the original architecture, with paneled doors, marble fireplaces, Persian rugs, velvet sofas, and crystal. All the comfortably furnished bedrooms have electric blankets and hot-beverage facilities; two rooms also feature four-posters.

An English and continental cuisine is served on Wedgwood china in the elegant dining room where home-prepared meals and a selection of table wines are offered. The cost is £12.50 ($18.80) and up. The restaurant is open only to hotel guests.

WELL HOUSE, St. Keyne, Liskeard, Cornwall PL14 4RN. Tel. 0579/ 342001. 10 rms (all with bath and shower), 1 suite. TV TEL **Directions:** From Liskeard, take the B3254 to St. Keyne, 3 miles away.
$ Rates (including continental breakfast): £60 ($90) single; £90–£105 ($135–$157.50) double; from £140 ($210) suite. MC, V. **Parking:** Free.
★ Well House is another of those *restaurants avec chambres* found occasionally in the West Country, and it's one of the best. Located 3 miles from Liskeard, it has 5 acres of gardens opening onto vistas of the Looe Valley. It offers beautifully furnished bedrooms, with many thoughtful extras, such as fresh flowers.

Dining/Entertainment: Guests flock here mainly for the cuisine, served daily 12:30 to 2pm and 7 to 9pm. A fixed-price luncheon goes for £21 ($31.50), with a five-course table d'hôte dinner offered for £25 ($37.50). You're ushered into an elegant dining room, where you can peruse the brief but imaginative and delectable menu. Carefully prepared and well presented, the dishes are made with tip-top ingredients that combine the best of British and continental cuisine.

Facilities: Swimming pool and all-weather tennis court.

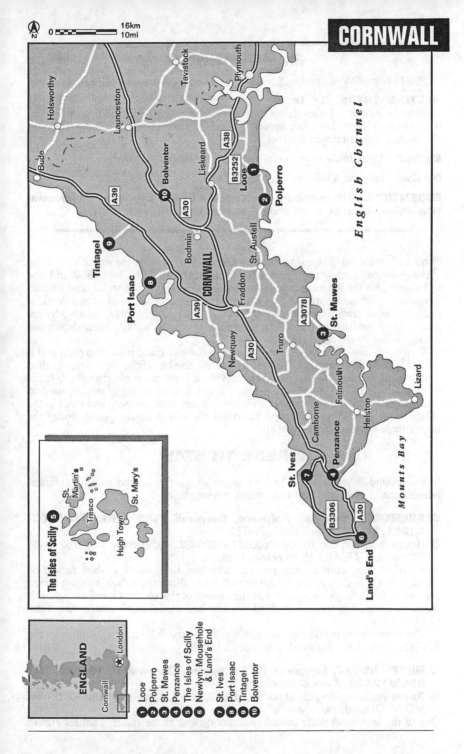

CORNWALL

0 ⊢━━━━┤ 16km
        10mi

N

English Channel

Plymouth
Tavistock
Holsworthy
Launceston
Bude
Bolventor
Liskeard
A38
B3252
Looe ①
Polperro ②
A30
A39
Tintagel ⑨
Bodmin
St. Austell
CORNWALL
A39
Port Isaac ⑧
Fraddon
A3078
St. Mawes ③
Newquay
Truro
A30
Falmouth
Lizard
Camborne
Helston
St. Ives
Penzance ④
⑦ St. Ives
B3306
A30
Land's End ⑥

Mounts Bay

The Isles of Scilly ⑤

St. Martin's
Tresco
Hugh Town
St. Mary's

ENGLAND

★ London
Cornwall

① Looe
② Polperro
③ St. Mawes
④ Penzance
⑤ The Isles of Scilly
⑥ Newlyn, Mousehole & Land's End
⑦ St. Ives
⑧ Port Isaac
⑨ Tintagel
⑩ Bolventor

2. POLPERRO

271 miles SW of London, 6 miles SW of Looe, 26 miles W of Plymouth

GETTING THERE   By Train   Most visitors arrive by car, but the nearest main-line station is at Liskeard, less than 4 hours from London's Paddington Station, with a branch line to Looe (see above). Taxis meet incoming trains to take visitors to the various little villages in the area.

By Bus   Local bus services are possible from Liskeard or Looe.

By Car   Take the A387 southwest from Looe.

ESSENTIALS   The **telephone area code** is 0503. There is no local **information office.** Ask at Looe (see above—summer only).

This ancient fishing village is reached by a steep descent from the top of a hill from the main road leading to Polperro. You can take the 4½-mile cliff walk from Looe to Polperro, but the less adventurous will want to drive. However, in July and August, motorists are forbidden to take cars into town unless they are booked at a hotel, in order to avoid traffic bottlenecks. There's a large parking area, which charges according to the length of your stay. For those unable to walk, a horse-drawn bus carries visitors to the town center.

Polperro is one of the handsomest villages in Cornwall, and it looks in parts as if it were still in the 17th century. The village is surrounded by cliffs, and a stream called the Pol runs through it. The heart of the village is its much photographed, much painted fishing harbor, where the pilchard boats, loaded to the gunwales, used to dock. At one time it was estimated that nearly every man, woman, and child in the village spent time salting down pilchards for the winter or smuggling. Today the tourist trade has replaced contraband.

WHERE TO STAY

In and around Polperro, you'll find a number of quite good and colorful cottages, houses, small hotels, and inns that receive paying guests.

CLAREMONT, Fore St., Polperro, Cornwall PL13 2RG. Tel. 0503/ 72241. 11 rms (all with bath). TV TEL
$ Rates (including English breakfast): £18–£26 ($27–$39) single; £32–£62 ($48–$93) double. AE, MC, V. **Parking:** Free.
This 17th-century cottage with postwar additions lies behind a white facade on the main street leading to the village center. It sits above the village, offering a view over its rooftops. Service and access to the owners of this pleasant hotel are probably the most compelling reasons to check in. The bedrooms are all comfortably furnished.

The owners serve genuine French cooking daily from 7:30 to 9pm, a dinner costing £11 ($16.50) and up. Bar meals begin at £5 ($7.50).

LANHAEL HOUSE, Langreek Rd., Polperro, Cornwall PL13 2PW. Tel. 0503/72428. 6 rms (2 with bath). TV
$ Rates (including English breakfast): £23 ($34.50) single; £35 ($52.50) double. MC, V. **Closed:** Nov–Mar.
One of the best moderately priced accommodations at the resort, Lanhael House,

situated off the road to Fowey, dates from the 17th century. Today it has many amenities, including a swimming pool and a terrace to capture the sun of the Cornish coast. The bedrooms are comfortable and attractively furnished, each with tea- or coffee-making equipment. An evening meal can be provided if arrangements are made in advance.

WHERE TO DINE

THE KITCHEN, Fish na Bridge. Tel. 72780.
Cuisine: ENGLISH/SEAFOOD. **Reservations:** Required.
$ Prices: Appetizers £2.50–£4.10 ($3.80–$6.20); main courses £8.50–£12.90 ($12.80–$19.40). MC, V.
Open: Apr–Oct, dinner only, Wed–Mon daily 7–9:30pm. Nov–Feb, dinner only, Fri–Sat 7–9:30pm. **Closed:** Jan.

 This pink cottage about halfway down to the harbor from the parking area was once a wagon builder's shop; it's now a restaurant run by Vanessa and Ian Bateson (Vanessa makes all the desserts and bakes the bread). It offers good English cookery, with everything homemade from the best fresh ingredients available. The menu changes seasonally, and it features prominently local fresh fish. Typical dishes include Fowey sea trout with lemon and herb butter or breast of duckling with blueberry and Drambuie sauce. Many vegetarian dishes are offered as main courses.

NELSON'S RESTAURANT, Big Green. Tel. 72366.
Cuisine: SEAFOOD. **Reservations:** Required.
$ Prices: Appetizers £2.50–£7.50 ($3.80–$11.30); main courses £5.50–£14 ($8.30–$21); 3-course table d'hôte lunch or dinner £13 ($19.50). AE, MC, V.
Open: Lunch Wed–Fri and Sun noon–1:45pm; dinner Tues–Sun 7–9:45pm. **Closed:** Mid-Jan to mid-Feb.
Situated in the lower reaches of Polperro, near the spot where the local river meets the sea, this is the only specifically built restaurant in town. Established in 1937, with a recent reincarnation from Peter and Betty Nelson, it features succulent preparations of local fish that arrive fresh from local fishing boats. The menu specialties change with the availability of local ingredients, but usually include Dover sole Nelson, carpetbagger's steak (stuffed with scallops and prawns), turbot with an oyster cream sauce, lobster, and several preparations of mussels and fresh crab. The decor is nautical, with lots of ships' wheels, diving helmets, and seafaring paraphernalia.

IN NEARBY PELYNT & LANREATH

If you find the busy activity of the two little harbors of Looe and Polperro too much for you, the pace of the nearby communities of Pelynt and Lanreath may be just right. The sleepy little village of Pelynt is just 3 miles north of Polperro. Peaceful Lanreath lies just 6 miles away from Polperro off the road to West Looe. Buses from Looe are infrequent and most visitors arrive by car or taxi from the Looe train station. The two places listed here number among England's major inns of character.

JUBILEE INN, Jubilee Hill, Pelynt, near Looe, Cornwall PL13 2JZ. Tel.
0503/220312. Fax 0503/220920. 12 rms (all with bath). TV TEL
$ Rates (including English breakfast): £30.50 ($45.80) single; £52 ($78) double. MC, V. **Parking:** Free.
Built in the 16th century, this inn takes its name from Queen Victoria's Jubilee celebration, when it underwent restoration. It's a comment on, rather than a

monument to, the past. The location is 4 miles from Looe and 3 miles from Polperro. The lounge has a hooded fireplace, with a raised hearth, Windsor armchairs, antique porcelain, and copper bowls filled with flowers cut from the garden behind the building. A glass-enclosed circular staircase takes you to the bedrooms. Fitting onto the outside, the winding stairway has been built to serve as a combined tower and hothouse. All but the three newest bedrooms have excellent 19th-century furnishings.

The dining room is elegantly Victorian, with mahogany chairs and tables. Vegetables come fresh from the inn's own garden. Both lunch and dinner are served in the bar, where bar snacks cost £3.50 to £6 ($5.30 to $9) per platter, or in the dignified dining room. There, à la carte meals cost around £15 to £25 ($22.50 to $37.50) each.

PUNCH BOWL INN, Lanreath, near Looe, Cornwall PL13 2NX. Tel. 0503/220218. 14 rms (12 with bath). TV **Directions:** From Polperro, take the B3359 north.
$ Rates (including English breakfast): £22.50 ($33.80) single without bath, £30 ($45) single with bath; £44 ($66) double without bath, £57 ($85.50) double with bath. MC, V. **Parking:** Free.

First licensed in 1620, the Punch Bowl has since served as a courthouse, coaching inn, and rendezvous for smugglers. Today its old fireplaces and high-backed settles, as well as its bedrooms (some with four-posters), provide hospitality. There is a modern lounge, TV room, air-conditioned cocktail bar, and an additional bedroom wing.

Even if you're not stopping over, you may sample the fare or drinks in one of the kitchens (really bars, among the few "kitchens" licensed in Britain as "bars"). In the Stable Restaurant, with its Tudor beams and fireplace, you order à la carte, from a bowl of soup to steak. Meals cost £10 ($15). Food is served from noon to 2pm and 7 to 9:30pm daily.

3. ST. MAWES

300 miles SW of London, 2 miles E of Falmouth, 18 miles S of Truro

GETTING THERE **By Train** Trains leave from London's Paddington Station for Truro several times a day, requiring 4½ hours for the trip. Passengers transfer at Truro to one of the two buses that make the 45-minute bus trip from Truro to St. Mawes. Much easier and better is to hire a taxi from either Truro or, even better, from the village of St. Austell, which is the train stop *before* Truro.

By Bus Buses depart from London's Victoria Coach Station several times a day for Truro, requiring 6 hours for the trip. Most visitors prefer the train.

By Car To reach St. Mawes, turn left off the A390 (the main road along the southern coast of Cornwall), at a junction 4 miles past St. Austell onto the Tregony road which will take you into St. Mawes.

By Ferry There is a ferry traveling to St. Mawes from both Falmouth and Truro, but schedules are erratic, varying with the tides and the weather conditions.

ESSENTIALS The **telephone area code** is 0326.

Overlooking the mouth of the Fal River, St. Mawes is often compared to a port on the French Riviera—it's sheltered from northern winds, and subtropical plants can grow here. From the town quay, you can take a boat to Frenchman's Creek and

Helford River, as well as other places. St. Mawes is noted for its sailing, boating, fishing, and yachting, and half a dozen sandy coves lie within 15 minutes by car from the port. The town, built on the Roseland Peninsula, makes for interesting walks, with its colorful cottages and sheltered harbor. On Castle Point, Henry VIII ordered the construction of St. Mawes Castle.

WHERE TO STAY & DINE

THE IDLE ROCKS, Tredenham Rd., St. Mawes, Cornwall TR2 5AN. Tel. 0326/270771. Fax 0326/270062. 24 rms (all with bath). TV TEL
$ Rates (including half board): £62–£78 ($93–$117) single; £114–£116 ($171–$174) double. MC, V. **Parking:** Free.
This solid old building right on the seawall sports gaily colored umbrellas and tables lining the terrace. Water laps at the wall, and the site opens onto views over the river and the constant traffic of sailing boats and dinghies. The bar serves tasty lunch snacks, including fresh seafood caught locally. Most of the bedrooms have sea or river views, and they're equipped with central heating, hot-beverage facilities, radios, intercoms, and private baths or showers. The 15 units in the main hotel building charge higher rates; there are nine more rooms in an annex. Golf is available at the Truro Golf Club at reduced greens fees.

THE RISING SUN, The Square, St. Mawes, Cornwall TR2 5DJ. Tel. 0326/270233. 12 rooms (all with bath). TV TEL
$ Rates (including English breakfast): £37 ($55.50) per person, single or double. AE, MC, V. **Parking:** Free.
Converted from a quartet of 17th-century fishing cottages, with a flower-draped flagstone terrace out in front, this colorful seafront inn in the center of town oozes charm. Known as one of Cornwall's best inns and owned by the Austell Breweries, it devotes at least some of its ground floor to one of St. Mawes's busiest pubs. This is a rustically appealing place with stone accents, a fireplace, and bar snacks priced at £1.85 to £9 ($2.80 to $13.50). The inn's restaurant—a dignified room adjacent to the pub—has a reputation for good food, and you might want to patronize it even if you don't stay at the hotel. Table d'hôte meals begin at £18.50 ($27.80) each and feature a variety of fish dishes. The inn's bedrooms are functional and cozy, and each is equipped with tea- and coffee-making facilities, color TV, and phone.

THE TRESANTON, 27 Lower Castle Rd., St. Mawes, Cornwall TR2 5DR. Tel. 0326/270544. Fax 0326/270002. 21 rms (all with bath), 1 suite. TV TEL
Directions: Follow the road along the harbor to St. Mawes Castle; the hotel is 250 yards from the castle.
$ Rates (including half board): £63 ($94.50) single; £90–£116 ($135–$174) double; £92 ($138) per person in a suite. MC, V. **Parking:** Free. **Closed:** Oct 31–Dec 23 and Jan–Mar 1.
★ This hotel is composed of what were originally three 18th- and 19th-century private houses, one beside the road and the other halfway up the hill. (The third building houses the hotel's genial staff.) The largest of the three buildings lies away from the traffic and has spacious veranda terraces, with many places to sit outside among the many flowers, looking across the bay. One reader wrote: "It's quite simply the most charming and delightful hotel I have ever stayed in." The bedrooms are fresh and bright, furnished for the most part in the French country-house manner, and are stocked with sewing kits, tissues, and books; all have a private bath and face the sea. The lounge has an open fireplace and comfortable chairs.
The dining room, also overlooking the sea, has attractive murals and a decor designed to carry the eye from the house to the sun terraces, the subtropical gardens,

and the sea beyond. The menu wisely emphasizes fish dishes and serves à la carte dinners for around £16 ($24) each.

---

4. PENZANCE

280 miles SW of London, 77 miles SW of Plymouth

GETTING THERE   By Train   British Rail runs 10 daily express trains from Paddington Station in London to Penzance (trip time: 5 hr.) and the one-way cost is £58 ($87).

By Bus   The Rapide, run by National Express from Victoria Coach Station in London (tel. 071/730-0202), costs £29 ($43.50) for the one-way trip from London, about 8 hours. The buses have toilets and reclining seats, and a hostess dispenses coffee, tea, and sandwiches.

By Car   Continue southwest across Cornwall on the A30 all the way to Penzance.

ESSENTIALS   The **telephone area code** is 0736. The **Tourist Information Centre** is on Station Road (tel. 0736/62207).

This little harbor town, which Gilbert and Sullivan made famous, is at the end of the Cornish Riviera. It is noted for its moderate climate (it's one of the first towns in England to blossom with spring flowers), and summer throngs descend for fishing, sailing, and swimming. Overlooking Mount's Bay, Penzance is graced in places with subtropical plants, including palm trees.

Those pirates in *The Pirates of Penzance* were not entirely fictional. The town was raided by Barbary pirates, destroyed in part by Cromwell's troops, sacked and burned by the Spaniards, and bombed by the Germans. In spite of its turbulent past, it offers tranquil resort living today.

The most westerly town in England, Penzance makes a good base for exploring Land's End, the Lizard peninsula, St. Michael's Mount, the old fishing ports and artists' colonies of St. Ives, Newlyn, and Mousehole—even the Isles of Scilly.

WHAT TO SEE & DO

CASTLE, on St. Michael's Mount, Mount's Bay. Tel. 710507.

⭐ Rising about 250 feet from the sea, St. Michael's Mount is topped by a partially medieval, partially 17th-century castle; it's 3 miles east of Penzance, and is reached at low tide by a causeway. At high tide the mount becomes an island, reached only by motor launch from Marazion. A Benedictine monastery, the gift of Edward the Confessor, stood on this spot in the 11th century. The castle, with its collections of armor and antique furniture, is open, weather and tide permitting, from the beginning of April to the end of October, Monday through Friday from 10:30am to 4:45pm. In winter, you can go over only when the causeway is dry. There is a tea garden on the island, as well as a National Trust restaurant, both open in summer. The steps up to the castle are steep and rough, so wear sturdy shoes. To avoid disappointment, it's a good idea to call the number listed above to learn the state of the tides, especially during the cooler months.

Admission: £3 ($4.50) adults, £1.50 ($2.30) children.

Open: Apr–Oct, Mon–Fri 10:30am–4:45pm; Nov–Mar, Mon, Wed, and Fri by conducted tour only leaving at 11am, noon, 2pm, and 3pm, weather and tide permitting. **Bus:** 20, 21, or 22 from Penzance to Marazion, the town opposite St. Michael's Mount.

MINACK THEATRE, Porthcurno. Tel. 810694.
At this unique theater, located 9 miles from Penzance, 750 people can watch the show, usually a play or musical, in the amphitheater, and also see the rocky coast beyond the stage. There's also an exhibition hall that houses a permanent record of the life and work of Rowena Cade, creator of the theater, and gives you the opportunity to visit the theater outside of performance times.

Admission: Tickets, £5 ($7.50). Tours, £1.50 ($2.30), given daily 10am–5:30pm.
Open: Exhibition hall, Easter–Oct 30. Performances, end of May to mid-Sept, matinees at 2pm, evening shows at 8pm. **Directions:** Leave Penzance on the A30 heading toward Land's End. After 3 miles, bear left onto the B3283 and follow the signs to Porthcurno.

WHERE TO STAY

ABBEY HOTEL, Abbey St., Penzance, Cornwall TR18 4AR. Tel. 0736/66906. Fax 0736/51163. 7 rms (all with bath), 1 suite. TV
$ Rates (including English breakfast): £60–£65 ($90–$97.50) single; £75–£110 ($112.50–$165) double; from £120 ($180) suite. AE, MC, V. **Parking:** Free.
A well-preserved place dating back to 1660, the Abbey is frequented by discerning guests. The bonus is its situation—on a narrow side street on several terraces directly overlooking Penzance Harbour. The bedrooms are stylishly furnished. The owners, Michael and Jean Cox, bring vitality, style, and charm to the hotel business. Mrs. Cox is the former international model, Jean Shrimpton.

You can take a room and breakfast at the Abbey, or have dinner in the restaurant downstairs. Behind the hotel is a tiny formal garden on two tiers, each with a view of the water. Here the herbs are grown that are used to spice the delicately flavored meats in the restaurant downstairs. Sample dinner dishes include homemade soups, mackerel pâté, fresh local fish dishes, and generally a roast joint. Everything is fresh and delicately cooked; dinner begins at £21.50 ($32.30).

THE GEORGIAN HOUSE, 20 Chapel St., Penzance, Cornwall TR18 4AE. Tel. 0736/65664. 12 rms (6 with bath or shower). TV TEL
$ Rates (including English breakfast): £18 ($27) single without bath, £24 ($36) single with bath; £30 ($45) double without bath, £37 ($55.50) double with bath. AE, MC, V. **Parking:** Free.
The former home of the mayors of Penzance, reputedly haunted by the ghost of a Mrs. Baines, who owned it hundreds of years ago, has been completely renovated into an intimate hotel, whose bright, cozy rooms all have hot and cold water basins, and tea and coffee makers. The house is centrally heated, with a comfortable reading lounge, a licensed bar with a nautical motif, and an intimate dining room, where good Cornish meals are served from April to October. The house takes guests all year.

TARBERT HOTEL, 11 Clarence St., Penzance, Cornwall TR18 2NU. Tel. 0736/63758. 12 rms (all with bath). TV TEL
$ Rates (including English breakfast): £30 ($45) single; £60 ($90) double. Half board £43 ($64.50) per person. AE, DC, MC, V. **Parking:** Free.
In the center of town, this Georgian town-house hotel is one of the better choices in Penzance. It's small and popular, so reservations are always advisable for a summer visit. The well-furnished and comfortable bedrooms are well maintained. Only two singles are available. The hotel also serves an evening meal, costing from £13 ($19.50),

but arrangements should be made in advance. Bar lunches are also served but for residents only.

WHERE TO DINE

BERKELEY, Abbey St. Tel. 62541.
   Cuisine: ENGLISH. **Reservations:** Recommended.
$ **Prices:** Appetizers £2.75–£5 ($4.10–$7.50); main courses £6.50–£14.50 ($9.80–$21.80). AE, MC, V.
   Open: July–Sept, dinner only, Mon–Sat 7:30pm–1am. Oct–June, dinner only, Thurs–Sat 7:30pm–1am.

On a side street off Chapel Street near the Abbey Hotel, at the rear of Admiral Benbow's Restaurant and Bar, this sophisticated rendezvous has exposed stone, plush banquettes, and touches of glitter. Some of the taped jazz music and much of the atmosphere evokes a setting of some 50 years ago. You get good honest cookery here, not flights of fancy. Try, for example, the whole Dover sole cooked in butter with lemon juice, filet steak with a creamy garlic-and-pepper sauce, or perhaps scallops Breton style.

HARRIS'S RESTAURANT, 46 New St. Tel. 64408.
   Cuisine: FRENCH/ENGLISH. **Reservations:** Recommended.
$ **Prices:** Appetizers £3.25–£6.50 ($4.90–$9.80); main courses £9.50–£15.50 ($14.30–$23.30). AE, DC, MC, V.
   Open: Lunch Tues–Sat noon–1:45pm; dinner Mon–Sat 7–10pm. **Closed:** Nov.

Down a narrow cobblestone street off Market Jew Street, opposite Lloyds Bank, this warm, candlelit place has a relaxed atmosphere. Light lunches, served upstairs, include crab Florentine, lobster salad, and salade niçoise. Dinner is more elaborate, offering breast of duckling in a port wine sauce, filet steak with a red wine and wild-mushroom sauce, and lamb with crabapple jelly and rosemary.

---

5. THE ISLES OF SCILLY

27 miles WSW of Land's End

GETTING THERE   By Plane or Helicopter   Isles of Scilly Skybus, Ltd. (tel. 0736/62009) operates between two and eight flights per day, depending on the season, between Penzance's Land's End Airport and Hugh Town on St. Mary's Island. Flight time on the eight-passenger fixed-wing planes is 20 minutes each way. The round-trip fare costs £50 ($75) for same-day return, and £76 ($114) if you plan to stay over for the night.

There's also a helicopter service maintained by British International Helicopters at the Penzance Heliport (tel. 0736/63871), which operates, weather permitting, between 2 and 12 daily helicopter flights between Penzance and both St. Mary's and the less populated island of Tresco. Flight time is 20 minutes from Penzance to either island. A same-day round-trip fare costs £52 ($78), rising to £80 ($120) if you spend a night or more on the island. A bus, whose timing coincides with the departure of each helicopter flight, runs to the heliport from the railway station in Penzance for a cost of £1 ($1.50) per person each way.

By Rail   The rail line ends in Penzance (see above).

By Ship   Slower but perhaps more romantic, you can travel via the Isles of Scilly Steamship Co., Ltd., Quay Street, Penzance (tel. 0736/62009), which offers daily runs between Penzance and the Scillies between April and October. The trip from Penzance to Hugh Town, St. Mary's, takes 2 hours 40 minutes, with continuing service on to Tresco. Steamships depart Monday to Friday at 9:15am, returning from St. Mary's at 4:30pm. Saturday schedules vary according to the time of year, sometimes with two sailings a day. In winter, service is much more limited. A same-day round-trip ticket from Penzance to St. Mary's costs £29 ($43.50) for adults, £15 ($22.50) for children under 15. An onward ticket from St. Mary's to Tresco costs an additional £6 ($9).

ESSENTIALS The **telephone area code** is 0720. For information about Tresco's boat schedules, possible changes in hours and prices at the Abbey Gardens, and other matters, call 0720/22849. St. Mary's **Tourist Information Office** is at Porthcressa Bank, St. Mary's (tel. 0720/22536).

I t's only a short trip from Penzance to the Isles of Scilly, which lie off the Cornish coast. There are five inhabited and more than 100 uninhabited islands in the group. Some are only a few square miles, while others, such as the largest, St. Mary's, encompass some 30 square miles. Three of these islands—Tresco, St. Mary's, and St. Agnes—attract visitors from the mainland. Early flowers are the main export and tourism the main industry.

The Isles of Scilly were known to the early Greeks and the Romans, and in Celtic legend they were inhabited entirely by holy men. There are more ancient burial mounds on these islands than anywhere else in southern England, and artifacts have clearly established that people lived here more than 4,000 years ago. Today there is little left of this long history for the visitor to see.

St. Mary's is the capital, with about seven-eighths of the total population of all the islands, and it is here that the ship from the mainland docks at Hugh Town. However, if you wish to make this a day visit, I recommend the helicopter flight from Penzance to Tresco, the neighboring island, where you can enjoy a day's walk through the 735 acres, mostly occupied by the Abbey Gardens.

TRESCO

No cars or motorbikes are allowed on Tresco, but bikes can be rented by the day; the hotels use a special wagon towed by a farm tractor to transport guests and luggage from the harbor.

The ✿ **Abbey Gardens** are the most outstanding features of Tresco, started by Augustus Smith in the mid-1830s. When he began his work, the area was a barren hillside, a fact visitors now find hard to believe.

The gardens are a nature-lover's dream, with more than 5,000 species of plants from some 100 different countries. The old abbey, or priory, now in ruins, is said to have been founded by Benedictine monks in the 11th century, although some historians date it from 964. Of special interest in the gardens is Valhalla, a collection of nearly 60 figureheads from ships wrecked around the islands; these gaily painted figures from the past have a rather eerie quality, each one a ghost with a different story to tell. Hours are 10am to 4pm daily. Admission is £3 ($4.50) for adults, £1.50 ($2.30) for children under 14.

After a visit to the gardens, take a walk through the fields, along paths, and across dunes thick with heather. Flowers, birds, shells, and fish are abundant. Birds are so unafraid that they land within a foot or so of you and feed happily. You can call 0720/22849 for information about the abbey.

WHERE TO STAY

THE ISLAND HOTEL, Old Grimsby, Tresco, Isles of Scilly, Cornwall TR24 OPU. Tel. 0720/22883. Fax 0720/23008. 39 rms (all with bath), 1 suite. MINIBAR TV TEL

$ Rates (including half board): £80–£95 ($120–$142.50) single; £140–£220 ($210–$330) double; £190–£240 ($285–$360) suite. AE, MC, V. **Closed:** Nov–Mar.

⭐ This is considered the finest hotel in the Scillies, located at Old Grimsby near the northeastern shore of Tresco. It was established in 1960, when a late 19th-century stone cottage was enlarged with conservatory-style windows and a series of long and low extensions. Today, the plant-filled interior provides a feeling not unlike what you might experience in the Caribbean, with water views and lots of inside greenery. Some rooms overlook the sea, others face inland, and all were renovated in 1990. All are comfortably furnished with easy chairs, storage spaces, and drying racks. The hotel is noted for its subtropical garden. Nonresidents pay around £25 ($37.50) for a five-course evening meal.

NEW INN, Tresco, Isles of Scilly, Cornwall TR24 0QQ. Tel. 0720/ 22844. Fax 0720/22939. 12 rms (all with bath). TEL
$ Rates (including half board): £35–£56 ($52.50–$84) per person, single or double occupancy, depending on the season. MC, V.
Composed of an interconnected row of 19th-century fishermen's cottages and shops, much enlarged since its transformation into a hotel, this establishment lies in the center of the island, beside its unnamed main road. Much of its income derives from its status as a pub, which offers an outdoor area for those who wish to picnic or drink a glass of ale. Inside, the bar is a meeting place for locals and visitors alike. Lunch snacks are available, and a bar meal costs £5 ($7.50) and up for two courses. Fixed-price dinners cost £16.50 ($24.80) and are served nightly between 7:30 and 8:30pm. The pictures in the bar show many of the ships that sank or foundered around the islands in the past, as well as some of the gigs used in pilotage, rescue, smuggling, and pillage. The inn has a heated outdoor swimming pool.

ST. MARY'S

GETTING AROUND Cars are available but hardly necessary. The **Island Bus Service** has a basic charge of £1 ($1.50) from one island point to another. Children ride for half fare.

Bicycles are one of the most practical means of transport. **Buccabu Bicycle Rentals,** Porthcressa, St. Mary's (tel. 22289), is the major rental agency. The cost, depending on the type of bicycle you want, starts at £4.50 ($6.80) per day for a mountain bike.

WHAT TO SEE & DO

The **Isles of Scilly Museum** illustrates the history of the Scillies from 2500 B.C. with drawings, artifacts from wrecked ships, and assorted relics discovered on the islands. The museum is located on Church Street in St. Mary's (tel. 22337). It's open March through October daily from 10am to noon and 1:30 to 4:30pm. From June through September it is also open from 7:30 to 9pm. In the off-season, it's open Wednesday from 2 to 4pm only. Admission is 75p ($1.10) for adults, 10p (20¢) for children.

WHERE TO STAY

CARNWETHERS COUNTRY HOUSE, Pelistry Bay, St. Mary's, Isles of Scilly, Cornwall TR21 0NX. Tel. 0720/22415. 10 rms (all with bath or shower).

$ Rates (including half board): £38–£48 ($57–$72) per person. No credit cards. **Closed:** Oct–Mar.

 Pelistry Bay, a secluded part of St. Mary's island, northeast of the airport, has a well-sheltered sandy beach, and this modernized farmhouse stands on top of a hill looking down to fields, beach, and the sea. You can walk at low tide across to the nearby uninhabited island of Tolls. The guesthouse rooms are spotless, warm, and comfortable. The main lounge is in two parts, one for conversation and reading, the other containing a library full of books about the island.

At dinner a limited choice of traditional English fare is offered. Dinner, served at 6:30pm, includes fresh local produce and homegrown vegetables. Breakfast is a substantial meal, the marmalade being a particular pride of the house. There is a well-stocked bar. The house has its own grounds and a croquet lawn. A heated outdoor swimming pool is in operation from May to September. Sauna and a games room are also available.

STAR CASTLE HOTEL, The Garrison, St. Mary's, Isles of Scilly TR21 0JA. Tel. 0720/22317. Fax 0720/22343. 24 rms (all with bath). TV TEL
$ Rates (including half board): £45–£65 ($67.50–$97.50) per person. No credit cards. **Parking:** Free. **Closed:** Mid-Oct to mid-Mar.
This hotel was originally built as a castle in 1593 in the shape of an eight-pointed star, to defend the Isles of Scilly against Spanish attacks in retaliation for the 1588 defeat of the armada. Because of the purpose of the original building, the hotel has views out to sea as well as over the town and the harbor. The great kitchen has a huge fireplace where a whole ox could be roasted. A young Prince of Wales (later King Charles II) took shelter here in 1643 when he was being hunted by Cromwell and his parliamentary forces. In 1933 another Prince of Wales officiated at the opening of the castle as a hotel—the man who succeeded to the throne as King Edward VIII but was never crowned.

The 16 bedrooms in the garden annex are extra-large units, each with bath and each opening directly onto the gardens. Eight double rooms are in the castle. There is a glass-covered, heated swimming pool, and the garden has many sheltered places for you to relax. Lunches tend to be simple pub-style platters whose orders are accepted in the cellar bar. Dinners are more elaborate, with most of the vegetables coming from the hotel's large gardens. Nonresidents who wish to dine pay £17.50 ($26.30) for a four-course dinner.

6. NEWLYN, MOUSEHOLE & LAND'S END

Newlyn: 1 mile S of Penzance
Mousehole: 3 miles S of Penzance, 2 miles S of Newlyn
Land's End: 9 miles W of Penzance

GETTING THERE **By Train** From London, journey first to Penzance (see above), then rely on local buses for the rest of the journey.

By Bus From Penzance, take bus A to Mousehole and bus no. 1 to Land's End. There is frequent service throughout the day.

By Car After reaching Penzance, cut south along the B3315.

ESSENTIALS The **telephone area code** is 0736.

NEWLYN

From Penzance, a promenade leads to Newlyn, another fishing village of infinite charm on Mount's Bay. In fact, its much-painted harbor seems to have more fishing craft than that of Penzance. Stanhope Forbes, now dead, founded an art school in Newlyn, and in the past few years the village has gained an increasing reputation for its artists' colony, attracting both serious painters and Sunday sketchers. From Penzance, the old fishing cottages and crooked lanes of Newlyn are reached by bus.

WHERE TO STAY & DINE

HIGHER FAUGAN HOTEL, Chywoone Hill, Newlyn, Penzance, Cornwall TR18 5NS. Tel. 0736/62076. 12 rms (all with bath). TV TEL **Directions:** Take the B3315 three-quarters of a mile south of Penzance.

$ Rates (including English breakfast): £38–£45 ($57–$67.50) single; £76–£94 ($114–$141) double. Children under 12 stay free in parents' room. AE, DC, MC, V. **Parking:** Free.

The structure was built in 1904 by painter Alexander Stanhope Forbes, whose work is now in demand, as is that of his wife, Elizabeth Adela Forbes, and many other artists from the "Newlyn" school. The spacious building's granite walls, big windows, and steep roofs are surrounded by 10 acres of lawn, garden, and woodland, all of which can be covered on foot by adventurous visitors. Amenities include a heated outdoor swimming pool, a putting green, a hard tennis court, a billiards room, and a dining room serving beautifully prepared English and continental specialties. Rooms are traditionally furnished and well maintained.

MOUSEHOLE

The Cornish fishing village of Mousehole attracts hordes of tourists, who, fortunately, haven't changed it too much. The cottages still sit close to the harbor wall; the fishermen still bring in the day's catch; the salts sit around smoking tobacco, talking about the good old days; and the lanes are as narrow as ever. About the most exciting thing to happen here was the arrival in the late 16th century of the Spanish galleons, whose sailors sacked and burned the village. In a sheltered cove of Mount's Bay, Mousehole (pronounced "*Mou*-sel") today has developed as the nucleus of an artists' colony.

WHERE TO STAY & DINE

CARN DU HOTEL, Raginnis Hill, Mousehole, Cornwall TR19 6SS. Tel. 0736/731233. 7 rms (all with bath). TV **Directions:** Take the B3315 from Newlyn past the village of Sheffield (1½ miles) and bear left toward Castallack; after a few hundred yards, turn left to Mousehole, indicated by a sign; coming down the hill, Carn Du is on the left facing the sea.

$ Rates (including English breakfast): £28 ($42) single; £56 ($84) double. AE, MC, V. **Parking:** Free.

Twin bay windows gaze over the top of the village onto the harbor with its bobbing fishing vessels. The hotel's bedrooms (all doubles or twins) offer radios and much comfort. Single occupancy of a double room carries a £5 ($7.50) surcharge. The owners will arrange sporting options for active vacationers but won't mind if you prefer to sit and relax.

The meals, going for £13.50 ($20.30), are straightforward and fresh, usually accompanied by a bottle of wine from the cellars. You might precede your meal with a drink in one of the lounges.

TAVIS VOR HOTEL, The Parade, Mousehole, Cornwall TR19 6PR. Tel. 0736/731306. 6 rms (3 with bath). TV
$ Rates (including English breakfast): £23.50 ($35.30) single without bath; £47 ($70.50) double without bath, £50 ($75) double with bath. No credit cards. **Parking:** Free.

Tavis Vor is set on its own half-acre garden and has a marvelous view overlooking the harbor and St. Michael's Mount. Almost directly opposite is a small island with the remains of a monastery. There is direct access to the beach from the grounds.

The hotel, which remains open all year, specializes in fresh seafood. Meals begin at £10 ($15) for three courses.

In Nearby Lamorna Cove

LAMORNA COVE HOTEL, Lamorna Cove, Cornwall TR19 6XH. Tel. 0736/731411. 18 rms (all with bath), 2 suites. TV TEL **Transportation:** Take a taxi from Penzance.
$ Rates (including English breakfast): £48.50–£58.50 ($72.80–$87.80) single; £67–£110 ($100.50–$165) double; from £120 ($180) suite. MC, V. **Parking:** Free.

Set near one of the most perfect coves in Cornwall, only 5 miles south of Penzance but seemingly inaccessible down a winding, narrow road, this hotel was skillfully terraced—after months of blasting—into a series of rocky ledges that drop down to the sea. Originally built as a chapel for Cornish miners, with a bell tower that has been saved despite numerous enlargements and improvements, the hotel offers a rocky garden that clings to the cliffsides and surrounds a small swimming pool and a sun terrace overlooking the sea. Bedrooms are comfortable and cozy with sea views. The hotel's bar is in the original chapel. Nearby, a long and narrow dining room runs the length of the building, and a public lounge is furnished with comfortable chairs, centered around a wintertime log fire.

If you don't have the time to stay at the hotel, stop in for one of its well-recommended meals. Bar snacks cost £2.50 to £5.75 ($3.80 to $8.60), and a full meal in the restaurant begins at around £17.50 ($26.30).

LAND'S END

Craggy Land's End is where England comes to an end. America's coast is 3,291 miles west of the rugged rocks that tumble into the sea beneath Land's End. Some enjoyable cliff walks and spectacular views are available here.

WHERE TO STAY & DINE

STATE HOUSE HOTEL, Land's End, Sennen, Cornwall TR19 7AA. Tel. 0736/871844. Fax 0736/871812. 34 rms (all with bath). TV TEL
$ Rates (including English breakfast): £35–£60 ($52.50–$90) single; £70–£120 ($105–$180) double. AE, MC, V. **Parking:** Free.

Situated behind a white facade in a complex of buildings rising from the scrubby landscape at the very tip of England, at the end of the main A30 road, this hotel has a panoramic clifftop position, exposed to the wind and sea spray. The rooms are attractively furnished and well maintained.

Much of the hotel's business comes from the many day visitors who stop by for a snack or cup of coffee in one of the three eating areas. Bar meals are served daily from noon to 2pm, and a cafeteria remains open all day. In the evening, more formal meals are served, mostly to residents, who pay between £15 ($22.50) and £20 ($30) for a fixed-price dinner.

7. ST. IVES

319 miles SW of London, 21 miles NE of Land's End, 10 miles N of Penzance

GETTING THERE By Train There is frequent service throughout the day between London's Paddington Station and the rail terminal at St. Ives (trip time: 5½ hr.).

By Bus Several coaches a day run from London's Victoria Coach Station to St. Ives (trip time: 7 hr.).

By Car Take the A30 across Cornwall, cutting northwest at the junction with the B3306, leading to St. Ives on the coast. During the summer months many of the streets in the center of town are closed to vehicles. You may want to leave your car in the Lelant Saltings Car Park, 3 miles from St. Ives on the A3074, and take the regular train service into town, an 11-minute journey. Departures are every half hour. It's free to all car passengers and drivers, and the parking charge is £3.50 ($5.30) per day. You can also use the large Trenwith Car Park, close to the town center, for 50p (80¢) and then walk down to the shops and harbor or take a bus costing 30p (50¢) for adults and 15p (20¢) for children.

ESSENTIALS The **telephone area code** is 0736. The **Tourist Information Centre** is at The Guildhall, Street-an-Pol (tel. 0736/796297).

This north-coast fishing village, with its sandy beaches, is England's most famous artists' colony. It's a village of narrow streets and well-kept cottages. The artists settled in many years ago and have integrated with the fishers and their families.

The artists' colony has been established long enough to have developed several schools or "splits," and they almost never overlap—except in a pub where the artists hang out, or where classes are held. The old battle continues between the followers of the representational and the devotees of the abstract in art, with each group recruiting young artists all the time. In addition, there are the potters, weavers, and other craftspeople—all working, exhibiting, and selling in this area.

A word of warning: St. Ives becomes virtually impossible to visit in August, when you're likely to be trampled underfoot by busloads of tourists, mostly the English themselves. However, in spring and early fall, the pace is much more relaxed, and a visitor can have the true experience of the art colony.

WHAT TO SEE & DO

TATE GALLERY, Portmeor Beach. Tel. 796226.
   This new branch of London's famed Tate Gallery exhibits changing groups of work from the Tate Gallery's preeminent collection of St. Ives painting and sculpture, dating from about 1925 to 1975. The gallery is administered jointly with the Barbara Hepworth Museum (see below). The collection includes examples of works by artists associated with St. Ives, including Alfred Wallis, Ben Nicholson, Barbara Hepworth, Naum Gabo, Peter Lanyon, Terry Frost, Patrick Heron, and Roger Hilton. The untutored Alfred Wallis, for example, was said to have had a profound influence on the work of Ben Nicholson. All the artists whose works are shown here had a decisive

effect on the development of painting in the U.K. in the second half of the 20th century. Forty to 50 works are on display at all times. The new museum occupies a spectacular site overlooking Portmeor Beach, close to the home of Alfred Wallis and to the studios used by many of the St. Ives artists. The museum is a three-story building, backing directly onto the cliff face and exploiting the dramatic sea views offered by the site.

Admission: £2.50 ($3.80) per adult, including one child under 11.

Open: Sept–May, Sun 1–5pm, Tues 11am–7pm, Wed–Sat 11am–5pm. June–Aug, Sun 1–7pm; Mon, Wed, Fri–Sat 11am–7pm; Tues and Thurs 11am–9pm.

Closed: Dec 24–26 and Jan 1.

THE BARBARA HEPWORTH MUSEUM AND GARDEN, Barnoon Hill. Tel. 796226.

Dame Barbara Hepworth lived at Trewyn from 1949 until her death in 1975 at the age of 72. In her will she asked that her working studio be turned into a museum where visitors for years to come could see where she lived and created her world-famed sculpture. Today the museum and garden are virtually just as she left them. On display are about 47 sculptures and drawings, covering the period from 1928 to 1974, as well as photographs, documents, and other Hepworth memorabilia. You can also visit her workshops, housing a selection of tools and some unfinished carvings. The museum is administered jointly with the Tate Gallery (see above).

Admission: Included in Tate Gallery admission (see above).

Open: Sept–May, Sun 1–5pm, Tues–Sat 11am–5pm. June–Aug, Sun 1–7pm; Mon, Wed, Fri–Sat 11am–7pm; Tues and Thurs 11am–9pm. **Closed:** Dec 24–26 and Jan 1.

WHERE TO STAY

GARRACK HOTEL, Burthallan Lane, Higher Ayr, St. Ives, Cornwall TR26 3AA. Tel. 0736/796199. Fax 0736/798955. 18 rms (all with bath or shower). TV TEL **Directions:** Take the B3306 to the outskirts of St. Ives; after passing a gas station on the left, take the third road left toward Portmeor Beach and Ayr (red telephone kiosk in fork) and after 200 yards look for the hotel sign. **Bus:** 16 or 17A.
$ Rates (including English breakfast): £33.50–£53.50 ($50.30–$80.30) per person. AE, DC, MC, V. **Parking:** Free.

 This vine-covered little hotel, once a private home, commands a panoramic view of St. Ives and Portmeor Beach from its 2-acre knoll at the head of a narrow lane. It's one of the friendliest and most efficiently run small, medium-priced hotels on the entire coast, with every room furnished in a warm, homelike manner. The atmosphere in the living room is inviting, with a log-burning fireplace, antiques, and comfortable chairs.

The Garrack belongs to Mr. and Mrs. Kilby, who are proud of their meals (see my dining recommendation, below). They have added a wooden leisure building to the hotel with a swimming pool that has a Jacuzzi whirlpool and swim jet, a solarium, and a sauna, all with changing rooms and a small bar overlooking the lovely bay. On a patio, you can sunbathe. There is a launderette.

PEDN-OLVA HOTEL, The Warren, St. Ives, Cornwall TR26 2EA. Tel. 0736/796222. Fax 0736/797710. 35 rms (33 with bath).
$ Rates (including English breakfast): £38–£40 ($57–$60) single; £76–£80 ($114–$120) double. MC, V. **Parking:** £2 ($3).
You'll pass through the lobby to the lounges and restaurant before coming to the magnificent view over the bay that is the outstanding feature of this establishment, which was originally built in the 1870s as the home of the paymaster for the local mines, then transformed into a hotel in the 1930s. The bedrooms are well furnished

and maintained in modern style. The two single rooms with a shared bath cost exactly the same as those with a private bath. There are sun terraces with lounges and umbrellas and a swimming pool for those who don't want to walk down the rocky path to Porthminster Beach. If you crave solitude, however, scramble down the rocks to sunbathe just above the gentle rise and fall of the sea. A dinner costs £14.50 ($21.80) and up.

PORTHMINSTER HOTEL, The Terrace, St. Ives, Cornwall TR26 2BN. Tel. 0736/795221. Fax 0736/797043. 49 rms (all with bath). TV TEL
$ Rates (including English breakfast): £48–£55 ($72–$82.50) single; £92–£108 ($138–$162) double. AE, DC, V. **Parking:** Free.
This leading Cornish Riviera resort stands on the main road into town amid a beautiful garden and within easy walking distance of Porthminster Beach. Large and imposing, Porthminster is a traditional choice for visitors to St. Ives. With its staunchly Victorian architecture, it's warm and inviting. The bedrooms are spacious and well furnished.

Facilities include a sun lounge, a solarium, and a sauna, as well as a swimming pool that sees action from June to September. Bar lunches go for £7 ($10.50), with dinners costing £17.50 ($26.30) and up.

WHERE TO DINE

OLIVER'S RESTAURANT, in the Garrack Hotel, Burthallan Lane, Higher Ayr. Tel. 796199.
Cuisine: ENGLISH/INTERNATIONAL. **Reservations:** Recommended. **Directions:** See the Garrack Hotel, above. **Bus:** No. 16 or 17A.
$ Prices: Fixed-price dinner £15 ($22.50). AE, DC, MC, V.
Open: Dinner only, daily 7–8:30pm.

 The dining room at the Garrack Hotel, the domain of Mr. and Mrs. Kilby (see "Where to Stay," above), produces an excellent cuisine and, whenever possible, uses fresh ingredients from their own garden. The hotel dining room, open to nonresidents, offers regular à la carte listings, plus a cold buffet or snacks at the bar. The menu features some of the finest of English dishes, such as roast shoulder of lamb with mint sauce, fried filet of plaice, and a wide sampling of continental fare, such as filet of bass meunière, and escalopes de veau Cordon Bleu. Live lobsters swim in the Kilbys' seawater tank until removed for preparation and cooking to order. Of course, if you order cold lobster salad, a little prior notice is required. Cheese and dessert trolleys are at your service.

8. PORT ISAAC

266 miles SW of London, 14 miles SW of Tintagel, 9 miles N of Wadebridge

GETTING THERE By Train Bodmin is the nearest railway station. It lies on the main line from London (Paddington Station) to Penzance (about a 4- or 4½-hour trip). From Bodmin, many hotels will send a car to pick up guests. If you reject the idea of a taxi and insist on taking a bus from Bodmin, you must change buses at Wadebridge, and connections are not good. Driving time from Bodmin to Port Isaac is 40 minutes. Taxis charge £20 ($30), but most hoteliers can arrange to have you picked up for £15 ($22.50).

By Bus A bus to Wadebridge goes to Port Isaac about six times a day. It's maintained by the Prout Brothers Bus Co. Wadebridge is a local bus junction to many other places within the rest of England.

By Car From London, take the M4 west, then cut south onto the M5. Head west again at the junction of the A39, continuing to the junction with the B3267, which you follow until you reach the signposted cutoff for Port Isaac.

ESSENTIALS The **telephone area code** is 0208.

Port Isaac remains the most unspoiled fishing village on the north Cornish coastline, in spite of large numbers of summer visitors. By all means wander through its winding, narrow lanes, gazing at the whitewashed fishing cottages with their rainbow trims.

WHERE TO STAY & DINE

PORT GAVERNE HOTEL, Port Gaverne, Port Isaac, Cornwall PL29 3SQ. Tel. 0208/880244. Fax 0208/880151. 18 rms (all with bath). TV TEL
$ Rates (including English breakfast): £39–£45 ($58.50–$67.50) per person. AE, DC, MC, V. **Parking:** Free. **Closed:** Mid-Jan to mid-Feb.

Built in the 17th century as a coastal inn for fishermen who needed a rest from their seagoing labors, the Port Gaverne, half a mile east of Port Isaac, today caters to vacationing families and couples. The bedrooms are well furnished with traditional styling and each has a radio. The hotel boasts a sheltered cove for boating and swimming, and can arrange shark fishing, pony trekking, and country hikes. Its painted facade is draped with vines, and inside you'll find a trio of comfortably atmospheric bars for relaxing beside a fireplace (one of them is a modified baking oven). Clusters of antiques, stained glass, and early photographs of Cornwall add sometimes bittersweet grace notes.

Dinners are served by candlelight and include locally caught lobster, fish, or crab in season, as well as locally raised lamb and beef. Bar snacks are also available, with dinners costing from £15 to £20 ($22.50 to $30).

SLIPWAY HOTEL, The Harbour Front, Port Isaac, Cornwall PL29 3RH. Tel. 0208/880264. 10 rms (5 with bath). TEL
$ Rates (including English breakfast): £19 ($28.50) single without bath; £38 ($57) double without bath, £52 ($78) double with bath. AE, MC, V. **Parking:** Free. **Closed:** Feb.

Originally built in 1527, with major additions in the early 1700s, this waterside building has seen more uses than any other structure in town, serving as everything from fishing cottages to the headquarters of the first bank here. Once the building was a lifeboat station for rescuing sailors stranded on stormy seas. The bedrooms are comfortable and cozy.

The hotel is better known for its restaurant. Its main dining room has a minstrel's gallery that occupies the cellar and part of the ground floor. At lunch, only bar snacks are available, but dinner is served nightly in the restaurant from 7:30 to 9:30pm, a three-course meal costing £20 ($30) and up.

---

9. TINTAGEL

264 miles SW of London, 49 miles W of Plymouth

GETTING THERE **By Train** The nearest railway station is in Bodmin, which lies on the main rail lines from London to Penzance. From Bodmin, you'll have to drive or take a taxi for 30 minutes to get to Tintagel, costing around £15 to £18 ($22.50 to $27). There is no bus service from Bodmin to Tintagel.

By Bus If you insist on taking the bus, passengers usually travel from London to Plymouth by bus or by train. In Plymouth, the bus and rail stations are almost adjacent to one another. There is a bus traveling from Plymouth to Tintagel, departing once a day, at 4:20pm, but it takes twice the time (2 hr.) that is required for a private car, which only takes about 50 minutes, since the bus stops at dozens of small hamlets along the way.

By Car From Exeter, head across Cornwall on the A30, continuing west at the junction with the A395. From this highway, various secondary roads (all signposted) lead to Tintagel.

ESSENTIALS The **telephone area code** is 0840.

On a wild stretch of the Atlantic coast, Tintagel is forever linked with the legends of King Arthur, Lancelot, and Merlin. If you become excited by tales of Knights of the Round Table, you can go to **Camelford**, 5 miles inland from Tintagel. The market hall there dates from 1790, but more interestingly, the town has claims to being Camelot.

WHAT TO SEE & DO

TINTAGEL CASTLE, half a mile northwest of Tintagel. Tel. 770328.
These 13th-century ruins of a castle—built on the foundations of a Celtic monastery from the 6th century—are popularly known as King Arthur's Castle. Standing 300 feet above the sea on a rocky promontory, to get to them you must take a long, steep, tortuous walk from the car park. In summer, many visitors make the ascent to **Arthur's lair**, up 100 rock-cut steps. You can also visit **Merlin's Cave.**
Admission: £2 ($3) adults, £1 ($1.50) children.
Open: Good Friday–Sept, daily 10am–6pm; Oct–Mar, Tues–Sun 10am–4pm.

THE OLD POST OFFICE, 3–4 Tintagel Center. Tel. 0208/4281.
This National Trust property was once a 14th-century manor, but since the 19th century it has had connections with the post office. It has a genuine Victorian post room.
Admission: £1.80 ($2.70) adults, 90p ($1.40) children.
Open: Apr–Sept, daily 11am–5:30pm; Oct, daily 11am–4:45pm.

WHERE TO STAY & DINE

BOSSINEY HOUSE HOTEL, Bossiney Rd., Bossiney, Tintagel, Cornwall PL34 0AX. Tel. 0840/770240. Fax 0840/770501. 20 rms (all with bath or shower). **Directions:** Take the B3263 half a mile northeast of Tintagel.
$ Rates (including English breakfast): £39.50–£41 ($59.30–$61.50) single; £63–£68 ($94.50–$102) double. MC, V. **Parking:** Free. **Closed:** Nov–Mar.
The hotel, in its inviting location, is comfortable, with a TV lounge and a well-stocked bar/lounge, which has a fine view of surrounding meadows marching right up to the tops of the cliff as well as the wide expanse of lawn with a putting green. A big English breakfast and other well-prepared meals are served in the dining room, which offers a lovely view out over the lawns. On the grounds is a Scandinavian log chalet with a heated swimming pool, a sauna, and a solarium. The bedrooms have streamlined modern styling.

OLD BOROUGH HOUSE, Bossiney, Tintagel, Cornwall PL34 0AY. Tel. 0840/770475. 5 rms (2 with bath).
$ Rates (including English breakfast): £24.50 ($36.80) single without bath, £27.50

($41.30) single with bath; £29 ($43.50) double without bath, £35 ($52.50) double with bath. No credit cards.

 Run by the Rayner family, this charming Cornish house has thick stone walls, small windows, low ceiling beams, and an illustrious history dating back to 1558. Most of what stands today was completed in the late 1600s, when it served as the residence for the mayor of Bossiney, the hamlet in which it is situated. (Bossiney was the seat from which Sir Francis Drake was elected for a brief period to the English Parliament.) To reach this house, walk north from the ruins of Tintagel Castle for 10 minutes. Accommodations are cozy, low-ceilinged, antique, and very comfortable. There's a sitting room with a TV for use by guests, and evening meals are available if advance notice is given for £9.50 ($14.30).

TREBREA LODGE, Trenale, near Tintagel, Cornwall PL34 0HR. Tel. 0840/770410. 8 rms (all with bath or shower). TV TEL **Directions:** From Tintagel, take the Boscastle road and turn right at the Roman Catholic church; take another right at the top of the lane.
$ Rates (including English breakfast): £37.50–£44 ($56.30–$66) single; £56–£66 ($84–$99) double. AE, MC, V. **Parking:** Free.

From the outside a stately home, on the inside this is an old (1315) Cornish farmhouse, lived in by the same family for more than 600 years. It looks straight out across fields to the sea, and each bedroom has a good view. The bedrooms come in many sizes, each with a radio. The original first-floor drawing room has been restored, and there is a traditional Victorian smoking room in addition to the bar. You can have drinks in another lounge with a fireplace. Dining is most informal, and all food is prepared on the premises from true English recipes. The lodge is open all year.

10. BOLVENTOR

260 miles SW of London, 20 miles E of Newquay

GETTING THERE   By Train   Trains whose final destination is Penzance leave London's Paddington Station, pass through Plymouth, then (several stations later) stop at Liskeard and then at Bodmin. Either of these stations lies close enough to Bolventor so that a taxi could be rented for the 20-minute ride on to Bolventor.

By Bus   There are no buses going to Bolventor.

By Car   Take the A30 across Cornwall to Launceston and follow the signs.

ESSENTIALS   The **telephone area code** is 0566.

This village east of Tintagel near Launceston is often visited by the fans of Daphne du Maurier since this was the setting for her novel *Jamaica Inn* (see below). The inn is named for the Caribbean island where the one-time owner of the inn had become prosperous from sugar on his plantation there. Opposite the inn, a small road leads to Dozmary Pool where the "waves wap and the winds wan" into which Sir Bedivere threw Excalibur at King Arthur's behest.

WHERE TO STAY & DINE

JAMAICA INN, Bolventor, Launceston, Cornwall, PL15 7TS. Tel. 0566/

86250. 6 rms (all with bath). TV **Directions:** Take the A30; the inn is between Bodmin and Launceston.

$ Rates (including English breakfast): £27.50–£35 ($41.30–$52.50) single; £45–£65 ($67.50–$97.50) double. MC, V. **Parking:** Free.

This long, low building was built in 1547 as a coaching inn. Today it has a room dedicated to the memory of Daphne du Maurier and her novel *Jamaica Inn*. The bedrooms include one four-poster room. The hotel has a bar (open all day) and a grill restaurant (open only in the evening). Snacks are available daily from 9:30am to 10pm.

WILTSHIRE, SOMERSET & AVON

For our final look at the "West Countree," we move now into Wiltshire, Somerset, and Avon, the most antiquity-rich shires of England. When we reach this area of pastoral woodland, London seems far removed from the bucolic life here.

When you cross into **Wiltshire,** you'll be entering a county of chalky, grassy uplands and rolling plains. Much of the shire is agricultural, and a large part is devoted to pastureland. Wiltshire produces an abundance of England's dairy products and is noted for its sheep raising. Here you'll traverse the Salisbury Plain, the Vale of Pewsey, and the Marlborough Downs (the latter making up the greater part of the landmass).

Most people agree that the West Country, a loose geographical term, begins at Salisbury, with its Early English cathedral. Nearby is Stonehenge, England's oldest prehistoric monument. Both Stonehenge and Salisbury are in Wiltshire.

The western shire of **Somerset** is composed of some of the most beautiful scenery in England. The undulating limestone hills of Mendip and the irresistible Quantocks are especially lovely in spring and fall. Somerset opens onto the Bristol Channel, with Minehead its chief resort.

Somerset is rich in legend and history, with particularly fanciful associations with King Arthur and Queen Guinevere, Camelot, and Alfred the Great. Its villages are noted for the tall towers of their parish churches.

You may end up in a vine-covered old inn, talking with the regulars, or you'll find a large estate in the woods surrounded by bridle paths and sheep walks (Somerset was once a great wool center); or maybe you'll settle down in a 16th-century thatched stone farmhouse set in the midst of orchards in a vale. By the way, Somerset is reputed to have the best cider anywhere.

Avon is the name that has been given to the area around the old port of Bristol, an area that used to be in Somerset. In addition to Bristol's seaports, the old Roman city of Bath is the main point of interest.

SEEING WILTSHIRE, SOMERSET & AVON
GETTING THERE

The M4 from London provides fast access to the region. British Rail maintains frequent service from London's Paddington Station, taking 70 to 90 minutes to reach Bath, for example. National Express coaches from London's Victoria Coach Station also service the area conveniently, taking 2½ hours, for example, to reach Bath.

WHAT'S SPECIAL ABOUT WILTSHIRE, SOMERSET & AVON

Great Towns/Villages

☐ Bath, a Georgian spa city beside the River Avon, known for its abbey and spa waters.

☐ Glastonbury, with its famed abbey, a country town with many religious and historical links—associated with the legends of King Arthur.

Ancient Monuments

☐ Stonehenge, a huge circle of lintels and megalithic pillars, 3,500 to 5,000 years old—the most important prehistoric monument in Britain.

☐ Old Sarum, outside Salisbury, the remains of an Iron Age fortification.

Buildings

☐ Glastonbury Abbey, the oldest Christian foundation and once the most important abbey in England.

☐ Wells Cathedral, one of the best examples of the Early English style of architecture, known for the medieval sculpture of its west front.

☐ Salisbury Cathedral, just as John Constable painted it, with its 404-foot pinnacle, the tallest in England.

Natural Spectacles

☐ Exmoor National Park, once the English royal hunting preserve, stretching for 265 square miles on the north coast of Devon and Somerset.

Palaces

☐ Wilton House, at Wilton, the magnificent home of the Earl of Pembroke, with 17th-century state rooms by Inigo Jones.

A SUGGESTED ITINERARY

Day 1: From London, head first for Salisbury to see its cathedral and spend the afternoon exploring the monument of Stonehenge.

Day 2: Head west in the morning for a visit to the abbey at Glastonbury, journeying to Wells in the north to see its cathedral. Stay overnight in Wells.

Day 3: Transfer to Bath for a full day of sightseeing.

Day 4: Head west for Bristol to see its attractions and spend the night.

---

1. SALISBURY

91 miles SW of London, 53 miles SE of Bristol

GETTING THERE   By Train   A Network Express train departs hourly from Waterloo Station in London bound for Salisbury (trip time: 2 hr.), and British Rail's Sprinter trains make a speedy journey from Portsmouth, Bristol, and South Wales, likewise departing hourly. There is also direct rail service from Exeter, Plymouth, Brighton, and Reading.

By Bus   Five National Express buses per day run from London Monday through Friday. On Saturday and Sunday four buses depart Victoria Coach Station heading for Salisbury (trip time: 2½ hr.).

By Car   From London, head west on the M3 to the end of the run, continuing the rest of the way along the A30.

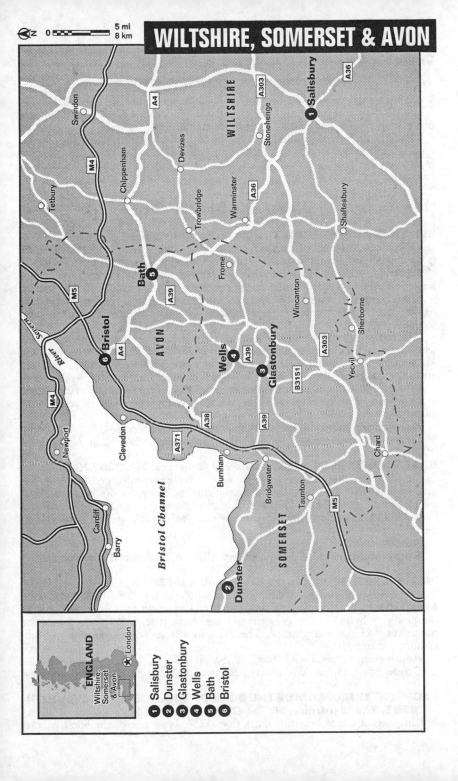

ESSENTIALS The **telephone area code** is 0722. The **Tourist Information Centre** is at Fish Row (tel. 0722/334956).

Long before you've even entered Salisbury, the spire of Salisbury Cathedral comes into view—just as John Constable painted it so many times. The 404-foot pinnacle of the Early English and Gothic cathedral is the tallest in England.

Salisbury, or New Sarum, lies in the valley of the Avon River, and is a fine base for touring such sights as Stonehenge. Filled with Tudor inns and tearooms, it is known to readers of Thomas Hardy as Melchester and to fans of Anthony Trollope as Barchester.

WHAT TO SEE & DO

SALISBURY CATHEDRAL, The Close. Tel. 328726.

You can search all of England, but you'll find no better example of the Early English, or pointed, style than Salisbury Cathedral. Construction was begun as early as 1220 and took 38 years to complete, which was fast in those days (it was customary for cathedral-building to take three centuries at least). The soaring spire was completed at the end of the 13th century. Despite an ill-conceived attempt at renovation in the 18th century, the architectural integrity of the cathedral has been retained.

The cathedral's 13th-century octagonal chapter house (note the fine sculpture), which is especially attractive, possesses one of the four surviving original texts of the Magna Carta, along with treasures from the diocese of Salisbury and manuscripts and artifacts belonging to the cathedral. The cloisters enhance the beauty of the cathedral, and the exceptionally large close, with at least 75 buildings in its compound (some from the early 18th century and others predating that), sets off the cathedral most effectively.

Admission: Cathedral, £1.50 ($2.30); chapter house, 50p (80¢).
Open: May–Aug, daily 8:30am–8:30pm; Sept–Apr, daily 8:30am–6:30pm.

BRASS RUBBING CENTRE, Cathedral Cloisters. Tel. 328726.

Here you can choose from a variety of exact replicas molded perfectly from the original brasses: local medieval and Tudor knights and ladies, famous historical faces, even Celtic designs. The £3 ($4.50) average charge made for each rubbing includes materials and instruction. You can also buy ready-made rubbings and historical gift items.

Admission: Free.
Open: Mid-June to late Sept, Mon–Sat 10am–6pm, Sun 11:15am–4pm.

MOMPESSON HOUSE, in the Close. Tel. 335659.

This is one of the most distinguished houses in the area. Built by Charles Mompesson in 1701, while he was Member of Parliament for Old Sarum, it is an outstandingly beautiful example of the Queen Anne style, well known for its fine plasterwork ceilings and paneling. There is also a magnificent collection of 18th-century drinking glasses.

Admission: £3 ($4.50) adults, £1.50 ($2.30) children.
Open: Apr–Oct, Sat–Wed noon–5:30pm or dusk.

REGIMENTAL MUSEUM OF THE DUKE OF EDINBURGH'S ROYAL REGIMENT, The Wardrobe, 58 The Close. Tel. 414536.

This elegant house originally dates from 1254. Now one of the finest military museums in the country, it has exhibits covering nearly 250 years of this famous regiment, including uniforms, pictures, weapons, and other militaria.

Admission: £1.50 ($2.30) adults, 70p ($1.10) children.

Open: Feb–Mar and Nov, Mon–Fri 10am–4:30pm; Apr–Oct, daily 10am–4:30pm.

WHERE TO STAY

EXPENSIVE

RED LION HOTEL, 4 Milford St., Salisbury, Wiltshire SP1 2AN. Tel. 0722/323334. Fax 0722/325756. 56 rms. TV TEL

$ Rates (including English breakfast): £60–£70 ($90–$105) single; £80–£125 ($120–$187.50) double. AE, DC, MC, V. **Parking:** Free.

Since the 1300s the Red Lion has been accommodating wayfarers who rumbled in stagecoaches from London across the Salisbury Plain to the West Country. Cross under its arch into a courtyard with a hanging, much-photographed creeper, a red lion, and a half-timbered facade, and you'll be transported back to an earlier era. However, the Red Lion has stayed abreast of the times, even installing an elevator. Each comfortable bedroom also has a radio, hot-beverage facilities, and hairdryer. The most expensive rooms feature a four-poster bed.

Many patronize the hotel for its continental and English cuisine. An à la carte luncheon begins at £9.50 ($14.30), and a three-course dinner goes for £14.50 ($21.80). The restaurant has a wattle-and-daub wall dating from 1230, and the antique-filled hotel is also noted for its clocks, including a skeleton organ clock in the reception hall. Meals are served daily from 12:30 to 1:45pm and 7 to 9pm.

THE ROSE AND CROWN, Harnham Rd., Salisbury, Wiltshire SP2 8JQ. Tel. 0722/327908, or toll free 0800/289330 in England. Fax 0722/339816. 28 rms, 1 suite. TV TEL **Directions:** Take the A3094 1½ miles from the center of town.

$ Rates (including English breakfast): £60–£70 ($90–$105) single; £90–£100 ($135–$150) double; from £135 ($202.50) suite. AE, DC, MC, V. **Parking:** Free.

This half-timbered, 13th-century gem stands with its feet almost in the River Avon, and beyond the water you can see the tall spire of the cathedral. You can easily walk over the arched stone bridge to the center of Salisbury from here in 10 minutes or so. The lawns and gardens between the inn and the river are shaded by old trees, and chairs are set out so you can enjoy the view and count the swans. The inn, part of the Queens Moat House Hotels chain, is made up of both a new and an old wing. The new wing is modern, but to me the old wing is more appealing, with its sloping ceilings and antique fireplaces and furniture. Each bedroom has a radio and hot-beverage facilities.

You can dine on English fare while overlooking the river. A luncheon goes for £10 to £14 ($15 to $21) and a dinner costs £15 ($22.50) and up. Across the courtyard are two taverns.

WHITE HART, 1 St. John St., Salisbury, Wiltshire SP1 2SD. Tel. 0722/327476, or toll free 800/435-4542 in the U.S. Fax 0722/412761. 68 rms, 2 suites. TV TEL

$ Rates: £75 ($112.50) single; £95 ($142.50) double; from £110 ($165) suite. Breakfast £7.95 ($11.90) extra. AE, DC, MC, V. **Parking:** Free.

Combining the best of old and new, the White Hart has been a Salisbury landmark since Georgian times. Its classic facade is intact, with tall columns crowning a life-size effigy of a hart. The older accommodations are traditional, and a new section has been added in the rear, opening onto a large parking area—like a motel. New-wing units are tastefully conceived and decorated. You can have your before-dinner drink in Wavell's Bar, followed by a meal in the Shire's Restaurant for £15.95 ($23.90).

MODERATE

GRASMERE, 70 Harnham Rd., Salisbury, Wiltshire SP2 8JN. Tel. 0722/ 338388. Fax 0722/339816. 5 rms (all with bath). TV TEL **Directions:** Take the A3094 1½ miles from the center of town.
$ Rates (including English breakfast): £45 ($67.50) single; £65 ($97.50) double. AE, DC, MC, V. **Parking:** Free.

 Operated by the Rose and Crown, also recommended, Grasmere stands near the confluence of the Nadder and Avon Rivers on 1½ acres of grounds. Constructed in 1896 for Salisbury merchants, the house still suggests a family home. Architectural features were retained as much as possible, including a "calling box" for servants in the dining room. Three of the luxurious bedrooms overlook the cathedral.

KING'S ARMS HOTEL, 9–11 St. John St., Salisbury, Wiltshire SP1 2SB. Tel. 0722/327629. Fax 0722/414246. 15 rms (all with bath or shower), 1 suite. TV TEL
$ Rates (including English breakfast): £45–£55 ($67.50–$82.50) single; £68–£88 ($102–$132) double; £98 ($147) suite. AE, DC, MC, V. **Parking:** Free.
You'll recognize this former coaching inn in black-and-white Tudor style by its leaded-glass windows, an old pub sign out front, and a covered entrance for alighting coach passengers. It is unsophisticated without being self-consciously so. A special feature is the William and Mary four-poster suite. The other bedrooms are cozy and well kept, with traditional styling. No one seems to know the age of the inn, although it's generally recognized that it was built before the cathedral. Conspirators helping Charles II flee to France were thought to have met here in the mid-17th century. The hotel features a good restaurant, fine old oak beams, the original ironwork, a priest's hiding hole, and an Elizabethan fireplace. Have a pint of ale in the oak-beamed pub, sitting in a high-backed settle, warming yourself in front of the open fire.

THE NEW INN, 41–43 New St., Salisbury, Wiltshire SP1 2PH. Tel. 0722/327679. 8 rms (all with bath). TV TEL
$ Rates (including buffet breakfast): £35–£55 ($52.50–$82.50) single; £45–£65 ($67.50–$97.50) double. MC, V. **Parking:** Free.

This upmarket B&B is one of the finest in Salisbury but, despite its name, it isn't new at all. It's a 15th-century building whose walled garden backs up to the cathedral close wall. Bedrooms are cozy, heavily beamed, and evocative of an earlier century. The center of the inn is the serving bar, which is a common center for three outer rooms: one, a tiny sitting area; another, a tavern with high-backed settles and a fireplace; and the third, a lounge. Food and drink are available to nonresidents. In the pub, appetizers range from £2.45 to £5 ($3.70 to $7.50), with main courses costing from £5 to £10 ($7.50 to $15). Adjacent to the main building, The Old House Restaurant, with a Victorian decor, offers set lunches and four-course dinners costing from £15 to £20 ($22.50 to $30).

IN NEARBY DINTON

HOWARD'S HOUSE, Teffont Evias, Dinton, near Salisbury, Wiltshire SP3

5RJ. Tel. 0722/716392. Fax 0722/716820. 9 rms (all with bath). TV TEL
Directions: Take the A36 and A30 west of Salisbury for 10½ miles; it's on the
B3089.
$ Rates (including English breakfast): £70 ($105) single; £90 ($135) double. AE,
MC, V. **Parking:** Free.

★ On a lane opposite the Black Horse, this partial 17th-century dower house
stands in a medieval hamlet. It has been turned into one of the most appealing
small hotels and restaurants in the area. The Ford and Firmin families
combined their talent and money to convert this building into an exceptional
accommodation. The bedrooms are carefully furnished and great attention was given
to the decoration and comfort of the place. Plenty of towels are provided, for
example.

Even if you don't stay here, consider stopping by for a meal (but call for a table
first). Dinner is served nightly from 7 to 10pm, costing £28 ($42) and up for a
fixed-price meal. There are ample choices on the fixed-price menu. Try such dishes as
pigeon breasts with truffle gravy or a curry with chicken and mango. Toffee pecan pie
with crème fraîche makes a splendid dessert. A fixed-price lunch for £17.50 ($26.30) is
also served on Sunday from noon to 2pm. The hotel has attractive gardens, and on
chilly nights log fires burn.

WHERE TO DINE

CRUSTACEANS, 2–4 Ivy St. Tel. 333948.
Cuisine: SEAFOOD. **Reservations:** Recommended.
$ Prices: Appetizers £3.25–£8 ($4.90–$12); main courses £8.50–£21.50
($12.80–$32.30); 3-course lunch £13.95 ($20.90); 4-course dinner £19.50
($29.30). MC, V.
Open: Lunch Mon–Sat 11:30am–2pm; dinner Mon–Sat 7–10:30pm.
The best restaurant in town specializes in fish, from the north of Scotland all the way
to the Isles of Scilly (off the coast of Cornwall). Lemon and Dover sole are specialties,
but you'll find a complete array of seafood here, everything from langoustines and
tiger prawns to Devonshire turbot. Vegetarians will also be pleased with the menu. A
comprehensive wine list includes California wines.

HARPER'S RESTAURANT, 7–9 Ox Row, Market Sq. Tel. 333118.
Cuisine: ENGLISH. **Reservations:** Recommended.
$ Prices: Appetizers £1.70–£4.70 ($2.60–$7.10); main courses £7.90–£10.90
($11.90–$16.40); 3-course fixed-price meals £7.30 ($11) at lunch, £13.50
($20.30) at dinner. DC, MC, V.
Open: Lunch Mon–Sat noon–2pm; dinner Mon–Sat 6:30–10pm, Sun (Easter–
Oct) 6:30–9:30pm.
The chef-owner prides himself on specializing in "real food," homemade and
wholesome. The pleasantly decorated restaurant offers such à la carte selections as
homemade tuna cakes or Italian pasta diavolo, perhaps *lentejas* (a provincial Spanish
dish made with lentils, cumin, potatoes, and chorizo sausage). Luscious desserts
complete the menu. Special menus for children include fish fingers, beefburgers, or
sausages, all with french fries, beans, and ice cream.

SALISBURY HAUNCH OF VENISON, 1 Minster St. Tel. 322024.
Cuisine: ENGLISH. **Reservations:** Recommended.
$ Prices: Appetizers £1.50–£4 ($2.30–$6); main courses £8.50–£12 ($12.80–
$18); 3-course fixed-price menu £10.50 ($15.80); bar platters for lunches, light
suppers, and snacks £3–£5 ($4.50–$7.50). AE, DC, MC, V.
Open: Lunch daily noon–2pm; dinner daily 7–10:30pm. Pub, Mon–Sat 11am–

11pm, Sun noon–3pm and 7–10:30pm. **Closed:** Christmas–Easter, Mon–Wed for dinner.

Right in the heart of Salisbury, this creaky-timbered, 1320 chophouse serves excellent dishes, especially English roasts and grills. Stick to its specialties and you'll rarely go wrong. Diners with more adventurous palates will sample a bowl of game soup. The pièce de résistance of the inn is its local New Forest haunch of venison, with chestnut purée and red-currant jelly. For a bargain lunch, enjoy the bar snacks, including game pie made with venison.

The centuries have given a gleam to the oak furnishings, and years of polishing have worn down the brass. Twisting steps lead to tiny, cozy rooms (there is one small room with space for about four to sit, where you can saturate yourself in the best of England's yesterdays and todays). Two windows of the bar room overlook St. Thomas's cloisters.

IN NEARBY PITTON

SILVER PLOUGH, White Hill, Pitton, near Salisbury. Tel. 0722/72266.
   Cuisine: ENGLISH. **Reservations:** Recommended. **Directions:** Take the A30 5 miles east of Salisbury; it's at the southern end of the hamlet of Pitton.
$ Prices: Lunch bar snacks £4–£6 ($6–$9); 3-course fixed-price lunch £12.50 ($18.80); fixed-price dinner £16.95 ($25.40) for 2 courses, £19.95 ($29.90) for 3 courses. AE, DC, MC, V.
   Open: Restaurant, lunch daily noon–2pm; dinner Mon–Sat 7–10pm, Sun 7–9pm. Pub, Mon–Sat 11am–3pm and 6–11pm, Sun noon–3pm and 6–11pm. **Closed:** Dec 25–26 and Jan 1.

Built as a stone-sided farmhouse 150 years ago, the Silver Plough is now a charming and accommodating country pub with an attached restaurant. Specializing in wines and English cheeses, it contains heavily beamed ceilings hung with tankards, coachhorns, and other country-inspired memorabilia. Snacks available in the bar include, among others, ratatouille au gratin and grilled sardines with garlic butter and freshly baked bread. In the somewhat more formal dining room, the chef prepares such dishes as fresh Dorset mussels in a white wine, garlic, and cream sauce, sliced breast of duck in cracked pepper or orange sauce, and roast guinea fowl in a sharp strawberry sauce. The Silver Plough has known many famous visitors, but apart from displaying a signed letter from Queen Victoria thanking the women of England for their concern after the death of her husband, Albert, the management prefers to stick to its quiet, country atmosphere and to concentrate on making its guests feel at home.

EASY EXCURSIONS

OLD SARUM ✪ About 2 miles north of Salisbury off the A345 is Old Sarum, Castle Rd. (tel. 0722/335398), the remains of what is believed to have been an Iron Age fortification. The earthworks were known to the Romans as Sorbiodunum, and later to the Saxons. The Normans built a cathedral and a castle here in what was then a Middle Ages walled town. Parts of the old cathedral were taken down to erect the cathedral at New Sarum. Admission is £1.30 ($2) for adults, 65p ($1) for children. It's open from Good Friday to September, Tuesday through Sunday from 10am to 6pm; other times, Tuesday through Sunday from 10am to 4pm. Bus no. 5 runs every 15 minutes during the day from the Salisbury bus station.

WILTON HOUSE ✪ In the town of Wilton, 2½ miles to the west of Salisbury, is one of England's great country estates, the home of the earls of Pembroke. Wilton House in Wilton, on the A30 (tel. 0722/743115), dates from the 16th century, but has undergone numerous alterations, most recently in Victoria's day. It's noted for its 17th-century state rooms by the celebrated architect Inigo Jones. Many famous personages have either lived at or visited Wilton; it is believed that Shakespeare's troupe entertained here. Plans for the D-day landings at Normandy were laid out here in utmost secrecy by Eisenhower and his advisers.

The house is filled with beautifully maintained furnishings, and displays world-class art, including works by Sir Anthony Van Dyck, Rembrandt, Rubens, and Reynolds. An exhibition, "Times Past—Times Present," is a documentary film on the lives and times of the earls of Pembroke. Some 7,000 model soldiers are displayed in diorama scenes, along with the Pembroke Palace dollhouse and a true-to-life reconstruction of a Tudor kitchen. Kids will enjoy a huge adventure playground.

Growing on the 20-acre estate are giant cedars of Lebanon, the oldest of which were planted in 1630. The Palladian Bridge was built in 1737 by the ninth Earl of Pembroke and Roger Morris. You can walk through with guides in attendance; however, guided tours are by appointment only.

An inclusive ticket to the house, grounds, and exhibitions is £5 ($7.50) for adults, £3.50 ($5.30) for children under 16. A ticket to the grounds only is £2 ($3) for adults, £1.50 ($2.30) for children. Wilton House is open April to mid-October, daily 11am to 6pm. Last admission is 4:45pm. To get here from Salisbury, take bus no. 60 or 61.

STONEHENGE ✪ Two miles west of Amesbury and about 9 miles north of Salisbury, at the junction of the A303 and the A344/A360, is the renowned Stonehenge, Stone Circle (tel. 0980/623108), believed to be anywhere from 3,500 to 5,000 years old. This huge circle of lintels and megalithic pillars is the most important prehistoric monument in Britain.

Some Americans are disappointed when they see that Stonehenge is nothing more than concentric circles of stones. Perhaps they do not understand that Stonehenge represents an amazing engineering feat since many of the boulders, the bluestones in particular, were moved many miles (perhaps from southern Wales) to this site.

The widely held view of the 18th- and 19th-century romantics that Stonehenge was the work of the Druids is without foundation. The boulders, many weighing several tons, are believed to have predated the arrival in Britain of that Celtic cult. Recent excavations continue to bring new evidence to bear on the origin and purpose of Stonehenge. Controversy surrounds the prehistoric site especially since the publication of *Stonehenge Decoded* by Gerald S. Hawkins and John B. White, which maintains that Stonehenge was an astronomical observatory—that is, a Neolithic "computing machine" capable of predicting eclipses.

Your ticket permits you to go inside the fence surrounding the site that protects the stones from vandals and souvenir hunters. You can go all the way up to a short rope barrier about 50 feet from the stones. If you don't have a car, you can take a bus from the Salisbury train station. The first bus—marked STONEHENGE—leaves Salisbury at 8:40am. The last bus back from Stonehenge is 4:15pm. Trip time is 40 minutes.

Admission is £2.70 ($4.10) for adults, £1.30 ($2) for children. Stonehenge is open April to September, daily from 10am to 6pm; October to March, daily from 10am to 4pm.

NETHER WALLOP On a country road between the A343 and the A30 east of Salisbury is the little village of Nether Wallop (not to be confused with Over Wallop or Middle Wallop in the same vicinity). Aficionados of television's "Mystery" series about Agatha Christie's Miss Marple will be interested in this village, used as Miss Christie's fictitious St. Mary Mead, home of Miss Marple. Visitors to Nether Wallop can easily identify the sites in many of the TV movies.

The village is about 12 miles from Stonehenge, 8 miles from Salisbury, and 10 miles from Winchester.

2. DUNSTER

3 miles SE of Minehead, 184 miles W of London

GETTING THERE   By Train   The best rail link is to Minehead via Taunton, which is easily reached on the main London-Penzance line from Paddington Station in London. From Minehead you have to reach Dunster by either taxi or coach.

By Bus   At Taunton, you can take one of the seven Southern National coaches (no. 28), leaving hourly Monday through Saturday; there is only one bus on Sunday. Trip time is 1 hour and 10 minutes. Buses (no. 38 or 39) from Minehead stop in Dunster Village at the rate of one per hour, but only from June to September. Off-season visitors have to take a taxi.

By Car   From London, head west along the M4, cutting south at the junction with the M5 until you reach the junction with the A39 going west to Minehead. Before your final approach to Minehead, cut south to Dunster along the A396.

ESSENTIALS   The **telephone area code** is 0643. Dunster doesn't have an official tourist office, but an **Exmoor National Park Information Centre** is found at Dunster Steep Car Park (tel. 0643/821835), 2 miles east of Minehead. It's open March to mid-November, from 10am to 5pm.

The village of Dunster in Somerset is near the eastern edge of Exmoor National Park (see below). It grew up around the original Dunster Castle, constructed as a fortress for the de Mohun family, whose progenitor came to England with William the Conqueror. The village, about 4 miles from the Cistercian monastery at Cleeve, has an ancient priory church and dovecote, a 17th-century gabled yarn market, and little cobbled streets dotted with whitewashed cottages.

WHAT TO SEE & DO

DUNSTER CASTLE, on the A396, just off the A39 in Dunster. Tel. 821314.

The castle is on a tor (high hill), from which you can see the Bristol Channel, and it stands on the site of a Norman castle granted to William de Mohun of Normandy by William the Conqueror shortly after the conquest of England. The 13th-century gateway built by the de Mohuns is all that remains of the original fortress. In 1376 the castle and its lands were bought by Lady Elizabeth Luttrell and belonged to her family until given to the National Trust in 1976, together with 30 acres of surrounding parkland. The first castle was largely demolished during the Civil War, and the present Dunster Castle is a Jacobean house built in the lower ward of the original fortifications in 1620, then rebuilt in 1870 to look like a castle. From the terraced walks and gardens you'll have good views of Exmoor and the Quantock Hills.

Some of the outstanding artifacts within are the 17th-century panels of embossed painted and gilded leather depicting the story of Antony and Cleopatra, and a remarkable allegorical 16th-century portrait of Sir John Luttrell shown wading naked through the sea with a female figure of peace and a wrecked ship in the background. The 17th-century plasterwork ceilings of the dining room, and the finely carved staircase balustrade of cavorting huntsmen, hounds, and stags are also noteworthy.

Admission: Castle and grounds, £4.50 ($6.80) adults, £2.20 ($3.30) children; grounds only, £2.50 ($3.80) adults, £1.20 ($1.80) children.

Open: Apr 3–Oct 3, Sat–Wed 11am–5pm; Oct 4–31, Sat–Wed noon–4pm. **Bus:** 38 or 39 from Minehead.

WHERE TO STAY & DINE

LUTTRELL ARMS, 36 High St., Dunster, Somerset TA24 6SG. Tel. 0643/821555, or toll free 800/435-4542 in the U.S. Fax 0643/821567. 27 rms (all with bath or shower). TV TEL

$ Rates: £70 ($105) single; £90 ($135) double. Breakfast £7.95 ($11.90) extra. AE, DC, MC, V.

On the site of what has been a hostelry for weary travelers for more than 600 years, this hotel is the outgrowth of a guesthouse the Cistercian abbots at Cleeve had built in the village of Dunster. It was named for the Luttrell lords of the manor, who bought Dunster Castle and the property attached to it in the 14th century. It has, of course, been provided with the amenities expected by modern travelers, but from its stone porch to the 15th-century Gothic hall with hammer-beam roof (now divided) it still retains a feeling of antiquity. The bedrooms are comfortably appointed and attractively decorated in keeping with the hotel's long history; four of them have four-poster beds.

A lounge is upstairs, while downstairs you can enjoy a drink in the timbered Tudor bar, with its large inglenook fireplace. This was once the kitchen of the hostelry. A meal in the dining room, costing £15.95 ($23.90) and up, can be ordered from a varied menu. Depending on the season, you might choose guinea fowl or baked sugared ham with Somerset cider sauce. A buffet lunch is offered Monday through Saturday, and you can also order bar food.

EASY EXCURSIONS

COMBE SYDENHAM HALL, Monksilver. Tel. 0984/56284.

This hall was the home of Elizabeth Sydenham, wife of Sir Francis Drake, and it stands on the ruins of monastic buildings that were associated with nearby Cleeve Abbey. Here you can see a cannon ball that legend says halted the wedding of Lady Elizabeth to a rival suitor in 1585. The gardens include Lady Elizabeth's Walk, which circles ponds originally laid out when the knight was courting his bride-to-be. The valley ponds are fed by springwater full of rainbow trout (ask about getting fly-fishing instruction). Woodland walks are possible to Long Meadow with its host of wildflowers. Also to be seen are a deserted hamlet, whose population reputedly was wiped out by the Black Death, and a historic corn mill. In the hall's tearoom, smoked trout and pâté are produced on oak chips, as in days of yore, and there are a shop and car park.

Incidentally, it was from Watchet, a few miles east of Minehead along the coast, that Coleridge's Ancient Mariner sailed.

Admission: £3.50 ($5.30) adults, £1.50 ($2.30) children.

Open: Hall, July–Sept, Mon–Fri 11am–4pm; Apr–June and Oct, Mon–Fri 11am–3pm. Country park, July–Sept, Mon–Fri 11am–6pm; Apr–June and Oct, Mon–Fri 11am–5pm. **Directions:** Drive 5 miles south of Watchet on the B3188 road between Monksilver and Elsworthy.

COLERIDGE COTTAGE, Nether Stowey, near Bridgwater. Tel. 0278/ 732662.

The hamlet of Nether Stowey is on the A39, north of Taunton across the Quantock Hills to the east of Exmoor. The cottage is at the west end of Nether Stowey on the south side of the A39 and 8 miles west of Bridgwater. Here you can visit the home of Samuel Taylor Coleridge when he wrote *The Rime of the Ancient*

Mariner. During his 1797–1800 sojourn here, he and his friends, William Words-worth and sister Dorothy, enjoyed exploring the Quantock woods. The parlor and reading room of this National Trust property are open to visitors.

Admission: £2.50 ($3.80) adults, £1 ($1.50) children.

Open: Apr–Sept, Tues–Thurs and Sun 2–5pm.

EXMOOR NATIONAL PARK

The far west of Somerset forms most of Exmoor National Park, a wooded area abounding in red deer and wild ponies, with much of its moorland 1,200 feet above sea level. The remainder of the park is in Devon. In addition to the heather-covered moor, the park includes the wooded valleys of the Rivers Exe and Barle, the Brendon Hills, and the sweeping stretch of coast from Minehead to the boundary of Devon. This is more of the land of Blackmore's *Lorna Doone.* You can walk up Badgworthy Water from Malmsmead to Doone Valley, divided by the Somerset-Devon line. The moors, which rise to 1,707 feet at Dunkery Beacon, are inviting to walkers and pony trekkers, with ponies and wild deer roaming freely.

Visit England's smallest complete church at **Culbone** and the centuries-old clapper bridge over the River Barle at **Tarr Steps.** Some of England's prettiest villages are within the national park, and some lie along its borders. **Selworthy,** an idyllic little town, is in Exmoor, as is **Allerford,** with its packhorse bridge preserved by the National Trust.

Minehead, a fine resort, is just outside the park's northeastern boundary, but in some ways the little villages that have that town as a focal point have more charm. Bus service in and around the park is erratic; it's better to explore by car. Buses run by Southern National (tel. 0823/272033 for information) are the most reliable means of transport. More information is available at Dunster Steep.

3. GLASTONBURY

136 miles SW of London, 26 miles S of Bristol, 6 miles SW of Wells

GETTING THERE By Train Go to Taunton, which is on the London-Penzance line leaving frequently from London's Paddington Station; at Taunton, proceed the rest of the way by bus. Or leave London's Paddington Station for Bristol Temple Meads, and go the rest of the way by Badgerline bus no. 376.

By Bus From Taunton, take the Southern National bus (no. 17) to Glastonbury Monday through Saturday. There are one to three departures per day (trip time: 1 hr.). A Badgerline bus (no. 376) runs from Bristol via Wells to Glastonbury every hour Monday through Saturday; on Sunday, the schedule is reduced to every 2 hours. Trip time is 1½ hours. For information about bus schedules of Badgerline, call 0749/73084; for data about Southern National, call 0823/272033. One National Express bus a day (no. 602) leaves London's Victoria Coach Station at 5:30pm and arrives in Glastonbury at 9:40pm.

By Car Take the M4 west from London, then cut south on the A4 going via Bath to Glastonbury.

ESSENTIALS The **telephone area code** is 0458. The summer-only **Tourist Information Centre** is at 1 Marchant's Buildings, Northload Street (tel. 0458/832954).

Glastonbury may be one of the oldest inhabited sites in Britain. Excavations have revealed Iron Age lakeside villages on its periphery, and some of the discoveries dug up may be viewed in a little museum on the High Street. After the destruction of its once-great abbey, the town lost prestige; today it is a market town. The ancient gatehouse entry to the abbey is a museum, and its principal exhibit is a scale model of the abbey and its community buildings as they stood in 1539, at the time of the dissolution.

WHAT TO SEE & DO

GLASTONBURY ABBEY, Abbey Gatehouse. Tel. 832267.

What was once one of the wealthiest and most prestigious monasteries in England is no more than a ruined sanctuary today; but it provides Glastonbury's claim to historical greatness, an assertion augmented by legendary links to such figures as Joseph of Arimathea, King Arthur, Queen Guinevere, and St. Patrick.

It is said that Joseph of Arimathea journeyed to what was then the Isle of Avalon, with the Holy Grail in his possession. According to tradition, he buried the chalice at the foot of the conical Glastonbury Tor and a stream of blood burst forth. You can scale this more than 500-foot-high hill today, on which rests a 15th-century tower.

Joseph, so it goes, erected a church of wattle in Glastonbury. (The town, in fact, may have had the oldest church in England, as excavations have shown.) And at one point the saint is said to have leaned against his staff, which was immediately transformed into a fully blossoming tree; a cutting alleged to have survived from the Holy Thorn can be seen on the abbey grounds today—it blooms at Christmastime. Some historians have traced this particular story back to Tudor times.

The most famous link—popularized for Arthurian fans in the Victorian era by Tennyson—concerns the burial of King Arthur and Queen Guinevere on the abbey grounds. In 1191 the monks dug up the skeletons of two bodies on the south side of the lady chapel, said to be those of the king and queen. In 1278, in the presence of Edward I, the bodies were removed and transferred to a black marble tomb in the choir. Both the burial spot and the shrine are marked today.

A large Benedictine Abbey of St. Mary grew out of the early wattle church. St. Dunstan, who was born nearby, was the abbot in the 10th century and later became archbishop of Canterbury. Edmund, Edgar, and Edmund "Ironside," three early English kings, were buried at the abbey.

In 1184 a fire destroyed most of the abbey and its vast treasures. It was eventually rebuilt after much difficulty, only to be dissolved by Henry VIII. Its last abbot, Richard Whiting, was hanged at Glastonbury Tor. Like the Roman forum, the abbey for years was used as a stone quarry.

Today you can visit the ruins of the chapel, linked by an Early English "Galilee" to the nave of the abbey. The best-preserved building on the grounds is a 14th-century octagonal Abbot's Kitchen, where oxen were once roasted whole to feed the wealthier of the pilgrims.

Admission: £2 ($3) adults, £1.20 ($1.80) children under 16.
Open: Daily 9:30am–6pm or dusk.

SOMERSET RURAL LIFE MUSEUM, Abbey Farm, Chilkwell St., Glastonbury. Tel. 831197.

The history of the Somerset countryside since the early 19th century is illustrated in this museum based in the abbey farm. The centerpiece of the museum is the abbey barn, built around 1370. The magnificent timbered room, stone tiles, and sculptural details (including the head of Edward III) make it special. There is also a Victorian farmhouse comprising exhibits illustrating farming in Somerset during the "horse age" and domestic and social life in Victorian times. In summer, there are demonstrations of buttermaking, weaving, basketwork, and many other traditional craft and farming activities, which are rapidly disappearing. There is a museum shop and tearoom.

Admission: £1.20 ($1.80) adults, 30p (50¢) children.
Open: Easter–Oct, Mon–Fri 10am–5pm, Sat–Sun 2–6pm; Nov–Mar, Mon–Fri 10am–5pm, Sat 11am–4pm.

WHERE TO STAY

THE GEORGE & PILGRIMS INN, 1 High St., Glastonbury, Somerset BA6 9DP. Tel. 0458/831146. Fax 0458/832252. 13 rms (all with bath). TV TEL
$ Rates (including English breakfast): £52–£65 ($78–$97.50) single; £70–£90 ($105–$135) double. AE, DC, MC, V.

One of the few pre-Reformation hostelries still left in England, this inn once offered hospitality to Glastonbury pilgrims; now it accepts modern travelers. In the center of town, the inn has a facade that looks like a medieval castle, with stone-mullioned windows with leaded glass. Some of the bedrooms were formerly monks' cells; others have four-posters, veritable carved monuments of oak. You may be given the Henry VIII Room, from which the king watched the burning of the abbey in 1539.

The old kitchen is now the Pilgrim's Bar, with old oak beams. Even if you don't stay over, stop in for dinner in the Georgian Restaurant to enjoy the à la carte or table d'hôte menus, both of which feature traditional local dishes, or homemade fare in the snack bar. Dinners begin at £16 ($24).

WHERE TO DINE

NUMBER 3 RESTAURANT AND HOTEL, 3 Magdalene St., Glastonbury, Somerset BA6 9EW. Tel. 0458/832129.
Cuisine: ENGLISH/FRENCH. **Reservations:** Required.
$ Prices: Fixed-price dinner from £26 ($39). MC, V.
Open: Dinner only, Tues–Sat 7:30–9pm. **Closed:** Jan.

★ Only a fixed-priced dinner is served in this pleasant, family-run restaurant and hotel. That makes an evening meal here something of an event for the loyal clientele of its Georgian-style dining room. Specialties include several lobster dishes (they have their own tanks), scallops in Smitain sauce topped with langoustine, loin of Somerset lamb served with orange-and-ginger sauce, venison with blackberry and port wine sauce, and wild Scottish salmon with lime sauce. There are also special vegetarian dishes. A super wine list contains descriptions of each of the carefully selected vintages. There are two outdoor tables for warm-weather dining.

The restaurant also has six double bedrooms, tastefully and individually decorated, with private baths, TVs, and phones, costing £55 ($82.50) daily in a single and £75 ($112.50) in a double, breakfast included.

4. WELLS

21 miles SW of Bath, 123 miles SW of London

GETTING THERE   By Train   Take the train to Bath (see below) and continue the rest of the way by bus.

By Bus   Wells has good bus connections with its surrounding towns and cities. Badgerline bus no. 175 links Wells with Bath. Departures are every hour Monday through Saturday and every 2 hours on Sunday. Both no. 376 and 378 buses run between Bristol and Glastonbury every hour Monday through Saturday and every 2 hours on Sunday.

By Car   Take the M4 west from London, cutting south on the A4 toward Bath and continuing along the A39 into Wells.

ESSENTIALS   The **telephone area code** is 0749. The **Tourist Information Centre** is at the Town Hall, Market Place (tel. 0749/672552).

To the south of the Mendip Hills, the cathedral town of Wells is a medieval gem. Wells was a vital link in the Saxon kingdom of Wessex—that is to say, it was important in England long before the arrival of William the Conqueror. Once the seat of a bishopric, it was eventually toppled from its ecclesiastical hegemony by the rival city of Bath. But the subsequent loss of prestige has paid off handsomely in Wells today: After experiencing the pinnacle of prestige, it fell into a slumber—hence, much of its old look remains. Wells was named after wells in the town, which were often visited by pilgrims to Glastonbury in the hope that their gout could be eased by its supposedly curative waters.

WHAT TO SEE & DO

Begun in the 12th century, **Wells Cathedral** (tel. 674483), in the center of town, is a well-preserved example of the Early English style of architecture. The medieval sculpture (six tiers of hundreds of statues recently restored) of its west front is without equal. The western facade was completed in the mid-13th century. The landmark central tower was erected in the 14th century, with the fan vaulting attached later. The inverted arches were added to strengthen the top-heavy structure.

Much of the stained glass dates from the 14th century. The fan-vaulted lady chapel, also from the 14th century, is in the Decorated style. To the north is the vaulted chapter house, built in the 13th century. Look also for a medieval astronomical clock in the north transept. There is no charge to enter the cathedral; however, visitors are asked to make voluntary donations of £2.50 ($3.80) for adults, 75p ($1.10) for students and children. The Cloister Restaurant and Cathedral Shop are adjacent to the cathedral.

After a visit to the cathedral, walk along its cloisters to the moated **Bishop's Palace.** The Great Hall, built in the 13th century, is in ruins. Finally, the street known as the **Vicars' Close** is one of the most beautifully preserved streets in Europe. The cathedral is usually open from 7:15am to 6pm or until dusk in summer.

WHERE TO STAY

STAR HOTEL, 18 High St., Wells, Somerset BA5 2SQ. Tel. 0749/ 673055. Fax 0749/672654. 12 rms (all with bath or shower). TV
$ Rates: £22.50–£39 ($33.80–$58.50) single; £45–£54 ($67.50–$81) double. Breakfast £6.50 ($9.80) extra. AE, DC, MC, V.

   The Star had its origins sometime in the 16th century, but is most closely associated with the great coaching era, though the hotel front was restored in the Georgian period. The cobbled carriageway is still a feature and leads to the dining room—once the stables. The hotel bedrooms have been modernized, yet retain their old charm. Copper and brass are extensively used for decoration, and several original stone walls and timbers have been exposed. The inn has a reputation for good food; a fixed-price dinner begins at £15 ($22.50).

THE SWAN HOTEL, 11 Sadler St., Wells, Somerset BA5 2RX. Tel. 0749/678877. Fax 0749/677647. 38 rms (all with bath). TV TEL

$ Rates (including English breakfast): £59–£64.50 ($88.50–$96.80) single; £79.50–£87 ($119.30–$130.50) double. AE, DC, MC, V. **Parking:** Free.

Set behind a stucco facade on one of the town's main arteries, this place was originally built in the 15th century as a coaching inn. It faces the west front of Wells Cathedral. Several of the well-furnished accommodations contain four-poster beds. The spacious and elegant public rooms stretch out to the left and right of the entrance as you enter. Both ends contain a blazing and baronial fireplace, beamed ceilings, and paneling. The Swan Hotel Restaurant is recommended separately (see below).

WHERE TO DINE

SWAN HOTEL RESTAURANT, in the Swan Hotel, 11 Sadler St. Tel. 678877.

Cuisine: TRADITIONAL ENGLISH. **Reservations:** Recommended.

$ Prices: Appetizers £2.25–£6.50 ($3.40–$9.80); main courses £11.50–£14 ($17.30–$21); fixed-price lunch or dinner £15.50 ($23.30). AE, DC, MC, V.

Open: Daily 11am–11pm.

Owned and operated by this previously recommended hotel, this restaurant is decorated in a traditional English style. It offers both table d'hôte and à la carte meals, a classic English repertoire of dishes. Begin perhaps with the chef's homemade pâté, then follow with grilled lamb cutlets, roast Somerset chicken with bacon, or roast duckling with apple sauce. All dishes are served with potatoes and fresh vegetables. You can order a dessert from the "sweet trolley," or make a selection from the cheese board. Wine is sold by the glass.

AN EASY EXCURSION

Easily reached by heading west out of Wells, the **Caves of Mendip** are two exciting natural sightseeing attractions in Somerset—the great caves of Cheddar and Wookey Hole.

WOOKEY HOLE CAVES & PAPER MILL, Wookey Hole, near Wells. Tel. 0749/672243.

Just 2 miles from Wells, you'll first come to the source of the Axe River. In the first chamber of the caves, as legend has it, is the Witch of Wookey turned to stone. These caves are believed to have been inhabited by prehistoric people at least 60,000 years ago. A tunnel opened in 1975 leads to the chambers unknown in early times and previously accessible only to divers.

Leaving the caves, you follow a canal path to the mill, where paper has been made by hand since the 17th century. Here you can watch the best-quality paper being made by skilled workers according to the traditions of their ancient craft. Also in the mill is a "Fairground Memories" exhibition, a colorful assembly of relics from the world's fairgrounds, and an Edwardian Penny Pier Arcade where new pennies can be exchanged for old ones with which to play the original machines.

Free parking is provided, and visitors can use the self-service restaurant and picnic area.

Admission: 2-hour tour, £5.20 ($7.80) adults, £3 ($4.50) children 16 and under.

Open: Apr–Oct, daily 9:30am–5:30pm; Nov–Mar, daily 10:30am–4:30pm. **Closed:** Dec 17–25. **Directions:** Follow the signs from the center of Wells for 2 miles. **Bus:** 172 from Wells.

CHEDDAR SHOW CAVES, Cheddar Gorge. Tel. 0934/742343.

A short distance from Bath, Bristol, and Wells is the village of Cheddar, home of

Open: Apr–Oct, Mon–Sat 9am–6pm; Nov–Mar, Mon–Sat 9am–4:30pm; year-round, Sun 1–2:30pm and 4:30–5:30pm.

PUMP ROOM AND ROMAN BATHS, Abbey Churchyard. Tel. 461111, ext. 2785.

✪ Founded in A.D. 75 by the Romans, the baths were dedicated to the goddess Sulis Minerva; in their day they were an engineering feat. Even today they're considered among the finest Roman remains in the country, and are still fed by Britain's most famous hot spring water. After centuries of decay, the original baths were rediscovered in Victoria's reign. The site of the Temple of Sulis Minerva has been excavated and is now open to view. The museum contains many interesting objects from Victorian and recent digs (look for the head of Minerva). Coffee, lunch, and tea, usually with music from the Pump Room Trio, can be enjoyed in the 18th-century pump room, overlooking the hot springs. There's also a drinking fountain with hot mineral water.

Admission: £4 ($6) adults, £2 ($3) children.
Open: Mar–Oct, daily 9am–6pm; Nov–Feb, Mon–Sat 9am–5pm, Sun 10am–5pm. Evenings in Aug 8–10pm.

THEATRE ROYAL, Sawclose. Tel. 448844.

The Theatre Royal, located next to the new Seven Dials development, has been restored and refurbished with plush red velvet seats, red carpets, and a painted proscenium arch and ceiling, and is now thought to be the most beautiful theater in Britain. It is a 1,000-seat theater with a small pit and grand tiers rising to the upper circle. Beneath the theater, reached from the back of the stalls or by a side door, are the theater vaults, where you will find a bar in one of the curved vaults with stone walls. In the next vault is a brasserie.

The theater advertises a list of forthcoming events with a repertoire that includes, among other offerings, West End shows.

Admission: Tickets, £7–£22 ($10.50–$33) adults, £1 ($1.50) children.
Open: Box office, Mon–Sat 9:30am–8pm. Shows, Mon–Wed at 7:30pm, Thurs–Sat at 8pm, Wed matinee at 2:30pm, Sat matinee at 4:30pm. For credit-card bookings, call 0225/448861.

NO. 1 ROYAL CRESCENT, 1 Royal Crescent. Tel. 428126.

The interior of this Bath town house has been redecorated and furnished by the Bath Preservation Trust to appear as it might have looked toward the end of the 18th century. The house is positioned at one end of Bath's most magnificent crescent, west of the Circus.

Admission: £3 ($4.50) adults, £2 ($3) children.
Open: Mar–Oct, Tues–Sat 11am–5pm, Sun 2–5pm; Nov–Christmas, Tues–Sat 11am–3pm (last admission 30 minutes before closing).

THE AMERICAN MUSEUM, Claverton Manor, Bathwick Hill. Tel. 460503.

Some 2½ miles outside Bath, you can get an idea of what life was like in America up until Lincoln's day. It was the first American museum established outside the United States. In a Greek Revival house (Claverton Manor) designed by a Georgian architect, the museum sits proudly on extensive grounds high above the Avon valley. Among the authentic exhibits—shipped over from the States—are a New Mexico room, a Conestoga wagon, an early American beehive oven (try gingerbread baked from the recipe of George Washington's mother), the dining room of a New York town house of the early 19th century, and (on the grounds) a copy of Washington's flower garden at Mount Vernon. There is a permanent exhibition in the New Gallery of the Dallas Pratt Collection of Historical Maps, and there is an American arboretum on the grounds.

Admission: £4.50 ($6.80) adults, £2.50 ($3.80) children.
Open: Late Mar–late Oct, Tues–Sun 2–5pm. **Bus:** 18.

WHERE TO STAY

EXPENSIVE

BATH SPA HOTEL, Sydney Rd., Bath, Avon BA2 6JF. Tel. 0225/444424.
Fax 0225/444006. 103 rms, 7 suites. MINIBAR TV TEL **Directions:** Lies east of
the city off the A36.
$ Rates: £120 ($180) single occupancy of double room; £150–£185 ($225–
$277.50) double; from £225 ($337.50) suite for two. Breakfast £11.25 ($16.90)
extra. AE, DC, MC, V. **Parking:** Free.

This restored 19th-century mansion is a 10-minute walk from the center of Bath.
Behind a facade of Bath stone, it lies at the end of a tree-lined drive on 7 acres of
landscaped grounds, with a Victorian grotto and a Grecian temple. Winston Churchill
visited when it was the headquarters of the Admiralty in World War II. In its long
history, it had served many purposes (once a hostel for nurses) before being returned
to its original grandeur. The drawing room of what once was an English general's
house (he served in India) is today restored. It is representative of the new style of the
hotel, which uses log fireplaces, elaborate moldings, oak paneling, and staircases to
create country-house charm. Rooms are handsomely furnished with the best of
English furniture and well-chosen and coordinated fabrics. Most are spacious.

Dining/Entertainment: The former owner called his home Vellore House, and
the name is today remembered in the restaurant where a continental cuisine is served.
You're given immaculate service and superb food and wine at a cost of £33 ($49.50)
for a fixed-price dinner served from 7 to 10pm daily. A second restaurant, the Alfresco
Restaurant, is also popular, offering a Mediterranean-style menu. In summer, guests
can dine outside in an informal garden with a fountain.

Services: 24-hour room service, valet and laundry service, beauty treatments.

Facilities: Indoor swimming pool, gymnasium, tennis court, sauna and whirlpool
bath, croquet lawn.

**FOUNTAIN HOUSE, 9–11 Fountain Buildings, Lansdown Rd., Bath,
Avon BA1 5DV. Tel. 0225/338622.** Fax 0225/445855. 15 suites. MINIBAR
TV TEL
$ Rates (including continental breakfast): £120–£168 ($180–$252) one-bedroom
suite for two people; £168–£202 ($252–$303) two-bedroom suite for four people.
AE, DC, MC, V. **Parking:** £10 ($15).

The three buildings that comprise this hotel are a trio of Georgian neoclassic, natural
stone-fronted structures dating from 1735. British entrepreneur Robin Bryan created
an all-suite hotel that has been favorably compared to the most prestigious in England.
Each suite contains original or reproduction antiques, lots of color-coordinated
chintz, at least one bedroom, a sitting room, private bath, and all the electronic
equipment you'd expect in such an elegant hotel. The hotel stands within 100 yards of
Milsom Street, the city's main shopping and historic thoroughfare. It doesn't serve a
formal breakfast. Instead, all ingredients are delivered in a basket to the door and
guests prepare their own breakfasts at their own pace.

**THE PRIORY HOTEL, Weston Rd., Bath, Avon BA1 2XT. Tel. 0225/
331922.** Fax 0225/448276. 21 rms. TV TEL
$ Rates: £90 ($135) single; £160 ($240) standard double; £195 ($292.50) deluxe
room for two. English breakfast £10 ($15) extra. MC, V. **Parking:** Free.

Converted from one of Bath's Georgian houses in 1969, the Priory is situated
on 2 acres of formal and award-winning gardens with manicured lawns and
flowerbeds, a swimming pool, and a croquet lawn. The bedrooms are

individually decorated and furnished with antiques; my personal favorite is Clivia (all rooms are named after flowers or shrubs), a nicely appointed duplex in a circular turret.

The restaurant consists of three separate dining rooms, one in a small salon in the original building; the others have views over the garden. The menu is varied and reflects seasonal availability. Grouse, partridge, hare, and venison are served in season in several recipes, as is the succulent best end of lamb roasted with herb-flavored breadcrumbs. The average dinner price is £30 ($45). A three-course luncheon is offered for £22 ($33), and on Sunday traditional roasted meats are featured. The Priory is known for its wine list.

QUEENSBERRY HOTEL, Russel St., Bath, Avon BA1 2QF. Tel. 0225/ 447928, or toll free 800/323-5463 in the U.S. Fax 0225/446065. 22 rms. TV TEL
$ Rates (including continental breakfast): £88 ($132) single; £90–£149 ($135– $223.50) double. AE, MC, V. **Parking:** 50p (80¢) per hour; free on the street.

★ Much of the beauty of this place derives from the many original fireplaces, ornate ceilings, and antiques, which the creators of the property, Stephen and Penny Ross, have preserved. Each of three interconnected town houses that form this hotel was constructed in the early Georgian era. Today each bedroom has antique furniture and carefully chosen upholstery, in keeping with the character of the house. Open since 1988, the Queensberry has become one of Bath's most important hotels.

At the hotel you can dine at the Olive Tree, offering a contemporary English cuisine. See separate recommendation in "Where to Dine," below.

ROYAL CRESCENT HOTEL, 16 Royal Crescent, Bath, Avon BA1 2LS. Tel. 0225/319090, or toll free 800/525-4800 in the U.S. Fax 0225/339401. 28 rms, 14 suites. TV TEL
$ Rates (including continental breakfast): £98 ($147) single; £165–£195 ($247.50– $292.50) double; from £265 ($397.50) suite. AE, DC, MC, V. **Parking:** Free.
A special place, standing proudly in the center of the famed Royal Crescent, the Georgian colonnade of town houses was designed by John Wood the Younger in 1767. Long regarded as Bath's premier hotel, it has attracted the rich and famous. Crystal chandeliers, period furniture, and paintings add to the rich adornment. The bedrooms, including the Jane Austen Suite, are often lavishly decorated with such trappings as four-poster beds and Jacuzzi baths. Each bedroom is not only individually designed, but features such amenities as trouser press, hairdryer, bathrobes, bottled mineral water, remote-control TV, direct-dial phone, fruit plates, and other special touches. Excellent English cuisine is served in the Dower House Restaurant. Reservations are essential for rooms or meals.

MODERATE

APSLEY HOUSE HOTEL, 141 Newbridge Hill, Bath, Avon BA1 3PT. Tel. 0225/336966. Fax 0225/425462. 7 rms (all with bath or shower). TV TEL
Directions: Take the A4 to Upper Bristol Rd. and fork right at the traffic signals into Newbridge Hill.
$ Rates (including continental breakfast): £60–£90 ($90–$135) single; £80–£110 ($120–$165) double. AE, MC, V. **Parking:** Free.
This charming building, just a mile west of the center of Bath, dates back to 1830—the reign of William IV. It's set in its own gardens, stately, with a square tower, arched windows, and a walled garden with south views. Bedrooms have traditional furnishings and fine English fabrics.

If you'd like to have dinner in the handsome dining room, expect to spend £18.50 ($27.80) for the three-course menu. Drinks are served in an intimate cocktail bar, and there's a comfortable lounge.

DUKES HOTEL, 53–54 Great Pulteney St., Bath, Avon BA2 4DN. Tel. 0225/463512. Fax 0225/483733. 22 rms (all with bath). TV TEL **Bus:** 18.
$ Rates (including English breakfast): £45–£60 ($67.50–$90) single; £55–£75 ($82.50–$112.50) double; £65–£80 ($97.50–$120) family rm. AE, MC, V. **Parking:** £8 ($12).

A short walk from the heart of Bath, this building dates from 1780 but has been completely restored and rather elegantly furnished and modernized, both in its public rooms and its bedrooms. Many of the original Georgian features, including cornices and moldings, have been retained. Amenities include electric trouser presses and hairdryers. Guests can relax in a refined drawing room or patronize the cozy bar. A traditional English menu is also offered, costing £15.50 ($23.30) for a four-course meal.

FRANCIS HOTEL, Queen Sq., Bath, Avon BA1 2HH. Tel. 0225/424257, or toll free 800/435-4542 in the U.S. Fax 0225/319715. 93 rms (all with bath), 3 suites. TV TEL
$ Rates: £80 ($120) single; £108 ($162) double; from £125 ($187.50) suite. English breakfast £8.50 ($12.80) extra. AE, DC, MC, V. **Parking:** Free.

An integral part of Queen Square, the first major development of John Wood, architect and creator of Bath's most prestigious buildings, the Francis is an example of 18th-century taste. Originally six private residences dating from 1729, the Francis was opened as a private hotel by Emily Francis in 1884 and has offered guests first-class service for more than 100 years. Many of the well-furnished and traditionally styled bedrooms overlook Queen Square—named in honor of George II's consort, Caroline. The public rooms contain shell-shaped niches, moldings, some 18th-century antiques, a cocktail bar, and the Edgar Restaurant, which offers a wide array of both British and international food; a fixed-price meal costs £16.95 ($25.40).

LANSDOWN GROVE HOTEL, Lansdown Rd., Bath, Avon, BA1 5EH. Tel. 0225/315891. Fax 0225/448092. 45 rms (all with bath or shower). MINIBAR TV TEL
$ Rates (including English breakfast): £70–£85 ($105–$127.50) single; £105–£115 ($157.50–$172.50) double. AE, DC, MC, V. **Parking:** Free.

A well-run hotel outside the center of the city, the Lansdown Grove is situated on the northern slopes with good views. Its drawing room is informal, with flowering chintz draperies, a large gilt-and-marble console, and comfortable armchairs. The well-furnished bedrooms all have hairdryers and trouser presses. It's a pleasure to eat in the sunny dining room, with its bay window that opens onto the garden. Before-dinner drinks are available in the cocktail bar.

PRATT'S HOTEL, South Parade, Bath, Avon BA2 4AB. Tel. 0225/460441. Fax 0225/448807. 46 rms (all with bath). TV TEL
$ Rates (including English breakfast): £42.95 ($64.40) single; £65.90 ($98.90) double. Children under 15 sharing a room with two adults stay free. AE, DC, MC, V. **Parking:** £5.40 ($8.10).

Once the home of Sir Walter Scott, Pratt's is conveniently located for sightseeing. Several elegant terraced Georgian town houses were joined into a comfortable place with warm, cheerful lounges, a bar, and a high-ceilinged dining room. The attractive cuisine is served in the dining room, where fixed-price dinners cost £13.50 to £17 ($20.30 to $25.50).

INEXPENSIVE

ARDEN HOTEL, 73 Great Pulteney St., Bath, Avon BA2 4DL. Tel. 0225/466601. Fax 0225/465548. 10 rms (all with bath). TV TEL

$ Rates (including English breakfast): £49–£54 ($73.50–$81) single; £54–£74 ($81–$111) double. MC, V.

 Built in 1785 of Bath sandstone, this hotel sits on a historic street of similarly elegant facades near the town center. The Arden, owned by Eric and Jacqueline Newbigin, has recently been entirely refurbished. The hotel, in a Georgian building off Laura Place, is fully licensed, and all the beautifully decorated bedrooms have hot-beverage facilities. The establishment stands on one of Bath's most famous streets, a few minutes' walk from the major sights.

LAURA PLACE HOTEL, 3 Laura Place, Great Pulteney St., Bath, Avon BA2 4BH. Tel. 0225/463815. Fax 0225/310222. 7 rms (all with bath or shower). TEL **Bus:** 18 or 19.

$ Rates (including English breakfast): £50 ($75) single; £60–£75 ($90–$112.50) double. AE, MC, V. **Parking:** Free.

 Built the year of the French Revolution (1789), this hotel has won a civic award for the restoration of its stone facade. Set on a corner of a residential street overlooking a public fountain, it lies within a 2-minute walk of the Roman Baths and Bath Abbey. The hotel has been skillfully decorated with antique furniture and fabrics evocative of the 18th century.

NUMBER NINETY THREE, 93 Wells Rd., Bath, Avon BA2 3AN. Tel. 0225/317977. 5 rms (all with bath). TV **Bus:** 3, 13, 14, 17, 23, or 33.

$ Rates (including English breakfast): £25–£30 ($37.50–$45) single; £38–£42.50 ($57–$63.80) double. AE, MC, V.

This well-run guesthouse is a traditional B&B, British style: small but immaculately kept and well maintained. The elegant Victorian house serves a traditional English breakfast, and the location is within walking distance of the city center. An evening meal can be arranged at 6:30pm. Parking can be difficult in Bath, but the hotel will advise.

SYDNEY GARDENS HOTEL, Sydney Rd., Bath, Avon BA2 6NT. Tel. 0225/464818. 6 rms (all with bath). TV TEL

$ Rates (including English breakfast): £59–£65 ($88.50–$97.50) single; £69 ($103.50) double. MC, V. **Parking:** Free.

 This spot is reminiscent of the letters of Jane Austen, who wrote to friends about the long walks she enjoyed in Sydney Gardens, a public park just outside the city center. In 1852 an Italianate Victorian villa was constructed here of gray stone on a lot immediately adjacent to the gardens. Three rooms have twin beds and the other three have 5-foot-wide double beds. Each accommodation is individually decorated with an English country-house charm. Amenities include radio alarm clocks, hairdryers, and beverage-making facilities. No meals other than breakfast are served, since the center of town with its many dining spots lies within a 10-minute walk. There's also a footpath running beside a canal for an additional pedestrian adventure. No smoking is allowed.

IN NEARBY HINTON CHARTERHOUSE

HOMEWOOD PARK, Hinton Charterhouse, Bath, Avon BA3 6BB. Tel. 0225/723731. Fax 0225/723820. 15 rms (all with bath). TV TEL **Directions:** Take the A36 Bath-Warminster road 6 miles south of Bath.

$ Rates (including English breakfast): £90–£130 ($135–$195) single; £99–£140 ($148.50–$210) double. AE, DC, MC, V. **Parking:** Free.

This small, family-run hotel, set on 10 acres of grounds, was built in the 18th century and enlarged in the 19th. Overlooking the Limpley Stoke Valley, it's a large Victorian house with grounds adjoining the 13th-century ruin of Hinton Priory. You can play tennis and croquet in the garden. Riding and golfing are available nearby, and beautiful walks in the Limpley Stoke Valley lure guests. Each of the bedrooms is luxuriously decorated, with a particularly good use of color-coordinated fabrics, and each is furnished with taste and charm. Most of the rooms overlook the gardens and grounds or have views of the valley.

Most visitors come here for the cuisine, served in a dining room facing south, overlooking the gardens. The French and English cooking is prepared with skill and flair, and you should expect to spend from £24.50 ($36.80) for dinner.

IN NEARBY STON EASTON

STON EASTON PARK, Ston Easton, Somerset BA3 4DF. Tel. 0761/ 241631. Fax 0761/241377. 21 rms (all with bath), 2 suites. TV
$ Rates (including continental breakfast): £95 ($142.50) single occupancy of double room; £135 ($202.50) double; from £320 ($480) suite. Children under 7 not accepted. AE, DC, MC, V. **Parking:** Free.

From the moment you pass a collection of stone outbuildings and the century-old beeches of the 30-acre park—just up the road from Farrington Gurney—you know you've come to a very special place. The mansion was created in the mid-1700s from the shell of an existing Elizabethan house, and in 1793 Sir Humphry Repton designed the landscape. In 1977, after long years of neglect, Peter and Christine Smedley acquired the property and poured money, love, and labor into its restoration. Now it's one of the great country hotels of England. A pair of carved mahogany staircases ringed with ornate plaster detailing might be considered works of sculpture. The sheer volume of antiques filling the place is staggering. There's a manorial library, as well as a drawing room suitable for a diplomatic reception. The tasteful bedrooms are filled with flowers, plus upholstery and antiques.

A sunflower-colored formal dining room displays museum-quality oil portraits, grandeur, and exquisite attention to detail. The chef prepares superb food, offering imaginative menus. A lunch costs £22 ($33), and a dinner goes for £35 ($52.50). Guests who return early from sightseeing enjoy tea on the terrace at the front of the hotel.

IN NEARBY HUNSTRETE

HUNSTRETE HOUSE, Hunstrete, Chelwood, near Bristol, Avon BS18 4NS. Tel. 0761/490490. Fax 0761/490732. 24 rms (all with bath), 1 suite. TV TEL **Directions:** Take the A4 8½ miles west of Bath.
$ Rates (including English breakfast): £95–£100 ($142.50–$150) single; £120–£200 ($180–$300) double; from £235 ($352.50) suite. MC, V. **Parking:** Free.
This fine Georgian house, a Relais & Châteaux, is situated on 90 acres of private parkland. The existence of the village of Hunstrete was first recorded in 936 when King Athelstan passed through on his way to the abbey in Glastonbury. Six units are in the Courtyard House, attached to the main structure and overlooking a paved courtyard with its Italian fountain and flower-filled tubs. Swallow Cottage, which adjoins the main house, has its own private sitting room, double bedroom, and bath. Units in the main house are individually decorated and furnished in attractive colors. A heated swimming pool lies in a sheltered corner of the walled garden.

Part of the pleasure of staying at Hunstrete is the contemporary and classic cuisine. A three-course dinner at £29.50 ($44.30) gives diners a wide and delectable choice.

WHERE TO DINE

BEAUJOLAIS, 5A Chapel Row, Queen Sq. Tel. 423417.

Cuisine: FRENCH. **Reservations:** Recommended.

$ Prices: Appetizers £3.25–£5 ($4.90–$7.50); main courses £8.50–£13.50 ($12.80–$20.30); fixed-price lunch £10.50 ($15.80). MC, V.

Open: Lunch Mon–Sat noon–2pm; dinner Mon–Sat 7–10:30pm.

This is perhaps the best-known bistro in Bath, maintaining its old habitutés but also attracting new admirers every year. Diners are drawn to the good, honest cookery and the decent value. One area of the restaurant is reserved for nonsmokers. The disabled (wheelchair access), children (special helpings), and vegetarians will all find comfort here. The house wines are modestly priced from £9 ($13.50) per bottle. Begin with a salad made with goat cheese and warm spinach leaves, followed perhaps with a delectable onion-flavored veal chop.

THE MOON AND SIXPENCE, 6A Broad St. Tel. 460962.

Cuisine: INTERNATIONAL. **Reservations:** Recommended.

$ Prices: Appetizers £3.25–£5.80 ($4.90–$8.70); main courses £9.25–£11.75 ($13.90–$17.60); fixed-price lunch £11.95 ($17.90). AE, MC, V.

Open: Lunch daily noon–2:30pm; dinner daily 5:30–10:30pm.

 One of the leading restaurants and wine bars of Bath, the Moon and Sixpence occupies a stone structure east of Queen Square, with an extended conservatory and sheltered patio. Just off Broad Street, it has a cobbled passageway leading you past a fountain into its courtyard.

At lunch a large cold buffet with a selection of hot dishes is featured in the wine bar section. In the upstairs restaurant overlooking the bar, full service is offered. Main courses are likely to include such dishes as filet of lamb with caramelized garlic or médaillons of beef filet with a fresh-herb and shallot hollandaise. Look for the daily specials on the continental menu.

THE OLIVE TREE, in the Queensberry Hotel, Russel St. Tel. 446065.

Cuisine: ENGLISH/MEDITERRANEAN. **Reservations:** Recommended.

$ Prices: Appetizers £3.75–£5.50 ($5.60–$8.30); main courses £9.50–£12.95 ($14.30–$19.40); 3-course fixed-price lunch £10.50 ($15.80). AE, DC, MC, V.

Open: Lunch Tues–Sat noon–2pm; dinner Tues–Sat 7–10:30pm.

In the basement of this previously recommended hotel, Stephen and Penny Ross operate one of the most sophisticated little restaurants in Bath with a white-tile floor and black wood chairs. Stephen uses the best of local produce, with an emphasis on freshness. The menu is changed to reflect the season, with game and fish being the specialties. You might begin with a Provençal fish soup or a pheasant lentil soup, unless the marinade of Mediterranean vegetables, olive toast, and feta cheese tempts you instead. Then you could go on to try seafood risotto or the breast of pheasant flavored with apple and ginger. Stephen is also known for his desserts, which are likely to include such treats as a hot chocolate soufflé or a prune-and-Armagnac tart.

PINO'S HOLE IN THE WALL, 16 George St. Tel. 425242.

Cuisine: ITALIAN. **Reservations:** Required.

$ Prices: Appetizers £3.80–£9.50 ($5.70–$14.30); main courses £10.50–£20 ($15.80–$30). AE, DC, MC, V.

Open: Lunch Mon–Sat noon–2:30pm; dinner Mon–Sat 6:30–11:15pm.

You enter what looks like the living room of a Georgian town house, where a hostess greets you, takes your name and drink order, and presents you with the impressive menu—and even helps plan your meal, if you prefer. All the selections are especially prepared for you. When your table is ready, you descend into an old-world dining room, with an attractive decor including a great fireplace. The benches, tables, and chairs are antiques.

The menu is changed frequently. Try the veal parmigiana or the breast of chicken covered with ham or mozzarella. The superb use of fresh ingredients and fresh fish is notable. The menu is à la carte and daily specials are also available.

POPJOY'S, in the Beau Nash House, Sawclose. Tel. 460494.
 Cuisine: ENGLISH/INTERNATIONAL. **Reservations:** Required.
$ **Prices:** Appetizers £4–£6.50 ($6–$9.80); main courses £4.60–£12.50 ($6.90–$18.80); fixed-price dinner £25 ($37.50). AE, MC, V.
 Open: Lunch Tues–Sun noon–2pm; dinner Tues–Sat 6–10:30pm.

Housed in a 1720 Georgian building at the south end of Barton Street that was once the home of Beau Nash (the "King of Bath"), the restaurant is named after Julianna Popjoy, Nash's last mistress, whose ghost is said to haunt the drawing room. In 1982 Popjoy's was restored to exactly the way it had been in 1720, even down to scraping away centuries of paint from the walls to discover the original colors.

Everything is freshly prepared in the basement kitchen. Meat comes from Devon, fish daily from Cornwall, and fresh vegetables from local farmers. Menus lean toward the new way of cooking, using less fat, less cream, and no flour in sauces. The wine list (they buy their wine from 16 different wine merchants) is more than 100 strong. The menu is changed every 8 weeks, and ever since the place reopened in 1983, there has hardly been an empty seat. The menu is divided into two separate groups, the first offering traditional English fare suitable for light meals and pre- or posttheater suppers. Menu items include Lancashire hot pot, braised oxtail, and homemade faggots (a minced version of offal of pork). More glamorous items on the second part of the menu are grilled sea bass, suprême of salmon, and filets of lemon sole in an orange butter sauce. The house wine is bottled in France and imported for the restaurant.

WOODS, 9–13 Alfred St. Tel. 314812.
 Cuisine: ENGLISH. **Reservations:** Recommended.
$ **Prices:** Appetizers £3–£4.25 ($4.50–$6.40); main courses £6.50–£14 ($9.80–$21); fixed-price lunch £8–£10 ($12–$15); fixed-price dinner £12–£18 ($18–$27). AE, MC, V.
 Open: Lunch Mon–Sat noon–2:30pm; dinner Mon–Sat 6:30–10:30pm.

This restaurant in a converted Georgian building gives you a choice of dining in a more formal room or a brasserie, with tables placed out on the street. Attracting a lot of young people, the restaurant is run by horse-racing enthusiast David Price, along with his French wife, Claude. A talented kitchen staff turns out some of the finest food in Bath. Look for the blackboard of changing daily specials. These might include such dishes as escalope of salmon lightly poached with tomatoes and spices, or breast of chicken stuffed with a basil-and-pinenut mousse served with a Pernod-and-fennel sauce. Or you might find cod with ginger and orange on the menu. Their selection of "puds" (desserts) is also tempting.

EASY EXCURSIONS

LONGLEAT HOUSE

Between Bath and Salisbury, Longleat House, Warminster, in Wiltshire (tel. 0985/844551), owned by the seventh marquess of Bath, lies 4 miles southwest of Warminster and 4½ miles southeast of Frome on the A362. The first view of this magnificent Elizabethan house, built in the early Renaissance style, is romantic enough, but the wealth of paintings and furnishings in its lofty rooms is enough to dazzle.

From the Elizabethan Great Hall to the library, the state rooms, and the grand staircase, the house is filled with variety. The state dining room is full of silver and plate, and fine tapestries and paintings adorn the walls in profusion. The library represents the finest private collection in the country. The Victorian kitchens are open, offering a glimpse of life below the stairs in a well-ordered country home. Various exhibitions are mounted in the stable yard. Events are staged frequently on the grounds, and the Safari Park has a vast array of animals in open parklands, including Britain's only white tiger.

The Maze, believed to be the largest in the world, was added to the attractions by Lord Weymouth. It has more than 1½ miles of paths. The first part is comparatively easy, but the second part is rather complicated.

Admission to Longleat House is £3.50 ($5.30) for adults, £1.50 ($2.30) for children; admission to Safari Park, £5 ($7.50) for adults, £3.50 ($5.30) for children. Special exhibitions and rides require separate admission tickets. It's open Easter to September, daily from 10am to 6pm; October to Easter, daily from 10am to 4pm. The park is open mid-March to early November, daily from 10am to 6pm (last cars are admitted at 5:30pm or sunset).

STOURHEAD

After Longleat, you can drive 6 miles down the B3092 to Stourton, a village just off the highway, 3 miles northwest of Mere (A303). A Palladian house, Stourhead (tel. 0747/840348) was built in the 18th century by the banking family of Hoare. The magnificent gardens, which blended art and nature, became known as *le jardin anglais*. Set around an artificial lake, the grounds are decorated with temples, bridges, islands, and grottoes, as well as statuary.

Admission to the house, open from April 3 to October 31, Saturday through Wednesday from noon to 5:30pm, is £4 ($6) for adults, £2 ($3) for children. Admission to the gardens from April to October is £3.60 ($5.40) for adults, £1.70 ($2.60) for children; from November to February, £4 ($6) for adults, £2 ($3) for children. The gardens are open all year, daily from 8am to 7pm or sunset if earlier. You'll need a car (see above for directions).

AVEBURY

One of the largest prehistoric sites in Europe, Avebury lies on the Kennet River 7 miles west of Marlborough. Unlike at Stonehenge, visitors here can walk around the 28-acre site at Avebury, winding in and out of the circle of more than 100 stones, some weighing up to 50 tons. The stones are made of sarsen, a sandstone found in Wiltshire. Inside this large circle are two smaller ones, each with about 30 stones standing upright. Native Neolithic tribes are believed to have built these circles.

Avebury is on the A361 between Swindon and Devizes and a mile from the A4 London-Bath road. The closest rail station is at Swindon, some 12 miles away, which is served by the main rail line from London to Bath. A limited bus service (no. 49) runs from Swindon to Devizes through Avebury.

What to See and Do

AVEBURY MUSEUM, Avebury. Tel. 06723/250.

Founded by Alexander Keiller, this museum houses one of Britain's most important archeological collections. It began with Keiller's material from excavations at Windmill Hill and Avebury, and now includes artifacts from other prehistoric digs at West Kennet, Long Barrow, Silbury Hill, West Kennet Avenue, and the Sanctuary.

Admission: £1.30 ($2) adults, 65p ($1) children.

Open: Good Friday–Sept, daily 10am–6pm; Oct–Maundy Thursday, daily 10am–4pm.

THE GREAT BARN MUSEUM OF WILTSHIRE RURAL LIFE, Avebury. Tel. 06723/555.

Housed in a 17th-century thatched barn is a center for the display and interpretation of Wiltshire life during the last three centuries. There are displays on cheese making, blacksmithing, thatching, sheep and shepherds, the wheelwright, and other rural crafts, as well as local geology and domestic life.

Admission: £1 ($1.50) adults, 50p (80¢) children.

Open: Mid-Mar to Oct, daily 10am–5:30pm; Nov to mid-Mar, Sat 1–4:30pm, Sun 11am–4:30pm.

Where to Dine

STONES RESTAURANT, High St. Tel. 06723/514.

Cuisine: INTERNATIONAL. **Reservations:** Not accepted.

$ Prices: Appetizers £2.10–£2.50 ($3.20–$3.80); main courses £4.75–£5.25 ($7.10–$7.90); afternoon cream teas £2.95 ($4.40). No credit cards.

Open: Apr–Oct, daily 10am–6pm (hot food noon–2:30pm); Nov–Mar, Sat–Sun 10am–5pm.

This restaurant has made an impact since its opening in 1984 by two trained archeologists, Dr. Hilary Howard and her husband, Michael Pitts. They specialize in freshly made food grown organically without artificial additives, which is prepared in original ways and sold at reasonable prices. Pastries, coffee, fruit juices, bottled beer, cold quiche, snacks, and an array of Welsh and English cheeses are available throughout the day. Especially attractive is the midafternoon cream tea served with whole-wheat scones and clotted cream imported from Cornwall. The owners travel abroad every winter, bringing back their culinary inspirations.

---

6. BRISTOL

13 miles W of Bath, 121 miles W of London

GETTING THERE By Plane   The Bristol Airport (tel. 0272/027587) is conveniently situated beside the main A38 road, just over 7 miles from the city center. Flights arrive during the day from London.

By Train   Rail services to and from the area are among the fastest and most efficient in Britain. British Rail runs hourly service from London's Paddington Station to each of Bristol's two main stations: Temple Meads in the center of Bristol, and Parkway on the city's northern outskirts (trip time: 1½ hr.).

By Bus   National Express buses depart every hour during the day from London's Victoria Coach Station (trip time: 2½ hr.).

By Car   Head west from London along the M4.

ESSENTIALS   The **telephone area code** is 0272. The **Tourist Information Centre** is at 14 Narrow Quay (tel. 0272/260767).

Bristol, the largest city in the West Country, is just across the Bristol Channel from Wales and is a good center for touring western Britain. This historic inland port is linked to the sea by 7 miles of the navigable Avon River. Bristol has long been rich in seafaring traditions and has many links with the early colonization of America. In fact, some claim that the new continent was named after a Bristol town clerk, Richard

Ameryke. In 1497, John Cabot sailed from Bristol, which led to the discovery of the northern half of the New World.

WHAT TO SEE & DO

Guided walking tours are conducted in summer and last about 1½ hours. The tours depart from Neptune's Statue on Saturday at 2:30pm and on Thursday at 7pm. Guided tours are also conducted through Clifton, a suburb of Bristol, which has more Georgian houses than Bath.

SS *GREAT BRITAIN,* City Docks, Great Western Dock. Tel. 260680.
In Bristol, the world's first iron steamship and luxury liner has been partially restored to its 1843 appearance, although it's still a long way from earning its old title of a "floating palace." This vessel, which weighs 3,443 tons, was designed by Isambard Brunel, a Victorian engineer.
Incidentally, in 1831 (at the age of 25), Brunel began a Bristol landmark, Suspension Bridge, over the 250-foot-deep Avon Gorge at Clifton.
Admission: £2.90 ($4.40) adults, £1.90 ($2.90) children.
Open: June–Sept, daily 10am–6pm; Oct–May, daily 10am–5pm. **Bus:** 511 from city center, a rather long haul.

BRISTOL CATHEDRAL, College Green. Tel. 264879.
Construction of the cathedral, once an Augustinian abbey, was begun in the 12th century, and the central tower was added in 1466. The chapter house and gatehouse are good examples of late Norman architecture, and the choir is magnificent. The cathedral's interior was singled out for praise by Sir John Betjeman, the late poet laureate.
Admission: Free; requested donation £2 ($3).
Open: Daily 8am–6pm. **Bus:** 8 or 9.

ST. MARY REDCLIFFE, 10 Redcliffe Parade West. Tel. 291487.
This church was called "the fairest, the goodliest, and most famous parish church in England" by none other than Elizabeth I. Built in the 14th century, it has been carefully restored. One of the chapels is called "The American Chapel," where the kneelers show the emblems of all the states of the U.S.A. The tomb and armor of Adm. Sir William Penn, father of the founder of Pennsylvania, are in the church. The location is 400 yards from the Temple Meads Station.
Admission: Free.
Open: June–Sept, daily 8am–8pm; Oct–May, daily 8am–6pm. **Bus:** 20, 21, or 22.

THEATRE ROYAL, King St. Tel. 250250 for the box office or 277466 for the administration.
Built in 1776, this is now the oldest working playhouse in the United Kingdom. It is the home of the Bristol Old Vic. Backstage tours leave from the foyer.
Tours: Fri–Sat at noon; £2 ($3) adults, £1.50 ($2.30) children and students under 19.
Admission: Tickets, £4–£16 ($6–$24).
Open: Call the box office for the current schedule. **Bus:** 48, 49, 51, or 52.

WHERE TO STAY

BRISTOL HILTON, Redcliffe Way, Bristol, Avon BS1 6NJ. Tel. 0272/

260041, or toll free 800/445-8667 in the U.S. Fax 0272/230089. 201 rms (all with bath), 8 suites. MINIBAR TV TEL **Bus:** 1 or 2.
$ Rates: £90–£95 ($135–$142.50) single; £95–£115 ($142.50–$172.50) double; from £160 ($240) suite. Breakfast £10.25 ($15.40) extra. AE, DC, MC, V. **Parking:** Free.

Situated conveniently amid the commercial bustle of the center of town, this modern hotel offers an imaginative decor. Many bedrooms are outfitted in pastels, and all have private baths, radios, in-house video, and tea and coffee makers.

Its split-level restaurant is located inside the brick-lined walls of a former 16th-century glass kiln refurbished in the style of a French brasserie, offering English and French specialties. Dinner begins at £19.50 ($29.30).

BRISTOL MARRIOTT, Lower Castle St., Bristol, Avon BS1 3AD. Tel. 0272/294281, or toll free 800/228-9290 in the U.S. Fax 0272/225838. 290 rms (all with bath), 7 suites. A/C TV TEL **Bus:** 8 or 9.
$ Rates: £65–£125 ($97.50–$187.50) single or double; from £175 ($262.50) suite. Breakfast £10.25 ($15.40) extra. AE, DC, MC, V. **Parking:** Free.

This modern hotel is ideal for the business traveler, but also suitable for the visitor to this part of the West Country. The heated swimming pool is impressive, and the foyer is spacious. Public areas are comfortable and stylish, in the tradition of the popular chain. The Brasserie serves an à la carte menu as well as snacks from 7am to 10pm. The bedrooms are uniformly furnished, bright, and cheerful, with double beds (doubles have two) and good tile bathrooms.

GRAND HOTEL, Broad St., Bristol, Avon BS1 2EL. Tel. 0272/291645. Fax 0272/227619. 178 rms (all with bath), 3 suites. TV TEL **Bus:** 8 or 9.
$ Rates: £72 ($108) single; £95 ($142.50) double; from £125 ($187.50) suite. Breakfast £8 ($12) extra. AE, DC, MC, V.

This Victorian grand hotel sits on a street in the commercial heart of town. The architectural detailing that led to its reputation as one of the most noteworthy hotels in town includes rows of fan-shaped windows, intricate exterior corniches, lavishly ornate crystal chandeliers, two bars (one in a nautical mode), and a pair of comfortable restaurants, including the Brass Nails, which serves good food. Dinner costs £15.50 ($23.30) and up. Bedrooms are traditionally furnished and well maintained.

WHERE TO DINE

HARVEY'S RESTAURANT, 12A Denmark St. Tel. 277665.
Cuisine: FRENCH. **Reservations:** Required.
$ Prices: Appetizers £5.50–£9 ($8.30–$13.50); main courses £15–£19 ($22.50–$28.50); fixed-price lunch £16.50 ($24.80); fixed-price dinner £30 ($45). AE, DC, MC, V.
Open: Lunch Mon–Fri noon–1:45pm; dinner Mon–Sat 7–10:45pm.

⭐ Harvey's Restaurant is situated in medieval cellars that have belonged to Harvey's of Bristol, famous for Harvey's Bristol Cream sherry, since 1796.

Today, Harvey's is one of the top restaurants in Bristol and the West Country, serving contemporary British food based upon classical methods. The philosophy of head chef Ramon Farthing is to respect the natural flavor of every ingredient, however humble or exotic, with a constant reappraisal of cooking methods and presentation. The à la carte is complemented by an extensive wine list with the red wines of Bordeaux a specialty.

The rest of the historic cellars accommodate Harvey's Wine Museum, with collections of English 18th-century drinking glasses, antique decanters, corkscrews, bottles, silverware, and furniture. The museum is open daily, and there are regular guided tours with tutored tastings. It is usually possible for restaurant customers to browse in the museum prior to lunch or dinner.

LETTONIE, 9 Druid Hill, Stoke Bishop. Tel. 686456.
   Cuisine: FRENCH. **Reservations:** Required. **Bus:** 40.
$ **Prices:** Fixed-price meals £15.95 ($23.90) at lunch, £29.95 ($44.90) at dinner. AE, MC, V.
   Open: Lunch Tues–Sat noon–2pm; dinner Tues–Sat 7–9:30pm.
Martin and Sian Blunos imbue their subtle restaurant with a simple elegance, and they are known for producing some of the most memorable fixed-price meals in the area. Try, for example, guinea fowl in a prune-and-brandy sauce, followed by one of their luscious desserts, perhaps a terrine of mixed chocolates. Service is top-rate, as is the welcome. The wine list is carefully selected and moderate in price.

MICHAEL'S, 129 Hotwell Rd., Bristol, Avon BS8 4RU. Tel. 0272/ 276190.
   Cuisine: CONTINENTAL. **Reservations:** Required for Sat dinner. **Directions:** Take the A370 west; then turn north and go over the suspension bridge.
$ **Prices:** 3-course fixed-price menus £12.50 ($18.80) at lunch, £22.50 ($33.80) at dinner. MC, V.
   Open: Lunch Tues–Fri 12:30–2:30pm; dinner Tues–Sat 7–11:30pm.
   This charming and well-patronized restaurant is near Clifton on a highway leading toward the Avon Gorge. In its pleasant bar, decorated like an Edwardian parlor, an open fire burns. The dining room is also bright and inviting. The fixed-price menus are imaginative and change according to the availability of seasonal produce. The service is informal and enthusiastic. Always call for a table. There's no smoking in the dining room. If you want a cigarette, stick to the bar.
   Michael offers simple accommodations in a five-story Regency house overlooking the Avon Gorge and the suspension bridge. The rooms have hot and cold running water, and guests can use a kitchen and communal lounge. Two rooms with showers are available. The price begins at £22 ($33) per person per night.

EASY EXCURSIONS

THORNBURY

Twelve miles north of Bristol, Thornbury is known for its castle (now a hotel; see below). Many of the crenellations and towers were built in 1511 as the last defensible castle ever constructed in England. Its owner was beheaded by Henry VIII for certain words spoken in haste. Henry confiscated the lands and, to celebrate, stayed here for 10 days with Anne Boleyn in 1535. Later, Mary Tudor spent 3 years of her adolescence here.

Where to Stay and Dine

THORNBURY CASTLE, Thornbury, near Bristol, Avon BS12 1HH. Tel. 0454/281182. Fax 0454/416188. 18 rms (all with bath), 1 suite. TV TEL
   Directions: From Bristol, approach Thornbury on the B4061; continue downhill to the monumental water pump, bear left, and continue for 300 yards.
$ **Rates** (including continental breakfast): £80 ($120) single; £100–£195 ($150–$292.50) double; from £200 ($300) suite. AE, DC, MC, V. **Parking:** Free.
   A genuine Tudor castle (built in 1511) and once owned by Henry VIII, it is surrounded by trees and thick stone walls. The rooms are superbly fitted with fine furniture and many amenities; eight have four-posters.
   French and English dishes highlight the menus at the hotel's two dining rooms. A three-course lunch begins at £17.75 ($26.60) per person and is served from noon to

2pm daily. A three-course dinner, from £31 ($46.50) per person, is served from 7 to 9:30pm. Although the menu changes, some of the regular offerings include: suprême of pheasant roasted with herbs and served on a bed of artichoke purée and a wild mushroom and truffle reduction; goujons of chicken sautéed with red onions and flavored with Pernod; or whole lemon sole grilled with tomato and dill butter. A vegetarian menu is also available.

CHAPTER 15

T IE COTSWOLD

- **WHAT'S SPECIAL ABOUT THE COTSWOLDS**
1. **TETBURY**
2. **CIRENCESTER & PAINSWICK**
3. **CHELTENHAM**
4. **BIBURY**
5. **BURFORD**
6. **BOURTON-ON-THE-WATER**
7. **STOW-ON-THE-WOLD**
8. **MORETON-IN-MARSH**
9. **BROADWAY**
10. **CHIPPING CAMPDEN**

The Cotswolds, a stretch of limestone hills sometimes covered by grass and many barren plateaus known as wolds, is a pastoral land dotted by ancient villages and deep wooded ravines. This bucolic scene in the middle of southwest England, about a 2-hour drive west of London, is found mainly in Gloucestershire, with portions in Oxfordshire, Wiltshire, and Worcestershire. The wolds or plateaus led to this area's being given the name Cotswold, Old English for "God's high open land."

Cotswold lambs used to produce so much wool that they made their owners very rich—wealth they invested in some of the finest domestic architecture in Europe, made out of honey-brown Cotswold stone. The wool-rich gentry didn't neglect their church contributions either. Often the simplest of villages will have a church that in style and architecture detail seems far beyond the means of the hamlet.

If possible, try to explore the area by car. That way, you can spend hours surveying the land of winding goat paths, rolling hills, and sleepy hamlets, with names such as Stow-on-the Wold, Wotton-under-Edge, Moreton-in-Marsh, Old Sodbury, Chipping Campden, Shipton-under-Wychwood, Upper and Lower Swell, and Upper and Lower Slaughter, often called "the Slaughters."

SEEING THE COTSWOLDS
GETTING THERE

Motorists take the M4 from London to Gloucestershire for a tour of the Cotswolds. At Exit 20, take the M5 north to enter the area, perhaps beginning in or around Cheltenham. You can also take Exit 15 along the M4, then the A361 to enter the Cotswolds. British Rail serves the western part of the region from London's Paddington Station. For example, it takes only 1 hour and 50 minutes to reach Moreton-in-Marsh from London. However, the train does not connect with the most beautiful and charming villages. Once you arrive at a station, you'll have to take a connecting bus to reach a particular village. National Express coaches from London's Victoria Coach Station service the major cities of the region, such as Cheltenham (trip time: 2 hr., 40 min.). Once at one of the major centers you'll have to rely on local bus services with somewhat erratic schedules to explore some of the more remote villages.

A SUGGESTED ITINERARY

Day 1: From London, visit Cheltenham for an overnight stop, strolling its Promenade and tasting its spa waters.

Day 2: Detour south from Cheltenham to Painswick for a morning visit and a

WHAT'S SPECIAL ABOUT THE COTSWOLDS

Great Towns/Villages

☐ Broadway, called "the show village of England," with 16th-century stone houses and cottages.

☐ Painswick, considered by some the prettiest village in England, with a 15th-century parish church.

☐ Bibury, vying with Painswick for the title of England's prettiest village; noted for its 15th-century Arlington Row of cottages.

☐ Stow-on-the-Wold, an attractive Cotswold wool town with a large marketplace and some fine old houses.

Architectural Highlights

☐ The High Street of Broadway, representing some of the finest domestic architecture in Britain, with honey-colored stone buildings.

☐ The High Street of Chipping Campden—historian G. M. Trevelyan called it "the most beautiful village street now left in the island."

Museums

☐ Corinium Museum, Cirencester, one of the finest collections of Roman antiquities in Britain.

Spa Retreats

☐ Cheltenham, one of England's most fashionable spas, with Regency architecture of ironwork, balconies, and verandas; its Promenade is called "the most beautiful thoroughfare in England."

Cool for Kids

☐ Birdland, Bourton-on-the-Water, a garden set on 8½ acres with some 1,200 birds of 361 different species.

---

luncheon stopover, followed by an overnight stay in Cirencester after a walk to the Corinium Museum.

Day 3: From Cirencester, head west for Bibury—perhaps a luncheon stopover—followed by an overnight stop in Burford.

Day 4: From Burford, visit Bourton-on-the-Water in the northwest; then continue northeast to Stow-on-the-Wold for an overnight stop.

Day 5: From Stow-on-the-Wold, head north to Moreton-in-Marsh for a luncheon stopover, followed by a walk along the High Street in Chipping Campden, staying overnight in Broadway.

---

1. TETBURY

113 miles W of London, 27 miles NE of Bristol

GETTING THERE   By Train   There is no direct service from London. Frequent daily trains run from London's Paddington Station to Kemble, 7 miles east of Tetbury. There is adequate bus service between Kemble and Tetbury.

By Bus   National Express buses leave from London's Victoria Coach Station with direct service to Cirencester, 10 miles northeast of Tetbury. From Cirencester, several buses a day run to Tetbury.

By Car   From London, take the M40 northwest to Oxford, continuing along the A40 to the junction with the A429. Cut south to Cirencester, where you connect with the A433 southwest into Tetbury.

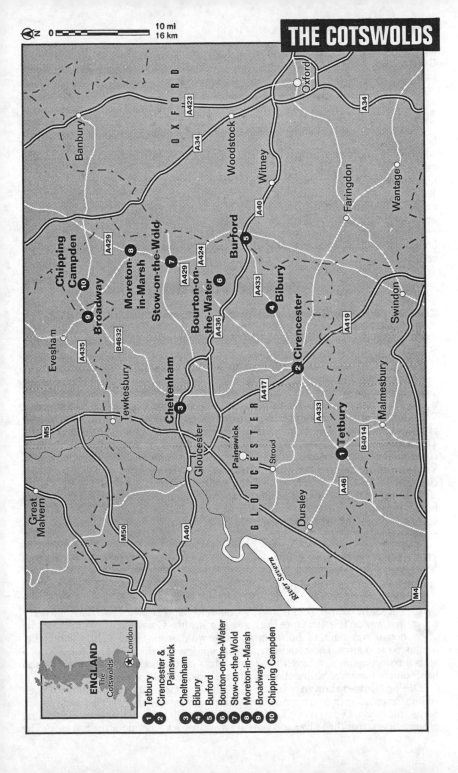

THE COTSWOLDS

0   10 mi
    16 km

ENGLAND
The Cotswolds
London

1 Tetbury
2 Cirencester & Painswick
3 Cheltenham
4 Bibury
5 Burford
6 Bourton-on-the-Water
7 Stow-on-the-Wold
8 Moreton-in-Marsh
9 Broadway
10 Chipping Campden

ESSENTIALS The **telephone area code** is 0666. The **Tourist Information Centre** is in The Old Court House, 63 Long St. (tel. 0666/503552); it's open only June to September.

In the rolling Cotswolds, Tetbury never used to be in the mainstream of tourism like Oxford or Stratford-upon-Avon; however, after a famous royal man and his lovely bride took up residence in the Macmillan place, a Georgian building on nearly 350 acres, it began drawing crowds from all over the world. Prince Charles could be seen riding horses, and perhaps tourists could spot Princess Di shopping in the village. The nine-bedroom Windsor mansion, **Highgrove,** lies just outside town on the way to Westonbirt Arboretum. It cannot be seen from the road. Princess Di is no longer in residence, although Prince Charles is. He's often seen around Tetbury today with his neighbor and friend, Camilla Parker-Bowles.

The town has a 17th-century market hall and a lot of antiques shops, along with boutiques. Its inns, even before royalty moved in, were not cheap, and the prices certainly have not dropped since that time.

WHERE TO STAY

CALCOT MANOR, Calcot, near Tetbury, Gloucestershire GL8 8YJ. Tel. 0666/890391, or toll free 800/544-4970 in the U.S. Fax 0666/890394. 15 rms (all with bath). TV TEL **Directions:** Take the A4135 3½ miles west of Tetbury.

$ Rates (including early-morning tea and English breakfast): £75 ($112.50) single; £85–£135 ($127.50–$202.50) double. Children under 12 not accepted. AE, DC, MC, V. **Parking:** Free.

⭐ On the grounds of this former farmhouse is a 14th-century tithe barn, among the oldest in Britain. The thick stone walls of the main house shelter a flowering terrace where tea and drinks are served in good weather. Tastefully decorated public rooms mix touches of modernism with clusters of flowers and English antiques. The bedrooms are furnished with antiques, rich fabrics, private baths, and modern conveniences; four are equipped with whirlpool baths, and one has a four-poster bed. Views from many of the rooms encompass a sweep of lawn and the Cotswold countryside. Facilities include an open-air swimming pool.

Dining/Entertainment: Meals are relaxing, with continental touches gathered from the proprietors' catering experience in Switzerland and France. The food is the finest served in the area, featuring fixed-price menus. Dinner, daily from 7:30 to 9:30pm, goes for £18 to £26 ($27 to $39).

THE CLOSE, 8 Long St., Tetbury, Gloucestershire GL8 8AQ. Tel. 0666/ 502272. Fax 0666/504401. 15 rms (all with bath). TV TEL

$ Rates (including English breakfast): £65–£120 ($97.50–$180) single; £75–£135 ($112.50–$202.50) double. AE, DC, MC, V. **Parking:** Free.

⭐ The Close, which dates from 1596, takes its name from a Cistercian monastery that was on this site. Once the home of a wealthy Cotswold wool merchant, the house was built of honey-brown Cotswold stone, with gables and stone-mullioned windows. The ecclesiastical-type windows in the rear overlook a garden with a reflecting pool, a haven for doves. Most of the bedrooms are spacious and handsomely furnished with antiques; all have private bathrooms.

Dining/Entertainment: Inside, you'll find a Georgian room with a domed ceiling (once an open courtyard), where before-dinner drinks are served and you can peruse the menu. Dining is in one of two rooms. Candlelight on winter evenings, floral arrangements, sparkling silver and glass are just the background for the fine food. The cooking is superb, and an à la carte menu offers specialty dishes. A fixed-price dinner costs £24 ($36) and up per person. Fixed-price menus are offered at lunch for £17.50 ($26.30).

THE SNOOTY FOX, Market Place, Tetbury, Gloucestershire GL8 8DD. Tel. 0666/502436. Fax 0666/503479. 12 rms (all with bath). TV TEL
$ Rates (including continental breakfast): £60–£76 ($90–$114) single; £80–£130 ($120–$195) double. AE, DC, MC, V.
This desirable hotel in the commercial heart of Tetbury was originally a 16th-century coaching inn. The Victorians added a high front porch under which flowers grow in what used to be watering troughs for horses. A stone-walled lounge with comfortable chairs and a Gothic fireplace opens off the reception area. Three bedrooms contain antique beds with canopies, and the rest are comfortably and tastefully furnished in a more modern style. Each has radio, hairdryer, trouser press, and hot-beverage facilities.
   Dining/Entertainment: There's a popular bar inside, with an amusing caricature of a Snooty Fox in full riding regalia and one of the most elegant restaurants in town, with meals beginning at £16 ($24). In warm weather, tables are set at the edge of the market square beneath the 19th-century iron overhang.

2. CIRENCESTER & PAINSWICK

CIRENCESTER

89 miles W of London, 16 miles S of Cheltenham,
17 miles SE of Gloucester, 36 miles W of Oxford

GETTING THERE   By Train   Because Cirencester has no railway station of its own, passengers usually get off at the nearby town of Kemble, 4 miles to the southwest. Trains depart several times a day from London's Paddington Station for Kemble (trip time: 80 min.). Passengers sometimes (but not always) must transfer trains at Swindon. From Kemble, a bus travels to Cirencester four to five times a day.

By Bus   National Express buses leave from London's Victoria Coach Station with direct service to Cirencester. From Cirencester, you can visit Painswick by one of the local bus services.

By Car   From London, take the M40 northwest to Oxford, continuing along the A40 to the junction with the A429. Cut south on the A429 to Cirencester.

ESSENTIALS   The **telephone area code** is 0285. The **Tourist Information Centre** is at Corn Hall, Market Place (tel. 0285/653939).

Don't worry about how to pronounce the name of the town. There's disagreement even among the English. Say "*Siren*-cess-ter" and you won't be too far off.
   Cirencester is often considered the unofficial capital of the Cotswolds, probably a throwback to its reputation in the Middle Ages, when it flourished as the center of the

great Cotswold wool industry. In Roman Britain, five roads converged on Cirencester, which was called Corinium in those days. In size, it ranked second only to London. Today it is chiefly a market town, and a good base for touring.

WHAT TO SEE & DO

CORINIUM MUSEUM, Park St. Tel. 655611.

The museum houses one of the finest collections of archeological remains from the Roman occupation, found locally in and around Cirencester. Mosaic pavements found here on Dyer Street in 1849 and other mosaics are the most important exhibits. Provincial Roman sculpture, including such figures as Minerva and Mercury, pottery, and artifacts salvaged from long-decayed buildings, provide a link with the remote civilization that once flourished here. The museum has been completely modernized to include full-scale reconstructions and special exhibitions on local history and conservation.

Admission: £1.25 ($1.90) adults, 75p ($1.10) children.
Open: Mon–Sat 10am–5pm, Sun 2–5pm.

CIRENCESTER PARISH CHURCH, Market Place. Tel. 653142.

Dating back to Norman times and Henry I is the Church of John the Baptist, overlooking the Market Place in the town center. (Actually, a church may have stood on this spot in Saxon times.) In size, the Cirencester church appears to be a cathedral—not a mere parish church. The present building represents a variety of styles, largely Perpendicular, as in the early-15th-century tower. Among the treasures inside are a 15th-century pulpit and a silver-gilt cup given to Queen Anne Boleyn 2 years before her execution.

Admission: Free; donations invited.
Open: Mon–Fri 9:30am–5pm, Sun 12:30–6pm.

WHERE TO STAY & DINE

THE FLEECE RESORT HOTEL, Market Place, Cirencester, Gloucester-shire GL7 2NZ. Tel. 0285/658507. Fax 0285/651017. 28 rms (all with bath), 2 suites. TV TEL
$ **Rates:** Mon–Thurs, £55 ($82.50) single; £65 ($97.50) double; £75 ($112.50) suite. Fri–Sun English breakfast £7.50 ($11.30) extra. Fri–Sun (including English breakfast): £28 ($42) per person, single or double occupancy. Half board £40 ($60) per person, single or double occupancy. AE, DC, MC, V. **Parking:** £5 ($7.50).

Its half-timbered facade hints at its origins as an Elizabethan coaching inn. Later it was enlarged by the Georgians. On warm days its flowering courtyard offers one of the most pleasant dining spots in town. Inside, a handful of open fireplaces warm the beamed interior whenever it's chilly. The comfortably modern bedrooms feature old-fashioned hints of yesteryear, such as quilted bedcoverings, and radio and coffee-making facilities.

The staff offers clients French-inspired dinners. Dinner is served in a formal dining room, where fixed-price menus cost £12.95 ($19.40) for three courses. A la carte lunches are offered in Shepherd's Bar where platters range from £4.95 to £6.95 ($7.40 to $10.40).

STRATTON HOUSE HOTEL, Gloucester Rd., Cirencester, Gloucester-shire GL7 2LE. Tel. 0285/651761. Fax 0285/640024. 41 rms (all with bath or shower). TV TEL **Directions:** Take the A417 1¼ miles northwest of Cirencester.
$ **Rates** (including English breakfast): £45–£50 ($67.50–$75) single; £60–£80 ($90–$120) double. AE, DC, MC, V. **Parking:** Free.

Built in several stages throughout the 18th century, with a discreetly designed modern wing added in the 1990s, this is an inviting and comfortable country house whose design is part Jacobean and part Georgian. It is surrounded by beautiful grounds with a walled garden and herbaceous borders. The large and well-furnished bedrooms have hairdryers and trouser presses. In the dining and drawing rooms, some fine antique furniture and oil paintings may be seen. A well-served dinner is provided, with a choice of British dishes costing £14 to £17 ($21 to $25.50) for a fixed-price menu. There is a timbered-beam bar, and in winter log fires blaze in this bar and in the main hall.

In Nearby Purton

THE PEAR TREE AT PURTON, Church End, Purton, near Swindon, Wiltshire SN5 9ED. Tel. 0793/772100. Fax 0793/772369. 18 rms (all with bath), 2 suites. TV TEL
$ Rates (including English breakfast): £92–£102 ($138–$153) single or double; from £130 ($195) suite. AE, DC, MC, V. **Parking:** Free. **Closed:** Dec 26–30.
This English country restaurant, 3 miles from Junction 16 of the M4 and 5 miles from Swindon, offers well-furnished, individually decorated rooms with hairdryers, trouser presses, and free sherry and mineral water, that open onto views of the garden and countryside. Each accommodation—three with four-poster beds—is named after a famous Purtonian, such as Anne Hyde, mother of Queen Mary and Queen Anne. The Cotswold stone house was formerly the vicarage for the twin-towered parish Church of St. Mary; set in 7½ acres, it looks out over a traditional Victorian garden and beyond the rolling hills to the source of the Thames.

Dining/Entertainment: The owners, Francis and Anne Young, run the best restaurant in the area. The cuisine is inspired by France, although the recipes and cooking are distinctly English. The best seasonal produce is featured, including local beef, lamb, and pork. Seafood is brought fresh from Devon, and many of the herbs used to flavor the dishes come from the establishment's own garden. Dining is in an attractive conservatory, and service is daily from noon to 2:30pm and 7 to 9:30pm (until 10pm on Friday and Saturday). A fixed-price lunch goes for £15 ($22.50) and a fixed-price dinner for £25 ($37.50). Reservations are necessary.

PAINSWICK

4 miles NE of Stroud, 107 miles W of London, 10 miles S of Cheltenham

GETTING THERE **By Train** The nearest railway station is at Stroud, 3 miles away. Trains depart from London's Paddington Station several times a day, sometimes (but not always) requiring a change of train at Swindon (trip time: 90–120 min., depending on the train). From Stroud, buses run to Painswick, some as frequently as once every hour. There are also many taxis waiting at the Stroud railway station.

By Bus Buses depart from Bath in the direction of Cheltenham twice a day, stopping in Painswick (and many other small towns) along the way. The train is really much more convenient.

By Car From Cirencester (see above), continue west along the A419 to Stroud; then head north along the B4073.

ESSENTIALS The **telephone area code** is 0452. The summer-only **Tourist Information Centre** is at the Painswick Library, Stroud Road (tel. 0452/813552).

The sleepy little town of Painswick is considered a model village. All its houses, although erected at different periods, blend harmoniously because the builders used only Cotswold stone as their building material. The one distinctive feature on the Painswick skyline is the spire of its 15th-century parish church. It's also known for its annual Clipping Feast (when the congregation joins hands and circles around the church as if it were a maypole, singing hymns as they do). Ancient tombstones dot the churchyard.

WHERE TO STAY

PAINSWICK HOTEL, Kemps Lane, Painswick, Gloucestershire GL6 6YB. Tel. 0452/812160. Fax 0452/814059. 20 rms (all with bath). TV TEL
$ Rates (including English breakfast): £60 ($90) single; £89–£120 ($133.50–$180) double. AE, MC, V. **Parking:** Free.
Completely refurbished, this beautiful Georgian house behind the Painswick parish church, with a 19th-century facade, was once a vicarage and is encircled by terraces of formal gardens. Many readers have reported it to be the highlight of their Cotswold tour. In rooms, cuisine, and service, it merits a major detour from wherever else you were going. The hotel has high standards of cuisine and service in its half-paneled dining room, where meals begin at £22.50 ($33.80) for three courses. The bedrooms are comfortably and attractively furnished.

THORNE, Friday St., Painswick, Gloucestershire GL6 6QJ. Tel. 0452/ 812476. Fax 0452/812912. 2 rms (all with bath). TV **Transportation:** Free transfers from the rail station.
$ Rates (including half board, wine, and cocktails): £42–£44 ($63–$66) per person. No credit cards. **Parking:** Free.

Before Columbus sailed on his quest for a new route to China, there was a market hall in Painswick, supported by stone pillars. In Shakespeare's time, Gloucestershire stonemasons turned the hall into one of the most beautiful houses in the town. Today, right in the middle of Painswick, that market hall is the home of Barbara Blatchley. This handsome, beautifully appointed, centrally heated house has only two twin guest rooms. A qualified "Blue Badge Guide," Barbara will arrange trips to Bath, Stratford-upon-Avon, Oxford, and Stonehenge.

Meals are served in the beam-ceilinged dining room, where two of the market pillars dating from 1400 are part of the wall. Top-quality farm produce and fresh vegetables are used in preparation of meals. If you arrive at the railway station in Stroud, Barbara will arrange to have you picked up at no extra charge.

WHERE TO DINE

THE COUNTRY ELEPHANT, New St. Tel. 813564.
   Cuisine: INTERNATIONAL. **Reservations:** Required.
$ Prices: Appetizers £2.85–£5 ($4.30–$7.50); main courses £9.85–£16.50 ($14.80–$24.80). DC, MC, V.
   Open: Lunch May–Sept only, Tues–Sun 12:30–2pm; dinner year-round, Tues–Sat 7–10pm.
Housed in a centrally located building crafted from Cotswold stone, this excellent restaurant serves some of the most imaginative (and finest) food in town. Owned by the Edwards and Gibson families, it boasts walls dating from the 14th century (in the kitchens) and the 17th century (in the dining rooms). Many guests enjoy a predinner drink near the open fireplace of the heavily beamed bar. The cuisine includes such dishes as a hot pot of Cornish fish in a cream sauce served on a bed of deep-fried leeks, thin slices of home-smoked beef bound together with a shallot-flavored mayonnaise

sauce, grilled filet steak served with potato and horseradish pancakes and a red wine sauce, and brill gently braised with a lemon and crabmeat sauce and served with fresh asparagus. Desserts might include a hot chocolate pudding with Kahlúa sauce—a spectacular concoction originally invented by Michel Guérard.

3. CHELTENHAM

99 miles NW of London, 9 miles E of Gloucester, 43 miles W of Oxford

GETTING THERE By Train Twenty-one trains from London's Paddington Station arrive daily (trip time: 2 hr., 15 min., often involving a change of trains at Bristol or Swindon). Trains between Cheltenham and Bristol take only an hour, with continuing service to Bath.

By Bus National Express offers nine buses daily from London's Victoria Coach Station to Cheltenham (trip time: 2 hr., 35 min.).

By Car From London, head northwest along the M40 to Oxford, continuing along the A40 to Cheltenham.

ESSENTIALS The **telephone area code** is 0242. The **Tourist Information Centre** is at 77 Promenade (tel. 0242/522878).

SPECIAL EVENTS The **International Festival of Music** and the **Festival of Literature** take place each year in July and October, respectively, and attract internationally acclaimed performers and orchestras.

In a sheltered area between the Cotswolds and the Severn Vale, a mineral spring was discovered by chance. Legend has it that the Cheltenham villagers noticed pigeons drinking from a spring and observed how healthy they were—which is why the pigeon has been incorporated into the town's crest.

Always seeking a new spa, George III arrived in 1788 and launched the town. The Duke of Wellington came to ease his liver disorder. Even Lord Byron came this way, proposing marriage to Miss Millbanke.

Cheltenham is one of England's most fashionable spas. It is also the winner of a contest, "Beautiful Britain in Bloom," and many visitors come here just to see its gardens from spring to autumn.

The architecture is mainly Regency, with lots of ironwork, balconies, and verandas. Attractive parks and open spaces of greenery make the town especially inviting. The main street, the Promenade, has been called "the most beautiful thoroughfare in Britain." Rather similar are such thoroughfares as Lansdowne Place and Montpellier Parade. The design for the dome of the Rotunda was based on the Pantheon in Rome. Montpellier Walk, with its shops separated by caryatids, is one of the most interesting shopping centers in England.

WHAT TO SEE & DO

Escorted coach tours of the Cotswolds take place every Tuesday, Thursday, and Sunday from June through December; for details, call the information center listed above.

PITTVILLE PUMP ROOM, West Approach Dr., Pittville Park. Tel. 512470.

Cheltenham Waters are the only natural, consumable alkaline waters in Great Britain, and are still taken from one of the spa's finest Regency buildings. On every Sunday from the end of May until the end of September, the Pittville Pump Room is open for a host of activities, including Sunday brunch, afternoon cream teas, live classical music, landau carriage rides around the city, and brass bands playing in Pittville Park—it's real traditional England. The Gallery of Fashion is also situated in the pump room, and depicts the social history of Cheltenham Spa. Memorabilia include photographs and prints of when the U.S. Army was stationed at Pittville in the 1940s.

Admission: Pump room, free; gallery, 65p ($1).

Open: Pump room, Tues–Sat 10:30am–5pm. Gallery, Apr–Oct, Tues–Sun 10:30am–5pm. **Directions:** From the center, take Portland St. and Evesham Rd.

CHELTENHAM ART GALLERY & MUSEUM, Clarence St. Tel. 237431.

The gallery houses one of the foremost collections of the arts-and-crafts movement, notably the fine furniture of William Morris and his followers. One section is devoted to Edward Wilson, Cheltenham's native son who died with Captain Scott on the Antarctic Expedition of 1913. The gallery is located near Royal Crescent and the Coach Station.

Admission: Free.

Open: Mon–Sat 10am–5:20pm.

EVERYMAN THEATRE, Regent St. Tel. 572573.

Cheltenham is the cultural center of the Cotswolds, and this restored theater is the only professional repertory theater in Gloucestershire. In the center near the Imperial Gardens, it offers a mixed program of musicals, dramas, comedies, and classics. Pick up a free copy of the monthly *What's On* from the tourist office (see above).

Admission: Depends on the event, but tickets generally £5–£14 ($7.50–$21).

Open: Box office, Mon–Sat 10am–8pm.

WHERE TO STAY

GREENWAY, Shurdington, near Cheltenham, Gloucestershire GL51 5UG. Tel. 0242/862352, or toll free 800/543-4135 in the U.S. Fax 0242/862780. 19 rms (all with bath). TV TEL **Directions:** Take the A46 less than 4 miles southwest of Cheltenham.

$ Rates (including English breakfast): £85 ($127.50) single; £120–£175 ($180–$262.50) double. AE, DC, MC, V. **Parking:** Free.

An elegant and beautifully furnished Cotswold country house in a garden setting, this is an ivy-clad Cotswold showpiece. Restored with sensitivity and decorated and furnished to a high standard, Greenway rents rooms in both its main house and in a converted coach house, all with private bath or shower. Original paintings and antiques abound throughout the hotel. On a chilly day, open fires beckon. Guests are almost assured of comfort here.

Dining/Entertainment: The dining room is elegantly appointed with an extension added in the Victorian conservatory style. The cooking is superb, using quality produce and good, fresh ingredients that are handled deftly. Lunch is served from 12:30 to 2pm Sunday through Friday, and dinner is from 7:30 to 9:30pm Monday through Saturday; on Sunday, at 7:30pm only. Lunches begin at £16 ($24), and a table d'hôte dinner goes for £25 ($37.50). Service is formal, on target, and polite, all at the same time.

HOTEL DE LA BERE AND COUNTRY CLUB, Southam, Cheltenham, Gloucestershire GL52 3NH. Tel. 0242/237771, or toll free 800/225-

5843 in the U.S. Fax 0242/236016. 57 rms (all with bath). TV TEL **Directions:** Take the A46 3 miles northeast of town.
$ Rates: £75 ($112.50) single; £85–£100 ($127.50–$150) double. Breakfast £8.50 ($12.80) extra. AE, DC, MC, V. **Parking:** Free.

The building on this property dates from 1500. Constructed of Cotswold stone, it stands near the racecourse. Owned by the De la Bere family for three centuries, it was converted into a hotel in 1972, and every effort has been made to ensure that the original charm of the building still remains. Five of the rooms boast double four-poster beds, and all have hot-beverage facilities and private baths; they are tastefully decorated and furnished to preserve their individual charm and character.

Dining/Entertainment: The restaurant, the Elizabethan Room, and the Royalist Room are all paneled in oak, and there is also a Great Hall, complete with minstrel's gallery. The menu is impressive, and there are some interesting first courses. Dinner à la carte begins at £22 ($33), with a fixed-price menu available for £13 ($19.50) at lunch and for £18 ($27) at dinner.

HOTEL ON THE PARK, Evesham Rd., Cheltenham, Gloucestershire GL52 2AH. Tel. 0242/518898. Fax 0242/511526. 9 rms (all with bath), 3 suites. TV TEL
$ Rates (including English breakfast): £74.50 ($111.80) single· £89 ($133.50) double; £109 ($163.50) suite. AE, DC, MC, V.

Opened in 1991 in what was formerly the private villa of a local building contractor in the 1830s, this is the newest and most-talked-about hotel in town. It is located among similar terraced buildings in the once-prominent village of Pittville Spa, a half mile north of the town center of Cheltenham. Owned and operated by Darryl and Lesley-Anne Gregory, who undertook most of the Regency-inspired interior design, it has received several awards since its opening. The bedrooms are each named after one or another of the prominent 19th-century visitors who came calling here shortly after the villa was built. Comfortable and high-ceilinged, they have stylish accessories and a tasteful assortment of antique and reproduction furniture. The hotel is noteworthy for its restaurant, Epicurean, which is recommended separately (see "Where to Dine, below).

QUEEN'S HOTEL, Promenade, Cheltenham, Gloucestershire GL50 1NN. Tel. 0242/514724, or toll free 800/225-5843 in the U.S. Fax 0242/224145. 74 rms (all with bath). TV TEL
$ Rates: £85 ($127.50) single; £105–£140 ($157.50–$210) double. Breakfast £9.50 ($14.30) extra. AE, DC, MC, V. **Parking:** £5 ($7.50).

At the head of the Regency Promenade, this hotel looks down on the Imperial Gardens. Architecturally it is imposing, built in 1838 in the style of Rome's temple of Capitoline Jupiter. The distinguished interior boasts a Regency decor and an unusually fine staircase. The attractively furnished bedrooms at the back are quieter, and all have private bath. Everything is well furnished, although decidedly old-fashioned. Meals cost £18.50 to £28.50 ($27.80 to $42.80).

WHERE TO DINE

LE CHAMPIGNON SAUVAGE, 24–26 Suffolk Rd. Tel. 573449.
Cuisine: FRENCH/ENGLISH. **Reservations:** Required.
$ Prices: Appetizers £4.75–£7 ($7.10–$10.50); main courses £9.50–£16.50 ($14.30–$24.80); fixed-price meals £17.50 ($26.30) at lunch, £24 ($36) at dinner. AE, MC, V.
Open: Lunch Mon–Fri 12:30–1:30pm; dinner Mon–Sat 7:30–9:15pm. **Closed:** 2 weeks in June

This is one of the leading restaurants of this old spa. David Everitt-Matthias, a chef of considerable talent, wisely limits the selection of dishes every night for better quality control. On some nights he allows his imagination to roam a bit, so dining here is always a surprise, a pleasant one usually. He might stuff a wild rabbit with herbs or stuff a lamb with eggplant. To dine à la carte costs £31 ($46.50) and up per person.

EPICUREAN, in the Hotel on the Park, Evesham Rd. Tel. 518898.
   Cuisine: CONTINENTAL. **Reservations:** Required.
$ Prices: Lunch fixed-price menus £15–£32.50 ($22.50–$48.80); dinner fixed-price menus £22.50–£45 ($33.80–$67.50). AE, DC, MC, V.
   Open: Lunch Tues–Sun 12:30–2pm; dinner Mon–Thurs 7–10:15pm, Fri–Sat 6–10:45pm.

Located on the street level of the previously recommended hotel, this is one of the most elaborate and ambitious restaurants in the district. Guests enjoy an apéritif at the bar before heading to one of only 30 seats in the yellow-and-gray-toned dining room. (One of the room's most memorable features is a polychromed plaster cornice whose motif of grape vines was meticulously restored by the new owners.)

Food is presented in a series of fixed-price formats that allow a broad choice of appetizers, main courses, and desserts within each category. Most elaborate of all, available only in the evening, is an eight-course "tasting menu," priced at £45 ($67.50), which is recommended only for very serious eaters with ample amounts of time. The elegant but uncluttered cuisine of partner and chef Patrick MacDonald changes with the season but is likely to include roasted foie gras with shallots, chicken and scallops with sauterne sauce, stuffed pigs' trotters, ravioli of fish with celeriac pancakes, baby onions with café au lait sauce, and, for dyed-in-the-wool Anglophiles, a filet of beef served with clapshot and haggis. Desserts might include a trifle made from "winter fruits" (i.e., dried fruits) in aspic, or perhaps a calvados soufflé.

---

4. BIBURY

86 miles W of London, 30 miles W of Oxford, 26 miles E of Gloucester

GETTING THERE By Train About five trains per day depart from London's Paddington Station for Kemble (trip time: 1 hr., 10 min.). Some of these will require a rapid change of train in Swindon (just across the tracks to another waiting train). From Kemble, 13 miles south of Bibury, there are no buses, but most hoteliers will arrange for a car to meet guests if you make arrangements in advance.

By Bus From London's Victoria Coach Station, you can take one of the five daily buses that depart for Cirencester, 7 miles from Bibury. There are no buses into Bibury, but, once again, local hotels will send a car and there are many taxis.

By Car Take the M4 from London, getting off at Exit 15 toward Cirencester. Then, take the A33 (which on some maps is still designated as the B4425) on to Bibury.

ESSENTIALS The **telephone area code** is 0285.

On the road from Burford to Cirencester, Bibury is one of the loveliest spots in the Cotswolds. In fact, the utopian romancer of Victoria's day, poet William Morris, called it England's most beautiful village. On the banks of the tiny Coln River, Bibury is noted for **Arlington Row,** a gabled group of 15th-century cottages, its biggest and most-photographed attraction, which is protected by the National Trust.

WHERE TO STAY & DINE

BIBURY COURT HOTEL, Bibury, Gloucestershire GL7 5NT. Tel. 0285/ 740337. Fax 0285/740660. 20 rms (all with bath), 1 suite. TV TEL
$ Rates (including continental breakfast): £43–£53 ($64.50–$79.50) single; £72–£74 ($108–$111) double; from £93 ($139.50) suite. AE, DC, MC, V. **Parking:** Free.

⭐ This Jacobean manor house was built by Sir Thomas Sackville in 1633 (parts of it date from Tudor times). You enter the 8 acres of grounds through a large gateway, and the lawn extends to the Coln River. The house was privately owned until it was turned into a hotel in 1968. The structure is built of Cotswold stone, with many gables, huge chimneys, leaded-glass stone-mullioned windows, and a formal graveled entryway. Inside, there are many country manor furnishings and antiques, as well as an open stone log-burning fireplace. Many of the rooms have four-poster beds, original oak paneling, and antiques. Meals are an event, with dinners priced from £20 ($30). Lunchtime bar meals begin at £5 ($7.50). After tea and biscuits in the drawing room, walk across the lawn along the river where you'll find a little church.

---

5. BURFORD

76 miles NW of London, 20 miles W of Oxford

GETTING THERE By Train The nearest station is at Oxford. Many trains depart from London to Oxford every day (trip time: 45 min.). From Oxford, passengers walk a very short distance to the entrance of the Taylor Institute, from which about three or four buses per day make the 30-minute run to Burford.

By Bus A National Express coach runs from London's Victoria Coach Station to Burford several times a day, with many stops along the way (trip time: 2 hr.).

By Car From Oxford, head west along the A40 to Burford.

ESSENTIALS The **telephone area code** is 0993. The **Tourist Information Centre** is at the Old Brewery, Sheep Street (tel. 0993/3558).

In Oxfordshire is Burford, an unspoiled medieval town built of Cotswold stone that serves as a gateway to the Cotswolds and is largely famous for its early Norman church (ca. 1116) and its High Street lined with coaching inns. Oliver Cromwell passed this way, as (in a happier day) did Charles II and his mistress, Nell Gwynne. Burford was one of the last of the great wool centers, the industry bleating out its last breath as late as Victoria's day. You may want to photograph the bridge across the Windrush River where Queen Elizabeth I once stood. Burford is definitely equipped for tourists, as the antique shops along the High will testify.

Minster Lovell is visited because of **Minster Lovell Hall** (tel. 0993/775315), which lies in ruins and dates from the 1400s. The medieval dovecote with nesting boxes survives. An early Lovell is said to have hidden in the moated manor house and subsequently starved to death after a battle in the area. The legend of the mistletoe bough originated in the village by the Windrush River. Minster Lovell is mainly built of Cotswold stone, with thatch or stone-slate roofs. It's a pity that there is a forest of TV antennas, but the place is still attractive to photographers. Admission is £1 ($1.50) for adults, 50p (80¢) for children. It's open from Good Friday to September, from 10am to 6pm. Minster Lovell lies 2½ miles west of Witney. To reach Minster Lovell from Burford, take the A40 to Oxford, cutting northwest along the secondary road signposted to Minster Lovell.

WHERE TO STAY & DINE

BAY TREE HOTEL, 12–14 Sheep St., Burford, Oxfordshire OX18 6LW. Tel. 0993/822791. Fax 0993/823008. 20 rms (all with bath), 3 suites. TV TEL
$ Rates (including English breakfast): £75 ($112.50) single; £105–£115 ($157.50–$172.50) double; £145–£185 ($217.50–$277.50) suite. AE, DC, MC, V. **Parking:** Free.

⭐ The house was built for Sir Lawrence Tanfield, the unpopular Lord Chief Baron of the Exchequer to Elizabeth I, definitely not noted for his hospitality. But time has erased his bad memory, and the splendor of this Cotswold manor house remains, even more so after a major overhaul. The house has oak-paneled rooms with stone fireplaces, where logs burn in chilly weather. There is a high-beamed hall with a minstrel's gallery. Room after room is furnished tastefully and individually decorated. The 20th-century comforts have been discreetly installed, and the beds are a far cry from the old rope-bottom contraptions of the days of Queen Elizabeth I. Try to get one of the rooms overlooking the terraced gardens at the rear of the house. The hotel has a country-style bar, "The Woolsack," offering guests and visitors a choice of light meals at lunchtime and in the evening. The head chef is well known for his tempting menus, with dishes based on local and seasonal produce. The 65-seat oak-beamed restaurant, which overlooks the gardens, retains all its original charm. Fixed-price lunches begin at £12.95 ($19.40); fixed-price dinners cost £21.50 to £23 ($32.30 to $34.50). The delightful conservatory is now the residents' lounge.

GOLDEN PHEASANT HOTEL, 91 High St., Burford, Oxfordshire OX8 4RJ. Tel. 0993/823223. Fax 0993/822621. 12 rms (all with bath or shower). TV TEL
$ Rates (including English breakfast): £58 ($87) single; £92 ($138) double. AE, MC, V. **Parking:** Free.
On the principal street, the Golden Pheasant has the oldest set of property deeds surviving in Burford. In the 1400s it was the home of a prosperous wool merchant, but began serving food and drink in the 1730s when it used both to brew and serve beer. Like many of its neighbors, it is capped with a slate roof and fronted with light gray hand-chiseled stones. Inside, within view of dozens of old beams and a blazing fireplace, a candlelit restaurant serves both French and English specialties. The rooms are comfortable and cozy; one has a four-poster bed.

LAMB INN, Sheep St., Burford, Oxfordshire OX18 4LR. Tel. 0993/823155. Fax 0993/822228. 15 rms (all with bath). TV TEL
$ Rates (including English breakfast): £40 ($60) single; £80 ($120) double. MC, V.
This thoroughly Cotswold house was built solidly in 1430 with thick stones, mullioned and leaded windows, many chimneys and gables, and a slate roof now mossy with age. It opens onto a stone-paved rear garden, with a rose-lined walk and a shaded lawn. The bedrooms are a mixture of today's comforts, such as good beds and plentiful hot water, and antiques. The public living rooms contain heavy oak beams, stone floors, window seats, Oriental rugs, and fine antiques (Chippendale, Tudor, Adam, Georgian, Jacobean).
In the drinking lounge, a special beer, made in an adjoining brewery, is served.

Light lunches and snacks are served in the bars and lounges, or in the garden in summer. Dinner as well as a traditional Sunday lunch are offered in the beamed dining room with a garden view. Dinners begin at £17.50 ($26.30). If you're dining here in the right season, you can feast on treats of the rivers or forest, such as salmon, trout, and venison.

---

6. BOURTON-ON-THE-WATER

85 miles NW of London, 36 miles NW of Oxford

GETTING THERE   By Train   Trains go from Paddington Station in London to nearby Moreton-in-Marsh (trip time: 2 hr.). From Moreton-in-Marsh, Pulhams Bus Company runs buses for the 15-minute (6-mile) journey on to Bourton-on-the-Water. Other cities that also have train service into London include Cheltenham or Kingham, and both of those, while somewhat more distant, also have bus connections into Bourton-on-the-Water.

By Bus   National Express coaches, from Victoria Coach Station in London, travel to both Cheltenham and Stow-on-the-Wold. From either of those towns, Pulhams Bus Company operates about four buses per day into Bourton-on-the-Water.

By Car   From Oxford, head west along the A40, until you reach the junction with the A429 (Fosse Way). Take it northeast to Bourton-on-the-Water.

ESSENTIALS   The **telephone area code** is 0451.

In this scenic Cotswold village, you may feel like Gulliver, voyaging to Lilliput. Bourton-on-the-Water lies on the banks of the tiny Windrush River. Its mellow stone houses, its village greens on the banks of the water, and its bridges have earned it the title of the Venice of the Cotswolds. But that label tends to obscure its true charm.

WHAT TO SEE & DO

OLD NEW INN, High St. Tel. 820467.

To see Lilliput, you have to visit this inn on the main street. In the garden is a near-perfect and most realistic model village.

Admission: £1.20 ($1.80) adults, 90p ($1.40) children.
Open: Daily 9:30am–6pm or dusk.

BIRDLAND, Rissington Rd. Tel. 820689.

Established in 1958 on 8½ acres of field and forests about a mile east of Bourton-on-the-Water, this is a handsomely designed homage to the ornithological splendors of the world. It contains about 1,200 birds representing 361 species. Included is the largest and most varied collection of penguins in any zoo, with glass-walled tanks that allow observers to appreciate their agile underwater movements. There's also an enviable collection of hummingbirds. Many of the birds contained here are on exhibition for the first time.

Admission: £3 ($4.50) for adults; £2 ($3) for children 14 and under.
Open: Mar–Nov, daily 10am–6pm; Dec–Feb, daily 10am–4pm.

A NEARBY ATTRACTION

COTSWOLD COUNTRYSIDE COLLECTION, Fosse Way, Northleach, Cheltenham (Cotswold District Council). Tel. 0451/860715.

Opened in 1981, this museum of rural life displays is off the A40 between Burford and Cheltenham. You can see the Lloyd-Baker collection of agricultural history, including wagons, horse-drawn implements, and tools, as well as a seasons-of-the-year display. A Cotswold gallery records the social history of the area. Below Stairs is an exhibition of laundry, dairy, and kitchen implements. The museum was once a house of correction, and its history is displayed in the reconstructed cellblock and courtroom.

Admission: £1.25 ($1.90) adults, 75p ($1.10) children.
Open: Apr–Oct, Mon–Sat 10:30am–5:30pm, Sun 2–5pm.

WHERE TO STAY & DINE

CHESTER HOUSE HOTEL AND MOTEL, Victoria St., Bourton-on-the-Water, Cheltenham, Gloucestershire GL54 2BU. Tel. 0451/820286. Fax 0451/820471. 23 rms (all with bath or shower). TV TEL
$ Rates (including buffet breakfast): £42.25–£46.50 ($63.40–$69.80) single; £65.50–£77 ($98.30–$115.50) double. AE, DC, MC, V. **Parking:** Free. **Closed:** Dec to mid-Feb.

This weathered, 300-year-old, Cotswold-stone house built on the banks of the Windrush River is conveniently located in the center of town. It blends an old building with a row of stables converted into a hotel with comfortable bedrooms. The hotel also has an intimate bar and a stone-walled restaurant with a full restaurant license for serving drinks. Diners are served a reliable English cuisine, including Cotswold lamb. Meals begin at £16.80 ($25.20).

OLD MANSE HOTEL, Bridge End Walk, Bourton-on-the-Water, Cheltenham, Gloucestershire GL54 2BX. Tel. 0451/820082. Fax 0451/810381. 12 rms (all with bath or shower), 1 suite. TV TEL
$ Rates (including English breakfast): £43.50 ($65.30) single; £67–£95 ($100.50–$142.50) double; from £110 ($165) suite. MC, V. **Parking:** Free. **Closed:** First week in Jan.

An architectural gem reminiscent of the setting of Nathaniel Hawthorne's *Mosses from an Old Manse,* this hotel in the center of town is by the slow-moving river that wanders through the village green. Built of Cotswold stone in 1748, with chimneys, dormers, and small-paned windows, it has been modernized inside. Bedrooms have recently been refurbished to a high standard. The inn's best feature is the stone fireplace in the dining room, and the wood-paneled bar is cozy too. Dining is a treat here. Meals cost £13.95 ($20.90).

OLD NEW INN, High St., Bourton-on-the-Water, Cheltenham, Gloucestershire GL54 2AF. Tel. 0451/820467. Fax 0451/810236. 17 rms (6 with bath). TV
$ Rates (including English breakfast): £30 ($45) single without bath, £36 ($54) single with bath; £52 ($78) double without bath, £64 ($96) double with bath. MC, V. **Parking:** Free.

 The Old New Inn can lay claim to being the landmark hostelry in the village. On the main street, overlooking the river, it's a good example of Queen Anne design (the miniature model village in its garden was referred to earlier). Hungry or tired travelers are drawn to the old-fashioned comforts and cuisine of this most English inn. The rooms are comfortable, with homelike furnishings and soft beds.

Nonresidents are also welcome here for meals, with lunches at £10 ($15) and dinner from £15 ($22.50). You may want to spend an evening in the pub lounge, playing darts or chatting with the villagers.

EN ROUTE TO STOW-ON-THE-WOLD

Midway between Bourton-on-the-Water and Stow-on-the-Wold are the twin villages of **Upper and Lower Slaughter.** Don't be put off by the name—these are two of the prettiest villages in the Cotswolds. Actually the name "Slaughter" is a corruption of "de Sclotre," the name of the original Norman landowner. The houses are constructed of honey-colored Cotswold stone, and a stream meanders right through the street, providing a home for the ducks that wander freely about, begging scraps from kindly visitors. In Upper Slaughter you can visit a fine example of a 17th-century Cotswold manor house.

WHERE TO STAY & DINE

LORDS OF THE MANOR HOTEL, Upper Slaughter, near Cheltenham, Gloucestershire GL54 2JD. Tel. 0451/820243, or toll free 800/322-2408 in the U.S. Fax 0451/820696. 29 rms (all with bath). TV TEL **Directions:** Take the A429 2¾ miles from Cheltenham.

$ Rates (including English breakfast): £75–£90 ($112.50–$135) single; £90–£120 ($135–$180) standard double; £160 ($240) four-poster rm. AE, DC, MC, V. **Parking:** Free.

A 17th-century house standing on several acres of rolling fields, the Lords of the Manor has gardens with a stream and fishing for brown trout. Modernized in its amenities, the hotel has still been successful in maintaining the quiet country-house atmosphere of 300 years ago. Half the bedrooms are in a sympathetically converted old barn and granary, and many have views of the Cotswold hills; all have private baths.

The walls in the lounge bar are hung with family portraits of the original lords of the manor. Another bar overlooks the garden, and chintz and antiques are everywhere. The country atmosphere is carried into the dining room as well, with its antiques and mullioned windows. All the well-prepared dishes are fresh and home-cooked. You'll pay an average of about £29 ($43.50) for an à la carte dinner with dessert and coffee. The cooking is modern English with some French influence.

LOWER SLAUGHTER MANOR, Lower Slaughter, near Cheltenham, Gloucestershire GL54 2HP. Tel. 0451/820456. Fax 0451/822150. 15 rms (all with bath). TV TEL **Directions:** Take the A429 3 miles east of Cheltenham.

$ Rates (including half board): £125 ($187.50) single; £170–£250 ($255–$375) double. No children under 10 admitted. AE, MC, V. **Parking:** Free.

Steeped in 1,000 years of history, Lower Slaughter Manor still offers the facilities of a modern first-class hotel. Even before the Norman Conquest a manor house stood on this spot, becoming at some period a convent housing the nuns of the Bridgetine Order of Syon for a few centuries. A reminder of those days is a decorated ceiling on which pious words are used as a motif. After the breakup of religious houses and expulsion of the nuns, the house was given to the high sheriff of Gloucestershire in 1608, and he rebuilt it much as it is today. The west wing was added, as was the stable block with its central clock tower and great stone fireplace. All the excellent bedrooms are doubles, and some have four-poster beds.

In the manor's restaurant you can enjoy traditional English country cooking, with each meal cooked fresh using locally grown produce, herbs from the house's gardens, honey from Cotswold bees, local free-range eggs, and homemade preserves. Nonresidents who reserve a table can also dine here. Fixed-price menus are £15.95 ($23.90) at lunch or £29.50 ($44.30) at dinner. Guests can use the heated indoor swimming pool with a sauna and a solarium, or in good weather, the croquet lawn and tennis court. There is also an outdoor pool.

7. STOW-ON-THE-WOLD

9 miles SE of Broadway, 10 miles S of Chipping Campden,
4 miles S of Moreton-in-Marsh, 21 miles S of Stratford-upon-Avon

GETTING THERE   By Train   From London, take a train to Moreton-in-Marsh (see below) from London's Paddington Station, a service possible several times a day. From Moreton-in-Marsh, continue by a Pulhams bus for the 10-minute ride to Stow-on-the-Wold.

By Bus   National Express coaches also run daily from London's Victoria Coach Station to Moreton-in-Marsh, where a Pulhams Bus Company coach goes the rest of the way to Stow-on-the-Wold. Several Pulhams coaches also run daily to Stow-on-the-Wold from Cheltenham.

By Car   From Oxford, take the A40 west to the junction with the A424, near Burford. Head northwest along the A424 to Stow-on-the-Wold.

ESSENTIALS   The **telephone area code** is 0451. The **Tourist Information Centre** is at Hollis House, The Square (tel. 0451/31082).

Stow-on-the-Wold is an unspoiled Cotswold market town, in spite of the busloads of tourists who stop off en route to Broadway and Chipping Campden. The town is the loftiest in the Cotswolds, built on a wold (rolling hill) about 800 feet above sea level. In its open market square you can still see the stocks where offenders in days gone by were jeered at and punished by the townspeople, who threw rotten eggs at the accused. The final battle between the Roundheads and the Royalists took place in Stow-on-the-Wold. The town, which is really like a village, is used by many as a base for exploring the Cotswold wool towns, as well as Stratford-upon-Avon.

WHERE TO STAY & DINE

FOSSE MANOR HOTEL, Fosse Way, Stow-on-the-Wold, Cheltenham, Gloucestershire GL54 1JX. Tel. 0451/830354. Fax 0451/832486. 20 rms (all with bath or shower), 2 suites. TV TEL **Directions:** Take the A429 1¼ miles south of Stow-on-the-Wold.
$ Rates (including English breakfast): £45 ($67.50) single; £90 ($135) double; from £124 ($186) suite. AE, DC, MC, V. **Parking:** Free.
The hotel lies near the site of an ancient Roman road that used to bisect England, its stone walls and Neo-Gothic gables almost concealed by strands of ivy. From some of the high stone-sided windows you can enjoy a view of a landscaped garden with a sunken lily pond, flagstone walks, and an old-fashioned sundial. Inside, the interior is conservatively modernized with such touches as a padded and upholstered bar and a dining room. The bedrooms are homelike, with matching fabrics and wallpaper, and two of the rooms are favorites of honeymooners.

THE GRAPEVINE HOTEL, Sheep St., Stow-on-the-Wold, Cheltenham, Gloucestershire GL54 1AU. Tel. 0451/830344, or toll free 800/528-1234 in the U.S. Fax 0451/832278. 23 rms (all with bath or shower). TV TEL
$ Rates (including English breakfast): £66–£89 ($99–$133.50) single; £92–£138 ($138–$207) double. AE, DC, MC, V. **Parking:** Free. **Closed:** Dec 24–Jan 10.
The Grapevine, facing the village green, mingles urban sophistication with reasonable prices, rural charm, and intimacy. Known for both its hotel and its restaurant, this is

one of the most innovative and charming places to stay in this much-visited village. It was named after the ancient vine whose tendrils shade and shelter the beautiful conservatory restaurant. Each bedroom has tasteful furnishings, radio, hairdryer, and a tea and coffee maker. Six rooms have a minibar.

The reading room, comfortable lounge, and cozy bar with Victorian accessories create a warm ambience for tea, bar snacks, or dinner. Full meals feature English, French, and Italian cuisine and are served from 7 to 9:30pm daily. Bar snacks are served at midday. The hotel has won an AA Rosette for its cuisine. Dinners are more elaborate, beginning at £15.95 ($23.90) and including, perhaps, turkey scallops with white wine sauce, beef filet topped with Stilton, or, for the vegetarian, garlic mushroom mille-feuilles.

STOW LODGE HOTEL, The Square, Stow-on-the-Wold, Cheltenham, Gloucestershire GL54 1AB. Tel. 0451/830485. 20 rms (all with bath). TV
$ Rates (including English breakfast): £45–£55 ($67.50–$82.50) single; £55–£80 ($82.50–$120) double. AE, DC. **Parking:** Free.

 Stow Lodge dominates the marketplace, but is set back far enough to maintain its aloofness. Its gardens, honeysuckle growing over the stone walls, diamond-shaped windows, gables, and many chimneys capture the best of country living, while letting you anchor right into the heart of town. The ample, well-furnished bedrooms have radios, central heating, and hot-beverage facilities. Arrange to have your afternoon tea out back by the flower garden. The owners discovered an old (ca. 1770) open stone fireplace in their lounge and offer log fires as an added attraction.

WYCK HILL HOUSE, Burford Rd., Stow-on-the-Wold, Cheltenham, Gloucestershire GL54 1HY. Tel. 0451/831936. Fax 0451/832243. 30 rms (all with bath), 3 suites. TV TEL **Directions:** Head 2½ miles south of Stow-on-the-Wold on the A424.
$ Rates (including English breakfast): £77–£130 ($115.50–$195) single; £135 ($202.50) double; from £170 ($255) suite. AE, DC, MC, V. **Parking:** Free.

Wyck Hill House dates from 1720 when its stone walls were begun as a manor house. One wing of the manor house, it was discovered in the course of recent restoration, rested on the foundations of a Roman villa. Today, Wyck Hill is one of the most sophisticated country hotels in the region, lying on 100 acres of grounds and gardens. The opulent interior pays attention to 18th-century authenticity with room after room leading to paneled libraries and Adam sitting rooms. The well-furnished bedrooms are in the main hotel, in the coach-house annex, or in the orangery.

Excellent food is also served, a three-course luncheon costing £15 ($22.50); an à la carte dinner goes for £36 ($54).

IN NEARBY LOWER SWELL

THE OLD FARMHOUSE HOTEL, Lower Swell, Stow-on-the-Wold, Cheltenham, Gloucestershire GL54 1LF. Tel. 0451/830232. Fax 0451/870962. 14 rms (12 with bath). TV TEL **Directions:** Take the B4068 1¼ miles west of Stow-on-the-Wold.
$ Rates (including English breakfast): £22 ($33) single without bath, £43 ($64.50) single with bath; £44 ($66) double without bath, £65 ($97.50) double with bath. MC, V. **Parking:** Free. **Closed:** Jan 1–14.

This small, intimate hotel in the heart of the Cotswolds was converted from a 16th-century farmhouse. The hotel has been completely refurbished and the original fireplaces restored, once again blazing with log fires.

The relaxed atmosphere, together with excellent food and wine, has made this a popular stop for visitors, so reserving a room before arrival is strongly recommended. Two accommodations under the eaves share a bath, and all units are different because of the building's farmhouse origin. Dinner is served daily from 7pm, with last orders taken at 9pm. The table d'hôte menu is changed daily, costing £14.50 ($21.80). The hotel has a secluded walled garden and ample private parking.

8. MORETON-IN-MARSH

83 miles NW of London, 8 miles N of Bourton-on-the-Water,
4 miles N of Stow-on-the-Wold, 8 miles W of Broadway,
7 miles S of Chipping Campden, 17 miles S of Stratford-upon-Avon

GETTING THERE   By Train   From London's Paddington Station, British Rail provides daily service to Moreton-in-Marsh (trip time: 1 hr., 50 min.).

By Bus   National Express coaches run from London's Victoria Coach Station to Moreton-in-Marsh daily.

By Car   From Stow-on-the-Wold (see above), take the A429 4 miles north.

ESSENTIALS   The **telephone area code** is 0608. The nearest **tourist office** is at Stow-on-the-Wold (see above).

M oreton-in-Marsh is an important center for British Rail passengers headed for the Cotswolds because it's near many villages of interest. Incidentally, don't take the name "Moreton-in-Marsh" too literally. "Marsh" derives from an old word meaning "border." Look for the 17th-century market hall and the old curfew tower, and then walk down the High (the main street), where Roman legions trudged centuries ago. The town once lay on the ancient Fosse Way.

WHERE TO STAY

MANOR HOUSE HOTEL, High St., Moreton-in-Marsh, Gloucestershire GL56 0LJ. Tel. 0608/50501, or toll free 800/876-9480 in the U.S. Fax 0608/51481. 38 rms (all with bath or shower), 1 suite. TV TEL
$ Rates (including English breakfast): £63.50 ($95.30) single; £83–£98 ($124.50–$147) double; from £128 ($192) suite. AE, DC, MC, V. **Parking:** Free.
The Manor House comes complete with its own ghost, a priest's hiding hole, a secret passage, and a moot room used centuries ago by local merchants to settle arguments over wool exchanges. On the main street, it's a formal yet gracious house, and its rear portions reveal varying architectural periods of design. Here, the vine-covered walls protect the garden. Inside are many living rooms, one especially intimate with leather chairs and a fireplace-within-a-fireplace, ideal for drinks and the exchange of "bump-in-the-night" stories. The hotel has a heated indoor pool, a spa bath, and a sauna. Bedrooms are tastefully furnished, often with antiques or fine reproductions. Many have fine old desks set in front of window ledges, with a view of the garden and ornamental pond.
   A favorite nook is the bar, with its garden view through leaded Gothic windows. Evening meals in the two-level dining room are candlelit. A table d'hôte lunch goes for £12 ($18), and dinner is £17.50 ($26.30).

REDESDALE ARMS, High St., Moreton-in-Marsh, Gloucestershire GL56 0AW. Tel. 0608/50308. Fax 0608/51843. 15 rms (all with bath), 2 suites. TV TEL
$ Rates (including English breakfast): £47 ($70.50) single; £60 ($90) double or suite. AE, MC, V. **Parking:** Free.

This is one of the largest and best-preserved coaching inns in Gloucestershire. Originally established around 1774 as the Unicorn Hotel, it functioned around 1840 as an important link in the Bath-to-Lincoln stagecoach routes, offering food and accommodations to both humans and horses during the arduous journey. In 1891, it was renamed in honor of Baron Redesdale, donor of Moreton's unusual town hall, which still stands a few steps away.

Since then, the inn has been considerably upgraded, with modernized and comfortably furnished bedrooms, and much of the old-fashioned charm still intact. Guests gravitate to the bar, where drinks are served in front of a 6-foot-high stone fireplace. During clement weather, tables are set up in a sheltered courtyard.

The inn is especially well known for its meals and its English and French cuisine. A three-course dinner costs £15 ($22.50). Lunches usually consist of simpler platters, priced from £2.25 to £6.50 ($3.40 to $9.80), which are usually served in the bar.

THE WHITE HART ROYAL HOTEL, High St., Moreton-in-Marsh, Gloucestershire GL56 0BA. Tel. 0608/50731. Fax 0608/50880. 18 rms (all with bath). TV TEL

$ Rates (including English breakfast): £55 ($82.50) single; £70–£75 ($105–$112.50) double. AE, DC, MC, V. **Parking:** Free.

A mellow old Cotswold inn once graced by Charles I (in 1644), the inn provides modern amenities without compromising the personality of yesteryear. The well-furnished bedrooms all have hot and cold running water, innerspring mattresses, and a few antiques intermixed with basic 20th-century pieces. The bar is built of irregular Cotswold stone. You can have drinks in front of the 10-foot open fireplace. Lunches are informal affairs served in the hotel's pub, where platters priced from £2.25 to £6.50 ($3.40 to $9.80) are featured. Dinners are more elaborate sit down events, with four-course table d'hôte menus priced at £14 ($21) each. The hotel passed from ownership by one of Britain's largest chains, the Forte Group, into private hands in 1992.

WHERE TO DINE

After long years of slumber, the restaurant picture in Moreton-in-Marsh has awakened—in fact, the town is now known as "the dining center of the Cotswolds." That reputation is based entirely on the two restaurants previewed below.

ANNIE'S, 3 Oxford St. Tel. 51981.
   Cuisine: ENGLISH/FRENCH COUNTRY COOKING. **Reservations:** Recommended.
$ Prices: Appetizers £3.60–£6.50 ($5.40–$9.80); main courses £13.50–£17.50 ($20.30–$26.30); fixed-price 3-course dinner £19 ($28.50); fixed-price 3-course Sun lunch £16 ($24). AE, DC, MC, V.
   Open: Lunch, Sun only, noon–2pm; dinner Mon–Sat 7–10pm.
   Closed: 2 weeks in late Jan.

Situated in the heart of town, on a side street that merges with Fosse Way (the old Roman road), lies a stone-sided three-story house whose walls range from 300 to 400 years of age. Here David and Anne Ellis, along with Milly Kent, prepare ample portions of English and French country cuisine which have won an enthusiastic response from weekending Londoners escaping from their careers in television and the West End theater district.

Specialties include a warm salad of pan-fried pigeon breast on a bed of greens with pan-fried mushrooms, bacon, and warm balsamic vinaigrette; a feuilleté of smoked haddock lined with spinach in a Stilton-flavored cream sauce; saddle of venison with a port wine and juniperberry sauce served with a phyllo parcel and puréed vegetables; filet of lamb with a sauce of young leeks and pink peppercorns; and a gourmet version of steak-and-kidney pie. Desserts include a brown-sugar meringue filled with rose-petal cream and tropical fruits, and such perennial English favorites as treacle tart and spotted dick.

MARSH GOOSE, High St. Tel. 52111.
   Cuisine: MODERN BRITISH. **Reservations:** Recommended.
$ **Prices:** Lunch appetizers £2.25–£6 ($3.40–$9); lunch main courses £9–£13 ($13.50–$19.50); fixed-price 3-course dinners £21.50 ($32.30). MC, V.
   Open: Lunch Tues–Sun 12:30–2:30pm; dinner Tues–Sat 7:30–9:45pm.

⭐ Despite its antique allure and country-house elegance, this is very much an outpost of young and sophisticated Londoners seeking temporary respite in a tranquil area. The premises were formerly the stables for a coaching inn, then served as a shoe shop until their recent transformation. Today, you'll dine amid exposed Cotswold stone, a medley of autumn colors, and many of the accessories of the English country life.

The unusual cuisine is modern British, with goodly doses of Caribbean style thrown in. Examples include a curried parsnip soup; calves' liver with mangoes and Dubonnet sauce; breast of roasted guinea fowl with a creamy mustard sauce and prunes wrapped in bacon; and a suprême of salmon with mussels and a saffron-flavored cream sauce. The most talked-about dessert is a black-coffee jelly in a brownie-snap basket with butterscotch sauce and clotted cream. There's an exceptionally cozy bar area with ceiling beams and an open fireplace for before-dinner drinks.

---

9. BROADWAY

15 miles SW of Stratford-upon-Avon, 93 miles NW of London,
15 miles NE of Cheltenham

GETTING THERE By Train Connections are possible from London's Paddington Station via Oxford. The nearest railway stations are at Moreton-in-Marsh (7 miles away) or at Evesham (5 miles away). Frequent buses arrive from Evesham, but one has to take a taxi from Moreton.

By Bus From London's Victoria Coach Station, one coach daily runs to Broadway, taking 2½ hours.

By Car From Oxford, head west along the A40 until you reach Cheltenham and the junction with the A46 going northeast to Broadway.

ESSENTIALS The **telephone area code** is 0386. The **Tourist Information Centre** is at 1 Cotswold Court (tel. 0386/852937), open June to September only.

Many of the prime attractions of the Cotswolds, as well as the Shakespeare Country, lie within easy reach of Broadway, which is near Evesham at the southern tip of Hereford and Worcester. The best-known Cotswold village, Broadway has a wide and beautiful High Street flanked with honey-colored stone buildings, remarkable for their harmony of style and design. Overlooking the Vale of Evesham, it's a major stopover for bus tours and is mobbed in summer; however, it manages to retain its charm in spite of the invasion.

WHERE TO STAY

For lodgings, Broadway has the dubious distinction of having some of the most expensive inns in the Cotswolds. The guesthouses can also command a good price—and get it.

BROADWAY HOTEL, The Green, Broadway, Hereford and Worcester WR12 7AA. Tel. 0386/852401. Fax 0386/853879. 19 rms (all with bath or shower). TV TEL

$ **Rates** (including English breakfast): £57 ($85.50) single; £86–£92 ($129–$138) double. AE, DC, MC, V. **Parking:** Free.

Right on the village green, perhaps one of the most colorful places in Broadway, is this converted 15th-century house, formerly used by the abbots of Pershore, combining the half-timbered look of the Vale of Evesham with the stone of the Cotswolds. While keeping its old-world charm, the hotel has been modernized and converted to provide comforts. All the pleasantly furnished rooms have hot-beverage facilities and central heating. One of the rooms with full private bath has a four-poster bed. The cooking is fine, the service personal, the dining room attractive. The comfortable cocktail bar is well stocked. Locals claim that the best luncheon stopover in Broadway, if you're keeping an eye on costs, is the bar at this hotel. Lunches are served daily from noon to 2pm, with bar platters priced from £3.50 to £6 ($5.30 to $9). Dinner in the main dining room is served daily, featuring English specialties such as fish, duckling, or venison. A table d'hôte three-course meal costs £19.45 ($29.20), whereas à la carte main courses range from £9.50 to £15 ($14.30 to $22.50).

BUCKLAND MANOR, Buckland, near Broadway, Gloucestershire WR12 7LY. Tel. 0386/852626. Fax 0386/853557. 13 rms (all with bath). TV TEL **Directions:** Take the B4632 about 2 miles south of Broadway, across the county line in Gloucestershire.

$ **Rates** (including early-morning tea and English breakfast): £135–£260 ($202.50–$390) single occupancy in a double; £145–£270 ($217.50–$405) double. Children under 12 not accepted. AE, MC, V. **Parking:** Free.

This imposing slate-roofed manor house is ringed with fences of Cotswold stone, green lawns, lambs, and daffodils. Its jutting chimneys rise a few steps from the Buckland church, with its darkened stone tower. The core of the manor house was erected in the 13th century, with wings added in succeeding centuries, especially the 19th. The Oak Room, with a four-poster bed and burnished paneling, occupies what used to be a private library. In each of the rooms, leaded windows overlook gardens and grazing land with Highland cattle and Jacob sheep. Even the oversize bathrooms each contain at least one antique, as well as carpeting and modern plumbing. French-inspired meals, served in the elegant dining room with a baronial fireplace, cost £25 ($37.50) and up. Meals are served to nonresidents as well as residents. Service is daily from noon to 2pm and 7:30 to 9pm.

COLLIN HOUSE HOTEL AND RESTAURANT, Collin Lane, Broadway, Hereford and Worcester WR12 7PB. Tel. 0386/858354. 7 rms (all with bath). **Directions:** From Broadway, follow the signs to Evesham before turning right onto Collin Lane; the hotel is a mile west of Broadway off the A44.

$ **Rates** (including English breakfast): £45 ($67.50) single; £86–£99 ($129–$148.50) double. MC, V. **Parking:** Free.

A 16th-century Cotswold stone farmhouse has been transformed into a hotel, sitting on a country lane amid 8 acres of gardens and orchards. The cozy bedrooms are named for flowers that grow here in profusion. Large structural timbers, tasteful wallpaper, private baths, and mullioned windows make them attractive; Wild Rose, with its sloped ceiling, is probably the most romantic. A bar offers seating beside an inglenook fireplace.

Traditional English food, flavorfully and freshly prepared, is served in the evening by candlelight in a room with stone-rimmed windows and ceiling beams. Lunch is served daily from noon to 2:30pm, either in the bar (cheaply), or in the more formal dining room where a four-course fixed-price menu goes for £14.50 ($21.80). Dinner is served nightly from 7 to 9pm, costing from £17 to £23 ($25.50 to $34.50) for set menus.

DORMY HOUSE, Willersey Hill, Broadway, Hereford and Worcester WR12 7LF. Tel. 0386/852711. Fax 0386/858636. 49 rms (all with bath), 3 suites. TV TEL **Directions:** Take the A44 2 miles southeast of Broadway.

$ Rates (including English breakfast): £58–£74 ($87–$111) single; £110–£135 ($165–$202.50) double; from £140 ($210) suite. AE, DC, MC, V. **Parking:** Free.

This manor house high on a hill above the village boasts views in all directions. Its spectacular position has made it a favorite place for those who desire a meal, afternoon tea, or lodgings. Halfway between Broadway and Chipping Campden, it was created from a sheep farm. The owners transformed it, furnishing the 17th-century farmhouse with a few antiques, good soft beds, and full central heating, extending these amenities to an old adjoining timbered barn, which they converted into studio rooms, with open-beamed ceilings. Bowls of fresh flowers adorn tables and alcoves throughout the hotel.

The establishment serves excellent cuisine. A table d'hôte luncheon costs £16.50 ($24.80), and a fixed-price dinner goes for £26 ($39), both with coffee included. The cellar contains a superb selection of wines. Bar meals range from around £6 ($9).

LYGON ARMS, High St., Broadway, Hereford and Worcester WR12 7DU. Tel. 0386/852255. Fax 0386/858611. 60 rms (all with bath), 5 suites. TV TEL

$ Rates (including continental breakfast): £110–£130 ($165–$195) single; £130–£176 ($195–$264) double; from £208 ($312) suite. AE, DC, MC, V. **Parking:** Free.

This many-gabled structure, its mullioned windows looking right out on the road in the center of town, basks in its reputation as one of the greatest old English inns. In the rear it opens onto a private garden, with 3 acres of lawns, trees, and borders of flowers, stone walls with roses, and nooks for tea or sherry. The oldest portions date from 1532 or earlier, but builders many times since have made their additions. King Charles I reputedly drank with his friends in one of the oak-lined chambers, and later, his enemy, Oliver Cromwell, slept here on the night before the Battle of Worcester. Today an earlier century is evoked by the almost overwhelmingly charming cluster of antique-laden public rooms. These include cavernous fireplaces, smoke-stained paneling, 18th-century pieces, and polished brass. Many but not all the rooms are in the antique style; a new wing offers a more 20th-century environment. Each room contains a radio, hairdryer, and trouser press.

Dining/Entertainment: You dine in the oak-paneled Great Hall, with a Tudor fireplace, a vaulted ceiling, and a minstrels' gallery. Meals range from £29 to £43 ($43.50 to $64.50).

Services: 24-hour room service, laundry service.

Facilities: A country club adjoins the old inn. The club building was created from an 18th-century abattoir, formerly owned by pie makers and the site of the only butchery in England run by a clergyman. Many health and leisure facilities are available here, including a large swimming pool, a sauna, beauty therapy facilities, and a gym. Guests receive a complimentary membership.

WHERE TO DINE

HUNTER'S LODGE RESTAURANT, 48 High St. Tel. 853247.
 Cuisine: CONTINENTAL. **Reservations:** Required.
$ Prices: Appetizers £2.85–£7.50 ($4.30–$11.30); main courses £9.50–£13 ($14.30–$19.50); fixed-price menu £15 ($22.50). AE, DC, MC, V.
 Open: Lunch Sat–Sun 12:30–2pm; dinner Wed–Sat 7:30–9:45pm.

Housed in a historic building that dates back to 1650, this restaurant is set back from the main street of town, surrounded by lawns, flowerbeds, and shady trees. The stone gables are partially covered with ivy, the windows are deep-set with mullions and leaded panes, and the formal entrance has a small foyer furnished with antiques. The

English-Swiss owners prepare a sophisticated array of dishes that might include mushroom Stroganoff in a sour cream sauce, a salad of king prawns with bacon, boned and roasted quail in a cider-cream sauce, monkfish with courgettes (zucchini) and herbs, grilled salmon with tomatoes and ginger, and a deviled rack of lamb with mustard glaze and an herb-flavored crust. The establishment's most popular dessert is an almond meringue with an apricot sauce.

10. CHIPPING CAMPDEN

36 miles NW of Oxford, 12 miles S of Stratford-upon-Avon,
93 miles NW of London

GETTING THERE   By Train   Trains depart from London's Paddington Station for Moreton-in-Marsh, requiring about 90 to 120 minutes for the transit. At Moreton-in-Marsh, a bus operated by Barry's Coaches travels the 7 miles to Chipping Campden only 2 days a week. Most visitors get a taxi at Moreton-in-Marsh for the continuation on to Chipping Campden.

By Bus   The largest and most important nearby bus depot is Cheltenham, which receives service several times a day from London's Victoria Coach Station. From Cheltenham, however, bus service (again by Barry's Coaches) is infrequent and uncertain, departing at the most only three times per week.

By Car   From Oxford, take the A40 west to the junction with the A424 which you take northwest, passing by Stow-on-the-Wold. The route becomes the A44 until you reach the junction with the B4081, which you take northeast to Chipping Campden.

ESSENTIALS   The **telephone area code** is 0386. The summer-only **Tourist Information Centre** is at Woolstaplers Hall Museum, High Street (tel. 0386/840101).

The English, regardless of how often they visit the Cotswolds, are attracted in great numbers to this town, once a great wool center. Off the main road, it's easily accessible to major points of interest, and double-decker buses frequently run through here on their way to Oxford or Stratford-upon-Avon.

On the northern edge of the Cotswolds above the Vale of Evesham, Campden, a Saxon settlement, was recorded in the *Domesday Book*. In medieval times, rich merchants built homes of Cotswold stone along its model High Street, described by historian G. M. Trevelyan as "the most beautiful village street now left in the island." The houses have been so well preserved that Chipping Campden to this day remains a gem of the Middle Ages. Its church dates from the 15th century, and its old market hall is the loveliest in the Cotswolds. Look, also, for its almshouses, which, along with the market hall, were built by a great wool merchant, Sir Baptist Hicks, whose tomb is in the church.

WHERE TO STAY & DINE

COTSWOLD HOUSE HOTEL, The Square, Chipping Campden, Gloucestershire GL55 6AN. Tel. 0386/840330. Fax 0386/840310. 15 rms (all with bath). TV TEL

$ Rates (including half board): £84.50–£95.50 ($126.80–$143.30) single; £151–£193 ($226.50–$289.50) double. AE, DC, V. **Parking:** Free.

A stately, formal Regency house dating from 1800, right in the heart of the village, opposite the old wool market, Cotswold House sits amid 1½ acres of tended, walled garden with shaded seating. Note the fine winding Regency staircase in the reception hall. Bedrooms are furnished with themes ranging from Gothic to French to military, with many others included along the way.

You can dine in the restaurant, which serves first-class English and French food in a formal, elegant room, or in Greenstocks All-Day Eaterie, open daily from 9:30am to the last orders at 9:30pm. Here light dishes and meals are served.

KINGS ARMS HOTEL, The Square, Chipping Campden, Gloucestershire GL55 6AW. Tel. 0386/840256. 15 rms (7 with bath). TEL
$ Rates (including English breakfast): £20 ($30) single without bath, £30 ($45) single with bath; £40 ($60) double without bath, £60 ($90) double with bath. MC, V. **Parking:** Free.

 Partly Georgian, partly much older, this pretty house in the center of town has a large garden from which come the fresh vegetables for your good dinner. All the accommodations are well furnished and spotlessly clean. Only the rooms with private bath have a TV.

This hotel has a high reputation for its cooking, and over the years has won many awards. The traditional English-style Sunday lunch is offered at £9.50 ($14.30). However, a regular fixed-price dinner is featured at £12 ($18). Bar snacks, incidentally, are an inexpensive way to sample some gourmet dishes here.

NOEL ARMS HOTEL, High St., Chipping Campden, Gloucestershire GL55 6AT. Tel. 0386/840317, or toll free 800/528-1234 in the U.S. Fax 0386/841136. 26 rms (all with bath). TV TEL
$ Rates (including English breakfast): £58–£68 ($87–$102) single; £78–£88 ($117–$132) double. AE, MC, V. **Parking:** Free.
Dating back to the 14th century, the Noel Arms is a famous establishment. The food here always draws praise. Lunch averages £9 ($13.50) and dinner runs £12.75 to £14.75 ($19.10 to $22.10), if you order from the à la carte menu. The food is traditional English: poached salmon, roast sirloin of beef with Yorkshire pudding, roast leg of lamb with onion sauce, steak hollandaise, apple and loganberry pie.

There's a private sitting room for residents, but you may prefer the lounge, with its 12-foot-wide fireplace. The adjoining room is the public tavern—public in the sense that it's frequented by the locals. It's almost too quaint: old worn curved settles where you can drink beer from mugs of pewter, and soak up an atmosphere enhanced by racks of copper, brass pans, medallions, and oak tables and chairs worn from centuries of use. There are bedrooms in both the main building and a modern extension built of Cotswold stone. The rooms are comfortably furnished and well kept.

IN NEARBY CHARINGWORTH

CHARINGWORTH MANOR HOTEL, Charingworth, near Chipping Campden, Gloucestershire GL55 6NS. Tel. 038678/555, or toll free 800/525-4800 in the U.S. Fax 038678/353. 25 rms (all with bath), 1 suite. TV TEL
Directions: Take the B4035 3¼ miles east of Chipping Campden.
$ Rates: £85 ($127.50) single; £110–£175 ($165–$262.50) double; from £210 ($315) suite. AE, DC, MC, V. **Parking:** Free.

A manor has stood on this spot since the time of the *Domesday Book*. The present Tudor-Jacobean house, in honey-colored stone with slate roofs, sits on 55 acres of grounds, and in the 1930s was host to such illustrious guests as T. S. Eliot. The old-world charm of the place has been preserved, in spite of modernization, and log fires and well-chosen antiques create a delightful country-house ambience. Each room is individually decorated and luxuriously furnished, both in its use of antiques and English fabrics. Amenities include a hairdryer, trouser press, and room safe. Many of the period rooms contain four-poster beds. Guests can also wander through a well-manicured garden.

Dining/Entertainment: A fixed-price lunch is offered for £13.50 ($20.30) and a fixed-price dinner for £32.50 ($48.80) in the elegant restaurant of the hotel, which lies under low ceiling beams. Excellent ingredients are deftly handled in the kitchen to create a French and English menu. Game is often featured. The wine list is carefully chosen. Lunch is served daily from noon to 2pm and dinner daily from 7 to 9:30pm.

Services: 24-hour room service, laundry service.

Facilities: A Leisure Spa opened in 1992 consisting of a luxurious indoor heated pool built in Romanesque style, a sauna, steam room, solarium, and billiards room. There is also an all-weather tennis court on the grounds.

STRATFORD-UPON-AVON & WARWICK

Shakespeare Country in the heart of England is, after London, the district most visited by North Americans. Many who don't recognize the county name, Warwickshire, know its foremost tourist town, Stratford-upon-Avon, birthplace of England's greatest writer. Other places that attract overseas visitors include Warwick and Kenilworth castles, as well as Coventry Cathedral.

The county and its neighboring shires form a land of industrial cities, green fields, and market towns dotted with buildings, some of which have changed little since Shakespeare's time.

SEEING STRATFORD-UPON-AVON & WARWICK

GETTING THERE

Motorists from London take the M40 toward Oxford, continuing along the A34 to reach Stratford. British Rail has services to Stratford-upon-Avon, involving changes at Oxford and Leamington Spa. Service to Coventry is from London's Euston Station. At Coventry, connections are made to Stratford. National Express coaches leaving from London's Victoria Coach Station also serve both Stratford and Warwick.

A SUGGESTED ITINERARY

Days 1–2: Spend 2 days in Stratford, taking in the literary-pilgrimage centers. Spend Day 2 visiting Ragley Hall and perhaps George Washington's Sulgrave Manor—as much as can be done in a single day. Take in as much theater as you can.

Days 3–4: While staying overnight in Warwick, visit Warwick Castle in the morning, and explore the ruins of Kenilworth Castle in the early afternoon before a late-afternoon visit to Coventry Cathedral.

---

1. STRATFORD-UPON-AVON

91 miles NW of London, 40 miles NW of Oxford, 8 miles S of Warwick

GETTING THERE **By Train** The train from London's Paddington Station takes you here in 2 hours, 15 minutes; call 071/262-6767 for schedules. Standard round-trip tickets cost £25 ($37.50).

✓ WHAT'S SPECIAL ABOUT STRATFORD-UPON-AVON & WARWICK

Castles

☐ Warwick Castle, between Stratford and Coventry, regarded as England's finest medieval castle.

☐ Kenilworth Castle, in magnificent ruins, the setting of Sir Walter Scott's romance *Kenilworth.*

Literary Shrines

☐ Shakespeare's Birthplace, Stratford, where the Bard was born on April 23, 1564.

☐ Anne Hathaway's Cottage, a mile from Stratford, a wattle-and-daub cottage where Anne Hathaway lived before marrying Shakespeare.

Buildings

☐ Ragley Hall, built in 1680 outside Stratford, home of the Marquess of Hertford and restored to its original look.

☐ Coventry Cathedral, consecrated in 1962, was designed by Sir Basil Spence in a modern style that aroused the opposition of traditional architectural devotees.

Theatrical Events

☐ Attending a performance at the Royal Shakespeare Theatre on the River Avon in Stratford.

By "Road & Rail Link" This Shakespeare Connection by train and bus is a sure way to attend the Royal Shakespeare Theatre and return to London on the same day. It leaves from London's Euston Station (tel. 071/387-7070) Monday through Friday at 9:10am, 10:40am, 4:55pm, and 5:15pm, and on Saturday at 9:10am, 10:30am, 5pm, and 5:15pm. If you only want to attend the evening performance at the theater, the best train to catch is the 5pm. Travel is by train to Coventry, then bus to Stratford. Returns to London are scheduled according to theater performances, with departures at 11:15pm. The "Road & Rail Link" is operated by British Rail and Guide Friday. The Guide Friday office in Stratford is at Civic Hall, 14 Rother St. (tel. 0789/294466). Prices are £22 ($33) for a one-way ticket or £25 ($37.50) for a round-trip ticket valid for 3 months. Ask for a Shakespeare Connection ticket at London's Euston Station or at any British Rail London Travel Centre. BritRail pass holders using the service simply pay the bus fare to Stratford from Coventry, costing £6 ($9) one way or £7.50 ($11.30) round-trip.

By Bus Eight National Express coaches from Victoria Coach Station in London (tel. 071/730-0202) run daily to Stratford-upon-Avon (trip time: 3 hrs., 20 min.). A single-day round-trip ticket costs £15.50 ($23.30), or £12.75 ($19.10) if you return on the same day.

By Car Take the M40 toward Oxford and continue to Stratford-upon-Avon on the A34.

ESSENTIALS The **telephone area code** is 0789. The **Tourist Information Centre,** Bridgefoot (tel. 0789/293127), has all the details about the Shakespeare properties. It's open March to October, Monday through Saturday from 9am to 5:30pm and on Sunday from 2 to 5pm; November to February, Monday through Saturday from 10:30am to 4pm.

To contact the **Shakespeare Birthplace Trust,** which administers many of the attractions, send a self-addressed envelope and International Reply Coupon to the Director, the Shakespeare Centre, Henley Street, Stratford-upon-Avon, Warwickshire CV37 6QW (tel. 0789/204016).

Tourism is responsible for the magnitude of traffic to this market town on the Avon River. Actor David Garrick really launched the shrine in 1769, when he organized the first of the Bard's commemorative birthday celebrations. William Shakespeare, of course, was born in Stratford-upon-Avon. Little is known about his early life, and many of the stories connected with Shakespeare's days in Stratford are largely fanciful, invented to amuse and entertain the vast number of literary fans who make the pilgrimage.

Another magnet for tourists today is the Royal Shakespeare Theatre, where Britain's foremost actors perform during a long season that lasts from Easter until late January. Stratford-upon-Avon is also a good center for trips to Warwick Castle, Kenilworth Castle, Sulgrave Manor (ancestral home of George Washington), and Coventry Cathedral.

WHAT TO SEE & DO
THE THEATER

★ The **Royal Shakespeare Company** has a major showcase in Stratford-upon-Avon, the Royal Shakespeare Theatre, Waterside (tel. 0789/295623), on the banks of the Avon. Seating 1,500 patrons, the theater has a season that runs from March to December. The company has some of the finest actors on the British stage. In an average season, five Shakespearean plays are staged.

Usually, you'll need reservations. There are two successive booking periods, each one opening about 2 months in advance. You can pick these up from a North American or an English travel agent. If you wait until your arrival in Stratford, it may be too late to get a good seat. Tickets can be booked through New York agents Edwards and Edwards or Keith Prowse, or direct with the theater box office with payment by major credit card. Call the box office at the number listed above. The box office is open Monday through Saturday from 9:30am to 8pm. The price of seats generally ranges from £6 to £39 ($9 to $58.50). A small number of tickets are always held for sale on the day of a performance. You can make a credit-card reservation and pick up your ticket on the day it is to be used, but you can't cancel once your reservation is made.

The **Swan Theatre** (same address and phone as Royal Shakespeare Theatre) opened in 1986. It seats 430, and stages many plays by Shakespeare and later playwrights. The interior of the Swan Theatre is in the style of an Elizabethan playhouse. The Swan was erected after the Victorian-style Memorial Theatre, dating from 1879, was destroyed by fire in 1926. The original art gallery, library, and the collections escaped the fire, and now the Swan has displays on stagecraft from medieval mummers to the present day, as well as costumes, props, and photographs from Royal Shakespeare Company productions. The Swan Theatre, which uses the same box office as the Royal Shakespeare Theatre, presents a repertoire of five plays each season, with tickets ranging from £8 to £27 ($12 to $40.50).

The RSC Collection is an exhibition of the memorabilia, costumes, and paintings of the famous participants and actors associated with the theater in Stratford. It is open all year (except Christmas and December 26) Monday through Saturday from 9:15am to 8pm and on Sunday from noon to 5pm (November to March, on Sunday from 11am to 4pm). Admission is £1.70 ($2.60) for adults, £1.20 ($1.80) for children. Theater tours of the Royal Shakespeare and Swan Theatres are at 1:30pm and 5:30pm (excluding matinee days) and four times on Sunday, production schedules permitting. Tours cost £3.50 ($5.30) for adults and £2.50 ($3.80) for children.

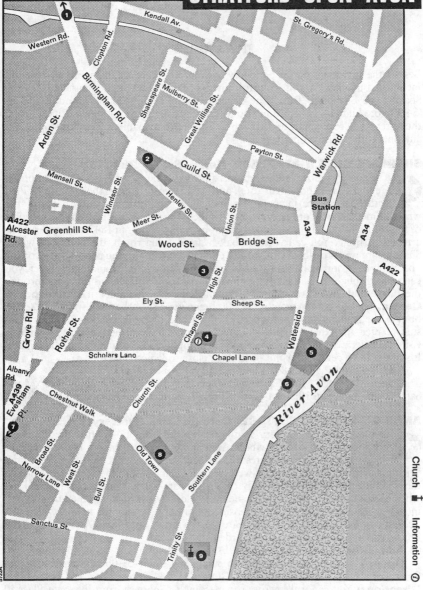

STRATFORD–UPON–AVON

Mary Arden's House and the
   Shakespeare Countryside Museum ❶
Hall's Croft ❽
Harvard House ❸
Anne Hathaway's Cottage ❼

Holy Trinity Church ❾
New Place/Nash's House ❹
Royal Shakespeare Theatre ❺
Shakespeare's Birthplace ❷
Swan Theatre ❻

Church ✝

Information ⊖

For information on the RSC Collection and Theatre Tours, call 0789/296655, ext. 421.

THE SIGHTS

Besides the attractions on the periphery of Stratford, there are many Elizabethan and Jacobean buildings in this colorful town—many of them administered by the Shakespeare Birthplace Trust. One ticket—costing £7.50 ($11.30) for adults, £3.25 ($4.90) for children—will permit you to visit the five most important sights. Pick up the ticket if you're planning to do much sightseeing (obtainable at your first stopover at any one of the Trust properties).

SHAKESPEARE'S BIRTHPLACE, Henley St. Tel. 204016.

The son of a glover and whittawer (leather worker), the Bard was born on St. George's day (April 23) in 1564, and died 52 years later on the same day. Filled with Shakespeare memorabilia, including a portrait and furnishings of the writer's time, the Trust property is a half-timbered structure, dating from the first part of the 16th century. The house was bought by public donors in 1847 and preserved as a national shrine. You can visit the oak-beamed living room, the bedroom where Shakespeare was probably born, a fully equipped kitchen of the period (look for the "babyminder"), and a Shakespeare Museum, illustrating his life and times. Later, you can walk through the garden. It's estimated that some 660,000 visitors pass through the house annually. Next door to the birthplace is the modern **Shakespeare Centre,** built to commemorate the 400th anniversary of the Bard's birth. It serves both as the administrative headquarters of the Birthplace Trust and as a library and study center. An extension to the original center, which opened in 1981, includes a visitors' center, which acts as a reception area for all those coming to the birthplace. It's in the town center near the post office close to Union Street.

Admission: £2.50 ($3.80) adults, £1.10 ($1.70) children.

Open: Mar–Oct, Mon–Sat 9am–5:30pm, Sun 10am–5:30pm; Nov–Feb, Mon–Sat 9:30am–4pm, Sun 10:30am–4pm. **Closed:** Jan 1, Good Friday, and Dec 24–26.

ANNE HATHAWAY'S COTTAGE, Cottage Lane, Shottery. Tel. 292100.

In the hamlet of Shottery 1 mile from Stratford-upon-Avon is the thatched, wattle-and-daub cottage where Anne Hathaway lived before her marriage to the poet. It's the most interesting and seemingly the most photographed of the Trust properties. The Hathaways were yeoman farmers, and the cottage provides a rare insight into the life of a family of Shakespeare's day. Shakespeare married her when he was only 18 years old, and she much older. Many of the original furnishings, including the courting settle and utensils, are preserved inside the house, which was occupied by descendants of Shakespeare's wife's family until 1892. After a visit to the house, you'll want to linger in the garden and orchard.

Admission: £2.10 ($3.20) adults, £1 ($1.50) children.

Open: Mar–Oct, Mon–Sat 9am–5:30pm, Sun 10am–5:30pm; Nov–Feb, Mon–Sat 9:30am–4pm, Sun 10:30am–4pm. **Closed:** Jan 1, Good Friday, and Dec 24–26.

Directions: You can walk across the meadow to Shottery from Evesham Place in Stratford (pathway marked), or take a bus from Bridge St.

NEW PLACE/NASH'S HOUSE, Chapel St. Tel. 204016.

This is where Shakespeare retired in 1610, a prosperous man to judge from the standards of his day. He died here 6 years later, at the age of 52. Regrettably, only the site of his former home remains today, since the house was torn down. You enter the gardens through Nash's House (Thomas Nash married Elizabeth Hall, a granddaughter of the poet). Nash's House has 16th-century period rooms and an exhibition illustrating the history of Stratford. The popular Knott Garden adjoins the site, and represents the style of a fashionable Elizabethan garden. New Place has its own great garden, which once belonged to Shakespeare. Here, the Bard planted a mulberry tree, so popular with latter-day visitors to Stratford that the cantankerous owner of the garden chopped it down. The mulberry tree that grows there today is said to have been planted from a cutting of the original tree.

Admission: £1.70 ($2.60) adults, 70p ($1.10) children.

Open: Mar–Oct, Mon–Sat 9:30am–5pm, Sun 10:30am–5:30pm; Nov–Feb, Mon–Sat 10am–4pm. **Closed:** Jan 1, Good Friday, and Dec 24–26. **Directions:** Walk west down High St.; Chapel St. is a continuation of High St.

MARY ARDEN'S HOUSE AND THE SHAKESPEARE COUNTRYSIDE MUSEUM, Wilmcote. Tel. 293455.

This Tudor farmstead, with its old stone dovecote and various outbuildings, was the girlhood home of Shakespeare's mother. It's situated at Wilmcote, 3½ miles from Stratford. The house contains rare pieces of country furniture and domestic utensils. In the barns, stable, cowshed, and farmyard you'll find an extensive collection of farming implements illustrating life and work in the local countryside from Shakespeare's time to the present.

Visitors also see the neighboring **Glebe Farm,** whose interior evokes farm life in late Victorian and Edwardian times. Light refreshments are available, and there is a picnic area.

Admission: £3 ($4.50) adults, £1.20 ($1.80) children.

Open: Mar–Oct, Mon–Sat 9:30am–5pm, Sun 10:30am–5pm; Nov–Feb, Mon–Sat 10am–4pm, Sun 1:30–4pm. **Closed:** Jan 1, Good Friday, and Dec 24–26. **Directions:** Take the A34 (Birmingham) road for 3½ miles.

HALL'S CROFT, Old Town. Tel. 297848.

This house is on Old Town (the name of a street), not far from the parish church, Holy Trinity. It was here that Shakespeare's daughter Susanna lived with her husband, Dr. John Hall. Hall's Croft is an outstanding Tudor house with a beautiful walled garden, furnished in the style of a middle-class home of the time. Dr. Hall was widely respected and he built up a large medical practice in the area. Exhibits illustrating the theory and practice of medicine in Dr. Hall's time are on view. Visitors to the house are welcome to use the adjoining Hall's Croft Club, which serves morning coffee, lunch, and afternoon tea.

Admission: £1.70 ($2.60) adults, 70p ($1.10) children.

Open: Mar–Oct, Mon–Sat 9:30am–5pm, Sun 10:30am–5:30pm; Nov–Feb, Mon–Sat 10am–4pm, Sun 1:30–4pm. **Closed:** Jan 1, Good Friday, and Dec 24–26. **Directions:** To reach Hall's Croft, walk west from High St., which becomes Chapel St. and Church St. At the intersection with Old Town, go left.

HOLY TRINITY CHURCH, Old Town. Tel. 266316.

In an attractive setting near the Avon river is the parish church where Shakespeare is buried ("and curst be he who moves my bones"). The Parish Register records his baptism in 1564 and burial in 1616 (copies of the original). The church has been described as one of the most beautiful parish churches in England.

Admission: Church, free; Shakespeare's tomb, 50p (80¢) adults, 30p (50¢) students.

Open: Apr–Oct, Mon–Sat 8:30am–6pm, Sun 2–5pm; Nov–Mar, Mon–Sat 8:30am–4pm, Sun 2–5pm. **Directions:** Continue past the Royal Shakespeare Theatre with the river on your left; the church is reached after a 4-minute walk.

HARVARD HOUSE, High St. Tel. 204507.

Harvard House is a fine example of an Elizabethan town house. Rebuilt in 1596, it was once the home of Katherine Rogers, mother of John Harvard, founder of Harvard University. In 1909 the house was purchased by Chicago millionaire Edward Morris, who presented it as a gift to the American university. It's the most ornate house in Stratford. The rooms are filled with period furniture, and floors are made of the local flagstone. Look for the Bible Chair, used for hiding the Bible during the days of Tudor persecution.

Admission: £1 ($1.50) adults, 50p (80¢) students and children.
Open: June–Sept, Mon–Sat 10am–4pm. **Closed:** Oct–May.

THE ROYAL SHAKESPEARE THEATRE SUMMER HOUSE, Avonbank Gardens. Tel. 297671.

This is a brass-rubbing center, where medieval and Tudor brasses illustrate the knights and ladies, scholars, merchants, and priests of a bygone era. The Stratford collection contains a large assortment of exact replicas of brasses. The charge made for the rubbings includes the paper and wax, and any instruction you might need.

Admission: Free.
Open: Apr–Sept, daily 10am–6pm; Oct, daily 11am–4pm.

TOURS

Guided tours of Stratford-upon-Avon leave from the **Guide Friday Tourism Centre,** Civic Hall, Rother Street (tel. 0789/294466) daily. In summer, departures of open-top double-decker buses are every 15 minutes from 9:30am to 5:30pm. You can take a 1-hour ride without stops, or you can get off at any or all of the Shakespeare's Birthplace Trust properties. Anne Hathaway's Cottage and Mary Arden's House are the two logical stops to make outside the town. Tour tickets are valid all day so you can hop on and off the buses. The price for these tours is £6 ($9) for adults or £1.50 ($2.30) for children.

NEARBY ATTRACTIONS

RAGLEY HALL, Alcester. Tel. 0789/762090.

A magnificent 115-room Palladian country house, Ragley Hall, built in 1680, is the home of the Earl and Countess of Yarmouth. It's located in Alcester, 9 miles from Stratford-upon-Avon. The house has been restored and appears much as it did during the early 1700s. Great pains have been taken to duplicate colors, and, in some cases, the original wallpaper patterns. The pictures, furniture, and works of art that fill the vast and spacious rooms represent 10 generations of collecting by the Seymour family. Ragley Hall may be a private home, but it has a museumlike quality, and many of its artifacts have great historical importance. Perhaps the most spectacular attraction is the lavishly painted south staircase hall. Muralist Graham Rust painted a modern trompe l'oeil work depicting the Temptation.

Admission: House, garden, and park, £4.50 ($6.80) adults, £3.50 ($5.30) children; park and gardens only, £3.50 ($5.30) adults, £2.50 ($3.80) children.
Open: Easter–Sept, Tues–Thurs and Sat–Sun, house noon–5pm; gardens 10am–6pm. **Closed:** Oct–Easter. **Directions:** Since there is no suitable bus service, visitors arrive by car. Ragley Hall is located on the A435 to Evesham, about 1½ miles west of the town of Alcester. There is easy access from the main motorway network, including the M40 from London, some 100 miles away.

Coventry

Coventry, 19 miles north of Stratford-upon-Avon, has long been noted in legend as the ancient market town through which Lady Godiva took her famous ride—giving rise to a new expression in English, *Peeping Tom*. The veracity of the Lady Godiva story is hard to ascertain. It's been suggested that the good lady never appeared nude in town, but was the victim of scandalmongers. Coventry today is a Midlands industrial city. The city was partially destroyed during the Blitz in the early '40s, but the restoration is miraculous.

COVENTRY CATHEDRAL, Priory Row, Coventry. Tel. 0203/227597.

Sir Basil Spence's controversial cathedral (consecrated in 1962) is the city's main attraction. The cathedral is on the same site as the 14th-century Perpendicular building, and you can visit the original tower. Many locals have maintained that the structure is more likely to be appreciated by the foreign visitor, as the Britisher is more attached to traditional cathedral design.

Outside is Sir Jacob Epstein's bronze masterpiece, *St. Michael Slaying the Devil*. Inside, the outstanding feature is the 70-foot-high altar tapestry by Graham Sutherland, said to be the largest in the world. The floor-to-ceiling abstract stained-glass windows are the work of the Royal College of Art. The West Window is most interesting, with its engraved glass depicting rows of stylized saints and prophets with angels flying around between them.

In the undercroft of the cathedral is a visitor center, the **Spirit of Coventry.** There you can see the Walkway of Holograms, three-dimensional images created with laser light, depicting the Stations of the Cross. The treasures of the cathedral are on show. An audiovisual exhibit on the city and church includes the fact that 450 aircraft dropped 40,000 firebombs on the city in 1 day.

After visiting the cathedral, you may want to have tea in Fraters Restaurant nearby.

Admission: Cathedral, free, but suggested donation £2 ($3); tower, £1 ($1.50) adults, 80p ($1.20) children; visitor center, £1.25 ($1.90) adults, 75p ($1.10) children 6–16.

Open: June–Sept, daily 9:30am–7pm; Oct–May, daily 9:30am–5:30pm. **Bus:** Local buses from Stratford-upon-Avon run north to Coventry every 20 minutes during the day.

⭐ SULGRAVE MANOR, Manor Rd., Sulgrave, Banbury. Tel. 0295/760205.

American visitors especially will be interested in this small mid-16th-century Tudor manor. As a part of Henry VIII's plan to dissolve the monasteries, he sold the priory-owned manor in 1539 to Lawrence Washington, who had been mayor of Northampton; George Washington was a direct descendant of Lawrence (seven generations removed). The Washington family occupied Sulgrave for more than a century, and in 1656, Col. John Washington left for the New World.

In 1914 the manor was purchased by a group of English people in honor of the friendship between Britain and America. Over the years, major restoration has taken place, with an eye toward returning it as much as possible to its original state. The Colonial Dames have been largely responsible for raising the money. From both sides of the Atlantic, the appropriate furnishings were donated, including a number of portraits—even a Gilbert Stuart original of the first president. On the main doorway is the Washington family coat-of-arms—two bars and a trio of mullets—which is believed to have been the inspiration for the "Stars and Stripes."

Admission: £3 ($4.50) adults, £1.50 ($2.30) children 5–16, free for children under 5.

Open: Mar and Oct–Dec, Thurs–Tues 10:30am–1pm and 2–4pm; Apr–Sept, Thurs–Tues 10:30am–1pm and 2–5:30pm. **Closed:** Jan–Feb. **Directions:** You'll need a car. From Stratford-upon-Avon, take the A422 via Banbury (whose famous cross entered nursery rhyme fame) and continue to Brackley. Six miles from Brackley, leave the A422 and join the B4525, which goes to the tiny village of Sulgrave. Signs will lead you to Sulgrave Manor.

WHERE TO STAY

During the long theater season, you may run into difficulty if you arrive without a reservation. However, you can go to the **Tourist Information Centre,** Bridgefoot, Stratford-upon-Avon, Warwickshire, CV37 6GW (tel. 0789/293127), from March to October, Monday through Saturday from 9am to 6pm and on Sunday from 2 to 5pm; and November to February, Monday through Saturday from 10:30am to 4pm. A staff person who is experienced in finding accommodations for travelers in all budget categories will try to book a room for you in your desired price range. The fee for room reservations made is 10% of the first night's stay (bed-and-breakfast charges only). It's also possible to reserve accommodations if you write well in advance. If you do write, be sure to specify the price range and the number of beds required. The booking charge is £3.15 ($4.70).

EXPENSIVE

ALVESTON MANOR HOTEL, Clopton Bridge, Stratford-upon-Avon, Warwickshire CV37 7HP. Tel. 0789/204581, or toll free 800/225-5843 in the U.S. Fax 0789/414095. 103 rms, 5 suites. TV TEL
$ Rates: £95 ($142.50) single; £115 ($172.50) double; from £165 ($247.50) suite. Breakfast £9.50 ($14.30) extra. AE, DC, MC, V. **Parking:** Free.
This black-and-white timbered manor is perfect for theatergoers—it's just a 2-minute walk from the Avon off the B4066. It has a wealth of chimneys and gables, and everything from an Elizabethan gazebo to Queen Anne windows. Mentioned in the *Domesday Book,* the building predates the arrival of William the Conqueror. Rooms in the manor house will appeal to those who appreciate old slanted floors, overhead beams, and antique furnishings. Some triples or quads are available in the modern section, which is connected by a covered walk through the rear garden. Rooms here have built-in pieces and a color-coordinated decor. The lounges are in the manor; and guests gather in the Cedar Room with a view of the centuries-old tree at the top of the garden—said to have been the background for the first presentation of *A Midsummer Night's Dream.* In the main living room, with its linenfold paneling, logs burn in the Tudor fireplace.
  Dining/Entertainment: Meals are served in the softly lit Tudor Restaurant amid oak beams and leaded-glass windows. A fixed-price dinner costs £21.50 ($32.30).
  Services: 24-hour room service, laundry, valet, babysitting.

MOAT HOUSE INTERNATIONAL, Bridgefoot, Stratford-upon-Avon, Warwickshire CV37 6YR. Tel. 0789/414411. Fax 0789/298589. 245 rms, 2 suites. TV TEL
$ Rates (including English breakfast): £95 ($142.50) single; £125 ($187.50) double; from £190 ($285) suite. AE, DC, MC, V. **Parking:** Free.
A four-star hotel, the Moat House International stands on 5 acres of landscaped lawns on the banks of the River Avon near Clopton Bridge. It is one of the flagships of Queens Moat Houses, a British hotel chain. The hotel has recently been refurbished, and now every bedroom has a high standard of comfort. Amenities include bathrooms with generous shelf space, large mirrors, and hairdryer.
  Dining/Entertainment: The Warwick Grill features a British and continental menu, and the Riverside Restaurant offers a carvery of hot and cold roasts, costing £14.25 ($21.40). You can drink in the Tavern Pub and in the Actors, which doubles as a nightclub.
  Services: 24-hour room service, hairdresser, laundry service.
  Facilities: Leisure complex with a swimming pool, sauna, solarium, minigym, and Jacuzzi.

SHAKESPEARE, Chapel St., Stratford-upon-Avon, Warwickshire CV37 6ER. Tel. 0789/294771, or toll free 800/435-4542 in the U.S. Fax 0789/415411. 62 rms, 1 suite. MINIBAR TV TEL
$ Rates: £85 ($127.50) single; £110 ($165) double; £135 ($202.50) suite. AE, DC, MC, V. **Parking:** Free.

Filled with historical associations, the original core of this hotel dates from the 1400s, but it has seen many additions in its long life. It's been called both the Four Gables Hotel and the Five Gables Hotel. In the 1700s a demure facade of Regency brick was added to conceal the intricate timber framing, but in the 1880s, with a rash of Shakespearean revivals, the hotel was restored to its original Tudor look. Residents relax in the post-and-timber-studded public rooms, within sight of fireplaces and playbills from 19th-century productions of Shakespeare's plays.

Many of the bedrooms were named by the noted actor David Garrick. The oldest are capped with hewn timbers, and all have modern comforts. Even the newer accommodations are at least 40 to 50 years old and have rose and thistle patterns carved into many of their exposed timbers. The rooms are equipped with hairdryers.

Dining/Entertainment: The hotel restaurant serves well-prepared lunches and dinners, and one of the most charming pubs in town, the Froth and Elbow, is on the hotel's street level.

Services: 24-hour room service, laundry service.

Facilities: Bar billiards.

WELCOMBE HOTEL, Warwick Rd., Stratford-upon-Avon, Warwickshire CV37 ONR. Tel. 0789/295252. Fax 0789/414666. 67 rms, 9 suites. TV TEL
Directions: Take the A439 1½ miles northeast of the town center.
$ Rates (including English breakfast): £105 ($157.50) single; £145–f195 ($217.50–$292.50) double; £160–£350 ($240–$525) suite. AE, DC, MC, V.
Parking: Free.

One of England's great Jacobean country houses, this hotel is a 10-minute ride from the heart of Stratford-upon-Avon. The home once belonged to Sir Archibald Flower, the philanthropic brewer who helped create the Shakespeare Memorial Theatre. Converted into a hotel, it is surrounded by 157 acres of grounds and has a formal entrance on Warwick Road, a winding driveway leading to the main hall. Guests gather for afternoon tea or drinks on the rear terrace, with its Italian-style garden and steps leading down to flowerbeds. The public rooms are heroic in size, with high mullioned windows providing views of the park. The bedrooms—some big enough for tennis matches—have pleasant furnishings.

Dining/Entertainment: The hotel's restaurant offers table d'hôte or à la carte menus. A fixed-price lunch goes for £17 ($25.50), with a fixed-price dinner costing £27.50 ($41.30).

Services: 24-hour room service, laundry service.

Facilities: 18-hole 6,202-yard golf course, tennis courts, putting green.

MODERATE

ARDEN THISTLE HOTEL, 44 Waterside, Stratford-upon-Avon, Warwickshire CV37 6BA. Tel. 0789/294949. Fax 0789/415874. 63 rms (all with bath). TV TEL
$ Rates (including English breakfast): £59 ($88.50) single; £79 ($118.50) double; £38 ($57) per person, single or double occupancy, for stays of 2 or more nights. AE, DC, MC, V. **Parking:** Free.

Across the street from the main entrance of the Royal Shakespeare and Swan Theatres, the interior of this hotel was completely gutted and rebuilt in 1993 after its purchase by the Thistle chain. Its red-brick main section dates from the Regency period, although over the years a handful of adjacent buildings were included and a modern extension was added. Today, the refurbished interior has a well-upholstered cocktail lounge and pub, a dining room with big front windows, a covered garden terrace, and comfortable bedrooms with hot-beverage facilities. A fixed-price dinner in the restaurant costs £15 ($22.50).

DUKES, Payton St., Stratford-upon-Avon, Warwickshire CV37 6UA. Tel. 0789/269300. Fax 0789/414700. 22 rms (all with bath or shower). TV TEL
$ Rates (including English breakfast): £50 ($75) single; £65–£105 ($97.50–$157.50) double. AE, DC, MC, V. **Parking:** Free.
Located in the center of Stratford north of Guild Street, this little charmer was formed when two Georgian town houses were united and restored. The family-operated inn has a large garden and is close to Shakespeare's birthplace. The public areas and bedrooms are attractive, having been restored to an impressive degree of comfort and coziness. The furniture is tasteful, much of it antique. Dukes also serves a good English and continental cuisine, with meals costing £15 ($22.50) and up.

FALCON, Chapel St., Stratford-upon-Avon, Warwickshire CV37 6HA. Tel. 0789/205777. Fax 0789/414260. 73 rms (all with bath). TV TEL
$ Rates (including English breakfast): £75 ($112.50) single; £85–£99 ($127.50–$148.50) double. AE, DC, MC, V. **Parking:** Free.
The Falcon is a blending of the very old and the very new. At the rear of a black-and-white timbered inn, licensed a quarter of a century after Shakespeare's death, is a contemporary bedroom extension, joined by a glass-covered passageway. In the heart of Stratford, the inn faces the Guild Chapel and the New Place Gardens. You arrive at the rear portion to unload luggage, just as horse-drawn coaches once dispatched their passengers. The bedrooms in the mellowed part have oak beams, diamond leaded-glass windows, some antique furnishings, and good reproductions. Each room includes a radio, electric trouser press, and hot-beverage facilities.
The lounges are comfortable—some of the finest in the Midlands. In the intimate Merlin Lounge is an open copper-hooded fireplace where coal and log fires are kept burning under beams salvaged from old ships (the walls are a good example of wattle and daub, typical of Shakespeare's day). The Oak Lounge Bar is a forest of weathered beams, and on either side of the stone fireplace is the paneling removed from the poet's last home, New Place. A fixed-price luncheon or dinner begins at £14.50 ($21.80).

GROSVENOR HOUSE HOTEL, 12–14 Warwick Rd., Stratford-upon-Avon, Warwickshire CV37 6YT. Tel. 0789/269213. Fax 0789/266087. 38 rms (all with bath or shower), 2 suites. TV TEL
$ Rates (including English or continental breakfast): £68 ($102) single; £91 ($136.50) double; £112 ($168) suite. AE, DC, MC, V. **Parking:** Free in large hotel lot.
A pair of Georgian town houses, built in 1832 and 1843, respectively, were joined together to form this hotel. Situated in the center of town, with lawns and gardens to the rear, it is a short stroll from the intersection of Bridge Street and Waterside, allowing easy access to the Avon River, Bancroft Gardens, and the Royal Shakespeare Theatre. All bedrooms have radios and tea and coffee makers. The informal bar (open until midnight) and terrace offer relaxation before or after you lunch or dine in the large restaurant, whose floor-to-ceiling windows face the gardens.

STRATFORD HOUSE, 18 Sheep St., Stratford-upon-Avon, Warwickshire CV37 6EF. Tel. 0789/268288. Fax 0789/295580. 11 rms (all with bath or shower), 1 family rm. TV TEL
$ Rates (including English breakfast): £60–£65 ($90–$97.50) single; £69–£82 ($103.50–$123) double; from £100 ($150) family rm. AE, DC, MC, V. **Parking:** £2.50 ($3.80).

S This Georgian house stands 100 yards from the River Avon and the Royal Shakespeare Theatre. The staff of this small hotel extends a warm welcome to North American guests. The house is furnished tastefully and with style, somewhat like a private home, with books and pictures along with a scattering of antiques. Everything is spotlessly maintained. There is a walled courtyard on the side with flowering plants. All bedrooms have tea and coffee makers. Both hotel guests and outsiders can dine in the garden restaurant, Shepherd's, recommended separately (see "Where to Dine," below).

WHITE SWAN, Rother St., Stratford-upon-Avon, Warwickshire CV37 6NH. Tel. 0789/297022, or toll free 800/435-4542 in the U.S. Fax 0789/ 268773. 37 rms (all with bath or shower). TV TEL

$ Rates: £70–£80 ($105–$120) single; £90–£110 ($135–$165) double. Breakfast £8.50 ($12.80) extra. AE, DC, MC, V. **Parking:** Free.

This cozy, intimate hotel is one of the most atmospheric in Stratford and is, in fact, considered the oldest building there. It was in business for more than 100 years before Shakespeare appeared on the scene. The gabled medieval front would present the Bard with no surprises, but the modern comforts inside would surely astonish him, even though many of the rooms have been preserved. Paintings dating from 1550 hang on the lounge walls. All the bedrooms are well appointed; the amenities include a radio, trouser press, and hairdryer. The hostelry has a spacious restaurant where good food is served. The oak-beamed bar is a popular meeting place (see "Pubs" in "Where to Dine," below).

INEXPENSIVE

FORTE POSTHOUSE, Bridgefoot, Stratford-upon-Avon, Warwickshire CV37 7LT. Tel. 0789/266761, or toll free 800/435-4542 in the U.S Fax 0789/414547. 60 rms (all with bath). TV TEL

$ Rates: Sun–Thurs, £53.50 ($80.30) single or double; Fri–Sat, £41.50 ($62.30) single or double. English breakfast £6.95 ($10.40) extra. AE, DC, MC, V. **Parking:** Free.

An 18th-century Georgian facade with tall, narrow windows fronts this hotel, which looks out over the swans of Avon near Clopton Bridge. The complex is surrounded by gardens on a low, flat area beside a canal, a 5-minute drive south of the Royal Shakespeare Theatre leading toward Oxford. The bedrooms are comfortably modern and filled with tasteful furnishings; most are located in a modern, red-brick extension. Amenities include a radio and hot-beverage facilities.

The River Bar offers a view of the planting outside. The Swans Nest Restaurant serves food in a room lined with early 19th-century paintings. A la carte dinners cost around £15 ($22.50).

SEQUOIA HOUSE, 51–53 Shipston Rd., Stratford-upon-Avon, Warwick-shire CV37 7LN. Tel. 0789/268852. Fax 0789/414559. 24 rms (20 with bath or shower). TV TEL

$ Rates (including English breakfast): £30 ($45) single without bath, £39 ($58.50) single with bath; £39 ($58.50) double without bath, £69 ($103.50) double with bath. AE, DC, MC, V. **Parking:** Free

This privately run hotel has its own beautiful garden on three-quarters of an acre across the Avon, conveniently located for visiting the major Shakespeare properties of the National Trust. It's also within easy walking distance of the theater. In fact, the hotel is just across the Avon River opposite the theater. Renovation has vastly improved the house, which was created from two late Victorian buildings. Today it offers rooms with beverage-making equipment and hot and cold running water.

Guests gather in a lounge that has a licensed bar and an open Victorian fireplace. The hotel also has a private parking area.

STRATHEDEN HOTEL, 5 Chapel St., Stratford-upon-Avon, Warwickshire CV37 6EP. Tel. 0789/297119. Fax 0789/297119. 9 rms (all with bath). TV TEL

$ Rates (including English breakfast): £30–£34 ($45–$51) single; £48–£56 ($72–$84) double. MC, V.

Tucked away in a desirable position on a plot of land that was first mentioned in a property deed in 1333, a short walk north of the Royal Shakespeare Theatre, is the Stratheden Hotel. Built in 1673 (and today the oldest-remaining brick building in the town center), it has a tiny rear garden and top-floor rooms with slanted, beamed ceilings. Under the ownership of the Wells family for the past quarter century, it has improved in both decor and comfort with the addition of fresh paint, new curtains, and good beds. The glass cupboard in the entry hallway holds family heirlooms and collector's items. The dining room, with a bay window, has an overscale sideboard that once belonged to the "insanely vain" Marie Corelli, an eccentric novelist, poet, and mystic, and a favorite author of Queen Victoria. The Victorian novelist (1855–1924) was noted for her passion for pastoral settings and objets d'art. You can see an example of her taste: a massive mahogany tester bed in Room 4.

VICTORIA SPA LODGE, Bishopton Lane, Stratford-upon-Avon, Warwickshire CV37 9QY. Tel. 0789/267985. Fax 0789/204728. 7 rms (5 with bath or shower). TV

$ Rates (including English breakfast): £37 ($55.50) single without bath; £39–£50 ($58.50–$75) single or double with bath. MC, V. **Parking:** Free.

Situated by a canal, 1½ miles north of the center of town where the A3400 intersects the A46, this large 1837 lodge was originally a spa, and once housed Queen Victoria's eldest daughter, Princess Vicky, as well as the famous cartoonist, Bruce Bairnsfather. Accommodating hosts Paul and Dreen Tozer offer tastefully decorated bedrooms with Laura Ashley wallpaper and matching quilts. Hot-beverage makers are in all rooms. A full English breakfast is served in a cheerful dining room filled with antiques, and meals and light refreshments are available on request.

IN NEARBY ALDERMINSTER

ETTINGTON PARK HOTEL, Alderminster, near Stratford-upon-Avon, Warwickshire CV37 8BS. Tel. 0789/450123. Fax 0789/450472. 41 rms (all with bath), 9 suites. TV TEL **Directions:** Don't go to the village of Ettington—instead, head along the A34 between Stratford-upon-Avon and Oxford to the village of Alderminster (it's signposted).

$ Rates (including English breakfast): £110 ($165) single; £140–£155 ($210–$232.50) double; from £180 ($270) suite. AE, DC, MC, V. **Parking:** Free.

This Victorian Gothic mansion is one of the most sumptuous retreats in Shakespeare Country. It opened as a hotel in 1985, but has a history that spans over nine centuries. The land is a legacy of the Shirley family, whose 12th-century burial chapel stands near the hotel. Like a grand private home, the hotel boasts baronial fireplaces, a conservatory, and a charming staff. The Adam ceilings, stone carvings, and ornate staircases have all been beautifully restored. A new wing, assembled with the same stone and Neo-Gothic carving of the original house, stretches toward a Renaissance-style arbor entwined with vines. The giant sequoias, ancient yews, and cedars are surrounded by lawns and terraced gardens, whose flowers and ferns cascade toward a rock-lined stream. The bedrooms conjure memories of another era, yet the most modern comforts are concealed behind antique facades.

Dining/Entertainment: In the dining room, the Shirley family crest is inlaid in hundreds of marquetry depictions in the carved and burnished paneling. The cuisine is a medley of English and French specialties, a fixed-price dinner costing £15.75 to £28 ($23.60 to $42).

Services: 24-hour room service, laundry service.

Facilities: Jacuzzi, indoor swimming pool, sauna, tennis.

IN NEARBY WILMCOTE

SWAN HOUSE HOTEL, The Green, Wilmcote, Stratford-upon-Avon, Warwickshire CV37 9XJ. Tel. 0789/267030. Fax 0789/204875. 12 rms (all with bath or shower). TV **Directions:** Take the A3400 3½ miles northwest of Stratford.

$ Rates (including English breakfast): £36–£42 ($54–$63) single; £60–£70 ($90–$105) double. AE, MC, V. **Parking:** Free.

 Shakespeare's mother, Mary Arden, lived in this tiny village where you'll find the tranquil Swan House. Really an upgraded village pub-hotel, it offers not only appealing and well-furnished bedrooms at low prices, but good meals as well. Amenities include hot-beverage makers, and a four-poster bed is available.

Homemade hot and cold bar snacks are served in the popular beamed bar with an open fire and the original well. The bar offers four real ales at lunch and in the evening. In the hotel restaurant, "Hot Rocks," you cook your own dinner over a hot stove placed at your table.

WHERE TO DINE

THE BOX TREE RESTAURANT, in the Royal Shakespeare Theatre, Waterside. Tel. 293226.
   Cuisine: FRENCH/ITALIAN/ENGLISH. **Reservations:** Required.
$ Prices: Dinner £21.70 ($32.60) Mon–Sat; matinee lunch £13.50 ($20.30). AE, MC, V.
   Open: Lunch matinees Thurs–Sat noon–2:30pm, dinner Mon–Sat 5:45pm–midnight.

This place is in the best location in town, right in the theater itself, with walls of glass providing an unobstructed view of the Avon and its swans. During intermission there is a snack feast of smoked salmon and champagne. After each evening's performance you can dine by flickering candlelight. There's a special phone for reservations in the theater lobby. You might begin with pigeon and venison pâté, or Scottish smoked salmon, then follow with guinea fowl suprême Grand Marnier or roast saddle of venison. The dessert menu always features a specialty of the day.

GIOVANNI, 8 Ely St. Tel. 297999.
   Cuisine: ITALIAN. **Reservations:** Required.
$ Prices: Appetizers 95p–£6.80 ($1.40–$10.20); main courses £6–£13.80 ($9–$20.70). MC, V.
   Open: Lunch Mon–Sat noon–2pm; dinner Mon–Sat 6:30–11:30pm.

Actors favor this intimate restaurant housed in a yellow-brick cottage with an Italianate facade. The trattoria includes a cocktail lounge with antiques. The classic Italian menu begins with minestrone and includes such pasta dishes as lasagne and cannelloni, as well as offerings like escalope piemontese and scampi provençal. A good Italian dessert is the zabaglione, although at least two diners must order it. A selection of excellent continental ices is also featured, everything from Italian cassata to mela stregata.

HUSSAIN'S, 6A Chapel St. Tel. 267506.
Cuisine: INDIAN. **Reservations:** Recommended.
$ Prices: Appetizers £2.50–£4.50 ($3.80–$6.80); main courses £6.50–£9 ($9.80–$13.50); fixed-price lunch £5.95–£15.50 ($8.90–$23.30); fixed-price dinner £15.50 ($23.30). AE, DC, MC, V.
Open: Lunch daily noon–2pm; dinner daily 5:15–11:45pm.

 Dining here has been compared to a visit to a private Indian home. The restaurant has many admirers—some consider it one of the brighter spots on the culinary landscape. At least it pleased actor Ben Kingsley. The owner has selected a well-trained, alert staff, who welcome guests, advising them about special dishes. Against a setting of pink crushed-velvet paneling, you can select from an array of dishes from northern India. Herbs and spices are blended imaginatively in the kitchen to give dishes a distinctive flavor. Many tandoori dishes are offered, along with various curries with lamb or prawn. Hussain's is across from the Shakespeare Hotel and historic New Place.

THE RIVER TERRACE RESTAURANT, in the Royal Shakespeare Theatre, Waterside. Tel. 293226.
Cuisine: ENGLISH. **Reservations:** Required.
$ Prices: Fixed-price meals £13.50 ($20.30) at lunch, £21.25 ($31.90) at dinner. MC, V.
Open: Lunch Mon–Sat noon–2:30pm; dinner Mon–Sat 5:45–10pm. **Closed:** 2 weeks in Mar.

 Also in the theater overlooking the Avon, this coffee shop and licensed restaurant is open to the general public as well as to theatergoers. This self-service establishment offers typical English and pasta dishes, as well as morning coffee and afternoon tea. You might begin with onion soup flavored with sweet cider, or game pâté with a Cumberland sauce. A lobster and salmon "duo" terrine is also served. For a main course, try Dover sole, suprême of guinea fowl, or Scottish filet of beef. Vegetarian dishes are also served. Dessert might be caramel blood oranges soaked with brandy.

SHEPHERD'S GARDEN RESTAURANT, in the Stratford House Hotel, 18 Sheep St. Tel. 268288.
Cuisine: ENGLISH/FRENCH. **Reservations:** Recommended.
$ Prices: Fixed-price menus £14.50–£17.50 ($21.80–$26.30). AE, DC, MC, V.
Open: Lunch Tues–Sun noon–2pm; dinner Tues–Sat 5:45–9:30pm.

 Light and airy, the Shepherd's Garden has a skylit conservatory look, with cascading vines and plants, and windows opening onto a walled garden. It's appropriately stylish for its role as host to many of the directors and actors from the Royal Shakespeare Theatre. The British and French cuisine served here is among the finest in Stratford-upon-Avon. For an appetizer, you might begin with smoked chicken and mango with a curried mayonnaise, going on to either fresh salmon with chive-and-butter sauce or roast rack of lamb with a mild garlic sauce. The fixed-price menus, based on the use of fresh ingredients, changes frequently.

SIR TOBY'S, 8 Church St. Tel. 268822.
Cuisine: INTERNATIONAL. **Reservations:** Recommended.
$ Prices: Appetizers £2.50–£7 ($3.80–$10.50); main courses £8–£11 ($12–$16.50). AE, MC, V.
Open: Dinner only, Wed–Sat 5:30–9:30pm

Located away from the busy center, this brick restaurant is cozy and intimate, with limited seating. In summer, a few tables are placed outside for al fresco dining. Mr. and Mrs. Watkins take pride in their good home-cooking and also cater to the vegetarian palate, blending the best of the past with the cooking techniques of today. You might also visit for a pretheater meal because of its early opening. The menu changes frequently but might include such items as fresh salmon pickled with lemon-lime juice and dill, homemade bresaola (thinly sliced marinated beef), pan-fried chicken livers on a bed of salad greens. You might begin with a bowl of homemade wild mushroom soup.

PUBS

THE BLACK SWAN (also known as the Dirty Duck), Waterside. Tel. 297312.

Cuisine: ENGLISH. **Reservations:** Required.

$ Prices: Appetizers £1.35–£5 ($2–$7.50); main courses £6.25 ($9.40); bar snacks 95p–£3.50 ($1.40–$5.30); pint of ale £1.50 ($2.30). No credit cards.

Open: Pub, Mon–Sat 11am–11pm, Sun noon–3pm and 7–10:30pm. Restaurant, lunch Tues–Sun noon–2pm; dinner Mon–Sat 6–11pm.

Affectionately known as the Dirty Duck, this has been a popular hangout for Stratford players since the 18th century. The wall is lined with autographed photos of its patrons, some of long ago such as Lord Olivier. The front lounge and bar crackles with intense conversation. In the spring and fall an open fire blazes. In the Dirty Duck Grill Room, typical English grills, among other dishes, are featured. You'll be faced with a choice of a dozen appetizers, most of which would make a meal in themselves. Main dishes include braised kidneys or oxtails, roast chicken, or honey-roasted duck. In fair weather you can have drinks in the front garden and watch the swans on the Avon glide by.

THE GARRICK INN, 25 High St. Tel. 292186.

Cuisine: ENGLISH. **Reservations:** Not accepted.

$ Prices: Appetizers £1.55–£1.95 ($2.30–$2.90); main courses £4–£8 ($6–$12). MC, V.

Open: Lunch daily noon–3pm; dinner Mon–Sat 5–7:30pm. Pub, Mon–Sat 11am–11pm, Sun noon–3pm and 7–10:30pm.

This black-and-white timbered Elizabethan pub near Harvard House has an unpretentious charm. It's named after David Garrick, one of England's greatest actors. The front bar is decorated with tapestry-covered settles, an old oak refectory table, and an open fireplace which the locals gravitate to. The black bar has a circular fireplace with a copper hood and mementos of the triumphs of the English stage. Menu choices include samosas (curried vegetarian crêpes) a mixed farmhouse grill, grilled lamb chops, or a succulent version of rumpsteak.

THE WHITE SWAN, Rother St. Tel. 297022.

Cuisine: ENGLISH. **Reservations:** Recommended.

$ Prices: Bar snacks £2–£5.50 ($3–$8.30); 3-course fixed-price dinner £16.95 ($25.40). AE, DC, MC, V.

Open: Morning coffee daily 10am–noon; self-service bar snacks daily noon–2pm; afternoon tea daily 2–5pm; dinner Mon–Thurs 6–9pm, Fri–Sat 6–10pm, Sun 7–9pm.

This is one of the most atmospheric pubs in Stratford-upon-Avon, in the oldest building in town (see my hotel recommendation in "Where to Stay," above). Once you step inside, you're drawn into a world of cushioned leather armchairs, old oak settles, oak paneling, and fireplaces. It's believed that Shakespeare may have come here to drink back when it was called the Kings Head. At lunch you can partake of the hot dishes of the day, along with fresh salads and sandwiches.

2. WARWICK

92 miles NW of London, 8 miles N of Stratford-upon-Avon

GETTING THERE **By Train** Trains run frequently between Stratford-upon-Avon and Warwick.

By Bus One Midland Red bus per hour (no. 18 or X16) departs Stratford-upon-Avon during the day. Trip time is 15 to 20 minutes.

By Car You can approach Warwick via the A46 from Stratford-upon-Avon.

ESSENTIALS The **telephone area code** is 0926. The **Tourist Information Centre** is at the Court House, Jury Street (tel. 0926/492212).

Most visitors come to this town just to see Warwick Castle. Then they're off on their next adventure, usually to the ruins of Kenilworth Castle (see below). But the historic center of medieval Warwick has a lot more to offer.

In 1694 a fire swept through the heart of Warwick, destroying large parts of the town, but a number of Elizabethan and medieval buildings still survive, along with some fine Georgian structures from a later date. (Very few traces of the town walls remain, except the East and West Gates.) Warwick cites Ethelfleda, daughter of Alfred the Great, as its founder. But most of its history is associated with the earls of Warwick, a title created by the son of William the Conqueror in 1088. The story of those earls—the Beaumonts, the Beauchamps (such figures as "Kingmaker" Richard Neville)—makes for an exciting episode in English history but is too complicated to go into here.

WHAT TO SEE & DO

WARWICK CASTLE, Castle Hill. Tel. 408000.

Perched on a rocky cliff above the Avon in the town center, this stately late 17th-century–style mansion is surrounded by a magnificent 14th-century fortress. The importance of the site has long been recognized. The first significant fortifications at Warwick were built by Ethelfleda, daughter of Alfred the Great, in 915. Two years after the Norman Conquest in 1068, William the Conqueror ordered the construction of a motte and baily castle. The castle mound is all that remains today of the Norman castle, as this was sacked by Simon de Montfort in the Barons' War of 1264.

The Beauchamp family, the most illustrious medieval earls of Warwick, are responsible for the way the castle looks today, and much of the external structure remains unchanged from the mid-14th century. When the castle was granted to Sir Fulke Greville by James I in 1604, he spent £20,000 (an enormous sum in those days) converting the existing castle buildings into a luxurious mansion. The Grevilles have held the Earl of Warwick title since 1759, when it passed from the Rich family.

The state rooms and Great Hall house fine collections of paintings, furniture, arms, and armor. The armory, dungeon, torture chamber, ghost tower, clock tower, and Guy's tower create a vivid picture of the castle's turbulent past and its important role in the history of England.

The private apartments of Lord Brooke and his family, who in recent years sold the castle to Madame Tussaud's waxworks company, are open to visitors. They house a display of a carefully reconstructed Royal Weekend House Party of 1898. The major rooms contain wax models of important figures of the time: young Winston Churchill; the Duchess of Devonshire; Winston's widowed mother, Jennie; and Clara Butt, the celebrated singer, along with the Earl and Countess of Warwick and their family. In the Kenilworth bedroom, the Prince of Wales, later King Edward VII, reads a letter, and in the red bedroom the Duchess of Marlborough prepares for her bath. Among the most lifelike of the figures is a little uniformed maid, bending over a bathtub into which the water is running, to test the temperature. Surrounded by gardens, lawns, and woodland, where peacocks roam freely, and skirted by the Avon, Warwick Castle was described by Sir Walter Scott in 1828 as "that fairest monument of ancient and chivalrous splendor which yet remains uninjured by time."

Don't miss the Victorian rose garden, a re-creation of an original design from 1868 by Robert Marnock. The original garden had fallen into disrepair, and a tennis court had been built on the site. In 1980 it was decided to restore the garden, and as luck would have it, Marnock's original plans were discovered in the county records office. Close by the rose garden is a Victorian alpine rockery and water garden. The romantic castle is host to various colorful pageants.

Admission: £6.75 ($10.10) adults, £4.25 ($6.40) children.

Open: Mar–Sept, daily 10am–5:30pm; Oct–Feb, daily 10am–4:30pm. **Closed:** Christmas Day.

ST. MARY'S CHURCH, Warwick Parish Office, Old Sq. Tel. 400771.

Destroyed in part by the fire of 1694, this church with its rebuilt battlemented tower and nave is considered among the finest examples of late 17th- and early-18th-century architecture. The Beauchamp Chapel, spared from the flames, encases the Purbeck marble tomb of Richard Beauchamp, a well-known Earl of Warwick who died in 1439 and is commemorated by a gilded bronze effigy. The most powerful man in the kingdom, not excepting Henry V, Beauchamp has a tomb considered one of the finest remaining examples of Perpendicular-Gothic style from the mid-15th century. The tomb of Robert Dudley, Earl of Leicester, a favorite of Elizabeth I, is against the north wall. The Perpendicular-Gothic choir dates from the 14th century, as do the Norman crypt and the chapter house.

Admission: Free; donations accepted.

Open: Apr–Sept, 9am–6pm; Oct–Mar, 9am–4pm. **Directions:** All buses to Warwick stop at Old Sq.

LORD LEYCESTER HOSPITAL, High St. Tel. 491422.

At the West Gate, this group of half-timbered almshouses was also spared from the great fire. The buildings were erected about 1400, and the hospital was founded in 1571 by Robert Dudley, Earl of Leicester, as a home for old soldiers. It's in use by ex-service personnel and their spouses today. On top of the West Gate is the attractive little chapel of St. James, dating from the 12th century but renovated many times since.

Admission: £2 ($3) adults, 60p (90¢) children.

Open: June–Sept, Mon–Sat 10am–5:30pm; Oct–May, Mon–Sat 10am–4pm (last admission 15 minutes before closing).

WARWICK DOLL MUSEUM, Oken's House, Castle St. Tel. 495546.

In one of the most charming Elizabethan buildings in Warwick is this doll museum, located near St. Mary's Church. Its seven rooms contain an extensive collection of dolls in wood, wax, and porcelain. Off Jury Street in the center, the house once belonged to Thomas Oken, a great benefactor of Warwick.

Admission: £1 ($1.50) adults, 70p ($1.10) children.

Open: Easter–Sept, Mon–Sat 10am–5pm, Sun 2–5pm.

WARWICKSHIRE MUSEUM, Market Hall, The Market Place. Tel. 412500.

This museum was established in 1836 to house a collection of geological remains, fossils, and an exhibit of amphibians from the Triassic period. There are also displays illustrating the history, archeology, and natural history of the county, including the famous Sheldon tapestry map.

Admission: Free.

Open: Mon–Sat 10am–5:30pm, Sun (May–Sept) 2:30–5pm. **Directions:** From Jury St. in the center, take a right onto Swan St., which leads to the museum.

ST. JOHN'S HOUSE MUSEUM, St. John's. Tel. 412021.

At Coten End, not far from the castle gates, is this early 17th-century house with exhibits on Victorian domestic life. A schoolroom is furnished with original 19th-century school furniture and equipment. During the school term, Warwickshire children, dressed in period costumes, can be seen enjoying Victorian-style lessons. Groups of children also use the Victorian parlor and the kitchen. As it's impossible to display more than a small number of items at a time, a study room is available where you can see objects from the reserve collections. The costume collection is a particularly fine one, and visitors can study the drawings and photos that make up the costume catalog. These facilities are available by appointment only. Upstairs is a military museum, tracing the history of the Royal Warwickshire Regiment from 1674 to the present day. For more information and for appointments in the study room, telephone the Keeper of Social History at the number above. St. John's House is at the crossroads of the main Warwick-Leamington road (A425/A429), and the Coventry road (A429).

Admission: Free.

Open: Oct–Apr, Tues–Sat 10am–12:30pm and 1:30–5:30pm; May–Sept, Tues–Sat 10am–12:30pm and 1:30–5:30pm, Sun 2:30–5pm.

WHERE TO STAY

Many prefer to seek lodgings in Warwick and commute to Stratford-upon-Avon.

HILTON NATIONAL HOTEL, Warwick Bypass (A46 Stratford Rd.), Warwick, Warwickshire CV34 6RE. Tel. 0926/499555, or toll free 800/445-8667 in the U.S. Fax 0926/410020. 178 rms (all with bath), 2 suites. TV TEL

Directions: Take the A429 2 miles southwest of Warwick (7 miles north of Stratford).

$ Rates: £90 ($135) single; £120 ($180) double; £135 ($202.50) suite. English breakfast £9.55 ($14.30) extra. AE, DC, MC, V. **Parking:** Free.

This Hilton is at the elbow junction of a network of highways, making it popular with commercial travelers. It has a hutch-style, low-slung modern design of earth-colored brick, an octagonal dining room, and a series of interconnected bars, lounges, and public areas, as well as a heated indoor swimming pool. The establishment hosts many conferences and sales meetings for local companies. Foreign visitors find that its standardized comfort and easy-to-find location make it a good base for touring Warwick and the surrounding regions. The rooms are well furnished, and there is 24-hour room service.

LORD LEYCESTER HOTEL [CALOTELS], Jury St., Warwick, Warwickshire CV34 4EJ. Tel. 0926/491481. Fax 0926/491561. 52 rms (all with bath or shower). TV TEL

$ Rates (including English breakfast): £48 ($72) single; £69 ($103.50) double. AE, DC, MC, V. **Parking:** Free.

In 1726, this manor house belonged to Lord Archer of Umberslade. Years later it was converted into an inn under the sign of the three tuns (wine casks), and later still it once more became a private residence. In 1926 it was finally turned into a hotel. The comfortable bedrooms are equipped with a radio and hot-beverage maker. A small à la carte English menu is offered in the dining room, or you can have snacks in Alexander's Bar. Meals begin at £14.95 ($22.40). A large parking lot is found at the rear of the hotel, within walking distance of the castle and other historic buildings of Warwick.

TUDOR HOUSE INN & RESTAURANT, 90–92 West St., Warwick, Warwickshire CV34 6AW. Tel. 0926/495447. Fax 0926/492948. 11 rms (8 with bath or shower). TV TEL **Directions:** Take the A429 road toward Stratford; the inn is right outside town.
$ **Rates** (including English breakfast): £24 ($36) single without bath, £38 ($57) single with bath; £54 ($81) double with bath. AE, DC, MC, V. **Parking:** Free.

 At the edge of town is a black-and-white timbered inn built in 1472. It's one of the few buildings to escape the fire that destroyed High Street in 1694. Off the central hall are two large rooms, each of which could be the setting for an Elizabethan play. All bedrooms have washbasins, and two have doors only 4 feet high. In the corner of the lounge is an open turning staircase. A regular meal in the restaurant and steak bar costs £12 ($18) and up. Tudor House is on the main road from Stratford-upon-Avon leading to Warwick Castle.

WHERE TO DINE

NICOLINI'S BISTRO, 18 Jury St. Tel. 495817.
   Cuisine: ITALIAN. **Reservations:** Recommended.
$ **Prices:** Appetizers £2.20–£6.95 ($3.30–$10.40); main courses £5.50–£8.95 ($8.30–$13.40). AE, DC, MC, V.
   Open: Lunch Mon–Sat noon–2pm; dinner Mon–Sat 6–10:30pm. **Closed:** 2 weeks in June (dates vary).
This restaurant brings a touch of sunny Italy to staid Warwick. Lynne and Nicky, as they are known locally, welcome you into their pleasant restaurant decorated with greenery. Check out the crisp salads and luscious desserts. You're faced with an array of appetizers, including king prawns cooked in garlic butter or Nicky's polenta served with a napoletana sauce and baked in the oven. Pastas such as lasagne can be served either as an appetizer or a main course. Main courses include daily specialties, as well as such standard Italian fare as pork marsala or veal milanese. The restaurant stands in the center of town near the castle.

---

3. KENILWORTH

5 miles N of Warwick, 13 miles N of Stratford-upon-Avon,
102 miles NW of London

GETTING THERE   By Train   From London (both Paddington and Euston Stations) InterCity train lines make very frequent and fast connections to either Coventry or Stratford-upon-Avon, from which the Midland Red Line buses make regular connections into Kenilworth.

By Bus   Midland Red Line buses run frequently from either Stratford-upon-Avon or Coventry.

By Car   From Warwick (see above), drive to Kenilworth along the A46 on the road to Coventry.

ESSENTIALS The **telephone area code** is 0926. The **Tourist Information Centre** is at the Kenilworth Library, 11 Smalley Place (tel. 0926/52595).

The major attraction here is **Kenilworth Castle,** Kenilworth (tel. 52078), at one time with walls that enclosed an area of 7 acres, now in magnificent ruins. It is the subject of Sir Walter Scott's romance *Kenilworth*. In 1957 Lord Kenilworth presented the decaying castle to England, and limited restoration has since been carried out.

The castle was built by Geoffrey de Clinton, a lieutenant of Henry I. Caesar's Tower, with its 16-foot-thick walls, is all that remains of the original castle. Edward II was forced to abdicate at Kenilworth in 1327, before being carried off to Berkeley Castle in Gloucestershire, where he was undoubtedly murdered. In 1563 Elizabeth I gave the castle to her favorite, Robert Dudley, Earl of Leicester. The earl built the gatehouse, which the queen visited on several occasions. After the Civil War, the Roundheads were responsible for breaching the outer walls and towers, and blowing up the north wall of the keep. This was the only damage caused following the Earl of Monmouth's plea that it be "Slighted with as little spoil to the dwellinghouse as might be."

Admission is £1.70 ($2.60) for adults, 85p ($1.30) for children under 16. From Good Friday to the end of September, the castle is open daily from 10am to 6pm; in other months, Tuesday through Sunday from 10am to 4pm. The castle is closed January 1 and December 24–26.

WHERE TO STAY

CLARENDON HOUSE HOTEL, 6–8 Old High St., Kenilworth, Warwickshire CV8 1LZ. Tel. 0926/57668. Fax 0926/50669. 31 rms (all with bath or shower). TV TEL
$ Rates (including English breakfast): £49.50–£55 ($74.30–$82.50) single; £75 ($112.50) double. MC, V. **Parking:** Free.

A family-run hotel and restaurant, the Clarendon House is in the old part of Kenilworth. The oak tree around which the original ale house was built in 1430 is still supporting the roof of the building today. The present owners welcome guests to spend the night in one of the tastefully decorated rooms.

Dining/Entertainment: Before the evening meal, guests gather in the timbered and oak-paneled Royalist Retreat Bar and lounges. The hotel's Castle Tavern restaurant is housed in what was once the inn stable. The oddly timbered room is decorated with antique maps and armor, constant reminders that a Cromwellian garrison once stayed at the inn during a siege of Kenilworth Castle. Game is featured at the Clarendon House, and in season you may dine on such specialties as jugged hare, pheasant georgienne (marinated in madeira wine with oranges, grapes, and walnuts), grouse, or mallard (wild duck cooked in red wine, mushrooms, and fines herbes). Lunches at this establishment are always in the form of bar meals, priced from £1.50 to £5 ($2.30 to $7.50). Bar lunches are served Monday through Saturday from noon to 1:45pm. At Sunday lunch, a fixed-price menu is offered for £8.50 ($12.80) for three courses. A la carte meals, served in the more formal restaurant, range from £18 to £20 ($27 to $30), and service is from 7 to 9:30pm Sunday through Thursday and from 7 to 10pm on Friday and Saturday.

WHERE TO DINE

RESTAURANT BOSQUET, 97A Warwick Rd. Tel. 52463.
Cuisine: FRENCH. **Reservations:** Required.
$ Prices: Appetizers £6–£6.50 ($9–$9.80); main courses £14.50–£15.50 ($21.80–$23.30); fixed-price lunch or dinner £19.50 ($29.30). AE, MC, V.
Open: Dinner Tues–Sat 7–10pm. **Closed:** Last 3 weeks in July.

This tiny terraced town-house restaurant is a culinary oasis in Kenilworth. It's owned and operated by Bernard Lignier, a Frenchman, who does the cooking, and his English wife, Jane. The à la carte menu is changed with the seasons but consists mainly of French dishes, such as sweetbreads, loin of lamb with tarragon, fish according to the market, and game according to the season. There's a good selection of reasonably priced regional French wines.

CHAPTER 17

AST ANGLIA: CAMBRIDGESHIRE, ESSEX, SUFFOLK & NORFOLK

- **WHAT'S SPECIAL ABOUT EAST ANGLIA**
1. **CAMBRIDGE**
2. **ELY**
3. **SAFFRON WALDEN/THAXTED**
4. **DEDHAM**
5. **NEWMARKET**
6. **LONG MELFORD**
7. **LAVENHAM**
8. **WOODBRIDGE & ALDEBURGH**
9. **NORWICH**

The four counties of East Anglia—Essex, Suffolk, Norfolk, and Cambridgeshire—are essentially bucolic. East Anglia was an ancient Anglo-Saxon kingdom under domination of the Danes. Beginning in the 12th century, its cloth industry brought it prosperity, which is apparent today in the impressive spires of some of its churches. In part, it's a land of heaths, fens, marshes, and "broads" in Norfolk. Cambridge is the most-visited city in East Anglia, but don't neglect to pass through Suffolk and Essex, Constable Country, with some of the finest landscapes in England. Norwich, the seat of the dukes of Norfolk, is less popular, but the few who go that far toward the North Sea will be rewarded.

CAMBRIDGESHIRE Most visitors gravitate toward Cambridge, the center of Cambridgeshire, but those with more time may want to visit some of the county itself, especially the cathedral city of Ely. Cambridgeshire is in large part an agricultural region, with some distinct geographic features, including the black peat soil of the Fens, a district crisscrossed by dikes and drainage ditches. Many old villages and market towns abound, including Peterborough, which sits on the divide between the flat Fens and the "wolds" of the East Midlands. Birdwatchers, fishing enthusiasts, walkers, and cyclists are all drawn to the area.

Many famous figures in English history came from this land, including Oliver Cromwell (1699–1758), the Lord Protector during the English Civil War.

ESSEX Even though it's close to London and industrialized in places, Essex is a land of rolling fields that contains unspoiled rural areas and villages. Most motorists pass through it on the way to Cambridge. In the east there are many seaside towns and villages.

The major city is Colchester, in the east, known for its oysters and roses. Fifty miles from London, it was the first Roman city in Britain, the oldest-recorded town in the kingdom. Parts of its Roman fortifications remain. A Norman castle has been turned into a museum, housing a fine collection of Roman-British artifacts. Among the former residents of Colchester were King Cole, subject of the nursery rhyme, and Cunobelinus, the warrior king, Shakespeare's Cymbeline.

WHAT'S SPECIAL ABOUT EAST ANGLIA

Great Towns/Villages

☐ Cambridge, one of the world's oldest and greatest universities, on the River Cam with 31 colleges.

☐ Thaxted, a "classic" East Anglia small town with outstanding buildings, dominated by a hilltop medieval church.

☐ Long Melford, one of Suffolk's loveliest villages, remarkable for the length of its High Street.

☐ Lavenham, the showplace of Suffolk small towns, a symphony of color-washed buildings.

Castles

☐ Sandringham, the country home of British monarchs since the days of King Edward VII.

Architectural Highlights

☐ King's College Chapel, Cambridge, founded by the adolescent Henry VI in 1441; Henry James called it "the most beautiful in England."

Cathedrals

☐ Ely Cathedral, dating from 1081, a handsome example of the Perpendicular style.

☐ Norwich Cathedral, dating from 1096, with two-story cloisters—the only one of its type in England.

Buildings

☐ Audley End House, outside Saffron Walden, a Jacobean mansion, considered the finest in East Anglia.

However, Colchester is not the pathway of most visitors—so I have concentrated instead on tiny villages in the western part of Essex, including Saffron Walden and Thaxted, which represent the best part of the shire. You can explore all of East Anglia quite easily on your way to Cambridge or on your return trip to London. They lie roughly 25 to 30 miles south of Cambridge.

SUFFOLK The easternmost county of England, Suffolk is a refuge for artists, just as it was in the day of its famous native sons, Constable and Gainsborough. Through them, many of the Suffolk landscapes have ended up in museums on canvas.

A fast train can make it from London to East Suffolk in approximately 1½ hours. Still, its fishing villages, dozens of flint churches, historic homes, and national monuments remain far removed from mainstream tourism in England.

The major towns of Suffolk are Bury St. Edmunds, the capital of West Suffolk, and Ipswich in the east, a port city on the Orwell River. But to capture the true charm of Suffolk, you must explore its little market towns and villages. Beginning at the Essex border, we'll head toward the North Sea, highlighting the most scenic villages as we move eastward across the shire.

NORFOLK Bounded by the North Sea, Norfolk is the biggest of the East Anglian counties. It's a low-lying area, with fens, heaths, and salt marshes. An occasional dike or windmill makes you think you're in the Netherlands. One of the features of Norfolk is its network of Broads—miles and miles of lagoons, shallow in parts, connected by streams. Summer sports people flock to Norfolk to hire boats for sailing or fishing.

From Norwich itself, Wroxham, capital of the Broads, is easily reached, only 8 miles to the northeast. Motorboats regularly leave from this resort, taking parties on short trips. Some of the best scenery of the Broads is to be found on the periphery of Wroxham.

SEEING EAST ANGLIA

GETTING THERE

From London, motorists head north along the M11 to Cambridge. The M11 also connects with the A11 to Norwich. The A12 from London goes through East Suffolk via Colchester, Ipswich, and Great Yarmouth to reach some of the charming little villages. British Rail runs trains to Cambridge and East Anglia from London's Liverpool Street Station. National Express coaches from London's Victoria Coach Station service the area, taking about 2 hours to reach Cambridge or 3 hours to reach Norwich.

A SUGGESTED ITINERARY

Day 1: From London, head for Cambridge for an overnight stay. Visit its most interesting colleges and overnight there.

Day 2: Head north to Ely to see its cathedral in the morning before dipping south to explore the villages of Saffron Walden and Thaxted, where an overnight stopover is in order.

Day 3: From Thaxted or Saffron Walden, head east, enjoying a luncheon stopover in Long Melford, before visiting Lavenham for an overnight stay.

Day 4: From Lavenham, head northeast to Norwich, capital of Norfolk, for an overnight stopover.

Day 5: Visit Sandringham Castle, north of Norwich, before continuing on your way, perhaps back to London.

---

1. CAMBRIDGE

55 miles NE of London, 80 miles NE of Oxford

GETTING THERE   By Train   There is frequent rail service, with trains departing from Liverpool Street Station and King's Cross Station in London (trip time: 1 hr.). A same-day round-trip ticket is £11.20 ($16.80).

By Bus   National Express coaches run hourly between London's Victoria Coach Station, arriving at Drummer Street Station in Cambridge (trip time: 2 hr.). A one-way or same-day round-trip costs £8.50 ($12.80).

By Car   Head north on the M11 from London.

ESSENTIALS   The **telephone area code** is 0223.

Orientation   The center of Cambridge is made for pedestrians, so park your car at one of the many car parks (they get more expensive as you get nearer the city center), and take the opportunity to visit some of the colleges spread throughout the city. Follow the courtyards through to the "Backs" (the college lawns) and walk through to Trinity (where Prince Charles studied) and St. John's Colleges, including the Bridge of Sighs.

Information   The **Cambridge Tourist Information Centre,** Wheeler Street (tel. 0223/322640), is behind the Guildhall.

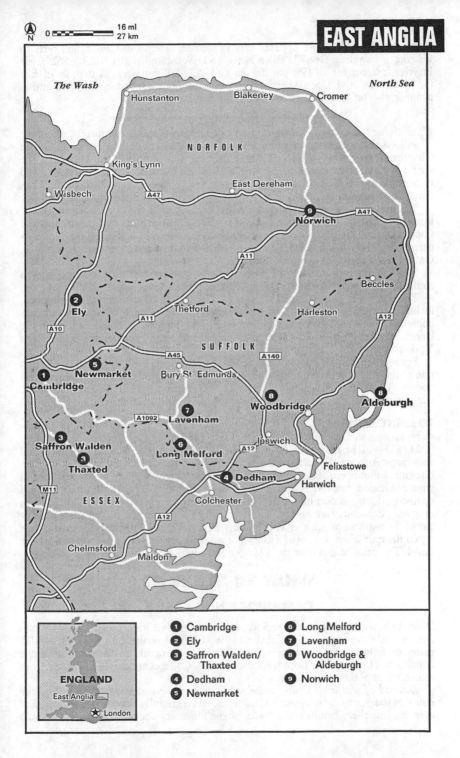

Fast Facts   The most popular way of getting around in Cambridge, next to walking, is bicycling. **Geoff's Bike Hire,** 65 Devonshire Rd. (tel. 0223/65629), has bicycles for rent for £6 ($9) per day or £15 ($22.50) per week. A deposit of £25 ($37.50) is required. Open Monday through Saturday from 9am to 5:30pm, and in summer also on Sunday from 9am to 5:30pm.

Cambridge is a collage of images: the Bridge of Sighs; spires and turrets; drooping willows that witness much punting; dusty secondhand bookshops; carol singing on Christmas Eve in King's College Chapel; dancing until sunrise at the May balls; the sound of Elizabethan madrigals; narrow lanes where Darwin, Newton, and Cromwell once walked; the Backs, where the lawns of the colleges sweep down to the Cam River; the tattered black robe of a hurrying upperclassman flying in the wind.

The university city of Cambridge, along with Oxford, is one of the ancient seats of learning in Britain. The city on the banks of the Cam River is also the county town of Cambridgeshire. In many ways the stories of Oxford and Cambridge are similar—particularly the age-old conflict between town and gown. But beyond the campus, Oxford has a thriving, high-tech industry.

There is much to explore in Cambridge—so give yourself time to wander, even aimlessly. For those who are pressed, I'll offer more specific direction.

There are many historic buildings in the city center, all within walking distance, including Great St. Mary's Church (from which the original Westminster chimes come), St. Benet's Church, the Round Church, the Fitzwilliam Museum (one of the largest and finest provincial museums), the Folk Museum, and the modern Kettles Yard Art Gallery.

For more insight into the life and times of Cambridge, both town and gown, join one of the guided tours from the Cambridge Tourist Information Centre (see address above). The center has a wide range of information, including data on public transportation in the area and on different sightseeing attractions.

TOURIST SERVICES   A tourist reception center for Cambridge and Cambridgeshire is operated by **Guide Friday Ltd.** at Cambridge Railway Station (tel. 0223/62444). The center, on the concourse of the railway station, sells brochures and sells maps. Also available is a full range of tourist services, including accommodations booking. In summer the center is open daily from 9am to 6:30pm; it closes at 3pm in winter. Guided tours of Cambridge leave the center daily. In summer, aboard open-top, double-decker buses, departures are every 15 minutes from 9:45am to 6pm; in winter, departures are hourly. The tour can be a 1-hour ride or you can get off at any of the many stops, such as King's College Chapel or the American Cemetery, then rejoin the tour when you wish. Tickets are valid all day for you to hop on and off the buses. The price of this tour is £5 ($7.50) for adults or £1.50 ($2.30) for children.

WHAT TO SEE & DO

CAMBRIDGE UNIVERSITY

Oxford University predates Cambridge, but by the early 13th century scholars began coming here too. Eventually, Cambridge won partial recognition from Henry III, rising or falling with the approval of subsequent English monarchs. Cambridge consists of 31 colleges for both men and women. Colleges are closed for exams from mid-April until the end of June.

A word of warning: Unfortunately, because of the disturbances caused by the influx of tourists to the university, Cambridge has regretfully had to limit visitors, and even exclude them from various parts of the university altogether. In some cases, a

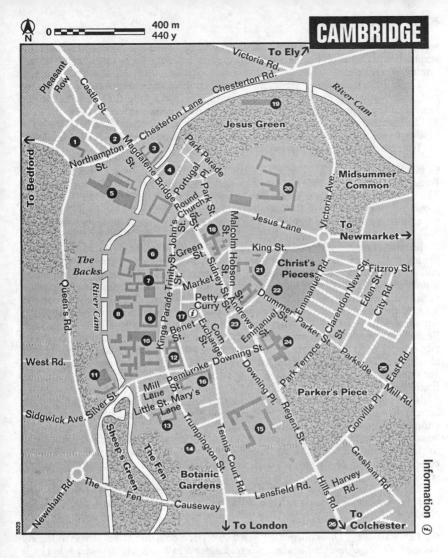

CAMBRIDGE

0 — 400 m
440 y

N

To Ely ↗

Victoria Rd.

Chesterton Rd.

River Cam

Pleasant Row

Castle St.

Chesterton Lane

Jesus Green

19

Northampton St.

Magdalene Bridge

Magdalene St.

Portugal Pl.

Park Parade

1

2

3

4

5

20

Midsummer Common

Victoria Ave.

To Newmarket →

Round Church St.

Park St.

St. John's St.

Trinity St.

Jesus Lane

Malcolm Holson St.

18

King St.

Christ's Pieces

Fitzroy St.

To Bedford ←

The Backs

Queen's Rd.

River Cam

6

7

Green St.

Sidney St.

King's Parade

Market St.

St. Andrews St.

21

Emmanuel Rd.

New Sq.

Eden St.

City Rd.

Clarendon St.

8

9

Benet St.

Petty Curry

Corn Exchange St.

Drummer St.

22

Emmanuel St.

Parker St.

West Rd.

10

11

Pembroke St.

Kings Parade

17 i

23

24

Park Terrace

Parkside

25

Mill Rd.

Gonville Pl.

East Rd.

Sidgwick Ave.

Silver St.

12

Mill Lane

Little St. Mary's Lane

16

Downing St.

Downing Pl.

Regent St.

Parker's Piece

Gresham Rd.

Sheep's Green

13

14

Trumpington St.

15

Tennis Court Rd.

Lensfield Rd.

Hills Rd.

Harvey Rd.

Newnham Rd.

The Fen

The Fen

Botanic Gardens

Causeway

↓ To London

To Colchester ↓

26

Information ⓘ

5523

British Rail Station **26**
Bus Station **22**
Christ's College **21**
Clare College **8**
Corpus Christi College **12**
Downing College **15**
Emmanuel College **24**
Fitzwilliam Museum **14**
Folk Museum **2**
General Post Office **23**

Gonville & Caius College **7**
Jesus College **20**
King's College **9**
Magdalene College **3**
Pembroke College **16**
Peterhouse College **13**
Police Station **25**
Punts **4**
Queens' College **11**

Sidney Sussex College **18**
St. Catharine's College **10**
St. John's College **5**
Swimming Pool **19**
Tourist Information Office **17**
Trinity College **6**
Westminster College **1**

small entry fee will be charged. Small groups of up to six people are generally admitted with no problem, and you can inquire from the local tourist office about visiting hours here.

These listings are only a representative selection of some of the more interesting colleges. If you're planning to stop in Cambridge for a long time, you might get around to the following: **Magdalene College** on Magdalene Street was founded in 1542, **Pembroke College** on Trumpington Street was founded in 1347, **Christ's College** on St. Andrew's Street was founded in 1505, and **Corpus Christi College** on Trumpington Street dates from 1352.

✪ **KING'S COLLEGE** The adolescent Henry VI founded the college on King's Parade (tel. 350411) in 1441. Most of its buildings today are from the 19th century. The Perpendicular **King's College Chapel,** dating from the Middle Ages, is its crowning glory and one of the architectural gems of England. The chapel, owing to the chaotic vicissitudes of English kings, wasn't completed until the early years of the 16th century.

Its most characteristic features are the magnificent fan vaulting—all of stone—and the great windows, most of which were fashioned by Flemish artisans between 1517 and 1531 (the west window, however, dates from the late Victorian period). The stained glass, in hues of red, blue, and amber, portray biblical scenes. The long range of the windows, from the first on the north side at the west end, all the way around the back of the chapel to the first on the south side, depicts the Birth of the Virgin; the Annunciation; the Birth of Christ; the Life, Ministry, and Death of Christ; the Resurrection; the Ascension; the Acts of the Apostles; and the Assumption. The upper range contains Old Testament parallels to these New Testament stories. The chapel also houses *The Adoration of the Magi* by Rubens. The rood screen is from the early 16th century. Henry James called King's College Chapel "the most beautiful in England."

It is open during vacation time Monday to Saturday, 9:30am to 5:45pm, and on Sunday from 10:30am to 5:45pm. During term time the public is welcome to attend choral services, which are at 5:30pm Tuesday to Saturday and at 10:30am and 3:30pm Sunday. In term the chapel is open to visitors Monday through Saturday from 9:30am to 3:45pm, and on Sunday from 1:30pm to 2:30pm and from 4:45pm to 5:45pm; closed December 26 to January 1. It may be closed at other times for recording sessions.

There is an exhibition in the seven northern side chapels showing why and how the chapel was built. Admission to the exhibition is £1 ($1.50) for adults, 50p (80¢) for children.

PETERHOUSE This college (tel. 338200) on Trumpington Street is visited largely because it's the oldest Cambridge college, founded in 1284. The founder was Hugh de Balsham, the bishop of Ely. Of the original buildings, only the hall remains, but this was restored in the 19th century and now boasts stained-glass windows by William Morris. Old Court, constructed in the 15th century, was renovated in 1754; the chapel dates from 1632. Ask permission to enter at the porter's desk.

TRINITY COLLEGE On Trinity Street, Trinity College (not to be confused with Trinity Hall) is the largest in Cambridge. It was founded in 1546 by Henry VIII, who consolidated a number of smaller colleges that had existed on the site. The courtyard is the most spacious in Cambridge, built when Thomas Nevile was master. Sir Christopher Wren designed the library. For admission to the college, apply at the porter's lodge, or call 338400 for information.

EMMANUEL COLLEGE On St. Andrew's Street, Emmanuel (tel. 334233) was founded in 1584 by Sir Walter Mildmay, a chancellor of the exchequer to Elizabeth I. It's of interest to Harvard students since John Harvard, founder of that university, studied here. You can take a good stroll around its attractive gardens. You might even visit the chapel designed by Sir Christopher Wren and consecrated in 1677. Both the chapel and college are open daily from 9:30am to 12:15pm and 2 to 6pm.

QUEEN'S COLLEGE   On Queen's Lane, Queens' College (tel. 335511) is thought by some to be the loveliest. Dating back to 1448, it was founded by two English queens, one the wife of Henry VI, the other the wife of Edward IV. Its second cloister is the most interesting, flanked by the early 16th-century half-timbered President's Lodge. Admission is 50p (80¢) and a short printed guide is issued. Normally, individual visitors are admitted daily from 1:45 to 4:30pm, but during July, August, and September the college is also open to visitors daily from 10:15am to 12:45pm. Entry and exit is by the old porters' lodge in Queens' Lane only. The old hall and chapel are usually open to the public when not in use.

✪ ST. JOHN'S COLLEGE   On St. John's Street, the college (tel. 338600) was founded in 1511 by Lady Margaret Beaufort, mother of Henry VII. A few years earlier she had founded Christ's College. Before her intervention, an old monk-run hospital had stood on the site of St. John's. The impressive gateway bears the Tudor coat-of-arms, and Second Court is a fine example of late Tudor brickwork. But its best-known feature is the Bridge of Sighs crossing the Cam, built in the 19th century, patterned after the bridge in Venice. It connects the older part of the college with New Court, a Gothic revival on the opposite bank from which there is an outstanding view of the famous "backs." The Bridge of Sighs is closed to visitors but can be viewed from the neighboring Kitchen Bridge. Wordsworth was an alumnus of St. John's College. The college is open daily from 10:30am to 5:30pm except in May and June. Admission is £1 ($1.50) for adults and 50p (80¢) for children, but it is charged only in April, July, August, and September. Visitors are welcome to attend choral services in the chapel.

OTHER SIGHTS

THE FITZWILLIAM MUSEUM, Trumpington St., near Peterhouse. Tel. 332900.
This museum was the gift of the Viscount Fitzwilliam, who in 1816 gave Cambridge University his paintings and rare books—along with £100,000 to build the house in which to display them. Other gifts have since been bequeathed to the museum, and now it's one of the finest in England. The collection has also been beefed up by loans and purchases. It's noted for its porcelain, old prints, antiquities, and oils (17th-century Italian, including Titian, Veronese, and Tintoretto; Rubens; Van Dyck; French impressionists; and a superb collection of 18th- and 19th-century British paintings). A gallery for Japanese prints opened in 1992.
Admission: Free.
Open: Tues–Sat 10am–5pm, Sun 2:15–5pm. **Closed:** Jan 1, Good Friday, and Dec 24–31.

GREAT ST. MARY'S, King's Parade. Tel. 350914.
The university church is built on the site of an 11th-century church, but the present building dates largely from 1478. It was closely associated with events of the Reformation. The cloth that covered the hearse of King Henry VII is on display in the church. A fine view of Cambridge may be obtained from the top of the tower.
Admission: £1 ($1.50) adults, 20p (30¢) children.
Open: Daily 9am–5pm.

TOURS

The person to know if you're in the Cambridge area is Mrs. Isobel Bryant, who operates **Heritage Tours** from her 200-year-old home, Manor Cottage, Swaffham

Prior CB5 0JZ (tel. 0638/741440). An expert on the region, she will arrange tours starting from your hotel or Cambridge railway station to Lavenham with its thatched and timbered houses, to the fine medieval churches of the Suffolk villages, to Ely Cathedral, or to one of the grand mansions nearby with their many treasures. The charge of £85 ($127.50) is for the day for up to four passengers and all travel expenses, including the service of the driver/guide. Lunch in a village pub and admission fees add £5 ($7.50) per person.

There are also walking tours around the colleges of Cambridge given by Mrs. Bryant, costing £15 ($22.50) for a family-size party and lasting about 2 hours. There is a tour of Newmarket, headquarters of the horse-racing industry. For a group of 12 or more, a whole-day tour costs £15 ($22.50) per person; a half-day tour goes for £8 ($12) per person. A shorter tour can be arranged for individuals or a family group. If you want lunch at a private manor house with Cordon Bleu cooking, the cost will be £10 ($15) per person, with wine included, for groups of 12 or more.

BOATING

Punting on the Cam is a traditional pursuit of students and visitors in Cambridge, but there are other types of boating available if you don't trust yourself to stand up and pole a punt under and around the weeping willow trees. Upriver, you can go a distance of about 2 miles to Grantchester, which was immortalized by poet Rupert Brooke. Downstream, you pass along the Backs behind the colleges of the university.

Scudamore's Boatyards, Granta Place (tel. 359750), by the Anchor Pub, has been in business since 1910. All craft rent for £6 ($9) per hour, including punts, canoes, and rowboats. A £40 ($60) deposit, payable with cash or a credit card, is required. There is a maximum of six persons per punt.

The **Cambridge Punt Company,** working out of The Anchor Pub, Silver Street (without number; tel. 357565), is well recommended for its hour-long rowboat tours. A guide (usually a Cambridge student) appropriately dressed in a boater (straw hat) and a blazer will both row and give running commentary to groups of between one and six persons. Tours, depending on their length, range from £16 to £20 ($24 to $30) per hour. Boats are moored near the base of the Anchor Pub (see "Where to Eat," below). Spokespeople from the company maintain a dialogue with the Anchor's service staff, any of whom can call a guide over to your table. Additionally, if you want to row yourself along the Cam, "unchauffeured" boats rent for £5 ($7.50) per hour. The company is open daily between Easter and October from 10am to 7pm, although if it rains or if winds get too high, everyone packs up and goes home.

WHERE TO STAY

MODERATE

CAMBRIDGESHIRE MOAT HOUSE, Huntingdon Rd., Bar Hill, Cambridge, Cambridgeshire CB3 8EU. Tel. 0954/780555. Fax 0954/780010. 100 rms (all with bath). TV TEL **Directions:** Take the A604 5½ miles northwest of the town center.

$ Rates (including English breakfast): £65 ($97.50) single; £78 ($117) double. AE, DC, MC, V. **Parking:** Free.

Built 20 years ago, this hotel enjoys an isolated location, sitting in wide open countryside surrounded by a golf course. This modern three-star hotel has a heated indoor swimming pool, sauna, three squash courts, two outdoor tennis courts, an 18-hole championship golf course, putting green, and helipad. The bedrooms, each comfortably furnished, are equipped with radios, hairdryers, trouser presses, and hot-beverage facilities. Guests can use the sports facilities free on weekdays. On weekends, greens fees range from £10 to £12.50 ($15 to $18.80), with the use of the solarium costing £4 ($6) per person. The restaurant offers both table d'hôte and à la carte menus. Table d'hôte dinners cost £15.50 ($23.30) except on Saturday night when the price is £16.75 ($25.10). Meals are also served daily in the bar.

THE GARDEN HOUSE, Granta Place, Cambridge, Cambridgeshire CB2 1RT. Tel. 0223/63421. Fax 0223/316605. 118 rms (all with bath), 7 suites. MINIBAR TV TEL
$ Rates (including continental breakfast): £90 ($135) single; £125–£170 ($187.50–$255) double; £295 ($442.50) suite. AE, DC, MC, V. **Parking:** Free.

This modern hotel is situated between the riverbank and a cobblestone street in the oldest part of town, a short stroll from the principal colleges. Next door is a boatyard where you can rent punts. The hotel has a series of outdoor terraces where drinks and afternoon tea are served in good weather. The earth-tone brick and stained-wood exterior harmonizes with the wall coverings in the bar and lounge, where visitors can relax on comfortable sofas and chairs. The well-furnished bedrooms are equipped with radios, soundproof windows, hot-beverage facilities, and hairdryers. Most rooms have balconies and river views. River-view rooms cost £12 ($18) extra.

The hotel's Le Jardin Restaurant, which overlooks the river and gardens, offers fixed-price and à la carte menus, including vegetarian meals, at lunch and dinner. A three-course fixed-price menu costs £21 ($31.50). The Riverside Lounge provides a selection of hot and cold light meals, accompanied in the evening by piano music. When weather permits, the Cocktail Bar serves drinks on the terrace and lawn. The hotel has ample parking.

UNIVERSITY ARMS HOTEL, Regent St., Cambridge, Cambridgeshire CB2 1AD. Tel. 0223/351241. Fax 0223/315256. 115 rms (all with bath), 1 suite. TV TEL **Bus:** 1.
$ Rates (including English breakfast): £55–£81 ($82.50–$121.50) single; £80–£110 ($120–$165) double; from £150 ($225) suite. AE, DC, MC, V. **Parking:** Free.

Built in 1834, this hotel maintains much of its antique charm and many of its original architectural features despite discreet modernizations through the years. Near the city center and the university, this traditional hotel offers tastefully decorated bedrooms with central heating, electric-razor outlets, and a radio. Most overlook Parker's Piece, where one of England's greatest cricketers, Sir Jack Hobbs, learned to play. The Octagon Lounge, with its stained-glass domed ceiling and open log fire, is a popular place to meet for tea. The spacious oak-paneled restaurant features both table d'hôte and à la carte menus. Dinner costs £16 ($24) and up.

Tip: The hotel porter can arrange a guided tour of the city for you.

INEXPENSIVE

ARUNDEL HOUSE, 53 Chesterton Rd., Cambridge, Cambridgeshire CB4 3AN. Tel. 0223/67701. Fax 0223/67721. 88 rms (all with bath). TV TEL **Bus:** 3 or 5.
$ Rates (including continental breakfast): £39–£53.50 ($58.50–$80.30) single; £54–£72.50 ($81–$108.80) double. AE, DC, MC, V. **Parking:** Free.

Occupying one of the finest sites in Cambridge, this hotel overlooks the River Cam and open parkland. It's only a few minutes' walk from the city center and the university colleges. The 19th-century terraced hotel's rooms are equipped with radios, hairdryers, and hot-beverage facilities. Assorted films as well as a videotaped guide to Cambridge can be viewed in the rooms. There is a cocktail bar and a small garden with outdoor tables and an attractive Victorian-style restaurant offering table d'hôte or à la carte menus. Bar meals are also available. A fixed-price three-course lunch is £8.50 ($12.80); a table d'hôte dinner, £14 ($21). There's a coin-operated launderette on the premises.

GONVILLE HOTEL, Gonville Place, Cambridge, Cambridgeshire CB1 1LY. Tel. 0223/66611, or toll free 800/435-4542 in the U.S. Fax 0223/315470. 62 rms (all with bath). TV TEL
$ Rates (including English breakfast): £65 ($97.50) single; £82 ($123) double. AE, DC, MC, V. **Parking:** Free.

Only a 5-minute walk from the center of town, this comfortable hotel and its grounds are opposite Parker's Piece. It's not unlike a country house—ivy covered, with shade trees and a formal car entry. In 1973 it was gutted and rebuilt as a commercial hotel, hoping to attract businesspeople as well as tourists in summer. The rooms are comfortable and furnished in a modern style. There is central heating throughout and air conditioning in the restaurant. A fixed-price lunch costs £11.50 ($17.30); dinner, £14.50 ($21.80). You can also order à la carte.

POST HOUSE HOTEL, Lakeview, Bridge Rd., Lakeview Bridge, Impington, Cambridge, Cambridgeshire CB4 4PH. Tel. 0223/237000, or toll free 800/435-4542 in the U.S. Fax 0223/233426. 118 rms (all with bath). TV TEL
Directions: Head 2 miles north of Cambridge on the B1049 to the A45 intersection. **Bus:** 104.
$ Rates: Sun–Thurs, £53.50 ($80.30) per person, single or double; Fri–Sat, £39.50 ($59.30) per person, single or double. English breakfast £6.95 ($10.40) extra. AE, DC, MC, V. **Parking:** Free.

Located a short walk from a small artificial lake, the wings of this hotel partially embrace a grassy courtyard. The ceilings of the lofty public rooms soar above dozens of sofas and chairs, ending in a peaked summit. The bedrooms have large windows with pleasant views, and baths. Facilities include a heated indoor swimming pool, Jacuzzi, sauna, and lobby bar. The hotel restaurant, the Churchill, has mahogany paneling and reproductions of paintings created by Sir Winston Churchill.

REGENT HOTEL, 41 Regent St., Cambridge, Cambridgeshire CB2 1AB. Tel. 0223/351470. Fax 0223/356220. 26 rms (all with bath). TV TEL
$ Rates (including English breakfast): £52.50 ($78.80) single; £69.50 ($104.30) double. AE, DC, MC, V.

 This is one of the nicest of the reasonably priced small hotels in Cambridge. Right in the city center, overlooking Parker's Piece, the house was built in the 1840s as the original site of Newham College. When the college outgrew its quarters, the building became a hotel. The attractive, comfortable bedrooms have radios, hairdryers, and trouser presses. There's a cocktail bar on the street level, and the restaurant serves seafood and international specialties.

WHERE TO DINE

BROWNS, 23 Trumpington St. Tel. 461655.
   Cuisine: ENGLISH/CONTINENTAL. **Reservations:** Not required. **Bus:** 2.
$ Prices: Main courses £5.95–£9.95 ($8.90–$14.90). AE, MC, V.
   Open: Mon–Sat 11am–11:30pm, Sun noon–11:30pm.

 Long a favorite at Oxford, it also became a sensation at Cambridge some time ago. With a neoclassical colonnade in front, it has all the grandeur of the Edwardian era. It was actually built in 1914 as the outpatient department of a hospital dedicated to Edward VII. Today it's the most lighthearted place for dining in the city, with wicker chairs, high ceilings, pre–World War I woodwork, and a long bar covered with bottles of wine. The extensive bill of fare includes various renditions of spaghetti, fresh salads, several selections of meat and fish (from charcoal-grilled leg of lamb with rosemary to fresh fish in season), hot sandwiches, and the chef's daily specials posted on a blackboard. If you drop by in the afternoon, you can also order thick milk shakes or natural fruit juices. There are no appetizers. In fair weather, outdoor seating is provided. The location is 5 minutes from King's College and opposite the Fitzwilliam Museum.

CHARLIE CHAN, 14 Regent St. Tel. 61763.

Cuisine: CHINESE. **Reservations:** Recommended.

$ Prices: Appetizers £3.50–£5 ($5.30–$7.50); main courses £7.50–£12.50 ($11.30–$18.80); fixed-price menus £10–£20 ($15–$30). AE, MC, V.

Open: Lunch daily noon–2:15pm; dinner daily 6–11:15pm.

Most people agree that this is the finest Chinese restaurant in Cambridge, and in my experience, Charlie Chan is reliable and capable in spite of its large selection of dishes. It's a long corridorlike restaurant, with pristine decor and tile floors. The specialties I've most enjoyed include an aromatic and crispy duck, lemon chicken, and prawn with garlic and ginger. It's best to go with a party—that way you can sample many different dishes. It's located on a busy commercial street.

MIDSUMMER HOUSE, Midsummer Common. Tel. 69299.

Cuisine: FRENCH. **Reservations:** Required.

$ Prices: Lunch £23 ($34.50) for 3 courses; dinner £30 ($45) for 3 courses. AE, DC, MC, V.

Open: Lunch Sun–Fri 12:15–2pm; dinner Mon–Sat 7:15–10pm.

Located near the River Cam, the Midsummer House is one of the dining discoveries of Cambridge. It lies within the Edwardian era cottage that once housed the groundskeeper for Midsummer Common, the largest of central Cambridge's several verdant squares. The preferred dining area is in an elegant conservatory, but you can also find a smartly laid table upstairs. The fixed-price menus are wisely limited, and quality control is much in evidence here. The chef/patron, Hans Schweitzer, knows the French school, except that every dish seems to bear his own special imprint—and that's quite good. Attired in funereal black, the waiters will come to your assistance as you peruse the menu for the freshest or most exciting selection on any given day. Specialties include délice of salmon, foie gras, terrine of summer vegetables, carré of lamb in jus, filet of turbot wrapped in a "pig's veil" (the membrane from a pig's stomach), salmon and turbot in puff pastry, and a *mille-feuille* of sweetbreads and kidneys.

RESTAURANT ANGELINE, 8 Market Passage. Tel. 60305.

Cuisine: FRENCH. **Reservations:** Not required.

$ Prices: Appetizers £2–£3 ($3–$4.50); main courses £8.60–£11.50 ($12.90–$17.30). MC, V.

Open: Lunch daily noon–2:30pm; dinner Mon–Sat 6–11pm.

 This restaurant above the Arts Cinema is set along a commercial passageway in the heart of town behind a narrow facade, found between Sidney and Market Streets just 2 blocks east of Trinity College. The multiple nationalities of its owners, coupled with its French chef, make this one of the most varied restaurants in town. The menu might include trout meunière, grilled Dover sole, fresh salmon, and several preparations of lamb. The price of a main course includes the soup of the day or a selection of hors d'oeuvres from the trolley, along with two vegetables, plus potatoes and French bread and butter.

TWENTY TWO, 22 Chesterton Rd. Tel. 351880.

Cuisine: ENGLISH/CONTINENTAL. **Reservations:** Required.

$ Prices: Fixed-price menu £21.50 ($32.30). MC, V.

Open: Dinner only, Tues–Sat 7:30–9:30pm.

Who would expect to find one of the best restaurants in Cambridge in this quiet residential and hotel district? In the vicinity of Jesus Green, it has up to now been an address jealously guarded by the locals who "don't want tourists to spoil it." Decorated in pink and gray tones, it's an exponent of the best of contemporary English and continental cookery, relying on the freshest ingredients in any season. The fixed-price menu is ever-changing, based on fresh produce at the market. Owners David Carter and Louise Crompton use time-tested recipes along with their own inspirations. Typical dishes include Stilton-and-bacon soup and local pan-fried venison with a cranberry sauce, followed by homemade ice cream.

PUBS

CAMBRIDGE ARMS, 4 King St. Tel. 359650.

Cuisine: ENGLISH. **Reservations:** Not accepted.
$ Prices: Bar snacks from £3 ($4.50). No credit cards.
Open: Mon–Sat noon–7pm, Sun noon–3pm. Pub, Mon–Sat 11am–11pm, Sun noon–3pm and 7–10:30pm.

This bustling, no-nonsense pub in the center of town has plenty of atmosphere, and dispenses endless platters of food to clients who order it over the bar's countertop. Menu possibilities include chef's daily specials, grilled steaks, lasagne, and an array of both hot and cold dishes.

THE GREEN MAN, 59 High St., Grantchester. Tel. 841178.

Cuisine: ENGLISH. **Reservations:** Not required. **Bus:** 118 from Cambridge.
$ Prices: Appetizers £1.95–£2.75 ($2.90–$4.10); main courses £3.95–£7.50 ($5.90–$11.30). AE, MC, V.
Open: Lunch daily noon–2:30pm; dinner daily 6:30–9:30pm.

Named in honor of Robin Hood, this 400-year-old inn is perhaps the most popular pub outing from Cambridge. It's set beside the A603, 2 miles south of Cambridge in the hamlet of Grantchester. The village was made famous by Rupert Brooke, the famed Edwardian-era poet best known for his sonnet "The Soldier." Grantchester is considered one of the shire's most beautiful villages, with an old church and gardens leading down to a series of peaceful meadows. Even if you've never heard of Brooke, you might enjoy spending a late afternoon here, wandering through the old church and then heading, as everybody does, to the Green Man. In winter you'll be welcomed with a crackling fire, but in summer you might want to retreat to the beer garden in back. From there, you can stroll to the edge of the River Cam. Place your food order at the counter, after which an employee will carry the food to your table. Menu choices include steak-and-Guinness pie, steak-and-mushroom pie, lasagne, fresh salads, English cheeses, and pâtés. A specialty is a 7-inch Yorkshire pudding stuffed with one of the chef's homemade pie fillings.

2. ELY

70 miles NE of London, 16 miles N of Cambridge

GETTING THERE By Train Ely is a major railway junction served by express trains to Cambridge. Service is frequent from London's Liverpool Street Station.

By Bus Frequent buses run between Cambridge and Ely.

By Car   From Cambridge, take the A10 north.

ESSENTIALS   The **telephone area code** is 0353. The **Tourist Information Centre** is at Oliver Cromwell's House, 29 St. Mary's St. (tel. 0353/662062).

The top attraction in the fen country, outside of Cambridge, is Ely Cathedral. Ely used to be known as the Isle of Ely, until the surrounding marshes and meres were drained. The last stronghold of Saxon England, Ely was defended by Hereward the Wake, until his capitulation to the Normans in 1071.

WHAT TO SEE & DO

ELY CATHEDRAL, The College. Tel. 667735.

The near-legendary founder of the cathedral was Etheldreda, the wife of a Northumbrian king who established a monastery on the spot in 673. The present structure dates from 1081. Visible for miles around, the landmark octagonal lantern is the crowning glory of the cathedral. Erected in 1322, following the collapse of the old tower, it represents a remarkable engineering achievement. Four hundred tons of lead and wood hang in space, held there by timbers reaching to the eight pillars.

You enter the cathedral through the Galilee West Door, a good example of the Early English style of architecture. The lantern tower and the Octagon are the most notable features inside, but visit the lady chapel too. Although its decor has deteriorated over the centuries, it's still a handsome example of the Perpendicular style, having been completed in the mid-14th century. The entry fee goes to help preserve the cathedral.

Admission: £2.60 ($3.90) adults, £2.10 ($3.20) children 12–16, free for children under 12.

Open: Apr–Oct, daily 7am–7pm; Nov–Mar, Mon–Sat 7:30am–6pm, Sun 7:30am–5pm.

ELY MUSEUM, 28C High St. Tel. 666655.

Artifacts from the area are displayed here, including a rare collection of 17th-century Ely trade tokens. A gallery presents old films of Ely and the surrounding fenland.

Admission: £1 ($1.50) adults, 50p (80¢) children 6–16.

Open: Tues–Sun 10:30am–1pm and 2:15–5pm.

NEARBY ATTRACTIONS

GRIME'S GRAVES, on the B1108, 2¾ miles northeast of Brandon, Norfolkshire. Tel. 0842/810656.

On the B1108, off the main A1065 road from Swaffham to Mildenhall east of Ely, and 2¾ miles northeast of Brandon (Norfolkshire), you can visit the largest group of Neolithic flint mines in the country. This is sparsely populated, fir-wooded country, and it's easy to imagine yourself transported back to ancient times. The mines are well signposted, and you'll soon find yourself at a small parking lot presided over by a custodian who will open up one or several of the shafts, allowing you to enter a remnant of ancient Britain, from a time even before that of the Anglo-Saxons. Restoration has been carried out, and it's now possible to see where work took place. If you're lucky, you may find a worked flint of your own to present to the custodian. It's best to have a flashlight handy. The steep climb down is only for the vigorous.

The mines are close to the air force bases so well known to countless American air crews during World War II.

Admission: £1.20 ($1.80) adults, 60p (90¢) children 5–15.

Open: Good Friday–Sept, daily 10am–1pm and 2–6pm; Oct–Maundy Thursday, Tues–Sun 10am–1pm and 2–4pm.

IMPERIAL WAR MUSEUM, Duxford Airfield, on the A505, at Junction 10 of the M11. Tel. 835000.

In this former Battle of Britain station and U.S. Eighth Air Force base in World War II, you'll find a huge collection of historic civil and military aircraft from both world wars, including the only B-29 Superfortress in Europe. Other exhibits include midget submarines, tanks, and a variety of field artillery pieces, as well as a historical display on the U.S. Eighth Air Force. Special charges are made for special events, and parking is free.

Admission: £5.80 ($8.70) adults, £2.90 ($4.40) children.

Open: Mid-Mar to Oct, daily 10am–6pm; Nov to mid-Mar, daily 10am–4pm. **Closed:** Jan 1 and Dec 25–26. **Directions:** Take the M11 to Junction 10, 8 miles south of Cambridge. **Bus:** Cambus no. 103 from Drummer Street Station in Cambridge.

WHERE TO STAY

LAMB HOTEL, 2 Lynn Rd., Ely, Cambridgeshire CB7 4EJ. Tel. 0353/ 663574. Fax 0353/666350. 32 rms (all with bath). TV TEL **Bus:** 109.

$ Rates (including English breakfast): £58 ($87) single; £75 ($112.50) double. AE, DC, MC, V.

Right in the center of town, this hotel is a former coaching inn. In the shadow of the cathedral, this Queens Moat House hotel offers renovated bedrooms with private baths or showers and hot-beverage facilities. In the 1400s this place was known as the "Holy Lambe," a stopping-off spot for wayfarers, often pilgrims, through East Anglia. A table d'hôte lunch or dinner costs £13.50 ($20.30) and up. During Sunday brunches, a roast topside of beef is wheeled out in the Merrie Olde England style.

WHERE TO DINE

THE OLD FIRE ENGINE HOUSE, 25 St. Mary's St. Tel. 662582.

Cuisine: ENGLISH. **Reservations:** Required. **Bus:** 109.

$ Prices: Appetizers £2.60–£3.20 ($3.90–$4.80); main courses £10.80–£12.10 ($16.20–$18.20). MC, V.

Open: Lunch daily 12:30–2pm; dinner Mon–Sat 7:30–9pm (last entry).

Opposite St. Mary's Church is one of the finer restaurants in East Anglia. It's worth making a detour to this converted fire station in a walled garden, in a complex of buildings that includes an art gallery. Soups are served in huge bowls, accompanied by coarse-grained crusty bread. Main dishes include duck with orange sauce, jugged hare, steak-and-kidney pie, baked stuffed pike, casserole of rabbit, and pigeon with bacon and black olives. Desserts include fruit pie and cream, although I'd recommend the syllabub, made with cream and liquor. In summer you can dine outside in the garden, even order a cream tea. It is owned and in large part run by Ann Ford, who still finds time to talk to customers.

3. SAFFRON WALDEN/THAXTED

43 miles N of London, 15 miles SE of Cambridge

GETTING THERE   By Train   Trains leave London's Liverpool Street Station in the direction of Cambridge several times a day. Two or three stations before Cambridge, passengers should get off in the hamlet of Audley End, 8 miles north of Thaxted and a mile from Saffron Walden. There is a circumvoluted bus from Audley End, but it meanders so wildly that most visitors opt for one of the many taxis instead.

By Bus Cambus no. 122 leaves Cambridge Monday through Saturday at 12:15pm, 2:40pm, and 5:35pm, heading for Saffron Walden. Cambus no. 9 departs only Sunday every 1½ hours between 10am to 6pm. The last bus back on Sunday departs Saffron Walden at 7:10pm. National Express buses leave London's Victoria Coach Station several times a day and stop at Saffron Walden, 6 miles north of Thaxted. From there, there are about three (at the very most) buses heading on to Thaxted. Most visitors opt instead for a taxi, which is a lot easier.

By Car From Cambridge, take the A1301 southeast, connecting with the B184 (also southeast) into Saffron Walden. The B184 also leads to the adjoining village of Thaxted.

ESSENTIALS The **telephone area code** is 0799 for Saffron Walden and 0371 for Thaxted. The **Tourist Information Centre** is at 1 Market Sq. (tel. 0799/ 524282), in Saffron Walden.

In the northern corner of Essex, a short drive from Thaxted, is the ancient market town of Walden, renamed Saffron Walden because of the fields of autumn crocus that used to grow around it. Despite its proximity to London, it isn't disturbed by heavy tourist traffic. Residents of Cambridge escape to this old borough for their weekends.

Many of the houses in Saffron Walden are distinctive in England, in that the 16th- and 17th-century builders faced their houses with parget—a kind of plasterwork (sometimes made with cow dung) used for ornamental facades. There are many 15th- and 16th-century timber-framed houses with pargetting, as well as the 14th-century Sun Inn, and the Perpendicular-style Church of Saffron Walden, the largest in Essex. Saffron Walden is one of the few market towns in England which still has its original medieval street pattern.

WHAT TO SEE & DO

One mile west of Saffron Walden (on the B1383) is **Audley End House,** "Brunketts," Wendens Ambo, near Saffron Walden (tel. 0799/522842), considered one of the finest mansions in all of East Anglia. This Jacobean house was begun by Sir Thomas Howard, treasurer to the king, in 1605, built on the foundation of a monastery. James I is reported to have said, "Audley End is too large for a king, though it might do for a lord treasurer." Among the house's outstanding features is an impressive Great Hall with an early 17th-century screen at the north end, considered one of the most beautiful ornamental screens in England. Rooms decorated by Robert Adam contain fine furniture and works of art. A "Gothick" chapel and a charming Victorian ladies' sitting room are among the attractions. The park surrounding the house was landscaped by Capability Brown. It has a lovely rose garden, a river and cascade, and a picnic area. In the stables, built at the same time as the mansion, is a collection of agricultural machinery, as well as a Victorian coach, old wagons, and the estate fire wagon. From April 1 until the end of September, the house and grounds are open Wednesday through Sunday. House hours are from 1 to 5pm, and the grounds are open from noon to 6pm. A ticket for the house and grounds costs £4.90 ($7.40) for adults and £2.40 ($3.60) for children 5 to 16. To visit just the grounds costs only £2.70 ($4.10) for adults and £1.30 ($2) for children.

The location is 1¼ miles (a 20-minute walk) from Audley End Station where trains arrive from Cambridge.

WHERE TO STAY & DINE

SAFFRON HOTEL, 10–18 High St., Saffron Walden, Essex CB10 1AY. Tel. 0799/522676. Fax 0799/513979. 17 rms (all with bath). TV TEL
$ Rates (including English breakfast): £45 ($67.50) single; £55–£65 ($82.50–$97.50) double. MC, V. **Parking:** Free.

In the center of this Cromwellian market town stands the Saffron Hotel, dating from the 16th century. The hotel combines modern comforts with old-world charm, as reflected by its individually designed and decorated rooms. Amenities include tea and coffee makers, and central heating. Most rooms overlook High Street or the inner courtyard with its patio garden. Stories abound in the area about the Saffron Hotel ghost.

The hotel's restaurant, which is well known locally, is decorated in the Regency style. Dining is by candlelight overlooking a floodlit patio garden. A fixed-price lunch costs £10 ($15) and a fixed-price dinner goes for £15 ($22.50), each consisting of three courses. The menu is more sophisticated than ever under new ownership at the inn, a combination of modern British cuisine with classical French. A specialty is filet of sole Saffron. Lunch is served Sunday through Friday from noon to 2pm and dinner Monday through Saturday from 7:30 to 9:30pm.

AN EXCURSION TO THAXTED

Sitting on the crest of a hill 43 miles north of London, the Saxon town of Thaxted contains the most beautiful small church in England, whose graceful spire can be seen for miles around. Its bells ring out special chimes to parishioners who attend their church. Dating back to 1340, the church is a nearly perfect example of religious architecture. Thaxted also has a number of well-preserved Elizabethan houses and a wooden-pillared Jacobean guildhall.

WHERE TO STAY & DINE

WHITEHALL, Church End, Broxted, Thaxted, Essex CM6 2BZ. Tel. 0279/850603. Fax 0279/850385. 25 rms (all with bath). TV TEL **Directions:** Take the B1052 about 4 miles southwest of Thaxted.
$ Rates (including English breakfast): £75 ($112.50) single; £105–£155 ($157.50–$232.50) double. AE, DC, MC, V. **Parking:** Free.

In the 18th century this property was attached to almost 28,000 acres of prime farmland. By the 1900s the Countess of Warwick, then its mistress, entertained King Edward VII within these baronial walls. Today, in an elegantly simplified format, guests are still entertained more or less royally. The bedrooms are each uniquely furnished in 18th-century style; all have thoughtful extras and views of the 300-year-old yew trees in the ancient walled garden. A medieval brewhouse with a soaring ceiling is the setting for specialties prepared with fresh ingredients. A tempting fixed-price dinner is offered for £33.50 ($50.30).

---

4. DEDHAM

63 miles N of London, 8 miles NE of Colchester

GETTING THERE **By Train** Trains depart every 20 minutes from London's Liverpool Street Station for the 50-minute ride to Colchester. From Colchester, it's possible to take a taxi from the railway station to the bus station, then board a bus run by the Eastern National Bus Company for the 5-mile trip to Dedham. (Buses leave about once an hour.) Most people find this so inconvenient, however, that they instead opt for taking a taxi from Colchester directly to Dedham.

By Bus   National Express buses depart from London's Victoria Coach Station for Colchester, whereupon the connection just described above goes into effect. Again, many guests opt for a taxi instead of the connecting bus to Dedham.

By Car   From the London ring road, branch northeast along the A12 to Colchester, turning off at East Bergholt onto a small secondary road leading east to Dedham.

ESSENTIALS   The **telephone area code** is 0206.

Remember Constable's *Vale of Dedham?* In this little Essex village on the Stour River you're in the heart of Constable country. Flatford Mill is only a mile farther down the river. The village, with its Tudor, Georgian, and Regency houses, is set in the midst of the water meadows of the Stour. Constable painted its church and tower. Dedham is right on the Essex-Suffolk border and makes a good center for exploring both North Essex and the Suffolk border country.

WHAT TO SEE & DO

About three-quarters of a mile from the village center is **Castle House,** East Lane (tel. 322127), home of Sir Alfred Munnings, the president of the Royal Academy (1944–49) and painter extraordinaire of racehorses and other animals. The house and studio, which have sketches and other works, are open from early May to early October, on Sunday, Wednesday, and bank holidays, as well as on Thursday and Saturday in August, from 2 to 5pm. Admission is £2 ($3) for adults, 25p (40¢) for children.

The English landscape painter, John Constable (1776–1837), was born at East Bergholt, directly north of Dedham. Near the village is **Flatford Mill,** East Bergholt, (tel. 0206/298283), subject of one of his most renowned works. The mill, in a scenic setting, was given to the National Trust in 1943, and has since been leased to the Field Studies Council for use as a residential college.

Weekly courses are offered on all aspects of the countryside and the environment. None of the buildings has exhibits, nor are they open to the general public, but students of all ages are welcome to attend the courses. The fee for 1 week is inclusive of accommodation, meals, and tuition. Details may be obtained from Director of Studies, Field Studies Council, Flatford Mill Field Centre, East Bergholt, Colchester, Essex CO7 6UL.

WHERE TO STAY

DEDHAM VALE HOTEL, Stratford Rd., Dedham, Colchester, Essex CO7 6HW. Tel. 0206/322273, or toll free 800/635-3612 in the U.S. Fax 0206/322752. 6 rms (all with bath). TV TEL
$ Rates (including continental breakfast): £72–£77 ($108–$115.50) single; £87–£97 ($130.50–$145.50) double. AE, MC, V. **Parking:** Free.
Attractive bedrooms are offered at this vine-covered Edwardian house in a peaceful bucolic setting three-quarters of a mile west of the town center on Stratford Road. It's less glamorous than owner Gerald Milsom's other hotel—the nearby Maison

Talbooth, also previewed. Rooms include a radio and a comfortable collection of traditional furniture. One of Constable's great-nieces occupied one of the upstairs bedrooms here, when this was a convalescent home. The hotel is within easy reach of the ports of Harwich and Felixstowe for journeys to the Continent. On chilly mornings a fire blazes in the Regency-style fireplace in the sitting room.

Dining/Entertainment: The bar offers views of a flowering terrace and floor-to-ceiling murals of Constable's East Anglia. In the Terrace Restaurant, an Edwardian conservatory shelters the napery and cut flowers of an increasingly popular dining spot.

MAISON TALBOOTH, Stratford Rd., Dedham, Colchester, Essex CO7 6HN. Tel. 0206/322367. Fax 0206/322752. 10 suites. MINIBAR TV TEL **Directions:** Take Stratford Rd. half a mile west of the town center.

$ Rates (including continental or English breakfast): £82.50–£107.50 ($123.80–$161.30) single; £102.50–£137.50 ($153.80–$206.30) double. MC, V. **Parking:** Free.

This small and exclusive hotel is located in a handsomely restored Victorian country house. Accommodations here consist of spacious suites distinctively furnished by one of England's best-known decorators. High-fashion colors abound, antiques are mixed discreetly with reproductions, and the original architectural beauty has been preserved. A super-luxury suite has a sunken bath and a draped bed. Each suite has its own theme. When you arrive, you're welcomed and brought to your suite, where fresh flowers, fruit, and a private bar are standard. Guests meet in an informal, yet stylish, drawing room.

WHERE TO DINE

LE TALBOOTH, Gun Hill. Tel. 323150.
   Cuisine: ENGLISH/FRENCH. **Reservations:** Required.
$ Prices: Appetizers £6–£10 ($9–$15); main courses £13–£18 ($19.50–$27); fixed-price lunch £19.95 ($29.90). AE, MC, V.
   Open: Lunch daily noon–2pm; dinner daily 7–9pm.

A hand-hewn, half-timbered weaver's house is the setting for this restaurant standing amid beautiful gardens on the banks of the River Stour in Constable Country. Le Talbooth was featured in Constable's *Vale of Dedham.* You descend a sloping driveway leading past flowering terraces. A well-mannered staff will usher you to a low-ceilinged bar for an apéritif. Taller guests are cautioned to beware of low ceiling beams, which add a rich atmospheric note of another era. Owner Gerald Milsom has brought a high standard of cooking to this rustically elegant place, where a well-chosen wine list complements the good food. An à la carte menu changes six times a year, and special dishes change daily, as they reflect the best produce available at the market. Food is cooked to order to preserve natural flavors. Main dishes are likely to range from garlic-studded Scottish beef filet to roast Barbary duck.

---

5. NEWMARKET

62 miles NE of London, 13 miles NE of Cambridge

GETTING THERE   By Train Trains depart from London's Liverpool Street Station every 45 to 60 minutes for Cambridge. In Cambridge, passengers change trains and head in the direction of Mildenhall. Three stops later, they arrive at Newmarket.

By Bus About eight National Express buses depart from London's Victoria Coach Station for Norwich every day, stopping at Stratford, Stansted, and (finally) Newmarket along the way.

By Car From Cambridge, head east along the A133.

ESSENTIALS The **telephone area code** is 0638.

This old Suffolk town has been famous as a racing center since the time of King James I. Visitors can see Nell Gwynne's House, but mainly they come to visit Britain's first and only equestrian museum.

WHAT TO SEE & DO

NATIONAL HORSERACING MUSEUM, 99 High St. Tel. 667333.

The museum is housed in the old subscription rooms, early 19th-century rooms used for placing and settling bets. Visitors will be able to see the history of horse racing over a 300-year period. There are fine paintings of famous horses, paintings on loan from Queen Elizabeth II, and copies of old Parliamentary Acts governing races. There is also a replica of a weighing-in room, plus explanations of the signs used by the ticktack men who keep the on-course bookies informed of changes in the price of bets. A continuous 53-minute audiovisual presentation shows races and racchorses.

To make history come alive for the museum visitor, they also offer equine tours of this historic town. You are taken by a guide to watch morning gallops on the heath, through the town where you'll see bronzes of horses from the past, and other points of interest. An optional tour of a famous training establishment is offered, plus a visit to the Jockey Club rooms, known for its fine collection of paintings. Reservations are necessary, but the tour, which lasts a whole morning, is conducted April to October. The museum is closed from December to March, but those with a special interest in seeing it during those months can telephone.

Admission: £2.50 ($3.80) adults, 75p ($1.10) children.
Open: Apr–Nov, Tues–Sat 10am–5pm, Sun 2–5pm. **Closed:** Dec–Mar; Mon except bank holidays in Aug.

THE NATIONAL STUD, July Race Course. Tel. 663464.

Next to Newmarket's July Race Course, 2 miles southwest of the town, is the place for those who wish to see some of the world's finest horseflesh, as well as watch a working Thoroughbred breeding stud in operation. A tour lasting about 1¼ hours lets you see many mares and foals, plus horses in training for racing. Reservations for tours must be made at the National Stud office or by phoning the number given above.

Admission: £3 ($4.50) adults, £2 ($3) children.
Open: Mar 29–Sept 30, tours daily 11:15am and 2:30pm. **Closed:** Oct–Mar.

WHERE TO STAY & DINE

NEWMARKET MOAT HOUSE, Moulton Rd., Newmarket, Suffolk CB8 8DY. Tel. 0638/667171. Fax 0638/666533. 47 rms (all with bath or shower). TV TEL

$ Rates (including English breakfast): £66 ($99) single; £95–£150 ($142.50–$225) double. AE, DC, MC, V. **Parking:** Free.

The town's best inn, a member of Queens Moat Houses, lies near Newmarket Heath, close to the center of town. A favorite of the English horse-racing world, it houses many devotees of the "sport of kings." The bedrooms are well appointed and contemporary. The cuisine is a combination of English and French and full dinners cost £16 ($24) and up. You should arrive for dining no later than 9:30pm.

SWYNFORD PADDOCKS, Six Mile Bottom, Cambridgeshire CB8 0UE. Tel. 063870/234. Fax 063870/283. 15 rms (all with bath or shower), 4 suites. TV TEL **Directions:** Take the A1304 6 miles southwest of Newmarket.

$ Rates (including English breakfast): £72 ($108) single; £109 ($163.50) double; £130 ($195) suite. AE, DC, MC, V. **Parking:** Free.

This well-appointed country house, one of the finest in the area, lies on a 60-acre stud farm surrounded by beautiful grounds. Once a favorite retreat of Lord Byron, it has since been converted into a first-class hotel and restaurant (it is open to nonresidents, but you should call first). Many guests use it as a base for exploring not only Newmarket but Cambridge. The attractive bedrooms are handsomely equipped. The rates are expensive, but you get a lot of quality here. The restaurant serves a first-rate English and French cuisine, with dinners beginning at £22.50 ($33.80).

6. LONG MELFORD

61 miles NE of London, 34 miles E of Cambridge

GETTING THERE By Train From London's Liverpool Street Station, trains run toward Ipswich and on to Marks Tey. There you can take a shuttle train going back and forth between that junction and Sudbury. From the town of Sudbury, it's a 3-mile taxi ride to Long Melford.

By Bus From Cambridge, take a bus (maintained by Chambers Bus Company) to Bury St. Edmunds, then change buses for the final ride into Long Melford. Chambers runs these circumvoluted routes about once an hour throughout the day and early evening.

By Car From Newmarket (see above), continue east along the A45 to Bury St. Edmunds, but cut south along the A134 (toward Sudbury) to Long Melford.

ESSENTIALS The **telephone area code** is 0787. There is a **Tourist Information** office at Ipswich Town Hall, Princes Street (tel. 0473/258070) at Ipswich—24 miles away.

Long Melford has been famous since the days of the early clothmakers. Like Lavenham, it grew in prestige and importance in the Middle Ages. Of the old buildings remaining, the village church is often called "one of the glories of the shire." Along its 3-mile-long High Street—said to boast the highest concentration of antiques shops in Europe—are many private homes erected by wealthy wool merchants of yore. Of special interest are Long Melford's two stately homes.

WHAT TO SEE & DO

MELFORD HALL, on the east side of the A134, Long Melford. Tel. 880286.

Standing in Long Melford on the east side of the A134 was the ancestral home of Beatrix Potter, who often visited. Jemima Puddleduck still occupies a chair in one of the bedrooms upstairs, and other of her figures are on display. The house, built between 1554 and 1578, contains paintings, fine furniture, and Chinese porcelain. Melford Hall is a National Trust property.

Admission: £2.50 ($3.80) adults, £1.25 ($1.90) children.

Open: May–Sept, Wed–Thurs, Sat–Sun, and bank holidays 2–5:30pm; Apr and Oct, Sat–Sun 2–5:30pm.

KENTWELL HALL, on the A134 between Sudbury and Bury St. Edmunds. Tel. 310207.

At the end of an avenue of linden trees, the red-brick Tudor mansion surrounded by a broad moat has been restored by its owners, barrister Patrick Phillips and his wife. A 15th-century moat house, interconnecting gardens, a brick-paved maze, and a costume display are of interest, and there are also rare-breed farm animals to be seen. The hall hosts regular re-creations of Tudor domestic life including the well-known annual events for the weeks June 20 to July 18, and small events over holiday weekends.

Admission: £4 ($6) adults, £2.50 ($3.80) children.

Open: Easter weekend and mid-Apr to mid-June, Sun 2–6pm; mid-July to Sept, Wed–Sat 2–6pm; bank holidays 11am–6pm. **Directions:** The entrance is north of the green in Long Melford on the west side of the A134, about half a mile north of Melford Hall.

WHERE TO STAY

BLACK LION HOTEL, The Green, Long Melford, Suffolk CO10 9DN. Tel. 0787/312356. Fax 0787/374557. 8 rms (all with bath), 1 suite. TV TEL

$ **Rates** (including continental or English breakfast): £45–£55 ($67.50–$82.50) single; £65–£75 ($97.50–$112.50) double; £85 ($127.50) suite. MC, V. **Parking:** Free.

Since the 1100s, there has been some kind of an inn on this spot. Fourteenth-century documents mention it as the spot where drinks were dispensed to revolutionaries during one of the Peasants' Revolts. The present building dates from the early 1800s; it has been richly restored by its present owners. It overlooks one of the loveliest village greens in Suffolk. Each of the individually decorated bedrooms features a tea- and coffee-making facility. An added bonus is the hotel's well-patronized Countrymen restaurant, which offers excellent food and a well-chosen wine list. Fixed-price meals cost £11.25 ($16.90) at lunchtime, and £18.25 ($27.40) at dinner.

BULL HOTEL, Hall St., Long Melford, Sudbury, Suffolk CO10 9JG. Tel. 0787/378494, or toll free 800/435-4542 in the U.S. Fax 0787/880307. 25 rms (all with bath or shower), 2 suites. TV TEL

$ **Rates:** £75 ($112.50) single; £85–£95 ($127.50–$142.50) double. English breakfast £8.50 ($12.80) extra. AE, DC, MC, V. **Parking:** Free.

⭐ Here is an opportunity to experience life in one of the great old inns of East Anglia. Built by a wool merchant in 1540, this hotel is probably Long Melford's finest and best-preserved building. Improvements have been made and the interior has been modernized. Incorporated into the general hotel is a medieval weavers' gallery and the open hearth with Elizabethan brickwork. The bedrooms are a mix of old and new. The Cordell Room is the outstanding part of the Bull, with its high beamed ceilings, trestle tables, settles, and handmade chairs, as well as a 10-foot fireplace. English and continental food is served daily from noon to 2:30pm and 7 to 9:30pm. A fixed-price lunch costs £13.95 ($20.90); an à la carte dinner, £17.95 ($26.90).

WHERE TO DINE

CHIMNEYS, Hall St. Tel. 79806.

Cuisine: BRITISH. **Reservations:** Required.

$ **Prices:** Appetizers £4.50–£6.50 ($6.80–$9.80); main courses £11.50–£14.50 ($17.30–$21.80); fixed-price meals £13.95 ($20.90) at lunch, £17.50 ($26.30) at dinner. MC, V.

Open: Lunch Tues–Sun noon–2pm; dinner Tues–Sat 7–9pm.

The most highly rated restaurant in town, Chimneys offers an array of the best of English cuisine. Right in the heart of town, the restaurant has oak beams and brick walls. The house dates from the 16th century, and in the back is a "secret garden." This establishment offers modern British cookery at its best. Try, if featured, ravioli stuffed with smoked Scottish salmon, or perhaps a wild-mushroom soup given added zest with herbs and a dash of madeira. For a main course, sample such fare as a breast of guinea fowl with cabbage and bacon.

---

7. LAVENHAM

66 miles N of London, 7 miles N of Sudbury,
11 miles SE of Bury St. Edmunds, 35 miles SE of Cambridge

GETTING THERE **By Train** Board a train at London's North Street Station to Colchester. These depart at least once an hour, sometimes even more frequently. There, connect to the town of Sudbury (connections are good; only very short delays between trains). At Sudbury, there are about nine daily buses making the short run to Lavenham. These buses are maintained by Beeston's Coaches, Ltd. Total trip time from London is between 2 and 2½ hours.

By Car From Bury St. Edmunds, continue south on the A134 toward Long Melford (see above), but at the junction with the A1141 cut southeast to Lavenham.

ESSENTIALS The **telephone area code** is 0787. The summer-only **Tourist Information Centre** is at The Guildhall, Market Place (tel. 0787/248207).

Once a great wool center, Lavenham is considered a typical East Anglian village. It's filled with a number of half-timbered Tudor houses, washed in the characteristic Suffolk pink. The prosperity of the town in the days of wool manufacture is apparent in the guildhall, on the triangular main "square," built from wool-trading profits. Inside are exhibits on the textile industry of Lavenham, showing how yarn was spun, then "dyed in the wool" with woad (the plant used by the ancient Picts to dye themselves blue) and following on to the weaving process. There is also a display showing how half-timbered houses were constructed.

The Church of St. Peter and St. Paul, at the edge of Lavenham, contains interesting carvings on the misericords and the chancel screen, as well as ornate tombs. This is one of the "wool churches" of the area, built by pious merchants in the Perpendicular style with a landmark tower.

WHERE TO STAY

THE SWAN, High St., Lavenham, Sudbury, Suffolk CO10 9QA. Tel. 0787/247477, or toll free 800/435-4542 in the U.S. Fax 0787/248286. 44 rms (all with bath), 3 suites. MINIBAR TV TEL

$ Rates: £85–£110 ($127.50–$165) single; £110–£125 ($165–$187.50) double; £145 ($217.50) suite. English breakfast £8.95 ($13.40) extra. AE, DC, MC, V. **Parking:** Free.

⭐ Linked to the Middle Ages, this lavishly timbered inn is one of the oldest and best-preserved buildings in this relatively unmarred village. Its success has necessitated incorporating an adjoining ancient wool hall, which provides a high-ceilinged and timbered guesthouse and raftered, second-story bedrooms opening onto a tiny cloistered garden. The bedrooms vary in size, according to the eccentricities of the architecture. Most have beamed ceilings and a mixture of traditional pieces that blend well with the old. The more expensive rooms contain four-poster beds. There are nearly enough lounges for guests to try a different one every night of the week.

Dining/Entertainment: The Garden Bar opens onto yet another garden, with old stone walls and flowerbeds. Londoners often visit on weekends for dinner and chamber-music concerts, which are performed from September to March. Meals in the two-story-high dining room, where you sit on leather-and-oak chairs with brass studs, have their own drama. Even if you're not spending the night, you can sample the three-course lunch priced at £14.50 ($21.80). Evening table d'hôte dinners go for £19.95 ($29.90). From the à la carte menu, you can order such specialties as roast goose breast in a rich sauce with crispy bacon and mushrooms or rosettes of English lamb with avocado served with a fresh basil-wine sauce with chopped tomatoes. During World War II, Allied pilots (who made the Swan their second home) carved their signatures into the bar, a longish room with a timbered ceiling and a fine weapons collection.

WHERE TO DINE

THE GREAT HOUSE, Market Place, Lavenham, Sudbury, Suffolk CO10 9QZ. Tel. 0787/247431.
Cuisine: FRENCH. **Reservations:** Recommended.
$ Prices: Appetizers £3.25–£4.75 ($4.90–$7.10); main courses £6.95–£8.95 ($10.40–$13.40); fixed-price meals £14.95 ($22.40) at lunch, £14.95 ($22.40) at dinner (Tues–Fri). MC, V.
Open: Lunch Tues–Sun noon–2:30pm; dinner Tues–Sun 7–10:30pm. **Closed:** Jan.

 With its Georgian facade and location near the marketplace, the Great House is the finest place to dine. The interior is also attractively decorated, with Laura Ashley prints, an inglenook fireplace, and old oak beams. The owner, Régis Crépy, is also the chef de cuisine. He is assisted by his wife, Martine. He is an inventive cook, as reflected by such dishes as marinated smoked salmon with cucumber purée and sour cream, sauté of sweetbreads with a wild-mushroom sauce, and médaillons of lamb filet in lime sauce. The least expensive way to dine here is to order the fixed-price lunch.

The house also rents four elegantly decorated bedrooms (suites, actually) for £50 to £75 ($75 to $112.50) for a double. An English breakfast is included in the rates, and the rooms have private baths or showers, TVs, and phones.

8. WOODBRIDGE & ALDEBURGH

Woodbridge: 81 miles NE of London, 47 miles S of Norwich
Aldeburgh: 97 miles NE of London, 41 miles SE of Norwich

GETTING THERE By Train Aldeburgh doesn't have a rail station. Trains leave either London's Victoria Station or Liverpool Street Station (depending on the schedule) about six per day in the direction of the line's last stop, Lowestoft. Six stops after Ipswich, the train will stop in the hamlet of Saxmundham. From Saxmundham, there are about a half dozen buses traveling the 6 miles to Aldeburgh. These tend to be daytime (not nighttime) buses. Instead, many visitors hire a taxi at Saxmundham for the transit on to Aldeburgh. Woodbridge, larger and busier than Aldeburgh, has a railway station. The same line described above (to Lowestoft) stops at Woodbridge, which lies two stops after Ipswich.

By Bus   A National Express coach departs once per day from London's Victoria Coach Station for Great Yarmouth, and passes through Aldeburgh (and also through Woodbridge) along the way. Travel time to Aldeburgh is woefully long (4¼ hr.) because it visits every country town and virtually every narrow lane along the way.

Note that Aldeburgh and Woodbridge lie 15 miles from one another, and are interconnected frequently with bus no. 80/81, operated by the Eastern Counties Bus Company. Buses between the towns are frequent.

Many visitors reach both towns with the buses from Ipswich; there are about half a dozen per day, and are operated by the Eastern Counties Bus Company.

By Car   From London's ring road, the A12 runs northeast to Ipswich. From Ipswich, continue northeast on the A12 to Woodbridge or stay on the road until you reach the junction with the A1094, at which point you can head east to the North Sea and Aldeburgh at the end of the line.

ESSENTIALS   The **telephone area code** for Aldeburgh is 0728 and for Woodbridge it's 0394. The summer-only **Tourist Information Centre** is at the Cinema, High Street (tel. 0728/453637), in Aldeburgh.

The market town of Woodbridge is also a yachting center, situated on the Deben River. Its best-known, most famous resident was Edward Fitzgerald, Victorian poet and translator of the *Rubaiyat of Omar Khayyam*. The poet died in 1883 and was buried nearly four miles away at Boulge.

Woodbridge is a good base for exploring the East Suffolk coastline, particularly the small resort of Aldeburgh, noted for its moot hall.

Bordering on the North Sea, Aldeburgh is a favorite resort of educated travelers, and it attracts many Dutch, who make the sea crossing via Harwich and Felixstowe, now major entry ports for traffic from the Continent. It was the home of Benjamin Britten (1913–76), renowned composer of the operas *Peter Grimes* and *Billy Budd* as well as many orchestral works. Many of his compositions were first performed at the **Aldeburgh Festival,** which he founded in 1946. The festival takes place in June, featuring internationally known performers. There are other concerts and events throughout the year. Write or call the tourist office for details. The Snape Maltings Concert Hall nearby is generally regarded as one of the more successful of the smaller British concert halls, and it also contains the Britten-Pears School of Advanced Musical Studies, established in 1973.

The town dates from Roman times, and has long been known as a small port for North Sea fisheries. There are two golf courses, one at Aldeburgh and another at Thorpeness, 2 miles away. A yacht club is set on the River Alde 9 miles from the river's mouth. Two bird sanctuaries are also nearby, Minsmere and Havergate Island. Both are famous for their water fowl, and they are managed by the Royal Society for the Protection of Birds.

Constructed on a shelf of land at the level of the sea, the High, or main street, runs parallel to the often-turbulent waterfront. A cliff face rises some 55 feet above the main street. A major attraction is the 16th-century **Moot Hall Museum,** Market Cross Place, Aldeburgh (tel. 453295). The hall dates from the time of Henry VIII, but its tall twin chimneys are later additions. The timber-frame structure displays old maps, prints, and Anglo-Saxon burial urns. It is open July and August from 10:30am to 5pm; Easter to June and in September from 2:30 to 5pm. Admission is 35p (50¢) for adults, free for children.

Aldeburgh is also the site of the nation's northernmost martello tower, erected to protect the coast from a feared invasion by Napoléon.

WHERE TO STAY & DINE

NEAR WOODBRIDGE

SECKFORD HALL, along the A12, Woodbridge, Suffolk IP13 6NU. Tel. 0394/385678. Fax 0394/380610. 27 rms (all with bath), 7 suites. TV TEL
Directions: Take the A12 1¼ miles southwest of Woodbridge.
$ Rates (including English breakfast): £75–£85 ($112.50–$127.50) single; £90–£99 ($135–$148.50) double; £135 ($202.50) suite. AE, DC, MC, V. **Parking:** Free.

⭐ This ivy-covered brick estate captures the spirit of the days of Henry VIII and his strong-willed daughter, Elizabeth (the latter may have held court here), with its crowstepped gables, mullioned windows, and ornate chimneys—pure Tudor. It was built in 1530 by Sir Thomas Seckford, a member of one of Suffolk's first families. You enter through a heavy, studded Tudor door into a flagstone hallway with antiques. The butler will show you to your bedroom. Rooms often contain four-poster beds, and one of the four-posters is a monumental 1587 specimen. Owners Mr. and Mrs. Michael Bunn have seen to it that your stay is like a house party. Facilities include a heated indoor swimming pool.

If you arrive before sundown, you may want to stroll through a portion of the 34-acre gardens, which include a rose garden, herbaceous borders, and greenhouses. At the bottom of the garden is an ornamental lake, complete with weeping willows and paddling ducks. At 4pm, you can enjoy a complete tea in the Great Hall. Sip your brew slowly, savoring the atmosphere of heavy beams and a stone fireplace. Your chair may be Queen Anne, your table Elizabethan. Dinner will be announced by the butler. Good English meals are served in a setting of linenfold paneling and Chippendale and Hepplewhite chairs. After-dinner coffee and brandy are featured in the Tudor Bar. (Nonresidents can stop by for dinner, which is à la carte; it's best to phone first.) A fixed-price lunch costs £11.50 ($17.30), with à la carte dinners priced from £25 ($37.50). Seckford Hall is 1½ miles from the Woodbridge rail station.

IN ALDEBURGH

BRUDENELL HOTEL, The Parade, Aldeburgh, Suffolk IP15 5BU. Tel. 0728/452071, or toll free 800/435-4542 in the U.S. Fax 0728/454082. 47 rms (all with bath). TV TEL
$ Rates: £70–£85 ($105–$127.50) single; £75–£90 ($112.50–$135) double. English breakfast £8.50 ($12.80) extra. AE, DC, MC, V. **Parking:** Free.
Located on the waterfront, this hotel was built at the beginning of the 20th century. It has been remodeled and redecorated, and the interior is pleasant. Many of the bedrooms face the sea, and each has a radio, tea and coffee makers, central heating, and good beds. The dining room, with an all-glass wall overlooking the coast, is an ideal spot for a three-course luncheon costing £11 ($16.50). Dinner goes for £16 ($24).

WENTWORTH HOTEL, Wentworth Rd., Aldeburgh, Suffolk IP15 5BD. Tel. 0728/452312. 31 rms (28 with bath). TV TEL
$ Rates (including English breakfast): £45 ($67.50) single without bath, £50–£55 ($75–$82.50) single with bath; £80–£100 ($120–$150) double with bath. AE, DC, MC, V. **Parking:** Free. **Closed:** Dec 27–Jan 10.
A traditional country-house hotel with tall chimneys and gables, the Wentworth overlooks the sea. Built in the early 19th century as a private residence, it was converted into a hotel around 1900. Many rooms have lovely views. Since 1920, the Pritt family has welcomed the world to their hotel, including Sir Benjamin Britten and the novelist E. M. Forster. In summer tables are placed outside so guests can enjoy the sun, but in winter the open fires in the lounges, even the cozy bar, are a welcome sight. Many come here just to enjoy the good food and wine. Meals begin at £16.50

($24.80) for three courses. Others seeking accommodations are housed in any of 31 bedrooms, each well appointed.

---

9. NORWICH

109 miles NE of London, 20 miles W of the North Sea, 120 miles E of Nottingham

GETTING THERE **By Train** There is hourly service from London's Liverpool Street Station (trip time: 1 hr., 50 min.).

By Bus National Express buses depart London's Victoria Coach Station once each hour (trip time: 3 hr.).

By Car From London's ring road, head north to Cambridge on the M11, but turn northeast at the junction with the A11, which will carry you all the way to Norwich.

ESSENTIALS The **telephone area code** is 0603. There is a **Tourist Information Centre** at The Guildhall, Goal Hill (tel. 0603/666071).

Norwich still holds to its claim as the capital city of East Anglia. As the county town of Norfolk, Norwich is, despite its partial industrialization, a charming and historic city. It's the most important shopping center in East Anglia and has a lot to offer in the way of hotels and entertainment. In addition to its cathedral, it has more than 30 medieval parish churches built of flint.

There are many interesting hotels in the narrow streets and alleyways, and a big open-air market, busy every weekday, where fruit, flowers, vegetables, and other goods are sold from stalls with colored canvas roofs.

WHAT TO SEE & DO

NORWICH CATHEDRAL, 62 The Close. Tel. 764385.

Principally of Norman design, the cathedral dates from 1096. It is noted primarily for its long nave, with its lofty columns. Its spire, built in the late Perpendicular style, rises 315 feet; together with the keep of the castle, it forms a significant landmark on the Norwich skyline. On the vaulted ceiling are more than 300 bosses (knoblike ornamental projections) depicting biblical scenes. The impressive choir stalls with the handsome misericords date from the 15th century. Edith Cavell—"Patriotism is not enough"—an English nurse executed by the Germans in World War I, was buried on the cathedral's Life's Green. The quadrangular cloisters, which date back to the 13th century, are among the most spacious in England.

The cathedral visitors' center includes a refreshment area and an exhibition and film room with tape/slide shows about the cathedral. A short walk from the cathedral will take you to Tombland, one of the most interesting old squares in Norwich.

Admission: Cathedral, free; treasury, 50p (80¢).

Open: Oct–May, daily 7:30am–6pm; June–Sept, daily 7:30am–7pm.

NORWICH CASTLE (Norfolk Museums Service), Castle Meadow. Tel. 223624.

In the center of Norwich, on a partly artificial mound, sits the castle, formerly the county jail. Its huge 12th-century Norman keep and the later prison buildings are used as a civic museum and headquarters of the countywide Norfolk Museums Service.

The museum's art exhibits include an impressive collection of pictures by artists of the Norwich School, the most distinguished of whom were John Crome (b. 1768) and John Sell Cotman (b. 1782). The castle museum also has the best collection of British ceramic teapots in the world, and unrivaled collections of Lowestoft porcelain and Norwich silver. Rare prehistoric gold jewelry and other archeological finds help to illustrate Norfolk's wealth and importance and the life of its people. A set of dioramas shows Norfolk wildlife in its natural setting. You can also visit a geology gallery. The cafeteria is open Monday through Saturday from 10am to 4:30pm.

Admission: £1.60 ($2.40) adults, 60p (90¢) children.

Open: Museum, Mon–Sat 10am–5pm, Sun 2–5pm.

SAINSBURY CENTRE FOR VISUAL ARTS, University of East Anglia, Earlham Rd. Tel. 56060.

The center was the gift in 1973 of Sir Robert and Lady Sainsbury, who contributed their private collection to the University of East Anglia, 3 miles west of Norwich on Earlham Road. Together with their son David, they gave an endowment to provide a building to house the collection. The center, designed by Foster Associates, was opened in 1978, and since then the building has won many national and international awards. Features of the structure are its flexibility, allowing solid and glass areas to be interchanged, and the superb quality of light, which allows optimum viewing of works of art.

The Sainsbury Collection is one of the foremost in the country, including modern, ancient, classical, and ethnographic art. It is especially strong in works by Francis Bacon, Alberto Giacometti, and Henry Moore. Other displays at the center include the Anderson collection of art nouveau and the university holdings of 20th-century abstract art and design. There's also a regular program of special exhibitions. The restaurant on the premises offers a self-service buffet Monday through Friday from 10:30am to 2pm and a carvery service from 12:30 to 2pm. A conservatory coffee bar serves light lunches and refreshments Tuesday through Sunday from noon to 4:30pm.

Admission: £1 ($1.50) adults, 50p (80¢) children.

Open: Tues–Sun noon–5pm. **Bus:** 12, 14, 23, or 26 from Castle Meadow.

THE MUSTARD SHOP, 3 Bridewell Alley. Tel. 627889.

The Victorian-style Mustard Shop is a wealth of mahogany and shining brass. An old cash register records your purchase, and the standard of service and pace of life also reflect the personality and courtesy of a bygone age. In the Mustard Museum is a series of displays illustrating the history of the Colman Company and the making of mustard, its properties and origins. There are old advertisements, as well as packages and "tins." You can browse in the shop, selecting whichever of the mustards you prefer. Really hot, English-type mustards are sold, as well as the continental blends. Besides mustards, the shop sells aprons, tea towels, chopping boards, pottery mustard pots, and mugs.

Admission: Free.

Open: Mon–Sat 9am–5:30pm.

SECOND AIR DIVISION MEMORIAL LIBRARY, Bethel St. Tel. 223852.

A memorial room honoring the Second Air Division of the Eighth United States Army Air Force is part of the central library. A memorial fountain also honoring the United States airmen who were based in Norfolk and Suffolk during World War II—many of whom lost their lives in the line of duty—is in the library courtyard. The fountain incorporates the insignia of the Second Air Division and a stone from each state of the United States. Books, audiovisual materials, and records of the various bomber groups are in the library.

Admission: Free.

Open: Daily 9:30am–5pm.

WHERE TO STAY

EMBASSY LANSDOWNE HOTEL, 116 Thorpe Rd., Norwich, Norfolk NR1 1RU. Tel. 0603/620302. Fax 0603/761706. 45 rms (all with bath). TV TEL **Directions:** Take Thorpe Rd. half a mile east of the city center.

$ Rates: Mon–Thurs, £59 ($88.50) single; £69 ($103.50) double. Fri–Sun, £31.50 ($47.30) per person, single or double. English breakfast £8.50 ($12.80) extra. AE, DC, MC, V. **Parking:** Free.

 This hotel was originally constructed in the 18th century as a residence for the local lord mayor.

     Guests enjoy many modern conveniences, as well as high standards of service and atmosphere here. The refurbished bedrooms are situated in the main building, as well as two semidetached cottages. The cottages have bay windows and wooden beams as well as a private garden. The reception area's chandeliers light the way up the elegant staircase to the restaurant where a fixed-price lunch costs £8.50 ($12.80) and a fixed-price dinner, £12 ($18).

FORTE POST HOUSE HOTEL, Ipswich Rd., Norwich, Norfolk NR4 6EP. Tel. 0603/356431, or toll free 800/435-4542 in the U.S. Fax 0603/506400. 116 rms (all with bath). MINIBAR TV TEL **Directions:** Take the A140 Ipswich road 2 miles from city center and 1 mile from the A11/London road.

$ Rates: Sun–Thurs, £53.50 ($80.30) single or double; Fri–Sat, £39.50 ($59.30) single or double. English breakfast £6.95 ($10.40) extra. AE, DC, MC, V. **Parking:** Free.

The rooms in the Post House have sitting areas with sofas and armchairs. Amenities include radios and tea and coffee makers. Sturdy farm tools reflecting Norfolk's ties with agriculture decorate the wall of the coffee shop, which stays open till 10:30pm. The main restaurant specializes in traditional English fare, such as game in season, smoked fish, and potted meats. The Punch Bar is decorated with early *Punch* cartoons and drawings. Facilities include an activity center with indoor pool, gym, solarium, and sauna.

HOTEL NELSON, 121 Prince of Wales Rd., Norwich, Norfolk NR1 1DX. Tel. 0603/760260. Fax 0603/620008. 121 rms (all with bath), 3 suites. TV TEL

$ Rates (including English breakfast): £71–£76 ($106.50–$114) single; £82.50–£87.50 ($123.80–$131.30) double; from £97 ($145.50) suite. AE, DC, MC, V. **Parking:** Free.

This modern four-story hotel is located by the water, near Thorpe Station and Foundry Bridge. Each of the bedrooms has a view of either the river or a pleasant courtyard. A nautical theme prevails in most of the public rooms. One of the restaurants, the Quarterdeck, brings back memories of Norwich's most famous son, Horatio, Admiral Lord Nelson. This restaurant offers fast, cheerful service and a choice of dishes such as Cromer fish pie or beef-and-beer casserole with mushrooms and noodles. It's open daily from 10:30am for coffee and drinks, from noon to 2pm for lunch, and from 5:30 to 10:30pm for informal dinners, beginning at £12.50 ($18.80).

MAIDS HEAD HOTEL, Palace St., Tombland, Norwich, Norfolk NR3 1LB. Tel. 0603/761111. Fax 0603/613688. 80 rms (all with bath or shower), 7 suites. TV TEL

$ Rates (including English breakfast): £77 ($115.50) single; £89 ($133.50) double; £138 ($207) suite. AE, DC, MC, V. **Parking:** Free.

In business since 1272, the Maids Head claims to be the oldest continuously operated hotel in the United Kingdom. Located in the oldest part of the city, next to Norwich Cathedral, the hotel has two parts to its architecture: Elizabethan and Georgian. The Georgian section has a prim white entry and small-paned windows. The bedrooms have fresh fruit and newspapers, and traditional services, such as shoe cleaning, breakfast in bed, and afternoon cream teas, are offered. The four-poster Queen Elizabeth I Suite (where the Tudor monarch allegedly once slept) is much sought after. Lunch is served in the Courtyard Carvery, with an extensive buttery service all day. The Georgian paneled Minstrel Room offers dinner each night. Lunches begin at £10.50 ($15.80) and dinner, at £15 ($22.50).

IN NEARBY SHIPDHAM

SHIPDHAM PLACE, Church Close, Shipdham, Thetford, Norfolk 1P25 7LX. Tel. 0362/820303. 8 rms (all with bath). TV TEL **Directions:** Take the A1075 19 miles north of Thetford, a 20-mile drive southwest of Norwich.
$ Rates (including English breakfast): £30–£40 ($45–$60) single; £45–£65 ($67.50–$97.50) double. AE, MC, V. **Parking:** Free.

As you negotiate a sharp bend around the churchyard in Shipdham village, near Thetford, you come to an open gateway leading to the wide graveled front yard of this hotel. Ring the bell and you'll be welcomed into an old country house that was once the rectory. It dates back to the 17th century, with an elegant Regency block that was added in 1800. The bedrooms come in varying shapes and sizes, and some have sloping ceilings. All are decorated in pretty country prints, and fresh fruit and flowers are placed in your room on arrival. Located at the front of the house, the doubles are big, with large baths and walk-in closets.

Dining/Entertainment: There are two lounges with comfortable chairs and a drinks trolley. You help yourself and enter your drinks in a book for payment at departure. Guests can also wander in the garden behind the house and take coffee on the terrace on a warm summer evening. It is mainly for the cuisine that hosts Mr. and Mrs. Alan Poulton are known. Dishes are likely to include roast Norfolk partridge with bread sauce, potted Norfolk crab, and saddle of new-season English lamb. Lunch is served daily from noon to 1:30 pm and dinner is from 7:30 to 9:30pm. Lunch begins at £9 ($13.50); dinner, at £18.95 ($28.40).

WHERE TO DINE

ADLARD'S, 79 Upper St. Giles St. Tel. 633522.
  Cuisine: BRITISH. **Reservations:** Required.
$ Prices: Lunch £16.50 ($24.80) for 2 courses, £19 ($28.50) for 3 courses; dinner £28 ($42) for 3 courses, £32 ($48) for 4 courses. MC, V.
  Open: Lunch Tues–Fri 12:30–1:45pm; dinner Tues–Sat 7:30–9pm.

⭐ Chef and owner David Adlard is clearly the culinary star of Norwich. The stylish dining room has a clean crisp decor of green and white, with candlelit tables and a collection of paintings. David and his wife, Mary, see to it that service is correct in every way, but also relaxed enough to make diners comfortable. The chef specializes in modern British cookery, bringing his own interpretation to every dish. These are likely to include poached salmon suprême with a chive-flavored butter sauce, rosette of lamb with an artichoke mousse, or pheasant with a game mousse accompanied by madeira sauce.

BRASTED'S, 8–10 St. Andrews Hill. Tel. 625949.
  Cuisine: ENGLISH/FRENCH. **Reservations:** Required.
$ Prices: Appetizers £2.95–£7.50 ($4.40–$11.30); main courses £8.50–£17 ($12.80–$25.50). MC, V.
  Open: Lunch Mon–Fri noon–2pm; dinner Mon–Sat 7–10pm.

Within an easy stroll of both the cathedral and the castle, Brasted's is set in a lovely home in the oldest part of Norwich. After exploring the two major sights of Norwich, you can come here to sample the savory cooking of John Brasted, for whom the restaurant is named. The owner and chef de cuisine, Mr. Brasted, knows how to combine the best of yesterday with modern cooking techniques and innovations. As you enjoy the rather flamboyant interior, you can peruse the menu. You'll probably settle for one of the fresh fish dishes of East Anglia. Other dishes, including vegetables and desserts, seem equally well prepared.

GREEN'S SEAFOOD RESTAURANT, 82 Upper St. Giles St. Tel. 623733.
Cuisine: SEAFOOD. **Reservations:** Required.
$ Prices: Appetizers £2.95–£6.50 ($4.40–$9.80); main courses £9.80–£16 ($14.70–$24); fixed-price lunch £14 ($21); fixed-price dinner £26 ($39). MC, V.
Open: Lunch Tues–Fri 12:15–2:15pm; dinner Tues–Sat 7–10:45pm.

The finest fresh fish dishes in Norwich are served here by the glow of candlelight. Well-seasoned meat dishes are also available. You might begin with a flavorful fish soup, then follow with poached scallops in red wine sauce or turbot with a creamy prawn sauce. Grilled Dover sole is a perennial favorite.

MARCO'S, 17 Pottergate. Tel. 624044.
Cuisine: ITALIAN. **Reservations:** Required.
$ Prices: Appetizers £5.50–£7.50 ($8.30–$11.30); main courses £12.50–£13.50 ($18.80–$20.30); 3-course lunch £16 ($24). AE, DC, MC, V.
Open: Lunch Tues–Sat 12:30–2pm; dinner Tues–Sat 7:30–10pm. **Closed:** Sept and some holidays.

Marco's, a 2-minute walk from Market Place, serves the best Italian food in the region, accompanied by salad greens and herbs that owner Marco Vessalio grows in a nearby kitchen garden. The pasta is homemade and concocted into tempting specialties, including gnocchi and a range of tagliatelle. One of Signor Vessalio's chicken, veal, or beef dishes might follow a steaming bowl of minestrone or pasta.

EXCURSIONS FROM NORWICH

BLICKLING HALL, Blickling, near Aylsham. Tel. 0263/733084.
A long drive, bordered by massive yew hedges that frame your first view of this old house, leads you to Blickling Hall. A great Jacobean house built in the early 17th-century, it is perhaps one of the finest examples of such architecture in the country. The long gallery has an elaborate 17th-century ceiling, and the Peter the Great Room, decorated later, has a fine tapestry on the wall. The house is set in ornamental parkland with a formal garden and an orangery. Meals and snacks are available.
Admission: House and gardens, £4.90 ($7.40) adults, £2.40 ($3.60) children; gardens only, £2.50 ($3.80) adults, £1.25 ($1.90) children.
Open: Apr–Oct, Tues–Wed and Fri–Sun 1–5pm (gardens, shop, and restaurant noon–5pm). **Directions:** Blickling Hall lies 14 miles north of the city of Norwich, 1½ miles west of Aylsham on the B1354; take the A140 toward Cromer and follow the signs.

SANDRINGHAM, Sandringham, 8 miles northeast of King's Lynn (off the A149). Tel. 0553/772675.
Some 110 miles northeast of London, Sandringham has been the country home of four generations of British monarchs, ever since the Prince of Wales (later King Edward VII) purchased it in 1861. The son of Queen Victoria, along with his Danish wife, Princess Alexandra, rebuilt the house, standing on 7,000 acres of grounds, and in time it became a popular meeting place for British society. The red-brick, Victorian-Tudor mansion consists of more than 200 rooms, and in recent years some of the rooms have been opened to the public, including two drawing rooms and a dining room. Sandringham is now among the few British royal residences

that can be visited by the public. Guests can also view a lofty saloon with a minstrels' gallery.

A group of former coach houses has been converted into a museum of big-game trophies, plus a collection of cars, including the first vehicle purchased by a member of the royal family, a 1900 Daimler Tonneau that belonged to Edward VII. The house and grounds are open, except when the queen or members of the royal family are there. The 70-acre gardens are richly planted with azaleas, rhododendrons, hydrangeas, and camellias.

Admission: House and grounds, £3 ($4.50) adults, £1.50 ($2.30) children; grounds only, £2 ($3) adults, £1 ($1.50) children.

Open: Easter–Oct 3, Mon–Sat 11am–4:45pm, Sun noon–4:45pm. **Closed:** July 19–Aug 7. **Transportation/Directions:** Sandringham lies 50 miles east of Norwich and 8 miles northeast of King's Lynn (off the A149). King's Lynn is the end of the main train route from London's Liverpool Street Station that goes via Cambridge and Ely. Trains to King's Lynn arrive from London once every 2 hours (trip time: 2½ hr.). From Cambridge, the train ride takes only 1 hour. Buses from both Cambridge and Norwich run to King's Lynn, from which you can catch bus no. 411 to take you the rest of the way to Sandringham.

The great industrial shadow of the 19th century cast such a darkness over England's northwest that the area has been relatively neglected by foreign visitors. At best, most Americans rush through it heading for the glories of the Lake District and Scotland.

However, the northwest, in spite of its industry and bleak commercial areas, has much beauty for the tourist who is willing to seek it out. Manchester, Lancaster, Morecambe, and Southport—to name only a few—are all interesting cities, and much of the countryside is beautiful and is filled with inns, restaurants, and pubs, along with many sightseeing attractions.

I will concentrate, however, on only two of its more popular cities—Chester and Liverpool, followed by the most interesting towns and villages of the Lake District, such as Windermere.

Cheshire, the county in which Chester lies, is world renowned for its cheese. This low-lying northwestern county is largely agricultural, and, bordering Wales, it has had a turbulent history. The towns and villages of Cheshire offer a good base for touring North Wales, the most beautiful part of that little country. Chester, the capital of Cheshire, has a wealth of accommodations, and Nantwich, an easy excursion from Chester, is an old salt town.

Liverpool, home of the Beatles, has done much in recent years to revitalize its tourist industry, especially since the restoration of its waterfront, which today houses many museums and exhibitions. An extension of London's Tate Gallery also opened there in 1988, with a collection of modern art. Many people visit just to follow in the footsteps of the Beatles.

One of England's most popular summer retreats in Queen Victoria's day was the Lake District. In its time the district has lured such writers as Samuel Taylor Coleridge, Charlotte Brontë, Charles Lamb, Percy Bysshe Shelley, John Keats, Alfred Lord Tennyson, and Matthew Arnold.

The Lake District, called a "miniature Switzerland," is actually quite small, measuring about 35 miles wide. Most of the district is in Cumbria, although it begins in the northern part of Lancashire.

Driving in the wilds of this northwestern shire is fine for a start. But the best activity is walking, which is an art best practiced here with a crooked stick. Don't go out without a warning, however: There is a great deal of rain and heavy mist, and sunny days are few. When the mist starts to fall, try to be near an inn or pub, where you can drop by and warm yourself beside an open fireplace. You'll be carried back to the good old days, since many places in Cumbria have valiantly resisted change.

The far-northwestern part of the shire, bordering Scotland, used to be called Cumberland. Now part of Cumbria, it is generally divided geographically into a trio

WHAT'S SPECIAL ABOUT THE NORTHWEST

Great Towns/Villages
- Chester, a Roman and medieval walled city, famed for its Rows (galleried arcades reached by steps from the street).
- Liverpool, the home of the Beatles, a major 18th-century port for the trade of sugar and slaves.
- Windermere, major center for England's most beautiful lake and best resort for a Lake District base.

Natural Spectacles
- Scafell Pike, rising to a height of 3,210 feet, the tallest peak in England.
- Lake Windermere, the grandest of lakes, a recreational center in summer, attracting boaters.

Literary Shrines
- Rydal Mount, outside Ambleside, home of William Wordsworth from 1813 until his death in 1850.
- Brantwood, home of John Ruskin, the poet, artist, and towering figure of the Victorian age.

Cathedrals
- Cathedral Church of Christ, Liverpool, the last Gothic cathedral erected worldwide and the fifth-largest cathedral in the world.

Museums
- Tate Gallery, Liverpool, the great collection of 20th-century art in the north of England.

---

of segments: the Pennines, dominating the eastern sector (loftiest point at Cross Fell, nearly 3,000 feet high); the Valley of Eden; and the lakes and secluded valleys of the west, by far the most interesting. The area, so beautifully described by the romantic Lake Poets, enjoys many literary associations.

The largest town is Carlisle in the north—a possible base for explorations to Hadrian's Wall. Built in the 2nd century A.D. by the Romans, the 75-mile wall stretches from Wallsend in the east to Bowness on the Solway. Brockhole National Park Centre, between Ambleside and Windermere, is well worth a visit.

SEEING THE NORTHWEST

GETTING THERE

From London, the M1 and the M6 motorways head north and Chester and Liverpool are easily reached. The M6 continues north, with cutoffs to various villages and towns in the Lake District. British Rail serves the region from London's Euston Station. Change at the Oxenholme Lake District Station for branch lines into Windermere. It takes about 4½ hours to reach the Lake District from London. National Express coaches also service the region from London's Victoria Coach Station, arriving in Windermere in about 7½ hours.

A SUGGESTED ITINERARY

Day 1: Explore the walled city of Chester and spend the night.

Day 2: Take in the attractions of Liverpool, including the Tate Gallery and the restored waterfront, and spend the night.

Days 3–4: Spend the time in the Lake District, exploring literary shrines, while based in Windermere. Or use one of the neighboring villages as a center, perhaps Ambleside, Hawkshead, or Grasmere.

1. CHESTER

207 miles NW of London, 19 miles S of Liverpool,
91 miles NW of Birmingham

GETTING THERE By Train   About 21 trains per day from London's Euston Station depart every hour for Chester (trip time: 3 hr.). Trains also run every 30 minutes between Liverpool and Chester (trip time: 45 min.).

By Bus   One National Express bus every hour runs between Birmingham and Chester (trip time: 2 hr.). The same bus line also offers service between Liverpool and Chester. It's also possible to catch a National Express coach from London's Victoria Coach Station to Chester.

By Car   From London, head north on the M1, crossing onto the M6 at the junction. Continue northwest and turn onto the M54. Near the end of the M54 motorway, continue the final lap of the journey northwest on the A41.

ESSENTIALS   The **telephone area code** is 0244. The **Tourist Information Centre** is at the Town Hall, Northgate Street (tel. 0244/313126), and offers a hotel-reservation service as well as information. Arrangements can also be made for coach tours or walking tours of Chester (including a ghost hunter tour).

Chester is ancient, having been founded by a Roman legion on the Dee River in the 1st century A.D. It reached its pinnacle as a bustling port in the 13th and 14th centuries, but declined following the gradual silting up of the river. The upstart Liverpudlians captured the sea-trafficking business. While other walls of medieval cities of England were either torn down or badly fragmented, Chester still retains 2 miles of fortified city walls intact.

The main entrance into Chester is Eastgate, which dates from only the 18th century. Within the walls are half-timbered houses and shops; of course not all of them came from the days of the Tudors. Chester is unusual in that some of its builders used black-and-white timbered facades even during the Georgian and Victorian periods.

The Rows are double-decker layers of shops, one tier on the street level, the others stacked on top and connected by a footway. The upper tier is like a continuous galleried balcony—rain is never a problem. Shopping upstairs is much more adventurous than down on the street. Thriving establishments operate in this traffic-free paradise: tobacco shops, restaurants, department stores, china shops, jewelers, and antiques dealers. For the best look, take a walk on arcaded Watergate Street.

At the junction of Watergate, Northgate, and Bridge Streets, at noon and 3pm Tuesday through Saturday, April to September, at the City Cross, the town crier issues his news (local stuff on sales, exhibitions, and attractions in the city), to the accompaniment of a hand bell. Eastgate Street is now a pedestrian way, and musicians often play for your pleasure beside St. Peter's Church and the Town Cross.

WHAT TO SEE & DO

In a big Victorian building opposite the Roman amphitheater, the largest uncovered amphitheater in Britain, the **Chester Visitor Centre**, Vicars Lane (tel. 0244/

351609), offers a number of services to visitors. A visit to a life-size Victorian street complete with sounds and smells helps your appreciation of and orientation to Chester. The center has a gift shop, a licensed restaurant serving meals and snacks all day, and a currency exchange. Admission is free, and the center is open daily from 9am to 9pm, to 7pm in winter.

In the center of town, you'll see the much-photographed Eastgate clock. Climb the stairs near it to the top of the **city wall.** You can walk along it looking down on Chester. Passing through centuries of English history, you'll go by a cricket field, see the River Dee, formerly a major trade artery, and get a look at many old buildings of the 18th century. The wall also goes past some Roman ruins, and it's possible to leave the walkway to explore them. The walk is charming and free.

CHESTER CATHEDRAL, St. Werburgh St. Tel. 324756.

The present building, founded in 1092 as a Benedictine abbey, was created a cathedral church in 1541. Considerable architectural restorations were carried out in the 19th century, but older parts have been preserved. Notable features include the fine range of monastic buildings, particularly the cloisters and refectory, the chapter house, and the superb medieval wood carving in the quire (especially the misericords). Also worth seeing are the long south transept with its various chapels, the consistory court, and the medieval roof bosses in the lady chapel. A freestanding bell tower, the first to be built in England since the Reformation, was completed in 1975 and may be seen southeast of the main building. Facilities include a refectory, a bookshop, and an audiovisual presentation.

Admission: Free.
Open: Daily 7am–6:30pm.

CHESTER ZOO, off the A41, Upton-by-Chester, north of the center. Tel. 380280.

On the outskirts of Chester, 2 miles from the center of the city, the Chester Zoo is world famous for its wide collection of mammals, birds, reptiles, and fish. Many rare and endangered species breed freely in spacious enclosures, and the zoo is particularly renowned for the most successful group of chimpanzees and orangutans in Europe. The 110 acres of gardens are worth seeing in any season, with 160,000 plants in the spring and summer bedding displays alone. The waterbus, a popular summer feature, allows you to observe the hundreds of water birds that make their home here. The zoo has several facilities if you get hungry or thirsty during your visit: the licensed Oakfield Restaurant, the Jubilee self-service cafeteria, the Oasis snack bar, and the Rainbow kiosk for either meals or snacks and drinks.

Admission: £6 ($9) adults, £3.50 ($5.30) children 3–15.
Open: Daily 10am–dusk. **Closed:** Dec 25. **Directions:** From the center, head north along Liverpool Rd.

WHERE TO STAY

BLOSSOMS HOTEL, St. John's St., Chester, Cheshire CH1 1HL. Tel. 0244/323186, or toll free 800/435-4542 in the U.S. Fax 0244/346433. 64 rms (all with bath), 3 suites. TV TEL

$ Rates: £80 ($120) single; £90 ($135) double; from £110 ($165) suite. Breakfast £8.95 ($13.40) extra. AE, DC, MC, V. **Parking:** Free.

The Blossoms Hotel has been in business since the mid-17th century, although the present structure was rebuilt late in Victoria's day. Each of the traditionally furnished bedrooms is equipped with central heating, and all have private baths, radios, and coffee makers. The old open staircase in the reception room sets the tone of the hotel.

Dining/Entertainment: Dinner is served in the Brooks Restaurant from 7 to

9:30pm daily, offering both a table d'hôte dinner at £16.95 ($25.40) and an à la carte menu. These are available for lunch as well as dinner. The Snooty Fox, a traditional English pub with a hunting decor, is open for lunch Monday through Saturday from 11am to 2:30pm and on Sunday from noon to 2pm.

CHESTER GROSVENOR HOTEL, Eastgate St., Chester, Cheshire CH1 1DE. Tel. 0244/324024. Fax 0244/313246. 86 rms (all with bath), 8 suites. A/C MINIBAR TV TEL
$ Rates: £98–£115 ($147–$172.50) single; £150–£170 ($225–$255) double; from £235 ($352.50) suite. Breakfast £9.95 ($14.90) extra. AE, DC, MC, V. **Parking:** Free.

★ In a fine, half-timbered building in the heart of Chester is this hotel, one of the most luxurious in the north of England. Its reputation is well deserved. It is owned and named after the family of the dukes of Westminster, and its origin can be traced back to the reign of Queen Elizabeth I. Started as a Tudor inn, it became a political headquarters in Hanoverian days and later became a glittering mecca for the Regency and Victorian set, continuing to be a social center in the Edwardian era. Prince Albert visited here, and more recent guests have included Princess Diana and Prince Rainier.

The high-ceilinged, marble-floored foyer of the hotel, with its 200-year-old chandelier, carved wooden staircase, and antiques, sets the tone. The large, well-furnished bedrooms have radios and hairdryers.

Dining/Entertainment: This grand hotel has the finest drinking and dining facilities in the county. Its formal restaurant, Arkle, and its more informal La Brasserie will be reviewed later (see "Where to Dine," below).

Services: 24-hour room service, laundry.

Facilities: Sauna, gym, solarium, business center.

CRABWALL MANOR, Parkgate Rd., Mollington, Chester, Chesire CH1 6NE. Tel. 0244/851666, or toll free 800/525-4800 in the U.S. Fax 0244/851400. 42 rms (all with bath), 6 suites. TV TEL **Directions:** Take the A540 2¼ miles northwest of Chester. **Bus:** 22 or 23.
$ Rates: £87 ($130.50) single; £125 ($187.50) double; from £155 ($232.50) suite. Breakfast £8 ($12) extra. AE, DC, MC, V. **Parking:** Free.

★ Chester's only country-house hotel, Crabwall Manor traces its origins back to the 16th century. Most of the present building, however, dates from the early 1800s. Standing amid 11 acres of private grounds and gardens, the capably managed hotel rents well-furnished bedrooms, each with private bath or shower. Most of the rooms are quite large and show a certain flair in their decoration, and the bathrooms are first class, with bidets and separate showers for the most part.

The finest of contemporary English and French dishes are offered in a split-level restaurant. Nonresidents can also visit to enjoy the harmonious flavors, the subtle sauces, and the well-chosen meat, fowl, and fish that are served daily from 12:30 to 2pm and 7 to 9:30pm. Fixed-price lunches cost £14.75 ($22.10), and a table d'hôte dinner is offered for £27.50 ($41.30). You can also dine à la carte.

MOLLINGTON BANASTRE, Parkgate Rd., Chester, Chesire CH1 6NN. Tel. 0244/851471, or toll free 800/528-1234 in the U.S. Fax 0244/851165. 62 rms (all with bath), 2 suites. TV TEL **Directions:** Take the A540 2 miles northwest of the center of Chester.
$ Rates (including English breakfast): £80 ($120) single; £95 ($142.50) double; £110 ($165) suite. AE, DC, MC, V. **Parking:** Free.
This Victorian mansion has been successfully converted into one of the leading country-house hotels in Cheshire. It's affiliated with the Best Western reservation system. A gabled house, it offers a health and leisure complex, along with a trio of

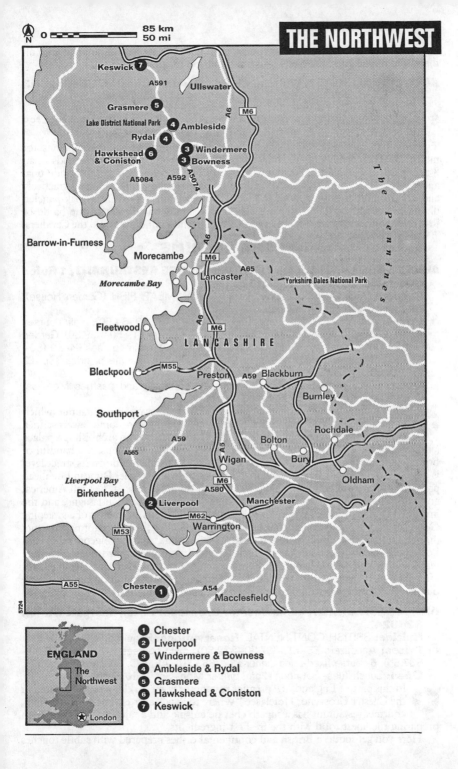

THE NORTHWEST

0 ——— 85 km / 50 mi

Keswick **7**

A591

Ullswater

Grasmere **5**

A6 M6

Lake District National Park **4** Ambleside

Rydal **4**

Hawkshead **6** **3** Windermere
& Coniston **3** Bowness

A5084 A592 A5074

The Pennines

Barrow-in-Furness

Morecambe

A6 M6

Lancaster

Morecambe Bay

A65

Yorkshire Dales National Park

Fleetwood

A6 M6

L A N C A S H I R E

M55

Blackpool

Preston A59 Blackburn

Burnley

Southport

A59

A565

Bolton Rochdale

A5

Wigan Bury

M6

Liverpool Bay

A580 Oldham

Birkenhead

2 Liverpool Manchester

M62

M53 Warrington

A55

Chester **1** A54

Macclesfield

ENGLAND

The
Northwest

★ London

1 Chester
2 Liverpool
3 Windermere & Bowness
4 Ambleside & Rydal
5 Grasmere
6 Hawkshead & Coniston
7 Keswick

restaurants and well-furnished bedrooms, each with private bath. Equipped with all the modern amenities, the hotel also has a pub on its grounds.

ROWTON HALL HOTEL, Whitchurch Rd., Rowton, Chester, Chesire CH3 6AD. Tel. 0244/335262. Fax 0244/335464. 42 rms (all with bath), 1 suite. TV TEL **Directions:** Take the A41 2 miles from the center to Whitchurch.
$ Rates (including English breakfast): £76–£86 ($114–$129) single; £90–£98 ($135–$147) double; £128 ($192) suite. AE, DC, MC, V. **Parking:** Free.

Two miles from Chester, this stately home offers overnight accommodations for motorists. The gracious house, built in 1779 with a wing added later, stands in an 8-acre garden, with a formal driveway entrance. The Hall has comfortable traditional and contemporary furnishings. All bedrooms have private baths and are attractively and comfortably furnished. The good English meals are served in an oak-paneled dining room with a Tudor fireplace. The hotel stands on the site of the battle of Rowton Moor, which was fought in 1643 between the Roundheads and the Cavaliers.

WHERE TO DINE

ABBEY GREEN RESTAURANT/GARDEN HOUSE RESTAURANT, 1 Rufus Court, Northgate St. Tel. 313251.
Cuisine: VEGETARIAN (Abbey Green)/GAME, MEAT, FISH (Garden House). **Reservations:** Recommended.
$ Prices: Abbey Green, lunch appetizers £1.60–£3 ($2.40–$4.50); main courses £3.75–£5.25 ($5.60–$7.90); 4-course fixed-price dinner £19.50 ($29.30). Garden House, lunch appetizers £3.25–£4.75 ($4.90–$7.10), main courses £4–£9 ($6–$13.50); 4-course fixed-price dinner £19.50 ($29.30). Teatime pastries 75p–£2 ($1.10–$3). DC, MC, V.
Open: Lunch Mon–Sat noon–2:30pm, afternoon tea and pastries Mon–Sat 2:30–6:30pm; dinner Mon–Sat 6:30–10pm.

★ This is the newest headquarters and site of an expansion of a restaurant which has repeatedly won many of Chester's civic and gastronomic awards. In a complex of Georgian buildings originally constructed as an archbishop's palace (and later occupied by the city's hangman), it lies within a few steps of a handful of boutiques and other restaurants. It's divided into two distinct sections: Its street level is devoted to the Abbey Green Vegetarian restaurant, where owner Duncan Lochhead prepares dishes inspired by his family's travels in the Middle East, Central America, and Australia. Examples include marinated mushrooms, vegetarian lasagne, and the imagined cuisine of some mythical South Sea island. Upstairs, at the top of a sweeping Georgian staircase, amid oil portraits and silver chandeliers, is a more formal gourmet (nonvegetarian) restaurant, where dishes might include smoked pigeon salad in a horseradish-cream sauce, terrine of duck flavored with juniperberries and red-wine jelly, and rack of Welsh lamb in a honey-rosemary sauce. Both areas are open for afternoon tea. These are sometimes consumed in the large outdoor garden, where pieces of sculpture are strategically placed amid the shrubberies.

ARKLE RESTAURANT, in the Chester Grosvenor Hotel, Eastgate St. Tel. 324024.
Cuisine: BRITISH/CONTINENTAL. **Reservations:** Required.
$ Prices: Appetizers £5–£15 ($7.50–$22.50); main courses £15–£25 ($22.50–$37.50); 6-course fixed-price dinner £37 ($55.50). AE, DC, MC, V.
Open: Lunch Tues–Sat noon–2pm; dinner Mon–Sat 7–10:30pm.

★ In this part of England, the premier restaurant is the Arkle, which is located in the Chester Grosvenor Hotel (see "Where to Stay," above). The 45-seat formal, gourmet restaurant has a superb chef de cuisine and a talented 40-strong team preparing the finest food with the freshest ingredients.

Here you get modern British and continental dishes prepared with subtle touches and a certain lightness, as reflected by the sauces and the cooking of meats and vegetables. You're likely to be served such entrées as roast filet of halibut with crab sausages or cutlet of Norfolk duckling with morels and shallot fondue. Desserts are equally luscious and tempting. The Arkle has an award-winning cheese selection and unique breads (a choice of at least six daily) and cheese biscuits are homemade.

LA BRASSERIE, in the Chester Grosvenor Hotel, Eastgate St. Tel. 324024.
Cuisine: ENGLISH/FRENCH. **Reservations:** Not required.
$ Prices: Appetizers £3–£5.50 ($4.50–$8.30); main courses £6–£12 ($9–$18). AE, DC, MC, V.
Open: Daily 6:30am–11:30pm.

In the same building as the prestigious Chester Grosvenor Hotel is this restaurant, perhaps the best all-around dining choice in Chester, not only for convenience but also for price and quality. In a delightful art nouveau setting, the Brasserie offers an extensive à la carte menu to suit most tastes and pocketbooks. Main dishes are likely to include poached filet of salmon with a dill sauce, roast guinea fowl with green cabbage, veal steak with marsala sauce, and other hearty brasserie food.

AN EASY EXCURSION TO NANTWICH

Fifteen miles east of Chester, this old market town on the Weaver River is particularly outstanding because of its black-and-white timbered houses. The most spectacular one, Churche's Mansion, is a dining recommendation.

WHERE TO STAY

ROOKERY HALL, Main Rd., Worleston, near Nantwich, Cheshire CW5 6DQ. Tel. 0270/610016. Fax 0270/626027. 45 rms (all with bath), 5 suites. TV TEL **Directions:** Take the A51 2½ miles north of Nantwich.
$ Rates (including English breakfast): £95 ($142.50) single; £115 ($172.50) double; £215 ($322.50) suite. AE, DC, MC, V. **Parking:** Free.

With its striking Italianate facade and massive proportions, this structure would appear at home in the Loire Valley in France. More château than manor house, it was built in the 1700s but radically altered in 1867 into the High Victorian design that stands today. Guests are welcomed to the handsomely furnished bedrooms, each with comfortable amenities.

While you enjoy panoramic views of the surrounding countryside, you can sample well-prepared food, a combination of English dishes and modern French cuisine. The lavishly paneled dining room is a suitable setting for meals based on traditional English cookery with a modern twist. Dinners begin at £25 ($37.50). The restaurant at the hotel has received many awards for its food and service. All dishes are freshly prepared and cooked to order. Meat and fish dishes are cooked lightly to preserve their natural flavors, and the freshest vegetables are prepared to retain their natural crispness. You might begin with breast of pigeon with autumn leaves, scallops, deep-fried vegetables, and a cranberry dressing, then follow with such dishes as best end of lamb with braised lentils and wild mushrooms or saddle of venison with port wine and a red currant sauce.

WHERE TO DINE

CHURCHE'S MANSION RESTAURANT, 150 Hospital St. Tel. 625933.

Cuisine: ENGLISH. **Reservations:** Recommended. **Directions:** Take the A534 half a mile east of the center, at the junction with the A52.

$ Prices: 2-course fixed-price lunch £9.50 ($14.30); 3-course fixed-price lunch £12.50 ($18.80); 4-course fixed-price dinner £20 ($30). DC, MC, V.

Open: Morning coffee daily 10–11:45am; lunch Tues–Sat noon–2pm; dinner Tues–Sat 7–10:30pm.

The most enchanting restaurant in Cheshire, Churche's Mansion lies in Nantwich at the junction of Newcastle Road and the Chester bypass. Many years ago, the late Dr. and Mrs. E. C. Myott learned that this historic home had been advertised for sale in America and asked the town council to step in and save it. Outbidding the American syndicate that wanted to transport it to the United States, they sought out the mysteries of the house: a window in the side wall, inlaid initials, a Tudor well in the garden, and a long-ago love knot with a central heart (a token of Richard Churche's affection for his young wife). At lunch you are likely to be served a selection of spring salad greens with tiger prawns and smoked duckling, ravioli of ricotta and spinach with walnuts and pesto, or partially smoked and pan-fried salmon with a warm salad of new potatoes. At dinner the chef is likely to prepare such typical dishes as a saddle of rabbit with a lemon and coriander sauce; roast breast of duck stuffed with apples, prunes, and raisins; or honey-grilled chicken with pecans and a lemon-chive sauce.

2. LIVERPOOL

219 miles NW of London, 103 miles NW of Birmingham,
35 miles W of Manchester

GETTING THERE **By Plane** Liverpool has its own airport, Spoke (tel. 051/486-8877), which has frequent daily flights from many parts of the United Kingdom, including London, the Isle of Man, and Ireland.

By Train Express trains from London's Euston Station arrive frequently at Liverpool (trip time: 2¼ hr.). There is also frequent service from Manchester (trip time: 1 hr.).

By Bus National Express buses from London's Victoria Coach Station depart every 2 hours (trip time: 4¼ hr.). Buses also arrive every hour from Manchester (trip time: 1 hr.).

By Car From London, head northwest on the M1, until it links with the M6. Continue northwest on the M6 until you reach the junction with the M62 heading west to Liverpool.

ESSENTIALS The **telephone area code** is 051. The **Tourist Information Centre** is at the Atlantic Pavilion, Albert Dock (tel. 051/708-8854).

Liverpool, with its famous waterfront on the River Mersey, is a great shipping port and industrial center that gave the world such famous figures as the fictional Fannie Hill and the Beatles. King John launched it on its road to glory when he granted it a charter in 1207. Before that, it had been a tiny 12th-century fishing village, but it quickly became a port for shipping men and materials to Ireland. In the 18th century its port grew to prominence as a result of the sugar, spice, and tobacco trade with the Americans. By the time Victoria came to the throne, Liverpool had become Britain's biggest commercial seaport. Recent refurbishing of the Albert Dock, establishment of a Maritime Museum, and the converting of warehouses into little stores similar to those in Ghirardelli Square in San Francisco have made this an up-and-coming area once again, with many attractions for visitors.

Liverpudlians are proud of their city, with its new hotels, two cathedrals, shopping and entertainment complexes, and parks and open spaces (2,400 acres in and around the city). Liverpool's main shopping street, Church, is traffic-free.

WHAT TO SEE & DO

Liverpool has a wealth of things for the visitor to see and enjoy—major cathedrals, waterfront glories restored, cultural centers, even the places where the Beatles began their meteoric rise to fame and fortune.

THE CATHEDRALS

CATHEDRAL CHURCH OF CHRIST, Saint James Mount. Tel. 709-6271.

The great new Anglican edifice was begun in 1903 and was largely completed 74 years later. On a rocky eminence overlooking the River Mersey, this might possibly be the last Gothic-style cathedral to be built worldwide. Dedicated in the presence of Queen Elizabeth II in 1978, it is the largest church in the country and is the fifth largest in the world: Its vaulting under the tower is 175 feet high, the highest in the world, and its length—619 feet—makes it one of the longest cathedrals in the world. The organ contains nearly 10,000 pipes, the most found in any church. The tower houses the highest (219 feet) and the heaviest (31 tons) bells in the world, and the Gothic arches are the highest ever built. From the tower, you can see into North Wales.

The architect, Giles Scott, after winning a competition in 1903 for the building's design, went on to rebuild the House of Commons, gutted by bombs, after World War II. He personally laid the last stone on the highest tower pinnacle.

In 1984 a Visitor Centre and Refectory was opened, and its dominant feature is an aerial sculpture of 12 huge sails, with a ship's bell, clock, and light that changes color on an hourly basis. Full meals may be taken in the charming refectory.

Admission: Cathedral, free; tower, £1.50 ($2.30) adults, 50p (80¢) children.
Open: Daily 9am–6pm.

ROMAN CATHOLIC METROPOLITAN CATHEDRAL OF CHRIST THE KING, Mount Pleasant. Tel. 709-9222.

Half a mile away from the Anglican cathedral stands the Roman Catholic cathedral—the two are joined by a road called Hope Street. The sectarian strife of earlier generations has ended, and a change in attitude, called by some the "Mersey Miracle," was illustrated clearly in 1982 when Pope John Paul II drove along Hope Street to pray in both cathedrals.

The construction of the cathedral, designed by Sir Edwin Lutyens, was started in 1930, but when World War II halted progress in 1939, not even the granite and brick vaulting of the crypt was complete. At the end of the war it was estimated that the cost of completing the structure as Lutyens had designed it would be some £27 million. Architects throughout the world were invited to compete to design a more realistic project to cost about £1 million and to be completed in 5 years. Sir Frederick Gibberd won the competition and was commissioned to oversee the construction of the circular cathedral in concrete and glass, pitched like a tent at one end of the piazza that covered all the original site, crypt included.

Between 1962 and 1967 construction was completed, and today the cathedral provides seating for a congregation of more than 2,000, all within 50 feet of the central altar. Above the altar rises a multicolored glass lantern weighing 2,000 tons and rising to a height of 290 feet. Called a "space age" cathedral, this has a bookshop, a tearoom, and tour guides.

Admission: Free.

Open: Mon–Sat 8am–6pm, Sun 8am–5pm.

SIGHTS ON THE WATERFRONT

A fun thing to do is to take the famous Mersey Ferry that travels from the Pier Head to both Woodside and Seacombe. Service operates daily from early morning to early evening throughout the year. For more information, contact the **Mersey Ferries,** Victoria Place, Seacombe, Wallasey (tel. 639-0609).

ALBERT DOCK, Albert Dock Co. Ltd. Tel. 708-7334.

Built of brick, stone, and cast iron, this showpiece development on Liverpool's waterfront opened in 1846, saw a long period of decline, and has been renovated and refurbished so that it's now England's largest Grade 1 Listed Building, a designation for landmark buildings. The dockland warehouses now contain quality shops, restaurants, cafés, an English pub, and a cellar wine bar. One pavilion houses the main building of the Merseyside Maritime Museum (see below) and another is the home of the Tate Gallery Liverpool, the National Collection of modern art in the north of England (see below). Parking is available.

Admission: Free.

Open: Shops, daily 10am–6pm. Bars and restaurants, daily 10am–11pm. **Bus:** "Albert Dock Shuttle" from the city center.

MERSEYSIDE MARITIME MUSEUM, Albert Dock. Tel. 207-0001.

✪ Set in the historic heart of Liverpool's magnificent waterfront, this large museum provides a unique blend of floating exhibits, craft demonstrations, working displays, and special events. In addition to restored waterfront buildings, exhibitions show the story of mass emigration through Liverpool in the last century, shipbuilding on Merseyside, and many other aspects of Liverpool's maritime heritage. One exhibition traces the story of the Beatles. You can see a restored piermaster's house and a working cooperage, and you can take a steamboat trip around the historic Albert Dock complex. A smörgåsbord restaurant, a coffee shop, a waterfront café, gift shops (open 7 days a week), and ample parking space are among the facilities. There is wheelchair access to all floors of the main museum building and most areas of the Maritime Park, and disabled visitors are made most welcome.

Admission: £1.50 ($2.30) adults, 75p ($1.10) children.

Open: Daily 10:30am–5:30pm (last admission at 4:30pm). **Bus:** "Albert Dock Shuttle" from the city center.

TATE GALLERY, Albert Dock. Tel. 709-0507.

✪ Opened in 1988, this gallery houses the National Collection of 20th-century Art in the North, a collection of London's Tate Gallery. "The Tate Gallery of the North" was opened to display part of the Tate's fastest growing collection, its ever increasing numbers of modern paintings. Some of the world's greatest artists, such as Picasso, Dalí, Magritte, and Chagall, are likely to be on display at any time, along with changing temporary exhibitions and events.

Admission: Free.

Open: Tues–Sun 10am–6pm. **Bus:** "Albert Dock Shuttle" from the city center.

WALKER ART GALLERY, William Brown St. Tel. 207-0001.

This gallery has one of the finest collections of paintings outside London and is known for its European pictures and sculptures from 1300 to the present.

Admission: Free.

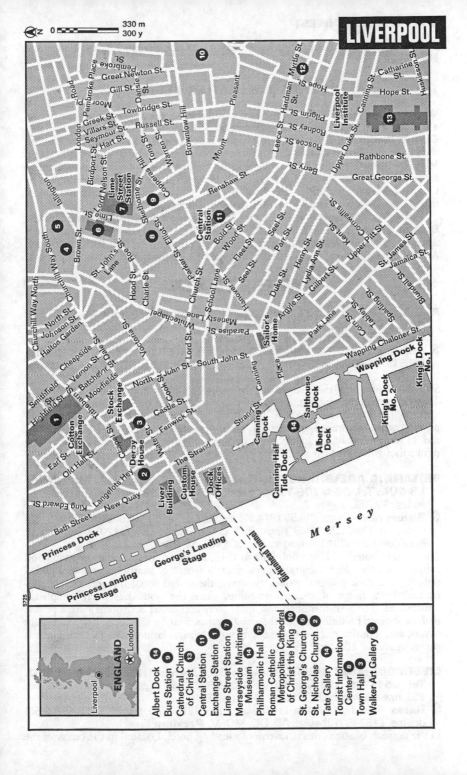

LIVERPOOL

330 m
300 y

Mersey

Princess Dock
George's Landing Stage
Princess Landing Stage

ENGLAND
London
Liverpool

Albert Dock 14
Bus Station 9
Cathedral Church of Christ 13
Central Station 11
Exchange Station 1
Lime Street Station 7
Merseyside Maritime Museum
Philharmonic Hall 12
Roman Catholic Metropolitan Cathedral of Christ the King 10
St. George's Church 6
St. Nicholas Church 2
Tate Gallery 14
Tourist Information Center 8
Town Hall 3
Walker Art Gallery 5

Open: Mon–Sat 10am–5pm, Sun noon–5pm. **Closed:** Jan 1, Good Friday, and Dec 24–26.

WHERE THE BEATLES BEGAN

Whether or not they're Beatles fans, most visitors who come to Liverpool want to take a look at where Beatlemania began. Mathew Street is the heart of Beatleland, and **Cavern Walks** (tel. 236-9082) is a shopping development and tour service built on the site of the former Cavern Club, where the Beatles performed almost 300 times. John Doubleday's statue of the group is in the central piazza of the Cavern complex, surrounded by shops and restaurants. The outside of Cavern Walks was decorated by Cynthia Lennon, John's first wife. Another statue of John, Paul, George, and Ringo, this one by Liverpool sculptor Arthur Dooley, is opposite the building facade.

Farther along Mathew Street is the **John Lennon Memorial Club** and the **Beatles Shop,** 31 Mathew St. (tel. 236-8066), open Monday through Saturday from 9:30am to 5:30pm, plus Sunday from April through December from 10:30am to 4pm. Around the corner on Stanley Street is a statue of Eleanor Rigby, seated on a bench.

WHERE TO STAY

ATLANTIC TOWER, 30 Chapel St., Liverpool, Merseyside L3 9RE. Tel. 051/227-4444, or toll free 800/847-4358 in the U.S. Fax 051/236-3973. 216 rms (all with bath), 10 suites. A/C TV TEL

$ Rates: £75–£85 ($112.50–$127.50) single; £85–£100 ($127.50–$150) double; £165 ($247.50) suite. Breakfast £8.25 ($12.40) extra. AE, DC, MC, V. **Parking:** £2 ($3).

Showcased in a high-rise that evokes the bows of a great luxury liner, the Atlantic Tower is considered one of the two or three top hotels in the city. You check into a spacious lobby and are shown to one of the well-furnished bedrooms, each with private bath or shower. The bedrooms often open onto views of the River Mersey, and 34 rooms contain a minibar. You can dine in the Stateroom Restaurant, enjoying drinks in a bar that resembles a Pullman coach.

BRITANNIA ADELPHI HOTEL, Ranalagh Place, Liverpool, Merseyside L3 5UL. Tel. 051/709-7200. Fax 051/708-8326. 391 rms (all with bath), 17 suites. TV TEL

$ Rates: Mon–Thurs, £49.50 ($74.30) single; £87 ($130.50) double, £110 ($165) suite. Fri–Sun, £28 ($42) single; £48 ($72) double; £80 ($120) suite. English breakfast £6.95 ($10.40) extra. AE, DC, MC, V. **Parking:** £2 ($3).

This "grand hotel" of Liverpool, built in 1914, is known for its fine rooms and good cuisine. Past the elegant entrance, you enter a world of marble corridors, molded ceilings, and dark polished wood. However, these traditional features are complemented by a range of modern amenities since the hotel has been completely refurbished. The well-furnished and attractively appointed bedrooms have a private bath or shower. Facilities include three restaurants, four bars, a disco, hair and beauty salons, and a health club with swimming pool, gym, solarium, and Jacuzzi. There is garage space for 100 cars.

LIVERPOOL MOAT HOUSE, Paradise St., Liverpool, Merseyside L1 8JD. Tel. 051/709-0181, or toll free 0800/289330 in England. Fax 051/709-2706. 251 rms (all with bath), 7 suites. A/C TV TEL

$ Rates (including English breakfast): £105 ($157.50) single; £135 ($202.50) double; £182 ($273) suite. AE, DC, MC, V. **Parking:** Free.

In the opinion of some, this is Liverpool's leading hotel. Located in the center of the city, it's one of the most comfortable, efficient hotels in Merseyside. The bedrooms are spread across seven floors, and each has a private bath or shower. Most often favored by businesspeople, the hotel also lures sightseers drawn to the attractions of "new Liverpool." The hotel's facilities include a solarium, gym, indoor swimming pool, and garden. Its coffee shop stays open until 10:30pm for late arrivals. It also offers the Garden Restaurant serving British and French dishes, with meals costing £15 ($22.50) and up.

TRIALS, 56–62 Castle St., Liverpool, Merseyside L2 7LQ. Tel. 051/ 227-1021. Fax 051/236-0110. 20 suites. MINIBAR TV TEL
$ Rates: £90–£100 ($135–$150) single; £120–£130 ($180–$195) double. AE, MC, V. **Parking:** £4.50 ($6.80).

A leading hotel of Liverpool, although it's small and only offers suites, is the Trials. Rather luxurious, this hotel of charm and character was created in 1986 from a centrally located Victorian structure that had once been a bank. Now beautifully converted, this hotel is often the choice of discriminating visitors to Liverpool. The plush accommodations are split-level, and have Jacuzzis, private baths or showers, trouser presses, and hairdryers. With a unique character, Trials Restaurant offers a grand cuisine served in first-class surroundings. Meals cost £12.95 ($19.40) and up. The hotel has 24-hour room service.

WHERE TO DINE

ARMADILLO, 20–22 Mathew St. Tel. 236-4123.
   Cuisine: BRITISH/FRENCH. **Reservations:** Required.
$ Prices: Lunch appetizers £2.50–£3 ($3.80–$4.50), lunch main courses £7–£7.50 ($10.50–$11.30); dinner appetizers £3–£3.75 ($4.50–$5.60), dinner main courses £10–£13.50 ($15–$20.30). MC, V.
   Open: Lunch Tues–Sat noon–3pm; dinner Tues–Sat 7:30–10:30pm.
One of the leading restaurants in Liverpool not associated with a hotel, this restaurant is housed within the solid stone walls of a converted Victorian warehouse, across the street from the site of the famous Cavern, where the Beatles got their start. The cuisine includes such dishes as pork filet with a honey-mango sauce, rack of lamb stuffed with sweetbreads and spinach and served with a black-olive vinaigrette sauce, and paupiettes of plaice with a tarragon-flavored hollandaise sauce. With a conservative modern decor and big windows, this restaurant seems to be near the top of everybody's list of favorites in Liverpool.

FAR EAST, 27–35 Berry St. Tel. 709-3141.
   Cuisine: CANTONESE. **Reservations:** Required.
$ Prices: Appetizers £1.65–£5.80 ($2.50–$8.70); main courses £4.70–£9.20 ($7.10–$13.80); fixed-price meals £5.80 ($8.70) at lunch, £12.50 ($18.80) at dinner. AE, DC, MC, V.
   Open: Daily noon–11:15pm.

Far East is considered the finest Chinese restaurant in town. Liverpool is famous for its Chinese restaurants, which is not surprising since the city has one of the largest Chinese populations in Europe and its own "Chinatown." Here you might enjoy a dim sum lunch, later returning in the evening for more haute Chinese fare. You face a bewildering array of Cantonese specialties, including chile-flavored large prawns. The chefs also do marvelous things with duck. However, you're likely to get carried away with the à la carte specialties and spend at least £15 ($22.50).

JENNY'S SEAFOOD RESTAURANT, Old Ropery, Fenwich St. Tel. 236- 0332.

Cuisine: SEAFOOD. **Reservations:** Required.
$ **Prices:** Appetizers £1.60–£7.95 ($2.40–$11.90); main courses £8.95–£23 ($13.40–$34.50); fixed-price lunch or dinner £15 ($22.50). MC, V.
Open: Lunch Mon–Fri noon–2:15pm; dinner Tues–Sat 7–10pm. **Closed:** Aug 15–31.

★ Consistently good food is served at this restaurant near the harbor; its basement room is both pleasantly decorated and softly illuminated. All this forms a backdrop for the good-tasting fresh seafood that's brought in daily, including halibut, scallops, scampi, and monkfish. Everything I've sampled has been of fine quality and well prepared. The service, on my latest rounds, was excellent.

3. WINDERMERE & BOWNESS

274 miles NW of London, 10 miles NW of Kendal

GETTING THERE   By Train   Trains to Windermere meet with the main line at Oxenholme for connections both north to Scotland and south to London. Information about rail services in the area can be obtained by calling the Oxenholme Railway Station (tel. 0539/720397). Frequent connections are possible throughout the day.

By Bus   The National Express bus link, originating at London's Victoria Coach Station, serves Windermere, with good connections also to Preston, Manchester, and Birmingham. Local buses to various villages and towns in the Lake District (see below) are operated mainly by Cumberland Motor Services (CMS) and go to Kendal, Ambleside, Grasmere, and Keswick. Information on various routings within the Lake District can be obtained by calling the Windermere Bus Station (tel. 09662/6499).

By Car   Head north from London, as if going toward Liverpool (see above), but stay on the M6 until you reach the A685 junction heading west to Kendal. From Kendal, the A591 continues west to Windermere.

By Ferry   There are boat cruises from Bowness, 1½ miles from Windermere, in summer. These are operated by the Bowness Bay Boating Company (tel. 05394/3360 for information). There's also a ferry service from Bowness across the lake to the western shore.

ESSENTIALS   The **telephone area code** for Windermere and Bowness is 05394. The **Tourist Information Centre** at Windermere is at 23 Victoria St. (tel. 05394/46499), and the **Tourist Information Centre** at Bowness is a summer-only office at The Glebe (tel. 05394/42895).

The largest lake in England is Windermere, whose shores wash up against the town of Bowness, with Windermere in close reach. Both these resorts lie on the eastern shore of the lake. A ferry service connects Hawkshead and Bowness. Windermere, the resort, is the end of the railway line.

From either town, you can climb Orrest Head in less than an hour for a panoramic view of England's lakeland. From that vantage point, you can even see **Scafell Pike,** rising to a height of 3,210 feet—the peak pinnacle in all of England.

The twin resorts of Windermere and Bowness are separated by 1½ miles. The rail station is at Windermere. To go to Bowness and its pier (from which you can catch a ferry across the lake), turn left from the rail terminal and traverse the center of Windermere until you reach New Road. This eventually changes its name to Lake

Road before it approaches the outskirts of Bowness. It's about a 20-minute walk downhill. The CMS Lakeland Experience bus also runs from the Windermere Station to Bowness every 20 minutes.

WHAT TO SEE & DO

There is regular steamer service around Windermere, the largest of the lakes, about 10½ miles long. It's also possible to take a steamer on Coniston Water, a small lake that Wordsworth called "a broken spoke sticking in the rim." Coniston Water is a smaller and less heavily traveled lake than Windermere. Ullswater, a lake measuring 7½ miles long, used to be called "Ulfr's Water." It is second in size to Lake Windermere and can also be traversed by lake steamer.

The **Windermere Steamboat Museum,** Rayrings Road, Windermere (tel. 45565), houses probably the finest collection of steamboats in the world. Important examples of these elegant Victorian and Edwardian steamboats have been preserved in working order.

The steamboats are exhibited in a unique wet dock where they are moored in their natural lakeside setting. The fine display of touring and racing motorboats in the dry dock links the heyday of steam with some of the most famous names of powerboat racing and record-breaking attempts on Windermere, including Sir Henry Segrave's world water speed record set in 1930.

All the boats have intriguing stories, including the veteran SL *Dolly,* built around 1850 and probably the oldest mechanically powered boat in the world. The vessel was raised from the lakebed in the early 1960s and ran for 10 years with its original boiler and steambox.

In the dry dock is the speedboat *Jane* dating from 1938, the first glider-plane to take off from the water (in 1943), and the hydroplane racer *Cookie.* There is also Beatrix Potter's rowing boat and the sailing dinghy *Amazon* from Arthur Ransome's classic story *Swallows and Amazons.*

Also displayed is the *Espérance,* an iron steam yacht registered with Lloyd's in 1869, and the SS *Raven* built in 1871 to carry everything from coal and timber to farm produce and beer to the scattered communities around the lake when the only alternative would be to transport these goods by horse and cart over very poor roads.

The museum is open daily from Easter to October, charging an admission of £2.80 ($4.20) for adults and £1.40 ($2.10) for children. The SL *Osprey* is regularly in steam and visitors can make a 50-minute trip on the lake, where tea and coffee will be made from the Windermere Steam Kettle and served by the crew.

ORGANIZED TOURS Windermere is the center of many interesting tours in the Lake District area. To provide a true appreciation of the Lake District and its many attractions, try **Mountain Goat Holidays,** Victoria Street, Windermere (tel. 45161). Begun in 1972 by Chris Taylor—who had a strong desire to start his own business after spending some years in Australia—it has become firmly established in the Lake District for touring or walking holidays. Mountain Goat also runs daily minibus tours that take you to many of the otherwise-inaccessible spots of the area.

These tours include trips to the Northern Lakes, Grasmere, Keswick, Buttermere, and Honister Pass, with a visit to Wordsworth's home in Grasmere, Rydal Mount. The cost of tours is from £18 ($27) per person.

WHERE TO STAY

CEDAR MANOR, Ambleside Rd., Windermere, Cumbria LA23 1AX. Tel. 05394/43192. 12 rms (all with bath). TV TEL **Directions:** Take the A591 Kendal-Ambleside road.

$ Rates (including half board): £40–£45 ($60–$67.50) single; £80–£90 ($120–$135) double. MC, V. **Parking:** Free.

One of the most desirable country-house hotels in the area is Cedar Manor. In Victoria's day it was an impressive home with gables and chimneys. But since those times it has been converted into a small hotel of exceptional merit. Each of the well-furnished bedrooms is equipped with a private bath or shower. A cedar tree, perhaps from India, has grown in the garden for some two centuries, and from that tree the hotel takes its name. Meals are good and wholesome. Typical dishes include roast leg of lamb, fresh Scottish salmon steak, and honey-roasted half duckling.

HOLBECK GHYLL, Holbeck Lane, Windermere, Cumbria LA23 1LU. Tel. 05394/32375. Fax 05394/34743. 14 rms (all with bath). TV TEL **Directions:** Take the A591 3¼ miles northwest of the town center.

$ Rates (including English breakfast and 5-course dinner): £50–£80 ($75–$120) per person. Children under 17 half price when sharing their parents' room. MC, V. **Parking:** Free. **Closed:** Jan.

Perhaps the most enchanting place to stay in the area, this country-house hotel was once a 19th-century hunting lodge owned by Lord Lonsdale, one of the richest men in Britain. It still has a wealth of oak paneling and stained glass. Overlooking Lake Windermere, this hotel not only offers the highest standards in decor, food, and service, but is excellent value for money. An inglenook fireplace welcomes visitors, as do the resident owners, David and Patricia Nicholson. Each bedroom is beautifully maintained and has a special decor in the English chintz and Laura Ashley tradition.

The hotel also operates one of the finest restaurants in the Lake District, where a five-course menu costs £27.50 ($41.30) for nonresidents. The menu changes every day and is never repeated. It's likely to include, as an appetizer, home oak-smoked Barbary duck breast with a plum-and-port sauce, followed by guinea fowl pot-roasted in the French style or loin of lamb studded with garlic and baked with lemon and thyme. Call for a reservation if you're not a resident of the hotel.

LANGDALE CHASE HOTEL, on the A591, Windermere, Cumbria LA23 1LW. Tel. 05394/32201. Fax 05394/32604. 31 rms (all with bath). TV TEL **Directions:** Take the A591 from Windermere toward Ambleside; it's 2 miles north of Windermere. **Bus:** 55.

$ Rates (including English breakfast): £47–£60 ($70.50–$90) single; £94–£130 ($141–$195) double. AE, DC, MC, V. **Parking:** Free.

A great, old, lakeside house built for grandeur, this hotel is comparable to a villa on Lake Como, Italy. The story goes back to 1930 when the dynamic Ms. Dalzell and her mother took over the country estate, with its handsomely landscaped gardens, and decided to accept paying guests while retaining an uncommercial house-party atmosphere. Waterskiing, rowing, lake bathing, tennis, croquet on the grounds, and fishing attract the sports-minded. The bedrooms have excellent furniture and private baths. The interior of the Victorian stone château, with its many gables, balconies, large mullioned windows, and terraces, is a treasure house of antiques. The main lounge hall looks like a setting for one of those English drawing-room comedies. The house was built in part with bits and pieces salvaged from the destruction of a nearby abbey and castle—hence, the ecclesiastical paneling. On the walls are distinctive paintings, mostly Italian primitives, although one is alleged to be a Van Dyck.

Dining/Entertainment: The dining room ranks among the finest in the Lake District—with guests selecting tables that are good vantage points for lake viewing. The cuisine is highly personal, mostly a liberated English fare, supported by a fine wine list. Open to nonresidents, the dining room charges from £12 ($18) for a fixed-price lunch, from £22 ($33) for a fixed-price dinner.

MILLER HOWE HOTEL, Rayrigg Rd., Windermere, Cumbria LA23 1EY. Tel. 05394/42536. Fax 05394/45664. 13 rms (all with bath). TV TEL **Directions:** From the center, take the A5074 (New Rd.)

$ Rates (including English breakfast and dinner): £95 ($142.50) single; £150–£250 ($225–$375) double. AE, DC, MC, V. **Parking:** Free. **Closed:** Mid-Dec to mid-Mar.

⭐ An international clientele comes to this inn bearing the unique imprint of its creator, former actor John Tovey. At the beginning of the 1970s he selected a country estate overlooking Lake Windermere, with views of the Langdale Peaks, and converted it to provide stylish accommodations and an exquisite cuisine. The house was built in 1916 in the Edwardian style, sitting on 4½ acres of statue-dotted garden and parkland. His large, graciously furnished rooms have names—no numbers—and he treats guests as if they were invited to a house party. Each room is supplied with binoculars to help guests fully enjoy the view; there are even copies of *Punch* from the 1890s. Each room also has a private bath or shower. Antiques are scattered lavishly throughout the house.

Dining/Entertainment: Dinner at Miller Howe is worth the drive up from London. While Tovey is famed as a pastry chef, he is equally known for his original appetizers and main dishes. Even if you can't stay overnight, at least consider a meal here, for which you must reserve. The fixed-price dinner of five courses will cost £32 ($48) per person, including coffee. Regional dishes using local produce are a special feature. You might try Hardwick lamb with rosemary sauce, game pies (in season), Lancashire cheese, and Cumbria sausage. Several interpretations of salmon are presented, including an award-winning version that is marinated in soy sauce, ginger, and orange, then coated with fresh herbs, pistachios, and capers, sautéed, and served over a bed of baked cucumbers. Men must wear coats and ties in the dining room. Dinners are served Sunday through Friday at 8:30pm only, at 7:30 and 9:30pm on Saturday.

WHERE TO DINE

ROGER'S, 4 High St., Windermere. Tel. 44954.
Cuisine: ENGLISH/INTERNATIONAL. **Reservations:** Required.
$ Prices: Appetizers £3.25–£6.95 ($4.90–$10.40); main courses £6.95–£12.95 ($10.40–$19.40); fixed-price dinner £12.50 ($18.80). AE, DC, MC, V.
Open: Dinner only, Mon–Sat 7–9:30pm.

⭐ The stellar French dining room of Cumbria, Roger's carries the name of its skilled chef de cuisine, Roger Pergl-Wilson. For almost a decade he has been going strong at this location (a part of England where restaurants seem to have a high mortality rate). That means he's doing something right. You can judge for yourself.

A table d'hôte dinner is a superb value, but you're most likely to be tempted to order à la carte. Homegrown ingredients go into the cookery whenever possible. Regardless, everything tastes fresh here, as care goes not only into the preparation but also into the presentation, which is polite and efficient without being overly formal. Deer from the field, salmon from the rivers, char from Lake Windermere, and quail from the air—everything seems deftly handled here.

AN EASY EXCURSION TO BOWNESS

A short way south of Windermere on Bowness Bay of the lake, the attractive town of Bowness has some interesting old architecture. This has been an important center for boating and fishing for a long time, and you can rent boats of all descriptions to explore the lake.

WHERE TO STAY

LINDETH FELL HOTEL, Lyth Valley Rd., along the A5074, Bowness-on-Windermere, Cumbria LA23 3JP. Tel. 05394/43286. 14 rms (all with bath or shower). TV TEL **Directions:** Take the A5074 1 mile south of Bowness.
$ Rates (including half board): £50 ($75) single; £92–£109 ($138–$163.50) double. MC, V. **Parking:** Free. **Closed:** Nov 16–Mar 14.

($) High above the town and the lake is a traditional large Lakeland house built of stone and brick in 1907, with many of its rooms overlooking the handsome gardens and the lake. The owners, the Kennedys, run the place more like a country house than a hotel, achieving an atmosphere of comfort in pleasingly furnished surroundings. The cooking is supervised by Diana Kennedy and a resident chef, with local produce used whenever possible to prepare a variety of Lakeland and traditional English dishes. In pursuit of the country-house atmosphere, the Kennedys offer tennis, croquet, and putting on the lawn, as well as a private tarn for fishing. All bedrooms have beverage-making facilities. It's open from March 15 to mid-November.

LINDETH HOWE, Longtail Hill, Storrs Park, Bowness-on-Windermere, Cumbria LA23 3JF. Tel. 05394/45759. Fax 05394/46368. 14 rms (all with bath or shower). TV **Directions:** Head south of the village on the B5284.
$ Rates (including English or continental breakfast): £46.50–£61.50 ($69.80–$92.30) single occupancy of a double room; £55–£75 ($82.50–$112.50) double. MC, V. **Parking:** Free. **Closed:** Dec 22–Jan 6.

($) This is a country house in a scenic position above Lake Windermere, standing on 6 acres of grounds. The house, part stone and part red brick with a roof of green Westmorland slate, was built for a wealthy mill owner in 1879, but its most famous owner was Beatrix Potter, who installed her mother here while she lived across the lake at Sawrey. The present owners, Eileen and Clive Baxter, have furnished it in fine style. Most of the bedrooms have lake views. They are comfortably furnished, with in-house movies, beverage-making facilities, and central heating. Two rooms have handsome four-poster beds. There are no singles. The dining room has two deep bay windows overlooking the lake. The lounge contains a brick fireplace with a solid oak mantel set in an oak-framed inglenook. The hotel has a sauna and solarium.

---

4. AMBLESIDE & RYDAL

278 miles NW of London, 14 miles NW of Kendal, 4 miles N of Windermere

GETTING THERE   By Train   Go to Windermere (see above); then continue the rest of the way by bus.

By Bus   Cumberland Motor Services (CMS) has hourly bus service from Grasmere and Keswick (see below) and from Windermere. All these buses into Ambleside are labeled either no. 555 or no. 557.

By Car   From Windermere (see above), continue northwest along the A591.

ESSENTIALS The **telephone area code** is 05394. The summer-only **Tourist Information Centre** is at Old Courthouse, Church Street (tel. 05394/32582).

An idyllic retreat, Ambleside is one of the major centers of the Lake District, attracting pony trekkers, fell hikers, and rock scalers. The charms are here all year, even in late autumn, when it's fashionable to sport a mackintosh. Ambleside is perched at the top of Lake Windermere. Just a small village and not filled with attractions, Ambleside is used primarily as a refueling stop or overnight stopover for those exploring the Lake District.

Between Ambleside and Wordsworth's former retreat at Grasmere is Rydal, a small village on one of the smallest lakes, Rydal Water. The village of Rydal is noted for its sheep-dog trials at the end of summer. The location is 1½ miles north of Ambleside on the A591.

WHAT TO SEE & DO

Rydal Mount, off the A591, 1½ miles north of Ambleside (tel. 33002), was the home of William Wordsworth from 1813 until his death in 1850. Part of the house was built as a farmer's lake cottage around 1575. A descendant of Wordsworth's still owns the property, now a museum displaying numerous portraits, furniture, and family possessions as well as mementos and books of the poet. The 3½-acre garden was landscaped by Wordsworth and contains rare trees, shrubs, and other features of interest. The house is open daily: 9:30am to 5pm from March to October, 10am to 4pm from November to February (closed Tuesday in winter). Admission is £2 ($3) for adults, 80p ($1.20) for children 5 to 16.

WHERE TO STAY & DINE

IN AMBLESIDE

KIRKSTONE FOOT, Kirkstone Pass Rd., Ambleside, Cumbria LA22 9EH. Tel. 05394/32232. Fax 05394/31110. 32 rms (all with bath). TV TEL **Directions:** Take Rydal Rd. north from the center, cutting right onto Kirkstone Pass Rd.
$ Rates (including English breakfast and dinner): £47.50–£52 ($71.30–$78) single; £95–£104 ($142.50–$156) double. MC, V. **Parking:** Free. **Closed:** Jan.

The facilities of this 17th-century manor house have been increased with the construction of several slate-roofed and self-catering apartments in the surrounding parklike grounds. The original building is encircled by a well-tended lawn, while the interior is cozily furnished with overstuffed chairs and English paneling. The comfortable accommodations, 16 in the main house and 16 in the outlying units, are tastefully decorated in a cozy family style, and have radios and private baths or showers.

The restaurant offers home-cooked English meals under the direction of the co-owner, Jane Bateman, who personally runs this fine establishment along with her husband, Simon. Fresh produce is used whenever possible. A five-course dinner costs £19.50 ($29.30) for nonresidents.

NANNY BROW HOTEL, Clappersgate, Ambleside, Cumbria LA22 9NF. Tel. 05394/32036. Fax 05394/32450. 15 rms (all with bath), 3 suites. TV TEL **Directions:** Take the A593 about a mile west of Ambleside.

$ Rates (including half board): Sun–Thurs, £55–£80 ($82.50–$120) per person; Fri–Sat, £115–£155 ($172.50–$232.50) per person. AE, MC, V. **Parking:** Free. **Closed:** 3 weeks in Jan.

Set on a hill, this former private home, built in 1904, has been turned into one of the most successful hotels in the Ambleside area. The Tudor-style gabled house is reached via a steep tree-flanked drive. Once you arrive, you find a country-house setting with a lovely sitting room with intricate cove moldings and, if the weather merits it, a log fire. The rooms are in both the main house and a garden wing, the latter offering first-rate accommodations (some of the suites have half-tester beds). The rooms feature private baths or showers, as well as coffee makers and lots of comfortable charm. The food is well prepared, using fresh ingredients. Meals begin at £22.50 ($33.80) for nonresidents. Other facilities include a solarium and a whirlpool bath.

RIVERSIDE HOTEL, near Rothay Bridge, Under Loughrigg, Ambleside, Cumbria LA22 9LJ. Tel. 05394/32395. Fax 05394/32395. 10 rms (all with bath). TV TEL **Directions:** See below.
$ Rates (including half board): £62 ($93) single; £94 ($141) double. MC, V. **Parking:** Free. **Closed:** Nov–Feb.

Ⓢ Secluded on a quiet lane, this small country hotel is set on the riverside. Away from traffic noise, it's still only a few minutes' walk from the center of Ambleside. The hotel is owned and run by Jim and Jean Hainey, who accommodate guests and provide good meals, costing £18 ($27) for nonresidents. All the well-furnished bedrooms have radios, hairdryers, and central heating. Each room is a double.

To get here, approaching Ambleside from Windermere on the A591, take the left fork at Waterhead toward Coniston. Follow the Coniston Road for about a mile until you come to the junction at Rothay Bridge. Turn left across the bridge and then immediately sharp right along the small lane signposted Under Loughrigg.

RIVERSIDE LODGE COUNTRY HOUSE, near Rothay Bridge, Ambleside, Cumbria LA22 0EH. Tel. 05394/34208. 6 rms (all with bath). TV TEL **Directions:** Take the A593 from Ambleside, which crosses Rothay Bridge.
$ Rates (including English breakfast): £48–£52 ($72–$78) double. MC, V. **Parking:** Free.

This early Georgian house is set on a riverbank, a short walk from the town center, near the foot of Loughrigg Fell on 3 acres of grounds. The property is run by Alan and Gillian Rhone and it's featured in the book *Famous Lakeland Homes* by Kathleen Eyres. Bonnie Prince Charlie rested here in 1745. The lodge has some beamed ceilings and offers well-furnished bedrooms, some with river views. Each room is a double. Have a drink in the intimate lounge with its open fire before going into the breakfast room overlooking the river.

ROTHAY MANOR, Rothay Bridge, Ambleside, Cumbria LA22 0EH. Tel. 05394/33605. Fax 05394/33607. 15 rms (all with bath), 3 suites. TV TEL **Directions:** Take the A593 half a mile south of Ambleside.
$ Rates (including English breakfast): £69–£75 ($103.50–$112.50) single; £108–£120 ($162–$180) double; £152 ($228) suite. AE, DC, MC, V. **Parking:** Free.

✪ At this spot reminiscent of a French country inn, the star is the cuisine, along with a dedicated chef in the kitchen, well-selected French wines, and comfortable, centrally heated bedrooms and suites. Each of the individually decorated units has a bath and shower, and most have shuttered French doors opening onto a sun balcony, with a mountain view. Throughout the estate you'll find an eclectic combination of antiques (some Georgian blended harmoniously with Victorian), flowers, and enticing armchairs.

Dining/Entertainment: The manor is also a restaurant open to nonresidents.

The spacious dining room is decked with antique tables and chairs. The flawless appointments include fine crystal, silver, and china. Buffet lunches are served from 12:30 to 2pm every day except Sunday when a traditional Sunday lunch is featured, always with a whole sirloin of roast beef with Yorkshire pudding, among other dishes, perhaps wild mallard duck breast sautéed in herb-flavored butter. Dinners, from 8 till 9pm, are more ambitious, costing £27 ($40.50) for five courses.

WATEREDGE HOTEL, Borrans Rd., Waterhead, Ambleside, Cumbria LA22 0EP. Tel. 05394/32332. Fax 05394/32332. 23 rms (all with bath). TV TEL **Directions:** Take the A591 1 mile south of Ambleside.
$ Rates (including half board): £68 ($102) single; £122–£156 ($183–$234) double. AE, MC, V. **Parking:** Free. **Closed:** Mid-Dec to early Feb.

The center of this hotel was formed long ago from two 17th-century fishing cottages. Wateredge was, in fact, listed as a lodging house as early as 1873, and further additions were made in the early 1900s. Set in beautiful gardens overlooking Lake Windermere, the hotel also serves some of the best food in the area. Public rooms contain many little nooks for reading and conversation, and there is also a cozy bar. However, on sunny days guests prefer to laze in one of the chairs on the lawn. The rooms vary in size and appointments; some are spacious, others much smaller. Each has a private bath or shower.

Dining/Entertainment: A six-course fixed-price dinner costs about £23.90 ($35.90) for nonresidents, and is offered nightly from 7 to 8:30pm. If hotel guests don't take all the tables, nonresidents can join the dining party. Fresh produce is used, and the quality of cooking is high. In winter a log fire will greet you.

IN RYDAL

GLEN ROTHAY HOTEL, along the A591, Rydal, Ambleside, Cumbria LA22 9LR. Tel. 05394/32524. 9 rms (all with bath or shower), 2 suites. TV TEL **Directions:** Take the A591 1½ miles northwest of Ambleside.
$ Rates (including English breakfast): £32–£35 ($48–$52.50) single; £62–£70 ($93–$105) double; £199 ($298.50) suite. AE, DC, MC, V. **Parking:** Free.

Built in the 17th century as a wayfarer's inn, this hotel adjoins Dora's Field, immortalized by Wordsworth. Set back from the highway, it has a stucco-and-flagstone facade added by Victorians. Inside, the place has been modernized, but original details remain, including beamed ceilings and paneling. There is a popular street-level pub, plus a more formal cocktail lounge, with a fireplace and comfortable armchairs, as well as a dining room serving solid English food. A table d'hôte meal costs £10 ($15) for residents and £17.50 ($26.30) for nonresidents. The comfortable bedrooms upstairs have private baths or showers, central heating, and coffee makers, and a few offer four-poster beds.

5. GRASMERE

282 miles NW of London, 18 miles NW of Kendal, 43 miles S of Carlisle

GETTING THERE   By Train   Go to Windermere (see above) and continue the rest of the way by bus.

By Bus   Cumberland Motor Services (CMS) runs hourly bus service to Grasmere from Keswick (see below) and Windermere (see above). Buses running in either direction are marked no. 555 or no. 557.

By Car   From Windermere (see above), continue along the A591 northwest.

ESSENTIALS The **telephone area code** is 05394. The summer-only **Tourist Information Centre** is on Red Bank Road (tel. 05394/35245).

On a lake that bears its name, Grasmere was the home of Wordsworth from 1799 to 1808. He called this area "the loveliest spot that man hath ever known." The nature poet lived with his sister, Dorothy (the writer and diarist), at **Dove Cottage,** which is now a museum administered by the Wordsworth Trust. Wordsworth, who followed Southey as poet laureate, died in the spring of 1850, and was buried in the graveyard of the village church at Grasmere. Another tenant of Dove Cottage was Thomas De Quincey *(Confessions of an English Opium Eater).* For a combined ticket costing £3.70 ($5.60) for adults, £1.85 ($2.80) for children, you can visit both **Dove Cottage** and the adjoining **Wordsworth Museum.** They're both on the A591 directly south of the village of Grasmere on the road to Kendal. The Wordsworth Museum houses manuscripts, paintings, and memorabilia. There are also various special exhibitions throughout the year, exploring the art and literature of English Romanticism. The property is open daily from 9:30am to 5:30pm; closed from mid-January to mid-February. For further information, call 05394/35544, 05394/35544 for Dove Cottage Restaurant information.

WHERE TO STAY & DINE

MICHAEL'S NOOK, ¼ mile east of the A591, Grasmere, Cumbria LA22 9RP. Tel. 05394/35496, or toll free 800/544-9941 in the U.S. Fax 05394/35765. 14 rms (all with bath), 3 suites. TV TEL **Directions:** Turn off the A591 at the Swan Hotel, half a mile northeast of Grasmere.

$ Rates (including English breakfast and dinner): £118 ($177) single; £185–£265 ($277.50–$397.50) double; from £320 ($480) suite. AE, DC, MC, V. **Parking:** Free.

This country-house hotel, once a private residence, stands amid its own secluded 3-acre garden. A lakeland home of stone (honoring a hill shepherd, Michael, subject of a Wordsworth poem), it is adorned with much fine mahogany woodwork and paneling, especially its elegant staircase. Throughout the house, owned by Grasmere antiques dealer Reg Gifford and his wife, Elizabeth, are many fine antiques, enhanced by the glow of log fires or vases of flowers. All the handsomely decorated bedrooms have baths and showers. Amenities include hairdryers and sandalwood sachets in drawers; one room has a four-poster bed. During some peak weekends, a minimum 3-night stay is requested, but shorter bookings are accommodated where possible.

Dining/Entertainment: Only about 20 people can be served in the intimate dining room, which accepts reservations from nonresidents for both lunch and dinner. Additional seating is available in the Oak Room. Meals are carefully prepared, with menus changing daily. You might choose poached prawns or sautéed calves' liver in shallot-and-vinegar sauce. Lunch is priced at £27.50 ($41.30) and is served at 12:30pm daily; dinner, at 7:30pm daily, costs £38 ($57) for nonresidents. In summer, dinner sittings on Saturday are at 7 and 9pm.

RED LION HOTEL, Red Lion Sq., Grasmere, Cumbria LA22 9SS. Tel. 05934/35456. Fax 05394/34157. 35 rms (all with bath or shower). TV TEL

$ Rates (including English breakfast): £38–£40.50 ($57–$60.80) single or double occupancy. AE, DC, MC, V. **Parking:** Free.

This 200-year-old coaching inn is only a short stroll from Wordsworth's Dove Cottage, and it's assumed that the poet often stopped here for a meal, drink, or to warm himself by the fire. Recently refurbished, the hotel offers comfortably furnished bedrooms with private baths. There's an elevator to all floors. Enjoy a drink or lunch in the light and airy surroundings of the Easdale Bar, or try the Lamb Inn and

Buttery for a more traditional pub atmosphere. In the dining room, you'll be served some of the finest fare in the district; a fixed-price meal starts at £16 ($24), or you can order à la carte.

SWAN HOTEL, on the A592, Grasmere, Cumbria LA22 9RF. Tel. 05394/ 35551, or toll free 800/225-5843 in the U.S. Fax 05394/35741. 36 rms (all with bath). TV TEL
$ Rates: £75 ($112.50) single; £100 ($150) double. English breakfast £7.95 ($11.90) extra. AE, DC, MC, V. **Parking:** Free.
Following a renovation, only the shell of this 1650 building remains. The hotel lies 400 yards outside Grasmere, beside the road leading to Keswick. Sir Walter Scott used to slip in for a secret drink early in the morning, and Wordsworth mentioned the place in "The Waggoner." In fact, the poet's tapestry chair is in one of the rooms. The restaurant serves daily from noon to 2pm and 7 to 9pm, providing both table d'hôte and à la carte meals. Dinners begin at £19.95 ($29.90).

WHITE MOSS HOUSE, along the A594, Rydal Water, Grasmere, Cumbria LA22 9SE. Tel. 05394/35295. 5 rms (all with bath), 1 cottage. TV TEL **Directions:** Take the A591 1½ miles south of town.
$ Rates (including English breakfast): £74–£110 ($111–$165) double; £120 ($180) cottage. MC, V. **Parking:** Free. **Closed:** Dec–Feb.
This old Lakeland cottage, once owned by Wordsworth, overlooks the lake and the fells. You'll be welcomed here by Peter and Susan Dixon who will pamper you with morning tea in bed, turn down your bedcovers at night, and cater to your culinary preferences. The rooms are comfortably furnished and well heated in nippy weather. Since there are only five double accommodations, advance booking is essential. All units have radios, trouser presses, hairdryers, and such bathroom amenities as soap, shampoo, and herbal bath salts. There's also Brockstone, their cottage annex, a 5-minute drive along the road, where two, three, or four guests can be accommodated in utter peace.
Dining/Entertainment: Dinner is a leisurely affair beginning at 8pm. You're served five courses likely to include a roast of lamb with an orange and red-currant sauce or quail with a chicken and brown-rice stuffing. For dessert, hope that Mrs. Beeton's chocolate pudding is featured. Dinner begins at £27.50 ($41.25), and you must reserve a table early.

WORDSWORTH HOTEL, Stock Lane, Grasmere, Cumbria LA22 9SW. Tel. 05394/35592. Fax 05394/35765. 37 rms (all with bath), 2 suites. TV TEL **Directions:** From the A591, turn left at the Grasmere Village sign and follow the road past the church, over the bridge, and around on an S-bend; the Wordsworth is on the right.
$ Rates (including English breakfast): £58 ($87) single; £98–£136 ($147–$204) double; £185 ($277.50) suite. AE, DC, MC, V. **Parking:** Free.
Reg Gifford of Michael's Nook Country House Hotel owns this hostelry in the heart of the village, set in a 3-acre garden. An old stone Lakeland house (once the hunting lodge of the Earl of Cadogan), the Wordsworth has been completely refurbished to provide luxuriously appointed bedrooms with views of the fells, as well as modern baths, radios, and trouser presses. Three rooms have a four-poster bed. The original master bedroom has a Victorian bathroom, with a brass towel rail and polished pipes and taps.
Dining/Entertainment: There are several lounges, with comfortable armchairs. A buffet lunch is served in the cocktail lounge, including the chef's hot dish of the day. A fixed-price four- or five-course dinner in the Prelude Restaurant at £29.50 ($44.25) is likely to include a light fruit or vegetable appetizer, soup, fish or meat course, dessert or cheese, and coffee and petit fours. Each dish is carefully explained on the menu so you know what you're getting. The cuisine is in the modern English style. Meals are

served Sunday through Thursday from 12:30 to 2pm and 7 to 9pm, to 9:30pm on Friday and Saturday.

Services: 24-hour room service, babysitting, laundry.

Facilities: The hotel has a large, heated swimming pool, a whirlpool, a sauna, a solarium, a games room, and a minigym.

---

6. HAWKSHEAD & CONISTON

263 miles NW of London, 52 miles S of Carlisle, 19 miles NW of Kendal

GETTING THERE   By Train   Go first to Windermere (see above) and proceed the rest of the way by bus.

By Bus   Cumberland Motor Services (CMS) runs buses from Windermere to Hawkshead and Coniston, three per day Monday through Saturday and two per day on Sunday. Take either bus no. 505 or no. 515 from Windermere.

By Car   From Windermere, proceed north along the A591 to Ambleside, cutting southwest on the B5285 to Hawkshead.

By Ferry   The Bowness Bay Boating Company in summer operates a ferry service from Bowness, directly south of Windermere, to Hawkshead. It reduces driving time considerably.

ESSENTIALS   The **telephone area code** for Hawkshead and Coniston is 05394. The **Tourist Information Centre** is at Hawkshead at the Main Car Park (tel. 05394/36525). It's open only in summer.

Discover for yourself the village of Hawkshead, with its 15th-century grammar school where Wordsworth went to school for 8 years (he carved his name on a desk that still remains). Near Hawkshead, in the vicinity of Esthwaite Water, is the 17th-century Hill Top Farm, former home of author Beatrix Potter.

At Coniston, 4 miles west of Hawkshead, you can visit the village famously associated with John Ruskin. Coniston is a good base for rock climbing. The Coniston "Old Man" towers in the background at 2,633 feet, giving mountain climbers one of the finest views of the Lake District.

WHAT TO SEE & DO

BRANTWOOD, Coniston. Tel. 41396.

John Ruskin, poet, artist, and critic, was one of the great figures of the Victorian age and a prophet of social reform, inspiring such diverse men as Proust, Frank Lloyd Wright, and Gandhi. He moved to his home, Brantwood, on the east side of Coniston Water, in 1872 and lived there until his death in 1900. The house today is open for visitors to view much Ruskiniana, including some 200 pictures by him. Also displayed are his coach and boat, the *Jumping Jenny*. A video program tells the story of Ruskin's life and work.

An exhibition illustrating the work of W. J. Linton is laid out in his old printing room. Linton was born in England in 1812 and died at New Haven, Connecticut, in 1897. Well known as a wood engraver and for his private press, he lived at Brantwood, where he set up his printing business in 1853. He published *The English Republic,* a newspaper and review, before sailing to America in 1866, where he set up his printing press in 1870. The house is owned and managed by the Education Trust, a self-supporting registered charity. Part of the 250-acre estate is open as a nature trail.

The Brantwood stables, designed by Ruskin, have been converted into a tearoom and restaurant, the Jumping Jenny. Also in the stable building is the Lakeland Guild Craft Gallery, which follows the Ruskin tradition in encouraging contemporary craft work of the finest quality.

Literary fans may want to pay a pilgrimage to the graveyard of the village church, where Ruskin was buried; his family turned down the invitation to have him interred at Westminster Abbey.

Admission: £2.80 ($4.20) adults, free for children; nature walk, £1 ($1.50) adults, free for children.

Open: Mid-Mar to mid-Nov, daily 11am–5:30pm; mid-Nov to mid-Mar, Wed–Sun 11am–5:30pm.

JOHN RUSKIN MUSEUM, Yewdale Rd., Coniston Village. Tel. 41387.

At this institute, in the center of the village, you can see Ruskin's personal possessions and mementos, pictures by him and his friends, letters, and a collection of mineral rocks he collected.

Admission: £1 ($1.50) adults, 50p (75¢) children.

Open: Easter–Oct, Sun–Fri 11am–1pm and 2–5pm. **Closed:** Nov–Easter.

WHERE TO STAY

IN HAWKSHEAD

HIGHFIELD HOUSE, Hawkshead Hill, Hawkshead, Ambleside, Cumbria LA22 0PM. Tel. 05394/36344. 11 rms (all with bath). TV

$ Rates (including English breakfast): £30.50 ($45.80) single; £54–£65 ($81–$97.50) double. MC, V.

This solidly built stone-sided house sits proudly on the side of a hill that enjoys sweeping views over the Lake District (at least on clear days) for a distance of up to 12 miles. Constructed around 1870, it lies three-quarters of a mile east of Hawkshead Village (on the road leading to Coniston), surrounded by 2½ acres of its own land. Operated by members of the Bennett family, it has cozy bedrooms, either with pastel colors or wallpaper inspired by the turn-of-the-century designs of William Morris. A four-course dinner can be prepared if advance notice is given for £14.50 ($21.80) per person.

IN CONISTON

CONISTON SUN HOTEL, Brow Hill, Coniston, Cumbria LA21 8HQ. Tel. 05394/41248. 11 rms (9 with bath). TV TEL

$ Rates (including English breakfast): £27 ($40.50) single without bath, £35 ($52.50) single with bath; £54 ($81) double without bath, £70 ($105) double with bath. MC, V. **Parking:** Free.

This is the most popular, traditional, and attractive pub, restaurant, and hotel in this Lakeland village. In reality it's a country-house hotel of much character, dating from 1902, although the inn attached to it is from the 16th century. Standing on its own beautiful grounds above the village, 150 yards from the town center off the A593, it lies at the foot of the Coniston "Old Man." Donald Campbell made this place his headquarters during his attempt to break the world water speed record. Each of the bedrooms is decorated with style and flair, and two of them have four-posters. Fresh local produce is used whenever possible in the candlelit restaurant. Log fires take the chill off a winter evening, and guests relax informally in the lounge, which is like a library. Many sports can be arranged.

WHERE TO DINE

GRIZEDALE LODGE, Grizedale, Hawkshead, Cumbria LA22 0QL. Tel. 05394/36532.
Cuisine: ENGLISH/FRENCH. **Reservations:** Recommended. **Directions:** About 500 yards before Hawkshead, turn left (signposted GRIZEDALE) and follow this road for 2 miles before coming to Grizedale Lodge Hotel.
$ Prices: Bar lunches from £6 ($9); fixed-price dinner £17.95 ($26.95). MC, V.
Open: Lunch daily 12:30–1:45pm; dinner daily 7–8pm. **Closed:** Jan 2–Feb 14.

The best place for food in the area is this country *restaurant avec chambres,* which was built in 1902 as a hunting lodge for the chairman of the Cunard Line. Many people come here just to dine because the cuisine is top-notch. Margaret Lamb is considered one of the finest chefs in the Lake District, and her considerable talents are reflected by her five-course evening meals. During the day guests order bar lunches, but at night they can enjoy a memorable meal in a tranquil setting. Service is personable.

Mrs. Lamb and her husband, Jack, also offer nine handsomely furnished bedrooms for guests, each with a private bath and TV. For half board, charges are £55 ($82.50) daily in a single, rising to £94 ($141) in a double.

---

7. KESWICK

22 miles NW of Windermere, 294 miles NW of London,
31 miles NW of Kendal

GETTING THERE By Train Go first to Windermere (see above) and proceed the rest of the way by bus.

By Bus Cumberland Motor Services (CMS) has hourly service from Windermere and Grasmere (bus no. 555 or no. 557).

By Car From Windermere, proceed northwest along the A591.

ESSENTIALS The **telephone area code** is 07687. The **Tourist Information Centre** is at Moot Hall, Market Square (tel. 07687/72645).

Keswick opens onto Derwentwater, one of the loveliest lakes in the district. It makes a good center for exploring the northern half of the Lake District National Park. The small town has two landscaped parks, and above the town is a historic Stone Circle thought to be some 4,000 years old.

St. Kentigern's Church dates from 553, and a weekly market held in the center of Keswick descends from a charter granted in the 13th century. It's a short walk to the classic view point of Friar's Crag on Derwentwater. The walk also takes you past boat landings with launches operating regularly on tours around the lake.

Around Derwentwater are many places with literary associations, evoking memories of Wordsworth, Robert Southey (poet laureate), Coleridge, and Hugh Walpole. Several of Beatrix Potter's stories were based at Keswick. The town also has a professional repertory theater offering shows in summer. There is a modern swimming pool, plus an 18-hole golf course at the foot of the mountains 4 miles away.

Close at hand are villages and lakes, including Borrowdale, Buttermere, and Bassenthwaite, while the open country of "John Peel" fame is to the north of the 3,053-foot Skiddaw.

WHERE TO STAY & DINE

BRUNDHOLME COUNTRY HOUSE, Brundholme Rd., Keswick, Cumbria CA12 4NL. Tel. 07687/74495. 12 rms (all with bath). TV TEL **Directions:** At the A66 Keswick Roundabout, turn left at the sign to Brundholme.
$ Rates (including English breakfast): £45–£55 ($67.50–$82.50) single; £90–£120 ($135–$180) double. MC, V. **Parking:** Free. **Closed:** Dec 21–Feb 14.
Coleridge wrote that this Regency villa (restored and opened as a choice hotel in 1988) was "in a delicious situation." He was referring to the views over Keswick to the enveloping hills. Wordsworth was also known to visit this house above the River Greta. Owner Ian Charlton is also the chef de cuisine. The well-chosen staff is one of the most helpful in the area. The well-furnished bedrooms are comfortable, and some are quite large. The hotel also has a garden.

Dining/Entertainment: This country-house hotel is known mainly for its French and English cuisine, using, when available, local produce such as char (a succulent fish found in Lake Windermere) or trout from Borrowdale. The local game from Cumberland is reputedly the best in England. Try such specialties as homemade soups, jugged hare, and Cumberland ham. Meals are served daily from 12:15 to 1:30pm and 7:30 to 8:30pm. A table d'hôte dinner is priced from £19.50 ($29.25). Reservations are important.

GRANGE COUNTRY HOUSE, Manor Brow, Ambleside Rd., Keswick, Cumbria CA12 4BA. Tel. 07687/72500. 10 rms (all with bath). TV TEL
Directions: On the southeast side of Keswick overlooking the town just off A591.
$ Rates (including English breakfast): £40.50–£44 ($66.75–$66) single; £69–£77 ($103.50–$115.50) double. MC, V. **Parking:** Free. **Closed:** Nov to mid-Mar.
A tranquil retreat, this charming hotel is located amid its own gardens on a hilltop. The hotel, which dates from the 1800s, is furnished in part with antiques. Guests enjoy the crackling log fires in chilly weather. Many of the attractively furnished, well-kept rooms open onto beautiful views of the lakeland hills. The hotel, run by Jane and Duncan Miller, also offers a first-rate cuisine. Guests can dine here for £17 ($25.50) in the evening.

SKIDDAW HOTEL, Main St., Keswick, Cumbria CA12 5BN. Tel. 07687/ 72071. Fax 07687/74850. 40 rms (all with bath). TV TEL
$ Rates: £32–£34 ($48–$51) single; £51–£55 ($76.50–$82.50) double. English breakfast £6 ($9) extra. AE, MC, V. **Parking:** Free.

 This hotel has an impressive facade and entrance marquee built right onto the sidewalk in the heart of Keswick at the market square. The owners have refurbished the interior, retaining the best features which they combined with modern facilities. The bedrooms, which are compact and eye-catching, have hot-beverage-making facilities.

Guests gather in the lounge or the popular cocktail bar with an art nouveau ambience. The meals feature well-prepared English and continental cuisine, available à la carte all day. In addition, a chef's special, such as Lancashire hot pot, is offered at lunch. Dinner costs £15 ($22.50). There is a wide selection of wines.

IN NEARBY BASSENTHWAITE LAKE

ARMATHWAITE HALL HOTEL, Bassenthwaite Lake, Keswick, Cumbria CA12 4RE. Tel. 07687/76551. Fax 07687/76220. 38 rms (all with bath), 4 studio suites. TV TEL **Directions:** Take the B5291 1½ miles west of the center of Bassenthwaite and 7 miles northwest of Keswick.

$ **Rates** (including English breakfast): £50–£70 ($75–$105) single; £100–£154 ($150–$231) double; £184 ($276) suite. AE, DC, MC, V. **Parking:** Free.

⭐ Rich in history, this hotel was originally built in the 1300s as a house for Benedictine nuns. During the Middle Ages it was plundered frequently, leaving the sisters wretchedly poor. By the 17th century a series of wealthy landowners had completed the severe Gothic design of its stately facade, and in 1844 an architecturally compatible series of wings were added. In the 1930s it was converted into a hotel, and Sir Hugh Walpole, who once stayed here, found it "a house of perfect and irresistible charm." Ringed with almost 400 acres of woodland, some of it bordering the lake, the place offers a magnificent entrance hall filled with hunting trophies and sheathed with expensive paneling. There's also a whimsically modern cocktail lounge whose veneer-clad, Gay '90s bar contrasts with one of the most neobaroque fireplaces in the district. A Victorian billiard room is lined with old engravings, and a first-class restaurant offers a view of the lake. A three-course fixed-price lunch costs £11.95 ($17.95), and a six-course fixed-price dinner goes for £16.95 ($18.45). An indoor swimming pool is ringed with stone walls and sheltered from the rain by a roof of wooden trusses. Each of the handsomely furnished bedrooms contains a private bath and radio. The hotel also provides the finest equestrian center in the area.

IN NEARBY BORROWDALE

BORROWDALE HOTEL, Borrowdale Rd. (B5289), Borrowdale, Keswick, Cumbria CA12 5UY. Tel. 07687/77224. Fax 07687/77338. 34 rms (all with bath). TV TEL **Directions:** Take the B5289 3½ miles south from Keswick.

$ **Rates** (including English breakfast): £29.20–£33.10 ($43.80–$49.65) per person, single or double. MC, V. **Parking:** Free.

When the weather is inclement, log fires welcome guests in this lakeland stone building (originally a coaching inn) circa 1866. The rooms are comfortable and many have fine views. All have private baths or showers, toilets, radios, intercom units, and hairdryers. Some traditional four-poster beds are available.

Dining/Entertainment: The main attraction here is the restaurant. A traditional English lunch on Saturday costs £9.90 ($14.85). During the rest of the week, bar lunches with a choice of 25 main courses cost in the £6 ($9) range. The seven-course dinner, consisting of appetizer, entrée, and dessert, each with a choice of at least six different dishes, starts at £17.90 ($26.85). Cuisine from all parts of the globe is offered, and the menu changes daily. If you wish to have the daily roast, the chef will carve it at your table from a silver trolley.

STAKIS LODORE SWISS HOTEL, Borrowdale Rd. (B5289), Borrowdale, Keswick, Cumbria CA12 5UX. Tel. 07687/77285. Fax 07687/77343. 67 rms (all with bath), 1 suite. A/C MINIBAR TV TEL **Directions:** Take the B5289 3½ miles south of Keswick.

$ **Rates** (including half board): £65–£72 ($97.50–$108) per person, single or double. AE, DC, MC, V. **Parking:** £3.50 ($5.25)

Since 1987, the Stakis hotel chain has run this hotel overlooking Derwentwater, amid fields where cows graze. With its spike-capped mansard tower, symmetrical gables, and balcony-embellished stone facade, it looks a lot like a hotel you might find in the foothills of Lake Geneva. When it was constructed in the 19th century, its owners were Swiss. The old tradition of good rooms, good food, and service continues today. The interior has been modernized, and each of the well-furnished bedrooms has a hairdryer, private bath, radio, and coffee maker.

Dining/Entertainment: The food is exceptional for the area, with a fixed-price dinner costing £25 ($37.50) for nonresidents. Dishes include roast topside of English beef with Yorkshire pudding, Morecambe Bay shrimp, and plaice sautéed in butter. Call for a reservation, especially at dinner. Food is served from 12:30 to 2pm and 7:30 to 9:30pm daily.

Services: 24-hour room service, laundry.

Facilities: Indoor and outdoor swimming pool, garden.

---

8. ULLSWATER

296 miles NW of London, 6 miles E of Penrith, 26 miles SE of Keswick

GETTING THERE   By Train   Penrith is the region's main rail junction. About three trains from London's Euston Station arrive daily in Penrith—usually a change of trains isn't necessary. Once in Penrith, passengers usually take a taxi to Ullswater.

By Bus   From June 24 to September 29, two buses operated by Cumberland Motor Services begin in Carlisle and end in Bowness-on-Windermere. They stop at the Penrith Rail Station, where passengers must take a taxi to Ullswater.

By Car   From Penrith, head southeast along the B5320.

ESSENTIALS   The **telephone area code** is 07684. The summer-only **Tourist Information Centre** for the lake is at The Square, Pooley Bridge (tel. 07684/ 86530).

A 7-mile expanse of water, stretching from Pooley Bridge to Patterdale, Ullswater is the second-largest lake in the district. Incidentally, it was on the shores of Ullswater that Wordsworth saw his "host of golden daffodils." While housed in the area, it's easy to explore several places of archeological interest, such as Hadrian's Wall, east of Carlisle, or Long Meg stone circle near Penrith.

WHERE TO STAY & DINE

SHARROW BAY COUNTRY HOUSE HOTEL, Howtown Rd., Lake Ullswater, near Penrith, Cumbria CA10 2LZ. Tel. 07684/86301. Fax 07684/86349. 22 rms (all with bath), 6 suites. TV TEL **Directions:** Take Howtown Rd. 2 miles south from Pooley Bridge.

$ Rates (including English breakfast and dinner): £120–£145 ($180–$217.50) single; £240 ($360) double; £290 ($435) suite. No credit cards. **Parking:** Free. **Closed:** Dec–Feb.

A Relais & Châteaux for the past quarter of a century, this hotel is the second-oldest member of that prestigious group in Britain. It's an unusual Victorian house that had been a private home until it was purchased by Francis Coulson in 1949. Realizing its potential, he began restoration work on the structure, with its low angled roof and wide eaves, sleeping on the floor while the work was in progress. Three years later he was joined by Brian Sack, and together they turned Sharrow into one of England's finest eating places. This was also the first Country House Hotel to be created in Great Britain. The hotel offers 28 antique-filled bedrooms, 16 of which are in the gatehouse and cottages. Some accommodations, as well as the drawing room, have views of the lakes, trees, or Martindale Fells. Each of the individually decorated bedrooms has a name rather than a number. Some of the rooms have a minibar.

Dining/Entertainment: The six-course £40 ($60) fixed-price menu presents a formidable list of choices. I recently counted 28 appetizers, including the chef's specialty, mousseline of fresh salmon with hollandaise sauce. The carefully chosen main courses seem designed to make the best of homegrown products, including roast Lancashire guinea fowl and Cumberland ham. The dessert selections are among the best you'll find in northwest England, including a fresh strawberry, hazelnut, and brandy-cream roulade. Also featured are Sharrow homemade cream ices, including prune and Armagnac. Brian Sack, the dining room host, has an efficient staff. If you're motoring through the area, call ahead and make a reservation for the £29.50 ($44.25) fixed-price luncheon. Meals are served from 1 to 1:45pm and 8 to 8:45pm daily. For either a meal or a room, you should write or call in advance.

CHAPTER 19
THE NORTHEAST

- **WHAT'S SPECIAL ABOUT THE NORTHEAST**
1. **LINCOLN**
2. **YORK**
3. **NORTH YORK MOORS NATIONAL PARK**
4. **HAWORTH**
5. **HEXHAM & HADRIAN'S WALL**

The northeast of England is rich in attractions, its most visited cities, Lincoln and York, lying on the "cathedral circuit."

Lincoln is the largest city of Lincolnshire, bordered on one side by the North Sea. Of all England's counties (or shires) of the East Midlands, Lincolnshire is the most interesting to visit. Within Lincolnshire, other than the cathedral city of Lincoln, the most interesting section is Holland.

Located in the southeast, Holland is a land known for its fields of tulips, marshes and fens, as well as windmills reminiscent of the Netherlands. Tourists, particularly North Americans, generally cross the tulip fields and pass by the busy port of Boston before making the swing north to Lincoln, which is inland.

Yorkshire, known to readers of *Wuthering Heights* and *All Creatures Great and Small,* embraces both the moors of North Yorkshire and the dales. With the radical changing of the old county boundaries, the shire is now divided into North Yorkshire (the most interesting from the tourist's point of view), West Yorkshire, South Yorkshire, and Humberside.

Away from the cities and towns that still carry the taint of the Industrial Revolution, the beauty is wild and remote, and is characterized by limestone crags, caverns along the Pennines, mountainous uplands, rolling hills, chalkland wolds, heather-covered moorlands, broad vales, and tumbling streams.

Yorkshire offers not only the beauty of its inland scenery, but its 100 miles of shoreline, with its rocky headlands, cliffs, sandy bays, rock pools, sheltered coves, fishing villages, bird sanctuaries, former smugglers' dens, and yachting havens, is definitely worth a visit.

Across this vast region came the Romans, the Anglo-Saxons, the Vikings, the monks of the Middle Ages, kings of England, lords of the manor, craftspeople, hill farmers, and wool growers, all leaving their own mark. You can still see Roman roads and pavements, great abbeys and castles, stately homes, open-air museums, and craft centers, along with parish churches, old villages, and cathedrals. In fact, Yorkshire's battle-scarred castles, Gothic abbeys, and great country manor houses (from all periods) are unrivaled anywhere in Britain.

Northumbria is made up of the counties of Northumberland, Cleveland, and Durham. Tyne and Wear is one of the more recently created counties, and has Newcastle upon Tyne as its center. The Saxons who came to northern England centuries ago carved out this kingdom, which at the time stretched from the Firth of Forth in Scotland to the banks of the Humber in Yorkshire. Vast tracts of that ancient kingdom remain natural and unspoiled. Again, this slice of England has more than its share of industrial towns, but as a visitor, you should set out to explore the wild hills and open spaces, and cross the dales of the eastern Pennines.

WHAT'S SPECIAL ABOUT THE NORTHEAST

Great Towns/Villages
- [ ] Lincoln, ancient city dominated by its towering 11th-century cathedral with triple towers.
- [ ] York, Roman walled city nearly 2,000 years old, with many medieval buildings.

Cathedrals
- [ ] York Cathedral, with a history spanning some 800 years; noted for its 100 stained-glass windows.
- [ ] Lincoln Cathedral, dating from the 12th century with a tower rising 271 feet, the second tallest in England.

Literary Shrines
- [ ] Haworth, where the Brontës lived.

Natural Spectacles
- [ ] Yorkshire Dales, some 700 square miles of water-carved wonderland preserved as a national park.
- [ ] Yorkshire Moors, heather-covered moorland; the 553-square-mile parkland borders the North Sea.

Ancient Monuments
- [ ] Hadrian's Wall, built by conquering Romans, and once considered a wonder of the Western world.

Buildings
- [ ] Castle Howard, near Malton in North Yorkshire, with lakes, fountains, extensive gardens, and the main location for the "Brideshead Revisited" TV series.

The whole area evokes ancient battles and bloody border raids. Space limitations prevent a proper exploration of this area, which is often overlooked by the rushed North American visitor. However, you should venture into the area at least to see Hadrian's Wall, a Roman structure that was considered one of the wonders of the Western world. The finest stretch of the wall lies within the Northumberland National Park, between the stony North Tyne River and the county boundary at Gilsland.

SEEING THE NORTHEAST

GETTING THERE

Although one of the more remote parts of England, the northeast is relatively easy to reach from London or points in the south. Motorists take the M1 from London; British Rail trains reach either Lincoln or York in about 2 hours. York is farther away but Lincoln takes the same amount of time because of a change of trains. National Express buses also cover the area from London's Victoria Coach Station, reaching York, for example, in about 4 hours.

A SUGGESTED ITINERARY

Day 1: Head for Lincoln for a day of sightseeing and a visit to its cathedral.

Days 2—4: Continue to York and remain there for 3 nights, using it as a center not only for its own attractions but for some starred sights in its vicinity, including Castle Howard and the Yorkshire Dales.

Day 5: Call on the literary shrines of the Brontës at Haworth in West Yorkshire and stay overnight there.

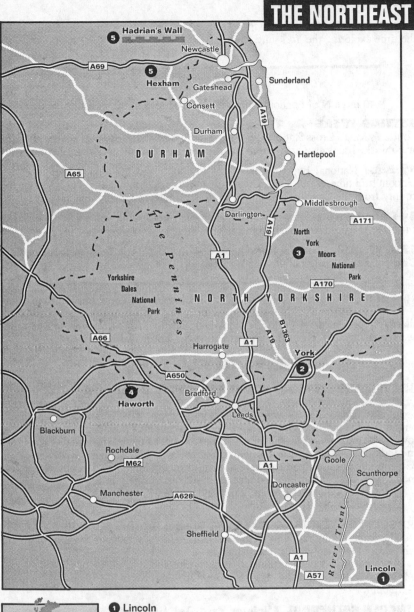

THE NORTHEAST

Hadrian's Wall

5

Newcastle

A69

5
Hexham

Gateshead

Sunderland

Consett

A19

Durham

D U R H A M

Hartlepool

A65

Middlesbrough

Darlington

A171

A19

North
York Moors
National
Park

3

A170

A1

Yorkshire
Dales
National
Park

The Pennines

N O R T H   Y O R K S H I R E

A66

Harrogate

A1

A19

B1363

York

2

A650

4
Haworth

Bradford

Leeds

Blackburn

Rochdale

M62

Goole

Scunthorpe

Manchester

A628

Doncaster

A1

River Trent

Sheffield

A1

Lincoln

1

A57

ENGLAND

★ London

1 Lincoln
2 York
3 North York Moors National Park
4 Haworth
5 Hexham & Hadrian's Wall

Day 6: Visit Thirsk of *All Creatures Great and Small* fame, and spend the rest of the time exploring the Yorkshire Moors.

1. LINCOLN

140 miles N of London, 94 miles N of Cambridge, 82 miles S of York

GETTING THERE   By Train   Trains arrive every hour during the day from London's King's Cross Station (trip time: 2 hr.), and usually involve a change of trains at Newark. Trains also arrive from Cambridge, again involving a change at Newark.

By Bus   National Express buses from London's Victoria Coach Station service Lincoln (trip time: about 3 hr.). Once in Lincoln, local and regional buses service the county from the City Bus Station, off St. Mary's Street, opposite the rail station.

By Car   From London, take the M1 motorway north until you reach the junction with the A57 heading east to Lincoln.

ESSENTIALS   The **telephone area code** is 0522. The **Tourist Information Centre** is at 9 Castle Hill (tel. 0522/529828).

One of the most ancient cities of England, Lincoln was known to the Romans as Lindum and some of the architectural glory of the Roman Empire still stands to charm the present-day visitor. The renowned Newport Arch (the North Gate) is the last remaining arch left in Britain that still spans a principal highway.

WHAT TO SEE & DO

GREYFRIARS CITY AND COUNTY MUSEUM, Broadgate. Tel. 530401.
Two years after the Battle of Hastings, William the Conqueror built a castle on the site of a Roman fortress. Now used for administrative purposes, parts of the castle still remain, including the walls, the 12th-century keep, and fragments of the gateway tower. The museum relates the history of Lincolnshire from prehistoric times to 1750. In addition, you can visit the High Bridge over the Witham River, with its half-timbered houses (you can have a meal in one of them); this is one of the few medieval bridges left in England that has buildings nestling on it.
Admission: 50p (80¢) adults, 25p (40¢) children.
Open: Mon–Sat 10am–5:30pm, Sun 2:30–5pm.

MUSEUM OF LINCOLNSHIRE LIFE, Burton Rd. Tel. 528448.
The largest folk museum in the area has displays ranging from a Victorian schoolroom to locally built steam engines.
Admission: £1 ($1.50) adults, 50p (80¢) children.
Open: May–Sept, daily 10am–5:30pm; Oct–Apr, Mon–Sat 10am–5:30pm, Sun 2–5:30pm.

LINCOLN CATHEDRAL, Minister Yard. Tel. 544544.
No other English cathedral dominates its surroundings as does Lincoln. Visible from up to 30 miles away, the central tower is 271 feet high, which makes it the second tallest in England. Lincoln's central tower once carried a huge spire, which, prior to heavy gale damage in 1549, made it the tallest in the world at 525 feet. Construction on the original Norman cathedral was begun in 1072, and it was consecrated 20 years later. It sustained a major fire and, in 1185, an earthquake. Only the central portion of the West Front and lower halves of the western towers survive

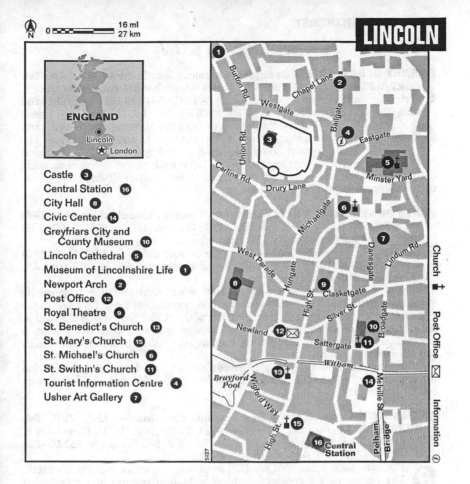

LINCOLN

0 ⊨⊨⊨⊨⊨ 16 ml / 27 km

ENGLAND
Lincoln
London

Castle ③
Central Station ⑯
City Hall ⑧
Civic Center ⑭
Greyfriars City and County Museum ⑩
Lincoln Cathedral ⑤
Museum of Lincolnshire Life ①
Newport Arch ②
Post Office ⑫
Royal Theatre ⑨
St. Benedict's Church ⑬
St. Mary's Church ⑮
St. Michael's Church ⑥
St. Swithin's Church ⑪
Tourist Information Centre ④
Usher Art Gallery ⑦

Church ✝
Post Office ⊠
Information ⓘ

from this period. The present cathedral is Gothic style, particularly the Early English and Decorated periods. The nave is 13th century, but the black font of Tournai marble originates from the 12th century. In the Great North Transept is a rose medallion window known as the Dean's Eye. Opposite it, in the Great South Transept, is its cousin, the Bishop's Eye. East of the high altar is the Angel Choir, consecrated in 1280, and so called after the sculpted angels high on the walls. The exquisite wood carving in St. Hugh's Choir dates from the 14th century. Lincoln's roof bosses, dating from the 13th and 14th centuries, are handsome, and a mirror trolley assists visitors in their appreciation of these features, which are some 70 feet above the floor. Oak bosses are in the cloister.

In the Seamen's Chapel (Great North Transept) is a window commemorating Lincolnshire-born Capt. John Smith, one of the pioneers of early settlement in America and the first governor of Virginia. The library and north walk of the cloister were built in 1674 to designs by Sir Christopher Wren. In the Treasury is fine silver plate from the churches of the diocese.

Admission: Suggested donation £1.50 ($2.30) adults, 50p (80¢) children.

Open: Cathedral, Nov–Mar, daily 7:15am–5pm; Apr–Oct, daily 7:15am–8pm. Treasury, daily 11am–3pm.

WHERE TO STAY

D'ISNEY PLACE HOTEL, Eastgate, Lincoln, Lincolnshire LN2 4AA. Tel. 0522/538881. Fax 0522/511321. 17 rms (all with bath), 1 suite. **Bus:** 1A or 8.
$ Rates (including English breakfast): £39–£49 ($58.50–$73.50) single; £57–£69 ($85.50–$103.50) double; £126 ($189) suite. AE, DC, MC, V. **Parking:** Free.

A family-owned hostelry, this hotel is close to the cathedral, the minster yard, the castle, and the Bailgate shops. It was built in 1735 and later enlarged. The southern boundary of the house gardens is formed by the wall of the cathedral close and towers, which were constructed in 1285. Each of the rooms is uniquely decorated and includes a radio and hot-beverage makers. Some units have four-poster beds and Jacuzzi baths. There is a parking lot.

FORTE POST HOUSE HOTEL, Eastgate, Lincoln, Lincolnshire LN2 1PN Tel. 0522/520341, or toll free 800/435-4542 in the U.S. Fax 0522/510780. 69 rms (all with bath), 1 suite. TV TEL **Bus:** 1A or 8.
$ Rates: Sun–Thurs, £53.50 ($80.30) single or double; Fri–Sat, £41.40 ($62.10) single or double; £107 ($160.50) suite. English breakfast £6.95 ($10.40) extra. AE, DC, MC, V. **Parking:** Free.

This hotel occupies a historic site: In fact, when workmen were digging its foundations in the mid-1960s, they discovered the remnants of the north tower of the East Gate of Roman Lincoln. A preserved part of the Roman city wall is included in the rear garden. The hotel faces Lincoln Cathedral and is attached to a Victorian mansion (now the Eastgate Bar). All the recently refurbished bedrooms have radios and hot-beverage makers.

Breakfast, lunch, and dinner are served in the Spires Restaurant, which also overlooks the cathedral. A la carte lunches go for £11 ($16.50), and à la carte dinners cost from £16 ($24).

GRAND HOTEL, St. Mary's St., Lincoln, Lincolnshire LN5 7EP. Tel. 0522/524211. Fax 0522/537661. 48 rms (all with bath). TV TEL **Bus:** 1A or 8.
$ Rates (including English breakfast): £42–£53 ($63–$79.50) single; £52.50–£58 ($78.80–$87) double. AE, DC, MC, V. **Parking:** Free.

This extensively remodeled hotel has suitable amenities and a cooperative staff. The bedrooms are compact, with many built-in features and coordinated colors. The Grand is easy to spot just opposite the bus depot and near the rail station. The West bar and the lounges are streamlined, but the Tudor bar pays homage to the past. The food is a top-notch bargain, in both price and taste. From 7 to 8:30pm, a four-course table d'hôte dinner is offered for £10.50 ($15.80). The food is not only good and typically English, but the portions are ample. You can also lunch at the Grand daily from noon to 2pm. A buttery is open from 11am to 10pm.

WHITE HART HOTEL, Bailgate, Lincoln, Lincolnshire LN1 3AR. Tel. 0522/526222, or toll free 800/435-4542 in the U.S. Fax 0522/531798. 37 rms (all with bath), 13 suites. TV TEL **Bus:** 1A.
$ Rates: £70 ($105) single; £90–£105 ($135–$157.50) double; £135 ($202.50) suite. English breakfast £7.95 ($11.90) extra. AE, DC, MC, V. **Parking:** £5 ($7.50).

Since Richard II visited this region shortly before this hotel's construction (and probably stayed at an inn on the site), the White Hart is named after his emblem. A letter written in 1460 by a London woman who paid sixpence for her room complains that her bed was lumpy. The facade covering the inn dates from the 1700s when it was a luxurious private home. Its life as a modern hotel began in 1913 when the live-in owners started accepting paying guests, but only if they came with ironclad references. The hotel also bears the honor of having hosted several meetings between Churchill and Eisenhower in the darkest days of World War II. Other guests have included Lloyd George, Edward VIII, and Margaret Thatcher.

Once through a revolving mahogany door, you enter a large and finely proportioned lounge filled with fine antiques, rare and unusual clocks, and display cabinets of rare silver, glass, and porcelain. The Georgian main dining room has elegant furnishings and well-prepared lunches and dinners. Each of the accommodations has some antique furniture, a well-accessorized bath, and views of the old city. To reach your room, you negotiate a labyrinth of narrow halls and stairways. The White Hart is surrounded by ancient cobblestone streets usually reserved for pedestrians. The cathedral and the oldest part of Lincoln lie a short walk from the doorstep.

WHERE TO DINE

JEWS HOUSE RESTAURANT, The Jews House, 15 The Strait. Tel. 524851.
    Cuisine: CONTINENTAL. **Reservations:** Required. **Bus:** 1A or 8.
$ Prices: Appetizers £2.25–£6.50 ($3.40–$9.80); main courses £9.50–£14.50 ($14.30–$21.80). AE, DC, MC, V.
    Open: Lunch Tues–Sat noon–2pm; dinner Mon–Sat 7–10pm. **Closed:** 2 weeks Feb–Mar (dates vary).

Originally built around 1150, this stone-fronted building is said by local historians to be the oldest lived-in house in Europe. The dining room has a low-beamed ceiling, a cast-iron fireplace, and an array of medieval features. Two of the massive ceiling beams are known to date from the construction of the original house. Seating only about 28 diners, the establishment is run by chef-proprietor Richard Gibbs and his wife, Sally. The menu features stylish dishes that change weekly according to market ingredients and the inspiration of the chef. Examples include grilled goat cheese served on a bed of fresh spinach with croutons and bacon, grilled mussels in their half-shells slathered with a hazelnut-butter sauce, roast rack of lamb with a basil and pine-nut crust, and such fish dishes as steamed turbot with a fennel and fresh tomato sauce.

WIG & MITRE, 29 Steep Hill. Tel. 535190.
    Cuisine: INTERNATIONAL. **Reservations:** Recommended. **Bus:** 1A or 8.
$ Prices: Appetizers £2–£6.75 ($3–$10.10); main courses £4–£12.50 ($6–$18.80), English breakfast £4.75 ($7.10), sandwiches £2.50–£5.50 ($3.80–$8.30). AE, DC, MC, V.
    Open: Daily 8am–midnight.

Run by Michael and Valerie Hope, this is not only one of the best pubs in old Lincoln, but its bill of fare is superior to that found in most restaurants. Sitting on the aptly named Steep Hill near the cathedral, redolent of an Old English atmosphere, the establishment operates somewhat like a café-brasserie. The main restaurant, behind the drinking section on the second floor, has oak timbers, Victorian armchairs, and settees. The 14th-century pub, which has been substantially restored over the years, also has a summer beer garden. If the restaurant is full, all dishes can be served in the bar downstairs. Blackboard specials change daily, and you are likely to be offered roast rack of lamb resting on onion-and-sage purée, fricassée of guinea fowl, and roast duck suprême garnished with pink grapefruit. A favorite dessert is chocolate roulade.

---

2. YORK

203 miles N of London, 26 miles NE of Leeds, 88 miles N of Nottingham

GETTING THERE   **By Plane**   British Midland flights arrive at Leeds/Bradford

Airport, a 50-minute flight from London's Heathrow Airport. Connecting buses at the airport take you east and the rest of the distance to York.

By Train From London's King's Cross Station, York-bound trains leave every 10 minutes (trip time: 2 hr).

By Bus Four National Express buses depart daily from London's Victoria Coach Station for York (trip time: 4½ hr.).

By Car From London, head north along the M1 motorway, cutting northeast below Leeds at the junction of the A64 heading east to York.

ESSENTIALS The **telephone area code** is 0904. The **Tourist Information Centre** is at De Grey Rooms, Exhibition Square (tel. 0904/621756).

Few cities in England are as rich in history as York. It is still encircled by its 13th- and 14th-century city walls—about 2½ miles long—with four gates. One of these, Micklegate, once grimly greeted visitors coming up from the south with the heads of traitors. To this day, you can walk on the footpath of the medieval walls.

The crowning achievement of York is its minster, or cathedral, which makes the city an ecclesiastical center equaled only by Canterbury. In spite of this, York is one of the most overlooked cities on the cathedral circuit. Perhaps foreign visitors are intimidated by the feeling that the great city of northeastern England is too far north. Actually, it lies about 203 miles north of London on the Ouse River and can easily be tied in with a motor trip to Edinburgh. Or, after visiting Cambridge, a motorist can make a swing through a too-often-neglected cathedral circuit: Ely, Lincoln, York, and Ripon.

There was a Roman York (Hadrian came this way), then a Saxon York, a Danish York, a Norman York (William the Conqueror slept here), a medieval York, a Georgian York, and a Victorian York (the center of a flourishing rail business). Today a large amount of 18th-century York remains, including Richard Boyle's restored Assembly Rooms.

At some point in your exploration, you may want to visit the Shambles, once the meat-butchering center of York that dates back before the Norman Conquest. This messy business has given way, but the ancient street survives and is filled with jewelry stores, cafés, and buildings that huddle so closely together that you can practically stand in the middle of the pavement, arms outstretched, and touch the houses on both sides of the street.

Recently interest has focused on discoveries of the Viking era, from 867 to 1066, when the city was known as Jorvik, the Viking capital and a major Scandinavian trade center (see below).

Incidentally, the suffix "gate" used for streets and sites in York derived from the Scandinavian word for "street"—a historical reminder of the earlier Viking period.

WHAT TO SEE & DO

To get to know York, start at York Minster and walk down past Youngs Hotel, the reputed birthplace of Guy Fawkes. Turn right onto Stonegate, a pedestrian area with old shops, a 12th-century house on the right, and some old coffeehouses. Continue across Davygate into St. Helen's Square to see the guildhall and Mansion House, then go left onto Coney Street and take a right onto Lower Ousegate.

At the beginning of Ouse Bridge, take the steps down to King's Staith, with a pub on the left for refreshment, before you continue on onto South Esplanade and St. George's Gardens beside the river. At the bridge, join the road again and turn left. In front of you stand the Castle Museum, the Assize Courts, and Clifford's Tower. Walk

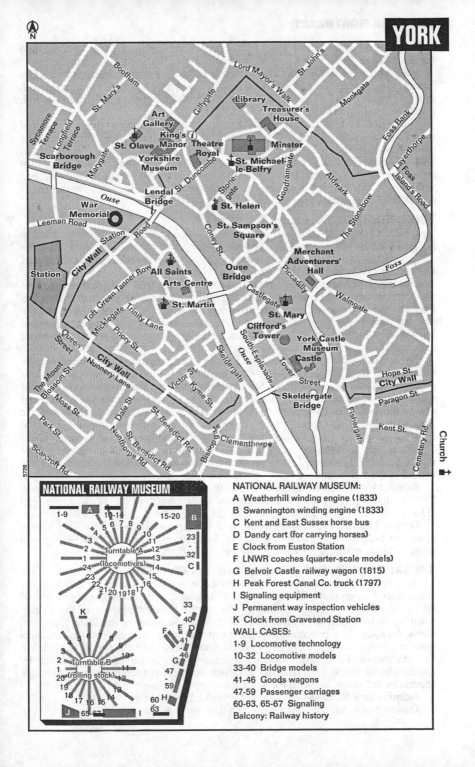

YORK

N

Bootham
Lord Mayor's Walk
St. John's
Monkgate
Sycamore Terrace
Longfield Terrace
St. Mary's
Gillygate
Library
Treasurer's House
Foss Bank
Scarborough Bridge
Maygate
Art Gallery
King's Manor
St. Olave
Theatre Royal
Minster
Goodramgate
Aldwark
Layerthorpe
Island's Road
Little Foss
Yorkshire Museum
St. Michael-le-Belfry
St. Duncombe
Stonegate
Ouse
War Memorial
Lendal Bridge
St. Helen
Leeman Road
Station Road
Coney St.
St. Sampson's Square
The Stonebow
Foss
Station
City Wall
Toft Green
Tanner Row
All Saints
Arts Centre
St. Martin
Ouse Bridge
Castlegate
Piccadilly
Merchant Adventurers' Hall
Walmgate
Mickgate
Trinity Lane
Priory St.
Queen Street
The Mount
Blossom St.
City Wall
Nunnery Lane
Victor St.
Kyme St.
Skeldergate
Ouse
South Esplanade
St. Mary
Clifford's Tower
York Castle Museum
Castle
Tower Street
Hope St.
City Wall
Paragon St.
Moss St.
Dale St.
St. Benedict Rd.
Skeldergate Bridge
Fishergate
Kent St.
Park St.
Nunthorpe Rd.
Bishopgate
Clementhorpe
Cemetery Rd.
Scarcroft Rd.
Church ■ †

NATIONAL RAILWAY MUSEUM

Turntable A (locomotives)
Turntable B (rolling stock)
A   B   C   K   F   E   D   G   H   I   J

NATIONAL RAILWAY MUSEUM:

A Weatherhill winding engine (1833)
B Swannington winding engine (1833)
C Kent and East Sussex horse bus
D Dandy cart (for carrying horses)
E Clock from Euston Station
F LNWR coaches (quarter-scale models)
G Belvoir Castle railway wagon (1815)
H Peak Forest Canal Co. truck (1797)
I Signaling equipment
J Permanent way inspection vehicles
K Clock from Gravesend Station

WALL CASES:

1-9 Locomotive technology
10-32 Locomotive models
33-40 Bridge models
41-46 Goods wagons
47-59 Passenger carriages
60-63, 65-67 Signaling
Balcony: Railway history

up Tower Street and Clifford Street to Nessgate. Turn right onto High Ousegate and continue across Parliament Street to the beginning of the Shambles on the left.

Walk up the Shambles past the attractive shops and ancient buildings to Kings Square, then bear right onto Goodramgate. Walk down Goodramgate and, at the end, cross Deangate onto College Street with St. William's College on the right. At the end, a narrow road leads to the Treasurer's House.

You're now behind the east end of the minster. Walk around to the west end and then up Bootham Bar, through the city gate, and turn left into Exhibition Square. The art gallery is on the right, the tourist information center to the left, and, beside it, York's Theatre Royal. Continue down St. Leonard's Street to the crossroads and turn right onto Museum Street. Cross the river and go right to join part of the old medieval wall, which you follow all the way to Skeldergate Bridge. Then follow the river's course upstream again to the center of York.

★ YORK MINSTER, Deangate. Tel. 624426.

One of the great cathedrals of the world, York Minster traces its origins back to the early 7th century; the present building, however, dates from the 13th century and stands at the converging point of several streets: Deangate, Duncombe Place, Minster Yard, and Petergate.

Like the cathedral at Lincoln, York Minster is characterized by three towers built in the 15th century. The central tower is lantern-shaped in the Perpendicular style and from the top of the tower on a clear day there are panoramic views of York and the Vale of York. It is a steep climb up a stone spiral staircase and not recommended for the very elderly, very young, or anyone with a heart condition or breathing difficulties.

Perhaps the most memorable distinguishing characteristic of the cathedral is its stained glass from the Middle Ages—in glorious Angelico blues, ruby reds, forest greens, and honey-colored ambers. See especially the Great East Window, the work of a 15th-century Coventry-based glass painter. In the north transept is an architectural gem of the mid-13th century—the Five Sisters Window with its five lancets in grisaille glass. The late 15th-century choir screen has an impressive lineup of historical figures—everybody from William the Conqueror to the overthrown Henry VI.

At a reception desk near the entrance to the minster, groups can arrange a guide, if one is available. Conducted tours are free but donations toward the upkeep of the cathedral are requested.

Admission: Chapter house, 70p ($1.10) adults, 30p (50¢) children; crypt, 60p (90¢) adults, 30p (50¢) children; foundations and treasury, £1.80 ($2.70) adults, 70p ($1.10) children; tower, £2 ($3) adults, £1 ($1.50) children.

Open: Chapter house, foundations and treasury, and tower, Mon–Sat 10am–6pm, Sun 1–6pm (closing time in winter 4:30pm). Crypt, Mon–Fri 10am–4:30pm (in winter 11am–3pm), Sat 10am–3:30pm, Sun 1–3:30pm.

TREASURER'S HOUSE, Minster Yard. Tel. 624247.

Treasurer's House stands on a site where a continuous succession of buildings has stood since Roman times. The main part of the house, built in 1620, was refurbished by Yorkshire industrialist Frank Green at the turn of the century; he used this elegant town house to display his collection of 17th- and 18th-century furniture, glass, and china. An audiovisual program and exhibit explain the work of the medieval treasures and the subsequent fascinating history of the house. It has an attractive small garden in the shadow of York Minster. Some summer evenings you can enjoy coffee by candlelight in the Great Hall. An attractive licensed restaurant, where Yorkshire specialties are served, is open the same hours as the house.

Admission: £2.80 ($4.20) adults, £1.40 ($2.10) children.

Open: Apr–Oct, daily 10:30am–5pm (last entry 4:30pm).

YORK CASTLE MUSEUM, Eye of York off Tower St. Tel. 653611.

★ On the site of York's Castle this is one of the finest folk museums in the country. Its unique feature is a re-creation of a Victorian cobbled street, Kirkgate, named for the museum's founder, Dr. John Kirk. He acquired his large collection while visiting his patients in rural Yorkshire at the beginning of this century. The period rooms range from a neoclassical Georgian dining room through an overstuffed and heavily adorned Victorian parlor, to the 1953 sitting room with a brand-new television set purchased to watch the coronation of Elizabeth II. In the Debtors' Prison, former prison cells display craft workshops. There is also a superb collection of arms and armor. In the Costume Gallery, displays are changed regularly to reflect the collection's variety. Half Moon Court is an Edwardian street, with a gypsy caravan and a pub (sorry, the bar's closed!). During the summer, you can visit a watermill on the bank of the River Foss. It's recommended that you allow at least 2 hours for a visit to this museum.

Admission: £3.75 ($5.60) adults, £2.75 ($4.10) children.
Open: Apr–Oct, Mon–Sat 9:30am–5:30pm, Sun 10am–5:30pm; Nov–Mar, Mon–Sat 9:30am–4:30pm, Sun 10am–4:30pm.

NATIONAL RAILWAY MUSEUM, Leeman Rd. Tel. 621261.

This was the first national museum to be built outside London, and it has attracted millions of visitors since it opened in 1975. Adapted from an original steam-locomotive depot, the museum gives visitors a chance to see how Queen Victoria traveled in luxury and to look under and inside steam locomotives. In addition, there's a collection of railway memorabilia, including an early 19th-century clock and penny machine for purchasing tickets on the railway platform. More than 40 locomotives are on display. One, the *Agenoria,* dates from 1829 and is a contemporary of Stephenson's well-known *Rocket.* Of several royal coaches, the most interesting is Queen Victoria's Royal Saloon; it's like a small hotel, with polished wood, silk, brocade, and silver accessories.

Admission: £3.95 ($5.90) adults, £2 ($3) children.
Open: Mon–Sat 10am–6pm, Sun 11am–6pm.

JORVIK VIKING CENTRE, Coppergate. Tel. 643211.

This Viking city, discovered many feet below the present ground level, was reconstructed exactly as it stood in 948. In a "time car," you travel back through the ages to 1067, when Normans sacked the city, and then ride slowly through the street market peopled by faithfully modeled Vikings. You also go through a house where a family lived and down to the river to see the ship chandlers at work and a Norwegian cargo ship unloading. At the end of the ride, you pass through the Finds Hut, where thousands of artifacts are displayed. The time train departs at regular intervals.

Admission: £3.50 ($5.30) adults, £1.75 ($2.60) children.
Open: Apr–Oct, daily 9am–7pm; Nov–Mar, daily 9am–5:30pm.

THEATRE ROYAL, St. Leonard's Place. Tel. 623568.

This old, traditional theater building has modern additions to house the box office, bars, and restaurant. It's worth inquiring about the current production as the Royal Shakespeare Company includes York in its tours; the Arts Council presents dance, drama, and opera; and visiting celebrities appear in classics. There is also an excellent resident repertory company.

Admission: Tickets, gallery seats £5 ($7.50), dress circle seats £13 ($19.50).
Open: Evening shows, daily at 7:30pm or 8pm; matinees, Wed at 2:30pm, Sat at 4pm. **Closed:** Mar 8–Apr 30.

AN ORGANIZED WALKING TOUR

The best way to see York is to go to the Tourist Information Centre, De Grey Rooms, Exhibition Square (tel. 0904/621756), where you'll be met by a volunteer guide who will take you on a free 1½-hour walking tour of the city. You'll learn about history and lore through numerous intriguing stories. Tours are given April through October, daily at 10:15am and 2:15pm, plus at 7pm from June to August; from November to March, a daily tour is given at 10:15am. The tour assembles across the road from the De Grey Rooms.

WHERE TO STAY

VERY EXPENSIVE

MIDDLETHORPE HALL HOTEL, Bishopthorpe Rd., York, North Yorkshire YO2 1QB. Tel. 0904/641241, or toll free 800/525-4800 in the U.S. Fax 0904/620176. 23 rms, 7 suites. TV TEL **Directions:** Take the A191 1½ miles south of York.

$ Rates: £83–£129 ($124.50–$193.50) single; £115–£165 ($172.50–$247.50) double; £189 ($283.50) suite. Breakfast £9.95 ($14.90) extra. AE, DC, MC, V. **Parking:** Free.

⭐ Set on a 26-acre park, this hotel is located on the outskirts of York, near the racecourse. Built in 1699, the stately, red-brick, William and Mary country house had fallen into disrepair as a nightclub before it was purchased by Historic House Hotels and beautifully restored, both inside and out. Fresh flowers are displayed profusely and lots of antiques provide the ambience of a classic manor house. As befits such a house, there is an elegant drawing room, plus a library. The rooms are individually decorated and all have up-to-date bathrooms. The rooms are divided between the main house and restored outbuildings. Guests find in their room such niceties as homemade cookies and bottles of Malvern water, as well as bathrobes.

Dining/Entertainment: Meals are served in two restaurants, one oak-paneled and one a grill room. A choice of either international or English traditional meals is offered, a table d'hôte dinner costing £30 ($45).

EXPENSIVE

ABBOTS MEWS HOTEL, 6 Marygate Lane, Bootham, York, North Yorkshire YO3 7DE. Tel. 0904/634866. Fax 0904/612848. 50 rms (all with bath). TV TEL **Directions:** Take Bootham west from the cathedral and cut left onto Marygate; Marygate Lane lies off Marygate.

$ Rates (including English breakfast): £58 ($87) single; £105 ($157.50) double. AE, DC, MC, V. **Parking:** Free.

The setting here, as the name suggests, is a mews. What was at one time a 19th-century Victorian coach house with stables is now a highly recommendable hotel and restaurant, the latter serving international food. The rooms are comfortably furnished, with both modern and traditional styling. The hotel is also well located, lying close to the historic district. Good food is served here as well—you can order dinner until 9:30pm. Meals begin a £20 ($30).

BILBROUGH MANOR, Bilbrough, near York, North Yorkshire YO2 3PH. Tel. 0937/834002. Fax 0937/834724. 11 rms, 1 suite. TV TEL **Directions:** Head 5 miles southwest of York on the A1036.

$ Rates (including English breakfast): £77–£100 ($115.50–$150 single; £85–£135 ($127.50–$202.50) double; £150 ($225) suite. AE, DC, MC, V. **Parking:** Free. **Closed:** Dec 25–30.

★ One of the loveliest places to stay—or dine—in the vicinity of York is this hotel near the village church. The imposing Neo-Gothic walls and multiple chimneys were built in 1901 as a replacement for a dilapidated manor house. However, its foundations go back to the 13th century.

The sumptuous public rooms have paneling and baronial fireplaces, along with deep chintz-covered sofas. Each of the individually furnished bedrooms is elegant and unique, with many thoughtful amenities, including a private bath or shower, radio, hairdryer, and trouser press.

Dining/Entertainment: Even if you don't spend the night, you might want to dine here, sampling superb viands the chef offers in the modern French and British tradition. The carefully prepared meals are served with flourish on Wedgwood dinnerware in a historic paneled dining room. The menu changes frequently, but fresh, quality ingredients are always used. Meals are served daily from noon to 1:45pm and 7 to 9:30pm. Dinner costs £25 ($37.50) and up; table d'hôte luncheons go for £14 ($21). Always call for a reservation.

JUDGES LODGING, 9 Lendal, York, North Yorkshire YO1 2AQ. Tel. 0904/638733. Fax 0904/679947. 13 rms. TV TEL
$ Rates (including English breakfast): £60–£70 ($90–$105) single; £110 ($165) double. AE, DC, MC, V. **Parking:** Free.

The earliest historical fact about this charming house is that it was the home of a certain Dr. Wintringham in 1710. At the beginning of the 19th century it is listed as having been a judges' lodging, used when they traveled north from the London Inns of Justice. You'll be greeted by the receptionist, who will register your name and then lead you up to a circular wooden staircase, the only one of its type in the United Kingdom. All bedrooms have private baths or showers and some have four-poster beds. If you want to spoil yourself, you can book the large Prince Albert room, a twin-bedded room with three large windows overlooking the minster (Prince Albert actually slept in the room once). Each room has a different decor and is named accordingly. One is known as the Queen Mother Room. Some of the rooms, however, aren't as grand and many have been converted from former staff quarters, so your opinion of this place will undoubtedly hinge on your room assignment.

Dining/Entertainment: There are two dining rooms, where candles flicker and the carefully trained staff will attend to your every need. Dinner costs £9.95 ($14.90) and up. All meat, fish, and vegetables are fresh. Down in the old cellars—where they found bits of Roman pottery, antique pieces of glass, and other relics of the house's varied past—there is a cocktail bar, open to the public.

MODERATE

DEAN COURT HOTEL, Duncombe Place, York, North Yorkshire YO1 2EF. Tel. 0904/625082, or toll free 800/528-1234 in the U.S. Fax 0904/620305. 40 rms. TV TEL
$ Rates (including English breakfast): £50–£60 ($75–$90) single; £75–£95 ($112.50–$142.50) double. AE, DC, MC, V. **Parking:** Free.

This 1850 building lies right beneath the towers of the minster. This privately owned hotel was originally constructed to provide housing for the clergy of York Minster and then converted to a hotel after World War I. All the well-furnished rooms have bathtubs or showers and radios. The owner has done a lot to bring the facilities up to standards expected today. Snacks are served in a coffee lounge from 10am to 8pm (to 10pm in summer). The restaurant serves both a traditional English and an international cuisine, offered daily from noon to 2pm and 6:30 to 9:30pm.

MOUNT ROYALE HOTEL, 119 The Mount, York, North Yorkshire YO2 2DA. Tel. 0904/628856. Fax 0904/611171. 17 rms, 6 suites. TV TEL
$ Rates (including English breakfast): £63.50–£88 ($95.30–$132) single; £73–£98

($109.50–$147) double; from £105 ($157.50) suite. AE, DC, MC, V. **Parking:** Free.

Located in a district of York known as The Mount, this hotel is excellent for the money, and it serves good food as well. Built in 1833, it is carefully furnished with both antiques and modern pieces. The owners took over the house next door to increase their room capacity. Each bedroom has a bath, and some have private terraces leading to the garden.

Dining/Entertainment: The restaurant's menu consists of roast joints with interesting accompaniments. The extensive fixed-price menu, costing £24 ($36), carries supplements for such items as fresh out-of-season asparagus or strawberries. Justifiably popular with locals, the restaurant requires advance reservations. The dining room opens onto an attractive garden.

Services: All-day room service, laundry.

Facilities: Outdoor swimming pool, exercise room, sauna.

VIKING HOTEL, North St., York, North Yorkshire YO1 1JF. Tel. 0904/ 659822. Fax 0904/641793. 188 rms, 2 suites. TV TEL

$ Rates (including English breakfast): £92.50–£102.50 ($138.80–$153.80) single; £112.50–£127.50 ($168.80–$191.30) double; £170 ($255) suite. AE, DC, MC, V. **Parking:** £5 ($7.50).

Within the ancient city walls, this modern hotel overlooks the River Ouse. Built in the 1970s, the hotel is today the largest in York. The attractions of York are only a short walk away. The well-furnished and modern bedrooms, many with views toward the minster, have trouser presses, hairdryers, and hot-beverage makers.

Dining/Entertainment: The hotel's two restaurants offer a variety of dining. The Regatta serves a fixed-price dinner for £13.50 ($20.30), and the Carvery offers a lunch for £9 ($13.50) and a set dinner for £13.50 ($20.30). Each eating place has a bar and offers a welcoming atmosphere.

INEXPENSIVE

BEECHWOOD CLOSE HOTEL, 19 Shipton Rd., Clifton, York, North Yorkshire YO3 6RE. Tel. 0904/658378. Fax 0904/647124. 14 rms (all with bath). TV TEL **Directions:** Take the A19 north of the city.

$ Rates (including English breakfast): £39.50 ($59.30) single; £62.50 ($93.80) double. AE, DC, MC, V. **Parking:** Free.

Beechwood is a large house surrounded by trees, a garden with a putting green, and a parking area. The Spinks and the Blythes run the small hotel which offers comfortable bedrooms with central heating and hot-beverage makers. Good dinners or bar meals are served in the dining room overlooking the garden. The hotel is a 15-minute walk to the minster, either by road or along the river.

COTTAGE HOTEL, 3 Clifton Green, York, North Yorkshire YO3 6LH. Tel. 0904/643711. Fax 0904/611230. 19 rms (all with bath). TV TEL

$ Rates (including English breakfast): £25–£40 ($37.50–$60) single; £45–£65 ($67.50–$97.50) double. AE, DC, MC, V. **Parking:** Free.

About a 10-minute walk north of York Minster, this hotel comprises two refurbished and extended Victorian houses overlooking the village green of Clifton. The hotel offers handsome bedrooms with hot-beverage makers. Some 400-year-old timber beams rescued from Micklegate grace the restaurant and bar. Among the beverages served in the bar are two kinds of hand-pulled real ale. The hotel provides parking for its guests.

HEWORTH COURT, 76–78 Heworth Green, York, North Yorkshire YO3 7TQ. Tel. 0904/425156. Fax 0904/415290. 26 rms (all with bath). TV TEL **Directions:** Take the A1036 to the east side of the city.

$ Rates (including English breakfast): £42 ($63) single; £72 ($108) double. AE, DC, MC, V. **Parking:** Free.

Of York's reasonably priced accommodations, this establishment is a 10- to 15-minute walk east of the center. It is a three-story red-brick Victorian structure, although many of its bedrooms are within a modern extension added during the 1980s. The rooms are agreeably furnished and some open onto the courtyard. The hotel also offers a commendable cuisine; you can order dinner until 9:30pm. Meals cost £9.50 ($14.25) and up.

HUDSON'S HOTEL, 60 Bootham, York, North Yorkshire YO3 7BZ. Tel. 0904/621267. Fax 0904/654719. 30 rms (all with bath). TV TEL
$ Rates (including English breakfast): £39 ($58.50) single; £55–£79 ($82.50–$118.50) double; £75 ($112.50) triple; £80 ($120) quad. AE, DC, MC, V. **Parking:** Free.

Just a short walk from the minster, this hotel offers personal service. The owner converted two Victorian houses into the main hotel building in 1981 and later added an extension in the Victorian style. All accommodations are comfortably furnished and have tea and coffee makers. Hudson's has its own large parking lot. Both bar food and an English/French menu are offered, with fixed-price meals starting at £14 ($21).

WHERE TO DINE

IVY RESTAURANT, in the Grange Hotel, Clifton, York, North Yorkshire YO3 6AA. Tel. 0904/644744.
Cuisine: FRENCH/ENGLISH. **Reservations:** Required.
$ Prices: Appetizers £4.80–£6.45 ($7.20–$9.70); main courses £15.50–£16.25 ($23.30–$24.40); fixed-price meals £13.50 ($20.30) at lunch, £22 ($33) at dinner. AE, DC, MC, V.
Open: Lunch Sun–Fri 12:30–2:30pm; dinner daily 7–10:15pm.

In a Regency town house that's also a hotel of 29 rooms (see below), Cara Baird is the chef at this exceptionally good restaurant. The setting is that of a typically English country-house hotel, and there is both the main restaurant and a brasserie for your dining choice.

Vegetarians will find dishes to their liking, but meat and seafood reign supreme. The menu depends on the season and availability. However, you're likely to be tempted with fresh Scottish salmon flavored with dill, perhaps saddle of venison in a delectable juniper sauce. The sauces, such as the madeira sauce that goes with the tender beef, are one of the reasons that make dining here a treat.

The Grange also rents well-furnished and comfortable bedrooms, costing from £90 ($135) in a single and £110 ($165) in a double, including breakfast. There is adequate parking and wheelchair access.

KITES, 13 Grape Lane. Tel. 641750.
Cuisine: INTERNATIONAL. **Reservations:** Required.
$ Prices: Appetizers £2.15–£3.95 ($3.20–$5.90); main courses £5.45–£9.75 ($8.20–$14.60). MC, V.
Open: Lunch Sat noon–1:45pm; dinner Mon–Sat 7–10:30pm.

About a 5-minute walk from the minster, this restaurant is in the heart of York, on a small street near Stonegate. To reach it, walk up a narrow staircase to the second floor. This is a simple York bistro where the food is good and the atmosphere and service, unpretentious. Kites has many devotees, attracted to its eclectic brand of cookery that's international in scope. For example, one recipe might have been a dish served in the Middle Ages in England (perhaps with adaptations) and another one from Thailand. The baked trout in tahini might have come from Beirut in the old days, or else the filet of beef flavored with tarragon from France. Fondues, fresh salads, and herbs from the owner's garden are part of the features here. Vegetarian meals are also served.

MELTON'S, 7 Scarcroft Rd. Tel. 634341.

Cuisine: FRENCH/ENGLISH. **Reservations:** Required.

$ Prices: Appetizers £3.50–£5.80 ($5.30–$8.70); main courses £9.50–£13.50 ($14.30–$20.30). MC, V.

Open: Lunch Tues–Sun 12:30–2pm; dinner Mon–Sat 5:30–10pm. **Closed:** Aug 31–Sept 7 and Dec 22–Jan 11.

⭐ Some local food critics claim that Michael and Lucy Hjort serve the finest food in York. The location of their small place is approximately a mile from the heart of the city on a Victorian terrace. Mr. Hjort trained with the famous Roux brothers of Le Gavroche in London but doesn't charge their astronomical prices. His cuisine reflects his own imprint, both in his choice of dishes and in the fresh ingredients.

In what has always been known as a sleepy culinary backwater of England, the city of York, the Hjorts have created some local excitement. Their menu changes frequently, based on the season and the chef's inspiration, but is likely to include such dishes as peppered roast rib of beef with beetroot pasta, rack of lamb with herbs, or sea bass with baked fennel in the style of the French Riviera. Vegetarian meals are also available, and families with children are welcome.

19 GRAPE LANE, 19 Grape Lane. Tel. 636366.

Cuisine: ENGLISH. **Reservations:** Recommended for dinner.

$ Prices: Appetizers £2.75–£7.50 ($4.10–$11.30); main courses £13.95–£15 ($20.90–$22.50); fixed-price dinner £18.95 ($28.40). MC, V.

Open: Lunch Tues–Sat noon–1:45pm; dinner Tues–Fri 7:30–10:30pm, Sat 7–10:30pm. **Closed:** First 2 weeks in Feb and last 2 weeks in Sept.

In the heart of York, this restaurant occupies two floors. With such a name, you expect a very British restaurant and you get that, but with a very contemporary touch. You might begin with monkfish salad with toasted pine kernels or fettuccine with salmon. This is followed by such main dishes as breast of guinea fowl or médaillons of hare with field mushrooms. The menus are wisely limited, so that every dish will be fresh. The wine list is ever growing, and service is thoughtful and considerate. The location is on a cobbled lane off Petergate.

PUBS

THE BLACK SWAN, Peaseholme Green. Tel. 625236.

Cuisine: ENGLISH. **Reservations:** Not required.

$ Prices: Appetizers all £1.50 ($2.30); main courses £3.75–£4.50 ($5.60–$6.80); beer from £1.40 ($2.10). No credit cards.

Open: Mon–Sat 11am–11pm, Sun noon–3pm and 7–10:30pm. Food daily 11:30am–2pm; dinner Mon–Thurs only, 5:30–8pm.

The Black Swan is a fine, timbered, frame house that was once the home of the lord mayor of York in 1417; the mother of Gen. James Wolfe of Québec also lived here. One of the oldest inns in the city, it offers pub meals, which can be enjoyed in front of a log fire in a brick inglenook. Food consists of sandwiches, homemade soups, and Yorkshire puddings filled with beef stew. There are two doubles with private bath, costing from £45 ($67.50), plus a single without bath—which is rented only if the other two are already taken, and then only to a single occupant—costing £20 ($30).

KINGS ARMS PUBLIC HOUSE, King's Staith. Tel. 659435.

Cuisine: ENGLISH. **Reservations:** Not accepted.

$ Prices: Appetizers £1.50 ($2.25); main courses £3.50–£4 ($5.25–$6); beer £1.20 ($1.80). No credit cards.

Open: Lunch Mon–Fri 11:30am–2:30pm, Sat 11:30am–2pm, Sun noon–2pm.

Situated at the base of the Ouse Bridge, a few steps from the edge of the river, this 16th-century pub is boisterous and fun. A historic monument in its own right, it's filled with charm and character, and has the ceiling beams, paneling, and weathered brickwork you'd expect. A board records various disastrous flood levels, the most recent of which inundated the place in 1990. In summer, rows of outdoor tables are placed beside the river. Your hosts serve a full range of draft and bottled beers, the most popular of which (Samuel Smith's) is still brewed in Tadcaster, only 10 miles away. Place your lunch food order at the counter for bar snacks, which could include burgers, homemade curries, soups, and steak-and-kidney pie.

YE OLD STARRE INNE, 40 Stonegate. Tel. 623063.

Cuisine: ENGLISH. **Reservations:** Not accepted.

$ Prices: Soup £1.50 ($2.30); main courses £3–£4.10 ($4.50–$6.20). AE, DC, MC, V.

Open: Lunch Mon–Sat 11:30am–3pm, Sun noon–2:30pm; dinner Mon–Thurs 5:30–8pm. Pub, Mon–Thurs 11am–11pm, Fri–Sat 11am–3:30pm and 7–11pm, Sun noon–3pm and 7–10:30pm.

On a pedestrian street in the heart of Old York, this dates back to 1644 and is York's oldest licensed pub. Some inn (of one kind or another) might have stood on this spot since 900. In a pub said to be haunted by an old woman, a little girl, and a cat, you enter into an atmosphere of cast-iron tables, an open fireplace, oak Victorian settles, and time-blackened beams. In addition to standard alcoholic beverages, the pub offers an array of such English staples as steak-and-kidney pie, several different versions of hot pots, lasagne, and platters of roast beef with Yorkshire pudding. A recent addition to the nationwide Chef & Brewer chain of pubs and restaurants, the establishment offers a duet of outdoor courtyards which guests enjoy during fine weather.

EASY EXCURSIONS

CASTLE HOWARD

In its dramatic setting of lakes, fountains, and extensive gardens, Castle Howard, at Malton in North Yorkshire (tel. 065384/333), the 18th-century palace designed by Sir John Vanbrugh, is undoubtedly the finest private residence in Yorkshire. The principal location for the TV series "Brideshead Revisited," this was the first major achievement of the architect who later created the lavish Blenheim Palace near Oxford. The Yorkshire palace was begun in 1699 for the third Earl of Carlisle, Charles Howard. The striking facade is topped by a painted and gilded dome, which reaches more than 80 feet into the air. The interior boasts a 192-foot-long gallery, as well as a chapel with magnificent stained-glass windows by the 19th-century artist Sir Edward Burne-Jones. Besides the collections of antique furniture, porcelains, and sculpture, the castle contains a number of important paintings, including a portrait of Henry VIII by Holbein, and works by Rubens, Reynolds, and Gainsborough.

The seemingly endless grounds around the palace also offer the visitor some memorable sights, including the domed Temple of the Four Winds, by Vanbrugh, and the richly designed family mausoleum by Hawksmoor. There are two rose gardens, one with old-fashioned roses, the other featuring modern creations. The stable court houses the Costume Galleries, the largest private collection of 18th- to 20th-century costumes in Britain. Authentically dressed mannequins are exhibited in period settings.

Castle Howard is open to the public daily from March 19 to October 1: The grounds are open from 10am to 5pm; the cafeteria, house, and Costume Galleries, from 11am to 5pm, with last admission to the house and galleries at 4:30pm. Admission is £5.50 ($8.30) for adults, £3 ($4.50) for children. You can enjoy sandwiches, hot dishes, and wines in the self-service cafeteria. It lies 15 miles northeast of York, 3 miles off the A64.

Reynard Pullman, Ltd., Bootham Tower, Exhibition Square, in York (tel. 0904/622992 for reservations), conducts an afternoon tour to Castle Howard.

HAREWOOD HOUSE & BIRD GARDEN

At the junction of the A61 and A659, midway between Leeds and Harrogate, stands Harewood House, Harewood, West Yorkshire (tel. 0532/886225), the home of the Earl and Countess of Harewood, one of England's great 18th-century houses, which has always been owned by the Lascelles family. The fine Adam interior has superb ceilings and plasterwork, and furniture made especially for Harewood by Chippendale. There are also important collections of English and Italian paintings and Sèvres and Chinese porcelain.

The gardens, designed by Capability Brown, include terraces, lakeside and woodland walks, and a 4½-acre bird garden with exotic species from all over the world, including penguins, macaws, flamingos, and snowy owls, as well as a tropical rain-forest exhibit. Other facilities include shops, a restaurant, and cafeteria. Parking is free, and there is a picnic area, plus an adventure playground for the children.

Admission to Harewood and its grounds is £5.75 ($8.60) for adults and £3 ($4.50) for children. The house, bird garden, and adventure playground are open Easter to October, daily from 10am to 5pm. The location is 7 miles south of Harrogate, 8 miles north of Leeds on the Leeds-Harrogate road (at the junction of the A61/A659) at Harewood Village; 5 miles from the A1 at Wetherby, and 22 miles west of York. From York, head west along the B1224 toward Wetherby and follow the signs to Harewood from there.

FOUNTAINS ABBEY & STUDLEY ROYAL

At Fountains, 4 miles southwest of Ripon off the B6265, stands Fountains Abbey and Studley Royal, Fountains (tel. 0765/620333), on the banks of the Silver Skell. The abbey was founded by Cistercian monks in 1132 and is the largest monastic ruin in Britain. In 1987 it was awarded World Heritage status. The ruins provide the focal point of the 18th-century landscape garden at Studley Royal, one of the few surviving examples of a Georgian green garden. It's known for its water gardens, ornamental temples, follies, and vistas. The garden is bounded at its northern edge by a lake and 400 acres of deer park.

Admission is £3.50 ($5.30) for adults and £1.60 ($2.40) for children 16 and under. The sight is open January through March, daily from 10am to 5pm (or dusk); April through June and in September, daily from 10am to 7pm; in July and August, daily from 10am to 8pm; in October, daily from 10am to 6pm (to dusk); in November and December, Saturday through Thursday from 10am to 5pm (or dusk). It's closed December 24–25.

It's best to visit the sight by private car, although it can be reached from York by public transportation. From York, take bus no. 143 leaving from the York Hall Station to Ripon, 23 miles to the northwest (the A59, A1, and B6265 lead to Ripon). From Ripon, it will be necessary to take a taxi 4 miles to the southwest, although some prefer to go on foot as it's a scenic walk.

HAWES

About 65 miles northwest of York on the A684, Hawes is the natural center of Yorkshire Dales National Park. On the Pennine Way, it's England's highest market town and the capital of Wensleydale, which is famous for its cheese. There are rail connections from York taking you to Garsdale, which is 5 miles from Hawes. From Garsdale, bus connections will take you into Hawes.

The **Dales Countryside Museum,** Station Yard (the old train station) (tel. 0969/667494), traces folk life in the area of the Upper Dales. Peat cutting and cheese making, among other occupations, are depicted. The museum is open April through October daily from noon to 5pm. Winter opening hours are not fixed; you'll have to check locally. Admission is £1.20 ($1.80) adults or 60p (90¢) for children.

Hawes is a good center for exploring the ✪ **Yorkshire Dales National Park,** some 700 square miles of water-carved country that have been designated as a national park. Before you visit England, you can write for information about the park from the Yorkshire & Humberside Tourist Board, 312 Tadcaster Rd., York, North Yorkshire YO2 2HF (tel. 0904/707961).

In the dales you'll find dramatic white limestone crags, roads and fields bordered by drystone walls, fast-running rivers, isolated sheep farms, and clusters of sandstone cottages—all hallmarks of the impressive Yorkshire Dales.

Malhamdale receives more visitors annually than any dale in Yorkshire. Two of the most interesting historic attractions are the 12th-century ruins of Bolton Priory and the 14th-century Castle Bolton, to the north in Wensleydale.

Richmond, the most frequently copied town name in the world, stands at the head of the dales and, like Hawes, makes a good center for touring the surrounding countryside.

Where to Stay and Dine

SIMONSTONE HALL, Hawes, North Yorkshire DL8 3LY. Tel. 0969/ 667255. Fax 0969/667741. 10 rms (all with bath). TV
$ Rates (including half board): £60–£80 ($90–$120) per person. MC, V. **Parking:** Free.

Constructed in 1733, this building has been restored and converted into a comfortable family-run, country-house hotel offering spacious bedrooms, each a double. It's the former home of the earls of Wharncliffe and is located in a rural but not isolated area 1½ miles north of Hawes on the road signposted to Muker. The place once attracted such guests as Lillie Langtry and Disraeli. Owners Mr. and Mrs. J. R. Jeffryes are happy to have guests relax in the large, south-facing, paneled drawing rooms, which have comfortable antique furnishings.

You can have drinks in the Tawny Owl Bar and enjoy good food in the hotel's dining room. Nonresidents can dine here for £21.25 ($31.90) per person for a five-course dinner. Dinner can be complemented with good wines from the extensive cellar.

3. NORTH YORK MOORS NATIONAL PARK

The moors, on the other side of the Vale of York, have a wild beauty all their own, quite different from that of the dales. This rather barren moorland blossoms in summer with purple heather. Bounded on the east by the North Sea, it embraces a

553-square-mile area which England has turned into a national park. For information before you go, especially good maps, contact the **Yorkshire & Humberside Tourist Board,** 312 Tadcaster Rd., York, North Yorkshire, YO2 2HF (tel. 0904/707961).

Bounded by the Cleveland and Hambleton hills, the moors are dotted with early burial grounds and ancient stone crosses. At Kilburn a white horse can be seen hewn out of the hillside.

Pickering and Northallerton, both market towns, serve as gateways to the moors. The most popular trek is the Lyke Wake Walk, a 40-mile hike over bog, heather, and stream from Mount Grace Priory to Ravenscar on the seacoast.

The isolation and the beauty of the landscape attracted the founders of three great abbeys: Rievaulx near Helmsley, Byland Abbey near the village of Wass, and Ampleforth Abbey near Coxwold, one of the most attractive villages in the moors. The Cistercian Rievaulx and Byland abbeys are in ruins, but Benedictine Ampleforth still functions as a monastery and well-known Roman Catholic boys' school. Although many of its buildings date from the 19th and 20th century, they do contain earlier artifacts.

Along the eastern boundary of the park, North Yorkshire's 45-mile coastline shelters such traditional seaside resorts as Filey, Whitby, and Scarborough, the latter claiming to be the oldest seaside spa in Britain, located supposedly on the site of a Roman signaling station. The spa was founded in 1622, when mineral springs with medicinal properties were discovered. In the 19th century its Grand Hotel, a Victorian structure, was acclaimed as the best in Europe. The Norman castle on big cliffs overlooks the twin bays.

You can drive through the moorland while still based in York, but if you'd like to be closer to the moors, there are many centers where you can stay, notably Thirsk (see below).

THIRSK

This old market town in the Vale of Mowbray, 24 miles north of York on the A19, is on the western fringe of the park. It has a fine parish church, but what makes it such a popular stopover is its association with James Herriot, author of *All Creatures Great and Small.* Mr. Herriot still practices veterinary medicine in Thirsk, and visitors can photograph his office and perhaps get a picture of his partner standing in the door.

WHERE TO STAY

BROOK HOUSE, Ingramgate, Thirsk, North Yorkshire YO7 1DD. Tel. 0845/522240. Fax 0845/523133. 3 rms (none with bath). TV
$ Rates (including English breakfast): £16 ($24) per person. Discount available for children. No credit cards. **Parking:** Free.

⑤ This large, brown-brick Victorian house, originally built in 1887, is situated on 2 acres of land and overlooks the Barbeck Brook (which flows through its front yard) and the open countryside. Despite its peace and isolation, the town's Market Square is only a 3-minute walk away. Mrs. Margaret McLauchlan, the owner, is charming and kind, and has even been known to do a batch of washing for guests at no extra cost (but, I can't promise that). She serves a good Yorkshire breakfast, hearty and filling, plus an English tea in the afternoon. Tea-making facilities are also available for the guests, and a spacious and comfortable living room has color TV. The house is centrally heated, and in the guests' drawing room there is an open log fire in cool weather. There is ample parking for cars. The experience of knowing John and Margaret McLauchlan and enjoying their hospitality will remain long in your memory.

Note in advance that the modern brick-sided bungalow set adjacent to Brook House's driveway also accepts overnight guests, but it is not associated in any way with the McLauchlan family or its enterprises.

ST. JAMES HOUSE, 36 The Green, Thirsk, North Yorkshire YO7 1AQ. Tel. 0845/524120. 4 rms (2 with bath or shower). TV
$ Rates (including English breakfast): £26 ($39) single without bath; £32 ($48) double without bath, £40 ($60) double with bath. No credit cards. **Parking:** Free.
Closed: Nov–Mar.

 This lovely three-story, 18th-century Georgian brick house on the village green is near the former maternity home where James Herriot's children were born. The guesthouse, operated by Mrs. Liz Ogleby, is tastefully furnished, with some antiques. The attractive bedrooms, each a double, have such touches as good bone china to use with the hot-beverage facilities.

---

4. HAWORTH

45 miles W of York, 21 miles W of Leeds

GETTING THERE   By Train   To reach Haworth by rail, catch the train from Leeds to Keighley. Leeds has rail connections to York if you're visiting from there. At Keighley, board a privately run train, the Keighley and Worth Valley Railway, for the trip to Haworth. Some five to seven trains per day run between Keighley and Haworth in July and August. From March to June and in September and October, seven trains per day make the trip. For information, call 0535/43629.

By Bus   Yorkshire Rider, a private company, offers bus service between Hebden Bridge (which has rail links to Leeds and York) and Haworth. Bus no. 500 makes the trip between Hebden Bridge and Haworth from June through September only, four per day Sunday through Friday and one per day on Saturday. For information, call 0274/732237.

By Car   From York, head west for Leeds along the A64. After traversing the Leeds industrial area, continue west along the A650 to Keighley, dipping south on the B6143 to Haworth.

ESSENTIALS   The **telephone area code** is 0535. The **Tourist Information Centre,** 2-4 West Lane in Haworth (tel. 0535/642329), is open April through October, daily from 9:30am to 5:30pm; November to March, daily from 9:30am to 5pm.

Famous as the home of the Brontës, this village is in West Yorkshire, a county that might easily be overlooked otherwise. On the high moors of the Pennines, it's the most visited literary shrine in England after Stratford-upon-Avon. Anne Brontë wrote two novels, *The Tenant of Wildfell Hall* and *Agnes Grey;* Charlotte wrote two masterpieces, *Jane Eyre* and *Villette,* which depicted her experiences as a teacher; and Emily is the author of *Wuthering Heights,* a novel of passion and haunting melancholy. Charlotte and Emily are buried in the family vault under the Church of St. Michael, and the parsonage where they lived has been preserved as the **Brontë Parsonage Museum,** Church Street (tel. 0535/642323), which houses their furniture, personal treasures, pictures, books, and manuscripts. It may be visited April to September, daily from 10am to 5pm; October to March, daily from 11am to 4:30pm. It's closed from January 10 to February 4, and at Christmas. Admission is £3.50 ($5.30) for adults and £1 ($1.50) for children.

WHERE TO STAY

OLD WHITE LION HOTEL, 6 West Lane, Haworth, near Keighley, West Yorkshire BD22 8DU. Tel. 0535/642313. Fax 0535/646222. 14 rms (all with bath). TV TEL **Bus:** 664 or 665.

$ Rates (including English breakfast): £30.50 ($45.80) single; £49.50 ($74.30) double. AE, DC, MC, V. **Parking:** Free.

At the top of a cobblestone street, this hotel was built around 1700 with a solid stone roof. It's almost next door to the church where the Reverend Brontë preached, as well as the parsonage where the family lived. Joyce and Keith Bradford welcome tourists from all over the world to their warm, cheerful, and comfortable hotel. The bedrooms are attractively furnished. Although full of old-world charm, all rooms are fully up-to-date.

Dinners are à la carte; the good meals featuring fresh vegetables cost £11 ($16.50) in the evenings. Bar snacks include the usual favorites—ploughman's lunch, hot pies, fish, and sandwiches.

WHERE TO DINE

WEAVER'S RESTAURANT, 15 West Lane. Tel. 643822.
Cuisine: BRITISH. **Reservations:** Recommended.
$ Prices: Appetizers £2.50–£4.95 ($3.80–$7.40); main courses £8.50–£12.95 ($12.80–$19.40); fixed-price lunch or dinner £13.50 ($20.30). AE, DC, MC, V.
Open: Lunch (Oct–Mar only) Sun noon–1:30pm; dinner Tues–Sat 7–9:30pm.

The best restaurant in the Brontë hometown, this spot once housed weavers. British to the core, it not only has an inviting atmosphere but it serves excellent food made with fresh ingredients. Jane and Colin Rushworth have much talent in the kitchen. Lunch is served in the winter only. Dinners might include such classic dishes as Yorkshire pudding with gravy. Try, if featured, one of the Gressingham ducks, which are widely praised in the U.K. for the quality of their meat. For your final course, you might select a Yorkshire cheese or one of the homemade desserts. The style of the place is informal. The restaurant is likely to be closed for vacation for a certain period each summer, so call in advance to check.

---

5. HEXHAM & HADRIAN'S WALL

304 miles N of London, 37 miles E of Carlisle,
21 miles W of Newcastle upon Tyne

GETTING THERE   By Train   Take one of the many daily trains from London's Kings Cross Station to Newcastle upon Tyne. At Newcastle, change trains and take one in the direction of Carlisle. The fifth or sixth (depending on the schedule) stop after Newcastle will be Hexham. Hexham lies 14 miles southeast of Hadrian's Wall.

Visitors interested in the wall rather than in Hexham should get off the Carlisle-bound train at the second stop (Bardon Mill) or at the third stop (Haltwhistle), which lie 4 miles and 2½ miles, respectively, from the wall. At either of these hamlets, you can take a taxi on to whichever part of the wall you care to visit. Taxis line up freely at the railway station in Hexham, less frequently at the hamlets. If you get off in one of the above-mentioned hamlets and don't see a taxi, you can call 0434/344272 for the local taxis, and they will come to get you. Many visitors request their taxi to return at a prearranged time (which they gladly do) to pick them up after their excursion on the windy ridges near the wall.

By Bus   Once again, bus passengers headed for Hexham from both York and London will need to transfer at Newcastle upon Tyne onto a Northumbria Bus Lines bus which heads for Carlisle every hour or so throughout the day. The bus follows the same route as the above-mentioned train line, stopping in the hamlets mentioned above (and also in Hexham).

By Car From Newcastle upon Tyne, head west along the A69 until you see the cutoff south to Hexham.

ESSENTIALS The **telephone area code** is 0434. The **Tourist Information Centre** at Hexham is at the Manor Office, Hallgate (tel. 0434/605225).

Above the Tyne River, this historic old market town has narrow streets, an old market square, a fine abbey church, and a moot hall. It makes a good base for exploring Hadrian's Wall (see below) and the Roman supply base of Corstopitum at Corbridge-on-Tyne, the ancient capital of Northumberland. The tourist office (see above), has masses of information on the wall for walkers, drivers, campers, and picnickers.

The **Abbey Church of St. Wilfrid** is full of ancient relics. The Saxon font, the misericord carvings on the choir stalls, Acca's Cross, and St. Wilfrid's chair are well worth seeing.

WHAT TO SEE & DO

⭐ **HADRIAN'S WALL** Hadrian's Wall, which extends for 73 miles across the north of England, from the North Sea to the Irish Sea, is particularly interesting for a stretch of 10 miles west of Housesteads, which lies 2¾ miles northeast of Bardon Mill on the B6318. Only the lower courses of the wall are preserved intact; the rest were reconstructed in the 19th century using the original stones. From the wall, there are incomparable views north to the Cheviot Hills along the Scottish border and south to the Durham moors.

The wall was built in A.D. 122 after the visit of the emperor Hadrian, who was inspecting far frontiers of the Roman Empire and wished to construct a dramatic line between the empire and the barbarians. Legionnaires were ordered to build a wall across the width of the island of Britain, stretching for 73½ miles, beginning at the North Sea and ending at the Irish Sea.

The wall is a major Roman attraction in Europe. The western end can be reached from Carlisle, which also has a good museum of Roman artifacts; the eastern end can be reached from Newcastle upon Tyne (where some remains can be seen on the city outskirts; there's also a good museum at the university).

Along the wall are several **Roman forts.** The one at Housesteads was built about A.D. 130 to house an infantry of 1000 men. The fort was called Vercovicium. Admission is £2 ($3) for adults, £1 ($1.50) for children. It's open April to September, daily from 10am to 6pm; October to March, daily from 10am to 4pm. For information, call 0434/344363.

Just west of Housesteads, **Vindolanda** (tel. 0434/344277) is another well-preserved fort south of the wall. It is located on a minor road 1¼ miles southeast of Twice Brewed off the B6318. There is also an excavated civilian settlement outside the fort with an interesting museum of artifacts of everyday Roman life. Admission is £3 ($4.50) for adults, £1.75 ($2.60) for children. It's open daily February through November 10am to 5pm (or dusk).

Near Vindolanda at the garrison fort at Carvoran, near the village of Greenhead, the **Roman Army Museum** (tel. 06977/47485) traces the growth and influence of Rome from its early beginnings to the development and expansion of the empire, with special emphasis on the role of the Roman army and the garrisons of Hadrian's Wall. A barracks room shows basic army living conditions. Realistic life-size figures make this a strikingly visual museum experience. Admission is £2.50 ($3.80) for adults, £1.50 ($2.30) for children. It's open April to September, daily from 10am to 5:30pm;

in March and October, daily from 10am to 5pm. It's located at the junction of the A69 and the B6318, 18 miles west of Hexham.

Within easy walking distance of the Roman Army Museum lies one of the most imposing and high-standing sections of Hadrian's Wall, Walltown Crags, where the height of the wall and magnificent views to north and south are impressive.

Visiting the Wall   From July 24 to September 5, the Tynedale Council and the Northumberland National Park run a bus service departing daily from a point near the railway station in Hexham at 10am, noon, 2pm, and 4pm—except on Sunday when service is only at 12:20pm. The bus visits every important site along the wall, then turns around in the village of Haltwhistle and returns to Hexham. The cost is £4 ($6) for an all-day ticket. Many visitors take one bus out, then return on a subsequent bus 2, 4, or 6 hours later. Every Sunday a national park warden leads a 2½-hour walking tour of the wall, in connection with the bus service. The Hexham tourist office (see above) will provide further details.

NEARBY PLACES TO STAY & DINE

The best accommodations are found not in Hexham itself, but in satellite villages and small towns.

ANCHOR HOTEL, John Martin St., Haydon Bridge, Northumberland NE47 6AB. Tel. 0434/684227. Fax 0434/684586. 12 rms (10 with bath). TV TEL **Directions:** Take the A69 6 miles west of Hexham.
$ Rates (including English breakfast): £35–£39 ($52.50–$58.50) single without bath, £44–£47 ($66–$70.50) single with bath; £46–£49 ($69–$73.50) double without bath, £52–£60 ($78–$90) double with bath. AE, DC, MC, V. **Parking:** Free.
Ideally situated for visitors to the wall and its surroundings, between Haltwhistle (9 miles away) and Hexham (6 miles), this riverside village pub was once a coaching inn on the route from Newcastle to Carlisle. The building, which was constructed in 1700 near the edge of the North Tyne river (which still flows within a few feet of its foundations), sits in the heart of the tiny village of Haydon Bridge. The cozy bar is much used by locals. In the country dining room, wholesome evening meals are served. Dinner begins at £16 ($24). The bedrooms are comfortably furnished.

GEORGE HOTEL, Chollerford, Humshaugh, near Hexham, Northumberland NE46 4EW. Tel. 0434/681611. Fax 0434/681727. 50 rms (all with bath). MINIBAR TV TEL **Directions:** Take the A6079 directly north from Hexham.
$ Rates (including English breakfast): £77.50 ($116.30) single; £98.50 ($147.80) double. AE, DC, MC, V. **Parking:** Free.
Standing on the banks of the Tyne, this creeper-covered country hotel has gardens leading to the riverbank. It's a convenient base for visiting Hadrian's Wall. The hotel dates from the 18th century, when the original structure was built of Roman stone. The hotel has been extensively refurbished in recent months to an extremely high standard, with conference facilities and a leisure club. All bedrooms are luxuriously furnished and equipped, including such amenities as fully stocked minibars with fresh milk daily for the beverage-making equipment, an iron and ironing board, hairdryer, TV, and radio.

The Fisherman's Bar is where locals gather for a traditional pub welcome and bar snacks served at lunch. A fixed-price buffet luncheon in the Riverside Restaurant begins at £13.50 ($20.30); dinner, at £19.50 ($29.30). An à la carte menu is also available, complemented by a large wine list.

HADRIAN HOTEL, Wall, near Hexham, Northumberland NE46 4EE. Tel. 0434/681232. 6 rms (4 with bath, 2 with shower but no toilet). TV TEL

$ Rates (including English breakfast): £30 ($45) single with shower and sink, £35 ($52.50) single with bath; £42 ($63) double with shower and sink, £49 ($73.50) double with bath. DC, MC, V. **Parking:** Free.

Considered an ideal hotel for stopovers along Hadrian's Wall, the Hadrian lies on the only street of the hamlet of Wall, 3½ miles north of Hexham. It's an ivy-covered 18th-century building erected of stones gathered long ago from the site of the ancient wall. The owners have carefully refurbished the place, which now has two Jacobean-style bars serving bar meals priced between £6 ($9) and £9 ($13.50). Each of the attractive bedrooms is furnished with a radio alarm and hot-beverage facility. The hotel maintains a private garden for the use of its residents, and a beer garden that serves as a warm-weather extension of its pub.

LANGLEY CASTLE HOTEL, Langley, Hexham, Northumberland NE47 5LU. Tel. 0434/688888. Fax 0434/684019. 8 rms (all with bath), 1 suite. TV TEL **Directions:** From Hexham, go west on the A69 to Haydon Bridge, then head south on the A686 for 2 miles.

$ Rates (including English breakfast): £35–£79 ($52.50–$118.50) single; £70–£118 ($105–$177) double; £158 ($237) suite. AE, DC, MC, V. **Parking:** Free.

For a stay in a stately home, I recommend this hotel standing on 10 acres of woodland on the edge of Northumberland National Park, southwest of Haydon Bridge and about 7 miles west of Hexham. It's the only medieval fortified castle home in England that receives paying guests. The castle, built in 1350, was mainly uninhabited after being damaged in 1400 in the English-Scottish war, until its purchase in the late 19th century by Cadwallader Bates, a historian, who spent the rest of his life carefully restoring the property to its original beauty. Medieval features here include the 1350 spiral staircase, stained-glass windows, huge open fireplaces, seven-foot-thick walls, and many turrets. The luxuriously appointed bedrooms are of varying size; all have radios and some have whirlpools or saunas; the rates vary according to the features of the room. The hotel has an elegant drawing room, with an adjoining oak-paneled bar. Local specialties are served in the intimate restaurant, where meals cost £17.95 ($26.90) and up.

A. METRIC MEASURES

LENGTH

1 millimeter (mm)	=	.04 inches (*or* less than 1/16 in.)
1 centimeter (cm)	=	.39 inches (*or* just under ½ in.)
1 meter (m)	=	39 inches (*or* about 1.1 yards)
1 kilometer (km)	=	.62 miles (*or* about ⅔ of a mile)

To convert kilometers to miles, multiply the number of kilometers by .62. Also use to convert kilometers per hour (kmph) to miles per hour (m.p.h.).
To convert miles to kilometers, multiply the number of miles by 1.61. Also use to convert from m.p.h. to kmph.

CAPACITY

1 liter (l)	=	33.92 fluid ounces	=	2.1 pints	=	1.06 quarts
	=	.26 U.S. gallons				
1 imperial gallon	=	1.2 U.S. gallons				

To convert liters to U.S. gallons, multiply the number of liters by .26.
To convert U.S. gallons to liters, multiply the number of gallons by 3.79.
To convert imperial gallons to U.S. gallons, multiply the number of imperial gallons by 1.2.
To convert U.S. gallons to imperial gallons, multiply the number of U.S. gallons by .83.

WEIGHT

1 gram (g)	=	.035 ounces (*or* about a paperclip's weight)
1 kilogram (kg)	=	35.2 ounces
	=	2.2 pounds
1 metric ton	=	2,205 pounds (1.1 short ton)

To convert kilograms to pounds, multiply the number of kilograms by 2.2.
To convert pounds to kilograms, multiply the number of pounds by .45.

AREA

1 hectare (ha)	=	2.47 acres		
1 square kilometer (km²)	=	247 acres	=	.39 square miles

To convert hectares to acres, multiply the number of hectares by 2.47.
To convert acres to hectares, multiply the number of acres by .41.
To convert square kilometers to square miles, multiply the number of square kilometers by .39.
To convert square miles to square kilometers, multiply the number of square miles by 2.6.

TEMPERATURE

°C	−18°	−10		0		10		20		30		40
°F	0°	10	20	32	40	50	60	70	80	90	100

To convert degrees Celsius to degrees Fahrenheit, multiply °C by 9, divide by 5, and add 32 (example: 20°C × 9/5 + 32 = 68°F).

To convert degrees Fahrenheit to degrees Celsius, subtract 32 from °F, multiply by 5, then divide by 9 (example: 85°F − 32 × 5/9 = 29.4°C).

B. SIZE CONVERSIONS

The following charts should help you to choose the correct clothing sizes in England. However, sizes can vary, so the best guide is simply to try things on.

WOMEN'S DRESSES, COATS & SKIRTS

American	3	5	7	9	11	12	13	14	15	16	18
Continental	36	38	38	40	40	42	42	44	44	46	48
British	8	10	11	12	13	14	15	16	17	18	20

WOMEN'S BLOUSES & SWEATERS

American	10	12	14	16	18	20
Continental	38	40	42	44	46	48
British	32	34	36	38	40	42

WOMEN'S STOCKINGS

American	8	8½	9	9½	10	10½
Continental	1	2	3	4	5	6
British	8	8½	9	9½	10	10½

WOMEN'S SHOES

American	5	6	7	8	9	10
Continental	36	37	38	39	40	41
British	3½	4½	5½	6½	7½	8½

MEN'S SUITS

American	34	36	38	40	42	44	46	48
Continental	44	46	48	50	52	54	56	58
British	34	36	38	40	42	44	46	48

MEN'S SHIRTS

American	14½	15	15½	16	16½	17	17½	18
Continental	37	38	39	41	42	43	44	45
British	14½	15	15½	16	16½	17	17½	18

MEN'S SHOES

American	7	8	9	10	11	12	13
Continental	39½	41	42	43	44½	46	47
British	6	7	8	9	10	11	12

MEN'S HATS

American	6⅞	7⅛	7¼	7⅜	7½	7⅝
Continental	55	56	58	59	60	61
British	6¼	6⅞	7⅛	7¼	7⅜	7½

CHILDREN'S CLOTHING

American	3	4	5	6	6X
Continental	98	104	110	116	122
British	18	20	22	24	26

CHILDREN'S SHOES

American	8	9	10	11	12	13	1	2	3
Continental	24	25	27	28	29	30	32	33	34
British	7	8	9	10	11	12	13	1	2

INDEX

GENERAL INFORMATION

DESTINATIONS

Key to abbreviations: E = Expensive; I = Inexpensive; M = Moderate; VE = Very expensive; * = an author's favorite; $ = Super value choice.

Now Save Money on All Your Travels by Joining
FROMMER'S ™ TRAVEL BOOK CLUB
The World's Best Travel Guides at Membership Prices

FROMMER'S TRAVEL BOOK CLUB is your ticket to successful travel! Open up a world of travel information and simplify your travel planning when you join ranks with thousands of value-conscious travelers who are members of the FROMMER'S TRAVEL BOOK CLUB. Join today and you'll be entitled to all the privileges that come from belonging to the club that offers you travel guides for less to more than 100 destinations worldwide. Annual membership is only $25 (U.S.) or $35 (Canada and foreign).

The Advantages of Membership

1. Your choice of three FREE travel guides. You can select any **two** FROMMER'S COMPREHENSIVE GUIDES, FROMMER'S $-A-DAY GUIDES, *or* FROMMER'S FAMILY GUIDES—plus **one** FROMMER'S CITY GUIDE *or* FROMMER'S CITY $-A-DAY GUIDE.
2. Your own subscription to **TRIPS AND TRAVEL** quarterly newsletter.
3. You're entitled to a **30% discount** on your order of any additional books offered by FROMMER'S TRAVEL BOOK CLUB.
4. You're offered (at a small additional fee of $6.50) our **Domestic Trip-Routing Kits.**

Our quarterly newsletter **TRIPS AND TRAVEL** offers practical information on the best buys in travel, the "hottest" vacation spots, the latest travel trends, world-class events and much, much more.

Our **Domestic Trip-Routing Kits** are available for any North American destination. We'll send you a detailed map highlighting the best route to take to your destination—you can request direct or scenic routes.

Here's all you have to do to join:

Send in your membership fee of $25 ($35 Canada and foreign) with your name and address on the form below along with your selections as part of your membership package to **FROMMER'S TRAVEL BOOK CLUB, P.O. Box 473, Mt. Morris, IL 61054-0473.** Remember to select any **two** FROMMER'S COMPREHENSIVE GUIDES, FROMMER'S $-A-DAY GUIDES, *or* FROMMER'S FAMILY GUIDES—plus **one** FROMMER'S CITY GUIDE *or* FROMMER'S CITY $-A-DAY GUIDE.

If you would like to order additional books, please select the books you would like and send a check for the total amount (please add sales tax in the states noted below), plus $2 per book for shipping and handling ($3 per book for all foreign orders) to:

FROMMER'S TRAVEL BOOK CLUB
P.O. Box 473
Mt. Morris, IL 61054-0473
(815) 734-1104

[ ] **YES.** I want to take advantage of this opportunity to join FROMMER'S TRAVEL BOOK CLUB.
[ ] **My check is enclosed.** Dollar amount enclosed_____*

Name_____
Address_____
City_____ State_____ Zip_____

To ensure that all orders are processed efficiently, please apply sales tax in the following areas: CA, CT, FL, IL, NJ, NY, TN, WA and CANADA.

*With membership, shipping and handling will be paid by FROMMER'S TRAVEL BOOK CLUB for the three free books you select as part of your membership. Please add $2 per book for shipping and handling for any additional books purchased ($3 per book for foreign orders).

Allow 4–6 weeks for delivery. Prices of books, membership fee, and publication dates are subject to change without notice.

Please Send Me the Books Checked Below:

FROMMER'S COMPREHENSIVE GUIDES
(Guides listing facilities from budget to deluxe,
with emphasis on the medium-priced)

	Retail Price	Code		Retail Price	Code
☐ Acapulco/Ixtapa/Taxco 1993–94	$15.00	C120	☐ Jamaica/Barbados 1993–94	$15.00	C105
☐ Alaska 1994–95	$17.00	C130	☐ Japan 1992–93	$19.00	C020
☐ Arizona 1993–94	$18.00	C101	☐ Morocco 1992–93	$18.00	C021
☐ Australia 1992–93	$18.00	C002	☐ Nepal 1994–95	$18.00	C126
☐ Austria 1993–94	$19.00	C119	☐ New England 1993	$17.00	C114
☐ Belgium/Holland/ Luxembourg 1993–94	$18.00	C106	☐ New Mexico 1993–94	$15.00	C117
☐ Bahamas 1994–95	$17.00	C121	☐ New York State 1994–95	$19.00	C132
☐ Bermuda 1994–95	$15.00	C122	☐ Northwest 1991–92	$17.00	C026
☐ Brazil 1993–94	$20.00	C111	☐ Portugal 1992–93	$16.00	C027
☐ California 1993	$18.00	C112	☐ Puerto Rico 1993–94	$15.00	C103
☐ Canada 1992–93	$18.00	C009	☐ Puerto Vallarta/Manzanillo/ Guadalajara 1992–93	$14.00	C028
☐ Caribbean 1994	$18.00	C123	☐ Scandinavia 1993–94	$19.00	C118
☐ Carolinas/Georgia 1994– 95	$17.00	C128	☐ Scotland 1992–93	$16.00	C040
☐ Colorado 1993–94	$16.00	C100	☐ Skiing Europe 1989–90	$15.00	C030
☐ Cruises 1993–94	$19.00	C107	☐ South Pacific 1992–93	$20.00	C031
☐ DE/MD/PA & NJ Shore 1992–93	$19.00	C012	☐ Spain 1993–94	$19.00	C115
☐ Egypt 1990–91	$17.00	C013	☐ Switzerland/Liechtenstein 1992–93	$19.00	C032
☐ England 1994	$18.00	C129	☐ Thailand 1992–93	$20.00	C033
☐ Florida 1994	$18.00	C124	☐ U.S.A. 1993–94	$19.00	C116
☐ France 1994–95	$20.00	C131	☐ Virgin Islands 1994–95	$13.00	C127
☐ Germany 1994	$19.00	C125	☐ Virginia 1992–93	$14.00	C037
☐ Italy 1994	$19.00	C130	☐ Yucatán 1993–94	$18.00	C110

FROMMER'S $-A-DAY GUIDES
(Guides to low-cost tourist accommodations and facilities)

	Retail Price	Code		Retail Price	Code
☐ Australia on $45 1993–94	$18.00	D102	☐ Mexico on $45 1994	$19.00	D116
☐ Costa Rica/Guatemala/ Belize on $35 1993–94	$17.00	D108	☐ New York on $70 1992– 93	$16.00	D016
☐ Eastern Europe on $30 1993–94	$18.00	D110	☐ New Zealand on $45 1993–94	$18.00	D103
☐ England on $60 1994	$18.00	D112	☐ Scotland/Wales on $50 1992–93	$18.00	D019
☐ Europe on $50 1994	$19.00	D115	☐ South America on $40 1993–94	$19.00	D109
☐ Greece on $45 1993–94	$19.00	D100			
☐ Hawaii on $75 1994	$19.00	D113	☐ Turkey on $40 1992–93	$22.00	D023
☐ India on $40 1992–93	$20.00	D010	☐ Washington, D.C. on $40 1992–93	$17.00	D024
☐ Ireland on $40 1992–93	$17.00	D011			
☐ Israel on $45 1993–94	$18.00	D101			

FROMMER'S CITY $-A-DAY GUIDES
(Pocket-size guides with an emphasis on low-cost tourist accommodations and facilities)

	Retail Price	Code		Retail Price	Code
☐ Berlin on $40 1994–95	$12.00	D111	☐ Madrid on $50 1992–93	$13.00	D014
☐ Copenhagen on $50 1992–93	$12.00	D003	☐ Paris on $45 1994–95	$12.00	D117
☐ London on $45 1994–95	$12.00	D114	☐ Stockholm on $50 1992– 93	$13.00	D022

FROMMER'S WALKING TOURS
(With routes and detailed maps, these companion guides point out
the places and pleasures that make a city unique)

	Retail Price	Code		Retail Price	Code
☐ Berlin	$12.00	W100	☐ Paris	$12.00	W103
☐ London	$12.00	W101	☐ San Francisco	$12.00	W104
☐ New York	$12.00	W102	☐ Washington, D.C.	$12.00	W105

FROMMER'S TOURING GUIDES
(Color-illustrated guides that include walking tours, cultural and historic
sites, and practical information)

	Retail Price	Code		Retail Price	Code
☐ Amsterdam	$11.00	T001	☐ New York	$11.00	T008
☐ Barcelona	$14.00	T015	☐ Rome	$11.00	T010
☐ Brazil	$11.00	T003	☐ Scotland	$10.00	T011
☐ Florence	$ 9.00	T005	☐ Sicily	$15.00	T017
☐ Hong Kong/Singapore/			☐ Tokyo	$15.00	T016
Macau	$11.00	T006	☐ Turkey	$11.00	T013
☐ Kenya	$14.00	T018	☐ Venice	$ 9.00	T014
☐ London	$13.00	T007			

FROMMER'S FAMILY GUIDES

	Retail Price	Code		Retail Price	Code
☐ California with Kids	$18.00	F100	☐ San Francisco with Kids	$17.00	F004
☐ Los Angeles with Kids	$17.00	F002	☐ Washington, D.C. with Kids	$17.00	F005
☐ New York City with Kids	$18.00	F003			

FROMMER'S CITY GUIDES
(Pocket-size guides to sightseeing and tourist accommodations and
facilities in all price ranges)

	Retail Price	Code		Retail Price	Code
☐ Amsterdam 1993–94	$13.00	S110	☐ Montreál/Québec		
☐ Athens 1993–94	$13.00	S114	City 1993–94	$13.00	S125
☐ Atlanta 1993–94	$13.00	S112	☐ New Orleans 1993–94	$13.00	S103
☐ Atlantic City/Cape			☐ New York 1993	$13.00	S120
May 1993–94	$13.00	S130	☐ Orlando 1994	$13.00	S135
☐ Bangkok 1992–93	$13.00	S005	☐ Paris 1993–94	$13.00	S109
☐ Barcelona/Majorca/			☐ Philadelphia 1993–94	$13.00	S113
Minorca/Ibiza 1993–94	$13.00	S115	☐ Rio 1991–92	$ 9.00	S029
☐ Berlin 1993–94	$13.00	S116	☐ Rome 1993–94	$13.00	S111
☐ Boston 1993–94	$13.00	S117	☐ Salt Lake City 1991–92	$ 9.00	S031
☐ Cancún/Cozumel 1991–			☐ San Diego 1993–94	$13.00	S107
92	$ 9.00	S010	☐ San Francisco 1994	$13.00	S133
☐ Chicago 1993–94	$13.00	S122	☐ Santa Fe/Taos/		
☐ Denver/Boulder/Colorado			Albuquerque 1993–94	$13.00	S108
Springs 1993–94	$13.00	S131	☐ Seattle/Portland 1992–93	$12.00	S035
☐ Dublin 1993–94	$13.00	S128	☐ St. Louis/Kansas		
☐ Hawaii 1992	$12.00	S014	City 1993–94	$13.00	S127
☐ Hong Kong 1992–93	$12.00	S015	☐ Sydney 1993–94	$13.00	S129
☐ Honolulu/Oahu 1994	$13.00	S134	☐ Tampa/St.		
☐ Las Vegas 1993–94	$13.00	S121	Petersburg 1993–94	$13.00	S105
☐ London 1994	$13.00	S132	☐ Tokyo 1992–93	$13.00	S039
☐ Los Angeles 1993–94	$13.00	S123	☐ Toronto 1993–94	$13.00	S126
☐ Madrid/Costa del			☐ Vancouver/Victoria 1990–		
Sol 1993–94	$13.00	S124	91	$ 8.00	S041
☐ Miami 1993–94	$13.00	S118	☐ Washington, D.C. 1993	$13.00	S102
☐ Minneapolis/St.					
Paul 1993–94	$13.00	S119			

Other Titles Available at Membership Prices

SPECIAL EDITIONS

	Retail Price	Code		Retail Price	Code
☐ Bed & Breakfast North America	$15.00	P002	☐ Marilyn Wood's Wonderful Weekends (within a 250-mile radius of NYC)	$12.00	P017
☐ Bed & Breakfast Southwest	$16.00	P100	☐ National Park Guide 1993	$15.00	P101
☐ Caribbean Hideaways	$16.00	P103	☐ Where to Stay U.S.A.	$15.00	P102

GAULT MILLAU'S "BEST OF" GUIDES
(The only guides that distinguish the truly superlative from the merely overrated)

	Retail Price	Code		Retail Price	Code
☐ Chicago	$16.00	G002	☐ New England	$16.00	G010
☐ Florida	$17.00	G003	☐ New Orleans	$17.00	G011
☐ France	$17.00	G004	☐ New York	$17.00	G012
☐ Germany	$18.00	G018	☐ Paris	$17.00	G013
☐ Hawaii	$17.00	G006	☐ San Francisco	$17.00	G014
☐ Hong Kong	$17.00	G007	☐ Thailand	$18.00	G019
☐ London	$17.00	G009	☐ Toronto	$17.00	G020
☐ Los Angeles	$17.00	G005	☐ Washington, D.C.	$17.00	G017

THE REAL GUIDES
(Opinionated, politically aware guides for youthful budget-minded travelers)

	Retail Price	Code		Retail Price	Code
☐ Able to Travel	$20.00	R112	☐ Kenya	$12.95	R015
☐ Amsterdam	$13.00	R100	☐ Mexico	$11.95	R128
☐ Barcelona	$13.00	R101	☐ Morocco	$14.00	R129
☐ Belgium/Holland/ Luxembourg	$16.00	R031	☐ Nepal	$14.00	R018
☐ Berlin	$13.00	R123	☐ New York	$13.00	R019
☐ Brazil	$13.95	R003	☐ Paris	$13.00	R130
☐ California & the West Coast	$17.00	R121	☐ Peru	$12.95	R021
☐ Canada	$15.00	R103	☐ Poland	$13.95	R131
☐ Czechoslovakia	$15.00	R124	☐ Portugal	$16.00	R126
☐ Egypt	$19.00	R105	☐ Prague	$15.00	R113
☐ Europe	$18.00	R122	☐ San Francisco & the Bay Area	$11.95	R024
☐ Florida	$14.00	R006	☐ Scandinavia	$14.95	R025
☐ France	$18.00	R106	☐ Spain	$16.00	R026
☐ Germany	$18.00	R107	☐ Thailand	$17.00	R119
☐ Greece	$18.00	R108	☐ Tunisia	$17.00	R115
☐ Guatemala/Belize	$14.00	R127	☐ Turkey	$13.95	R027
☐ Hong Kong/Macau	$11.95	R011	☐ U.S.A.	$18.00	R117
☐ Hungary	$14.95	R118	☐ Venice	$11.95	R028
☐ Ireland	$17.00	R120	☐ Women Travel	$12.95	R029
☐ Italy	$18.00	R125	☐ Yugoslavia	$12.95	R030